CW00321378

LONDON

CONTENTS

Key to map pages 2-3

Key to map symbols 4-5

Central London maps 6-37

Main London maps 38-207

Theatres and cinemas map 208

Shopping map 209

Index to street names, place names,
and places of interest 210-376

Published by Collins
An imprint of HarperCollins*Publishers*
77-85 Fulham Palace Road, Hammersmith, London
W6 8JB

www.collins.co.uk

Copyright © HarperCollins*Publishers* Ltd 2003
Mapping generated from Collins/Bartholomew digital
databases

London Underground Map by permission of Transport
Trading Limited Registered User No. 02/3682

Collins® is a registered trademark of
HarperCollins*Publishers* Limited

The grid on this map is the National Grid taken from the
Ordnance Survey map with the permission of the
Controller of Her Majesty's Stationery Office.

Printed in China   QM11426/QM11427   CDM

ISBN 0 00 715532 8 (paperback) imp 002
ISBN 0 00 715531 X (spiral) imp 002
e-mail: roadcheck@harpercollins.co.uk

M1 A41
M25
WATFORD
Croxley Green
Bushey
Elstree
Borehamwood
Hadley Wood
New Barnet
BARNET

| 38 | 39 | 40 | 41 |

Rickmansworth
A1

Maple Cross

| 50 | 51 | 52 | 53 | 54 | 55 | 56 | 57 |

South Oxhey
Stanmore
A41
Edgware
A1
Finchley

Northwood

| 66 | 67 | 68 | 69 | 70 | 71 | 72 | 73 |

Harefield
Pinner
Wealdstone
Kingsbury
Hendon
HARROW
M1
Golders Green
A1
A406

Rayners Lane

| 84 | 85 | 86 | 87 | 88 | 89 | 90 | 91 |

Denham
A40
M40
Ruislip
Northolt
BRENT
Wembley
Willesden
Hampstead
A41
CAMDEN

UXBRIDGE

| 102 | 103 | 104 | 105 | 106 | 107 | 108 | 109 |

A40
HILLINGDON
Greenford
Perivale
Harlesden
Kilburn
A406
A40

| | | | | | | | 6 | 7 | 8 |

Hayes
Southall EALING

| 120 | 121 | 122 | 123 | 124 | 125 | 126 | 127 | 128 | 129 |

Iver
M25
West Drayton
Norwood Green
M4
HAMMERSMITH & FULHAM
Chiswick
KENSINGTON & CHELSEA

								14	15	1
								22	23	2
								30	31	3

Poyle
A4
Harmondsworth
Heston
Osterley
Brentford

| 140 | 141 | 142 | 143 | 144 | 145 | 146 | 147 | 148 | 149 |

M4
A4
London Heathrow
Hatton
Kew
Putney
WANDSWORTH
A21
Isleworth
A316

HOUNSLOW
Twickenham
RICHMOND UPON THAMES

| 160 | 161 | 162 | 163 | 164 | 165 | 166 | 167 |

Ham
Upper Tooting
A30
Ashford
A316
Teddington
KINGSTON UPON THAMES
A24

STAINES
A308
Hanworth
Wimbledon

| 178 | 179 | 180 | 181 | 182 | 183 | 184 | 185 |

M3
Sunbury
West Molesey
Thames Ditton
Surbiton
New Malden
MERTON
Mitcham
Morden
A24

Shepperton
Chertsey

| 194 | 195 | 196 | 197 | 198 | 199 |

Weybridge
ESHER
A309
A3
Worcester Park
A217
Carshalton
A232

M25
Addlestone
Chessington
Cheam
SUTTON

Byfleet
A3
Oxshott
EPSOM
A24
A240
Ewell
Belmont
A217

Chessington
A243

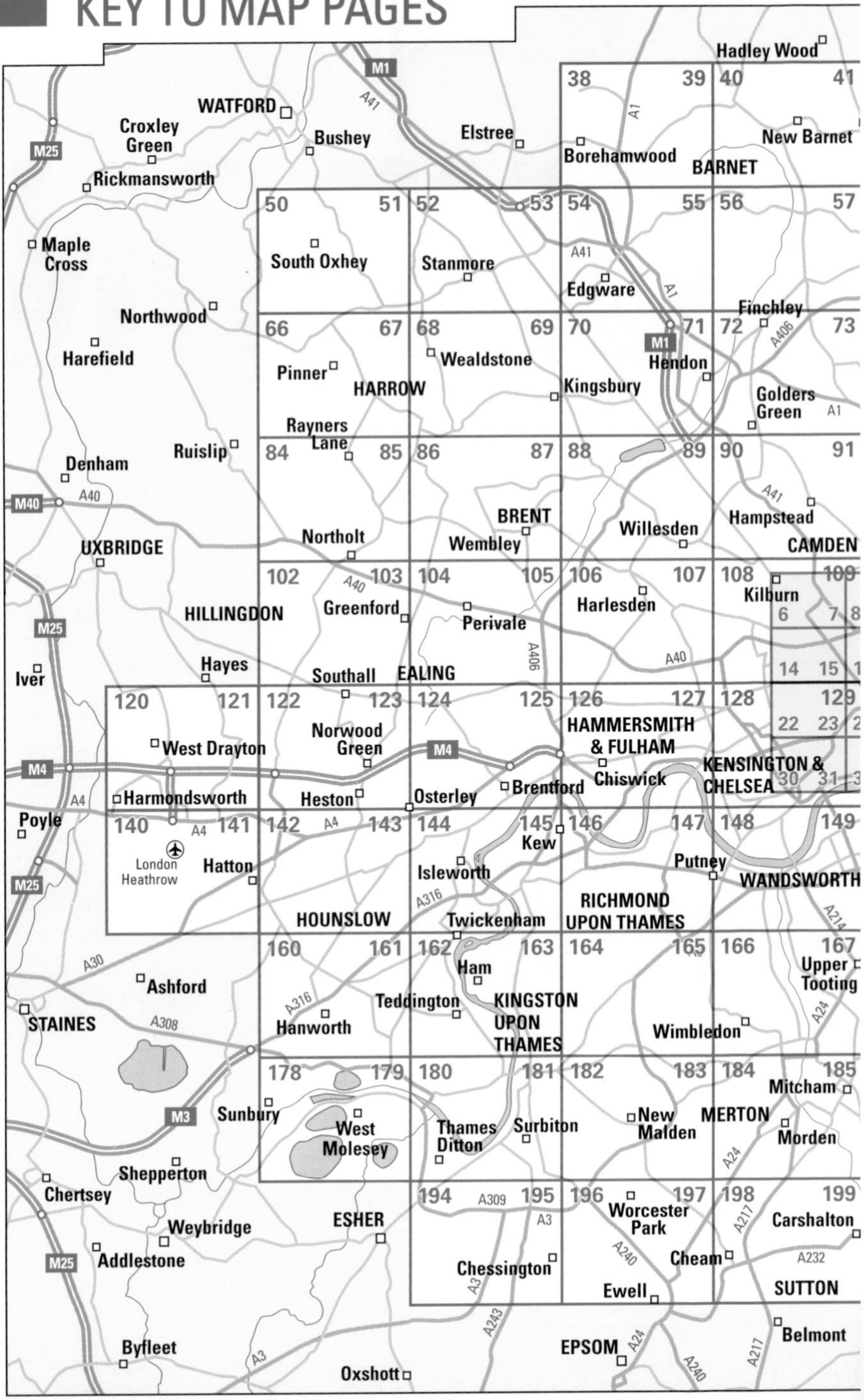

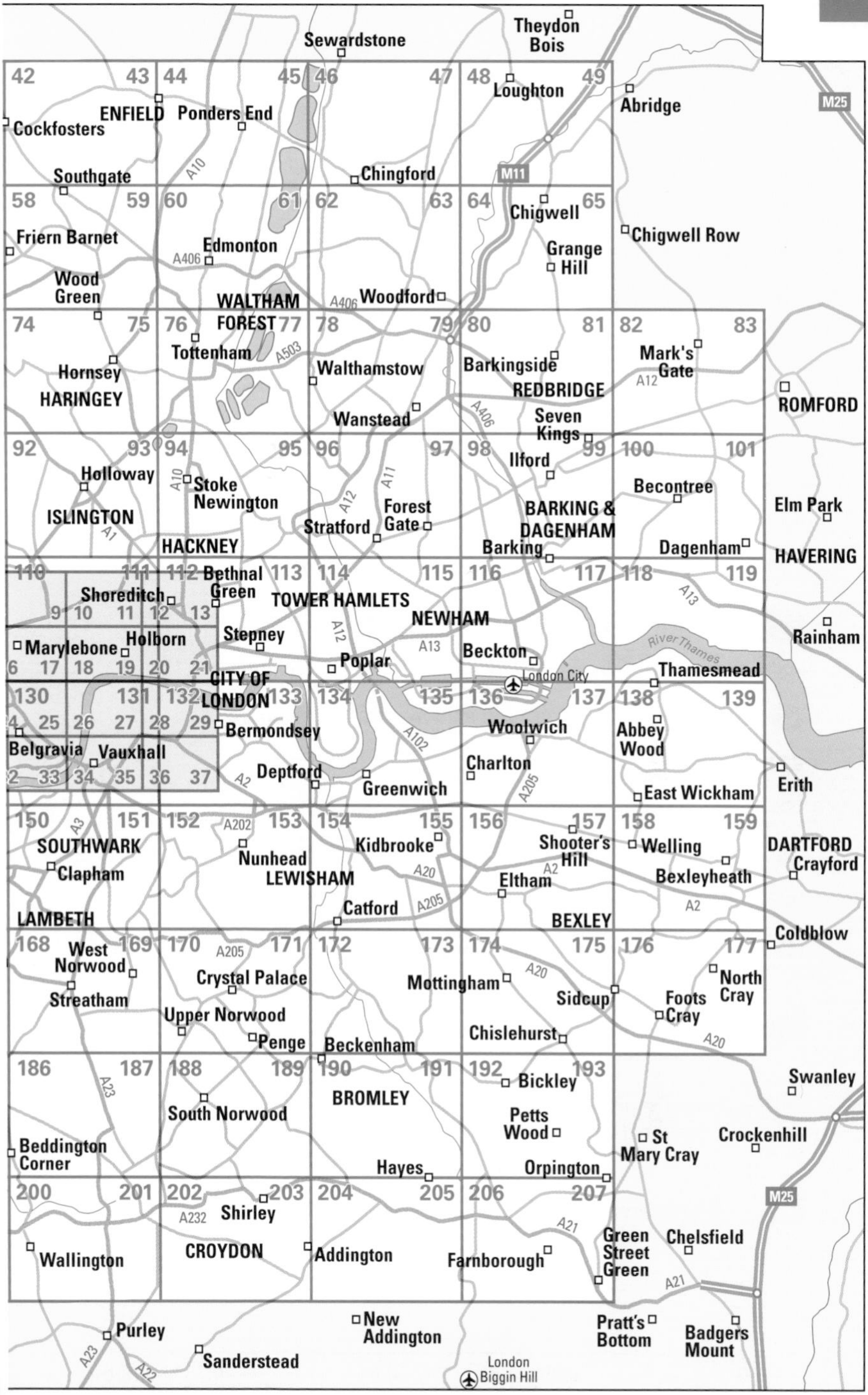

Sewardstone

Theydon
Bois

| 42 | 43 | 44 | 45 | 46 | 47 | 48 | 49 |

Loughton

Abridge

M25

ENFIELD   Ponders End

Cockfosters

Southgate

Chingford

M11

| 58 | 59 | 60 | 61 | 62 | 63 | 64 | 65 |

Chigwell

Chigwell Row

Friern Barnet

Edmonton

A406

Grange
Hill

Wood
Green

WALTHAM
FOREST

A406   Woodford

| 74 | 75 | 76 | 77 | 78 | 79 | 80 | 81 | 82 | 83 |

Tottenham

A503

Mark's
Gate

A12

Hornsey

Walthamstow

Barkingside

HARINGEY

Wanstead

REDBRIDGE

ROMFORD

Seven
Kings

| 92 | 93 | 94 | 95 | 96 | 97 | 98 | 99 | 100 | 101 |

Holloway

A10

Stoke
Newington

A12

A11

Ilford

Becontree

Elm Park

ISLINGTON

A1

Stratford

Forest
Gate

BARKING &
DAGENHAM

HAVERING

HACKNEY

Barking

Dagenham

| 110 | 111 | 112 | 113 | 114 | 115 | 116 | 117 | 118 | 119 |

Bethnal
Green

TOWER HAMLETS

A13

| 9 | 10 | 11 | 12 | 13 |

Shoreditch

NEWHAM

River Thames

Holborn

Stepney

A12

A13

Beckton

Rainham

| 6 | 17 | 18 | 19 | 20 | 21 |

Marylebone

Poplar

London City

Thamesmead

CITY OF
LONDON

| 130 | 131 | 132 | 133 | 134 | 135 | 136 | 137 | 138 | 139 |

Woolwich

Abbey
Wood

| 4 | 25 | 26 | 27 | 28 | 29 |

Bermondsey

A102

Belgravia   Vauxhall

Deptford

Charlton

A205

| 2 | 33 | 34 | 35 | 36 | 37 |

A2

Greenwich

East Wickham

Erith

| 150 | 151 | 152 | 153 | 154 | 155 | 156 | 157 | 158 | 159 |

A3

A202

Kidbrooke

Shooter's
Hill

Welling

DARTFORD

SOUTHWARK

Nunhead

A20

Crayford

Clapham

LEWISHAM

Eltham

Bexleyheath

LAMBETH

Catford

A205

BEXLEY

A2

Coldblow

| 168 | 169 | 170 | 171 | 172 | 173 | 174 | 175 | 176 | 177 |

West
Norwood

A205

A20

North
Cray

Streatham

Crystal Palace

Mottingham

Sidcup

Foots
Cray

Upper Norwood

Chislehurst

A20

Penge

Beckenham

| 186 | 187 | 188 | 189 | 190 | 191 | 192 | 193 |

A23

BROMLEY

Bickley

Swanley

South Norwood

Petts
Wood

St
Mary Cray

Crockenhill

Beddington
Corner

Hayes

Orpington

| 200 | 201 | 202 | 203 | 204 | 205 | 206 | 207 |

A232   Shirley

M25

Wallington

CROYDON

Addington

Farnborough

Green
Street
Green

Chelsfield

A21

Purley

New
Addington

Pratt's
Bottom

Badgers
Mount

A23

A22

Sanderstead

London
Biggin Hill

4

KEY TO CENTRAL MAP SYMBOLS

Dual **A4**	Primary route		Leisure & tourism
Dual **A40**	'A' road		Shopping
B504	'B' road		Administration & law
	Other road		Health & welfare
	Street market		Education
	Pedestrian street		Industry & commerce
	Access restriction		Public open space
	Track/Footpath		Park/Garden/Sports ground
→	One way street		Cemetery
	Ferry	▬ POL	Police station
CITY	Borough boundary	▬ Fire Sta	Fire station
EC2	Postal district boundary	▬ PO	Post Office
	Main railway station		Cinema
	Other railway station		Theatre
	London Underground station	☒	Major hotel
-DLR-	Docklands Light Railway station		Embassy
	Bus/Coach station	+	Church
P	Car park	☾	Mosque
WC	Public toilet	✡	Synagogue
i	Tourist information centre	Mormon ■	Other place of worship

Extent of London Congestion Charging Zone
For more information see website www.cclondon.com

The reference grid on this atlas coincides with the Ordnance Survey
National Grid system. The grid interval is 250 metres.

A Grid reference   Page continuation number

SCALE
1: 10,000 6.3 inches to 1 mile/10 cms to 1 km

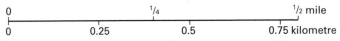

M4	Motorway
Dual A4	Primary route
Dual A40	'A' road
B504	'B' road
→	Other road/One way street
⊥	Toll
▬	Street market
▬	Restricted access road
▬	Pedestrian street
═	Cycle path
----	Track/Footpath
LC	Level crossing
V__P	Vehicle/Pedestian ferry
▬ ▬	County/Borough boundary
──	Postal district boundary
⊁	Main railway station
⊕	Other railway station
⊖	London Underground station
DLR	Docklands Light Railway station
⊖	Tramlink
⊖	Bus/Coach station
P	Car park

▮	Leisure & tourism
▮	Shopping
▮	Administration & law
▮	Health & welfare
▮	Education
▮	Industry & commerce
▮	Cemetery
▮	Golf course
▮	Public open space/Allotments
▮	Park/Garden/Sports ground
▮	Wood/Forest
USA	Embassy
Pol	Police station
Fire Sta	Fire station
PO/Lib	Post Office/Libary
▲	Youth hostel
□	Tower block
i	Tourist information centre
Ⓗ	Heliport
+	Church
☾	Mosque
✿	Synagogue

Extent of London Congestion Charging Zone
For more information see website www.cclondon.com

The reference grid on this atlas coincides with the Ordnance Survey National Grid system. The grid interval is 500 metres.

A Grid reference   **38** Page continuation number

SCALE
1:20,000 3.2 inches to 1 mile/5 cms to 1 km

35 OS National Grid kilometre square

0 — ¼ — ½ mile
0 — 0.25 — 0.5 — 0.75 — 1 kilometre

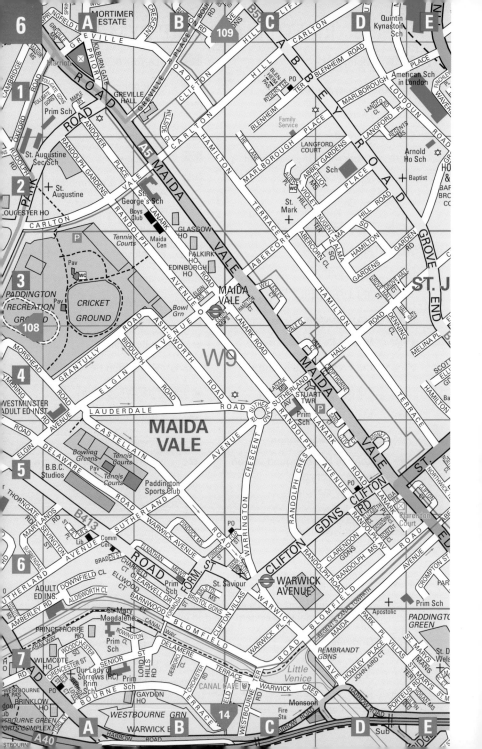

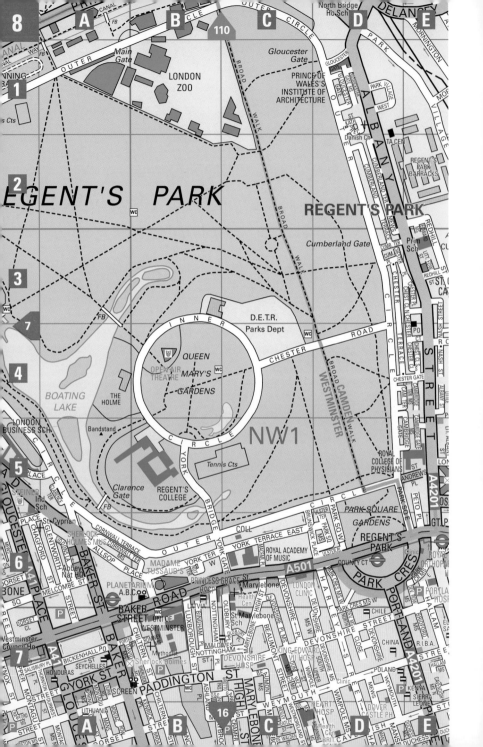

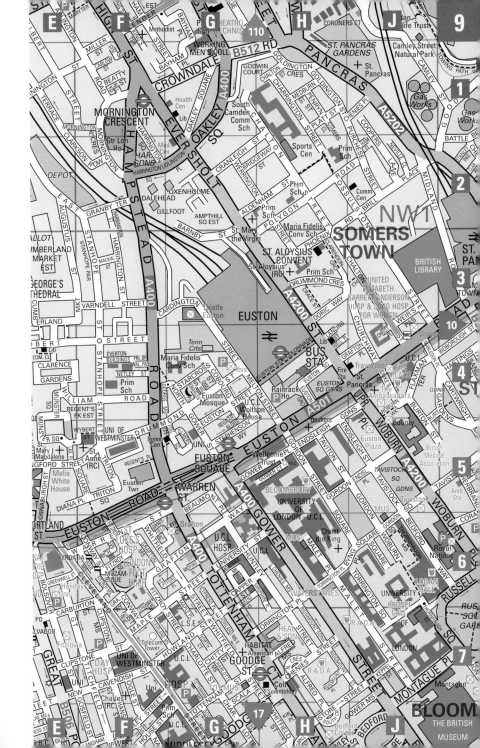

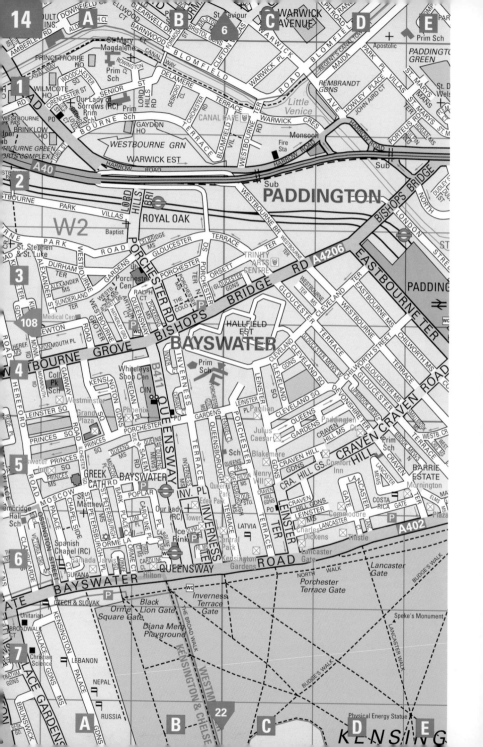

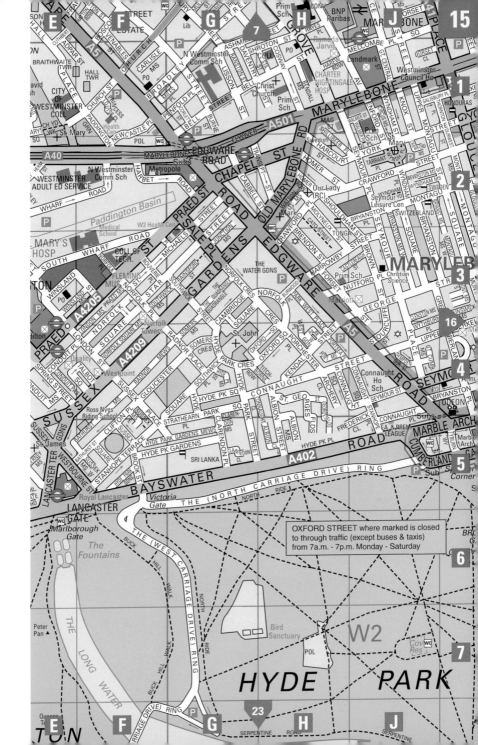

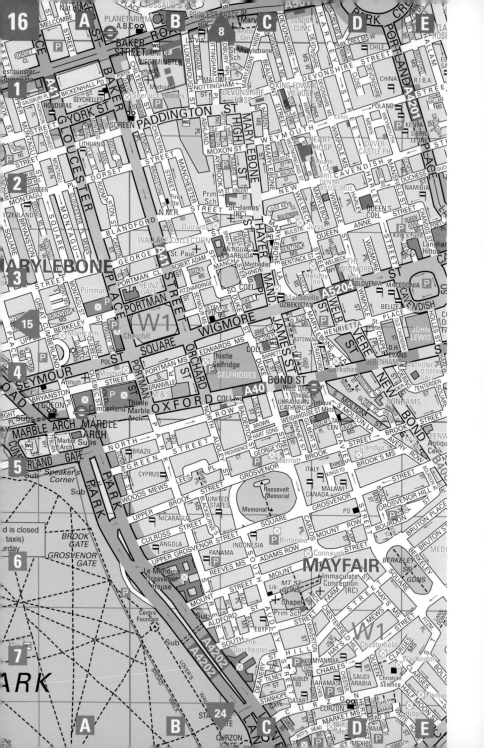

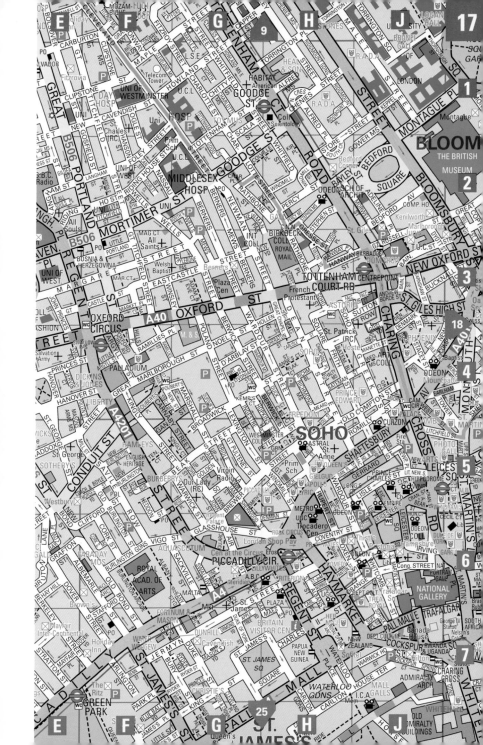

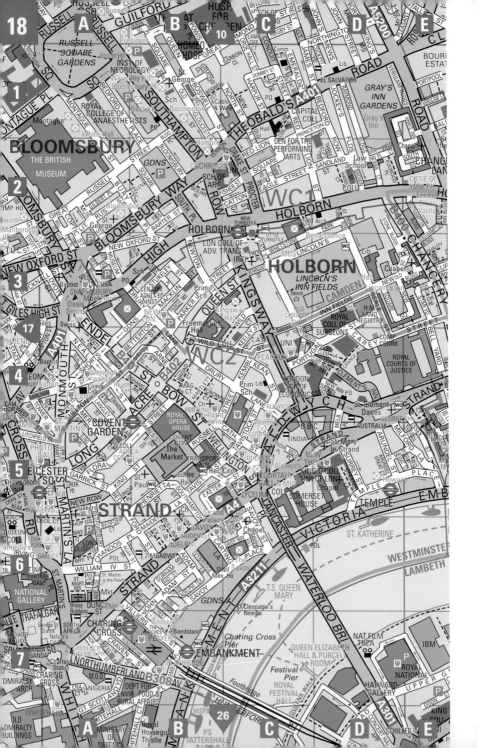

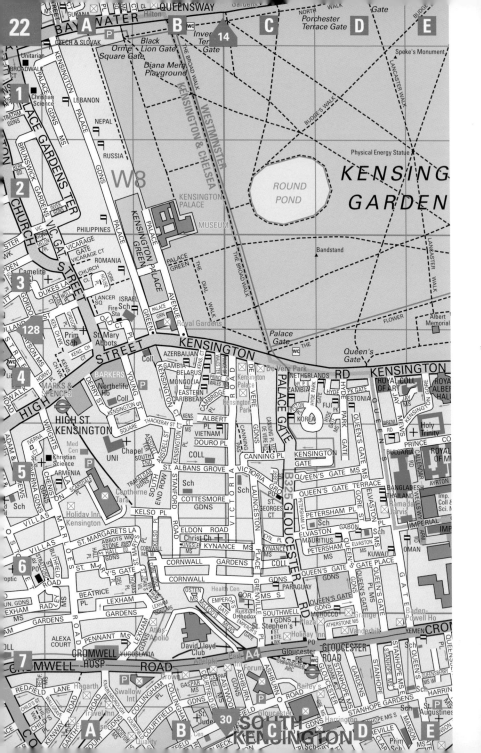

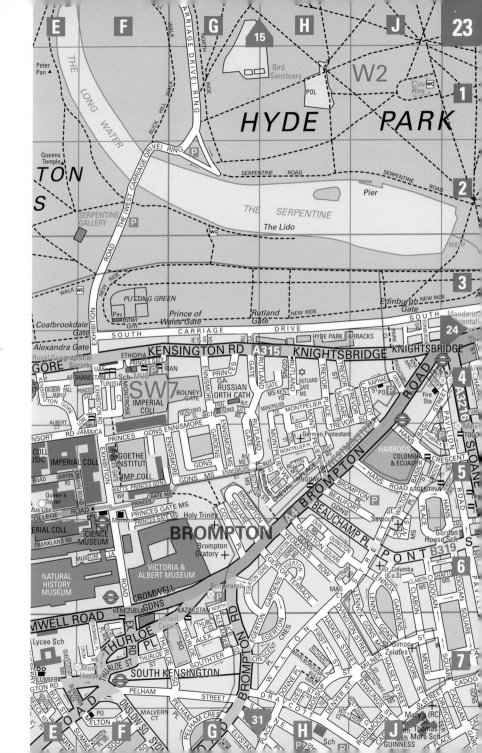

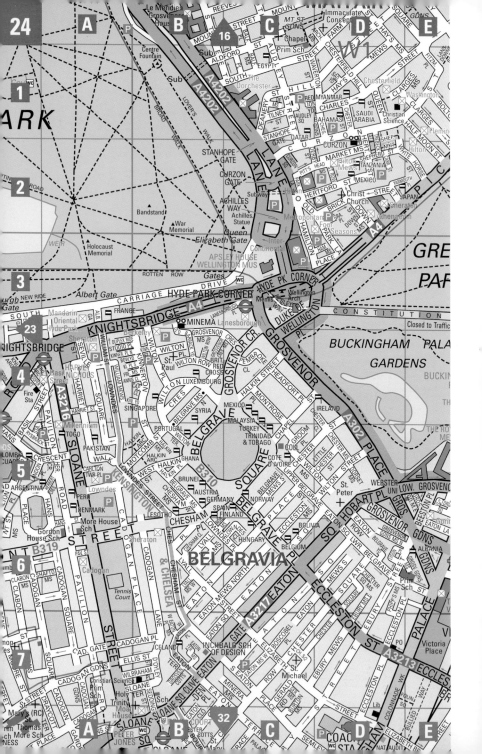

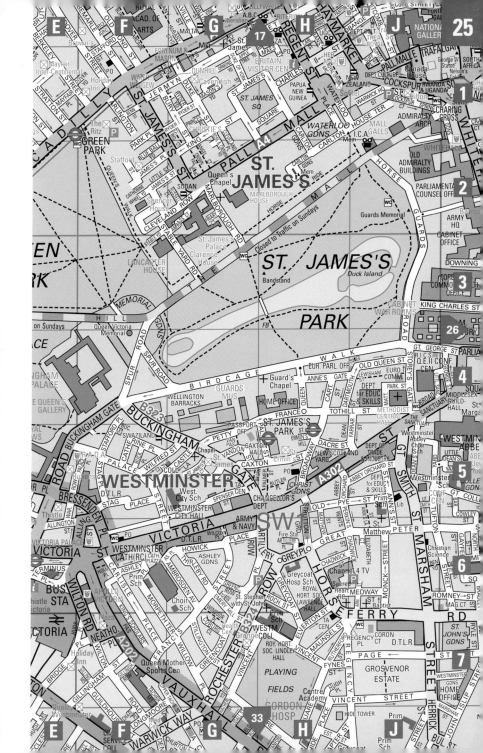

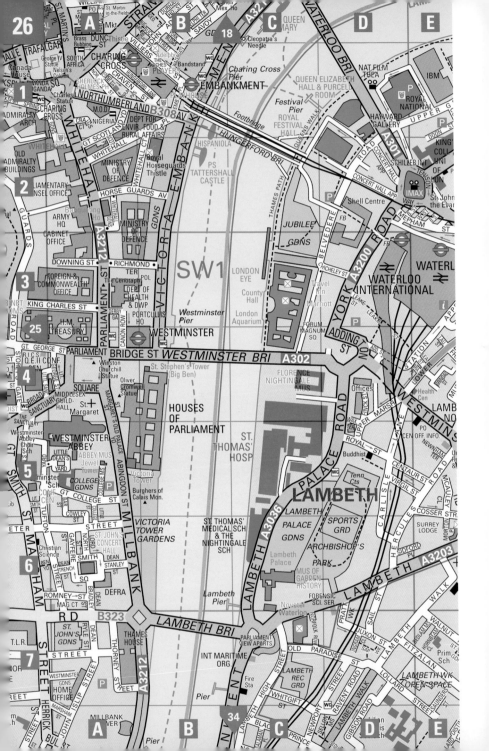

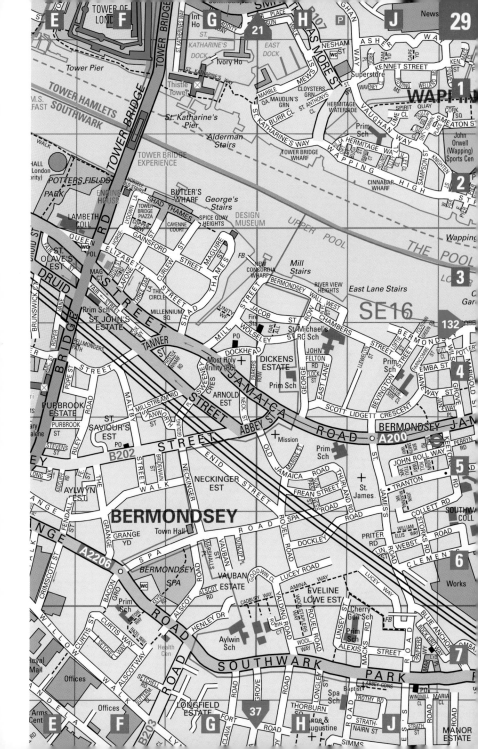

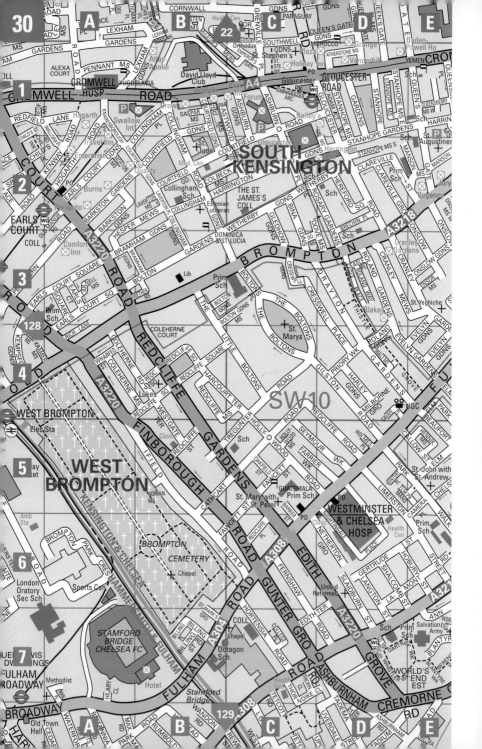

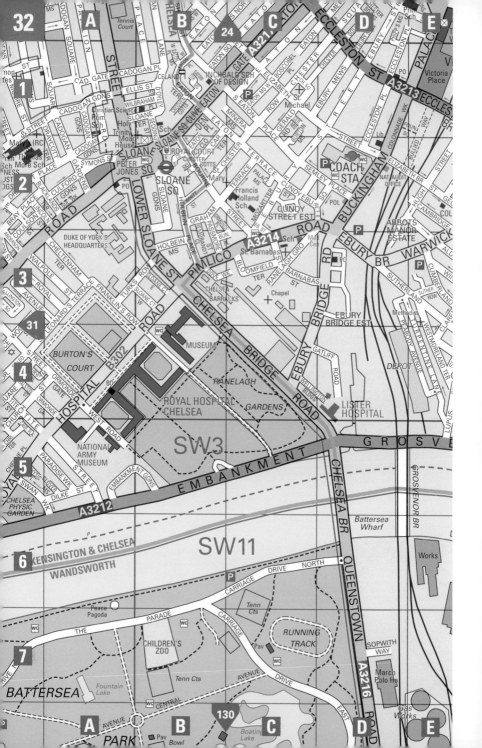

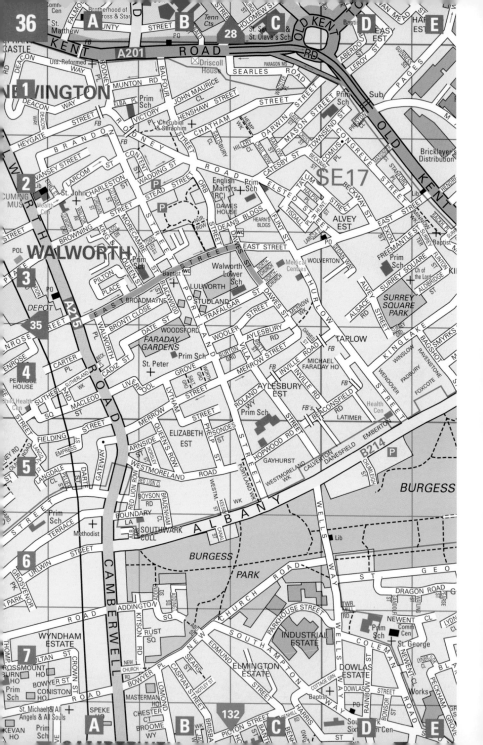

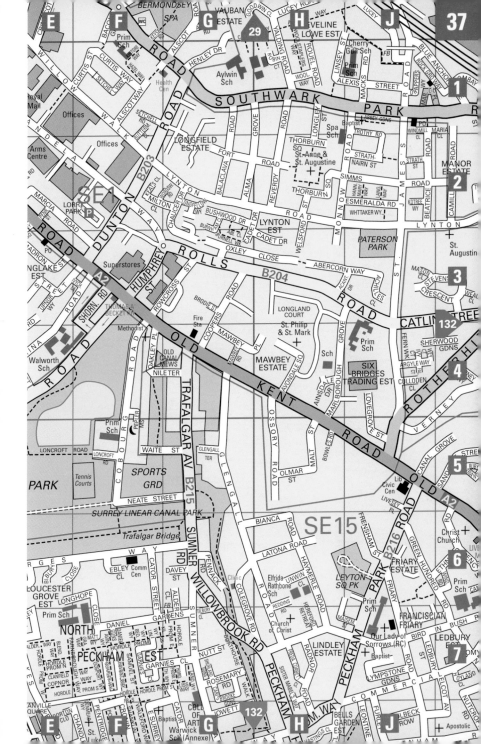

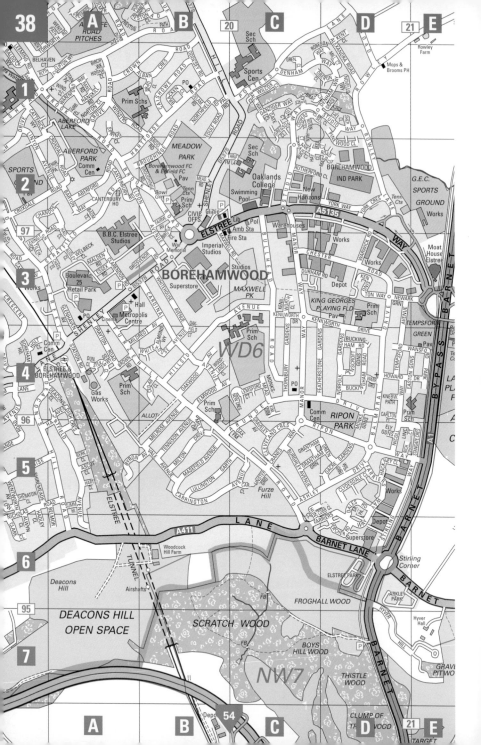

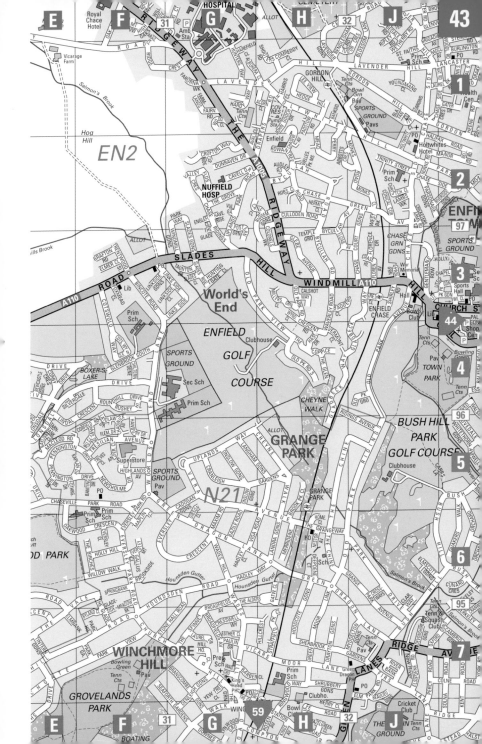

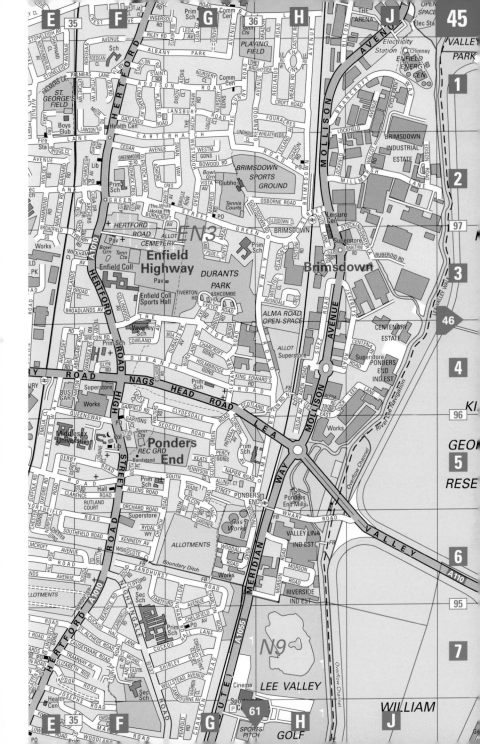

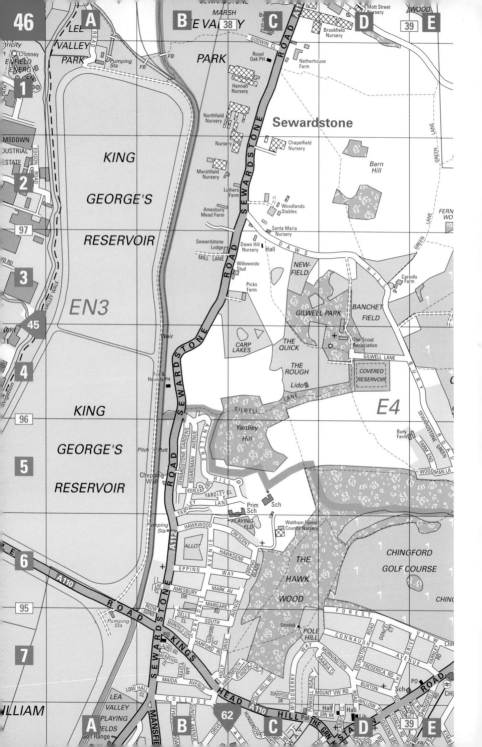

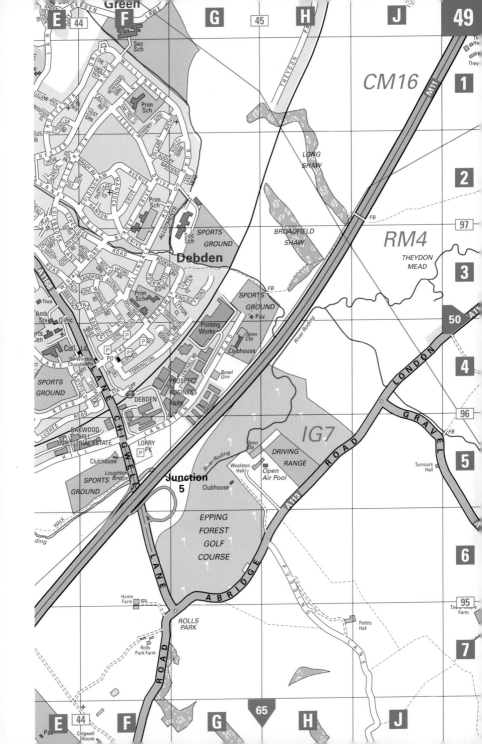

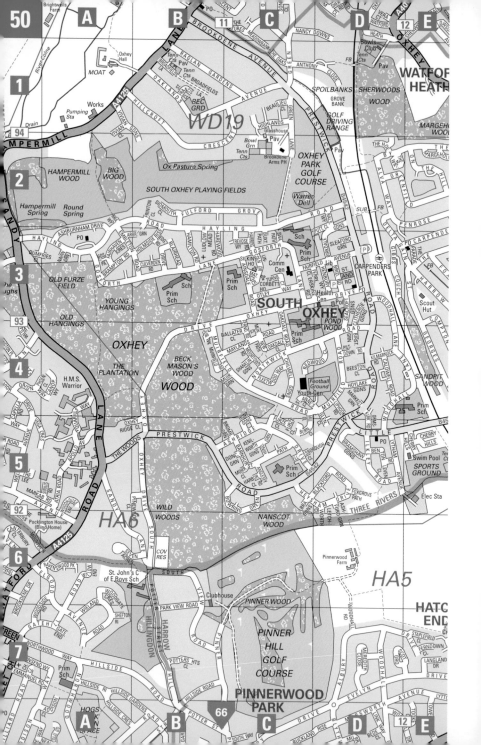

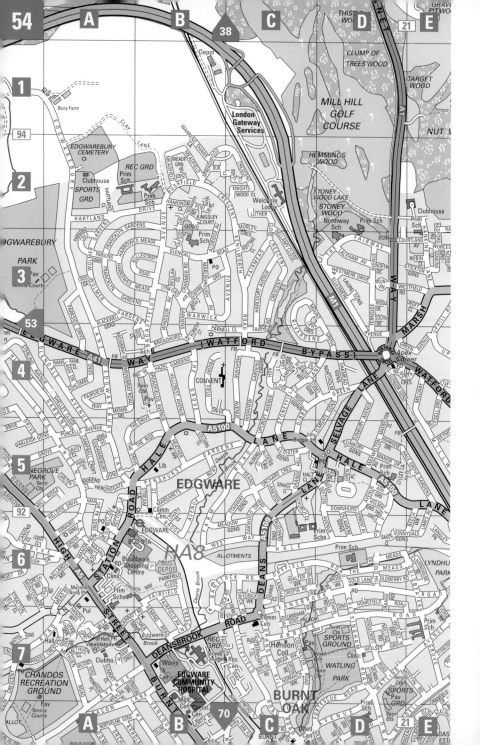

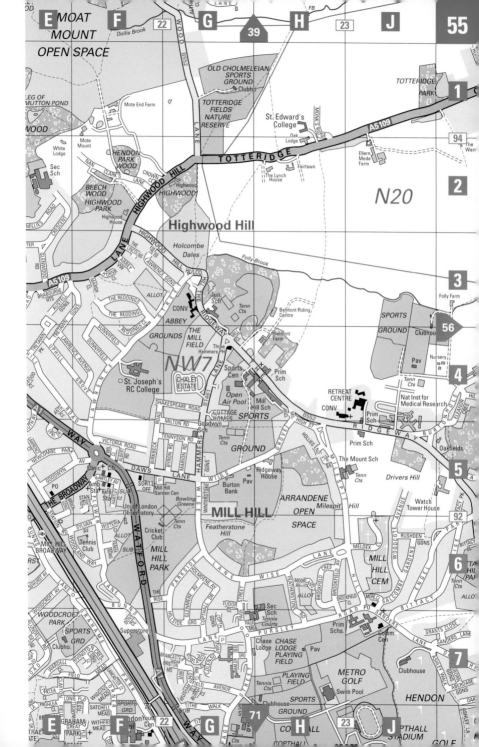

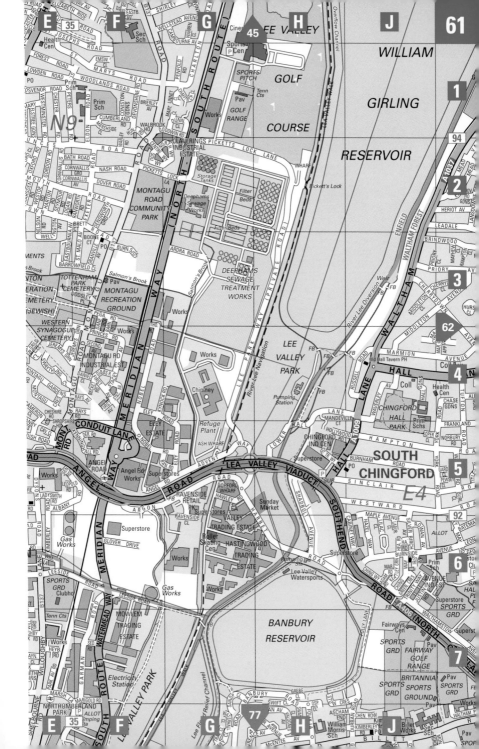

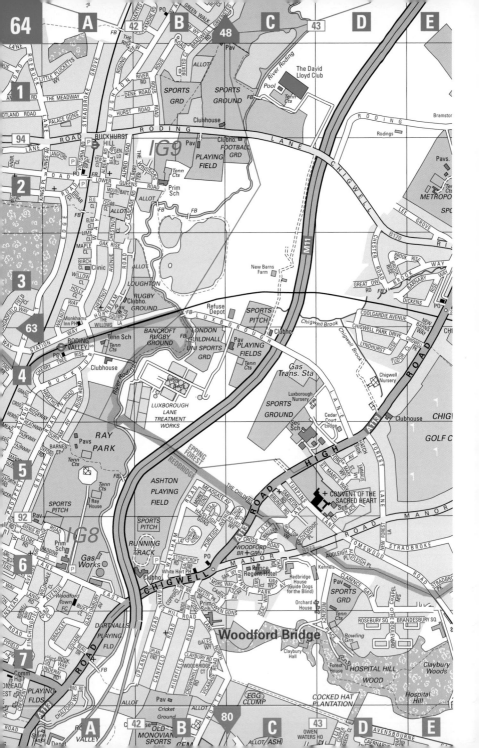

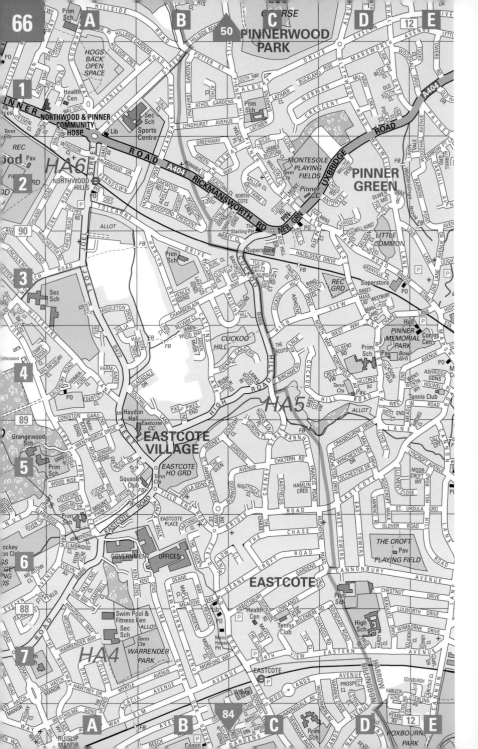

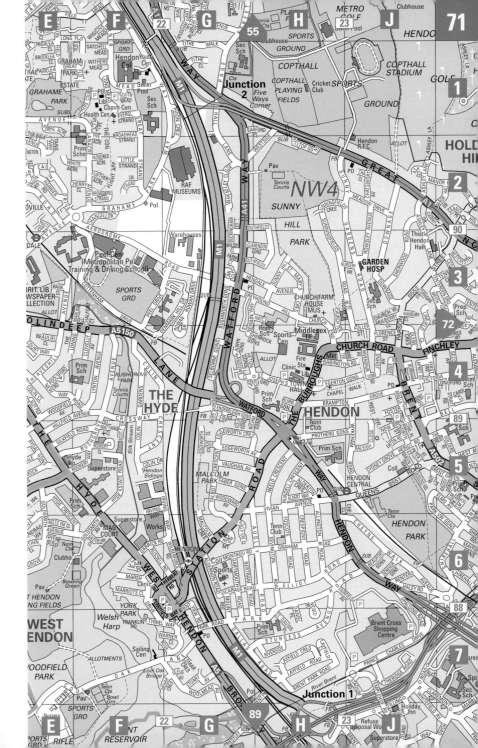

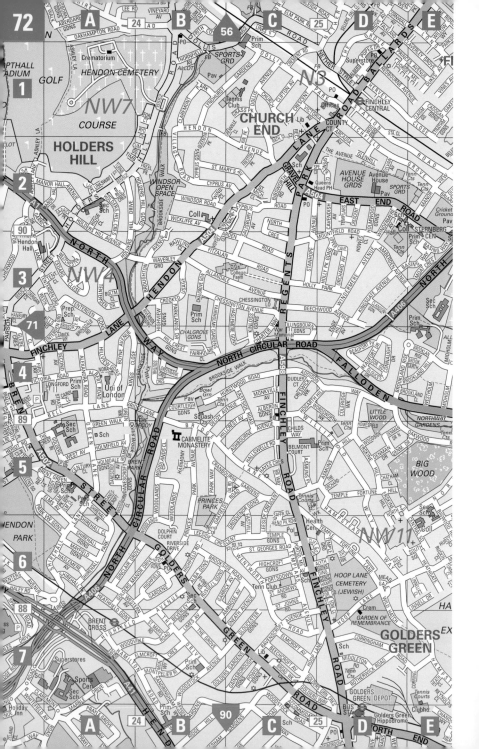

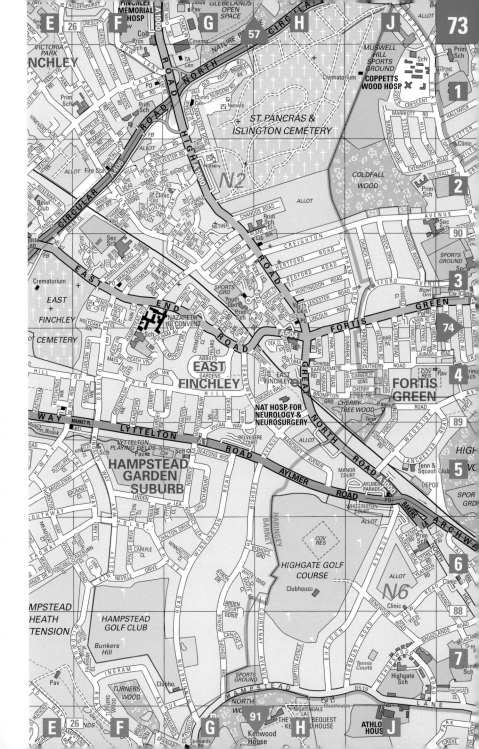

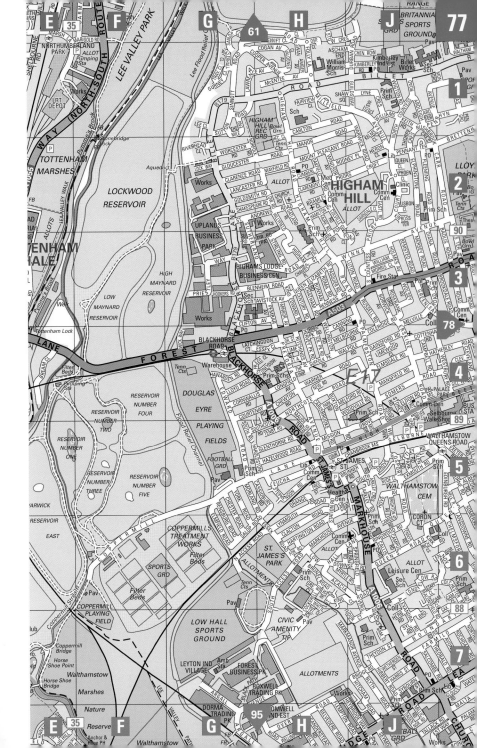

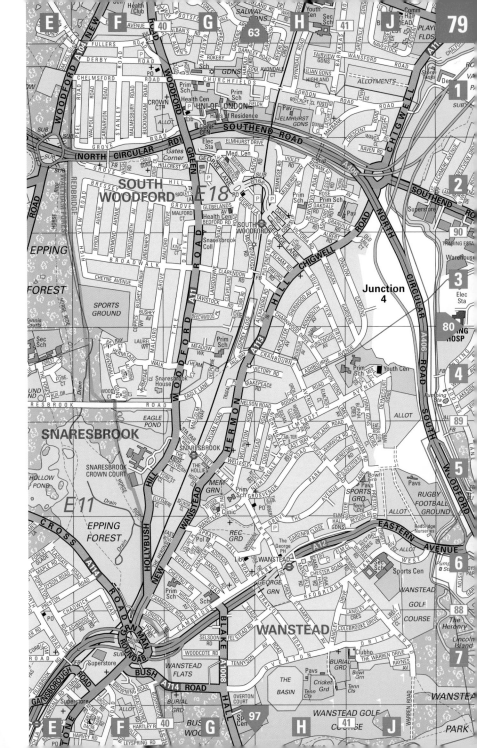

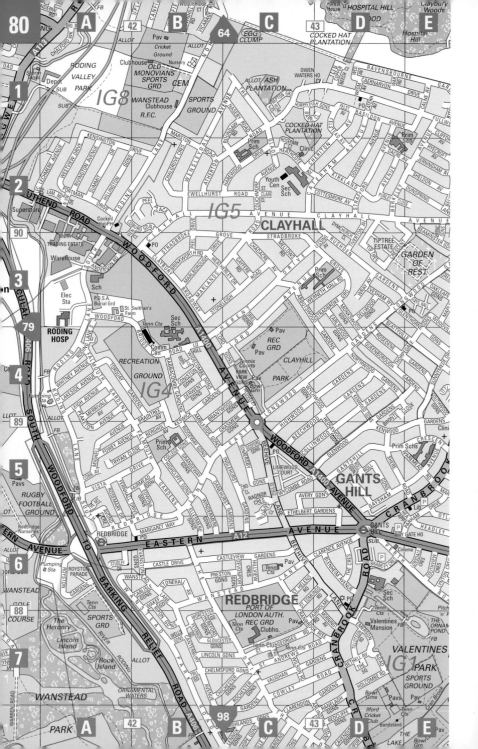

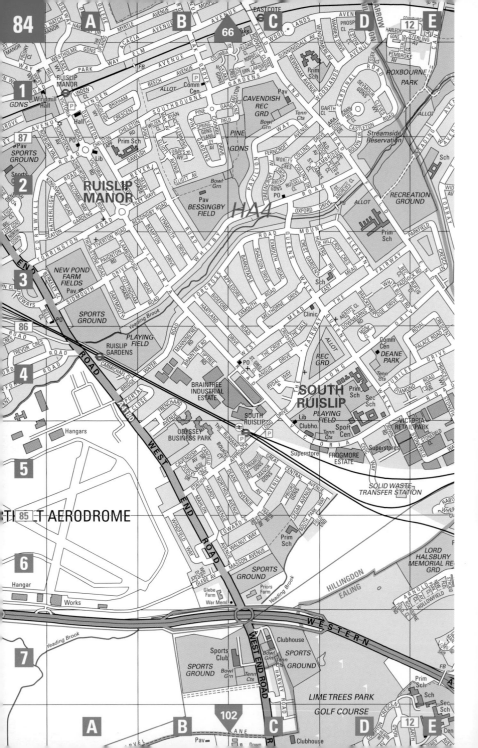

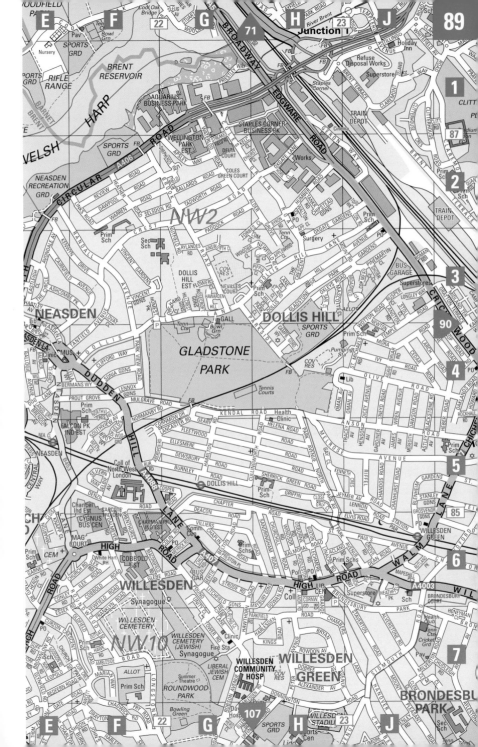

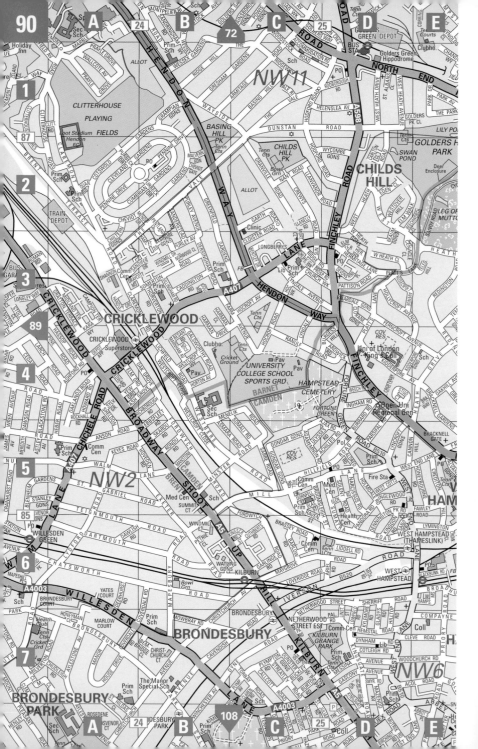

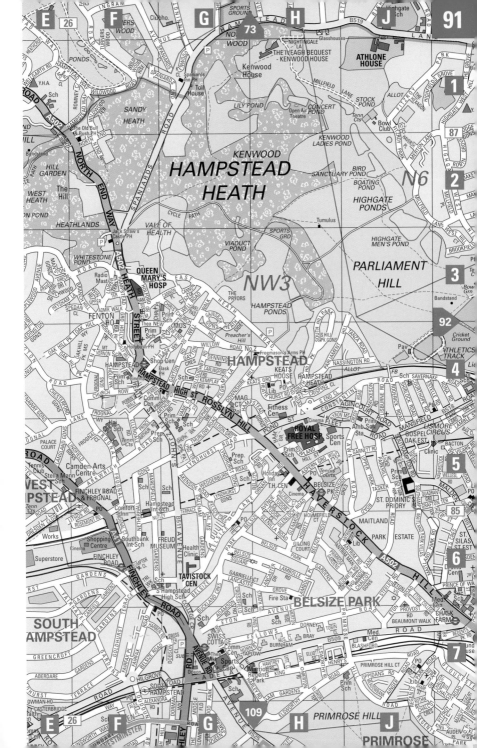

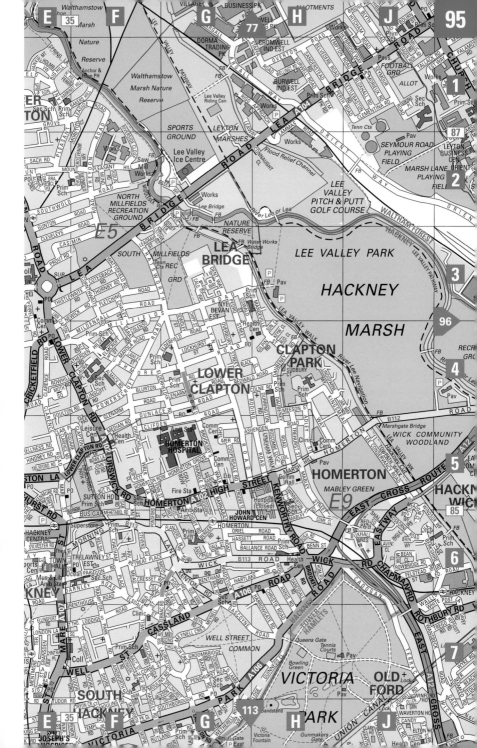

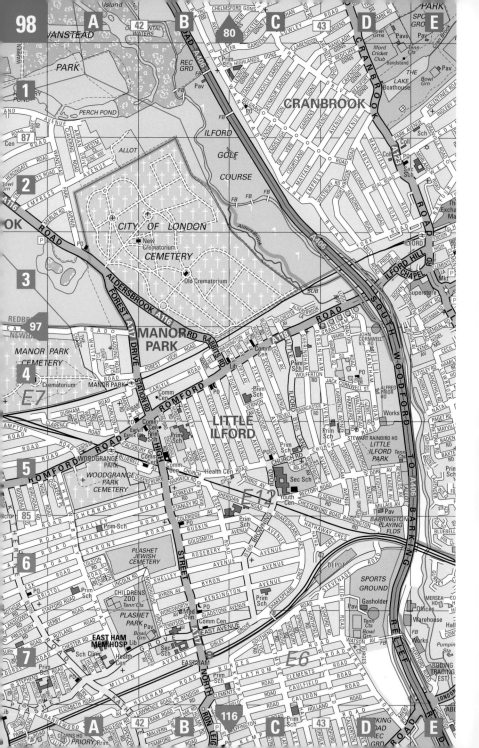

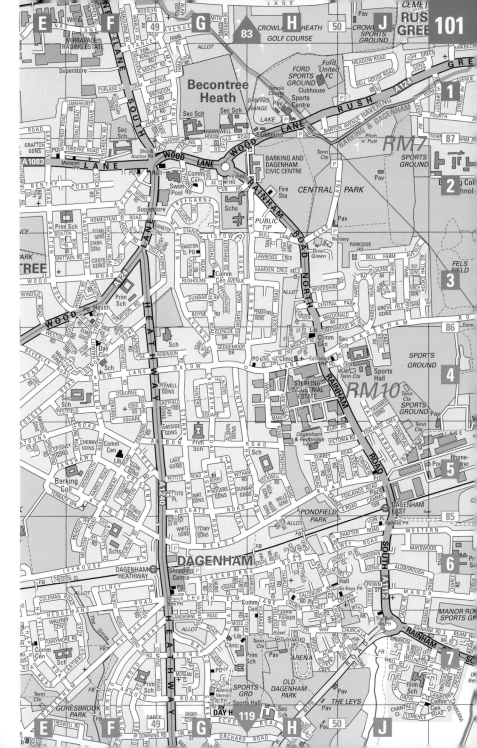

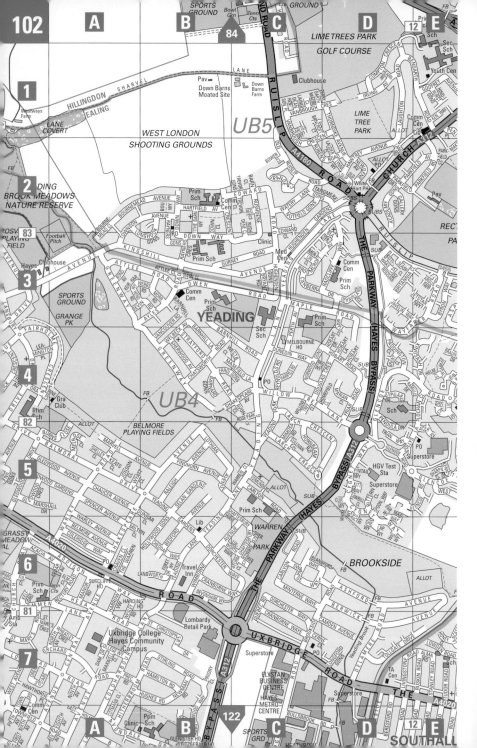

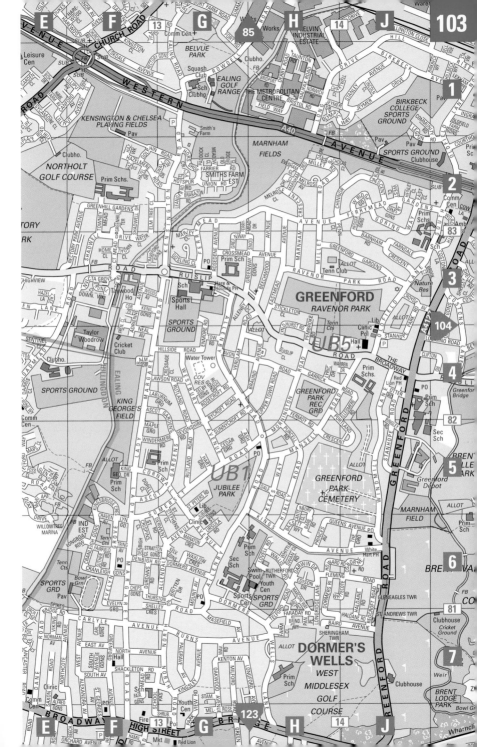

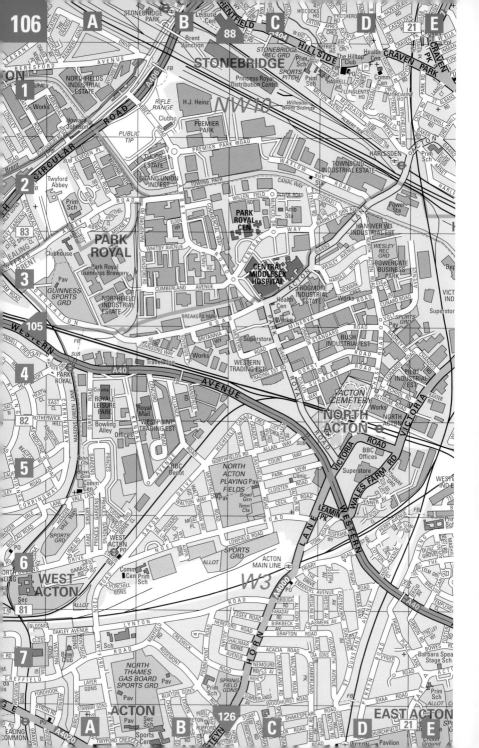

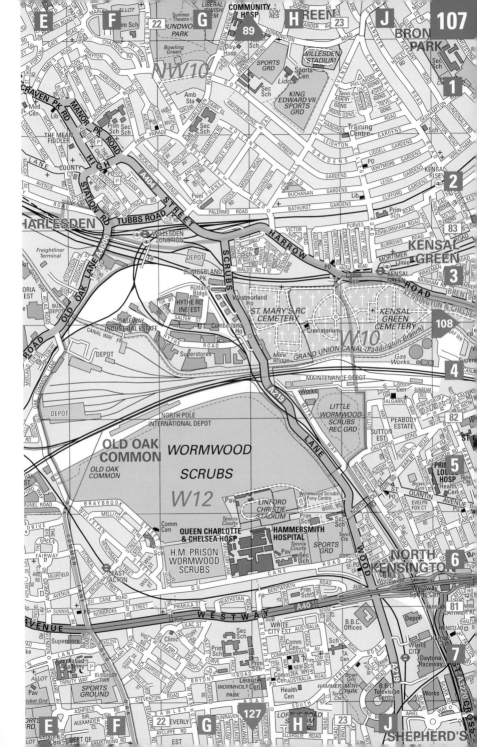

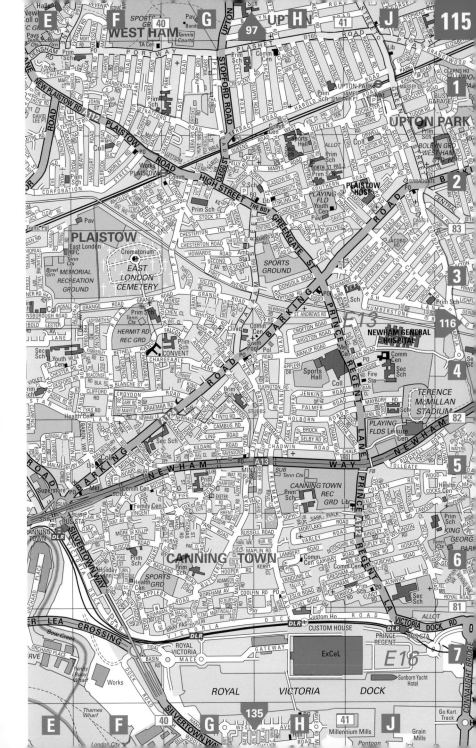

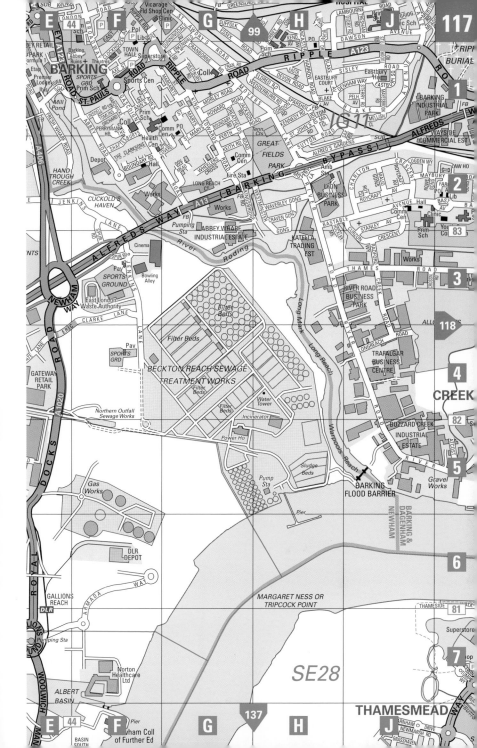

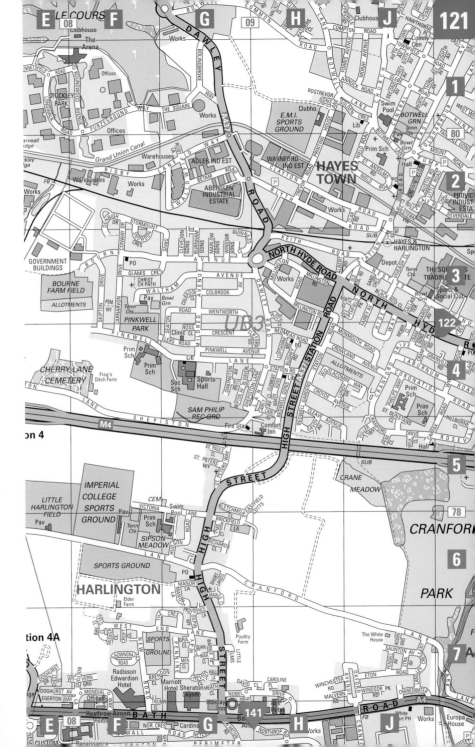

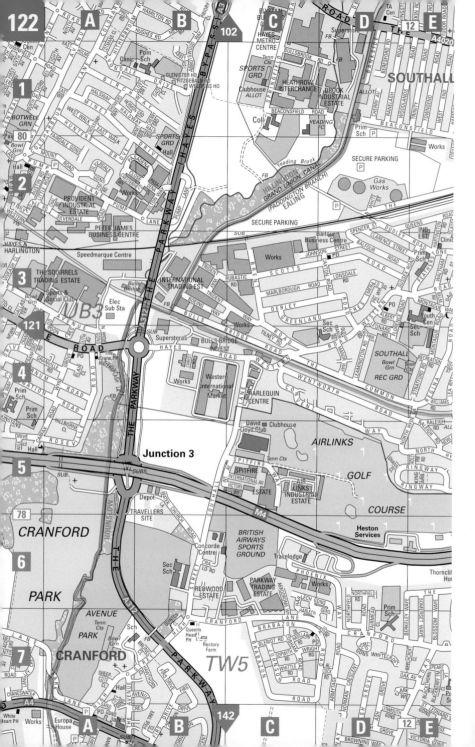

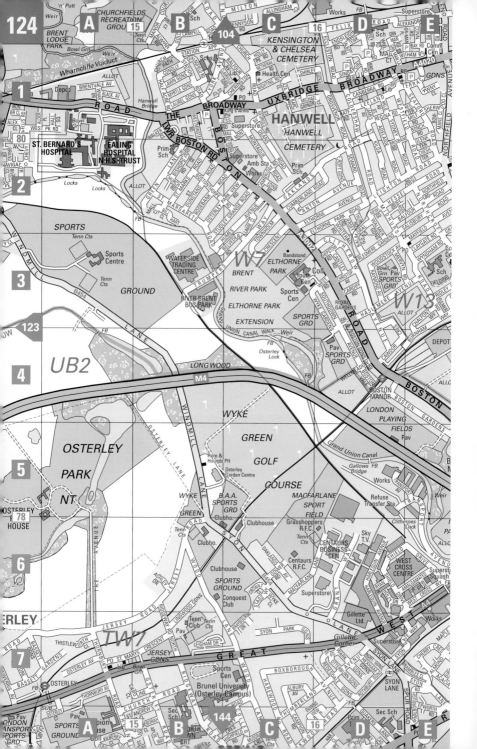

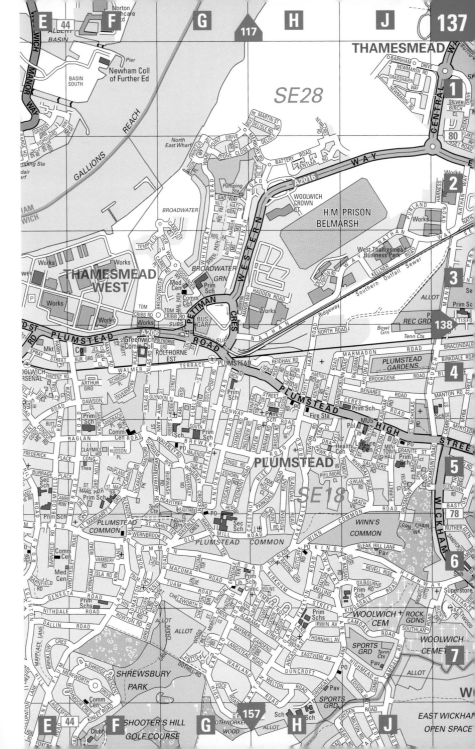

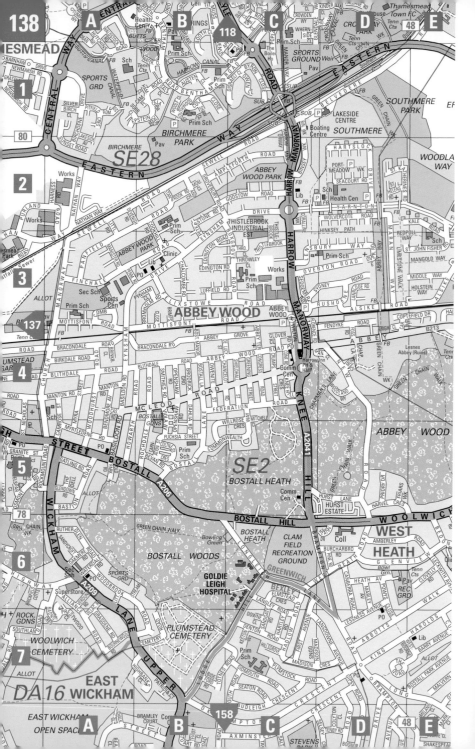

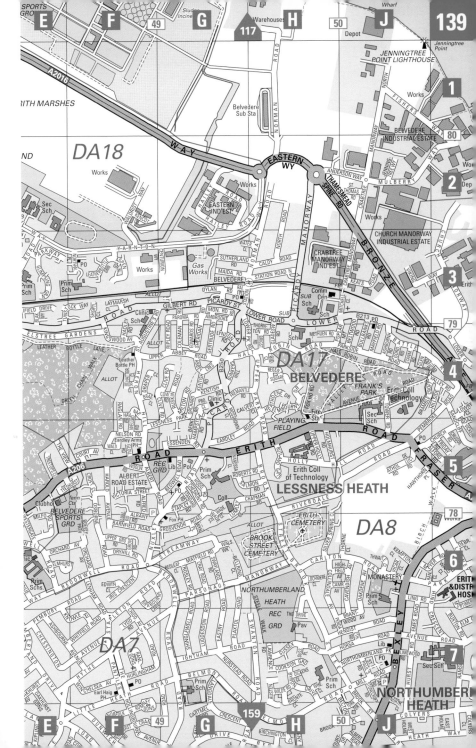

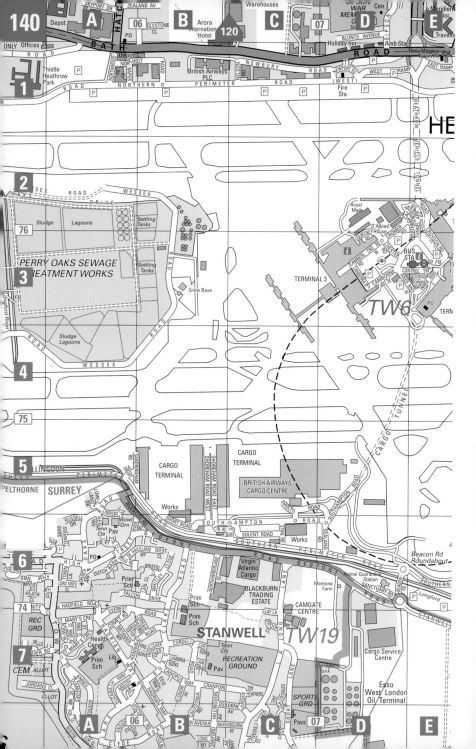

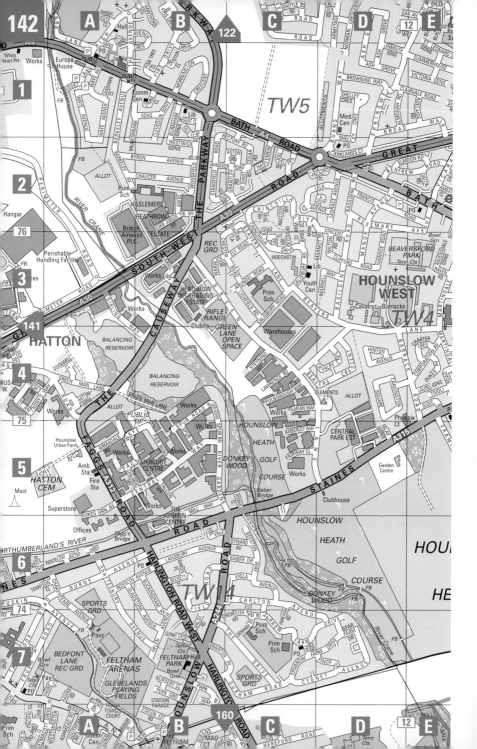

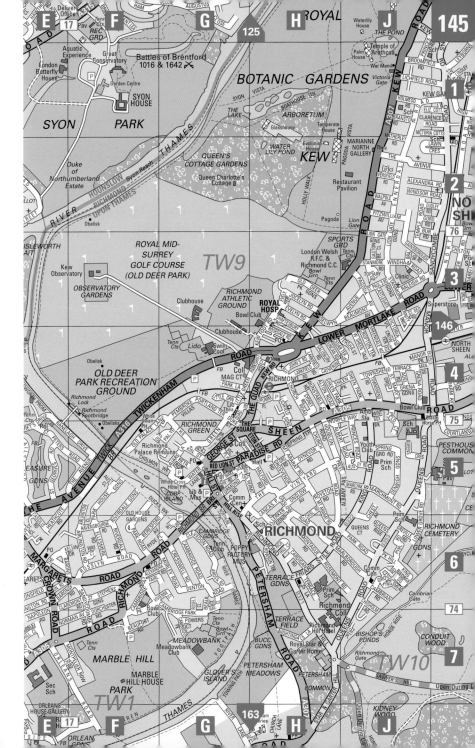

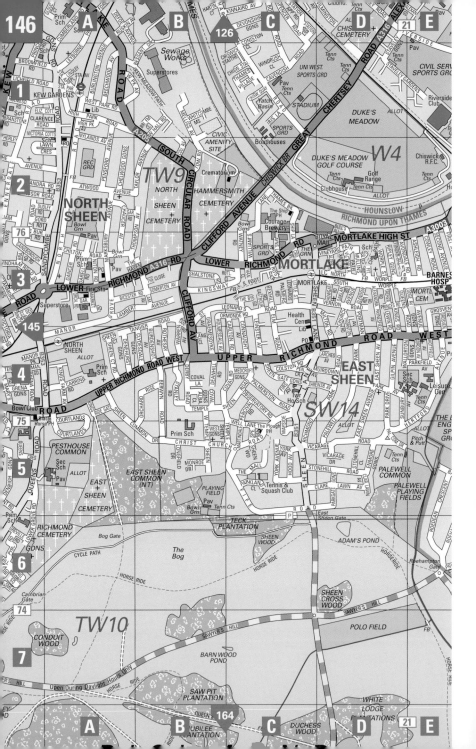

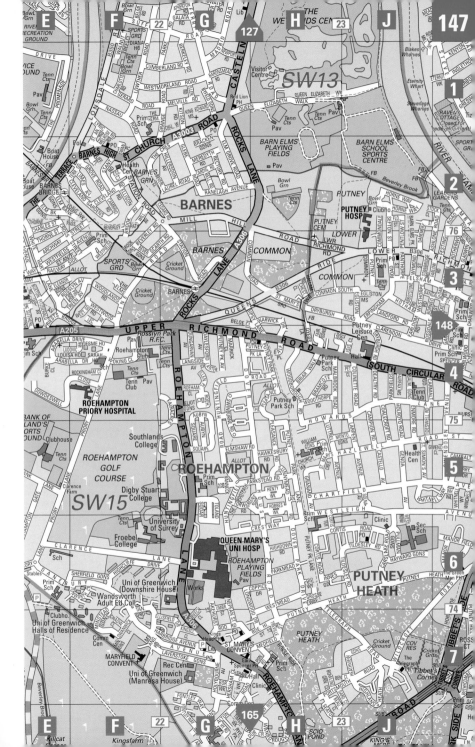

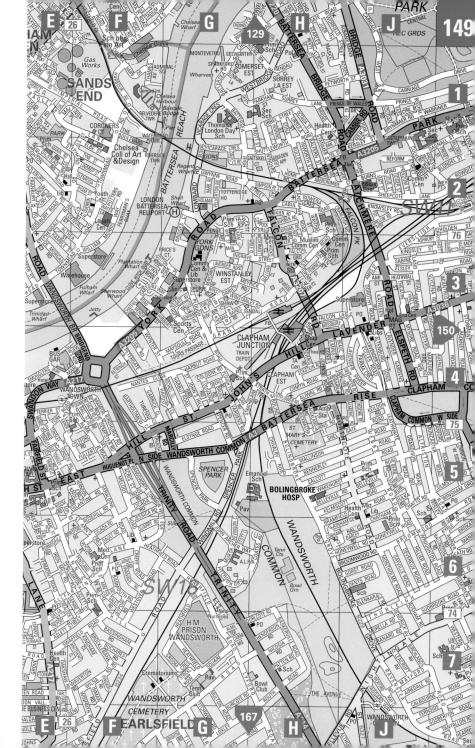

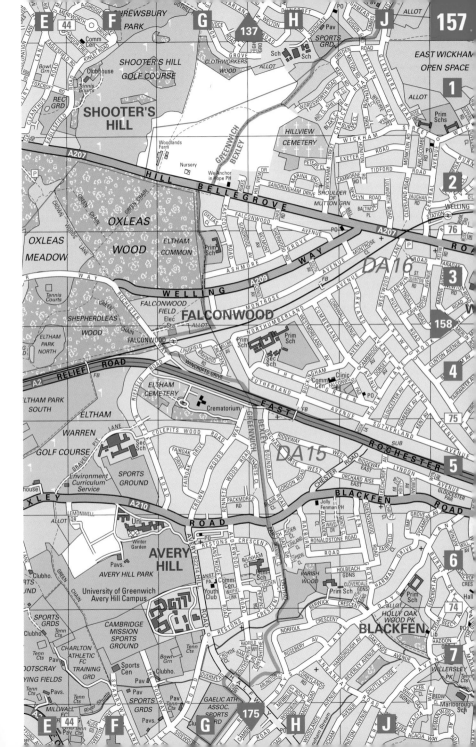

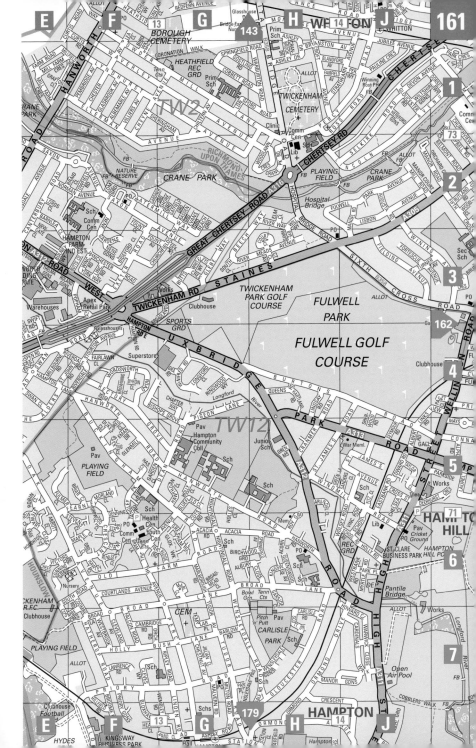

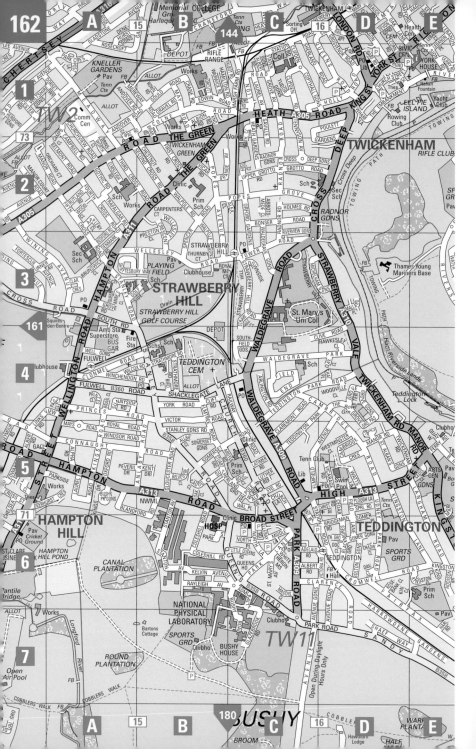

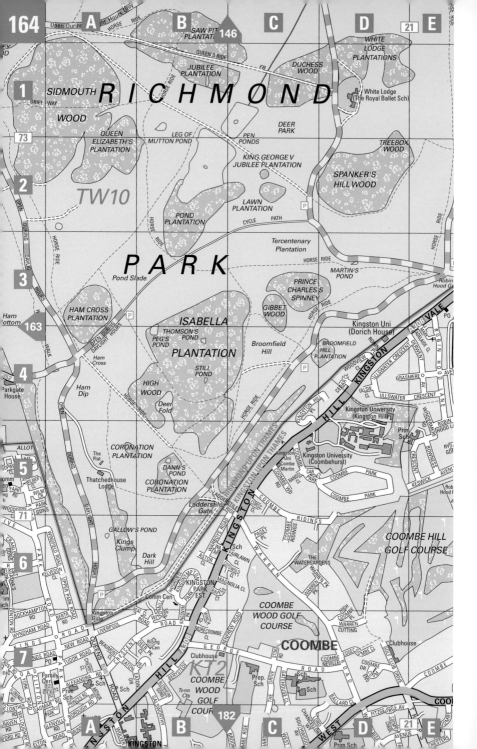

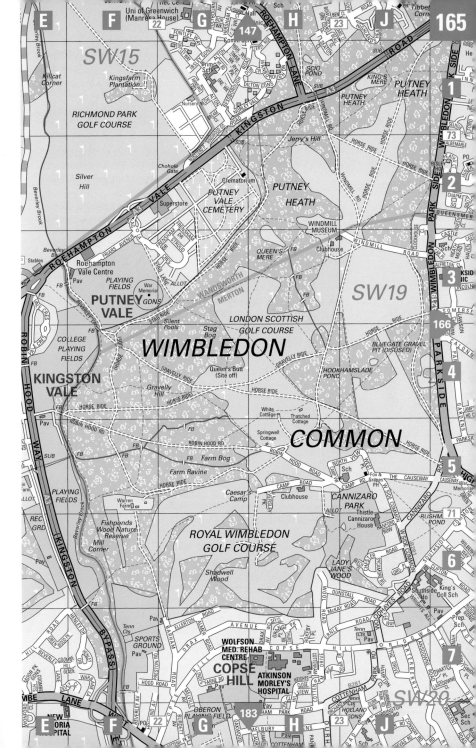

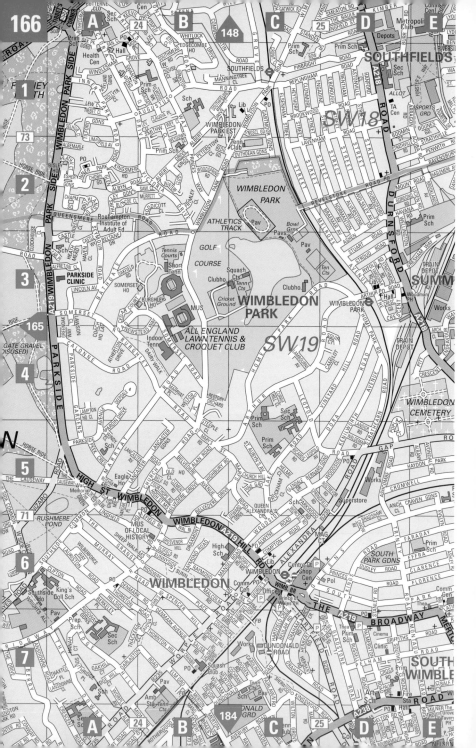

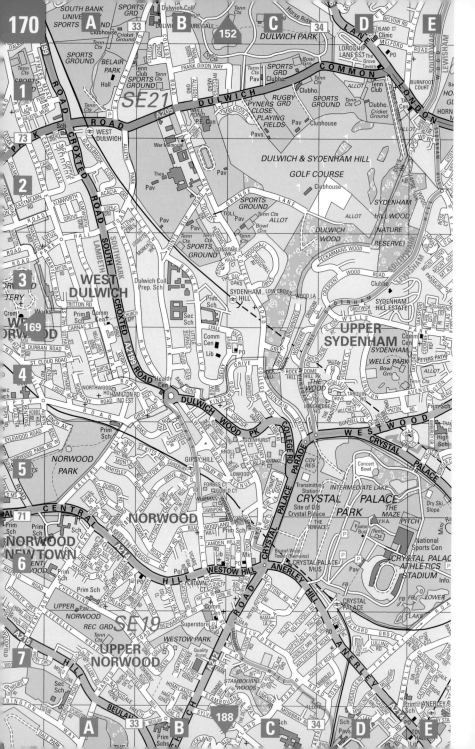

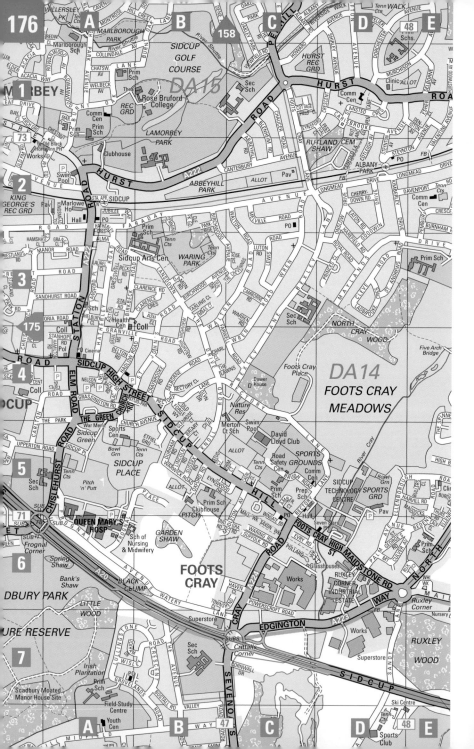

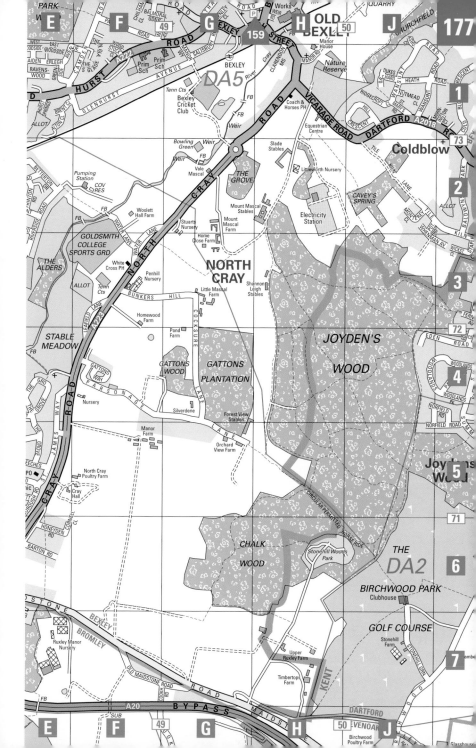

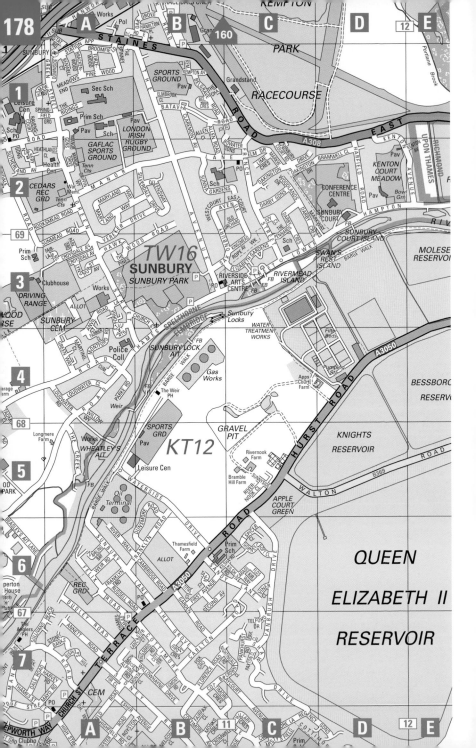

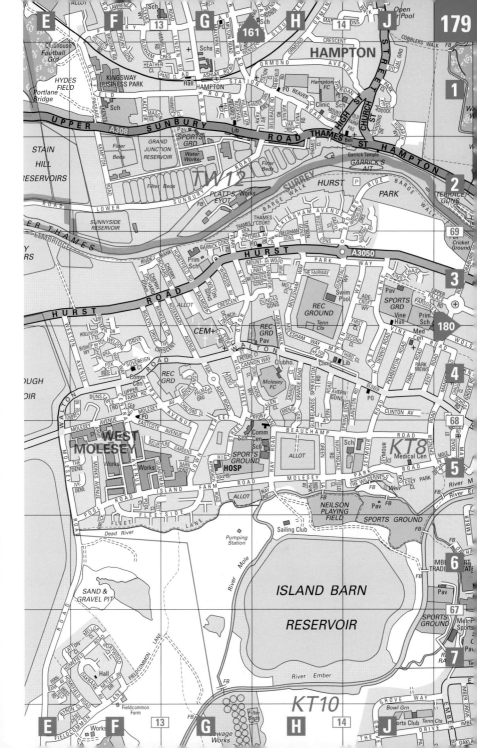

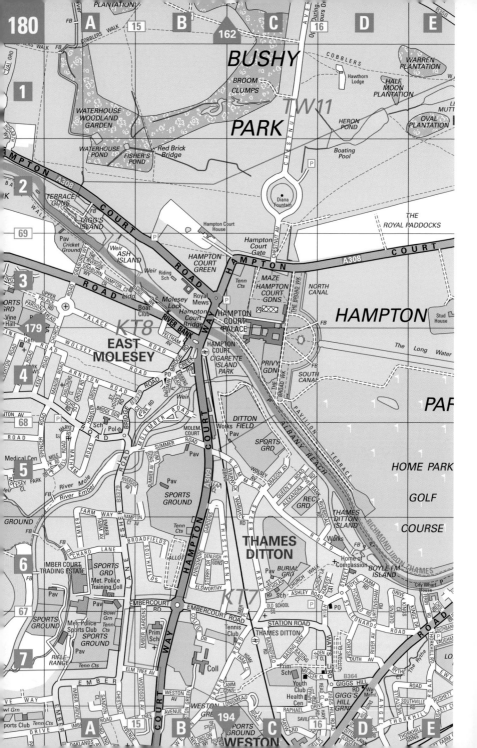

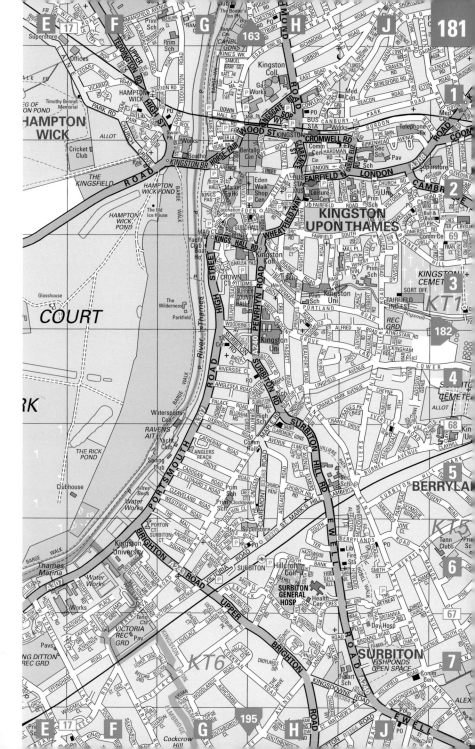

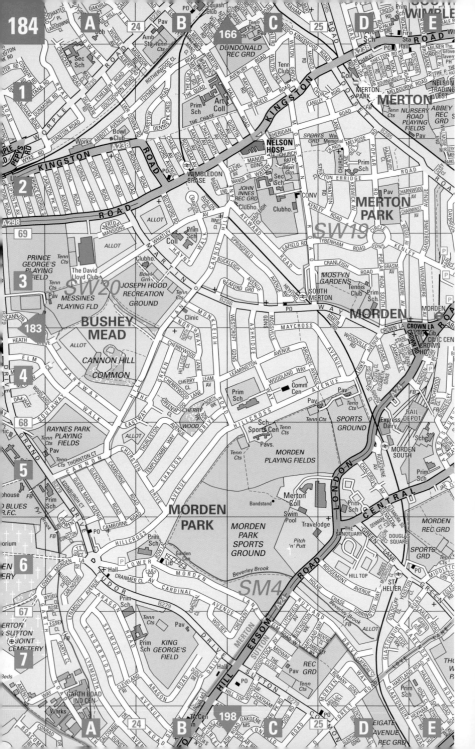

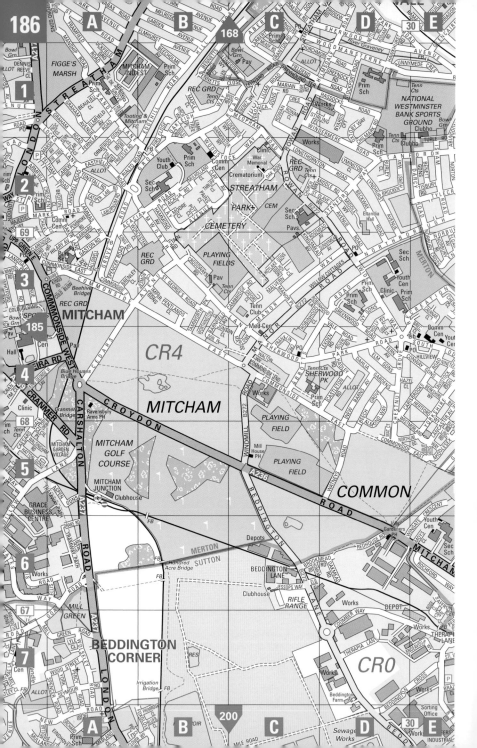

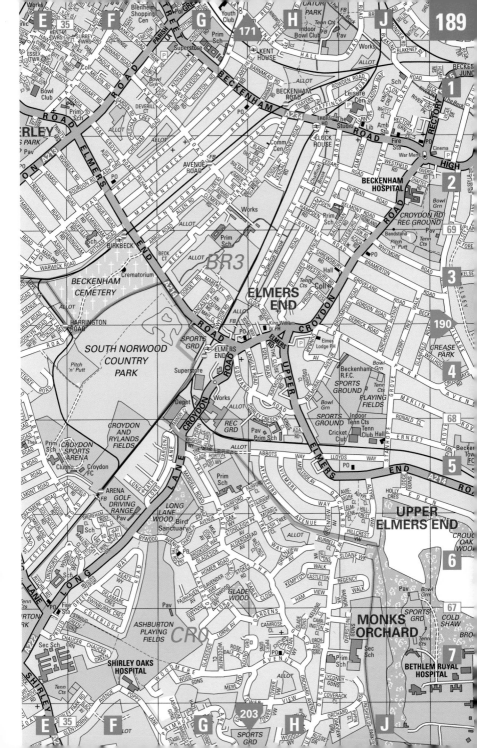

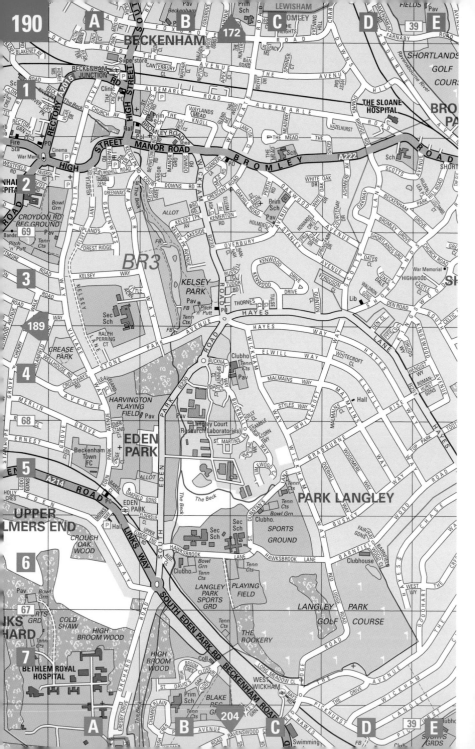

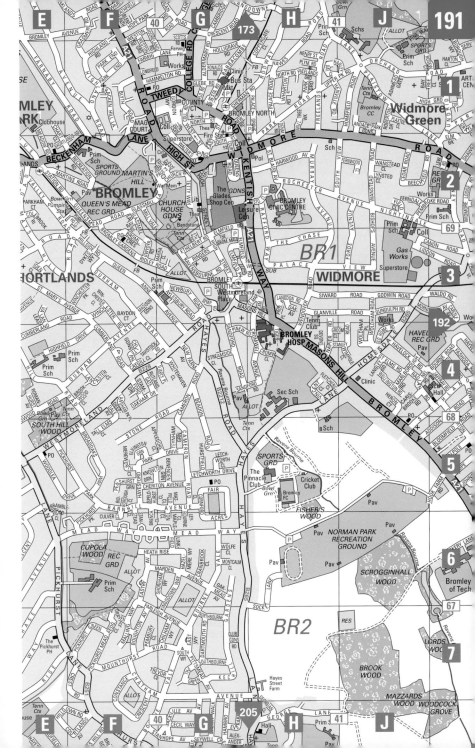

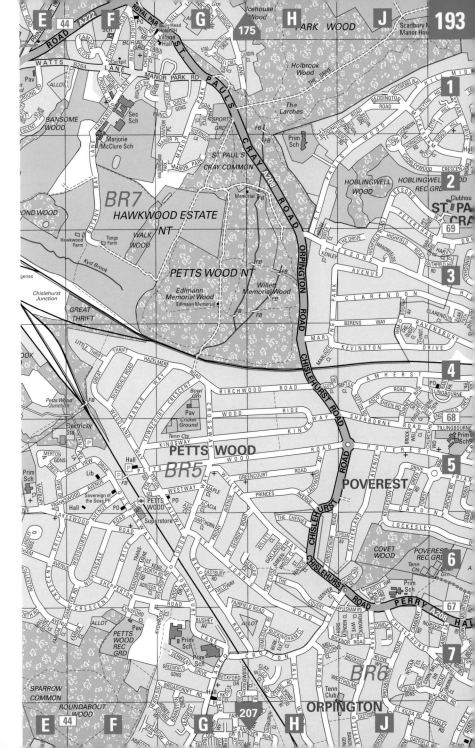

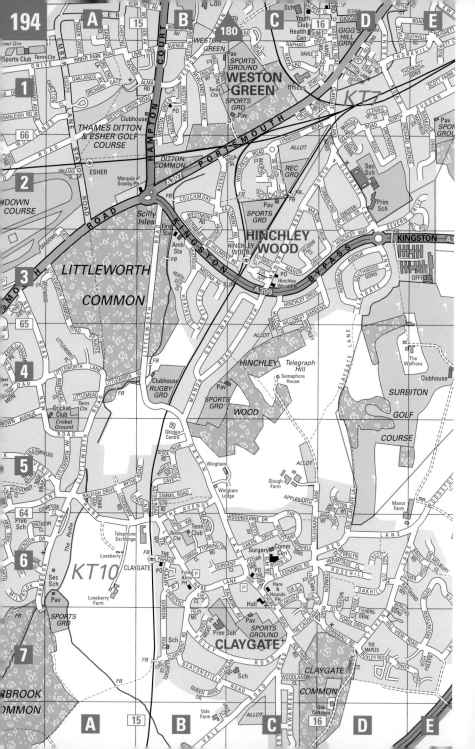

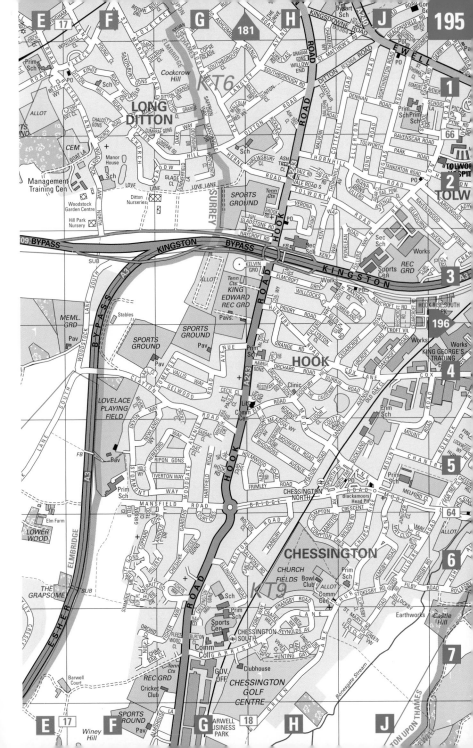

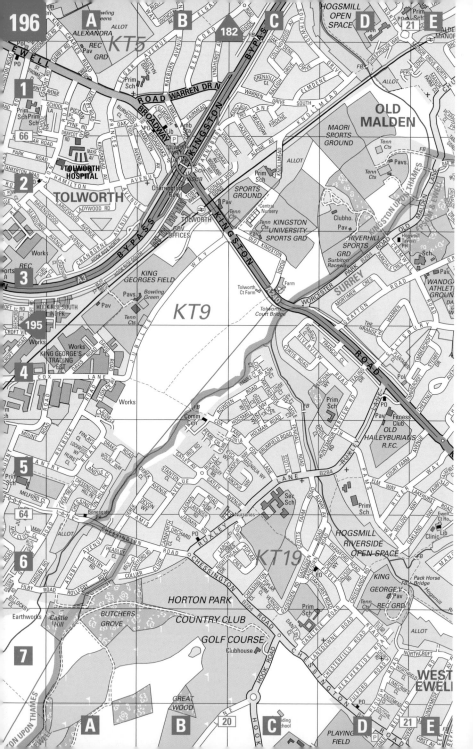

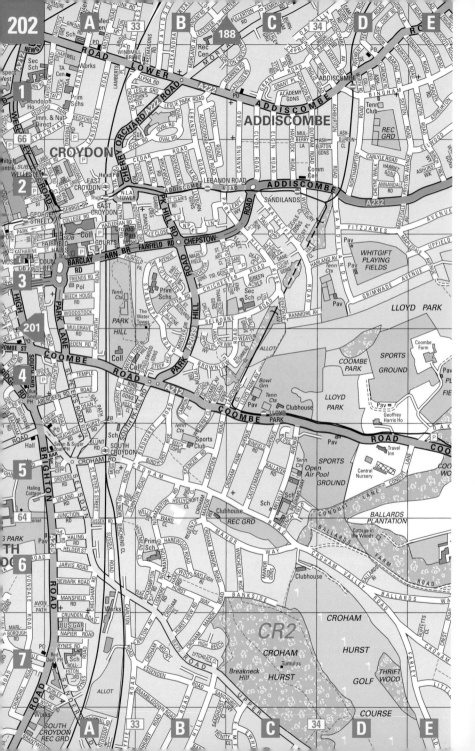

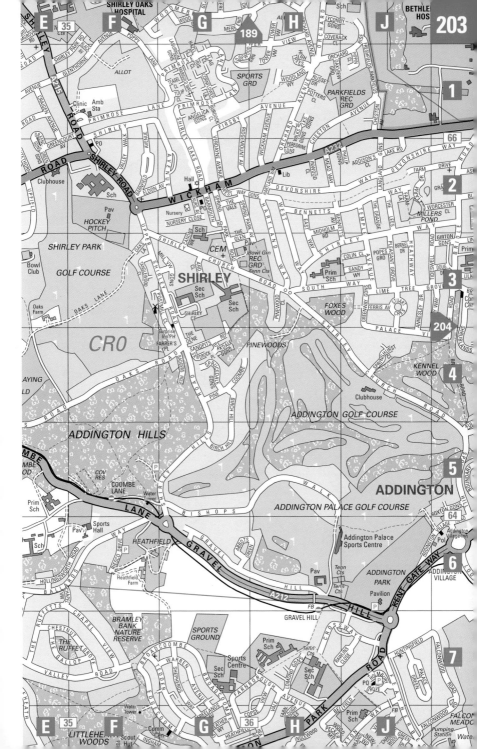

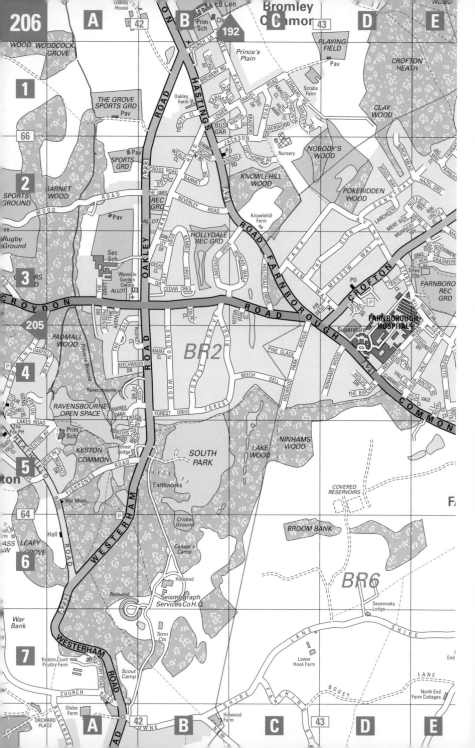

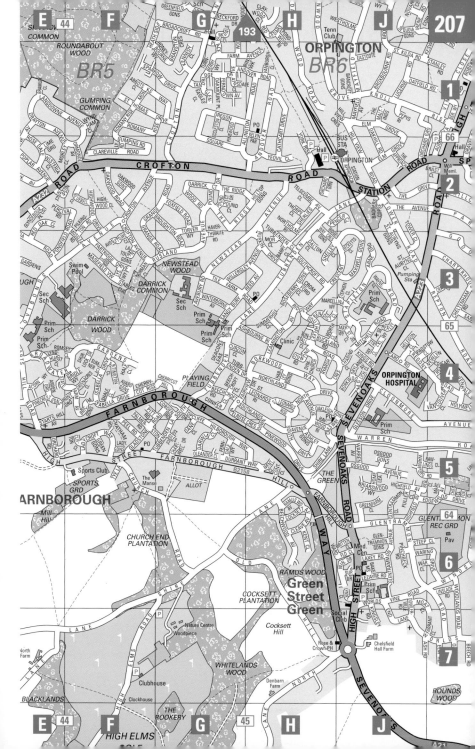

WEST END THEATRES & CINEMAS

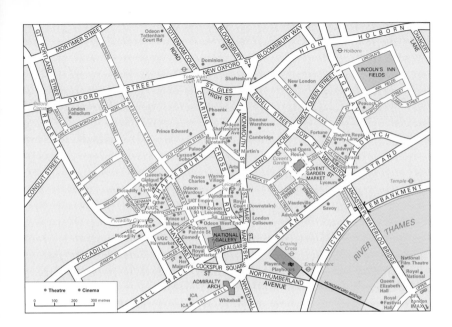

THEATRES

Adelphi *020 7344 0055*
Albery *020 7369 1730*
Aldwych *020 7836 5537*
Apollo *020 7494 5070*
Arts *020 7836 2132*
Cambridge *020 7494 5054*
Comedy *020 7369 1731*
Criterion *020 7839 8811*
Dominion *0870 6077400*
Donmar Warehouse
 020 7369 1732
Duchess *020 7494 5075*
Fortune *020 7369 1747*
Garrick *020 7494 5085*
Gielgud *020 7494 5065*
Her Majesty's *0870 8901 106*
ICA *020 7930 3647*
London Coliseum *020 7632 8300*
London Palladium *020 7494 5020*

Lyceum *0870 6063441*
Lyric *020 7494 5045*
New London *020 7405 0072*
Palace *020 7434 0909*
Peacock *020 7863 8222*
Phoenix *020 7369 1733*
Piccadilly *020 7478 8000*
Players *020 7839 1134*
Playhouse *020 7839 4401*
Prince Edward *020 7447 5400*
Prince of Wales *020 7839 5987*
Queen Elizabeth Hall
 020 7960 4242
Queen's *020 7494 5040*
Royal Court Theatre Downstairs
 (Duke of York) *020 7565 5000*
Royal Court Theatre Upstairs
 (Ambassadors)
 020 7565 5000

Royal Festival Hall
 020 7921 0600
Royal National *020 7452 3000*
Royal Opera House
 020 7304 4000
St. Martin's *020 7836 1443*
Savoy *020 7836 8888*
Shaftesbury *020 7379 5399*
Strand *020 7836 4144*
Theatre Royal, Drury Lane
 020 7494 5060
Theatre Royal, Haymarket
 020 7930 8890
Vaudeville *0870 8900511*
Whitehall *020 7321 5400*
Wyndhams *020 7369 1736*

CINEMAS

ABC Piccadilly *020 7437 3561*
BFI London IMAX
 020 7902 1234
Curzon Soho *020 7734 9209*
ICA *020 7930 3647*
National Film Theatre
 020 7928 3232
Odeon Leicester Sq
 08705 050007
Odeon Panton St
 08705 050007

Odeon Shaftesbury Avenue
 08705 050007
Odeon Tottenham Court Rd
 08705 050007
Odeon Wardour
 08705 050007
Odeon West End
 08705 050007
Other *020 7437 0757*
Prince Charles
 020 7437 7003

UCI Empire Leicester Sq
 08700 102030
UGC Haymarket *08709 070712*
UGC Trocadero *08709 070716*
Warner Village *08702 406020*

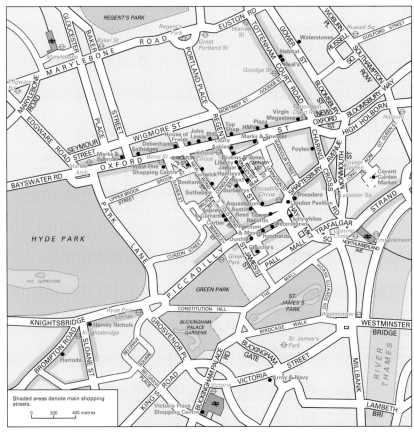

SHOPS

Aquascutum *020 7675 8200*
Army & Navy *020 7834 1234*
Asprey & Garrard
  020 7493 6767
Austin Reed *020 7534 7777*
BHS (Oxford St)
  020 7629 2011
Bonhams *020 7393 3900*
Burberrys *020 7734 4060*
Cartier *020 7408 5700*
Christie's *020 7839 9060*
Covent Garden Market
  020 7836 9136
Debenhams *020 7580 3000*
Dickins & Jones *020 7734 7070*
Dunhill *020 7290 8600*
Fenwick *020 7629 9161*
Fortnum & Mason
  020 7734 8040
Foyles *020 7437 5660*

Habitat (Tottenham Court Rd)
  020 7631 3880
Hamleys *0870 333 2455*
Harrods *020 7730 1234*
Harvey Nichols *020 7235 5000*
Hatchards *020 7439 9921*
Heal's *020 7636 1666*
HMV *020 7631 3423*
House of Fraser *020 7529 4700*
Jaeger *020 7734 8211*
John Lewis *020 7629 7711*
Laura Ashley (Regent St)
  020 7355 1363
Liberty *020 7734 1234*
Lillywhites *020 7930 3181*
London Pavilion
  020 7437 1838
Marks & Spencer
  (Marble Arch) *020 7935 4422*
Marks & Spencer Pantheon
  (Oxford St) *020 7437 7722*

Next (Regent St)
  020 7434 2515
Plaza Shopping Centre, Oxford
St
  020 7637 8811
Selfridges *0870 377377*
Sotheby's *020 7293 5000*
Top Shop & Top Man
  020 7636 7700
Tower Records *020 7439 2500*
Trocadero *09068 881100*
Victoria Place Shopping
  Centre *020 7931 8811*
Virgin Megastore
  020 7631 1234
Waterstones (Gower St)
  020 7636 1577
Waterstones (Picadilly)
  020 7851 2400

INDEX

How to use this index

This index combines entries for street names, place names and places of interest.

Place names are shown in capital letters,
e.g. **ACTON**, W3 . . . .**126** A1
These include towns, villages and localities within the area covered by this atlas.

Places of interest are shown with a star symbol,
e.g. ★ **British Mus**, WC1 . . . . .**18** A2
These include parks, museums, galleries, and other important buildings or locations of tourist interest.

All other entries are for street names. When there is more than one street with exactly the same name then that name is shown only once in the index. It is then followed by a list of entries for each postal district that contains a street with that same name. For example, there are three streets called Appleby Close in this atlas and the index entry shows that one of these is in London postal district E4, one is in London postal district N15 and one is in Twickenham, TW2.

Appleby Cl, E4 . . . .**62** C6
N15 . . . .**76** A5
Twickenham TW2 . . . . .**162** A2

All entries are followed by the page number and grid reference on which the name will be found. So, in the example above, **Appleby Close,** E4 will be found on page **62** in square C6. All entries are indexed to the largest scale map on which they are shown.

The index also contains some street names which are not actually shown on the maps because there is not enough space to name them. In these cases the adjoining or nearest named thoroughfare to such streets is shown in the index in *italics,* and the reference indicates where the unnamed street is located *off* the named thoroughfare.

e.g. **Bacton St**, E2
off Roman Rd **113** F3

This means that Bacton Street is not named on the map, but it is located *off* Roman Road on page **113** in square F3.

A strict letter-by-letter alphabetical order is followed in this index. All non-alphabetic characters such as spaces, hyphens or apostrophes are not included in the index order. For example Belle Vue Road and Bellevue Road will be found listed together.

Standard terms such as Avenue, Close, Rise and Road are abbreviated in the index but are ordered alphabetically as if given in full. So, for example, **Abbots Ri** comes before **Abbots Rd**.

Names beginning with a definite article (i.e. The) are indexed from their second word onwards with the article being placed at the end of the name,
e.g. **Avenue, The**, E4 . . . .**62** D6

The alphabetical order extends to include postal information so that where two or more streets have exactly the same name, London postal district references are given first in alpha-numeric order and are followed by non-London post town references in alphabetical order, e.g. Appleby Close, E4 is followed by Appleby Close, N15 and then Appleby Close, Twickenham TW2.

In cases where there are two or more streets of the same name in the same postal area, extra information is given in brackets to aid location. For example, High St, Orpington BR6 (Farnborough), and High St, Orpington BR6 (Green St Grn), distinguishes between two streets called High Street which are both in the post town of Orpington, within the same postal district of BR6.

Extra locational information is also given for some localities within large post towns. This is also to aid location.
e.g. **Alford Grn**, Croy. (New Adgtn.) CR0

This street is within the locality of New Addington which is part of the post town of Croydon, and it is within postal district CR0.

A full list of locality and post town abbreviations used in this atlas is given below.

General abbreviations

All	Alley	Cem	Cemetery	Cors	Corners
Allot	Allotments	Cen	Central, Centre	Cotts	Cottages
Amb	Ambulance	Cft	Croft	Cov	Covered
App	Approach	Cfts	Crofts	Crem	Crematorium
Arc	Arcade	Ch	Church	Cres	Crescent
Av	Avenue	Chyd	Churchyard	Ct	Court
Bdy	Broadway	Cin	Cinema	Cts	Courts
Bk	Bank	Circ	Circus	Ctyd	Courtyard
Bldgs	Buildings	Cl	Close	Dep	Depot
Boul	Boulevard	Co	County	Dev	Development
Bowl	Bowling	Coll	College	Dr	Drive
Br	Bridge	Comm	Community	Dws	Dwellings
C of E	Church of	Conv	Convent	E	East
	England	Cor	Corner	Ed	Education
Cath	Cathedral	Coron	Coroners	Elec	Electricity

Abbr	Expansion	Abbr	Expansion	Abbr	Expansion
Embk	Embankment	Lwr	Lower	Shop	Shopping
Est	Estate	Mag	Magistrates	Sq	Square
Ex	Exchange	Mans	Mansions	St.	Saint
Exhib	Exhibition	Mem	Memorial	St	Street
FB	Footbridge	Mkt	Market	Sta	Station
FC	Football Club	Mkts	Markets	Sts	Streets
Fld	Field	Ms	Mews	Sub	Subway
Flds	Fields	Mt	Mount	Swim	Swimming
Fm	Farm	Mus	Museum	TA	Territorial Army
Gall	Gallery	N	North	TH	Town Hall
Gar	Garage	NT	National Trust	Tenn	Tennis
Gdn	Garden	Nat	National	Ter	Terrace
Gdns	Gardens	PH	Public House	Thea	Theatre
Gen	General	PO	Post Office	Trd	Trading
Govt	Government	Par	Parade	Twr	Tower
Gra	Grange	Pas	Passage	Twrs	Towers
Grd	Ground	Pav	Pavilion	Uni	University
Grds	Grounds	Pk	Park	Vil	Villas
Grn	Green	Pl	Place	Vil	Villa
Grns	Greens	Pol	Police	Vw	View
Gro	Grove	Prec	Precinct	W	West
Gros	Groves	Prim	Primary	Wd	Wood
Gt	Great	Prom	Promenade	Wds	Woods
Ho	House	Pt	Point	Wf	Wharf
Hos	Houses	Quad	Quadrant	Wk	Walk
Hosp	Hospital	RC	Roman Catholic	Wks	Works
Hts	Heights	Rd	Road	Yd	Yard
Ind	Industrial	Rds	Roads		
Int	International	Rec	Recreation		
Junct	Junction	Res	Reservoir		
La	Lane	Ri	Rise		
Las	Lanes	S	South		
Lib	Library	Sch	School		
Lo	Lodge	Sec	Secondary		

Locality and post town abbreviations

In the list of abbreviations shown below, post towns are in **bold** type

Bark.	Barking	Harm.	Harmondsworth	Rich.	**Richmond**
Barn.	Barnet	Hatt.Cr.	Hatton Cross	Rod.Val.	Roding Valley
Barne.	Barnehurst	High Barn.	High Barnet	Rom.	**Romford**
Beck.	Beckenham	Highams Pk.	Highams Park	Ruis.	**Ruislip**
Bedd.	Beddington	Hinch.Wd.	Hinchley Wood	S.Croy.	**South Croydon**
Bedd.Cor.	Beddington Corner	Hmptn.	**Hampton**	S.Har.	South Harrow
Belv.	**Belvedere**	Hmptn.H.	Hampton Hill	S.Norwood	South Norwood
Bex.	**Bexley**	Hmptn.W.	Hampton Wick	S.Oxhey	South Oxhey
Bexh.	**Bexleyheath**	Houns.	**Hounslow**	S.Ruis.	South Ruislip
Borwd.	**Borehamwood**	Houns.W.	Hounslow West	Scad.Pk.	Scadbury Park
Brent.	**Brentford**	Hthrw.Air.	Heathrow Airport	Short.	Shortlands
Brom.	**Bromley**	Hthrw.Air.N.	Heathrow Airport North	Sid.	**Sidcup**
Buck.H.	**Buckhurst Hill**			St.P.Cray	St. Paul's Cray
Bushey Hth.	Bushey Heath	Ilf.	**Ilford**	Stai.	**Staines**
Carp.Pk.	Carpenders Park	Islw.	**Isleworth**	Stan.	**Stanmore**
Cars.	**Carshalton**	Kes.	**Keston**	Stanw.	Stanwell
Chad.Hth.	Chadwell Heath	Kings.T.	**Kingston upon Thames**	Sthl.	**Southall**
Chess.	**Chessington**			Sthl.Grn.	Southall Green
Chig.	**Chigwell**	Long Dit.	Long Ditton	Sun.	**Sunbury-on-Thames**
Chis.	**Chislehurst**	Loug.	**Loughton**		
Clay.	Claygate	Lt.Hth.	Little Heath	Surb.	**Surbiton**
Cockfos.	Cockfosters	Lwr. Sydenham	Lower Sydenham	Sutt.	**Sutton**
Coll.Row	Collier Row			T.Ditt.	**Thames Ditton**
Cran.	Cranford	Mitch.	**Mitcham**	Tedd.	**Teddington**
Croy.	**Croydon**	Mord.	**Morden**	Th.Hth.	**Thornton Heath**
Dag.	**Dagenham**	Mots.Pk.	Motspur Park	They.B.	Theydon Bois
Dart.	**Dartford**	N.Finchley	North Finchley	Tkgtn.	Tokyngton
E.Bed.	East Bedfont	N.Har.	North Harrow	Twick.	**Twickenham**
E.Croy.	East Croydon	N.Mal.	**New Malden**	Uxb.	**Uxbridge**
E.Mol.	**East Molesey**	New Adgtn.	New Addington	W.Croy.	West Croydon
Eastcote Vill.	Eastcote Village	New Barn.	New Barnet	W.Ewell	West Ewell
Edg.	**Edgware**	Northumb. Hth.	Northumberland Heath	W.Mol.	**West Molesey**
Elm.Wds.	Elmstead Woods	Norwood Junct.	Norwood Junction	W.Wick.	**West Wickham**
Enf.	**Enfield**			Wall.	**Wallington**
Epp.	**Epping**	Nthlt.	**Northolt**	Walt.	**Walton-on-Thames**
Farnboro.	Farnborough	Nthwd.	**Northwood**	Wat.	**Watford**
Felt.	**Feltham**	Orp.	**Orpington**	Wdf.Grn.	**Woodford Green**
Grn.St.Grn.	Green Street Green	Petts Wd	Petts Wood	Well.	**Welling**
Grnf.	**Greenford**	Pnr.	**Pinner**	Wem.	**Wembley**
Hackbr.	Hackbridge	Pond.End	Ponders End	West Dr.	**West Drayton**
Han.	Hanworth	Pot.B.	**Potters Bar**	Wldste.	Wealdstone
Har.	**Harrow**	Pur.	**Purley**	Woodside Pk.	Woodside Park
Har.Hill	Harrow on the Hill	Rain.	**Rainham**	Wor.Pk.	**Worcester Park**
Har.Wld.	Harrow Weald			Yiew.	Yiewsley

02 Shop Cen, NW3
off Finchley Rd 91 F6

A

Aaron Hill Rd, E6 . . . . . . .116 D5
Abberley Ms, SW4
off Cedars Rd 150 B3
Abbess Cl, E6
off Oliver Gdns 116 B5
SW2 . . . . .169 H1
Abbeville Rd, N8
off Barrington Rd 74 D4
SW4 . . . . .150 C6
Abbey Av, Wem. HA0 . . .105 H2
Abbey Business Cen, SW8
off Ingate Pl 150 B1
Abbey Cl, Hayes UB3 . .122 B1
Northolt UB5
off Invicta Gro 103 F3
Pinner HA5 . . . . .66 B3
Abbey Cres, Belv. DA17 .139 G4
Abbeydale Rd, Wem.
HA0 . . . . .106 A1
Abbey Dr, SW17
off Church La 168 A5
Abbeyfield Rd, SE16 . . .133 F4
Abbeyfields Cl, NW10 . .106 A2
Abbey Gdns, NW8 . . . . . . .6 C2
SE16 . . . . .37 J1
W6 . . . . .128 B6
Chislehurst BR7 . . . . .192 D1
Abbey Gro, SE2 . . . . . . .138 B4
Abbeyhill Rd, Sid. DA15 .176 C2
Abbey Ind Est, Mitch.
CR4 . . . . .185 J5
Wembley HA0 . . . . . . .105 J1
Abbey La, E15 . . . . .114 C2
Beckenham BR3 . . . . .172 A7
Abbey Ms, E17
off Leamington Av 78 A5
Abbey Orchard St, SW1 . .25 J5
Abbey Par, SW19
off Merton High St . . .167 F7
W5 off Hanger La 105 J3
Abbey Pk, Beck. BR3 . . .172 A7
Abbey Retail Pk, Bark.
IG11 . . . . .117 E1
Abbey Rd, E15 . . . . .114 E2
NW6 . . . . .90 E7
NW8 . . . . .109 F2
NW10 . . . . .106 B2
SE2 . . . . .138 D4
SW19 . . . . .167 F7
Barking IG11 . . . . .99 E2
Belvedere DA17 . . . . .138 D4
Bexleyheath DA7 . . . .159 E4
Croydon CR0 . . . . . . .201 H3
Enfield EN1 . . . . .44 B5
Ilford IG2 . . . . .81 G5
Abbey Rd Est, NW8 . . . .109 E1
Abbey St, E13 . . . . .115 G4
SE1 . . . . .28 E5
Abbey Ter, SE2 . . . . .138 C4
Abbey Vw, NW7 . . . . .55 F3
Abbey Wk, W.Mol. KT8 . .179 H3
Abbey Way, SE2 . . . . . . .138 D3
Abbey Wf Ind Est, Bark.
IG11 . . . . .117 G2
ABBEY WOOD, SE2 . . . .138 B3
Abbey Wd Rd, SE2 . . . . .138 B4
Abbotsbury Cl, E15 . . . .114 C2
W14
off Abbotsbury Rd . . .128 C2
Abbotsbury Gdns, Pnr.
HA5 . . . . .66 C6
Abbotsbury Ms, SE15 . .153 F3
Abbotsbury Rd, W14 . . .128 B2
Bromley BR2 . . . . . . .205 F2
Morden SM4 . . . . .184 E5
Abbots Cl, N1
off Alwyne Rd 93 J6
Orpington BR5 . . . . . .207 F1
Ruislip HA4 . . . . .84 D3
Abbots Dr, Har. HA2 . . . .85 G2
Abbotsford Av, N15 . . . . .75 J4
Abbotsford Gdns, Wdf.Grn.
IG8 . . . . .63 G7
Abbotsford Rd, Ilf. IG3 . .100 A3
Abbots Gdns, N2 . . . . . . .73 G4
W8 . . . . .22 A6
Abbots Grn, Croy. CR0 . .203 G6
Abbotshade Rd, SE16 . .133 G1
Abbotshall Av, N14 . . . . .58 C3
Abbotshall Rd, SE6 . . . .172 D1
Abbots La, SE1 . . . . .28 E2
Abbotsleigh Cl, Sutt.
SM2 . . . . .198 E7
Abbotsleigh Rd, SW16 .168 C4

Abbots Manor Est, SW1 . .32 D2
Abbotsmede Cl, Twick.
TW1 . . . . .162 C2
Abbots Pk, SW2 . . . . . . .169 G1
Abbot's Pl, NW6 . . . . . . .108 E1
Abbot's Rd, E6 . . . . .116 A1
Abbots Rd, Edg. HA8 . . . .54 C7
Abbots Ter, N8 . . . . .74 E6
Abbotstone Rd, SW15 . .147 J3
Abbot St, E8 . . . . .94 C6
Abbots Wk, W8 . . . . .22 A6
Abbots Way, Beck. BR3 .189 H5
Abbotswell Rd, SE4 . . . .153 J5
Abbotswood Cl, Belv. DA17
off Coptefield Dr .138/139 E3
Abbotswood Gdns, Ilf.
IG5 . . . . .80 C3
Abbotswood Rd, SE22 . .152 B4
SW16 . . . . .168 D3
Abbotswood Way, Hayes
UB3 . . . . .122 B1
Abbott Av, SW20 . . . . . .184 A2
Abbott Cl, Hmptn. TW12 .161 E6
Northolt UB5 . . . . .85 F6
Abbott Rd, E14 . . . . .114 C5
Abbotts Cl, SE28 . . . . . .118 C7
Romford RM7 . . . . .83 H3
Abbotts Cres, E4 . . . . . . .62 D4
Enfield EN2 . . . . .43 H2
Abbotts Dr, Wem. HA0 . . .86 E2
Abbotts Pk Rd, E10 . . . . .78 C7
Abbotts Rd, Barn. EN5 . . .40 E4
Mitcham CR4 . . . . . . .186 C4
Southall UB1 . . . . .123 E1
Sutton SM3 . . . . .198 C3
Abbotts Wk, Bexh. DA7 . .138 D7
Abchurch La, EC4 . . . . . . .20 C5
Abchurch Yd, EC4 . . . . . .20 B5
Abdale Rd, W12 . . . . .127 H1
Aberavon Rd, E3 . . . . . . .113 H3
Abercairn Rd, SW16 . . .168 C7
Aberconway Rd, Mord.
SM4 . . . . .184 E3
Abercorn Cl, NW7 . . . . . .56 B7
NW8 . . . . .6 C2
Abercorn Cres, Har. HA2 . .85 H1
Abercorn Gdns, Har. HA3 .69 G7
Romford RM6 . . . . .82 B6
Abercorn Pl, NW8 . . . . . . .6 C3
Abercorn Rd, NW7 . . . . . .56 B7
Stanmore HA7 . . . . . . .53 F7
Abercorn Way, SE1 . . . . .37 H3
Abercrombie Dr, Enf. EN1
off Linwood Cres 44 D1
Abercrombie St, SW11 . .149 H2
Aberdale Ct, SE16
off Poolmans St 133 G2
Aberdare Cl, W.Wick.
BR4 . . . . .204 C2
Aberdare Gdns, NW6 . . .91 E7
NW7 . . . . .56 A7
Aberdare Rd, Enf. EN3 . . .45 F4
Aberdeen La, N5 . . . . .93 H5
Aberdeen Par, N18
off Angel Rd 60/61 E5
Aberdeen Pk, N5 . . . . . . .93 H5
Aberdeen Pk Ms, N5 . . . .93 J4
Aberdeen Pl, NW8 . . . . . . .6 E6
Aberdeen Rd, N5 . . . . . . .93 J4
N18 . . . . .60 E5
NW10 . . . . .89 F5
Croydon CR0 . . . . . . .201 J4
Harrow HA3 . . . . .68 C2
Aberdeen Sq, E14
off Westferry Circ 133 J1
Aberdeen Ter, SE3 . . . . .154 D2
Aberdour Rd, Ilf. IG3 . . .100 B3
Aberdour St, SE1 . . . . . . .36 D1
Aberfeldy St, E14 . . . . . .114 C6
Aberford Gdns, SE18 . . .156 B1
Aberford Rd, Borwd.
WD6 . . . . .38 A2
Aberfoyle Rd, SW16 . . . .168 D6
Abergeldie Rd, SE12 . . . .155 H6
Aberglen Ind Est, Hayes
UB3 . . . . .121 G2
Abernethy Rd, SE13 . . . .154 E4
Abersham Rd, E8 . . . . . . .94 C5
Abery St, SE18 . . . . .137 H4
Abingdon Cl, NW1 . . . . . .92 D6
off Camden Sq 92 D6
SE1 . . . . .37 G3
SW19 . . . . .167 F6
Abingdon Rd, N3 . . . . . . .73 F2
SW16 . . . . .186 E2
W8 . . . . .128 D3
Abingdon St, SW1 . . . . . .26 A5
Abingdon Vil, W8 . . . . . . .128 D3
Abinger Cl, Bark. IG11 . .100 A4
Bromley BR1 . . . . . . .192 B3

Abinger Cl, Croy. CR0 . .204 C6
Wallington SM6 . . . . .201 E5
Abinger Gdns, Islw. TW7 .144 B3
Abinger Gro, SE8 . . . . . .133 J6
Abinger Ms, W9
off Warlock Rd 108 D4
Abinger Rd, W4 . . . . .127 E3
Ablett St, SE16 . . . . .133 F5
Abney Gdns, N16 off Stoke
Newington High St . . .94 C2
Aboyne Dr, SW20 . . . . . .183 G2
Aboyne Est, SW17 . . . . .167 G3
Aboyne Rd, NW10 . . . . . .88 E3
SW17 . . . . .167 G3
Abraham Cl, Wat. WD19
off Muirfield Rd 50 B4
Abridge Rd, Chig. IG7 . . .49 G6
Abridge Way, Bark. IG11 .118 B2
Abyssinia Cl, SW11
off Cairns Rd 149 H4
Abyssinia Rd, SW11
off Auckland Rd 149 H4
Acacia Av, N17 . . . . .60 A7
Brentford TW8 . . . . . .124 E7
Mitcham CR4
off Acacia Rd 186 B2
Ruislip HA4 . . . . .84 A1
Wembley HA9 . . . . . . .87 H5
SE20 off Selby Rd 188 D2
Orpington BR5 . . . . . .193 G5
Stanmore HA7 . . . . . . .52 B6
Acacia Dr, Sutt. SM3 . . .198 C1
Acacia Gdns, NW8 . . . . . .7 F1
West Wickham BR4 . .204 C2
Acacia Gro, SE21 . . . . . .170 A2
New Malden KT3 . . . . .182 D3
Acacia Ms, West Dr. UB7 .120 A6
Acacia Pl, NW8 . . . . .7 F1
Acacia Rd, E11 . . . . .97 E2
E17 . . . . .77 H6
N22 . . . . .75 G1
NW8 . . . . .7 F1
SE16 . . . . .187 E1
W3 . . . . .106 C7
Beckenham BR3 . . . . .189 J3
Enfield EN2 . . . . .44 A1
Hampton TW12 . . . . .161 G6
Mitcham CR4 . . . . . . .186 B2
Acacia Way, Sid. DA15 . .175 J1
Academy Gdns, Croy.
CR0 . . . . .202 C1
Northolt UB5 . . . . .102 D2
Academy Pl, SE18 . . . . . .156 C1
Academy Rd, SE18 . . . . .156 C1
Acanthus Dr, SE1 . . . . . .37 H3
Acanthus Rd, SW11 . . . .150 A3
Accommodation Rd,
NW11 . . . . .72 C7
A.C. Ct, T.Ditt. KT7
off Harvest La 180 D6
Acer Av, Hayes UB4 . . . . .102 E5
Acfold Rd, SW6 . . . . .148 E1
Achilles Cl, SE1 . . . . .37 J3
Achilles Rd, NW6 . . . . . . .90 D5
Achilles St, SE14 . . . . . .133 H7
Achilles Way, W1 . . . . . . .24 C2
Acklam Rd, W10 . . . . . . .108 C5
Acklington Dr, NW9 . . . . .70 E1
Ackmar Rd, SW6 . . . . . . .148 D1
Ackroyd Dr, E3 . . . . .113 J5
Ackroyd Rd, SE23 . . . . . .153 G7
Acland Cl, SE18
off Clothworkers Rd . .137 G7
Acland Cres, SE5 . . . . . .152 A4
Acland Rd, NW2 . . . . . . .89 H6
Acock Gro, Nthlt. UB5 . . .85 H4
Acol Cres, Ruis. HA4 . . . .84 B5
Acol Rd, NW6 . . . . .90 D7
Aconbury Rd, Dag. RM9 .118 B1
Acorn Cl, E4 . . . . .62 A5
Chislehurst BR7 . . . . .175 F5
Enfield EN2 . . . . .43 H1
Hampton TW12 . . . . .161 H6
Stanmore HA7 . . . . . . .53 E7
Acorn Ct, Ilf. IG2 . . . . . . .81 H6
Acorn Gdns, SE19 . . . . . .188 C1
W3 . . . . .106 D5
Acorn Gro, Hayes UB3 . .121 J7
Acorn Par, SE15
off Carlton Gro .132/133 E7
Acorns, The, Chig. IG7 . . .65 H4
Acorn Wk, SE16 . . . . .133 H1
Acorn Way, SE23 . . . . . .171 G3
Beckenham BR3 . . . . .190 C5
Orpington BR6 . . . . . .207 E4
Acre Dr, SE22 . . . . .152 D4
Acre La, SW2 . . . . .150 E4
Carshalton SM5 . . . . .200 A4
Wallington SM6 . . . . .200 A4

Acre Path, Nthlt. UB5
off Arnold Rd 84/85 E6
Acre Rd, SW19 . . . . .167 G6
Dagenham RM10 . . . .101 H7
Acre Rd, Kings.T. KT2 . . .181 H1
Acris St, SW18 . . . . .149 F5
ACTON, W3 . . . . .126 A1
Acton Cl, N9 . . . . .60 D2
Acton Hill Ms, W3
off Uxbridge Rd 126 B1
Acton La, NW10 . . . . . . .106 C2
W3 . . . . .126 C2
W4 . . . . .126 D3
Acton Ms, E8 . . . . .112 C1
Acton Pk Ind Est, W3 . . .126 D2
Acton St, WC1 . . . . .10 C4
Acuba Rd, SW18 . . . . . . .166 E2
Acworth Cl, N9
off Turin Rd 45 F7
Ada Gdns, E14 . . . . .114 D6
E15 . . . . .115 F1
Adair Cl, SE25 . . . . .188 E3
Adair Rd, W10 . . . . .108 B4
Adair Twr, W10
off Appleford Rd 108 B4
Adam & Eve Ct, W1 . . . . .17 G3
Adam & Eve Ms, W8 . . . .128 D3
Adam Cl, SE6 . . . . .171 J4
Adam Ct, SW7 . . . . .30 D1
Adam Pl, N16 off Stoke
Newington High St . . .94 C2
Adam Rd, E4 . . . . .61 J6
Adams Cl, N3
off Falkland Av 56 D7
NW9 . . . . .88 B2
Surbiton KT5 . . . . .181 J6
Adams Ct, EC2 . . . . .20 C3
Adams Gdns Est, SE16
off St. Marychurch St .133 F2
Adamson Rd, E16 . . . . . .115 G6
NW3 . . . . .91 G7
Adams Pl, N7
off George's Rd 93 F5
Adamsrill Cl, Enf. EN1 . . .44 A6
Adamsrill Rd, SE26 . . . . .171 H4
Adams Rd, N17 . . . . .76 B2
Beckenham BR3 . . . . .189 H5
Adams Row, W1 . . . . .16 C6
Adams Sq, Bexh. DA6
off Regency Way .158/159 E3
Adam St, WC2 . . . . .18 B6
Adams Wk, Kings.T. KT1 .181 H2
Adams Way, Croy. CR0 . .188 C6
Adam Wk, SW6 . . . . .127 J7
Ada Pl, E2 . . . . .112 D1
Adare Wk, SW16 . . . . . . .169 F3
Ada Rd, SE5 . . . . .132 B7
Wembley HA0 . . . . . . .87 G3
Adastral Est, NW9 . . . . . .70 E1
Ada St, E8 . . . . .112 E1
Adcock Wk, Orp. BR6
off Borkwood Pk 207 J4
Adderley Gdns, SE9 . . . .174 D4
Adderley Gro, SW11
off Culmstock Rd 150 A5
Adderley Rd, Har. HA3 . . .68 C1
Adderley St, E14 . . . . . . .114 C6
ADDINGTON, Croy. 203 J5
Addington Cl, SW14 . . . .146 D3
Addington Dr, N12 . . . . . .57 F6
Addington Gro, SE26 . . .171 H4
Addington Rd, E3 . . . . . .114 A3
E16 . . . . .115 E4
N4 . . . . .75 G6
Croydon CR0 . . . . . . .201 G1
West Wickham BR4 . .204 E2
Addington Sq, SE5 . . . . .36 A7
Addington St, SE1 . . . . . .26 D4
Addington Village Rd, Croy.
CR0 . . . . .204 A5
Addis Cl, Enf. EN3 . . . . . .45 G1
ADDISCOMBE, Croy. 202 C1
Addiscombe Av, Croy.
CR0 . . . . .188 D7
Addiscombe Cl, Har. HA3 .69 F5
Addiscombe Ct Rd, Croy.
CR0 . . . . .202 B1
Addiscombe Gro, Croy.
CR0 . . . . .202 A2
Addiscombe Rd, Croy.
CR0 . . . . .202 A1
Addison Av, N14 . . . . .42 B6
W11 . . . . .128 B1
Hounslow TW3 . . . . . .143 J1
Addison Br Pl, W14 . . . . .128 C4
Addison Cl, Nthwd. HA6 . .66 A1
Orpington BR5 . . . . . .193 F6
Addison Cres, W14 . . . . .128 B3
Addison Dr, SE12
off Eltham Rd 155 H5

Addison Gdns, W14 . . . . .128 A3
Surbiton KT5 . . . . . . .181 J4
Addison Gro, W4 . . . . . . .127 E3
Addison Pl, W11 . . . . . . .128 B1
Addison Pl, Southall UB1
    off Longford Av 103 G7
Addison Rd, E11 . . . . . .79 G6
E17 . . . . .78 B5
SE25 . . . . .188 D4
W14 . . . . .128 C3
Bromley BR2 . . . . . . .191 J5
Enfield EN3 . . . . .45 F1
Ilford IG6 . . . . .81 F1
Teddington TW11 . . . . .162 E6
Addison's Cl, Croy. CR0 .203 J2
Addison Way, NW11 . . . .72 C4
Hayes UB3 . . . . .102 A6
Addle Hill, EC4 . . . . . . .19 H5
Addle St, EC2 . . . . .20 A2
Adecroft Way, W.Mol.
    KT8 . . . . .179 J3
Adela Av, N.Mal. KT3 . .183 H5
Adelaide Av, SE4 . . . . . .153 J4
Adelaide Cl, Stan. HA7 . .52 D4
Adelaide Cotts, W7 . . . . .124 C2
Adelaide Gdns, Rom.
    RM6 . . . . .82 E5
Adelaide Gro, W12 . . . . .127 G1
Adelaide Rd, E10 . . . . . .96 B3
NW3 . . . . .91 G7
SW18
    off Putney Br Rd 148 D5
W13 . . . . .124 D1
Chislehurst BR7 . . . . .175 E5
Hounslow TW5 . . . . . .142 E1
Ilford IG1 . . . . .99 E2
Richmond TW9 . . . . . .145 J4
Southall UB2 . . . . . . .123 E4
Surbiton KT6 . . . . . . .181 H5
Teddington TW11 . . . . .162 C6
Adelaide St, WC2 . . . . . .18 A6
Adelaide Ter, Brent. TW8 .125 G5
Adelaide Wk, SW9
    off Sussex Wk 151 G4
Adela St, W10
    off Kensal Rd 108 B4
Adelina Gro, E1 . . . . . . .113 F5
Adelina Ms, SW12
    off King's Av 168 D1
Adeline Pl, WC1 . . . . . . .17 J2
Adeliza Cl, Bark. IG11
    off North St 98/99 E7
Adelphi Cl, SE16
    off Poolmans St 133 G2
Adelphi Ter, WC2 . . . . . .18 B6
Adeney Cl, W6 . . . . . . .128 A6
Aden Gro, N16 . . . . .94 A4
Adenmore Rd, SE6 . . . . .154 A6
Aden Rd, Enf. EN3 . . . . .45 H4
Ilford IG1 . . . . .81 E7
Aden Ter, N16 . . . . .94 A4
Adie Rd, W6 . . . . .127 J3
Adine Rd, E13 . . . . .115 H4
Adler Ind Est, Hayes
    UB3 . . . . .121 G2
Adler St, E1 . . . . .21 H3
Adley St, E5 . . . . .95 H5
Adlington Cl, N18 . . . . . .60 A5
Admaston Rd, SE18 . . . .137 F7
Admiral Ct, NW4
    off Barton Cl 71 G5
Admiral Ho, Tedd. TW11
    off Twickenham Rd . . .162 D4
Admiral Pl, SE16 . . . . . .133 H1
Admirals Cl, E18 . . . . . .79 H4
Admiral Seymour Rd,
    SE9 . . . . .156 C4
Admiral Sq, SW10 . . . . .149 G1
Admiral St, SE8 . . . . . .154 A2
Admirals Wk, NW3 . . . . .91 F3
Admirals Way, E14 . . . . .134 A2
★ Admiralty Arch, SW1 . .25 J1
Admiralty Cl, SE8
    off Reginald Sq 134 A7
Admiralty Rd, Tedd.
    TW11 . . . . .162 C6
Admiral Wk, W9 . . . . . . .108 D5
Adolf St, SE6 . . . . .172 B4
Adolphus Rd, N4 . . . . . .93 H2
Adolphus St, SE8 . . . . .133 J7
Adomar Rd, Dag. RM8 . . .100 D3
Adpar St, W2 . . . . .7 E6
Adrian Av, NW2
    off North Circular Rd . .89 H1
Adrian Ms, SW10 . . . . . .30 B5
Adrienne Av, Sthl. UB1 . .103 F4
Advance Rd, SE27 . . . . .169 J4
Advent Ct, Wdf.Grn. IG8
    off Wood La 63 F5
Advent Way, N18 . . . . . .61 G5

Adys Rd, SE15 . . . . . . .152 C3
Aerodrome Rd, NW4 . . . .71 F3
NW9 . . . . .71 F2
Aerodrome Way, Houns.
    TW5 . . . . .122 C6
Aeroville, NW9 . . . . .71 E2
Affleck St, N1 . . . . .10 D2
Afghan Rd, SW11 . . . . .149 H2
★ Africa Cen, WC2
    off King St 18 A5
Africa Ho, SE16 . . . . . . .133 E4
Agamemnon Rd, NW6 . . .90 C5
Agar Cl, Surb. KT6 . . . . .195 J2
Agar Gro, Est, NW1 . . . .92 C7
Agar Pl, NW1 . . . . .92 C7
Agar St, WC2 . . . . .18 A6
Agate Cl, E16 . . . . .116 A6
Agate Rd, W6 . . . . .127 J3
Agatha Cl, E1
    off Prusom St . . .132/133 E1
Agaton Rd, SE9 . . . . . . .175 F2
Agave Rd, NW2 . . . . . . .89 J4
Agdon St, EC1 . . . . .11 G5
Agincourt Rd, NW3 . . . . .91 J4
Agnes Av, Ilf. IG1 . . . . . .98 E4
Agnes Cl, E6 . . . . .116 D7
Agnesfield Cl, N12 . . . . .57 H6
Agnes Gdns, Dag. RM8 . .100 D4
Agnes Rd, W3 . . . . .127 F1
Agnes St, E14 . . . . .113 J6
Agnew Rd, SE23 . . . . . .153 G7
Agricola Cl, E3
    off Parnell Rd 113 J1
Aidan Cl, Dag. RM8 . . . .100 E4
Aileen Wk, E15 . . . . . . .97 F7
Ailsa Av, Twick. TW1 . . . .144 D5
Ailsa Rd, Twick. TW1 . . . .145 E5
Ailsa St, E14 . . . . .114 C5
Ainger Ms, NW3
    off Ainger Rd 91 J7
Ainger Rd, NW3 . . . . . . .91 J7
Ainsdale Cl, Orp. BR6 . . .207 G1
Ainsdale Cres, Pnr. HA5 . .67 G3
Ainsdale Dr, SE1 . . . . . .37 H4
Ainsdale Rd, W5 . . . . . .105 G4
Watford WD19 . . . . . .50 C3
Ainsley Av, Rom. RM7 . . .83 H6
Ainsley Cl, N9 . . . . .60 B1
Ainsley St, E2 . . . . .112 E3
Ainslie Wk, SW12 . . . . .150 B7
Ainslie Wd Cres, E4 . . . .62 B5
Ainslie Wd Gdns, E4 . . . .62 B4
Ainslie Wd Rd, E4 . . . . .62 A5
Ainsty Est, SE16 . . . . . .133 G2
Ainsworth Cl, NW2 . . . . .89 G3
SE15
    off Lyndhurst Gro 152 B2
Ainsworth Rd, E9 . . . . . .95 F7
Croydon CR0 . . . . . . .201 H2
Ainsworth Way, NW8 . . . .109 F1
Aintree Av, E6 . . . . .116 B1
Aintree Cres, Ilf. IG6 . . . .81 F2
Aintree Est, SW6
    off Dawes Rd 128 B7
Aintree Rd, Grnf. UB6 . . .105 E2
Aintree St, SW6 . . . . . .128 B7
Aird Ct, Hmptn. TW12
    off Oldfield Rd 179 F1
Airdrie Cl, N1 . . . . .93 F7
Hayes UB4
    off Glencoe Rd . . .102/103 E5
Airedale Av, W4 . . . . . . .127 F4
Airedale Av S, W4
    off Netheravon Rd S . .127 F5
Airedale Rd, SW12 . . . . .149 J7
W5 . . . . .125 F3
Airlie Gdns, W8 . . . . . . .128 D1
Ilford IG1 . . . . .99 E1
Air Links Ind Est, Houns.
    TW5 . . . . .122 C5
Air Pk Way, Felt. TW13 . .160 B2
Airport Roundabout, E16
    off Connaught Br 136 A1
Air St, W1 . . . . .17 G6
Airthrie Rd, Ilf. IG3 . . . . .100 B2
Aisgill Av, W14 . . . . . . .128 C5
Aisher Rd, SE28 . . . . . .118 C7
Aislibie Rd, SE12 . . . . . .155 E4
Aiten Pl, W6
    off Standish Rd 127 G4
Aitken Cl, E8
    off Pownall Rd 112 D1
Mitcham CR4 . . . . . . .185 J7
Aitken Rd, SE6 . . . . . . .172 B2
Barnet EN5 . . . . .39 J5
Ajax Av, NW9 . . . . .70 E3
Ajax Rd, NW6 . . . . .90 D5
Akabusi Cl, Croy. CR0 . .188 D6

Akehurst St, SW15 . . . . .147 G6
Akenside Rd, NW3 . . . . .91 G5
Akerman Rd, SW9 . . . . .151 H2
Surbiton KT6 . . . . . . .181 F6
Alabama St, SE18 . . . . .137 G7
Alacross Rd, W5 . . . . . .125 F2
Alandale Dr, Pnr. HA5 . . .66 B2
Aland Ct, SE16
    off Finland St 133 H3
Alander Ms, E17 . . . . . .78 C4
Alan Dr, Barn. EN5 . . . . .40 B6
Alan Gdns, Rom. RM7 . . .83 G7
Alan Hocken Way, E15 . .114 E2
Alan Rd, SW19 . . . . . . .166 B5
Alanthus Cl, SE12 . . . . .155 F6
Alaska St, SE1 . . . . .27 E2
Alba Cl, Hayes UB4
    off Ramulis Dr 102 D4
Albacore Cres, SE13 . . . .154 B6
Alba Gdns, NW11 . . . . . .72 B6
Alban Cres, Borwd.
    WD6 . . . . .38 B1
Alban Highwalk, EC2
    off London Wall 111 J5
Albany, W1 . . . . .17 F6
Albany, The, Wdf.Grn. IG8 .63 F4
Albany Cl, N15 . . . . .75 H4
SW14 . . . . .146 B4
Bexley DA5 . . . . .158 C7
Albany Ct, E4
    off Chelwood Cl 46 B6
Albany Ctyd, W1 . . . . . . .17 G6
Albany Cres, Edg. HA8 . . .54 A7
Esher (Clay.) KT10 . . . .194 B6
Albany Mans, SW11 . . . .129 H7
Albany Ms, N1
    off Barnsbury Pk 93 G7
SE5 . . . . .36 A6
Bromley BR1 . . . . . . .173 G6
Kingston upon Thames KT2
    off Albany Pk Rd 163 G6
Sutton SM1
    off Camden Rd . .198/199 E5
Albany Pk Av, Enf. EN3 . .45 F1
Albany Pk Rd, Kings.T.
    KT2 . . . . .163 H6
Albany Pas, Rich. TW10 . .145 J5
Albany Pl, N7 . . . .
    off Benwell Rd 93 G4
Brentford TW8
    off Albany Rd 125 H6
Albany Rd, E10 . . . . . . .78 A7
E12 . . . . .98 A4
E17 . . . . .77 H6
N4 . . . . .75 F6
N18 . . . . .61 E5
SE5 . . . . .36 B6
SW19 . . . . .166 E6
W13 . . . . .104 E7
Belvedere DA17 . . . . .139 F6
Bexley DA5 . . . . .158 C7
Brentford TW8 . . . . . .125 G6
Chislehurst BR7 . . . . .174 E5
New Malden KT3 . . . . .182 D4
Richmond TW10
    off Albert Rd 145 J5
Romford RM6 . . . . . . .83 F6
Albany St, NW1 . . . . . . .8 D1
Albany Ter, NW1
    off Marylebone Rd 110 B4
Albany Vw, Buck.H. IG9 . .63 G1
Alba Pl, W11
    off Portobello Rd 108 C6
Albatross St, SE18 . . . . .137 H7
Albatross Way, SE16 . . . .133 G2
Albemarle, SW19 . . . . . .166 A2
Albemarle App, Ilf. IG2 . . .81 E6
Albemarle Av, Twick.
    TW2 . . . . .161 F1
Albemarle Gdns, Ilf. IG2 . .81 E6
New Malden KT3 . . . . .182 D4
Albemarle Pk, Stan. HA7
    off Marsh La 53 F5
Albemarle Rd, Barn.
    EN4 . . . . .41 H7
Beckenham BR3 . . . . .190 B1
Albemarle St, W1 . . . . . .17 E6
Albemarle Way, EC1 . . . .11 G6
Alberon Gdns, NW11 . . . .72 C4
Alberta Av, Sutt. SM1 . . .198 B4
Alberta Est, SE17 . . . . . .35 H3
Alberta Rd, Enf. EN1 . . . .44 C6
Erith DA8 . . . . .159 J1
Alberta St, SE17 . . . . . .35 G3
Albert Av, E4 . . . . .62 A4
SW8 . . . . .131 F7
Albert Br, SW3 . . . . .31 H6
SW11 . . . . .31 H6
Albert Br Rd, SW11 . . . . .31 H7
Albert Carr Gdns, SW16 .168 E5

Albert Cl, E9
    off Northiam St 112/113 E1
N22 . . . . .74 D1
Albert Ct, SW7 . . . . .23 E4
Albert Cres, E4 . . . . .62 A4
Albert Dr, SW19 . . . . . . .166 B2
Albert Embk, SE1 . . . . . .34 B4
Albert Gdns, E1 . . . . . . .113 G6
Albert Gate, SW1 . . . . . .24 A3
Albert Gro, SW20 . . . . . .184 A1
Albert Hall Mans, SW7 . .23 E4
Albert Mans, SW11
    off Albert Br Rd 149 J1
★ Albert Mem, SW7 . . . .22 E3
Albert Ms, E14
    off Narrow St 113 H7
W8 . . . . .22 C5
Albert Pl, N3 . . . . .72 D1
N17 off High Rd 76 C3
W8 . . . . .22 B4
Albert Rd, E10 . . . . .96 C2
E16 . . . . .136 B1
E17 . . . . .78 A5
E18 . . . . .79 H3
N4 . . . . .93 F1
N15 . . . . .76 B6
N22 . . . . .74 C1
NW4 . . . . .72 A4
NW6 . . . . .108 C2
NW7 . . . . .55 F5
SE9 . . . . .174 B3
SE20 . . . . .171 G7
SE25 . . . . .188 D4
W5 . . . . .105 E4
Barnet EN4 . . . . .41 F4
Belvedere DA17 . . . . .139 F5
Bexley DA5 . . . . .159 G6
Bromley BR2 . . . . . . .192 A5
Buckhurst Hill IG9 . . . .64 A2
Dagenham RM8 . . . . .101 G1
Hampton (Hmptn.H.)
    TW12 . . . . .161 J5
Harrow HA2 . . . . .67 J3
Hayes UB3 . . . . .121 H3
Hounslow TW3 . . . . . .143 G4
Ilford IG1 . . . . .99 E3
Kingston upon Thames
    KT1 . . . . .181 J2
Mitcham CR4 . . . . . . .185 J3
New Malden KT3 . . . . .183 F4
Richmond TW10 . . . . .145 H5
Southall UB2 . . . . . . .122 D4
Sutton SM1 . . . . .199 G5
Teddington TW11 . . . .162 C6
Twickenham TW1 . . . . .162 C1
West Drayton UB7 . . . .120 B1
Albert Rd Est, Belv.
    DA17 . . . . .139 F5
Albert Sq, E15 . . . . .97 E5
SW8 . . . . .131 F7
Albert St, N12 . . . . .57 F5
NW1 . . . . .110 B1
NW10 . . . . .106 D1
Buckhurst Hill IG9 . . . .64 A2
Albert Ter Ms, NW1
    off Regents Pk Rd 110 A1
Albert Way, SE15 . . . . . .132 E7
Albion Av, N10 . . . . .74 A1
SW8 . . . . .150 D2
Albion Bldgs, EC1
    off Bartholomew Cl . .111 J5
Albion Cl, W2 . . . . .15 H5
Albion Dr, E8 . . . . .94 C7
Albion Est, SE16 . . . . . .133 G2
Albion Gdns, W6 . . . . . .127 H4
Albion Gro, N16 . . . . . . .94 B4
Albion Hill, SE13 . . . . . .154 B6
Loughton IG10 . . . . . .47 J5
Albion Ms, N1 . . . . .111 G1
NW6
    off Kilburn High Rd . . .90 C7
W2 . . . . .15 H4
W6 off Galena Rd 127 H4
Albion Par, N16
    off Albion Rd 94 A4
Albion Pk, Loug. IG10 . . .48 A5
Albion Pl, EC1 . . . . .19 G5
SE25 off High St 188 D3
W6 . . . . .127 H4
Albion Rd, E17 . . . . .78 C3
N16 . . . . .94 A4
N17 . . . . .76 C2
Bexleyheath DA6 . . . .159 F4
Hounslow TW3 . . . . . .143 G4
Kingston upon Thames
    KT2 . . . . .182 C1
Sutton SM2 . . . . .199 G6
Twickenham TW2 . . . .162 B1
Albion Sq, E8 . . . . .94 C7

Albion St, SE16 ....**133** F2
W2 ....**15** H4
Croydon CR0 ....**201** H1
Albion Ter, E8 ....**94** C7
Albion Vil Rd, SE26 .....**171** F3
Albion Way, EC1 ....**19** J2
SE13 ....**154** C4
Wembley HA9
off North End Rd **88** B3
Albrighton Rd, SE22 ....**152** B3
Albuhera Cl, Enf. EN2 ....**43** G1
Albury Av, Bexh. DA7 ...**158** E2
Isleworth TW7 ....**124** C7
Albury Cl, Hmptn. TW12 .**161** G6
Albury Ct, Sutt. SM1
off Ripley Gdns **199** F4
Albury Dr, Pnr. HA5 .....**50** D7
Albury Ms, E12 ....**97** J1
Albury Rd, Chess. KT9 ..**195** H5
Albury St, SE8 ....**134** A6
Albyfield, Brom. BR1 ....**192** C3
Albyn Rd, SE8 ....**154** A1
Alcester Cres, E5 ....**95** E2
Alcester Rd, Wall. SM6 ..**200** B4
Alcock Cl, Wall. SM6 ....**200** D7
Alcock Rd, Houns. TW5 ..**122** D7
Alconbury Rd, E5 ....**94** D2
Alcorn Cl, Sutt. SM3 ....**198** D2
Alcott Cl, W7
off Westcott Cres **104** C5
Alcuin Ct, Stan. HA7
off Old Ch La **53** F7
ALDBOROUGH HATCH,
Ilf. **81** H3
Aldborough Rd, Dag.
RM10 ....**101** J6
Aldborough Rd N, Ilf. IG2 .**81** J5
Aldborough Rd S, Ilf. IG3 .**99** H1
Aldbourne Rd, W12 .....**127** F1
Aldbridge St, SE17 ......**36** E3
Aldburgh Ms, W1 ....**16** C3
Aldbury Av, Wem. HA9 ...**88** B7
Aldbury Ms, N9 ....**44** A7
Aldebert Ter, SW8 ......**131** E7
Aldeburgh Cl, E5
off Southwold Rd ..**94/95** E2
Aldeburgh Pl, SE10
off Aldeburgh St **135** G4
Woodford Green IG8 ...**63** G4
Aldeburgh St, SE10 .....**135** G5
Alden Av, E15 ....**115** F3
Aldenham St, NW1 ....**9** G2
Aldensley Rd, W6 ......**127** H3
Alderbrook Rd, SW12 ...**150** B6
Alderbury Rd, SW13 ....**127** G6
Alder Cl, SE15 ....**37** G6
Alder Gro, NW2 ....**89** H2
Aldergrove Gdns, Houns. TW3
off Bath Rd **142/143** E2
Alderholt Way, SE15 .....**36** E7
Alderman Av, Bark. IG11 .**118** A3
Aldermanbury, EC2 ......**20** A3
Aldermanbury Sq, EC2 ...**20** A2
Alderman Judge Mall, Kings.T.
KT1 *off Eden St* **181** H2
Aldermans Hill, N13 .....**58** E4
Alderman's Wk, EC2 .....**20** D2
Aldermary Rd, Brom.
BR1 ....**191** G1
Alder Ms, N19
off Bredgar Rd **92** C2
Aldermoor Rd, SE6 .....**171** J3
Alderney Av, Houns.
TW5 ....**123** H7
Alderney Gdns, Nthlt.
UB5 ....**85** F7
Alderney Ms, SE1 ....**28** B5
Alderney Rd, E1 ....**113** G4
Alderney St, SW1 ....**32** E3
Alder Rd, SW14 ....**146** D3
Sidcup DA14 ....**175** J3
Alders, The, N21 ....**43** G6
Feltham TW13 ....**160** E4
Hounslow TW5 ....**123** F6
West Wickham BR4 ...**204** B1
Alders Av, Wdf.Grn. IG8 ..**62** E6
ALDERSBROOK, E12 .....**97** H2
Aldersbrook Av, Enf. EN1 .**44** B2
Aldersbrook Dr, Kings.T.
KT2 ....**163** J6
Aldersbrook La, E12 .....**98** C3
Aldersbrook Rd, E11 .....**97** H2
E12 ....**98** A3
Alders Cl, E11
off Aldersbrook Rd **97** H2
W5 ....**125** G3
Edgware HA8 ....**54** C5
Aldersey Gdns, Bark.
IG11 ....**99** G6
Aldersford Cl, SE4 ......**153** G5
Aldersgate St, EC1 ......**19** J3
Alders Gro, E.Mol. KT8
off Esher Rd **180** A5
Aldersgrove Av, SE9 ....**173** J3
Aldershot Rd, NW6 .....**108** C1
Aldersmead Av, Croy.
CR0 ....**189** G6
Aldersmead Rd, Beck.
BR3 ....**171** H7
Alderson Pl, Sthl. UB2 ..**123** J1
Alderson St, W10
off Kensal Rd **108** B4
Alders Rd, Edg. HA8 .....**54** C5
Alderton Cl, NW10 ......**88** D3
Loughton IG10 ....**48** D4
Alderton Cres, NW4 .....**71** H5
Alderton Hall La, Loug.
IG10 ....**48** D4
Alderton Hill, Loug. IG10 .**48** B5
Alderton Ms, Loug. IG10
off Alderton Hall La ...**48** D4
Alderton Ri, Loug. IG10 ..**48** D4
Alderton Rd, SE24 ......**151** J3
Croydon CR0 ....**188** C7
Alderton Way, NW4 ......**71** H5
Loughton IG10 ....**48** C5
Alderville Rd, SW6 .....**148** C2
Alder Wk, Ilf. IG1 ....**99** F5
Alderwick Dr, Houns.
TW3 ....**144** A3
Alderwood Rd, SE9 .....**157** G6
Aldford St, W1 ....**24** B1
Aldgate, EC3 ....**21** F4
Aldgate Av, E1 ....**21** F3
Aldgate Barrs Shop Cen,
E1 ....**21** G3
Aldgate High St, EC3 ....**21** F4
Aldine Ct, W12
off Aldine St **127** J1
Aldine Pl, W12
off Uxbridge Rd **127** J1
Aldine St, W12 ....**127** J2
Aldington Cl, Dag. RM8 ..**82** C7
Aldington Rd, SE18 .....**136** A3
Aldis Ms, SW17
off Aldis St **167** H5
Aldis St, SW17 ....**167** H5
Aldred Rd, NW6 ....**90** D5
Aldren Rd, SW17 ....**167** F3
Aldriche Way, E4 ....**62** C6
Aldrich Gdns, Sutt. SM3 .**198** C3
Aldrich Ter, SW18
off Lidiard Rd **167** F2
Aldridge Av, Edg. HA8 ...**54** B3
Ruislip HA4 ....**84** D2
Stanmore HA7 ....**69** H1
Aldridge Ri, N.Mal. KT3 .**182** E7
Aldridge Rd Vil, W11 ....**108** C5
Aldridge Wk, N14 ....**42** E7
Aldrington Rd, SW16 ....**168** C5
Aldsworth Cl, W9 ....**6** A6
Aldwick Cl, SE9 ....**175** G3
Aldwick Rd, Croy. CR0 ..**201** F3
Aldworth Gro, SE13 ....**154** C6
Aldworth Rd, E15 ....**96** E7
Aldwych, WC2 ....**18** C5
Aldwych Av, Ilf. IG6 ......**81** F4
Aldwych Underpass, WC2
off Kingsway **111** F6
Alers Rd, Bexh. DA6 ....**158** D5
Alesia Cl, N22
off Nightingale Rd .**58/59** E7
Alestan Beck Rd, E16 ...**116** A5
Alexa Ct, W8 ....**30** A1
Sutton SM2
off Mulgrave Rd **198** D6
Alexander Av, NW10 .....**89** H7
Alexander Cl, Barn. EN4 ..**41** G4
Bromley BR2 ....**205** G1
Sidcup DA15 ....**157** H5
Southall UB2 ....**123** J1
Twickenham TW2 .....**162** C2
Alexander Evans Ms, SE23
off Sunderland Rd ...**171** G1
★ **Alexander Fleming Laboratory Mus**, W2
off Praed St **15** F3
Alexander Ms, W2 ....**14** A3
Alexander Pl, SW7 ....**31** G1
Alexander Rd, N19 ....**92** E3
Bexleyheath DA7 .....**158** D2
Chislehurst BR7 ......**175** E5
Alexander Sq, SW3 ......**31** G1
Alexander St, W2 ....**108** D6
Alexandra Av, N22 ....**74** D1
SW11 ....**150** A1
W4 ....**126** D7
Harrow HA2 ....**85** F1
Southall UB1 ....**103** F7
Sutton SM1 ....**198** D3
Alexandra Cl, SE8 ......**133** J6
Harrow HA2
off Alexandra Av **85** G3
Alexandra Cotts, SE14 ..**153** J1
Alexandra Ct, N14 ....**42** C5
N16 *off Belgrade Rd* ...**94** C4
Wembley HA9 ....**87** J4
Alexandra Cres, Brom.
BR1 ....**173** F6
Alexandra Dr, SE19 .....**170** B5
Surbiton KT5 ....**182** A7
Alexandra Gdns, N10 ....**74** B4
W4 ....**126** D7
Hounslow TW3 ....**143** H2
Alexandra Gro, N4 ....**93** H1
N12 ....**57** E5
Alexandra Ms, N2
off Fortis Grn **73** J3
SW19
off Alexandra Rd **166** D6
★ **Alexandra Palace**, N22 .**74** D2
Alexandra Palace, N22 ...**74** D2
Alexandra Palace Way,
N22 ....**74** C3
Alexandra Pk Rd, N10 ....**74** B2
N22 ....**74** D2
Alexandra Pl, NW8 ......**109** F1
SE25 ....**188** A5
Croydon CR0
off Alexandra Rd **202** B1
Alexandra Rd, E6 ....**116** D3
E10 ....**96** C3
E17 ....**77** J6
E18 ....**79** H3
N8 ....**75** G3
N9 ....**44** E7
N10 ....**58** B6
N15 ....**76** A5
NW4 ....**72** A4
NW8 ....**91** F7
SE26 ....**171** G6
SW14 ....**146** D3
SW19 ....**166** C6
W4 ....**126** D2
Brentford TW8 ....**125** G6
Croydon CR0 ....**202** B1
Enfield EN3 ....**45** G4
Hounslow TW3 ....**143** H2
Kingston upon Thames
KT2 ....**164** A7
Mitcham CR4 ....**167** H7
Richmond TW9 ....**145** J2
Romford (Chad.Hth.)
RM6 ....**82** D6
Thames Ditton KT7 ...**180** C5
Twickenham TW1 .....**145** F6
Alexandra Sq, Mord.
SM4 ....**184** D5
Alexandra St, E16 ......**115** G5
SE14 ....**133** H7
Alexandra Wk, SE19 ....**170** B5
Alexandria Rd, W13 .....**104** D7
Alexis St, SE16 ....**37** H1
Alfearn Rd, E5 ....**95** F4
Alford Grn, Croy. (New Adgtn.)
CR0 ....**204** D6
Alford Pl, N1 ....**12** A2
Alford Rd, SW8 ....**150** D1
Alfoxton Av, N15 ....**75** H4
Alfreda St, SW11 ....**150** B1
Alfred Cl, W4
off Belmont Rd **126** D4
Alfred Gdns, Sthl. UB1 ..**103** E7
Alfred Ms, W1 ....**17** H1
Alfred Pl, WC1 ....**17** H1
Alfred Prior Ho, E12 .....**98** D4
Alfred Rd, E15 ....**97** F5
SE25 ....**188** D5
W2 ....**108** D5
W3 ....**126** C1
Belvedere DA17 ......**139** F5
Buckhurst Hill IG9 .....**64** A2
Feltham TW13 ....**160** C2
Kingston upon Thames
KT1 ....**181** H3
Sutton SM1 ....**199** F5
Alfred's Gdns, Bark. IG11 .**117** H2
Alfred St, E3 ....**113** J3
Alfreds Way, Bark. IG11 ..**117** F3
Alfreds Way Ind Est, Bark.
IG11 ....**118** A1
Alfreton Cl, SW19 ......**166** A3
Alfriston Av, Croy. CR0 ..**186** E7
Harrow HA2 ....**67** G6
Alfriston Cl, Surb. KT5 ..**181** J5
Alfriston Rd, SW11 .....**149** J5
Algar Cl, Islw. TW7
off Algar Rd **144** D3
Stanmore HA7 ....**52** C5
Algar Rd, Islw. TW7 .....**144** D3
Algarve Rd, SW18 ......**167** E1
Algernon Rd, NW4 ......**71** G6
NW6 ....**108** D1
Algernon Rd, SE13 .....**154** B4
Algers Cl, Loug. IG10 ....**48** A5
Algers Mead, Loug. IG10 .**48** A5
Algers Rd, Loug. IG10 ....**48** A5
Algiers Rd, SE13 ....**154** A4
Alibon Gdns, Dag. RM10 .**101** G5
Alibon Rd, Dag. RM9,
RM10 ....**101** F5
Alice Cl, Barn. EN5 ......**41** F4
Alice Ct, SW15
off Deodar Rd **148** C4
Alice Gilliatt Ct, W14 ....**128** C6
Alice La, E3 ....**113** J1
Alice Ms, Tedd. TW11
off Luther Rd **162** C5
Alice St, SE1 ....**28** D6
Alice Thompson Cl,
SE12 ....**173** J2
Alice Walker Cl, SE24
off Shakespeare Rd ..**151** H4
Alice Way, Houns. TW3 ..**143** H4
Alicia Av, Har. HA3 ......**69** E4
Alicia Cl, Har. HA3 ....**69** F4
Alicia Gdns, Har. HA3 ....**69** E4
Alie St, E1 ....**21** G4
Alington Cres, NW9 .....**88** C1
Alison Cl, E6 ....**116** D6
Croydon CR0
off Shirley Oaks Rd ..**203** G1
Aliwal Rd, SW11 ....**149** H4
Alkerden Rd, W4 ....**127** E5
Alkham Rd, N16 ....**94** C2
Allan Barclay Cl, N15
off High Rd **76** C6
Allan Cl, N.Mal. KT3 ....**182** D5
Allandale Av, N3 ....**72** B3
Allan Way, W3 ....**106** C5
Allard Cres, Bushey
(Bushey Hth.) WD23 ...**51** J1
Allard Gdns, SW4 ......**150** D5
Allardyce St, SW4 ......**151** F4
Allbrook Cl, Tedd. TW11 ..**162** B5
Allcroft Rd, NW5 ....**92** A5
Allenby Cl, Grnf. UB6 ...**103** G3
Allenby Rd, SE23 ....**171** H3
Southall UB1 ....**103** G6
Allen Cl, Mitch. CR4 .....**186** B1
Sunbury-on-Thames
TW16 ....**178** B1
Allen Ct, Grnf. UB6 ......**86** C5
Allendale Av, Sthl. UB1 ..**103** G6
Allendale Cl, SE5
off Daneville Rd **152** A1
SE26 ....**171** G5
Allendale Rd, Grnf. UB6 ..**86** E6
Allen Edwards Dr, SW8 .**150** E1
Allenford Ho, SW15
off Tunworth Cres **147** F6
Allen Pl, Twick. TW1
off Church St **162** D1
Allen Rd, E3 ....**113** J2
N16 ....**94** B4
Beckenham BR3 ......**189** G2
Croydon CR0 ....**187** F7
Sunbury-on-Thames
TW16 ....**178** B1
Allensbury Pl, NW1 ......**92** D7
Allens Rd, Enf. EN3 .....**45** F5
Allen St, W8 ....**128** D3
Allenswood Rd, SE9 ....**156** B3
Allerford Ct, Har. HA2 ....**67** H5
Allerford Rd, SE6 ......**172** B4
Allerton Ct, NW4
off Holders Hill Rd **72** A2
Allerton Rd, N16 ....**93** J2
Allerton Wk, N7
off Durham Rd **93** F2
Allestree Rd, SW6 ......**128** B7
Alleyn Cres, SE21 ......**170** A2
Alleyndale Rd, Dag.
RM8 ....**100** C2
Alleyn Pk, SE21 ....**170** A2
Southall UB2 ....**123** F4
Alleyn Rd, SE21 ....**170** A3
Allfarthing La, SW18 ....**149** E6
Allgood Cl, Mord. SM4 ..**184** A6
Allgood St, E2 ....**13** G2
Allhallows La, EC4 ......**20** B6
★ **All Hallows-on-the-Wall C of E Church**, EC2
off London Wall **20** C2
Allhallows Rd, E6 ......**116** B5
All Hallows Rd, N17 .....**76** B1
Alliance Cl, Wem. HA0 ...**87** G4
Alliance Ct, W3
off Alliance Rd **106** B4
Alliance Rd, E13 ....**115** J4

Alliance Rd, SE18 . . . . . .138 A6
W3 . . . . .106 B4
Allied Way, W3
off Larden Rd . . .126/127 E2
Allingham Cl, W7 . . . . . . .104 C7
Allingham Ms, N1 . . . . . . .11 J1
Allingham St, N1 . . . . . . .11 J1
Allington Av, N17 . . . . . . .60 B6
Allington Cl, SW19 off High St
Wimbledon 166 A5
Greenford UB6 . . . . .85 J7
Allington Ct, Enf. EN3 . . . .45 G5
Allington Rd, NW4 . . . . . .71 H5
W10 . . . . .108 B2
Harrow HA2 . . . . .67 J5
Orpington BR6 . . . . . . .207 G2
Allington St, SW1 . . . . . . .25 F6
Allison Cl, SE10
off Dartmouth Hill 154 C1
Allison Gro, SE21 . . . . . .170 B1
Allison Rd, N8 . . . . .75 G5
W3 . . . . .106 C6
Allitsen Rd, NW8 . . . . . . .7 G2
Allnutt Way, SW4 . . . . . .150 D5
Alloa Rd, SE8 . . . . .133 G5
Ilford IG3 . . . . .100 A2
Allonby Gdns, Wem.
HA9 . . . . .87 F1
Allotment Way, NW2
off Midland Ter 90 A3
Alloway Rd, E3 . . . . .113 H3
Allports Ms, E1
off Stepney Grn 113 F4
All Saints Cl, N9 . . . . .60 C2
SW8 off Lansdowne
Way 150/151 E1
All Saints Dr, SE3 . . . . . .155 E2
All Saints Ms, Har. HA3 . .52 B6
All Saints Pas, SW18
off Wandsworth
High St 148/149 E5
All Saints Rd, SW19 . . . .167 F7
W3 . . . . .126 C3
W11 . . . . .108 C5
Sutton SM1 . . . . .199 E3
All Saints St, N1 . . . . .10 C1
All Saints Ter, E10 . . . . . . .78 B7
Allsop Pl, NW1 . . . . .8 A6
All Souls Av, NW10 . . . . .107 H2
All Souls Pl, W1 . . . . .17 E2
Allum Way, N20 . . . . .57 F1
Allwood Cl, SE26 . . . . . .171 G4
Alma Av, E4 . . . . .62 C7
Almack Rd, E5 . . . . .95 F4
Alma Cres, Sutt. SM1 . . .198 B5
Alma Gro, SE1 . . . . .37 G2
Alma Pl, NW10
off Harrow Rd 107 H3
SE19 . . . . .170 C7
Thornton Heath CR7 . .187 G5
Alma Rd, N10 . . . . .58 A7
SW18 . . . . .149 F5
Carshalton SM5 . . . . . .199 H5
Enfield EN3 . . . . .45 H5
Esher KT10 . . . . .194 B1
Sidcup DA14 . . . . .176 A3
Southall UB1 . . . . .102 E7
Alma Row, Har. HA3 . . . . .68 A1
Alma Sq, NW8 . . . . .6 D3
Alma St, E15 . . . . .96 D6
NW5 . . . . .92 B6
Alma Ter, SW18 . . . . . . .149 G7
W8 off Allen St 128 D3
Almeida St, N1 . . . . .93 H7
Almeric Rd, SW11 . . . . . .149 J4
Almer Rd, SW20 . . . . . . .165 G2
Almington St, N4 . . . . . . .93 F1
Almond Av, W5 . . . . .125 H3
Carshalton SM5 . . . . . .199 J2
West Drayton UB7 . . . .120 D3
Almond Cl, SE15 . . . . . . .152 D2
Bromley BR2 . . . . .192 D7
Feltham TW13
off Highfield Rd 160 A1
Almond Gro, Brent. TW8 .124 E7
Almond Rd, N17 . . . . .60 D7
SE16 . . . . .133 E4
Almonds Av, Buck.H. IG9 .63 G2
Almond Way, Borwd.
WD6 . . . . .38 B4
Bromley BR2 . . . . .192 D7
Harrow HA2 . . . . .67 H2
Mitcham CR4 . . . . .186 D5
Almorah Rd, N1 . . . . .94 A7
Hounslow TW5 . . . . . . .142 D1
Alnwick Gro, Mord. SM4
off Bordesley Rd .184/185 E4
Alnwick Rd, E16 . . . . . . .115 J6
SE12 . . . . .155 H7
ALPERTON, Wem. 105 J1

Alperton La, Grnf. UB6 . .105 G3
Wembley HA0 . . . . .105 G3
Alperton St, W10 . . . . . . .108 B4
Alphabet Gdns, Cars.
SM5 . . . . .185 G6
Alphabet Sq, E3
off Hawgood St 114 A5
Alpha Cl, NW1 . . . . .7 H4
Alpha Gro, E14 . . . . .134 A2
Alpha Pl, NW6 . . . . .108 D2
SW3 . . . . .31 H5
Alpha Rd, E4 . . . . .62 B3
N18 . . . . .60 D6
SE14 . . . . .153 J1
Croydon CR0 . . . . .202 B1
Enfield EN3 . . . . .45 H4
Surbiton KT5 . . . . .181 J6
Teddington TW11 . . . . .162 A5
Alpha St, SE15 . . . . .152 D2
Alphea Cl, SW19
off Courtney Rd 167 H7
Alpine Av, Surb. KT5 . . . .196 C2
Alpine Business Cen, E6 .116 D5
Alpine Cl, Croy. CR0 . . . .202 B3
Alpine Copse, Brom.
BR1 . . . . .192 D2
Alpine Gro, E9 . . . . .95 F7
Alpine Rd, E10 . . . . .96 B2
SE16 . . . . .133 F4
Walton-on-Thames
KT12 . . . . .178 A7
Alpine Vw, Cars. SM5 . . .199 H5
Alpine Wk, Stan. HA7 . . . .52 B2
Alpine Way, E6 . . . . .116 D5
Alric Av, NW10 . . . . .88 D7
New Malden KT3 . . . . .183 E3
Alroy Rd, N4 . . . . .75 G7
Alsace Rd, SE17 . . . . .36 D3
Alscot Rd, SE1 . . . . .37 G1
Alscot Way, SE1 . . . . .37 F1
Alsike Rd, SE2 . . . . .138 D3
Erith DA18 . . . . .138 E3
Alsom Av, Wor.Pk. KT4 . .197 G4
Alston Cl, Surb. KT6 . . . .181 E7
Alston Rd, N18 . . . . .60 E5
SW17 . . . . .167 G4
Barnet EN5 . . . . .40 B3
Altair Cl, N17 . . . . .60 C6
Altash Way, SE9 . . . . . . .174 C2
Altenburg Av, W13 . . . . .125 E3
Altenburg Gdns, SW11 . .149 J4
Alt Gro, SW19
off St. George's Rd . .166 C7
Altham Rd, Pnr. HA5 . . . .51 E7
Althea St, SW6 . . . . .149 E3
Althorne Gdns, E18 . . . . .79 F4
Althorne Way, Dag.
RM10 . . . . .101 G2
Althorp Cl, Barn. EN5 . . . .39 G7
Althorpe Gro, SW11
off Westbridge Rd . . .149 G1
Althorpe Ms, SW11
off Westbridge Rd . . .149 G1
Althorpe Rd, Har. HA1 . . .67 J5
Althorp Rd, SW17 . . . . . .167 J1
Altmore Av, E6 . . . . .98 C7
Alton Cl, Bex. DA5 . . . . . .177 E1
Isleworth TW7 . . . . . . .144 C2
Alton Gdns, Beck. BR3 . .172 A7
Twickenham TW2 . . . . .144 A7
Alton Rd, N17 . . . . .76 A3
SW15 . . . . .165 G1
Croydon CR0 . . . . .201 G3
Richmond TW9 . . . . . . .145 H4
Alton St, E14 . . . . .114 B5
Altyre Cl, Beck. BR3 . . . .189 J5
Altyre Rd, Croy. CR0 . . . .202 A2
Altyre Way, Beck. BR3 . . .189 J5
Alvanley Gdns, NW6 . . . . .90 E5
Alva Way, Wat. WD19 . . . .50 D2
Alverstone Av, SW19 . . . .166 D2
Barnet EN4 . . . . .41 H7
Alverstone Gdns, SE9 . . .175 F1
Alverstone Rd, E12 . . . . . .98 D4
NW2 . . . . .89 J7
New Malden KT3 . . . . .183 F4
Wembley HA9 . . . . .87 J1
Alverston Gdns, SE25 . . .188 B5
Alverton St, SE8 . . . . . . .133 J5
Alveston Av, Har. HA3 . . . .68 E3
Alvey Est, SE17 . . . . .36 D2
Alvey St, SE17 . . . . .36 D3
Alvia Gdns, Sutt. SM1 . . .199 F4
Alvington Cres, E8 . . . . . .94 C5
Alway Av, Epsom KT19 . .196 C5
Alwold Cres, SE12 . . . . . .155 H6
Alwyn Av, W4 . . . . .126 D5
Alwyn Cl, Croy. (New Adgtn.)
CR0 . . . . .204 B7

Alwyne La, N1
off Alwyne Vil 93 H7
Alwyne Pl, N1 . . . . .93 J6
Alwyne Rd, N1 . . . . .93 J7
SW19 . . . . .166 C6
Alwyne Rd, W7 . . . . .104 B7
Alwyne Sq, N1 . . . . .93 J6
Alwyne Vil, N1 . . . . .93 H7
Alwyn Gdns, NW4 . . . . . .71 G4
W3 . . . . .106 B6
Alyth Gdns, NW11 . . . . . .72 D6
Alzette Ho, E2 . . . . .113 G3
Amalgamated Dr, Brent.
TW8 . . . . .124 D6
Amanda Cl, Chig. IG7 . . . .65 J6
Amanda Ms, Rom. RM7 . .83 J5
Amazon St, E1
off Hessel St 112/113 E6
Ambassador Cl, Houns.
TW3 . . . . .142 E2
Ambassador Gdns, E6 . .116 C5
Ambassador's Ct, SW1 . . .25 C5
Ambassador Sq, E14
off Cahir St 134 B4
Amber Av, E17 . . . . .77 H1
Amber Ct, SW17
off Brudenell Rd 168 A4
Amberden Av, N3 . . . . . . .72 D3
Ambergate St, SE17 . . . . .35 H3
Amber Gro, NW2
off Prayle Gro 90 A1
Amberley Cl, Orp. BR6
off Warnford Rd 207 J5
Pinner HA5 . . . . .67 F3
Amberley Ct, Sid. DA14 . .176 C5
Amberley Gdns, Enf. EN1 .44 B7
Epsom KT19 . . . . .197 F4
Amberley Gro, SE26 . . . .170 E4
Croydon CR0 . . . . .188 C2
Amberley Rd, E10 . . . . . . .78 B7
N13 . . . . .59 F2
SE2 . . . . .138 D6
W9 . . . . .108 D5
Buckhurst Hill IG9 . . . . .63 J1
Enfield EN1 . . . . .44 C7
Amberley Way, Houns.
TW4 . . . . .142 C5
Morden SM4 . . . . .184 C7
Romford RM7 . . . . .83 H4
Amber Ms, N22
off Brampton Pk Rd . . .75 G3
Amberside Cl, Islw. TW7 .144 A6
Amber St, E15
off Great Eastern Rd . .96 D6
Amberwood Cl, Wall. SM6
off The Chase . . .200/201 E5
Amberwood Ri, N.Mal.
KT3 . . . . .182 E6
Amblecote Cl, SE12 . . . .173 H3
Amblecote Meadows,
SE12 . . . . .173 H3
Amblecote Rd, SE12 . . . .173 H3
Ambler Rd, N4 . . . . .93 H3
Ambleside, Brom. BR1 . .172 D6
Ambleside Av, SW16 . . . .168 D4
Beckenham BR3 . . . . . .189 H5
Ambleside Cl, E9
off Churchill Wk 95 F5
E10 . . . . .78 B7
Ambleside Cres, Enf. EN3 .45 G4
Ambleside Gdns, SW16 .168 D5
Ilford IG4 . . . . .80 B4
Sutton SM2 . . . . .199 F6
Wembley HA9 . . . . .87 G1
Ambleside Pt, SE15
off Ilderton Rd 133 F7
Ambleside Rd, NW10 . . . .89 F7
Bexleyheath DA7 . . . . .159 G2
Ambrooke Rd, Belv.
DA17 . . . . .139 G3
Ambrosden Av, SW1 . . . . .25 G6
Ambrose Av, NW11 . . . . . .72 B7
Ambrose Cl, E6
off Lovage App 116 B5
Orpington BR6
off Stapleton Rd 207 J3
Ambrose Ms, SW11 . . . . .149 H2
Ambrose St, SE16 . . . . . .132 E4
Ambrose Wk, E3
off Malmesbury Rd . .114 A2
Amelia Cl, W3 . . . . .126 B1
Amelia St, SE17 . . . . .35 H3
Amen Cor, EC4 . . . . .19 H4
SW17 . . . . .167 J6
Amen Ct, EC4 . . . . .19 H3
Amenity Way, Mord.
SM4 . . . . .183 J7
America Sq, EC3 . . . . .21 F5
America St, SE1 . . . . .27 J2
Amerland Rd, SW18 . . . .148 C6

Amersham Av, N18 . . . . . .60 A6
Amersham Gro, SE14 . . .133 J7
Amersham Rd, SE14 . . . .133 J7
Croydon CR0 . . . . .187 J6
Amersham Vale, SE14 . . .133 J7
Amery Gdns, NW10 . . . . .107 H1
Amery Rd, Har. HA1 . . . . .86 D2
Amesbury Av, SW2 . . . . .169 E2
Amesbury Cl, Wor.Pk.
KT4 . . . . .197 J1
Amesbury Dr, E4 . . . . .46 B6
Amesbury Rd, Brom.
BR1 . . . . .192 A3
Dagenham RM9 . . . . . .100 D7
Feltham TW13 . . . . . . .160 D2
Amesbury Twr, SW8
off Westbury St 150 C2
Amethyst Rd, E15 . . . . . . .96 D4
Amherst Av, W13 . . . . . . .105 F6
Amherst Dr, Orp. BR5 . . .193 J4
Amherst Rd, W13 . . . . . . .105 F6
Amhurst Gdns, Islw.
TW7 . . . . .144 C1
Amhurst Par, N16
off Amhurst Pk 76 C7
Amhurst Pk, N16 . . . . .76 A7
Amhurst Pas, E8 . . . . .94 D5
Amhurst Rd, E8 . . . . .94 E5
N16 . . . . .94 C4
Amhurst Ter, E8 . . . . .94 D4
Amhurst Wk, SE28
off Pitfield Cres 138 A1
Amidas Gdns, Dag.
RM8 . . . . .100 B4
Amiel St, E1 . . . . .113 F4
Amies St, SW11 . . . . .149 J3
Amina Way, SE16 . . . . . . .29 H6
Amis Av, Epsom KT19 . . .196 B6
Amity Gro, SW20 . . . . . . .183 J1
Amity Rd, E15 . . . . .115 F1
Ammanford Grn, NW9
off Ruthin Cl 70/71 E6
Amner Rd, SW11 . . . . . . .150 A6
Amor Rd, W6 . . . . .127 J3
Amott Rd, SE15 . . . . .152 D3
Amoy Pl, E14 . . . . .114 A6
Ampere Way, Croy. CR0 .187 E7
Ampleforth Rd, SE2 . . . .138 B2
Ampthill Sq Est, NW1 . . . .9 G2
Ampton Pl, WC1 . . . . .10 C4
Ampton St, WC1 . . . . .10 C4
Amroth Cl, SE23 . . . . . . .171 E1
Amroth Grn, NW9
off Fryent Gro 70/71 E6
Amsterdam Rd, E14 . . . . .134 C3
Amundsen Ct, E14
off Napier Av 134 A5
Amwell Cl, Enf. EN2 . . . . .44 A5
Amwell Ct Est, N4 . . . . . . .93 J1
Amwell St, EC1 . . . . .11 E3
Amyand Cotts, Twick. TW1
off Amyand
Pk Rd 144/145 E6
Amyand La, Twick. TW1
off Marble Hill
Gdns 144/145 E7
Amyand Pk Gdns, Twick. TW1
off Amyand
Pk Rd 144/145 E7
Amyand Pk Rd, Twick.
TW1 . . . . .144 D7
Amy Cl, Wall. SM6
off Mollison Dr . .200/201 E7
Amyruth Rd, SE4 . . . . . . .154 A5
Amy Warne Cl, E6 off Evelyn
Denington Rd 116 B4
Anatola Rd, N19
off Dartmouth Pk Hill . .92 B2
Ancaster Cres, N.Mal.
KT3 . . . . .183 G6
Ancaster Ms, Beck. BR3 .189 G3
Ancaster Rd, Beck. BR3 .189 G3
Ancaster St, SE18 . . . . . .137 H7
Anchorage Cl, SW19 . . . .166 D5
Anchorage Pt, E14
off Cuba St 134 A2
Anchorage Pt Ind Est,
SE7 . . . . .135 J3
Anchor & Hope La, SE7 .135 H3
Anchor Dr, Bark. IG11 . . .118 B3
Anchor Ms, SW12
off Hazelbourne Rd . .150 B6
Anchor Retail Pk, E1 . . . .113 F4
Anchor St, SE16 . . . . . . .132 E4
Anchor Ter, E1
off Cephas Av 113 F4
Anchor Wf, E3
off Watts Gro 114 A5
Anchor Yd, EC1 . . . . .12 A5
Ancill Cl, W6 . . . . .128 B6

Ancona Rd, NW10 .....107 G2
SE18 .....137 G5
Andace Pk Gdns, Brom.
  BR1 .....191 J1
Andalus Rd, SW9 .....151 E3
Ander Cl, Wern. HA0 .....87 G4
Anderson Cl, N21 .....43 F5
Anderson Cl, W3 .....106 D6
  Sutton SM3 .....198 D1
Anderson Ho, Bark. IG11
  off The Coverdales 117 G2
Anderson Pl, Houns.
  TW3 .....143 H4
Anderson Rd, E9 .....95 G6
  Woodford Green IG8 ..80 A3
Andersons Sq, N1
  off Gaskin St 111 H1
Anderson St, SW3 ....31 J3
Anderson Way, Belv.
  DA17 .....139 H2
Anderton Cl, SE5 .....152 A3
Andmark Ct, Sthl. UB1
  off Herbert Rd 123 F1
Andover Av, E16
  off King George Av ...116 A6
Andover Cl, Grnf. UB6
  off Ruislip Rd 103 H4
Andover Pl, NW6 .....6 A1
Andover Rd, N7 .....93 F2
  Orpington BR6 .....207 G1
  Twickenham TW2 .....162 A1
Andre St, E8 .....94 D5
Andrew Borde St, WC2 ...17 J3
Andrew Cl, Ilf. IG6 .....65 G6
Andrewes Gdns, E6 .....116 B6
Andrewes Ho, EC2 .....20 A2
Andrew Pl, SW8
  off Cowthorpe Rd 150 D1
Andrew Reed Ho, SW18
  off Linstead Way 148 B7
Andrews Cl, E6
  off Linton Gdns 116 B6
  Buckhurst Hill IG9 .....63 J2
  Harrow HA1
  off Bessborough Rd ...68 A7
  Worcester Park KT4 ...198 A2
Andrews Crosse, WC2 ...18 E4
Andrews Pl, SE9 .....156 E6
Andrew's Rd, E8 .....112 E1
Andrew St, E14 .....114 C6
Andrews Wk, SE17 .....35 H6
Andwell Cl, SE2 .....138 B2
ANERLEY, SE20 .....188 E1
Anerley Gro, SE19 .....170 C7
Anerley Hill, SE19 .....170 C6
Anerley Pk, SE20 .....170 D7
Anerley Pk Rd, SE20 .....170 D7
Anerley Rd, SE19 .....170 D7
  SE20 .....170 D7
Anerley Sta Rd, SE20 ...188 E1
Anerley St, SW11 .....149 J2
Anerley Vale, SE19 .....170 C7
Anfield Cl, SW12
  off Belthorn Cres 150 C7
Angel All, E1 .....21 G3
Angel Cl, N18 .....60 C4
Angel Cor Par, N18
  off Fore St 60 D5
Angel Ct, EC2 .....20 C3
  SW1 .....25 G2
  SW17 .....167 J4
Angelfield, Houns.
  TW3 .....143 H4
Angel Gate, EC1 .....11 H3
Angel Hill, Sutt. SM1
  off Sutton Common
  Rd 198/199 E3
Angel Hill Dr, Sutt. SM1 .199 E3
Angelica Dr, E6 .....116 D5
Angelica Gdns, Croy.
  CR0 .....203 G1
Angel La, E15 .....96 D6
Angell Pk Gdns, SW9 ...151 G3
Angell Rd, SW9 .....151 G3
Angell Town Est, SW9 ...151 G2
Angel Ms, E1
  off Cable St 112 D7
  N1 .....11 F2
  SW16 off Roehampton
  High St 147 G7
Angel Pas, EC4 .....20 B6
Angel Pl, N18 .....60 D5
  SE1 .....28 B3
Angel Rd, N18 .....60 E5
  Harrow HA1 .....68 B6
  Thames Ditton KT7 ...180 D7
Angel Rd Works, N18 ....61 F5
Angel Sq, EC1 .....11 F2
Angel St, EC1 .....19 J3
Angel Wk, W6 .....127 J4

Angerstein La, SE3 .....135 F7
Angle Grn, Dag. RM8 .....100 C1
Anglers Cl, Rich. TW10
  off Locksmeade Rd ...163 F4
Angler's La, NW5 .....92 B6
Anglers Reach, Surb.
  KT6 .....181 G5
Anglesea Av, SE18 .....136 E4
Anglesea Ms, SE18
  off Anglesea Av ..136/137 E4
Anglesea Rd, SE18 .....136 E4
  Kingston upon Thames
  KT1 .....181 G4
Anglesea Ter, W6
  off Wellesley Av 127 H3
Anglesey Ct Rd, Cars.
  SM5 .....200 A6
Anglesey Gdns, Cars.
  SM5 .....200 A6
Anglesey Rd, Enf. EN3 ...45 E4
  Watford WD19 .....50 C5
Anglesmede Cres, Pnr.
  HA5 .....67 G3
Anglesmede Way, Pnr.
  HA5 .....67 F3
Angles Rd, SW16 .....169 E4
Anglia Cl, N17
  off Park La 60/61 E7
Anglia Ct, Dag. RM8
  off Spring Cl 100 D1
Anglia Ho, E14 .....113 H6
Anglian Rd, E11 .....96 D3
Anglia Wk, E6 .....116 C1
Anglo Rd, E3 .....113 J2
Angrave Ct, E8 .....112 C1
Angrave Pas, E8
  off Haggerston Rd ...112 C1
Angus Cl, Chess. KT9 ...196 A5
Angus Dr, Ruis. HA4 .....84 C4
Angus Gdns, NW9 .....70 D1
Angus Rd, E13 .....115 J3
Angus St, SE14 .....133 H7
Anhalt Rd, SW11 .....31 H7
Ankerdine Cres, SE18 ...136 D7
Anlaby Rd, Tedd. TW11 .162 B5
Anley Rd, W14 .....128 A2
Anmersh Gro, Stan. HA7 .69 G1
Annabel Cl, E14 .....114 B6
Anna Cl, E8 .....112 C1
Annandale Rd, SE10 ....135 F6
  W4 .....126 E4
  Croydon CR0 .....202 D2
  Sidcup DA15 .....157 H7
Anna Neagle Cl, E7
  off Dames Rd 97 G4
Anne Boleyn's Wk, Kings.T.
  KT2 .....163 H5
  Sutton SM3 .....198 A7
Anne Case Ms, N.Mal. KT3
  off Sycamore Gro 182 D3
Anne Compton Ms,
  SE12 .....155 F7
Annesley Av, NW9 .....70 D3
Annesley Cl, NW10 .....88 E3
Annesley Dr, Croy. CR0 .203 J3
Annesley Rd, SE3 .....155 H1
Annesley Wk, N19 .....92 C2
Anne St, E13 .....115 G4
Anne Taylor Ho, E12
  off Walton Rd 98 D4
Annette Cl, Har. HA3
  off Spencer Rd 68 B2
Annette Cres, N1
  off Essex Rd 93 J7
Annette Rd, N7 .....93 F4
Annett Rd, Walt. KT12 ...178 A7
Anne Way, Ilf. IG6 .....65 F6
  West Molesey KT8 ....179 H4
Annie Besant Cl, E3 .....113 J1
Anning St, EC2 .....13 E5
Annington Rd, N2 .....73 J3
Annis Rd, E9 .....95 H6
Ann La, SW10 .....30 E7
Ann Moss Way, SE16 ...133 F3
Ann's Cl, SW1 .....24 A4
Ann's Pl, E1 .....21 F2
Ann St, SE18 .....137 G4
Annsworthy Av, Th.Hth. CR7
  off Grange Pk Rd 188 A3
Annsworthy Cres, SE25
  off Grange Rd 188 A2
Ansdell Rd, SE15 .....153 F2
Ansdell St, W8 .....22 B5
Ansdell Ter, W8 .....22 B5
Ansell Gro, Cars. SM5 ..200 A1
Ansell Rd, SW17 .....167 H3
Anselm Cl, Croy. CR0
  off Park Hill Ri 202 C3
Anselm Rd, SW6 .....128 D6
  Pinner HA5 .....51 F7

Ansford Rd, Brom. BR1 .172 C5
Ansleigh Pl, W11 .....108 A7
Anson Cl, Rom. RM7 .....83 H2
Anson Pl, SE28 .....137 G2
Anson Rd, N7 .....92 C4
  NW2 .....90 A5
Anson Ter, Nthlt. UB5 ....85 H6
Anstey Rd, SE15 .....152 D3
Anstey Wk, N15 .....75 H4
Anstice Cl, W4 .....127 E7
Anstridge Path, SE9 ....157 G6
Anstridge Rd, SE9 .....157 G6
Antelope Rd, SE18 .....136 C3
Anthony Cl, NW7 .....55 E4
  Watford WD19 .....50 C1
★ Anthony d'Offay Gall,
  W1 .....16 E4
Anthony Rd, SE25 .....188 D6
  Greenford UB6 .....104 B2
  Welling DA16 .....158 A1
Anthony St, E1
  off Commercial Rd ..112/113 E6
Antigua Cl, E1
  off Salters Hill 170 A5
Antigua Wk, SE19 .....170 A5
Antill Rd, E3 .....113 H3
  N15 .....76 C4
Antill Ter, E1 .....113 G6
Antlers Hill, E4 .....46 B5
Anton Cres, Sutt. SM1 ..198 D3
Antoneys Cl, Pnr. HA5 ...66 D2
Anton Pl, Wem. HA9 .....88 B3
Anton St, E8 .....94 D5
Antrim Gro, NW3 .....91 J6
Antrim Mans, NW3 .....91 H6
Antrim Rd, NW3 .....91 J6
Antrobus Cl, Sutt. SM1 .198 C5
Antrobus Rd, W4 .....126 C4
Anvil Cl, SW16 .....168 C7
Anvil Rd, Sun. TW16 ....178 A3
Anworth Cl, Wdf.Grn.
  IG8 .....63 H6
Apex Cl, Beck. BR3 .....190 B1
Apex Cor, NW7 .....54 D4
Apex Ind Est, NW10
  off Hythe Rd 107 G3
Apex Retail Pk, Felt.
  TW13 .....161 F3
Apex Twr, N.Mal. KT3 ...182 E3
Aplin Way, Islw. TW7 ....144 B1
Apollo Av, Brom. BR1
  off Rodway Rd 191 H1
Apollo Cl, E11 .....96 E3
★ Apollo Hammersmith,
  W6 .....127 J5
Apollo Pl, E11 .....96 E3
  SW10 .....31 E7
★ Apollo Thea, W1
  off Shaftesbury Av 17 H5
★ Apollo Victoria Thea,
  SW1 .....25 F6
Apollo Way, SE28
  off Broadwater Rd ...137 G3
Apostle Way, Th.Hth.
  CR7 .....187 H2
Apothecary St, EC4 .....19 G4
Appach Rd, SW2 .....151 G6
Apple Blossom Ct, SW8
  off Pascal St 130 D7
Appleby Cl, E4 .....62 C6
  N15 .....76 A5
  Twickenham TW2 .....162 A2
Appleby Rd, E8 .....94 D7
  E16 .....115 F6
Appleby St, E2 .....13 F1
Appledore Av, Bexh.
  DA7 .....159 J1
  Ruislip HA4 .....84 B3
Appledore Cl, SW17 ....167 J2
  Bromley BR2 .....191 F5
  Edgware HA8 .....70 A1
Appledore Cres, Sid.
  DA14 .....175 H3
Appledore Way, NW7
  off Bittacy Hill 56 B7
Appleford Rd, W10 .....108 B4
Apple Garth, Brent. TW8 .125 G4
Applegarth, Croy. (New Adgtn.)
  CR0 .....204 B7
  Esher (Clay.) KT10 ...194 C5
Applegarth Dr, Ilf. IG2 ...81 J4
Applegarth Rd, SE28 ....138 B1
  W14 .....128 A3
Apple Gro, Chess. KT9 ..195 H4
  Enfield EN1 .....44 B3
Apple Mkt, Kings.T. KT1
  off Eden St 181 G2
Apple Rd, E11 .....96 E3
Appleton Gdns, N.Mal.
  KT3 .....183 G6

Appleton Rd, SE9 .....156 B3
  Loughton IG10 .....49 E3
Appleton Sq, Mitch. CR4
  off Silbury Av 185 H1
Appletree Cl, SE20
  off Jasmine Gro .188/189 E1
Appletree Gdns, Barn.
  EN4 .....41 H4
Apple Tree Yd, SW1 .....25 G1
Applewood Cl, N20 .....57 H1
  NW2 .....89 H3
Applewood Dr, E13 .....115 H4
Appold St, EC2 .....20 D1
Apprentice Way, E5
  off Clarence Rd ...94/95 E4
Approach, The, NW4 .....72 A5
  W3 .....106 D6
  Enfield EN1 .....44 E2
  Orpington BR6 .....207 J2
Approach Cl, N16
  off Cowper Rd 94 B5
Approach Rd, E2 .....113 F2
  SW20 .....183 J2
  Barnet EN4 .....41 G4
  West Molesey KT8 ...179 G5
Aprey Gdns, NW4 .....71 J4
April Cl, W7 .....104 B7
  Feltham TW13 .....160 A3
  Orpington BR6
  off Briarswood Way .207 J5
April Glen, SE23 .....171 G3
April St, E8 .....94 C4
Apsley Cl, Har. HA2 .....67 J5
★ Apsley Ho, Wellington Mus,
  W1 .....24 B3
Apsley Rd, SE25 .....188 E4
  New Malden KT3 .....182 C3
Apsley Way, NW2 .....89 G2
  W1 .....24 C3
Aquarius Business Pk,
  NW2 .....89 G1
Aquarius Way, Nthwd.
  HA6 .....50 A5
★ Aquatic Experience, Brent.
  TW8 .....145 E1
Aquila St, NW8 .....7 F1
Aquinas St, SE1 .....27 F2
Arabella Dr, SW15 .....147 E4
Arabia Cl, E4 .....46 D7
Arabin Rd, SE4 .....153 H4
Aragon Av, T.Ditt. KT7 ..180 B6
Aragon Cl, Brom. BR2 ..206 C1
  Loughton IG10 .....48 B6
Aragon Dr, Ilf. IG6 .....65 F7
  Ruislip HA4 .....84 D1
Aragon Rd, Kings.T. KT2 .163 H5
  Morden SM4 .....184 A6
Aragon Twr, SE8 .....133 J4
Arandora Cres, Rom.
  RM6 .....82 B7
Aran Dr, Stan. HA7 .....53 F4
Arbery Rd, E3 .....113 H3
Arbor Cl, Beck. BR3 .....190 B2
Arbor Ct, N16
  off Lordship Rd 94 A2
Arborfield Cl, SW2 .....169 F1
Arbor Rd, E4 .....62 D3
Arbour Rd, Enf. EN3 .....45 G4
Arbour Sq, E1 .....113 G6
Arbroath Grn, Wat. WD19 .50 A3
Arbroath Rd, SE9 .....156 B3
Arbury Ter, SE26
  off Oaksford Av ..170/171 E3
Arbuthnot La, Bex. DA5 .159 E6
Arbuthnot Rd, SE14 ....153 G2
Arbutus St, E8 .....112 B1
Arcade, The, EC2 .....20 D2
  Croydon CR0
  off High St 201 J3
Arcadia Av, N3 .....72 D1
Arcadia Cl, Cars. SM5 ..200 A4
Arcadian Av, Bex. DA5 ..158 E6
Arcadian Cl, Bex. DA5 ..158 E6
Arcadian Gdns, N22 .....59 F7
Arcadian Rd, Bex. DA5 .158 E6
Arcadia Shop Cen, W5 .105 G7
Arcadia St, E14 .....114 A6
Archangel St, SE16 .....133 G2
Archbishops Pl, SW2 ...151 F6
Archdale Pl, N.Mal. KT3 .182 B3
Archdale Rd, SE22 .....152 C5
Archel Rd, W14 .....128 C6
Archer Cl, Kings.T. KT2 .163 H7
Archer Ho, SW11
  off Vicarage Cres 149 G1
Archer Ms, Hmptn. (Hmptn.H.)
  TW12
  off Windmill Rd 161 J6
Archer Rd, SE25 .....188 E4
Archers Dr, Enf. EN3 ....45 F2

Archer Sq, SE14
off Chubworthy St ...133 H6
Archer St, W1 ....17 H5
Archery Cl, W2 ....15 H1
Harrow HA3 ....68 C3
Archery Rd, SE9 ....156 C5
Arches, The, SW6
off Munster Rd 148 C2
Arches, WC2 ....26 B1
Harrow HA2 ....85 H2
Archibald Ms, W1 ....24 C1
Archibald Rd, N7 ....92 D4
Archibald St, E3 ....114 A3
Archie Cl, West Dr. UB7 .120 D2
Archie St, SE1 ....29 E4
Arch St, SE1 ....27 J6
Archway Cl, N19
off St. Johns Way 92 C2
SW19 ....166 E4
W10 ....108 A5
Wallington SM6 ......200 D3
Archway Mall, N19
off Magdala Av 92 C2
Archway Ms, SW15
off Putney Br Rd 148 B4
Archway Rd, N6 ....74 A6
N19 ....92 C1
Archway St, SW13 ......147 E3
Arcola St, E8 ....94 C5
Arctic St, NW5
off Gillies St 92 A5
Arcus Rd, Brom. BR1 ...173 E6
Ardbeg Rd, SE24 ......152 A6
Arden Cl, Har. HA1 ......86 A3
Arden Ct Gdns, N2 ......73 G6
Arden Cres, E14 ....134 A4
Dagenham RM9 ......100 C7
Arden Est, N1 ....12 D2
Arden Gro, Orp. BR6 ...207 E4
Arden Ho, SW9
off Grantham Rd .150/151 E2
Arden Ms, E17 ....78 B5
Arden Mhor, Pnr. HA5 ...66 B4
Arden Rd, N3 ....72 B3
W13 ....105 F7
Ardent Cl, SE25 ....188 B3
Ardfern Av, SW16 ......187 G3
Ardfillan Rd, SE6 ......172 D1
Ardgowan Rd, SE6 ......154 E7
Ardilaun Rd, N5 ....93 J4
Ardingly Cl, Croy. CR0 .203 G3
Ardleigh Gdns, Sutt.
SM3 ....184 D7
Ardleigh Ho, Bark. IG11
off St. Ann's 117 F1
Ardleigh Ms, Ilf. IG1
off Bengal Rd 98/99 E3
Ardleigh Rd, E17 ....77 J1
N1 ....94 A6
Ardleigh Ter, E17 ....77 J1
Ardley Cl, NW10 ....88 E3
SE6 ....171 H3
Ardlui Rd, SE27 ....169 J2
Ardmay Gdns, Surb.
KT6 ....181 H5
Ardmere Rd, SE13 ......154 D6
Ardmore La, Buck.H. IG9 .47 H7
Ardmore Pl, Buck.H. IG9 .47 H7
Ardoch Rd, SE6 ....172 D2
Ardra Rd, N9 ....61 G3
Ardrossan Gdns, Wor.Pk.
KT4 ....197 G3
Ardshiel Cl, SW15
off Bemish Rd 148 A3
Ardwell Av, Ilf. IG6 ......81 F5
Ardwell Rd, SW2 ......168 E2
Ardwick Rd, NW2 ......90 D4
Arewater Grn, Erith DA18
off Kale Rd 138/139 E3
Argall Av, E10 ....77 G7
Argall Way, E10 ....95 G1
Argenta Way, NW10 ....88 B7
Argent St, SE1 ....27 H3
Argon Ms, SW6 ....128 D7
Argon Rd, N18 ....61 F5
Argosy La, Stai. (Stanw.)
TW19 ....140 A7
Argus Cl, Rom. RM7 ....83 H1
Argus Way, W3 ....126 B3
Northolt UB5 ....102 E3
Argyle Av, Houns.TW3 .143 G6
Argyle Cl, W13 ....104 D4
Argyle Pas, N17 ....76 C1
Argyle Pl, W6 ....127 H4
Argyle Rd, E1 ....113 G4
E15 ....96 E4
E16 ....115 J6
N12 ....56 D5
N17 ....76 D1

Argyle Rd, N18 ....60 D4
W13 ....104 D5
Barnet EN5 ....39 J4
Greenford UB6 ....104 C3
Harrow HA2 ....67 H6
Hounslow TW3 ....143 H5
Ilford IG1 ....98 D2
Teddington TW11 ......162 B5
Argyle Sq, WC1 ....10 B3
Argyle St, WC1 ....10 A3
Argyle Wk, WC1 ....10 B4
Argyle Way, SE16 ......37 J4
Argyll Av, Sthl. UB1 ...123 H1
Argyll Cl, SW9
off Dalyell Rd 151 F3
Argyll Gdns, Edg. HA8 ..70 B2
Argyll Rd, W8 ....128 D2
Argyll St, W1 ....17 F4
Arica Rd, SE4 ....153 H4
Ariel Rd, NW6 ....90 D6
Ariel Way, W12 ....127 J1
Hounslow TW4 ....142 B3
Aristotle Rd, SW4 ......150 D3
Arkell Gro, SE19 ......169 H7
Arkindale Rd, SE6 ......172 C3
ARKLEY, Barn. 39 G5
Arkley Cres, E17 ....77 J5
Arkley Dr, Barn. EN5 ....39 G4
Arkley La, Barn. EN5 ....39 G3
Arkley Pk, Barn. EN5 ....38 D6
Arkley Rd, E17 ....77 J5
Arkley Vw, Barn. EN5 ....39 H4
Arklow Ms, Surb. KT6
off Vale Rd S 195 H2
Arklow Rd, SE14 ....133 J6
Arkwright Rd, NW3 ......91 F5
Arlesey Cl, SW15
off Lytton Gro 148 B6
Arlesford Rd, SW9 ......151 E3
Arlingford Rd, SW2 ....151 G5
Arlington, N12 ....56 D3
Arlington Av, N1 ....111 J2
Arlington Cl, SE13 ......154 D6
Sidcup DA15 ....157 H7
Sutton SM1 ....198 D2
Twickenham TW1 ......145 F6
Arlington Ct, Hayes UB3
off Shepiston La 121 G5
Arlington Dr, Cars. SM5 .199 J2
Arlington Gdns, W4 ....126 C5
Ilford IG1 ....98 D1
Arlington Grn, NW7
off Bittacy Hill 56 B7
Arlington Lo, SW2 ......151 F4
Arlington Ms, Twick. TW1
off Arlington Rd 145 F6
Arlington Pl, SE10
off Greenwich S St ..134 C7
Arlington Rd, N14 ......58 B2
NW1 ....110 B1
W13 ....104 E6
Richmond TW10 ......163 G2
Surbiton KT6 ....181 G6
Teddington TW11 ......162 C4
Twickenham TW1 ......145 F6
Woodford Green IG8 ..79 G1
Arlington Sq, N1 ....111 J1
Arlington St, SW1 ......25 F1
Arlington Way, EC1 ......11 F3
Arliss Way, Nthlt. UB5 ..102 C1
Arlow Rd, N21 ....59 G1
Armada Ct, SE8
off Watergate St 134 A6
Armadale Cl, N17 ....76 E4
Armadale Rd, SW6 ......128 D7
Feltham TW14 ....142 A5
Armada St, SE8 ....134 A6
Armada Way, E6 ....117 F7
Armagh Rd, E3 ....113 J1
Armfield Cl, W.Mol. KT8 .179 F5
Armfield Cres, Mitch.
CR4 ....185 J2
Armfield Rd, Enf. EN2 ....44 A1
Arminger Rd, W12 ......127 H1
Armistice Gdns, SE25
off Penge Rd 188 D3
Armitage Rd, NW11 ......90 C1
SE10 ....135 F5
Armour Cl, N7
off Roman Way 93 F6
Armoury Rd, SE8 ......154 B2
Armoury Way, SW18 ...148 D5
Armstead Wk, Dag.
RM10 ....101 G7
Armstrong Av, Wdf.Grn.
IG8 ....62 E6
Armstrong Cl, E6
off Porter Rd 116 C6
Borehamwood WD6
off Manor Way 38 C3

Armstrong Cl, Dag. RM8
off Palmer Rd 100 D1
Armstrong Cl, Pnr. HA5 ..66 A6
Walton-on-Thames KT12
off Sunbury La 178 A6
Armstrong Cres, Barn.
EN4 ....41 G3
Armstrong Rd, SW7 ......22 E6
W3 ....127 F1
Armstrong Rd, Feltham
TW13 ....160 E5
Armstrong Way, Sthl.
UB2 ....123 H2
Armytage Rd, Houns.
TW5 ....122 D7
Arnal Cres, SW18 ......148 B7
Arncliffe Cl, N11
off Kettlewell Cl 58 A6
Arncroft Ct, Bark. IG11
off Renwick Rd 118 B3
Arndale Wk, SW18
off Garratt La 148/149 E5
Arne Gro, Orp. BR6 ....207 J3
Arne St, WC2 ....18 B4
Arnett Sq, E4
off Burnside Av 61 J6
Arne Wk, SE3 ....155 F4
Arneways Av, Rom. RM6 .82 D3
Arneway St, SW1 ....25 J6
Arnewood Cl, SW15 ....165 G1
Arney's La, Mitch. CR4 .186 A6
Arngask Rd, SE6 ....154 D7
Arnhem Pl, E14 ....134 A3
Arnhem Way, SE22
off East Dulwich Gro .152 B5
Arnhem Wf, E14
off Arnhem Pl 134 A3
Arnison Rd, E.Mol. KT8 .180 A4
Arnold Circ, E2 ....13 F4
Arnold Cres, Islw. TW7 .144 A5
Arnold Dr, Chess. KT9 ..195 G6
Arnold Est, SE1 ....29 G4
Arnold Gdns, N13 ....59 H5
Arnold Rd, E3 ....114 A3
N15 ....76 C3
SW17 ....167 J7
Dagenham RM9,
RM10 ....101 F7
Northolt UB5 ....84 D6
Arnos Gro, N14 ....58 D4
Arnos Rd, N11 ....58 C5
Arnott Cl, SE28
off Applegarth Rd ...118 C7
W4 off Fishers La 126 D4
Arnould Av, SE5 ....152 A4
Arnsberg Way, Bexh.
DA7 ....159 G4
Arnside Gdns, Wem. HA9 .87 G1
Arnside Rd, Bexh. DA7 .159 G1
Arnside St, SE17 ....36 A5
Arnulf St, SE6 ....172 B4
Arnulls Rd, SW16 ......169 G6
Arodene Rd, SW2 ......151 F6
Arosa Rd, Twick. TW1 ..145 G6
Arpley Sq, SE20
off High St 171 F7
Arragon Gdns, SW16 ..168 E7
West Wickham BR4 ..204 B3
Arragon Rd, E6 ....116 A1
SW18 ....166 E1
Twickenham TW1 ......144 D7
Arran Cl, Wall. SM6 ....200 B4
Arran Dr, E12 ....98 A1
Arran Grn, Wat. WD19
off Prestwick Rd 50 C1
Arran Ms, W5 ....125 J1
Arran Rd, SE6 ....172 B2
Arran Wk, N1 ....93 J7
Arras Av, Mord. SM4 ...185 F5
Arrol Rd, Beck. BR3 ....189 F3
Arrow Rd, E3 ....114 B3
Arrowscout Wk, Nthlt. UB5
off Argus Way ...102/103 E3
Arrowsmith Cl, Chig.
IG7 ....65 J5
Arrowsmith Path, Chig.
IG7 ....65 J5
Arrowsmith Rd, Chig. IG7 .65 H5
Loughton IG10 ....48 B3
Arsenal FC, N5 ....93 H3
Arsenal Rd, SE9 ....156 C2
Arterberry Rd, SW20 ...165 J7
Artesian Cl, NW10 ......88 D7
Artesian Gro, Barn. EN5 .41 F4
Artesian Rd, W2 ....108 D6
Artesian Wk, E11 ....96 E3
Arthingworth St, E15 ..114 E1
Arthur Ct, W2 ....14 A3
Arthurdon Rd, SE4 ......154 A5

Arthur Gro, SE18 ......137 F4
Arthur Henderson Ho,
SW6 ....148 C2
off Magpie Cl 97 F5
Arthur Rd, E6 ....116 C2
N7 ....93 F4
N9 ....60 C2
SW19 ....166 D3
Kingston upon Thames
KT2 ....164 A7
New Malden KT3 ......183 H5
Romford RM6 ....82 C7
Arthur St, EC4 ....20 C6
Artichoke Hill, E1
off Pennington
St 112/113 E7
Artichoke Pl, SE5
off Camberwell
Ch St 152 A1
Artillery Cl, Ilf. IG2
off Horns Rd 81 F5
Artillery La, E1 ....20 E2
W12 ....107 G6
Artillery Pas, E1 ....21 E2
Artillery Pl, SE18 ......136 C4
SW1 ....25 H6
Harrow HA3
off Chicheley Rd 51 J7
Artillery Row, SW1 ......25 H6
Artington Cl, Orp. BR6 .207 F4
Artisan Cl, E6
off Ferndale St ...116/117 E6
Artizan St, E1 ....21 E3
Arundel Av, Mord. SM4 .184 C4
Arundel Cl, E15 ....97 E4
SW11 off Chivalry Rd .149 H5
Bexley DA5 ....159 F6
Croydon CR0 ....201 H3
Hampton (Hmptn.H.)
TW12 ....161 H5
Arundel Ct, N12 ....57 H6
Harrow HA2 ....85 G4
Arundel Dr, Borwd. WD6 .38 C5
Harrow HA2 ....85 F4
Woodford Green IG8 ..63 G7
Arundel Gdns, N21 ......59 G1
W11 ....108 C7
Edgware HA8 ....54 D7
Ilford IG3 ....100 A2
Arundel Gt Ct, WC2 ....18 D5
Arundel Gro, N16 ....94 B5
Arundel Pl, N1 ....93 G6
Arundel Rd, Barn. EN4 ..41 H3
Croydon CR0 ....188 A6
Hounslow TW4 ....142 C3
Kingston upon Thames
KT1 ....182 B2
Sutton SM3 ....198 C2
Arundel Sq, N7 ....93 G6
Arundel St, WC2 ....18 D5
Arundel Ter, SW13 ......127 H6
Arvon Rd, N5 ....93 G5
Asbaston Ter, Ilf. IG1
off Buttsbury Rd 99 F5
Ascalon St, SW8 ......130 C7
Ascham Dr, E4
off Rushcroft Rd 62 B7
Ascham End, E17 ....77 H1
Ascham St, NW5 ....92 C5
Aschurch Rd, Croy. CR0 .188 C7
Ascot Cl, Borwd. (Elstree)
WD6 ....38 A5
Ilford IG6 ....65 H6
Northolt UB5 ....85 G5
Ascot Gdns, Sthl. UB1 .103 F5
Ascot Rd, E6 ....116 C3
N15 ....76 A5
N18 ....60 D4
SW17 ....168 A6
Orpington BR5 ....193 J4
Ascott Av, W5 ....125 H2
Ashbourne Av, E18 ......79 H4
N20 ....57 J2
NW11 ....72 C5
Bexleyheath DA7 ......139 E7
Harrow HA2 ....86 A2
Ashbourne Cl, N12 ......57 E4
W5 ....106 A5
Ashbourne Ct, E5
off Daubeney Rd 95 H4
Ashbourne Gro, NW7 ....54 D5
SE22 ....152 C5
W4 ....127 E5
Ashbourne Par, W5
off Ashbourne Rd 105 J4
Ashbourne Ri, Orp. BR6 .207 G4
Ashbourne Rd, W5 ......105 J5
Mitcham CR4 ....168 A6
Ashbourne Ter, SW19 ..166 D7

Ashbourne Way, NW11
  off Ashbourne Av 72 C5
Ashbridge Rd, E11 ......79 F7
Ashbridge St, NW8 ......7 G6
Ashbrook Rd, N19 ......92 D1
  Dagenham RM10 .....101 H3
Ashburn Gdns, SW7 ....30 C1
Ashburnham Av, Har.
  HA1 ....68 C6
Ashburnham Cl, N2 ....73 G3
  Watford WD19
  off Ashburnham Dr 50 A3
Ashburnham Dr, Wat.
  WD19 ....50 A3
Ashburnham Gdns, Har.
  HA1 ....68 C6
Ashburnham Gro, SE10 .134 B7
Ashburnham Pl, SE10 ..134 B7
Ashburnham Retreat,
  SE10 ....134 B7
Ashburnham Rd, NW10 .107 J3
  SW10 ....129 F7
  Belvedere DA17 .....139 J4
  Richmond TW10 .....163 E3
Ashburn Pl, SW7 ......30 C1
Ashburton Av, Croy.
  CR0 ....202 E1
  Ilford IG3 ....99 H4
Ashburton Cl, Croy.
  CR0 ....202 D1
Ashburton Ct, Pnr. HA5 .66 D3
Ashburton Gdns, Croy.
  CR0 ....202 D2
  Ruislip HA4 ....84 A2
Ashburton Ter, E13
  off Grasmere Rd 115 G2
Ashbury Gdns, Rom.
  RM6 ....82 D5
Ashbury Pl, SW19 .....167 F6
Ashbury Rd, SW11 .....149 J3
Ashby Av, Chess. KT9 ..196 A6
Ashby Gro, N1 ....93 J7
Ashby Ms, SE4 ....153 J2
Ashby Rd, N15 ....76 D5
  SE4 ....153 J2
Ashby St, EC1 ....11 H4
Ashby Wk, Croy. CR0 ..187 J6
Ashby Way, West Dr.
  UB7 ....120 D7
Ashchurch Gro, W12 ...127 G2
Ashchurch Pk Vil, W12 .127 G3
Ashchurch Ter, W12 ...127 G3
Ash Cl, SE20 ....189 F2
  Carshalton SM5 .....199 J2
  Edgware HA8 ....54 C4
  New Malden KT3 .....182 D2
  Orpington BR5 ......193 G5
  Sidcup DA14 ....176 B3
  Stanmore HA7 ....52 D6
Ashcombe Av, Surb.
  KT6 ....181 G7
Ashcombe Gdns, Edg.
  HA8 ....54 A4
Ashcombe Ho, Enf. EN3 .45 G3
Ashcombe Pk, NW2 ....89 E3
Ashcombe Rd, SW19 ...166 D5
  Carshalton SM5 .....200 A6
Ashcombe Sq, N.Mal.
  KT3 ....182 C3
Ashcombe St, SW6 ....148 E2
Ashcroft, Pnr. HA5 ....51 G6
Ashcroft Av, Sid. DA15 .158 A6
Ashcroft Ct, N20
  off Oakleigh Rd N 57 G2
Ashcroft Cres, Sid.
  DA15 ....158 A6
Ashcroft Rd, E3 ......113 H4
  Chessington KT9 .....195 J3
Ashcroft Sq, W6
  off King St 127 J4
Ashdale Cl, Twick. TW2 .143 J7
Ashdale Gro, Stan. HA7 .52 C6
Ashdale Rd, SE12 ....173 H1
Ashdale Way, Twick. TW2
  off Ashdale Cl 143 J7
Ashdene, SE15 ....152 E1
  Pinner HA5 ....66 B4
Ashdon Cl, Wdf.Grn. IG8 .63 H6
Ashdon Rd, NW10 ....107 E1
Ashdown Cl, Beck. BR3 .190 B2
  Bexley DA5 ....159 J7
Ashdown Cres, NW5
  off Queen's Cres 92 A5
Ashdown Est, E11
  off High Rd
  Leytonstone 96/97 E4

Ashdown Rd, Enf. EN3 ..45 F3
  Kingston upon Thames
  KT1 ....181 H2
Ashdown Wk, E14 .....134 A4
  Romford RM7 ....83 H2
Ashdown Way, SW17 ..168 A2
Ashen, E6
  off Downings 116 D6
Ashenden Rd, E5 ......95 G5
Ashen Gro, SW19 .....166 D3
Ashentree Ct, EC4 .....19 F4
Asher Loftus Way, N11 ..57 J6
Ashfield Av, Felt. TW13 .160 B1
Ashfield Cl, Beck. BR3 ..172 A7
  Richmond TW10 .....163 H1
Ashfield La, Chis. BR7 ..175 F6
Ashfield Par, N14 ......58 D1
Ashfield Rd, N4 ....75 J6
  N14 ....58 C3
  W3 ....127 F1
Ashfields, Loug. IG10 ..48 C2
Ashfield St, E1 ......112 E5
Ashfield Yd, E1
  off Ashfield St ..112/113 E5
Ashford Av, N8 ....74 E4
  Hayes UB4 ....102 D6
Ashford Cl, E17 ....77 J6
Ashford Cres, Enf. EN3 .45 F2
Ashford Grn, Wat. WD19 .50 D5
Ashford Ms, N17
  off Vicarage Rd 76 D1
Ashford Rd, E6 ....98 D6
  E18 ....79 H2
  NW2 ....90 A4
Ashford St, N1 ....12 D3
Ash Gro, E8 ....113 E1
  N13 ....59 J3
  NW2 ....90 A4
  SE20 ....189 F2
  W5 ....125 H2
  Enfield EN1 ....44 B7
  Hounslow TW5 .....142 D1
  Southall UB1 ....103 G5
  Wembley HA0 ....86 D4
  West Wickham BR4 ..204 C2
Ashgrove Rd, Brom.
  BR1 ....172 D6
  Ilford IG3 ....99 J1
Ash Hill Cl, Bushey
  WD23 ....51 H1
Ash Hill Dr, Pnr. HA5 ...66 C3
Ashingdon Cl, E4 ......62 C3
Ashington Rd, SW6 ...148 C2
Ash Island, E.Mol. KT8 .180 A3
Ashlake Rd, SW16 ....168 E4
Ashland Pl, W1 ....16 B1
Ashlar Pl, SE18
  off Masons Hill ..136/137 E4
Ashleigh Gdns, Sutt.
  SM1 ....198 E2
Ashleigh Pt, SE23
  off Dacres Rd 171 G3
Ashleigh Rd, SE20 ....189 E3
  SW14 ....146 E3
Ashley Av, Ilf. IG6 .....81 E2
  Morden SM4
  off Chalgrove Av 184 D5
Ashley Cl, NW4 ....71 J2
  Pinner HA5 ....66 B2
Ashley Cres, N22 ......75 G2
  SW11 ....150 A3
Ashley Dr, Borwd. WD6 .38 C5
  Isleworth TW7 ......124 B6
  Twickenham TW2 ....143 H7
Ashley Gdns, N13 .....59 J4
  SW1 ....25 G6
  Orpington BR6 ......207 H5
  Richmond TW10 .....163 G3
  Wembley HA9 ....87 H2
Ashley Gro, Loug. IG10
  off Staples Rd 48 B3
Ashley La, NW4 ....71 J2
  Croydon CR0 ....201 H4
Ashley Pl, SW1 ....25 F6
Ashley Rd, E4 ....62 A5
  E7 ....97 J7
  N17 ....76 D3
  N19 ....92 E1
  SW19 ....166 E6
  Enfield EN3 ....45 F2
  Hampton TW12 .....179 G1
  Richmond TW9
  off Jocelyn Rd 145 H3
  Thames Ditton KT7 ..180 C6
  Thornton Heath CR7 .187 F4
Ashley Wk, NW7 ......55 J7
Ashling Rd, Croy. CR0 .202 D1
Ashlin Rd, E15 ....96 D4
Ashlone Rd, SW15 ....147 J3

Ashlyns Way, Chess.
  KT9 ....195 G6
Ashmead, N14 ....42 C5
Ashmead Gate, Brom.
  BR1 ....191 J1
Ashmead Rd, SE14 ...154 A2
  Feltham TW14 ......160 A1
Ashmere Av, Beck. BR3 .190 D2
Ashmere Cl, Sutt. SM3 .197 J5
Ashmere Gro, SW2 ...150 E4
Ashmill St, NW1 ....15 G1
Ashmole Pl, SW8 ......34 E6
Ashmole St, SW8 ......34 D6
Ashmore Ct, Houns. TW5
  off Wheatlands 123 G6
Ashmore Gro, Well.
  DA16 ....157 G3
Ashmore Rd, W9 ....6 A6
Ashmount Est, N19
  off Ashmount Rd 74 D7
Ashmount Rd, N15 .....76 C5
  N19 ....74 C7
Ashmount Ter, W5
  off Murray Rd 125 G4
Ashneal Gdns, Har. HA1 .86 A3
Ashness Gdns, Grnf. UB6 .86 E6
Ashness Rd, SW11 ....149 J5
Ashridge Cl, Har. HA3 ..69 F6
Ashridge Cres, SE18 ..137 F7
Ashridge Dr, Wat. WD19 .50 C5
Ashridge Gdns, N13 ...58 D5
  Pinner HA5 ....66 E4
Ashridge Way, Mord.
  SM4 ....184 C3
  Sunbury-on-Thames
  TW16 ....160 A6
Ash Rd, E15 ....97 E5
  Croydon CR0 ....204 A2
  Orpington BR6 ......207 J7
  Sutton SM3 ....184 B7
Ash Row, Brom. BR2 ..192 D7
Ashtead Rd, E5 ....76 D7
Ashton Cl, Sutt. SM1 ..198 D4
Ashton Gdns, Houns.
  TW4 ....143 F4
  Romford RM6 ....83 E6
Ashton Rd, E15 ....96 D5
Ashton St, E14 ....114 C7
Ashtree Av, Mitch. CR4 .185 H2
Ash Tree Cl, Croy. CR0 .189 H6
Ashtree Cl, Orp. BR6
  off Broadwater
  Gdns 206/207 E4
Ash Tree Cl, Surb. KT6 .195 H1
Ash Tree Dell, NW9 ....70 C5
Ash Tree Way, Croy. CR0 .189 H5
Ashurst Cl, SE20 .....189 E1
Ashurst Dr, Ilf. IG2, IG6 ..81 E6
Ashurst Rd, N12 ......57 H5
  Barnet EN4 ....41 J5
Ashurst Wk, Croy. CR0 .202 E2
Ashvale Rd, SW17 ....167 J5
Ashville Rd, E11 ....96 D2
Ash Wk, SW2 ....169 F1
  Wembley HA0 ....87 F4
Ashwater Rd, SE12 ...173 G1
Ashwell Cl, E6
  off Northumberland
  Rd 116 B6
Ashwin St, E8 ....94 C6
Ashwood Gdns, Croy.
  (New Adgtn.) CR0 ...204 B6
  Hayes UB3
  off Cranford Dr 121 J4
Ashwood Rd, E4 ......62 D3
Ashworth Cl, SE5
  off Love Wk 152 A2
Ashworth Rd, W9 ....6 B3
Askern Cl, Bexh. DA6 ..158 D4
Aske St, N1 ....12 D3
Askew Cres, W12 .....127 F2
Askew Rd, W12 ....127 G1
Askham Ct, W12 .....127 G1
Askham Rd, W12 .....127 G1
Askill Dr, SW15
  off Keswick Rd 148 B5
Asland Rd, E15 ....114 E1
Aslett St, SW18 ......149 E7
Asmara Rd, NW2 ......90 B5
Asmuns Hill, NW11 ....72 D5
Asmuns Pl, NW11 .....72 C5
Asolando Dr, SE17 ....36 A2
Aspen Cl, N19
  off Hargrave Pk 92 C2
  W5 ....125 J2
  West Drayton UB7 ..120 C1
Aspen Copse, Brom.
  BR1 ....192 C2
Aspen Ct, Hayes UB3 ..121 H4
Aspen Dr, Wem. HA0 ...86 D4

Aspen Gdns, W6 ......127 H5
  Mitcham CR4 ....186 A5
Aspen Grn, Erith DA18 .139 F3
Aspen La, Nthlt. UB5 ..102 E3
Aspenlea Rd, W6 .....128 A6
Aspen Way, E14 ......114 A7
  Feltham TW13 ......160 B3
Aspern Gro, NW3 ......91 H5
Aspinall Rd, SE4 .....153 G3
Aspinden Rd, SE16 ...133 E4
Aspley Rd, SW18 .....149 E5
Asplins Rd, N17 ....76 D1
Asprey Pl, Brom. BR1
  off Chislehurst Rd ..192 A2
Asquith Cl, Dag. RM8 ..100 C1
Assam St, E1 ....21 H3
Assata St, N1
  off St. Paul's Rd 93 H6
Assembly Pas, E1 .....113 F5
Assembly Wk, Cars.
  SM5 ....185 H7
Ass Ho La, Har. HA3 ...51 H4
Assurance Cotts, Belv. DA17
  off Heron Hill 139 F5
Astall Cl, Har. HA3 .....68 B1
Astbury Rd, SE15 ....153 F1
Astell St, SW3 ....31 H3
Aste St, E14 ....134 C2
Asteys Row, N1
  off River Pl 93 H7
Asthall Gdns, Ilf. IG6 ...81 F4
Astle St, SW11 ......150 A2
Astley Av, NW2 ....89 J5
Aston Av, Har. HA3 ....69 F7
Aston Cl, Sid. DA14 ...176 A3
Aston Grn, Houns.
  TW4 ....142 C2
Aston Ms, Rom. RM6 ...82 C7
Aston Pl, SW16
  off Averil Gro 169 H6
Aston Rd, SW20 .....183 J2
  W5 ....105 G6
  Esher (Clay.) KT10 ...194 B6
Aston St, E14 ....113 H6
Aston Ter, SW12
  off Cathles Rd 150 B6
Astonville St, SW18 ..166 D1
Astor Av, Rom. RM7 ...83 J6
Astor Cl, Kings.T. KT2 ..164 B6
Astoria Wk, SW9 .....151 G3
Astrop Ms, W6 ....127 J3
Astrop Ter, W6 ....127 J3
Astwood Ms, SW7 ....30 C1
Asylum Rd, SE15 .....133 E7
Atalanta St, SW6 .....148 A1
Atbara Ct, Tedd. TW11 .163 E6
Atbara Rd, Tedd. TW11 .163 E6
Atcham Rd, Houns.
  TW3 ....143 J4
Atcost Rd, Bark. IG11 ..118 A5
Atheldene Rd, SW18 ..167 E1
Athelney St, SE6 .....172 A3
Athelstane Gro, E3 ....113 J2
Athelstane Ms, N4
  off Stroud Grn Rd ...93 G1
Athelstan Rd, Kings.T.
  KT1 ....181 J4
Athelstone Rd, Har. HA3 .68 A2
Athena Cl, Har. HA2
  off Byron Hill Rd 86 B2
  Kingston upon Thames
  KT1 ....181 J3
Athenaeum Pl, N10
  off Fortis Grn Rd 74 B3
Athenaeum Rd, N20 ...57 F1
Athenlay Rd, SE15 ...153 G5
Athens Gdns, W9
  off Harrow Rd 108 D4
Atherden Rd, E5 ....95 F4
Atherfold Rd, SW9 ...150 E3
Atherley Way, Houns.
  TW4 ....143 F7
Atherstone Ct, W2
  off Delamere Ter .108/109 E5
Atherstone Ms, SW7 ..30 D1
Atherton Dr, SW19 ...166 A4
Atherton Hts, Wem.
  HA0 ....87 F6
Atherton Ms, E7 ......97 F6
Atherton Pl, Har. HA2 ..68 A3
  Southall UB1
  off Longford Av 103 H7
Atherton Rd, E7 ....97 F5
  SW13 ....127 G7
  Ilford IG5 ....80 B2
Atherton St, SW11 ...149 H2
Athlone, Esher (Clay.)
  KT10 ....194 B6

Athlone Cl, E5
off Goulton Rd **94/95** E4
Athlone Rd, SW2 . . . . . .**151** F7
Athlone St, NW5 . . . .**92** A6
Athlon Rd, Wem. HA0 . . .**105** G2
Athol Cl, Pnr. HA5 . . . . . .**66** B1
Athole Gdns, Enf. EN1 . . .**44** B5
Athol Gdns, Pnr. HA5 . . . .**66** B1
Atholl Rd, Ilf. IG3 . . . .**82** A7
Athol Rd, Erith DA8 . . . .**139** J5
Athol Sq, E14 . . . .**114** C6
Atkins Dr, W.Wick. BR4 . .**204** D2
Atkinson Rd, E16 . . . .**115** J5
Atkins Rd, E10 . . . .**78** B6
   SW12 . . . .**150** D7
Atlantic Rd, SW9 . . . . . .**151** G4
Atlantis Cl, Bark. IG11 . . .**118** B3
Atlas Gdns, SE7 . . . .**135** J4
Atlas Ms, E8
off Tyssen St **94** C6
   N7 . . . .**93** F6
Atlas Rd, E13 . . . .**115** G2
   N11 . . . .**58** B6
   NW10 . . . .**107** E3
   Wembley HA9 . . . .**88** C4
Atley Rd, E3 . . . .**114** A1
Atlip Rd, Wem. HA0 . . . .**105** H1
Atney Rd, SW15 . . . .**148** B4
Atria Rd, Nthwd. HA6 . . . .**50** A5
Attenborough Cl, Wat. WD19
off Harrow Way **50/51** E3
Atterbury Rd, N4 . . . .**75** G6
Atterbury St, SW1 . . . . . .**33** J2
Attewood Av, NW10 . . . . .**88** E3
Attewood Rd, Nthlt. UB5 . .**85** E6
Attfield Cl, N20 . . . .**57** G2
Attlee Cl, Hayes UB4 . . . .**102** B3
   Thornton Heath CR7 . . .**187** J6
Attlee Rd, SE28 . . . .**118** B7
   Hayes UB4 . . . .**102** A3
Attlee Ter, E17 . . . .**78** B4
Attneave St, WC1 . . . .**10** E4
Atwater Cl, SW2 . . . .**169** G1
Atwell Cl, E10
off Belmont Pk Rd . . .**78** B6
Atwell Pl, T.Ditt. KT7 . . .**194** C1
Atwell Rd, SE15
off Rye La **152** D2
Atwood Av, Rich. TW9 . . .**146** A2
Atwood Rd, W6 . . . .**127** H4
Atwoods All, Rich. TW9
off Leyborne Pk **146** A1
Aubert Pk, N5 . . . .**93** H4
Aubert Rd, N5 . . . .**93** H4
Aubrey Pl, NW8 . . . .**6** C2
Aubrey Rd, E17 . . . .**78** A3
   N8 . . . .**75** E5
   W8 . . . .**128** C1
Aubrey Wk, W8 . . . .**128** C1
Auburn Cl, SE14 . . . .**133** H7
Aubyn Hill, SE27 . . . . . .**169** J4
Aubyn Sq, SW15 . . . . . .**147** G4
Auckland Cl, SE19 . . . . .**188** C1
Auckland Gdns, SE19 . . .**188** B1
Auckland Hill, SE27 . . . .**169** J4
Auckland Ri, SE19 . . . . .**188** B1
Auckland Rd, E10 . . . . . .**96** B3
   SE19 . . . .**188** C1
   SW11 . . . .**149** H4
   Ilford IG1 . . . .**99** E1
   Kingston upon Thames
   KT1 . . . .**181** J4
Auckland St, SE11 . . . . . .**34** C4
Auden Pl, NW1 . . . .**110** A1
   Sutton SM3
   off Wordsworth Dr . . .**197** J4
Audleigh Pl, Chig. IG7 . . . .**64** D6
Audley Cl, N10 . . . .**58** B7
   SW11 . . . .**150** A3
   Borehamwood WD6 . . . .**38** A3
Audley Ct, E18 . . . .**79** F4
   Pinner HA5
   off Rickmansworth Rd .**66** C2
Audley Dr, E16
off Wesley Av **135** H1
Audley Gdns, Ilf. IG3 . . . .**99** J2
   Loughton IG10 . . . .**49** F2
Audley Pl, Sutt. SM2 . . . .**198** D7
Audley Rd, NW4 . . . .**71** H6
   W5 . . . .**105** J5
   Enfield EN2 . . . .**43** H2
   Richmond TW10 . . . . . .**145** J5
Audley Sq, W1 . . . .**24** C1
Audrey Cl, Beck. BR3 . . .**190** B6
Audrey Gdns, Wem.
   HA0 . . . .**87** E2
Audrey Rd, Ilf. IG1 . . . . . .**98** E3
Audrey St, E2 . . . .**13** H1
Audric Cl, Kings.T. KT2 . .**182** A1
Augurs La, E13 . . . .**115** H3

Augusta Cl, W.Mol. KT8
off Freeman Dr **179** F3
Augusta Rd, Twick. TW2 .**161** J2
Augusta St, E14 . . . .**114** B6
Augustine Rd, W14 . . . . .**128** A3
   Harrow HA3 . . . .**67** H1
Augustus Cl, Brent. TW8 .**125** F7
Augustus Rd, SW19 . . . .**166** B1
Augustus St, NW1 . . . .**9** E2
Aultone Way, Cars. SM5 .**199** J3
   Sutton SM1 . . . .**199** E2
Aulton Pl, SE11 . . . .**35** F4
Aurelia Gdns, Croy. CR0 .**187** F5
Aurelia Rd, Croy. CR0 . . .**187** E6
Auriga Ms, N16 . . . .**94** A5
Auriol Cl, Wor.Pk. KT4
off Auriol Pk Rd . .**196/197** E3
Auriol Dr, Grnf. UB6 . . . . .**86** A7
Auriol Pk Rd, Wor.Pk.
   KT4 . . . .**197** E3
Auriol Rd, W14 . . . .**128** B4
Austell Gdns, NW7 . . . . . .**55** E3
Austen Cl, SE28 . . . .**138** B1
   Loughton IG10 . . . .**49** G3
Austen Ho, NW6 . . . .**108** D3
Austen Rd, Erith DA8 . . .**139** H7
   Harrow HA2 . . . .**85** H2
Austin Av, Brom. BR2 . . .**192** B5
Austin Cl, SE23 . . . .**153** J7
   Twickenham TW1 . . . . .**145** F5
Austin Ct, E6
off Kings Rd **115** J1
Austin Friars, EC2 . . . . . .**20** C3
Austin Friars Pas, EC2 . . .**20** C3
Austin Friars Sq, EC2 . . . .**20** C3
Austin Rd, SW11 . . . .**150** A1
   Hayes UB3 . . . .**121** J2
Austin St, E2 . . . .**13** F4
Austral Cl, Sid. DA15 . . . .**175** J3
Australia Rd, W12 . . . . . .**107** H7
Austral St, SE11 . . . .**35** G1
Austyn Gdns, Surb.
   KT5 . . . .**196** B1
Autumn Cl, SW19 . . . . . .**167** F6
   Enfield EN1 . . . .**44** D1
Autumn St, E3 . . . .**114** A1
Avalon Cl, SW20 . . . . . .**184** B2
   W13 . . . .**104** D5
   Enfield EN2 . . . .**43** G2
Avalon Rd, SW6 . . . .**148** E1
   W13 . . . .**104** D4
Avard Gdns, Orp. BR6 . . .**207** F4
Avarn Rd, SW17 . . . .**167** J6
Avebury Ct, N1
off Poole St **112** A1
Avebury Pk, Surb. KT6 . .**181** G7
Avebury Rd, E11
off Southwest Rd **96** D1
   SW19 . . . .**184** C1
   Orpington BR6 . . . .**207** G3
Avebury St, N1
off Poole St **112** A1
Aveline St, SE11 . . . .**34** E3
Aveling Pk Rd, E17 . . . . . .**78** A2
Ave Maria La, EC4 . . . . . .**19** H4
Avenell Rd, N5 . . . .**93** H3
Avening Rd, SW18
off Brathway Rd **148** D7
Avening Ter, SW18 . . . . .**148** D6
Avenons Rd, E13 . . . . . .**115** G4
Avenue, The, E4 . . . .**62** D6
Avenue Cl, N14 . . . .**42** C6
   NW8 . . . .**109** H1
   Hounslow TW5
   off The Avenue **142** A1
   West Drayton UB7 . . . .**120** A3
Avenue Cres, W3 . . . . . .**126** B2
   Hounslow TW5 . . . . . .**122** B7
Avenue Elmers, Surb.
   KT6 . . . .**181** H5
Avenue Gdns, SE25 . . . .**188** D3
   SW14 . . . .**146** E3
   W3 . . . .**126** B2
   Hounslow TW5
   off The Avenue **122** A7
   Teddington TW11 . . . . .**162** C7
Avenue Gate, Loug. IG10 .**47** J6
Avenue Ind Est, E4 . . . . . .**61** J6
Avenue Ms, N10 . . . .**74** B3
Avenue Pk Rd, SE27 . . . .**169** H2
Avenue Rd, E7 . . . .**97** H5
   N6 . . . .**74** C7
   N12 . . . .**57** F4
   N14 . . . .**42** B7
   N15 . . . .**76** A4
   NW3 . . . .**91** G7
   NW8 . . . .**91** G7
   NW10 . . . .**107** F2
   SE20 . . . .**189** F1
   SE25 . . . .**188** D2
   SW16 . . . .**186** D2
   SW20 . . . .**183** H2
   W3 . . . .**126** B2
   Beckenham BR3 . . . . . .**189** F1
   Belvedere DA17 . . . . . .**139** J4
   Bexleyheath DA7 . . . . .**158** E3
   Brentford TW8 . . . .**125** F5
   Erith DA8 . . . .**139** J7
   Hampton TW12 . . . . . .**179** H1
   Isleworth TW7 . . . .**144** C1
   Kingston upon Thames
   KT1 . . . .**181** H3
   New Malden KT3 . . . . .**182** E4
   Pinner HA5 . . . .**66** E3
   Romford (Chad.Hth.)
   RM6 . . . .**82** B7
   Southall UB1 . . . .**123** F2
   Teddington TW11 . . . . .**162** D7
   Wallington SM6 . . . . . .**200** C7
   Woodford Green IG8 . . . .**63** J6
Avenue S, Surb. KT5 . . . .**181** J7
Avenue Ter, N.Mal. KT3
off Kingston Rd **182** C3
Averil Gro, SW16 . . . . . .**169** H6
Averill St, W6 . . . .**128** A6
Avern Gdns, W.Mol. KT8 .**179** H4
Avern Rd, W.Mol. KT8 . . .**179** H5
Avery Fm Row, SW1 . . . . .**32** C2
Avery Gdns, Ilf. IG2 . . . . .**80** C5
AVERY HILL, SE9 . . . . . .**157** F6
★ Avery Hill Pk, SE9
   (Eltham) **157** F6
Avery Hill Rd, SE9 . . . . .**157** G6
Avery Row, W1 . . . .**16** D5
Avey La, Loug. IG10 . . . . .**47** H1
Aviary Cl, E16 . . . .**115** F5
Aviemore Cl, Beck. BR3 . .**189** J5
Aviemore Way, Beck.
   BR3 . . . .**189** H5
Avignon Rd, SE4 . . . .**153** G3
Avington Ct, SE1
off Old Kent Rd **132** B4
Avington Gro, SE20 . . . . .**171** F7
Avington Way, SE15 . . . . .**37** F7
Avion Cres, NW9 . . . .**71** G1
Avis Sq, E1 . . . .**113** G6
Avoca Rd, SW17 . . . .**168** A4
Avocet Ms, SE28 . . . . . .**137** G3
Avon Cl, Hayes UB4 . . . .**102** C4
   Sutton SM1 . . . .**199** F4
   Worcester Park KT4 . . .**197** G2
Avon Ct, Grnf. UB6
off Braund Av **103** H4
Avondale Av, N12 . . . .**56** E5

Avondale Av, NW2 . . . . . .**89** E3
   Barnet EN4 . . . .**57** J1
   Esher KT10 . . . .**194** D3
   Worcester Park KT4 . . .**197** F1
Avondale Cl, Loug. IG10 . .**48** C7
Avondale Ct, E11 . . . .**96** E1
   E16 *off Avondale*
   Rd **114/115** E5
   E18 . . . .**79** H3
Avondale Cres, Enf. EN3 . .**45** H3
   Ilford IG4 . . . .**80** A5
Avondale Dr, Hayes UB3 .**122** A1
   Loughton IG10 . . . .**48** C7
Avondale Gdns, Houns.
   TW4 . . . .**143** F5
Avondale Ms, Brom. BR1
off Avondale Rd **173** G6
Avondale Pk Gdns, W11 .**108** B7
Avondale Pk Rd, W11 . . .**108** B7
Avondale Pavement, SE1
off Avondale Sq **132** D5
Avondale Ri, SE15 . . . . . .**152** C3
Avondale Rd, E16 . . . . . .**115** E5
   E17 . . . .**78** A7
   N3 . . . .**73** F1
   N13 . . . .**59** G2
   N15 . . . .**75** H5
   SE9 . . . .**174** B2
   SW14 . . . .**146** D3
   SW19 . . . .**166** E5
   Bromley BR1 . . . .**173** E6
   Harrow HA3 . . . .**68** C3
   South Croydon CR2 . . .**201** J6
   Welling DA16 . . . .**158** C2
Avondale Sq, SE1 . . . .**37** H4
Avonley Rd, SE14 . . . . . .**133** F7
Avon Ms, Pnr. HA5 . . . . . .**67** F1
Avonmore Gdns, W14
off Avonmore Rd **128** B4
Avonmore Pl, W14
off Avonmore Rd **128** B4
Avonmore Rd, W14 . . . . .**128** C4
Avonmouth St, SE1 . . . . .**27** J5
Avon Path, S.Croy. CR2 . .**201** J6
Avon Pl, SE1 . . . .**28** A4
Avon Rd, E17 . . . .**78** D3
   SE4 . . . .**154** A3
   Greenford UB6 . . . . . .**103** G4
Avonstowe Cl, Orp. BR6 .**207** F3
Avon Way, E18 . . . .**79** G3
Avonwick Rd, Houns.
   TW3 . . . .**143** H2
Avril Way, E4 . . . .**62** C5
Avro Way, Wall. SM6 . . . .**201** E7
Awlfield Av, N17 . . . .**76** A1
Awliscombe Rd, Well.
   DA16 . . . .**157** J2
Axe St, Bark. IG11 . . . . . .**117** F1
Axholme Av, Edg. HA8 . . .**70** A1
Axminster Cres, Well.
   DA16 . . . .**158** C1
Axminster Rd, N7 . . . .**93** E3
Aybrook St, W1 . . . .**16** B2
Aycliffe Cl, Brom. BR1 . . .**192** C4
Aycliffe Rd, W12 . . . .**127** F1
Aylands Cl, Wem. HA9
off Preston Rd **87** H2
Aylesbury Cl, E7
off Atherton Rd **97** F6
Aylesbury Ct, Sutt. SM1
off Benhill Wd Rd . . .**199** F3
Aylesbury Est, SE17 . . . . .**36** C4
Aylesbury Rd, SE17 . . . . .**36** C4
   Bromley BR2 . . . .**191** G3
Aylesbury St, EC1 . . . .**11** G6
   NW10 . . . .**88** D3
Aylesford Av, Beck. BR3 .**189** H5
Aylesford St, SW1 . . . .**33** H3
Aylesham Cen, The,
   SE15 . . . .**152** D1
Aylesham Cl, NW7 . . . . . .**55** G7
Aylesham Rd, Orp. BR6 . .**193** J7
Ayles Rd, Hayes UB4 . . .**102** B3
Aylestone Av, NW6 . . . . .**108** A1
Aylett Rd, SE25 . . . .**188** E4
   Isleworth TW7 . . . .**144** B2
Ayley Cft, Enf. EN1 . . . . . .**44** D5
Ayliffe Cl, Kings.T. KT1
off Cambridge Gdns .**182** A2
Aylmer Cl, Stan. HA7 . . . .**52** D4
Aylmer Dr, Stan. HA7 . . . .**52** D4
Aylmer Par, N2 . . . .**73** J5
Aylmer Rd, E11 . . . .**97** F1
   N2 . . . .**73** H5
   W12 . . . .**127** F2
   Dagenham RM8 . . . . . .**100** E3
Ayloffe Rd, Dag. RM9 . . .**101** F6
Aylton Est, SE16
off Renforth St **133** F2
Aylward Rd, SE23 . . . . . .**171** G2

Aylward Rd, SW20 . . . . .184 C2
Aylwards Ri, Stan. HA7 . .52 D4
Aylward St, E1 . . . . .113 F6
Aylwyn Est, SE1 . . . . .29 F5
Aynhoe Rd, W14 . . . . .128 A4
Aynscombe La, SW14 . . .146 C3
Aynscombe Path, SW14
  off Thames Bk 146 C2
Ayr Ct, W3
  off Monks Dr 106 A5
Ayres Ct, E13 . . . . .115 G3
Ayres Cres, NW10 . . . . . . .88 D7
Ayres St, SE1 . . . . .28 A3
Ayrsome Rd, N16 . . . . . . .94 B3
Ayrton Rd, SW7 . . . . .23 E5
Aysgarth Ct, Sutt. SM1
  off Sutton Common
  Rd 198/199 E3
Aysgarth Rd, SE21 . . . .152 B6
Aytoun Pl, SW9 . . . . .151 F2
Aytoun Rd, SW9 . . . . . . .151 F2
Azalea Cl, W7 . . . . .124 C1
  Ilford IG1 . . . . .98 E5
Azalea Ct, Wdf.Grn. IG8
  off The Bridle Path .62/63 E7
Azalea Wk, Pnr. HA5 . . . . .66 B5
  Southall UB2
  off Navigator Dr 123 J2
Azania Ms, NW5
  off Cathcart St 92 B6
Azenby Rd, SE15 . . . . . . .152 C2
Azile Everitt Ho, SE18
  off Vicarage Pk 137 F5
Azof St, SE10 . . . . .135 E4

B

Baalbec Rd, N5 . . . . .93 H5
Babbacombe Cl, Chess.
  KT9 . . . . .195 G5
Babbacombe Gdns, Ilf.
  IG4 . . . . .80 B4
Babbacombe Rd, Brom.
  BR1 . . . . .191 G1
Baber Dr, Felt. TW14 . . . .142 C6
Babington Ri, Wem.
  HA9 . . . . .88 A6
Babington Rd, NW4 . . . . .71 H4
  SW16 . . . . .168 D5
  Dagenham RM8 . . . . . .100 C5
Babmaes St, SW1 . . . . . . .17 G6
Bacchus Wk, N1 . . . . .12 D2
Baches St, N1 . . . . .12 C4
Back Ch La, E1 . . . . .21 H5
Back Hill, EC1 . . . . .11 E6
Backhouse Pl, SE17 . . . . . .36 E2
Back La, N8 . . . . .74 E5
  NW3 off Heath St 91 F4
  Bexley DA5 . . . . .159 G7
  Brentford TW8 . . . . . . .125 G6
  Edgware HA8 . . . . .70 C1
  Richmond TW10 . . . . . .163 F3
  Romford RM6
  off St. Chad's Rd . .82/83 E7
Backley Gdns, SE25 . . . .188 D6
Back Rd, Sid. DA14 . . . . .176 A4
Bacon Gro, SE1 . . . . .29 F6
Bacon La, NW9 . . . . .70 B4
  Edgware HA8 . . . . .70 A1
Bacons La, N6 . . . . .92 A1
Bacon St, E1 . . . . .13 G5
  E2 . . . . .13 G5
Bacon Ter, Dag. RM8
  off Fitzstephen Rd . . .100 B5
Bacton, NW5 . . . . .92 A5
Bacton St, E2
  off Roman Rd 113 F3
Baddow Cl, Dag. RM10 . .119 G1
  Woodford Green IG8 . . .64 A6
Baddow Wk, N1 . . . . .111 J1
Baden Pl, SE1 . . . . .28 B3
Baden Powell Cl, Dag.
  RM9 . . . . .119 E1
  Surbiton KT6 . . . . .195 J2
Baden Rd, N8 . . . . .74 D4
  Ilford IG1 . . . . .98 E5
Badger Cl, Felt. TW13
  off Sycamore Cl 160 A3
  Hounslow TW4 . . . . . . .142 C3
  Ilford IG2 . . . . .81 F7
Badgers Cl, Enf. EN2 . . . . .43 H3
  Harrow HA1 . . . . .68 A6
Badgers Copse, Orp.
  BR6 . . . . .207 J2
  Worcester Park KT4 . . .197 F2
Badgers Cft, N20 . . . . .56 B1
  SE9 . . . . .174 D3
Badgers Hole, Croy. CR0 .203 G4
Badgers Wk, N.Mal. KT3 .182 E2

Badlis Rd, E17 . . . . .78 A2
Badminton Cl, Borwd.
  WD6 . . . . .38 A2
  Harrow HA1 . . . . .68 B4
Badminton Cl, Nthlt UB5 .85 G6
Badminton Ms, E16
  off Hanameel St 135 G1
Badminton Rd, SW12 . . .150 A6
Badric Ct, SW11
  off Yelverton Rd 149 G2
Badsworth Rd, SE5 . . . . .131 J7
Baffin Way, E14
  off Prestons Rd 114 C7
Bagley Cl, West Dr. UB7 .120 B2
Bagley's La, SW6 . . . . . . .149 E1
Bagleys Spring, Rom.
  RM6 . . . . .83 E4
Bagshot Ct, SE18
  off Prince Imperial
  Rd 156 D1
Bagshot Rd, Enf. EN1 . . . .44 C7
Bagshot St, SE17 . . . . .36 E4
Baildon St, SE8 . . . . .133 J7
Bailey Cl, E4 . . . . .62 C4
  N11 . . . . .58 D7
Bailey Pl, SE26 . . . . .171 G6
Baillies Wk, W5
  off Liverpool Rd 125 G2
Bainbridge Cl, Rich. TW10
  off Latchmere Cl 163 H5
Bainbridge Rd, Dag.
  RM9 . . . . .101 F4
Bainbridge St, WC1 . . . . . .17 J3
Baines Cl, S.Croy. CR2
  off Brighton Rd 201 J5
Baird Av, Sthl. UB1 . . . . .103 H7
Baird Cl, E10
  off Marconi Rd 96 A1
  NW9 . . . . .70 C6
Baird Gdns, SE19 . . . . . . .170 B4
Baird Rd, Enf. EN1 . . . . . .44 E4
Baird St, EC1 . . . . .12 A5
Baizdon Rd, SE3 . . . . .154 E2
Baker La, Mitch. CR4 . . . .186 A2
Baker Pas, NW10
  off Acton La 106/107 E1
Baker Rd, NW10 . . . . .106 E1
  SE18 . . . . .136 B7
Bakers Av, E17 . . . . .78 B6
Bakers Ct, SE25 . . . . .188 B3
Bakers End, SW20 . . . . . .184 B2
Bakers Fld, N7 . . . .
  off Crayford Rd 92 D4
Bakers Gdns, Cars. SM5 .199 H2
Bakers Hill, E5 . . . . .95 F1
  Barnet EN5 . . . . .41 E2
Bakers La, N6 . . . . .73 J5
Baker's Ms, W1 . . . . .16 B3
Bakers Ms, Orp. BR6 . . . .207 J6
Bakers Pas, NW3
  off Heath St 91 F4
Baker's Rents, E2 . . . . .13 F4
Bakers Row, E15 . . . . .114 E2
Baker's Row, EC1 . . . . .11 E6
Baker St, NW1 . . . . .8 A6
  W1 . . . . .16 A1
  Enfield EN1 . . . . .44 A3
Baker's Yd, EC1
  off Baker's Row 111 G4
Bakery Cl, SW9 . . . . .151 F1
Bakery Path, Edg. HA8
  off Station Rd 54 B6
Bakery Pl, SW11
  off Altenburg Gdns .149 J4
Bakewell Way, N.Mal.
  KT3 . . . . .182 E2
Balaams La, N14 . . . . .58 D2
Balaam St, E13 . . . . .115 G3
Balaclava Rd, SE1 . . . . . . .37 G2
  Surbiton KT6 . . . . .181 F7
Bala Grn, NW9
  off Snowdon Dr . . .70/71 E6
Balcaskie Rd, SE9 . . . . . .156 C5
Balchen Rd, SE3 . . . . .156 A2
Balchier Rd, SE22 . . . . . .152 E6
Balcombe Cl, Bexh.
  DA6 . . . . .158 D4
Balcombe St, NW1 . . . . . . .7 J6
Balcon Ct, W5
  off Boileau Rd 105 J6
Balcon Way, Borwd. WD6 .38 C1
Balcorne St, E9 . . . . .95 F7
Balder Ri, SE12 . . . . .173 H2
Balderton St, W1 . . . . .16 C4
Baldock St, E3 . . . . .114 B2
Baldry Gdns, SW16 . . . . .169 E6
Baldwin Cres, SE5 . . . . . .151 J1
Baldwin Gdns, Houns.TW3
  off Chamberlain
  Gdns 143 J1

Baldwin's Gdns, EC1 . . . . .18 E1
Baldwins Hill, Loug.
  IG10 . . . . .48 C2
Baldwin St, EC1 . . . . .12 B4
Baldwin Ter, N1 . . . . .11 J1
Baldwyn Gdns, W3 . . . . . .106 D7
Bale Rd, E1 . . . . .113 H5
Balfern Gro, W4 . . . . .127 E5
Balfern St, SW11 . . . . .149 H1
Balfe St, N1 . . . . .10 B2
Balfour Av, W7 . . . . .124 C1
Balfour Business Cen, Sthl.
  UB2 . . . . .122 D3
Balfour Gro, N20 . . . . .57 J3
Balfour Ho, W10
  off St. Charles Sq . . .108 A5
Balfour Ms, N9
  off The Broadway 60 D3
  W1 . . . . .24 C1
Balfour Pl, SW15 . . . . .147 H4
  W1 . . . . .16 C6
Balfour Rd, N5 . . . . .93 J4
  SE25 . . . . .188 D4
  SW19 . . . . .166 E7
  W3 . . . . .106 C5
  W13 . . . . .124 D2
  Bromley BR2 . . . . .192 A5
  Carshalton SM5 . . . . . .199 J7
  Harrow HA1 . . . . .68 A5
  Hounslow TW3 . . . . . . .143 H3
  Ilford IG1 . . . . .98 E2
  Southall UB2 . . . . .122 D3
Balfour St, SE17 . . . . .36 B1
Balfron Twr, E14
  off St. Leonards Rd . .114 C6
Balgonie Rd, E4 . . . . .62 D1
Balgowan Cl, N.Mal.
  KT3 . . . . .183 E5
Balgowan Rd, Beck.
  BR3 . . . . .189 H3
Balgowan St, SE18 . . . . .137 J4
BALHAM, SW12 . . . . .167 J1
Balham Continental Mkt,
  SW12 off Shipka Rd .168 B1
Balham Gro, SW12 . . . . . .150 A7
Balham High Rd, SW12 .168 A1
  SW17 . . . . .168 A2
Balham Hill, SW12 . . . . . .150 B7
Balham New Rd,
  SW12 . . . . .150 B7
Balham Pk Rd, SW12 . . . .167 J1
Balham Rd, N9 . . . . .60 D2
Balham Sta Rd, SW12 . . .168 B1
Balkan Wk, E1
  off Pennington
  St 112/113 E7
Balladier Wk, E14 . . . . . . .114 B5
Ballamore Rd, Brom.
  BR1 . . . . .173 G3
Ballance Rd, E9 . . . . .95 G6
Ballantine St, SW18 . . . . .149 F4
Ballard Cl, Kings.T. KT2 .164 D7
Ballards Cl, Dag. RM10 . .119 H1
Ballards Fm Rd, Croy.
  CR0 . . . . .202 D6
  South Croydon CR2 . . .202 D6
Ballards La, N3 . . . . .72 D1
  N12 . . . . .72 D1
Ballards Ms, Edg. HA8 . . . .54 A6
Ballards Ri, S.Croy. CR2 .202 D6
Ballards Rd, NW2 . . . . .89 G2
  Dagenham RM10 . . . . .119 H1
Ballards Way, Croy. CR0 .203 E6
  South Croydon CR2 . . .202 D6
Ballast Quay, SE10 . . . . . .134 D5
Ballater Rd, SW2 . . . . .151 E4
  South Croydon CR2 . . .202 C5
Ballina St, SE23 . . . . .153 G6
Ballingdon Rd, SW11 . . . .150 A6
Ballinger Pt, E3
  off Bromley High St . .114 B3
Balliol Av, E4 . . . . .62 D4
Balliol Rd, N17 . . . . .76 B1
  W10 . . . . .107 J6
  Welling DA16 . . . . .158 B2
Balloch Rd, SE6 . . . . .172 D1
Ballogie Av, NW10 . . . . . . .89 E4
Ballow Cl, SE5
  off Harris St 132 B7
Balls Pond Pl, N1
  off Balls Pond Rd 94 A6
Balls Pond Rd, N1 . . . . .94 A6
Balmain Cl, W5 . . . . .125 G1
Balmer Rd, E3 . . . . .113 J2
Balmes Rd, N1 . . . . .112 A1
Balmoral Av, N11 . . . . .58 A5
  Beckenham BR3 . . . . . .189 H4
Balmoral Cl, SW15
  off Westleigh Av 148 A6

Balmoral Ct, Wor.Pk.
  KT4 . . . . .197 H2
Balmoral Cres, W.Mol.
  KT8 . . . . .179 G3
Balmoral Dr, Borwd.
  WD6 . . . . .38 D5
  Southall UB1 . . . . .103 F4
Balmoral Gdns, W13 . . . .124 D3
  Bexley DA5 . . . . .159 F7
  Ilford IG3 . . . . .99 J1
Balmoral Gro, N7 . . . . .93 F6
Balmoral Ms, W12 . . . . . .127 F2
Balmoral Rd, E7 . . . . .97 J4
  E10 . . . . .96 B2
  NW2 . . . . .89 H6
  Harrow HA2 . . . . .85 G4
  Kingston upon Thames
  KT1 . . . . .181 J4
  Worcester Park KT4 . . .197 H3
Balmore Cl, E14 . . . . .114 C6
Balmore Cres, Barn. EN4 .42 A5
Balmore St, N19 . . . . .92 B2
Balmuir Gdns, SW15 . . . .147 J4
Balnacraig Av, NW10 . . . . .89 E4
Balniel Gate, SW1 . . . . . . .33 J3
Baltic Cl, SW19 . . . . .167 G7
Baltic Ct, SE16
  off Timber Pond Rd . .133 G2
Baltic Pl, N1
  off Kingsland Rd 112 B1
Baltic St E, EC1 . . . . .11 J6
Baltic St W, EC1 . . . . .11 J6
Baltimore Pl, Well.
  DA16 . . . . .157 J2
Balvaird Pl, SW1 . . . . .33 J4
Balvernie Gro, SW18 . . . .148 C7
Bamber Ho, Bark. IG11
  off St. Margarets 117 F1
Bamborough Gdns,W12 .127 J2
Bamford Av, Wem. HA0 . .105 J1
Bamford Ct, E15
  off Clays La 96 B5
Bamford Rd, Bark. IG11 . .99 F6
  Bromley BR1 . . . . .172 C5
Bampfylde Cl, Wall.
  SM6 . . . . .200 C3
Bampton Dr, NW7 . . . . .55 G7
Bampton Rd, SE23 . . . . . .171 G3
Banavie Gdns, Beck.
  BR3 . . . . .190 C1
Banbury Cl, Enf. EN2
  off Holtwhites Hill 43 H1
Banbury Ct, WC2 . . . . .18 A5
  Sutton SM2 . . . . .198 D7
Banbury Enterprise Cen,
  Croy. CR0
  off Factory La 201 H2
Banbury Rd, E9 . . . . .95 G7
  E17 . . . . .61 G7
Banbury St, SW11 . . . . . . .149 H2
Banbury Wk, Nthlt. UB5
  off Brabazon Rd 103 G2
Banchory Rd, SE3 . . . . . . .135 H7
Bancroft Av, N2 . . . . .73 H5
  Buckhurst Hill IG9 . . . . .63 G2
Bancroft Ct, Nthlt. UB5 . .102 C1
Bancroft Gdns, Har. HA3 . .67 J1
  Orpington BR6 . . . . . . .207 J1
Bancroft Rd, E1 . . . . .113 F3
  Harrow HA3 . . . . .67 J2
Bandon Ri, Wall. SM6 . . . .200 D5
Banfield Rd, SE15 . . . . . . .152 E4
Bangalore St, SW15 . . . . .147 J3
Bangor Cl, Nthlt. UB5 . . . . .85 H5
Banim St, W6 . . . . .127 H3
Banister Rd, W10 . . . . . . .108 A3
Bank, The, N6
  off Cholmeley Pk 92 B1
Bank Av, Mitch. CR4 . . . .185 G2
Bank End, SE1 . . . . .28 A1
Bankfoot Rd, Brom.
  BR1 . . . . .173 E4
Bankhurst Rd, SE6 . . . . . .153 J7
Bank La, SW15 . . . . .146 E5
  Kingston upon Thames
  KT2 . . . . .163 H7
Bank Ms, Sutt. SM1
  off Sutton Ct Rd 199 F6
★ Bank of England,
  EC2 . . . . .20 B4
★ Bank of England Mus,
  EC2 . . . . .20 C4
Banksian Wk, Islw.TW7 .144 B1
Banksia Rd, N18 . . . . .61 F5
Bankside, SE1 . . . . .19 J6
  Enfield EN2 . . . . .43 H1
  South Croydon CR2 . . .202 C6
  Southall UB1 . . . . .122 D1
Bankside Av, Nthlt. UB5
  off Townson Av 102 A2

Bankside Cl, Cars. SM5 . .199 H6
Isleworth TW7 . . . . .144 C4
Bankside Dr, T.Ditt. KT7 . .194 E1
★ Bankside Gall, SE1
    off Hopton St 19 H6
Bankside Rd, Ilf. IG1 . . . .99 F5
Bankside Way, SE19
    off Lunham Rd 170 B6
Banks La, Bexh. DA6 . . . .159 F4
Banks Rd, Borwd. WD6 . . .38 C2
Bank St, E14 . . . . .134 A1
Banks Way, E12
    off Grantham Rd 98 D4
Bankton Rd, SW2 . . . . . .151 G4
Bankwell Rd, SE13 . . . . .155 E4
Bannerman Ho, SW8 . . . .34 C6
Banner St, EC1 . . . . .12 A6
Banning St, SE10 . . . . . .134 E5
Bannister Cl, SW2
    off Ewen Cres 169 G1
Greenford UB6 . . . . .86 A5
Bannister Ho, E9
    off Homerton High St .95 G5
Bannockburn Rd, SE18 . .137 H4
★ Banqueting Ho, SW1 . .26 A2
Banstead Gdns, N9 . . . . .60 B3
Banstead Rd, Cars. SM5 .199 H6
Banstead St, SE15 . . . . .153 F3
Banstead Way, Wall.
    SM6 . . . . .201 E5
Banstock Rd, Edg. HA8 . . .54 B6
Banting Dr, N21 . . . . . . .43 F5
Banton Cl, Enf. EN1
    off Central Av 44/45 E2
Bantry St, SE5 . . . . .132 A7
Banwell Rd, Bex. DA5
    off Woodside La 158 D6
Banyard Rd, SE16
    off Southwark
    Pk Rd 132/133 E3
Baptist Gdns, NW5
    off Queen's Cres 92 A6
Barandon Wk, W11 . . . . .108 A7
Barbara Brosnan Ct, NW8 .7 E2
Barbara Hucklesby Cl, N22
    off The Sandlings 75 H2
Barbauld Rd, N16 . . . . . .94 B3
Barber Cl, N21 . . . . .43 G7
Barber's All, E13 . . . . . .115 H3
Barbers Rd, E15 . . . . . . .114 B2
BARBICAN, EC2 . . . . . . .19 J2
Barbican, The, EC2 . . . . .19 J1
★ Barbican Arts & Conf Cen,
    EC2 . . . . .20 A1
Barbican Rd, Grnf. UB6 . .103 H6
Barb Ms, W6 . . . . .127 J3
Barbon Cl, WC1 . . . . . . .18 C1
Barbot Cl, N9 . . . . .60 D3
Barchard St, SW18 . . . . .148 E5
Barchester Cl, W7 . . . . . .124 C1
Barchester Rd, Har. HA3 . .68 A2
Barchester St, E14 . . . . .114 B5
Barclay Cl, SW6 . . . . . . .128 D7
Barclay Oval, Wdf.Grn.
    IG8 . . . . .63 G4
Barclay Path, E17 . . . . . .78 C5
Barclay Rd, E11 . . . . . . .97 E1
E13 . . . . .115 J4
E17 . . . . .78 C5
N18 . . . . .60 A6
SW6 . . . . .128 D7
Croydon CR0 . . . . .202 A3
Barclay Way, SE22
    off Lordship La 152 D7
Barcombe Av, SW2 . . . . .169 E2
Barcombe Cl, Orp. BR5 . .193 J3
Barden St, SE18 . . . . . . .137 H7
Bardfield Av, Rom. RM6 . .82 D3
Bardney Rd, Mord. SM4 .185 E4
Bardolph Rd, N7 . . . . . . .92 E4
    Richmond TW9
    off St. Georges Rd . . .145 J3
Bard Rd, W10 . . . . .108 A7
Bardsey Pl, E1
    off Mile End Rd 113 F5
Bardsey Wk, N1
    off Clephane Rd 93 J6
Bardsley Cl, Croy. CR0 . .202 C3
Bardsley La, SE10 . . . . . .134 C6
Barfett St, W10 . . . . .108 C4
Barfield Av, N20 . . . . . . .57 H2
Barfield Rd, E11 . . . . . . .97 F1
    Bromley BR1 . . . . .192 D3
Barfields, Loug. IG10 . . . .48 D4
Barfields Gdns, Loug. IG10
    off Barfields 48 D4
Barfields Path, Loug.
    IG10 . . . . .48 D4
Barford Cl, NW4 . . . . . . .71 G1
Barford St, N1 . . . . .111 G1

Barforth Rd, SE15 . . . . . .153 E3
Barfreston Way, SE20 . . .189 E1
Bargate Cl, SE18 . . . . . . .137 J5
    New Malden KT3 . . . .183 G6
Barge Ho Rd, E16 . . . . . .136 E1
Barge Ho St, SE1 . . . . . . .27 F1
Bargery Rd, SE6 . . . . . . .172 B1
Barge Wk, E.Mol. KT8 . . .181 G2
    Kingston upon Thames
    KT1 . . . . .181 G1
    Walton-on-Thames
    KT12 . . . . .179 J2
Bargrove Cl, SE20 . . . . . .170 D7
Bargrove Cres, SE6
    off Elm La 171 J2
Barham Cl, Brom. BR2 . .206 B1
    Chislehurst BR7 . . . . .174 E5
    Romford RM7 . . . . . . .83 H2
    Wembley HA0 . . . . . . .87 E6
Barham Rd, SW20 . . . . . .165 G7
    Chislehurst BR7 . . . . .174 E5
    South Croydon CR2 . . .201 J5
Baring Cl, SE12 . . . . .173 G2
Baring Rd, SE12 . . . . . . .155 G7
    Barnet EN4 . . . . .41 G3
    Croydon CR0 . . . . . . .202 D1
Baring St, N1 . . . . .112 A1
Barkantine Shop Par, The, E14
    off The Quarterdeck . .134 A2
Barker Cl, N.Mal. KT3 . . .182 B4
Barker Dr, NW1 . . . . .92 C7
Barker Ms, SW4 . . . . . . .150 B4
Barker St, SW10 . . . . . . .30 C5
Barker Wk, SW16 . . . . . .168 D3
Barker Way, SE22
    off Dulwich Common .170 D1
Barkham Rd, N17 . . . . . .60 A7
Barkham Ter, SE1 . . . . . . .27 F5
BARKING 117 E1
Barking Ind Pk, Bark.
    IG11 . . . . .117 J1
Barking Rd, E6 . . . . .116 A2
    E13 . . . . .115 H4
    E16 . . . . .115 F5
BARKINGSIDE, Ilf. 81 E3
Bark Pl, W2 . . . . .14 A5
Barkston Gdns, SW5 . . . . .30 A3
Barkwood Cl, Rom.
    RM7 . . . . .83 J5
Barkworth Rd, SE16 . . . .133 E5
Barlborough St, SE14 . . .133 F7
Barlby Gdns, W10 . . . . . .108 A4
Barlby Rd, W10 . . . . .108 A5
Barleycorn Way, E14 . . . .113 J7
Barleyfields Cl, Rom.
    RM6 . . . . .82 B7
Barley La, Ilf. IG3 . . . . . .100 A1
    Romford RM6 . . . . . . .82 B6
Barley Mow Pas, EC1 . . . .19 H2
    W4 . . . . .126 D5
Barley Shotts Business Pk, W10
    off St. Ervans Rd 108 C5
Barlow Cl, Wall. SM6 . . .200 E7
Barlow Dr, SE18 . . . . . . .156 B1
Barlow Pl, W1 . . . . .17 E6
Barlow Rd, NW6 . . . . . . .90 C6
    W3 . . . . .126 B1
    Hampton TW12 . . . . .161 G7
Barlow St, SE17 . . . . .36 C2
Barmeston Rd, SE6 . . . . .172 B2
Barmor Cl, Har. HA2 . . . .67 H2
Barmouth Av, Grnf.
    UB6 . . . . .104 C2
Barmouth Rd, SW18 . . . .149 F6
    Croydon CR0 . . . . . . .203 G2
Barnabas Ct, N21
    off Cheyne Wk 43 G5
Barnabas Rd, E9 . . . . . . .95 G5
Barnaby Cl, Har. HA2 . . . .85 J2
Barnaby Pl, SW7 . . . . . . .31 E2
Barnaby Way, Chig. IG7 . .64 E3
Barnard Cl, SE18 . . . . . . .136 D4
    Chislehurst BR7 . . . . .193 G1
    Sunbury-on-Thames TW16
    off Oak Gro 160 B7
    Wallington SM6 . . . . .200 D7
Barnard Gdns, Hayes
    UB4 . . . . .102 B4
    New Malden KT3 . . . .183 G4
Barnard Gro, E15
    off Vicarage La 97 F7
Barnard Hill, N10 . . . . . .74 A2
Barnard Ms, SW11 . . . . .149 H4
Barnardo Dr, Ilf. IG6 . . . .81 F4
Barnardo Gdns, E1
    off Devonport St 113 G7
Barnardo St, E1
    off Devonport St 113 G6
Barnardos Village, Ilf.
    IG6 . . . . .81 F3

Barnard Rd, SW11 . . . . . .149 H4
    Enfield EN1 . . . . .45 E2
    Mitcham CR4 . . . . . . .186 A3
Barnard's Inn, EC1 . . . . . .19 F3
Barnby Sq, E15
    off Barnby St 114/115 E1
Barnby St, E15 . . . . .114 E1
    NW1 . . . . .9 G2
Barn Cl, Nthlt. UB5 . . . . .102 C2
Barn Cres, Stan. HA7 . . . .53 F6
Barncroft Cl, Loug. IG10 . .48 D5
Barncroft Grn, Loug.
    IG10 . . . . .48 D5
Barncroft Rd, Loug. IG10 . .48 D5
Barnehurst Av, Bexh.
    DA7 . . . . .159 J1
    Erith DA8 . . . . .159 J1
Barnehurst Cl, Erith
    DA8 . . . . .159 J1
Barnehurst Rd, Bexh.
    DA7 . . . . .159 J1
Barn Elms Pk, SW15 . . . .147 J2
Barnes All, Hmptn. TW12
    off Hampton Ct Rd . . .179 J2
Barnes Av, SW13 . . . . . .127 G7
    Southall UB2 . . . . . . .123 F4
Barnes Br, SW13 . . . . . . .147 E2
Barnesbury Ho, SW4 . . . .150 D5
Barnes Cl, E12 . . . . .98 A4
★ Barnes Common,
    SW13 . . . . .147 G3
Barnes Ct, E16
    off Ridgwell Rd 115 J5
    Woodford Green IG8 . . .64 A5
Barnes End, N.Mal. . . . . .
    KT3 . . . . .183 G5
Barnes High St, SW13 . . .147 F2
Barnes Ho, Bark. IG11
    off St. Marys 117 G1
Barnes Pikle, W5 . . . . . . .105 G7
Barnes Rd, N18 . . . . .61 F4
    Ilford IG1 . . . . .99 F5
Barnes St, E14 . . . . .113 H6
Barnes Ter, SE8 . . . . .133 J5
BARNET 40 C3
Barnet Bypass, Barn. . . . .
Barnet Dr, Brom. BR2 . . .206 B2
BARNET GATE, Barn. 39 F6
Barnet Gate La, Barn. . . . .
    EN5 . . . . .39 F6
Barnet Gro, E2 . . . . .13 H3
Barnet Hill, Barn. EN5 . . . .40 D4
Barnet Ho, N20 . . . . .57 F2
Barnet La, N20 . . . . .56 C1
    Barnet EN5 . . . . .40 C6
★ Barnet Mus, Barn. EN5
    off Wood St 40 B4
Barnet Rd, Barn. EN5 . . . .39 H5
Barnet Trd Est, Barn.
    EN5 . . . . .40 C3
    off Cannon St Rd .112/113 E6
Barnet Way, NW7 . . . . . . .38 D7
    BR2 . . . . .205 J2
Barney Cl, SE7 . . . . .135 J5
Barnfield, N.Mal. KT3 . . .182 E6
Barnfield Av, Croy. CR0 .203 F2
    Kingston upon Thames
    KT2 . . . . .163 H5
    Mitcham CR4 . . . . . . .186 B4
Barnfield Cl, N4
    off Crouch Hill 74/75 E7
    SW17 . . . . .167 F3
Barnfield Gdns, SE18
    off Plumstead
    Common Rd 136/137 E6
    Kingston upon Thames
    KT2 . . . . .163 H4
Barnfield Pl, E14 . . . . . . .134 A4
Barnfield Rd, SE18 . . . . .137 E6
    W5 . . . . .105 F4
    Belvedere DA17 . . . . .139 F6
    Edgware HA8 . . . . . . .70 C1
Barnfield Wd Cl, Beck.
    BR3 . . . . .190 D6
Barnfield Wd Rd, Beck.
    BR3 . . . . .190 D6
Barnham Dr, SE28 . . . . . .137 J1
Barnham Rd, Grnf. UB6 .103 J3
Barnham St, SE1 . . . . . . .28 E3
Barnhill, Pnr. HA5 . . . . . . .66 C5
Barn Hill, Wem. HA9 . . . .88 B2
Barnhill Av, Brom. BR2 . .191 F5
Barnhill La, Hayes UB4 . .102 B3
Barnhill Rd, Hayes UB4 . .102 B3
    Wembley HA9 . . . . . . .88 C3

Barnhurst Path, Wat.
    WD19 . . . . .50 C5
Barningham Way, NW9 . . .70 D6
Barnlea Cl, Felt. TW13 . . .161 E2
Barnmead Gdns, Dag. . . . .
    RM9 . . . . .101 F5
Barnmead Rd, Beck. . . . . .
    BR3 . . . . .189 H1
    Dagenham . . . .
    RM9 . . . . .101 F5
Barn Ms, Har. HA2 . . . . . .85 G3
Barn Ri, Wem. HA9 . . . . . .88 A1
BARNSBURY, N1 . . . . . . .93 F7
Barnsbury Cl, N.Mal. . . . . .
    KT3 . . . . .182 C4
Barnsbury Cres, Surb. . . . .
    KT5 . . . . .196 C1
Barnsbury Est, N1
    off Barnsbury Rd 111 G1
Barnsbury Gro, N7 . . . . . .93 F7
Barnsbury La, Surb. . . . . .
    KT5 . . . . .196 B2
Barnsbury Pk, N1 . . . . . . .93 G7
Barnsbury Rd, N1 . . . . . . .10 E1
Barnsbury Sq, N1 . . . . . . .93 G7
Barnsbury St, N1 . . . . . . .93 G7
Barnsbury Ter, N1 . . . . . . .93 F7
Barnscroft, SW20 . . . . . .183 H3
Barnsdale Av, E14 . . . . . .134 A4
Barnsdale Rd, W9 . . . . . .108 C4
Barnsley St, E1 . . . . .113 E4
Barnstaple Rd, Ruis. . . . . .
    HA4 . . . . .84 C3
Barnston Wk, N1
    off Popham St 111 J1
Barn St, N16
    off Stoke Newington
    Ch St 94 B3
Barn Way, Wem. HA9 . . . .88 A1
Barnwell Rd, SW2 . . . . . .151 G5
Barnwood Cl, W9 . . . . .6 A6
Baron Cl, N11 . . . .
    off Balmoral Av 58 A5
Baroness Rd, E2 . . . . .13 G3
Baronet Gro, N17 . . . .
    off St. Paul's Rd 76 D1
Baronet Rd, N17 . . . . .76 D1
Baron Gdns, Ilf. IG6 . . . . .81 F3
Baron Gro, Mitch. CR4 . .185 H4
Baron Rd, Dag. RM8 . . . .100 D1
Barons, The, Twick. . . . . .
    TW1 . . . . .145 E6
Barons Ct, Wall. SM6
    off Whelan Way 200 D3
Barons Ct Rd, W14 . . . . .128 B5
Baronsfield Rd, Twick. . . . .
    TW1 . . . . .145 E6
Barons Gate, Barn. EN4 . .41 H6
Barons Keep, W14 . . . . . .128 B5
Baronsmead Rd, SW13 . .147 G1
Baronsmede, W5 . . . . . . .125 J2
Baronsmere Rd, N2 . . . . . .73 H4
Barons Pl, SE1 . . . . .27 F4
Baron St, N1 . . . . .11 E1
Barons Wk, Croy. CR0 . . .189 H6
Baron Wk, E16 . . . . .115 F5
    Mitcham CR4 . . . . . . .185 H4
Barque Ms, SE8 . . . .
    off Watergate St 134 A6
Barrack Rd, Houns. TW4 .142 D4
Barracks La, Barn. EN5 . . . .
    off High St 40 B3
Barratt Av, N22 . . . . .75 F2
Barratt Ind Pk, Sthl. . . . . .
    UB1 . . . . .123 G2
Barratt Way, Har. HA3 . . . .
    off Tudor Rd 68 A3
Barrenger Rd, N10 . . . . . .73 J1
Barrett Rd, E17 . . . . .78 C4
Barretts Grn Rd, NW10 . .106 C2
Barretts Gro, N16 . . . . . . .94 B5
Barrhill Rd, SW2 . . . . . . .169 E2
Barriedale, SE14 . . . . . . .153 H2
Barrie Est, W2 . . . . .14 E5
Barrier App, SE7 . . . . . . .136 A3
Barrier Pt Rd, E16 . . . . . .136 A1
Barringer Sq, SW17 . . . . .168 A4
Barrington Cl, NW5 . . . . . .92 A5
    Ilford IG5 . . . . .80 C1
    Loughton IG10
    off Barrington Rd 49 F4
Barrington Grn, Loug.
    IG10 . . . . .49 F4
Barrington Rd, E12 . . . . . .98 D6
    N8 . . . . .74 D5
    SW9 . . . . .151 H3
    Bexleyheath DA7 . . . . .158 D2

Barrington Rd, Loug.
  IG10 . . . . .49 F3
  Sutton SM3 . . . . .198 D1
Barrington Vil, SE18 . . .156 D1
Barrow Av, Cars. SM5 . . .199 J7
Barrow Cl, N21 . . . . .59 H3
Barrowdene Cl, Pnr. HA5
Barrowell Grn, N21 . . . . .59 H2
Barrowfield Cl, N9 . . . . . .61 E3
Barrowgate Rd, W4 . . . .126 C5
Barrow Hedges Cl, Cars.
  SM5 . . . . .199 H7
Barrow Hedges Way, Cars.
  SM5 . . . . .199 H7
Barrow Hill, Wor.Pk.
  KT4 . . . . .196 E2
Barrow Hill Cl, Wor.Pk. KT4
  off Barrow Hill . . .196/197 E2
Barrow Hill Est, NW8
  off Barrow Hill Rd 109 H2
Barrow Hill Rd, NW8 . . . . .7 G2
Barrow Pt Av, Pnr. HA5 . . .66 E2
Barrow Pt La, Pnr. HA5 . . .66 E2
Barrow Rd, SW16 . . . . . .168 D6
  Croydon CR0 . . . . . . .201 G5
Barrow Wk, Brent. TW8
  off Glenhurst Rd 125 F5
Barrs Rd, NW10 . . . . . . .88 D7
Barry Av, N15
  off Craven Pk Rd 76 C6
  Bexleyheath DA7 . . . . .138 E7
Barry Cl, Orp. BR6 . . . . .207 H3
Barry Rd, E6 . . . . .116 B6
  NW10 . . . . .88 C7
  SE22 . . . . .152 D6
Barset Rd, SE15 . . . . . .153 F3
Barson Cl, SE20 . . . . . .171 F7
Barston Rd, SE27 . . . . . .169 J3
Barstow Cres, SW2 . . . .169 F1
Barter St, WC1 . . . . .18 B2
Barters Wk, Pnr. HA5
  off High St 66/67 E3
Bartholomew Cl, EC1 . . . .19 J2
  SW18 . . . . .149 F4
Bartholomew La, EC2 . . . .20 C4
Bartholomew Pl, EC1 . . . .19 J2
Bartholomew Rd, NW5 . . .92 C6
Bartholomew Sq, E1
  off Coventry Rd . . .112/113 E4
  EC1 . . . . .12 A5
Bartholomew St, SE1 . . . .28 B6
Bartholomew Vil, NW5 . . .92 C6
Barth Rd, SE18 . . . . . . .137 H4
Bartle Av, E6 . . . . .116 B2
Bartle Rd, W11 . . . . . . .108 B6
Bartlett Cl, E14 . . . . . . .114 A6
Bartlett Ct, EC4 . . . . .19 F3
Bartletts Pas, EC4 . . . . . .19 F3
Bartlett St, S.Croy. CR2 . .202 A5
Bartonway, NW8
  off Queen's Ter 109 G2
Barton Way, Borwd.
  WD6 . . . . .38 A2
Bartram Rd, SE4 . . . . . .153 H5
Barts Cl, Beck. BR3 . . . . .190 A5
Barville Cl, SE4
  off St. Norbert Rd 153 H4
Barwick Rd, E7 . . . . .97 H4
Barwood Av, W.Wick.
  BR4 . . . . .204 B1
Bascombe St, SW2 . . . . .151 G6
Basden Gro, Felt. TW13 . .161 G2
Basedale Rd, Dag. RM9 . .100 B7
Baseing Cl, E6 . . . . .116 D7
Basevi Way, SE8 . . . . . .134 B6
Bashley Rd, NW10 . . . . .106 D4
Basil Av, E6 . . . . .116 B2
Basildene Rd, Houns.
  TW4 . . . . .142 D2
Basildon Av, Ilf. IG5 . . . . .80 D1
Basildon Rd, SE2 . . . . . .138 A5
Basil Gdns, SE27 . . . . . .169 J5
  Croydon CR0
  off Primrose La 203 G1
Basilon Rd, Bexh. DA7 . .158 E2

Basil St, SW3 . . . . .23 J5
Basin App, E14
  off Commercial Rd . . .113 H6
Basing Cl, T.Ditt. KT7 . . .180 C7
Basing Ct, SE15 . . . . . . .152 C1
Basingdon Way, SE5 . . . .152 A4
Basing Dr, Bex. DA5 . . . .159 F6
Basingfield Rd, T.Ditt.
  KT7 . . . . .180 C7
Basinghall Av, EC2 . . . . . .20 B2
Basinghall St, EC2 . . . . . .20 B3
Basing Hill, NW11 . . . . . .90 C1
  Wembley HA9 . . . . . . .87 J2
Basing Ho, Bark. IG11
  off St. Margarets 117 G1
Basing Ho Yd, E2 . . . . . . .13 E3
Basing Pl, E2 . . . . .12 E3
Basing St, W11 . . . . .108 C6
Basing Way, N3 . . . . .72 D3
  Thames Ditton KT7 . . .180 C7
Basire St, N1 . . . . .111 J1
Baskerville Rd, SW18 . . .149 H7
Basket Gdns, SE9 . . . . . .156 B5
Baslow Cl, Har. HA3 . . . . .68 A1
Baslow Wk, E5
  off Overbury St 95 G4
Basnett Rd, SW11 . . . . .150 A3
Basque Ct, SE16
  off Poolmans St 133 G2
Bassano St, SE22 . . . . . .152 C5
Bassant Rd, SE18 . . . . . .137 J6
Bassein Pk Rd, W12 . . . .127 F2
Bassett Gdns, Islw. TW7 .123 J7
Bassett Ho, Dag. RM9 . . .118 B1
Bassett Rd, W10 . . . . . . .108 A6
Bassetts Cl, Orp. BR6 . . .206 E4
Bassett St, NW5 . . . . .92 A6
Bassetts Way, Orp. BR6 .206 E4
Bassett Way, Grnf. UB6 . .103 H6
Bassingham Rd, SW18 . . .149 F7
  Wembley HA0 . . . . . . .87 G6
Bassishaw Highwalk, EC2
  off London Wall 111 J5
Basswood Cl, SE15
  off Linden Gro . .152/153 E3
Bastable Av, Bark. IG11 . .117 H2
Bastion Highwalk, EC2
  off London Wall 111 J5
Bastion Ho, EC2
  off London Wall 111 J5
Bastion Rd, SE2 . . . . . . .138 A5
Baston Manor Rd, Brom.
  BR2 . . . . .205 H3
Baston Rd, Brom. BR2 . .205 H1
Bastwick St, EC1 . . . . . . .11 J5
Basuto Rd, SW6 . . . . . . .148 D1
Batavia Cl, Sun. TW16 . . .178 C1
Batavia Ms, SE14
  off Goodwood Rd 133 H7
Batavia Rd, SE14 . . . . . .133 H7
  Sunbury-on-Thames
  TW16 . . . . .178 B1
Batchelor St, N1 . . . . . . .11 E1
Bateman Cl, Bark. IG11
  off Glenny Rd 99 F6
Bateman Ho, SE17 . . . . . .35 G6
Bateman Rd, E4 . . . . .62 A6
Bateman's Bldgs, W1 . . . .17 H4
Bateman's Row, EC2 . . . .12 E5
Bateman St, W1 . . . . .17 H4
Bates Cres, SW16 . . . . . .168 C7
  Croydon CR0 . . . . . . .201 G5
Bateson St, SE18 . . . . . .137 H4
Bates Pt, E13
  off Pelly Rd 115 G1
Bate St, E14
  off Three Colt St 113 J7
Bath Cl, SE15
  off Asylum Rd . . .132/133 E7
Bath Ct, EC1 . . . . .11 E6
Bathgate Rd, SW19 . . . . .166 A3
Bath Ho Rd, Croy. CR0 . .200 E1
Bath Pas, Kings.T. KT1
  off St. James Rd 181 G2
Bath Pl, EC2 . . . . .12 D4
  Barnet EN5 . . . . .40 C3
Bath Rd, E7 . . . . .98 A6
  N9 . . . . .61 E2
  W4 . . . . .126 E4
  Hayes UB3 . . . . .141 F1
  Hounslow TW3, TW4,
  TW5, TW6 . . . . .142 D2
  Mitcham CR4 . . . . . . .185 G3
  Romford RM6 . . . . . . .82 E6
  West Drayton UB7 . . . .140 A1
Baths Rd, Brom. BR2 . . .192 A4
Bath St, EC1 . . . . .12 A4
Bath Ter, SE1 . . . . .27 J6
Bathurst Av, SW19
  off Brisbane Av . .184/185 E1

Bathurst Gdns, NW10 . . .107 H2
Bathurst Ms, W2 . . . . . . .15 E5
Bathurst Rd, Ilf. IG1 . . . . .98 E1
Bathurst St, W2 . . . . .15 E5
Batley Cl, Mitch. CR4 . . .185 J7
Batley Pl, N16 . . . . .94 C3
Batley Rd, N16
  off Stoke Newington
  High St 94 C3
Batley Rd, Enf. EN2 . . . . .43 J1
Batman Cl, W12 . . . . . . .127 H1
Batoum Gdns, W6 . . . . . .127 J3
Batson St, W12 . . . . .127 G2
Batsworth Rd, Mitch.
  CR4 . . . . .185 G3
Battenburg Wk, SE19
  off Brabourne Cl 170 B5
Batten Cl, E6
  off Savage Gdns 116 C6
Batten St, SW11 . . . . . . .149 H3
Battersby Rd, SE6 . . . . . .172 D2
BATTERSEA, SW11 . . . . .150 B1
Battersea Br, SW3 . . . . . .31 F7
  SW11 . . . . .31 F7
Battersea Br Rd, SW11 . .129 H7
Battersea Ch Rd, SW11 . .149 G1
★ Battersea Dogs Home,
  SW8 . . . . .130 B7
Battersea High St,
  SW11 . . . . .149 G1
★ Battersea Park,
  SW11 . . . . .31 J7
Battersea Pk, SW11 . . . . .31 J7
Battersea Pk Rd, SW8 . . .150 B1
  SW11 . . . . .149 H2
Battersea Ri, SW11 . . . . .149 H5
Battersea Sq, SW11
  off Battersea High St .149 G1
Battery Rd, SE28 . . . . . .137 H2
Battishill Gdns, N1
  off Waterloo Ter 93 H7
Battishill St, N1
  off Waterloo Ter 93 H7
Battlebridge Ct, N1
  off Wharfdale Rd 110 E2
Battle Br La, SE1 . . . . . . .28 D2
Battle Br Rd, NW1 . . . . . .10 A2
Battle Cl, SW19
  off North Rd 167 F6
Battledean Rd, N5 . . . . . .93 H5
Battle Rd, Belv. DA17 . . .139 J4
  Erith DA8 . . . . .139 J4
Batty St, E1 . . . . .21 J3
Baudwin Rd, SE6 . . . . . .172 E2
Baugh Rd, Sid. DA14 . . .176 C5
Baulk, The, SW18 . . . . . .148 D7
Bavant Rd, SW16 . . . . . .187 E2
Bavaria Rd, N19 . . . . .92 E2
Bavdene Ms, NW4
  off The Burroughs 71 H4
Bavent Rd, SE5 . . . . . . .151 J2
Bawdale Rd, SE22 . . . . . .152 C5
Bawdsey Av, Ilf. IG2 . . . . .81 J4
Bawtree Rd, SE14 . . . . . .133 H7
Bawtry Rd, N20 . . . . .57 J3
Baxendale, N20 . . . . .57 F2
Baxendale St, E2 . . . . . . .13 H3
Baxter Rd, E16 . . . . .115 J6
  N1 . . . . .94 A6
  N18 . . . . .60 E4
  Ilford IG1 . . . . .98 E5
Bay Ct, W5
  off Popes La 125 H3
Baycroft Cl, Pnr. HA5 . . . .66 C3
Baydon Ct, Brom. BR2 . .191 F3
Bayes Cl, SE26 . . . . .171 F5
Bayfield Rd, SE9 . . . . . . .156 A4
Bayford Ms, E8
  off Bayford St 94/95 E7
Bayford Rd, NW10 . . . . . .108 A3
Bayford St, E8 . . . . .95 E7
Bayham Pl, NW1 . . . . .9 F1
Bayham Rd, W4 . . . . . . .126 D3
  W13 . . . . .104 E7
  Morden SM4 . . . . . . .185 E4
Bayham St, NW1 . . . . . . .110 C1
Bayley St, WC1 . . . . .17 H2
Bayley Wk, SE2
  off Woolwich Rd .138/139 E5
Baylin Rd, SW18
  off Garratt La . . .148/149 E6
Baylis Rd, SE1 . . . . .27 E4
Bayliss Av, SE28 . . . . . . .118 D7
Bayliss Cl, N21 . . . . .43 E5
Bayne Cl, E6
  off Savage Gdns 116 C6
Baynes Cl, Enf. EN1 . . . . .44 D2

Baynes Ms, NW3
  off Belsize La 91 G6
Baynes St, NW1 . . . . .92 C7
Baynham Cl, Bex. DA5 . .159 F6
Bayonne Rd, W6 . . . . . . .128 B6
Bayshill Ri, Nthlt. UB5 . . .85 H6
Bayston Rd, N16 . . . . .94 C3
BAYSWATER, W2 . . . . . . .14 B4
Bayswater Rd, W2 . . . . . .15 F5
Baythorne St, E3 . . . . . . .113 J5
Bay Tree Cl, Brom. BR1 . .191 J1
Baytree Cl, Sid. DA15 . . .175 J1
Baytree Ho, E4
  off Dells Cl 46 B7
Baytree Rd, SW2 . . . . . . .151 F4
Bazalgette Cl, N.Mal.
  KT3 . . . . .182 D5
Bazalgette Gdns, N.Mal.
  KT3 . . . . .182 D5
Bazely St, E14 . . . . .114 C7
Bazile Rd, N21 . . . . .43 G6
Beacham Cl, SE7 . . . . . . .136 A5
Beachborough Rd, Brom.
  BR1 . . . . .172 C4
Beachcroft Rd, E11 . . . . .97 E3
Beachcroft Way, N19 . . . .92 D1
Beach Gro, Felt. TW13 . .161 G2
Beachy Rd, E3 . . . . .96 A7
Beacon Gate, SE14 . . . . .153 G3
Beacon Gro, Cars.
  SM5 . . . . .200 A4
Beacon Hill, N7 . . . . .92 E5
Beacon Rd, SE13 . . . . . .154 D6
  Hounslow (Hthrw.Air.)
  TW6 . . . . .140 D6
Beacon Rd Roundabout,
  Houns. (Hthrw.Air.)
  TW6 . . . . .140 E6
Beacons Cl, E6
  off Oliver Gdns 116 B5
Beaconsfield Cl, N11 . . . .58 A4
  SE3 . . . . .135 G6
  W4 . . . . .126 C5
Beaconsfield Par, SE9
  off Beaconsfield Rd . . .174 B4
Beaconsfield Rd, E10 . . . .96 C2
  E16 . . . . .115 F4
  E17 . . . . .77 J6
  N9 . . . . .60 D4
  N11 . . . . .58 A3
  N15 . . . . .76 B4
  NW10 . . . . .89 F6
  SE3 . . . . .135 F7
  SE9 . . . . .174 B2
  SE17 . . . . .36 C4
  W4 . . . . .126 D3
  W5 . . . . .125 F2
  Bromley BR1 . . . . . . .192 A3
  Croydon CR0 . . . . . . .188 A6
  Esher (Clay.) KT10 . . .194 B7
  Hayes UB4 . . . . .122 C1
  New Malden KT3 . . . .182 D2
  Southall UB1 . . . . . . .122 D1
  Surbiton KT5 . . . . . . .181 J7
  Twickenham TW1 . . . .144 E6
Beaconsfield Ter, Rom.
  RM6 . . . . .82 D6
Beaconsfield Ter Rd,
  W14 . . . . .128 B3
Beaconsfield Wk, E6
  off East Ham Manor
  Way 116 D6
  SW6 . . . . .148 C1
Beacontree Av, E17 . . . . .78 D1
Beacontree Rd, E11 . . . . .79 F7
Beadlow Cl, Cars. SM5
  off Olveston Wk 185 G6
Beadman Pl, SE27
  off Norwood High St .169 H4
Beadman St, SE27 . . . . . .169 H4
Beadnell Rd, SE23 . . . . . .171 G1
Beadon Rd, W6 . . . . .127 J4
  Bromley BR2 . . . . . . .191 G4
Beaford Gro, SW20 . . . . .184 B3
Beagle Cl, Felt. TW13 . . .160 B4
Beak St, W1 . . . . .17 G5
Beal Cl, Well. DA16 . . . . .158 A1
Beale Cl, N13 . . . . .59 H5
Beale Pl, E3 . . . . .113 J2
Beale Rd, E3 . . . . .113 J1
Beal Rd, Ilf. IG1 . . . . .98 D2
Beam Av, Dag. RM10 . . .119 H1
Beaminster Gdns, Ilf.
  IG6 . . . . .80 E2
Beamish Dr, Bushey
  (Bushey Hth.) WD23 . .51 J1
Beamish Rd, N9 . . . . .60 D1
Beanacre Cl, E9 . . . . .95 J6
Bean Rd, Bexh. DA6 . . . .158 D4
Beanshaw, SE9 . . . . .174 D4

Beansland Gro, Rom.
RM6 . . . . .83 E2
Bear All, EC4 . . . . .19 G3
Bear Cl, Rom. RM7 . . . . .83 H6
Beardell St, SE19 . . . . . .170 C6
Beardow Gro, N14 . . . . . .42 C6
Beard Rd, Kings.T.
KT2 . . . . .163 J5
Beardsfield, E13
off Valetta Gro 115 G1
Beard's Hill, Hmptn.
TW12 . . . . .179 G1
Beard's Hill Cl, Hmptn. TW12
TW12 . . . . .179 G1
Beardsley Ter, Dag. RM8
off Fitzstephen Rd 100 B5
Beardsley Way, W3 . . . . .126 D2
Bearfield Rd, Kings.T.
KT2 . . . . .163 H7
Bear Gdns, SE1 . . . . .27 J1
Bear La, SE1 . . . . .27 H1
Bear Rd, Felt. TW13 . . . .160 D5
Bearstead Ri, SE4 . . . . . .153 J5
Bearsted Ter, Beck. BR3 . .190 A1
Bear St, WC2 . . . . .17 J5
Beaton Cl, SE15
off Kelly Av 132 C7
Beatrice Av, SW16 . . . . .187 F3
Wembley HA9 . . . . .87 H5
Beatrice Cl, E13
off Chargeable La 115 G4
Pinner HA5
off Reid Cl 66 A4
Beatrice Ct, Buck.H.
IG9 . . . . .64 A2
Beatrice Pl, W8 . . . . .22 A6
Beatrice Rd, E17 . . . . . . .78 A5
N4 . . . . .75 G7
N9 . . . . .45 F7
SE1 . . . . .37 J2
Richmond TW10
off Albert Rd 145 J5
Southall UB1 . . . . .123 F1
Beatson Wk, SE16 . . . . . .133 H1
Beattock Ri, N10 . . . . . . .74 B4
Beatty Rd, N16 . . . . .94 B4
Stanmore HA7 . . . . .53 F6
Beatty St, NW1 . . . . .9 F1
Beattyville Gdns, Ilf. IG6 . .80 D3
Beauchamp Cl, W4
off Church Path 126 C3
Beauchamp Ct, Stan. HA7
off Hardwick Cl 53 F5
Beauchamp Pl, SW3 . . . . .23 H5
Beauchamp Rd, E7 . . . . . .97 H7
SE19 . . . . .188 A1
SW11 . . . . .149 H4
East Molesey KT8 . . . . .179 H5
Sutton SM1 . . . . .198 D5
Twickenham TW1 . . . . .144 D7
West Molesey KT8 . . . .179 H5
Beauchamp St, EC1 . . . . . .19 E2
Beauchamp Ter, SW15
off Dryburgh Rd 147 H3
Beauclerc Rd, W6 . . . . . .127 H3
Beauclerk Cl, Felt. TW13
off Florence Rd 160 B1
Beaudesert Ms, West Dr.
UB7 . . . . .120 B2
Beaufort, E6
off Newark Knok 116 D5
Beaufort Cl, E4
off Higham Sta Av 62 B6
SW15 . . . . .147 H7
W5 . . . . .105 J5
Romford RM7 . . . . .83 J4
Beaufort Ct, Rich. TW10
off Beaufort Rd 163 F4
Beaufort Dr, NW11 . . . . . .72 D4
Beaufort Gdns, NW4 . . . . .71 J6
SW3 . . . . .23 H5
SW16 . . . . .169 F7
Hounslow TW5 . . . . . .143 E1
Ilford IG1 . . . . .98 D1
Beaufort Ms, SW6
off Lillie Rd 128 C6
Beaufort Pk, NW11 . . . . . .72 D4
Beaufort Rd, W5 . . . . . . .105 J5
Kingston upon Thames
KT1 . . . . .181 H4
Richmond TW10 . . . . . .163 F4
Twickenham TW1 . . . . .145 F7
Beaufort St, SW3 . . . . . . .31 F6
Beaufort Way, Epsom
KT17 . . . . .197 G7
Beaufoy Rd, N17 . . . . .60 B7
Beaufoy Wk, SE11 . . . . . . .34 D2
Beaulieu Av, E16 . . . . . . .135 H1
SE26 . . . . .170 E4

Beaulieu Cl, NW9 . . . . . . .71 E4
SE5 . . . . .152 A3
Hounslow TW4 . . . . . .143 F5
Mitcham CR4 . . . . . . .186 A1
Twickenham TW1 . . . . .145 G7
Watford WD19 . . . . . . .50 C1
Beaulieu Dr, Pnr. HA5 . . . .66 D6
Beaulieu Gdns, N21 . . . . .43 J7
Beaulieu Pl, W4
off Rothschild Rd 126 C3
Beaumanor Gdns, SE9 . .174 D4
Beaumaris Dr, Wdf.Grn.
IG8 . . . . .64 A7
Beaumaris Grn, NW9
off Goldsmith Av . . .70/71 E6
Beaumont Av, W14 . . . . .128 C5
Harrow HA2 . . . . .67 H6
Richmond TW9 . . . . . .145 J3
Wembley HA0 . . . . .87 F5
Beaumont Cl, Kings.T.
KT2 . . . . .164 A7
Beaumont Cres, W14 . . . .128 C5
Beaumont Gdns, NW3 . . . .90 D3
Beaumont Gro, E1 . . . . . .113 G4
Beaumont Ms, W1 . . . . . . .16 C1
Beaumont Pl, W1 . . . . .9 G5
Barnet EN5 . . . . .40 C1
Isleworth TW7 . . . . . . .144 C5
Beaumont Ri, N19 . . . . . . .92 D1
Beaumont Rd, E10 . . . . . .78 B7
E13 . . . . .115 H3
SE19 . . . . .169 J6
SW19 . . . . .148 B7
W4 . . . . .126 C3
Orpington BR5 . . . . . . .193 G6
Beaumont Sq, E1 . . . . . .113 G4
Beaumont St, W1 . . . . . . .16 C1
Beaumont Wk, NW3 . . . . .91 J7
Beauvais Ter, Nthlt. UB5 .102 D3
Beauval Rd, SE22 . . . . . .152 C6
Beaverbank Rd, SE9 . . . .175 G1
Beaver Cl, SE20
off Lullington Rd 170 D7
Hampton TW12 . . . . . .179 H1
Beaver Gro, Nthlt. UB5
off Jetstar Way . . .102/103 E3
Beavers Cres, Houns.
TW4 . . . . .142 C4
Beavers La, Houns.
TW4 . . . . .142 C3
Beavers La Camp, Houns.
TW4 off Beavers La . . .142 C3
Beaverwood Rd, Chis. . . .175 H6
Beavor Gro, W6
off Beavor La 127 G4
Beavor La, W6 . . . . .127 G4
Bebbington Rd, SE18 . . . .137 H4
Bebletts Cl, Orp. BR6 . . . .207 J5
Beccles Dr, Bark. IG11 . . . .99 H6
Beccles St, E14 . . . . .113 J7
Bec Cl, Ruis. HA4 . . . . . . .84 D3
Beck Cl, SE13 . . . . .154 B1
Beck Ct, Beck. BR3 . . . . .189 G3
BECKENHAM 190 A1
Beckenham Business Cen,
Beck. BR3 . . . . .171 H6
Beckenham Gdns, N9 . . . .60 B3
Beckenham Gro, Brom.
BR2 . . . . .190 D2
Beckenham Hill Rd,
SE6 . . . . .172 B5
Beckenham BR3 . . . . . .172 B5
Beckenham La, Brom.
BR2 . . . . .191 E2
Beckenham Pl Pk, Beck.
BR3 . . . . .172 B7
Beckenham Rd, Beck.
BR3 . . . . .189 G1
West Wickham BR4 . . .190 B7
Beckers, The, N16
off Rectory Rd 94 D3
Becket Av, E6 . . . . .116 D3
Becket Cl, SE25 . . . . .188 D6
Becket Fold, Har. HA1
off Courtfield Cres 68 C5
Becket Rd, N18 . . . . .61 F4
Becket St, SE1 . . . . .28 B5
Beckett Cl, NW10 . . . . . . .88 D6
SW16 . . . . .168 D2
Belvedere DA17
off Tunstock Way . .138/139 E3
Becketts Cl, Felt. TW14 . .142 B6
Orpington BR6 . . . . . . .207 J3
Becketts Pl, Kings.T.
KT1 . . . . .181 G1
Beckett Wk, Beck. BR3 . .171 H6
Beckford Dr, Orp. BR5 . . .193 G7
Beckford Pl, SE17 . . . . . . .36 A4
Beckford Rd, Croy. CR0 . .188 C6

Beck La, Beck. BR3 . . . . .189 G3
Becklow Gdns, W12
off Becklow Rd 127 G2
Becklow Ms, W12
off Becklow Rd 127 F2
Becklow Rd, W12 . . . . . .127 G2
Beck River Pk, Beck.
BR3 . . . . .189 J1
Beck Rd, E8 . . . . .112 E1
Becks Rd, Sid. DA14 . . . .176 A3
BECKTON, E6 . . . . .116 D5
Beckton Pk Roundabout, E16
off Royal Albert Way . .116 C7
Beckton Retail Pk, E6 . . .116 C5
Beckton Rd, E16 . . . . . . .115 F5
Beck Way, Beck. BR3 . . . .189 J3
Beckway Rd, SW16 . . . . .186 D2
Beckway St, SE17 . . . . . . .36 C2
Beckwith Rd, SE24 . . . . .152 A6
Beclands Rd, SW17 . . . . .168 A6
Becmead Av, SW16 . . . . .168 D4
Harrow HA3 . . . . .68 E5
Becondale Rd, SE19 . . . .170 B5
BECONTREE, Dag. 100 E3
Becontree Av, Dag.
RM8 . . . . .100 B4
BECONTREE HEATH,
Dag. 101 G1
Bective Pl, SW15
off Bective Rd 148 C4
Bective Rd, E7 . . . . .97 G4
SW15 . . . . .148 C4
Becton Pl, Erith DA8 . . . .139 H7
Bedale St, SE1 . . . . .28 B2
BEDDINGTON, Wall. 200 D2
BEDDINGTON CORNER,
Mitch. 186 A7
Beddington Cross, Croy.
CR0 . . . . .200 D1
Beddington Fm Rd, Croy.
CR0 . . . . .200 D1
Beddington Gdns, Cars.
SM5 . . . . .200 A6
Wallington SM6 . . . . . .200 B6
Beddington Grn, Orp.
BR5 . . . . .193 J1
Beddington Gro, Wall.
SM6 . . . . .200 D5
Beddington La, Croy.
CR0 . . . . .186 C5
Beddington Path, Orp.
BR5 . . . . .193 J1
Beddington Rd, Ilf. IG3 . . . .81 J7
Orpington BR5 . . . . . . .193 H2
Beddington Trd Pk W, Croy.
CR0 . . . . .200 E1
Bede Cl, Pnr. HA5 . . . . . . .66 D7
Bedenham Way, SE15 . . . .37 F7
Bedens Rd, Sid. DA14 . . .176 E6
Bede Rd, Rom. RM6 . . . . .82 C6
Bedfont Cl, Felt. TW14 . . .141 F6
Mitcham CR4 . . . . . . .186 A2
Bedfont La, Felt. TW13,
TW14 . . . . .141 J7
Bedfont Rd, Stai. (Stanw).
TW19 . . . . .140 B6
Bedford Av, WC1 . . . . . . .17 J2
Barnet EN5 . . . . .40 C5
Hayes UB4 . . . . .102 B6
Bedfordbury, WC2 . . . . . .18 A5
Bedford Cl, N10 . . . . .58 A7
W4 . . . . .127 E6
Bedford Cor, W4
off The Avenue . . .126/127 E4
Bedford Ct, WC2 . . . . . . .18 A6
Bedford Gdns, W8 . . . . . .128 D1
Bedford Hill, SW12 . . . . .168 B1
SW16 . . . . .168 B1
★ Bedford Hill Gall,
SW12 . . . . .168 B1
Bedford Ho, SW4 . . . . . .150 E4
Bedford Ms, N2
off Bedford Rd 73 H3
BEDFORD PARK, W4 . . . .126 D3
Bedford Pk, Croy. CR0 . . .201 J1
Bedford Pk Cor, W4
off Bath Rd 126/127 E4
Bedford Pas, SW6
off Dawes Rd 128 B7
Bedford Pl, WC1 . . . . .18 A1
Croydon CR0 . . . . .202 A1
Bedford Rd, E6 . . . . .116 D1
E17 . . . . .78 A1
E18 . . . . .79 G2
N2 . . . . .73 H3
N8 . . . . .74 D6
N9 . . . . .44 E7
N15 . . . . .76 B4

Bedford Rd, N22 . . . . .74 E1
NW7 . . . . .54 E3
SW4 . . . . .150 E3
W4 . . . . .126 D3
W13 . . . . .104 E7
Harrow HA1 . . . . .67 J6
Ilford IG1 . . . . .99 E3
Sidcup DA15 . . . . .175 H3
Twickenham TW2 . . . . .162 A3
Worcester Park KT4 . . .197 J2
Bedford Row, WC1 . . . . . .18 D1
Bedford Sq, WC1 . . . . . . .17 J2
Bedford St, WC2 . . . . .18 A5
Bedford Ter, SW2
off Lyham Rd 150/151 E5
Bedford Way, WC1 . . . . . . .9 J6
Bedgebury Gdns, SW19 .166 B2
Bedgebury Rd, SE9 . . . . .156 A4
Bedivere Rd, Brom. BR1 .173 G3
Bedlam Ms, SE11 . . . . . . .34 D1
Bedlow Way, Croy. CR0 . .201 F4
Bedonwell Rd, SE2 . . . . .138 E6
Belvedere DA17 . . . . . .139 G6
Bexleyheath DA7 . . . . .139 G6
Bedser Cl, SE11 . . . . .34 D5
Thornton Heath CR7 . .187 J3
Bedser Dr, Grnf. UB6 . . . .86 A5
Bedster Gdns, W.Mol.
KT8 . . . . .179 H2
Bedwardine Rd, SE19 . . .170 B7
Bedwell Gdns, Hayes
UB3 . . . . .121 H5
Bedwell Rd, N17 . . . . .76 B1
Belvedere DA17 . . . . . .139 G5
Beeby Rd, E16 . . . . .115 H5
Beech Av, N20 . . . . .57 H1
W3 . . . . .126 E1
Brentford TW8 . . . . . . .125 E7
Buckhurst Hill IG9 . . . . .63 H2
Ruislip HA4 . . . . .84 B1
Sidcup DA15 . . . . .158 A7
Beech Cl, N9 . . . . .44 D6
SE8 off Clyde St 133 J6
SW15 . . . . .147 G7
SW19 . . . . .165 J6
Carshalton SM5 . . . . . .199 J2
Loughton IG10
off Cedar Dr 48/49 E2
Staines (Stanw.) TW19
off St. Mary's Cres . . .140 A7
Sunbury-on-Thames TW16
off Harfield Rd 178 D2
West Drayton UB7 . . . .120 D3
Beech Copse, Brom.
BR1 . . . . .192 C2
South Croydon CR2 . . .202 B5
Beech Ct, E17 . . . . .78 D3
SE9 . . . . .156 B6
Ilford IG1
off Riverdene Rd 98 D3
Surbiton KT6 . . . . .181 H7
Beechcroft, Chis. BR7 . . .174 D7
Beechcroft Av, NW11 . . . .72 C7
Harrow HA2 . . . . .67 G7
New Malden KT3 . . . . .182 C1
Southall UB1 . . . . .123 F1
Beechcroft Cl, Houns.
TW5 . . . . .122 E7
Orpington BR6 . . . . . . .207 G4
Beechcroft Gdns, Wem.
HA9 . . . . .87 J3
Beechcroft Lo, Sutt. SM2
off Devonshire Rd 199 F7
Beechcroft Rd, E18 . . . . . .79 H2
SW14 off Elm Rd 146 C3
SW17 . . . . .167 H2
Chessington KT9 . . . . .195 J3
Orpington BR6 . . . . . . .207 G4
Beechdale, N21 . . . . .59 F2
Beechdale Rd, SW2 . . . . .151 F6
Beech Dell, Kes. BR2 . . . .206 C4
Beech Dr, N2 . . . . .73 J3
Beechen Cliff Way, Islw. TW7
off Henley Cl 144 C1
Beechen Gro, Pnr. HA5 . . .67 F3
Beeches, The, Houns.
TW3 . . . . .143 H1
Beeches Av, Cars.
SM5 . . . . .199 H7
Beeches Cl, SE20
off Genoa Rd 189 F1
Beeches Rd, SW17 . . . . .167 H3
Sutton SM3 . . . . .198 B1
Beechfield Cotts, Brom. BR1
off Widmore Rd 191 J2
Beechfield Gdns, Rom.
RM7 . . . . .83 J7
Beechfield Rd, N4 . . . . . . .75 J6
SE6 . . . . .171 J1
Bromley BR1 . . . . .191 J2

Beech Gdns, EC2
 off Aldersgate St 111 J5
W5 . . . . .125 H2
Dagenham RM10 . . . . .101 H7
Beech Gro, Ilf. IG6 . . . . . .65 H6
Mitcham CR4 . . . . .186 D4
New Malden KT3 . . . . .182 D3
Beech Hall Cres, E4 . . . . .62 D7
Beech Hall Rd, E4 . . . . . .62 C7
Beechhill Rd, SE9 . . . . .156 D5
Beech Ho, Croy. CR0 . . . .204 B6
Beech Ho Rd, Croy.
 CR0 . . . . .202 A3
Beech La, Buck.H. IG9 . . .63 H2
Beech Lawns, N12 . . . . . .57 G5
Beechmont CI, Brom.
 BR1 . . . . .172 E5
Beechmore Gdns, Sutt.
 SM3 . . . . .198 A2
Beechmore Rd, SW11 . . .149 J1
Beechmount Av, W7 . . . .104 A5
Beecholme Av, Mitch.
 CR4 . . . . .186 B1
Beecholme Est, E5
 off Prout Rd 94/95 E3
Beech Rd, N11 . . . . .59 E6
SW16 . . . . .187 E2
Feltham TW14 . . . . . . .141 H7
Beech Row, Rich.TW10 . .163 H4
Beech St, EC2 . . . . .19 J1
Romford RM7 . . . . .83 J4
Beech Tree Glade, E4
 off Forest Side 63 F1
Beech Tree PI, Sutt. SM1
 off St. Nicholas
 Way 198/199 E5
Beechvale CI, N12 . . . . . .57 H5
Beech Wk, NW7 . . . . .54 E6
Beech Way, NW10 . . . . . .88 D7
Beechway, Bex. DA5 . . . .158 D6
Beech Way, Twick.TW2 . .161 G3
Beechwood Av, N3 . . . . . .72 C3
Greenford UB6 . . . . . .103 H3
Harrow HA2 . . . . .85 H3
Orpington BR6 . . . . . . .207 H5
Richmond TW9 . . . . . .146 A1
Sunbury-on-Thames
 TW16 . . . . .160 A6
Thornton Heath CR7 . .187 H4
Beechwood Circle, Har. HA2
 off Beechwood Gdns . .85 H3
Beechwood CI, NW7 . . . .54 D5
Beechwood Ct, Cars.
 SM5 . . . . .199 J4
Sunbury-on-Thames
 TW16 . . . . .160 A6
Beechwood Cres, Bexh.
 DA7 . . . . .158 D3
Beechwood Dr, Kes.
 BR2 . . . . .206 A4
Woodford Green IG8 . . .63 F5
Beechwood Gdns, NW10
 off St. Annes Gdns . . .105 J3
Harrow HA2 . . . . .85 H3
Ilford IG5 . . . . .80 C5
Beechwood Gro, W3
 off East Acton La .106/107 E1
Surbiton KT6 . . . . .181 F7
Beechwood Ms, N19 . . . . .60 D2
Beechwood Pk, E18 . . . . .79 G3
Beechwood Ri, Chis.
 BR7 . . . . .175 E4
Beechwood Rd, E8 . . . . . .94 C6
N8 . . . . .74 D4
Beechwoods Ct, SE19
 off Crystal Palace Par .170 C5
Beechworth CI, NW3 . . . .90 D2
Beecroft Rd, SE4 . . . . . .153 H5
Beehive CI, E8 . . . . .94 C7
Beehive La, Ilf. IG1, IG4 . .80 C6
Beehive Pas, EC3 . . . . . . .20 D4
Beehive PI, SW9 . . . . . . .151 G3
Beeken Dene, Orp. BR6
 off Isabella Dr 207 F4
Beeleigh Rd, Mord.
 SM4 . . . . .185 E4
Beeston CI, E8
 off Ferncliff Rd 94 D5
Watford WD19 . . . . .50 D4
Beeston PI, SW1 . . . . .24 E6
Beeston Rd, Barn. EN4 . . .41 G6
Beeston Way, Felt.
 TW14 . . . . .142 C6
Beethoven St, W10 . . . . .108 B3
Beeton CI, Pnr. HA5 . . . . .51 G7
Begbie Rd, SE3 . . . . .155 J1
Beggars Hill, Epsom
 KT17 . . . . .197 F7

Beggars Roost La, Sutt.
 SM1 . . . . .198 D6
Begonia CI, E6 . . . . .116 B5
Begonia PI, Hmptn.TW12
 off Gresham Rd 161 G6
Begonia Wk, W12
 off Du Cane Rd 107 F6
Beira St, SW12 . . . . .150 B7
Bekesbourne St, E14
 off Ratcliffe La 113 H6
Belcroft CI, Brom. BR1
 off Hope Pk 173 F7
Beldham Gdns, W.Mol.
 KT8 . . . . .179 H3
Belfairs Dr, Rom. RM6 . . .82 C7
Belfairs Grn, Wat. WD19
 off Heysham Dr 50 D5
Belfast Rd, N16 . . . . .94 C2
SE25 . . . . .188 E4
Belfont Wk, N7 . . . . .93 E4
Belford Gro, SE18 . . . . . .136 D4
Belfort Rd, SE15 . . . . . . .153 F2
Belfry CI, SE16 . . . . .72 E2
Belfry CI, SE16
 off Masters Dr . . .132/133 E5
Belgrade Rd, N16 . . . . . . .94 B4
Hampton TW12 . . . . . .179 H1
Belgrave CI, N14
 off Prince George Av . .42 C5
NW7 . . . . .54 D5
W3 off Avenue Rd 126 C2
Belgrave Ct, E14
 off Westferry Circ 134 A1
Belgrave Cres, Sun.
 TW16 . . . . .178 B1
Belgrave Gdns, N14 . . . . .42 D5
NW8 . . . . .109 E1
Stanmore HA7
 off Copley PI 53 F5
Belgrave Hts, E11 . . . . . . .97 G1
Belgrave Ms N, SW1 . . . . .24 B4
Belgrave Ms S, SW1 . . . . .24 C5
Belgrave Ms W, SW1 . . . . .24 B5
Belgrave PI, SW1 . . . . . . .24 C5
Belgrave Rd, E10 . . . . . . .96 C1
E11 . . . . .97 G2
E13 . . . . .115 J4
E17 . . . . .78 A5
SE25 . . . . .188 C4
SW1 . . . . .33 F2
SW13 . . . . .127 F7
Hounslow TW4 . . . . . .143 F3
Ilford IG1 . . . . .98 C1
Mitcham CR4 . . . . .185 G3
Sunbury-on-Thames
 TW16 . . . . .178 B1
Belgrave Sq, SW1 . . . . . .24 B5
Belgrave St, E1 . . . . .113 G6
Belgrave Ter, Wdf.Grn.
 IG8 . . . . .63 G3
Belgrave Wk, Mitch.
 CR4 . . . . .185 G3
Belgrave Yd, SW1 . . . . . .24 D6
BELGRAVIA, SW1 . . . . . . .24 B6
Belgravia CI, Barn.
 EN5 . . . . .40 C3
Belgravia Gdns, Brom.
 BR1 . . . . .172 E6
Belgravia Ho, SW4 . . . . .150 E6
Belgravia Ms, Kings.T.
 KT1 . . . . .181 G4
Belgrove St, WC1 . . . . . . .10 A3
Belham Wk, SE5
 off D'Eynsford Rd 152 A1
Belinda Rd, SW9 . . . . . . .151 H3
Belitha Vil, N1 . . . . .93 F7
Bellamy CI, E14
 off Byng St 134 A2
W14 off Aisgill Av 128 C5
Edgware HA8 . . . . .54 C3
Bellamy Dr, Stan. HA7 . . .68 E1
Bellamy Rd, E4 . . . . .62 B6
Enfield EN2 . . . . .44 A2
Bellamy St, SW12 . . . . . .150 B7
Bellasis Av, SW2 . . . . . . .168 E2
Bell Av, West Dr. UB7 . . .120 C4
Bell CI, Pnr. HA5 . . . . .66 C3
Bellclose Rd, West Dr.
 UB7 . . . . .120 B2
Bell Ct, Surb. KT5
 off Barnsbury La 196 B2
Bell Dr, SW18 . . . . .148 B7
Bellefields Rd, SW9 . . . .151 F3
Bellegrove CI, Well.
 DA16 . . . . .157 J2
Bellegrove Par, Well. DA16
 off Bellegrove Rd 157 J3
Bellegrove Rd, Well.
 DA16 . . . . .157 G2
Bellenden Rd, SE15 . . . .152 C2

Bellestaines Pleasaunce,
 E4 . . . . .62 A2
Belleville Rd, SW11 . . . . .149 J5
Belle Vue, Grnf. UB6 . . . .104 A1
Belle Vue Est, NW4
 off Bell La 71 J4
Belle Vue La, Bushey
 (Bushey Hth.) WD23 . .52 A1
Bellevue Ms, N11
 off Bellevue Rd 58 A5
Bellevue Par, SW17
 off Bellevue Rd 167 H1
Belle Vue Pk,Th.Hth.
 CR7 . . . . .187 J3
Bellevue PI, E1 . . . . .113 F4
Belle Vue Rd, E17 . . . . . . .78 D2
Bellevue Rd, N11 . . . . . . .58 A4
Belle Vue Rd, NW4
 off Bell La 71 J4
Bellevue Rd, SW13 . . . . .147 G2
SW17 . . . . .167 H1
W13 . . . . .104 E4
Bexleyheath DA6 . . . . .159 F5
Kingston upon Thames
 KT1 . . . . .181 H3
Bellew St, SW17 . . . . . . .167 F3
Bell Fm Av, Dag. RM10 . .101 J3
Bellfield Av, Har. HA3 . . . .51 J6
Bellflower CI, E6
 off Sorrel Gdns 116 B5
Bell Gdns, E10
 off Church Rd 96 A1
 E17 off Markhouse Rd . .77 J5
Bellgate Ms, NW5
 off York Ri 92 B3
BELL GREEN, SE6 . . . . . .171 J3
Bell Grn, SE26 . . . . .171 J3
Bell Grn La, SE26 . . . . . .171 H5
Bell Hill, Croy. CR0
 off Surrey St 201 J3
Bell Ho Rd, Rom. RM7 . . .101 J1
BELLINGHAM, SE6 . . . . .172 B3
Bellingham Ct, Bark. IG11
 off Renwick Rd 118 B3
Bellingham Grn, SE6 . . . .172 A3
Bellingham Rd, SE6 . . . . .172 B3
Bell Inn Yd, EC3 . . . . .20 C4
Bell La, E1 . . . . .21 F2
E16 . . . . .135 G1
NW4 . . . . .72 A4
Twickenham TW1
 off The Embankment .162 D1
Wembley HA9
 off Magnet Rd 87 G2
Bellmaker Ct, E3
 off St. Pauls Way 113 J5
Bell Meadow, SE19
 off Dulwich Wd Av . . .170 B4
Bello CI, SE24 . . . . .151 H7
Bellot Gdns, SE10 . . . . . .135 E5
Bellot St, SE10 . . . . .135 E5
Bellring CI, Belv. DA17 . . .139 G6
Bell Rd, E.Mol. KT8 . . . . .180 A5
Enfield EN1 . . . . .44 A1
Hounslow TW3 . . . . . .143 H4
Bells All, SW6 . . . . .148 D2
Bells Gdn Est, SE15
 off Buller CI 132 D7
Bells Hill, Barn. EN5 . . . . .40 A5
Bell St, NW1 . . . . .15 G1
SE18 . . . . .156 B1
Belltrees Gro, SW16 . . . .169 F5
Bell Water Gate, SE18 . . .136 D3
Bell Wf La, EC4 . . . . .20 A5
Bellwood Rd, SE15 . . . . .153 G4
Bell Yd, WC2 . . . . .18 E3
Belmarsh Rd, SE28
 off Western Way 137 H2
BELMONT, Har. 68 D2
Belmont Av, N9 . . . . .60 D1
N13 . . . . .59 E5
N17 . . . . .75 J3
Barnet EN4 . . . . .41 J5
New Malden KT3 . . . . .183 G5
Southall UB2 . . . . .122 E3
Welling DA16 . . . . .157 H3
Wembley HA0 . . . . . . .105 J1
Belmont Circle, Har.
 HA3 . . . . .68 E1
Belmont CI, E4 . . . . .62 D5
N20 . . . . .56 E1
SW4 . . . . .150 C3
Barnet EN4 . . . . .41 J4
Woodford Green IG8 . . .63 H4
Belmont Ct, NW11 . . . . . .72 D5
Belmont Gro, SE13 . . . . .154 D3
W4 off Belmont Rd 126 D4
Belmont Hall Ct, SE13
 off Belmont Gro 154 D3
Belmont Hill, SE13 . . . . .154 D3

Belmont La, Chis. BR7 . .175 F5
Stanmore HA7 . . . . . . .53 F7
Belmont Ms, SW19
 off Chapman Sq 166 A2
Belmont Pk, SE13 . . . . . .154 D4
Belmont Pk CI, SE13
 off Belmont Pk 154 D4
Belmont Pk Rd, E10 . . . . .78 B6
Belmont Ri, Sutt. SM2 . . .198 D7
Belmont Rd, N15 . . . . . . .75 J4
N17 . . . . .75 J4
SE25 . . . . .188 E5
SW4 . . . . .150 C3
W4 . . . . .126 D4
Beckenham BR3 . . . . .189 J2
Chislehurst BR7 . . . . .175 E5
Erith DA8 . . . . .139 G7
Harrow HA3 . . . . .68 C3
Ilford IG1 . . . . .99 F3
Twickenham TW2 . . . .162 A2
Wallington SM6 . . . . . .200 B5
Belmont St, NW1 . . . . . . .92 A7
Belmont Ter, W4
 off Belmont Rd 126 D4
Belmor, Borwd. (Elstree)
 WD6 . . . . .38 A5
Belmore Av, Hayes
 UB4 . . . . .102 A6
Belmore La, N7 . . . . .92 D5
Belmore St, SW8 . . . . . .150 D1
Beloe CI, SW15 . . . . .147 G3
Belper Ct, E5
 off Pedro St 95 G4
Belsham St, E9 . . . . .95 F6
Belsize Av, N13 . . . . .59 F6
NW3 . . . . .91 G6
W13 . . . . .125 E3
Belsize Ct, NW3
 off Belsize La 91 H5
Belsize Cres, NW3 . . . . . .91 G5
Belsize Gdns, Sutt.
 SM1 . . . . .199 E4
Belsize Gro, NW3 . . . . . . .91 H6
Belsize La, NW3 . . . . .91 G6
Belsize Ms, NW3
 off Belsize La 91 G6
BELSIZE PARK, NW3 . . . . .91 H6
Belsize Pk, NW3 . . . . .91 G6
Belsize Pk Gdns, NW3 . . .91 H6
Belsize Pk Ms, NW3
 off Belsize La 91 G6
Belsize PI, NW3
 off Belsize La 91 G6
Belsize Rd, NW6 . . . . . . .108 E1
Harrow HA3 . . . . .52 A7
Belsize Sq, NW3 . . . . .91 G6
Belsize Ter, NW3 . . . . . . .91 G6
Belson Rd, SE18 . . . . . . .136 C4
Beltane Dr, SW19 . . . . . .166 A3
Belthorn Cres, SW12 . . . .150 C7
Belton Rd, E7 . . . . .97 H7
E11 . . . . .96 E4
N17 . . . . .76 B3
NW2 . . . . .89 G4
Sidcup DA14 . . . . .176 A4
Belton Way, E3 . . . . .114 A5
Beltran Rd, SW6 . . . . . . .148 E2
Beltwood Rd, Belv.
 DA17 . . . . .139 J4
BELVEDERE 139 H4
Belvedere Av, SW19 . . . .166 B5
Ilford IG5 . . . . .80 E2
Belvedere Bldgs, SE1 . . . .27 H4
Belvedere CI, Tedd.
 TW11 . . . . .162 B5
Belvedere Ct, N2 . . . . . . .73 G5
Belvedere Dr, SW19 . . . .166 B5
Belvedere Gdns, W.Mol.
 KT8 . . . . .179 F5
Belvedere Gro, SW19 . . .166 B5
Belvedere Ho, Felt.
 TW13 . . . . .160 A1
Belvedere Ind Est, Belv.
 DA17 . . . . .139 J3
Belvedere Ms, SE3
 off Langton Way 155 F1
SE15 . . . . .153 E3
Belvedere PI, SE1 . . . . . . .27 H4
SW2 off Acre La 151 F4
Belvedere Rd, E10 . . . . . .95 H1
SE1 . . . . .26 D3
SE2 . . . . .138 D1
SE19 . . . . .170 C7
W7 . . . . .124 C3
Bexleyheath DA7 . . . . .159 F3
Belvedere Sq, SW19 . . . .166 B5
Belvedere Strand, NW9 . .71 F2
Belvedere Twr, The,
 SW10 . . . . .149 F1
Belvedere Way, Har. HA3 . .69 H6

Belvoir Cl, SE9 . . . . .174 B3
Belvoir Rd, SE22 . . . . . .152 D7
Belvue Cl, Nthlt. UB5 . . . .85 G7
Belvue Rd, Nthlt. UB5 . . . .85 G7
Bembridge Cl, NW6 . . . . . .90 B7
Bemerton Est, N1 . . . . . . .93 F7
Bemerton St, N1 . . . . . . .111 F1
Bemish Rd, SW15 . . . . . .148 A3
Bempton Dr, Ruis. HA4 . . .84 B2
Bemsted Rd, E17 . . . . .77 J3
Benares Rd, SE18 . . . . . .137 J4
Benbow Rd, W6 . . . . . . .127 H3
Benbow St, SE8 . . . . . . .134 A6
Benbury Cl, Brom. BR1 . .172 C5
Bench Fld, S.Croy. CR2 . .202 C6
Bencroft Rd, SW16 . . . . .168 C7
Bencurtis Pk, W.Wick.
  BR4 . . . . .204 D3
Bendall Ms, NW1 . . . . . . .15 H1
Bendemeer Rd, SW15 . . .148 A3
Bendish Rd, E6 . . . . .98 B7
Bendmore Av, SE2 . . . . .138 A5
Bendon Valley, SW18 . . .148 E7
Benedict Cl, Belv. DA17
  off Tunstock Way .138/139 E3
  Orpington BR6 . . . . . .207 H3
Benedict Dr, Felt. TW14 . .141 G7
Benedict Rd, SW9 . . . . . .151 F3
  Mitcham CR4 . . . . . . .185 G3
Benedict Way, N2 . . . . . . .73 F3
Benenden Grn, Brom.
  BR2 . . . . .191 G5
Benett Gdns, SW16 . . . .186 E2
Benfleet Cl, Sutt. SM1 . . .199 F3
Benfleet Way, N11 . . . . . .58 A2
Bengal Ct, EC3
  off Birchin La 112 A6
Bengal Rd, Ilf. IG1 . . . . . . .98 E4
Bengarth Dr, Har. HA3 . . .68 A2
Bengarth Rd, Nthlt.
  UB5 . . . . .102 D1
Bengeworth Rd, SE5 . . . .151 J3
  Harrow HA1 . . . . .86 D2
Ben Hale Cl, Stan. HA7 . . .52 E4
Benham Cl, SW11 . . . . . .149 G3
  Chessington KT9
  off Merritt Gdns 195 F6
Benham Gdns, Houns.
  TW4 . . . . .143 F5
Benham Rd, W7 . . . . . . .104 B5
Benhams Pl, NW3
  off Holly Wk 91 F4
Benhill Av, Sutt. SM1 . . . .199 E4
Benhill Rd, SE5 . . . . .132 A7
  Sutton SM1 . . . . .199 F3
Benhill Wd Rd, Sutt.
  SM1 . . . . .199 F3
BENHILTON, Sutt. 199 E2
Benhilton Gdns, Sutt.
  SM1 . . . . .199 E3
Benhurst Ct, SW16 . . . . .169 G5
Benhurst La, SW16 . . . . .169 G5
Benin St, SE13 . . . . .154 D7
Benjafield Cl, N18
  off Brettenham Rd .60/61 E4
Benjamin Cl, E8 . . . . . . .112 D1
Benjamin St, EC1 . . . . . . .19 G1
Benledi St, E14 . . . . .114 D6
Bennelong Cl, W12 . . . . .107 H7
Bennerley Rd, SW11 . . . .149 H5
Bennetsfield Rd, Uxb.
  UB11 . . . . .120 E1
Bennet's Hill, EC4 . . . . . . .19 H5
Bennett Cl, Kings.T.
  KT1 . . . . .181 F1
  Welling DA16 . . . . . . .158 A2
Bennett Gro, SE13 . . . . .154 B1
Bennett Pk, SE3 . . . . . . .155 F3
Bennett Rd, E13 . . . . . . .115 J4
  N16 . . . . .94 B4
  Romford RM6 . . . . .83 E6
Bennetts Av, Croy. CR0 . .203 H2
  Greenford UB6 . . . . . .104 B1
Bennetts Castle La, Dag.
  RM8 . . . . .100 C4
Bennetts Cl, N17 . . . . . . .60 C6
  Mitcham CR4 . . . . . . .186 B1
Bennetts Copse, Chis.
  BR7 . . . . .174 B6
Bennett St, SW1 . . . . .25 F1
  W4 . . . . .126 E6
Bennetts Way, Croy.
  CR0 . . . . .203 H2
Bennetts Yd, SW1 . . . . . . .25 J6
Benningholme Rd, Edg.
  HA8 . . . . .54 E6
Bennington Rd, N17 . . . . .76 B1
  Woodford Green IG8 . . .62 E7
Benn St, E9 . . . . .95 H6

Benn's Wk, Rich. TW9
  off Rosedale Rd 145 H4
Benrek Cl, Ilf. IG6 . . . . . . .81 F1
Bensbury Cl, SW15 . . . . .147 H7
Bensham Cl, Th.Hth.
  CR7 . . . . .187 J4
Bensham Gro, Th.Hth.
  CR7 . . . . .187 J2
Bensham La, Croy. CR0 .187 H7
  Thornton Heath CR7 . .187 H4
Bensham Manor Rd, Th.Hth.
  CR7 . . . . .187 J4
Bensington Ct, Felt.
  TW14 . . . . .141 G6
Bensley Cl, N11 . . . . .57 J5
Ben Smith Way, SE16 . . . .29 J5
Benson Av, E6 . . . . .115 J2
Benson Cl, Houns. TW3 .143 G4
Benson Quay, E1
  off Garnet St 113 F7
Benson Rd, SE23 . . . . . .171 F1
  Croydon CR0 . . . . . . .201 G3
Bentalls Cen, Kings.T.
  KT1 . . . . .181 H2
Bentfield Gdns, SE9
  off Aldersgrove Av . . .173 J3
Benthal Rd, N16 . . . . .94 D2
Bentham Ct, N1
  off Rotherfield St 93 J7
Bentham Rd, E9 . . . . .95 G6
  SE28 . . . . .118 B7
Bentham Wk, NW10 . . . . .88 C5
Ben Tillett Cl, Bark. IG11 .100 A7
Ben Tillett Cl, E16
  off Newland St 136 C1
Bentinck Ms, W1 . . . . . . .16 C3
Bentinck Pl, NW8 . . . . . . .7 G2
Bentinck Rd, West Dr.
  UB7 . . . . .120 A1
Bentinck St, W1 . . . . .16 C3
Bentley Dr, NW2 . . . . .90 C3
  Ilford IG2 . . . . .81 F6
Bentley Ms, Enf. EN1 . . . .44 A6
★ Bentley Priory, Stan.
  HA7 . . . . .52 B3
Bentley Rd, N1
  off Tottenham Rd 94 B6
Bentley Way, Stan. HA7 . .52 D5
  Woodford Green IG8 . . .63 G3
Benton Rd, Ilf. IG1 . . . . . .99 G1
  Watford WD19 . . . . .50 D5
Bentons La, SE27 . . . . . .169 J4
Bentons Ri, SE27 . . . . . .170 A5
Bentry Cl, Dag. RM8 . . . .101 E2
Bentry Rd, Dag. RM8 . . . .101 E2
Bentworth Rd, W12 . . . . .107 H6
Benwell Ct, Sun. TW16 . .178 A1
Benwell Rd, N7 . . . . .93 G4
Benwick Cl, SE16
  off Southwark
  Pk Rd 132/133 E3
Benworth St, E3 . . . . . . .113 J3
Benyon Rd, N1
  off Southgate Rd 112 A1
Berberis Wk, West Dr.
  UB7 . . . . .120 B4
Berber Pl, E14
  off Birchfield St 114 A7
Berber Rd, SW11 . . . . . .149 J5
Berberry Cl, Edg. HA8
  off Larkspur Gro 54 C4
Bercta Rd, SE9 . . . . .175 F2
Berenger Wk, SW10 . . . . .30 E7
Berens Rd, NW10 . . . . . .108 A3
Berens Way, Chis. BR7 . .193 J4
Beresford Av, N20 . . . . . . .57 J2
  W7 . . . . .104 A5
  Surbiton KT5 . . . . . . .196 B1
  Twickenham TW1 . . . .145 F6
  Wembley HA0 . . . . . . .105 J1
Beresford Dr, Brom.
  BR1 . . . . .192 A3
  Woodford Green IG8 . . .63 J4
Beresford Gdns, Enf.
  EN1 . . . . .44 B4
  Hounslow TW4 . . . . . .143 F5
  Romford RM6 . . . . .83 E5
Beresford Rd, E4 . . . . . . .62 E1
  E17 . . . . .78 B1
  N2 . . . . .73 H3
  N5 . . . . .93 J5
  N8 . . . . .75 G5
  Harrow HA1 . . . . .68 A5
  Kingston upon Thames
  KT2 . . . . .181 J1
  New Malden KT3 . . . .182 C4
  Southall UB1 . . . . . . .122 D1
  Sutton SM2 . . . . .198 C7
Beresford Sq, SE18 . . . .136 E4
Beresford St, SE18 . . . . .136 E3

Beresford Ter, N5 . . . . . . .93 J5
Berestede Rd, W6 . . . . . .127 F5
Bere St, E1
  off Cranford St 113 G7
Bergen Sq, SE16
  off Norway Gate 133 H3
Berger Cl, Orp. BR5 . . . .193 G6
Berger Rd, E9 . . . . .95 G6
Berghem Ms, W14
  off Blythe Rd 128 A3
Bergholt Av, Ilf. IG4 . . . . . .80 B5
Bergholt Cres, N16 . . . . . .76 B7
Bergholt Ms, NW1
  off Rossendale Way . . .92 C7
Berglen Ct, E14
  off Branch Rd 113 H6
Bering Sq, E14 . . . . .134 A5
Bering Wk, E16 . . . . .116 A6
Berisford Ms, SW18 . . . .149 F6
Berkeley Av, Bexh. DA7 . .158 D1
  Greenford UB6 . . . . . . .86 B6
  Hounslow TW4 . . . . . .142 A2
  Ilford IG5 . . . . .80 D2
Berkeley Cl, Borwd.
  (Elstree) WD6 . . . . . . .38 A5
  Kingston upon Thames
  KT2 . . . . .163 H7
  Orpington BR5 . . . . . .193 H7
  Ruislip HA4 . . . . .84 A3
Berkeley Ct, N14 . . . . .42 C6
  Wallington SM6 . . . . .200 C3
Berkeley Cres, Barn.
  EN4 . . . . .41 G5
Berkeley Dr, W.Mol.
  KT8 . . . . .179 F3
Berkeley Gdns, N21 . . . . .44 A7
  W8
  off Brunswick Gdns .128 D1
  Esher (Clay.) KT10 . . .194 D6
Berkeley Ho, E3 . . . . .114 A4
Berkeley Ms, W1 . . . . .16 A3
Berkeley Pl, SW19 . . . . .166 A6
Berkeley Rd, E12 . . . . .98 B5
  N8 . . . . .74 D5
  N9 . . . . .70 A4
  N15 . . . . .76 A6
  NW9 . . . . .70 A4
  SW13 . . . . .147 G1
Berkeley Sq, W1 . . . . .16 E6
Berkeley St, W1 . . . . .17 E6
Berkeley Wk, N7
  off Durham Rd 93 F2
Berkeley Waye, Houns.
  TW5 . . . . .122 D7
Berkhampstead Rd, Belv.
  DA17 . . . . .139 G5
Berkhamsted Av, Wem.
  HA9 . . . . .87 J6
Berkley Gro, NW1
  off Berkley Rd 91 J7
Berkley Rd, NW1 . . . . .91 J7
Berkshire Gdns, N13 . . . .59 G6
  N18 . . . . .60 E5
Berkshire Rd, E9 . . . . .95 J6
Berkshire Sq, Mitch. CR4
  off Berkshire
  Way 186/187 E4
Berkshire Way, Mitch.
  CR4 . . . . .186/187 E4
Bermans Way, NW10 . . . .89 E4
BERMONDSEY, SE1 . . . . .29 F6
★ Bermondsey Leather Mkt,
  SE1 . . . . .28 D4
Bermondsey Sq, SE1 . . . .28 E5
Bermondsey St, SE1 . . . .28 D2
Bermondsey Wall E,
  SE16 . . . . .29 J4
Bermondsey Wall W,
  SE16 . . . . .29 H3
Bernal Cl, SE28
  off Haldane Rd 118 D7
Bernard Ashley Dr,
  SE7 . . . . .135 H5
Bernard Av, W13 . . . . . . .124 E3
Bernard Cassidy St, E16 .115 F5
Bernard Gdns, SW19 . . .166 C5
Bernard Rd, N15 . . . . .76 C5
  Romford RM7 . . . . .83 J7
  Wallington SM6 . . . . .200 B4
Bernards Cl, Ilf. IG6 . . . . .65 F6
Bernard St, WC1 . . . . .10 A6
Bernays Cl, Stan. HA7 . . . .53 F6
Bernays Gro, SW9 . . . . .151 F4
Bernel Dr, Croy. CR0 . . . .203 J3
Berne Rd, Th.Hth. CR7 . .187 J5
Berners Dr, W13 . . . . . . .104 D6
Bernersmede, SE3
  off Blackheath Pk 155 G3
Berners Ms, W1 . . . . .17 G2
Berners Pl, W1 . . . . .17 G3

Berners Rd, N1 . . . . .11 F1
  N22 . . . . .75 G1
Berners St, W1 . . . . .17 G2
Berney Rd, Croy. CR0 . . .188 A7
Bernhardt Cres, NW8 . . . .7 G5
Bernhart Cl, Edg. HA8 . . . .54 C7
Bernville Way, Har. HA3
  off Kenton Rd 69 J5
Bernwell Rd, E4 . . . . .63 E3
Berridge Grn, Edg. HA8 . . .54 A7
Berridge Ms, NW6
  off Hillfield Rd 90 D5
Berridge Rd, SE19 . . . . .170 A5
Berriman Rd, N7 . . . . .93 F3
Berriton Rd, Har. HA2 . . . .85 F1
Berrybank Cl, E4
  off Greenbank Cl 62 C2
Berry Cl, N21 . . . . .59 H1
  NW10 . . . . .88 E7
  Dagenham RM10 . . . .101 G5
Berry Ct, Houns. TW4 . . .143 F5
Berrydale Rd, Hayes
  UB4 . . . . .102 E4
Berryfield Cl, E17 . . . . .78 B4
  Bromley BR1 . . . . . . .192 B1
Berryfield Rd, SE17 . . . . .35 H3
Berryhill, SE9 . . . . .156 E4
Berry Hill, Stan. HA7 . . . . .53 G4
Berryhill Gdns, SE9 . . . .156 E4
BERRYLANDS, Surb. 181 J5
Berrylands, SW20 . . . . . .183 J3
  Surbiton KT5 . . . . . . .182 A5
Berrylands Rd, Surb.
  KT5 . . . . .181 J6
Berry La, SE21 . . . . .170 A4
Berryman Cl, Dag. RM8
  off Bennetts Castle
  La 100 C3
Berrymans La, SE26 . . . .171 G4
Berrymead Gdns, W3 . . .126 C1
Berrymede Rd, W4 . . . . .126 D3
Berry Pl, EC1 . . . . .11 H4
Berry St, EC1 . . . . .11 H5
Berry Way, W5 . . . . .125 H3
Bertal Rd, SW17 . . . . . . .167 G4
Berthon St, SE8 . . . . . . .134 A7
Bertie Rd, NW10 . . . . .89 G6
  SE26 . . . . .171 G6
Bertram Cotts, SW19
  off Hartfield Rd 166 D7
Bertram Rd, NW4 . . . . . . .71 G6
  Enfield EN1 . . . . .44 D4
  Kingston upon Thames
  KT2 . . . . .164 A7
Bertram St, N19 . . . . .92 B2
Bertram Way, Enf. EN1 . . .44 C4
Bertrand St, SE13 . . . . . .154 B3
Bertrand Way, SE28 . . . . .118 B7
Bert Rd, Th.Hth. CR7 . . . .187 J5
Bert Way, Enf. EN1
  off Percival Rd 44 C4
Berwick Av, Hayes UB4 . .102 D6
Berwick Cl, Stan. HA7
  off Gordon Av 52 C7
Berwick Cres, Sid. DA15 .157 H6
Berwick Rd, E16 . . . . . . .115 H6
  N22 . . . . .75 H1
  Welling DA16 . . . . . . .158 B1
Berwick St, W1 . . . . .17 H4
Berwyn Av, Houns.
  TW3 . . . . .143 H1
Berwyn Rd, SE24 . . . . . .169 H1
  Richmond TW10 . . . . .146 B4
Beryl Av, E6 . . . . .116 B5
Beryl Ho, SE18
  off Spinel Cl 137 J5
Beryl Rd, W6 . . . . .128 A5
Berystede, Kings.T.
  KT2 . . . . .164 B7
Besant Ct, N1
  off Newington Grn Rd .94 A5
Besant Rd, NW2 . . . . .90 B4
Besant Wk, N7
  off Newington
  Barrow Way 93 F2
Besant Way, NW10 . . . . . .88 C5
Besley St, SW16 . . . . . . .168 C6
Bessant Dr, Rich. TW9 . .146 B1
Bessborough Gdns,
  SW1 . . . . .33 J3
Bessborough Pl, SW1 . . . .33 H3
Bessborough Rd, SW15 .165 G1
  Harrow HA1 . . . . .86 A2
Bessborough St, SW1 . . . .33 H3
Bessemer Rd, SE5 . . . . .151 J2
Bessie Lansbury Cl, E6 . .116 D6
Bessingby Rd, Ruis. HA4 . .84 A2
Bessingham Wk, SE4
  off Frendsbury Rd 153 G4
Besson St, SE14 . . . . . . .153 F1

Bessy St, E2
Bestwood St, SE8 .....**133** G4
Beswick Ms, NW6
  off Lymington Rd . **.90/91** E6
Betam Rd, Hayes UB3 . .**121** G2
Beta Pl, SW8
  off Santley St . . .**150/151** E4
Betchworth Cl, Sutt. SM1
  off Turnpike La **199** G5
Betchworth Rd, Ilf. IG3 . . .**99** H2
Betham Rd, Grnf. UB6 . .**104** A3
Bethany Waye, Felt.
  TW14 ....**141** H7
Bethecar Rd, Har. HA1 . . .**68** B5
Bethell Av, E16 ....**115** F4
  Ilford IG1 ....**80** D7
Bethel Rd, Well. DA16 . .**158** C3
Bethersden Cl, Beck.
  BR3 ....**171** J7
BETHNAL GREEN, E2 . . .**112** D2
Bethnal Grn Est, E2 . . . .**113** D2
★ Bethnal Green Mus of
  Childhood, E2 ....**113** E3
Bethnal Grn Rd, E1 . . . .**13** F5
  E2 ....**13** F5
Bethune Av, N11 ....**57** J4
Bethune Rd, N16 ....**76** A7
  NW10 ....**106** D4
Bethwin Rd, SE5 ....**35** H7
Betjeman Cl, Pnr. HA5 . . .**67** G4
Betony Cl, Croy. CR0
  off Primrose La **203** G1
Betoyne Av, E4 ....**62** E4
Betstyle Rd, N11 ....**58** B4
Betterton Dr, Sid.
  DA14 ....**177** E2
Betterton St, WC2 ....**18** A4
Bettons Pk, E15 ....**115** E1
Bettridge Rd, SW6 ....**148** C2
Betts Cl, Beck. BR3
  off Kendall Rd **189** H2
Betts Ms, E17
  off Queen's Rd **77** J6
Betts Rd, E16
  off Victoria Dock Rd . .**115** H7
Betts St, E1
  off The Highway . .**112/113** E7
Betts Way, SE20 ....**189** E1
  Surbiton KT6 ....**195** E1
Beulah Av, Th.Hth. CR7
  off Beulah Rd **187** F4
Beulah Cl, Edg. HA8 . . . .**54** B3
Beulah Cres, Th.Hth.
  CR7 ....**187** J2
Beulah Gro, Croy.
  CR0 ....**187** J6
Beulah Hill, SE19 ....**169** H6
Beulah Path, E17
  off Addison Rd **78** B5
Beulah Rd, E17 ....**78** B5
  SW19 ....**166** C2
  Sutton SM1 ....**198** D4
  Thornton Heath CR7 . .**187** J3
Bevan Av, Bark. IG11 . . .**100** A7
Bevan Ct, Croy. CR0 . . .**201** G5
Bevan Rd, SE2 ....**138** B5
  Barnet EN4 ....**41** J4
Bevan St, N1 ....**111** J1
Bev Callender Cl, SW8
  off Daley Thompson
  Way **150** B3
Bevenden St, N1 ....**12** C3
Bevercote Wk, Belv. DA17
  off Osborne Rd **139** F6
Beveridge Rd, NW10
  off Curzon Cres . . .**88/89** E7
Beverley Av, SW20 . . . .**183** F1
  Hounslow TW4 ....**143** F4
  Sidcup DA15 ....**157** J7
Beverley Cl, N21 ....**59** J1
  SW11 off Maysoule Rd **149** G4
  SW13 ....**147** F2
  Chessington KT9 . . . .**195** F4
  Enfield EN1 ....**44** B4
Beverley Cotts, SW15
  off Kingston Vale **164** D4
Beverley Ct, N14 ....**42** C7
  N20 off Farnham Cl . . .**41** F7
  SE4 ....**153** J3
Beverley Cres, Wdf.Grn.
  IG8 ....**79** H1
Beverley Dr, Edg. HA8 . . .**70** B3
Beverley Gdns, NW11 . . .**72** B7
  SW13 ....**147** F3
  Stanmore HA7 ....**68** D1
  Wembley HA9 ....**87** J1
  Worcester Park KT4
  off Green La **197** G1
Beverley Ho, NW8 ....**7** G4

Beverley La, SW15 .....**165** F3
  Kingston upon Thames
  KT2 ....**165** E7
Beverley Ms, E4
  off Beverley Rd **62** D6
Beverley Path, SW13 . . .**147** F2
Beverley Rd, E4 ....**62** D6
  E6 ....**116** A3
  SE20
  off Wadhurst Cl . .**188/189** E2
  SW13 ....**147** F3
  W4 ....**127** F5
  Bexleyheath DA7 .....**159** J2
  Bromley BR2 ....**206** B2
  Dagenham RM9 .....**101** E4
  Kingston upon Thames
  KT1 ....**181** F1
  Mitcham CR4 ....**186** D4
  New Malden KT3 . . . .**183** G4
  Ruislip HA4 ....**84** A2
  Southall UB2 ....**123** E3
  Worcester Park KT4 . .**197** J2
Beverley Trd Est, Mord. SM4
  off Garth Rd **184** A7
Beverley Way, SW20 . . .**183** F1
  New Malden KT3 . . . .**183** F1
Beversbrook Rd, N19 . . .**92** D3
Beverston Rd, SW2 . . . .**151** F5
  Thornton Heath CR7 . .**187** G4
Beverston Ms, W1 ....**15** J2
Bevill Allen Cl, SW17 . . .**167** J5
Bevill Cl, SE25 ....**188** D3
Bevin Cl, SE16
  off Stave Yd Rd **133** H1
Bevin Ct, WC1
  off Holford St **111** G3
Bevington Path, SE1
  off Tanner St **132** C2
Bevington Rd, W10 . . . .**108** B5
  Beckenham BR3 ......**190** B2
Bevington St, SE16 ....**29** J4
Bevin Rd, Hayes UB4 . . .**102** A3
Bevin Sq, SW17 ....**167** J3
Bevin Way, WC1 ....**10** E3
Bevis Marks, EC3 ....**20** E3
Bewcastle Gdns, Enf.
  EN2 ....**43** E4
Bewdley St, N1 ....**93** G7
Bewick St, SW8 ....**150** B2
Bewley St, E1
  off Dellow St . . .**112/113** E7
Bewley St, SW19
  off East Rd **167** F6
Bewlys Rd, SE27 ....**169** H5
Bexhill Cl, Felt. TW13 . . .**160** E2
Bexhill Rd, N11 ....**58** D5
  SE4 ....**153** J7
  SW14 ....**146** C3
Bexhill Wk, E15
  off Mitre Rd **114/115** E2
BEXLEY **159** G6
Bexley Gdns, N9 ....**60** A3
  Romford (Chad.Hth.)
  RM6 ....**82** B5
BEXLEYHEATH **159** F5
Bexley High St, Bex.
  DA5 ....**159** G7
Bexley La, Sid. DA14 . . .**176** C3
Bexley Rd, SE9 ....**156** E5
  Erith DA8 ....**139** J7
Beynon Rd, Cars. SM5 . .**199** J5
Bianca Ho, N1
  off Crondall St **112** B2
Bianca Rd, SE15 ....**37** H6
Bibsworth Rd, N3 ....**72** C2
Bibury Cl, SE15 ....**37** E6
Bicester Rd, Rich. TW9 . .**146** A3
Bickenhall St, W1 ....**16** A1
Bickersteth Rd, SW17 . . .**167** J6
Bickerton Rd, N19 ....**92** C2
BICKLEY, Brom. **192** C3
Bickley Cres, Brom.
  BR1 ....**192** B4
Bickley Pk Rd, Brom.
  BR1 ....**192** B4
Bickley Rd, E10 ....**78** B7
  Bromley BR1 ....**192** A2
Bickley St, SW17 ....**167** H5
Bicknell Rd, SE5 ....**151** J3
Bicknoller Rd, Enf. EN1 . .**44** C1
Bicknor Rd, Orp. BR6 . . .**193** H7
Bidborough Cl, Brom.
  BR2 ....**191** F5
Bidborough St, WC1 . . . .**10** A4
Biddenden Way, SE9 . . .**174** D4
Bidder St, E16 ....**114** E5
Biddestone Rd, N7 ....**93** F4
Biddulph Rd, W9 ....**6** A4
Bideford Av, Grnf.
  UB6 ....**104** E2

Bideford Cl, Edg. HA8 . . . .**70** A1
  Feltham TW13 ....**161** F3
Bideford Gdns, Enf. EN1 . .**44** B7
Bideford Rd, Brom.
  BR1 ....**173** F3
  Ruislip HA4 ....**84** B3
  Welling DA16 ....**138** B7
Bidwell Gdns, N11 ....**58** C7
Bidwell St, SE15 ....**153** E1
★ Big Ben (St. Stephens Twr),
  SW1 ....**26** B4
Bigbury Cl, N17
  off Weir Hall Rd **60** A7
Bigbury Rd, N17
  off Barkham Rd **60** B7
Biggerstaff Rd, E15 . . . .**114** C1
Biggerstaff St, N4 ....**93** G2
Biggin Av, Mitch. CR4 . . .**185** J1
Biggin Hill, SE19 ....**169** H7
Biggin Hill Cl, Kings.T.
  KT2 ....**163** F5
Biggin Way, SE19 ....**169** H7
Bigginwood Rd, SW16 . .**169** H7
Biggs Row, SW15
  off Felsham Rd **148** A3
Big Hill, E5 ....**95** E1
Bigland St, E1 ....**112** E6
Bignell Rd, SE18 ....**136** E5
Bignold Rd, E7 ....**97** G4
Bigwood Rd, NW11 ....**72** E5
Billet Cl, Rom. RM6 . . . .**82** D3
Billet Rd, E17 ....**77** G2
  Romford RM6 ....**82** B3
Billets Hart Cl, W7 . . . .**124** B2
Billet Wks, E17 ....**77** J1
Bill Hamling Cl, SE9 . . .**174** C2
Billingford Cl, SE4 . . . .**153** G4
Billing Pl, SW10 ....**30** B7
Billing Rd, SW10 ....**30** B7
Billings Cl, Dag. RM9
  off Ellerton Rd **100** C7
★ Billingsgate Fish Mkt,
  E14 ....**134** B1
Billing St, SW10 ....**30** B7
Billington Rd, SE14 . . . .**133** G7
Billiter Sq, EC3 ....**20** E5
Billiter St, EC3 ....**20** E4
Bill Nicholson Way, N17
  off High Rd **60** C7
Billockby Cl, Chess.
  KT9 ....**195** J6
Billson St, E14 ....**134** C4
Bilsby Gro, SE9 ....**174** A4
Bilton Rd, Grnf. UB6 . . .**105** E1
Bilton Way, Enf. EN3 . . . .**45** H1
  Hayes UB3 ....**122** B2
Bina Gdns, SW5 ....**30** C2
Bincote Rd, Enf. EN2 . . . .**43** F3
Binden Rd, W12 ....**127** F3
Bindon Grn, Mord.
  SM4 ....**185** E4
Binfield Rd, SW4 ....**151** E1
  South Croydon CR2 . .**202** C5
Bingfield St, N1 ....**111** E1
Bingham Ct, N1
  off Halton Rd **93** H7
Bingham Pl, W1 ....**16** B1
Bingham Pt, SE18
  off Whitworth Pl .**136/137** E4
Bingham Rd, Croy.
  CR0 ....**202** D1
Bingham St, N1 ....**94** A6
Bingley Rd, E16 ....**115** J6
  Greenford UB6 ......**103** J5
  Sunbury-on-Thames
  TW16 ....**160** A7
Binley Ho, SW15
  off Highcliffe Dr **147** G6
Binney St, W1 ....**16** C5
Binns Rd, W4 ....**126** E5
Binns Ter, W4
  off Binns Rd **126/127** E5
Binsey Wk, SE2 ....**138** C1
Binyon Cres, Stan. HA7 . .**52** C5
Birbetts Rd, SE9 ....**174** C2
Bircham Path, SE4
  off St. Norbert Rd . . .**153** G4
Birchanger Rd, SE25 . . .**188** D5
Birch Av, N13 ....**59** J3
Birch Cl, E16 ....**115** E5
  N19 off Hargrave Pk . . .**92** C2
  SE15
  off Bournemouth Rd . .**152** D2
  Brentford TW8 ....**124** E7
  Buckhurst Hill IG9 . . . .**64** A3
  Hounslow TW3 ....**144** A3
  Romford RM7 ....**83** H3
  Teddington TW11 . . . .**162** D5
Birchdale Gdns, Rom.
  RM6 ....**82** D7

Birchdale Rd, E7 ....**97** J5
Birchdene Dr, SE28 . . . .**138** A2
Birchen Cl, NW9 ....**88** D2
Birchend Cl, S.Croy.
  CR2 ....**202** A6
Birchen Gro, NW9 ....**88** D2
Birches, The, N21 ....**43** F6
  SE7 ....**135** H6
  Orpington BR6 ......**206** D4
Birches Cl, Mitch. CR4 . .**185** J3
  Pinner HA5 ....**66** E5
Birchfield St, E14 ....**114** A7
Birch Gdns, Dag. RM10 . .**101** J3
Birch Grn, NW9
  off Clayton Fld . . .**54/55** E7
Birch Gro, E11 ....**96** E3
  SE12 ....**155** F7
  W3 ....**126** A1
  Welling DA16 ....**158** A4
Birch Hill, Croy. CR0 . . .**203** G5
Birchington Cl, Bexh.
  DA7 ....**159** H1
Birchington Rd, N8 . . . .**74** D6
  NW6 ....**108** D1
  Surbiton KT5 ....**181** J7
Birchin La, EC3 ....**20** C4
Birchlands Av, SW12 . . .**149** J7
Birch Mead, Orp. BR6 . .**206** D2
Birchmead Av, Pnr. HA5 . .**66** C4
Birchmere Row, SE3 . . .**155** F2
Birchmore Wk, N5 ....**93** J3
Birch Pk, Har. HA3 ....**51** J7
Birch Rd, Felt. TW13 . . .**160** D5
  Romford RM7 ....**83** H3
Birch Row, Brom. BR2 . .**192** D7
Birch Tree Av, W.Wick.
  BR4 ....**205** F5
Birch Tree Way, Croy.
  CR0 ....**202** E2
Birchville Ct, Bushey
  (Bushey Hth.) WD23
  off Heathbourne Rd . .**52** B1
Birch Wk, Borwd. WD6 . .**38** A1
  Erith DA8 ....**139** J6
  Mitcham CR4 ....**186** B1
Birchway, Hayes UB3 . .**122** A1
Birchwood Av, N10 . . . .**74** A3
  Beckenham BR3 ......**189** J4
  Sidcup DA14 ....**176** B2
  Wallington SM6 . . . .**200** A3
Birchwood Cl, Mord.
  SM4 ....**184** E4
Birchwood Ct, N13 . . . .**59** H5
  Edgware HA8 ....**70** C2
Birchwood Dr, NW3 . . . .**91** E3
Birchwood Gro, Hmptn.
  TW12 ....**161** G6
Birchwood Rd, SW17 . .**168** B5
  Orpington BR5 ......**193** G4
Birdbrook Cl, Dag.
  RM10 ....**101** J7
Birdbrook Rd, SE3 ....**155** J3
Birdcage Wk, SW1 ....**25** G4
Birdham Cl, Brom. BR1 . .**192** B5
Birdhurst Av, S.Croy.
  CR2 ....**202** A4
Birdhurst Gdns, S.Croy.
  CR2 ....**202** A4
Birdhurst Ri, S.Croy.
  CR2 ....**202** B5
Birdhurst Rd, SW18 . . .**149** F4
  SW19 ....**167** H6
  South Croydon CR2 . .**202** B5
Bird in Bush Rd, SE15 . . .**37** J7
Bird-in-Hand La, Brom.
  BR1 ....**192** A2
Bird-in-Hand Pas, SE23
  off Dartmouth Rd . . .**171** F2
Birds Fm Av, Rom. RM5 . .**83** H1
Birdsfield La, E3 ....**113** J1
Bird St, W1 ....**16** C4
Bird Wk, Twick. TW2 . . .**161** F1
Birdwood Cl, Tedd.
  TW11 ....**162** B4
Birkbeck Av, W3 ....**106** C2
  Greenford UB6 ......**103** J1
Birkbeck Gdns, Wdf.Grn.
  IG8 ....**63** F2
Birkbeck Gro, W3 ....**126** D2
Birkbeck Hill, SE21 . . .**169** H2
Birkbeck Ms, E8
  off Sandringham Rd . .**94** C5
Birkbeck Pl, SE21 ....**169** J1
Birkbeck Rd, E8 ....**94** C5
  N8 ....**75** E4
  N12 ....**57** F5
  N17 ....**76** C1
  NW7 ....**55** F5
  SW19 ....**167** E5
  W3 ....**126** D1

Birkbeck Rd, W5 . . . . . .125 F4
  Beckenham BR3 . . . . . .189 F2
  Enfield EN2 . . . . .44 A1
  Ilford IG2 . . . . .81 G5
  Sidcup DA14 . . . . .176 A3
Birkbeck St, E2 . . . . . . .113 E3
Birkbeck Way, Grnf.
  UB6 . . . . .103 J1
Birkdale Av, Pnr. HA5 . . .67 G3
Birkdale Cl, SE16
  off Masters Dr 132/133 E5
  Orpington BR6 . . . . . . .193 G7
Birkdale Gdns, Croy.
  CR0 . . . . .203 G4
  Watford WD19 . . . . .50 D3
Birkdale Rd, SE2 . . . . . .138 A4
  W5 . . . . .105 H4
Birkenhead Av, Kings.T.
  KT2 . . . . .181 J2
Birkenhead St, WC1 . . . .10 B3
Birkhall Rd, SE6 . . . . . .172 D1
Birkwood Cl, SW12 . . . .150 D7
Birley Rd, N20 . . . . .57 F2
Birley St, SW11 . . . . . . .150 A2
Birnam Rd, N4 . . . . .93 F2
Birrell Ho, SW9
  off Stockwell Rd 151 F2
Birse Cres, NW10 . . . . . .89 E4
Birstall Grn, Wat. WD19 . .50 D4
Birstall Rd, N15 . . . . . . .76 B5
Biscay Rd, W6 . . . . .128 A5
Biscoe Cl, Houns. TW5 . .123 G6
Biscoe Way, SE13 . . . . . .154 D3
Bisenden Rd, Croy. CR0 .202 B2
Bisham Cl, Cars. SM5 . . .199 J1
Bisham Gdns, N6 . . . . . .92 A1
Bishop Butt Cl, Orp. BR6
  off Stapleton Rd 207 J3
Bishop Cl, W4 . . . . .126 C5
Bishop Fox Way, W.Mol.
  KT8 . . . . .179 F4
Bishop Ken Rd, Har.
  HA3 . . . . .68 C2
Bishop Kings Rd, W14 . .128 B4
Bishop Rd, N14 . . . . .42 B7
Bishop's Av, E13 . . . . . . .115 H1
  SW6 . . . . .148 A2
Bishops Av, Brom. BR1 . .191 J2
  Romford RM6 . . . . .82 C6
Bishops Av, The, N2 . . . .73 G7
Bishops Br, W2 . . . . .14 D2
Bishops Br Rd, W2 . . . . .14 B4
Bishops Cl, E17 . . . . . . .78 B4
  N19 off Wyndham Cres .92 C3
  SE9 . . . . .175 F2
  Barnet EN5 . . . . .40 A6
  Enfield EN1
    off Central Av 44/45 E2
  Richmond TW10 . . . . . .163 G3
Bishop's Cl, Sutt. SM1 . .198 D3
Bishop's Ct, EC4 . . . . . . .19 G3
  WC2 . . . . .18 E3
Bishops Dr, Felt. TW14 . .141 G6
  Northolt UB5 . . . . .103 E1
Bishopsford Rd, Mord.
  SM4 . . . . .185 F7
Bishopsgate, EC2 . . . . . .20 D4
Bishopsgate Arc, EC2 . . .20 E4
Bishopsgate Chyd, EC2 . .20 D3
Bishops Gro, N2 . . . . . . .73 G6
  Hampton TW12 . . . . . . .161 F4
Bishop's Hall, Kings.T.
  KT1 . . . . .181 G2
Bishops Hill, Walt. KT12 .178 A7
Bishop's Pk, SW6 . . . . . .148 A2
Bishop's Pk Rd, SW6 . . .148 A2
Bishops Pk Rd, SW16 . . .187 E1
Bishops Pl, Sutt. SM1
  off Lind Rd 199 F5
Bishops Rd, N6 . . . . .74 A6
  SW6 . . . . .148 C1
  W7 . . . . .124 B2
  Croydon CR0 . . . . .187 H7
Bishops Ter, SE11 . . . . . .35 F1
Bishopsthorpe Rd,
  SE26 . . . . .171 G4
Bishop St, N1 . . . . .111 J1
Bishops Wk, Chis. BR7 . .193 F1
  Croydon CR0 . . . . .203 G5
Bishop's Wk, Pnr. HA5
  off High St 66/67 E3
Bishops Way, E2 . . . . . . .113 E2
Bishopswood Rd, N6 . . . .73 J7
Bishop Way, NW10 . . . . .88 E7
Bishop Wilfred Wd Cl, SE15
  off Moncrieff St 152 D2
Bisley Cl, Wor.Pk. KT4 . .197 J1
Bisley Ho, SW19 . . . . . . .166 A2
Bispham Rd, NW10 . . . . .105 J3
Bisson Rd, E15 . . . . .114 C2

Bisterne Av, E17 . . . . . . .78 D3
Bittacy Cl, NW7 . . . . . . .56 A6
Bittacy Hill, NW7 . . . . . .56 A6
Bittacy Pk Av, NW7 . . . .56 A6
Bittacy Ri, NW7 . . . . . . .55 J6
Bittacy Rd, NW7 . . . . . . .56 A6
Bittern Cl, Hayes UB4 . .102 D5
Bittern St, SE1 . . . . .27 J4
Bittoms, The, Kings.T.
  KT1 . . . . .181 G3
Bixley Cl, Sthl. UB2 . . . .123 F4
Blackall St, EC2 . . . . . . .12 D5
Blackberry Fm Cl, Houns.
  TW5 . . . . .122 E7
Blackbird Hill, NW9 . . . .88 C2
Blackbird Yd, E2 . . . . . . .13 G3
Blackborne Rd, Dag.
  RM10 . . . . .101 G6
Black Boy La, N15 . . . . .75 J5
Blackbrook La, Brom. BR1,
  BR2 . . . . .192 D3
Blackburne's Ms, W1 . . .16 B5
Blackburn Rd, NW6 . . . . .90 E6
Blackburn Trd Est, Stai.
  (Stanw.) TW19 . . . . . . .140 C6
Blackbush Av, Rom.
  RM6 . . . . .82 D5
Blackbush Cl, Sutt.
  SM2 . . . . .199 E7
Blackdown Cl, N2 . . . . . .73 F2
Blackdown Ter, SE18
  off Prince Imperial
  Rd 136 D7
Blackett St, SW15 . . . . .148 A3
Black Fan Cl, Enf. EN2 . . .43 J1
BLACKFEN, Sid. 157 J7
Blackfen Rd, Sid. DA15 . .157 H5
Blackford Rd, Wat.
  WD19 . . . . .50 D5
Blackford's Path, SW15
  off Roehampton
  High St 147 G7
Blackfriars Br, EC4 . . . . .19 G5
  SE1 . . . . .19 G5
Black Friars Ct, EC4 . . . .19 G5
Black Friars La, EC4 . . . .19 G5
Blackfriars Pas, EC4 . . . .19 G5
Blackfriars Rd, SE1 . . . . .27 G4
Black Gates, Pnr. HA5
  off Church La 67 F3
BLACKHEATH, SE3 . . . .155 E1
★ Blackheath, SE3 . . . . .154 C1
Blackheath Av, SE10 . . . .134 D7
Blackheath Gro, SE3 . . . .155 F2
Blackheath Hill, SE10 . . .154 C1
BLACKHEATH PARK,
  SE3 . . . . .155 F4
Blackheath Pk, SE3 . . . .155 F3
Blackheath Ri, SE13 . . . .154 C2
Blackheath Rd, SE10 . . . .154 B1
Blackheath Vale, SE3 . . . .155 E2
Blackheath Village,
  SE3 . . . . .155 F2
Black Horse Ct, SE1 . . . .28 C5
Blackhorse La, E17 . . . . .77 G4
  Croydon CR0 . . . . .188 D7
Blackhorse Ms, E17
  off Blackhorse La 77 G3
Blackhorse Rd, E17 . . . . .77 G4
  SE8 . . . . .133 H5
  Sidcup DA14 . . . . .176 A4
Blacklands Dr, Hayes UB4
Blacklands Rd, SE6 . . . . .172 C4
Blacklands Ter, SW3 . . . .31 J2
Black Lion La, W6 . . . . . .127 G4
Black Lion Ms, W6
  off Black Lion La 127 G4
Blackmans Yd, E2
  off Cheshire St 112 D4
Blackmore Av, Sthl.
  UB1 . . . . .124 A1
Blackmore Rd, Buck.H.
  IG9 . . . . .48 B7
Blackmores Gro, Tedd.
  TW11 . . . . .162 D6
Black Path, E10 . . . . .77 G7
Blackpool Rd, SE15 . . . .152 E2
Black Prince Rd, SE1 . . . .34 C2
  SE11 . . . . .34 D2
Black Rod Cl, Hayes
  UB3 . . . . .121 J3
Blackshaw Pl, N1
  off Hertford Rd 94 B7
Blackshaw Rd, SW17 . . .167 F4
Blacksmiths Cl, Rom.
  RM6 . . . . .82 C6
Blacks Rd, W6
  off Queen Caroline
  St 127 J4
Blackstock Ms, N4
  off Blackstock Rd 93 H2

Blackstock Rd, N4 . . . . . .93 H2
  N5 . . . . .93 H2
Blackstone Est, E8 . . . . . .94 E7
Blackstone Rd, NW2 . . . .89 J5
Black Swan Yd, SE1 . . . .28 E3
Blackthorn Av, West Dr.
  UB7 . . . . .120 D4
Blackthorn Ct, Houns.
  TW5 . . . . .122 E7
Blackthorne Av, Croy.
  CR0 . . . . .189 F7
Blackthorne Dr, E4 . . . . .62 D4
Blackthorn Gro, Bexh.
  DA7 . . . . .158 D3
Blackthorn St, E3 . . . . . .114 A4
Blacktree Ms, SW9 . . . . .151 G3
Blackwall La, SE10 . . . . .135 E5
Blackwall Pier, E14 . . . . .114 E7
Blackwall Trd Est, E14 . .114 D5
Blackwall Tunnel, E14 . . .134 D1
Blackwall Tunnel App,
  SE10 . . . . .134 E2
Blackwall Tunnel
  Northern App, E3 . . . .114 A2
  E14 . . . . .114 A2
Blackwall Way, E14 . . . . .114 C7
Blackwater Cl, E7 . . . . . .97 F4
Blackwater Rd, Sutt. SM1
  off High St 198/199 E4
Blackwater St, SE22 . . . .152 C5
Blackwell Cl, E5 . . . . . . .95 G4
  Harrow HA3 . . . . .52 A7
Blackwell Gdns, Edg.
  HA8 . . . . .54 A3
Blackwell Rd, SE17 . . . . .36 B3
Blade Ms, SW15
  off Deodar Rd 148 C4
Blades Ct, SW15
  off Deodar Rd 148 C4
Bladindon Dr, Bex. DA5 .158 C7
Bladon Gdns, Har. HA2 . .67 H6
Blagdens Cl, N14 . . . . . . .58 C2
Blagdens La, N14 . . . . . .58 D2
Blagdon Rd, SE13 . . . . . .154 B6
  New Malden KT3 . . . . .183 F4
Blagdon Wk, Tedd. TW11 .163 F6
Blagrove Rd, W10 . . . . . .108 B5
Blair Av, NW9 . . . . .70 E7
Blair Cl, N1 . . . . .93 J6
  Hayes UB3 . . . . .122 A4
  Sidcup DA15 . . . . .157 H5
Blairderry Rd, SW2 . . . . .169 E2
Blairhead Dr, Wat. WD19 .50 B3
Blair St, E14 . . . . .114 C6
Blake Av, Bark. IG11 . . . .117 H1
Blake Cl, W10 . . . . .107 J5
  Carshalton SM5 . . . . . .185 H7
  Welling DA16 . . . . .157 H1
Blakeden Dr, Esher (Clay.)
  KT10 . . . . .194 C6
Blake Gdns, SW6 . . . . . .148 E1
Blake Hall Cres, E11 . . . .97 G1
Blake Hall Rd, E11 . . . . . .79 G7
Blakehall Rd, Cars. SM5 .199 J6
Blake Ho, Beck. BR3 . . . .172 A6
Blakeley Cotts, SE10
  off Tunnel Av 134 D2
Blakemore Rd, SW16 . . .168 E3
  Thornton Heath CR7 . . .187 F5
Blakemore Way, Belv.
  DA17 . . . . .139 E3
Blakeney Av, Beck. BR3 . .189 J1
Blakeney Cl, E8 . . . . .94 D5
  N20 . . . . .57 F1
  NW1
    off Rossendale Way . . .92 D7
Blakeney Rd, Beck. BR3 .171 J7
Blakenham Rd, SW17 . . .167 J4
Blaker Ct, SE7
  off Fairlawn 135 J7
Blake Rd, E16 . . . . .115 F4
  N11 . . . . .58 C7
  Croydon CR0 . . . . .202 B2
  Mitcham CR4 . . . . .185 H3
Blaker Rd, E15 . . . . .114 C1
Blakes Av, N.Mal. KT3 . .183 F5
Blake's Grn, W.Wick.
  BR4 . . . . .204 C1
Blakesley Av, W5 . . . . . .105 F6
Blakesley Wk, SW20
  off Kingston Rd 184 C2
Blakes Rd, SE15 . . . . . . .36 E7
Blakes Ter, N.Mal. KT3 . .183 G5
Blake St, SE8
  off Watergate St 134 A6
Blakesware Gdns, N9 . . . .44 A7
Blakewood Cl, Felt.
  TW13 . . . . .160 C4

Blanchard Cl, SE9 . . . . . .174 B3
Blanchard Way, E8 . . . . . .94 D6
Blanch Cl, SE15
  off Culmore Rd 133 F7
Blanchedowne, SE5 . . . .152 A4
Blanche St, E16 . . . . . . .115 F4
Blanchland Rd, Mord.
  SM4 . . . . .184 E5
Blandfield Rd, SW12 . . . .150 A6
Blandford Av, Beck.
  BR3 . . . . .189 H2
  Twickenham TW2 . . . . .161 H1
Blandford Cl, N2 . . . . . . .73 F4
  Croydon CR0 . . . . .201 E3
  Romford RM7 . . . . .83 H4
Blandford Cres, E4 . . . . . .46 C7
Blandford Rd, W4 . . . . . .126 E3
  W5 . . . . .125 G2
  Beckenham BR3 . . . . . .189 F2
  Southall UB2 . . . . .123 G4
  Teddington TW11 . . . . .162 A5
Blandford Sq, NW1 . . . . .7 H6
Blandford St, W1 . . . . . . .16 A3
Blandford Waye, Hayes
  UB4 . . . . .102 C6
Bland St, SE9 . . . . .156 A4
Blaney Cres, E6 . . . . .116 E3
Blanmerle Rd, SE9 . . . . .174 E1
Blann Cl, SE9 . . . . .156 A6
Blantyre St, SW10 . . . . . .30 E7
Blantyre Wk, SW10 . . . . .30 E7
Blashford, NW3 . . . . .91 J7
Blashford St, SE13 . . . . .154 D7
Blasker Wk, E14 . . . . . . .134 A5
Blawith Rd, Har. HA1 . . . .68 B4
Blaydon Cl, N17 . . . . .60 E7
Blaydon Wk, N17 . . . . . . .60 E7
Bleak Hill La, SE18 . . . . .137 J6
Blean Gro, SE20 . . . . . . .171 F7
Bleasdale Av, Grnf.
  UB6 . . . . .104 D3
Blechynden St, W10
  off Bramley Rd 108 A7
Bleddyn Cl, Sid. DA15 . . .158 C6
Bledlow Cl, SE28 . . . . . . .118 C7
Bledlow Ri, Grnf. UB6 . . .103 J2
Bleeding Heart Yd, EC1 . .19 F2
Blegborough Rd, SW16 . .168 C6
Blendon Dr, Bex. DA5 . . .158 D6
Blendon Path, Brom.
  BR1 . . . . .173 F7
Blendon Rd, Bex. DA5 . . .158 D6
Blendon Ter, SE18 . . . . . .137 F5
Blendworth Pt, SW15
  off Wanborough Dr . . .165 H1
Blendworth Way, SE15 . . .37 E7
Blenheim Av, Ilf. IG2 . . . .80 D6
Blenheim Cl, N21
  off Elm Pk Rd 59 J1
  SE12 off Guibal Rd . . .173 H1
  SW20 . . . . .183 J3
  Greenford UB6
    off Leaver Gdns 104 A2
  Romford RM7 . . . . .83 J4
  Wallington SM6 . . . . . .200 C7
Blenheim Ct, N19
  off Marlborough
  Rd 92/93 E2
  Sidcup DA14 . . . . .175 G3
  Sutton SM2
    off Wellesley Rd 199 F6
  Woodford Green IG8
    off Navestock Cres . . .63 J7
Blenheim Cres, W11 . . . .108 B6
  South Croydon CR2 . . .201 J7
Blenheim Dr, Well.
  DA16 . . . . .157 J1
Blenheim Gdns, NW2 . . . .89 J5
  SW2 . . . . .151 F6
  Kingston upon Thames
  KT2 . . . . .164 B7
  Wallington SM6 . . . . . .200 C6
  Wembley HA9 . . . . .87 H3
Blenheim Gro, SE15 . . . .152 D2
Blenheim Pas, NW8 . . . . .6 C1
Blenheim Ri, N15
  off Talbot Rd 76 C4
Blenheim Rd, E6 . . . . . . .116 A3
  E15 . . . . .97 E4
  E17 . . . . .77 G3
  NW8 . . . . .6 C1
  SE20 off Maple Rd . . .171 F7
  SW20 . . . . .183 J3
  W4 . . . . .126 E3
  Barnet EN5 . . . . .40 A3
  Bromley BR1 . . . . .192 B4
  Harrow HA2 . . . . .67 H6
  Northolt UB5 . . . . .85 H6
  Sidcup DA15 . . . . .176 C1
  Sutton SM1 . . . . .198 D3

Blenheim Shop Cen,
SE20 . . . .**171** F7
Blenheim St, W1 . . . .**16** D4
Blenheim Ter, NW8 . . . .**6** C1
Blenheim Way, Islw.
TW7 . . . .**144** A3
Blenkarne Rd, SW11 . . . . .**149** J6
Bleriot Rd, Houns. TW5 . .**122** C7
Blessbury Rd, Edg. HA8 . .**70** C1
Blessington Ct, SE13 . . . .**154** D3
Blessington Rd, SE13 . . . .**154** D3
Blessing Way, Bark. IG11 .**118** C3
Bletchingley Cl, Th.Hth.
CR7 . . . .**187** H4
Bletchley Ct, N1 . . . .**12** B2
Bletchley St, N1 . . . .**12** A2
Bletchmore Cl, Hayes
UB3 . . . .**121** G5
Bletsoe Wk, N1 . . . .**12** A1
Blewbury Ho, SE2
off Yarnton Way **138** D2
Blincoe Cl, SW19 . . . .**166** A6
Blind La, Loug. (High Beach)
IG10 . . . .**46** E2
Bliss Cres, SE13
off Coldbath St **154** B2
Blissett St, SE10 . . . .**154** C1
Bliss Ms, W10
off Third Av **108** B3
Blisworth Cl, Hayes UB4
off Braunston Dr .**102/103** E4
Blithbury Rd, Dag.
RM9 . . . .**100** B6
Blithdale Rd, SE2 . . . .**138** A4
Blithfield St, W8 . . . .**22** A6
Blockley Rd, Wem. HA0 . .**86** E2
Bloemfontein Av, W12 . . .**127** H1
Bloemfontein Rd, W12 . . .**107** H7
Blomfield Rd, W9 . . . .**14** C1
Blomfield St, EC2 . . . .**20** C2
Blomfield Vil, W2 . . . .**14** B2
Blomville Rd, Dag. RM8 .**101** E3
Blondell Cl, West Dr.
UB7 . . . .**120** A6
Blondel St, SW11 . . . .**150** A2
Blondin Av, W5 . . . .**125** F4
Blondin St, E3 . . . .**114** A2
Bloomburg St, SW1 . . . . . .**33** G2
Bloomfield Cres, Ilf. IG2 . .**81** E6
Bloomfield Pl, W1 . . . .**16** E5
Bloomfield Rd, N6 . . . .**74** A6
SE18 . . . .**137** E5
Bromley BR2 . . . .**192** A5
Kingston upon Thames
KT1 . . . .**181** H4
Bloomfield Ter, SW1 . . . . .**32** C3
Bloom Gro, SE27 . . . .**169** H3
Bloomhall Rd, SE19 . . . . .**170** A5
Bloom Pk Rd, SW6 . . . . .**128** C7
BLOOMSBURY, WC1 . . . .**17** J2
Bloomsbury Cl, W5 . . . . .**105** J7
Bloomsbury Ct, WC1 . . . . .**18** B2
Pinner HA5 . . . .**67** F3
Bloomsbury Ho, SW4 . . .**150** D6
Bloomsbury Pl, SW18
off Fullerton Rd **149** F5
WC1 . . . .**18** B1
Bloomsbury Sq, WC1 . . . . .**18** B2
Bloomsbury St, WC1 . . . . .**17** J2
Bloomsbury Way, WC1 . . .**18** A3
Blore Cl, SW8
off Thessaly Rd **150** D1
Blore Ct, W1 . . . .**17** H4
Blossom Cl, W5
off Almond Av **125** H2
Dagenham RM9 . . . . . .**119** F1
South Croydon CR2 . . .**202** C5
Blossom La, Enf. EN2 . . . .**43** J1
Blossom Pl, E1 . . . .**13** E6
Blossom St, E1 . . . .**21** E1
Blossom Way, West Dr.
UB7 . . . .**120** D4
Blossom Waye, Houns.
TW5 . . . .**122** E7
Blount St, E14 . . . .**113** H6
Bloxam Gdns, SE9 . . . . . .**156** B5
Bloxhall Rd, E10 . . . .**95** J1
Bloxham Cres, Hmptn.
TW12 . . . .**161** F7
Bloxworth Cl, Wall. SM6 .**200** C3
Blucher Rd, SE5 . . . .**131** J7
Blue Anchor All, Rich. TW9
off Kew Rd **145** H4
Blue Anchor La, SE16 . . . .**37** J1
Blue Anchor Yd, E1 . . . . . .**21** H5
Blue Ball Yd, SW1 . . . .**25** F2
Bluebell Av, E12 . . . .**98** A5
Bluebell Cl, E9
off Moulins Rd **113** F1
SE26 . . . .**170** C4

Bluebell Cl Orp. BR6 . . . .**207** F2
Wallington SM6 . . . . . .**200** B1
Bluebell Way, Ilf. IG1 . . . .**98** E6
Blueberry Cl, Wdf.Grn.
IG8 . . . .**63** G6
Bluebird La, Dag. RM10 . .**101** G7
Bluebird Way, SE28 . . . . .**137** G2
Bluefield Cl, Hmptn.
TW12 . . . .**161** G5
Bluegates, Epsom (Ewell)
KT17 . . . .**197** G2
Bluehouse Rd, E4 . . . .**63** E3
Blundell Rd, E10 . . . .**78** D1
Blundell St, N7 . . . .**92** E7
Blunden Cl, Dag. RM8 . . .**100** C1
Blunt Rd, S.Croy. CR2 . .**202** A5
Blunts Av, West Dr. UB7 .**120** D7
Blunts Rd, SE9 . . . .**156** D5
Blurton Rd, E5 . . . .**95** F4
Blyth Cl, E14
off Manchester Rd . . .**134** D4
Twickenham TW1
off Grimwood Rd **144** C6
Blythe Cl, SE6 . . . .**153** J7
Blythe Hill, SE6 . . . .**153** J7
Orpington BR5 . . . .**193** J1
Blythe Hill La, SE6 . . . . .**153** J7
Blythe Rd, W14 . . . .**128** A3
Blythe St, E2 . . . .**112** E3
Blythe Vale, SE6 . . . .**171** J1
Blyth Rd, E17 . . . .**77** J7
SE28 . . . .**118** C7
Bromley BR1 . . . .**191** F1
Hayes UB3 . . . .**121** H2
Blyth's Wf, E14
off Narrow St **113** H7
Blythswood Rd, Ilf. IG3 . .**100** A1
Blyth Wd Pk, Brom. BR1
off Blyth Rd **191** F1
Blythwood Rd, N4 . . . .**75** E7
Pinner HA5 . . . .**66** D1
Boades Ms, NW3
off New End **91** G4
Boadicea St, N1
off Copenhagen St . . .**111** F1
Boakes Cl, NW9 . . . .**70** C4
Boardman Av, E4 . . . .**46** B5
Boardman Cl, Barn. EN5 . .**40** B5
Boardwalk Pl, E14 . . . . . .**134** C1
Boar's Head Yd, Brent. TW8
off Brent Way **125** G2
Boathouse Wk, SE15 . . . . .**37** G7
Richmond TW9 . . . .**145** H1
Boat Lifter Way, SE16
off Sweden Gate **133** H4
Bob Anker Cl, E13
off Chesterton Rd **115** G3
Bobbin Cl, SW4 . . . .**150** C3
Bobby Moore Way, N10 . .**57** J7
Bob Marley Way, SE24
off Mayall Rd **151** G4
Bockhampton Rd, Kings.T.
KT2 . . . .**163** J7
Bocking St, E8 . . . .**112** E1
Boddicott Cl, SW19 . . . . .**166** B2
Bodiam Cl, Enf. EN1 . . . . .**44** A2
Bodiam Rd, SW16 . . . . . .**168** D7
Bodicea Ms, Houns.
TW4 . . . .**143** F7
Bodley Cl, N.Mal. KT3 . .**182** E5
Bodley Manor Way, SW2
off Papworth Way **151** G7
Bodley Rd, N.Mal. KT3 . .**182** D6
Bodmin Cl, Har. HA2 . . . .**85** F3
Bodmin Gro, Mord.
SM4 . . . .**185** E5
Bodmin St, SW18 . . . . . .**166** D1
Bodnant Gdns, SW20 . . .**183** G3
Bodney Rd, E8 . . . .**94** E5
Boeing Way, Sthl. UB2 . .**122** B3
Boevey Path, Belv.
DA17 . . . .**139** F6
Bogey La, Orp. BR6 . . . .**206** D7
Bognor Gdns, Wat. WD19
off Bowring Grn **50** C5
Bognor Rd, Well. DA16 . .**158** D1
Bohemia Pl, E8 . . . .**95** E6
Bohn Rd, E1 . . . .**113** H5
Bohun Gro, Barn. EN4 . . .**41** H6
Boileau Par, W5
off Boileau Rd **105** J6
Boileau Rd, SW13 . . . . . .**127** G7
W5 . . . .**105** J6
Bolden St, SE8 . . . .**154** B2
Bolderwood Way, W.Wick.
BR4 . . . .**204** B2

Boldmere Rd, Pnr. HA5 . . .**66** C7
Boleyn Av, Enf. EN1 . . . . .**44** E1
Boleyn Cl, E17 . . . .**78** A4
Loughton IG10
off Roding Gdns **48** B6
Boleyn Ct, Buck.H. IG9 . . .**63** G1
Boleyn Dr, Ruis. HA4 . . . .**84** D2
West Molesey KT8 . . . .**179** F3
Boleyn Gdns, Dag.
RM10 . . . .**101** J7
West Wickham BR4 . . .**204** B2
Boleyn Gro, W.Wick.
BR4 . . . .**204** C2
Boleyn Rd, E6 . . . .**116** A2
E7 . . . .**97** G7
N16 . . . .**94** B5
Boleyn Way, Barn. EN5 . . .**41** F3
Ilford IG6 . . . .**65** F6
Bolina Rd, SE16 . . . .**133** F5
Bolingbroke Gro, SW11 . .**149** H4
Bolingbroke Rd, W14 . . .**128** A3
Bolingbroke Wk, SW11 . .**129** G7
Bolingbroke Way, Hayes
UB3 . . . .**121** G1
Bolliger Ct, NW10
off Park Royal Rd **106** C4
Bollo Br Rd, W3 . . . .**126** B3
Bollo La, W3 . . . .**126** B2
W4 . . . .**126** C4
Bolney Gate, SW7 . . . . . .**23** G4
Bolney St, SW8 . . . .**131** F7
Bolney Way, Felt. TW13 . .**161** E3
Bolsover St, W1 . . . .**9** E6
Bolstead Rd, Mitch.
CR4 . . . .**186** B1
Bolt Ct, EC4 . . . .**19** F4
Boltmore Cl, NW4 . . . .**72** A3
Bolton Cl, SE20
off Selby Rd **188** D2
Chessington KT9 . . . . .**195** G6
Bolton Cres, SE5 . . . .**35** F6
Bolton Gdns, NW10 . . . .**108** A2
SW5 . . . .**30** A3
Bromley BR1 . . . .**173** F6
Teddington TW11 . . . . .**162** D6
Bolton Gdns Ms, SW10 . .**30** C3
Bolton Rd, E15 . . . .**97** F6
N18 . . . .**60** C5
NW8 . . . .**109** E1
NW10 . . . .**107** E1
W4 . . . .**126** C7
Chessington KT9 . . . . .**195** G6
Harrow HA1 . . . .**67** J4
Boltons, The, SW10 . . . . .**30** C3
Wembley HA0 . . . .**86** C4
Woodford Green IG8 . . .**63** G4
Boltons La, Hayes UB3 . .**121** F7
Boltons Pl, SW5 . . . .**30** C3
Bolton St, W1 . . . .**24** E1
Bolton Wk, N7
off Durham Rd **93** F2
Bombay St, SE16 . . . . . .**132** E4
Bomer Cl, West Dr. UB7 .**120** D7
Bomore Rd, W11 . . . .**108** A7
Bonar Pl, Chis. BR7 . . . .**174** B7
Bonar Rd, SE15 . . . .**132** D7
Bonchester Cl, Chis.
BR7 . . . .**174** D7
Bonchurch Cl, Sutt.
SM2 . . . .**199** E7
Bonchurch Rd, W10 . . . .**108** B5
W13 . . . .**124** E1
Bond Ct, EC4 . . . .**20** B4
Bondfield Av, Hayes
UB4 . . . .**102** A3
Bondfield Rd, E6
off Lovage App **116** B5
Bond Gdns, Wall. SM6 . .**200** C4
Bonding Yd Wk, SE16
off Finland St **133** H3
Bond Rd, Mitch. CR4 . . .**185** H2
Surbiton KT6 . . . .**195** J2
Bond St, E15 . . . .**96** E5
W4 . . . .**126** E4
W5 . . . .**105** G2
Bondway, SW8 . . . .**34** B5
Boneta Rd, SE18 . . . .**136** C3
Bonfield Rd, SE13 . . . . . .**154** C4
Bonham Gdns, Dag.
RM8 . . . .**100** D2
Bonham Rd, SW2 . . . . . .**151** F5
Dagenham RM8 . . . . .**100** D2
Bonheur Rd, W4 . . . .**126** D2
Bonhill St, EC2 . . . .**12** C6
Boniface Gdns, Har. HA3 .**51** H7
Boniface Wk, Har. HA3 . .**51** H7
Bonington Ho, Enf. EN1
off Ayley Cft **44** D5
Bon Marche Ter Ms, SE27
off Gipsy Rd **170** B4

Bonner Hill Rd, Kings.T.
KT1 . . . .**181** J3
Bonner Rd, E2 . . . .**113** F2
Bonnersfield Cl, Har.
HA1 . . . .**68** C6
Bonnersfield La, Har.
HA1 . . . .**68** D6
Bonner St, E2 . . . .**113** F2
Bonneville Gdns, SW4 . .**150** C6
Bonnington Sq, SW8 . . . .**34** C5
Bonnington Twr, Brom.
BR2 . . . .**192** B6
Bonny St, NW1 . . . .**92** C7
Bonser Rd, Twick. TW1 . .**162** C2
Bonsor St, SE5 . . . .**132** B7
Bonville Gdns, NW4
off Handowe Cl **71** G4
Bonville Rd, Brom. BR1 . .**173** F5
Bookbinders' Cotts, N20
off Manor Dr **57** J3
Booker Cl, E14
off Wallwood St **113** J5
Booker Rd, N18 . . . .**60** D5
Book Ms, WC2 . . . .**17** J4
Boone Ct, N9 . . . .**61** F3
Boones Rd, SE13 . . . . . .**155** E4
Boone St, SE13 . . . .**155** E4
Boord St, SE10 . . . .**135** E3
Boothby Rd, N19 . . . .**92** D2
Booth Cl, E9
off Victoria Pk Rd .**112/113** E1
SE28 . . . .**118** B7
Booth Rd, NW9 . . . .**70** E2
Croydon CR0
off Waddon New Rd . .**201** H2
Booth's Pl, W1 . . . .**17** G2
Boot St, N1 . . . .**12** D4
Bordars Rd, W7 . . . .**104** B5
Bordars Wk, W7 . . . .**104** B5
Borden Av, Enf. EN1 . . . . .**44** A6
Border Cres, SE26 . . . . .**170** E5
Border Gdns, Croy. CR0 .**204** B4
Bordergate, Mitch. CR4 . .**185** H1
Border Rd, SE26 . . . .**171** E5
Borders La, Loug. IG10 . .**48** D4
Bordesley Rd, Mord.
SM4 . . . .**185** E4
Bordon Wk, SW15 . . . . . .**147** G7
Boreas Wk, N1 . . . .**11** H2
Boreham Av, E16 . . . .**115** G6
Boreham Cl, E11
off Hainault Rd **96** C1
Boreham Rd, N22 . . . .**75** J2
BOREHAMWOOD **38** B3
Borehamwood Ind Pk, Borwd.
WD6 . . . .**38** D2
Borgard Rd, SE18 . . . . . .**136** B4
Borkwood Pk, Orp. BR6 .**207** J4
Borkwood Way, Orp.
BR6 . . . .**207** H4
Borland Rd, SE15 . . . . . .**153** F4
Teddington TW11 . . . . .**162** E6
Borneo St, SW15 . . . .**147** J3
BOROUGH, THE, SE1 . . . .**27** J4
Borough High St, SE1 . . . .**27** J4
Borough Hill, Croy. CR0 .**201** H3
★ Borough Mkt, SE1 . . . .**28** B2
Borough Rd, SE1 . . . .**27** G5
Isleworth TW7 . . . .**144** B1
Kingston upon Thames
KT2 . . . .**182** A1
Mitcham CR4 . . . .**185** H2
Borough Sq, SE1 . . . .**27** J4
Borrett Cl, SE17 . . . .**35** J4
Borrodaile Rd, SW18 . . .**149** E6
Borrowdale Av, Har.
HA3 . . . .**68** D2
Borrowdale Cl, Ilf. IG4 . . .**80** B4
Borrowdale Ct, Enf. EN2 . .**43** J1
Borthwick Ms, E15
off Borthwick Rd . . .**96/97** E4
Borthwick Rd, E15 . . . . . .**96** E4
NW9
off West Hendon Bdy . .**71** F6
Borthwick St, SE8 . . . . . .**134** A5
Borwick Av, E17 . . . .**77** J3
Bosbury Rd, SE6 . . . .**172** C3
Boscastle Rd, NW5 . . . . . .**92** B3
Boscobel Pl, SW1 . . . .**32** C1
Boscobel St, NW8 . . . .**7** F6
Bosco Cl, Orp. BR6
off Strickland Way . . .**207** J4
Boscombe Av, E10 . . . . . .**78** D7
Boscombe Cl, E5 . . . .**95** H5
Boscombe Gdns,
SW16 . . . .**169** E6
Boscombe Rd, SW17 . . . .**168** A6
SW19 . . . .**184** E1
W12 . . . .**127** G2
Worcester Park KT4 . . .**197** J1

Bose Cl, N3
off Claremont Pk **72** B1
Bosgrove, E4 . . . . **62** C1
Boss St, SE1 . . . . **29** F3
Bostall Heath, SE2 . . . . . **138** C5
Bostall Hill, SE2 . . . . **138** A5
Bostall La, SE2 . . . . **138** B5
Bostall Manorway,
SE2 . . . . **138** B4
Bostall Pk Av, Bexh.
DA7 . . . . **138** E7
Bostall Rd, Orp. BR5 . . . . **176** B7
Bostal Row, Bexh. DA7
off Harlington Rd **159** F3
Boston Gdns, W4 . . . . . . **127** E6
W7 . . . . **124** D4
Brentford TW8 . . . . **124** D4
★ **Boston Manor**, Brent.
TW8 . . . . **125** E5
Boston Manor Rd, Brent.
TW8 . . . . **124** E4
Boston Pk Rd, Brent.
TW8 . . . . **125** F5
Boston Pl, NW1 . . . . **7** J6
Boston Rd, E6 . . . . **116** B3
E17 . . . . **78** A6
W7 . . . . **124** B1
Croydon CR0 . . . . **187** F6
Edgware HA8 . . . . **54** C7
Boston St, E2 . . . . **13** H1
Bostonthorpe Rd, W7 . . . **124** B2
Boston Vale, W7 . . . . **124** D4
Bosun Cl, E14
off Byng St **134** A2
Boswell Ct, WC1 . . . . **18** B1
Boswell Path, Hayes UB3
off Croyde Av **121** J4
Boswell Rd, Th.Hth. CR7 . **187** J4
Boswell St, WC1 . . . . **18** B1
Bosworth Cl, E17 . . . . **77** J1
Bosworth Rd, N11 . . . . **58** D6
W10 . . . . **108** B4
Barnet EN5 . . . . **40** D3
Dagenham RM10 . . . . . **101** G4
Botany Bay La, Chis.
BR7 . . . . **193** F3
Botany Cl, Barn. EN4 . . . . **41** H4
Boteley Cl, E4 . . . . **62** D2
Botham Cl, Edg. HA8
off Pavilion Way **54** C7
Botha Rd, E13 . . . . **115** H5
Bothwell Cl, E16 . . . . **115** F5
Bothwell St, W6
off Delorme St **128** A6
Botolph All, EC3 . . . . **20** D5
Botolph La, EC3 . . . . **20** D5
Botsford Rd, SW20 . . . . . **184** B2
Botts Ms, W2
off Chepstow Rd **108** D6
Botts Pas, W2
off Chepstow Rd **108** D6
Botwell La, Hayes UB3 . . **121** H1
Boucher Cl, Tedd. TW11 . . **162** C5
Boughton Av, Brom.
BR2 . . . . **191** F7
Boughton Rd, SE28 . . . . . **137** H3
Boulcott St, E1 . . . . **113** G6
Boulevard, The, SW6 . . . . **149** F1
SW17
off Balham High Rd . . **168** A2
Pinner HA5
off Pinner Rd **67** G4
Woodford Green IG8 . . . **64** D7
Boulevard 25 Retail Pk, Borwd.
WD6 . . . . **38** A3
Boulogne Rd, Croy.
CR0 . . . . **187** J6
Boulton Ho, Brent. TW8
off Green Dragon La . **125** H5
Boulton Rd, Dag. RM8 . . . **101** E3
Boultwood Rd, E6 . . . . . . **116** B6
Bounces La, N9 . . . . **60** E2
Bounces Rd, N9 . . . . **60** E1
Boundaries Rd, SW12 . . . **167** J2
Feltham TW13 . . . . **160** C1
Boundary Av, E17 . . . . **77** J7
Boundary Cl, SE20
off Haysleigh Gdns . . **188** D2
Barnet EN5 . . . . **40** C1
Ilford IG3
off Loxford La **99** H4
Kingston upon Thames
KT1 . . . . **182** B3
Southall UB2 . . . . **123** G5
Boundary La, E13 . . . . . . **116** A3
SE17 . . . . **36** A6
Boundary Pas, E2 . . . . **13** F5
Boundary Rd, E13 . . . . . . **115** J2
E17 . . . . **77** J7
N9 . . . . **45** F6
Boundary Rd, N22 . . . . **75** H3
NW8 . . . . **109** E1
SW19 . . . . **167** G6
Barking IG11 . . . . **117** F2
Carshalton SM5 . . . . . . **200** B6
Pinner HA5 . . . . **66** D6
Sidcup DA15 . . . . **157** H5
Wallington SM6 . . . . . . **200** B6
Wembley HA9 . . . . **87** H3
Boundary Row, SE1 . . . . . **27** G3
Boundary St, E2 . . . . **13** F4
Boundary Way, Croy.
CR0 . . . . **204** A5
Boundfield Rd, SE6 . . . . . **172** E3
Bounds Grn Rd, N11 . . . . . **58** C6
N22 . . . . **58** C6
Bourchier St, W1 . . . . **17** H5
Bourdon Pl, W1 . . . . **16** E5
Bourdon Rd, SE20 . . . . . . **189** F2
Bourdon St, W1 . . . . **16** E5
Bourke Cl, NW10
off Mayo Rd **88/89** E6
SW4 . . . . **150** E6
Bourlet Cl, W1 . . . . **17** F2
Bourn Av, N15 . . . . **76** A4
Barnet EN4 . . . . **41** G5
Bournbrook Rd, SE3 . . . . **156** A3
Bourne, The, N14 . . . . **58** D1
Bourne Av, N14 . . . . **58** E2
Hayes UB3 . . . . **121** F3
Ruislip HA4 . . . . **84** C5
Bourne Cl, T.Ditt. KT7 . . . . **194** C2
Bourne Ct, Ruis. HA4 . . . . **84** B5
Bourne Dr, Mitch. CR4 . . **185** G2
Bourne Est, EC1 . . . . **18** E1
Bourne Gdns, E4 . . . . **62** B4
Bourne Hill, N13 . . . . **58** E1
Bournemead Av, Nthlt.
UB5 . . . . **102** A2
Bournemead Cl, Nthlt.
UB5 . . . . **102** A2
Bournemead Way, Nthlt.
UB5 . . . . **102** B2
Bournemouth Cl, SE15 . . **152** D2
Bournemouth Rd, SE15 . **152** D2
SW19 . . . . **184** D1
Bourne Pl, W4
off Dukes Av **126** D5
Bourne Rd, E7 . . . . **97** F3
N8 . . . . **75** E6
Bexley DA5 . . . . **159** H6
Bromley BR2 . . . . **192** A4
Dartford DA1 . . . . **159** J6
Bourneside Cres, N14 . . . . **58** D1
Bourneside Gdns, SE6 . . **172** C5
Bourne St, SW1 . . . . **32** B2
Croydon CR0
off Waddon New Rd . . **201** H2
Bourne Ter, W2 . . . . **14** A1
Bourne Vale, Brom. BR2 . **191** G7
Bournevale Rd, SW16 . . . **168** E4
Bourne Vw, Grnf. UB6 . . . **86** C6
Bourne Way, Brom. BR2 . **205** F2
Epsom KT19 . . . . **196** C4
Sutton SM1 . . . . **198** C5
Bournewood Rd, SE18 . . **138** A7
Bournville Rd, SE6 . . . . . **154** A7
Bournwell Cl, Barn. EN4 . . **41** J3
Bourton Cl, Hayes UB3
off Avondale Dr **122** A1
Bousfield Rd, SE14 . . . . . **153** G2
Boutflower Rd, SW11 . . . **149** H4
Bouverie Gdns, Har.
HA3 . . . . **69** G6
Bouverie Ms, N16
off Bouverie Rd **94** B2
Bouverie Pl, W2 . . . . **15** F3
Bouverie Rd, N16 . . . . **94** B2
Harrow HA1 . . . . **67** J7
Bouverie St, EC4 . . . . **19** F4
Boveney Rd, SE23 . . . . . . **153** G7
Bovill Rd, SE23 . . . . **153** G7
Bovingdon Av, Wem.
HA9 . . . . **88** A6
Bovingdon Cl, N19
off Brookside Rd **92** C2
Bovingdon La, NW9 . . . . . **71** E1
Bovingdon Rd, SW6 . . . . **148** E1
Bovingdon Sq, Mitch. CR4
off Leicester Av . . **186/187** E4
BOW, E3 . . . . **113** J2
Bowater Cl, NW9 . . . . **70** D5
SW2 . . . . **150** E6
Bowater Gdns, Sun.
TW16 . . . . **178** B2
Bowater Pl, SE3 . . . . **135** H7
Bowater Rd, SE18 . . . . . . **136** A3
Bow Br Est, E3 . . . . **114** B3
Bow Chyd, EC4 . . . . **20** A4
Bow Common La, E3 . . . **113** J4
Bowden St, SE11 . . . . **35** F4
Bowditch, SE8 . . . . **133** J5
Bowdon Rd, E17 . . . . **78** A7
Bowen Dr, SE21 . . . . **170** B3
Bowen Rd, Har. HA1 . . . . . **67** J7
Bowen St, E14 . . . . **114** B6
Bower Av, SE10 . . . . **154** E1
Bower Cl, Nthlt. UB5 . . . . **102** C2
Bowerdean St, SW6 . . . . **148** E1
Bowerman Av, SE14 . . . . **133** H6
Bower St, E1 . . . . **113** G6
Bowers Wk, E6 . . . . **116** B6
Bowes Cl, Sid. DA15 . . . . **158** B6
BOWES PARK, N22 . . . . . . **59** E6
Bowes Rd, N11 . . . . **58** B5
N13 . . . . **58** E5
W3 . . . . **106** E7
Dagenham RM8 . . . . . . **100** C4
Bowfell Rd, W6 . . . . **127** J6
Bowford Av, Bexh. DA7 . . **158** E1
Bowhill Cl, SW9 . . . . **131** G7
Bowie Cl, SW4 . . . . **150** D7
Bow Ind Pk, E15 . . . . **96** A7
Bowland Rd, SW4 . . . . . . **150** D4
Woodford Green IG8 . . . **63** J6
Bowland Yd, SW1 . . . . **24** A4
Bow La, EC4 . . . . **20** A4
N12 . . . . **73** F1
Morden SM4 . . . . **184** B6
Bowl Ct, EC2 . . . . **12** E6
Bowles Rd, SE1 . . . . **37** H5
Bowley Cl, SE19 . . . . **170** C6
Bowley La, SE19 . . . . **170** C5
Bowling Grn Cl, SW15 . . . **147** H7
Bowling Grn La, EC1 . . . . . **11** F5
Bowling Grn Pl, SE1 . . . . . **28** B3
Bowling Grn Row, SE18
off Samuel St **136** C3
Bowling Grn St, SE11 . . . . **35** E5
Bowling Grn Wk, N1 . . . . . **12** D3
Bowls, The, Chig. IG7 . . . . **65** H4
Bowls Cl, Stan. HA7 . . . . . **52** E5
Bowman Av, E16 . . . . **115** F7
Bowman Ms, SW18 . . . . . **166** C1
Bowmans Cl, W13 . . . . . . **124** E1
Bowmans Lea, SE23 . . . . **153** F7
Bowmans Meadow, Wall.
SM6 . . . . **200** B3
Bowmans Ms, E1 . . . . **21** H5
N7 *off Seven Sisters*
Rd **92/93** E3
Bowmans Pl, N7
off Holloway Rd . . . **92/93** E3
Bowman's Trd Est, NW9
off Westmoreland Rd . . **69** J3
Bowmead, SE9 . . . . **174** C2
Bowmore Wk, NW1
off St. Paul's Cres **92** D7
Bowness Cl, E8
off Beechwood Rd **94** C6
Bowness Cres, SW15 . . . **164** E5
Bowness Dr, Houns.
TW4 . . . . **143** E4
Bowness Rd, SE6 . . . . . . **154** B7
Bexleyheath DA7 . . . . . **159** H2
Bowood Rd, SW11 . . . . . . **150** A4
Enfield EN3 . . . . **45** G2
Bowring Grn, Wat. WD19 . **50** C5
Bow Rd, E3 . . . . **113** J3
Bowrons Av, Wem. HA0 . . **87** G7
Bowsley Ct, Felt. TW13
off Highfield Rd **160** A1
Bowsprit Pt, E14 . . . . **134** A3
Bow St, E15 . . . . **96** E5
WC2 . . . . **18** B4
Bowyer Cl, E6 . . . . **116** C5
Bowyer Pl, SE5 . . . . **36** A7
Bowyer St, SE5 . . . . **35** J7
Boxall Rd, SE21 . . . . **152** B6
Boxgrove Rd, SE2 . . . . . . **138** C3
Box La, Bark. IG11 . . . . . . **118** B2
Boxley Rd, Mord. SM4 . . **185** F4
Boxley St, E16 . . . . **135** H1
Boxmoor Rd, Har. HA3 . . . **68** E4
Boxoll Rd, Dag. RM9 . . . . **101** F4
Boxted Cl, Buck.H. IG9 . . . **64** B1
Boxtree La, Har. HA3 . . . . **67** J1
Boxtree Rd, Har. HA3 . . . . **52** A7
Boxwood Cl, West Dr. UB7
off Hawthorne Cres . . **120** C2
Boxworth Cl, N12 . . . . **57** G5
Boxworth Gro, N1
off Richmond Av **111** F1
Boyard Rd, SE18 . . . . **136** E5
Boyce St, SE1 . . . . **26** D2
Boyce Way, E13 . . . . **115** G4
Boycroft Av, NW9 . . . . **70** C6
Boyd Av, Sthl. UB1 . . . . . **123** F1
Boyd Cl, Kings.T. KT2
off Crescent Rd **164** A7
Boydell Ct, NW8
off St. John's Wd Pk . . . **91** G7
Boyd Rd, SW19 . . . . **167** G6
Boyd St, E1 . . . . **21** H4
Boyfield St, SE1 . . . . **27** H4
Boyland Rd, Brom. BR1 . **173** F5
Boyle Av, Stan. HA7 . . . . . **52** D6
Boyle Fm Island, T.Ditt.
KT7 . . . . **180** D6
Boyle Fm Rd, T.Ditt. KT7 . **180** D6
Boyle St, W1 . . . . **17** F5
Boyne Av, NW4 . . . . **72** A4
Boyne Rd, SE13 . . . . **154** C3
Dagenham RM10 . . . . . **101** G3
Boyne Ter Ms, W11 . . . . . **128** C1
Boyseland Ct, Edg. HA8 . . **54** C2
Boyson Rd, SE17 . . . . **36** B5
Boyton Cl, E1
off Stayner's Rd **113** G4
N8 . . . . **75** E3
Boyton Rd, N8 . . . . **75** E3
Brabant Ct, EC3 . . . . **20** D5
Brabant Rd, N22 . . . . **75** F2
Brabazon Av, Wall. SM6 . **200** E7
Brabazon Rd, Houns.
TW5 . . . . **122** C7
Northolt UB5 . . . . **103** G2
Brabazon St, E14 . . . . **114** B6
Brabourne Cl, SE19 . . . . . **170** B5
Brabourne Cres, Bexh.
DA7 . . . . **139** F6
Brabourne Hts, NW7 . . . . . **55** E3
Brabourne Ri, Beck. BR3 . **190** C5
Brabourn Gro, SE15 . . . . **153** F2
Bracewell Av, Grnf. UB6 . . **86** C5
Bracewell Rd, W10 . . . . . **107** J5
Bracewood Gdns, Croy.
CR0 . . . . **202** C3
Bracey Ms, N4
off Bracey St **92/93** E2
Bracey St, N4 . . . . **93** E2
Bracken, The, E4
off Hortus Rd **62** C2
Bracken Av, SW12 . . . . . . **150** A6
Croydon CR0 . . . . **204** B3
Brackenbridge Dr, Ruis.
HA4 . . . . **84** D3
Brackenbury Gdns, W6 . . **127** H3
Brackenbury Rd, N2 . . . . . **73** F3
W6 . . . . **127** H3
Bracken Cl, E6 . . . . **116** C5
Borehamwood WD6 . . . . **38** B1
Twickenham TW2
off Hedley Rd **143** G7
Brackendale, N21 . . . . **59** F2
Brackendale Cl, Houns.
TW3 . . . . **143** H1
Bracken Dr, Chig. IG7 . . . . **65** E6
Bracken End, Islw. TW7 . . **144** A5
Brackenfield Cl, E5
off Tiger Way **94/95** E4
Bracken Gdns, SW13 . . . **147** G2
Bracken Hill Cl, Brom. BR1
off Bracken Hill La . . . **191** F1
Bracken Hill La, Brom.
BR1 . . . . **191** F1
Bracken Ind Est, Ilf. IG6 . . . **65** J7
Bracken Ms, E4
off Hortus Rd **62** C2
Romford RM7 . . . . **83** G6
Brackens, The, Enf. EN1 . . **44** B7
Brackenwood, Sun.
TW16 . . . . **178** A1
Brackley Cl, Wall. SM6 . . **201** E7
Brackley Rd, W4 . . . . **127** E5
Beckenham BR3 . . . . . . **171** J7
Brackley Sq, Wdf.Grn.
IG8 . . . . **64** A7
Brackley St, EC1 . . . . **19** J1
Brackley Ter, W4 . . . . **127** E5
Bracklyn Cl, N1 . . . . **12** B1
Bracklyn Ct, N1 . . . . **12** B1
Bracklyn St, N1 . . . . **12** B1
Bracknell Cl, N22 . . . . **75** G1
Bracknell Gdns, NW3 . . . . **90** E4
Bracknell Gate, NW3 . . . . **90** E5
Bracknell Way, NW3 . . . . . **90** E4
Bracondale Rd, SE2 . . . . **138** A4
Bradbourne Rd, Bex.
DA5 . . . . **159** G7
Bradbourne St, SW6 . . . . **148** D2
Bradbury Cl, Borwd.
WD6 . . . . **38** B1
Southall UB2 . . . . **123** F4
Bradbury Ms, N16
off Bradbury St **94** B5
Bradbury St, N16 . . . . **94** B5
Braddock Cl, Islw. TW7 . . **144** C3
Braddon Rd, Rich. TW9 . . **145** J3
Braddyll St, SE10 . . . . . . **134** E5

Bradenham Av, Well.
DA16 . . . . .158 A4
Bradenham Cl, SE17 . . . .36 B5
Bradenham Rd, Har. HA3 .68 E4
Braden St, W9 . . . . .6 A2
Bradfield Dr, Bark. IG11 . .100 A5
Bradfield Rd, E16 . . . . . .135 G2
Ruislip HA4 . . . . .85 E5
Bradford Cl, N17
off Commercial Rd 60 B6
SE26 off Coombe
Rd 170/171 E4
Bromley BR2 . . . . .206 C1
Bradford Dr, Epsom
KT19 . . . . .197 F6
Bradford Rd, W3
off Warple Way . .126/127 E2
Ilford IG1 . . . . .99 G1
Bradgate Rd, SE6 . . . . . .154 A6
Brading Cres, E11 . . . . . .97 H2
Brading Rd, SW2 . . . . . .151 F7
Croydon CR0 . . . . .187 F6
Bradiston Rd, W9 . . . . . .108 C3
Bradley Cl, N7
off Sutterton St 93 F6
Bradley Gdns, W13 . . . . .104 E6
Bradley Ms, SW17
off Bellevue Rd 167 J1
Bradley Rd, N22 . . . . . . .75 F2
SE19 . . . . .169 J6
Bradley's Cl, N1 . . . . .11 F1
Bradley Stone Rd, E6 . .116 C5
Bradman Row, Edg. HA8
off Pavilion Way 54 C7
Bradmead, SW8 . . . . . . .130 B7
Bradmore Pk Rd, W6 . . .127 H3
Bradshaw Cl, SW19 . . . .166 D6
Bradshaw Dr, NW7
off Bittacy Hill 56 B7
Bradshaws Cl, SE25 . . . .188 D3
Bradstock Rd, E9 . . . . . . .95 G6
Epsom KT17 . . . . .197 G5
Brad St, SE1 . . . . .27 F2
Bradwell Av, Dag. RM10 .101 G2
Bradwell Cl, E18 . . . . . . .79 F4
Bradwell Ms, N18
off Lyndhurst Rd 60 D4
Bradwell Rd, Buck.H. IG9 .64 B1
Bradwell St, E1 . . . . . . .113 G3
Brady Av, Loug. IG10 . . . .49 F2
Bradymead, E6 . . . . . . .116 D6
Brady St, E1 . . . . .112 E4
Braemar Av, N22 . . . . . . .75 E1
NW10 . . . . .88 D3
SW19 . . . . .166 D2
Bexleyheath DA7 . . . . .159 J4
Thornton Heath CR7 . .187 G3
Wembley HA0 . . . . .87 G7
Braemar Gdns, NW9 . . . .70 D1
Sidcup DA15 . . . . .175 G3
West Wickham BR4 . . .204 C1
Braemar Rd, E13 . . . . . .115 F4
N15 . . . . .76 B5
Brentford TW8 . . . . . . .125 H6
Worcester Park KT4 . . .197 H3
Braeside, Beck. BR3 . . . .172 A5
Braeside Av, SW19 . . . . .184 B1
Braeside Cl, Pnr. HA5
off The Avenue 51 G2
Braeside Cres, Bexh.
DA7 . . . . .159 J4
Braeside Rd, SW16 . . . . .168 C7
Braes St, N1 . . . . .93 H7
Braesyde Cl, Belv. DA17 .139 F4
Brafferton Rd, Croy. CR0 .201 J4
Braganza St, SE17 . . . . .35 G3
Bragg Cl, Dag. RM8
off Porters Av 100 B6
Braham St, E1 . . . . .21 G3
Braid Av, W3 . . . . .106 E6
Braid Cl, Felt. TW13 . . . .161 F2
Braid Ct, W4
off Lawford Rd 126 C7
Braidwood Pas, EC1
off Aldersgate St 111 J5
Braidwood Rd, SE6 . . . .172 D1
Braidwood St, SE1 . . . . .28 D2
Brailsford Cl, Mitch. CR4 .167 H7
Brailsford Rd, SW2 . . . .151 G5
Brainton Av, Felt. TW14 .142 B7
Braintree Av, Ilf. IG4 . . . .80 B4
Braintree Ind Est, Ruis.
HA4 . . . . .84 B4
Braintree Rd, Dag. RM10 .101 G3
Ruislip HA4 . . . . .84 B4
Braintree St, E2 . . . . . . .113 F3
Braithwaite Av, Rom.
RM7 . . . . .83 G7
Braithwaite Gdns, Stan.
HA7 . . . . .69 F1

Braithwaite Rd, Enf. EN3 .45 J3
Braithwaite Twr, W2 . . . . .15 E1
Bramah Grn, SW9 . . . . .151 G1
★ Bramah Mus, SE1 . . . .29 G3
Bramalea Cl, N6 . . . . . . .74 A6
Bramall Cl, E15
off Idmiston Rd 97 F5
Bramber Ct, Brent. TW8
off Sterling Pl 125 H4
Bramber Rd, N12 . . . . . . .57 H5
W14 . . . . .128 C6
Brambleacres Cl, Sutt.
SM2 . . . . .198 D7
Bramblebury Rd, SE18 . .137 F5
Bramble Cl, Beck. BR3 . .190 C5
Croydon CR0 . . . . . . .204 A4
Stanmore HA7 . . . . . . .53 G7
Bramble Cft, Erith DA8 . .139 J4
Brambledown Cl, W.Wick.
BR4 . . . . .191 E5
Brambledown Rd, Cars.
SM5 . . . . .200 A7
South Croydon CR2 . . .202 B7
Wallington SM6 . . . . . .200 B7
Bramble Gdns, W12
off Wallflower St 107 F7
Bramble La, Hmptn.
TW12 . . . . .161 F6
Brambles, The, Chig. IG7
off Clayside 65 F5
West Drayton UB7 . . . .120 B4
Brambles Cl, Islw. TW7 . .124 E7
Bramblewood Cl, Cars.
SM5 . . . . .199 H1
Bramblings, The, E4 . . . .62 D4
Bramcote Av, Mitch.
CR4 . . . . .185 J4
Bramcote Ct, Mitch. CR4
off Bramcote Av 185 J4
Bramcote Gro, SE16 . . . .133 F5
Bramcote Rd, SW15 . . . .147 H4
Bramdean Cres, SE12 . . .173 G1
Bramdean Gdns, SE12 . .173 G1
Bramerton Rd, Beck.
BR3 . . . . .189 J3
Bramerton St, SW3 . . . . .31 G5
Bramfield Ct, N4
off Queens Dr 93 J2
Bramfield Rd, SW11 . . . .149 H6
Bramford Ct, N14 . . . . . . .58 D2
Bramford Rd, SW18 . . . .149 F4
Bramham Gdns, SW5 . . . .30 A3
Chessington KT9 . . . . .195 G4
Bramhope La, SE7 . . . . .135 H6
Bramlands Cl, SW11 . . . .149 H3
Bramley Cl, E17 . . . . .77 H2
N14 . . . . .42 B5
Hayes UB3
off Orchard Rd 102 A7
Orpington BR6 . . . . . . .207 E1
South Croydon CR2 . . .201 H5
Twickenham TW2 . . . . .143 J6
Bramley Ct, Well. DA16 . .158 B1
Bramley Cres, SW8 . . . . .33 J7
Ilford IG2 . . . . .80 D6
Bramley Gdns, Wat.
WD19 . . . . .50 C5
Bramley Hill, S.Croy.
CR2 . . . . .201 H5
Bramley Ho, SW15
off Tunworth Cres 147 F6
Bramley Rd, N14 . . . . . . .42 B5
W5 . . . . .125 F3
W10 . . . . .108 A7
Sutton SM1 . . . . .199 G5
Bramley Way, Houns.
TW4 . . . . .143 F5
West Wickham BR4 . . .204 B2
Brampton Cl, E5 . . . . .95 E2
Brampton Gdns, N15
off Brampton Rd 75 J5
Brampton Gro, NW4 . . . .71 H4
Harrow HA3 . . . . .68 D4
Wembley HA9 . . . . .88 A1
Brampton La, NW4 . . . . .71 J4
Brampton Pk Rd, N22 . . .75 G3
Brampton Rd, E6 . . . . . .116 A3
N15 . . . . .75 J5
NW9 . . . . .70 A4
SE2 . . . . .138 C6
Bexleyheath DA7 . . . . .138 D7
Croydon CR0 . . . . . . .188 C7
Watford WD19 . . . . . . .50 A3
Bramshaw Gdns, Wat.
WD19 . . . . .50 D5
Bramshaw Ri, N.Mal.
KT3 . . . . .183 E6
Bramshaw Rd, E9 . . . . . .95 G6
Bramshill Cl, Chig. IG7
off Tine Rd 65 H5

Bramshill Gdns, NW5 . . . .92 B3
Bramshill Rd, NW10 . . . .107 F2
Bramshot Av, SE7 . . . . . .135 G6
Bramshot Way, Wat.
WD19 . . . . .50 A2
Bramston Cl, Ilf. IG6 . . . . .65 J6
Bramston Rd, NW10 . . . .107 G2
SW17 . . . . .167 F3
Bramwell Cl, Sun. TW16 .178 D2
Bramwell Ms, N1 . . . . . .111 F1
Brancaster Dr, NW7 . . . . .55 F7
Brancaster Pl, Loug.
IG10 . . . . .48 C3
Brancaster Rd, E12 . . . . .98 C4
SW16 . . . . .168 E3
Ilford IG2 . . . . .81 G6
Brancepeth Gdns, Buck.H.
IG9 . . . . .63 G2
Branch Hill, NW3 . . . . . . .91 F3
Branch Pl, N1 . . . . .112 A1
Branch Rd, E14 . . . . .113 H7
Branch St, SE15 . . . . . . .132 B7
Brancker Cl, Wall. SM6
off Brown Cl 200/201 E7
Brancker Rd, Har. HA3 . . .69 G3
Brancroft Way, Enf. EN3 . .45 H1
Brand Cl, N4 . . . . .93 H1
Brandesbury Sq, Wdf.Grn.
IG8 . . . . .64 D7
Brandlehow Rd, SW15 . .148 C4
Brandon Est, SE17 . . . . . .35 H6
Brandon Ms, EC2
off The Barbican 111 J5
Brandon Rd, E17 . . . . . . .78 C3
N7 . . . . .92 E7
Southall UB2 . . . . .123 F5
Sutton SM1 . . . . .198 E4
Brandon St, SE17 . . . . . .36 A2
Brandram Ms, SE13
off Brandram Rd .154/155 E3
Brandram Rd, SE13 . . . .154 E3
Brandreth Rd, E6 . . . . . .116 C6
SW17 . . . . .168 B2
Brandries, The, Wall.
SM6 . . . . .200 D3
Brand St, SE10 . . . . .134 C7
Brandville Gdns, Ilf. IG6 . .81 E4
Brandville Rd, West Dr.
UB7 . . . . .120 B2
Brandy Way, Sutt. SM2 . .198 D7
Brangbourne Rd, Brom.
BR1 . . . . .172 C5
Brangton Rd, SE11 . . . . . .34 D4
Brangwyn Cres, SW19 . .185 G1
Branksea St, SW6 . . . . . .128 B7
Branksome Av, N18 . . . . .60 C5
Branksome Cl, Tedd.
TW11 . . . . .162 A4
Branksome Rd, SW2 . . . .151 E5
SW19 . . . . .184 D1
Branksome Way, Har.
HA3 . . . . .69 H6
New Malden KT3 . . . . .182 C1
Bransby Rd, Chess. KT9 .195 H6
Branscombe Gdns, N21 . .43 G7
Branscombe St, SE13 . . .154 B3
Bransdale Cl, NW6
off West End La . .108/109 E1
Bransgrove Rd, Edg. HA8 .69 J1
Branston Cres, Orp. BR5 .207 G1
Branstone Rd, Rich. TW9 .145 J1
Brants Wk, W7 . . . . .104 B4
Brantwood Av, Erith
DA8 . . . . .139 J7
Isleworth TW7 . . . . . . .144 D4
Brantwood Cl, E17 . . . . . .78 B3
Brantwood Gdns, Enf.
EN2 . . . . .42 E4
Ilford IG4 . . . . .80 B4
Brantwood Rd, N17 . . . . .60 C6
SE24 . . . . .151 J5
Bexleyheath DA7 . . . . .159 H2
Brasenose Dr, SW13 . . . .127 J6
Brasher Cl, Grnf. UB6 . . . .86 A5
Brassett Pt, E15 . . . . . . .114 E1
Brassey Cl, Felt. TW14 . .160 A1
Brassey Rd, NW6 . . . . . . .90 C6
Brassey Sq, SW11 . . . . .150 A3
Brassie Av, W3 . . . . .106 E6
Brass Tally All, SE16
off Middleton Dr 133 G2
Brasted Cl, SE26 . . . . . . .171 F4
Bexleyheath DA6 . . . . .158 D5
Brathway Rd, SW18 . . . .148 D7
Bratley St, E1 . . . . .13 H6
Braund Av, Grnf. UB6 . . .103 H4
Braundton Av, Sid.
DA15 . . . . .175 J1
Braunston Dr, Hayes
UB4 . . . . .102 E4

Bravington Pl, W9
off Bravington Rd 108 C4
Bravington Rd, W9 . . . . .108 C2
Brawne Ho, SE17 . . . . . . .35 G6
Braxfield Rd, SE4 . . . . . .153 H4
Braxted Pk, SW16 . . . . . .169 F6
Bray, NW3 . . . . .91 H7
Brayards Rd, SE15 . . . . .152 E2
Braybourne Dr, Islw.
TW7 . . . . .124 C7
Braybrooke Gdns, SE19
off Fox Hill 170 C7
Braybrook St, W12 . . . . .107 F5
Brayburne Av, SW4 . . . . .150 C2
Bray Cl, Borwd. WD6 . . . .38 C1
Braycourt Av, Walt.
KT12 . . . . .178 B7
Bray Cres, SE16 . . . . . . .133 G2
off Marlow Way 133 G2
Braydon Rd, N16 . . . . . . .94 C1
Bray Dr, E16 . . . . .115 F7
Brayfield Ter, N1
off Lofting Rd 93 G7
Brayford Sq, E1
off Summercourt Rd .113 F6
Bray Pas, E16 . . . . .115 G7
Bray Pl, SW3 . . . . .31 J2
Bray Rd, NW7 . . . . .56 A6
Brayton Gdns, Enf. EN2 . .42 D4
Braywood Rd, SE9 . . . . .157 G4
Brazil Cl, Croy. (Bedd.)
CR0 . . . . .186 E7
Breach La, Dag. RM9 . . .119 G3
Bread St, EC4 . . . . .20 A4
Breakspears Ms, SE4
off Breakspears Rd . . .154 A2
Breakspears Rd, SE4 . . .153 J3
Bream Cl, N17 . . . . .77 E4
Bream Gdns, E6 . . . . . . .116 D3
Breamore Cl, SW15 . . . .165 G1
Breamore Rd, Ilf. IG3 . . . .99 J2
Bream's Bldgs, EC4 . . . . .18 E3
Bream St, E3 . . . . .96 A7
Breamwater Gdns, Rich.
TW10 . . . . .163 E3
Brearley Cl, Edg. HA8
off Pavilion Way 54 C7
Breasley Cl, SW15 . . . . .147 H4
Brechin Pl, SW7 . . . . .30 D2
Brecknock Rd, N7 . . . . . .92 C4
N19 . . . . .92 C4
Brecknock Rd Est, N7 . . . .92 C4
Breckonmead, Brom. BR1
off Wanstead Rd 191 J2
Brecon Cl, Mitch. CR4 . . .186 E3
Worcester Park KT4 . . .197 J2
Brecon Grn, NW9
off Goldsmith Av . .70/71 E6
Brecon Rd, W6 . . . . .128 B6
Enfield EN3 . . . . .45 F4
Brede Cl, E6 . . . . .116 D3
Bredgar, SE13 . . . . .154 C5
Bredgar Rd, N19 . . . . . . .92 C2
Bredhurst Cl, SE20 . . . . .171 F6
Bredon Rd, SE5 . . . . . . .151 J3
Croydon CR0 . . . . . . .188 C7
Breer St, SW6 . . . . .148 E3
Breezers Hill, E1 . . . . . . .21 J6
Brember Rd, Har. HA2 . . .85 J2
Bremer Ms, E17
off Church La 78 B4
Bremner Rd, SW7 . . . . . .22 D4
Brenchley Cl, Brom. BR2 .191 F6
Chislehurst BR7 . . . . . .192 D1
Brenchley Gdns, SE23 . .153 F6
Brenchley Rd, Orp. BR5 .193 J1
Brenda Rd, SW17 . . . . . .167 J2
Brende Gdns, W.Mol.
KT8 . . . . .179 H4
Brendon Av, NW10 . . . . . .89 E4
Brendon Cl, Hayes UB3 .121 F7
Brendon Gdns, Har. HA2 .85 H4
Ilford IG2 . . . . .81 H5
Brendon Gro, N2 . . . . . . .73 F2
Brendon Rd, SE9 . . . . . .175 G2
Dagenham RM8 . . . . . .101 F1
Brendon St, W1 . . . . .15 H3
Brendon Way, Enf. EN1 . .44 B7
Brenley Cl, Mitch. CR4 . .186 A3
Brenley Gdns, SE9 . . . . .156 A4
Brent Cl, Bex. DA5 . . . . .177 E1
Brentcot Cl, W13 . . . . . .104 E4
Brent Cres, NW10 . . . . . .105 J2
Brent Cross Gdns, NW4
off Haley Rd 72 A6
Brent Cross Shop Cen,
NW4 . . . . .71 J7
Brentfield, NW10 . . . . . . .88 B7
Brentfield Cl, NW10
off Normans Mead 88 D6

Brentfield Gdns, NW2
off Hendon Way 72 A7
Brentfield Rd, NW10 ....88 D6
BRENTFORD 125 G6
Brentford Business Cen, Brent.
TW8 ....125 F7
Brentford Cl, Hayes UB4 .102 D4
★ Brentford FC, Brent.
TW8 ....125 G6
Brent Grn, NW4 ....71 J5
Brent Grn Wk, Wem. HA9 .88 C3
Brentham Way, W5 .....105 G4
Brenthouse Rd, E9 ......95 E7
Brenthurst Rd, NW10 ....89 F6
Brent Lea, Brent.TW8 ..125 F7
Brentmead Cl, W7 .....104 B7
Brentmead Gdns, NW10 .105 J2
Brentmead Pl, NW11
off North Circular Rd .72 A6
Brenton St, E14 ....113 H6
Brent Pk, NW10 ....88 D5
Brent Pk Rd, NW4 ....71 H7
NW9 ....89 G1
Brent Pl, Barn. EN5 .....40 D5
Brent Rd, E16 ....115 G5
SE18 ....136 E7
Brentford TW8 ....125 F6
Southall UB2 ....122 C3
Brent Side, Brent.TW8 .125 F6
Brentside Cl, W13 .....104 D4
Brentside Executive Cen, Brent.
TW8 ....125 E6
Brent St, NW4 ....71 J4
Brent Ter, NW2 ....89 J2
Brentvale Av, Sthl. UB1 .124 A1
Wembley HA0 ....105 J1
Brent Vw Rd, NW9 ......71 G7
Brent Way, N3 ....56 D6
Brentford TW8 ....125 G7
Wembley HA9 ....88 B6
Brentwick Gdns, Brent.
TW8 ....125 H4
Brentwood Cl, SE9 .....175 F1
Brentwood Ho, SE18
off Shooter's Hill Rd ..136 A7
Brereton Rd, N17 ....60 C7
Bressenden Pl, SW1 .....25 E5
Bressey Av, Enf. EN1 ....44 D1
Bressey Gro, E18 ....79 F2
Brett Cl, N16
off Yoakley Rd 94 B2
Northolt UB5
off Broomcroft Av 102 D3
Brett Ct, N9 ....61 F2
Brett Cres, NW10 ....88 D7
Brettell St, SE17 ....36 C4
Brettenham Av, E17 .....78 A1
Brettenham Rd, E17 .....78 A2
N18 ....60 E4
Brett Gdns, Dag. RM9 ..100 E7
Brett Ho Cl, SW15
off Putney Heath La ..148 A6
Brett Pas, E8
off Kenmure Rd 94/95 E5
Brett Rd, E8 ....95 E5
Barnet EN5 ....39 J5
Brewer's Grn, SW1 .....25 H5
Brewers Hall Gdns, EC2 .20 A2
Brewers La, Rich.TW9 ..145 G5
Brewer St, W1 ....17 G5
Brewery Cl, Wem. HA0 ...86 D5
Brewery La, Twick. TW1 .144 C7
Brewery Rd, N7 ....92 E7
SE18 ....137 G5
Bromley BR2 ....206 B1
Brewery Sq, SE1
off Horselydown La ..132 C1
Brewhouse La, E1 ......133 E1
Brewhouse Rd, SE18 ...136 C4
Brewhouse St, SW15 ...148 B3
Brewhouse Wk, SE16 ..133 H1
Brewhouse Yd, EC1 .....11 G5
Brewood Rd, Dag. RM8 .100 B6
Brewster Gdns, W10 ...107 J5
Brewster Ho, E14 ......113 J7
Brewster Rd, E10 ....96 B1
Brian Rd, Rom. RM6 .....82 C5
Briants Cl, Pnr. HA5 .....67 F2
Briant St, SE14 ....153 G1
Briar Av, SW16 ....169 F7
Briarbank Rd, W13 .....104 D6
Briar Cl, N2 ....73 E3
N13 ....59 J3
Buckhurst Hill IG9 .....64 A2
Hampton TW12 ....161 F5
Isleworth TW7 ....144 C5
Briar Ct, Sutt. SM3 .....197 J4
Briar Cres, Nthlt. UB5 ...85 H6
Briardale Gdns, NW3 ....90 D3
Briarfield Av, N3 ....72 E2

Briar Gdns, Brom. BR2 ..205 F1
Briaris Cl, N17 ....60 E7
Briar La, Croy. CR0 ....204 B4
Briar Pas, SW16 ....187 E3
Briar Pl, SW16 ....187 F3
Briar Rd, NW2 ....89 J4
SW16 ....187 E3
Harrow HA3 ....69 F5
Twickenham TW2 .....162 B1
Briarswood Way, Orp.
BR6 ....207 J5
Briar Wk, SW15 ....147 H4
W10 off Droop St 108 B4
Edgware HA8 ....54 C7
Briar Way, West Dr. UB7 .120 D2
Briarwood Cl, NW9 ......70 C6
Briarwood Dr, Nthwd.
HA6 ....66 A2
Briarwood Rd, SW4 ....150 D5
Epsom KT17 ....197 G6
Briary Cl, NW3
off Fellows Rd 91 H7
Briary Ct, Sid. DA14 ....176 B5
Briary Gdns, Brom. BR1 .173 H5
Briary Gro, Edg. HA8 ....70 B2
Briary La, N9 ....60 C3
Brick Ct, EC4 ....18 E4
Brick Fm Cl, Rich. TW9 .146 B1
Brickfield Cl, Brent.
TW8 ....125 F7
Brickfield Cotts, SE18 ..137 J6
Brickfield La, Barn. EN5 .39 F6
Hayes UB3 ....121 G6
Brickfield Rd, SW19 ...167 E4
Thornton Heath CR7 .187 H1
Brickfields, Har. HA2 ....86 A2
Brickfields Way, West Dr.
UB7 ....120 C3
Brick La, E1 ....13 G6
E2 ....13 G4
Enfield EN1, EN3 .....44 E2
Stanmore HA7
off Honeypot La 53 G7
Bricklayer's Arms Distribution
Cen, SE1 ....36 E2
Bricklayer's Arms Roundabout,
SE1 off Old Kent Rd ..132 A3
Brick St, W1 ....24 D2
Brickwood Cl, SE26 ....171 E3
Brickwood Rd, Croy.
CR0 ....202 B2
Brideale Cl, SE15
off Colegrove Rd 132 C7
Bride Ct, EC4 ....19 G4
Bride La, EC4 ....19 G4
Bridel Ms, N1
off Colebrooke Row ..111 H1
Bride St, N7 ....93 F6
Bridewain St, SE1 ......29 F5
Bridewell Pl, E1
off Brewhouse
La 132/133 E1
EC4 ....19 G4
Bridford Ms, W1 ....16 E1
Bridge, The, Har. HA3 ...68 B3
Bridge App, NW1 ....92 A7
Bridge Av, W6 ....127 J5
W7 ....104 A5
Bridge Cl, W10
off Kingsdown Cl 108 A6
Enfield EN1 ....45 E2
Teddington TW11
off Shacklegate La ..162 C4
Bridge Dr, N13 ....59 F4
Bridge End, E17 ....78 C1
Bridgefield Rd, Sutt.
SM1 ....198 D6
Bridgefoot, SE1 ....34 A4
Bridge Gdns, E.Mol.
KT8 ....180 A4
Bridge Gate, N21
off Ridge Av 43 J7
Bridge Ho Quay, E14
off Prestons Rd 134 C1
Bridgeland Rd, E16 ...115 G7
Bridge La, NW11 ....72 B5
SW11 ....149 H1
Bridgeman Rd, N1 ......93 F7
Teddington TW11 ....162 D6
Bridgeman St, NW8 ......7 G2
Bridge Meadows, SE14 .133 G6
Bridgend Rd, SW18 ....149 F4
Bridgenhall Rd, Enf. EN1 .44 C1
Bridgen Rd, Bex. DA5 ..158 E6
Bridge Pk, SW18 ......148 D5
Bridge Pl, SW1 ....33 E1
Croydon CR0 ....188 A7
Bridgeport Pl, E1 ....29 J1

Bridge Rd, E6 ....98 C7
E15 ....96 D7
E17 ....77 J7
N9 off The Broadway ..60 D3
N22 ....74 E1
NW10 ....88 E6
Beckenham BR3 .....171 J7
Bexleyheath DA7 ....159 E2
Chessington KT9 ....195 H5
East Molesey KT8 ....180 B4
Hounslow TW3 ......144 A2
Isleworth TW7 ....144 A3
Southall UB2 ....123 F2
Sutton SM2 ....199 E6
Twickenham TW1 ....144 E6
Wallington SM6 .....200 C5
Wembley HA9 ....88 A3
Bridge Row, Croy. CR0
off Cross Rd 202 A1
Bridges Cl, SW11 .....149 G3
Bridges La, Croy. CR0 ..200 E4
Bridges Pl, SW6 ....148 C1
Bridges Rd, SW19 ....166 E6
Stanmore HA7 ....52 C5
Bridges Rd Ms, SW19
off Bridges Rd ...166/167 E6
Bridge St, SW1 ....26 A4
W4 ....126 D4
Pinner HA5 ....66 D3
Richmond TW9 ......145 G5
Bridge Ter, E15
off Bridge Rd 96 D7
Bridgetown Cl, SE19
off St. Kitts Ter 170 B5
Bridge Vw, W6 ....127 J5
Bridgeview Ct, Ilf. IG6 ...65 G6
Bridgewater Cl, Chis.
BR7 ....193 H3
Bridgewater Gdns, Edg.
HA8 ....69 J2
Bridgewater Rd, Ruis.
HA4 ....84 A4
Wembley HA0 ....87 F7
Bridgewater Sq, EC2 ....19 J1
Bridgewater St, EC2 ....19 J1
Bridge Way, N11
off Pymmes Grn Rd ...58 C3
NW11 ....72 C5
Bridgeway, Bark. IG11 ...99 J7
Bridge Way, Twick. TW2 .143 J7
Bridgeway, Wem. HA0 ...87 H7
Bridgeway St, NW1 ......9 H2
Bridge Wf Rd, Islw. TW7
off Church St 144/145 E3
Bridgewood Cl, SE20 ..170 E7
Bridgewood Rd, SW16 .168 D7
Worcester Park KT4 .197 G4
Bridgford St, SW18 ....167 F3
Bridgman Rd, W4 .....126 C3
Bridgwater Rd, E15 ...114 C1
Bridle Cl, Epsom KT19 .196 D5
Kingston upon Thames
KT1 ....181 G4
Sunbury-on-Thames TW16
off Forge La 178 A3
Bridle La, W1 ....17 G5
Twickenham TW1
off Crown Rd 144/145 E6
Bridle Path, Croy. CR0 ..201 F3
Bridle Path, The, Wdf.Grn.
IG8 ....62 E7
Bridle Rd, Croy. CR0 ...204 A3
Esher (Clay.) KT10 ..194 E6
Pinner HA5 ....66 C6
Bridle Way, Croy. CR0 ..204 A5
Orpington BR6 ....207 F4
Bridleway, The, Wall.
SM6 ....200 C4
Bridlington Rd, N9 ......44 E7
Watford WD19 ....50 D3
Bridport Av, Rom. RM7 ..83 H6
Bridport Pl, N1 ....12 C1
Bridport Rd, N18 ....60 B5
Greenford UB6 ....103 H1
Thornton Heath CR7 .187 G3
Bridport Ter, SW8
off Wandsworth Rd ..150 D1
Bridstow Pl, W2
off Talbot Rd 108 D6
Brief St, SE5 ....151 H1
Brierley, Croy. (New Adgtn.)
CR0 ....204 B6
Brierley Av, N9 ....61 F1
Brierley Cl, SE25 ......188 D4
Brierley Rd, E11 ....96 D4
SW12 ....168 C2
Brierly Gdns, E2
off Royston St 113 F2
Brigade Cl, Har. HA2 ....86 A2

Brigade St, SE3
off Royal Par 155 F2
Brigadier Av, Enf. EN2 ...43 J1
Briggeford Cl, E5
off Geldeston Rd 94 D2
Briggs Rd, Mitch. CR4 ..186 B1
Bright Cl, Belv. DA17 ...138 D4
Brightfield Rd, SE12 ...155 F5
Brightling Rd, SE4 ....153 J6
Brightlingsea Pl, E14 ..113 J7
Brightman Rd, SW18 ..167 G1
Brighton Av, E17 ....77 J5
Brighton Dr, Nthlt. UB5 ..85 G6
Brighton Rd, E6 ....116 D3
N2 ....73 F2
N16 ....94 B4
South Croydon CR2 ..201 J5
Surbiton KT6 ....181 F6
Brighton Ter, SW9 .....151 F4
Brightside, Enf. EN3 ....45 G1
Brightside Rd, SE13 ...154 D6
Bright St, E14 ....114 B6
Brightwell Cl, Croy. CR0
off Sumner Rd 201 G1
Brightwell Cres, SW17 .167 J5
Brig Ms, SE8
off Watergate St 134 A6
Brigstock Rd, Belv.
DA17 ....139 H4
Thornton Heath CR7 .187 G5
Brill Pl, NW1 ....9 J2
Brim Hill, N2 ....73 F4
Brimpsfield Cl, SE2 ....138 B3
BRIMSDOWN, Enf. 45 H3
Brimsdown Av, Enf. EN3 .45 H2
Brimsdown Ind Est, Enf.
EN3 ....45 H3
Brindle Gate, Sid. DA15 .175 H1
Brindley Cl, Bexh. DA7 .159 H3
Wembley HA0 ....105 F1
Brindley Ho, SW2
off New Pk Rd 150/151 E7
Brindley St, SE14 .....153 J1
Brindley Way, Brom.
BR1 ....173 G5
Southall UB1 ....103 H7
Brinkburn Cl, SE2 .....138 A4
Edgware HA8 ....70 B2
Brinkburn Gdns, Edg.
HA8 ....70 A3
Brinkley, Kings.T. KT1
off Burritt Rd 182 A2
Brinkley Rd, Wor.Pk. KT4 .197 H2
Brinklow Cres, SE18 ...137 E7
Brinklow Ho, W2 ....14 A1
Brinkworth Rd, Ilf. IG5 ..80 B3
Brinkworth Way, E9 .....95 J6
Brinsdale Rd, NW4 ......72 A4
Brinsley Rd, Har. HA3 ...68 A2
Brinsley St, E1
off Watney St 112/113 E6
Brinsworth Cl, Twick.
TW2 ....162 A2
Brinton Wk, SE1 ....27 G2
Brion Pl, E14 ....114 C5
Brisbane Av, SW19 ....184 E1
Brisbane Ct, N10
off Sydney Rd 58 B7
Brisbane Rd, E10 ....96 B2
W13 ....124 D2
Ilford IG1 ....81 E7
Brisbane St, SE5 ......132 A7
Briscoe Cl, E11 ....97 F2
Briscoe Rd, SW19 .....167 G6
Briset Rd, SE9 ....156 A3
Briset St, EC1 ....19 G1
Briset Way, N7 ....93 F2
Bristol Cl, Stai. (Stanw.)
TW19 ....140 B6
Bristol Gdns, SW15
off Portsmouth Rd ..147 J7
W9 ....6 B6
Bristol Ms, W9 ....6 B6
Bristol Pk Rd, E17 ......77 H4
Bristol Rd, E7 ....97 J6
Greenford UB6 ....103 H1
Morden SM4 ....185 F5
Briston Gro, N8 ....75 E6
Briston Ms, NW7 ....55 G7
Bristow Rd, SE19 ......170 B5
Bexleyheath DA7 ....159 E1
Croydon CR0 ....200 E4
Hounslow TW3 ......143 J3
★ Britain at War Experience,
SE1 ....28 D2
Britannia Cl, SW4
off Bowland Rd 150 D4
Northolt UB5 ....102 D3
Britannia Gate, E16 ...135 G1

Britannia La, Twick. TW2 .143 J7
Britannia Rd, E14 ......134 A4
N12 ....57 F3
SW6 ....128 E7
Ilford IG1 ....98 E3
Surbiton KT5 ....181 J7
Britannia Row, N1 ......111 H1
Britannia St, WC1 ....10 C3
Britannia Wk, N1 ....12 B3
Britannia Way, NW10 ....106 B4
SW6 off Britannia
Rd 148/149 E1
Staines (Stanw.) TW19 .140 A7
★ British Dental Association
Mus, W1
off Wimpole St 16 D2
British Gro, W4 ....127 F5
British Gro Pas, W4 ....127 F5
British Gro S, W4
off British Gro Pas ...127 F5
British Legion Rd, E4 ....63 F2
★ British Lib, NW1 ....9 J3
★ British Lib Newspaper
Collection, NW9 ......71 E3
★ British Medical Association,
WC1 ....9 J5
★ British Mus, WC1 ......18 A2
British St, E3 ....113 J3
Brittain Rd, Dag. RM8 ...101 E3
Britten Cl, NW11 ....90 E1
Brittenden Cl, Orp. BR6 .207 H6
Britten St, Sthl. UB1 ...103 G6
Britten St, SW3 ....31 G4
Britton Cl, SE6
off Brownhill Rd 154 D7
Britton St, EC1 ....11 G6
Brixham Cres, Ruis. HA4 ..84 A1
Brixham Gdns, Ilf. IG3 ...99 H5
Brixham Rd, Well. DA16 .158 D1
Brixham St, E16 ....136 C1
BRIXTON, SW2 ....151 H4
★ Brixton Academy, The,
SW9 ....151 F3
Brixton Est, Edg. HA8 ...70 B2
Brixton Hill, SW2 ....151 F7
Brixton Hill Pl, SW2
off Brixton Hill ...150/151 E7
Brixton Oval, SW2 ......151 G4
Brixton Rd, SW9 ....151 G2
Brixton Sta Rd, SW9 ....151 G4
Brixton Water La, SW2 ..151 F5
Broadbent Cl, N6 ....92 B1
Broadbent St, W1 ....16 D5
Broadberry Ct, N18 .....60 E5
Broadbridge Cl, SE3 ...135 G7
Broadcoombe, S.Croy.
CR2 ....203 F7
Broad Ct, WC2 ....18 B4
Broadcroft Av, Stan. HA7 .69 G2
Broadcroft Rd, Orp. BR5 .193 G7
Broadeaves Cl, S.Croy.
CR2 ....202 B5
Broadfield Cl, NW2 ......89 J3
Croydon CR0
off Progress Way 201 F2
Broadfield Ct, Bushey
(Bushey Hth.) WD23 ..52 B2
Broadfield La, NW1 ......92 E7
Broadfield Rd, SE6 .....154 E7
Broadfields, E.Mol. KT8 .180 A6
Harrow HA2 ....67 H2
Broadfields Av, N21 .....43 G7
Edgware HA8 ....54 B4
Broadfields Hts, Edg.
HA8 ....54 B4
Broadfields La, Wat.
WD19 ....50 B1
Broadfield Sq, Enf. EN1 ..45 E2
Broadfields Way, NW10 ..89 F5
Broadfield Way, Buck.H.
IG9 ....63 J3
BROADGATE, EC2 ....20 C1
Broadgate, E13 ....115 J2
EC2 off Liverpool St ...112 B5
Broadgate Circle, EC2 ...20 D1
Broadgate Rd, E16 .....116 A6
Broadgates Av, Barn.
EN4 ....41 E1
Broadgates Rd, SW18
off Ellerton Rd 167 G1
BROAD GREEN, Croy. ...187 G6
Broad Grn Av, Croy.
CR0 ....187 H7
Broadhead Strand, NW9 ..71 F1
Broadheath Dr, Chis.
BR7 ....174 C5
Broadhinton Rd, SW4 ..150 B3
Broadhurst Av, Edg.
HA8 ....54 B4
Ilford IG3 ....99 J4

Broadhurst Cl, NW6
off Broadhurst Gdns ..91 F6
Richmond TW10
off Lower Gro Rd 145 J5
Broadhurst Gdns, NW6 ..90 E6
Chigwell IG7 ....65 F4
Ruislip HA4 ....84 C2
Broadlands, Felt. TW13 .161 F3
Broadlands Av, SW16 ...168 E2
Enfield EN3 ....45 E3
Broadlands Cl, N6 ......74 A7
SW16 ....168 E2
Enfield EN3 ....45 E3
Broadlands Rd, N6 ......73 J7
Bromley BR1 ....173 H4
Broadlands Way, N.Mal.
KT3 ....183 F6
Broad La, EC2 ....20 D1
N8 off Tottenham La ...75 F5
N15 ....76 C4
Hampton TW12 ......161 G6
Broad Lawn, SE9 ......174 D2
Broadlawns Ct, Har. HA3 .68 C1
Broadley St, NW8 ....15 F1
Broadley Ter, NW1 ......7 H6
Broadmayne, SE17 ......36 B3
Broadmead Av, Wor.Pk.
KT4 ....183 G7
Broadmead Cl, Hmptn.
TW12 ....161 G6
Pinner HA5 ....51 E7
Broadmead Est, Wdf.Grn.
IG8 ....63 J7
Broadmead Rd, Hayes
UB4 ....102 E4
Northolt UB5 ....102 E4
Woodford Green IG8 ...63 G6
Broad Oak, Wdf.Grn. IG8 .63 H5
Broad Oak Cl, E4
off Royston Av 62 A5
Broadoaks, Surb. KT6 ..196 B1
Broadoaks Way, Brom.
BR2 ....191 F5
Broad Sanctuary, SW1 ..25 J4
Broadstone Pl, W1 ......16 B2
Broad St, Dag. RM10 ...101 G7
Teddington TW11 .....162 C6
Broad St Av, EC2 ....20 D2
Broad St Pl, EC2 ....20 C2
Broad Vw, NW9 ....70 A6
Broadview Rd, SW16 ...168 D7
Broadwalk, E18 ....79 F3
Broad Wk, N21 ....59 F2
NW1 ....8 D4
SE3 ....155 J3
W1 ....24 B1
Broadwalk, Har. HA2 ....67 G5
Broad Wk, Houns. TW5 .142 D7
Richmond TW9 ......125 J7
Broad Wk, The, W8 .....14 B6
East Molesey KT8 ....180 C3
Broadwalk Ct, W8 .....128 D1
Broad Wk La, NW11 .....72 C7
Broadwalk Shop Cen, Edg.
HA8 ....54 B6
Broadwall, SE1 ....27 F1
Broadwater Gdns, Orp.
BR6 ....207 E4
Broadwater Rd, N17 ....76 B1
SE28 ....137 G3
SW17 ....167 H4
Broadway, E15 ....96 D7
SW1 ....25 H5
W13 ....124 D1
Barking IG11 ....99 F7
Bexleyheath DA6 .....159 E4
Surbiton KT6 ....196 B1
Broadway, The, E4 .....62 C6
E13 ....115 H2
N8 ....74 E6
N9 ....60 D3
N14
off Winchmore Hill Rd .58 D1
N22 ....75 G2
NW7 ....55 E5
SW13
off The Terrace ...146/147 E2
SW19 ....166 C6
W5 ....105 G7
W7 ....124 B1
Croydon CR0
off Croydon Rd ..200/201 E4
Dagenham RM8 ......101 F2
Greenford UB6 ......103 J4
Harrow HA2 ....68 B2
Loughton IG10 ....49 F4
Pinner HA5 ....51 F7
Southall UB1 ....102 D7
Stanmore HA7 ....53 F5

Broadway, The, Sutt (Cheam)
SM3 ....198 B6
Thames Ditton KT7
off Hampton Ct Way . .194 B1
Wembley HA9
off East La 87 H3
Woodford Green IG8 ...63 H6
Broadway Av, Croy. CR0 .188 A5
Twickenham TW1 .....144 E6
Broadway Cl, Wdf.Grn.
IG8 ....63 H6
Broadway Ct, SW19
off The Broadway 166 D6
Broadway Gdns, Mitch.
CR4 ....185 H4
Broadway Ho, Brom. BR1
off Elmfield Pk 191 G3
Broadway Mkt, E8 .....112 E1
Broadway Mkt Ms, E8
off Brougham Rd 112 D1
Broadway Ms, E5 ......76 C7
N13 off Elmdale Rd ...59 F5
N21 off Compton Rd ..59 H1
Broadway Par, N8 ......74 E6
Hayes UB3
off Coldharbour La . .122 A1
Broadway Pl, SW19
off Hartfield Rd 166 C6
Broadway Shop Cen, W6
off Hammersmith
Bdy 127 J4
Bexleyheath DA6 .....159 G4
Broadwick St, W1 ......17 G5
Broadwood Ter, W8
off Pembroke Rd 128 C4
Broad Yd, EC1 ....11 G6
Brocas Cl, NW3
off Fellows Rd 91 H7
Brockbridge Ho, SW15 .147 F6
Brockdish Av, Bark. IG11 .99 J5
Brockenhurst, W.Mol.
KT8 ....179 F6
Brockenhurst Av, Wor.Pk.
KT4 ....197 E1
Brockenhurst Gdns, NW7 .55 E5
Ilford IG1 ....99 F5
Brockenhurst Ms, N18
off Lyndhurst Rd 60 D4
Brockenhurst Rd, Croy.
CR0 ....188 E7
Brockenhurst Way,
SW16 ....186 D2
Brocket Cl, Chig. IG7
off Burrow Rd 65 J5
Brocket Way, Chig. IG7 ..65 H5
Brockham Cl, SW19 ....166 C5
Brockham Cres, Croy.
(New Adgtn.) CR0 ...204 D7
Brockham Dr, SW2
off Fairview Pl 151 F7
Ilford IG2 ....81 E6
Brockham St, SE1 ......28 A5
Brockhurst Cl, Stan. HA7 .52 C6
Brocklill Cres, SE4 .....153 H4
Brocklebank Rd, SE7 ...135 H4
SW18 ....149 F7
Brocklehurst St, SE14 ..133 G7
Brocklesby Rd, SE25 ...188 E4
BROCKLEY, SE4 ....153 H5
Brockley Av, Stan. HA7 ..53 H3
Brockley Cl, Stan. HA7 ..53 H4
Brockley Cross, SE4
off Endwell Rd 153 H3
Brockley Footpath, SE15 .153 F4
Brockley Gdns, SE4 ....153 J2
Brockley Gro, SE4 .....153 J5
Brockley Hall Rd, SE4 ..153 H6
Brockley Hill, Stan. HA7 .53 F1
Brockley Ms, SE4 .....153 H5
Brockley Pk, SE23 .....153 H7
Brockley Ri, SE23 .....153 H6
Brockley Rd, SE4 ......153 J3
Brockleyside, Stan. HA7 .53 G4
Brockley Vw, SE23 ....153 H7
Brockley Vw, SE4 .....153 G5
Brockman Ri, Brom.
BR1 ....172 D4
Brock Pl, E3 ....114 B4
Brock Rd, E13 ....115 H5
Brocks Dr, Sutt. SM3 ...198 B3
Brockshot Cl, Brent.
TW8 ....125 G6
Brock St, SE15
off Evelina Rd 153 F3
Brockway Cl, E11 ......97 E1
Brockwell Cl, Orp. BR5 .193 J5
★ Brockwell Park, SE24 .151 H6
Brockwell Pk Gdns,
SE24 ....151 G7

Brockwell Pk Row, SW2 .151 G6
Brodewater Rd, Borwd.
WD6 ....38 B2
Brodia Rd, N16 ....94 B3
Brodie Rd, E4 ....62 C1
Brodie St, SE1 ....37 G3
Brodlove La, E1 ....113 G7
Brodrick Gro, SE2 .....138 B4
Brodrick Rd, SW17 ....167 H2
Brograve Gdns, Beck.
BR3 ....190 B2
Broken Wf, EC4 ....19 J5
Brokesley St, E3 ......113 J4
Broke Wk, E8 ....112 D1
Bromar Rd, SE5 ....152 B3
Bromborough Grn, Wat.
WD19 ....50 C5
Bromefield, Stan. HA7 ..69 F1
Bromehead Rd, E1 .....113 F6
Bromehead St, E1
off Commercial Rd . .113 F6
Bromell's Rd, SW4 ....150 C4
Brome Rd, SE9 ....156 C3
Bromfelde Rd, SW4 ....150 D2
Bromfelde Wk, SW4 ....150 D2
Bromfield St, N1 ....11 F1
Bromhall Rd, Dag. RM8,
RM9 ....100 B6
Bromhedge, SE9 ......174 C3
Bromholm Rd, SE2 ....138 B3
Bromleigh Ct, SE23
off Lapse Wd Wk .170/171 E2
BROMLEY 191 F2
BROMLEY, E3 ....114 B4
Bromley Av, Brom. BR1 .173 E7
BROMLEY COMMON,
Brom. 192 C7
Bromley Common, Brom.
BR2 ....191 J4
Bromley Cres, Brom.
BR2 ....191 F3
Bromley Gdns, Brom.
BR2 ....191 F3
Bromley Gro, Brom.
BR2 ....190 D2
Bromley Hall Rd, E14 ...114 C5
Bromley High St, E3 ...114 B3
Bromley Hill, Brom. BR1 .172 E5
Bromley La, Chis. BR7 ..175 F7
Bromley Mall, The, Brom.
BR1 ....191 G3
BROMLEY PARK, Brom. .190 E1
Bromley Pk, Brom. BR1
off London Rd 191 F1
Bromley Pl, W1 ....17 F1
Bromley Rd, E10 ......78 B6
E17 ....78 A2
N17 ....60 A3
N18 ....76 C1
SE6 ....172 B1
Beckenham BR3 .....190 B1
Bromley (Downham)
BR1 ....172 C4
Bromley (Short.) BR2 .190 C2
Chislehurst BR7 ......192 E1
Bromley St, E1 ....113 G5
BROMPTON, SW3 ....23 G6
Brompton Arc, SW3 ....23 J4
Brompton Cl, SE20
off Selby Rd 188 D2
Hounslow TW4 ......143 F5
Brompton Gro, N2 .....73 H4
★ Brompton Oratory, SW7
off Brompton Rd 23 G6
Brompton Pk Cres, SW6 .30 A6
Brompton Pl, SW3 .....23 H5
Brompton Rd, SW1 ....23 H5
SW3 ....31 G1
SW7 ....23 G6
Brompton Sq, SW3 ....23 G5
Brompton Ter, SE18
off Prince Imperial Rd .156 D1
Bromwich Av, N6 ......92 A2
Bromyard Av, W3 ......127 E1
Bromyard Ho, SE15 ...132 E7
BRONDESBURY, NW2 ...90 B7
Brondesbury Ct, NW2 ..89 J6
Brondesbury Ms, NW6
off Willesden La 90 D7
BRONDESBURY PARK,
NW6 ....89 J7
Brondesbury Pk, NW2 ..89 H6
NW6 ....90 A7
Brondesbury Rd, NW6 ..108 C2
Brondesbury Vil, NW6 ..108 C2
Bronsart Rd, SW6 .....128 B7
Bronson Rd, SW20 ....184 A2
Bronte Cl, E7
off Bective Rd 97 G4
Erith DA8 ....139 H7

Bronte Cl, Ilf. IG2 . . . . **.80** D5
Bronte Ho, NW6 . . . . . **.108** D3
Bronti Cl, SE17 . . . .**.36** A4
Bronze Age Way, Belv.
  DA17 . . . .**.139** J3
  Erith DA8 . . . .**.139** J3
Bronze St, SE8 . . . .**.134** A7
Brook Av, Dag. RM10 . . . .**.101** H7
  Edgware HA8 . . . .**.54** B6
  Wembley HA9 . . . .**.88** A3
Brookbank Av, W7 . . . . . .**.104** A5
Brookbank Rd, SE13 . . . .**.154** A3
Brook Cl, NW7
  off Frith Ct . . . .**.56** B7
  SW17 . . . .**.168** A2
  SW20 . . . .**.183** H3
  W3 *off West Lo Av* . . . .**.126** A1
  Borehamwood WD6 . . . .**.38** B3
  Staines (Stanw.) TW19 .**.140** C7
Brook Ct, Buck.H. IG9 . . . .**.63** H1
Brook Cres, E4 . . . .**.62** A4
  N9 . . . .**.60** E4
Brookdale, N11 . . . .**.58** C4
Brookdale Rd, E17 . . . . . .**.78** A3
  SE6 . . . .**.154** B6
  Bexley DA5 . . . .**.159** E6
Brookdene Rd, SE18 . . . .**.137** J4
Brook Dr, SE11 . . . .**.27** F6
  Harrow HA1 . . . .**.67** J4
Brooke Av, Har. HA2 . . . . .**.85** J3
Brookehowse Rd, SE6 . . .**.172** B3
Brookend Rd, Sid. DA15 . .**.175** H1
Brooke Rd, E5 . . . .**.94** D3
  E17 . . . .**.78** C4
  N16 . . . .**.94** C3
Brooke's Ct, EC1 . . . .**.19** E1
Brookes Mkt, EC1 . . . . . .**.19** F1
Brooke St, EC1 . . . .**.19** E2
Brookfield, N6 . . . .**.92** A3
Brookfield Av, E17 . . . . . .**.78** C4
  NW7 . . . .**.55** H6
  W5 . . . .**.105** G4
  Sutton SM1 . . . .**.199** G4
Brookfield Cl, NW7 . . . . . .**.55** H6
Brookfield Ct, Grnf.
  UB6 . . . .**.103** J3
  Harrow HA3 . . . .**.69** G5
Brookfield Cres, NW7 . . . .**.55** H6
  Harrow HA3 . . . .**.69** G5
Brookfield Gdns, Esher (Clay.)
  KT10 . . . .**.194** C6
Brookfield Pk, NW5 . . . . .**.92** B3
Brookfield Path, Wdf.Grn.
  IG8 . . . .**.62** E6
Brookfield Rd, E9 . . . .**.95** H6
  N9 . . . .**.60** D3
  W4 . . . .**.126** D2
Brookfields, Enf. EN3 . . . .**.45** G4
Brookfields Av, Mitch.
  CR4 . . . .**.185** H6
Brook Gdns, E4 . . . .**.62** B4
  SW13 . . . .**.147** F3
  Kingston upon Thames
  KT2 . . . .**.182** C1
Brook Gate, W1 . . . .**.16** A6
Brook Grn, W6 . . . .**.128** A4
Brookhill Cl, SE18 . . . . . .**.136** E5
  Barnet EN4 . . . .**.41** H5
Brookhill Rd, SE18 . . . . .**.136** E5
  Barnet EN4 . . . .**.41** H5
Brookhouse Gdns, E4 . . . .**.62** E4
Brook Ind Est, Hayes
  UB4 . . . .**.122** D1
Brooking Rd, E7 . . . .**.97** G5
Brookland Cl, NW11 . . . . .**.72** E4
Brookland Garth, NW11 . . .**.72** E4
Brookland Hill, NW11 . . . .**.72** D4
Brookland Ri, NW11 . . . . .**.72** D4
Brooklands Av, SW19 . . . .**.166** E2
  Sidcup DA15 . . . .**.175** G2
Brooklands Dr, Grnf.
  UB6 . . . .**.105** G3
Brooklands Pk, SE3 . . . . .**.155** G3
Brooklands Rd, T.Ditt.
  KT7 . . . .**.194** C1
Brook La, SE3 . . . .**.155** H2
  Bexley DA5 . . . .**.158** D6
  Bromley BR1 . . . .**.173** G6
Brook La N, Brent. TW8 . .**.125** G5
Brooklea Cl, NW9 . . . .**.71** E1
Brooklyn Av, SE25 . . . . .**.189** E4
  Loughton IG10 . . . .**.48** B4
Brooklyn Cl, Cars. SM5 . .**.199** H2
Brooklyn Gro, SE25 . . . .**.189** E4
Brooklyn Rd, SE25 . . . . .**.188** E4
  Bromley BR2 . . . .**.192** A5
Brooklyn Way, West Dr.
  UB7 . . . .**.120** A3
Brookmarsh Ind Est, SE10
  off Norman Rd . . . . . .**.134** B7

Brook Mead, Epsom
  KT19 . . . .**.197** E6
Brookmead Av, Brom.
  BR1 . . . .**.192** C5
Brook Meadow, N12 . . . . .**.56** E4
Brook Meadow Cl, Wdf.Grn.
  IG8 . . . .**.62** E6
Brookmeade Rd, Croy.
  CR0 . . . .**.186** C6
Brookmeads Est, Mitch.
  CR4 . . . .**.185** H5
Brook Ms N, W2 . . . .**.14** D5
Brookmill Rd, SE8 . . . . .**.154** A1
Brook Par, Chig. IG7
  off High Rd . . . . . .**.64/65** E3
Brook Pk Cl, N21 . . . .**.43** H6
Brook Path, Loug. IG10 . . .**.48** B4
Brook Pl, Barn. EN5 . . . . .**.40** D5
Brook Ri, Chig. IG7 . . . . . .**.64** D3
Brook Rd, N8 . . . .**.74** E4
  N22 . . . .**.75** F3
  NW2 . . . .**.89** G2
  Borehamwood WD6 . . . .**.38** A2
  Buckhurst Hill IG9 . . . . .**.63** G2
  Ilford IG2 . . . .**.81** H6
  Loughton IG10 . . . .**.48** B5
  Surbiton KT6 . . . .**.195** H2
  Thornton Heath CR7 . .**.187** J4
  Twickenham TW1 . . . .**.144** D6
Brook Rd S, Brent. TW8 . .**.125** G6
Brooks Av, E6 . . . .**.116** C4
Brooksbank St, E9 . . . . . .**.95** G6
Brooksby Ms, N1
  off Brooksby St . . . . .**.93** G7
Brooksby St, N1 . . . .**.93** G7
Brooksby's Wk, E9 . . . . . .**.95** G5
Brooks Cl, SE9 . . . .**.174** D2
Brooks Ct, E15
  off Clays La . . . .**.96** B5
Brookscroft Rd, E17 . . . . .**.78** B1
Brookshill, Har. HA3 . . . . .**.52** A5
Brookshill Av, Har. HA3 . . .**.52** A5
Brookshill Dr, Har. HA3 . . .**.52** A5
Brookside, N21 . . . .**.43** F6
  Barnet EN4 . . . .**.41** H6
  Carshalton SM5 . . . . .**.200** A5
  Ilford IG6 . . . .**.65** F6
  Orpington BR6 . . . . . .**.193** J7
Brookside Cl, Barn. EN5 . .**.40** B6
  Feltham TW13
  off Sycamore Cl . . . .**.160** A3
  Harrow (Kenton) HA2 . .**.69** G5
  Harrow (S.Har.) HA3 . . .**.85** E4
Brookside Cres, Wor.Pk. KT4
  off Green La . . . . . .**.197** G1
Brookside Rd, N9 . . . .**.60** E4
  N19 . . . .**.92** C2
  NW11 . . . .**.72** B6
  Hayes UB4 . . . .**.102** C7
Brookside S, Barn. EN4 . . .**.42** A7
Brookside Wk, N3 . . . .**.72** B2
  N12 . . . .**.56** D6
  NW4 . . . .**.72** B4
  NW11 . . . .**.72** B4
Brookside Way, Croy.
  CR0 . . . .**.189** G6
Brooks La, W4 . . . .**.126** A6
Brook's Ms, W1 . . . .**.16** D5
Brook Sq, SE18
  off Shooter's Hill Rd .**.156** B1
Brooks Rd, E13 . . . .**.115** G1
  W4 . . . .**.126** A5
Brook St, N17
  off High Rd . . . .**.76** C2
  W1 . . . .**.16** C5
  W2 . . . .**.15** F5
  Belvedere DA17 . . . . .**.139** H5
  Erith DA8 . . . .**.139** H5
  Kingston upon Thames
  KT1 . . . .**.181** H2
Brooksville Av, NW6 . . . .**.108** B1
Brook Vale, Erith DA8 . . .**.159** H1
Brookview Rd, SW16 . . . .**.168** C5
Brookville Rd, SW6 . . . . .**.128** C7
Brook Wk, N2 . . . .**.73** G1
  Edgware HA8 . . . .**.54** D6
Brookway, SE3 . . . .**.155** G3
Brook Way, Chig. IG7 . . . .**.64** D3
Brookwood Av, SW13 . . .**.147** F2
Brookwood Cl, Brom.
  BR2 . . . .**.191** F4
Brookwood Rd, SW18 . . .**.166** C1
  Hounslow TW3 . . . . . .**.143** H1
Broom Cl, Brom. BR2 . . . .**.192** B6
  Teddington TW11 . . . .**.163** G7
Broomcroft Av, Nthlt.
  UB5 . . . .**.102** C3
Broome Rd, Hmptn.
  TW12 . . . .**.161** F7
Broome Way, SE5 . . . . . .**.131** J7

Broomfield, E17 . . . .**.77** J7
  Sunbury-on-Thames
  TW16 . . . .**.178** A1
Broomfield Av, N13 . . . . . .**.59** F5
  Loughton IG10 . . . .**.48** C6
Broomfield La, N13 . . . . . .**.59** F4
Broomfield Pl, W13
  *off Broomfield
  Rd* . . . .**.124/125** E1
Broomfield Rd, N13 . . . . . .**.59** E5
  W13 . . . .**.125** E1
  Beckenham BR3 . . . . .**.189** H3
  Bexleyheath DA6 . . . .**.159** G5
  Richmond TW9 . . . . . .**.145** J1
  Romford RM6 . . . .**.82** D7
  Surbiton KT5 . . . .**.195** J1
  Teddington TW11
  off Melbourne Rd . . .**.163** F6
Broomfield St, E14 . . . . .**.114** A5
Broom Gdns, Croy. CR0 .**.204** A3
Broomgrove Gdns, Edg.
  HA8 . . . .**.70** A1
Broomgrove Rd, SW9 . . .**.151** F2
Broomhill Ct, Wdf.Grn. IG8
  off Broomhill Rd . . . . .**.63** G6
Broomhill Ri, Bexh. DA6 .**.159** G5
Broomhill Rd, SW18 . . . .**.148** D5
  Ilford IG3 . . . .**.100** A2
  Woodford Green IG8 . . .**.63** G6
Broomhill Wk, Wdf.Grn.
  IG8 . . . .**.63** F7
Broomhouse La, SW6 . . .**.148** D2
Broomhouse Rd, SW6 . . .**.148** D2
Broomloan La, Sutt.
  SM1 . . . .**.198** D2
Broom Lock, Tedd. TW11 .**.163** F6
Broom Mead, Bexh.
  DA6 . . . .**.159** G5
Broom Pk, Tedd. TW11 . .**.163** G7
Broom Rd, Croy. CR0 . . .**.204** A3
  Teddington TW11 . . . .**.163** F6
Broomsleigh St, NW6 . . . .**.90** C5
Broom Water, Tedd.
  TW11 . . . .**.163** F6
Broom Water W, Tedd.
  TW11 . . . .**.163** F5
Broomwood Cl, Croy.
  CR0 . . . .**.189** G5
Broomwood Rd, SW11 . . .**.149** J6
Broseley Gro, SE26 . . . .**.171** H5
Broster Gdns, SE25 . . . .**.188** C3
Brougham Rd, E8 . . . . . .**.112** D1
  W3 . . . .**.106** C6
Brougham St, SW11 . . . .**.149** J2
Brough Cl, SW8
  off Kenchester Cl .**.130/131** E7
  Kingston upon Thames
  KT2 . . . .**.163** G5
Broughinge Rd, Borwd.
  WD6 . . . .**.38** B2
Broughton Av, N3 . . . .**.72** B3
  Richmond TW10 . . . . .**.163** E3
Broughton Dr, SW9 . . . .**.151** G4
Broughton Gdns, N6 . . . . .**.74** C6
Broughton Rd, SW6 . . . .**.148** E2
  W13 . . . .**.105** E7
  Orpington BR6 . . . . . .**.207** H2
  Thornton Heath CR7 . .**.187** G6
Broughton Rd App, SW6
  *off Wandsworth
  Br Rd* . . . .**.148/149** A2
Broughton St, SW8 . . . . .**.150** A2
Brouncker Rd, W3 . . . . .**.126** C2
Browells La, Felt. TW13 . .**.160** B2
Brown Cl, Wall. SM6 . . . .**.200** E7
Brownfield St, E14 . . . . .**.114** B6
Browngraves Rd, Hayes
  UB3 . . . .**.121** F7
Brown Hart Gdns, W1 . . . .**.16** C5
Brownhill Rd, SE6 . . . . .**.154** B7
Browning Av, W7 . . . . . .**.104** C6
  Sutton SM1 . . . .**.199** H4
  Worcester Park KT4 . .**.197** H1
Browning Cl, E17 . . . .**.78** C4
  W9 . . . .**.6** D6
  Hampton TW12 . . . . .**.161** F4
  Welling DA16 . . . .**.157** H1
Browning Ho, W12
  off Wood La . . . .**.107** J4
Browning Ms, W1 . . . .**.16** D2
Browning Rd, E11 . . . .**.79** F7
  E12 . . . .**.98** C6
Browning St, SE17 . . . . . .**.36** A3
Browning Way, Houns.
  TW5 . . . .**.142** D1
Brownlea Gdns, Ilf. IG3 . .**.100** A2
Brownlow Ms, WC1 . . . . .**.10** D6
Brownlow Rd, E7
  off Woodford Rd . . . . .**.97** H4
  E8 . . . .**.112** C1

Brownlow Rd, N3 . . . .**.56** E7
  N11 . . . .**.58** E6
  NW10 . . . .**.89** E7
  W13 . . . .**.124** D1
  Borehamwood WD6 . . .**.38** A4
  Croydon CR0 . . . .**.202** B4
Brownlow St, WC1 . . . . . .**.18** D2
Brown's Bldgs, EC3 . . . . .**.20** E4
Brownsea Wk, NW7
  off Sanders La . . . . . .**.56** A6
Browns La, NW5 . . . .**.92** B5
Brownspring Dr, SE9 . . .**.175** E4
Browns Rd, E17 . . . .**.78** A3
  Surbiton KT5 . . . .**.181** J7
Brown St, W1 . . . .**.15** J3
Brownswell Rd, N2 . . . . . .**.73** G2
Brownswood Rd, N4 . . . . .**.93** H3
Broxash Rd, SW11 . . . . .**.150** A6
Broxbourne Av, E18 . . . . .**.79** H4
Broxbourne Rd, E7 . . . . . .**.97** G3
  Orpington BR6 . . . . . .**.193** J7
Broxholm Rd, SE27 . . . .**.169** G3
Broxted Rd, SE6 . . . . . .**.171** J2
Broxwood Way, NW8 . . .**.109** H1
★ Bruce Castle Mus, N17
  (Tottenham) . . . .**.76** B1
Bruce Castle Rd, N17 . . . .**.76** C1
Bruce Cl, W10
  off Ladbroke Gro . . .**.108** B5
  Welling DA16 . . . .**.158** B1
Bruce Gdns, N20
  off Balfour Gro . . . . . .**.57** J3
Bruce Gro, N17 . . . .**.76** B1
Bruce Hall Ms, SW17
  off Brudenell Rd . . . .**.168** A4
Bruce Rd, E3 . . . .**.114** B3
  NW10 . . . .**.88** D7
  SE25 . . . .**.188** A4
  Barnet EN5
  off St. Albans Rd . . . .**.40** B3
  Harrow HA3 . . . .**.68** B2
  Mitcham CR4 . . . .**.168** A7
Bruckner St, W10 . . . . . .**.108** C3
Brudenell Rd, SW17 . . . .**.167** J3
Bruffs Meadow, Nthlt.
  UB5 . . . .**.85** E6
Bruges Pl, NW1
  off Randolph St . . . . .**.92** C7
Brumfield Rd, Epsom
  KT19 . . . .**.196** C5
Brummel Cl, Bexh. DA7 . .**.159** J3
★ Brunei Gall, WC1
  off Russell Sq . . . .**.9** J6
Brunel Cl, SE19 . . . .**.170** C6
  Hounslow TW5 . . . . . .**.122** B7
  Northolt UB5 . . . .**.103** F3
★ Brunel Engine Ho,
  SE16 . . . .**.133** F2
Brunel Est, W2 . . . .**.108** D5
Brunel Pl, Sthl. UB1 . . . .**.103** H6
Brunel Rd, E17 . . . .**.77** H6
  SE16 . . . .**.133** F2
  W3 . . . .**.106** E5
  Woodford Green IG8 . . .**.64** C5
Brunel St, E16 . . . .**.115** F6
  off Victoria Dock Rd . .**.115** F6
Brunel Wk, N15 . . . .**.76** B4
  Twickenham TW2
  off Stephenson Rd . .**.143** G7
Brune St, E1 . . . .**.21** F2
Brunner Cl, NW11 . . . . . .**.73** F5
Brunner Rd, E17 . . . .**.77** J5
  W5 . . . .**.105** G4
Bruno Pl, NW9 . . . .**.88** C2
Brunswick Av, N11 . . . . . .**.58** A3
Brunswick Cl, Bexh.
  DA6 . . . .**.158** D4
  Pinner HA5 . . . .**.67** E6
  Thames Ditton KT7 . . .**.194** C1
  Twickenham TW2 . . . .**.162** A3
Brunswick Ct, EC1
  off Northampton Sq . .**.111** H3
  SE1 . . . .**.29** E4
  Barnet EN4 . . . .**.41** G5
Brunswick Cres, N11 . . . .**.58** A3
Brunswick Gdns, W5 . . . .**.105** H3
  W8 . . . .**.128** D1
  Ilford IG6 . . . .**.65** F7
Brunswick Gro, N11 . . . . .**.58** A3
Brunswick Ind Pk, N11 . . .**.58** B4
Brunswick Ms, SW16
  off Potters La . . . . . .**.168** D6
BRUNSWICK PARK, N11 . .**.57** J2
Brunswick Pk, SE5 . . . . .**.152** A1
Brunswick Pk Gdns, N11 . .**.58** A2
Brunswick Pk Rd, N11 . . . .**.58** A2
Brunswick Pl, N1 . . . .**.12** C4
  NW1 . . . .**.8** C5
  SE19 . . . .**.170** D7

Brunswick Quay, SE16 . .**133** G3
Brunswick Rd, E10 . . . . . .**96** C1
E14 *off Blackwall Tunnel*
  Northern App **114** C6
N15 . . . .**76** B5
W5 . . . .**105** G4
Bexleyheath DA6 . . . . .**158** D4
Kingston upon Thames
  KT2 . . . .**182** A1
Sutton SM1 . . . .**199** E4
Brunswick Shop Cen,
WC1 . . . .**10** A5
Brunswick Sq, N17 . . . . .**60** C6
WC1 . . . .**10** B6
Brunswick St, E17 . . . . . .**78** C5
Brunswick Vil, SE5 . . . .**152** B1
Brunswick Way, N11 . . . .**58** B4
Brunton Pl, E14 . . . .**113** H6
Brushfield St, E1 . . . .**20** E2
Brussels Rd, SW11 . . . .**149** G4
Bruton Cl, Chis. BR7 . . .**174** C7
Bruton La, W1 . . . .**16** E6
Bruton Pl, W1 . . . .**16** E6
Bruton Rd, Mord. SM4 .**185** F5
Bruton St, W1 . . . .**16** E6
Bruton Way, W13 . . . . . .**104** D5
Bryan Av, NW10 . . . .**89** H7
Bryan Cl, Sun. TW16 . . .**160** A7
Bryan Rd, SE16 . . . .**133** J2
Bryan's All, SW6
  off Wandsworth
  Br Rd **148/149** E2
Bryanston Av, Twick.
  TW2 . . . .**161** H1
Bryanston Cl, Sthl.
  UB2 . . . .**123** F4
Bryanstone Ct, Sutt. SM1
  off Oakhill Rd **199** F4
Bryanstone Rd, N8 . . . . .**74** D5
Bryanston Ms E, W1 . . . .**15** J2
Bryanston Ms W, W1 . . . .**15** J2
Bryanston Pl, W1 . . . .**15** J2
Bryanston Sq, W1 . . . . . .**15** J2
Bryanston St, W1 . . . . . .**15** J4
Bryant Cl, Barn. EN5 . . . .**40** C5
Bryant Ct, E2 . . . .**13** F1
Bryant Rd, Nthlt. UB5 . .**102** C3
Bryant St, E15 . . . .**96** D7
Bryantwood Rd, N7 . . . . .**93** G5
Brycedale Cres, N14 . . . .**58** D4
Bryce Rd, Dag. RM8 . . . .**100** C4
Bryden Cl, SE26 . . . .**171** H5
Brydges Pl, WC2 . . . .**18** A6
Brydges Rd, E15 . . . .**96** D5
Brydon Wk, N1
  off Outram Pl **110/111** E1
Bryer Ct, EC2
  off Aldersgate St **111** J5
Bryett Rd, N7 . . . .**93** E3
Brymay Cl, E3 . . . .**114** A2
Brynmaer Rd, SW11 . . . .**149** J1
Bryn-y-Mawr Rd, Enf.
  EN1 . . . .**44** C4
Bryony Cl, Loug. IG10 . . .**48** E4
Bryony Rd, W12 . . . .**107** G7
Buchanan Cl, N21 . . . . . .**43** F5
Buchanan Ct, Borwd.
  WD6 . . . .**38** C2
Buchanan Gdns, NW10 . .**107** H2
Buchan Rd, SE15 . . . . . .**153** F3
Bucharest Rd, SW18 . . .**149** F7
Buckden Cl, N2
  off Southern Rd **73** J4
SE12 *off Upwood Rd* . .**155** F6
Buckfast Rd, Mord. SM4 .**185** E4
Buckfast St, E2 . . . .**13** J4
Buck Hill Wk, W2 . . . .**15** F6
Buckhold Rd, SW18 . . . .**148** D6
Buckhurst Av, Cars.
  SM5 . . . .**199** H1
BUCKHURST HILL **47** H7
Buckhurst St, E1 . . . . . .**113** E4
Buckhurst Way, Buck.H.
  IG9 . . . .**64** A4
Buckingham Arc, WC2 . . .**18** B6
Buckingham Av, N20 . . . .**41** F7
Feltham TW14 . . . .**142** B6
Greenford UB6 . . . .**104** D1
Thornton Heath CR7 . .**187** G1
Welling DA16 . . . .**157** H4
West Molesey KT8 . . . .**179** H3
Buckingham Cl, W5 . . . .**105** F5
Enfield EN1 . . . .**44** B2
Hampton TW12 . . . . . .**161** F5
Orpington BR5 . . . .**193** H7
Buckingham Ct, NW4 . . . .**71** G3
Loughton IG10
  off Rectory La **48** D2
Buckingham Dr, Chis.
  BR7 . . . .**175** E5

Buckingham Gdns, Edg.
  HA8 . . . .**53** J7
Thornton Heath CR7 . .**187** G2
West Molesey KT8
  off Buckingham Av . . .**179** H2
Buckingham Gate, SW1 . .**25** F4
Buckingham La, SE23 . .**153** H7
Buckingham Ms, N1
  off Buckingham Rd **94** B6
NW10
  off Buckingham Rd . . .**107** F2
SW1 . . . .**25** F5
★ Buckingham Palace,
  SW1 . . . .**24** E4
Buckingham Palace Rd,
  SW1 . . . .**32** D2
Buckingham Pl, SW1 . . . .**25** F5
Buckingham Rd, E10 . . . .**96** B3
E11 . . . .**79** J5
E15 . . . .**97** F5
E18 . . . .**79** F1
N1 . . . .**94** B6
N22 . . . .**74** E1
NW10 . . . .**107** F2
Borehamwood WD6 . . . .**38** D4
Edgware HA8 . . . .**53** J7
Hampton TW12 . . . . . .**161** F4
Harrow HA1 . . . .**68** A5
Ilford IG1 . . . .**99** G2
Kingston upon Thames
  KT1 . . . .**181** J4
Mitcham CR4 . . . .**186** E5
Richmond TW10 . . . . .**163** G2
Buckingham St, WC2 . . . .**18** B6
Buckland Cres, NW3 . . . .**91** G7
Buckland Ri, Pnr. HA5 . . .**66** C1
Buckland Rd, E10 . . . . . .**96** C2
Chessington KT9 . . . . .**195** J5
Orpington BR6 . . . .**207** H4
Bucklands Rd, Tedd.
  TW11 . . . .**163** F6
Buckland St, N1 . . . .**12** C2
Buckland Wk, W3 . . . . . .**126** C2
Morden SM4 . . . .**185** F4
Buckland Way, Wor.Pk.
  KT4 . . . .**197** J1
Buck La, NW9 . . . .**70** D5
Buckleigh Av, SW20 . . . .**184** B3
Buckleigh Rd, SW16 . . .**168** D6
Buckleigh Way, SE19 . .**188** C1
Buckler Gdns, SE9
  off Southold Ri **174** C3
Bucklers All, SW6 . . . . .**128** C6
Bucklersbury, EC4 . . . . . .**20** B4
Bucklersbury Pas, EC4 . . .**20** B4
Bucklers Way, Cars.
  SM5 . . . .**199** J3
Buckles Ct, Belv. DA17
  off Fendyke Rd **138** D3
Buckle St, E1 . . . .**21** G3
Buckley Rd, NW6 . . . .**90** C7
Buckley St, SE1 . . . .**26** E2
Buckmaster Cl, SW9
  off Stockwell Pk Rd . .**151** F3
Buckmaster Rd, SW11 . .**149** H4
Bucknall St, WC2 . . . .**17** J3
Bucknall Way, Beck. BR3 .**190** B4
Bucknell Cl, SW2 . . . . . .**151** F4
Buckner Rd, SW2 . . . . . .**151** F4
Buckrell Rd, E4 . . . .**62** D2
Buckstone Cl, SE23 . . . .**153** F6
Buckstone Rd, N18 . . . . .**60** D6
Buck St, NW1 . . . .**92** B7
Buckters Rents, SE16 . .**133** H1
Buckthorne Rd, SE4 . . . .**153** H6
Buck Wk, E17
  off Wood St **78** D4
Budd Rd, N12 . . . .**57** E4
Buddings Circle, Wem.
  HA9 . . . .**88** C3
Budd's All, Twick. TW1
  off Arlington St **145** F5
Budd Cl, E17 . . . .**77** J5
Budge La, Mitch. CR4 . .**185** J7
Budge Row, EC4 . . . .**20** B5
Budge's Wk, W2 . . . .**22** C1
Budleigh Cres, Well.
  DA16 . . . .**158** C1
Budoch Ct, Ilf. IG3 . . . . .**100** A2
Budoch Dr, Ilf. IG3 . . . . .**100** A2
Buer Rd, SW6 . . . .**148** B2
Bugsby's Way, SE7 . . . .**135** G4
SE10 . . . .**135** F4
Bulganak Rd, Th.Hth.
  CR7 . . . .**187** J4
Bulinga St, SW1 . . . .**33** J2
Bullace Row, SE5 . . . . . .**132** A7
Bull All, Well. DA16
  off Welling High St . . .**158** B3
Bullards Pl, E2 . . . .**113** G3

Bullbanks Rd, Belv.
  DA17 . . . .**139** J4
Bullen St, SW11 . . . .**149** H2
Buller Cl, SE15 . . . .**132** D7
Buller Rd, N17 . . . .**76** D2
N22 . . . .**75** G2
NW10
  off Chamberlayne Rd .**108** A3
Barking IG11 . . . .**99** H1
Thornton Heath CR7 . .**188** A2
Bullers Cl, Sid. DA14 . . .**176** E5
Bullers Wd Dr, Chis. BR7 .**174** B7
Bullescroft Rd, Edg. HA8 .**54** A3
Bullhead Rd, Borwd.
  WD6 . . . .**38** C3
Bullied Way, SW1 . . . .**32** E2
Bull Inn Ct, WC2 . . . .**18** B6
Bullivant St, E14 . . . . . .**114** C7
Bull La, N18 . . . .**60** B5
Chislehurst BR7 . . . . . .**175** G7
Dagenham RM10 . . . . .**101** H3
Bull Rd, E15 . . . .**115** F2
Bullrush Cl, Croy. CR0 . .**188** E6
Bull's All, SW14 . . . .**146** D2
Bulls Br Ind Est, Sthl.
  UB2 . . . .**122** B4
Bulls Br Rd, Sthl. UB2 . .**122** B3
Bullsbrook Rd, Hayes
  UB4 . . . .**122** C1
Bulls Gdns, SW3 . . . .**31** H1
Bull's Head Pas, EC3 . . . .**20** D4
Bull Wf La, EC4 . . . .**20** A5
Bulmer Gdns, Har. HA3 . .**69** G7
Bulmer Ms, W11
  off Ladbroke Rd **108** D7
Bulmer Pl, W11 . . . .**128** D1
Bulow Est, SW6
  off Broughton
  Rd **148/149** E2
Bulrush Cl, Cars. SM5
  off Fellowes Rd **199** H2
Bulstrode Av, Houns.
  TW3 . . . .**143** F2
Bulstrode Gdns, Houns.
  TW3 . . . .**143** F3
Bulstrode Pl, W1 . . . .**16** C2
Bulstrode Rd, Houns.
  TW3 . . . .**143** G3
Bulstrode St, W1 . . . .**16** C3
Bulwer Ct Rd, E11 . . . . . .**96** D1
Bulwer Gdns, Barn. EN5
  off Bulwer Rd **41** F4
Bulwer Rd, E11 . . . .**78** D7
N18 . . . .**60** B4
Barnet EN5 . . . .**41** E4
Bulwer St, W12 . . . .**127** J1
Bunces La, Wdf.Grn. IG8 . .**63** F7
Bungalow Rd, SE25 . . . .**188** B4
Bungalows,The, SW16 . .**168** B7
Wallington SM6 . . . . . .**200** B5
Bunhill Row, EC1 . . . .**12** B5
Bunhouse Pl, SW1 . . . . . .**32** B3
Bunkers Hill, NW11 . . . . .**73** F7
Belvedere DA17 . . . . . .**139** G4
Sidcup DA14 . . . .**177** F3
Bunning Way, N7 . . . .**93** E7
Bunns La, NW7 . . . .**55** F6
Bunsen St, E3
  off Kenilworth Rd **113** H2
Buntingbridge Rd, Ilf. IG2 .**81** G5
Bunting Cl, N9
  off Dunnock Rd **61** G1
Mitcham CR4 . . . .**185** J5
Bunton St, SE18 . . . . . .**136** D3
Bunyan Ct, EC2
  off Beech St **111** J5
Bunyan Rd, E17 . . . .**77** H3
Buonaparte Ms, SW1 . . . .**33** H3
Burbage Cl, SE1 . . . .**28** B6
Burbage Rd, SE21 . . . . .**152** A6
SE24 . . . .**151** J6
Burberry Cl, N.Mal.
  KT3 . . . .**182** E2
Burbridge Way, N17 . . . . .**76** C2
Burcham St, E14 . . . . . .**114** B6
Burcharbro Rd, SE2 . . . .**138** D6
Burchell Rd, E10 . . . .**96** B1
SE15 . . . .**153** E1
Burchett Way, Rom.
  RM6 . . . .**83** F6
Burcote Rd, SW18 . . . . .**167** G1
Burden Cl, Brent. TW8 . .**125** F5
Burdenshott Av, Rich.
  TW10 . . . .**146** B4
Burden Way, E11
  off Brading Cres **97** H2
Burder Cl, N1 . . . .**94** B6
Burder Rd, N1
  off Balls Pond Rd **94** B6
Burdett Av, SW20 . . . . . .**183** G1

Burdett Cl, W7
  off Cherington Rd . . .**124** C2
Sidcup DA14 . . . .**176** E5
Burdett Ms, NW3
  off Belsize Cres **91** G6
W2 . . . .**14** A3
Burdett Rd, E3 . . . .**113** J4
E14 . . . .**113** J4
Croydon CR0 . . . .**188** A6
Richmond TW9 . . . . . .**145** J3
Burdetts Rd, Dag. RM9 .**119** F1
Burdett St, SE1 . . . .**27** E5
Burdock Cl, Croy. CR0 . .**203** G1
Burdock Rd, N17 . . . .**76** D3
Burdon La, Sutt. SM2 . .**198** B7
Burfield Cl, SW17 . . . . . .**167** G4
Burford Cl, Dag. RM8 . .**100** C2
Ilford IG6 . . . .**81** F4
Burford Gdns, N13 . . . . . .**59** F3
Burford Rd, E6 . . . .**116** B3
E15 . . . .**96** D7
SE6 . . . .**171** J2
Brentford TW8 . . . .**125** H5
Bromley BR1 . . . .**192** B4
Sutton SM1 . . . .**198** D2
Worcester Park KT4 . . .**183** F7
Burford Wk, SW6
  off Cambria St . . .**128/129** E7
Burford Way, Croy.
  (New Adgtn.) CR0 . . . .**204** C6
Burges Ct, E6 . . . .**98** D7
Burges Gro, SW13 . . . . .**127** H7
Burges Rd, E6 . . . .**98** B7
Burgess Av, NW9 . . . .**70** D6
Burgess Cl, Felt. TW13 . .**160** E4
Burgess Hill, NW2 . . . . . .**90** D4
Burgess Rd, E15 . . . .**96** E4
Sutton SM1 . . . .**198** E4
Burgess St, E14 . . . .**114** A5
Burge St, SE1 . . . .**28** C6
★ Burgh Ho (Hampstead Mus),
  NW3 . . . .**91** G4
Burghill Rd, SE26 . . . . . .**171** H4
Burghley Av, Borwd.
  WD6 . . . .**38** C5
New Malden KT3 . . . . .**182** D1
Burghley Hall Cl, SW19 .**148** B7
Burghley Ho, SW19 . . . .**166** B3
Burghley Pl, Mitch. CR4 .**186** A5
Burghley Rd, E11 . . . .**97** E1
N8 . . . .**75** G3
NW5 . . . .**92** B5
SW19 . . . .**166** A4
Burghley Twr, W3 . . . . . .**107** F7
Burgh St, N1 . . . .**11** H1
Burgon St, EC4 . . . .**19** H4
Burgos Cl, Croy. CR0 . . .**201** G6
Burgos Gro, SE10 . . . . .**154** B1
Burgoyne Rd, N4 . . . .**75** H6
SE25 . . . .**188** C4
SW9 . . . .**151** F3
Burham Cl, SE20
  off Maple Rd **171** F7
Burhill Gro, Pnr. HA5 . . . .**66** E2
Burke Cl, SW15 . . . .**147** E4
Burke St, E16 . . . .**115** F6
Burket Cl, Sthl. UB2
  off Kingsbridge Rd . . .**123** F4
Burland Rd, SW11 . . . . .**149** J5
Burleigh Av, Sid. DA15 . .**157** J5
Wallington SM6 . . . . . .**200** A3
Burleigh Gdns, N14 . . . . .**58** C1
Burleigh Ho, W10
  off St. Charles Sq . . .**108** A5
Burleigh Pl, SW15 . . . . .**148** A5
Burleigh Rd, Enf. EN1 . . .**44** B4
Sutton SM3 . . . .**198** B1
Burleigh St, WC2 . . . .**18** C5
Burleigh Wk, SE6
  off Muirkirk Rd **172** C1
Burleigh Way, Enf. EN2
  off Church St **44** A3
Burley Cl, E4 . . . .**62** A5
SW16 . . . .**186** D2
Burley Rd, E16 . . . .**115** J6
Burlington Arc, W1 . . . . . .**17** F6
Burlington Av, Rich. TW9 .**146** A1
Romford RM7 . . . .**83** H6
Burlington Cl, E6 . . . . . .**116** B6
  off Northumberland
  Rd **108** A5
W9 . . . .**108** C4
Feltham TW14 . . . .**141** G7
Orpington BR6 . . . .**206** E2
Pinner HA5 . . . .**66** B3
Burlington Gdns, W1 . . . .**17** F6
W3 . . . .**126** C1
W4 . . . .**126** C5
Romford RM6 . . . .**83** E7
Burlington La, W4 . . . . .**126** E7

Burlington Ms, SW15 . . .148 C5
W3 . . . . .126 C1
Burlington Pl, SW6
  off Burlington Rd 148 B2
Woodford Green IG8 . .63 G3
Burlington Ri, Barn. EN4 . .57 H1
Burlington Rd, N10
  off Tetherdown 74 A2
N17 . . . . .76 D1
SW6 . . . . .148 B2
W4 . . . . .126 C5
Enfield EN2 . . . . .44 A1
Isleworth TW7 . . . . .144 A1
New Malden KT3 . . . . .183 G4
Thornton Heath CR7 . .187 J2
Burma Rd, N16 . . . . .94 A4
Burmester Rd, SW17 . . .167 F3
Burnaby Cres, W4 . . . . . .126 B6
Burnaby Gdns, W4 . . . . .126 C6
Burnaby St, SW10 . . . . .129 F7
Burnbrae Cl, N12 . . . . . . .57 E6
Burnbury Rd, SW12 . . . .168 C1
Burncroft Av, Enf. EN3 . . .45 F2
Burne Jones Ho, W14 . . .128 C4
Burnell Av, Rich. TW10 .163 F5
Welling DA16 . . . . .158 A2
Burnell Gdns, Stan. HA7 . .69 G1
Burnell Rd, Sutt. SM1 . .199 E4
Burnell Wk, SE1 . . . . .37 G3
Burnels Av, E6 . . . . .116 D3
Burness Cl, N7
  off Roman Way 93 F6
Burne St, NW1 . . . . .15 G1
Burnett Cl, E9 . . . . .95 F5
Burney Av, Surb. KT5 . . .181 J5
Burney Dr, Loug. IG10 . . .49 E2
Burney St, SE10 . . . . . . .134 C7
Burnfoot Av, SW6 . . . . . .148 B1
Burnfoot Ct, SE22 . . . . .170 E1
Burnham, NW3 . . . . .91 H7
Burnham Cl, NW7 . . . . . .55 G7
SE1 . . . . .37 G2
Harrow (Wldste.) HA3 . .68 D4
Burnham Cres, E11 . . . . .79 J4
Burnham Dr, Wor.Pk.
KT4 . . . . .198 A2
Burnham Gdns, Croy.
CR0 . . . . .188 C7
Hayes UB3 . . . . .121 G3
Hounslow TW4 . . . . . .142 B1
Burnham Rd, E4 . . . . .61 J5
Dagenham RM9 . . . . .100 B7
Morden SM4 . . . . .185 E5
Sidcup DA14 . . . . .176 E2
Burnham St, E2 . . . . .113 F3
Kingston upon Thames
KT2 . . . . .182 A1
Burnham Way, SE26 . . . .171 J5
W13 . . . . .124 E4
Burnhill Rd, Beck. BR3 . .190 A2
Burnley Cl, Wat. WD19 . . .50 C5
Burnley Rd, NW10 . . . . . .89 G5
SW9 . . . . .151 F2
Burnsall St, SW3 . . . . .31 H3
Burns Av, Felt. TW14 . . .142 A6
Romford (Chad.Hth.)
RM6 . . . . .82 C7
Sidcup DA15 . . . . .158 B6
Southall UB1 . . . . .103 G7
Burns Cl, E17 . . . . .78 C4
SW19 . . . . .167 G6
Welling DA16 . . . . .157 J1
Burn Side, N9 . . . . .61 F3
Burnside Av, E4 . . . . .61 J6
Burnside Cl, SE16 . . . . . .133 G1
Barnet EN5 . . . . .40 D3
Twickenham TW1 . . . .144 D6
Burnside Cres, Wem.
HA0 . . . . .105 G5
Burnside Rd, Dag. RM8 .100 C2
Burnt Ash Hill, SE12 . . .155 F6
Burnt Ash La, Brom. BR1 173 G6
Burnt Ash Rd, SE12 . . . .155 F5
Burnthwaite Rd, SW6 . .128 D7
BURNT OAK, Edg. 54 C7
Burnt Oak Bdy, Edg. HA8 .54 B7
Burnt Oak Flds, Edg. HA8 .54 C7
Burnt Oak La, Sid. DA15 .158 A6
Burntwood Cl, SW18 . . .167 G1
Burntwood Gra Rd,
SW18 . . . . .167 G1
Burntwood La, SW17 . . .167 H2
Burntwood Vw, SE19
  off Bowley La 170 C5

Buross St, E1
  off Commercial
  Rd 112/113 E6
Burrage Gro, SE18 . . . . .137 F4
Burrage Pl, SE18 . . . . . .137 E5
Burrage Rd, SE18 . . . . . .137 F6
Burrard Rd, E16 . . . . .115 H6
NW6 . . . . .90 D7
Burr Cl, E1 . . . . .29 H1
Bexleyheath DA7 . . . . .159 F3
Burrell Cl, Croy. CR0 . . .189 H6
Edgware HA8 . . . . .54 B2
Burrell Row, Beck. BR3
  off High St 190 A2
Burrell St, SE1 . . . . .27 G1
Burrells Wf Sq, E14 . . . .134 B5
Burrell Twr, E10 . . . . .78 A7
Burritt Rd, Kings.T. KT1 .182 A2
Burroughs, The, NW4 . . .71 H5
Burroughs Gdns, NW4 . . .71 H4
Burroughs Par, NW4
  off The Burroughs 71 H4
Burrow Cl, Chig. IG7
  off Burrow Rd 65 J5
Burrow Grn, Chig. IG7 . . .65 J5
Burrow Rd, SE22 . . . . . .152 B4
Chigwell IG7 . . . . .65 J5
Burrows Ms, SE1 . . . . . . .27 G3
Burrows Rd, NW10 . . . . .107 J3
Burrow Wk, SE21
  off Rosendale Rd 151 J7
Burr Rd, SW18 . . . . .148 D7
Bursar St, SE1 . . . . .28 D2
Bursdon Cl, Sid. DA15 . .175 J2
Burslem Rd, Enf. EN3 . . .45 G4
Burslem St, E1 . . . . .21 J4
Burstock Rd, SW15 . . . .148 B4
Burston Rd, SW15 . . . . .148 A5
Burston Vil, SW15
  off St. John's Av 148 A5
Burstow Rd, SW20 . . . . .184 B1
Burtenshaw Rd, T.Ditt.
KT7 . . . . .180 D7
Burtley Cl, N4 . . . . .93 J1
Burton Cl, Chess. KT9 . .195 G2
Thornton Heath CR7 . .188 A3
Burton Ct, SW3
  off Franklin's Row 129 J5
Burton Gdns, Houns.
TW5 . . . . .143 F1
Burton Gro, SE17 . . . . . . .36 B4
Burtonhole Cl, NW7 . . . . .56 A4
Burtonhole La, NW7 . . . . .56 B4
Burton La, SW9 . . . . .151 G2
Burton Ms, SW1 . . . . .32 C2
Burton Pl, WC1 . . . . .9 J4
Burton Rd, E18 . . . . .79 H3
NW6 . . . . .90 C7
SW9 . . . . .151 H2
Kingston upon Thames
KT2 . . . . .163 H7
Loughton IG10 . . . . .49 F4
Burtons Rd, Hmptn.
(Hmptn.H.) TW12 . . . .161 H4
Burton St, WC1 . . . . .9 J4
Burt Rd, E16 . . . . .135 J1
Burtwell La, SE27 . . . . . .170 A4
Burwash Ho, SE1 . . . . . . .28 C4
Burwash Rd, SE18 . . . . .137 G5
Burwell Av, Grnf. UB6 . . .86 B6
Burwell Cl, E1
  off Bigland St 112/113 E6
Burwell Ind Est, E10 . . . .95 H1
Burwell Rd, E10 . . . . .95 H1
Burwell Wk, E3 . . . . .114 A4
Burwood Av, Brom.
BR2 . . . . .205 H2
Pinner HA5 . . . . .66 C5
Burwood Cl, Surb. KT6 .196 A1
Burwood Pl, W2 . . . . .15 H3
Bury Cl, SE16
  off Rotherhithe St . . .133 G1
Bury Ct, EC3 . . . . .20 E3
Bury Gro, Mord. SM4 . . .184 E5
Bury Pl, WC1 . . . . .18 A2
Bury Rd, E4 . . . . .47 E5
N22 . . . . .75 G3
Dagenham RM10 . . . .101 H5
Bury St, EC3 . . . . .20 E4
N9 . . . . .60 D1
SW1 . . . . .25 F1
Bury St W, N9 . . . . .44 A7
Bury Wk, SW3 . . . . .31 G2
Busbridge Ho, E14
  off Brabazon St 114 A5
Busby Ms, NW5
  off Torriano Av 92 D6
Busby Pl, NW5 . . . . .92 D6
Busby St, E2 . . . . .13 G5
Bushbaby Cl, SE1 . . . . . . .28 D6

Bushberry Rd, E9 . . . . . . .95 H6
Bush Cl, Ilf. IG2 . . . . .81 G5
Bush Cotts, SW18
  off Putney Br Rd 148 D5
Bush Ct, W12
  off Shepherds Bush
  Grn 128 A2
Bushell Cl, SW2 . . . . .169 F2
Bushell Grn, Bushey
(Bushey Hth.) WD23 . .52 A2
Bushell St, E1 . . . . .29 J2
Bushell Way, Chis. BR7 . .174 D5
Bushey Av, E18 . . . . .79 F3
Orpington BR5 . . . . . . .193 G7
Bushey Cl, E4 . . . . .62 C3
Bushey Ct, SW20 . . . . . .183 H2
Bushey Down, SW12
  off Bedford Hill 168 B2
BUSHEY HEATH, Bushey .52 B1
Bushey Hill Rd, SE5 . . . .152 B1
Bushey La, Sutt. SM1 . . .198 D4
Bushey Lees, Sid. DA15
  off Fen Gro 157 J6
BUSHEY MEAD, SW20 . .184 A3
Bushey Rd, E13 . . . . .115 J2
N15 . . . . .76 B6
SW20 . . . . .183 H3
Croydon CR0 . . . . .204 A2
Hayes UB3 . . . . .121 H4
Sutton SM1 . . . . .198 E4
Bushey Way, Beck. BR3 .190 D6
Bushfield Cl, Edg. HA8 . .54 B3
Bushfield Cres, Edg. HA8 .54 B3
Bushfields, Loug. IG10 . .48 D5
Bush Gro, NW9 . . . . .70 C7
Stanmore HA7 . . . . .69 G1
Bushgrove Rd, Dag.
RM8 . . . . .100 D4
Bush Hill, N21 . . . . .43 J7
BUSH HILL PARK, Enf. . .44 B5
Bush Hill Rd, N21 . . . . . . .44 A6
Harrow HA3 . . . . .69 J6
Bush Ind Est, NW10 . . . .106 D4
Bush La, EC4 . . . . .20 B5
Bushmead Cl, N15
  off Copperfield Dr 76 C4
Bushmoor Cres, SE18 . .137 F7
Bushnell Rd, SW17 . . . .168 B2
Bush Rd, E8 . . . . .112 E1
E11 . . . . .79 F7
SE8 . . . . .133 G4
Buckhurst Hill IG9 . . . . .64 A4
Richmond TW9 . . . . . .125 J6
Bushway, Dag. RM8 . . . .100 D4
Bushwood, E11 . . . . .97 F1
Bushwood Dr, SE1 . . . . . .37 G2
Bushwood Rd, Rich.
TW9 . . . . .126 A6
★ Bushy Park, Tedd. 180 C1
Bushy Pk, Hmptn.
(Hmptn.H.) TW12 . . . .180 C1
Teddington TW11 . . . .180 C1
Bushy Pk Gdns, Tedd.
TW11 . . . . .180 C1
Bushy Pk Rd, Tedd.
TW11 . . . . .163 E7
Bushy Rd, Tedd. TW11 . .162 C6
★ Business Design Cen,
N1 . . . . .111 G1
Butcher Row, E1 . . . . . . .113 G7
E14 . . . . .113 G7
Butchers Rd, E16 . . . . . .115 G6
Bute Av, Rich. TW10 . . . .163 H2
Bute Ct, Wall. SM6
  off Bute Rd 200 C5
Bute Gdns, W6 . . . . .128 A4
Wallington SM6 . . . . . .200 C5
Bute Gdns W, Wall. SM6 .200 C5
Bute Ms, NW11
  off Northway 73 F4
Bute Rd, Croy. CR0 . . . . .201 G1
Ilford IG6 . . . . .81 E5
Wallington SM6 . . . . . .200 C5
Bute St, SW7 . . . . .31 E1
Bute Wk, N1
  off Marquess Rd 94 A6
Butler Av, Har. HA1 . . . . .68 A7
Butler Cl, Wem. HA0
  off Harrow Rd 86 D4
Butler Pl, SW1 . . . . .25 H5
Butler Rd, NW10
  off Curzon Cres 89 F7
Dagenham RM8 . . . . .100 B4
Harrow HA1 . . . . .67 J7
Butler St, E2
  off Knottisford St 113 F3
Butlers Wf, SE1 . . . . .29 G2
Butterfield Cl, N17
  off Devonshire Rd 59 J6

Butterfield Cl, SE16
  off Wilson Gro 132/133 E2
Twickenham TW1
  off Rugby Rd 144 C6
Butterfields, E17 . . . . .78 C5
Butterfield Sq, E6
  off Harper Rd 116 C6
Butterfly La, SE9 . . . . . . .156 E6
Butterfly Wk, SE5
  off Denmark Hill 152 A1
Butter Hill, Cars. SM5 . .200 A3
Wallington SM6 . . . . . .200 A3
Butteridges Cl, Dag.
RM9 . . . . .119 F1
Buttermere Cl, E15 . . . . . .96 D4
SE1 . . . . .37 F1
Morden SM4 . . . . .184 A6
Buttermere Dr, SW15 . . .148 B5
Buttermere Wk, E8 . . . . . .94 C6
Butterwick, W6 . . . . .127 J4
Butterworth Gdns, Wdf.Grn.
IG8 . . . . .63 G6
Buttesland St, N1 . . . . . . .12 C3
Buttfield Cl, Dag. RM10 .101 H6
Buttmarsh Cl, SE18 . . . .137 E5
Butts, The, Brent. TW8 . .125 G6
Sunbury-on-Thames TW16
  off Elizabeth Gdns . . .178 C3
Buttsbury Rd, Ilf. IG1 . . .99 F5
Butts Cotts, Felt. TW13 . .161 F3
Butts Cres, Felt. TW13 . .161 G3
Butts Piece, Nthlt. UB5
  off Longhook Gdns . . .102 B2
Butts Rd, Brom. BR1 . . .173 E5
Buxhall Cres, E9 . . . . .95 J6
Buxted Rd, E8 . . . . .94 C7
N12 . . . . .57 H5
SE22 . . . . .152 B4
Buxton Cl, Wdf.Grn. IG8 . .64 A6
Buxton Ct, N1 . . . . .12 A3
Buxton Cres, Sutt. SM3 .198 B4
Buxton Dr, E11 . . . . .79 E4
New Malden KT3 . . . . .182 D2
Buxton Gdns, W3 . . . . . .106 B7
Buxton Path, Wat. WD19 . .50 C3
Buxton Rd, E4 . . . . .46 D7
E6 . . . . .116 B3
E15 . . . . .96 E5
E17 . . . . .77 H4
N19 . . . . .92 D1
NW2 . . . . .89 H6
SW14 . . . . .147 E3
Ilford IG2 . . . . .81 H6
Thornton Heath CR7 . .187 H5
Buxton St, E1 . . . . .13 G6
Buzzard Creek Ind Est, Bark.
IG11 . . . . .117 J5
Byam St, SW6 . . . . .149 F2
Byards Cft, SW16 . . . . . .186 D1
Byatt Wk, Hmptn. TW12
  off Victors Dr 160/161 E6
Bychurch End, Tedd. TW11
  off Church Rd 162 C5
Bycroft Rd, Sthl. UB1 . . .103 G4
Bycroft St, SE20
  off Parish La 171 G7
Bycullah Av, Enf. EN2 . . .43 H3
Bycullah Rd, Enf. EN2 . . .43 H3
Bye, The, W3 . . . . .107 E6
Byegrove Rd, SW19 . . . .167 G6
Byeway, The, SW14 . . . .146 C3
Bye Way, The, Har. HA3 . .68 B1
Byeways, Twick. TW2 . . .161 H3
Byeways, The, Surb.
KT5 . . . . .182 A5
Byfeld Gdns, SW13 . . . .147 G1
Byfield Cl, SE16 . . . . .133 H2
Byfield Pas, Islw. TW7 . .144 D3
Byfield Rd, Islw. TW7 . . .144 D3
Byford Cl, E15 . . . . .97 E7
Bygrove, Croy. (New Adgtn.)
CR0 . . . . .204 B6
Bygrove St, E14 . . . . .114 B6
Byland Cl, N21 . . . . .43 F7
Bylands Cl, SE2
  off Finchale Rd 138 B3
SE16
  off Rotherhithe St . . .133 G1
Byne Rd, SE26 . . . . .171 F6
Carshalton SM5 . . . . .199 H2
Bynes Rd, S.Croy. CR2 . .202 A7
Byng Pl, WC1 . . . . .9 H6
Byng Rd, Barn. EN5 . . . . .40 A3
Byng St, E14 . . . . .134 A2
Bynon Av, Bexh. DA7 . . .159 E3
Byre, The, N14
  off Farm La 42 B6
Byre Rd, N14
  off Farm La 42 A6
Byrne Rd, SW12 . . . . . . .168 B1

Byron Av, E12 . . . . .98 B6
  E18 . . . . .79 F3
  NW9 . . . . .70 B4
Borehamwood WD6 . . . .38 A5
Hounslow TW4 . . . . .142 A2
New Malden KT3 . . . . . . .183 G5
Sutton SM1 . . . . .199 G4
Byron Av E, Sutt. SM1 . .199 G4
Byron Cl, E8 . . . . .112 D1
  SE26
    off Porthcawe Rd 171 H4
  SE28 . . . . .138 C1
  Hampton TW12 . . . . . . .161 F4
Byron Ct, W9
  off Lanhill Rd 108 D4
  Enfield EN2
    off Bycullah Rd 43 H2
  Harrow HA1 . . . . .68 B6
Byron Dr, N2 . . . . .73 G6
  Erith DA8 . . . . .139 H7
Byron Gdns, Sutt. SM1 . .199 G4
Byron Hill Rd, Har. HA2 . .86 A1
Byron Ho, Beck. BR3 . . . .172 A6
Byron Ms, NW3 . . . . .91 H5
  W9 off Shirland Rd 108 D4
Byron Rd, E10 . . . . .96 B1
  E17 . . . . .78 A3
  NW2 . . . . .89 H2
  NW7 . . . . .55 G5
  W5 . . . . .125 J1
  Harrow HA1 . . . . .68 B6
  Harrow (Wldste.) HA3 . .68 C2
  Wembley HA0 . . . . .87 F3
Byron St, E14
    off St. Leonards Rd . .114 C6
Byron Ter, N9 . . . . .45 F7
Byron Way, Nthlt. UB5 . .102 E3
  West Drayton UB7 . . . .120 C4
Bysouth Cl, N15 . . . . .76 A4
  Ilford IG5 . . . . .80 E1
By the Wd, Wat. WD19 . . .50 D2
Bythorn St, SW9 . . . . . . .151 F3
Byton Rd, SW17 . . . . . . .167 J6
Byward Av, Felt. TW14 . .142 C6
Byward St, EC3 . . . . .20 E6
Bywater Pl, SE16 . . . . . . .133 H1
Bywater St, SW3 . . . . . . .31 J3
Byway, The, Epsom
  KT19 . . . . .197 F4
Bywell Pl, W1 . . . . .17 F2
Bywood Av, Croy. CR0 . .189 F6
Byworth Wk, N19
    off Courtauld Rd 92 D1

C

Cabbell St, NW1 . . . . .15 G2
★ Cabinet War Rooms,
  SW1 . . . . .25 J3
Cabinet Way, E4 . . . . .61 J6
Cable Pl, SE10
    off Diamond Ter 154 C1
Cable St, E1 . . . . .21 H5
Cable Trade Pk, SE7 . . . .135 J4
Cabot Pl, E14 . . . . .134 A1
Cabot Sq, E14 . . . . .134 A1
Cabot Way, E6
    off Parr Rd 116 A1
Cabul Rd, SW11 . . . . .149 H2
Cactus Cl, SE15
    off Lyndhurst Gro 152 B2
Cactus Wk, W12
    off Du Cane Rd 107 F6
Cadbury Cl, Islw. TW7 . .144 D1
Cadbury Way, SE16 . . . . .29 G6
Caddington Cl, Barn.
  EN4 . . . . .41 H5
Caddington Rd, NW2 . . . .90 B3
Caddis Cl, Stan. HA7
    off Daventer Dr 52 C7
Cadell Cl, E2 . . . . .13 G2
Cade Rd, SE10 . . . . .154 D1
Cader Rd, SW18 . . . . . . .149 F6
Cadet Dr, SE1 . . . . .37 G3
Cadet Pl, SE10 . . . . .134 E5
Cadiz Rd, Dag. RM10 . . .101 J7
Cadiz St, SE17 . . . . .36 A4
Cadley Ter, SE23 . . . . . . .171 F2
Cadman Cl, SW9
    off Langton Rd 131 H7
Cadmer Cl, N.Mal. KT3 . .182 E4
Cadmus Cl, SW4
    off Aristotle Rd 150 D3
Cadnam Pt, SW15
    off Dilton Gdns 165 H1
Cadogan Cl, E9
    off Cadogan Ter 95 J7
  Beckenham BR3
    off Albemarle Rd 190 D1

Cadogan Cl, Har. HA2 . . .85 H4
  Teddington TW11 . . . . .162 B5
Cadogan Ct, Sutt. SM2 . .199 E6
Cadogan Gdns, E18 . . . . .79 H3
Cadogan Gdns, N3 . . . . . .72 E1
  N21 . . . . .43 G5
  SW3 . . . . .32 A1
Cadogan Gate, SW1 . . . . .32 A1
Cadogan La, SW1 . . . . . . .24 B6
Cadogan Pl, SW1 . . . . . . .24 A5
Cadogan Rd, Surb. KT6 .181 G5
Cadogan Sq, SW1 . . . . . . .24 A6
Cadogan St, SW3 . . . . . . .31 J2
Cadogan Ter, E9 . . . . .95 J6
Cadoxton Av, N15 . . . . . . .76 C6
Cadwallon Rd, SE9 . . . . .175 E2
Caedmon Rd, N7 . . . . .93 F4
Caerleon Cl, Sid. DA14 . .176 C5
Caerleon Ter, SE2
    off Blithdale Rd 138 B4
Caernarvon Cl, Mitch.
  CR4 . . . . .186 E3
Caernarvon Dr, Ilf. IG5 . . .80 D1
Caesars Wk, Mitch. CR4 .185 J5
Cahill St, EC1 . . . . .12 A6
Cahir St, E14 . . . . .134 B4
Cains La, Felt. TW14 . . . .141 H5
Caird St, W10 . . . . .108 B3
Cairn Av, W5 . . . . .125 G1
Cairndale Cl, Brom. BR1 .173 F7
Cairnes Ms, SE18
    off Shooter's Hill Rd . .156 B1
Cairnfield Av, NW2 . . . . . .89 E3
Cairngorm Cl, Tedd. TW11
    off Vicarage Rd 162 D5
Cairns Av, Wdf.Grn. IG8 . .64 B6
Cairns Rd, SW11 . . . . . . .149 H5
Cairn Way, Stan. HA7 . . . .52 C6
Cairo New Rd, Croy.
  CR0 . . . . .201 H2
Cairo Rd, E17 . . . . .78 A4
Caishowe Rd, Borwd.
  WD6 . . . . .38 B1
Caistor Ms, SW12
    off Caistor Rd 150 B7
Caistor Pk Rd, E15 . . . . .115 F1
Caistor Rd, SW12 . . . . . .150 B7
Caithness Gdns, Sid.
  DA15 . . . . .157 J6
Caithness Rd, W14 . . . . .128 A4
  Mitcham CR4 . . . . .168 B7
Calabria Rd, N5 . . . . .93 H6
Calais Gate, SE5
    off Calais St 151 H1
Calais St, SE5 . . . . .151 H1
Calbourne Rd, SW12 . . .149 J7
Calcott Wk, SE9 . . . . . . .174 A4
Caldbeck Av, Wor.Pk.
  KT4 . . . . .197 G2
Caldecot Rd, SE5 . . . . . .151 J2
Caldecott Way, E5 . . . . . . .95 G3
Calder Av, Grnf. UB6 . . . .104 C2
Calder Cl, Enf. EN1 . . . . . .44 B3
Calder Gdns, Edg. HA8 . . .70 A3
Calderon Pl, W10
    off St. Quintin Gdns . .107 J5
Calderon Rd, E11 . . . . . . .96 C4
Calder Rd, Mord. SM4 . .185 F5
Caldervale Rd, SW4 . . . .150 D5
Calderwood St, SE18 . . .136 D4
Caldicot Gm, NW9
    off Snowdon Dr . . .70/71 E6
Caldwell Rd, Wat.
  WD19 . . . . .50 D4
Caldwell St, SW9 . . . . . .131 F7
Caldwell Yd, EC4
    off Upper Thames St . .111 J7
Caldy Rd, Belv. DA17 . . .139 H3
Caldy Wk, N1
    off Clephane Rd 93 J6
Caleb St, SE1 . . . . .27 J3
Caledonian Cl, Ilf. IG3 . .100 B1
Caledonian Rd, N1 . . . . . .10 B2
  N7 . . . . .93 F5
Caledonian Wf, E14 . . . .134 D4
Caledonia St, N1 . . . . .10 B2
Caledon Rd, E6 . . . . .116 B1
  Wallington SM6 . . . . . .200 A4
Cale St, SW3 . . . . .31 G3
Caletock Way, SE10 . . . .135 F5
Calico Row, SW11
    off York Pl 149 F3
Calidore Cl, SW2
    off Endymion Rd 151 F6
California La, Bushey
  (Bushey Hth.) WD23 . . .52 A1
California Rd, N.Mal.
  KT3 . . . . .182 C4
Callaby Ter, N1
    off Wakeham St 94 A6

Callaghan Cl, SE13
    off Glenton Rd . .154/155 E4
Callander Rd, SE6 . . . . . .172 B2
Callard Av, N13 . . . . .59 H5
Callcott Rd, NW6 . . . . .90 C7
Callcott St, W8
    off Hillgate Pl 128 D1
Callendar Rd, SW7 . . . . . .22 E5
Callingham Cl, E14
    off Wallwood St 113 J5
Callis Fm Cl, Stai. (Stanw.)
  TW19 off Bedfont Rd .140 B6
Callis Rd, E17 . . . . .77 J6
Callow St, SW3 . . . . .30 D5
Calmont Rd, Brom. BR1 .172 D6
Calne Av, Ilf. IG5 . . . . .80 E1
Calonne Rd, SW19 . . . . .166 A4
Calshot Rd, Houns.
  (Hthrw.Air.) TW6 . . . . .140 D2
Calshot St, N1 . . . . .10 C1
Calshot Way, Enf. EN2 . . .43 H3
  Hounslow (Hthrw.Air.) TW6
    off Calshot Rd 140/141 D2
Calthorpe Gdns, Edg. HA8
    off Jesmond Way 53 H5
  Sutton SM1 . . . . .199 F3
Calthorpe St, WC1 . . . . . .10 D5
Calton Av, SE21 . . . . .152 B5
Calton Rd, Barn. EN5 . . . .41 F6
Calverley Cl, Beck. BR3 .172 B6
Calverley Cres, Dag.
  RM10 . . . . .101 G2
Calverley Gdns, Har. HA3 .69 G7
Calverley Gro, N19 . . . . . .92 D1
Calverley Rd, Epsom
  KT17 . . . . .197 G6
Calvert Av, E2 . . . . .13 E4
Calvert Cl, Belv. DA17 . .139 G4
  Sidcup DA14 . . . . .176 E6
Calverton, SE5 . . . . .36 C5
Calverton Rd, E6 . . . . . . .116 D1
Calvert Rd, SE10 . . . . . . .135 F5
  Barnet EN5 . . . . .40 A2
Calvert's Bldgs, SE1 . . . .28 B2
Calvert St, NW1
    off Chalcot Rd 110 A1
Calvin St, E1 . . . . .13 F6
Calydon Rd, SE7 . . . . . . .135 H5
Calypso Way, SE16 . . . . .133 J3
Camac Rd, Twick. TW2 . .162 A1
Cambalt Rd, SW15 . . . . .148 A5
Camberley Av, SW20 . . .183 H2
  Enfield EN1 . . . . .44 B4
Camberley Rd, Houns.
  (Hthrw.Air.) TW6 . . . . .140 D3
Cambert Way, SE3 . . . . . .155 H4
CAMBERWELL, SE5 . . . .151 J7
Camberwell Ch St, SE5 .152 A1
Camberwell Glebe, SE5 .152 A1
Camberwell Grn, SE5 . . .152 A1
Camberwell Gro, SE5 . . .152 A1
Camberwell New Rd,
  SE5 . . . . .35 E6
Camberwell Pas, SE5
    off Camberwell Grn . .151 J1
Camberwell Rd, SE5 . . . . .36 A6
Camberwell Sta Rd, SE5 .151 J1
Cambeys Rd, Dag. RM10 .101 H5
Camborne Av, W13 . . . . .125 E2
Camborne Cl, Houns.
  (Hthrw. Air.) TW6
    off Camborne Rd S . .140 D3
Camborne Ms, W11
    off St. Marks Rd 108 B6
Camborne Rd, SW18 . . .148 D7
  Croydon CR0 . . . . .188 D7
  Morden SM4 . . . . .184 A5
  Sidcup DA14 . . . . .176 C3
  Sutton SM2 . . . . .198 D7
  Welling DA16 . . . . .157 J2
Camborne Rd N, Houns.
  (Hthrw. Air.) TW6
    off Camborne Rd S . .140 D3
Camborne Rd S, Houns.
  (Hthrw. Air.) TW6 . . . . .140 D3
Camborne Way, Houns.
  TW5 . . . . .143 G1
  Hounslow (Hthrw.Air.) TW6
    off Camborne Rd S . .140 D3
Cambourne Av, N9 . . . . . .45 G7
Cambray Rd, SW12 . . . . .168 C1
  Orpington BR6 . . . . . . .193 J7
Cambria Cl, Houns.TW3 .143 G4
  Sidcup DA15 . . . . .175 G1
Cambria Ct, Felt.TW14
    off Hounslow Rd 142 B7
Cambria Gdns, Stai.
  TW19 . . . . .140 B7
Cambria Rd, Ilf. IG2 . . . . .81 H5

Cambrian Cl, SE27 . . . . .169 H3
Cambrian Grn, NW9
    off Snowdon Dr . . .70/71 E5
Cambrian Rd, E10 . . . . . . .78 A7
  Richmond TW10 . . . . . .145 J6
Cambria Rd, SE5 . . . . . . .151 J3
Cambria St, SW6 . . . . . . .129 E7
Cambridge Av, NW6 . . . .108 D2
  Greenford UB6 . . . . .86 C5
  New Malden KT3 . . . . .183 F2
  Welling DA16 . . . . .157 J4
Cambridge Barracks Rd,
  SE18 . . . . .136 C4
Cambridge Circ, WC2 . . . .17 J4
Cambridge Cl, E17 . . . . . .77 J6
  N22 off Pellatt Gro 75 G1
  NW10
    off Lawrence Way 88 C3
  SW20 . . . . .183 H1
  Hounslow TW4 . . . . . . .143 E4
  West Drayton UB7 . . . .120 A6
Cambridge Cotts, Rich.
  TW9 . . . . .126 A6
Cambridge Cres, E2 . . . .112 E2
  Teddington TW11 . . . . .162 D5
Cambridge Dr, SE12 . . . .155 G5
  Ruislip HA4 . . . . .84 C2
Cambridge Gdns, N10 . . .74 B1
  N13 . . . . .59 G5
  N17 off Great Cambridge
    Rd 60 A7
  N21 . . . . .44 A7
  NW6 . . . . .108 D2
  W10 . . . . .108 B6
  Enfield EN1 . . . . .44 D2
  Kingston upon Thames
  KT1 . . . . .182 A2
Cambridge Gate, NW1 . . .8 E4
Cambridge Gate Ms, NW1 .8 E4
Cambridge Grn, SE9 . . . .174 E1
Cambridge Gro, SE20 . . .188 E1
  W6 . . . . .127 H4
Cambridge Gro Rd, Kings.T.
  KT1 . . . . .182 A2
Cambridge Heath Rd, E1 .113 E2
  E2 . . . . .113 E2
Cambridge Mans, SW11
    off Cambridge Rd 149 J1
Cambridge Par, Enf. EN1
    off Great Cambridge
    Rd 44 D1
Cambridge Pk, E11 . . . . . .79 G7
  Twickenham TW1 . . . . .145 G7
Cambridge Pk Rd, E11
    off Cambridge Pk 79 F7
Cambridge Pl, W8 . . . . . . .22 B4
Cambridge Rd, E4 . . . . . . .62 D1
  E11 . . . . .79 F6
  NW6 . . . . .108 D3
  SE20 . . . . .188 E3
  SW11 . . . . .149 J1
  SW13 . . . . .147 F2
  SW20 . . . . .183 G1
  W7 . . . . .124 C2
  Barking IG11 . . . . .99 F7
  Bromley BR1 . . . . .173 G7
  Carshalton SM5 . . . . . .199 H6
  Hampton TW12 . . . . . .161 F7
  Harrow HA2 . . . . .67 G5
  Hounslow TW4 . . . . . . .143 E4
  Ilford IG3 . . . . .99 H1
  Kingston upon Thames
  KT1 . . . . .181 J2
  Mitcham CR4 . . . . .186 C3
  New Malden KT3 . . . . .182 E4
  Richmond TW9 . . . . . . .126 A7
  Sidcup DA14 . . . . .175 H4
  Southall UB1 . . . . .123 F1
  Teddington TW11 . . . . .162 C4
  Twickenham TW1 . . . . .145 G6
  Walton-on-Thames
  KT12 . . . . .178 B6
  West Molesey KT8 . . . .179 F4
Cambridge Rd N, W4 . . .126 B5
Cambridge Rd S, W4 . . .126 B5
Cambridge Row, SE18 . .137 E5
Cambridge Sq, W2 . . . . . .15 G3
Cambridge St, SW1 . . . . .32 E2
Cambridge Ter, N13 . . . . .59 G5
  NW1 . . . . .8 E4
Cambridge Ter Ms, NW1 . .8 E4
Cambstone Cl, N11 . . . . . .58 A2
Cambus Cl, Hayes UB4 .103 E5
Cambus Rd, E16 . . . . . . .115 G5
Camdale Rd, SE18 . . . . . .137 J7
★ Camden Arts Cen,
  NW3 . . . . .91 E5
Camden Av, Felt.TW13 . .160 C2
  Hayes UB4 . . . . .102 C7
Camden Cl, Chis. BR7 . . .175 F7

Camden Gdns, NW1
off Kentish Town Rd . . .92 B7
Sutton SM1 . . . . .198 E5
Thornton Heath CR7 . .187 H3
Camden Gro, Chis. BR7 .175 E6
Camden High St, NW1 . .110 B1
Camden Hill Rd, SE19 . . .170 B6
Camdenhurst St, E14 . . .113 H6
Camden La, N7
off Rowstock Gdns . . .92 C6
★ Camden Lock Mkt &
Waterbuses, NW1 . . . . . .92 B7
Camden Lock Pl, NW1
off Chalk Fm Rd 92 B7
Camden Ms, NW1 . . . . . . .92 D6
Camden Pk Rd, NW1 . . . .92 D6
Chislehurst BR7 . . . . . .174 C7
Camden Pas, N1 . . . . . . .111 H1
Camden Rd, E11 . . . . .79 H6
E17 . . . . .77 J6
N7 . . . . .92 D5
NW1 . . . . .92 C7
Bexley DA5 . . . . .177 F1
Carshalton SM5 . . . . . . .199 J4
Sutton SM1 . . . . .198 D5
Camden Row, SE3 . . . . .155 E2
Camden Sq, NW1 . . . . . . .92 D6
SE15 off Watts St 152 C1
Camden St, NW1 . . . . . . .92 C7
Camden Ter, NW1
off North Vil 92 D6
CAMDEN TOWN, NW1 . .110 C1
Camden Wk, N1 . . . . . . .111 H1
Camden Way, Chis.
BR7 . . . . .174 C7
Thornton Heath CR7 . .187 H3
Camelford Wk, W11
off Lancaster Rd 108 B6
Camel Gro, Kings.T.
KT2 . . . . .163 G5
Camellia Ct, Wdf.Grn. IG8
off The Bridle Path .62/63 E7
Camellia Pl, Twick. TW2 . .143 H7
Camellia St, SW8 . . . . . .130 E7
Camelot Cl, SE28 . . . . . .137 G2
SW19 . . . . .166 D4
Camelot Ho, N9
off Salisbury Rd 60 D3
Camelot St, SE15
off Bird in Bush
Rd 132/133 E7
Camel Rd, E16 . . . . .136 A1
Camera Pl, SW10 . . . . . . .30 E5
Cameron Cl, N18 . . . . . . .61 E4
N20 off Myddelton Pk . .57 H2
Cameron Pl, E1
off Varden St 112/113 E6
Cameron Rd, SE6 . . . . . .171 J2
Bromley BR2 . . . . .191 G4
Croydon CR0 . . . . .187 H6
Ilford IG3 . . . . .99 H1
Cameron Sq, Mitch.
CR4 . . . . .185 H1
Camerton Cl, E8
off Buttermere Wk 94 C6
Camgate Cen, Stai. (Stanw.)
TW19 . . . . .140 C6
Camilla Rd, SE16 . . . . . .132 E4
Camille Cl, SE25 . . . . . . .188 D3
Camlan Rd, Brom. BR1 . .173 F4
Camlet St, E2 . . . . .13 F5
Camlet Way, Barn. EN4 . . .40 D2
Camley St, NW1 . . . . .9 J1
★ Camley St Natural Pk,
NW1 . . . . .9 J1
Camm Gdns, Kings.T. KT1
off Church Rd 181 J2
Thames Ditton KT7 . . .180 B7
Camms Ter, Dag. RM10 .101 J5
Camomile Av, Mitch.
CR4 . . . . .185 J1
Camomile St, EC3 . . . . . .20 D3
Campana Rd, SW6 . . . . .148 D1
Campbell Av, Ilf. IG6 . . . .81 F4
Campbell Cl, SE18
off Moordown 156 D1
SW16 . . . . .168 D4
Ruislip HA4 . . . . .66 A6
Twickenham TW2 . . . . .162 A2
Campbell Ct, N17 . . . . . . .76 C1
Campbell Cft, Edg. HA8 . .54 A5
Campbell Gordon Way,
NW2 . . . . .89 H4
Campbell Rd, E3 . . . . . . .114 A3
E6 . . . . .116 B1
E15 off Trevelyan Rd . . .97 F4
E17 . . . . .77 J4
N17 . . . . .76 D1
W7 . . . . .104 B7
Croydon CR0 . . . . .187 H7

Campbell Rd, East Molesey KT8
off Hampton Ct Rd . . .180 C3
Twickenham TW2 . . . . .162 A2
Campbell Wk, N1
off Outram Pl 110/111 E1
Campdale Rd, N7 . . . . . . .92 D3
Campden Cres, Dag.
RM8 . . . . .100 B4
Wembley HA0 . . . . .87 E2
Campden Gro, W8 . . . . . .128 D2
Campden Hill Ct, W8
off Campden Hill Rd . .128 D2
Campden Hill Gdns, W8 .128 D1
Campden Hill Gate, W8
off Duchess of
Bedford's Wk 128 D2
Campden Hill Pl, W11
off Holland Pk Av 128 C1
Campden Hill Rd, W8 . . .128 D1
Campden Hill Sq, W8 . . .128 C1
Campden Hill Twrs, W11
off Notting Hill Gate .128 D1
Campden Ho Cl, W8
off Hornton St 128 D2
Campden Rd, S.Croy.
CR2 . . . . .202 B5
Campden St, W8 . . . . . . .128 D1
Campen Cl, SW19
off Queensmere Rd .166 B2
Camperdown St, E1 . . . . .21 G4
Campfield Rd, SE9 . . . . .156 A7
Campion Cl, E6 . . . . .116 C7
Croydon CR0 . . . . .202 B4
Harrow HA3 . . . . .69 J6
Campion Gdns, Wdf.Grn.
IG8 . . . . .63 G5
Campion Pl, SE28 . . . . . .138 B1
Campion Rd, SW15 . . . . .147 J4
Isleworth TW7 . . . . . . .144 C1
Campion Ter, NW2 . . . . . .90 A3
Campion Way, Edg. HA8 . .54 C4
Camplin Rd, Har. HA3 . . .69 H5
Camplin St, SE14 . . . . . .133 G7
Camp Rd, SW19 . . . . . . .165 J5
Campsbourne, The, N8
off High St 74/75 E4
Campsbourne Rd, N8 . . .75 E3
Campsey Gdns, Dag.
RM9 . . . . .100 B7
Campsey Rd, Dag. RM9 .100 B7
Campsfield Rd, N8
off Campsbourne
Rd 74/75 E3
Campshill Pl, SE13
off Campshill Rd 154 C5
Campshill Rd, SE13 . . . .154 C5
Campus Rd, E17 . . . . .77 J6
Campus Way, NW4
off Greyhound Hill 71 H3
Camp Vw, SW19 . . . . . . .165 H5
Cam Rd, E15 . . . . .114 D1
Camrose Av, Edg. HA8 . . .69 J1
Erith DA8 . . . . .139 H6
Feltham TW13 . . . . .160 B4
Camrose Cl, Croy. CR0 . .189 H7
Morden SM4 . . . . .184 D4
Camrose St, SE2 . . . . . . .138 A5
Canada Av, N18 . . . . .59 J6
Canada Cres, W3 . . . . . .106 C5
Canada Est, SE16 . . . . . .133 F3
Canada Gdns, SE13 . . . .154 C5
Canada Rd, W3 . . . . .106 C4
Canada Sq, E14 . . . . .134 B1
Canada St, SE16 . . . . . . .133 G2
Canada Way, W12 . . . . . .107 H7
Canadian Av, SE6 . . . . . .172 B1
Canal App, SE8 . . . . .133 H6
Canal Cl, E1 . . . . .113 H4
W10 . . . . .108 A4
Canal Gro, SE15 . . . . .37 J5
Canal Path, E2 . . . . .112 C1
Canal St, SE5 . . . . .36 B6
Canal Wk, N1 . . . . .112 A1
SE26 . . . . .171 F5
Croydon CR0 . . . . .188 B6
Canal Way, N1
off Packington Sq 111 J2
NW1 . . . . .7 G4
NW8 . . . . .7 F5
NW10 . . . . .107 F4
W10 . . . . .108 A4
Canal Way Wk, W10 . . . .108 A4
Canberra Cl, NW4 . . . . . . .71 G3
Canberra Dr, Hayes UB4 .102 C3
Northolt UB5 . . . . .102 C3
Canberra Rd, E6
off Barking Rd 116 C1
SE7 . . . . .135 J6
W13 . . . . .124 D1
Bexleyheath DA7 . . . . .138 D6

Canberra Rd, Houn. (Hthrw.Air.)
TW6 . . . . .140 D3
Canbury Av, Kings.T.
KT2 . . . . .181 J1
Canbury Ms, SE26
off Wells Pk Rd 170 D3
Canbury Pk Rd, Kings.T.
KT2 . . . . .181 H1
Canbury Pas, Kings.T.
KT2 . . . . .181 G1
Cancell Rd, SW9 . . . . . . .151 G1
Candahar Rd, SW11 . . . .149 H2
Candler St, N15 . . . . .76 A6
Candover Cl, West Dr.
UB7 . . . . .120 A7
Candover St, W1 . . . . .17 F2
Candy St, E3 . . . . .113 J1
Cane Cl, Wall. SM6 . . . . .201 E7
Caney Ms, NW2
off Claremont Rd 90 A2
Canfield Dr, Ruis. HA4 . . .84 B5
Canfield Gdns, NW6 . . . . .91 F7
Canfield Pl, NW6
off Canfield Gdns 91 F6
Canfield Rd, Wdf.Grn.
IG8 . . . . .64 B7
Canford Av, Nthlt. UB5 . .103 E1
Canford Cl, Enf. EN2 . . . .43 G2
Canford Gdns, N.Mal.
KT3 . . . . .182 D6
Canford Pl, Tedd. TW11 .163 E6
Canford Rd, SW11 . . . . . .150 A5
Canham Rd, SE25 . . . . . .188 B3
W3 . . . . .126 E2
Canmore Gdns, SW16 . .168 C7
Cann Hall Rd, E11 . . . . . . .96 E4
Canning Cres, N22 . . . . . .75 F1
Canning Cross, SE5 . . . .152 B2
Canning Pas, W8 . . . . . . .22 C5
Canning Pl, W8 . . . . .22 C5
Canning Pl Ms, W8 . . . . . .22 C5
Canning Rd, E15 . . . . . . .114 E2
E17 . . . . .77 H4
N5 . . . . .93 H3
Croydon CR0 . . . . .202 C2
Harrow HA3 . . . . .68 C3
Cannington Rd, Dag.
RM9 . . . . .100 C6
CANNING TOWN, E16 . .115 G6
Cannizaro Rd, SW19 . . . .165 J6
Cannonbury Av, Pnr. HA5 .66 D6
Cannon Cl, SW20 . . . . . .183 J3
Hampton TW12
off Hanworth Rd 161 H6
Cannon Dr, E14 . . . . .114 A7
Cannon Hill, N14 . . . . .58 D3
NW6 . . . . .90 D5
Cannon Hill La, SW20 . .184 B3
Cannon La, NW3 . . . . .91 G3
Pinner HA5 . . . . .84 E1
Cannon Pl, NW3 . . . . .91 G3
SE7 . . . . .136 B5
Cannon Rd, N14 . . . . .58 E3
Bexleyheath DA7 . . . . .159 E1
Cannon St, EC4 . . . . .19 J4
Cannon St Rd, E1 . . . . . .112 E6
Cannon Trd Est, Wem.
HA9 . . . . .88 B4
Cannon Way, W.Mol.
KT8 . . . . .179 G4
Cannon Wf Business Cen,
SE8 . . . . .133 H4
Cannon Workshops, E14
off Cannon Dr 114 A7
Canon Av, Rom. RM6 . . . .82 C5
Canon Beck Rd, SE16 . . .133 F2
Canonbie Rd, SE23 . . . . .153 F7
CANONBURY, N1 . . . . . . .93 J6
Canonbury Cres, N1 . . . . .93 J7
Canonbury Gro, N1 . . . . . .93 J7
Canonbury La, N1 . . . . . . .93 H7
Canonbury Pk N, N1 . . . . .93 J6
Canonbury Pk S, N1 . . . . .93 J6
Canonbury Pl, N1 . . . . . . .93 H6
Canonbury Rd, N1 . . . . . . .93 H6
Enfield EN1 . . . . .44 B1
Canonbury Sq, N1 . . . . . . .93 H7
Canonbury St, N1 . . . . . . .93 J7
Canonbury Vil, N1 . . . . . . .93 H7
Canonbury Yd, N1
off New N Rd 111 J1
Canonbury Yd W, N1
off Compton Rd 93 H6
Canon Mohan Cl, N14
off Farm La 42 B6
Canon Rd, Brom. BR1 . .191 J3
Canon Row, SW1 . . . . . . .26 A4
Canons Cl, N2 . . . . .73 G7
Edgware HA8 . . . . .53 J6
Canons Cor, Edg. HA8 . . .53 H4

Canons Dr, Edg. HA8 . . . .53 H6
Canonsleigh Rd, Dag.
RM9 . . . . .100 B7
CANONS PARK, Edg. 53 H7
Canons Pk Cl, Edg. HA8
off Donnefield Av 53 H7
Canon St, N1 . . . . .111 J1
Canons Wk, Croy. CR0 . .203 G3
Canopus Way, Nthwd.
HA6 . . . . .50 A4
Staines TW19 . . . . .140 B7
Canrobert St, E2 . . . . . . .112 E3
Cantelowes Rd, NW1 . . . .92 D6
Canterbury Av, Ilf. IG1 . . .80 B7
Sidcup DA15 . . . . .176 C2
Canterbury Cl, E6
off Harper Rd 116 C6
Beckenham BR3 . . . . . .190 B1
Chigwell IG7 . . . . .65 J3
Greenford UB6 . . . . . .103 H6
Canterbury Cres, SW9 . .151 G3
Canterbury Gro, SE27 . .169 H3
Canterbury Ho, Borwd.
WD6 . . . . .38 A2
Canterbury Pl, SE17 . . . . .35 H2
Canterbury Rd, E10 . . . . .78 C7
NW6 . . . . .108 D2
Borehamwood WD6 . . .38 A2
Croydon CR0 . . . . .187 F7
Feltham TW13 . . . . . . .161 E3
Harrow HA1, HA2 . . . . .67 H5
Morden SM4 . . . . .185 F5
Canterbury Ter, NW6 . . .108 D2
Cantley Gdns, SE19 . . . .188 C1
Ilford IG2 . . . . .81 F6
Cantley Rd, W7 . . . . .124 D3
Canton St, E14 . . . . .114 A6
Cantrell Rd, E3 . . . . .113 J4
Cantwell Rd, SE18 . . . . .136 E7
Canute Gdns, SE16 . . . . .133 G4
Canvey St, SE1 . . . . .27 H1
Cape Cl, Bark. IG11
off North St 99 F6
Capel Av, Wall. SM6 . . . .201 F5
Capel Cl, N20 . . . . .57 F3
Bromley BR2 . . . . .206 B1
Capel Ct, EC2 . . . . .20 C4
SE20 off Melvin Rd . . .189 F1
Capel Gdns, Ilf. IG3 . . . . .99 J4
Pinner HA5 . . . . .67 F4
Capel Pt, E7 . . . . .97 H4
Capel Rd, E7 . . . . .97 H4
E12 . . . . .97 J4
Barnet EN4 . . . . .41 H6
Capener's Cl, SW1 . . . . . .24 B4
Capern Rd, SW18
off Cargill Rd 167 F1
Cape Rd, N17
off High Cross Rd 76 D3
Cape Yd, E1 . . . . .29 J1
Capital Business Cen, Wem.
HA0 . . . . .105 G2
Capital Ind Est, Mitch. CR4
off Willow La 185 J5
Capital Interchange Way,
Brent. TW8 . . . . .126 A5
Capitol Ind Pk, NW9 . . . . .70 C3
Capitol Way, NW9 . . . . . . .70 C3
Capland St, NW8 . . . . .7 F5
Caple Par, NW10
off Harley Rd 106/107 E2
Caple Rd, NW10 . . . . . . .107 F2
Capper St, WC1 . . . . .9 G6
Caprea Cl, Hayes UB4
off Triandra Way 102 D5
Capri Rd, Croy. CR0 . . . .202 C1
Capstan Cl, Rom. RM6 . . .82 B6
Capstan Ride, Enf. EN2 . . .43 G2
Capstan Rd, SE8 . . . . . . .133 J4
Capstan Sq, E14 . . . . . . .134 C2
Capstan Way, SE16 . . . . .133 H1
Capstone Rd, Brom. BR1 .173 F4
Capthorne Av, Har. HA2 . .85 E1
Capuchin Cl, Stan. HA7 . .52 E6
Capulet Ms, E16
off Hanover Av 135 G1
Capworth St, E10 . . . . . . .96 A1
Caradoc Cl, W2 . . . . .108 D6
Caradoc St, SE10 . . . . . . .134 E5
Caradon Cl, E11
off Brockway Cl . . .96/97 E2
Caradon Way, N15 . . . . . .76 A4
Caravel Cl, E14
off Tiller Rd 134 A3
Caravelle Gdns, Nthlt. UB5
off Javelin Way 102 D3
Caravel Ms, SE8
off Watergate St 134 A6
Caraway Cl, E13 . . . . .115 H5
Caraway Pl, Wall. SM6 . .200 B3

Carberry Rd, SE19 . . . . . . .170 B6
Carbery Av, W3 . . . . .125 J2
Carbis Cl, E4 . . . . .62 D1
Carbis Rd, E14 . . . . .113 J6
Carbuncle Pas Way, N17 . .76 D2
Carburton St, W1 . . . . .17 E1
Cardale St, E14
   off Plevna St 134 C3
Carden Rd, SE15 . . . . .152 E3
Cardiff Rd, W7 . . . . .124 D3
   Enfield EN3 . . . . .45 E4
Cardiff St, SE18 . . . . .137 H7
Cardigan Gdns, Ilf. IG3 . . .100 A2
Cardigan Rd, E3 . . . . .113 J2
   SW13 . . . . .147 G2
   SW19 off Haydons Rd .167 F6
   Richmond TW10 . . . . . .145 H6
Cardigan St, SE11 . . . . . . .34 E3
Cardigan Wk, N1
   off Ashby Gro 93 J7
Cardinal Av, Borwd. WD6 .38 B3
   Kingston upon Thames
   KT2 . . . . .163 H5
   Morden SM4 . . . . .184 B6
Cardinal Bourne St, SE1 . .28 C6
Cardinal Cl, Chis. BR7 . . .193 G1
   Edgware HA8
   off Abbots Rd 54 D7
   Morden SM4 . . . . .184 B7
   Worcester Park KT4 . . .197 G4
Cardinal Ct, Borwd.WD6
   off Cardinal Av 38 B3
Cardinal Cres, N.Mal.
   KT3 . . . . .182 C2
Cardinal Dr, Ilf. IG6 . . . . . .65 F6
Cardinal Hinsley Cl,
   NW10 . . . . .107 G2
Cardinal Pl, SW15 . . . . . . .148 A4
Cardinal Rd, Felt. TW13 . .160 B1
   Ruislip HA4 . . . . .84 D1
Cardinals Wk, Hmptn.
   TW12 . . . . .161 J7
Cardinals Way, N19 . . . . . .92 D1
Cardinal Way, Har. HA3
   off Wolseley Rd 68 B3
Cardine Ms, SE15 . . . . . . .132 E7
Cardington Sq, Houns.
   TW4 . . . . .142 D4
Cardington St, NW1 . . . . . .9 F3
Cardinham Rd, Orp.
   BR6 . . . . .207 J4
Cardozo Rd, N7 . . . . .93 E5
Cardrew Av, N12 . . . . .57 G5
Cardrew Cl, N12 . . . . .57 H5
Cardross St, W6 . . . . .127 H3
Cardwell Rd, N7 . . . . .92 E4
Carew Cl, N7 . . . . .93 F2
Carew Rd, N17 . . . . .76 D2
   W13 . . . . .125 F2
   Mitcham CR4 . . . . .186 A2
   Thornton Heath CR7 . . .187 H3
   Wallington SM6 . . . . . .200 C6
Carew St, SE5 . . . . .151 J2
Carew Way, Wat. WD19 . .51 F3
Carey Ct, Bexh. DA6 . . . . .159 H5
Carey Gdns, SW8 . . . . . . .150 C1
Carey La, EC2 . . . . .19 J3
Carey Pl, SW1 . . . . .33 H2
Carey Rd, Dag. RM9 . . . . .101 E4
Carey St, WC2 . . . . .18 D4
Carey Way, Wem. HA9 . . . .88 B4
Carfax Pl, SW4
   off Holwood Pl 150 D4
Carfax Rd, Hayes UB3 . . .121 J5
Carfree Cl, N1
   off Bewdley St 93 G7
Cargill Rd, SW18 . . . . . . .167 E1
Cargreen Pl, SE25
   off Cargreen Rd 188 C4
Cargreen Rd, SE25 . . . . . .188 C4
Carholme Rd, SE23 . . . . . .171 J1
Carisbrooke Av, Bex.
   DA5 . . . . .176 C1
Carisbrooke Cl, Enf. EN1 . .44 C1
   Stanmore HA7 . . . . . . .69 G2
Carisbrooke Gdns, SE15 . .37 G7
Carisbrooke Rd, E17 . . . . .77 H4
   Bromley BR2 . . . . .191 J4
   Mitcham CR4 . . . . .186 D4
Carker's La, NW5 . . . . .92 B5
Carleton Cl, Esher
   KT10 . . . . .194 A4
Carleton Rd, N7 . . . . .92 D5
Carleton Vil, NW5
   off Leighton Gro 92 C5
Carlile Cl, E3 . . . . .113 J2
Carlina Gdns, Wdf.Grn.
   IG8 . . . . .63 H5
Carlingford Gdns, Mitch.
   CR4 . . . . .167 J7

Carlingford Rd, N15 . . . . . .75 H3
   NW3 . . . . .91 G4
   Morden SM4 . . . . .184 A6
Carlisle Av, EC3 . . . . .21 E4
   W3 . . . . .106 E6
Carlisle Cl, Kings.T. KT2 . .182 A1
   Pinner HA5 . . . . .66 E7
Carlisle Gdns, Har. HA3 . . .69 G7
   Ilford IG1 . . . . .80 B6
Carlisle La, SE1 . . . . .26 D6
Carlisle Ms, NW8 . . . . .15 F1
Carlisle Pl, N11 . . . . .58 B4
   SW1 . . . . .25 F6
Carlisle Rd, E10 . . . . .96 A1
   N4 . . . . .75 G7
   NW6 . . . . .108 B1
   NW9 . . . . .70 C3
   Hampton TW12 . . . . . .161 H7
   Sutton SM1 . . . . .198 C5
Carlisle St, W1 . . . . .17 H4
Carlisle Wk, E8
   off Laurel St 94 C6
Carlisle Way, SW17 . . . . . .168 A5
Carlos Pl, W1 . . . . .16 C6
Carlow St, NW1 . . . . .9 F1
Carlton Av, N14 . . . . .42 D5
   Feltham TW14 . . . . . . .142 C6
   Harrow HA3 . . . . .68 E5
   Hayes UB3 . . . . .121 H4
   South Croydon CR2 . . .202 B7
Carlton Av E, Wem. HA9 . .87 H1
Carlton Av W, Wem. HA0 . .86 E2
Carlton Cl, NW3 . . . . .90 D2
   Borehamwood WD6 . . .38 D4
   Chessington KT9 . . . . .195 G6
   Edgware HA8 . . . . .54 A5
   Northolt UB5
   off Whitton Av W 85 J5
Carlton Ct, SW9 . . . . .151 H1
   Ilford IG6 . . . . .81 G3
Carlton Cres, Sutt. SM3 . .198 B4
Carlton Dr, SW15 . . . . .148 B5
   Ilford IG6 . . . . .81 G3
Carlton Gdns, SW1 . . . . . .25 H2
   W5 . . . . .105 F6
Carlton Gro, SE15 . . . . . . .152 E1
Carlton Hill, NW8 . . . . . . .109 E2
Carlton Ho, Felt. TW14 . . .141 J7
Carlton Ho Ter, SW1 . . . . .25 H2
Carlton Pk Av, SW20 . . . . .183 J2
Carlton Rd, E11 . . . . .97 F1
   E12 . . . . .98 A4
   E17 . . . . .77 H1
   N4 . . . . .75 G7
   N11 . . . . .58 A5
   SW14 . . . . .146 C3
   W4 . . . . .126 D2
   W5 . . . . .105 F7
   Erith DA8 . . . . .139 H6
   New Malden KT3 . . . . .182 E2
   Sidcup DA14 . . . . .175 J5
   South Croydon CR2 . . .202 A4
   Walton-on-Thames
   KT12 . . . . .178 D2
   Welling DA16 . . . . .158 B3
Carlton Sq, E1
   off Argyle Rd 113 G4
Carlton St, SW1 . . . . .17 H6
Carlton Ter, E11 . . . . .79 H5
   N18 . . . . .60 A3
   SE26 . . . . .171 F3
Carlton Twr Pl, SW1 . . . . .24 A5
Carlton Vale, NW6 . . . . . . .108 E2
Carlton Vil, SW15
   off St. John's Av 147 J5
Carlwell St, SW17 . . . . . . .167 H5
Carlyle Av, Brom. BR1 . . .192 A3
   Southall UB1 . . . . .103 F7
Carlyle Cl, N2 . . . . .73 F6
   NW10 . . . . .106 D1
   West Molesey KT8 . . . .179 H2
Carlyle Gdns, Sthl. UB1 . .103 F7
Carlyle Lo, Barn. (New Barn.)
   EN5 off Richmond Rd .41 D5
Carlyle Ms, E1
   off Alderney Rd 113 G4
Carlyle Pl, SW15 . . . . .148 A4
Carlyle Rd, E12 . . . . .98 B4
   SE28 . . . . .118 B7
   W5 . . . . .125 F5
   Croydon CR0 . . . . .202 D2
★ Carlyle's Ho, SW3 . . . . .31 G6
Carlyle Sq, SW3 . . . . .31 F4
Carlyon Av, Har. HA2 . . . . .85 F4
Carlyon Cl, Wem. HA0 . . .105 H1
Carlyon Rd, Hayes UB4 . .102 C6
   Wembley HA0 . . . . . . .105 H2
Carmalt Gdns, SW15 . . . .147 J4
Carmarthen Grn, NW9
   off Snowdon Dr . . .70/71 E6

Carmel Ct, W8 . . . . .22 A3
   Wembley HA9 . . . . . . .88 B2
Carmelite Cl, Har. HA3 . . .67 J1
Carmelite Rd, Har. HA3 . . .67 J1
Carmelite St, EC4 . . . . . . .19 F5
Carmelite Wk, Har. HA3 . .67 J1
Carmelite Way, Har. HA3 .67 J2
Carmen St, E14 . . . . .114 B6
Carmichael Cl, SW11
   off Darien Rd 149 G3
   Ruislip HA4 . . . . .84 A4
Carmichael Ms, SW18 . . .149 G7
Carmichael Rd, SE25 . . . .188 D5
Carminia Rd, SW17 . . . . . .168 B2
Carnaby St, W1 . . . . .17 F4
Carnac St, SE27 . . . . .170 A4
Carnanton Rd, E17 . . . . . .78 D1
Carnarvon Av, Enf. EN1 . . .44 C3
Carnarvon Dr, Hayes
   UB3 . . . . .121 F3
Carnarvon Rd, E10 . . . . . . .78 C6
   E15 . . . . .97 F6
   E18 . . . . .79 F1
   Barnet EN5 . . . . .40 B3
Carnation St, SE2 . . . . . . .138 B5
Carnbrook Rd, SE3 . . . . . .156 A3
Carnecke Gdns, SE9 . . . . .156 B5
Carnegie Cl, Surb. KT6
   off Fullers Av 195 J2
Carnegie Pl, SW19 . . . . . .166 A3
Carnegie St, N1 . . . . .111 F1
Carnforth Cl, Epsom
   KT19 . . . . .196 B6
Carnforth Rd, SW16 . . . . .168 D7
Carnie Lo, SW17
   off Manville Rd 168 B3
Carnoustie Dr, N1 . . . . . . .93 F7
Carnwath Rd, SW6 . . . . . .148 D3
Carol Cl, NW4 . . . . .72 A4
Carolina Cl, E15 . . . . .96 E5
Carolina Rd, Th.Hth. CR7 .187 H2
Caroline Cl, N10
   off Alexandra Pk Rd . . .74 B2
   SW16 . . . . .169 F4
   W2 . . . . .14 B6
   Croydon CR0
   off Brownlow Rd 202 B4
   Isleworth TW7 . . . . . . .124 A7
   West Drayton UB7 . . . .120 A2
Caroline Ct, Stan. HA7
   off The Chase 52 D6
Caroline Gdns, SE15 . . . . .132 E7
Caroline Pl, SW11 . . . . . . .150 A2
   W2 . . . . .14 B5
   Hayes UB3 . . . . .121 H7
Caroline Pl Ms, W2 . . . . . .14 B6
Caroline Rd, SW19 . . . . . .166 C7
Caroline St, E1 . . . . .113 G6
Caroline Ter, SW1 . . . . . . .32 B2
Caroline Wk, W6 . . . . .128 B6
Carol St, NW1 . . . . .110 C1
Carpenders Av, Wat.
   WD19 . . . . .50 E3
CARPENDERS PARK,
   Wat. 51 F2
Carpenders Pk, Wat.
   WD19 . . . . .51 E2
Carpenter Gdns, N21 . . . . .59 H2
Carpenters Arms Path, SE9
   off Eltham High St . . .156 C6
Carpenters Ct, Twick.
   TW2 . . . . .162 B2
Carpenters Pl, SW4 . . . . . .150 D4
Carpenters Rd, E15 . . . . . .96 B6
Carpenter St, W1 . . . . .16 D6
Carrara Wk, SW9 . . . . .151 H4
Carrara Wf, SW6 . . . . .148 B3
Carr Gro, SE18 . . . . .136 B4
Carriage Dr E, SW11 . . . . .32 B7
Carriage Dr N, SW11 . . . . .32 C6
Carriage Dr S, SW11 . . . . .149 J1
Carriage Dr W, SW11 . . . . .129 J7
Carriage Ms, Ilf. IG1 . . . . .99 F2
Carriage Pl, N16 . . . . .94 A3
   SW16 off Eardley Rd . .168 C5
Carrick Cl, Islw. TW7 . . . .144 D3
Carrick Dr, Ilf. IG6 . . . . . . .81 F1
Carrick Gdns, N17
   off Flexmere Rd 60 B7
Carrick Ms, SE8
   off Watergate St 134 A6
Carrill Way, Belv. DA17 . .138 D4
Carrington Av, Borwd.
   WD6 . . . . .38 B5
   Hounslow TW3 . . . . . .143 H5
Carrington Cl, Barn. EN5 . .39 G5
   Borehamwood WD6 . . .38 C4
   Croydon CR0 . . . . .189 H7
   Kingston upon Thames
   KT2 . . . . .164 C5

Carrington Gdns, E7
   off Woodford Rd 97 H4
Carrington Rd, Rich.
   TW10 . . . . .146 A4
Carrington Sq, Har. HA3 . .51 J7
Carrington St, W1 . . . . . . .24 D2
Carrol Cl, NW5 . . . . .92 B4
Carroll Cl, E15 . . . . .97 F5
Carroll Hill, Loug. IG10 . . .48 C3
Carronade Pl, SE28 . . . . . .137 F3
Carron Cl, E14 . . . . .114 B6
Carroun Rd, SW8 . . . . .34 C7
Carroway La, Grnf. UB6
   off Cowgate Rd 104 A3
Carrow Rd, Dag. RM9 . . . .100 B7
Carr Rd, E17 . . . . .77 J2
   Northolt UB5 . . . . .85 G6
Carrs La, N21 . . . . .43 J5
Carr St, E14 . . . . .113 H5
CARSHALTON 199 G4
Carshalton Gro, Sutt.
   SM1 . . . . .199 G4
Carshalton Pk Rd, Cars.
   SM5 . . . . .199 J5
Carshalton Pl, Cars.
   SM5 . . . . .200 A4
Carshalton Rd, Cars.
   SM5 . . . . .199 F5
   Mitcham CR4 . . . . .186 A4
   Sutton SM1 . . . . .199 F5
Carslake Rd, SW15 . . . . . .147 J6
Carson Rd, E16 . . . . .115 G4
   SE21 . . . . .170 A2
   Barnet EN4 . . . . .41 J4
Carstairs Rd, SE6 . . . . . . .172 C3
Carston Cl, SE12 . . . . .155 F5
Carswell Cl, Ilf. IG4
   off Roding La S 80 A4
Carswell Rd, SE6 . . . . .154 C7
Carter Cl, Wall. SM6 . . . . .200 D7
Carter Ct, EC4
   off Carter La 111 H6
Carteret St, SW1 . . . . .25 H4
Carteret Way, SE8 . . . . . . .133 H4
Carterhatch La, Enf. EN1 . .44 D2
Carterhatch Rd, Enf. EN3 .45 F2
Carter La, EC4 . . . . .19 H4
Carter Pl, SE17 . . . . .36 A4
Carter Rd, E13 . . . . .115 H1
   SW19 . . . . .167 G6
Carters Cl, Wor.Pk. KT4 . .198 A2
Carters Hill Cl, SE9 . . . . . .173 J1
Carters La, SE23 . . . . .171 H2
Carter St, SE17 . . . . .35 J5
Carters Yd, SW18
   off Wandsworth
   High St 148 D5
Carthew Rd, W6 . . . . .127 H3
Carthew Vil, W6 . . . . .127 H3
Carthusian St, EC1 . . . . . .19 J1
Cartier Circle, E14 . . . . . . .134 B1
Carting La, WC2 . . . . .18 B6
Cart La, E4 . . . . .46 D7
Cartmel Cl, N17
   off Heybourne Rd . .60/61 E7
Cartmel Gdns, Mord.
   SM4 . . . . .185 F5
Cartmel Rd, Bexh. DA7 . .159 G1
Carton St, W1 . . . . .16 A3
Cartwright Gdns, WC1 . . .10 A4
Cartwright Rd, Dag.
   RM9 . . . . .101 F7
Cartwright St, E1 . . . . .21 G5
Cartwright Way, SW13 . . .127 H7
Carver Cl, W4 . . . . .126 C3
Carver Rd, SE24 . . . . .151 J6
Carville Cres, Brent.
   TW8 . . . . .125 H4
Cary Rd, E11 . . . . .97 E4
Carysfort Rd, N8 . . . . .74 D5
   N16 . . . . .94 A3
Cascade Av, N10 . . . . .74 C4
Cascade Cl, Buck.H. IG9
   off Cascade Rd 64 A2
Cascade Rd, Buck.H. IG9 . .64 A2
Casella Rd, SE14 . . . . .133 G7
Casewick Rd, SE27 . . . . . .169 H4
Casey Cl, NW8 . . . . .7 G4
Casimir Rd, E5 . . . . .95 E3
Casino Av, SE24 . . . . .151 J5
Caspian St, SE5 . . . . .36 B7
Caspian Wk, E16 . . . . .116 A6
Caspian Wf, E3
   off Violet Rd 114 B5
Cassandra Cl, Nthlt.
   UB5 . . . . .86 A4
Casselden Rd, NW10 . . . . .88 E7
Cassidy Rd, SW6 . . . . .128 D7
Cassilda Rd, SE2 . . . . .138 A4
Cassilis Rd, Twick. TW1 . .145 E5

Cassiobury Av, Felt. TW14 **141** J6
Cassiobury Rd, E17 **77** G5
Cassis Ct, Loug. IG10 **49** F4
Cassland Rd, E9 **95** F7
Thornton Heath CR7 **188** A4
Casslee Rd, SE6 **153** J7
Casson St, E1 **21** H2
Castalia Sq, E14
off Roserton St **134** C2
Castalia St, E14
off Plevna St **134** C2
Castellain Rd, W9 **6** C6
Castellane Cl, Stan. HA7
off Daventer Dr **52** C7
Castello Av, SW15 **147** J5
Castell Rd, Loug. IG10 **49** F1
CASTELNAU, SW13 **127** G6
Castelnau, SW13 **127** H6
Castelnau Gdns, SW13
off Arundel Ter **127** H6
Castelnau Pl, SW13
off Castelnau **127** H6
Castelnau Row, SW13
off Lonsdale Rd **127** H6
Casterbridge, NW6 **109** E1
Casterbridge Rd, SE3 **155** G3
Casterton St, E8
off Wilton Way **94/95** E6
Castile Rd, SE18 **136** D4
Castillon Rd, SE6 **172** E2
Castlands Rd, SE6 **171** J2
Castle Av, E4 **62** D5
Castlebar Hill, W5 **105** E5
Castlebar Ms, W5 **105** F5
Castlebar Pk, W5 **105** E4
Castlebar Rd, W5 **105** F5
Castle Baynard St, EC4 **19** H5
Castlebrook Cl, SE11 **35** G1
Castle Cl, E9
off Swinnerton St **95** H5
SW19 **166** A3
W3 **126** B2
Bromley BR2 **190** E3
Castlecombe Dr, SW19 **148** A7
Castlecombe Rd, SE9 **174** B4
Castle Ct, EC3 **20** C4
SE26 *off Champion Rd* **171** H4
Castledine Rd, SE20 **170** E7
Castle Dr, Ilf. IG4 **80** B6
Castleford Av, SE9 **174** E1
Castleford Cl, N17 **60** C6
Castlegate, Rich. TW9 **145** J3
Castlehaven Rd, NW1 **92** B7
Castle La, SW1 **25** G5
Castleleigh Ct, Enf. EN2 **44** A5
Castlemaine Av, S.Croy. CR2 **202** C5
Castlemaine Twr, SW11 **149** J1
Castle Ms, N12
off Castle Rd **57** F5
NW1 *off Castle Rd* **92** B6
Castle Par, Epsom KT17
off Ewell Bypass **197** G7
Castle Pl, NW1 **92** B6
W4 *off Windmill Rd* **126/127** E4
Castle Pt, E13 **115** J2
Castlereagh St, W1 **15** J3
Castle Rd, N12 **57** F5
NW1 **92** B6
Dagenham RM9 **118** B1
Enfield EN3 **45** H1
Isleworth TW7 **144** C2
Northolt UB5 **85** H6
Southall UB2 **123** F3
Castle St, E6 **115** J2
Kingston upon Thames KT1 **181** H2
Castleton Av, Wem. HA9 **87** H4
Castleton Cl, Croy. CR0 **189** H6
Castleton Gdns, Wem. HA9 **87** H3
Castleton Rd, E17 **78** D2
SE9 **174** A4
Ilford IG3 **100** A1
Mitcham CR4 **186** D4
Ruislip HA4 **84** D1
Castletown Rd, W14 **128** B5
Castleview Cl, N4 **93** J1
Castleview Gdns, Ilf. IG1 **80** B6
Castle Wk, Sun. TW16
off Elizabeth Gdns **178** C3
Castle Way, SW19 **166** A3
Feltham TW13 **160** C4
Castlewood Dr, SE9 **156** C2
Castlewood Rd, N15 **76** D6
N16 **76** D7
Barnet EN4 **41** G3
Castle Yd, N6
off North Rd **74** A7
SE1 **27** H1
Richmond TW10
off Hill St **145** G5
Castor La, E14 **114** B7
Caterham Av, Ilf. IG5 **80** C2
Caterham Rd, SE13 **154** C3
Catesby St, SE17 **36** C2
CATFORD, SE6 **172** B1
Catford Bdy, SE6 **154** B7
Catford Hill, SE6 **171** J2
Catford Ms, SE6
off Holbeach Rd **154** B7
Catford Rd, SE6 **154** A7
Cathall Rd, E11 **96** D3
Cathay St, SE16 **133** E2
Cathay Wk, Nthlt. UB5
off Brabazon Rd **103** G2
Cathcart Dr, Orp. BR6 **207** H2
Cathcart Hill, N19 **92** C3
Cathcart Rd, SW10 **30** B5
Cathcart St, NW5 **92** B6
Cathedral Piazza, SW1 **25** F6
Cathedral Pl, EC4 **19** J3
Cathedral St, SE1 **28** B1
Catherall Rd, N5 **93** J3
Catherine Cl, Loug. IG10
off Roding Gdns **48** C6
Catherine Ct, N14
off Conisbee Ct **42** C5
Catherine Dr, Rich. TW9 **145** H4
Catherine Gdns, Houns. TW3 **144** A4
Catherine Griffiths Ct, EC1 **11** F5
Catherine Gro, SE10 **154** B1
Catherine Pl, SW1 **25** F5
Harrow HA1 **68** C5
Catherine Rd, Surb. KT6 **181** G5
Catherine's Cl, West Dr. UB7
off Money La **120** A3
Catherine St, WC2 **18** C5
Catherine Wheel All, E1 **20** E2
Catherine Wheel Rd, Brent. TW8 **125** G7
Catherine Wheel Yd, SW1 **25** F2
Cat Hill, Barn. EN4 **41** H6
Cathles Rd, SW12 **150** B6
Cathnor Rd, W12 **127** H2
Catling Cl, SE23 **171** F3
Catlins La, Pnr. HA5 **66** B3
Catlin St, SE16 **37** J3
Cator La, Beck. BR3 **189** J2
Cato Rd, SW4 **150** D3
Cator Rd, SE26 **171** G6
Carshalton SM5 **199** J5
Cator St, SE15 **37** F6
Cato St, W1 **15** H2
Catterick Cl, N11 **58** A6
Cattistock Rd, SE9 **174** B5
Cattley Cl, Barn. EN5
off Wood St **40** B4
Catton St, WC1 **18** C2
Caulfield Rd, E6 **98** C7
SE15 **153** E2
Causeway, The, N2 **73** H4
SW18 **148** E4
SW19 **166** A5
Carshalton SM5 **200** A3
Chessington KT9 **195** H4
Esher (Clay.) KT10 **194** C7
Feltham TW14 **142** A4
Hounslow TW4 **142** A4
Teddington TW11
off Broad St **162** C6
Causeyware Rd, N9 **45** E7
Causton Rd, N6 **74** B7
Causton Sq, Dag. RM10 **101** G7
Causton St, SW1 **33** J2
Cautley Av, SW4 **150** C5
Cavalier Cl, Rom. RM6 **82** D4
Cavalry Barracks, Houns. TW4 **142** D3
Cavalry Cres, Houns. TW4 **142** D4
Cavalry Gdns, SW15 **148** B5
Cavaye Pl, SW10 **30** D4
Cavell Dr, Enf. EN2 **43** G2
Cavell Rd, N17 **60** A7
Cavell St, E1 **113** E5
Cavendish Av, N3 **72** D2
NW8 **7** F2
W13 **104** D5
Erith DA8 **139** J6
Harrow HA1 **86** A4
New Malden KT3 **183** H5
Ruislip HA4 **84** B5
Sidcup DA15 **158** A7
Cavendish Av, Well. DA16 **157** J3
Woodford Green IG8 **79** H1
Cavendish Cl, N18 **61** E5
NW6 *off Cavendish Rd* **90** C7
NW8 **7** F3
Cavendish Ct, EC3 **20** E3
Cavendish Cres, Borwd. (Elstree) WD6 **38** A4
Cavendish Dr, E11 **96** D1
Edgware HA8 **53** J6
Cavendish Dr, Esh (Clay.) KT10 **194** B5
Cavendish Gdns, Bark. IG11 **99** H5
Ilford IG1 **98** D1
Romford RM6 **83** E5
Cavendish Ms N, W1 **16** E1
Cavendish Ms S, W1 **16** E2
Cavendish Par, Houns. TW4
off Bath Rd **142/143** E2
Cavendish Pl, W1 **16** E3
Cavendish Rd, E4 **62** C6
N4 **75** G6
N18 **60** E5
NW6 **90** B7
SW12 **150** B6
SW19 **167** G7
W4 **146** C1
Barnet EN5 **39** J3
Croydon CR0 **201** H1
New Malden KT3 **183** F5
Sutton SM2 **199** F7
Cavendish Sq, W1 **16** E3
Cavendish St, N1 **12** B2
Cavendish Ter, Felt. TW13
off High St **160** A2
Cavendish Way, W.Wick. BR4 **204** B1
Cavenham Gdns, Ilf. IG1 **99** G3
Caverleigh Way, Wor.Pk. KT4 **197** G1
Cave Rd, E13 **115** H2
Richmond TW10 **163** F4
Caversham Av, N13 **59** G3
Sutton SM3 **198** B2
Caversham Ct, N11 **58** A3
Caversham Flats, SW3 **31** J5
Caversham Rd, N15 **75** J4
NW5 **92** C6
Kingston upon Thames KT1 **181** J2
Caversham St, SW3 **31** J5
Caverswall St, W12 **107** J6
Caveside Cl, Chis. BR7 **192** D1
Cave St, N1 **10** D1
Cawdor Cres, W7 **124** D4
Cawnpore St, SE19 **170** B5
Caxton Gro, E3 **114** A3
★ **Caxton Hall**, SW1 **25** G5
Caxton Ms, Brent. TW8
off The Butts **125** G6
Caxton Rd, N22 **75** F2
SW19 **167** F5
W12 **128** A2
Southall UB2 **122** D3
Caxton St, SW1 **25** G5
Caxton St N, E16
off Victoria Dock Rd **115** F7
Cayenne Ct, SE1 **29** G2
Caygill Cl, Brom. BR2 **191** F4
Cayley Cl, Wall. SM6 **200** E7
Cayley Rd, Sthl. UB2
off McNair Rd **123** H3
Cayton Pl, EC1 **12** B4
Cayton Rd, Grnf. UB6 **104** B2
Cayton St, EC1 **12** B4
Cazenove Rd, E17 **78** A1
N16 **94** C2
Cearns Ho, E6 **116** A1
Cecil Av, Bark. IG11 **99** G7
Enfield EN1 **44** C4
Wembley HA9 **87** J5
Cecil Cl, W5
off Helena Rd **105** G5
Chessington KT9 **195** G4
Cecil Ct, WC2 **17** J6
Barnet EN5 **40** A3
Cecile Pk, N8 **75** E6
Cecilia Cl, N2 **73** F3
★ **Cecilia Coleman Gall**, NW8
off St. John's Wd High St **7** F1
Cecilia Rd, E8 **94** D5
Cecil Pk, Pnr. HA5 **67** E4
Cecil Pl, Mitch. CR4 **185** J5
Cecil Rd, E11 **97** E3
E13 **115** G1
E17 **78** A1
N10 **74** B2
Cecil Rd, N14 **58** C1
NW9 **70** E3
NW10 **106** E1
SW19 **166** E7
W3 **106** C5
Croydon CR0 **187** F6
Enfield EN2 **44** A4
Harrow HA3 **68** B3
Hounslow TW3 **143** J2
Ilford IG1 **98** E4
Romford RM6 **82** D7
Cecil Rd, Sutt. SM1 **198** C6
★ **Cecil Sharp Ho**, NW1 **110** A1
Cecil Way, Brom. BR2 **205** G1
Cedar Av, Barn. EN4 **41** H7
Enfield EN3 **45** F2
Hayes UB3 **102** A6
Romford RM6 **82** E5
Ruislip HA4 **84** C6
Sidcup DA15 **158** A7
Twickenham TW2 **143** H6
West Drayton UB7 **120** C1
Cedar Cl, SE21 **169** J1
SW15 **164** D4
Borehamwood WD6 **38** B4
Bromley BR2 **206** B3
Buckhurst Hill IG9 **64** A2
Carshalton SM5 **199** J6
East Molesey KT8
off Cedar Rd **180** B4
Romford RM7 **83** J4
Cedar Copse, Brom. BR1 **192** C2
Cedar Ct, E11
off Grosvenor Rd **79** H5
N1 *off Essex Rd* **93** J7
SE9 **156** B6
SW19 **166** A3
Cedar Cres, Brom. BR2 **206** B3
Cedarcroft Rd, Chess. KT9 **195** J4
Cedar Dr, N2 **73** H4
Loughton IG10 **49** E2
Pinner HA5 **51** G6
Cedar Gdns, Sutt. SM2 **199** F6
Cedar Gro, W5 **125** H3
Bexley DA5 **158** C6
Southall UB1 **103** G5
Cedar Hts, Rich. TW10 **163** H1
Cedar Ho, Croy. CR0 **204** B6
Cedarhurst, Brom. BR1
off Elstree Hill **172/173** E7
Cedarhurst Dr, SE9 **155** J5
Cedar Lawn Av, Barn. EN5 **40** B5
Cedar Mt, SE9 **174** A1
Cedarne Rd, SW6 **128** E7
Cedar Pk, Chig. IG7
off High Rd **64/65** E4
Cedar Pk Gdns, Rom. RM6 **82** D7
Cedar Pl, SE7
off Floyd Rd **135** J5
Cedar Ri, N14 **42** A7
Cedar Rd, N17 **76** C1
NW2 **89** J4
Bromley BR1 **191** J2
Croydon CR0 **202** B2
East Molesey KT8 **180** B4
Hounslow TW4 **142** C2
Romford RM7 **83** J4
Sutton SM2 **199** F6
Teddington TW11 **162** D5
Cedars, The, E15
off Portway **115** F1
W13 *off Heronsforde* **105** F6
Buckhurst Hill IG9 **63** G1
Teddington TW11
off Adelaide Rd **162** C6
Cedars Av, E17 **78** A5
Mitcham CR4 **186** A4
Cedars Cl, NW4 **72** A3
Cedars Ct, N9
off Church St **60** B2
Cedars Ms, SW4
off Cedars Rd **150** B4
Cedars Rd, E15 **97** E6
N9 *off Church St* **60** D2
N21 **59** H2
SW4 **150** B3
SW13 **147** F2
W4 **126** C5
Beckenham BR3 **189** H2
Croydon CR0 **201** E3
Kingston upon Thames KT1 **181** F1
Morden SM4 **184** D4
Cedar Ter, Rich. TW9 **145** H4
Cedar Tree Gro, SE27 **169** H5
Cedarville Gdns, SW16 **169** F6

Cedar Vista, Rich. TW9
  off Kew Rd 145 H1
Cedar Wk, Esher (Clay.)
  KT10 . . . . .194 C6
Cedar Way, NW1 . . . . .92 D7
Cedra Ct, N16 . . . . .94 D1
Cedric Rd, SE9 . . . . .175 F3
Celadon Cl, Enf. EN3 . . . . .45 H3
Celandine Cl, E14 . . . . . .114 A5
Celandine Dr, E8 . . . . .94 C7
  SE28 . . . . .138 B1
Celandine Way, E15 . . . . .115 E3
Celbridge Ms, W2 . . . . . . .14 B3
Celestial Gdns, SE13 . . . .154 D4
Celia Rd, N19 . . . . .92 C4
Celtic Av, Brom. BR2 . . . .190 E3
Celtic St, E14 . . . . .114 B5
Cemetery La, Ilf. IG6 . . . .136 B6
Cemetery Rd, E7 . . . . .97 F4
  N17 . . . . .60 B7
  SE2 . . . . .138 B7
Cenacle Cl, NW3 . . . . .90 D3
★ Cenotaph, The, SW1 . . .26 A3
Centaurs Business Cen, Islw.
  TW7 . . . . .124 D6
Centaur St, SE1 . . . . .26 D5
Centenary Est, Enf. EN3 . .45 J4
Centenary Rd, Enf. EN3 . . .45 J4
Centenary Wk, Loug.
  IG10 . . . . .47 H3
Central Av, E11 . . . . .96 D2
  N2 . . . . .73 G2
  N9 . . . . .60 B3
  SW11 . . . . .129 J7
  Enfield EN1 . . . . .44 E2
  Hayes UB3 . . . . .102 A7
  Hounslow TW3 . . . . . . .143 J4
  Pinner HA5 . . . . .67 F6
  Wallington SM6 . . . . . . .201 E5
  Welling DA16 . . . . .157 J2
  West Molesey KT8 . . . .179 F4
Central Circ, NW4
  off Hendon Way 71 H5
★ Central Criminal Ct
  (Old Bailey), EC4 . . . . . . .19 H3
Central Gdns, Mord. SM4
  off Central Rd 184/185 E5
Central Hill, SE19 . . . . . . .170 A5
Central Mkts, EC1 . . . . . . .19 H2
Central Par, Felt. TW14 . . .142 C7
  Greenford UB6 . . . . . . .104 D3
  Hounslow TW5
    off Heston Rd 123 G7
  Surbiton KT6
    off St. Mark's Hill 181 H6
Central Pk Av, Dag.
  RM10 . . . . .101 H3
Central Pk Est, Houns.
  TW4 . . . . .142 D5
Central Pk Rd, E6 . . . . . . .116 A2
Central Pl, SE25
  off Portland Rd . .188/189 E4
Central Rd, Mord. SM4 . . .184 D5
  Wembley HA0 . . . . .86 E5
  Worcester Park KT4 . . . .197 G2
Central Sch Footpath,
  SW14 . . . . .146 C3
Central Sq, NW11 . . . . .72 E6
  Wembley HA9
    off Station Gro 87 H5
  West Molesey KT8 . . . .179 F4
Central St, EC1 . . . . .11 J4
Central Way, NW10 . . . . . .106 C3
  SE28 . . . . .118 A7
  Carshalton SM5 . . . . . . .199 H7
  Feltham TW14 . . . . .142 B5
Centre, The, Felt.
  TW13 . . . . .160 A2
Centre at the Circ, W1 . . . .17 G6
Centre Av, W3 . . . . .126 D1
  W10 off Harrow Rd 107 J3
Centre Common Rd, Chis.
  BR7 . . . . .175 F6
Centre Ct Shop Cen,
  SW19 . . . . .166 C6
Centrepoint, WC1 . . . . .17 J3
Centre Rd, E7 . . . . .97 G2
  E11 . . . . .97 G2
  Dagenham RM10 . . . . . .119 H2
Centre St, E2 . . . . .113 E2
Centre Way, E17 . . . . .62 C7
  N9 . . . . .61 F2
Centreway, Ilf. IG1 . . . . . . .99 F2
Centric Cl, NW1
  off Oval Rd 110 B1
Centurion Cl, N7 . . . . .93 F7
Centurion Ct, Wall. SM6
  off Wandle Rd 200 B2
Centurion La, E3
  off Libra Rd 113 J2

Centurion Way, Erith
  DA18 . . . . .139 G3
Century Cl, NW4 . . . . .72 A5
Century Ms, E5
  off Lower Clapton Rd . . .95 F4
Century Rd, E17 . . . . .77 H3
Cephas Av, E1 . . . . .113 F4
Cephas St, E1 . . . . .113 F4
Ceres Rd, SE18 . . . . .137 J4
Cerise Rd, SE15 . . . . .152 D1
Cerne Cl, Hayes UB4 . . . .102 D7
Cerne Rd, Mord. SM4 . . . .185 F6
Cerney Ms, W2 . . . . .15 C5
Cervantes Ct, W2 . . . . .14 B4
Cester St, E2
  off Whiston Rd 112 D1
Ceylon Rd, W14 . . . . .128 A3
Chadacre Av, Ilf. IG5 . . . . .80 C3
Chadacre Rd, Epsom
  KT17 . . . . .197 H6
Chadbourn St, E14 . . . . . .114 B5
Chadd Dr, Brom. BR1 . . . .192 B3
Chadd Grn, E13 . . . . .115 G1
Chadview Ct, Rom.
  (Chad.Hth.) RM6 . . . . . .82 D7
Chadville Gdns, Rom.
  RM6 . . . . .82 D5
Chadway, Dag. RM8 . . . . .100 C1
Chadwell Av, Rom. RM6 . . .82 B7
CHADWELL HEATH, Rom. .82 D6
Chadwell Heath La, Rom.
  RM6 . . . . .82 B5
Chadwell St, EC1 . . . . .11 F3
Chadwick Av, E4 . . . . .62 D4
  N21 . . . . .43 F5
  SW19 . . . . .166 D6
Chadwick Cl, SW15 . . . . . .147 F7
  W7 off Westcott Cres . . .104 C5
  Teddington TW11 . . . . . .162 D6
Chadwick Pl, Surb. KT6 . .181 F7
Chadwick Rd, E11 . . . . .79 E7
  NW10 . . . . .107 F1
  SE15 . . . . .152 C2
  Ilford IG1 . . . . .99 E3
Chadwick St, SW1 . . . . . . .25 J6
Chadwick Way, SE28 . . . . .118 D7
Chadwin Rd, E13 . . . . .115 H5
Chadworth Way, Esher (Clay.)
  KT10 . . . . .194 A5
Chaffinch Av, Croy. CR0 . .189 G6
Chaffinch Cl, N9 . . . . .61 G1
  Croydon CR0 . . . . .189 G6
  Surbiton KT6 . . . . .196 A3
Chaffinch Rd, Beck. BR3 . .189 H1
Chafford Way, Rom. RM6 . .82 C4
Chagford St, NW1 . . . . .7 J6
Chailey Av, Enf. EN1 . . . . . .44 C2
Chailey Cl, Houns. TW5
  off Springwell Rd 142 D1
Chailey St, E5 . . . . .95 F3
Chalbury Wk, N1 . . . . .111 F2
Chalcombe Rd, SE2 . . . . .138 B3
Chalcot Cl, Sutt. SM2 . . . .198 D7
Chalcot Cres, NW1 . . . . . .109 J1
Chalcot Gdns, NW3 . . . . . .91 J6
Chalcot Ms, SW16 . . . . . .168 E3
Chalcot Rd, NW1 . . . . .92 A7
Chalcot Sq, NW1 . . . . .92 A7
Chalcott Gdns, Surb.
  KT6 . . . . .195 F1
Chalcroft Rd, SE13 . . . . . .154 E5
Chaldon Path, Th.Hth.
  CR7 . . . . .187 H4
Chaldon Rd, SW6 . . . . . . .128 B7
Chale Rd, SW2 . . . . .150 E6
Chalet Est, NW7 . . . . .55 G4
Chalfont Av, Wem. HA9 . . .88 B6
Chalfont Ct, NW9 . . . . .71 F3
Chalfont Grn, N9 . . . . .60 B3
Chalfont Rd, N9 . . . . .60 B3
  SE25 . . . . .188 C3
  Hayes UB3 . . . . .122 A2
Chalfont Wk, Pnr. HA5
  off Willows Cl 66 C2
Chalfont Way, W13 . . . . . .124 E3
Chalford Cl, W.Mol.
  KT8 . . . . .179 G4
Chalford Rd, SE21 . . . . . .170 A4
Chalford Wk, Wdf.Grn.
  IG8 . . . . .80 A1
Chalgrove Av, Mord.
  SM4 . . . . .184 D5
Chalgrove Cres, Ilf. IG5 . . .80 B2
Chalgrove Gdns, N3 . . . . . .72 B3
Chalgrove Rd, N17 . . . . . . .76 E1
  Sutton SM2 . . . . .199 G7
Chalice Cl, Wall. SM6
  off Lavender Vale 200 D6
Chalkenden Cl, SE20 . . . .170 E7
Chalk Fm Rd, NW1 . . . . . . .92 A7

Chalk Hill Rd, W6
  off Shortlands 128 A4
Chalkhill Rd, Wem. HA9 . . .88 B3
Chalklands, Wem. HA9 . . . .88 C3
Chalk La, Barn. EN4 . . . . . .41 J4
Chalkley Cl, Mitch. CR4 . .185 J2
Chalkmill Dr, Enf. EN1 . . . .44 E3
Chalk Pit Way, Sutt.
  SM1 . . . . .199 F5
Chalk Rd, E13 . . . . .115 H5
Chalkstone Cl, Well.
  DA16 . . . . .158 A1
Chalkwell Pk Av, Enf.
  EN1 . . . . .44 B4
Challice Way, SW2 . . . . . .169 F1
Challin St, SE20 . . . . .189 F1
Challis Rd, Brent. TW8 . . .125 G5
Challoner Cl, N2 . . . . .73 G2
Challoner Cres, W14
  off Challoner St 128 C5
Challoners Cl, E.Mol.
  KT8 . . . . .180 A4
Challoner St, W14 . . . . . . .128 C5
Chalmers Wk, SE17 . . . . . .35 H6
Chalmers Way, Felt.
  TW14 . . . . .142 A5
Chaloner Ct, SE1 . . . . .28 B3
Chalsey Rd, SE4 . . . . .153 J4
Chalton Dr, N2 . . . . .73 F6
Chalton St, NW1 . . . . .9 J3
Chamberlain Cl, SE28
  off Broadwater Rd . . .137 G3
Chamberlain Cotts, SE5
  off Camberwell Gro . . .152 A1
Chamberlain Cres, W.Wick.
  BR4 . . . . .204 B1
Chamberlain Gdns, Houns.
  TW3 . . . . .143 J1
Chamberlain La, Pnr.
  HA5 . . . . .66 A4
Chamberlain Pl, E17 . . . . . .77 H3
Chamberlain Rd, N2 . . . . . .73 F2
  N9 . . . . .60 D3
  W13 off Midhurst Rd . . .124 D2
Chamberlain St, NW1
  off Regents Pk Rd 91 J7
Chamberlain Wk, Felt. TW13
  off Burgess Cl . . .160/161 E4
Chamberlain Way, Pnr.
  HA5 . . . . .66 B3
  Surbiton KT6 . . . . .181 H7
Chamberlayne Av, Wem.
  HA9 . . . . .87 H2
Chamberlayne Rd,
  NW10 . . . . .108 A3
Chambers Gdns, N2 . . . . . .73 G1
Chambers La, NW10 . . . . . .89 H7
Chambers Pl, S.Croy. CR2
  off Rolleston Rd 202 A7
Chambers Rd, N7 . . . . .92 E4
Chambers St, SE16 . . . . . .29 H3
Chamber St, E1 . . . . .21 G5
Chambon Pl, W6
  off Beavor La 127 G4
Chambord St, E2 . . . . .13 G4
Champion Cres, SE26 . . . .171 H4
Champion Gro, SE5 . . . . . .152 A3
Champion Hill, SE5 . . . . . .152 A3
Champion Hill Est, SE5 . .152 B3
Champion Pk, SE5 . . . . . . .152 A2
Champion Pk Est, SE5
  off Denmark Hill 152 A3
Champion Rd, SE26 . . . . . .171 H4
Champness Cl, SE27
  off Rommany Rd 170 A4
Champness Rd, Bark.
  IG11 . . . . .99 J6
Champneys Cl, Sutt.
  SM2 . . . . .198 C7
Chancellor Gro, SE21 . . . .169 J2
Chancellor Pas, E14
  off South Colonnade .133 J1
Chancellor Pl, NW9 . . . . . .71 F2
Chancellors Rd, W6 . . . . . .127 J5
Chancellors St, W6 . . . . . .127 J5
Chancelot Rd, SE2 . . . . . .138 B4
Chancel St, SE1 . . . . .27 G1
Chancery La, WC2 . . . . . . .18 E3
  Beckenham BR3 . . . . . .190 B2
Chancery Ms, SW17 . . . . .167 H2
Chance St, E1 . . . . .13 F5
  E2 . . . . .13 F5
Chanctonbury Cl, SE9 . . . .175 E3
Chanctonbury Gdns,
  Sutt. SM2 . . . . .198 E7
Chanctonbury Way, N12 . .56 C4
Chanctonbury Way, N12 . .56 C4
Chandler Av, E16 . . . . .115 G5
Chandler Cl, Hmptn.
  TW12 . . . . .179 G1
Chandler Rd, Loug. IG10 . .49 E1

Chandlers Cl, Felt. TW14 .141 J7
Chandlers Ms, E14 . . . . . .134 A2
Chandler St, E1
  off Wapping La . . .132/133 E1
Chandlers Way, SW2 . . . . .151 G7
Chandler Way, SE15 . . . . .132 C7
Chandon Lo, Sutt. SM2
  off Devonshire Rd 199 F7
Chandos Av, E17 . . . . .78 A2
  N14 . . . . .58 C3
  N20 . . . . .57 F1
  W5 . . . . .125 F4
Chandos Cl, Buck.H. IG9 . .63 H2
Chandos Cres, Edg. HA8 . .53 J7
Chandos Par, Edg. HA8
  off Chandos Cres 53 J7
Chandos Pl, WC2 . . . . .18 A6
Chandos Rd, E15 . . . . .96 D5
  N2 . . . . .73 G2
  N17 . . . . .76 B2
  NW2 . . . . .89 J5
  NW10 . . . . .106 E4
  Harrow HA1 . . . . .67 J5
  Pinner HA5 . . . . .66 C7
Chandos St, W1 . . . . .16 E2
Chandos Way, NW11 . . . . . .90 E1
Change All, EC3 . . . . .20 C4
Channel Cl, Houns. TW5 .143 G1
Channel Gate Rd, NW10
  off Old Oak La 107 F3
Channelsea Rd, E15 . . . . . .96 D7
Chantress Cl, Dag. RM10 .119 J1
Chantrey Rd, SW9 . . . . . . .151 F3
Chantry Cl, NW7
  off Hendon Wd La 39 F6
  W9 off Elgin Av 108 C4
  Harrow HA3 . . . . .69 J5
  Sidcup DA14
    off Ellenborough
    Rd 176/177 E5
  Sunbury-on-Thames
    TW16 . . . . .160 A7
Chantry Ct, Cars. SM5 . . .199 H3
Chantry La, Brom. BR2
  off Bromley
    Common 192 A5
Chantry Pl, Har. HA3 . . . . . .67 H1
Chantry Rd, Chess. KT9 . .195 J5
  Harrow HA3 . . . . .67 H1
Chantry Sq, W8
  off St. Mary's Pl .128/129 E3
Chantry St, N1 . . . . .111 H1
Chantry Way, Mitch.
  CR4 . . . . .185 G3
Chant Sq, E15 . . . . .96 D7
Chant St, E15 . . . . .96 D7
Chapel Ct, N2 . . . . .73 H3
  SE1 . . . . .28 B3
Chapel Fm Rd, SE9 . . . . . .174 C3
Chapel Ho St, E14 . . . . . . .134 B5
Chapel La, Chig. IG7 . . . . . .65 J3
  Pinner HA5 . . . . .66 D3
  Romford RM6 . . . . .82 D7
Chapel Mkt, N1 . . . . .10 E1
Chapel Ms, Wdf.Grn. IG8 . .64 D6
Chapelmount Rd, Wdf.Grn.
  IG8 . . . . .64 C6
Chapel Path, E11 . . . . .79 G6
Chapel Pl, EC2 . . . . .12 D4
  N1 . . . . .11 F1
  N17
    off White Hart La 60 C7
  W1 . . . . .16 D4
Chapel Rd, SE27 . . . . .169 H4
  W13 . . . . .125 E1
  Bexleyheath DA7 . . . . . .159 G4
  Hounslow TW3 . . . . . . .143 H3
  Ilford IG1 . . . . .98 D3
  Twickenham TW1 . . . . . .145 E7
Chapel Side, W2 . . . . .14 A5
Chapel Stones, N17 . . . . . .76 C1
Chapel St, NW1 . . . . .15 G2
  SW1 . . . . .24 C6
  Enfield EN2 . . . . .43 J3
Chapel Ter, Loug. IG10
  off Forest Rd 48 B4
Chapel Vw, S.Croy. CR2 .203 E6
Chapel Wk, NW4 . . . . .71 H4
  Croydon CR0
    off Wellesley Rd 201 J2
Chapel Way, N7
  off Sussex Way 93 F3
Chapel Yd, SW18
  off Wandsworth
    High St 148 D5
Chaplin Cl, SE1 . . . . .27 F3
Chaplin Rd, E15 . . . . .115 E2
  N17 . . . . .76 C3
  NW2 . . . . .89 G6
  Dagenham RM9 . . . . . .101 E7

Chaplin Rd, Wem. HA0 . . .87 F6
Chaplin Sq, N12 . . . . . . .57 G7
Chapman Cl, West Dr.
    UB7 . . . . .120 C3
Chapman Cres, Har. HA3 .69 H5
Chapman Pk Ind Est,
    NW10 . . . . .89 F6
Chapman Pl, N4 . . . . . . .93 H2
Chapman Rd, E9 . . . . . . .95 J6
    Belvedere DA17 . . . . . .139 G5
    Croydon CR0 . . . . .201 G1
Chapman's La, SE2 . . . . .138 C4
    Belvedere DA17 . . . . . .138 D4
Chapman Sq, SW19 . . . .166 A2
Chapman St, E1 . . . . . . .112 E7
Chapone Pl, W1 . . . . . . .17 H4
Chapter Cl, W4
    off Beaumont Rd 126 C3
Chapter Ho Ct, EC4 . . . . .19 J4
Chapter Rd, NW2 . . . . . .89 G5
    SE17 . . . . .35 H4
Chapter St, SW1 . . . . . . .33 H2
Chapter Way, Hmptn.
    TW12 . . . . .161 G4
Chara Pl, W4 . . . . .126 D6
Charcot Ho, SW15
    off Highcliffe Dr 147 F6
Charcroft Gdns, Enf.
    EN3 . . . . .45 G4
Chardin Rd, W4
    off Elliott Rd 126/127 E4
Chardmore Rd, N16 . . . . .94 D1
Chard Rd, Houns. (Hthrw.Air.)
    TW6 off Heathrow
    Tunnel App 140 D3
Chardwell Cl, E6
    off Northumberland
    Rd 116 B6
Charecroft Way, W12 . . .128 A2
Charfield Ct, W9 . . . . .6 A6
Charford Rd, E16 . . . . . .115 G5
Chargeable La, E13 . . . . .115 F4
Chargeable St, E16 . . . . .115 F4
Chargrove Cl, SE16
    off Marlow Way 133 G2
Charing Cl, Orp. BR6 . . .207 J4
Charing Cross, SW1 . . . . .26 A1
Charing Cross Rd, WC2 . .17 J3
Charlbert St, NW8 . . . . . .7 G1
Charlbury Av, Stan. HA7 . .53 G5
Charlbury Gdns, Ilf. IG3 . .99 J2
Charlbury Gro, W5 . . . . .105 F6
Charldane Rd, SE9 . . . . .174 E3
Charlecote Gro, SE26 . . .171 E3
Charlecote Rd, Dag.
    RM8 . . . . .100 E3
Charlemont Rd, E6 . . . . .116 C3
Charles Babbage Cl, Chess.
    KT9 . . . . .195 F7
Charles Barry Cl, SW4 . .150 C3
Charles Burton Ct, E5
    off Ashenden Rd 95 H5
Charles Cl, Sid. DA14 . . .176 B4
Charles Cobb Gdns, Croy.
    CR0 . . . . .201 G5
Charles Coveney Rd,
    SE15 . . . . .152 C1
Charles Cres, Har. HA1 . . .68 A7
Charles Dickens Ho, E2 . .112 E3
Charles Dickens Ter, SE20
    off Maple Rd 171 F7
Charlesfield, SE9 . . . . . .173 J3
Charles Flemwell Ms, E16
    off Hanameel St 135 G1
Charles Grinling Wk,
    SE18 . . . . .136 D4
Charles Haller St, SW2
    off Tulse Hill 151 G7
Charles Ho, N17
    off Love La 60 C1
Charles La, NW8 . . . . .7 F2
Charles Pl, NW1 . . . . .9 G4
Charles Rd, E7
    off Lens Rd 97 J7
    SW19 . . . . .184 D1
    W13 . . . . .104 D6
    Romford RM6 . . . . . . .82 D7
Charles II Pl, SW3
    off King's Rd 129 J5
Charles II St, SW1 . . . . . .25 H1
Charles Sevright Dr,
    NW7 . . . . .56 A5
Charles Sq, N1 . . . . .12 C4
Charles Sq Est, N1
    off Pitfield St 112 A3
Charles St, E16 . . . . . . .136 A1
    SW13 . . . . .147 E2
    W1 . . . . .24 D1
    Croydon CR0 . . . . .201 J3
    Enfield EN1 . . . . .44 C5

Charles St, Houns. TW3 .143 F2
Charleston Cl, Felt. TW13
    off Vineyard Rd 160 A3
Charleston St, SE17 . . . . .36 A2
Charles Townsend Ho,
    EC1 . . . . .11 F4
Charles Whincup Rd,
    E16 . . . . .135 H1
Charleville Circ, SE26 . . .170 D5
Charleville Rd, W14 . . . .128 B5
Charlie Chaplin Wk, SE1
    off Waterloo Rd 131 G1
Charlieville Rd, Erith DA8
    off Northumberland
    Pk 139 J7
Charlmont Rd, SW17 . . .167 J6
Charlotte Cl, Bexh. DA6 .158 E5
    Ilford IG6
    off Connor Cl 81 F1
Charlotte Despard Av,
    SW11 . . . . .150 A1
Charlotte Ms, W1 . . . . . .17 G1
    W10 . . . . .108 A6
    W14 off Munden St . . .128 B4
Charlotte Pl, NW9
    off Uphill Dr 70 C5
    SW1 . . . . .33 F2
    W1 . . . . .17 G2
Charlotte Rd, EC2 . . . . . .12 D5
    SW13 . . . . .147 F1
    Dagenham RM10 . . . .101 H6
    Wallington SM6 . . . . .200 C6
Charlotte Row, SW4 . . . .150 C3
Charlotte Sq, Rich.TW10
    off Greville Rd 145 J6
Charlotte St, W1 . . . . . . .17 G1
Charlotte Ter, N1 . . . . . .111 F1
Charlow Cl, SW6
    off Townmead Rd 149 F2
Charlton Ch La, SE7 . . . .135 J6
CHARLTON, SE7 . . . . . . .135 J6
★ Charlton Athletic FC,
    SE7 . . . . .135 J5
Charlton Ch La, SE7 . . . .135 J5
Charlton Cres, Bark.
    IG11 . . . . .117 J2
Charlton Dene, SE7 . . . .135 J7
Charlton Kings Rd, NW5 . .92 D5
Charlton La, SE7 . . . . . .136 A5
Charlton Pk La, SE7 . . . .136 A4
Charlton Pk Rd, SE7 . . . .136 A6
Charlton Pl, N1 . . . . .11 G1
Charlton Rd, N9 . . . . . . .61 G1
    NW10 . . . . .107 E1
    SE3 . . . . .135 G7
    SE7 . . . . .135 H7
    Harrow HA3 . . . . .69 G4
    Wembley HA9 . . . . . . .87 J1
Charlton Way, SE3 . . . . .154 E1
Charlwood Cl, Har. HA3
    off Kelvin Cres 52 B7
Charlwood Pl, SW1 . . . . .33 G2
Charlwood Rd, SW15 . . .148 A3
Charlwood Sq, Mitch.
    CR4 . . . . .185 G3
Charlwood St, SW1 . . . . .33 G3
Charlwood Ter, SW15
    off Cardinal Pl 148 A4
Charmian Av, Stan. HA7 . .69 G3
Charminster Av, SW19 . .184 E2
Charminster Ct, Surb.
    KT6 . . . . .181 G7
Charminster Rd, SE9 . . .174 A4
    Worcester Park KT4 . . .198 A1
Charmouth Rd, Well.
    DA16 . . . . .158 C1
Charnock Rd, E5 . . . . . . .94 E3
Charnwood Av, SW19 . . .184 D2
Charnwood Cl, N.Mal.
    KT3 . . . . .183 E4
Charnwood Dr, E18 . . . . .79 H3
Charnwood Gdns, E14 . .134 A4
Charnwood Pl, N20 . . . . .57 F3
Charnwood Rd, SE25 . . .188 A5
Charnwood St, E5 . . . . . .94 D2
Charrington Rd, Croy. CR0
    off Drayton Rd 201 H2
Charrington St, NW1 . . . . .9 H1
Charsley Rd, SE6 . . . . . .172 B2
Chart Cl, Brom. BR2 . . . .191 E1
    Croydon CR0
    off Stockbury Rd 189 F6
Charter Av, Ilf. IG2 . . . . . .99 G1
Charter Ct, N.Mal. KT3 . .182 E3
Charter Cres, Houns.
    TW4 . . . . .142 E4
Charter Dr, Bex. DA5 . . .158 E7
★ Chartered Insurance
    Institutes Mus, EC2
    off Aldermanbury 20 A3
★ Charterhouse, EC1 . . .19 H1

Charterhouse Av, Wem.
    HA0 . . . . .87 F4
Charterhouse Bldgs, EC1 .11 H6
Charterhouse Ms, EC1 . . .19 H1
Charterhouse Sq, EC1 . . .19 H1
Charterhouse St, EC1 . . .19 F2
Charteris Rd, N4 . . . . . . .93 G1
    NW6 . . . . .108 C1
    Woodford Green IG8 . .63 H7
Charter Rd, Kings.T.
    KT1 . . . . .182 B3
Charter Rd, The, Wdf.Grn.
    IG8 . . . . .62 E6
Charters Cl, SE19 . . . . . .170 B5
Charter Sq, Kings.T.
    KT1 . . . . .182 B2
Charter Way, N3 . . . . . . .72 C4
    N14 . . . . .42 C6
Chartfield Av, SW15 . . . .147 H5
Chartfield Sq, SW15 . . . .148 A5
Chartham Gro, SE27
    off Royal Circ 169 G3
Chartham Rd, SE25 . . . .188 E3
Chart Hills Cl, SE28
    off Fairway Dr . . .118/119 E6
Chartley Av, NW2 . . . . . .88 E3
    Stanmore HA7 . . . . . . .52 C6
Charton Cl, Belv. DA17
    off Nuxley Rd 139 F6
Chartridge Cl, Barn. EN5 . .39 G5
Chart St, N1 . . . . .12 C3
Chartwell Cl, SE9 . . . . . .175 F2
    Croydon CR0 . . . . .202 A1
    Greenford UB6 . . . . . .103 H1
Chartwell Dr, Orp. BR6 . .207 G5
Chartwell Gdns, Sutt.
    SM3 . . . . .198 B4
    Sutton SM3 . . . . .198 C4
Chartwell Way, SE20 . . . .188 E1
Charwood, SW16 . . . . . .169 G4
Chase, The, E12 . . . . . . .98 A4
    SW4 . . . . .150 B3
    SW16 . . . . .169 F7
    SW20 . . . . .184 B1
    Bexleyheath DA7 . . . . .159 H3
    Bromley BR1 . . . . .191 H3
    Chigwell IG7 . . . . .65 F4
    Edgware HA8 . . . . .70 B1
    Loughton IG10 . . . . . . .47 J7
    Pinner HA5 . . . . .67 F4
    Pinner (Eastcote) HA5 . .66 C6
    Romford (Chad.Hth.)
    RM6 . . . . .82 E6
    Stanmore HA7 . . . . . . .52 D5
    Sunbury-on-Thames
    TW16 . . . . .178 B1
    Wallington SM6 . . . . .200 E5
Chase Ct Gdns, Enf. EN2 .43 J3
Chasefield Rd, SW17 . . .167 J4
Chase Gdns, E4 . . . . . . .62 A4
    Twickenham TW2 . . . .144 A6
Chase Grn, Enf. EN2 . . . .43 J3
Chase Grn Av, Enf. EN2 . .43 J3
Chase Hill, Enf. EN2 . . . . .43 J3
Chase La, Ilf. IG6 . . . . . . .81 G5
Chaseley Dr, W4
    off Wellesley Rd 146 B1
Chaseley St, E14 . . . . . .113 H6
Chasemore Cl, Mitch.
    CR4 . . . . .185 J7
Chasemore Gdns, Croy. CR0
    off Thornelow Gdns . .201 H5
Chase Ridings, Enf. EN2 . .43 G2
Chase Rd, N14 . . . . .42 C6
    NW10 . . . . .106 D4
    W3 . . . . .106 D4
Chase Side, N14 . . . . . . .42 A6
    Enfield EN2 . . . . .43 J3
Chase Side Av, SW20 . . .184 B1
    Enfield EN2 . . . . .43 J2
Chase Side Cres, Enf.
    EN2 . . . . .43 J1
Chase Side Pl, Enf. EN2
    off Chase Side 43 J2
Chaseville Pk Rd, N21 . . .43 E5
Chase Way, N14 . . . . . . .58 B2
Chasewood Av, Enf. EN2 . .43 H2
Chasewood Pk, Har. HA1 .86 C3
Chatfield Rd, SW11 . . . . .149 F3
    Croydon CR0 . . . . .201 H1
Chatham Av, Brom. BR2 .191 F7
Chatham Cl, NW11 . . . . .72 D5
    Sutton SM3 . . . . .184 C7
Chatham Pl, E9 . . . . .95 F6
Chatham Rd, E17 . . . . . . .77 H3
    E18 off Grove Hill 79 F2
    SW11 . . . . .149 J6
    Kingston upon Thames
    KT1 . . . . .182 A2

Chatham Rd, Orp. BR6 . .207 F5
Chatham St, SE17 . . . . . .36 B1
Chatsfield Pl, W5 . . . . . .105 H6
Chatsworth Av, NW4 . . . .71 J2
    SW20 . . . . .184 B1
    Bromley BR1 . . . . .173 H4
    Sidcup DA15 . . . . .176 A1
    Wembley HA9 . . . . . . .87 J5
Chatsworth Cl, NW4 . . . .71 J2
    Borehamwood WD6 . . .38 A3
    West Wickham BR4 . . .205 F2
Chatsworth Ct, W8 . . . . .128 D4
    Stanmore HA7
    off Marsh La 53 F5
Chatsworth Cres, Houns.
    TW3 . . . . .144 A4
Chatsworth Dr, Enf. EN1 .44 D7
Chatsworth Est, E5
    off Elderfield Rd 95 G4
Chatsworth Gdns, W3 . . .106 B7
    Harrow HA2 . . . . .85 H1
    New Malden KT3 . . . . .183 F5
Chatsworth Par, Orp. BR5
    off Queensway 193 F5
Chatsworth Pl, Mitch.
    CR4 . . . . .185 J3
    Teddington TW11 . . . .162 D4
Chatsworth Ri, W5 . . . . .105 J4
Chatsworth Rd, E5 . . . . . .95 F3
    E15 . . . . .97 F5
    NW2 . . . . .90 A6
    W4 . . . . .126 C6
    W5 . . . . .105 J4
    Croydon CR0 . . . . .202 A4
    Hayes UB4 . . . . .102 B4
    Sutton SM3 . . . . .198 A5
Chatsworth Way, SE27 . .169 H3
Chatterton Ms, N4
    off Chatterton Rd 93 H3
Chatterton Rd, N4 . . . . . .93 H3
    Bromley BR2 . . . . .192 A4
Chatto Rd, SW11 . . . . . .149 J5
Chaucer Av, Hayes UB4 .102 A5
    Hounslow TW4 . . . . . .142 B2
    Richmond TW9 . . . . . .146 A2
Chaucer Cl, N11 . . . . . . .58 C5
    Chaucer Ct, N16 . . . . . .94 B4
Chaucer Dr, SE1 . . . . . . .37 G2
Chaucer Gdns, Sutt.
    SM1 . . . . .198 D3
Chaucer Grn, Croy. CR0 .189 E7
Chaucer Ho, Sutt. SM1 . .198 D3
Chaucer Rd, E7 . . . . .97 G6
    E11 . . . . .79 G6
    E17 . . . . .78 C2
    SE24 . . . . .151 G5
    W3 . . . . .126 C1
    Sidcup DA15 . . . . .176 C1
    Sutton SM1 . . . . .198 D4
    Welling DA16 . . . . . . .157 H1
Chaucer Way, SW19 . . . .167 G6
Chauncey Cl, N9 . . . . . . .60 D3
Chaundrye Cl, SE9 . . . . .156 B6
Chauntler Cl, E16 . . . . . .115 H6
CHEAM, Sutt. 198 A6
Cheam Common Rd, Wor.Pk.
    KT4 . . . . .197 H2
Cheam Mans, Sutt.
    SM3 . . . . .198 B7
Cheam Pk Way, Sutt.
    SM3 . . . . .198 B6
Cheam Rd, Sutt. SM1 . . .198 C6
Cheam St, SE15
    off Evelina Rd . . .152/153 E3
Cheapside, EC2 . . . . .20 A4
    N13 off Taplow Rd 59 J4
Cheddar Cl, N11
    off Martock Gdns 58 A6
Cheddar Rd, Houns. (Hthrw.Air.)
    TW6 off Cromer Rd . .140 D2
Cheddar Waye, Hayes
    UB4 . . . . .102 B6
Cheddington Rd, N18 . . . .60 B3
Chedworth Cl, E16
    off Hallsville Rd 115 F6
Cheeseman Cl, Hmptn.
    TW12 . . . . .161 G6
Cheesemans Ter, W14 . .128 C5
Cheldon Av, NW7
    off Bittacy Hill 56 B7
Chelford Rd, Brom. BR1 .172 D5
Chelmer Cres, Bark. IG11 .118 B2
Chelmer Rd, E9 . . . . .95 G5
Chelmsford Cl, E6
    off Guildford Rd 116 C6
    W6 . . . . .128 A6
Chelmsford Gdns, Ilf. IG1 .80 B7
Chelmsford Rd, E11 . . . . .96 D1
    E17 . . . . .78 A6
    E18 . . . . .79 F1

Chelmsford Rd, N14 . . . . .**42** C7
Chelmsford Sq, NW10 . . .**107** J1
CHELSEA, SW3 . . . .**31** E5
★ Chelsea Antique Mkt,
  SW3 . . . .**31** F5
Chelsea Br, SW1 . . . .**32** D5
  SW8 . . . .**32** D5
Chelsea Br Rd, SW1 . . . . .**32** B3
Chelsea Cloisters, SW3
  off Lucan Pl **129** H4
Chelsea Cl, NW10
  off Winchelsea Rd **106** D1
  Edgware HA8 . . . .**70** A2
  Hampton (Hmptn.H.)
  TW12 . . . .**161** J5
  Worcester Park KT4 . . .**183** G7
Chelsea Cres, SW10
  off Harbour Av **149** F1
★ Chelsea FC, SW6 . . . . . .**30** A7
★ Chelsea Gdns, W13
  off Hathaway Gdns . .**104** C5
  Sutton SM3 . . . .**198** B4
Chelsea Harbour, SW10 .**149** F1
Chelsea Harbour Dr,
  SW10 . . . .**149** F1
Chelsea Manor Ct, SW3 . .**31** H5
Chelsea Manor Gdns,
  SW3 . . . .**31** G5
Chelsea Manor St, SW3 . .**31** G4
Chelsea Pk Gdns, SW3 . .**30** E5
★ Chelsea Physic Gdn,
  SW3 . . . .**31** J5
Chelsea Sq, SW3 . . . .**31** F3
Chelsea Wf, SW10 . . . . . .**129** G7
Chelsfield Av, N9 . . . .**45** G7
Chelsfield Gdns, SE26 . .**171** F3
Chelsfield Grn, N9
  off Chelsfield Av **45** G7
Chelsham Rd, SW4 . . . . .**150** D3
  South Croydon CR2 . .**202** A6
Chelston App, Ruis. HA4 . .**84** A2
Chelston Rd, Ruis. HA4 . .**84** A1
Chelsworth Dr, SE18 . . . .**137** G6
Cheltenham Av, Twick.
  TW1 . . . .**144** D7
Cheltenham Cl, N.Mal. KT3
  off Northcote Rd **182** C3
  Northolt UB5 . . . .**85** H6
Cheltenham Gdns, E6 . . .**116** B2
  Loughton IG10 . . . .**48** B6
Cheltenham Pl, W3 . . . . .**126** B1
  Harrow HA3 . . . .**69** H4
Cheltenham Rd, E10 . . . .**78** C6
  SE15 . . . .**153** F4
Cheltenham Ter, SW3 . . . .**32** A3
Chelverton Rd, SW15 . . .**148** A4
Chelwood, N20
  off Oakleigh Rd N **57** G2
Chelwood Cl, E4 . . . .**46** B6
Chelwood Gdns, Rich.
  TW9 . . . .**146** A2
Chelwood Gdns Pas, Rich. TW9
  off Chelwood Gdns . .**146** A2
Chelwood Wk, SE4 . . . . .**153** H4
Chenappa Cl, E13 . . . . . .**115** G3
Chenduit Way, Stan. HA7 .**52** C5
Cheney Rd, NW1 . . . .**10** A2
Cheney Row, E17 . . . .**77** J1
Cheneys Rd, E11 . . . .**97** E3
Cheney St, Pnr. HA5 . . . . .**66** C5
Chenies, The, Orp. BR6 . .**193** H6
Chenies Ms, WC1 . . . .**9** H6
Chenies Pl, NW1 . . . .**9** J1
Chenies St, WC1 . . . .**17** H1
Cheniston Gdns, W8 . . . .**22** A5
Chepstow Cl, SW15
  off Lytton Gro **148** B6
  Ilford IG3 . . . .**81** H6
Chepstow Gdns, Sthl.
  UB1 . . . .**103** F6
Chepstow Pl, W2 . . . . . .**108** D6
Chepstow Ri, Croy. CR0 .**202** B3
Chepstow Rd, W2 . . . . . .**108** D6
  W7 . . . .**124** D3
  Croydon CR0 . . . .**202** B3
Chepstow Vil, W11 . . . . .**108** C7
Chepstow Way, SE15 . . .**132** C7
Chequers, Buck.H. IG9
  off Hills Rd **63** H1
Chequers Cl, NW9 . . . . . .**70** E3
  Orpington BR5 . . . . . .**193** J4
Chequers Gdns, N13 . . . .**59** H5
Chequers La, Dag. RM9 . .**119** F4
Chequers Par, SE9
  off Eltham High St . . .**156** C6
Chequers Rd, Loug. IG10 .**48** D5
Chequer St, EC1 . . . .**12** A6
Chequers Way, N13 . . . . .**59** J5

Cherbury Cl, SE28 . . . . .**118** D6
Cherbury Ct, N1 . . . .**12** C2
Cherbury St, N1 . . . .**12** C2
Cherchefelle Ms, Stan.
  HA7 . . . .**52** E5
Cherimoya Gdns, W.Mol. KT8
  off Kelvinbrook **179** H3
Cherington Rd, W7 . . . . .**124** C1
Cheriton Av, Brom. BR2 .**191** F5
  Ilford IG5 . . . .**80** C2
Cheriton Cl, W5 . . . .**105** F5
  Barnet EN4 . . . .**41** J3
Cheriton Dr, SE18 . . . . . .**137** G7
Cheriton Sq, SW17 . . . .**168** A2
Cherry Av, Sthl. UB1 . . . .**122** D1
Cherry Blossom Cl, N13 . .**59** H5
Cherry Cl, E17
  off Eden Rd **78** B4
  NW9 . . . .**71** E2
  SW2 off Tulse Hill **151** G7
  W5 . . . .**125** G3
  Carshalton SM5 . . . . .**199** J2
  Morden SM4 . . . .**184** B4
Cherrycot Hill, Orp. BR6 .**207** G4
Cherrycot Ri, Orp. BR6 . .**207** F4
Cherry Cres, Brent. TW8 .**124** E7
Cherrycroft Gdns, Pnr. HA5
  off Westfield Pk **51** F7
Cherrydown Av, E4 . . . . . .**61** J3
Cherrydown Cl, E4 . . . . . .**61** J3
Cherrydown Rd, Sid.
  DA14 . . . .**176** D2
Cherrydown Wk, Rom.
  RM7 . . . .**83** H2
Cherry Gdns, Dag. RM9 .**101** F5
  Northolt UB5 . . . .**85** H7
Cherry Gdn St, SE16 . . . .**132** E2
Cherry Garth, Brent.
  TW8 . . . .**125** G4
Cherry Gro, Hayes UB3 .**122** B1
Cherry Hill, Barn. EN5 . . . .**41** E6
  Harrow HA3 . . . .**52** B6
Cherry Hill Gdns, Croy.
  CR0 . . . .**201** F4
Cherry Hills, Wat. WD19 . .**50** E5
Cherrylands Cl, NW9 . . . .**88** C2
Cherry La, West Dr. UB7 .**120** C4
Cherry La Roundabout,
  West Dr. UB7 . . . .**120** E4
Cherry Laurel Wk, SW2
  off Beechdale Rd **151** F6
Cherry Orchard, West Dr.
  UB7 . . . .**120** B2
Cherry Orchard Gdns, Croy.
  CR0 off Oval Rd **202** A2
  West Molesey KT8 . . .**179** F3
Cherry Orchard Rd, Brom.
  BR2 . . . .**206** B2
  Croydon CR0 . . . .**202** A2
  West Molesey KT8 . . .**179** G3
Cherry Tree Cl, E9
  off Moulins Rd **113** F1
  Wembley HA0 . . . .**86** C4
Cherry Tree Ct, NW9 . . . .**70** C4
Cherry Tree Dr, SW16 . . .**169** E3
Cherry Tree Ri, Buck.H.
  IG9 . . . .**63** J4
Cherry Tree Rd, E15
  off Wingfield Rd . . .**96/97** E4
  N2 . . . .**73** J4
  Beckenham BR3 . . . . .**189** J4
  West Wickham BR4 . .**205** J4
Cherry Tree Way, Stan.
  HA7 . . . .**53** E6
Cherry Wk, Brom. BR2 .**205** G1
Cherry Way, Epsom
  KT19 . . . .**196** D6
Cherrywood Cl, E3 . . . . .**113** H3
  Kingston upon Thames
  KT2 . . . .**164** A7
Cherrywood Dr, SW15 . .**148** A5
Cherrywood La, Mord.
  SM4 . . . .**184** B4
Cherry Wd Way, W5
  off Hanger Vale La . .**106** A5
Cherston Gdns, Loug. IG10
  off Cherston Rd **48** D4
Cherston Rd, Loug. IG10 . .**48** D4
Chertsey Dr, Sutt. SM3 .**198** B2
Chertsey Rd, E11 . . . .**96** D2
  Ilford IG1 . . . .**99** G4
  Twickenham TW1,
  TW2 . . . .**144** C6
Chertsey St, SW17 . . . . .**168** A5
Chervil Cl, Felt. TW13 . . .**160** A3
Chervil Ms, SE28 . . . . . .**138** B1
Cherwell Ct, Epsom
  KT19 . . . .**196** C4
Cheryls Cl, SW6 . . . .**149** E1

Cheseman St, SE26 . . . .**171** E3
Chesfield Rd, Kings.T.
  KT2 . . . .**163** H7
Chesham Av, Orp. BR5 . .**192** E6
Chesham Cl, SW1 . . . .**24** B6
Chesham Cres, SE20 . . .**189** F2
Chesham Ms, SW1 . . . . . .**24** B5
Chesham Pl, SW1 . . . .**24** B6
Chesham Rd, SE20 . . . . .**189** F2
  SW19 . . . .**167** G5
  Kingston upon Thames
  KT1 . . . .**182** A1
Chesham St, NW10 . . . . .**88** D3
  SW1 . . . .**24** B6
Chesham Ter, W13 . . . . . .**124** C2
Cheshire Cl, E17 . . . .**78** B1
  SE4 . . . .**153** J2
  Mitcham CR4 . . . .**186** E3
Cheshire Ct, EC4 . . . .**19** F4
Cheshire Gdns, Chess.
  KT9 . . . .**195** G6
Cheshire Ho, N18 . . . .**61** E4
Cheshire Rd, N22 . . . .**59** F7
Cheshire St, E2 . . . .**13** G5
Chesholm Rd, N16 . . . . . .**94** B3
Cheshunt Rd, E7 . . . .**97** H6
  Belvedere DA17 . . . . .**139** G5
Chesil Ct, E2 . . . .**113** F2
Chesilton Rd, SW6 . . . . .**148** C1
Chesley Gdns, E6 . . . . . .**116** A2
Chesney Cres, Croy.
  (New Adgtn.) CR0 . . .**204** C7
Chesney St, SW11 . . . . .**150** A1
Chesnut Est, N17 . . . .**76** C3
Chesnut Gro, N17
  off Chesnut Rd **76** C3
Chesnut Rd, N17 . . . .**76** C3
CHESSINGTON **195** H6
Chessington Av, N3 . . . . .**72** B3
  Bexleyheath DA7 . . . .**139** E7
Chessington Cl, Epsom
  KT19 . . . .**196** C6
Chessington Ct, Pnr. HA5 .**67** F4
Chessington Hall Gdns,
  Chess. KT9 . . . .**195** G7
Chessington Hill Pk, Chess.
  KT9 . . . .**196** A5
Chessington Lo, N3 . . . . .**72** C3
Chessington Way, W.Wick.
  BR4 . . . .**204** B2
Chesson Rd, W14 . . . . . .**128** C6
Chesswood Way, Pnr.
  HA5 . . . .**66** D2
Chester Av, Rich. TW10 .**145** J5
  Twickenham TW2 . . . .**161** F1
Chester Cl, SW1 . . . .**24** C4
  SW13 . . . .**147** H3
  Loughton IG10 . . . .**49** F1
  Sutton SM1 . . . .**198** D2
Chester Cl N, NW1 . . . .**8** E3
Chester Cl S, NW1 . . . .**8** E4
Chester Cotts, SW1 . . . . .**32** B2
  SE5 . . . .**132** A7
Chester Cres, E8
  off Ridley Rd **94** C6
Chester Dr, Har. HA2 . . . . .**67** F6
Chesterfield Dr, Esher
  KT10 . . . .**194** D2
Chesterfield Gdns, N4 . . .**75** H5
  SE10 off Crooms Hill .**134** D7
  W1 . . . .**24** D1
Chesterfield Gro, SE22 .**152** C5
Chesterfield Hill, W1 . . . . .**16** D6
Chesterfield Ms, N4
  off Chesterfield Gdns . .**75** H5
Chesterfield Rd, E10 . . . .**78** C6
  N3 . . . .**56** D6
  W4 . . . .**126** C6
  Barnet EN5 . . . .**40** A5
  Epsom KT19 . . . .**196** D7
Chesterfield St, W1 . . . . .**24** D1
Chesterfield Wk, SE10 . .**154** D1
Chesterfield Way, SE15 .**133** F7
  Hayes UB3 . . . .**122** A2
Chesterford Gdns, NW3 .**91** E4
Chesterford Ho, SE18
  off Shooter's Hill Rd .**136** A7
Chesterford Rd, E12 . . . . .**98** C5
Chester Gdns, En3 . . . . .**104** D6
  Enfield EN3 . . . .**45** E6
  Morden SM4 . . . .**185** F6
Chester Gate, NW1 . . . . . .**8** D4
Chester Grn, Loug. IG10 . .**49** F1
Chester Ms, SW1 . . . .**24** D5
Chester Path, Loug. IG10 .**49** F1
Chester Pl, NW1 . . . .**8** E3
Chester Rd, E7 . . . .**98** A7
  E11 . . . .**79** H6
  E16 . . . .**115** E4

Chester Rd, E17 . . . .**77** G5
  N9 . . . .**61** E1
  N17 . . . .**76** A3
  N19 . . . .**92** B2
  NW1 . . . .**8** C4
  SW19 . . . .**165** J6
  Borehamwood WD6 . . .**38** C3
  Chigwell IG7 . . . .**64** D3
  Hounslow TW4 . . . . . .**142** B3
  Hounslow (Hthrw.Air.)
  TW6 . . . .**140** D3
  Ilford IG3 . . . .**99** J1
  Loughton IG10 . . . .**48** E2
  Sidcup DA15 . . . .**157** H5
Chester Row, SW1 . . . . . .**32** B2
Chesters, The, N.Mal.
  KT3 . . . .**182** E1
Chester Sq, SW1 . . . .**32** D1
Chester Sq Ms, SW1 . . . .**24** D6
Chester St, E2 . . . .**13** J5
  SW1 . . . .**24** C5
Chester Ter, NW1 . . . .**8** D3
Chesterton Cl, SW18
  off Ericcson Cl **148** D5
  Greenford UB6 . . . . . .**103** H2
Chesterton Rd, E13 . . . .**115** G3
  W10 . . . .**108** A5
Chesterton Sq, W8
  off Pembroke Rd **128** C4
Chesterton Ter, E13 . . . .**115** G3
  Kingston upon Thames
  KT1 . . . .**182** A2
Chester Way, SE11 . . . . . .**35** F2
Chesthunte Rd, N17 . . . . .**75** J1
Chestnut All, SW6
  off Lillie Rd **128** C6
Chestnut Av, E7 . . . .**97** H4
  N8 . . . .**74** E5
  SW14 off Thornton Rd .**146** D3
  Brentford TW8 . . . . . .**125** G4
  Buckhurst Hill IG9 . . . . .**64** A3
  East Molesey KT8 . . .**180** C3
  Edgware HA8 . . . .**53** H6
  Epsom KT19 . . . .**196** E4
  Esher KT10 . . . .**180** A7
  Hampton TW12 . . . . . .**161** G7
  Teddington TW11 . . . .**180** C2
  Wembley HA0 . . . .**86** B4
  West Wickham BR4 . .**205** E5
Chestnut Av N, E17 . . . . . .**78** C4
Chestnut Av S, E17 . . . . . .**78** C4
Chestnut Cl, N14 . . . .**42** C5
  N16 off Lordship Gro . .**94** A3
  SE6 . . . .**172** C5
  SE14
  off Shardeloes Rd . . .**153** J3
  SW16 . . . .**169** G4
  Buckhurst Hill IG9 . . . . .**64** A2
  Carshalton SM5 . . . . .**199** J1
  Sidcup DA15 . . . .**176** A1
  West Drayton UB7 . . .**121** E7
Chestnut Ct, SW6
  off North End Rd **128** C6
  Surbiton KT6
  off Penners Gdns . . .**181** H7
Chestnut Dr, E11 . . . .**79** G6
  Bexleyheath DA7 . . . .**158** D3
  Harrow HA3 . . . .**52** C7
  Pinner HA5 . . . .**66** D6
Chestnut Gro, SE20 . . . .**171** F7
  SW12 . . . .**150** A7
  W5 . . . .**125** G3
  Barnet EN4 . . . .**41** J5
  Ilford IG6 . . . .**65** H6
  Isleworth TW7 . . . . . .**144** D4
  Mitcham CR4 . . . .**186** D4
  New Malden KT3 . . . .**182** D3
  South Croydon CR2 . .**203** E7
  Wembley HA0 . . . .**86** B4
Chestnut La, N20 . . . .**56** B1
Chestnut Ms, SE18 . . . . .**137** C6
Chestnut Rd, E20 . . . . . .**169** H3
  SW20 . . . .**184** A2
  Kingston upon Thames
  KT2 . . . .**163** H7
  Twickenham TW2 . . . .**162** B2
Chestnut Row, N3
  off Nether St **56** D7
Chestnuts, The, SE14 . . .**153** J1
Chestnut Wk, Wdf.Grn.
  IG8 . . . .**63** G5
Chestnut Way, Felt.
  TW13 . . . .**160** B3
Cheston Av, Croy. CR0 . .**203** H2
Chettle Cl, SE1 . . . .**28** B5
Chettle Ct, N8 . . . .**75** G6
Chetwode Ho, NW8
Chetwode Rd, SW17 . . .**167** J2
Chetwode Wk, E6 . . . . . .**116** B6
Chetwynd Av, Barn. EN4 . .**57** J1
Chetwynd Rd, NW5 . . . . .**92** B4

Chevalier Cl, Stan. HA7 . . .53 H4
Cheval Pl, SW7 . . . . .23 H5
Cheval St, E14 . . . . . . .134 A3
Cheveney Wk, Brom. BR2
 off Marina Cl 191 G3
Chevening Rd, NW6 . . . .108 A2
 SE16 . . . . .135 F5
 SE19 . . . . .170 A6
Chevenings, The, Sid.
 DA14 . . . . .176 C3
Cheverton Rd, N19 . . . . .92 D1
Chevet St, E9
 off Kenworthy Rd 95 H5
Cheviot Cl, Enf. EN1 . . . .44 A2
 Hayes UB3 . . . . .121 G7
Cheviot Gdns, NW2 . . . . .90 A2
 SE27 . . . . .169 H4
Cheviot Gate, NW2 . . . . .90 B2
Cheviot Rd, SE27 . . . . .169 G5
Cheviot Way, Ilf. IG2 . . . .81 H4
Chevron Cl, E16 . . . . . .115 G6
Chevy Rd, Sthl. UB2 . . . .123 J2
Chewton Rd, E17 . . . . . .77 H4
Cheyne Av, E18 . . . . . . .79 F3
 Twickenham TW2 . . . . .161 F1
Cheyne Cl, NW4 . . . . . . .71 J5
 Bromley BR2
 off Cedar Cres 206 B3
Cheyne Ct, SW3 . . . . . . .31 J5
Cheyne Gdns, SW3 . . . . .31 H5
Cheyne Hill, Surb. KT5 . .181 J4
Cheyne Ms, SW3 . . . . . . .31 H5
Cheyne Path, W7 . . . . . .104 C5
Cheyne Pl, SW3 . . . . . . .31 J5
Cheyne Row, SW3 . . . . . .31 G6
Cheyne Wk, N21 . . . . . . .43 H5
 NW4 . . . . .71 J6
 SW3 . . . . .31 H6
 SW10 . . . . .30 E7
 Croydon CR0 . . . . . . .202 D2
Cheyneys Av, Edg. HA8 . . .53 G6
Chichele Gdns, Croy. CR0
 off Brownlow Rd 202 C4
Chichele Rd, NW2 . . . . . .90 A5
Chicheley Gdns, Har. HA3 .51 J7
Chicheley Rd, Har. HA3 . . .51 J7
Chicheley St, SE1 . . . . . .26 D3
Chichester Cl, E6 . . . . . .116 B6
 SE3 . . . . .155 J1
 Hampton TW12
 off Maple Cl 161 F6
Chichester Ct, Stan. HA7 . .69 H3
Chichester Gdns, Ilf. IG1 . .80 B7
Chichester Ms, SE27 . . . .169 G4
Chichester Rents, WC2 . . .18 E3
Chichester Rd, E11 . . . . . .97 E3
 N9 . . . . .60 D1
 NW6 . . . . .108 D2
 W2 . . . . .14 B1
 Croydon CR0 . . . . . . .202 B3
Chichester St, SW1 . . . . .33 G4
Chichester Way, E14 . . . .134 D4
 Feltham TW14 . . . . . . .142 B7
Chicksand St, E1 . . . . . . .21 G2
Chiddingfold, N12 . . . . . .56 D3
Chiddingstone Av, Bexh.
 DA7 . . . . .139 F7
Chiddingstone St, SW6 . .148 D2
Chieveley Rd, Bexh.
 DA7 . . . . .159 H4
Chignell Pl, W13
 off Broadway 124 D1
CHIGWELL 65 E3
Chigwell Hill, E1
 off Pennington
 St 112/113 E7
Chigwell Hurst Ct, Pnr.
 HA5 . . . . .66 D3
Chigwell La, Loug. IG10 . . .49 F6
Chigwell Pk, Chig. IG7 . . .64 E4
Chigwell Pk Dr, Chig. IG7 .64 D3
Chigwell Ri, Chig. IG7 . . . .64 D2
Chigwell Rd, E18 . . . . . . .79 H3
 Woodford Green IG8 . . .79 J2
Chilcombe Ho, SW15
 off Fontley Way 147 G7
Chilcot Cl, E14
 off Grundy St 114 B6
Childebert Rd, SW17 . . . .168 B2
Childeric Rd, SE14 . . . . .133 H7
Childerley, Kings.T. KT1
 off Burritt Rd 182 A3
Childerley St, SW6
 off Fulham Palace Rd .148 A1
Childers, The, Wdf.Grn.
 IG8 . . . . .64 C5
Childers St, SE8 . . . . . . .133 H6
Child La, SE10 . . . . .135 F3
CHILDS HILL, NW2 . . . . . .90 D2
Childs Hill Wk, NW2 . . . . .90 C3

Childs La, SE19
 off Westow St 170 B6
Child's Ms, SW5
 off Child's Pl 128 D4
Child's Pl, SW5 . . . . . . .128 D4
Child's St, SW5 . . . . . . .128 D4
Child's Wk, SW5
 off Child's St 128 D4
Childs Way, NW11 . . . . . .72 C5
Chilham Cl, Bex. DA5 . . .159 F7
 Greenford UB6 . . . . . .104 D2
Chilham Rd, SE9 . . . . . .174 B4
Chilham Way, Brom.
 BR2 . . . . .191 G7
Chillerton Rd, SW17 . . . .168 A5
Chillingworth Gdns,Twick.
 TW1 off Tower Rd 162 C3
Chillingworth Rd, N7 . . . .93 F5
Chilmark Gdns, N.Mal.
 KT3 . . . . .183 F7
Chilmark Rd, SW16 . . . .186 D2
Chiltern Av, Twick. TW2 . .161 G1
Chiltern Cl, Croy. CR0 . . .202 B3
 Worcester Park KT4
 off Cotswold Way 197 J2
Chiltern Dene, Enf. EN2 . .43 F4
Chiltern Dr, Surb. KT5 . . .182 B5
Chiltern Gdns, NW2 . . . . .90 A3
 Bromley BR2 . . . . . . .191 F4
Chiltern Rd, E3 . . . . . . .114 A4
 Ilford IG2 . . . . .81 H4
 Pinner HA5 . . . . .66 C5
Chiltern St, W1 . . . . .16 B1
Chiltern Way, Wdf.Grn.
 IG8 . . . . .63 G3
Chilthorne Cl, SE6
 off Ravensbourne
 Pk Cres 153 J7
Chilton Av, W5 . . . . .125 G4
Chilton Gro, SE8 . . . . . .133 G4
Chiltonian Ind Est, SE12 .155 F6
Chilton Rd, Edg. HA8
 off Manor Pk Cres 54 A6
 Richmond TW9 . . . . . .146 A3
Chiltons, The, E18
 off Grove Hill 79 G2
Chilton St, E2 . . . . .13 G5
Chilver St, SE10 . . . . . . .135 F5
Chilwell Gdns, Wat.
 WD19 . . . . .50 C4
Chilworth Ct, SW19 . . . . . .
 off Windlesham Gro . .166 A1
Chilworth Gdns, Sutt.
 SM1 . . . . .199 F3
Chilworth Ms, W2 . . . . . .14 D4
Chilworth St, W2 . . . . . . .14 D4
Chimes Av, N13 . . . . .59 G5
China Ms, SW2
 off Craster Rd 151 F7
★ Chinatown, W1
 off Gerrard St 17 H5
Chinbrook Cres, SE12 . . .173 H3
Chinbrook Est, SE9 . . . . .174 A3
Chinbrook Rd, SE12 . . . .173 H3
Chinchilla Dr, Houns.
 TW4 . . . . .142 C2
Chine, The, N10 . . . . .74 C4
 N21 . . . . .43 H6
 Wembley HA0 . . . . .87 E5
Ching Ct, WC2 . . . . .18 A4
Chingdale Rd, E4 . . . . . . .62 E3
CHINGFORD, E4 . . . . .62 B1
Chingford Av, E4 . . . . . . .62 B3
CHINGFORD GREEN, E4 . .63 F1
CHINGFORD HATCH, E4 . .62 D4
Chingford Ind Est, E4 . . . .61 H5
Chingford La, Wdf.Grn.
 IG8 . . . . .62 E4
Chingford Mt Rd, E4 . . . . .62 A4
Chingford Rd, E4 . . . . . . .62 A6
 E17 . . . . .78 B1
Chingley Cl, Brom. BR1 . .173 E6
Ching Way, E4 . . . . .61 J6
Chinnor Cres, Grnf. UB6 .103 H2
Chipka St, E14 . . . . .134 C2
Chipley St, SE14 . . . . . . .133 H6
Chipmunk Gro, Nthlt. UB5
 off Argus Way 102/103 E3
Chippendale St, E5 . . . . . .95 G3
Chippenham Av, Wem.
 HA9 . . . . .88 B5
Chippenham Gdns,
 NW6 . . . . .108 D3
Chippenham Ms, W9 . . . .108 D4
Chippenham Rd, W9 . . . .108 D4
CHIPPING BARNET, Barn. .40 B4
Chipping Cl, Barn. EN5
 off St. Albans Rd 40 B3
Chipstead Av, Th.Hth.
 CR7 . . . . .187 H4

Chipstead Cl, SE19 . . . . .170 C7
Chipstead Gdns, NW2 . . . .89 H2
Chipstead St, SW6 . . . . .148 D1
Chip St, SW4 . . . . .150 D3
Chirk Cl, Hayes UB4
 off Braunston Dr .102/103 E4
Chisenhale Rd, E3 . . . . . .113 H2
Chisholm Rd, Croy. CR0 .202 B2
 Richmond TW10 . . . . .145 J6
CHISLEHURST 174 D7
Chislehurst Av, N12 . . . . .57 F7
★ Chislehurst Caves, Chis.
 BR7 off Caveside Cl . .192 D1
Chislehurst Rd, Brom.
 BR1 . . . . .192 A2
 Orpington BR5, BR6 . .193 H4
 Richmond TW10 . . . . .145 H6
 Sidcup DA14 . . . . . . .176 A5
CHISLEHURST WEST,
 Chis. 174 C5
Chislet Cl, Beck. BR3
 off Abbey La 172 A7
Chisley Rd, N15 . . . . .76 B6
Chiswell Sq, SE3
 off Brook La 155 H2
Chiswell St, EC1 . . . . . . .20 A1
CHISWICK, W4 . . . . .126 D6
Chiswick Br, SW14 . . . . .146 C2
 W4 . . . . .146 C2
Chiswick Cl, Croy. CR0 . .201 F3
Chiswick Common Rd,
 W4 . . . . .126 D4
Chiswick Ct, Pnr. HA5 . . . .67 F3
Chiswick Grn Studios, W4
 off Evershed Wk 126 C4
Chiswick High Rd, W4 . . .126 D4
 Brentford TW8 . . . . . .125 J5
★ Chiswick Ho, W4 . . . . .126 D6
Chiswick Ho Grds, W4 . . .126 D6
Chiswick La, W4 . . . . . . .127 E5
Chiswick La S, W4 . . . . .127 F5
Chiswick Mall, W4 . . . . .127 F6
 W6 . . . . .127 F6
Chiswick Quay, W4 . . . . .146 C1
Chiswick Rd, N9 . . . . . . .60 D2
 W4 . . . . .126 C4
Chiswick Roundabout, W4
 off Chiswick High Rd .126 A5
Chiswick Sq, W4
 off Hogarth
 Roundabout 126/127 E6
Chiswick Staithe, W4 . . .146 C1
Chiswick Ter, W4
 off Acton La 126 C4
Chiswick Village, W4 . . . .126 B5
Chiswick Wf, W4 . . . . . . .127 F6
Chitterne Gate, West Dr.
 UB7 . . . . .120 D7
Chitty's La, Dag. RM8 . . .100 D2
Chitty St, W1 . . . . .17 G1
Chivalry Rd, SW11 . . . . .149 H5
Chivenor Gro, Kings.T.
 KT2 . . . . .163 G5
Chivers Rd, E4 . . . . .62 B3
Choats Manor Way, Bark.
 IG11 . . . . .118 C4
Choats Rd, Bark. IG11 . . .118 C2
 Dagenham RM9 . . . . .118 E2
Chobham Gdns, SW19 . . .166 A2
Chobham Rd, E15 . . . . . . .96 D5
Cholmeley Cres, N6 . . . . .74 B7
Cholmeley Pk, N6 . . . . . . .92 B1
Cholmley Gdns, NW6
 off Fortune Grn Rd 90 D5
Cholmley Rd, T.Ditt.
 KT7 . . . . .180 E6
Cholmondeley Av,
 NW10 . . . . .107 G2
Cholmondeley Wk, Rich.
 TW9 . . . . .145 F5
Choppins Ct, E1
 off Wapping La . .132/133 E1
Chopwell Cl, E15 . . . . . . .96 D7
Chorleywood Cres, Orp.
 BR5 . . . . .193 J2
Choumert Gro, SE15 . . . .152 D2
Choumert Rd, SE15 . . . .152 C3
Choumert Sq, SE15 . . . .152 D2
Chow Sq, E8
 off Arcola St 94 C5
Chrislaine Cl, Stai. (Stanw.)
 TW19 off High St 140 A6
Chrisp St, E14 . . . . .114 B5
Christchurch Av, N12 . . . .57 F6
 NW6 . . . . .90 B7
 Harrow HA3 . . . . .69 E4
 Teddington TW11 . . . .162 D5
 Wembley HA0 . . . . . . .87 H6

Christchurch Cl, SW19 . .167 G7
 Enfield EN2 . . . . .43 J2
Christchurch Ct, NW6 . . . .90 B7
Christchurch Gdns, Har.
 HA3 . . . . .68 D4
Christchurch Grn, Wem.
 HA0 . . . . .87 H6
Christchurch Hill, NW3 . . .91 G3
Christchurch La, Barn.
 EN5 . . . . .40 B2
Christchurch Pk, Sutt.
 SM2 . . . . .199 F7
Christ Ch Pas, EC1 . . . . . .19 H3
Christchurch Pas, NW3 . . .91 F3
 Barnet EN5 . . . . .40 B3
Christ Ch Path, Hayes
 UB3 . . . . .121 F3
Christchurch Rd, N8 . . . . .74 E6
 SW2 . . . . .169 F1
 SW14 . . . . .146 B5
 SW19 . . . . .185 G1
Christ Ch Rd, Beck. BR3
 off Fairfield Rd 190 A2
Christchurch Rd, Houns.
 (Hthrw.Air.) TW6
 off Courtney Rd 140 D3
 Ilford IG1 . . . . .99 E1
 Sidcup DA15 . . . . . . .175 J4
Christ Ch Rd, Surb. KT5 .181 J6
Christchurch Sq, E9
 off Victoria Pk Rd 113 F1
Christchurch St, SW3 . . . .31 J5
Christchurch Ter, SW3 . . .31 J5
Christchurch Way, SE10 .135 E4
Christian Cl, SE16 . . . . . .133 J1
Christian Flds, SW16 . . . .169 G7
Christian St, E1 . . . . .21 J3
Christie Dr, Croy. CR0 . . .188 D5
Christie Gdns, Rom. RM6 .82 B6
Christie Rd, E9 . . . . .95 H6
Christina Sq, N4
 off Adolphus St 93 H1
Christina St, EC2 . . . . . . .12 D5
Christine Worsley Cl, N21
 off Highfield Rd 59 H2
Christopher Av, W7 . . . . .124 D3
Christopher Cl, SE16 . . . .133 G2
 Sidcup DA15 . . . . . . .157 J5
Christopher Gdns, Dag. RM9
 off Wren Rd 100 D5
Christopher Pl, NW1 . . . . . .9 J4
Christopher Rd, Sthl.
 UB2 . . . . .122 B4
Christopher's Ms, W11
 off Penzance St 128 B1
Christopher St, EC2 . . . . .12 C6
Chryssell Rd, SW9 . . . . .131 G7
Chubworthy St, SE14 . . .133 H6
Chudleigh Cres, Ilf. IG3 . . .99 H4
Chudleigh Gdns, Sutt.
 SM1 . . . . .199 F3
Chudleigh Rd, NW6 . . . . .90 A7
 SE4 . . . . .153 J5
 Twickenham TW2 . . . .144 C7
Chudleigh St, E1 . . . . . . .113 G6
Chudleigh Way, Ruis.
 HA4 . . . . .84 A1
Chulsa Rd, SE26 . . . . . . .170 E5
Chumleigh St, SE5 . . . . . .36 D5
Chumleigh Wk, Surb.
 KT5 . . . . .181 J4
Church All, Croy. CR0 . . .201 G1
Church App, SE21 . . . . . .170 A3
 Staines (Stanw.) TW19 .140 A6
Church Av, E4 . . . . .62 D6
 NW1
 off Kentish Town Rd . . .92 B6
 SW14 . . . . .146 D3
 Beckenham BR3 . . . . .190 A1
 Northolt UB5 . . . . .85 F7
 Pinner HA5 . . . . .67 E6
 Sidcup DA14 . . . . . . .176 A5
 Southall UB2 . . . . . . .123 E3
Churchbury Cl, Enf. EN1 . .44 B2
Churchbury La, Enf. EN1 . .44 A3
Churchbury Rd, SE9 . . . .156 A7
 Enfield EN1 . . . . .44 A2
Church Cl, N20 . . . . .57 H3
 W8 . . . . .22 A3
 Edgware HA8 . . . . .54 C5
 Loughton IG10 . . . . . . .48 C2
 West Drayton UB7 . . . .120 B3
Church Ct, Rich. TW9
 off George St 145 G5
Church Cres, E9 . . . . .95 G7
 N3 . . . . .72 C1
 N10 . . . . .74 B4
 N20 . . . . .57 H3
Churchcroft Cl, SW12
 off Endlesham Rd 150 A7

Churchdown, Brom.
BR1 . . . . .173 E4
Church Dr, NW9 . . . . . . .88 D1
Harrow HA2 . . . . .67 F6
West Wickham BR4 . .205 E3
Church Elm La, Dag.
RM10 . . . . .101 G6
CHURCH END, N3 . . . . . .72 C1
CHURCH END, NW10 . . . .88 E6
Church End, E17 . . . . . . .78 B4
NW4 . . . . .71 H3
Church Entry, EC4 . . . . . .19 H4
★ Church Farm Ho Mus,
NW4 (Hendon) 71 H3
Church Fm La, Sutt.
SM3 . . . . .198 B6
Churchfield Av, N12 . . . .57 F6
Churchfield Cl, Har. HA2 . .67 J4
Churchfield Rd, W3 . . . .126 C1
W7 . . . . .124 B2
W13 . . . . .125 E1
Welling DA16 . . . . . . .158 A3
Churchfields, E18 . . . . . .79 G1
SE10 off Roan Rd 134 C6
Loughton IG10 . . . . . . .48 B4
West Molesey KT8 . . .179 G3
Churchfields Av, Felt.
TW13 . . . . .161 F3
Churchfields Rd, Beck.
BR3 . . . . .189 G2
Church Gdns, W5 . . . . .125 G2
Wembley HA0 . . . . . . .86 D4
Church Gate, SW6 . . . . .148 B3
Church Gro, SE13 . . . . .154 B4
Kingston upon Thames
KT1 . . . . .181 F1
Church Hill, E17 . . . . . . .78 A4
N21 . . . . .43 F7
SE18 . . . . .136 C3
SW19 . . . . .166 C5
Carshalton SM5 . . . . .199 J5
Harrow HA1 . . . . .86 B1
Loughton IG10 . . . . . . .48 B3
Church Hill Rd, E17 . . . . .78 B4
Barnet EN4 . . . . .41 J7
Surbiton KT6 . . . . . . .181 H5
Sutton SM3 . . . . .198 A4
Church Hill Wd, Orp.
BR5 . . . . .193 J5
Church Hyde, SE18
off Old Mill Rd 137 H6
Churchill Av, Har. HA3 . . .68 E6
Churchill Ct, W5 . . . . . .105 J4
Northolt UB5 . . . . .85 G5
Churchill Gdns, SW1 . . . .33 F4
W3 . . . . .106 A6
Churchill Gdns Rd, SW1 . .33 E4
off High Rd
Churchill Grn 63 F6
Harrow HA1
off Sandridge Cl 68 B4
Churchill Rd, E16 . . . . . .115 J6
NW2 . . . . .89 H6
NW5 . . . . .92 B4
Edgware HA8 . . . . .53 J6
South Croydon CR2 . .201 J7
Churchill Ter, E4 . . . . . . .62 A4
Churchill Wk, E9 . . . . . . .95 F5
Churchill Way, Brom. BR1
off Ethelbert Rd 191 G3
Sunbury-on-Thames
TW16 . . . . .160 A5
Church La, E11 . . . . .96 E1
E17 . . . . .78 B4
N2 . . . . .73 G3
N8 . . . . .75 F4
N9 . . . . .60 D2
N17 . . . . .76 B1
NW9 . . . . .88 C2
SW17 . . . . .168 B4
SW19 . . . . .184 C1
W5 . . . . .125 F2
Bromley BR2 . . . . . . .206 B1
Chessington KT9 . . . .195 J6
Chislehurst BR7 . . . . .193 F1
Dagenham RM10 . . . .101 H6
Enfield EN1 . . . . .44 A3
Harrow HA3 . . . . .68 C1
Loughton IG10 . . . . . . .48 C3
Pinner HA5 . . . . .67 E3
Richmond TW10 . . . . .163 H1
Teddington TW11 . . . .162 C5
Thames Ditton KT7 . . .180 C6
Twickenham TW1 . . . .162 D1
Wallington SM6 . . . . .200 D3
Churchley Rd, SE26 . . . .171 E4
Church Manor Est, SW9
off Vassall Rd 131 G7

Church Manorway, SE2 .137 J4
Church Manorway Ind Est,
Erith DA8 . . . . .139 J3
Churchmead Cl, Barn.
EN4 . . . . .41 H6
Church Meadow, Surb.
KT6 . . . . .195 F2
Churchmead Rd, NW10 . .89 G6
Churchmore Rd, SW16 . .186 C1
Church Mt, N2 . . . . .73 G5
Church Paddock Ct, Wall.
SM6 . . . . .200 D3
Church Pas, EC2
off Gresham St 111 J6
Barnet EN5
off Wood St 40 C4
Surbiton KT6 . . . . . . .181 H5
Church Path, E11 . . . . . . .79 G5
E17 off St. Mary Rd . . .78 B4
N12 . . . . .57 F5
N17 off White Hart La . .60 B7
N20 . . . . .57 F4
NW10 . . . . .89 E7
SW14 . . . . .146 D3
SW19 . . . . .184 D2
W4 . . . . .126 C3
W7 . . . . .124 B1
Mitcham CR4 . . . . . . .185 H3
Southall UB1 . . . . . . .123 G1
Southall (Sthl.Grn.)
UB2 . . . . .123 F3
Church Pl, SW1 . . . . .17 G6
W5 off Church Gdns . .125 G2
Mitcham CR4 . . . . . . .185 H3
Twickenham TW1
off Church La 162/163 E1
Church Ri, SE23 . . . . . . .171 G1
Chessington KT9 . . . .195 J6
Church Rd, E10 . . . . .96 B2
E12 . . . . .98 B5
E17 . . . . .77 H2
N6 . . . . .74 A4
N17 . . . . .76 B1
NW4 . . . . .71 H4
NW10 . . . . .89 E6
SE19 . . . . .188 B1
SW13 . . . . .147 F2
SW19 (Wimbledon) . . .166 B4
W3 . . . . .126 C2
W7 . . . . .124 C1
Barking IG11 . . . . .99 F6
Bexleyheath DA7 . . . .159 F2
Bromley BR2 . . . . . . .191 G2
Bromley (Short.) BR2 . .190 E3
Buckhurst Hill IG9 . . . .63 H1
Croydon CR0 . . . . . . .201 H3
East Molesey KT8 . . . .180 A4
Enfield EN3 . . . . .45 F6
Epsom (W.Ewell) KT19 .196 D7
Esher (Clay.) KT10 . . .194 C6
Feltham TW13 . . . . . .160 D5
Hayes UB3 . . . . .121 J1
Hounslow (Cran.) TW5 .122 B5
Hounslow (Heston)
TW5 . . . . .123 G7
Ilford IG2 . . . . .81 G6
Isleworth TW7 . . . . . .144 A1
Keston BR2 . . . . .206 A7
Kingston upon Thames
KT1 . . . . .181 J2
Loughton (High Beach)
IG10 . . . . .47 H2
Mitcham CR4 . . . . . . .185 G2
Northolt UB5 . . . . .85 F7
Orpington (Farnboro.)
BR6 . . . . .207 F5
Richmond TW9, TW10 .145 H5
Richmond (Ham) TW10 .163 J5
Sidcup DA14 . . . . . . .176 A4
Southall UB2 . . . . . . .123 F3
Stanmore HA7 . . . . . . .53 E5
Surbiton KT6 . . . . . . .195 F2
Sutton SM3 . . . . .198 B6
Teddington TW11 . . . .162 B4
Wallington SM6 . . . . .200 C3
Welling DA16 . . . . . . .158 B2
West Drayton UB7 . . . .120 A3
Worcester Park KT4 . .196 E1
Church Rd Merton,
SW19 . . . . .185 G1
Church Rd Twr Block, Stan.
HA7 off Church Rd . . .53 F5
Church Row, NW3 . . . . . .91 F4
Chislehurst BR7 . . . . .175 F7
Church St, E15 . . . . .115 E1
E16 . . . . .136 E1
N9 . . . . .60 B2
NW8 . . . . .15 F1
W2 . . . . .15 F1
W4 . . . . .127 E6

Church St, Croy. CR0 . . .201 J2
Dagenham RM10 . . . .101 H6
Enfield EN2 . . . . .44 A3
Hampton TW12 . . . . . .179 J1
Isleworth TW7 . . . . . .144 E3
Kingston upon Thames
KT1 . . . . .181 G2
Sunbury-on-Thames
TW16 . . . . .178 B3
Sutton SM1 . . . . .198/199 E5
Twickenham TW1 . . . .162 D1
Church St Est, NW8 . . . . .7 F6
Church St N, E15 . . . . . .115 E1
Church St Pas, E15
off Church St 114/115 E1
Church Stretton Rd, Houns.
TW3 . . . . .143 J5
Church Ter, NW4 . . . . . . .71 H3
SE13 . . . . .154 E3
SW8 . . . . .150 D2
Richmond TW10 . . . . .145 G5
Church Vale, N2 . . . . . . .73 J3
SE23 . . . . .171 F2
Churchview Rd, Twick.
TW2 . . . . .162 A1
Church Wk, N6 . . . .
off Swains La 92 A3
N16 . . . . .94 A4
NW2 . . . . .90 C3
NW4 . . . . .71 J3
NW9 . . . . .88 D2
SW13 . . . . .147 G1
SW15 . . . . .147 H5
SW16 . . . . .186 C2
SW20 . . . . .183 J3
Brentford TW8 . . . . . .125 F6
Enfield EN2
off Church La 44 A3
Richmond TW9
off Red Lion St 145 G5
Thames Ditton KT7 . . .180 C6
Church Way, N20 . . . . . . .57 G3
Churchway, NW1 . . . . . . .9 J3
Church Way, Barn. EN4 . . .41 J4
Edgware HA8 . . . . .54 A6
Churchwell Path, E9 . . . . .95 F5
Churchwood Gdns, Wdf.Grn.
IG8 . . . . .63 G4
Churchyard Row, SE11 . . .35 H1
Church Yd Wk, W2 . . . . . .15 E1
Churston Av, E13 . . . . . .115 H1
Churston Cl, SW2
off Tulse Hill 169 H1
SM4 . . . . .184 A5
Churston Dr, Mord.
SM4 . . . . .184 A5
Churston Gdns, N11 . . . . .58 C6
Churton Pl, SW1 . . . . . . .33 G2
Churton St, SW1 . . . . . . .33 G2
Chusan Pl, E14 . . . .
off Commercial Rd . . .113 J6
Chyngton Cl, Sid. DA15 .175 J3
Cibber Rd, SE23 . . . . . .171 G2
Cicada Rd, SW18 . . . . . .149 F5
Cicely Rd, SE15 . . . . . . .152 D1
Cinderella Path, NW11
off North End Rd . . .90/91 E1
Cinderford Way, Brom.
BR1 . . . . .173 E4
Cinema Par, W5
off Ashburne Rd 105 J4
Cinnabar Wf, E1 . . . . . . .29 J2
Cinnamon Cl, Croy. CR0 .186 E7
Cinnamon Row, SW11 . .149 F3
Cintra Pk, SE19 . . . . . . .170 C7
Circle, The, NW2 . . . . . . .89 E3
NW7 . . . . .54 D5
SE1 . . . . .29 F3
Circle Gdns, SW19 . . . . .184 D2
Circuits, The, Pnr. HA5 . . .66 C4
Circular Rd, N17 . . . . . . .76 C3
Circular Way, SE18 . . . . .136 C6
Circus Ms, W1 . . . . .15 J1
Circus Pl, EC2 . . . . .20 C2
Circus Rd, NW8 . . . . .6 E3
Circus St, SE10 . . . . . . .134 C7
Cirencester St, W2 . . . . . .14 A1
Cissbury Ring N, N12 . . . .56 C5
Cissbury Ring S, N12 . . . .56 C5
Cissbury Rd, N15 . . . . . . .76 A5
Citadel Pl, SE11 . . . . .34 C3
Citizen Ho, N7
off Harvist Est 93 G4
Citizen Rd, N7 . . . . .93 G4
C.I. Twr, N.Mal. KT3 . . . .183 E3
Citron Ter, SE15
off Nunhead La . . .152/153 E3
City Forum, EC1 . . . . . . .11 J3
City Gdn Row, N1 . . . . . . .11 H2

City Gate Ho, Ilf. IG2 . . . .80 E6
City Ho, Croy. CR0 . . . . .187 H7
★ City of Westminster
Archives Cen, SW1
off St. Ann's St 25 J5
City Pt, EC2 . . . . .20 B2
City Rd, EC1 . . . . .11 G2
★ City Uni, EC1 . . . . . . .11 G4
Civic Way, Ilf. IG6 . . . . . . .81 F4
Ruislip HA4 . . . . .84 D5
Clabon Ms, SW1 . . . . . . .23 J6
Clack St, SE16 . . . . .133 F2
Clacton Rd, E6 . . . . .116 A3
E17 . . . . .77 H6
N17 off Sperling Rd . . .76 C2
Claigmar Gdns, N3 . . . . . .72 E1
Claire Ct, N12 . . . . .57 F3
Bushey (Bushey Hth.)
WD23 . . . . .52 A1
Pinner HA5
off Westfield Pk 51 F7
Claire Gdns, Stan. HA7 . . .53 F5
Claire Pl, E14 . . . . .134 A3
Clairvale Rd, Houns.
TW5 . . . . .142 D1
Clairview Rd, SW16 . . . .168 B5
Clairville Gdns, W7 . . . . .124 C1
Clairville Pt, SE23 . . . . . .171 G3
Clamp Hill, Stan. HA7 . . .52 A4
Clancarty Rd, SW6 . . . . .148 D2
Clandon Cl, W3
off Avenue Rd 126 B2
Epsom KT17 . . . . .197 F6
Clandon Gdns, N3 . . . . . .72 D3
Clandon Rd, Ilf. IG3 . . . . .99 H2
Clandon St, SE8 . . . . . . .154 A2
Clanfield Way, SE15 . . . . .37 E7
Clanricarde Gdns, W2 . . .108 D7
CLAPHAM, SW4 . . . . . . .150 B3
★ Clapham Common,
SW4 . . . . .150 A4
Clapham Common N Side,
SW4 . . . . .150 B4
Clapham Common S Side,
SW4 . . . . .150 B5
Clapham Common W Side,
SW4 . . . . .150 A4
Clapham Cres, SW4 . . . .150 D4
Clapham Est, SW11 . . . .149 H4
Clapham High St, SW4 . .150 D4
Clapham Manor St,
SW4 . . . . .150 C3
CLAPHAM PARK, SW4 . .150 D6
Clapham Pk Est, SW4 . . .150 D6
Clapham Pk Rd, SW4 . . .150 D4
Clapham Rd, SW9 . . . . .150 E3
Clapham Rd Est, SW4 . . .150 D3
Clap La, Dag. RM10 . . . .101 H3
Claps Gate La, E6 . . . . . .116 E4
Clapton Common, E5 . . . .76 C7
CLAPTON PARK, E5 . . . . .95 H4
Clapton Pk Est, E5
off Blackwell Cl 95 H4
Clapton Pas, E5 . . . . .95 F5
Clapton Sq, E5 . . . . .95 F5
Clapton Ter, N16
off Oldhill St 94 D1
Clapton Way, E5 . . . . . . .94 D4
Clara Pl, SE18 . . . . .136 D4
Clare Cl, N2
off Thomas More Way . .73 F3
Clare Cor, SE9 . . . . .156 E7
Claredale St, E2 . . . . .13 J2
Clare Gdns, E7 . . . . .97 G4
W11 off Westbourne
Pk Rd 108 B6
Barking IG11 . . . . .99 J6
Clare Ho, E3 . . . . .113 J1
Clare La, N1 . . . . .93 J7
Clare Lawn Av, SW14 . . .146 D5
Clare Mkt, WC2 . . . . .18 C4
Clare Ms, SW6
off Waterford Rd .128/129 E7
Claremont Av, Har. HA3 . .69 H5
New Malden KT3 . . . .183 G5
Sunbury-on-Thames
TW16 . . . . .178 B1
Claremont Cl, E16 . . . . . .136 D1
N1 . . . . .11 F2
SW2 off Streatham
Hill 168/169 E1
Orpington BR6 . . . . . .206 D4
Claremont Ct, Surb. KT6
off St. James Rd 181 G6
Claremont Gdns, Ilf. IG3 . .99 H2
Surbiton KT6 . . . . . . .181 H5
Claremont Gro, W4
off Edensor
Gdns 126/127 E7
Woodford Green IG8 . . .63 J6

Claremont Pk, N3 . . . . .72 B1
Claremont Rd, E7 . . . . .97 H5
  E17 . . . . .77 H2
  N6 . . . . .74 C7
  NW2 . . . . .90 A3
  W9 . . . . .108 B2
  W13 . . . . .104 D5
  Bromley BR1 . . . . . . .192 B4
  Croydon CR0 . . . . . . .202 D1
  Esher (Clay.) KT10 . . .194 B7
  Harrow HA3 . . . . .68 B2
  Surbiton KT6 . . . . . . .181 H6
  Teddington TW11 . . . .162 C5
  Twickenham TW1 . . . .145 F6
Claremont Sq, N1 . . . . .10 E2
Claremont St, E16 . . . . .136 D1
  N18 . . . . .60 D6
  SE10 . . . . .134 B6
Claremont Way, NW2 . . .89 J1
Clarence Av, SW4 . . . . .150 D6
  Bromley BR1 . . . . . . .192 B4
  Ilford IG2 . . . . .80 D6
  New Malden KT3 . . . . .182 C2
Clarence Cl, Barn. EN4 . .41 G5
Clarence Cres, SW4 . . . .150 D6
  Sidcup DA14 . . . . . . .176 B3
Clarence Gdns, NW1 . . . .9 E4
Clarence Gate, Wdf.Grn.
  IG8 . . . . .64 D6
Clarence Gate Gdns, NW1
  off Glentworth St 109 J4
★ Clarence Ho, SW1 . . . .25 J3
Clarence La, SW15 . . . .147 E6
Clarence Ms, E5 . . . . . .95 E5
  SE16 . . . . .133 G1
  SW12 . . . . .150 B7
Clarence Pas, NW1 . . . .10 A2
Clarence Pl, E5 . . . . . . .95 E5
Clarence Rd, E5 . . . . . . .95 E4
  E12 . . . . .98 A5
  E16 . . . . .115 E4
  E17 . . . . .77 G2
  N15 . . . . .75 J5
  N22 . . . . .59 E7
  NW6 . . . . .90 C7
  SE9 . . . . .174 B2
  SW19 . . . . .166 E6
  W4 . . . . .126 A5
  Bexleyheath DA6 . . . .158 E4
  Bromley BR1 . . . . . . .192 A3
  Croydon CR0 . . . . . . .188 A7
  Enfield EN3 . . . . .45 E5
  Richmond TW9 . . . . . .145 J1
  Sidcup DA14 . . . . . . .176 B3
  Sutton SM1 . . . . .198 E4
  Teddington TW11 . . . .162 C6
  Wallington SM6 . . . . .200 B5
Clarence St, Kings.T.
  KT1 . . . . .181 H2
  Richmond TW9 . . . . . .145 H4
  Southall UB2 . . . . . . .122 D3
Clarence Ter, NW1 . . . . .8 A5
  Hounslow TW3 . . . . . .143 H4
Clarence Wk, SW4 . . . . .150 E2
Clarence Way, NW1 . . . .92 B7
Clarence Way Est, NW1 . .92 B7
Clarendon Cl, E9 . . . . . .95 F7
  W2 . . . . .15 G5
Clarendon Cres, Twick.
  TW2 . . . . .162 A3
Clarendon Cross, W11
  off Portland Rd 108 B7
Clarendon Dr, SW15 . . .147 J4
Clarendon Gdns, NW4 . . .71 H3
  W9 . . . . .6 D6
  Ilford IG1 . . . . .98 C1
  Wembley HA9 . . . . . . .87 H4
Clarendon Gro, NW1 . . . .9 H3
  Mitcham CR4 . . . . . . .185 J3
Clarendon Ms, W2 . . . . .15 G5
  Bexley DA5 . . . . .177 H1
  Borehamwood WD6
    off Clarendon Rd 38 A3
Clarendon Pl, W2 . . . . . .15 G5
Clarendon Ri, SE13 . . . .154 C3
Clarendon Rd, E11 . . . . .96 D1
  E17 . . . . .78 B6
  E18 . . . . .79 G3
  N8 . . . . .75 F3
  N15 . . . . .75 H4
  N18 . . . . .60 D6
  N22 . . . . .75 F2
  SW19 . . . . .167 H7
  W5 . . . . .105 H4
  W11 . . . . .108 B7
  Borehamwood WD6 . . .38 A3
  Croydon CR0 . . . . . . .201 H2
  Harrow HA1 . . . . .68 B6
  Hayes UB3 . . . . .121 J2
  Wallington SM6 . . . . .200 C6

Clarendon St, SW1 . . . . .32 E4
Clarendon Ter, W9 . . . . .6 D5
Clarendon Wk, W11 . . . .108 B6
Clarendon Way, N21 . . . .43 J6
  Chislehurst BR7 . . . . .193 J3
  Orpington BR5 . . . . . .193 J3
Clarens St, SE6 . . . . . . .171 J2
Clare Pl, SW15
  off Minstead Gdns 147 F7
Clare Pt, NW2
  off Claremont Rd 90 A1
Clare Rd, E11 . . . . .78 D6
  NW10 . . . . .89 G7
  SE14 . . . . .153 J1
  Greenford UB6 . . . . . .86 A6
  Hounslow TW4 . . . . . .143 F3
  Staines (Stanw.)TW19 .140 B7
Clare St, E2 . . . . .113 E2
Claret Gdns, SE25 . . . . .188 B4
Clareville Gro, SW7 . . . .30 D2
Clareville Rd, Orp. BR5 . .207 F2
Clareville St, SW7 . . . . .30 D2
Clare Way, Bexh. DA7 . . .158 E1
Clarewood Wk, SW9
  off Somerleyton Rd . . .151 G4
Clarges Ms, W1 . . . . . . .24 D1
Clarges St, W1 . . . . . . .24 E1
Claribel Rd, SW9 . . . . . .151 H2
Claridge Rd, Dag. RM8 . .100 D1
Clarina Rd, SE20
  off Evelina Rd 171 G7
Clarissa Rd, Rom. RM6 . .82 D7
Clarissa St, E8 . . . . . . .112 C1
Clarke Ms, N9
  off Plevna Rd 60 E3
Clarke Path, N16 . . . . . .94 D1
Clarkes Av, Wor.Pk. KT4 .198 A1
Clarke's Ms, W1 . . . . . .16 C1
Clark Lawrence Ct, SW11
  off Winstanley Rd 149 G3
Clarkson Rd, E16 . . . . . .115 F6
Clarkson Row, NW1 . . . .9 E2
Clarksons,The, Bark.
  IG11 . . . . .117 F2
Clarkson St, E2 . . . . . . .112 E3
Clarks Pl, EC2 . . . . .20 D3
Clarks Rd, Ilf. IG1 . . . . . .99 G2
Clark St, E1 . . . . .113 E5
Clark Way, Houns.TW5 . .122 D7
Classon Cl, West Dr.
  UB7 . . . . .120 B2
Claude Rd, E10 . . . . . . .96 C2
  E13 . . . . .115 H1
  SE15 . . . . .152 E2
Claude St, E14 . . . . . . .134 A4
Claudia Jones Way,
  SW2 . . . . .150 E6
Claudia Pl, SW19 . . . . . .166 B1
Claughton Rd, E13 . . . . .115 J2
Clauson Av, Nthlt. UB5 . .85 H5
Clavell St, SE10 . . . . . . .134 C6
Claverdale Rd, SW2 . . . .151 F7
Clavering Av, SW13 . . . .127 H6
Clavering Cl, Twick. TW1 .162 D4
Claverings Ind Est, N9 . . .61 G2
Claverley Gro, N3 . . . . . .56 D7
Claverley Vil, N3
  off Claverley Gro . .56/57 E7
Claverton St, SW1 . . . . .33 G4
Clave St, E1
  off Cinnamon St .132/133 E1
Claxton Gro, W6 . . . . . .128 A5
Clay Av, Mitch. CR4 . . . .186 B2
Claybank Gro, SE13
  off Algernon Rd 154 B3
Claybourne Ms, SE19
  off Church Rd 170 B7
Claybridge Rd, SE12 . . . .173 J4
Claybrook Cl, N2 . . . . . .73 G3
Claybrook Rd, W6 . . . . .128 A6
Claybury Bdy, Ilf. IG5 . . . .80 B3
Claybury Rd, Wdf.Grn.
  IG8 . . . . .64 B7
Claydon Dr, Croy. CR0 . .201 E4
Claydon Ms, SE18
  off Woolwich New Rd .136 D5
Clayfarm Rd, SE9 . . . . .175 F2
CLAYGATE, Esher 194 B7
Claygate Cres, Croy.
  (New Adgtn.) CR0 . . . .204 C6
Claygate La, Esher KT10 .194 D2
  Thames Ditton KT7 . . .194 D1
Claygate Lo Cl, Esher
  (Clay.) KT10 . . . . . . .194 B7
Claygate Rd, W13 . . . . .124 E3
CLAYHALL, Ilf. 80 C2
Clayhall Av, Ilf. IG5 . . . . .80 B3
Clayhill, Surb. KT5 . . . . .182 A5
Clayhill Cres, SE9 . . . . .174 A4

Claylands Pl, SW8 . . . . . .34 E7
Claylands Rd, SW8 . . . . .34 D6
Clay La, Edg. HA8 . . . . . .54 A1
  Staines (Stanw.)TW19 .140 C7
Claymill Ho, SE18 . . . . .137 F5
Claymore Cl, Mord. . . . . .
  SM4 . . . . .184 D7
Claymore Ct, E17
  off Billet Rd 77 H1
Claypole Dr, Houns. . . . . .
  TW5 . . . . .143 E1
Claypole Rd, E15 . . . . . .114 C2
Clayponds Av, Brent. . . . . .
  TW8 . . . . .125 H4
Clayponds Gdns, W5 . . .125 G4
Clayponds La, Brent. . . . . .
  TW8 . . . . .125 H5
Clay Rd,The, Loug. IG10 . .48 B1
Clayside, Chig. IG7 . . . . .65 F6
Clays La, E15 . . . . .96 B5
Clay's La, Loug. IG10 . . . .48 D1
Clays La Cl, E15 . . . . . . .96 B5
Clay St, W1 . . . . .16 A2
Clayton Av, Wem. HA0 . . .87 H7
Clayton Cl, E6
  off Brandreth Rd 116 C6
Clayton Cres, N1 . . . .
  off Havelock St 110 E1
  BrentfordTW8 . . . . . . .125 G5
Clayton Fld, NW9 . . . . . .55 E7
Clayton Ms, SE10 . . . . . .154 D1
Clayton Rd, SE15 . . . . . .152 D1
  Chessington KT9 . . . . .195 F4
  Hayes UB3 . . . . .121 H2
  IsleworthTW7 . . . . . . .144 B3
  Romford RM7 . . . . . . .101 J1
Clayton St, SE11 . . . . . . .34 E5
Clayton Ter, Hayes UB4
  off Jollys La 102 D5
Claywood Cl, Orp. BR6 . .193 H7
Clayworth Cl, Sid. DA15 .158 B6
Cleanthus Cl, SE18
  off Cleanthus Rd .156/157 E1
Cleanthus Rd, SE18 . . . .157 E1
Clearbrook Way, E1
  off West Arbour St 113 G6
Clearwater Ter, W11
  off Lorne Gdns 128 A2
Clearwell Dr, W9 . . . . . . .6 A6
Cleave Av, Hayes UB3 . . .121 H4
  Orpington BR6 . . . . . .207 H6
Cleaveland Rd, Surb. . . . . .
  KT6 . . . . .181 G5
Cleaverholme Cl, SE25 . .188 E6
Cleaver Sq, SE11 . . . . . .35 F3
Cleaver St, SE11 . . . . . . .35 F3
Cleeve Hill, SE23 . . . . . .171 E1
Cleeve Pk Gdns, Sid. . . . . .
  DA14 . . . . .176 B2
Cleeve Way, SW15
  off Danebury Av 147 F7
Clegg Ho, SE3 . . . .
  off Pinto Way 155 H4
Clegg St, E1
  off Prusom St . . .132/133 E1
  E13 . . . . .115 G2
Cleland Path, Loug. IG10 . .49 E1
Clematis Gdns, Wdf.Grn.
  IG8 . . . . .63 G5
Clematis St, W12 . . . . . .107 F7
Clem Attlee Ct, SW6 . . . .128 C6
Clem Attlee Est, SW6
  off Lillie Rd 128 C6
Clem Attlee Par, SW6
  off Clem Attlee Ct 128 C6
Clemence Rd, Dag.
  RM10 . . . . .119 J1
Clemence St, E14 . . . . . .113 J5
Clement Av, SW4 . . . . . .150 D4
Clement Cl, NW6 . . . . . . .89 J7
  W4 off Acton La 126 D4
Clement Gdns, Hayes
  UB3 . . . . .121 H4
Clementhorpe Rd, Dag.
  RM9 . . . . .100 C6
Clementina Rd, E10 . . . . .95 J1
Clementine Cl, W13
  off Balfour Rd . . .124/125 E2
Clement Rd, SW19 . . . . .166 B5
  Beckenham BR3 . . . . .189 G2
Clements Av, E16 . . . . . .115 G7
Clements Cl, Houns. . . . . .
  TW4 . . . . .142 D4
  Ilford IG1
    off Clements La . .98/99 E3
Clement's Inn, WC2 . . . . .18 D4
Clement's Inn Pas, WC2 . .18 D4
Clements La, EC4 . . . . . . .20 C5
  Ilford IG1 . . . . .98 E3
Clements Pl, Brent.TW8 .125 G5

Clements Rd, E6 . . . . . . .98 C7
  SE16 . . . . .29 J6
  Ilford IG1 . . . . .98 E3
Clendon Way, SE18
  off Polthorne Gro 137 G4
Clennam St, SE1 . . . . . . .28 A3
Clensham Ct, Sutt. SM1
  off Sutton Common
    Rd 198 D2
Clensham La, Sutt. SM1 .198 D2
Clenston Ms, W1 . . . . . . .15 J3
★ Cleopatra's Needle,
  WC2 . . . . .18 C6
Clephane Rd, N1 . . . . . . .93 J6
Clere St, EC2 . . . . .12 C5
CLERKENWELL, EC1 . . . .11 G6
Clerkenwell Cl, EC1 . . . . .11 F5
Clerkenwell Grn, EC1 . . . .11 F6
Clerkenwell Rd, EC1 . . . .10 E6
Clerks Piece, Loug. IG10 . .48 C3
Clermont Rd, E9 . . . . . . .113 F1
Clevedon Cl, N16
  off Smalley Cl 94 C3
Clevedon Gdns, Hayes
  UB3 . . . . .121 G3
  HounslowTW5 . . . . . .142 B1
Clevedon Rd, SE20 . . . . .189 G1
  Kingston upon Thames
    KT1 . . . . .182 A2
  Twickenham TW1 . . . .145 G6
Cleveland Av, SW20 . . . .184 C2
  W4 . . . . .127 F4
  Hampton TW12 . . . . . .161 F7
Cleveland Cres, Borwd. . . . . .
  WD6 . . . . .38 C5
Cleveland Gdns, N4 . . . . .75 J5
  NW2 . . . . .90 A2
  SW13 . . . . .147 F2
  W2 . . . . .14 C4
  Worcester Park KT4 . . .197 E2
Cleveland Gro, E1
  off Cleveland Way 113 F4
Cleveland Ms, W1 . . . . . .17 F1
Cleveland Pk, Stai. TW19
  off Northumberland
    Cl 140 B6
Cleveland Pk Av, E17 . . . .78 A4
Cleveland Pk Cres, E17 . . .78 A4
Cleveland Pl, SW1 . . . . . .25 G1
Cleveland Ri, Mord. . . . . .
  SM4 . . . . .184 A7
Cleveland Rd, E18 . . . . . .79 G3
  N1 . . . . .94 A7
  N9 . . . . .45 E7
  SW13 . . . . .147 F2
  W4 off Antrobus Rd . . .126 C3
  W13 . . . . .104 E5
  Ilford IG1 . . . . .99 E3
  IsleworthTW7 . . . . . . .144 D4
  New Malden KT3 . . . . .182 E4
  Welling DA16 . . . . . . .157 J2
  Worcester Park KT4 . . .197 E2
Cleveland Row, SW1 . . . .25 F2
Cleveland Sq, W2 . . . . . .14 C4
Cleveland St, W1 . . . . . . .9 F6
Cleveland Ter, W2 . . . . . .14 D3
Cleveland Way, E1 . . . . .113 F4
Cleveley Cl, SE7 . . . . . . .136 A4
Cleveley Cres, W5 . . . . . .105 H2
Cleveleys Rd, E5 . . . . . . .95 E3
Cleverly Est, W12 . . . . . .127 G1
Cleve Rd, NW6 . . . . .90 D7
  Sidcup DA14 . . . . . . .176 D3
Cleves Cl, Loug. IG10 . . . .48 B6
Cleves Rd, E6 . . . . .116 A1
  RichmondTW10 . . . . .163 F3
Cleves Wk, Ilf. IG6 . . . . . .65 F7
Cleves Way, Hmptn. . . . . .
  TW12 . . . . .161 F7
  Ruislip HA4 . . . . .84 D1
Clewer Cres, Har. HA3 . . .68 A1
Clewer Ho, SE2
  off Wolvercote Rd 138 D2
Clichy Est, E1 . . . . .113 F5
Clifden Rd, E5 . . . . .95 F5
  BrentfordTW8 . . . . . . .125 G6
  Twickenham TW1 . . . .162 C1
Cliffe Rd, S.Croy. CR2 . . .202 A5
Cliffe Wk, Sutt. SM1
  off Turnpike La 199 F5
Clifford Av, SW14 . . . . . .146 B3
  Chislehurst BR7 . . . . .174 C6
  Ilford IG5 . . . . .80 E1
  Wallington SM6 . . . . .200 C4
Clifford Cl, Nthlt. UB5 . . .103 E1
Clifford Dr, SW9 . . . . . . .151 H4
Clifford Gdns, NW10 . . . .107 J2
  Hayes UB3 . . . . .121 G4
Clifford Rd, E16 . . . . . . .115 F4
  E17 . . . . .78 C2

Clifford Rd, N9 .... 45 F6
SE25 .... 188 D4
Barnet EN5 .... 41 E3
Hounslow TW4 .... 142 D3
Richmond TW10 .... 163 G2
Wembley HA0 .... 105 G1
Clifford's Inn Pas, EC4 .... 19 E4
Clifford St, W1 .... 17 F6
Clifford Way, NW10 .... 89 F4
Cliff Rd, NW1 .... 92 D6
Cliff Ter, SE8 .... 154 A2
Cliffview Rd, SE13 .... 154 A3
Cliff Vil, NW1 .... 92 D6
Cliff Wk, E16 .... 115 F5
Clifton Av, E17 .... 77 G3
N3 .... 72 C1
W12 .... 127 F1
Feltham TW13 .... 160 C3
Stanmore HA7 .... 69 E2
Wembley HA9 .... 87 J6
Clifton Cl, Orp. BR6 .... 207 F5
Clifton Ct, N4
off Playford Rd 93 G2
NW8 .... 6 E5
Woodford Green IG8
off Snakes La W 63 G6
Clifton Cres, SE15 .... 133 E7
Clifton Est, SE15
off Consort Rd 152/153 E1
Clifton Gdns, N15 .... 76 C6
NW11 .... 72 C6
W4 *off Dolman Rd* 126 D4
W9 .... 6 C6
Enfield EN2 .... 42 E4
Clifton Gro, E8 .... 94 D6
Clifton Hill, NW8 .... 109 E2
Clifton Pk Av, SW20 .... 183 J2
Clifton Pl, SE16
off Canon Beck Rd 133 F2
W2 .... 15 F5
Clifton Ri, SE14 .... 133 H7
Clifton Rd, E7 .... 98 A6
E16 .... 115 E5
N3 .... 73 F1
N8 .... 74 D6
N22 .... 74 C1
NW10 .... 107 G2
SE25 .... 188 B4
SW19 .... 166 A6
W9 .... 6 D5
Greenford UB6 .... 103 J4
Harrow HA3 .... 69 J5
Hounslow (Hthrw.Air.) TW6
off Inner Ring E 140/141 E3
Ilford IG2 .... 81 G6
Isleworth TW7 .... 144 A2
Kingston upon Thames
KT2 .... 163 J7
Loughton IG10 .... 48 B4
Sidcup DA14 .... 175 H4
Southall UB2 .... 123 E4
Teddington TW11 .... 162 B4
Wallington SM6 .... 200 B5
Welling DA16 .... 158 C3
Clifton St, EC2 .... 20 D1
Clifton Ter, N4 .... 93 G2
Clifton Vil, W9 .... 14 B1
Clifton Wk, E6 .... 116 B6
W6 *off King St* 127 H4
Clifton Way, SE15 .... 133 E7
Borehamwood WD6 .... 38 A1
Wembley HA0 .... 105 H1
Clinch Ct, E16 .... 115 G5
Cline Rd, N11 .... 58 C6
Clinger Ct, N1
off Pitfield St 112 B1
★ **Clink Prison Mus**, SE1 .28 B1
Clink St, SE1 .... 28 A1
Clinton Av, E.Mol. KT8 .. 179 J4
Welling DA16 .... 157 J4
Clinton Cres, Ilf. IG6 .... 65 H6
Clinton Rd, E3 .... 113 H3
E7 .... 97 G4
N15 .... 76 A4
Clinton Ter, Sutt. SM1
off Manor La 199 F4
Clipper Cl, SE16
off Kinburn St 133 G2
Clipper Way, SE13 .... 154 C4
Clippesby Cl, Chess.
KT9 .... 195 J7
Clipstone Ms, W1 .... 9 F6
Clipstone Rd, Houns.
TW3 .... 143 G3
Clipstone St, W1 .... 17 E1
Clissold Cl, N2 .... 73 J3
Clissold Ct, N4 .... 93 J2
Clissold Cres, N16 .... 94 A3
Clissold Rd, N16 .... 94 A3
Clitheroe Av, Har. HA2 .. 85 G1
Clitheroe Gdns, Wat.
WD19 .... 50 D3
Clitheroe Rd, SW9 .... 151 E2
Clitherow Av, W7 .... 124 D3
Clitherow Pas, Brent.
TW8 .... 125 F5
Clitherow Rd, Brent.
TW8 .... 125 F5
Clitterhouse Cres, NW2 .. 89 J1
Clitterhouse Rd, NW2 .... 89 J1
Clive Av, N18
off Claremont St 60 D6
Clive Ct, W9 .... 6 D5
Cliveden Cl, N12
off Woodside Av 57 F4
Cliveden Pl, SW1 .... 32 B1
Cliveden Rd, SW19 .... 184 C1
Clivedon Ct, W13 .... 104 E5
Clivedon Rd, E4 .... 62 E5
Clive Pas, SE21
off Clive Rd 170 A3
Clive Rd, SE21 .... 170 A3
SW19 .... 167 H6
Belvedere DA17 .... 139 G4
Enfield EN1 .... 44 D4
Feltham TW14 .... 142 A6
Twickenham TW1 .... 162 C4
Clivesdale Dr, Hayes
UB3 .... 122 B1
Clive Way, Enf. EN1 .... 44 D4
Cloak La, EC4 .... 20 A5
Clockhouse Av, Bark.
IG11 .... 117 F1
Clockhouse Cl, SW19 .... 165 J3
Clockhouse Pl, SW15 .... 148 B5
Clock Ho Rd, Beck. BR3 .. 189 H3
★ **Clockmakers Company Collection, The, Guildhall Lib**,
EC2 .... 20 A3
Clock Twr Ms, N1
off Arlington Av 111 J1
SE28 .... 118 B7
Clock Twr Pl, N7 .... 92 E6
Clock Twr Rd, Islw. TW7 .144 C3
Cloister Cl, Tedd. TW11 .. 162 E5
Cloister Gdns, SE25 .... 188 E6
Edgware HA8 .... 54 C5
Cloister Rd, NW2 .... 90 C3
W3 .... 106 C5
Cloisters Av, Brom. BR2 .192 C5
Cloisters Business Cen, SW8
off Battersea Pk Rd .. 130 B7
Cloisters Mall, Kings.T. KT1
off Union St 181 G2
Clonard Way, Pnr. HA5 ... 51 G6
Clonbrock Rd, N16 .... 94 B4
Cloncurry St, SW6 .... 148 A2
Clonmel Cl, Har. HA2 .... 86 A1
Clonmell Rd, N17 .... 76 A3
Clonmel Rd, SW6 .... 128 C7
Teddington TW11 .... 162 A4
Clonmore St, SW18 .... 166 C1
Cloonmore Av, Orp.
BR6 .... 207 J4
Clorane Gdns, NW3 .... 90 D3
Close, The, E4
off Beech Hall Rd 62 C7
N14 .... 58 D2
N20 .... 56 C2
SE3 *off Heath La* 154 D2
Barnet EN4 .... 41 J6
Beckenham BR3 .... 189 H4
Bexley DA5 .... 159 G6
Harrow HA2 .... 67 J2
Isleworth TW7 .... 144 A2
Mitcham CR4 .... 185 J4
New Malden KT3 .... 182 C2
Orpington BR5 .... 193 H6
Pinner (Eastcote) HA5 .. 66 C7
Pinner (Rayners La)
HA5 .... 67 F7
Richmond TW9 .... 146 B3
Romford RM6 .... 82 E6
Sidcup DA14 .... 176 B5
Sutton SM3 .... 184 C7
Wembley (Barnhill Rd)
HA9 .... 88 C3
Wembley (Lyon Pk Av)
HA0 .... 87 H6
Cloth Ct, EC1 .... 19 H2
Cloth Fair, EC1 .... 19 H2
Clothier St, E1 .... 21 E3
Cloth St, EC1 .... 19 J1
Clothworkers Rd, SE18 .137 G7
Cloudesdale Rd, SW17 .. 168 B2
Cloudesley Pl, N1 .... 111 G1
Cloudesley Rd, N1 .... 111 G1
Bexleyheath DA7 .... 159 F1
Cloudesley Sq, N1 .... 111 G1
Cloudesley St, N1 .... 111 G1
Clouston Cl, Wall. SM6 .. 200 E5
Clova Rd, E7 .... 97 F6
Clove Cres, E14 .... 114 D7
Clove Hitch Quay,
SW11 .... 149 F3
Clovelly Av, NW9 .... 71 F4
Clovelly Cl, Pnr. HA5 .... 66 B3
Clovelly Gdns, SE19 .... 188 C1
Enfield EN1 .... 44 B7
Romford RM7 .... 83 H1
Clovelly Rd, N8 .... 74 D4
W4 .... 126 C2
W5 .... 125 F2
Bexleyheath DA7 .... 138 E6
Hounslow TW3 .... 143 G2
Clovelly Way, E1
off Jamaica St 113 F6
Harrow HA2 .... 85 F2
Orpington BR6 .... 193 J6
Clover Cl, E11
off Norman Rd 96 D2
Cloverdale Gdns, Sid.
DA15 .... 157 J6
Cloverleys, Loug. IG10 ... 48 A5
Clover Ms, SW3 .... 31 J5
Clover Way, Wall. SM6 .. 200 A1
Clove St, E13
off Barking Rd 115 G4
Clowders Rd, SE6 .... 171 J3
Clowser Cl, Sutt. SM1
off Turnpike La 199 F5
Cloysters Grn, E1 .... 29 H1
Cloyster Wd, Edg. HA8 ... 53 G7
Club Gdns Rd, Brom.
BR2 .... 191 G7
Club Row, E1 .... 13 F5
E2 .... 13 F5
Clunbury Av, Sthl. UB2 .. 123 F5
Clunbury St, N1 .... 12 C2
Cluny Est, SE1 .... 28 D5
Cluny Ms, SW5 .... 128 D4
Cluny Pl, SE1 .... 28 D5
Cluse Ct, N1 .... 11 J1
Clutton St, E14 .... 114 B5
Clydach Rd, Enf. EN1 .... 44 C4
Clyde Circ, N15 .... 76 B4
Clyde Pl, E10 .... 78 B7
Clyde Rd, N15 .... 76 B4
N22 .... 74 D1
Croydon CR0 .... 202 C1
Sutton SM1 .... 198 D5
Wallington SM6 .... 200 C5
Clydesdale, Enf. EN3 .... 45 G4
Clydesdale Av, Stan. HA7 .69 G3
Clydesdale Cl, Borwd.
WD6 .... 38 D5
Isleworth TW7 .... 144 C3
Clydesdale Gdns, Rich.
TW10 .... 146 B4
Clydesdale Ho, Erith DA18
off Kale Rd 138/139 E2
Clydesdale Rd, W11 .... 108 C6
Clyde St, SE8 .... 133 J6
Clyde Ter, SE23 .... 171 F2
Clyde Vale, SE23 .... 171 F2
Clymping Dene, Felt.
TW14 .... 142 B7
Clyston St, SW8 .... 150 C2
Coach & Horses Yd, W1 .. 17 E5
Coach Ho La, N5
off Highbury Hill 93 H4
SW19 .... 166 A4
Coach Ho Ms, SE14
off Waller Rd 153 G2
Coachhouse Ms, SE20 .. 170 E7
Coach Ho Ms, SE23 .... 153 G6
Coach Ho Yd, SW18
off Ebner St 148/149 E4
Coachmaker Ms, SW4
off Fenwick Pl 150/151 E3
Coach Yd Ms, N19
off Trinder Rd 92/93 E1
Coaldale Wk, SE21
off Lairdale Cl 151 J7
Coalecroft Rd, SW15 .... 147 J4
Coal Wf Rd, W12
off Sterne St 128 A2
Coates Av, SW18 .... 149 H6
Coates Hill Rd, Brom.
BR1 .... 192 D2
Coate St, E2 .... 13 J2
Coates Wk, Brent. TW8 .. 125 H5
Cobb Cl, Borwd. WD6 .... 38 C5
Cobbett Rd, SE9 .... 156 B3
Twickenham TW2 .... 161 G1
Cobbetts Av, Ilf. IG4 .... 80 A5
Cobbett St, SW8 .... 131 F7
Cobble La, N1
off Edwards Ms 93 H7
Cobble Ms, N5 .... 93 J3
Cobblers Wk, E.Mol. KT8 .180 D1
Hampton TW12 .... 161 J7
Kingston upon Thames
KT2 .... 180 D1
Teddington TW11 .... 180 D1
Cobblestone Pl, Croy. CR0
off Oakfield Rd 201 J1
Cobbold Est, NW10 .... 89 F6
Cobbold Ms, W12
off Cobbold Rd 127 F2
Cobbold Rd, E11 .... 97 F3
NW10 .... 89 F6
W12 .... 127 E2
Cobb's Ct, EC4
off Carter La 111 H6
Cobb's Rd, Houns. TW4 .. 143 F4
Cobb St, E1 .... 21 F2
Cobden Rd, E11 .... 97 E3
SE25 .... 188 D5
Orpington BR6 .... 207 G4
Cobham Av, N.Mal.
KT3 .... 183 G5
Cobham Cl, SW11 .... 149 H6
Bromley BR2 .... 192 B7
Edgware HA8 .... 70 B2
Enfield EN1 .... 44 D3
Sidcup DA15
off Park Mead 158 B6
Wallington SM6 .... 200 E6
Cobham Ho, Bark. IG11
off St. Margarets 117 F1
Cobham Ms, NW1
off Agar Gro 92 D7
Cobham Pl, Bexh. DA6 .. 158 D5
Cobham Rd, E17 .... 78 C1
N22 .... 75 H3
Hounslow TW5 .... 122 C7
Ilford IG3 .... 99 H2
Kingston upon Thames
KT1 .... 182 A1
Cobland Rd, SE12 .... 173 J4
Coborn Rd, E3 .... 113 J3
Coborn St, E3 .... 113 J3
Cobourg Rd, SE5 .... 37 F5
Cobourg St, NW1 .... 9 G4
Coburg Cl, SW1 .... 33 G1
Coburg Cres, SW2 .... 169 F1
Coburg Gdns, Ilf. IG5 .... 80 A2
Coburg Rd, N22 .... 75 F3
Cochrane Ms, NW8 .... 7 F2
Cochrane Rd, SW19 .... 166 C7
Cochrane St, NW8 .... 7 F2
Cockayne Way, SE8 .... 133 H5
Cockerell Rd, E17 .... 77 H7
COCKFOSTERS, Barn. 41 H4
Cockfosters Rd, Barn.
EN4 .... 41 J2
Cock Hill, E1 .... 21 E2
Cock La, EC1 .... 19 G2
Cockpit Steps, SW1 .... 25 J4
Cockpit Yd, WC1 .... 18 D1
Cocks Cres, N.Mal. KT3 .. 183 F4
Cocksett Av, Orp. BR6 ... 207 H6
Cockspur Ct, SW1 .... 25 J1
Cockspur St, SW1 .... 25 J1
Cocksure La, Sid. DA14 .. 177 G3
Code St, E1 .... 13 G6
Codicote Ter, N4
off Green Las 93 J2
Codling Cl, E1 .... 29 J1
Codling Way, Wem. HA0 .. 87 G4
Codrington Hill, SE23 ... 153 H7
Codrington Ms, W11
off Blenheim Cres ... 108 B6
Cody Cl, Har. HA3 .... 69 G3
Wallington SM6
off Alcock Cl 200 D7
Cody Rd, E16 .... 114 D4
Cody Rd Business Cen,
E16 .... 114 D4
Coe Av, SE25 .... 188 D6
Coe's All, Barn. EN5
off Wood St 40 B4
Cogan Av, E17 .... 77 H1
Coin St, SE1 .... 27 E1
Coity Rd, NW5 .... 92 A6
Cokers La, SE21
off Perifield 170 A1
Coke St, E1 .... 21 H3
Colas Ms, NW6
off Birchington Rd ... 108 D1
Colbeck Ms, SW7 .... 30 B2
Colbeck Rd, Har. HA1 .... 67 J7
Colberg Pl, N16 .... 76 B7
Colborne Way, Wor.Pk.
KT4 .... 197 J3
Colbrook Av, Hayes UB3 .121 G3
Colbrook Cl, Hayes UB3 .121 G3
Colburn Av, Pnr. HA5 .... 51 E6
Colburn Way, Sutt. SM1 .199 G3

Colby Ms, SE19
off Gipsy Hill 170 B5
Colby Rd, SE19 ....170 B5
Colchester Av, E12 ....98 C3
Colchester Dr, Pnr. HA5 ..66 D5
Colchester Rd, E10 ....78 C7
E17 ....78 A6
Edgware HA8 ....54 C7
Northwood HA6 ......66 A2
Colchester St, E1 .....21 G3
Coldbath Sq, EC1 ......11 E5
Coldbath St, SE13 ....154 B1
COLDBLOW, Bex. 177 J2
Cold Blow La, SE14 ...133 G7
Cold Blows, Mitch. CR4 .186 A3
Coldershaw Rd, W13 ..124 D1
Coldfall Av, N10 ....73 J2
Cold Harbour, E14 ....134 C2
Coldharbour Crest, SE9
off Great Harry Dr ...174 D3
Coldharbour La, SE5 ..151 G4
SW9 ....151 G4
Hayes UB3 ....102 A7
Coldharbour Pl, SE5
off Denmark Hill 151 J2
Coldharbour Rd, Croy.
CR0 ....201 G5
Coldstream Gdns,
SW18 ....148 C6
Colebeck Ms, N1 ....93 H6
Colebert Av, E1 ....113 F4
Colebrook Cl, NW7
off Bittacy Hill 56 B7
SW15 off West Hill ..148 A7
Colebrooke Av, W13 ...104 E6
Colebrooke Dr, E11 ....79 H7
Colebrooke Pl, N1
off St. Peters St 111 H1
Colebrooke Ri, Brom.
BR2 ....191 E2
Colebrooke Row, N1 ...11 G2
Colebrook Gdns, Loug.
IG10 ....49 E2
Colebrook Ho, E14
off Brabazon St 114 B6
Colebrook La, Loug.
IG10 ....49 E2
Colebrook Path, Loug.
IG10 ....49 E2
Colebrook Rd, SW16 ..187 E1
Colebrook Way, N11 ...58 B5
Coleby Path, SE5
off Harris St 132 A7
Coledale Dr, Stan. HA7 ..69 F1
Coleford Rd, SW18 ....149 F5
Cole Gdns, Houns. TW5 .122 A7
Colegrave Rd, E15 .....96 D5
Colegrove Rd, SE15 ....37 G6
Coleherne Ct, SW5 .....30 B4
Coleherne Ms, SW10 ...30 A4
Coleherne Rd, SW10 ...30 A4
Colehill Gdns, SW6
off Fulham Palace Rd.148 B2
Colehill La, SW6 ......148 B1
Coleman Cl, SE25 .....188 D2
Coleman Flds, N1 .....111 J1
Coleman Rd, SE5 ......36 D7
Belvedere DA17 .....139 G4
Dagenham RM9 .....101 E6
Colemans Heath, SE9 ..174 E3
Coleman St, EC2 ......20 A3
Colenso Dr, NW7 ......55 G7
Colenso Rd, E5 ....95 F4
Ilford IG2 ....99 H1
Cole Pk Gdns, Twick.
TW1 ....144 D6
Cole Pk Rd, Twick. TW1 .144 D6
Cole Pk Vw, Twick. TW1
off Hill Vw Rd 144 D6
Colepits Wd Rd, SE9 ..157 F5
Coleraine Rd, N8 ......75 G3
SE3 ....135 F6
Coleridge Av, E12 .....98 B6
Sutton SM1 ....199 H4
Coleridge Cl, SW8 ....150 B2
Coleridge Gdns, NW6
off Fairhazel Gdns ..91 F7
Coleridge La, N8
off Coleridge Rd ...74/75 E6
Coleridge Rd, E17 .....77 J4
N4 ....93 G2
N8 ....74 D6
N12 ....57 F5
Croydon CR0 ....189 F7
Coleridge Sq, W13
off Berners Dr 104 D6
Coleridge Wk, NW11 ...72 D4

Coleridge Way, Hayes
UB4 ....102 A6
West Drayton UB7 ...120 C4
Cole Rd, Twick. TW1 ..144 D6
Colesburg Rd, Beck. BR3 .189 J3
Coles Cres, Har. HA2 ..85 H2
Coles Grn, Bushey
(Bushey Hth.) WD23 ..51 J1
Loughton IG10 ....48 D1
Coles Grn Ct, NW2 ....89 G2
Coles Grn Rd, NW2 ....89 G1
Coleshill Rd, Tedd. TW11 .162 B6
Colestown St, SW11 ...149 H2
Cole St, SE1 ....28 A4
Colet Cl, N13 ....59 H6
Colet Gdns, W14 ......128 A4
Coley St, WC1 ....10 D6
Colfe Rd, SE23 ....171 H1
Colham Av, West Dr.
UB7 ....120 B1
Colham Mill Rd, West Dr.
UB7 ....120 A2
Colina Ms, N15
off Harringay Rd 75 H5
Colina Rd, N15 ....75 H5
Colin Cl, NW9 ....71 E4
Croydon CR0 ....203 J3
West Wickham BR4 ..205 F3
Colin Cres, NW9 ......71 F4
Colindale Av, NW9 ....70 D3
Colindale Business Pk,
NW9 ....70 C3
Colindeep Gdns, NW4 ..71 G5
Colindeep La, NW4 ....70 E3
NW9 ....70 E3
Colin Dr, NW9 ....71 F5
Colinette Rd, SW15 ...147 J4
Colin Gdns, NW9 ......71 F5
Colin Par, NW9
off Edgware Rd ...70/71 E4
Colin Pk Rd, NW9 .....70 E4
Colin Rd, NW10 ....89 G6
Colinton Rd, Ilf. IG3 ..100 B2
★ Coliseum, The, WC2 ..18 A6
Coliston Pas, SW18
off Coliston Rd 148 D7
Coliston Rd, SW18 ....148 D7
Collamore Av, SW18 ..167 H1
Collapit Cl, Har. HA1 ..67 H5
Collard Av, Loug. IG10 ..49 F2
Collard Grn, Loug. IG10
off Collard Av 49 F2
Collard Pl, NW1
off Harmood St 92 B7
College App, SE10 ....134 C6
College Av, Har. HA3 ..68 B1
College Cl, E9
off Median Rd 95 F5
N18 ....60 C5
SE21 ....170 B1
SW17 ....167 H2
Enfield EN2 ....44 A1
Ilford IG4 ....80 B5
New Malden KT3 ....183 F5
College Cres, NW3 ....91 G6
College Cross, N1 .....93 G7
College Dr, Ruis. HA4 ..66 A7
Thames Ditton KT7 ..180 B7
College Gdns, E4 ......46 B7
N18 ....60 C5
SE21 ....170 B1
SW17 ....167 H2
Enfield EN2 ....44 A1
Ilford IG4 ....80 B5
New Malden KT3 ....183 F5
College Grn, SE19 ....170 B7
College Gro, NW1
off St. Pancras Way ..110 D1
College Hill, EC4 ......20 A5
College Hill Rd, Har. HA3 .68 C1
College La, NW5 ......92 B4
College Ms, SW1 ......26 A5
SW18 off St. Ann's
Hill 148/149 E5
★ College of Arms, EC4 ..19 H5
College Pk Cl, SE13 ..154 D4
College Pk Rd, N17
off College Rd 60 C6
College Pl, E17 ....78 E4
NW1 ....110 C1
SW10 ....30 C7
College Pt, E15 ....97 F6
College Rd, E17 ....78 C5
N17 ....60 C6
N21 ....59 G2
NW10 ....107 J2
SE19 ....170 C5
SE21 ....152 B7
SW19 ....167 G6
W13 ....104 E6
Bromley BR1 ....173 G7
Croydon CR0 ....202 A2

College Rd, Enf. EN2 ...44 A2
Harrow (Har.Hill) HA1 ..68 B6
Harrow (Har.Wld.) HA3 ..68 B1
Isleworth TW7 ....144 C1
Wembley HA9 ....87 G1
College Row, E9 ......95 G5
College Slip, Brom. BR1 .191 G1
College St, EC4 ....20 A5
College Ter, E3 ....113 J3
N3 off Hendon La ...72 C2
College Vw, SE9 ......174 A1
College Wk, Kings.T. KT1
off Grange Rd 181 H2
College Way, Hayes UB3 .102 A7
College Yd, NW5
off College La 92 B4
Collent St, E9 ....95 F6
Colless Rd, N15 ....76 C5
Collett Rd, SE16 ......29 J6
Collett Way, Sthl. UB2 ..123 H1
Collier Cl, E6
off Trader Rd ...116/117 E6
Epsom KT19 ....196 A6
Collier Dr, Edg. HA8 ..70 A2
COLLIER ROW, Rom. ...83 G1
Collier Row Rd, Rom.
RM5 ....83 F1
Colliers Shaw, Kes. BR2 .206 A4
Collier St, N1 ....10 C2
Colliers Water La, Th.Hth.
CR7 ....187 G5
COLLIER'S WOOD,
SW19 ....167 G7
Collindale Av, Erith DA8 .139 H6
Sidcup DA15 ....176 A1
Collingbourne Rd, W12 .127 H1
Collingham Gdns, SW5 ..30 B2
Collingham Pl, SW5 ...30 A2
Collingham Rd, SW5 ..30 B1
Collings Cl, N22
off Whittington Rd ..59 F6
Collingtree Rd, SE26 ..171 F4
Collingwood Av, N10 ..74 A3
Surbiton KT5 ....196 C1
Collingwood Cl, SE20 ..189 E1
Twickenham TW2 ....143 G6
Collingwood Rd, E17 ..78 A6
N15 ....76 B4
Mitcham CR4 ....185 H2
Sutton SM1 ....198 D3
Collingwood St, E1 ...113 E4
Collins Av, Stan. HA7 ..69 H2
Collins Dr, Ruis. HA4 ..84 C2
Collinson St, SE1 .....27 J4
Collinson Wk, SE1 .....27 J4
Collins Rd, N5 ....93 J4
Collins Sq, SE3
off Tranquil Vale ...155 F2
Collins St, SE3 ....155 F2
Collin's Yd, N1
off Islington Grn ...111 H1
Collinwood Av, Enf. EN3 .45 F3
Collinwood Gdns, Ilf. IG5 .80 C5
Collis All, Twick. TW2
off The Green 162 B1
Colls Rd, SE15 ....153 F1
Collyer Av, Croy. CR0 ..200 E4
Collyer Pl, SE15
off Peckham High St .152 D1
Collyer Rd, Croy. CR0 ..201 E4
Colman Rd, E16 ....115 J5
Colmar Cl, E1
off Alderney Rd 113 G4
Colmer Pl, Har. HA3 ...52 A7
Colmer Rd, SW16 .....187 E1
Colmore Ms, SE15 ....153 E1
Colmore Rd, Enf. EN3 ..45 F4
Colnbrook St, SE1 .....27 G6
Colne Ct, Epsom KT19 .196 C4
Colne Ho, Bark. IG11 ..99 E6
Colne Rd, E5 ....95 H4
N21 ....44 A7
Twickenham TW1,
TW2 ....162 B1
Colne St, E13
off Grange Rd 115 G3
Colney Hatch La, N10 ..58 A7
N11 ....57 J6
Cologne Rd, SW11 ....149 G4
Colombo Rd, Ilf. IG1 ..99 F1
Colombo St, SE1 ......27 G2
Colomb St, SE10 .....135 E5
Colonels Wk, Enf. EN2 ..43 H3
Colonial Av, Twick. TW2 .143 J5
Colonial Rd, Felt. TW14 .141 H7
Colonnade, WC1 ......10 A6
Colonnades, The, W2 ..14 B3
Colonnade Wk, SW1 ...32 D2
Colosseum Ter, NW1
off Albany St 110 B4

Colson Gdns, Loug. IG10
off Colson Rd 48/49 E4
Colson Path, Loug. IG10 ..48 D4
Colson Rd, Croy. CR0 ..202 B2
Loughton IG10 ....48 E4
Colson Way, SW16 ....168 C4
Colsterworth Rd, N15 ..76 C4
Colston Av, Cars. SM5 ..199 H4
Colston Cl, Cars. SM5
off West St 199 J4
Colston Rd, E7 ....98 A6
SW14 ....146 C4
Colthurst Cres, N4 ....93 J2
Colthurst Dr, N9
off Plevna Rd 60 E3
Coltness Cres, SE2 ....138 B5
Colton Gdns, N17 .....75 J3
Colton Rd, Har. HA1 ..68 B5
Columbia Av, Edg. HA8 ..70 B1
Ruislip HA4 ....84 B1
Worcester Park KT4 ..183 F7
Columbia Pt, SE16
off Moodkee St 133 F3
Columbia Rd, E2 ......13 F3
E13 ....115 F4
Columbia Sq, SW14
off Upper Richmond
Rd W 146 C4
Columbine Av, E6 .....116 B5
South Croydon CR2 ..201 H7
Columbine Way, SE13 ..154 C2
Columbus Ct, SE16
off Rotherhithe St ..133 F1
Columbus Ctyd, E14
off West India Av ...134 A1
Columbus Gdns, Nthwd.
HA6 ....66 A1
Colva Wk, N19
off Chester Rd 92 B2
Colvestone Cres, E8 ..94 C5
Colview Ct, SE9
off Mottingham La ..174 A1
Colville Est, N1 ....112 B1
Colville Gdns, W11 ...108 C6
Colville Hos, W11 .....108 C6
Colville Ms, W11
off Lonsdale Rd 108 C6
Colville Pl, W1 ....17 G2
Colville Rd, E11 ....96 C3
E17 ....77 H2
N9 ....60 E1
W3 ....126 B3
W11 ....108 C6
Colville Sq, W11 ......108 C6
Colville Ter, W11 ......108 C6
Colvin Cl, SE26 ....171 F5
Colvin Gdns, E4 ....62 C3
E11 ....79 H4
Ilford IG6 ....81 F1
Colvin Rd, E6 ....98 B7
Thornton Heath CR7 ..187 G5
Colwall Gdns, Wdf.Grn.
IG8 ....63 G5
Colwell Rd, SE22 .....152 C5
Colwick Cl, N6 ....74 D7
Colwith Rd, W6 ....127 J6
Colwood Gdns, SW19 .167 G7
Colworth Gro, SE17 ...36 A2
Colworth Rd, E11 .....78 E6
Croydon CR0 ....202 D1
Colwyn Av, Grnf. UB6 ..104 C2
Colwyn Cl, SW16 .....168 C5
Colwyn Cres, Houns.
TW3 ....143 J1
Colwyn Grn, NW9
off Snowdon Dr ...70/71 E6
Colwyn Rd, NW2 ......89 H3
Colyer Cl, N1 ....10 D1
SE9 ....175 E2
Colyers La, Erith DA8 ..159 J1
Colyton Cl, Well. DA16 .158 D1
Wembley HA0
off Bridgewater Rd ..87 F6
Colyton Rd, SE22 .....153 E5
Colyton Way, N18 .....60 D6
Combe Av, SE3 ....135 F7
Combedale Rd, SE10 ..135 G5
Combe Lo, SE7
off Elliscombe Rd ...135 J6
Combe Martin, Kings.T.
KT2 ....164 C5
Combemartin Rd, SW18 .148 B7
Combe Ms, SE3 ....135 F7
Comber Cl, NW2 ......89 H3
Comber Gro, SE5 .....151 J1
Combermere Rd, SW9 .151 F3
Morden SM4 ....185 E6
Comberton Rd, E5 .....95 E2
Combeside, SE18 .....137 J7
Combwell Cres, SE2 ..138 A3

Comely Bk Rd, E17 . . . . . .78 C5
Comeragh Ms, W14 . . . . .128 B5
Comeragh Rd, W14 . . . . .128 B5
Comer Cres, Sthl. UB2
  off Windmill Av 123 J2
Comerford Rd, SE4 . . . . .153 H4
Comet Cl, E12 . . . . .98 A4
Comet Pl, SE8 . . . . .134 A7
Comet Rd, Stai. (Stanw.)
  TW19 . . . . .140 A7
Comet St, SE8 . . . . .134 A7
Comfort St, SE15
  off St. Georges Way . .132 C6
Commerce Rd, N22 . . . . . .75 F1
Brentford TW8 . . . . . . .125 F7
Commerce Way, Croy.
  CR0 . . . . .201 F2
Commercial Rd, E1 . . . . . .21 H3
  E14 . . . . .113 F6
  N17 . . . . .60 B6
  N18 . . . . .60 B5
Commercial St, E1 . . . . . .13 F6
Commercial Way, NW10 .106 B2
  SE15 . . . . .132 C7
Commerell St, SE10 . . . .135 E5
Commodity Quay, E1 . . . .21 G6
Commodore St, E1 . . . . .113 H4
Common, The, E15 . . . . . .97 E6
  W5 . . . . .105 H7
  Richmond TW10 . . . . .163 G3
  Southall UB2 . . . . . . .122 C4
  Stanmore HA7 . . . . . . .52 B2
Commondale, SW15 . . . .147 J3
Commonfield La, SW17
  off Tooting Gro 167 H5
Common La, Esher (Clay.)
  KT10 . . . . .194 D7
Common Mile Cl, SE4
  off Crescent La 150 D5
Common Rd, SW13 . . . . .147 J3
  Esher (Clay.) KT10 . . .194 D6
  Stanmore HA7 . . . . . . .52 A4
Commonside, Kes. BR2 .205 J4
Commonside E, Mitch.
  CR4 . . . . .185 J3
Commonside W, Mitch.
  CR4 . . . . .185 J3
Commonwealth Av,
  W12 . . . . .107 H7
★ Commonwealth Institute,
  W8 . . . . .128 C3
Commonwealth Rd, N17 .60 D7
Commonwealth Way,
  SE2 . . . . .138 B5
Community Cl, Houns.
  TW5 . . . . .142 B1
Community La, N7 . . . . . .92 D5
Community Rd, E15 . . . . .96 D5
  Greenford UB6 . . . . . .103 J1
Como Rd, SE23 . . . . . . .171 H2
Compass Hill, Rich.
  TW10 . . . . .145 G6
Compass Ho, SW18
  off Smugglers
  Way 148/149 E4
Compayne Gdns, NW6 . . .90 E7
Compton Av, E6 . . . . . . .116 A2
  N1 . . . . .93 H6
  N6 . . . . .73 H7
Compton Cl, E3 . . . . . . .114 A5
  NW1 . . . . .9 E4
  NW11 off The Vale 90 A3
  W13 . . . . .104 D6
  Edgware HA8
  off Pavilion Way 54 C7
  Esher KT10 . . . . .194 A5
Compton Ct, SE19
  off Victoria Cres 170 B5
Compton Cres, N17 . . . . .59 J7
  W4 . . . . .126 C6
  Chessington KT9 . . . .195 H6
  Northolt UB5 . . . . . . .102 D1
Compton Pas, EC1 . . . . . .11 H5
Compton Pl, WC1 . . . . . . .10 A5
  Watford WD19 . . . . . . .50 E3
Compton Ri, Pnr. HA5 . . .67 E5
Compton Rd, N1 . . . . .93 H6
  N21 . . . . .59 G1
  NW10 . . . . .108 A3
  SW19 . . . . .166 C6
  Croydon CR0 . . . . . . .202 E1
Compton St, EC1 . . . . . . .11 G5
Compton Ter, N1 . . . . . . .93 H6
Computer Ho, Brent.
  TW8 . . . . .125 F6
Comreddy Cl, Enf. EN2 . . .43 H1
Comus Pl, SE17 . . . . .36 D2
Comyn Rd, SW11 . . . . . .149 H4
Comyns, The, Bushey
  (Bushey Hth.) WD23 . . .51 J1

Comyns Cl, E16 . . . . . . .115 F5
Comyns Rd, Dag. RM9 . .101 G7
Conant Ms, E1 . . . . .21 H5
Concanon Rd, SW2 . . . . .151 F4
Concert Hall App, SE1 . . .26 D2
Concord Cl, Nthlt. UB5
  off Britannia Cl 102 D3
Concorde Cl, Houns. TW3
  off Lampton Rd 143 H2
Concorde Dr, E6 . . . . . . .116 C5
Concord Rd, W3 . . . . . . .106 B4
  Enfield EN3 . . . . .45 F5
Concourse, The, N9
  off New Rd 60 D2
  NW9 . . . . .71 F1
Condell Rd, SW8 . . . . . . .150 C1
Conder St, E14
  off Salmon La 113 H6
Conderton Rd, SE5 . . . . .151 J3
Condor Path, Nthlt. UB5
  off Brabazon Rd 103 G2
Condover Cres, SE18 . . .136 E7
Condray Pl, SW11 . . . . . .129 H7
Conduit Av, SE10
  off Crooms Hill 154 D1
Conduit Ct, WC2 . . . . . . .18 A5
Conduit La, N18 . . . . .61 F5
  Croydon CR0 . . . . . . .202 D5
  Enfield EN3
  off Morson Rd 45 H6
  South Croydon CR2 . .202 D5
Conduit Ms, SE18 . . . . . .137 E5
  W2 . . . . .14 E4
Conduit Pas, W2 . . . . . . .15 E4
Conduit Pl, W2 . . . . .15 E4
Conduit Rd, SE18 . . . . . .137 E5
Conduit St, W1 . . . . .17 E5
Conduit Way, NW10 . . . . .88 C7
Conewood St, N5 . . . . . . .93 H3
Coney Acre, SE21 . . . . . .169 J1
Coney Burrows, E4
  off Wyemead Cres .62/63 E2
Coneygrove Path, Nthlt. UB5
  off Arnold Rd 84/85 E6
CONEY HALL, W.Wick. .205 F3
Coney Hill Rd, W.Wick.
  BR4 . . . . .205 E2
Coney Way, SW8 . . . . . . .34 D6
Conference Cl, E4
  off Greenbank Cl 62 C2
★ Conference Forum, The,
  E1 . . . . .21 H3
Conference Rd, SE2 . . . .138 C4
Congleton Gro, SE18 . . .137 F5
Congo Rd, SE18 . . . . . . .137 G5
Congress Rd, SE2 . . . . . .138 C4
Congreve Rd, SE9 . . . . . .156 C3
Congreve St, SE17 . . . . . .36 D1
Congreve Wk, E16 . . . . . .116 A5
Conical Cor, Enf. EN2 . . . .43 J2
Conifer Cl, Orp. BR6 . . . .207 G4
Conifer Gdns, SW16 . . . .169 E3
  Enfield EN1 . . . . .44 B6
  Sutton SM1 . . . . .198 E2
Conifers Cl, Tedd. TW11 .163 E7
Conifer Way, Wem. HA0 . .87 F3
Coniger Rd, SW6 . . . . . . .148 D2
Coningham Ms, W12
  off Percy Rd 127 G1
Coningham Rd, W12 . . . .127 H2
Coningsby Cotts, W5
  off Coningsby Rd 125 G2
Coningsby Gdns, E4 . . . . .62 B6
Coningsby Rd, N4 . . . . . . .75 H7
  W5 . . . . .125 F2
Conington Rd, SE13 . . . .154 B2
Conisbee Ct, N14 . . . . . . .42 C5
Conisborough Cres, SE6 .172 C3
Coniscliffe Cl, Chis. BR7 .192 D1
Coniscliffe Rd, N13 . . . . .59 J3
Coniston Av, Bark. IG11 . .99 H7
  Greenford UB6 . . . . . .105 E3
  Welling DA16 . . . . . . .157 H3
Coniston Cl, N20 . . . . . . .57 F3
  SW13 off Lonsdale Rd .127 F7
  SW20 . . . . .184 A6
  W4 . . . . .146 C1
  Barking IG11
  off Coniston Av 99 H7
  Bexleyheath DA7 . . . .159 J1
Conistone Way, N7 . . . . . .93 E7
Coniston Gdns, N9 . . . . . .61 F1
  NW9 . . . . .70 D5
  Ilford IG4 . . . . .80 B4
  Pinner HA5 . . . . .66 A4
  Sutton SM2 . . . . .199 G6
  Wembley HA9 . . . . . . .87 F1
Coniston Ho, SE5 . . . . . . .35 J7
Coniston Rd, N10 . . . . . . .74 B2
  N17 . . . . .60 D6

Coniston Rd, Bexh. DA7 .159 J1
  Bromley BR1 . . . . .172 E6
  Croydon CR0 . . . . . . .188 D7
  Twickenham TW2 . . . .143 H6
Coniston Wk, E9
  off Clifden Rd 95 F5
Coniston Way, Chess.
  KT9 . . . . .195 H3
Conlan St, W10 . . . . .108 B4
Conley Rd, NW10 . . . . . . .89 E6
Conley St, SE10
  off Pelton Rd . . .134/135 E5
Connaught Av, E4 . . . . . . .46 D7
  SW14 . . . . .146 C3
  Barnet EN4 . . . . .57 J1
  Enfield EN1 . . . . .44 B2
  Hounslow TW4 . . . . . .143 E5
  Loughton IG10 . . . . . . .48 A4
Connaught Br, E16 . . . . .136 A1
Connaught Business Cen,
  Mitch. CR4
  off Wandle Way 185 J5
Connaught Cl, E10 . . . . . .95 H2
  W2 . . . . .15 G4
  Enfield EN1 . . . . .44 B2
  Sutton SM1 . . . . .199 G2
Connaught Ct, E17
  off Orford Rd 78 B4
  Buckhurst Hill IG9 . . . .63 H1
Connaught Dr, NW11 . . . .72 D4
Connaught Gdns, N10 . . .74 B5
  N13 . . . . .59 H4
  Morden SM4 . . . . .185 F4
Connaught Hill, Loug.
  IG10 . . . . .48 A4
Connaught La, Ilf. IG1
  off Connaught Rd 99 G2
Connaught Ms, SE18 . . .136 D5
  Ilford IG1
  off Connaught Rd 99 G2
Connaught Pl, W2 . . . . . . .15 J5
Connaught Rd, E4 . . . . . . .46 E7
  E11 . . . . .96 D1
  E16 . . . . .136 A1
  E17 . . . . .78 A5
  N4 . . . . .75 G7
  NW10 . . . . .107 E1
  SE18 . . . . .136 D5
  W13 . . . . .104 E7
  Barnet EN5 . . . . .40 A6
  Harrow HA3 . . . . .68 C1
  Ilford IG1 . . . . .99 G2
  New Malden KT3 . . . . .183 E4
  Richmond TW10
  off Albert Rd 145 J5
  Sutton SM1 . . . . .199 G2
  Teddington TW11 . . . .162 A5
Connaught Roundabout, E16
  off Connaught Br 116 A7
Connaught Sq, W2 . . . . . .15 J4
Connaught St, W2 . . . . . . .15 G4
Connaught Way, N13 . . . .59 H4
Connell Cres, W5 . . . . . . .105 J4
Connemara Cl, Borwd. WD6
  off Percheron Rd 38 D6
Connington Cres, E4 . . . . .62 D3
Connor Cl, E11 . . . . .78 E7
  Ilford IG6 . . . . .81 E1
Connor Rd, Dag. RM9 . . .101 F4
Connor St, E9
  off Lauriston Rd 113 G1
Conolly Rd, W7 . . . . .124 B1
Conrad Dr, Wor.Pk. KT4 .197 J1
Conrad Ho, N16 . . . . .94 B5
Consfield Av, N.Mal.
  KT3 . . . . .183 G4
Consort Ms, Islw. TW7 . .144 A5
Consort Rd, SE15 . . . . . .152 E1
Cons St, SE1 . . . . .27 F3
Constable Av, E16
  off Wesley Av 135 H1
Constable Cl, NW11 . . . . .73 E6
Constable Cres, N15 . . . . .76 D5
Constable Gdns, Edg.
  HA8 . . . . .70 A1
  Isleworth TW7 . . . . . .144 A5
Constable Ms, Dag. RM8
  off Stonard Rd 100 B4
Constance Cres, Brom.
  BR2 . . . . .191 F7
Constance Rd, Croy.
  CR0 . . . . .187 H7
  Enfield EN1 . . . . .44 B6
  Sutton SM1 . . . . .199 F4
  Twickenham TW2 . . . .143 H7
Constance St, E16
  off Albert Rd 136 B1
Constantine Rd, NW3 . . . .91 H4
Constitution Hill, SW1 . . .24 D3

Constitution Ri, SE18 . . .156 D1
Consul Av, Dag. RM9 . . . .119 J3
Content St, SE17 . . . . .36 A2
Contessa Cl, Orp. BR6 . . .207 F5
Control Twr Rd, Houns.
  (Hthrw.Air.) TW6 . . . . .140 D3
Convair Wk, Nthlt. UB5
  off Kittiwake Rd 102 D3
Convent Cl, Beck. BR3 . .172 C7
Convent Gdns, W5 . . . . . .125 F4
  W11 off Kensington
  Pk Rd 108 C6
Convent Hill, SE19 . . . . . .169 J6
Convent Way, Sthl. UB2 .122 C4
Conway Cl, Stan. HA7 . . . .52 D6
Conway Cres, Grnf. UB6 .104 B2
  Romford RM6 . . . . .82 C7
Conway Dr, Hayes UB3 . .121 F3
  Sutton SM2 . . . . .198 E6
Conway Gdns, Mitch.
  CR4 . . . . .186 D4
  Wembley HA9 . . . . . . .69 F7
Conway Gro, W3 . . . . . . .106 D5
Conway Ms, W1 . . . . .9 F6
Conway Rd, N14 . . . . .59 E3
  N15 . . . . .75 H5
  NW2 . . . . .89 J2
  SE18 . . . . .137 G4
  SW20 . . . . .183 J1
  Feltham TW13 . . . . . . .160 D5
  Hounslow TW4 . . . . . .143 F7
  Hounslow (Hthrw.Air.) TW6
  off Inner Ring E . .140/141 E3
Conway St, E13 . . . . .115 G4
  W1 . . . . .9 F6
Conway Wk, Hmptn. TW12
  off Fearnley Cres 161 F6
Conybeare, NW3
  off King Henry's Rd . . .91 H7
Conyers Cl, Wdf.Grn. IG8 .62 E6
Conyers Rd, SW16 . . . . . .168 D5
Conyer St, E3 . . . . .113 H2
Conyers Way, Loug. IG10 .49 E3
Cooden Cl, Brom. BR1
  off Plaistow La 173 H7
Cook Ct, SE16
  off Rotherhithe St . . .133 F1
Cooke Cl, E14
  off Cabot Sq 134 A1
Cookes Cl, E11 . . . . .97 F2
Cookes La, Sutt. SM3 . . .198 B6
Cookham Cl, Sthl. UB2 . .123 H2
Cookham Cres, SE16
  off Marlow Way 133 G2
Cookham Dene Cl, Chis.
  BR7 . . . . .193 G1
Cookham Rd, Sid. DA14 .177 G7
Cookhill Rd, SE2 . . . . . . .138 B2
Cook Rd, Dag. RM9 . . . . .118 E1
Cooks Cl, Rom. RM5 . . . . .83 J1
Cookson Gro, Erith DA8 .139 H7
Cook's Rd, E15 . . . . .114 B2
Cooks Rd, SE17 . . . . .35 G5
Coolfin Rd, E16 . . . . .115 G6
Coolgardie Av, E4 . . . . . . .62 C5
  Chigwell IG7 . . . . .64 D3
Coolhurst Rd, N8 . . . . .74 D6
Cool Oak La, NW9 . . . . . . .71 E7
Coomassie Rd, W9
  off Bravington Rd 108 C4
COOMBE, Kings.T. 164 C7
Coombe Av, Croy. CR0 . .202 B4
Coombe Bk, Kings.T.
  KT2 . . . . .182 E1
Coombe Cl, Edg. HA8 . . . .69 J2
  Hounslow TW3 . . . . . .143 G4
Coombe Cor, N21 . . . . . . .59 H1
Coombe Cres, Hmptn.
  TW12 . . . . .161 E7
Coombe Dr, Kings.T.
  KT2 . . . . .164 D7
  Ruislip HA4 . . . . .84 B1
Coombe End, Kings.T.
  KT2 . . . . .164 D7
Coombefield Cl, N.Mal.
  KT3 . . . . .183 E5
Coombe Gdns, SW20 . . .183 G2
  New Malden KT3 . . . . .183 F4
Coombe Hts, Kings.T.
  KT2 . . . . .165 E7
Coombe Hill Glade, Kings.T.
  KT2 . . . . .165 E7
Coombe Hill Rd, Kings.T.
  KT2 . . . . .164 E7
Coombe Ho Chase, N.Mal.
  KT3 . . . . .182 D1
Coombehurst Cl, Barn.
  EN4 . . . . .41 J2
Coombe La, SW20 . . . . . .183 G1
  Croydon CR0 . . . . . . .202 E5

Coombe La W, Kings.T.
KT2 . . . . .164 E7
Coombe Lea, Brom.
BR1 . . . . .192 B3
Coombe Neville, Kings.T.
KT2 . . . . .164 D7
Coombe Pk, Kings.T.
KT2 . . . . .164 D5
Coombe Ridings, Kings.T.
KT2 . . . . .164 C5
Coombe Ri, Kings.T.
KT2 . . . . .182 C1
Coombe Rd, N22 . . . . . . .75 G1
NW10 . . . . .88 D3
SE26 . . . . .170 E4
W4 . . . . .127 E5
W13 off Northcroft
Rd 124/125 E3
Croydon CR0 . . . . . . .202 A4
Hampton TW12 . . . . . .161 F6
Kingston upon Thames
KT2 . . . . .182 A1
New Malden KT3 . . . . .182 E2
Coomber Way, Croy.
CR0 . . . . .186 D7
Coombes Rd, Dag. RM9 .119 F1
Coombe Wk, Sutt. SM1 . .198 E3
Coombewood Dr, Rom.
RM6 . . . . .83 F6
Coombe Wd Rd, Kings.T.
KT2 . . . . .164 C5
Coombs St, N1 . . . . .11 H2
Coomer Ms, SW6
off Coomer Pl 128 C6
Coomer Pl, SW6 . . . . . . .128 C6
Coomer Rd, SW6
off Coomer Pl 128 C6
Cooms Wk, Edg. HA8
off East Rd 70 C1
Cooperage Cl, N17
off Brantwood Rd 60 C6
Cooper Av, E17 . . . . .77 G1
Cooper Cl, SE1 . . . . .27 F4
Cooper Ct, E15
off Clays La 96 B5
Cooper Cres, Cars. SM5 .199 J3
Cooper Rd, NW4 . . . . . . .72 A6
NW10 . . . . .89 G5
Croydon CR0 . . . . . . .201 G4
Coopersale Rd, E9 . . . . . .95 G5
Coopersall Cl, Wdf.Grn. IG8
off Navestock Cres . . .63 J7
Coopers Cl, E1 . . . . .113 F4
Dagenham RM10 . . . . .101 H6
Coopers Cres, Borwd.
WD6 . . . . .38 C1
Coopers La, E10 . . . . .96 B1
NW1 . . . . .9 J1
Cooper's La, SE12 . . . . . .173 H2
Coopers Rd, SE1 . . . . . . .37 G4
Cooper's Row, EC3 . . . . .21 F5
Cooper St, E16
off Lawrence St 115 F5
Coopers Wk, E15
off Maryland St 96 D5
Cooper's Yd, SE19
off Westow Hill 170 B6
Coote Gdns, Dag. RM8 . .101 F3
Coote Rd, Bexh. DA7 . . .159 F1
Dagenham RM8 . . . . . .101 F3
Copeland Dr, E14 . . . . . .134 A4
Copeland Rd, E17 . . . . . .78 B5
SE15 . . . . .152 D2
Copeman Cl, SE26 . . . . .171 F5
Copenhagen Gdns, W4 .126 C2
Copenhagen Pl, E14 . . . .113 J6
Copenhagen St, N1 . . . . .111 E1
Cope Pl, W8 . . . . .128 D3
Copers Cope Rd, Beck.
BR3 . . . . .171 J6
Cope St, SE16 . . . . .133 G4
Copford Cl, Wdf.Grn. IG8 .64 B6
Copford Wk, N1
off Popham St 111 J1
Copgate Path, SW16 . . . .169 F6
Copley Dene, Brom.
BR1 . . . . .192 A1

Copley Pk, SW16 . . . . . .169 F6
Copley Rd, Stan. HA7 . . . .53 F5
Copley St, E1 . . . . .113 G5
Copnor Way, SE15 . . . . . .37 E7
Coppard Gdns, Chess.
KT9 . . . . .195 F6
Copped Hall, SE21
off Glazebrook Cl 170 A2
Coppelia Rd, SE3 . . . . . .155 F4
Coppen Rd, Dag. RM8 . . .83 F7
Copperas St, SE8 . . . . . .134 B6
Copperbeech Cl, NW3
off Akenside Rd 91 G5
Copper Beech Cl, NW3
off Daleham Ms 91 G6
Ilford IG5 . . . . .80 D1
Copper Beech Ct, Loug.
IG10 . . . . .48 D1
Copper Beeches, Islw. TW7
off Eversley Cres 144 A1
Copper Cl, SE19
off Auckland Rd 170 C7
Copperdale Rd, Hayes
UB3 . . . . .122 A2
Copperfield, Chig. IG7 . . .65 G6
Copperfield App, Chig.
IG7 . . . . .65 G6
Copperfield Ct, Pnr. HA5
off Copperfield Way . . .67 F4
Copperfield Dr, N15 . . . . .76 C4
Copperfield Ms, N18 . . . . .60 B5
Copperfield Rd, E3 . . . . .113 H4
SE28 . . . . .118 C6
Copperfield St, SE1 . . . . .27 H3
Copperfield Way, Chis.
BR7 . . . . .175 F6
Pinner HA5 . . . . .67 F4
Coppergate Cl, Brom.
BR1 . . . . .191 H1
Copper Mead Cl, NW2 . . .89 J3
Copper Mill Dr, Islw.
TW7 . . . . .144 C2
Coppermill La, E17 . . . . . .77 F6
Copper Mill La, SW17 . . .167 F4
Copper Row, SE1 . . . . . . .29 F2
Coppetts Cl, N12 . . . . . . .57 H7
Coppetts Rd, N10 . . . . . . .74 A2
Coppice, The, Enf. EN2 . . .43 H4
Coppice Cl, SW20 . . . . . .183 J3
Beckenham BR3 . . . . .190 B4
Stanmore HA7 . . . . . . .52 C6
Coppice Dr, SW15 . . . . .147 H6
Coppice Wk, N20 . . . . . . .56 D3
Coppice Way, E18 . . . . . .79 F4
Coppies Gro, N11 . . . . . . .58 A4
Copping Cl, Croy. CR0
off Tipton Dr 202 B4
Coppins, The, Croy.
(New Adgtn.) CR0 . . . .204 B6
Harrow HA3 . . . . .52 B6
Coppock Cl, SW11 . . . . .149 H2
Coppsfield, W.Mol. KT8
off Hurst Rd 179 G3
Copse, The, E4 . . . . .63 F1
Copse Av, W.Wick. BR4 . .204 B3
Copse Cl, SE7 . . . . .135 H6
West Drayton UB7 . . . .120 A3
Copse Glade, Surb. KT6 .195 G1
COPSE HILL, SW20 . . . .165 F7
Copse Hill, SW20 . . . . . .165 H7
Sutton SM2 . . . . .199 E7
Copsewood Cl, Sid.
DA15 . . . . .157 H6
Coptefield Dr, Belv.
DA17 . . . . .138 D3
Copthall Av, EC2 . . . . . . .20 C3
Copthall Bldgs, EC2 . . . . .20 B3
Copthall Cl, EC2 . . . . . . .20 B3
Copthall Ct, EC2 . . . . . . .112 A6
Copthall Gdns, NW7 . . . . .55 G7
Twickenham TW1 . . . . .162 C1
Copthorne Av, SW12 . . . .150 D7
Bromley BR2 . . . . .206 D1
Ilford IG6 . . . . .65 E6
Copthorne Ms, Hayes
UB3 . . . . .121 H4
Coptic St, WC1 . . . . .18 A2
Copwood Cl, N12 . . . . . . .57 G4
Coral Cl, Rom. RM6 . . . . .82 C4
Coraline Cl, Sthl. UB1 . . .103 F3
Coralline Wk, SE2 . . . . . .138 C2
Coral Row, SW11
off Gartons Way 149 F3
Coral St, SE1 . . . . .27 E4
Coram St, WC1 . . . . .10 A6
Coran Cl, N9 . . . . .45 G7
Corban Rd, Houns.TW3 .143 G3
Corbden Cl, SE15 . . . . . .152 C1
Corbet Cl, Wall. SM6 . . . .200 A1

Corbet Ct, EC3 . . . . .20 C4
Corbet Pl, E1 . . . . .21 F1
Corbett Gro, N22 . . . . . . .58 E7
Corbett Ho, Wat. WD19 . . .50 C3
Corbett Rd, E11 . . . . .79 J6
E17 . . . . .78 C3
Corbetts La, SE16
off Rotherhithe
New Rd 133 F4
Corbetts Pas, SE16
off Rotherhithe
New Rd 133 F4
Corbicum, E11 . . . . .79 E7
Corbiere Ct, SW19
off Thornton Rd 166 A6
Corbiere Ho, N1 . . . . . . .112 B1
Corbins La, Har. HA2 . . . . .85 H3
Corbridge Cres, E2 . . . . .112 E2
Corby Cres, Enf. EN2 . . . .43 E4
Corbylands Rd, Sid.
DA15 . . . . .157 H7
Corbyn St, N4 . . . . .93 E1
Corby Rd, NW10 . . . . . . .106 D2
Corby Way, E3
off Knapp Rd 114 A4
Cordelia Cl, SE24 . . . . . .151 H4
Cordelia Gdns, Stai.
TW19 . . . . .140 B7
Cordelia Rd, Stai.TW19 . .140 B7
Cordelia St, E14 . . . . . . .114 B6
Cordell Ho, N15
off Newton Rd 76 C5
Cording St, E14
off Chrisp St 114 B5
Cordova Rd, E3 . . . . .113 H3
Cordwainers Wk, E13
off Clegg St 115 G2
Cord Way, E14
off Mellish St 134 A3
Cordwell Rd, SE13 . . . . .154 E5
Corefield Cl, N11
off Benfleet Way 58 A2
Corelli Rd, SE3 . . . . .156 B2
Corfe Av, Har. HA2 . . . . . .85 G4
Corfe Cl, Borwd. WD6
off Chester Rd 38 D3
Hayes UB4 . . . . .102 C6
Corfe Twr, W3 . . . . .126 B2
Corfield Rd, N21 . . . . .43 F5
Corfield St, E2 . . . . .113 E3
Corfton Rd, W5 . . . . .105 H6
Coriander Av, E14 . . . . . .114 D6
Cories Cl, Dag. RM8 . . . .100 D2
Corinium Cl, Wem. HA9 . .87 J4
Corinne Rd, N19 . . . . .92 C4
Corinthian Way, Stai. (Stanw.)
TW19 off Clare Rd 140 A7
Corker Wk, N7 . . . . .93 F2
Corkran Rd, Surb. KT6 . . .181 G7
Corkscrew Hill, W.Wick.
BR4 . . . . .204 D2
Cork Sq, E1
off Smeaton St . .132/133 E1
Cork St, W1 . . . . .17 F6
Cork St Ms, W1 . . . . .17 F6
Cork Tree Way, E4 . . . . . .61 H5
Corlett St, NW1 . . . . .15 G1
Cormont Rd, SE5 . . . . . .151 H1
Cormorant Cl, E17
off Banbury Rd 77 G1
Cormorant Ho, Enf. EN3
off Alma Rd 45 G5
Cormorant Pl, Sutt. SM1
off Sandpiper Rd 198 C5
Cormorant Rd, E7 . . . . . . .97 F4
Cornbury Rd, Edg. HA8 . . .53 G7
Cornelia St, N7 . . . . .93 F6
Cornell Cl, Sid. DA14 . . . .177 E6
Corner Grn, SE3 . . . . . . .155 G2
Corner Ho St, WC2 . . . . . .26 A1
Corner Mead, NW9 . . . . . .55 F7
Corney Reach Way, W4 . .127 E7
Corney Rd, W4 . . . . .127 E6
Cornflower La, Croy.
CR0 . . . . .203 G1
Cornflower Ter, SE22 . . . .152 E6
Cornford Cl, Brom. BR2 . .191 G5
Cornford Gro, SW12 . . . .168 B2
Cornhill, EC3 . . . . .20 C4
Cornish Cl, N9 . . . . .44 E7
Cornish Gro, SE20 . . . . . .171 E7
Cornish Ho, SE17 . . . . . . .35 G6
Brentford TW8
off Green Dragon La .125 J5
Corn Mill Dr, Orp. BR6 . .193 J7
Cornmill La, SE13 . . . . . .154 B3
Cornmow Dr, NW10 . . . . .89 F5
Cornshaw Rd, Dag.
RM8 . . . . .100 D1
Cornthwaite Rd, E5 . . . . . .95 F3

Cornwall Av, E2 . . . . .113 F3
N3 . . . . .56 D7
N22 . . . . .75 E1
Esher (Clay.) KT10
off The Causeway 194 C7
Southall UB1 . . . . .103 F5
Welling DA16 . . . . .157 H3
Cornwall Cl, Bark. IG11 . . .99 J6
Cornwall Cres, W11 . . . . .108 B7
Cornwall Dr, Orp. BR5 . . .176 C7
Cornwall Gdns, NW10 . . . .89 H6
SW7 . . . . .22 B6
Cornwall Gdns Wk, SW7 . .22 B6
Cornwall Gro, W4 . . . . . . .127 E5
Cornwallis Av, N9 . . . . . . .61 E2
SE9 . . . . .175 G2
Cornwallis Gro, N9 . . . . . .61 E2
Cornwallis Rd, E17 . . . . . .77 G4
N9 . . . . .61 E2
N19 . . . . .92 E2
Dagenham RM9 . . . . . .100 D4
Cornwallis Sq, N19 . . . . . .92 E2
Cornwallis Wk, SE9 . . . . .156 C3
Cornwall Ms S, SW7 . . . . .22 C6
Cornwall Ms W, SW7 . . . . .22 B6
Cornwall Rd, N4 . . . . .75 G7
N15 . . . . .76 A5
N18 off Fairfield Rd 60 D5
SE1 . . . . .26 E1
Croydon CR0 . . . . . . .201 H2
Esher (Clay.) KT10 . . . .194 D7
Harrow HA1 . . . . .67 J6
Pinner HA5 . . . . .51 F7
Sutton SM2 . . . . .198 C7
Twickenham TW1 . . . . .162 D1
Cornwall Sq, SE11 . . . . . .35 G3
Cornwall St, E1
off Watney St 112/113 E7
Cornwall Ter, NW1 . . . . . . .8 A6
Cornwall Ter Ms, NW1 . . . .8 A6
Corn Way, E11 . . . . .96 D3
Cornwood Cl, N2 . . . . .73 G5
Cornwood Dr, E1 . . . . . . .113 F6
Cornworthy Rd, Dag.
RM8 . . . . .100 C5
Corona Rd, SE12 . . . . . . .155 G7
Coronation Av, N16
off Victorian Rd 94 C3
Coronation Cl, Bex.
DA5 . . . . .158 D6
Ilford IG6 . . . . .81 F4
Coronation Rd, E13 . . . . .115 J3
NW10 . . . . .105 J3
Hayes UB3 . . . . .121 J4
Coronation Wk, Twick.
TW2 . . . . .161 F1
Coronet St, N1 . . . . .12 D4
Corporation Av, Houns.
TW4 . . . . .142 E4
Corporation Row, EC1 . . . .11 F5
Corporation St, E15 . . . . .115 E2
N7 . . . . .92 E5
Corrance Rd, SW2 . . . . . .151 E4
Corri Av, N14 . . . . .58 D4
Corrib Dr, Sutt. SM1 . . . .199 H5
Corrigan Cl, NW4 . . . . . . .71 J3
Corringham Ct, NW11
off Corringham Rd .72/73 E7
Corringham Rd, NW11 . . .72 D7
Wembley HA9 . . . . .88 A2
Corringway, NW11 . . . . . .72 E7
W5 . . . . .106 A4
Corris Grn, NW9
off Snowdon Dr 70/71 E6
Corsair Cl, Stai.TW19 . . .140 A7
Corsair Rd, Stai.TW19 . . .140 B7
Corscombe Cl, Kings.T.
KT2 . . . . .164 C5
Corsehill St, SW16 . . . . .168 C6
Corsham St, N1 . . . . .12 C4
Corsica St, N5 . . . . .93 H6
Cortayne Rd, SW6 . . . . . .148 C2
Cortis Rd, SW15 . . . . . . .147 H6
Cortis Ter, SW15 . . . . . . .147 H6
Corunna Rd, SW8 . . . . . .150 C1
Corunna Ter, SW8 . . . . . .150 C1
Corvette Sq, SE10
off Feathers Pl 134 D6
Coryton Path, W9
off Ashmore Rd 108 C4
Cosbycote Av, SE24 . . . . .151 J5
Cosdach Av, Wall. SM6 . .200 D7
Cosedge Cres, Croy.
CR0 . . . . .201 G5
Cosgrove Cl, N21 . . . . . . .59 J2
Hayes UB4
off Kingsash Dr . .102/103 E4
Cosmo Pl, WC1 . . . . .18 B1
Cosmur Cl, W12 . . . . . . .127 F3
Cossall Wk, SE15 . . . . . .153 E1

Cossar Ms, SW2
off Tulse Hill 151 G6
Cosser St, SE1 . . . . .26 E5
Costa St, SE15 . . . . . . .152 D2
Costons Av, Grnf. UB6 . .104 A3
Costons La, Grnf. UB6 . .104 A3
Coston Wk, SE4
off Frendsbury Rd . . .153 G4
Cosway St, NW1 . . . . . . .15 H1
Cotall St, E14 . . . . .114 A6
Coteford Cl, Loug. IG10 . .48 E2
Pinner HA5 . . . . .66 A5
Coteford St, SW17 . . . . .167 J4
Cotelands, Croy. CR0 . . .202 B3
Cotesbach Rd, E5 . . . . . . .95 F3
Cotesmore Gdns, Dag.
RM8 . . . . .100 C4
Cotford Rd, Th.Hth. CR7 .187 J4
Cotham St, SE17 . . . . . . .36 A2
Cotherstone Rd, SW2 . . .169 F1
Cotleigh Av, Bex. DA5 . .176 D2
Cotleigh Rd, NW6 . . . . . .90 D7
Cotman Cl, NW11 . . . . . . .73 F6
SW15 off Westleigh Av .148 A6
Cotman Gdns, Edg. HA8 . .70 A2
Cotman Ms, Dag. RM8
off Highgrove Rd 100 C5
Cotmans Cl, Hayes UB3 .122 A1
Coton Rd, Well. DA16 . . .158 A3
Cotsford Av, N.Mal. KT3 .182 C5
Cotswold Cl, Esher
KT10 . . . . .194 C3
Kingston uponThames
KT2 . . . . .164 B6
Cotswold Ct, EC1 . . . . . .11 J5
N11 . . . . .58 A4
Cotswold Gdns, E6 . . . .116 A3
NW2 . . . . .90 A2
Ilford IG2 . . . . .81 G7
Cotswold Gate, NW2
off Cotswold Gdns 90 B1
Cotswold Grn, Enf. EN2
off Cotswold Way 43 F4
Cotswold Ms, SW11
off Battersea High St .149 G1
Cotswold Ri, Orp. BR6 . .193 J6
Cotswold Rd, Hmptn.
TW12 . . . . .161 G6
Cotswold St, SE27
off Norwood High St .169 H4
Cotswold Way, Enf. EN2 . .43 F4
Worcester Park KT4 . . .197 J2
Cottage Av, Brom. BR2 . .206 B1
Cottage Fld Cl, Sid.
DA14 . . . . .176 C1
Cottage Grn, SE5 . . . . . .36 C7
Cottage Gro, SW9 . . . . .150 E3
Surbiton KT6 . . . . . . .181 G6
Cottage Homes, NW7 . . .55 G4
Cottage Pl, SW3 . . . . . . .23 G5
Cottage Rd, Epsom
KT19 . . . . .196 D7
Cottage St, E14 . . . . . . .114 B7
Cottage Wk, N16
off Smalley Cl 94 C3
Cottenham Dr, NW9 . . . .71 F3
SW20 . . . . .165 H7
Cottenham Par, SW20
off Durham Rd 183 H2
COTTENHAM PARK,
SW20 . . . . .183 H1
Cottenham Pk Rd,
SW20 . . . . .183 H1
Cottenham Pl, SW20 . . .165 H7
Cottenham Rd, E17 . . . . .77 J4
Cotterill Rd, Surb. KT6 . .195 H2
Cottesbrook St, SE14
off Nynehead St 133 H7
Cottesloe Ms, SE1 . . . . . .27 F5
Cottesmore Av, Ilf. IG5 . . .80 D3
Cottesmore Gdns, W8 . . .22 B5
Cottimore Cres, Walt.
KT12 . . . . .178 B7
Cottimore Ter, Walt.
KT12 . . . . .178 B7
Cottingham Chase, Ruis.
HA4 . . . . .84 A3
Cottingham Rd, SE20 . . .171 G7
SW8 . . . . .34 D6
Cottington Rd, Felt.
TW13 . . . . .160 D4
Cottington St, SE11 . . . . .35 F3
Cottle Way, SE16
off St. Marychurch St .133 F2
Cotton Av, W3 . . . . .106 D6
Cotton Cl, Dag. RM9
off Flamstead Rd 100 C7
Cottongrass Cl, Croy. CR0
off Cornflower La 203 G1
Cotton Hill, Brom. BR1 . .172 D4

Cotton Row, SW11 . . . . .149 F3
Cottons Gdns, E2 . . . . . .13 E3
Cottons La, SE1 . . . . .28 C1
Cotton St, E14 . . . . .114 C7
Cottrell Cl, SE10
off Greenroof Way . . .135 F3
Cotts Cl, W7
off Westcott Cres 104 C5
Couchmore Av, Esher
KT10 . . . . .194 B2
Ilford IG5 . . . . .80 C2
Coulgate St, SE4 . . . . . .153 H3
Coulson Cl, Dag. RM8 . . .82 C7
Coulson St, SW3 . . . . . . .31 J3
Coulter Cl, Hayes UB4
off Berrydale Rd .102/103 E4
Coulter Rd, W6 . . . . . . .127 H3
Councillor St, SE5 . . . . .131 J7
Counter Cl, SE1
off Southwark St 132 A1
Counter St, SE1 . . . . .28 D2
Countess Rd, NW5 . . . . . .92 C5
Countisbury Av, Enf. EN1 .44 C7
Country Way, Felt. TW13 .160 B7
Sunbury-on-Thames
TW16 . . . . .160 B7
County Gate, SE9 . . . . . .175 F3
Barnet EN5 . . . . .41 E6
County Gro, SE5 . . . . . .151 J1
★ County Hall, SE1 . . . . . .26 C3
County Rd, E6 . . . . .116 E5
Thornton Heath CR7 . .187 H2
County St, SE1 . . . . .28 A6
Coupland Pl, SE18 . . . . .137 F5
Courcy Rd, N8 . . . . .75 G3
Courier Rd, Dag. RM9 . . .119 J4
Courland Gro, SW8 . . . .150 D1
Courland St, SW8 . . . . . .150 D1
Course, The, SE9 . . . . . .174 D3
Courtauld Cl, SE28
off Pitfield Cres 138 A1
★ Courtauld Gall, WC2 . . .18 C5
Courtauld Rd, N19 . . . . . .92 D1
Court Av, Belv. DA17 . . . .139 F5
Court Cl, Har. HA3 . . . . . .69 H3
Twickenham TW2 . . . .161 H3
Wallington SM6 . . . . . .200 D7
Court Cl Av, Twick. TW2 .161 H3
Court Cres, Chess. KT9 . .195 G5
Court Downs Rd, Beck.
BR3 . . . . .190 B2
★ Court Dress Collection
Kensington Palace,
W8 . . . . .22 B2
Court Dr, Croy. CR0 . . . .201 F4
Stanmore HA7 . . . . . . .53 H4
Sutton SM1 . . . . .199 H4
Courtenay Av, N6 . . . . . . .73 H7
Harrow HA3 . . . . .67 J1
Courtenay Dr, Beck. BR3 .190 D2
Courtenay Gdns, Har.
HA3 . . . . .67 J2
Courtenay Ms, E17
off Cranbrook Ms 77 H5
Courtenay Pl, E17 . . . . . .77 H5
Courtenay Rd, E11 . . . . . .97 F3
E17 . . . . .77 G4
SE20 . . . . .171 G7
Wembley HA9 . . . . .87 G3
Worcester Park KT4 . . .197 J3
Courtenay Sq, SE11 . . . . .34 E4
Courtenay St, SE11 . . . . .34 E3
Courtens Ms, Stan. HA7 . .53 F7
Court Fm Av, Epsom
KT19 . . . . .196 D5
Court Fm Rd, SE9 . . . . . .174 A2
Northolt UB5 . . . . .85 G7
Courtfield, W5
off Castlebar Hill 105 F5
Courtfield Av, Har. HA1 . .68 C5
Courtfield Cres, Har. HA1 .68 C5
Courtfield Gdns, SW5 . . . .30 B1
W13 . . . . .104 D6
Courtfield Ms, SW5 . . . . .30 C2
Courtfield Ri, W.Wick.
BR4 . . . . .204 D3
Courtfield Rd, SW7 . . . . . .30 B2
Court Gdns, N7 . . . . .93 G6
Courthill Rd, SE13 . . . . .154 C4
Courthope Rd, NW3 . . . . .91 J4
SW19 . . . . .166 B5
Greenford UB6 . . . . . .104 A2
Courthope Vil, SW19 . . .166 B7
Court Ho Gdns, N3 . . . . . .56 D6
Courthouse Rd, N12 . . . . .56 E6
Courtland Av, E4 . . . . . . .63 F2
NW7 . . . . .54 D3
SW16 . . . . .169 F7
Ilford IG1 . . . . .98 C2

Courtland Dr, Chig. IG7 . .65 E3
Courtland Gro, SE28 . . . .118 D7
Courtland Rd, E6
off Harrow Rd 116 B1
Courtlands, Rich. TW10 .146 A4
Courtlands Av, SE12 . . . .155 H5
Bromley BR2 . . . . .205 F1
Hampton TW12 . . . . . .161 F6
Richmond TW9 . . . . . .146 B2
Courtlands Dr, Epsom
KT19 . . . . .197 E6
Courtlands Rd, Surb.
KT5 . . . . .182 A7
Court La, SE21 . . . . .152 B6
Court La Gdns, SE21 . . . .152 B7
Courtleet Dr, Erith DA8 . .159 H1
Courtleigh Gdns, NW11 . .72 B4
Courtman Rd, N17 . . . . . .59 J7
Court Mead, Nthlt. UB5 .103 F3
Courtmead Cl, SE24 . . . .151 J6
Courtnell St, W2 . . . . . . .108 D6
Courtney Cl, SE19 . . . . . .170 B6
Courtney Cres, Cars.
SM5 . . . . .199 J7
Courtney Pl, Croy. CR0 . .201 G3
Courtney Rd, N7
off Bryantwood Rd 93 G5
SW19 . . . . .167 H7
Croydon CR0 . . . . .201 G3
Hounslow (Hthrw.Air.)
TW6 . . . . .140 D3
Courtney Way, Houns.
(Hthrw.Air.) TW6
off Courtney Rd 140 D2
Court Par, Wem. HA0 . . . .86 E3
Courtrai Rd, SE23 . . . . . .153 H6
Court Rd, SE9 . . . . .174 B2
SE25 . . . . .188 C2
Southall UB2 . . . . .123 F4
Courtside, N8 . . . . .74 D6
Court St, E1
off Durward St . . .112/113 E5
Bromley BR1 . . . . .191 G2
Court Way, NW9 . . . . .71 E4
W3 . . . . .106 C5
Ilford IG6 . . . . .81 F3
Twickenham TW2 . . . .144 C7
Courtway, Wdf.Grn. IG8 . .63 J5
Courtway, The, Wat.
WD19 . . . . .51 E2
Court Yd, SE9 . . . . .156 B6
Courtyard, The, N1 . . . . . .93 F7
Cousin La, EC4 . . . . .20 B6
Couthurst Rd, SE3 . . . . .135 H6
Coutts Av, Chess. KT9 . .195 H5
Coutts Cres, NW5 . . . . . .92 A3
Coval Gdns, SW14 . . . . .146 B4
Coval La, SW14 . . . . . . .146 B4
Coval Rd, SW14 . . . . . . .146 C4
Covelees Wall, E6 . . . . . .116 D6
Covell Ct, SE8
off Reginald Sq 134 A7
★ Covent Gdn, WC2 . . . . .18 B5
Covent Gdn, WC2 . . . . . .18 B5
Coventry Cl, E6
off Harper Rd 116 C6
NW6
off Kilburn High Rd . .108 D1
Coventry Cross, E3
off Gillender St 114 C4
Coventry Rd, E1 . . . . . . .113 E4
E2 . . . . .113 E4
SE25 . . . . .188 D4
Ilford IG1 . . . . .98 E1
Coventry St, W1 . . . . .17 H6
Coverack Cl, N14 . . . . . . .42 C6
Croydon CR0 . . . . .189 H7
Coverdale Cl, Stan. HA7 . .53 E5
Coverdale Gdns, Croy. CR0
off Park Hill Ri 202 C3
Coverdale Rd, N11 . . . . . .58 A6
NW2 . . . . .90 A7
W12 . . . . .127 H1
Coverdales, The, Bark.
IG11 . . . . .117 G2
Coverley Cl, E1 . . . . .21 J1
Covert, The, Orp. BR6 . . .193 H6
Coverton Rd, SW17 . . . . .167 H5
Covert Rd, Ilf. IG6 . . . . . . .65 J6
Covert Way, Barn. EN4 . . .41 F2
Covet Wd Cl, Orp. BR5
off Lockesley Dr 193 J6
Covey Cl, SW19 . . . . . . .184 E2
Covington Gdns, SW16 .169 H7
Covington Way, SW16 . .169 F6
Cowan Cl, E6
off Oliver Gdns 116 B5
Cowbridge La, Bark. IG11 .98 E7
Cowbridge Rd, Har. HA3 . .69 J4
Cowcross St, EC1 . . . . . .19 G1

Cowdenbeath Path, N1 . .111 F1
Cowden Rd, Orp. BR6 . . .193 J7
Cowden St, SE6 . . . . . . .172 A4
Cowdrey Cl, Enf. EN1 . . . .44 B2
Cowdrey Rd, SW19 . . . . .167 E5
Cowdry Rd, E9
off Wick Rd 95 H6
Cowen Av, Har. HA2 . . . . .85 J2
Cowgate Rd, Grnf. UB6 .104 A2
Cowick Rd, SW17 . . . . . .167 J4
Cowings Mead, Nthlt.
UB5 . . . . .85 E7
Cowland Av, Enf. EN3 . . . .45 F4
Cow La, Grnf. UB6 . . . . .104 A2
Cow Leaze, E6 . . . . .116 D6
Cowleaze Rd, Kings.T.
KT2 . . . . .181 H1
Cowley La, E11
off Cathall Rd 96/97 E3
Cowley Pl, NW4 . . . . .71 J5
Cowley Rd, E11 . . . . .79 H5
SW9 . . . . .151 G1
SW14 . . . . .146 E3
W3 . . . . .127 F1
Ilford IG1 . . . . .80 C7
Cowley St, SW1 . . . . .26 A5
Cowling Cl, W11
off Wilsham St 128 B1
Cowper Av, E6 . . . . .98 B7
Sutton SM1 . . . . .199 G4
Cowper Cl, Brom. BR2 . .192 A4
Welling DA16 . . . . . . .158 A5
Cowper Gdns, N14 . . . . . .42 C6
Wallington SM6 . . . . . .200 C6
Cowper Rd, N14 . . . . .58 B1
N16 . . . . .94 B5
N18 . . . . .60 D5
SW19 . . . . .167 F6
W3 . . . . .126 D1
W7 . . . . .104 C7
Belvedere DA17 . . . . . .139 G4
Bromley BR2 . . . . .192 A4
Kingston uponThames
KT2 . . . . .163 J5
Cowper St, EC2 . . . . .12 C5
Cowper Ter, W10
off St. Marks Rd 108 A5
Cowslip Rd, E18 . . . . .79 H2
Cowthorpe Rd, SW8 . . . .150 D1
Coxe Pl, Har. (Wldste.)
HA3 . . . . .68 D4
Cox La, Chess. KT9 . . . . .195 J4
Epsom KT19 . . . . .196 B5
Coxmount Rd, SE7 . . . . .136 A5
Coxson Way, SE1 . . . . . . .29 F4
Cox's Wk, SE21 . . . . . . .170 D1
Coxwell Rd, SE18 . . . . . .137 G5
SE19 . . . . .170 B7
Coxwold Path, Chess. KT9
off Garrison La 195 H7
Crabbs Cft Cl, Orp. BR6
off Ladycroft Way 207 F5
Crab Hill, Beck. BR3 . . . .172 D7
Crabtree Av, Rom. RM6 . .82 D4
Wembley HA0 . . . . . . .105 H2
Crabtree Cl, E2 . . . . .13 F2
Crabtree Ct, E15
off Clays La 96 B5
Crabtree La, SW6 . . . . . .128 A7
Crabtree Manorway Ind Est,
Belv. DA17 . . . . .139 H3
Crabtree Manorway N, Belv.
DA17 . . . . .139 J2
Crabtree Manorway S, Belv.
DA17 . . . . .139 J3
Crace St, NW1 . . . . .9 H3
Craddock Rd, Enf. EN1 . . .44 C3
Craddock St, NW5
off Prince of Wales Rd .92 A6
Cradley Rd, SE9 . . . . . . .175 G1
★ Crafts Council, N1 . . . . .11 F2
Craigen Av, Croy. CR0 . . .203 E1
Craigerne Rd, SE3 . . . . .135 H7
Craig Gdns, E18 . . . . .79 F2
Craigholm, SE18 . . . . . .156 D2
Craigmuir Pk, Wem.
HA0 . . . . .105 J1
Craignair Rd, SW2 . . . . .151 G7
Craignish Av, SW16 . . . .187 F2
Craig Pk Rd, N18 . . . . . . .60 E5
Craig Rd, Rich. TW10 . . .163 F4
Craigs Ct, SW1 . . . . .26 A1
Craigton Rd, SE9 . . . . . .156 C4
Craigweil Cl, Stan. HA7 . .53 G5
Craigweil Dr, Stan. HA7 . .53 G5
Craigwell Av, Felt.
TW13 . . . . .160 A3
Craik Ct, NW6
off Carlton Vale 108 C2
Crail Row, SE17 . . . . .36 C2

Cramer Ct, N.Mal. KT3
off Warwick Rd 182 C3
Cramer St, W1 ....16 C2
Cramond Cl, W6 ....128 B6
Crampton Rd, SE20 ...171 F6
Crampton St, SE17 .....35 J2
Cranberry Cl, Nthlt. UB5
off Parkfield Av 102 D2
Cranberry La, E16 ....114 E4
Cranborne Av, Sthl. UB2 .123 G4
Surbiton KT6 ....196 A3
Cranborne Rd, Bark.
IG11 ....117 G1
Cranborne Waye, Hayes
UB4 ....102 C7
Cranbourne Av, E11 ...79 H4
Cranbourne Cl, SW16 .187 E3
Cranbourne Dr, Pnr. HA5 .66 D5
Cranbourne Gdns, NW11 .72 B5
Ilford IG6 ....81 F3
Cranbourne Rd, E12
off High St N 98 B5
E15 ....96 C4
N10 ....74 B2
Cranbourn Pas, SE16
off Marigold St .132/133 E2
Cranbourn St, WC2 ....17 J5
CRANBROOK, Ilf. 98 C1
Cranbrook Cl, Brom.
BR2 ....191 G6
Cranbrook Dr, Twick.
TW2 ....161 H1
Cranbrook Ms, E17 ....77 H5
Cranbrook Pk, N22 .....75 F1
Cranbrook Ri, Ilf. IG1 ..80 C7
Cranbrook Rd, SE8 ...154 A1
SW19 ....166 B7
W4 ....127 E5
Barnet EN4 ....41 G6
Bexleyheath DA7 ....159 F1
Hounslow TW4 ......143 F4
Ilford IG1, IG2, IG6 ...80 D7
Thornton Heath CR7 .187 J2
Cranbrook St, E2
off Mace St 113 G2
Cranbury Rd, SW6 ....149 E2
Crane Av, W3 ....106 C7
Isleworth TW7 ......144 D5
Cranebrook, Twick. TW2
off Manor Rd 161 J2
Crane Cl, Dag. RM10 ..101 G6
Harrow HA2 ....85 J3
Crane Ct, EC4 ....19 F4
Epsom KT19 ....196 C4
Craneford Cl, Twick. TW2 .144 C7
Craneford Way, Twick.
TW2 ....144 B7
Crane Gdns, Hayes UB3 .121 J4
Crane Gro, N7 ....93 G6
Crane Lo Rd, Houns.
TW5 ....122 B6
Crane Mead, SE16 ....133 G4
Crane Pk Rd, Twick. TW2 .161 H2
Crane Rd, Twick. TW2 .162 B1
Cranesbill Cl, NW9
off Colindale Av 70 D3
Cranes Dr, Surb. KT5 .181 H4
Cranes Pk, Surb. KT5 .181 H4
Cranes Pk Av, Surb. KT5 .181 H4
Cranes Pk Cres, Surb.
KT5 ....181 J4
Crane St, SE10 ....134 D5
SE15 ....152 C1
Craneswater, Hayes
UB3 ....121 J7
Craneswater Pk, Sthl.
UB2 ....123 F5
Cranes Way, Borwd.
WD6 ....38 C5
Crane Way, Twick. TW2 .143 J7
Cranfield Cl, SE27
off Dunelm Gro 169 J3
Cranfield Dr, NW9 .....54 E7
Cranfield Rd, SE4 ....153 J3
Cranfield Row, SE1 ....27 F5
CRANFORD, Houns. ...122 A7
Cranford Av, N13 ......59 E5
Staines TW19 ....140 B7
Cranford Cl, SW20 ....183 H1
Staines TW19
off Canopus Way ...140 B7
Cranford Cotts, E1
off Cranford St 113 G7
Cranford Dr, Hayes UB3 .121 J4
Cranford La, Hayes UB3 .121 G6
Hounslow (Hthrw.Air.)
TW6 ....141 J3
Hounslow (Hthrw.Air.N.)
TW6 ....141 J1

Cranford La, Houns.
(Heston) TW5 ......122 D7
Cranford Pk Rd, Hayes
UB3 ....121 J4
Cranford St, E1 ......113 G7
Cranford Way, N8 .....75 F5
Cranhurst Rd, NW2 ....89 J5
Cranleigh Cl, SE20 ...188 E2
Bexley DA5 ....159 H6
Cranleigh Gdns, N21 ..43 G5
SE25 ....188 B3
Barking IG11 ....99 G7
Harrow HA3 ....69 H5
Kingston upon Thames
KT2 ....163 J6
Loughton IG10 ......48 C6
Southall UB1 ....103 F6
Sutton SM1 ....198 E2
Cranleigh Gdns Ind Est, Sthl.
UB1 off Cranleigh
Gdns 103 F6
Cranleigh Ms, SW11 ..149 H2
Cranleigh Rd, N15 .....75 J5
SW19 ....184 D3
Cranleigh St, NW1 .....9 G2
Cranley Dene Ct, N10 ..74 B4
Cranley Dr, Ilf. IG2 ....81 F7
Cranley Gdns, N10 ....74 C4
N13 ....59 F3
SW7 ....30 D3
Wallington SM6 ....200 C7
Cranley Ms, SW7 .....30 D3
Cranley Par, SE9
off Beaconsfield Rd .174 B4
Cranley Pl, SW7 ....31 E2
Cranley Rd, E13 ......115 H5
Ilford IG2 ....81 F6
Cranmer Av, W13 .....124 E3
Cranmer Cl, Mord. SM4 .184 A6
Ruislip HA4 ....84 D1
Stanmore HA7 ....53 F7
Cranmer Ct, SW3 .....31 H2
SW4 ....150 D3
Hampton (Hmptn.H.) TW12
off Cranmer Rd 161 H5
Cranmer Fm Cl, Mitch.
CR4 ....185 J4
Cranmer Gdns, Dag.
RM10 ....101 J4
Cranmer Rd, E7 ....97 H4
SW9 ....35 F7
Croydon CR0 ....201 H3
Edgware HA8 ....54 B3
Hampton (Hmptn.H.)
TW12 ....161 H5
Kingston upon Thames
KT2 ....163 H5
Mitcham CR4 ....185 J4
Cranmer Ter, SW17 ...167 G5
Cranmore Av, Islw. TW7 .123 J7
Cranmore Rd, Brom. BR1 .173 E3
Chislehurst BR7 .....174 C5
Cranmore Way, N10 ...74 C4
Cranston Cl, Houns. TW3 .143 E2
Cranston Est, N1 ......12 C2
Cranston Gdns, E4 ....62 B5
Cranston Rd, SE23 ....171 H1
Cranswick Rd, SE16 ..133 E5
Crantock Rd, SE6 ....172 B2
Cranwell Cl, E3 ......114 B4
Cranwich Av, N21 .....44 A7
Cranwich Rd, N16 .....76 A7
Cranwood St, EC1 .....12 B4
Cranworth Cres, E4 ....62 D1
Cranworth Gdns, SW9 .151 G1
Craster Rd, SW2 .....151 F7
Crathie Rd, SE12 .....155 H6
Cravan Av, Felt. TW13 .160 A2
Craven Av, W5 ....105 F7
Southall UB1 ....103 F5
Craven Cl, Hayes UB4 ..102 A6
Craven Gdns, SW19 ..166 D5
Barking IG11 ....117 H2
Ilford IG6 ....81 G2
Craven Hill, W2 ....14 D5
Craven Hill Gdns, W2 ..14 C5
Craven Hill Ms, W2 ....14 D5
Craven Ms, SW11
off Taybridge Rd ...150 A3
Craven Pk, NW10 ....106 E1
Craven Pk Ms, NW10 .106 E1
Craven Pk Rd, N15 ....76 C6
NW10 ....106 E1
Craven Pas, WC2 ......26 A1
Craven Rd, NW10 ....106 D1
W2 ....14 D5
W5 ....105 F7
Croydon CR0 ....202 E1
Kingston upon Thames
KT2 ....181 J1

Craven St, WC2 ....26 A1
Craven Ter, W2 ....14 D5
Craven Wk, N16 ....76 D7
Crawford Av, Wem.
HA0 ....87 G5
Crawford Cl, Islw. TW7 .144 B2
Crawford Est, SE5 ....151 J2
Crawford Gdns, N13 ...59 H3
Northolt UB5 ....103 F3
Crawford Ms, W1 ......15 J2
Crawford Pas, EC1 ....11 E6
Crawford Pl, W1 ....15 H3
Crawford Rd, SE5 ....151 J1
Crawford St, NW10
off Fawood Av 88 D7
W1 ....15 J2
Crawley Rd, E10 ....96 B1
N22 ....75 J2
Enfield EN1 ....44 B7
Crawshay Ct, SW9
off Eythorne Rd 151 G1
Crawthew Gro, SE22 .152 C4
Craybrooke Rd, Sid.
DA14 ....176 B4
Craybury End, SE9 ...175 F2
Crayford Cl, E6
off Neatscourt Rd ...116 B5
Crayford Rd, N7 ....92 D4
Crayke Hill, Chess. KT9 .195 H7
Cray Rd, Belv. DA17 ..139 G6
Sidcup DA14 ....176 C7
Crealock Gro, Wdf.Grn.
IG8 ....63 F5
Crealock St, SW18 ...149 E6
Creasy Est, SE1 ....28 D6
Crebor St, SE22 .....152 D6
Credenhall Dr, Brom.
BR2 ....206 C1
Credenhill St, SW16 ..168 C6
Crediton Hill, NW6 ....90 E5
Crediton Rd, E16
off Pacific Rd 115 G6
NW10 ....108 A1
Crediton Way, Esher (Clay.)
KT10 ....194 D5
Credon Rd, E13 ......115 J2
SE16 ....133 E5
Creechurch La, EC3 ...20 E4
Creechurch Pl, EC3 ...21 E4
Creed Ct, EC4
off Ludgate Hill 111 H6
Creed La, EC4 ....19 H4
Creek, The, Sun. TW16 .178 A5
CREEKMOUTH, Bark. .118 A4
Creek Rd, SE8 ....134 A6
SE10 ....134 A6
Barking IG11 ....117 J3
East Molesey KT8 ...180 B4
Creekside, SE8 ......134 B7
Creeland Gro, SE6
off Catford Hill 171 J1
Crefeld Cl, W6 ....128 A6
Creffield Rd, W3 .....105 J7
W5 ....105 J7
Creighton Av, E6 .....116 A2
N2 ....73 H3
N10 ....73 H3
Creighton Cl, W12
off Bloemfontein Rd .107 H7
Creighton Rd, N17 ....60 B7
NW6 ....108 A2
W5 ....125 G3
Cremer St, E2 ....13 F2
Cremorne Est, SW10 ..31 E7
Cremorne Rd, SW10 ..129 F7
Crescent, EC3 ....21 F5
Crescent, The, E17 ....77 H5
N11 ....57 J4
NW2 ....89 H3
SW13 ....147 F2
SW19 ....166 D3
W3 ....106 E6
Barnet EN5 ....40 E3
Beckenham BR3 ....190 A1
Bexley DA5 ....158 C7
Croydon CR0 ....188 A5
Harrow HA2 ....86 A1
Hayes UB3 ....121 F7
Ilford IG2 ....80 D6
Loughton IG10 ......48 A5
New Malden KT3 ...182 C2
Sidcup DA14 ....175 J4
Southall UB1 ....123 F2
Surbiton KT6 ....181 H5
Sutton SM1 ....199 G4
Wembley HA0 ....86 E2
West Molesey KT8 ..179 G4
West Wickham BR4 .190 B6
Crescent Ct, Surb. KT6 .181 G5
Crescent Dr, Orp. BR5 .193 E6

Crescent Gdns, SW19 .166 D3
Ruislip HA4 ....66 B6
Crescent Gro, SW4 ...150 C4
Mitcham CR4 ....185 H4
Crescent Ho, SE13
off Ravensbourne Pl .154 B2
Crescent La, SW4 ....150 D5
Crescent Ms, N22
off Palace Gates Rd .74/75 E1
Crescent Pl, SW3 ......31 G1
Crescent Ri, N22 ......74 D1
Barnet EN4 ....41 H5
Crescent Rd, E4 ....47 E7
E6 ....115 J1
E10 ....96 B2
E13 ....115 G1
E18 ....79 J2
N3 ....72 C1
N8 ....74 D7
N9 ....60 D1
N11 ....57 J4
N15 off Carlingford Rd .75 H3
N22 ....74 D1
SE18 ....136 E5
SW20 ....184 A1
Barnet EN4 ....41 H5
Beckenham BR3 ....190 B2
Bromley BR1 ....173 G7
Dagenham RM10 ...101 H4
Enfield EN2 ....43 H3
Kingston upon Thames
KT2 ....164 A7
Sidcup DA15 ....175 J3
Crescent Row, EC1 ....11 J6
Crescent Stables, SW15
off Upper Richmond
Rd 148 B4
Crescent St, N1 ....93 F7
Crescent Vw, Loug. IG10 .48 A6
Crescent Way, N12 ....57 H6
SE4 ....154 A3
SW16 ....169 F7
Orpington BR6 .....207 H5
Crescent Wd Rd, SE26 .170 D3
Cresford Rd, SW6 ....148 E1
Crespigny Rd, NW4 ...71 H6
Cressage Cl, Sthl. UB1 .103 G4
Cresset Rd, E9 ....95 F6
Cresset St, SW4 .....150 D3
Cressfield Cl, NW5 ....92 A5
Cressida Rd, N19 ......92 C1
Cressingham Gro, Sutt.
SM1 ....199 F4
Cressingham Rd, SE13 .154 C3
Edgware HA8 ....54 D6
Cressington Cl, N16
off Wordsworth Rd ...94 B5
Cresswell Gdns, SW5 ..30 C3
Cresswell Pk, SE3 ....155 F3
Cresswell Pl, SW10 ....30 C3
Cresswell Rd, SE25 ..188 D4
Feltham TW13 ......160 E4
Twickenham TW1 ...145 G6
Cresswell Way, N21 ...43 G7
Cressy Ct, E1
off Cressy Rd 113 F5
W6 ....127 H3
Cressy Pl, E1 ....113 F5
Cressy Rd, NW3 ....91 J5
Crest, The, N13 ....59 G4
NW4 ....71 J5
Surbiton KT5 ....182 A5
Crestbrook Av, N13 ....59 H3
Crestbrook Pl, N13 ....59 H3
Crestfield St, WC1 .....10 B3
Crest Gdns, Ruis. HA4 ..84 C3
Creston Way, Wor.Pk.
KT4 ....198 A1
Crest Rd, NW2 ....89 F3
Bromley BR2 ....191 F7
South Croydon CR2 .202 E7
Crest Vw, Pnr. HA5 ....66 D4
Crest Vw Dr, Orp. BR5 .193 E5
Crestway, SW15 ......147 H6
Crestwood Way, Houns.
TW4 ....143 F5
Creswick Rd, W3 .....106 B7
Creswick Wk, E3
off Malmesbury Rd ..114 A3
NW11 ....72 C4
Creton St, SE18 .....136 D3
Crewdson Rd, SW9 ...131 G7
Crewe Pl, NW10 ......107 F3
Crews St, E14 ....134 A4
Crewys Rd, NW2 ......90 C2
SE15 ....153 E2
Crichton Av, Wall. SM6 .200 D5
Crichton Rd, Cars. SM5 .199 J6
Crichton St, SW8
off Westbury St 150 C2

Cricketers Arms Rd, Enf.
 EN2 . . . . .43 J2
Cricketers Cl, N14 . . . . .42 C7
 Chessington KT9 . . . . .195 G4
Cricketers Ct, SE11 . . . .35 G2
Cricketers Ms, SW18
 off East Hill 148/149 E5
 off Wrythe La 199 H3
Cricketfield Rd, E5 . . . . .94 E4
Cricket Grn, Mitch. CR4 .185 J3
Cricket Grd Rd, Chis.
 BR7 . . . . .192 E1
Cricklade Av, SW2 . . . . .169 E2
Cricklade Av, SW2 . . . .169 E2
CRICKLEWOOD, NW2 . . .90 A3
Cricklewood Bdy, NW2 . .90 A3
Cricklewood La, NW2 . . .90 A4
Cridland St, E15
 off Church Rd 115 F1
Crieff Ct, Tedd. TW11 . . .163 F7
Crieff Rd, SW18 . . . . . .149 F6
Criffel Av, SW2 . . . . . . .168 D2
Crimscott St, SE1 . . . . . .29 E6
Crimsworth Rd, SW8 . . .150 D1
Crinan St, N1 . . . . .10 B1
Cringle St, SW8 . . . . . . .33 F7
Cripplegate St, EC2 . . . . .19 J1
Cripps Ho, Hayes UB4
 off Stratford Rd 102 B4
Crispe Ho, Bark. IG11
 off Dovehouse Mead .117 G2
Crispen Rd, Felt. TW13 . .160 E4
Crispian Cl, NW10 . . . . .89 E4
Crispin Cl, Croy. CR0
 off Harrington Cl .200/201 E2
Crispin Cres, Croy. CR0 .200 D3
Crispin Rd, Edg. HA8 . . .54 C6
Crispin St, E1 . . . . .21 F2
Crisp Rd, W6 . . . . .127 J5
Cristowe Rd, SW6 . . . . .148 C2
Criterion Ms, N19 . . . . . .92 D2
Crittall's Cor, Sid. DA14 .176 C7
Crockerton Rd, SW17 . . .167 J2
Crockham Way, SE9 . . . .174 D4
Crocus Cl, Croy. CR0
 off Cornflower La . . .203 G1
Crocus Fld, Barn. EN5 . . .40 C6
Croft, The, E4 . . . . .62 E2
 NW10 . . . . .107 F2
 W5 . . . . .105 H5
 Barnet EN5 . . . . .40 A4
 Hounslow TW5 . . . . . .123 E6
 Loughton IG10 . . . . . . .48 D2
 Pinner HA5
 off Rayners La 67 F7
 Ruislip HA4 . . . . .84 C4
 Wembley HA0 . . . . . . .87 F5
Croft Av, W.Wick. BR4 . .204 C1
Croft Cl, NW7 . . . . .54 E3
 Belvedere DA17 . . . . .139 F5
 Chislehurst BR7 . . . . .174 C4
 Hayes UB3 . . . . .121 F7
Croft Ct, Borwd. WD6
 off Kensington Way . . .38 D3
Croftdown Rd, NW5 . . . .92 A3
Croft End Cl, Chess. KT9
 off Ashcroft Rd 195 J3
Crofters Cl, Islw. TW7
 off Ploughmans End .144 A5
Crofters Ct, SE8
 off Croft St 133 H4
Crofters Way, NW1 . . . .110 D1
Croft Gdns, W7 . . . . . . .124 D2
Croft Lo Cl, Wdf.Grn. IG8 .63 H6
Croft Ms, N12 . . . . .57 F3
Crofton Av, W4 . . . . . . .126 D7
 Bexley DA5 . . . . .158 D7
 Orpington BR6 . . . . . .207 F2
Croftongate Way, SE4 . .153 H5
Crofton Gro, E4 . . . . . . .62 D4
Crofton La, Orp. BR5,
 BR6 . . . . .193 G2
Crofton Pk Rd, SE4 . . . .153 J6
Crofton Rd, E13 . . . . . . .115 H4
 SE5 . . . . .152 B1
 Orpington BR6 . . . . . .206 D3
Crofton Ter, E5
 off Studley Cl 95 H5
 Richmond TW9 . . . . . .145 J4
Crofton Way, Barn. EN5
 off Wycherley Cres .40/41 E6
 Enfield EN2 . . . . .43 G2
Croft Rd, SW16 . . . . . . .187 G1
 SW19 . . . . .167 F7
 Bromley BR1 . . . . . . .173 G6
 Enfield EN3 . . . . .45 H1
 Sutton SM1 . . . . .199 H5
Croftside, SE25
 off Sunny Bk 188 D3

Crofts La, N22
 off Glendale Av 59 G7
Crofts Rd, Har. HA1 . . . .68 D6
Crofts St, E1 . . . . .21 H6
Croft St, SE8 . . . . .133 H4
Croftway, NW3 . . . . .90 D4
 Richmond TW10 . . . . .163 E3
Croft Way, Sid. DA15 . . .175 H3
Crogsland Rd, NW1 . . . . .92 A7
Croham Cl, S.Croy. CR2 .202 B6
Croham Manor Rd, S.Croy.
 CR2 . . . . .202 B5
Croham Mt, S.Croy. CR2 .202 B7
Croham Pk Av, S.Croy.
 CR2 . . . . .202 C5
Croham Rd, S.Croy.
 CR2 . . . . .202 A5
Croham Valley Rd, S.Croy.
 CR2 . . . . .202 C6
Croindene Rd, SW16 . . .187 E1
Cromartie Rd, N19 . . . . .74 D7
Cromarty Rd, Edg. HA8 . .54 B2
Crombie Cl, Ilf. IG4 . . . . .80 C5
Crombie Rd, Sid. DA15 . .175 G1
Cromer Pl, Orp. BR6
 off Andover Rd 207 G3
Cromer Rd, E10
 off James La 78 D6
 N17 . . . . .76 D2
 SE25 . . . . .188 E3
 SW17 . . . . .168 A6
 Barnet EN5 . . . . .41 F4
 Hounslow (Hthrw.Air.)
 TW6 . . . . .140 D3
 Romford RM7 . . . . . . .83 J6
 Romford (Chad.Hth.)
 RM6 . . . . .83 E6
 Woodford Green IG8 . .63 G4
Cromer Rd W, Houns.
 (Hthrw.Air.) TW6 . . . .140 D3
Cromer St, WC1 . . . . . . .10 B4
Cromer Ter, E8
 off Ferncliff Rd 94 D5
Cromer Vil Rd, SW18 . . .148 C6
Cromford Cl, Orp. BR6 .207 H3
Cromford Path, E5
 off Overbury St 95 G4
Cromford Rd, SW18 . . . .148 D5
Cromford Way, N.Mal.
 KT3 . . . . .182 D1
Cromlix Cl, Chis. BR7 . . .192 E2
Crompton St, W2 . . . . . . .6 E6
Cromwell Av, N6 . . . . . . .92 B1
 W6 . . . . .127 H5
 Bromley BR2 . . . . . . .191 H4
 New Malden KT3 . . . . .183 F5
Cromwell Cl, E1
 off Vaughan Way 132 D1
 N2 . . . . .73 G4
 W3 off High St 126 C1
 Bromley BR2 . . . . . . .191 H4
Cromwell Cres, SW5 . . .128 D4
Cromwell Gdns, SW7 . . .23 F6
Cromwell Gro, W6 . . . . .127 J3
Cromwell Highwalk, EC2
 off Beech St 111 J5
Cromwell Ind Est, E10 . .95 H1
Cromwell Ms, SW7 . . . . .31 F1
Cromwell Pl, N6 . . . . . . .92 B1
 SW7 . . . . .31 F1
 SW14 . . . . .146 C3
 W3 off Grove Pl 126 C1
Cromwell Rd, E7 . . . . . . .97 J7
 E17 . . . . .78 C5
 N3 . . . . .73 F1
 N10 . . . . .58 A7
 SW5 . . . . .128 E4
 SW7 . . . . .30 E1
 SW9 . . . . .151 H1
 SW19 . . . . .166 D5
 Beckenham BR3 . . . . .189 H2
 Croydon CR0 . . . . . . .188 A7
 Feltham TW13 . . . . . .160 B1
 Hounslow TW3 . . . . . .143 G4
 Kingston upon Thames
 KT2 . . . . .181 H1
 Teddington TW11 . . . .162 D6
 Wembley HA0 . . . . . . .105 H2
 Worcester Park KT4 . .196 D3
Cromwell St, Houns.
 TW3 . . . . .143 G4
Cromwell Twr, EC2 . . . . .20 A1
Crondace Rd, SW6 . . . . .148 D1
Crondall Ct, N1 . . . . .12 D2
Crondall Ho, SW15
 off Fontley Way 165 G1
Crondall St, N1 . . . . .12 C2
Cronin St, SE15 . . . . . . .132 C7
Crooked Billet, SW19
 off Woodhayes Rd . . .165 J6

Crooked Billet Roundabout,
 E17 . . . . .62 A7
Crooked Billet Yd, E2
 off Kingsland Rd 112 B3
Crooked Usage, N3 . . . . .72 B3
Crooke Rd, SE8 . . . . . . .133 H5
Crookham Rd, SW6 . . . .148 C1
Crookston Rd, SE9 . . . . .156 D3
Croombs Rd, E16 . . . . . .115 J5
Crooms Hill, SE10 . . . . .134 D7
Crooms Hill Gro, SE10 . .134 C7
Cropley Ct, N1 . . . . .12 B1
Cropley St, N1 . . . . .12 B1
Croppath Rd, Dag.
 RM10 . . . . .101 G4
Cropthorne Ct, W9 . . . . . .6 D4
Crosby Cl, Felt. TW13 . . .160 E4
Crosby Ct, SE1 . . . . .28 B3
Crosby Rd, E7 . . . . .97 G6
 Dagenham RM10 . . . .119 H2
Crosby Row, SE1 . . . . . . .28 B4
Crosby Sq, EC3 . . . . .20 D4
Crosby Wk, E8
 off Laurel St 94 C6
 SW2 . . . . .151 G7
Crosier Cl, SE3 . . . . .156 B1
Crosier Rd, Uxb.
 off Taybridge Rd 150 A3
Cross Av, SE10 . . . . .134 D6
Crossbow Rd, Chig. IG7 . .65 J5
Crossbrook Rd, SE3 . . . .156 B2
Cross Cl, SE15
 off Gordon Rd . . .152/153 E1
Cross Deep, Twick. TW1 .162 C2
Cross Deep Gdns, Twick.
 TW1 . . . . .162 C2
Crossfield Rd, N17 . . . . .75 J3
 NW3 . . . . .91 G7
Crossfields, Loug. IG10 . .48 E5
Crossfield St, SE8 . . . . . .134 A7
Crossford St, SW9 . . . . .151 F2
Crossgate, Edg. HA8 . . . .54 A3
 Greenford UB6 . . . . . . .87 E6
Cross Keys Cl, N9
 off Balham Rd 60 D2
 W1 . . . . .16 C2
Cross Keys Sq, EC1 . . . . .19 J2
Cross Lances Rd, Houns.
 TW3 . . . . .143 H4
Crossland Rd, Th.Hth.
 CR7 . . . . .187 H6
Crosslands Av, W5 . . . . .125 J1
 Southall UB2 . . . . . . .123 F5
Crosslands Rd, Epsom
 KT19 . . . . .196 D6
Cross La, EC3 . . . . .20 D6
 N8 . . . . .75 F4
 Bexley DA5 . . . . .159 F7
Crosslet St, SE17 . . . . . . .36 C1
Crosslet Vale, SE10 . . . .154 B1
Crossley St, N7 . . . . .93 G6
Crossmead, SE9 . . . . . . .174 C1
Crossmead Av, Grnf.
 UB6 . . . . .103 G3
Crossmount Ho, SE5 . . . .35 J7
Crossness La, SE28 . . . .118 D7
★ Crossness Pumping Sta,
 SE2 . . . . .119 E6
Crossness Rd, Bark.
 IG11 . . . . .117 J3
Cross Rd, E4 . . . . .62 D1
 N11 . . . . .58 B5
 N22 . . . . .59 G5
 SE5 . . . . .152 B2
 SW19 . . . . .166 D7
 Bromley BR2 . . . . . . .206 B2
 Croydon CR0 . . . . . . .202 A1
 Enfield EN1 . . . . .44 B4
 Feltham TW13 . . . . . .160 E4
 Harrow HA1 . . . . .68 A4
 Harrow (S.Har.) HA2 . .85 H3
 Harrow (Wldste.) HA3 . .68 D2
 Kingston upon Thames
 KT2 . . . . .163 J7
 Romford RM7 . . . . . . .83 G3
 Romford (Chad.Hth.)
 RM6 . . . . .82 C7
 Sidcup DA14
 off Sidcup Hill 176 B4
 Sutton SM2 . . . . .199 G5
 Woodford Green IG8 . .64 C6
Cross Rds, Loug. (High Beach)
 IG10 . . . . .47 H2
Cross St, N1 . . . . .111 H1
 SW13 . . . . .147 E2
 Hampton (Hmptn.H.)
 TW12 . . . . .161 J5
Crossthwaite Av, SE5 . . .152 A4
Crosswall, EC3 . . . . .21 F5

Crossway, N12 . . . . .57 G6
 N16 . . . . .94 B5
 NW9 . . . . .71 F4
 SE28 . . . . .118 C6
 SW20 . . . . .183 J4
 W13 . . . . .104 D4
 Dagenham RM8 . . . . .100 C3
 Enfield EN1 . . . . .44 B7
 Hayes UB3 . . . . .122 A1
 Orpington BR5 . . . . . .193 G4
 Pinner HA5 . . . . .66 B2
 Ruislip HA4 . . . . .84 C4
 Woodford Green IG8 . .63 J4
Crossway, The, N22 . . . .59 H7
 SE9 . . . . .174 A2
Cross Way, The, Har. HA3 .68 B2
Crossways, N21 . . . . . . .43 J6
 South Croydon CR2 . .203 H7
Crossways, The, Houns.
 TW5 . . . . .123 F7
 Wembley HA9 . . . . . . .88 A2
Crossways Rd, Beck.
 BR3 . . . . .190 A4
 Mitcham CR4 . . . . . . .186 B3
Croston St, E8 . . . . .112 D1
Crothall Cl, N13 . . . . . . .59 F3
Crouch Av, Bark. IG11 . .118 B2
Crouch Cl, Beck. BR3
 off Abbey La 172 A6
Crouch Cft, SE9 . . . . . . .174 D3
CROUCH END, N8 . . . . . .74 C6
Crouch End Hill, N8 . . . .74 D7
Crouch Hall Rd, N8 . . . . .74 D6
Crouch Hill, N4 . . . . .74 E6
 N8 . . . . .74 E6
Crouchman's Cl, SE26 . .170 C3
Crouch Rd, NW10 . . . . . .88 D7
Crowborough Path, Wat. WD19
 off Prestwick Rd 50 D4
Crowborough Rd, SW17 .168 A6
Crowden Way, SE28 . . . .118 C7
Crowder St, E1 . . . . .112 E7
Crowfoot Cl, E9
 off Lee Conservancy
 Rd 95 J5
Crowhurst Cl, SW9 . . . . .151 G2
Crowland Av, Hayes
 UB3 . . . . .121 H4
Crowland Gdns, N14 . . . .42 E7
Crowland Rd, N15 . . . . . .76 C5
 Thornton Heath CR7 . .188 A4
Crowlands Av, Rom.
 RM7 . . . . .83 H5
Crowland Ter, N1 . . . . . . .94 A7
Crowland Wk, Mord.
 SM4 . . . . .185 E6
Crow La, Rom. RM7 . . . . .83 F7
Crowley Cres, Croy. CR0 .201 G5
Crowline Wk, N1
 off Clephane Rd 94 A6
Crowmarsh Gdns, SE23
 off Tyson Rd 153 F7
Crown Arc, Kings.T. KT1
 off Union St 181 G2
Crown Cl, E3 . . . . .114 A1
 NW6 . . . . .90 E6
 NW7 . . . . .55 F2
 Hayes UB3 . . . . .121 J2
 Walton-on-Thames
 KT12 . . . . .178 C7
Crown Ct, EC2 . . . . .20 A4
 SE12 . . . . .155 H6
 WC2 . . . . .18 B4
 Bromley BR2
 off Victoria Rd 192 A5
Crown Dale, SE19 . . . . . .169 H6
Crowndale Rd, NW1 . . . . .9 F1
Crownfield Av, Ilf. IG2 . . .81 H5
Crownfield Rd, E15 . . . . .96 D5
Crown Hill, Croy. CR0
 off Church St 201 J2
Crownhill Rd, NW10 . . . .107 F1
 Woodford Green IG8 . .64 B7
Crown Ho, Bark. IG11
 off Linton Rd 99 F7
Crown La, N14 . . . . .58 C1
 SW16 . . . . .169 G5
 Bromley BR2 . . . . . . .192 A5
 Chislehurst BR7 . . . . .193 F1
 Morden SM4 . . . . . . .184 E3
Crown La Gdns, SW16
 off Crown La 169 G5
Crown La Spur, Brom.
 BR2 . . . . .192 A6
Crownmead Way, Rom.
 RM7 . . . . .83 H4
Crown Ms, E13
 off Waghorn Rd 115 J1
 W6 . . . . .127 G4
Crown Office Row, EC4 . .19 E5

Crown Pas, SW1 . . . . .25 G2
Kingston upon Thames KT1
  off Church St 181 G2
Crown Pl, EC2 . . . . .20 D1
NW5
  off Kentish Town Rd . . .92 B6
Crown Pt Par, SE19
  off Beulah Hill 169 H6
Crown Rd, N10 . . . . .58 A7
Borehamwood WD6 . . .38 A1
Enfield EN1 . . . . .44 E4
Ilford IG6 . . . . .81 G4
Morden SM4 . . . . .184 E4
New Malden KT3 . . . . .182 C1
Ruislip HA4 . . . . .84 D5
Sutton SM1 . . . . .198 E4
Twickenham TW1 . . . .145 E6
Crownstone Rd, SW2 . .151 G5
Crown St, SE5 . . . . .36 A7
W3 . . . . .126 B1
Dagenham RM10 . . . . .101 J6
Harrow HA2 . . . . .86 A1
Crown Ter, Rich. TW9 . . .145 J4
Crowntree Cl, Islw. TW7 .124 C6
Crown Wk, Wem. HA9 . . .87 J3
Crown Way, West Dr.
UB7 . . . . .120 C1
Crown Wds La, SE9 . . . .157 E2
SE18 . . . . .157 E2
Crown Wds Way, SE9 . .157 G5
Crown Wks, E2
  off Temple St 112/113 E2
Crown Yd, Houns. TW3
  off High St 143 J3
Crowshott Av, Stan. HA7 .69 F1
Crows Rd, E15 . . . . .114 D3
Barking IG11 . . . . .99 E6
Crowther Av, Brent. TW8 .125 H4
Crowther Rd, SE25 . . . .188 D4
Crowthorne Cl, SW18 . .166 C1
Crowthorne Rd, W10 . . .108 A6
Croxden Cl, Edg. HA8 . . .69 J3
Croxden Wk, Mord. SM4 .185 F6
Croxford Gdns, N22 . . . .59 H7
Croxley Rd, W9 . . . . . . .108 C3
Croxted Cl, SE21 . . . . . .151 J7
Croxted Rd, SE21 . . . . .151 J7
SE24 . . . . .151 J7
Croyde Av, Grnf. UB6 . . .103 J3
Hayes UB3 . . . . .121 H4
Croyde Cl, Sid. DA15 . . .157 G7
CROYDON 202 A2
Croydon Flyover, Croy.
CRO 201 H4
Croydon Gro, Croy. CRO .201 H1
★ Croydon Mus, Croy.
CRO 201 J3
Croydon Rd, E13 . . . . . .115 F4
SE20 . . . . .188 E2
Beckenham BR3 . . . . .189 H4
Bromley BR2 . . . . .205 F3
Croydon (Bedd.) CRO . .201 E4
Hounslow (Hthrw.Air.)
TW6 . . . . .140 E2
Keston BR2 . . . . .205 J3
Mitcham CR4 . . . . . . .186 A4
Wallington SM6 . . . . .200 B4
West Wickham BR4 . . .204 E3
Croyland Rd, N9 . . . . . . .60 D1
Croylands Dr, Surb. KT6 .181 H7
Croysdale Av, Sun.
TW16 . . . . .178 A3
Crozier Ho, SE3
  off Ebdon Way 155 H3
Crozier Ter, E9 . . . . .95 G5
Crucible Cl, Rom. RM6 . .82 B6
Crucifix La, SE1 . . . . .28 D3
Cruden Ho, SE17 . . . . . . .35 G6
Cruden St, N1 . . . . .111 H1
Cruikshank Rd, E15 . . . . .97 E4
Cruikshank St, WC1 . . . .10 E3
Crummock Gdns, NW9 . .70 E5
Crumpsall St, SE2 . . . . .138 C4
Crundale Av, NW9 . . . . . .70 A5
Crunden Rd, S.Croy.
CR2 . . . . .202 A7
Crusader Gdns, Croy. CRO
  off Cotelands 202 B3
Crusoe Ms, N16 . . . . . . .94 A2
Crusoe Rd, Mitch. CR4 . .167 J7
Crutched Friars, EC3 . . .21 E5
Crutchley Rd, SE6 . . . . .173 E2
Crystal Ct, SE19
  off College Rd 170 C5
Crystal Ho, SE18
  off Spinel Cl 137 J5
★ Crystal Palace FC,
SE25 . . . . .188 B4
★ Crystal Palace National
Sport Cen, SE19 . . .170 D6

Crystal Palace Par,
SE19 . . . . .170 C6
★ Crystal Palace Pk,
SE19 . . . . .170 C5
Crystal Palace Pk Rd,
SE26 . . . . .170 D5
Crystal Palace Sta Rd, SE19
  off Anerley Hill 170 D6
Crystal Ter, SE19 . . . . .170 A6
Crystal Vw Ct, Brom. BR1
  off Winlaton Rd 172 D4
Crystal Way, Dag. RM8 .100 C1
Harrow HA1 . . . . .68 C5
Cuba Dr, Enf. EN3 . . . . . .45 F2
Cuba St, E14 . . . . .134 A2
Cubitt Sq, Sthl. UB2
  off Windmill Av 123 J1
Cubitt Steps, E14
  off Cabot Sq 133 J1
Cubitt St, WC1 . . . . .10 C4
Croydon CR0 . . . . . . .201 F5
Cubitts Yd, WC2 . . . . . . .18 B5
Cubitt Ter, SW4 . . . . . . .150 C3
CUBITT TOWN, E14 . . . .134 C3
Cuckoo Av, W7 . . . . . . .104 B4
Cuckoo Dene, W7 . . . . .104 A5
Cuckoo Hall La, N9 . . . . .45 F7
Cuckoo Hill, Pnr. HA5 . . .66 C3
Cuckoo Hill Dr, Pnr. HA5 .66 C3
Cuckoo Hill Rd, Pnr. HA5 .66 C4
Cuckoo La, W7 . . . . . . .104 B7
Cudas Cl, Epsom KT19 .197 F4
Cuddington Av, Wor.Pk.
KT4 . . . . .197 F3
Cudham St, SE6 . . . . . .154 C7
Cudworth St, E1 . . . . . .113 E4
Cuff Cres, SE9 . . . . . . .156 A6
Cuff Pt, E2 . . . . .13 F3
Culford Gdns, SW3 . . . . .32 A2
Culford Gro, N1 . . . . .94 B6
Culford Ms, N1
  off Culford Rd 94 B6
Culford Rd, N1 . . . . .94 B7
Culgaith Gdns, Enf. EN2 .42 E4
Cullen Way, NW10 . . . .106 C4
Culling Rd, SE16
  off Lower Rd 133 F3
Cullington Cl, Har. HA3 . .68 D4
Cullingworth Rd, NW10 . .89 G5
Culloden Cl, SE16 . . . . . .37 J4
Culloden Rd, Enf. EN2 . . .43 H2
Culloden St, E14 . . . . . .114 C6
Cullum St, EC3 . . . . .20 D5
Culmington Rd, W13 . . .125 F2
Culmore Cross, SW12 . .168 B1
Culmore Rd, SE15 . . . . .133 E7
Culmstock Rd, SW11 . . .150 A5
Culpeper Cl, Ilf. IG6 . . . . .65 E6
Culross Cl, N15 . . . . .75 J4
Culross St, W1 . . . . .16 B6
Culsac Rd, Surb. KT6 . . .195 H2
Culverden Rd, SW12 . . .168 C2
Watford WD19 . . . . . . .50 B3
Culver Gro, Stan. HA7 . . .69 F2
Culverhouse Gdns,
SW16 . . . . .169 F3
Culverlands Cl, Stan. HA7 .52 E4
Culverley Rd, SE6 . . . . .172 B1
Culvers Av, Cars. SM5 . .199 J2
Culvers Retreat, Cars.
SM5 . . . . .199 J1
Culverstone Cl, Brom.
BR2 . . . . .191 F6
Culvers Way, Cars. SM5 .199 J2
Culvert Pl, SW11 . . . . . .150 A2
Culvert Rd, N15 . . . . .76 B5
SW11 . . . . .149 J2
Culworth St, NW8 . . . . . . .7 G2
Cumberland Av, NW10 .106 B3
Welling DA16 . . . . . . .157 H3
Cumberland Cl, E8 . . . . .94 C6
SW20 off Lansdowne
Rd 166 A7
Ilford IG6
  off Carrick Dr 81 F1
Twickenham TW1
  off Westmorland
Cl 144/145 E6
Cumberland Cres, W14 .128 B4
Cumberland Dr, Bexh.
DA7 . . . . .138 D7
Chessington KT9 . . . .195 J3
Esher KT10 . . . . .194 D2
Cumberland Gdns, NW4 .72 B2
WC1 . . . . .10 D3
Cumberland Gate, W1 . . .15 J5
Cumberland Mkt, NW1 . . .9 E3
Cumberland Mkt Est, NW1 .9 E3

Cumberland Mills Sq, E14
  off Saunders Ness
Rd 134 D5
Cumberland Pk, NW10 .107 G3
W3 . . . . .106 C7
Cumberland Pl, NW1 . . . . .8 D3
SE6 . . . . .173 F1
Sunbury-on-Thames
TW16 . . . . .178 A4
Cumberland Rd, E12 . . . .98 A4
E13 . . . . .115 H5
E17 . . . . .77 H2
N9 . . . . .61 F1
N22 . . . . .75 F2
SE25 . . . . .189 E6
SW13 . . . . .147 F1
W3 . . . . .106 C7
W7 . . . . .124 C7
Bromley BR2 . . . . . . .190 E4
Harrow HA1 . . . . .67 H5
Richmond TW9 . . . . . .126 A7
Stanmore HA7 . . . . . . .69 J3
Cumberland St, SW1 . . . .32 E3
Staines-upon-Thames
TW18 . . . .
Cumberland Ter, NW1 . . . .8 D3
Cumberland Ter Ms, NW1 . .8 D2
Cumberland Vil, W3
  off Cumberland Rd . . .106 C7
Cumberlow Av, SE25 . . .188 C3
Cumberton Rd, N17 . . . . .76 A1
Cumbrae Gdns, Surb.
KT6 . . . . .195 G2
Cumbria Ho, SE26
  off High Level Dr . . .170 D4
Cumbrian Gdns, NW2 . . .90 A2
★ Cuming Mus, SE17 . . .35 J2
Cumming St, N1 . . . . . . .10 C2
Cumnor Gdns, Epsom
KT17 . . . . .197 G6
Cumnor Rd, Sutt. SM2 . .199 F6
Cunard Cres, N21 . . . . . .44 A6
Cunard Pl, EC3 . . . . .20 E4
Cunard Rd, NW10 . . . . .106 D3
Cunard St, SE5
  off Albany Rd 132 B6
Cunard Wk, SE16 . . . . . .133 H4
Cundy Rd, E16 . . . . .115 J6
Cundy St, SW1 . . . . .32 C2
Cundy St Est, SW1 . . . . .32 C2
Cunliffe Rd, Epsom
KT19 . . . . .197 F4
Cunliffe St, SW16 . . . . .168 C6
Cunningham Cl, Rom.
RM6 . . . . .82 C5
West Wickham BR4 . . .204 B2
Cunningham Pk, Har.
HA1 . . . . .67 J5
Cunningham Pl, NW8 . . . .7 E5
Cunningham Rd, N15 . . .76 D4
Cunnington St, W4 . . . .126 C3
Cupar Rd, SW11 . . . . . .150 A1
Cupola Cl, Brom. BR1 . .173 H5
Cureton St, SW1 . . . . . . .33 J2
Curfew Ho, Bark. IG11
  off St. Ann's 117 F1
Curie Gdns, NW9 . . . . . .
  off Pasteur Cl 70/71 E2
Curlew Cl, SE28 . . . . . . .118 D7
Curlew Ct, Surb. KT6 . . .195 J3
Curlew Ho, Enf. EN3
  off Allington Ct 45 G5
Curlew St, SE1 . . . . .29 F3
Curlew Ter, Ilf. IG5
  off Tiptree Cres 80 B3
Curlew Way, Hayes UB4 .102 D5
Curnick's La, SE27
  off Chapel Rd 169 J4
Curnock Est, NW1
  off Plender St 110 C1
Curran Av, Sid. DA15 . . .157 J5
Wallington SM6 . . . . .200 A3
Currey Rd, Grnf. UB6 . . .86 A6
Curricle St, W3 . . . . . . .126 E1
Currie Hill Cl, SW19 . . .166 C4
Curry Ri, NW7 . . . . .56 A6
Cursitor St, EC4 . . . . . . .18 E3
Curtain Pl, EC2
  off Curtain Rd 112 B3
Curtain Rd, EC2 . . . . . . .12 D6
Curthwaite Gdns, Enf.
EN2 . . . . .42 D4
Curtis Dr, W3 . . . . .106 D6
Curtis Fld Rd, SW16 . . .169 F4
Curtis La, Wem. HA0
  off Montrose Cres . . .87 H6
Curtis Rd, Epsom KT19 .196 C4
Hounslow TW4 . . . . . .143 F7
Curtis St, SE1 . . . . .37 F1
Curtis Way, SE1 . . . . . . .37 F1
SE28 off Tawney Rd . .118 B7
Curve, The, W12 . . . . . .107 G7

Curwen Av, E7
  off Woodford Rd 97 H4
Curwen Rd, W12 . . . . . .127 G2
Curzon Av, Enf. EN3 . . . .45 G5
Stanmore HA7 . . . . . . .68 D1
Curzon Cl, Orp. BR6 . . .207 G4
Curzon Cres, NW10 . . . . .89 F7
Barking IG11 . . . . . . .117 J2
Curzon Gate, W1 . . . . . . .24 C2
Curzon Pl, Pnr. HA5 . . . .66 C5
Curzon Rd, N10 . . . . .74 B2
W5 . . . . .105 E4
Thornton Heath CR7 . .187 G6
Curzon Sq, W1 . . . . .24 C2
Curzon St, W1 . . . . .24 C2
Cusack Cl, Twick. TW1
  off Waldegrave Rd . .162 C4
CUSTOM HOUSE, E16 . .116 A6
★ Custom House, EC3 . .20 D6
Custom Ho Quay, EC3
  off Lower Thames St .112 B7
Custom Ho Reach, SE16 .133 J2
Custom Ho Wk, EC3 . . . .20 D6
Cut, The, SE1 . . . . .27 F3
Cutcombe Rd, SE5 . . . . .151 J2
Cuthberga Cl, Bark. IG11
  off George St 99 F7
Cuthbert Gdns, SE25 . . .188 B3
Cuthbert Rd, E17 . . . . . . .78 C3
N18 off Fairfield Rd . . .60 D5
Croydon CR0 . . . . . . .201 H2
Cuthbert St, W2 . . . . . . .15 E1
Cuthill Wk, SE5 . . . . . . .152 A1
Cutlers Gdns, E1 . . . . . . .21 E3
Cutlers Gdns Arc, EC2
  off Cutler St 112 B6
Cutlers Sq, E14
  off Britannia Rd 134 A4
Cutlers Ter, N1
  off Balls Pond Rd 94 A6
Cutler St, E1 . . . . .21 E3
Cutthroat All, Rich. TW10
  off Ham St 163 F2
★ Cutty Sark, SE10 . . .134 C6
Cutty Sark Gdns, SE10
  off King William Wk .134 C6
Cuxton Cl, Bexh. DA6 . .158 E5
Cyclamen Cl, Hmptn. TW12
  off Gresham Rd 161 G6
Cyclamen Way, Epsom
KT19 . . . . .196 B5
Cyclops Ms, E14 . . . . . .134 A4
Cygnet Av, Felt. TW14 . .142 C7
Cygnet Cl, NW10 . . . . . . .88 D7
Borehamwood WD6 . . .38 C1
Cygnets, The, Felt. TW13 .160 E4
Cygnet St, E1 . . . . .13 G5
Cygnet Way, Hayes
UB4 . . . . .102 D5
Cygnus Business Cen,
NW10 . . . . .89 F6
Cymbeline Ct, Har. HA1 . .68 C6
Cynthia St, N1 . . . . .10 D2
Cyntra Pl, E8 . . . . .95 E7
Cypress Av, Twick. TW2 .143 J7
Cypress Gro, Ilf. IG6 . . . .65 H6
Cypress Pl, W1 . . . . .9 G6
Cypress Rd, SE25 . . . . .188 B2
Harrow HA3 . . . . .68 A2
Cypress Tree Cl, Sid. DA15
  off White Oak Gdns . .157 J7
Cyprus Av, N3 . . . . .72 B3
Cyprus Cl, N4
  off Atterbury Rd 75 H6
Cyprus Gdns, N3 . . . . . . .72 B2
Cyprus Pl, E2 . . . . .113 F2
E6 . . . . .116 D7
Cyprus Rd, N3 . . . . .72 C2
N9 . . . . .60 C2
Cyprus Roundabout, E16
  off Royal Albert Way . .116 D7
Cyprus St, E2 . . . . .113 F2
Cyrena Rd, SE22 . . . . . .152 C6
Cyril Mans, SW11 . . . . .149 J1
Cyril Rd, Bexh. DA7 . . . .159 E2
Cyrus St, EC1 . . . . .11 H5
Czar St, SE8 . . . . .134 A6

D

Dabbs Hill La, Nthlt.
UB5 . . . . .85 H5
Dabin Cres, SE10 . . . . .154 C1
Dacca St, SE8 . . . . .133 J6
Dace Rd, E3 . . . . .96 A7
Dacre Av, Ilf. IG5 . . . . . . .80 D2
Dacre Cl, Chig. IG7 . . . . .65 F4
Greenford UB6 . . . . . .103 H2
Dacre Gdns, SE13 . . . . .154 E4

Dacre Gdns, Borehamwood WD6 38 D5
Chigwell IG7 65 F4
Dacre Pk, SE13 155 E3
Dacre Pl, SE13 154 E3
Dacre Rd, E11 97 F1
E13 115 H1
Croydon CR0 187 E7
Dacres Rd, SE23 171 G3
Dacre St, SW1 25 H5
Dade Way, Sthl. UB2 123 F5
Daerwood Cl, Brom. BR2 206 C1
Daffodil Cl, Croy. CR0 *off Primrose La* 203 G1
Daffodil Gdns, Ilf. IG1 98 E5
Daffodil Pl, Hmptn. TW12 *off Gresham Rd* 161 G6
Daffodil St, W12 107 F7
Dafforne Rd, SW17 168 A3
DAGENHAM 101 G6
Dagenham Av, Dag. RM9 118 E1
Dagenham Rd, E10 95 J1
Dagenham RM10 101 J4
Dagmar Av, Wem. HA9 87 J4
Dagmar Gdns, NW10 108 A2
Dagmar Ms, Sthl. UB2 *off Dagmar Rd* 122/123 E3
Dagmar Pas, N1 *off Cross St* 111 H1
Dagmar Rd, N4 75 G7
N15 *off Cornwall Rd* 76 A4
N22 74 D1
SE5 152 B1
SE25 188 B5
Dagenham RM10 101 J7
Kingston upon Thames KT2 181 J1
Southall UB2 122 E3
Dagmar Ter, N1 111 H1
Dagnall Pk, SE25 188 B6
Dagnall Rd, SE25 188 B5
Dagnall St, SW11 149 J2
Dagnan Rd, SW12 150 B7
Dagonet Gdns, Brom. BR1 173 G3
Dagonet Rd, Brom. BR1 173 G3
Dahlia Gdns, Ilf. IG1 99 E6
Mitcham CR4 186 D4
Dahlia Rd, SE2 138 B4
Dahomey Rd, SW16 168 C6
Daimler Way, Wall. SM6 200 E7
Daines Cl, E12 *off Colchester Av* 98 C3
Dainford Cl, Brom. BR1 172 D5
Dainton Cl, Brom. BR1 191 H1
Daintry Cl, Har. HA3 68 D4
Daintry Way, E9 *off Osborne Rd* 95 J6
Dairsie Rd, SE9 156 D3
Dairy Cl, NW10 107 G1
Thornton Heath CR7 187 J2
Dairy La, SE18 136 C4
Dairyman Cl, NW2 *off Claremont Rd* 90 B3
Dairy Ms, SW9 151 E3
Dairy Wk, SW19 166 B4
Daisy Cl, Croy. CR0 *off Primrose La* 203 G1
Daisy Dobbins Wk, N19 *off Hillrise Rd* 74/75 E7
Daisy La, SW6 148 D3
Daisy Rd, E16 *off Cranberry La* 114/115 E4
E18 79 H2
Dakota Cl, Wall. SM6 *off Handley Page Rd* 201 F7
Dakota Gdns, E6 116 B4
Northolt UB5 *off Argus Way* 102/103 E3
Dalberg Rd, SW2 151 G5
Dalberg Way, SE2 *off Lanridge Rd* 138 D3
Dalby Rd, SW18 149 F4
Dalby St, NW5 92 B6
Dalcross Rd, Houns. TW4 142 E2
Dale, The, Kes. BR2 206 A4
Dale Av, Edg. HA8 69 J1
Hounslow TW4 143 E3
Dalebury Rd, SW17 167 H2
Dale Cl, SE3 155 G3
Barnet EN5 41 E6
Pinner HA5 66 B1
Dale Gdns, Wdf.Grn. IG8 63 H4
Dale Grn Rd, N11 58 B3
Dale Gro, N12 57 F5
Daleham Gdns, NW3 91 G5
Daleham Ms, NW3 91 G6
Dalehead, NW1 9 F2
Dalemain Ms, E16 *off Hanover Av* 135 G1
Dale Pk Av, Cars. SM5 199 J2
Dale Pk Rd, SE19 187 J1
Dale Rd, NW5 *off Grafton Rd* 92 A5
SE17 35 H6
Greenford UB6 103 H5
Sutton SM1 198 C4
Dale Row, W11 *off St. Marks Rd* 108 B6
Daleside Gdns, Chig. IG7 65 F3
Daleside Rd, SW16 168 B5
Epsom KT19 196 D6
Dales Path, Borwd. WD6 *off Farriers Way* 38 D5
Dales Rd, Borwd. WD6 38 D5
Dale St, W4 126 E5
Dale Vw Av, E4 62 C2
Dale Vw Cres, E4 62 C2
Dale Vw Gdns, E4 62 D3
Daleview Rd, N15 76 B6
Dalewood Gdns, Wor.Pk. KT4 197 H2
Dale Wd Rd, Orp. BR6 193 H7
Daley St, E9 95 G6
Daley Thompson Way, SW8 150 B2
Dalgarno Gdns, W10 107 J5
Dalgarno Way, W10 107 J4
Dalgleish St, E14 113 H6
Daling Way, E3 113 H1
Dalkeith Gro, Stan. HA7 53 G5
Dalkeith Rd, SE21 169 J1
Ilford IG1 99 F3
Dallas Rd, NW4 71 G7
SE26 170 E4
W5 105 J5
Sutton SM3 198 B6
Dallas Ter, Hayes UB3 121 J3
Dallinger Rd, SE12 155 F6
Dalling Rd, W6 127 H3
Dallington Sq, EC1 *off Dallington St* 111 H4
Dallington St, EC1 11 H5
Dallin Rd, SE18 137 E7
Bexleyheath DA6 158 D4
Dalmain Rd, SE23 171 G1
Dalmally Rd, Croy. CR0 188 C7
Dalmeny Av, N7 92 D4
SW16 187 G2
Dalmeny Cl, Wem. HA0 87 F6
Dalmeny Cres, Houns. TW3 144 A4
Dalmeny Rd, N7 92 D3
Barnet EN5 41 F6
Carshalton SM5 200 A7
Erith DA8 159 H1
Worcester Park KT4 197 H3
Dalmeyer Rd, NW10 89 F6
Dalmore Av, Esher (Clay.) KT10 194 C6
Dalmore Rd, SE21 169 J2
Dalrymple Cl, N14 42 D7
Dalrymple Rd, SE4 153 H4
DALSTON, E8 94 D7
Dalston Cross Shop Cen, E8 94 C6
Dalston Gdns, Stan. HA7 69 H1
Dalston La, E8 94 C6
Dalton Av, Mitch. CR4 185 H2
Dalton Cl, Orp. BR6 207 H3
Dalton Rd, Har. (Har.Wld.) HA3 68 A2
Dalton St, SE27 169 H2
Dalwood St, SE5 152 B1
Daly Ct, E15 *off Clays La* 96 C5
Dalyell Rd, SW9 151 F3
Damascene Wk, SE21 *off Lovelace Rd* 169 J1
Damask Cres, E16 *off Cranberry La* 114/115 E4
Damer Ter, SW10 *off Tadema Rd* 129 F7
Dames Rd, E7 97 G3
Dame St, N1 11 J1
Damien St, E1 113 E6
Damon Cl, Sid. DA14 176 B3
Damson Dr, Hayes UB3 102 A7
Damsonwood Rd, Sthl. UB2 123 G3
Danbrook Rd, SW16 187 E1
Danbury Cl, Rom. RM6 82 D3
Danbury Ms, Wall. SM6 200 B4
Danbury Rd, Loug. IG10 48 B7
Danbury St, N1 11 H1
Danbury Way, Wdf.Grn. IG8 63 J6
Danby St, SE15 152 C3
Dancer Rd, SW6 148 C1
Richmond TW9 146 A3
Dando Cres, SE3 155 H3
Dandridge Cl, SE10 135 F5
Danebury, Croy. (New Adgtn.) CR0 204 B6
Danebury Av, SW15 147 E6
Daneby Rd, SE6 172 B3
Dane Cl, Bex. DA5 159 G7
Orpington BR6 207 G5
Danecourt Gdns, Croy. CR0 202 C3
Danecroft Rd, SE24 151 J5
Danehill Wk, Sid. DA14 *off Hatherley Rd* 176 A3
Danehurst Gdns, Ilf. IG4 80 B5
Danehurst St, SW6 148 B1
Daneland, Barn. EN4 41 J6
Danemead Gro, Nthlt. UB5 85 H5
Danemere St, SW15 147 J3
Dane Pl, E3 *off Roman Rd* 113 H2
Dane Rd, N18 61 F3
SW19 185 F1
W13 125 F1
Ilford IG1 99 F5
Southall UB1 103 E7
Danesbury Rd, Felt. TW13 160 B1
Danescombe, SE12 *off Winn Rd* 173 G1
Danes Ct, Wem. HA9 88 B3
Danescourt Cres, Sutt. SM1 199 F2
Danescroft, NW4 72 A5
Danescroft Av, NW4 72 A5
Danescroft Gdns, NW4 72 A5
Danesdale Rd, E9 95 H6
Danesfield, SE5 36 D5
Danes Gate, Har. HA1 68 B3
Danes Rd, Rom. RM7 83 J7
Dane St, WC1 18 C2
Daneswood Av, SE6 172 C3
Danethorpe Rd, Wem. HA0 87 G6
Danetree Cl, Epsom KT19 196 C7
Danetree Rd, Epsom KT19 196 C7
Danette Gdns, Dag. RM10 101 F2
Daneville Rd, SE5 152 A1
Dangan Rd, E11 79 G6
Daniel Bolt Cl, E14 *off Uamvar St* 114 B5
Daniel Cl, N18 61 F4
SW17 167 H6
Hounslow TW4 *off Harvey Rd* 143 F7
Daniel Gdns, SE15 37 F7
Daniell Way, Croy. CR0 201 E1
Daniel Pl, NW4 71 H6
Daniel Rd, W5 105 J7
Daniels Ms, SE4 153 J4
Daniels Rd, SE15 153 F3
Dan Leno Wk, SW6 *off Britannia Rd* 128/129 E7
Dansey Pl, W1 17 H5
Dansington Rd, Well. DA16 158 A4
Danson Cres, Well. DA16 158 B3
Danson La, Well. DA16 158 A4
Danson Mead, Well. DA16 158 C3
★ **Danson Park**, Well. DA16 158 C4
Danson Pk, Bexh. DA6 158 C4
Danson Rd, Bex. DA5 158 D5
Bexleyheath DA6 158 D5
Danson Underpass, Sid. DA15 *off Danson Rd* 158 C6
Dante Pl, SE11 35 H1
Dante Rd, SE11 35 G1
Danube St, SW3 31 H3
Danvers Rd, N8 74 D4
Danvers St, SW3 31 F6
Danziger Way, Borwd. WD6 38 C1
Daphne Gdns, E4 *off Gunners Gro* 62 C3
Daphne St, SW18 149 F6
Daplyn St, E1 21 H1
D'Arblay St, W1 17 G4
Darby Cres, Sun. TW16 178 C2
Darby Gdns, Sun. TW16 178 C2
Darcy Av, Wall. SM6 200 C4
Darcy Cl, N20 57 G2
D'Arcy Dr, Har. HA3 69 G4
Darcy Gdns, Dag. RM9 119 F1
D'Arcy Gdns, Har. HA3 69 H4
D'Arcy Pl, Brom. BR2 191 G4
Darcy Rd, SW16 186 E2
Isleworth TW7 *off London Rd* 144 D1
D'Arcy Rd, Sutt. SM3 198 A4
Dare Gdns, Dag. RM8 *off Grafton Rd* 100/101 E3
Darell Rd, Rich. TW9 146 A3
Darenth Rd, N16 76 C7
Welling DA16 158 A1
Darfield Rd, SE4 153 J5
Darfield Way, W10 108 A6
Darfur St, SW15 148 A3
Dargate Cl, SE19 *off Chipstead Cl* 170 C7
Darien Rd, SW11 149 G3
Dark Ho Wk, EC3 *off King William St* 112 B7
Darlands Dr, Barn. EN5 40 A5
Darlan Rd, SW6 128 C7
Darlaston Rd, SW19 166 A7
Darley Cl, Croy. CR0 189 H6
Darley Dr, N.Mal. KT3 182 D2
Darley Gdns, Mord. SM4 185 E6
Darley Rd, N9 60 C1
SW11 149 J6
Darling Rd, SE4 154 A3
Darling Row, E1 113 E4
Darlington Rd, SE27 169 H5
Darmaine Cl, S.Croy. CR2 *off Churchill Rd* 201 J7
Darnaway Pl, E14 *off Abbott Rd* 114 C6
Darndale Cl, E17 77 J2
Darnley Ho, E14 113 H6
Darnley Rd, E9 95 E6
Woodford Green IG8 79 G1
Darnley Ter, W11 *off St. James's Gdns* 128 B1
Darrell Rd, SE22 152 D5
Darren Cl, N4 75 F7
Darrick Wd Rd, Orp. BR6 207 G2
Darris Cl, Hayes UB4 103 E4
Darsley Dr, SW8 150 E1
Dartford Av, N9 45 F6
Dartford Gdns, Rom. (Chad.Hth.) RM6 *off Heathfield Pk Dr* 82 B6
Dartford Rd, Bex. DA5 177 J1
Dartford St, SE17 36 A5
Dartmoor Wk, E14 *off Charnwood Gdns* 134 A4
Dartmouth Cl, W11 108 C6
Dartmouth Gro, SE10 154 C1
Dartmouth Hill, SE10 154 C1
DARTMOUTH PARK, NW5 92 B3
Dartmouth Pk Av, NW5 92 B3
Dartmouth Pk Hill, N19 92 B1
NW5 92 B1
Dartmouth Pk Rd, NW5 92 B4
Dartmouth Pl, SE23 *off Dartmouth Rd* 171 F2
W4 127 E6
Dartmouth Rd, E16 *off Fords Pk Rd* 115 G6
NW2 90 A6
NW4 71 G6
SE23 171 F3
SE26 171 F3
Bromley BR2 191 G7
Ruislip HA4 84 A3
Dartmouth Row, SE10 154 C2
Dartmouth St, SW1 25 H4
Dartmouth Ter, SE10 154 D1
Dartnell Rd, Croy. CR0 188 C7
Dartrey Wk, SW10 30 D7
Dart St, W10 108 B3
Darville Rd, N16 94 C3
Darwell Cl, E6 116 D2
Darwin Cl, N11 58 B3
Orpington BR6 207 G5
Darwin Dr, Sthl. UB1 103 H6
Darwin Gdns, Wat. WD19 *off Barnhurst Path* 50 C5
Darwin Rd, N22 75 H1
W5 125 F5
Welling DA16 157 J3
Darwin St, SE17 36 C1
Daryngton Dr, Grnf. UB6 104 A2
Dashwood Cl, Bexh. DA6 159 G5
Dashwood Rd, N8 75 F6
Dassett Rd, SE27 169 H5

Datchelor Pl, SE5 . . . . . .**152** A1
Datchet Rd, SE6 . . . .**171** J3
Datchworth Ct, N4
Date St, SE17 . . . .**36** B4
Daubeney Gdns, N17 . . . .**59** J7
Daubeney Rd, E5 . . . .**95** H4
N17 . . . .**59** J7
Daubeney Twr, SE8 . . . . .**133** J4
Dault Rd, SW18 . . . .**149** F6
Davema Cl, Chis. BR7
off Brenchley Cl **192** D1
Davenant Rd, N19 . . . . . .**92** D2
Croydon CR0
off Duppas Hill Rd . .**201** H4
Davenant St, E1 . . . .**21** J2
Davenport Cl, Tedd.
TW11 . . . .**162** D6
Davenport Rd, SE6 . . . . .**154** B6
Sidcup DA14 . . . . . .**176** D2
Daventer Dr, Stan. HA7 . .**52** C7
Daventry Av, E17 . . . .**78** A5
Daventry St, NW1 . . . . . .**15** G1
Davern Cl, SE10 . . . .**135** F4
Davey Cl, N7 . . . .**93** F6
Davey Rd, E9 . . . .**96** A7
Davey St, SE15 . . . .**37** G6
David Av, Grnf. UB6 . . . . .**104** B3
David Cl, Hayes UB3 . . . .**121** G7
Davidge St, SE1 . . . .**27** G4
David Lee Pt, E15 . . . . . .**115** E1
David Ms, W1 . . . .**16** A1
David Rd, Dag. RM8 . . . . .**100** E2
Davidson Gdns, SW8 . . .**130** E7
Davidson La, Har. HA1
off Grove Hill **68** C7
Davidson Rd, Croy. CR0 .**188** C6
Davids Rd, SE23 . . . .**171** F1
David St, E15 . . . .**96** D6
David's Way, Ilf. IG6 . . . . .**65** H7
David Twigg Cl, Kings.T.
KT2 . . . .**181** H1
Davies Cl, Croy. CR0 . . . .**188** D6
Davies La, E11 . . . .**97** E2
Davies Ms, W1 . . . .**16** D5
Davies St, W1 . . . .**16** D5
Davington Gdns, Dag.
RM8 . . . .**100** B6
Davington Rd, Dag.
RM8 . . . .**100** B6
Davinia Cl, Wdf.Grn. IG8
off Deacon Way **64** C6
Davis Rd, W3 . . . .**127** F1
Chessington KT9 . . . .**196** A4
Davis St, E13 . . . .**115** H2
Davisville Rd, W12 . . . . . .**127** G2
Dawes Av, Islw. TW7 . . . .**144** D5
Dawes Ho, SE17 . . . .**36** C2
Dawes Rd, SW6 . . . .**128** B7
Dawes St, SE17 . . . .**36** C3
Dawley Rd, Hayes UB3 . .**121** H3
Dawlish Av, N13 . . . .**58** E4
SW18 . . . .**166** E2
Greenford UB6 . . . . .**104** D2
Dawlish Dr, Ilf. IG3 . . . . . .**99** H4
Pinner HA5 . . . .**67** E5
Ruislip HA4 . . . .**84** A2
Dawlish Rd, E10 . . . .**96** C2
N17 . . . .**76** D3
NW2 . . . .**90** A6
Dawnay Gdns, SW18 . . .**167** G2
Dawnay Rd, SW18 . . . . .**167** F2
Dawn Cl, Houns. TW4 . . .**143** E3
Dawn Cres, E15
off Bridge Rd **114** D1
Dawpool Rd, NW2 . . . . . .**89** F2
Daws Hill, E4 . . . .**46** C3
Daws La, NW7 . . . .**55** F5
Dawson Av, Bark. IG11 . . .**99** H7
Dawson Cl, SE18 . . . . . .**137** F4
Dawson Gdns, Bark. IG11
off Dawson Av **99** J7
Dawson Hts Est, SE22 . .**152** D7
Dawson Pl, W2 . . . .**108** D7
Dawson Rd, NW2 . . . .**89** J5
Kingston upon Thames
KT1 . . . .**181** J3
Dawson St, E2 . . . .**13** G2
Dax Ct, Sun. TW16
off Thames St **178** C3
Daybrook Rd, SW19 . . . .**184** E2
Daylesford Av, SW15 . . .**147** G4
Daymer Gdns, Pnr. HA5 . .**66** B4
Daysbrook Rd, SW2 . . . .**169** F1
Days La, Sid. DA15 . . . . .**157** H7
Dayton Gro, SE15 . . . . . .**153** F1
Deacon Ms, N1 . . . .**94** A7
Deacon Rd, NW2 . . . .**89** G5
Kingston upon Thames
KT2 . . . .**181** J1

Deacons Cl, Borwd. (Elstree)
WD6 . . . .**38** A4
Pinner HA5 . . . .**66** B2
Deacons Leas, Orp. BR6 .**207** G4
Deacons Ri, N2 . . . .**73** G5
Deacons Wk, Hmptn. TW12
off Bishops Gro **161** F4
Deacon Way, SE17 . . . . . .**35** J1
Woodford Green IG8 . .**64** C7
Deal Ms, W5
off Darwin Rd **125** G4
Deal Porters Way, SE16 .**133** F3
Deal Rd, SW17 . . . .**168** A6
Deal's Gateway, SE10
off Blackheath Rd . . .**154** B1
Deal St, E1 . . . .**21** H1
Dealtry Rd, SW15 . . . . . .**147** J4
Deal Wk, SW9
off Mandela St **131** G7
Dean Bradley St, SW1 . . .**26** A6
Dean Cl, E9
off Churchill Wk **95** F5
SE16
off Surrey Water Rd . .**133** G1
Dean Ct, Wem. HA0 . . . . .**87** E3
Deancross St, E1 . . . .**113** F6
Dean Dr, Stan. HA7 . . . . . .**69** H2
Deane Av, Ruis. HA4 . . . . .**84** C5
Deane Cft Rd, Pnr. HA5 . . .**66** B6
Deanery Cl, N2 . . . .**73** H4
Deanery Ms, W1 . . . .**24** C1
Deanery Rd, E15 . . . .**97** E6
Deanery St, W1 . . . .**24** C1
Deane Way, Ruis. HA4 . . . .**66** B6
Dean Farrar St, SW1 . . . .**25** H5
Dean Gdns, E17 . . . .**78** D4
W13 off Northfield
Av **124/125** E1
Deanhill Rd, SW14 . . . . .**146** B4
Dean Rd, NW2 . . . .**89** J6
SE28 . . . .**118** A7
Croydon CR0 . . . . . .**202** A4
Hampton TW12 . . . . .**161** G5
Hounslow TW3 . . . . .**143** H5
Dean Ryle St, SW1 . . . . . .**34** A1
Deansbrook Cl, Edg.
HA8 . . . .**54** C7
Deansbrook Rd, Edg.
HA8 . . . .**54** C6
Deans Bldgs, SE17 . . . . . .**36** B2
Deans Cl, W4 . . . .**126** B6
Dean's Cl, Croy. CR0 . . . .**202** C3
Deans Ct, EC4 . . . .**19** H4
Deanscroft Av, NW9 . . . . .**88** C1
Deans Dr, N13 . . . .**59** H6
Edgware HA8 . . . .**54** D5
Dean's Gate Cl, SE23 . . .**171** G3
Deans La, W4 . . . .**126** B6
Edgware HA8 . . . .**54** C6
Deans Ms, W1 . . . .**16** E3
Dean's Pl, SW1 . . . .**33** H3
Dean Rd, W7 . . . .**124** C1
Sutton SM1 . . . .**198** E3
Dean Stanley St, SW1 . . .**26** A6
Dean St, E7 . . . .**97** G5
W1 . . . .**17** H3
Deansway, N2 . . . .**73** G4
N9 . . . .**60** B3
Deans Way, Edg. HA8 . . . .**54** C5
Dean's Yd, SW1 . . . .**25** J5
Dean Trench St, SW1 . . . .**26** A6
Dean Wk, Edg. HA8
off Deansbrook Rd . . .**54** C6
Dean Way, Sthl. UB2 . . . .**123** H2
Dearne Cl, Stan. HA7 . . . .**52** D5
De'Arn Gdns, Mitch.
CR4 . . . .**185** H3
Dearsley Rd, Enf. EN1 . . . .**44** D3
Deason St, E15
off High St **114** C1
De Barowe Ms, N5
off Leigh Rd **93** H4
DEBDEN, Loug. **49** G3
Debden Cl, Kings.T. KT2 .**163** G5
Woodford Green IG8 . .**63** J7
De Beauvoir Cres, N1 . . .**112** B1
De Beauvoir Est, N1 . . . .**112** A1
De Beauvoir Rd, N1 . . . . .**112** B1
De Beauvoir Sq, N1 . . . . . .**94** B7
DE BEAUVOIR TOWN,
N1 . . . .**112** A1
Debnams Rd, SE16
off Rotherhithe
New Rd **133** F4
De Bohun Av, N14 . . . .**42** B6
Deborah Cl, Islw. TW7 . . .**144** B1
De Brome Rd, Felt.
TW13 . . . .**160** C1
Deburgh Rd, SW19 . . . . .**167** F7

Decima St, SE1 . . . .**28** D5
Deck Cl, SE16
off Thame Rd **133** G2
Decoy Av, NW11 . . . .**72** B5
De Crespigny Pk, SE5 . .**152** A2
Deeley Rd, SW8 . . . .**150** D1
Deena Cl, W3 . . . .**105** J6
Deepdale, SW19 . . . .**166** A4
Deepdale Av, Brom. BR2 .**191** F4
Deepdale Cl, N11
off Ribblesdale Av . . .**58** A6
Deepdene, W5 . . . .**105** J4
Deepdene Av, Croy. CR0 .**202** C3
Deepdene Cl, E11 . . . .**79** G4
Deepdene Ct, N21 . . . .**43** H6
Deepdene Gdns, SW2 . . .**151** F7
Deepdene Path, Loug.
IG10 . . . .**48** D4
Deepdene Pt, SE23
off Dacres Rd **171** G3
Deepdene Rd, SE5 . . . . .**152** A4
Loughton IG10 . . . . . .**48** D4
Welling DA16 . . . . . .**158** A3
Deepwell Cl, Islw. TW7 . .**144** D1
Deepwood La, Grnf. UB6
off Cowgate Rd **104** A3
Deerbrook Rd, SE24 . . . .**169** H1
Deerdale Rd, SE24 . . . . .**151** J4
Deerhurst Cl, Felt. TW13 .**160** A4
Deerhurst Cres, Hmptn.
(Hmptn.H.) TW12 . . . .**161** J5
Deerhurst Rd, NW2 . . . . . .**90** A6
SW16 . . . .**169** F5
Deerings Dr, Pnr. HA5 . . . .**66** A5
Deerleap Gro, E4 . . . .**46** B5
Dee Rd, Rich. TW9 . . . . . .**145** J4
Deer Pk Cl, Kings.T. KT2 .**164** B7
Deer Pk Gdns, Mitch.
CR4 . . . .**185** G3
Deer Pk Rd, SW19 . . . . .**185** E2
Deer Pk Way, W.Wick.
BR4 . . . .**205** F2
Deeside Rd, SW17 . . . . .**167** G3
Dee St, E14 . . . .**114** C6
Defiance Wk, SE18 . . . . .**136** C3
Defiant Way, Wall. SM6 .**200** E7
Defoe Av, Rich. TW9 . . . .**126** A7
Defoe Cl, SE16
off Vaughan St **133** J2
SW17 . . . .**167** H6
Defoe Ho, EC2 . . . .**20** A1
Defoe Pl, EC2
off Beech St **111** J5
SW17
off Lessingham Av . .**167** J4
Defoe Rd, N16 . . . .**94** B2
De Frene Rd, SE26 . . . . .**171** G4
De Gama Pl, E14
off Maritime Quay . .**134** A5
Degema Rd, Chis. BR7 . .**174** E5
Dehar Cres, NW9 . . . .**71** F7
Dehavilland Cl, Nthlt.
UB5 . . . .**102** D3
De Havilland Rd, Edg.
HA8 . . . .**70** B2
Hounslow TW5 . . . . .**122** C7
Wallington SM6 . . . .**201** E7
De Havilland Way, Stai.
(Stanw.) TW19 . . . . .**140** A6
Dekker Rd, SE21 . . . .**152** B6
Delacourt Rd, SE3
off Old Dover Rd . . .**135** H7
Delafield Rd, SE7 . . . . . .**135** H5
Delaford Rd, SE16 . . . . .**133** E5
Delaford St, SW6 . . . . . .**128** B7
Delamare Cres, Croy.
CR0 . . . .**189** F6
Delamere Gdns, NW7 . . . .**54** D6
Delamere Rd, SW20 . . . .**184** A1
W5 . . . .**125** H1
Borehamwood WD6 . .**38** B3
Hayes UB4 . . . .**102** D7
Delamere Ter, W2 . . . .**14** B1
Delancey Pas, NW1
off Delancey St **110** B1
Delancey St, NW1 . . . . . .**110** B1
De Laune St, SE17 . . . . . .**35** G4
Delaware Rd, W9 . . . .**6** A5
Delawyk Cres, SE24 . . . .**151** J6
Delcombe Av, Wor.Pk.
KT4 . . . .**197** J1
Delft Way, SE22
off East Dulwich Gro .**152** B5
Delhi Rd, Enf. EN1 . . . .**44** C7
Delhi St, N1 . . . .**111** E1
Delia St, SW18 . . . .**149** E7
Delisle Rd, SE28 . . . .**137** H1
Delius Gro, E15 . . . .**114** D2
Dell, The, SE2 . . . .**138** A5
SE19 . . . .**188** C1

Dell, The, Brentford TW8 .**125** F6
Feltham TW14
off Harlington Rd W .**142** B7
Pinner HA5 . . . .**66** D2
Wembley HA0 . . . .**87** E5
Dell, The, Wdf. Grn. IG8 . .**63** H3
Della Path, E5
off Napoleon Rd . . .**94/95** E3
Dellbow Rd, Felt. TW14
off Central Way **142** B5
Dell Cl, E15 . . . .**114** D1
Wallington SM6 . . . .**200** D4
Woodford Green IG8 . .**63** H3
Dellfield Cl, Beck. BR3
off Foxgrove Rd **172** C7
Dell La, Epsom KT17 . . .**197** G5
Dellors Cl, Barn. EN5 . . . .**40** A5
Dellow Cl, Ilf. IG2 . . . .**81** G7
Dellow St, E1 . . . .**113** E7
Dell Rd, Epsom KT17 . . .**197** G6
West Drayton UB7 . . .**120** C3
Dells Cl, E4 . . . .**46** B7
Teddington TW11
off Middle La **162** C6
Dell's Ms, SW1 . . . .**33** G2
Dellwood Gdns, Ilf. IG5 . .**80** D3
Delmare Cl, SW9
off Brighton Ter **151** F4
Delme Cres, SE3 . . . .**155** H2
Delmey Cl, Croy. CR0
off Radcliffe Rd **202** C3
Deloraine St, SE8 . . . . . .**154** A1
Delorme St, W6 . . . .**128** A6
Delta Cl, Wor.Pk. KT4 . . .**197** F3
Delta Ct, NW2 . . . .**89** G2
Delta Gain, Wat. WD19 . . .**50** D2
Delta Gro, Nthlt. UB5 . . .**102** D3
Delta Rd, Wor.Pk. KT4 . .**197** F3
Delta St, E2 . . . .**13** H3
De Luci Rd, Erith DA8 . . .**139** J5
De Lucy St, SE2 . . . .**138** B4
Delvan Cl, SE18
off Ordnance Rd . . .**136** D7
Delvers Mead, Dag.
RM10 . . . .**101** J4
Delverton Rd, SE17 . . . . . .**35** H4
Delvino Rd, SW6 . . . .**148** D1
De Mandeville Gate, Enf. EN1
off Southbury Rd **44** D4
Demesne Rd, Wall. SM6 .**200** D5
Demeta Cl, Wem. HA9 . . . .**88** C3
De Montfort Par, SW16
off Streatham
High Rd **168/169** E3
De Montfort Rd, SW16 . .**168** E3
De Morgan Rd, SW6 . . . .**149** E3
Dempster Cl, Surb. KT6 .**195** F1
Dempster Rd, SW18 . . . .**149** F5
Denbar Par, Rom. RM7
off Mawney Rd **83** J4
Denberry Dr, Sid. DA14 . .**176** B3
Denbigh Cl, NW10 . . . .**88** E7
W11 . . . .**108** C7
Chislehurst BR7 . . . .**174** C6
Southall UB1 . . . . . .**103** F6
Sutton SM1 . . . .**198** C5
Denbigh Dr, Hayes UB3 .**121** F2
Denbigh Gdns, Rich.
TW10 . . . .**145** J5
Denbigh Ms, SW1 . . . .**33** F2
Denbigh Pl, SW1 . . . .**33** F3
Denbigh Rd, E6 . . . .**116** A3
W11 . . . .**108** C7
W13 . . . .**105** E7
Hounslow TW3 . . . . .**143** H2
Southall UB1 . . . . . .**103** F6
Denbigh St, SW1 . . . .**33** F2
Denbigh Ter, W11 . . . . . .**108** C7
Denbridge Rd, Brom.
BR1 . . . .**192** C2
Den Cl, Beck. BR3 . . . . . .**190** D3
Croydon CR0 . . . . . .**203** G4
Wembley HA9 . . . .**87** H4
West Molesey KT8 . .**179** F5
Dene Av, Houns. TW3 . . .**143** F3
Sidcup DA15 . . . . . .**158** B7
Dene Cl, SE4 . . . .**153** H3
Bromley BR2 . . . . . .**205** F1
Worcester Park KT4 . .**197** F2
Dene Ct, Stan. HA7
off Marsh La **53** F5
Dene Gdns, Stan. HA7 . . .**53** F5
Thames Ditton KT7 . .**194** D2
Denehurst Gdns, NW4 . . .**71** J6
W3 . . . .**126** B1
Richmond TW10 . . . .**146** A4
Twickenham TW2 . . .**144** A7

Denehurst Gdns, Wdfd. Grn.
IG8 . . . . .63 H4
Dene Rd, N11 . . . . .57 J1
Buckhurst Hill IG9 . . . . .64 A1
Denewood, Barn. EN5 . . .41 F5
Denewood Rd, N6 . . . . . .73 J6
Dengie Wk, N1
off Basire St 111 J1
Denham CI, Well. DA16
off Park Vw Rd 158 C3
Denham Cres, Mitch.
CR4 . . . . .185 J4
Denham Dr, Ilf. IG2 . . . . .81 F6
Denham Rd, N20 . . . . . . .57 J3
Feltham TW14 . . . . . . .142 C6
Denham St, SE10 . . . . .135 G5
Denham Way, Bark. IG11 .111 H1
Borehamwood WD6 . . .38 D1
Denholme Rd, W9 . . . . .108 C3
Denison CI, N2 . . . . .73 F3
Denison Rd, SW19 . . . . .167 G6
W5 . . . . .105 F4
Deniston Av, Bex. DA5 .176 E1
Denleigh Gdns, N21 . . . .59 G1
Thames Ditton KT7 . .180 B6
Denman Dr, NW11 . . . . .72 D5
Esher (Clay.) KT10 . . .194 D5
Denman Dr N, NW11 . . . .72 D5
Denman Dr S, NW11 . . . .72 D5
Denman PI, W1
off Great Windmill St .110 D7
Denman Rd, SE15 . . . . .152 C1
Denman St, W1 . . . . . . .17 H6
Denmark Av, SW19 . . . .166 B7
Denmark Ct, Mord. SM4 .184 D5
Denmark Gdns, Cars.
SM5 . . . . .200 A3
Denmark Gro, N1 . . . . . .11 E1
Denmark Hill, SE5 . . . . .152 A1
Denmark Hill Dr, NW9 . . .71 F4
Denmark Hill Est, SE5 . .152 A4
Denmark PI, WC2 . . . . . .17 J3
Denmark Rd, N8 . . . . . . .75 F4
NW6 . . . . .108 C2
SE5 . . . . .151 J1
SE25 . . . . .188 D5
SW19 . . . . .166 A6
W13 . . . . .105 E7
Bromley BR1 . . . . . . .191 H1
Carshalton SM5 . . . . .199 J3
Kingston upon Thames
KT1 . . . . .181 H3
Twickenham TW2 . . . .162 A3
Denmark St, E11
off High Rd
Leytonstone 96/97 E3
E13 . . . . .115 H5
N17 . . . . .76 E1
WC2 . . . . .17 J4
Denmark Wk, SE27 . . . .169 J4
Denmead Ho, NW9
off Highcliffe Dr 147 F6
Denmead Rd, Croy. CR0 .201 H1
Denmead Way, SE15 . . . .37 F7
Dennan Rd, Surb. KT6 . .195 J1
Dennard Way, Orp. BR6 .206 E4
Denner Rd, E4 . . . . .62 A2
Denne Ter, E8 . . . . .112 C1
Dennett Rd, Croy. CR0 .201 G1
Dennetts Gro, SE14
off Dennetts Rd 153 G2
Dennetts Rd, SE14 . . . .153 F1
Denning Av, Croy. CR0 .201 G4
Denning CI, NW8 . . . . . . .6 D3
Hampton TW12 . . . . .161 F6
Denning Rd, NW3 . . . . . .91 G4
Dennington CI, E5
off Detmold Rd 94/95 E2
Dennington Pk Rd, NW6 .90 D6
Denningtons, The, Wor.Pk.
KT4 . . . . .197 E2
Dennis Av, Wem. HA9 . . .87 J5
Dennis Gdns, Stan. HA7 .53 F5
Dennis La, Stan. HA7 . . .52 E3
Dennison Pt, E15 . . . . . .96 C7
Dennis Pk Cres, SW20 .184 B1
Dennis Reeve CI, Mitch.
CR4 . . . . .185 J1
Dennis Rd, E.Mol. KT8 .179 J4
Dennis Way, Croy.
off Gauden Rd 150 D3
Denny CI, E6
off Linton Gdns 116 B5
Denny Cres, SE11 . . . . . .35 F2
Denny Gdns, Dag. RM9
off Canonsleigh Rd . . .100 B7
Denny Rd, N9 . . . . .60 E1
Denny St, SE11 . . . . .35 F3
Den Rd, Brom. BR2 . . . .190 D3
Densham Rd, E15 . . . . .115 E1

Densole CI, Beck. BR3
off Kings Hall Rd 189 H1
Densworth Gro, N9 . . . . .61 F2
Denton CI, Barn. EN5 . . .39 J5
Denton Rd, N8 . . . . .75 F5
N18 . . . . .60 B4
Denton Rd, Twick. TW1 .145 G6
Welling DA16 . . . . . . .138 C7
Denton St, SW18 . . . . .149 E6
Denton Way, E5 . . . . . . .95 G3
Dents Rd, SW11 . . . . . .149 J6
Denver CI, Orp. BR6 . . .193 H6
Denver Rd, N16 . . . . . . .76 B7
Denyer St, SW3 . . . . . . .31 H2
Denzil Rd, NW10 . . . . . .89 F5
Deodara CI, N20 . . . . . . .57 H3
Deodar Rd, SW15 . . . . .148 B4
★ Department for Environment,
Food & Rural Affairs (DEFRA),
SW1 . . . . .26 A1
★ Department for Transport,
Local Government &
Regions (DTLR), SW1 .25 F5
★ Department of Health &
Department for Work &
Pensions (DWP), SW1 .26 A3
Depot App, NW2 . . . . . . .90 A4
Depot Rd, Houns. TW3 . .144 A3
DEPTFORD, SE8 . . . . . .133 J5
Deptford Br, SE8 . . . . . .154 A1
Deptford Bdy, SE8 . . . . .154 A1
Deptford Ch St, SE8 . . .134 A6
Deptford Ferry Rd, E14 .134 A4
Deptford Grn, SE8 . . . . .134 A6
Deptford High St, SE8 . .134 A6
Deptford Strand, SE8 . .133 J4
Deptford Wf, SE8 . . . . .133 J4
De Quincey Ms, E16
off Wesley Av 135 G1
De Quincey Rd, N17 . . . .76 A1
Derby Av, N12 . . . . .57 F5
Harrow HA3 . . . . .68 A1
Romford RM7 . . . . . . .83 J6
Derby Ct, E5
off Overbury St 95 G4
Derby Gate, SW1 . . . . . .26 A3
Derby Hill, SE23 . . . . . .171 F2
Derby Hill Cres, SE23 . .171 F2
Derby Rd, E7 . . . . .97 J7
E9 . . . . .113 G1
E18 . . . . .79 F1
N18 . . . . .61 F5
SW14 . . . . .146 B4
SW19 off Russell Rd . .166 D7
Croydon CR0 . . . . . . .201 H2
Enfield EN3 . . . . .45 E5
Greenford UB6 . . . . . .103 H1
Hounslow TW3 . . . . . .143 H4
Surbiton KT5 . . . . . . .196 A1
Sutton SM1 . . . . .198 C6
Derbyshire St, E2 . . . . . .13 J4
Derby St, W1 . . . . .24 C2
Dereham PI, EC2 . . . . . .12 E4
Dereham Rd, Bark. IG11 .99 J6
Derek Av, Epsom
KT19 . . . . .196 A5
Wallington SM6 . . . . .200 B4
Wembley HA9 . . . . . . .88 B7
Derek CI, Epsom (Ewell)
KT19 . . . . .196 B5
Derek Walcott CI, SE24
off Shakespeare Rd . .151 H5
Dericote St, E8 . . . . . . .112 D1
Deridene CI, Stai. (Stanw.)
TW19 off Bedfont Rd .140 B6
Derifall CI, E6 . . . . .116 C5
Dering PI, Croy. CR0 . . .201 J4
Dering Rd, Croy. CR0 . .201 J4
Dering St, W1 . . . . .16 D4
Derinton Rd, SW17 . . . .167 J4
Derley Rd, Sthl. UB2 . . .122 C3
Dermody Gdns, SE13 . .154 D5
Dermody Rd, SE13 . . . .154 D5
Deronda Rd, SE24 . . . . .169 H1
Deroy CI, Cars. SM5 . . .199 J6
Derrick Gdns, SE7
off Anchor &
Hope La 135 J4
Derrick Rd, Beck. BR3 . .189 J3
Derry Rd, Croy. CR0 . . .200 E3
Derry St, W8 . . . . .22 A4
Dersingham Av, E12 . . . .98 D5
Dersingham Rd, NW2 . . .90 B3
Derwent Av, N18 . . . . . . .60 A5
NW7 . . . . .54 D5
SW15 . . . . .164 E4
Barnet EN4 . . . . .57 J1
Pinner HA5 . . . . .51 E6
Derwent CI, Esher (Clay.)
KT10 . . . . .194 B6

Derwent Cres, N20 . . . . .57 F3
Bexleyheath DA7 . . . .159 G2
Stanmore HA7 . . . . . . .69 F2
Derwent Dr, NW9 . . . . . .70 E5
Orpington BR5 . . . . . .193 G7
Derwent Gdns, Ilf. IG4 . .80 B4
Wembley HA9 . . . . . . .69 F7
Derwent Gro, SE22 . . . .152 C4
Derwent Ri, NW9 . . . . . .70 E6
Derwent Rd, N13 . . . . . .59 F4
SE20 . . . . .188 D2
SW20 . . . . .184 A6
W5 . . . . .125 F3
Southall UB1 . . . . . . .103 G6
Twickenham TW2 . . . .143 H6
Derwent St, SE10 . . . . .134 E5
Derwent Wk, Wall. SM6 .200 B7
Derwentwater Rd, W3 . .126 C1
Derwent Yd, W5
off Northfield Av 125 F3
Desborough CI, W2 . . . . .14 B1
Desborough St, W2 . . . . .14 A1
Desenfans Rd, SE21 . . .152 B6
Desford Ms, E16
off Desford Rd . . .114/115 E4
Desford Rd, E16 . . . . . .115 E4
★ Design Mus, SE1 . . . .29 G2
Desmond St, SE14 . . . .133 H6
Despard Rd, N19 . . . . . .92 C1
Detling Rd, Brom. BR1 .173 G5
Detmold Rd, E5 . . . . . . .95 F2
Devalls CI, E6 . . . . .116 D7
Devana End, Cars. SM5 .199 J3
Devas Rd, SW20 . . . . . .183 J1
Devas St, E3 . . . . .114 B4
Devenay Rd, E15 . . . . . .97 F7
Devenish Rd, SE2 . . . . .138 A2
Deventer Cres, SE22 . . .152 B5
De Vere Cotts, W8
off Canning PI 129 F3
De Vere Gdns, W8 . . . . .22 C4
Ilford IG1 . . . . .98 C2
Deverell St, SE1 . . . . . . .28 B6
De Vere Ms, W8 . . . . . . .22 C5
Devereux CI, WC2 . . . . . .18 E4
Devereux La, SW13 . . . .127 H7
Devereux Rd, SW11 . . . .149 J6
Deverill Ct, SE20 . . . . . .189 F1
Devey CI, Kings.T. KT2 .165 E7
Devizes St, N1
off Poole St 112 A1
Devon Av, Twick. TW2 . .161 J1
Devon CI, N17 . . . . .76 C3
Buckhurst Hill IG9 . . . .63 H2
Greenford UB6 . . . . . .105 F1
Devon Ct, Buck.H. IG9 . .63 H1
Devoncroft Gdns, Twick.
TW1 . . . . .144 D7
Devon Gdns, N4 . . . . . . .75 H6
Devonhurst PI, W4
off Heathfield Ter 126 D5
Devonia Gdns, N18 . . . . .59 J6
Devonia Rd, N1 . . . . . . .11 H1
Devonport Gdns, Ilf. IG1 .80 C6
Devonport Ms, W12
off Devonport Rd 127 H1
Devonport Rd, W12 . . . .127 H2
Devonport St, E1 . . . . . .113 F6
Devon Ri, N2 . . . . .73 G4
Devon Rd, Bark. IG11 . .117 H1
Devons Est, E3 . . . . . . .114 B3
Devonshire Av, Sutt.
SM2 . . . . .199 F7
Devonshire CI, E15 . . . . .97 E4
N13 . . . . .59 G4
W1 . . . . .16 D1
Devonshire Cres, NW7 . .56 A7
Devonshire Dr, SE10 . . .134 B7
Surbiton KT6 . . . . . . .195 G1
Devonshire Gdns, N17 . .59 J6
N21 . . . . .43 J7
W4 . . . . .126 C7
Devonshire Gro, SE15 . .133 E6
Devonshire Hill La, N17 . .59 J6
Devonshire Ho, Sutt. SM2
off Devonshire Av 199 F7
Devonshire Ms, SW10
off Park Wk 129 G6
W4 off Glebe St .126/127 E5
Devonshire Ms N, W1 . . .16 D1
Devonshire Ms S, W1 . . .16 D1
Devonshire Ms W, W1 . . .8 D6
Devonshire Pas, W4 . . . .126 E5
Devonshire PI, NW2 . . . .90 D3
W1 . . . . .8 C6
W4 . . . . .126 E5
W8 . . . . .22 A6
Devonshire PI Ms, W1 . . .8 C6
Devonshire Rd, E16 . . . .115 H6
E17 . . . . .78 A6

Devonshire Rd, N9 . . . . .61 F1
N13 . . . . .59 F4
N17 . . . . .59 J6
NW7 . . . . .56 A7
SE9 . . . . .174 B2
SE23 . . . . .171 F1
SW19 . . . . .167 H7
Devonshire Rd, W4 . . . .126 E5
W5 . . . . .125 F3
Bexleyheath DA6 . . . .159 E4
Carshalton SM5 . . . . .200 A4
Croydon CR0 . . . . . . .188 A7
Feltham TW13 . . . . . .160 E3
Harrow HA1 . . . . .68 A6
Ilford IG2 . . . . .81 G7
Pinner (Eastcote) HA5 .66 C6
Pinner (Hatch End) HA5 .67 F1
Southall UB1 . . . . . . .103 G5
Sutton SM2 . . . . .199 F7
Devonshire Row, EC2 . . .20 E2
Devonshire Row Ms, W1 .8 E6
Devonshire Sq, EC2 . . . .20 E3
Bromley BR2 . . . . . . .191 H4
Devonshire St, W1 . . . . .16 C1
W4 . . . . .126 E5
Devonshire Ter, W2 . . . . .14 D4
Devonshire Way, Croy.
CR0 . . . . .203 H2
Hayes UB4 . . . . .102 B6
Devons Rd, E3 . . . . .114 A5
Devon St, SE15 . . . . . . .132 E6
Devon Way, Chess. KT9 .195 F5
Epsom KT19 . . . . .196 B5
Devon Waye, Houns.
TW5 . . . . .123 F7
De Walden St, W1 . . . . . .16 C2
Dewar St, SE15 . . . . . . .152 D3
Dewberry Gdns, E6 . . . .116 B5
Dewberry St, E14 . . . . .114 C5
Dewey Rd, N1 . . . . .10 E1
Dagenham RM10 . . . .101 H6
Dewey St, SW17 . . . . . .167 J5
Dewhurst Rd, W14 . . . . .128 A3
Dewlands Ct, NW4
off Holders Hill Rd 72 A2
Dewsbury CI, Pnr. HA5 . .67 F6
Dewsbury Ct, W4
off Chiswick Rd 126 C4
Dewsbury Gdns, Wor.Pk.
KT4 . . . . .197 G3
Dewsbury Rd, NW10 . . . .89 G5
Dewsbury Ter, NW1
off Camden High St . .110 B1
Dexter Ho, Erith DA18
off Kale Rd 138/139 E3
Dexter Rd, Barn. EN5 . . .40 A6
Deyncourt Rd, N17 . . . . .75 J1
Deynecourt Gdns, E11 . .79 J4
D'Eynsford Rd, SE5 . . . .152 A1
Diadem Ct, W1 . . . . .17 H4
Dial Wk, The, W8 . . . . . .22 B3
Diamedes Av, Stai. (Stanw.)
TW19 . . . . .140 A7
Diameter Rd, Orp. BR5 .193 E7
Diamond CI, Dag. RM8 .100 C1
Diamond Rd, Ruis. HA4 . .84 D4
Diamond St, NW10
off Fawood Av 88 D7
SE15 . . . . .132 B7
Diamond Ter, SE10 . . . .154 C1
Diamond Way, SE8
off Deptford High St . .134 A7
Diana CI, E18 . . . . .79 H1
SE8 off Staunton St . . .133 J6
Diana Gdns, Surb. KT6 .195 J2
Diana Ho, SW13 . . . . . .147 F1
Diana PI, NW1 . . . . .9 E5
Diana Rd, E17 . . . . .77 J3
Dianne Way, Barn. EN4 . .41 H5
Dianthus CI, SE2
off Carnation St 138 B5
Dibden Row, SE1
off Gerridge St 131 G3
Dibden St, N1 . . . . .111 H1
Dibdin CI, Sutt. SM1 . . .198 D3
Dibdin Rd, Sutt. SM1 . .198 D3
Dicey Av, NW2 . . . . .89 J5
Dickens Av, N3 . . . . .73 F1
Dickens CI, Erith DA8 . .139 H7
Hayes UB3
off Croyde Av 121 H4
Richmond TW10 . . . . .163 H2
Dickens Dr, Chis. BR7 . .175 F6
Dickens Est, SE1 . . . . . .29 H4
SE16 . . . . .29 H4
★ Dickens Ho, WC1 . . . .10 D6
Dickens Ho, NW6 . . . . .108 D3
Dickens La, N18 . . . . . . .60 B5
Dickenson CI, N9
off Croyland Rd 60 D1

Dickenson Rd, N8 . . . . . .75 E7
Feltham TW13 . . . . .160 C5
Dickensons La, SE25 . . . .188 D5
Dickensons Pl, SE25 . . . .188 D6
Dickenson St, NW5
off Dalby St 92 B6
Dickens Ri, Chig. IG7 . . . .64 D3
Dickens Rd, E6 . . . . .116 A2
Dickens Sq, SE1 . . . . .28 A5
Dickens St, SW8 . . . . . . .150 B2
Dickenswood Cl, SE19 . .169 H7
Dickerage La, N.Mal.
KT3 . . . . .182 C3
Dickerage Rd, Kings.T.
KT1 . . . . .182 C1
New Malden KT3 . . . . .182 C1
Dickson Fold, Pnr. HA5 . .66 D4
Dickson Rd, SE9 . . . . . . .156 B3
Dick Turpin Way, Felt.
TW14 . . . . .141 J4
Didsbury Cl, E6
off Barking Rd 116 C1
Digby Cres, N4 . . . . .93 J2
Digby Gdns, Dag. RM10 .119 G1
Digby Pl, Croy. CR0 . . . .202 C3
Digby Rd, E9 . . . . .95 G6
Barking IG11 . . . . .99 J7
Digby St, E2 . . . . .113 F3
Diggon St, E1
off Stepney Way 113 G5
Dighton Ct, SE5 . . . . .35 J6
Dighton Rd, SW18 . . . . .149 F5
Dignum St, N1
off Cloudesley Rd 111 G2
Digswell St, N7
off Holloway Rd 93 G6
Dilhorne Cl, SE12 . . . . . .173 H3
Dilke St, SW3 . . . . .32 A5
Dilloway Yd, Sthl. UB2
off The Green 122/123 E2
Dillwyn Cl, SE26 . . . . . . .171 H4
Dilston Cl, Nthlt. UB5
off Yeading La 102 C3
Dilston Gro, SE16
off Abbeyfield Rd 133 F4
Dilton Gdns, SW15 . . . . .165 G1
Dilwyn Ct, E17
off Hillyfield 77 H3
Dimes Pl, W6
off King St 127 H4
Dimmock Dr, Grnf.
UB6 . . . . .86 A5
Dimond Cl, E7 . . . . .97 G4
Dimsdale Dr, NW9 . . . . . .88 C1
Enfield EN1 . . . . .44 D6
Dimsdale Wk, E13
off Stratford Rd 115 G1
Dimson Cres, E3 . . . . . . .114 A4
Dingle Cl, Barn. EN5 . . . . .39 F6
Dingle Gdns, E14 . . . . . .114 A7
Dingley La, SW16 . . . . . .168 D2
Dingley Pl, EC1 . . . . .12 A4
Dingley Rd, EC1 . . . . .11 J4
Dingwall Av, Croy. CR0 . .201 J2
Dingwall Gdns, NW11 . . .72 D6
Dingwall Rd, SW18 . . . . .149 F7
Croydon CR0 . . . . .202 A2
Dinmont St, E2
off Coate St 112/113 E2
Dinsdale Gdns, SE25 . . . .188 B5
Barnet EN5 . . . . .41 E5
Dinsdale Rd, SE3 . . . . . .135 F6
Dinsmore Rd, SW12 . . . .150 B7
Dinton Rd, SW19 . . . . . .167 G6
Kingston upon Thames
KT2 . . . . .163 J7
Diploma Av, N2 . . . . .73 H4
Diploma Ct, N2
off Diploma Av 73 H4
Dirleton Rd, E15 . . . . . . .115 F1
Disbrowe Rd, W6 . . . . . .128 B6
Discovery Business Pk, SE16
off St. James's Rd 132 D3
Discovery Wk, E1 . . . . . .132 E1
Dishforth La, NW9 . . . . . .70 E1
Disney Ms, N4
off Chesterfield Gdns . .75 H5
Disney Pl, SE1 . . . . .28 A3
Disney St, SE1 . . . . .28 A3
Dison Cl, Enf. EN3 . . . . . .45 G1
Disraeli Cl, SE28 . . . . . . .138 C1
W4 off Acton La 126 D4
Disraeli Gdns, SW15
off Fawe Pk Rd 148 C4
Disraeli Rd, E7 . . . . .97 G6
NW10 . . . . .106 C2
SW15 . . . . .148 B4
W5 . . . . .125 G1
Diss St, E2 . . . . .13 F3
Distaff La, EC4 . . . . .19 J5

Distillery La, W6
off Fulham Palace Rd .127 J5
Distillery Rd, W6 . . . . . .127 J5
Distillery Wk, Brent.
TW8 . . . . .125 H6
Distin St, SE11 . . . . .34 E2
District Rd, Wem. HA0 . . .86 E5
Ditch All, SE10 . . . . .154 B1
Ditchburn St, E14 . . . . . .114 C7
Ditchfield Rd, Hayes
UB4 . . . . .102 E4
Dittisham Rd, SE9 . . . . . .174 B4
Ditton Cl, T.Ditt. KT7 . . . .180 D7
Dittoncroft Cl, Croy. CR0 .202 B4
Ditton Gra Cl, Surb. KT6 .195 G1
Ditton Gra Dr, Surb.
KT6 . . . . .195 G1
Ditton Hill, Surb. KT6 . . .195 F1
Ditton Hill Rd, Surb.
KT6 . . . . .195 F1
Ditton Lawn, T.Ditt. KT7 . .194 D1
Ditton Pl, SE20 . . . . .189 E1
Ditton Reach, T.Ditt. KT7 .180 E6
Ditton Rd, Bexh. DA6 . . .158 D5
Southall UB2 . . . . .123 F4
Surbiton KT6 . . . . .195 H1
Divis Way, SW15 . . . . . .147 H6
Dixon Clark Ct, N1
off Canonbury Rd 93 H6
Dixon Cl, E6
off Brandreth Rd 116 C6
Dixon Ho, W10 . . . . .108 A6
Dixon Pl, W.Wick. BR4 . .204 B1
Dixon Rd, SE14 . . . . .153 H1
SE25 . . . . .188 B3
Dixon's All, SE16 . . . . . . .132 E2
Dobbin Cl, Har. HA3 . . . . .68 D2
Dobell Rd, SE9 . . . . .156 C5
Dobree Av, NW10 . . . . . . .89 H7
Dobson Cl, NW6 . . . . .91 G7
Dockers Tanner Rd, E14 . .134 A3
Dockhead, SE1 . . . . .29 G4
Dock Hill Av, SE16 . . . . . .133 G2
Dockland St, E16 . . . . . . .136 D1
Dockley Rd, SE16 . . . . . . .29 H6
Dock Rd, E16 . . . . .115 F7
Brentford TW8 . . . . . . .125 G7
Dock St, E1 . . . . .21 H5
Dockwell Cl, Felt. TW14 . .142 A4
Dockyard Ind Est, SE18
off Woolwich Ch St . . .136 B3
Doctor Johnson Av,
SW17 . . . . .168 B3
★ Doctor Johnson's Ho,
EC4 . . . . .19 F4
Doctors Cl, SE26 . . . . . . .171 F5
Docwra's Bldgs, N1 . . . . .94 B6
Dodbrooke Rd, SE27 . . . .169 G3
Doddington Gro, SE17 . . .35 G5
Doddington Pl, SE17 . . . .35 G5
Dodsley Pl, N9 . . . . .61 E3
Dodson St, SE1 . . . . .27 F4
Dod St, E14 . . . . .113 J6
Doebury Wk, SE18
off Prestwood Cl 138 A6
Doel Cl, SW19 . . . . .167 F7
Doggets Ct, Barn. EN4 . . .41 H5
Doggett Rd, SE6 . . . . . . .154 A7
Doghurst Av, Hayes
UB3 . . . . .121 E7
Doghurst Dr, West Dr.
UB7 . . . . .121 E7
Dog Kennel Hill, SE22 . . .152 B3
Dog Kennel Hill Est,
SE22 . . . . .152 B3
Dog La, NW10 . . . . .89 E4
Doherty Rd, E13 . . . . . . .115 G4
Dokal Ind Est, Sthl. UB2
off Hartington
Rd 122/123 E3
Dolben St, SE1 . . . . .27 G2
Dolby Ct, EC4 . . . . .20 A5
Dolby Rd, SW6 . . . . .148 C2
Dolland St, SE11 . . . . .34 D4
Dollis Av, N3 . . . . .72 C1
Dollis Brook Wk, Barn.
EN5 . . . . .40 B6
Dollis Cres, Ruis. HA4 . . . .84 C1
DOLLIS HILL, NW2 . . . . . .89 H3
Dollis Hill Av, NW2 . . . . . .89 H3
Dollis Hill Est, NW2 . . . . .89 G3
Dollis Hill La, NW2 . . . . . .89 H3
Dollis Ms, N3
off Dollis Pk 72 C1
Dollis Pk, N3 . . . . .72 C1
Dollis Rd, N3 . . . . .56 B7
NW7 . . . . .56 B7
Dollis Valley Grn Wk, N20
off Totteridge La 57 F2
Barnet EN5 . . . . .40 B6

Dollis Valley Way, Barn.
EN5 . . . . .40 C6
Dolman Cl, N3
off Avondale Rd 73 F2
Dolman Rd, W4 . . . . .126 D4
Dolman St, SW4 . . . . . . .151 F4
Dolphin Cl, SE16
off Kinburn St 133 G2
SE28 . . . . .118 D6
Dolphin Cl, Surb. KT6 . . .181 G6
Dolphin Ct, NW11 . . . . . .72 B6
Dolphin Ho, SW18
off Smugglers
Way 148/149 E4
Dolphin La, E14 . . . . .114 B7
Dolphin Rd, Nthlt. UB5 . .103 F2
Dolphin Sq, SW1 . . . . . . .33 G4
W4 . . . . .126 E2
Dolphin St, Kings.T. KT1 .181 H1
Dolphin Twr, SE8
off Abinger Gro 133 J6
Dombey St, WC1 . . . . . . .18 C1
★ Dome, The, SE10 . . . . .134 E1
Dome Hill Pk, SE26 . . . . .170 C4
Domett Cl, SE5 . . . . .152 A4
Domfe Pl, E5
off Rushmore Rd 95 F4
Domingo St, EC1 . . . . . . .11 J5
Dominica Cl, E13 . . . . . . .115 J2
Dominion Rd, Croy. CR0 .188 C2
Southall UB2 . . . . .123 E3
Dominion St, EC2 . . . . . . .20 C1
★ Dominion Thea, W1 . . .17 J3
Domonic Dr, SE9 . . . . . . .174 E4
Domville Cl, N20 . . . . .57 G2
Donald Dr, Rom. RM6 . . . .82 C5
Donald Rd, E13 . . . . .115 H1
Croydon CR0 . . . . .187 F6
Donaldson Rd, NW6 . . . .108 C1
SE18 . . . . .156 D1
Donald Wds Gdns, Surb.
KT5 . . . . .196 B2
Doncaster Dr, Nthlt.
UB5 . . . . .85 F5
Doncaster Gdns, N4
off Stanhope Gdns 75 J6
Northolt UB5 . . . . .85 F5
Doncaster Grn, Wat.
WD19 . . . . .50 C5
Doncaster Rd, N9 . . . . . . .44 E7
Doncel Ct, E4 . . . . .46 D7
Donegal St, N1 . . . . .10 D2
Doneraile St, SW6 . . . . . .148 A2
Dongola Rd, E1 . . . . .113 H5
E13 . . . . .115 H3
N17 . . . . .76 B3
Dongola Rd W, E13
off Balaam St 115 H3
Donington Av, Ilf. IG6 . . . .81 F5
Donkey All, SE22 . . . . . . .152 D7
Donkey La, Enf. EN1 . . . . .44 D2
Donne Ct, SE24 . . . . .151 J6
Donnefield Av, Edg. HA8 .53 H7
Donne Pl, SW3 . . . . .31 H1
Mitcham CR4 . . . . .186 B4
Donne Rd, Dag. RM8 . . . .100 C2
Donnington Rd, NW10 . . .89 H7
Harrow HA3 . . . . .69 G5
Worcester Park KT4 . . .197 G2
Donnybrook Rd, SW16 . . .168 C7
Donovan Av, N10 . . . . . . .74 B2
Don Phelan Cl, SE5 . . . . .152 A1
Doone Cl, Tedd. TW11 . . .162 D6
Doon St, SE1 . . . . .26 E2
Doral Way, Cars. SM5 . . .199 J5
Dorando Cl, W12 . . . . . . .107 H7
Doran Gro, SE18 . . . . . . .137 H7
Doran Wk, E15 . . . . .96 C7
Dora Rd, SW19 . . . . .166 D5
Dora St, E14 . . . . .113 J6
Dorchester Av, N13 . . . . .59 J4
Bexley DA5 . . . . .176 D1
Harrow HA2 . . . . .67 H6
Dorchester Cl, Nthlt. UB5 .85 H5
Orpington BR5
off Grovelands Rd 176 A7
Dorchester Ct, N14 . . . . . .42 B7
SE24 . . . . .151 J5
Dorchester Dr, SE24 . . . .151 J5
Feltham TW14 . . . . . . .141 H6
Dorchester Gdns, E4 . . . .62 A4
NW11 . . . . .72 D4
Dorchester Gro, W4 . . . . .127 E5
Dorchester Ms, N.Mal. KT3
off Elm Rd 182 D4
Twickenham TW1 . . . . .145 F7
Dorchester Rd, Mord.
SM4 . . . . .185 E7
Northolt UB5 . . . . .85 H5
Worcester Park KT4 . . .197 J1

Dorchester Way, Har.
HA3 . . . . .69 J6
Dorchester Waye, Hayes
UB4 . . . . .102 C6
Dorcis Av, Bexh. DA7 . . . .158 E2
Dordrecht Rd, W3 . . . . . .127 E1
Dore Av, E12 . . . . .98 D5
Doreen Av, NW9 . . . . .88 D1
Dore Gdns, Mord. SM4 . .185 E7
Dorell Cl, Sthl. UB1 . . . . .103 F5
Doria Rd, SW6 . . . . .148 C2
Doric Way, NW1 . . . . .9 H3
Dorien Rd, SW20 . . . . . . .184 A2
Doris Av, Erith DA8 . . . . .159 J1
Doris Rd, E7 . . . . .97 G7
Dorking Cl, SE8 . . . . .133 J6
Worcester Park KT4 . . .198 A2
Dorlcote Rd, SW18 . . . . .149 H7
Dorman Pl, N9
off Balham Rd 60 D2
Dorman Wk, NW10
off Garden Way 88 D5
Dorman Way, NW8 . . . . .109 G1
Dorma Trd Pk, E10 . . . . . .95 G1
Dormay St, SW18 . . . . . .148 E5
Dormer Cl, E15 . . . . .97 F6
Barnet EN5 . . . . .40 A5
Dormers Av, Sthl. UB1 . . .103 G6
Dormers Ri, Sthl. UB1 . . .103 H6
DORMER'S WELLS,
Sthl. 103 H7
Dormers Wells La, Sthl.
UB1 . . . . .103 G6
Dornberg Cl, SE3 . . . . . . .135 G7
Dornberg Rd, SE3
off Banchory Rd 135 H7
Dorncliffe Rd, SW6 . . . . .148 B2
Dorney, NW3 . . . . .91 H7
Dorney Ri, Orp. BR5 . . . .193 J4
Dorney Way, Houns.
TW4 . . . . .143 E5
Dornfell St, NW6 . . . . . . .90 C5
Dornton Rd, SW12 . . . . . .168 B2
South Croydon CR2 . . .202 A5
Dorothy Av, Wem. HA0 . . .87 H7
Dorothy Evans Cl, Bexh.
DA7 . . . . .159 H4
Dorothy Gdns, Dag.
RM8 . . . . .100 B4
Dorothy Rd, SW11 . . . . . .149 J3
Dorrell Pl, SW9
off Brixton Rd 151 G4
Dorrien Wk, SW16 . . . . . .168 D2
Dorrington Ct, SE25 . . . . .188 B2
Dorrington Pt, E3
off Bromley High St . .114 B3
Dorrington St, EC1 . . . . . .19 E1
Dorrit Ms, N18 . . . . .60 B4
Dorrit Way, Chis. BR7 . . .175 F6
Dors Cl, NW9 . . . . .88 D1
Dorset Av, Sthl. UB2 . . . .123 G4
Welling DA16 . . . . .157 J4
Dorset Bldgs, EC4 . . . . . .19 G4
Dorset Cl, NW1 . . . . .15 J1
Dorset Dr, Edg. HA8 . . . . .53 J6
Dorset Est, E2 . . . . .13 G3
Dorset Gdns, Mitch.
CR4 . . . . .187 F4
Dorset Ms, N3 . . . . .72 D1
SW1 . . . . .24 D5
Dorset Pl, E15 . . . . .96 D6
SW1 . . . . .33 H3
Dorset Ri, EC4 . . . . .19 G4
Dorset Rd, E7 . . . . .97 J7
N15 . . . . .76 A4
N22 . . . . .75 E1
SE9 . . . . .174 B2
SW8 . . . . .34 B7
SW19 . . . . .184 D1
W5 . . . . .125 F3
Beckenham BR3 . . . . . .189 G3
Harrow HA1 . . . . .67 J6
Mitcham CR4 . . . . .185 H2
Dorset Sq, NW1 . . . . .7 J6
Dorset St, W1 . . . . .16 A2
Dorset Way, Twick.
TW2 . . . . .162 A1
Dorset Waye, Houns.
TW5 . . . . .123 F7
Dorton Cl, SE15
off Chandler Way 132 C7
Dorville Cres, W6 . . . . . . .127 H3
Dorville Rd, SE12 . . . . . .155 F5
Dothill Rd, SE18 . . . . .137 G7
Douai Gro, Hmptn.
TW12 . . . . .179 J1
Doubleday Rd, Loug.
IG10 . . . . .49 F2
Doughty Ms, WC1 . . . . . . .10 C5
Doughty St, WC1 . . . . . . .10 C5

Douglas Av, E17 . . . . .78 A1
New Malden KT3 . . . . .183 H4
Wembley HA0 . . . . .87 H7
Douglas Cl, Stan. HA7 . . .52 D5
Wallington SM6 . . . . . .201 E7
Douglas Cres, Hayes
UB4 . . . . .102 C4
Douglas Dr, Croy. CR0 . .204 A3
Douglas Est, N1 . . . . . . .93 J6
Douglas Ms, NW2 . . . . . .90 B3
Douglas Rd, E4 . . . . .47 E7
E16 . . . . .115 G5
N1 . . . . .93 J7
N22 . . . . .75 G1
NW6 . . . . .108 C1
Hounslow TW3 . . . . . .143 H3
Ilford IG3 . . . . .82 A6
Kingston upon Thames
KT1 . . . . .182 B2
Staines (Stanw.) TW19 .140 A6
Surbiton KT6 . . . . . . .195 J2
Welling DA16 . . . . . . .158 B1
Douglas Sq, Mord. SM4 .184 D6
Douglas St, SW1 . . . . . . .33 H2
Douglas Ter, E17
off Douglas Av 78 A1
Douglas Way, SE8 . . . . .133 J7
Doulton Ms, NW6
off Lymington Rd . .90/91 E6
Dounesforth Gdns,
SW18 . . . . .166 E1
Douro Pl, W8 . . . . .22 B5
Douro St, E3 . . . . .114 A2
Douthwaite Sq, E1 . . . . . .29 J1
Dove App, E6 . . . . .116 B5
Dove Cl, NW7
off Bunns La 55 F7
Northolt UB5
off Wayfarer Rd . . .102 D4
Wallington SM6
off Hurricane Rd 201 F7
Dovecot Cl, Pnr. HA5 . . . .66 B5
Dovecote Av, N22 . . . . . .75 G3
Dovecote Gdns, SW14
off Avondale Rd 146 D3
Dove Ct, EC2 . . . . .20 B4
Dovedale Av, Har. HA3 . . .69 F6
Ilford IG5 . . . . .80 D2
Dovedale Cl, Well. DA16 .158 A2
Dovedale Ri, Mitch. CR4 .167 J7
Dovedale Rd, SE22 . . . .153 E5
Dovedon Cl, N14 . . . . . . .58 E2
Dove Ho Gdns, E4 . . . . . .62 A2
Dovehouse Mead, Bark.
IG11 . . . . .117 G2
Dovehouse St, SW3 . . . . .31 G3
Dove Ms, SW5 . . . . .30 C2
Dove Pk, Pnr. HA5 . . . . . .51 G7
Dover Cl, NW2
off Brent Ter 90 A2
Romford RM5 . . . . .83 J2
Dovercourt Av, Th.Hth.
CR7 . . . . .187 G4
Dovercourt Est, N1 . . . . . .94 A6
Dovercourt Gdns, Stan.
HA7 . . . . .53 H5
Dovercourt La, Sutt.
SM1 . . . . .199 F3
Dovercourt Rd, SE22 . . .152 B6
Doverfield Rd, SW2 . . . .151 E6
Dover Flats, SE1
off Old Kent Rd 132 B4
Dover Gdns, Cars. SM5 .199 J3
Dover Ho Rd, SW15 . . . .147 G4
Doveridge Gdns, N13 . . . .59 H4
Dove Rd, N1 . . . . .94 A6
Dove Row, E2 . . . . .112 D1
Dover Pk Dr, SW15 . . . .147 H6
Dover Patrol, SE3
off Kidbrooke Way . . .155 H2
Dover Rd, E12 . . . . .97 J2
N9 . . . . .61 F2
SE19 . . . . .170 A6
Romford RM6 . . . . .82 E6
Dover St, W1 . . . . .17 E6
Dover Yd, W1 . . . . .25 F1
Doves Cl, Brom. BR2 . . .206 B2
Doves Yd, N1 . . . . .111 G1
Doveton Rd, S.Croy.
CR2 . . . . .202 A5
Doveton St, E1
off Malcolm Rd 113 F4
Dove Wk, SW1 . . . . .32 B3
Dowanhill Rd, SE6 . . . . .172 D1
Dowdeswell Cl, SW15 . .147 E4
Dowding Pl, Stan. HA7 . . .52 D6
Dowdney Cl, NW5 . . . . . .92 C5
Dowgate Hill, EC4 . . . . . .20 B5
Dowland St, W10 . . . . . .108 B2
Dowlas Est, SE5 . . . . . . .36 D7

Dowlas St, SE5 . . . . .36 D7
Dowlerville Rd, Orp.
BR6 . . . . .207 J6
Dowman Cl, SW19
off Nelson Gro
Rd 184/185 E1
Downage, NW4 . . . . .71 J3
Downalong, Bushey
(Bushey Hth.) WD23 . .52 A1
Downbarns Rd, Ruis.
HA4 . . . . .84 D3
Downbury Ms, SW18
off Merton Rd 148 D6
Down Cl, Nthlt. UB5 . . . .102 B2
Downderry Rd, Brom.
BR1 . . . . .172 D3
Downe Cl, Well. DA16 . . .138 C7
Downend, SE18
off Moordown . . .136/137 E7
Downe Rd, Mitch. CR4 . .185 J2
Downers Cotts, SW4
off The Pavement . . .150 C4
Downes Cl, Twick. TW1
off St. Margarets
Rd 144/145 E6
Downes Ct, N21 . . . . .59 G1
Downfield, Wor.Pk. KT4 .197 F1
Downfield Cl, W9 . . . . .6 A6
Down Hall Rd, Kings.T.
KT2 . . . . .181 G1
DOWNHAM, Brom. 173 F5
Downham La, Brom. BR1
off Downham Way . . .172 D5
Downham Rd, N1 . . . . . . .94 A7
Downham Way, Brom.
BR1 . . . . .172 D5
Downhills Av, N17 . . . . . .76 A3
Downhills Pk Rd, N17 . . . .75 J3
Downhills Way, N17 . . . . .75 J3
Downhurst Av, NW7 . . . . .54 D5
Downing Cl, Har. HA2 . . . .67 J3
Downing Dr, Grnf. UB6 . .104 A1
Downing Rd, Dag. RM9 . .119 F1
Downings, E6 . . . . .116 D6
Downing St, SW1 . . . . . . .26 A3
Downland Cl, N20 . . . . . .57 F1
Downleys Cl, SE9 . . . . . .174 B2
Downman Rd, SE9 . . . . .156 B3
Down Pl, W6 . . . . .127 H4
Down Rd, Tedd. TW11 . . .163 E6
Downs, The, SW20 . . . . .166 A7
Downs Av, Chis. BR7 . . . .174 C5
Pinner HA5 . . . . .67 F6
Downs Br Rd, Beck. BR3 .190 D1
Downsbury Ms, SW18
off Merton Rd 148 D5
Downsell Rd, E15 . . . . . .96 C4
Downsfield Rd, E17 . . . . .77 H6
Downshall Av, Ilf. IG3 . . . .81 H6
Downs Hill, Beck. BR3 . .172 D7
Downshire Hill, NW3 . . . .91 G4
Downside, Sun. TW16 . . .178 A1
Twickenham TW1 . . . .162 C3
Downside Cl, SW19 . . . . .167 F6
Downside Cres, NW3 . . . .91 H5
W13 . . . . .104 D4
Downside Rd, Sutt. SM2 .199 G6
Downside Wk, Nthlt.
UB5 . . . . .103 F3
Downs La, E5
off Downs Rd 94/95 E4
Downs Pk Rd, E5 . . . . . . .94 D5
E8 . . . . .94 C5
Downs Rd, E5 . . . . .94 D4
Beckenham BR3 . . . . .190 B2
Enfield EN1 . . . . .44 B4
Thornton Heath CR7 . .187 J1
Down St, W1 . . . . .24 D2
West Molesey KT8 . . . .179 G5
Down St Ms, W1 . . . . . . .24 D2
Downs Vw, Islw. TW7 . . .124 C7
Downsview Gdns, SE19 .169 H7
Downsview Rd, SE19 . . .169 J7
Downsway, Orp. BR6 . . . .207 H5
Downton Av, SW2 . . . . . .169 E2
Downtown Rd, SE16 . . . .133 H2
Downway, N12 . . . . .57 H7
Down Way, Nthlt. UB5 . . .102 B3
Dowrey St, N1
off Richmond Av 111 G1
Dowsett Rd, N17 . . . . . . .76 C2
Dowson Cl, SE5 . . . . . . .152 A4
Doyce St, SE1 . . . . .27 J3
Doyle Gdns, NW10 . . . . .107 G1
Doyle Rd, SE25 . . . . .188 D4
D'Oyley St, SW1 . . . . .32 B1
Doynton St, N19 . . . . .92 B2
Draco St, SE17 . . . . .35 J5
Dragonfly Cl, E13
off Hollybush St 115 H3

Dragon Rd, SE15 . . . . . . .36 D6
Dragoon Rd, SE8 . . . . . .133 J5
Dragor Rd, NW10 . . . . . .106 C4
Drake Cl, SE16
off Middleton Dr 133 G2
Drake Ct, SE19 . . . . .170 C5
W12 . . . . .127 J2
Harrow HA2 . . . . .85 F1
Drake Cres, SE28 . . . . . .118 C6
Drakefell Rd, SE4 . . . . . .153 G2
SE14 . . . . .153 G2
Drakefield Rd, SW17 . . .168 A3
Drakeley Ct, N5
off Highbury Hill 93 H4
Drake Rd, SE4 . . . . .154 A3
Chessington KT9 . . . .196 A5
Croydon CR0 . . . . .187 F7
Harrow HA2 . . . . .85 F2
Mitcham CR4 . . . . .186 A6
Drakes Ctyd, NW6 . . . . . .90 C7
Drake St, WC1 . . . . .18 C2
Enfield EN2 . . . . .44 A1
Drakes Wk, E6 . . . . .116 C1
Drakewood Rd, SW16 . . .168 D7
Draper Cl, Belv. DA17 . . .139 F4
Isleworth TW7 . . . . . . .144 A2
Draper Pl, N1
off Dagmar Ter 111 H1
Drapers Gdns, EC2
off Copthall Av 112 A6
Drapers Rd, E15 . . . . . . .96 D4
N17 . . . . .76 C3
Enfield EN2 . . . . .43 H2
Drappers Way, SE16 . . . . .37 J1
Draven Cl, Brom. BR2 . .191 F7
Drawdock Rd, SE10 . . . .134 D1
Drawell Cl, SE18 . . . . . . .137 H5
Drax Av, SW20 . . . . .165 H7
Draxmont, SW19 . . . . . .166 B6
Draycot Rd, E11 . . . . .79 H6
Surbiton KT6 . . . . .196 A1
Draycott Av, SW3 . . . . . . .31 H1
Harrow HA3 . . . . .69 E6
Draycott Cl, NW2 . . . . . . .90 A3
Harrow HA3 . . . . .69 E6
Draycott Ms, SW6
off New Kings Rd 148 C2
Draycott Pl, SW3 . . . . . . .31 J2
Draycott Ter, SW3 . . . . . .32 A1
Drayford Cl, W9 . . . . . . .108 C4
Dray Gdns, SW2 . . . . . . .151 F5
Draymans Way, Islw.
TW7 . . . . .144 C3
Drayside Ms, Sthl. UB2
off Kingston Rd 123 F2
Drayson Ms, W8 . . . . . . .128 D2
Drayton Av, W13 . . . . . . .104 D7
Loughton IG10 . . . . . . .48 C6
Orpington BR6 . . . . . .207 E1
Drayton Br Rd, W7 . . . . .104 C7
W13 . . . . .104 C7
Drayton Cl, Houns. TW4
off Bramley Way 143 F5
Ilford IG1 . . . . .99 G1
Drayton Gdns, N21 . . . . . .43 H7
SW10 . . . . .30 D3
W13 . . . . .104 D7
West Drayton UB7 . . . .120 B2
Drayton Grn, W13 . . . . . .104 D7
Drayton Grn Rd, W13 . . .104 E7
Drayton Gro, W13 . . . . . .104 D7
Drayton Pk, N5 . . . . .93 G5
Drayton Pk Ms, N5
off Drayton Pk 93 G5
Drayton Rd, E11 . . . . .96 D1
N17 . . . . .76 B2
NW10 . . . . .107 F1
W13 . . . . .104 D7
Borehamwood WD6 . . . .38 A4
Croydon CR0 . . . . .201 H2
Drayton Waye, Har. HA3 . .69 E6
Dresden Cl, NW6 . . . . . . .91 E6
Dresden Rd, N19 . . . . . . .92 C1
Dressington Av, SE4 . . . .154 A6
Drew Av, NW7 . . . . .56 B6
Drew Gdns, Grnf. UB6 . . .86 C6
Drew Rd, E16 . . . . .136 B1
Drewstead Rd, SW16 . . .168 D2
Driffield Rd, E3 . . . . .113 H2
Drift, The, Brom. BR2 . . .206 A3
Drift Way, Rich. TW10 . . .163 J1
Driftway, The, Mitch.
CR4 . . . . .186 A1
Drinkwater Rd, Har. HA2 .85 H2
Drive, The, E4 . . . . .46 D7
E17 . . . . .78 B4
E18 . . . . .79 G3
N3 . . . . .56 D7
N6 . . . . .73 J5
N11 . . . . .58 C6

Drive, The, NW10
off Longstone Av 107 F1
NW11 . . . . .72 B7
SW6 off Fulham Rd . . .148 B2
SW16 . . . . .187 F3
SW20 . . . . .165 J7
W3 . . . . .106 C6
Barking IG11 . . . . .99 J7
Barnet (High Barn.)
EN5 . . . . .40 B3
Barnet (New Barn.)
EN5 . . . . .41 F6
Beckenham BR3 . . . . .190 A2
Bexley DA5 . . . . .158 C6
Buckhurst Hill IG9 . . . .47 J7
Chislehurst BR7 . . . . .193 J3
Chislehurst (Scad.Pk.)
BR7 . . . . .193 H1
Edgware HA8 . . . . .54 A5
Enfield EN2 . . . . .44 A1
Epsom KT19 . . . . .197 F6
Erith DA8 . . . . .139 H7
Feltham TW14 . . . . . . .142 C7
Harrow HA2 . . . . .67 G7
Hounslow TW3 . . . . . .144 A2
Ilford IG1 . . . . .98 C1
Isleworth TW7 . . . . . . .144 A2
Kingston upon Thames
KT2 . . . . .164 C7
Loughton IG10 . . . . . . .48 B3
Morden SM4 . . . . .185 G5
Orpington BR6 . . . . . .207 J2
Romford (Coll.Row)
RM5 . . . . .83 J1
Sidcup DA14 . . . . .176 B3
Surbiton KT6 . . . . .181 H7
Thornton Heath CR7 . .188 A4
Wembley HA9 . . . . .88 C2
West Wickham BR4 . . .190 D7
Driveway, The, E17
off Hoe St 78 B6
Droitwich Cl, SE26 . . . . .170 D3
Dromey Gdns, Har. HA3 . .52 C7
Dromore Rd, SW15 . . . . .148 B6
Dronfield Gdns, Dag.
RM8 . . . . .100 C5
Droop St, W10 . . . . .108 B4
Drover La, SE15 . . . . . . .133 E7
Drovers Pl, SE15 . . . . . . .133 E7
Drovers Rd, S.Croy. CR2 .202 A5
Droveway, Loug. IG10 . . . .49 E2
Druce Rd, SE21 . . . . .152 B6
Druid St, SE1 . . . . .28 E3
Druids Way, Brom. BR2 . .190 D4
Drumaline Ridge, Wor.Pk.
KT4 . . . . .197 E2
Drummond Cen, Croy.
CR0 . . . . .201 J2
Drummond Cres, NW1 . . . .9 H3
Drummond Dr, Stan. HA7 .52 C7
Drummond Gate, SW1 . . .33 J3
Drummond Pl, Rich.
TW9 . . . . .145 H4
Twickenham TW1 . . . .144 E6
Drummond Rd, E11 . . . . .79 J6
SE16 . . . . .132 E3
Croydon CR0 . . . . .201 J2
Drummonds, The, Buck.H.
IG9 . . . . .63 H2
Drummond St, NW1 . . . . . .9 F5
Drum St, E1 . . . . .21 G3
Drury Cres, Croy. CR0 . . .201 G2
Drury La, WC2 . . . . .18 B4
Drury Rd, Har. HA1 . . . . . .67 J7
Drury Way, NW10 . . . . . . .88 D5
Drury Way Ind Est, NW10 .88 D5
Dryad St, SW15 . . . . . . .148 A3
Dryburgh Gdns, NW9 . . . .70 A3
Dryburgh Rd, SW15 . . . .147 H3
Dryden Av, W7 . . . . .104 C6
Dryden Cl, Ilf. IG6 . . . . . . .65 J6
Dryden Ct, SE11 . . . . .35 F2
Dryden Rd, SW19 . . . . . .167 F6
Enfield EN1 . . . . .44 B6
Harrow HA3 . . . . .68 C1
Welling DA16 . . . . .157 H1
Dryden St, WC2 . . . . .18 B4
Dryfield Cl, NW10 . . . . . . .88 C6
Dryfield Rd, Edg. HA8 . . . .54 C6
Dryfield Wk, SE8
off New King St 134 A6
Dryhill Rd, Belv. DA17 . . .139 F6
Dryland Av, Orp. BR6 . . .207 J4
Drylands Rd, N8 . . . . .75 E6
Drysdale Av, E4 . . . . .46 B7
Drysdale Pl, N1 . . . . .12 E3
Drysdale St, N1 . . . . .12 E3
Dublin Av, E8 . . . . .112 D1
Du Burstow Ter, W7 . . . .124 B2
Ducal St, E2 . . . . .13 G4

Du Cane Cl, W12 . . . . .107 J6
Du Cane Ct, SW17 . . . . . . .168 A1
Du Cane Rd, W12 . . . . .107 F6
Duchess Cl, N11 . . . . .58 B5
  Sutton SM1 . . . . .199 F4
Duchess Gro, Buck.H. IG9 .63 H2
Duchess Ms, W1 . . . . .16 E2
Duchess of Bedford's Wk,
  W8 . . . . .128 D2
Duchess St, W1 . . . . .16 E2
Duchy St, SE1 . . . . .27 F1
Ducie St, SW4 . . . . .151 F4
Duckett Ms, N4
  off Duckett Rd 75 H6
Duckett Rd, N4 . . . . .75 H6
Duckett St, E1 . . . . .113 G4
Duck La, W1 . . . . .17 H4
Duck Lees La, Enf. EN3 . . .45 H4
DUCKS ISLAND, Barn. . . .40 A6
Ducks Wk, Twick. TW1 . .145 F5
Du Cros Dr, Stan. HA7 . . .53 G6
Du Cros Rd, W3
  off The Vale 126/127 E1
Dudden Hill La, NW10 . . . .89 F4
Duddington Cl, SE9 . . . . . .174 A4
Dudley Av, Har. HA3 . . . . . .69 F3
Dudley Ct, NW11 . . . . .72 C4
Dudley Dr, Mord. SM4 . . .184 B7
  Ruislip HA4 . . . . .84 B5
Dudley Gdns, W13 . . . . . . .125 E2
  Harrow HA2 . . . . .86 A1
Dudley Ms, SW2
  off Bascombe St 151 G6
Dudley Rd, E17 . . . . .78 A2
  N3 . . . . .72 E2
  NW6 . . . . .108 B2
  SW19 . . . . .166 D6
  Harrow HA2 . . . . .85 J2
  Ilford IG1 . . . . .99 E4
  Kingston upon Thames
  KT1 . . . . .181 J3
  Richmond TW9 . . . . .145 J2
  Southall UB2 . . . . .122 D2
  Walton-on-Thames
  KT12 . . . . .178 A6
Dudley St, W2 . . . . .14 E2
Dudlington Rd, E5 . . . . .95 F2
Dudmaston Ms, SW3 . . . . .31 F3
Dudsbury Rd, Sid.
  DA14 . . . . .176 B6
Dudset La, Houns. TW5 . .142 A1
Dufferin Av, EC1 . . . . .12 B6
Dufferin St, EC1 . . . . .12 A6
Duffield Cl, Har. HA1 . . . . .68 C5
Duffield Dr, N15
  off Copperfield Dr 76 C4
Duff St, E14 . . . . .114 B6
Dufour's Pl, W1 . . . . .17 G4
Dugard Way, SE11 . . . . .35 G1
Duke Gdns, Ilf. IG6
  off Duke Rd 81 G4
Duke Humphrey Rd,
  SE3 . . . . .155 E1
Duke of Cambridge Cl, Twick.
  TW2 . . . . .144 A6
Duke of Edinburgh Rd, Sutt.
  SM1 . . . . .199 G2
Duke of Wellington Pl,
  SW1 . . . . .24 C3
Duke of York St, SW1 . . . .25 G1
Duke Rd, W4 . . . . .126 D5
  Ilford IG6 . . . . .81 G4
Dukes Av, N3 . . . . .72 E1
  N10 . . . . .74 C3
  W4 . . . . .126 D5
  Edgware HA8 . . . . .53 J6
  Harrow HA1 . . . . .68 B4
  Harrow (N.Har.) HA2 . . . .67 F6
  Hounslow TW4 . . . . .142 E4
  Kingston upon Thames
  KT2 . . . . .163 F4
  New Malden KT3 . . . . . .183 F4
  Northolt UB5 . . . . .85 E7
  Richmond TW10 . . . . . . .163 F4
Dukes Cl, Hmptn. TW12 .161 F5
Dukes Ct, E6 . . . . .116 D1
Dukes Grn Av, Felt.
  TW14 . . . . .142 A5
Dukes Head Yd, N6
  off Highgate High St . .92 B1
Duke Shore Pl, E14
  off Narrow St 113 J7
Duke Shore Wf, E14
  off Narrow St 113 J7
Dukes La, W8 . . . . .128 D2
Duke's Meadows, W4
  off Great Chertsey Rd.146 C4
Dukes Ms, N10
  off Dukes Av 74 B3
Duke's Ms, W1 . . . . .16 C3

Dukes Orchard, Bex.
  DA5 . . . . .177 J1
Duke's Pas, E17 . . . . .78 C4
Dukes Pl, EC3 . . . . .21 E4
Dukes Rd, E6 . . . . .116 D1
  W3 . . . . .106 A5
Duke's Rd, WC1 . . . . .9 J4
Dukesthorpe Rd, SE26 . . .171 G4
Duke St, SW1 . . . . .25 G1
  W1 . . . . .16 C3
  Richmond TW9 . . . . .145 G4
  Sutton SM1 . . . . .199 G4
Duke St Hill, SE1 . . . . .28 C1
Dukes Way, W.Wick.
  BR4 . . . . .205 E3
Duke's Yd, W1 . . . . .16 C5
Dulas St, N4
  off Everleigh St 93 F1
Dulford St, W11 . . . . .108 B7
Dulka Rd, SW11 . . . . .149 J5
Dulverton Rd, SE9 . . . . . . .175 F2
  Ruislip HA4 . . . . .84 A1
DULWICH, SE21 . . . . .152 B7
★ Dulwich Coll Picture Gall,
  SE21 . . . . .152 B7
Dulwich Common, SE21 .170 B1
  SE22 . . . . .170 B1
Dulwich Lawn Cl, SE22
  off Colwell Rd 152 C5
Dulwich Oaks, The,
  SE21 . . . . .170 B3
Dulwich Rd, SE24 . . . . . . .151 G5
Dulwich Village, SE21 . . .152 B6
Dulwich Wd Av, SE19 . . . .170 B4
Dulwich Wd Pk, SE19 . . .170 B4
Dumbarton Rd, SW2 . . . . .151 E6
Dumbleton Cl, Kings.T. KT1
  off Gloucester Rd 182 B1
Dumbreck Rd, SE9 . . . . . .156 C4
Dumont Rd, N16 . . . . .94 B3
Dumpton Pl, NW1
  off Gloucester Av 92 A7
Dunbar Av, SW16 . . . . .187 G2
  Beckenham BR3 . . . . . . .189 H4
  Dagenham RM10 . . . . . .101 G3
Dunbar Cl, Hayes UB4 . . .102 A5
Dunbar Ct, Sutt. SM1 . . . .199 G5
Dunbar Gdns, Dag.
  RM10 . . . . .101 G5
Dunbar Rd, E7 . . . . .97 G6
  N22 . . . . .75 G1
  New Malden KT3 . . . . . .182 C4
Dunbar St, SE27 . . . . .169 J3
Dunblane Cl, Edg. HA8
  off Tayside Dr 54 B2
Dunblane Rd, SE9 . . . . . . .156 B3
Dunboyne Rd, NW3 . . . . . . .91 J5
Dunbridge Ho, SW15
  off Highcliffe Dr 147 F6
Dunbridge St, E2 . . . . .13 J5
Duncan Cl, Barn. EN5 . . . .41 F4
Duncan Gro, W3 . . . . .106 E6
Duncannon St, WC2 . . . . . .18 A6
Duncan Rd, E8 . . . . .112 E1
  Richmond TW9 . . . . .145 H4
Duncan St, N1 . . . . .11 G1
Duncan Ter, N1 . . . . .11 G2
Dunch St, E1
  off Watney St 112/113 E6
Duncombe Hill, SE23 . . . .153 H7
Duncombe Rd, N19 . . . . . . .92 D1
Duncrievie Rd, SE13 . . . . .154 D6
Duncroft, SE18 . . . . .137 H7
Dundalk Rd, SE4 . . . . .153 H3
Dundas Gdns, W.Mol.
  KT8 . . . . .179 H3
Dundas Rd, SE15 . . . . .153 F2
Dundee Rd, E13 . . . . .115 H2
  SE25 . . . . .188 E5
Dundee St, E1 . . . . .132 E1
Dundee Way, Enf. EN3 . . .45 H3
Dundela Gdns, Wor.Pk.
  KT4 . . . . .197 H4
Dundonald Cl, E6
  off Northumberland
  Rd 116 B6
Dundonald Rd, NW10 . . .108 A1
  SW19 . . . . .166 B7
Dunedin Ho, E16
  off Manwood St 136 C1
Dunedin Rd, E10 . . . . .96 B3
  Ilford IG1 . . . . .99 F1
Dunedin Way, Hayes
  UB4 . . . . .102 C4
Dunelm Gro, SE27 . . . . . . .169 J4
Dunelm St, E1 . . . . .113 G6
Dunfield Gdns, SE6 . . . . . .172 B4
Dunfield Rd, SE6 . . . . .172 B5
Dunford Rd, N7 . . . . .93 F4
Dungarvan Av, SW15 . . . .147 G4

Dunheved Cl, Th.Hth.
  CR7 . . . . .187 G6
Dunheved Rd N, Th.Hth.
  CR7 . . . . .187 G6
Dunheved Rd S, Th.Hth.
  CR7 . . . . .187 G6
Dunheved Rd W, Th.Hth.
  CR7 . . . . .187 G6
Dunhill Pt, SW15
  off Dilton Gdns 165 H1
Dunholme Grn, N9 . . . . . . .60 C3
Dunholme La, N9
  off Dunholme Rd 60 C3
Dunholme Rd, N9 . . . . .60 C3
Dunkeld Rd, SE25 . . . . . . .188 A4
  Dagenham RM8 . . . . . . .100 B2
Dunkery Rd, SE9 . . . . .174 A4
Dunkirk St, SE27
  off Waring St 169 J4
Dunlace Rd, E5 . . . . .95 F4
Dunleary Cl, Houns.
  TW4 . . . . .143 F7
Dunley Dr, Croy. (New Adgtn.)
  CR0 . . . . .204 B7
Dunlin Ho, W13 . . . . .104 C4
Dunloe Av, N17 . . . . .76 A3
Dunloe St, E2 . . . . .13 F2
Dunlop Pl, SE16 . . . . .29 G5
Dunmore Pt, E2 . . . . .13 F4
Dunmore Rd, NW6 . . . . . . .108 B1
  SW20 . . . . .183 J1
Dunmow Cl, Felt. TW13 . .160 E4
  Loughton IG10 . . . . .48 B6
  Romford RM6 . . . . .82 C5
Dunmow Ho, Dag. RM9 .118 B1
Dunmow Rd, E15 . . . . .96 D4
Dunmow Wk, N1
  off Popham St 111 J1
Dunnage Cres, SE16
  off Plough Way 133 H4
Dunn Mead, NW9
  off Field Mead 55 F7
Dunnock Cl, N9 . . . . .61 G1
  Borehamwood WD6 . . . .38 A4
Dunnock Rd, E6 . . . . .116 B6
Dunns Pas, WC1 . . . . .18 B3
Dunn St, E8 . . . . .94 C5
Dunollie Pl, NW5
  off Dunollie Rd 92 C5
Dunollie Rd, NW5 . . . . .92 C5
Dunoon Rd, SE23 . . . . .153 F7
Dunraven Dr, Enf. EN2 . . .43 G2
Dunraven Rd, W12 . . . . . . .127 G1
Dunraven St, W1 . . . . .16 A5
Dunsany Rd, W14 . . . . .128 A3
Dunsfold Way, Croy.
  (New Adgtn.) CR0 . . . . .204 B7
Dunsford Way, SW15
  off Dover Pk Dr 147 H6
Dunsmore Cl, Hayes UB4
  off Kingsash Dr . .102/103 E4
Dunsmore Rd, Walt.
  KT12 . . . . .178 B6
Dunsmure Rd, N16 . . . . . . .94 B1
Dunspring La, Ilf. IG5 . . . .80 E2
Dunstable Ms, W1 . . . . .16 C1
Dunstable Rd, Rich.
  TW9 . . . . .145 H4
  West Molesey KT8 . . . . .179 F4
Dunstall Rd, SW20 . . . . . .165 H6
Dunstall Way, W.Mol.
  KT8 . . . . .179 H3
Dunstan Cl, N2
  off Thomas More Way .73 F3
Dunstan Rd, NW11 . . . . . . .90 C1
Dunstans Gro, SE22 . . . . .152 E6
Dunstans Rd, SE22 . . . . . .152 D7
Dunster Av, Mord. SM4 . .198 A1
Dunster Cl, Barn. EN5 . . . .40 A4
  Romford RM5 . . . . .83 J2
Dunster Ct, EC3 . . . . .20 D5
  Borehamwood WD6
  off Kensington Way . .38 D3
Dunster Dr, NW9 . . . . .88 C1
Dunster Gdns, NW6 . . . . . .90 C7
Dunsterville Way, SE1 . . . .28 C4
Dunster Way, Har. HA2 . . .85 E3
  Wallington SM6
  off London Rd 200 A1
Dunston Rd, E8 . . . . .112 C1
  SW11 . . . . .150 A2
Dunston St, E8 . . . . .112 C1
Dunton Cl, Surb. KT6 . . . .195 H1
Dunton Rd, E10 . . . . .78 B7
  SE1 . . . . .37 F3
Duntshill Rd, SW18 . . . . . .167 E1
Dunvegan Cl, W.Mol.
  KT8 . . . . .179 H4
Dunvegan Rd, SE9 . . . . . . .156 C4
Dunwich Rd, Bexh. DA7 .159 F1

Dunworth Ms, W11
  off Portobello Rd 108 C6
Duplex Ride, SW1 . . . . .24 A4
Dupont Rd, SW20 . . . . .184 A2
Duppas Av, Croy. CR0
  off Violet La 201 H4
Duppas Hill La, Croy. CR0
  off Duppas Hill Rd . .201 H4
Duppas Hill Rd, Croy.
  CR0 . . . . .201 H4
Duppas Hill Ter, Croy.
  CR0 . . . . .201 H3
Duppas Rd, Croy. CR0 . .201 G3
Dupree Rd, SE7 . . . . .135 H5
Dura Den Cl, Beck. BR3 . .172 B7
Durand Cl, Cars. SM5 . . . .199 J1
Durand Gdns, SW9 . . . . . .151 F1
Durands Wk, SE16 . . . . . . .133 J2
Durand Way, NW10 . . . . . . .88 C7
Durants Pk Av, Enf. EN3 . .45 G4
Durants Rd, Enf. EN3 . . . . .45 F4
Durant St, E2 . . . . .13 H3
Durban Gdns, Dag.
  RM10 . . . . .101 J7
Durban Rd, E15 . . . . .114 E3
  E17 . . . . .77 J1
  N17 . . . . .60 B6
  SE27 . . . . .169 J4
  Beckenham BR3 . . . . . . .189 J2
  Ilford IG2 . . . . .99 H1
Durbin Rd, Chess. KT9 . . .195 H4
Durdans Rd, Sthl. UB1 . . .103 F6
Durell Gdns, Dag. RM9 . .100 D5
Durell Rd, Dag. RM9 . . . . .100 D5
Durford Cres, SW15 . . . . .165 H1
Durham Av, Brom. BR2 . .191 F4
  Hounslow TW5 . . . . .123 F5
  Woodford Green IG8 . . . .64 A5
Durham Cl, SW20
  off Durham Rd 183 H2
Durham Hill, Brom. BR1 .173 F4
Durham Ho St, WC2 . . . . . .18 B6
Durham Pl, SW3 . . . . .31 J4
  Ilford IG1
  off Eton Rd 99 F4
Durham Ri, SE18 . . . . .137 F5
Durham Rd, E12 . . . . .98 A4
  E16 . . . . .115 E4
  N2 . . . . .73 H3
  N7 . . . . .93 F2
  N9 . . . . .60 D2
  SW20 . . . . .183 H1
  W5 . . . . .125 G3
  Borehamwood WD6 . . . .38 C4
  Bromley BR2 . . . . .191 F3
  Dagenham RM10 . . . . . .101 J5
  Feltham TW14 . . . . .142 C7
  Harrow HA1 . . . . .67 H5
  Sidcup DA14 . . . . .176 B5
Durham Row, E1 . . . . .113 H5
Durham St, SE11 . . . . .34 C4
Durham Ter, W2 . . . . .14 A3
Durham Wf, Brent. TW8
  off London Rd 125 F7
Durham Yd, E2
  off Teesdale St . . .112/113 E3
Durley Av, Pnr. HA5 . . . . . .67 E7
Durley Rd, N16 . . . . .76 B7
Durlston Rd, E5 . . . . .94 D2
  Kingston upon Thames
  KT2 . . . . .163 H6
Durnell Way, Loug. IG10 . .48 D3
Durnford St, N15 . . . . .76 B5
  SE10
  off Greenwich Ch St .134 C6
Durning Rd, SE19 . . . . .170 A5
Durnsford Av, SW19 . . . . .166 D2
Durnsford Rd, N11 . . . . .74 D1
  SW19 . . . . .166 D2
Durrant Way, Orp. BR6 . .207 G5
Durrell Rd, SW6 . . . . .148 C1
Durrington Av, SW20 . . . .183 J1
Durrington Pk Rd, SW20 .165 J7
Durrington Rd, E5 . . . . .95 H4
Durrington Twr, SW8
  off Westbury St 150 C2
Dursley Cl, SE3 . . . . .155 J2
Dursley Gdns, SE3 . . . . . .156 A1
Dursley Rd, SE3 . . . . .155 J2
Durward St, E1 . . . . .112 E5
Durweston Ms, W1 . . . . . . .16 A1
Durweston St, W1 . . . . .16 A1
Dury Rd, Barn. EN5 . . . . . . .40 C1
Dutch Barn Cl, Stai. (Stanw.)
  TW19 . . . . .140 A6
Dutch Gdns, Kings.T. KT2
  off Windmill Ri 164 B6
Dutch Yd, SW18
  off Wandsworth
  High St 148 D5

Duthie St, E14
off Prestons Rd 114 C7
Dutton St, SE10 ....154 C1
Duxberry Cl, Brom. BR2
off Southborough La .192 B5
Duxford Ho, SE2
off Wolvercote Rd ...138 D2
Dwight Ct, SW6
off Burlington Rd 148 B2
Dye Ho La, E3 ....114 A1
Dyer's Bldgs, EC1 ......19 E2
Dyers Hall Rd, E11 .....96 E1
Dyers La, SW15 ....147 H4
Dykes Way, Brom. BR2 .191 F3
Dylan Rd, SE24 ....151 H4
Belvedere DA17 ....139 G3
Dylan Thomas Ho, N8 ...75 F4
Dylways, SE5 ....152 A4
Dymchurch Cl, Ilf. IG5 ...80 D2
Orpington BR6 ....207 H4
Dymes Path, SW19
off Queensmere Rd ..166 A2
Dymock St, SW6 .....148 E3
Dymond Est, SW17
off Glenburnie Rd ...167 H3
Dyneley Rd, SE12 .....173 J4
Dyne Rd, NW6 ....90 C7
Dynevor Rd, N16 ....94 B3
Richmond TW10 ......145 H5
Dynham Rd, NW6 ......90 D7
Dyott St, WC1 ....18 A3
Dysart Av, Kings.T. KT2 .163 F5
Dysart St, EC2 ....12 D6
Dyson Rd, E11 ....79 E6
E15 ....97 F6
Dysons Rd, N18 ....61 E5

E

Eade Rd, N4 ....75 J4
Eagans Cl, N2
off Market Pl 73 H3
Eagle Av, Rom. RM6 ....82 E6
Eagle Cl, SE16
off Varcoe Rd 133 F5
Enfield EN3 ....45 F4
Wallington SM6 ......201 E6
Eagle Ct, EC1 ....19 G1
Eagle Dr, NW9 ....71 E2
Eagle Hill, SE19 ......170 A6
Eagle La, E11 ....79 G4
Eagle Ms, N1
off Tottenham Rd 94 B6
Eagle Pl, SW1 ....17 G6
SW7 ....30 D3
Eagle Rd, Wem. HA0 ....87 G7
Eaglesfield Rd, SE18 ..137 E7
Eagle St, WC1 ....18 C2
Eagle Ter, Wdf.Grn. IG8 ..63 H7
off Willow La 185 J6
Eagle Wf, E14
off Broomfield St 114 B5
Eagle Wf Rd, N1 ....12 A1
Ealham Sq, SE9 ......155 J4
EALING, W5 ....105 F7
Ealing Bdy Shop Cen,
W5 ....105 G7
Ealing Cl, Borwd. WD6 ..38 D1
★ Ealing Common, W5 .125 H1
Ealing Downs Ct, Grnf. UB6
off Perivale La 104 D3
Ealing Grn, W5 ....125 G1
Ealing Pk Gdns, W5 ...125 F4
Ealing Rd, Brent. TW8 .125 G5
Northolt UB5 ....85 G7
Wembley HA0 ....105 H1
Ealing Village, W5 ....105 H6
Eamont Rd, NW8 ....7 G1
Eardley Cres, SW5 ....128 C5
Eardley Pt, SE18
off Wilmount St ..136/137 E4
Eardley Rd, SW16 ....168 C5
Belvedere DA17 ......139 G5
Earl Cl, N11 ....58 B5
Earldom Rd, SW15 ....147 J4
Earle Gdns, Kings.T. KT2 .163 H6
Earlham Gro, E7 ....97 F5
N22 ....59 F7
Earlham St, WC2 ....17 J4
Earl Ri, SE18 ....137 G4
Earl Rd, SW14 ....146 C4
off Elm Rd
EARLS COURT, SW5 ...128 C5
★ Earls Court Exhibition Cen,
SW5 ....128 D5
Earls Ct Gdns, SW5 ....30 A3
Earls Ct Rd, SW5 .....128 D4
W8 ....128 D3

Earls Ct Sq, SW5 ....30 A3
Earls Cres, Har. HA1 ...68 B4
Earlsdown Ho, Bark. IG11
off Wheelers Cross ..117 G2
Earlsferry Way, N1 .....93 F7
EARLSFIELD, SW18 ....167 F1
Earlsfield Rd, SW18 ...167 F1
Earlshall Rd, SE9 ....156 C4
Earlsmead, Har. HA2 ...85 F4
Earlsmead Rd, N15 ....76 C5
NW10 ....107 J2
Earl's Path, Loug. IG10 ..47 J2
Earls Ter, W8 ....128 C3
Earlsthorpe Ms, SW12 .150 A6
Earlsthorpe Rd, SE26 .171 G4
Earlstoke St, EC1 ......11 G3
Earlston Gro, E9 .....113 E1
Earl St, EC2 ....20 D1
Earls Wk, W8 ....128 D3
Dagenham RM8 ......100 B4
Earls Way, Orp. BR6
off Station Rd 207 J2
Earlswood Av, Th.Hth.
CR7 ....187 G5
Earlswood Cl, SE10
off Earlswood St .134/135 E5
Earlswood Gdns, Ilf. IG5 ..80 D3
Earlswood St, SE10 ...135 E5
Early Ms, NW1
off Arlington Rd 110 B1
Earnshaw St, WC2 .....17 J3
Earsby St, W14 ......128 B4
Easby Cres, Mord. SM4 .185 E6
Easebourne Rd, Dag.
RM8 ....100 C5
Easedale Ho, Islw. TW7
off Summerwood Rd .144 C5
Eashing Pt, SW15
off Wanborough Dr ..165 H1
Easley's Ms, W1 ....16 C3
EAST ACTON, W3 .....126 D1
East Acton La, W3 ....106 E7
East Arbour St, E1 ...113 G6
East Av, E12 ....98 B7
E17 ....78 B4
Hayes UB3 ....121 J2
Southall UB1 ....103 F7
Wallington SM6 .....201 F5
East Bk, N16 ....76 B7
Eastbank Rd, Hmptn.
(Hmptn.H.) TW12 ..161 J5
EAST BARNET, Barn. ...41 H6
East Barnet Rd, Barn.
EN4 ....41 H6
Eastbourne Av, W3 ...106 D6
Eastbourne Gdns, SW14 .146 C3
Eastbourne Ms, W2 ....14 D3
Eastbourne Rd, E6 ....116 D3
E15 ....115 E1
N15 ....76 B6
SW17 ....168 A6
W4 ....126 C6
Brentford TW8 ......125 F5
Feltham TW13 ......160 D2
Eastbourne Ter, W2 ....14 D3
Eastbournia Av, N9 ....61 E3
Eastbrook Av, N9 ......45 F7
Dagenham RM10 ....101 J4
Eastbrook Rd, SE3 ....135 H7
Eastbury Av, Bark. IG11 .117 H1
Enfield EN1 ....44 B1
Eastbury Ct, Bark. IG11 .117 H1
Eastbury Gro, W4 ....127 E5
★ Eastbury Ho, Bark.
IG11 ....117 J1
Eastbury Ho, Bark. IG11 .117 J1
Eastbury Rd, E6 .....116 D4
Kingston upon Thames
KT2 ....163 H7
Orpington BR5 ......193 G6
Eastbury Sq, Bark. IG11 .117 J1
Eastbury Ter, E1 .....113 G4
Eastcastle St, W1 ......17 F3
Eastcheap, EC3 ....20 C5
East Churchfield Rd, W3 .126 D1
Eastchurch Rd, Houns.
(Hthrw.Air.)TW6 ....141 H2
East Cl, W5 ....106 A4
Barnet EN4 ....42 A4
Greenford UB6 ......103 J2
Eastcombe Av, SE7 ...135 H6
EASTCOTE, Pnr. 66 C6
Eastcote, Orp. BR6 ....207 J1
Eastcote Av, Grnf. UB6 ..86 D5
Harrow HA2 ....85 H2
West Molesey KT8 ...179 F5
Eastcote La, Har. HA2 ...85 G3
Northolt UB5 ....85 G7
Eastcote La N, Nthlt. UB5 .85 F6
Eastcote Pl, Pnr. HA5 ...66 B6

Eastcote Rd, Har. HA2 ..85 J3
Pinner HA5 ....66 D5
Pinner (Eastcote Vill.)
HA5 ....66 A6
Eastcote Rd, Well.
DA16 ....157 G2
Eastcote St, SW9 .....151 F2
Eastcote Vw, Pnr. HA5 ..66 C4
EASTCOTE VILLAGE, Pnr. .66 B5
Eastcourt, Sun. TW16 .178 C2
East Ct, Wem. HA0 ....87 F2
East Cres, N11 ....57 J4
Enfield EN1 ....44 C5
Eastcroft Rd, Epsom
KT19 ....197 E7
East Cross Cen, E15 ...96 A6
East Cross Route, E3 ...95 J7
E9 ....95 J6
East Duck Lees La, Enf.
EN3 ....45 H4
EAST DULWICH, SE22 .152 D6
East Dulwich Gro, SE22 .152 B6
East Dulwich Rd, SE15 .152 C4
SE22 ....152 C4
East End Rd, N2 ....73 F3
N3 ....72 D2
East End Way, Pnr. HA5 .67 E3
East Entrance, Dag.
RM10 ....119 H2
Eastern Av, E11 ....79 J6
Ilford IG2, IG4 ....80 B6
Pinner HA5 ....66 D7
Romford RM6 ....82 C4
Eastern Av W, Rom. RM1, RM5,
RM6, RM7 ....82 E4
Eastern Ind Est, Erith
DA18 ....139 G2
Eastern Perimeter Rd, Houns.
(Hthrw.Air.)TW6 ....141 J3
Eastern Rd, E13 .....115 H2
E17 ....78 C5
N2 ....73 J3
N22 ....75 E1
SE4 ....154 A4
Easternville Gdns, Ilf. IG2 .81 F6
Eastern Way, SE2 .....138 B1
SE28 ....138 A2
Belvedere DA17 .....139 H2
Erith DA18 ....138 D1
East Ferry Rd, E14 ...134 B3
Eastfield Cotts, Hayes
UB3 ....121 H5
Eastfield Gdns, Dag.
RM10 ....101 G4
Eastfield Rd, E17 ......78 A4
N8 ....74 E3
Dagenham RM9,
RM10 ....101 G4
Eastfields Rd, W3 ....106 C5
Mitcham CR4 ....186 A2
Eastfields, Pnr. HA5 ...66 C5
Eastfield St, E14 .....113 H5
EAST FINCHLEY, N2 ....73 G4
East Gdns, SW17 ....167 H6
Eastgate Cl, SE28 ....118 D6
Eastglade, Pnr. HA5 ...67 E3
EAST HAM, E6 ....116 B2
Eastham Cl, Barn. EN5 ..40 B5
East Ham Ind Est, E6 ..116 B4
East Ham Manor Way,
E6 ....116 D6
off Myrtle Rd 116 B1
East Harding St, EC4 ...19 F3
East Heath Rd, NW3 ...91 G3
East Hill, SW18 ......149 E5
Wembley HA9 ....88 A2
Eastholm, NW11 ....73 E4
East India Dock Rd, E14 .114 A6
Eastlake Rd, SE5 .....151 H2
Eastlands Cres, SE21 .152 C6
East La, SE16 ....29 H4
Kingston upon Thames KT1
off High St 181 G3
Wembley HA0, HA9 ...87 G3

East Mascalls, SE7
off Mascalls Rd 135 J2
East Mead, Ruis. HA4 ...84 D3
Eastmead Av, Grnf. UB6 .103 H3
Eastmead Cl, Brom.
BR1 ....192 B2
Eastmearn Rd, SE21 ..169 J2
EAST MOLESEY 180 A4
Eastmont Rd, Esher
KT10 ....194 B2
Eastmoor Pl, SE7
off Eastmoor St 136 A3
Eastmoor St, SE7 ....136 A3
East Mt St, E1 ....113 E5
Eastney Rd, Croy. CR0 .201 H1
Eastney St, SE10 ....134 D5
Eastnor Rd, SE9 .....175 F1
Easton Gdns, Borwd.
WD6 ....38 D4
Easton St, WC1 ....10 E4
East Pk Cl, Rom. RM6 ...82 D5
East Parkside, SE10 ..135 E2
East Pas, EC1 ....19 H1
East Pier, E1
off Wapping High
St 132/133 E1
East Pl, SE27
off Pilgrim Hill 169 J4
East Poultry Av, EC1 ...19 G2
East Ramp, Houns. (Hthrw.Air.)
TW6 ....140 E1
East Rd, E15 ....115 G1
N1 ....12 B4
SW19 ....167 F6
Barnet EN4 ....58 A1
Edgware HA8 ....70 B1
Feltham TW14 ......141 G7
Kingston upon Thames
KT2 ....181 H1
Romford (Chad.Hth.)
RM6 ....82 E5
Welling DA16 ....158 B2
West Drayton UB7 ...120 C4
East Rochester Way,
SE9 ....157 H4
Bexley DA5 ....159 J7
Sidcup DA15 ....157 H4
East Row, E11 ....79 G6
W10 ....108 B4
Eastry Av, Brom. BR2 .191 F6
Eastry Rd, Erith DA8 ..139 G7
EAST SHEEN, SW14 ..146 D4
East Sheen Av, SW14 .146 D4
Eastside Rd, NW11 ....72 C4
East Smithfield, E1 ....21 G6
East St, SE17 ....36 A3
Barking IG11 ....99 F7
Bexleyheath DA7 ...159 G4
Brentford TW8 ......125 F7
Bromley BR1 ....191 G2
East Surrey Gro, SE15 .132 C7
East Tenter St, E1 .....21 G4
East Twrs, Pnr. HA5 ...66 D5
East Vw, E4 ....62 C5
Barnet EN5 ....40 C3
Eastview Av, SE18 ...137 H7
Eastville Av, NW11 ....72 C6
East Wk, Barn. EN4 ....42 A7
Hayes UB3 ....122 A1
Eastway, E9 ....95 J6
East Way, E11 ....79 H5
Bromley BR2 ....191 G7
Croydon CR0 ......203 H2
Hayes UB3 ....122 A1
Eastway, Mord. SM4 ..184 A5
East Way, Ruis. HA4 ...84 A1
Eastway, Wall. SM6 ..200 C4
Eastway Commercial Cen,
E9 ....96 A5
Eastwell Cl, Beck. BR3 .189 H1
Eastwick Ct, SW19
off Victoria Dr 166 A1
EAST WICKHAM, Well. .138 A7
Eastwood Cl, E18
off George La 79 G2
N7 off Eden Gro 93 G5
N17
off Northumberland
Gro 60/61 E7
Eastwood Rd, E18 .....79 G2
N10 ....74 A2
Ilford IG3 ....82 A7
West Drayton UB7 ...120 D2
East Woodside, Bex.
DA5 ....177 E1
Eastwood St, SW16 ..168 C6
Eatington Rd, E10 .....78 D5
Eaton Cl, SW1 ....32 B2
Stanmore HA7 ....53 E4
Eaton Dr, SW9 ......151 H4

Eaton Dr, Kings.T.
  KT2 . . . . .164 A7
Eaton Gdns, Dag. RM9 . .100 E7
Eaton Gate, SW1 . . . . .32 B1
Eaton Ho, E14
  off Westferry Circ 134 A1
Eaton La, SW1 . . . . .24 E6
Eaton Ms N, SW1 . . . . . . .32 B1
Eaton Ms S, SW1 . . . . . . .32 C1
Eaton Ms W, SW1 . . . . . . .32 C1
Eaton Pk Rd, N13 . . . . . . .59 G2
Eaton Pl, SW1 . . . . .24 B6
Eaton Ri, E11 . . . . .79 J5
  W5 . . . . .105 G6
Eaton Rd, NW4 . . . . .71 J5
  Enfield EN1 . . . . .44 B3
  Hounslow TW3 . . . . . . .144 A4
  Sidcup DA14 . . . . .176 D2
  Sutton SM2 . . . . .199 G6
Eaton Row, SW1 . . . . .24 D6
Eatons Mead, E4 . . . . .62 A2
Eaton Sq, SW1 . . . . .24 D5
Eaton Ter, SW1 . . . . .32 B1
Eaton Ter Ms, SW1 . . . . . .32 B1
Eatonville Rd, SW17 . . . . .167 J2
Eatonville Vil, SW17
  off Eatonville Rd 167 J2
Ebbisham Dr, SW8 . . . . . . .34 C5
Ebbisham Rd, Wor.Pk.
  KT4 . . . . .197 J2
Ebbsfleet Rd, NW2 . . . . . . .90 B4
Ebdon Way, SE3 . . . . .155 H3
Ebenezer Ho, SE11 . . . . . . .35 F2
Ebenezer St, N1 . . . . .12 B3
Ebenezer Wk, SW16 . . . . .186 C1
Ebley Cl, SE15 . . . . .37 F6
Ebner St, SW18 . . . . .149 E5
Ebor St, E1 . . . . .13 F5
Ebrington Rd, Har. HA3 . . .69 G6
Ebsworth St, SE23 . . . . . .153 G7
Eburne Rd, N7 . . . . .93 E3
Ebury Br, SW1 . . . . .32 D3
Ebury Br Est, SW1 . . . . . . .32 D3
Ebury Br Rd, SW1 . . . . . . .32 C4
Ebury Cl, Kes. BR2 . . . . . .206 B3
Ebury Ms, SE27 . . . . .169 H3
  SW1 . . . . .32 C1
Ebury Ms E, SW1 . . . . .32 D1
Ebury Sq, SW1 . . . . .32 C2
Ebury St, SW1 . . . . .32 D1
Ecclesbourne Cl, N13 . . . . .59 G5
Ecclesbourne Gdns, N13 . .59 G5
Ecclesbourne Rd, N1 . . . . .93 J7
  Thornton Heath CR7 . . .187 J5
Eccles Rd, SW11 . . . . .149 J4
Eccleston Br, SW1 . . . . . . .32 E1
Eccleston Cl, Barn. EN4 . . .41 J4
  Orpington BR6 . . . . . . .207 G1
Eccleston Cres, Rom.
  RM6 . . . . .82 A7
Ecclestone Ct, Wem. HA9
  off St. John's Rd 87 H5
Ecclestone Pl, Wem. HA9 . .87 J5
Eccleston Ms, SW1 . . . . . . .24 C6
Eccleston Pl, SW1 . . . . .32 D1
Eccleston Rd, W13 . . . . . . .104 D7
Eccleston Sq, SW1 . . . . . . .32 E2
Eccleston Sq Ms, SW1 . . . .33 F2
Eccleston St, SW1 . . . . . . .24 D6
Echo Hts, E4
  off Mount Echo Dr 62 B1
Eckersley St, E1
  off Buxton St 112 D4
Eckford St, N1 . . . . .10 E1
Eckington Ho, N15
  off Fladbury Rd 76 A6
Eckstein Rd, SW11 . . . . . .149 H4
Eclipse Rd, E13 . . . . .115 H5
Ector Rd, SE6 . . . . .172 E2
Edbrooke Rd, W9 . . . . .108 D4
Eddiscombe Rd, SW6 . . . .148 C2
Eddy Cl, Rom. RM7 . . . . . .83 H6
Eddystone Rd, SE4 . . . . . .153 H5
Eddystone Twr, SE8 . . . . .133 H4
Eddystone Wk, Stai.
  TW19 . . . . .140 B7
Ede Cl, Houns. TW3 . . . . .143 F3
Edenbridge Cl, SE16
  off Masters Dr . . .132/133 E5
Edenbridge Rd, E9 . . . . . . .95 G7
  Enfield EN1 . . . . .44 B6
Eden Cl, NW3 . . . . .90 D2
  W8
  off Adam & Eve Ms . .128 D3
  Wembley HA0 . . . . . . .105 G1
Edencourt Rd, SW16 . . . . .168 B6
Edenfield Gdns, Wor.Pk.
  KT4 . . . . .197 F3
Eden Gro, E17 . . . . .78 B5
  N7 . . . . .93 F5

Edenham Way, W10
  off Elkstone Rd 108 C5
Edenhurst Av, SW6 . . . . . .148 C3
Eden Ms, SW17
  off Huntspill St 167 F3
EDEN PARK, Beck. 190 A5
Eden Pk Av, Beck. BR3 . . .189 H4
Eden Rd, E17 . . . . .78 B5
  SE27 . . . . .169 H5
  Beckenham BR3 . . . . . .189 H4
  Bexley DA5 . . . . .177 J4
  Croydon CR0 . . . . .202 A4
Edensor Gdns, W4 . . . . . . .127 E7
Edensor Rd, W4 . . . . .126 E7
Eden St, Kings.T. KT1 . . . .181 G2
Edenvale Cl, Mitch. CR4
  off Edenvale Rd 168 A7
Edenvale Rd, Mitch. CR4 .168 A7
Edenvale St, SW6 . . . . . . .149 E2
Eden Wk, Kings.T. KT1
  off Eden St 181 H2
Eden Wk Shop Cen, Kings.T.
  KT1 . . . . .181 H2
Eden Way, Beck. BR3 . . . .189 J5
Ederline Av, SW16 . . . . . .187 F3
Edgar Kail Way, SE22 . . . .152 B4
Edgarley Ter, SW6 . . . . . .148 B1
Edgar Rd, E3 . . . . .114 B3
  Hounslow TW4 . . . . . . .143 F7
  Romford RM6 . . . . .82 D7
Edgbaston Rd, Wat.
  WD19 . . . . .50 B3
Edgeborough Way, Brom.
  BR1 . . . . .174 A7
Edgebury, Chis. BR7 . . . . .175 E4
Edgebury Wk, Chis. BR7 . .175 F4
Edgecombe Ho, SW19 . . . .166 B1
Edgecombe, S.Croy.
  CR2 . . . . .203 F7
Edgecoombe Cl, Kings.T.
  KT2 . . . . .164 D7
Edgecote Cl, W3
  off Cheltenham Pl 126 C1
Edgecot Gro, N15
  off Oulton Rd 76 A5
Edgefield Av, Bark. IG11 . .99 J7
Edge Hill, SE18 . . . . .136 E6
  SW19 . . . . .166 A7
Edge Hill Av, N3 . . . . .72 D3
Edge Hill Ct, SW19 . . . . . .166 A7
Edgehill Gdns, Dag.
  RM10 . . . . .101 G4
Edgehill Rd, W13 . . . . .105 F5
  Chislehurst BR7 . . . . . .175 F3
  Mitcham CR4 . . . . .186 B1
Edgeley La, SW4
  off Edgeley Rd 150 D3
Edgeley Rd, SW4 . . . . .150 D3
Edgel St, SW18
  off Ferrier St 148/149 E4
Edgepoint Cl, SE27
  off Knights Hill 169 H5
Edge St, W8
  off Kensington Ch St . .128 D1
Edgewood Dr, Orp. BR6 . .207 J5
Edgewood Grn, Croy.
  CR0 . . . . .203 G1
Edgeworth Av, NW4 . . . . . .71 G5
Edgeworth Cl, NW4 . . . . . .71 G5
Edgeworth Cres, NW4 . . . .71 G5
Edgeworth Rd, SE9 . . . . . .155 J4
  Barnet EN4 . . . . .41 H4
Edgington Rd, SW16 . . . . .168 D6
Edgington Way, Sid. 176 C7
EDGWARE 54 B5
Edgwarebury Gdns, Edg.
  HA8 . . . . .54 A5
Edgwarebury La, Edg.
  HA8 . . . . .54 A4
Edgware Ct, Edg. HA8
  off Cavendish Dr 54 A6
Edgware Rd, NW2 . . . . . . .89 H1
  NW9 . . . . .70 D3
  W2 . . . . .15 H3
Edgware Rd Subway, W2
  off Edgware Rd 109 H5
Edgware Way, Edg. HA8 . .53 J4
Edinburgh Cl, E2
  off Russia La 113 F2
  Pinner HA5 . . . . .66 D7
Edinburgh Ct, SW20 . . . . .184 A5
Edinburgh Dr, Rom. RM7
  off Eastern Av W 83 J4
Edinburgh Gate, SW1 . . . .23 J3
Edinburgh Ho, W9 . . . . . . .6 B3
Edinburgh Rd, E13 . . . . . .115 H2
  E17 . . . . .78 A5
  N18 . . . . .60 D5
  W7 . . . . .124 C2

Edinburgh Rd, Sutt.
  SM1 . . . . .199 F2
Edington Rd, SE2 . . . . . . .138 B3
  Enfield EN3 . . . . .45 F2
Edison Cl, E17
  off Exeter Rd 78 A5
Edison Ct, SE10
  off Greenroof Way 135 F3
Edison Dr, Sthl. UB1 . . . . .103 H6
  Wembley HA9 . . . . .87 H2
Edison Gro, SE18 . . . . . . .137 J7
Edison Rd, N8 . . . . .74 D6
  Bromley BR2 . . . . .191 G2
  Enfield EN3 . . . . .45 J2
  Welling DA16 . . . . .157 J1
Edis St, NW1 . . . . .110 A1
Edith Cavell Cl, N19
  off Hornsey Ri Gdns . .74 D7
Edith Gdns, Surb. KT5 . . .182 B7
Edith Gro, SW10 . . . . .30 C6
Edithna St, SW9 . . . . .151 E3
Edith Rd, E6 . . . . .98 A7
  E15 off Chandos Rd 96 D5
  N11 . . . . .58 D7
  SE25 . . . . .188 A5
  SW19 . . . . .167 E6
  W14 . . . . .128 B4
  Romford RM6 . . . . .82 D6
Edith Row, SW6 . . . . .149 E1
Edith St, E2 . . . . .13 H1
Edith Summerskill Ho, SW6
  off Clem Attlee Ct 128 C7
Edith Ter, SW10 . . . . .30 C7
Edith Vil, SW15
  off Bective Rd 148 B4
  W14 . . . . .128 C4
Edith Yd, SW10 . . . . .30 D7
Edmansons Cl, N17
  off Bruce Gro 76 B1
Edmeston Cl, E9 . . . . .95 H6
Edmond Halley Way,
  SE10 . . . . .134 E2
Edmonds Ct, W.Mol. KT8
  off Avern Rd 179 H4
EDMONTON, N9 . . . . .60 D4
Edmonton Grn, N9
  off Hertford Rd 60/61 E2
Edmund Gro, Felt. TW13 .161 F2
Edmund Hurst Dr, E6 . . . .116 E5
Edmund Rd, Mitch. CR4 . .185 H3
  Welling DA16 . . . . .158 A3
Edmunds Cl, Hayes UB4 .102 C5
Edmund St, SE5 . . . . .36 B7
Edmunds Wk, N2 . . . . .73 H4
Edna Rd, SW20 . . . . .184 A2
Edna St, SW11 . . . . .149 H1
Edrich Ho, SW4 . . . . .150 E1
Edrick Rd, Edg. HA8 . . . . .54 C6
Edrick Wk, Edg. HA8 . . . . .54 C6
Edric Rd, SE14 . . . . .133 G7
Edridge Rd, Croy. CR0 . . .201 J3
Edulf Rd, Borwd. WD6 . . .38 B1
Edward Av, E4 . . . . .62 B6
  Morden SM4 . . . . .185 G5
Edward Cl, N9 . . . . .44 C7
  NW2 . . . . .90 A4
  Hampton (Hmptn.H.) TW12
  off Edward Rd 161 J5
  Northolt UB5 . . . . .102 C2
Edward Ct, E16
  off Alexandra St 115 G5
Edwardes Pl, W8
  off Edwardes Sq 128 C3
Edwardes Sq, W8 . . . . . . .128 D3
Edward Gro, Barn. EN4 . .41 G5
Edward Ms, NW1 . . . . .8 E2
Edward Pl, SE8 . . . . .133 J6
Edward Rd, E17 . . . . .77 G4
  SE20 . . . . .171 G7
  Barnet EN4 . . . . .41 G5
  Bromley BR1 . . . . .173 H7
  Chislehurst BR7 . . . . . .175 E5
  Croydon CR0 . . . . .188 B7
  Feltham TW14 . . . . . . .141 G6
  Hampton (Hmptn.H.)
  TW12 . . . . .161 J5
  Harrow HA2 . . . . .67 J3
  Northolt UB5 . . . . .102 C2
  Romford RM6 . . . . .82 E6
Edward's Av, Ruis.
  HA4 . . . . .84 B6
Edwards Cl, Wor.Pk.
  KT4 . . . . .198 A2
Edwards Cotts, N1
  off Compton Av 93 H6
Edwards Dr, N11
  off Gordon Rd 58 D7
Edwards La, N16 . . . . .94 A2
Edwards Ms, N1 . . . . .93 G7
  W1 . . . . .16 B4

Edward Sq, N1
  off Caledonian Rd 111 F1
  SE16
  off Rotherhithe St . . .133 H1
Edwards Rd, Belv. DA17 .139 G4
Edward St, E16 . . . . .115 G4
  SE8 . . . . .133 J6
  SE14 . . . . .133 H7
Edwards Yd, Wem. HA0
  off Mount Pleasant . . .105 H1
Edward Temme Av, E15 . .97 F7
Edward Tyler Rd, SE12 . .173 H2
Edwina Gdns, Ilf. IG4 . . . .80 B5
Edwin Av, E6 . . . . .116 D2
Edwin Cl, Bexh. DA7 . . . . .139 F6
Edwin Pl, Croy. CR0
  off Cross Rd 202 A1
Edwin Rd, Edg. HA8 . . . . .54 D6
  Twickenham TW1,
  TW2 . . . . .162 C1
Edwin's Mead, E9
  off Lindisfarne Way . . .95 H4
Edwin St, E1 . . . . .113 F4
  E16 . . . . .115 G5
Edwyn Cl, Barn. EN5 . . . . .39 J6
Eel Brook Studios, SW6
  off Moore Pk Rd 128 D7
Eel Pie Island, Twick.
  TW1 . . . . .162 E1
Effie Pl, SW6 . . . . .128 D7
Effie Rd, SW6 . . . . .128 D7
Effingham Cl, Sutt. SM2 .199 E7
Effingham Rd, N8 . . . . .75 G5
  SE12 . . . . .155 E5
  Croydon CR0 . . . . .187 F7
  Surbiton KT6 . . . . .181 E7
Effort St, SW17 . . . . .167 H5
Effra Par, SW2 . . . . .151 G5
Effra Rd, SW2 . . . . .151 G4
  SW19 . . . . .166 E6
Egbert St, NW1 . . . . .110 A1
Egbury Ho, SW15
  off Tangley Gro 147 F6
Egerton Cl, Pnr. HA5 . . . . .66 A4
Egerton Cres, SW3 . . . . . .31 H1
Egerton Dr, SE10 . . . . . . .154 B1
Egerton Gdns, NW4 . . . . . .71 H4
  NW10 . . . . .107 J1
  SW3 . . . . .23 G6
  W13 . . . . .105 E6
  Ilford IG3 . . . . .99 J3
Egerton Gdns Ms, SW3 . .23 H6
Egerton Pl, SW3 . . . . .23 H6
Egerton Rd, N16 . . . . .76 C7
  SE25 . . . . .188 B3
  New Malden KT3 . . . . .183 F4
  Twickenham TW2 . . . . .144 B7
  Wembley HA0 . . . . .87 J7
Egerton Ter, SW3 . . . . .23 H6
Egerton Way, Hayes
  UB3 . . . . .121 E7
Eggardon Ct, Nthlt. UB5
  off Lancaster Rd 85 J6
Egham Cl, SW19
  off Winterfold Cl 166 B2
  Sutton SM3 . . . . .198 B2
Egham Cres, Sutt. SM3 . .198 A3
Egham Rd, E13 . . . . .115 H5
Eglantine Rd, SW18 . . . . .149 F5
Egleston Rd, Mord.
  SM4 . . . . .184 E6
Eglington Ct, SE17 . . . . . .35 J5
Eglington Rd, E4 . . . . .46 D7
Eglinton Hill, SE18 . . . . . .137 E6
Eglinton Rd, SE18 . . . . . . .136 D6
Egliston Ms, SW15 . . . . . .147 J3
Egliston Rd, SW15 . . . . . .147 J3
Eglon Ms, NW1
  off Berkley Rd 91 J7
Egmont Av, Surb. KT6 . . .195 J1
Egmont Rd, N.Mal. KT3 . .183 F4
  Surbiton KT6 . . . . .195 J1
  Sutton SM2 . . . . .199 F7
  Walton-on-Thames
  KT12 . . . . .178 B7
Egmont St, SE14 . . . . .133 G7
Egremont Ho, SE13
  off Conington Rd 154 B2
Egremont Rd, SE27 . . . . .169 G3
Egret Way, Hayes UB4 . . .102 D5
Eider Cl, E7 . . . . .97 F5
  Hayes UB4
  off Cygnet Way 102 D5
Eighteenth Rd, Mitch.
  CR4 . . . . .186 E4
Eighth Av, E12 . . . . .98 C4
  Hayes UB3 . . . . .122 A1
Eileen Rd, SE25 . . . . .188 A5
Eindhoven Cl, Cars.
  SM5 . . . . .200 A1

Eisenhower Dr, E6 . . . . .**116** B5
Elaine Gro, NW5 . . . .**92** A5
Elam Cl, SE5 . . . .**151** H2
Elam St, SE5 . . . .**151** H2
Eland Pl, Croy. CR0
  off Eland Rd **201** H3
Eland Rd, SW11 . . . .**149** G3
  Croydon CR0 . . . .**201** H3
Elba Pl, SE17 . . . .**36** A1
Elberon Av, Croy. CR0 . .**186** C6
Elbe St, SW6 . . . .**149** F2
Elborough Rd, SE25 . . . .**188** D5
Elborough St, SW18 . . . .**166** D1
Elbury Dr, E16 . . . .**115** G6
Elcho St, SW11 . . . .**129** H7
Elcot Av, SE15 . . . .**132** E7
Elder Av, N8 . . . .**74** E5
  off Linton Gro **169** J5
Elderberry Rd, W5 . . . . .**125** H2
Elder Cl, N20 . . . .**56** E2
  Sidcup DA15 . . . .**175** J1
Elder Rd, Bushey (Bushey Hth.)
  WD23 . . . .**52** B2
Elderfield Pl, SW17 . . . .**168** B4
Elderfield Rd, E5 . . . .**95** F4
Elderfield Wk, E11 . . . . . .**79** H5
Elderflower Way, E15 . . . .**96** E7
Elder Gdns, SE27
  off Gladstone Ter **169** J4
Elder Oak Cl, SE20 . . . . .**188** E1
Elder Rd, SE27 . . . .**169** J5
Elderslie Cl, Beck. BR3 . .**190** B5
Elderslie Rd, SE9 . . . . . .**156** D5
Elder St, E1 . . . .**21** F1
Elderton Rd, SE26 . . . . . .**171** H4
Eldertree Pl, Mitch. CR4
  off Eldertree Way . . .**186** C1
Eldertree Way, Mitch.
  CR4 . . . .**186** B1
Elder Wk, N1
  off Essex Rd **111** H1
Elderwood Pl, SE27
  off Elder Rd **169** J5
Eldon Av, Borwd. WD6 . . .**38** A2
  Croydon CR0 . . . .**203** F2
  Hounslow TW5 . . . . . .**123** G7
Eldon Gro, NW3 . . . .**91** G5
Eldon Pk, SE25 . . . .**188** E4
Eldon Rd, E17 . . . .**77** J4
  N9 . . . .**61** F2
  N22 . . . .**75** H1
  W8 . . . .**22** B6
Eldon St, EC2 . . . .**20** C2
Eldon Way, NW10 . . . . . .**106** B2
Eldred Rd, Bark. IG11 . . .**117** H1
Eldridge Cl, Felt. TW14 . .**160** A1
Eleanor Cl, N15
  off Arnold Rd **76** C3
  SE16 . . . .**133** G2
Eleanor Cres, NW7 . . . . . .**56** A4
Eleanor Gdns, Barn. EN5 .**40** A5
  Dagenham RM8 . . . . .**101** F3
Eleanor Gro, SW13 . . . . .**147** E3
Eleanor Rd, E8 . . . .**94** E7
  E15 . . . .**97** F6
  N11 . . . .**58** E6
Eleanor St, E3 . . . .**114** A3
Eleanor Wk, SE18
  off Samuel St **136** C4
Electric Av, SW9 . . . .**151** G4
Electric La, SW9 . . . .**151** G4
Electric Par, E18
  off George La **79** G2
  Surbiton KT6 . . . .**181** G6
Elephant & Castle, SE1 . . .**27** H6
Elephant & Castle Shop Cen,
  SE1 *off Elephant &*
  Castle **131** J4
Elephant La, SE16 . . . . . .**133** F2
Elephant Rd, SE17 . . . . . .**35** J1
Elers Rd, W13 . . . .**125** F2
  Hayes UB3 . . . .**121** G4
Eleven Acre Ri, Loug.
  IG10 . . . .**48** C3
Eley Est, N18 . . . .**61** F5
Eley Rd, N18 . . . .**61** G5
Elfindale Rd, SE24 . . . . .**151** J5
Elfin Gro, Tedd. TW11
  off Broad St **162** C5
Elford Cl, SE3 . . . .**155** H4
Elfort Rd, N5 . . . .**93** G4
Elfrida Cres, SE6 . . . .**172** A4
Elf Row, E1 . . . .**113** F7
Elfwine Rd, W7 . . . .**104** B5
Elgal Cl, Orp. BR6
  off Orchard Rd . .**206/207** E5
Elgar Av, NW10
  off Mitchellbrook Way .**88** D6
  SW16 . . . .**186** E3

Elgar Av, W5 . . . .**125** H2
  Surbiton KT5 . . . .**182** B7
Elgar Cl, E13
  off Bushey Rd **115** J2
Elgar Cl, SE8
  off Comet St **134** A7
  Buckhurst Hill IG9 . . . . .**64** A2
Elgar St, SE16 . . . .**133** H3
Elgin Av, W9 . . . .**6** A4
  Harrow HA3 . . . .**68** E2
Elgin Cres, W11 . . . .**108** C6
  Hounslow (Hthrw.Air.) TW6
  off Eastern Perimeter
  Rd **141** J2
Elgin Ms, W11
  off Ladbroke Gro **108** B6
Elgin Ms N, W9 . . . .**6** B3
Elgin Ms S, W9 . . . .**6** B3
Elgin Rd, N22 . . . .**74** C2
  Croydon CR0 . . . .**202** C1
  Ilford IG3 . . . .**99** H1
  Sutton SM1 . . . .**199** F3
  Wallington SM6 . . . . . .**200** C6
Elgood Av, Nthwd. HA6 . . .**50** A6
Elgood Cl, W11
  off Avondale Pk Rd . .**108** B7
Elham Cl, Brom. BR1 . . . .**174** A7
Elia Ms, N1 . . . .**11** G2
Elia St, N1 . . . .**11** G2
Elibank Rd, SE9 . . . .**156** D4
Elim Est, SE1 . . . .**28** D5
Elim St, SE1 . . . .**28** D5
Eliot Bk, SE23 . . . .**170** E2
Eliot Cotts, SE3
  off Eliot Pl **154/155** E2
Eliot Ct, N15
  off Tynemouth Rd **76** C4
Eliot Dr, Har. HA2 . . . .**85** H2
Eliot Gdns, SW15 . . . . . .**147** G4
Eliot Hill, SE13 . . . .**154** C2
Eliot Ms, NW8 . . . .**6** D2
Eliot Pk, SE13 . . . .**154** C3
Eliot Pl, SE3 . . . .**154** E2
Eliot Rd, Dag. RM9 . . . . .**100** D4
Eliot Vale, SE3 . . . .**154** D2
Elizabethan Cl, Stai. (Stanw.)
  TW19 *off Elizabethan*
  Way **140** A7
Elizabethan Way, Stai. (Stanw.)
  TW19 . . . .**140** A7
Elizabeth Av, N1 . . . .**93** J7
  Enfield EN2 . . . .**43** H3
  Ilford IG1 . . . .**99** G2
Elizabeth Blackwell Ho, N22
  off Progress Way **75** G1
Elizabeth Br, SW1 . . . .**32** D2
Elizabeth Cl, E14
  off Grundy St **114** B6
  W9 . . . .**6** D6
  Barnet EN5 . . . .**40** A3
  Romford RM7 . . . .**83** H1
  Sutton SM1 . . . .**198** C4
Elizabeth Clyde Cl, N15 . .**76** B4
Elizabeth Cotts, Rich.
  TW9 . . . .**145** J1
Elizabeth Ct, SW1 . . . .**25** J6
  Woodford Green IG8
  off Navestock Cres . . .**63** J7
Elizabeth Est, SE17 . . . . . .**36** B5
Elizabeth Fry Cl, SE18 . .**156** B3
Elizabeth Fry Rd, E8
  off Lamb La **94/95** E7
Elizabeth Gdns, W3 . . . .**127** F1
  Stanmore HA7 . . . .**53** F6
  Sunbury-on-Thames
  TW16 . . . .**178** C3
Elizabeth Ms, NW3 . . . . . .**91** H6
Elizabeth Pl, N15 . . . .**76** A4
Elizabeth Ride, N9 . . . .**45** E7
Elizabeth Rd, E6 . . . .**116** A1
  N15 . . . .**76** B5
Elizabeth Sq, SE16
  off Rotherhithe St . . .**113** H7
Elizabeth St, SW1 . . . .**32** C1
Elizabeth Ter, SE9 . . . . . .**156** C6
Elizabeth Way, SE19 . . . .**170** A7
  Feltham TW13 . . . .**160** C4
Elkanette Ms, N20
  off Ridgeview Rd **57** F2
Elkington Rd, E13 . . . . . .**115** H4
Elkstone Rd, W10 . . . . . .**108** C5
Ellaline Rd, W6 . . . .**128** A6
Ellanby Cres, N18 . . . .**60** E5
Elland Rd, SE15 . . . .**153** F4
Ella Rd, N8 . . . .**75** E7
Ellement Cl, Pnr. HA5 . . . .**66** D5
Ellenborough Pl, SW15 . .**147** G4
Ellenborough Rd, N22 . . . .**75** J1
  Sidcup DA14 . . . .**176** D5

Ellen Cl, Brom. BR1 . . . . .**192** A3
Ellen Ct, N9
  off Densworth Gro **61** F2
Ellen St, E1 . . . .**21** J4
Ellen Webb Dr, Har. (Wldste.)
  HA3 . . . .**68** B3
Elleray Rd, Tedd. TW11 . .**162** C6
Ellerby St, SW6 . . . .**148** A1
Ellerdale Cl, NW3
  off Ellerdale Rd **91** F4
Ellerdale Rd, NW3 . . . .**91** F5
Ellerdale St, SE13 . . . . . .**154** B4
Ellerdine Rd, Houns.
  TW3 . . . .**143** J4
Ellerker Gdns, Rich.
  TW10 . . . .**145** H6
Ellerman Av, Twick. TW2 .**161** F1
Ellerslie Gdns, NW10 . . .**107** G1
Ellerslie Rd, W12 . . . .**127** H1
Ellerslie Sq Ind Est,
  SW2 . . . .**150** E5
Ellerton Gdns, Dag.
  RM9 . . . .**100** C7
Ellerton Rd, SW13 . . . . . .**147** G1
  SW18 . . . .**167** G1
  SW20 . . . .**165** G7
  Dagenham RM9 . . . . .**100** C7
  Surbiton KT6 . . . .**195** J2
Ellery Rd, SE19 . . . .**170** A7
Ellery St, SE15 . . . .**152** E2
Ellesborough Cl, Wat.
  WD19 . . . .**50** C5
Ellesmere Av, NW7 . . . . . .**54** D3
  Beckenham BR3 . . . . .**190** B2
Ellesmere Cl, E11 . . . .**79** F5
Ellesmere Gdns, Ilf. IG4 . .**80** B5
Ellesmere Gro, Barn.
  EN5 . . . .**40** C5
Ellesmere Rd, E3 . . . .**113** H2
  NW10 . . . .**89** G5
  W4 . . . .**126** D6
  Greenford UB6 . . . . . .**103** J4
  Twickenham TW1 . . . .**145** F6
Ellesmere St, E14 . . . . . .**114** B6
Ellingfort Rd, E8 . . . .**95** E7
Ellingham Rd, E15 . . . .**96** D4
  W12 . . . .**127** G2
  Chessington KT9 . . . . .**195** G6
Ellington Rd, N10 . . . .**74** B4
  Hounslow TW3 . . . . . .**143** H2
  Feltham TW13 . . . .**160** D4
Ellington St, N7 . . . .**93** G6
Elliot Cl, E15 . . . .**96** E7
Elliot Rd, NW4 . . . .**71** H6
  Stanmore HA7 . . . .**52** D6
Elliott Av, Ruis. HA4 . . . . .**84** B2
Elliott Cl, Wem. HA9 . . . . .**87** J3
Elliott Rd, SW9 . . . .**131** H7
  W4 . . . .**126** E4
  Bromley BR2 . . . .**192** A4
  Thornton Heath CR7 . .**187** H4
Elliott's Pl, N1
  off St. Peters St **111** H1
Elliott Sq, NW3 . . . .**91** H7
Elliotts Row, SE11 . . . .**35** G1
Ellis Cl, NW10
  off High Rd **89** H6
  SE9 . . . .**175** F2
Elliscombe Rd, SE7 . . . . .**135** J5
Ellis Ct, W7 . . . .**104** C5
Ellisfield Dr, SW15 . . . . . .**147** F7
Ellis Ms, SE7 . . . .**135** J6
Ellison Gdns, Sthl. UB2 . .**123** F4
Ellison Ho, SE13
  off Lewisham Rd **154** C2
Ellison Rd, SW13 . . . .**147** F2
  SW16 . . . .**168** D7
  Sidcup DA15 . . . .**175** G1
Ellis Rd, Mitch. CR4 . . . . .**185** J6
  Southall UB2 . . . .**123** J1
Ellis St, SW1 . . . .**32** A1
Elliston Ho, SE18 . . . .**136** D4
Ellora Rd, SW16 . . . .**168** D5
Ellsworth St, E2 . . . .**113** E3
Ellwood Ct, W9 . . . .**6** A6
Elmar Rd, N15 . . . .**76** A4
Elm Av, W5 . . . .**125** H1
  Ruislip HA4 . . . .**84** A1
Elmbank, N14 . . . .**43** E7
Elm Bk, Brom. BR1 . . . . .**192** A1
Elmbank Av, Barn. EN5 . . .**39** J4
Elm Bk Gdns, SW13 . . . .**147** E2
Elmbank Way, W7 . . . . . .**104** A5
Elmbourne Dr, Belv.
  DA17 . . . .**139** H4
Elmbourne Rd, SW17 . . .**168** A3
Elmbridge Av, Surb. KT5 .**182** B5
Elmbridge Cl, Ruis. HA4 . .**66** A6
Elmbridge Wk, E8
  off Wilman Gro **94** D7
Elmbrook Cl, Sun. TW16 .**178** B1

Elmbrook Gdns, SE9 . . . .**156** B4
Elmbrook Rd, Sutt. SM1 .**198** C4
Elm Cl, E11 . . . .**79** H6
  N19 *off Hargrave Pk* . .**92** C2
Elm Cl, NW4 . . . .**72** A5
  SW20 *off Grand Dr* . .**183** J4
  Buckhurst Hill IG9 . . . . .**64** A2
  Carshalton SM5 . . . . . .**199** J1
  Harrow HA2 . . . .**67** H6
  Hayes UB3 . . . .**102** A6
  Romford RM7 . . . .**83** H2
  South Croydon CR2 . .**202** B6
  Surbiton KT5 . . . .**182** C7
  Twickenham TW2 . . . .**161** H2
Elm Ct, EC4 . . . .**19** E5
  Mitcham CR4
  off Armfield Cres **185** J2
Elmcourt Rd, SE27 . . . . .**169** H2
Elm Cres, W5 . . . .**125** H1
  Kingston upon Thames
  KT2 . . . .**181** H1
Elmcroft, N8 . . . .**75** F5
Elmcroft Av, E11 . . . .**79** H5
  N9 . . . .**44** E6
  NW11 . . . .**72** C7
  Sidcup DA15 . . . .**157** J6
Elmcroft Cl, E11 . . . .**79** H4
  W5 . . . .**105** G6
  Chessington KT9 . . . . .**195** H3
  Feltham TW14 . . . .**141** J6
Elmcroft Cres, NW11 . . . .**72** B7
  Harrow HA2 . . . .**67** G3
Elmcroft Dr, Chess.
  KT9 . . . .**195** H3
Elmcroft Gdns, NW9 . . . . .**70** A5
Elmcroft St, E5 . . . .**95** F4
Elmdale Rd, N13 . . . .**59** F5
Elmdene, Surb. KT5 . . . . .**196** C1
Elmdene Cl, Beck. BR3 . .**189** J5
Elmdene Rd, SE18 . . . . . .**136** E5
Elmdon Rd, Houns. TW4 .**142** D2
  Hounslow (Hatt.Cr.)
  TW6 . . . .**141** J3
Elm Dr, Har. HA2 . . . .**67** H6
  Sunbury-on-Thames
  TW16 . . . .**178** C2
Elmer Cl, Enf. EN2 . . . .**43** F3
Elmer Gdns, Edg. HA8 . . .**54** B7
  Isleworth TW7 . . . .**144** A3
Elmer Rd, SE6 . . . .**154** C7
Elmers Dr, Tedd. TW11
  off Kingston Rd . .**162/163** E6
ELMERS END, Beck. **189** H3
Elmers End Rd, SE20 . . .**189** F1
  Beckenham BR3 . . . . .**189** F2
Elmerside Rd, Beck. BR3 .**189** H4
Elmers Rd, SE25 . . . .**188** D7
Elmfield Av, N8 . . . .**74** E5
  Mitcham CR4 . . . .**186** A1
  Teddington TW11 . . . .**162** C5
Elmfield Cl, Har. HA1 . . . . .**86** B2
Elmfield Pk, Brom. BR1 . .**191** G3
Elmfield Rd, E4 . . . .**62** C2
  E17 . . . .**77** G6
  N2 . . . .**73** G3
  SW17 . . . .**168** A2
  Bromley BR1 . . . .**191** G3
  Southall UB2 . . . .**123** E3
Elmfield Way, W9 . . . . . .**108** D5
Elm Friars Wk, NW1 . . . . .**92** D7
Elm Gdns, N2 . . . .**73** F3
  Esher (Clay.) KT10 . . .**194** C6
  Mitcham CR4 . . . .**186** D4
Elmgate Av, Felt. TW13 . .**160** B3
Elmgate Gdns, Edg. HA8 .**54** D5
Elm Grn, W3 . . . .**106** E6
Elmgreen Cl, E15
  off Church St N . .**114/115** E1
Elm Gro, N8 . . . .**75** E6
  NW2 . . . .**90** A4
  SE15 . . . .**152** C2
  SW19 . . . .**166** B7
  Harrow HA2 . . . .**67** G7
  Kingston upon Thames
  KT2 . . . .**181** H1
  Orpington BR6 . . . . . .**207** J1
  Sutton SM1 . . . .**199** E4
  Woodford Green IG8 . . .**63** F5
Elmgrove Cres, Har. HA1 .**68** C5
Elmgrove Gdns, Har.
  HA1 . . . .**68** D5
Elm Gro Par, Wall. SM6
  off Butter Hill **200** A3
Elm Gro Rd, SW13 . . . . .**147** G2
  W5 . . . .**125** H2
Elmgrove Rd, Croy.
  CR0 . . . .**188** E7
  Harrow HA1 . . . .**68** C5
Elm Hall Gdns, E11 . . . . . .**79** H5
Elmhurst, Belv. DA17 . . . .**139** E6

Elmhurst Av, N2	73 G3
Mitcham CR4	168 B7
Elmhurst Dr, E18	79 G2
Elmhurst Gdns, E18	
off Elmhurst Dr	79 H1
Elmhurst Rd, E7	97 H7
N17	76 C2
SE9	174 B2
Elmhurst St, SW4	150 D3
Elmhurst Vil, SE15	
off Cheltenham Rd	153 F4
Elmhurst Way, Loug.	
IG10	48 C7
Elmington Cl, Bex. DA5	159 H6
Elmington Est, SE5	36 C7
Elmington Rd, SE5	152 A1
Elmira St, SE13	154 B3
Elm La, SE6	171 J2
Elmlee Cl, Chis. BR7	174 C6
Elmley Cl, E6	
off Northumberland	
Rd	116 B5
Elmley St, SE18	137 G4
Elm Ms, Rich. TW10	
off Grove Rd	145 J6
Elmore Cl, Wem. HA0	105 H2
Elmore Rd, E11	96 C3
Enfield EN3	45 G1
Elmores, Loug. IG10	48 D3
Elmore St, N1	93 J7
Elm Pk, SW2	151 F6
Stanmore HA7	53 E5
Elm Pk Av, N15	76 C5
Elm Pk Ct, Pnr. HA5	66 C3
Elm Pk Gdns, NW4	72 A5
SW10	31 E4
Elm Pk La, SW3	30 E4
Elm Pk Mans, SW10	30 D5
Elm Pk Rd, E10	95 H1
N3	56 C7
N21	43 J7
SE25	188 C3
SW3	30 E5
Pinner HA5	66 C2
Elm Pl, SW7	31 E3
Elm Quay Ct, SW8	33 H5
Elm Rd, E7	97 F6
E11	96 D2
E17	78 C5
N22 off Granville Rd	75 H1
SW14	146 C3
Barnet EN5	40 C4
Beckenham BR3	189 J2
Chessington KT9	195 H4
Epsom KT17	197 F6
Esher (Clay.) KT10	194 C6
Kingston upon Thames	
KT2	181 J1
New Malden KT3	182 D4
Romford RM7	83 H2
Sidcup DA14	176 A4
Thornton Heath CR7	188 A4
Wallington SM6	200 A1
Wembley HA9	87 H5
Elm Rd W, Sutt. SM3	184 C7
Elm Row, NW3	91 F3
Elms, The, SW13	147 F3
Elms Av, N10	74 B3
NW4	72 A5
Elmscott Gdns, N21	43 J6
Elmscott Rd, Brom.	
BR1	173 F5
Elms Ct, Wem. HA0	86 C4
Elms Cres, SW4	150 C6
Elmsdale Rd, E17	77 J4
Elms Gdns, Dag. RM9	101 F4
Wembley HA0	86 D4
Elmshaw Rd, SW15	147 G5
Elmshurst Cres, N2	73 G4
Elmside, Croy. (New Adgtn.)	
CR0	204 B6
Elmside Rd, Wem. HA9	88 A3
Elms La, Wem. HA0	86 C3
Elmsleigh Av, Har. HA3	69 E4
Elmsleigh Ct, Sutt. SM1	198 E3
Elmsleigh Rd, Twick.	
TW2	162 A2
Elmslie Cl, Wdf.Grn. IG8	64 C6
Elmslie Pt, E3	113 J5
Elms Ms, W2	14 E5
Elms Pk Av, Wem. HA0	86 D4
Elms Rd, SW4	150 C5
Harrow HA3	52 B7
ELMSTEAD, Chis.	174 A5
Elmstead Av, Chis. BR7	174 C5
Wembley HA9	87 H1
Elmstead Cl, N20	56 D2
Epsom KT19	197 E5
Elmstead Cres, Well.	
DA16	138 C6

Elmstead Gdns, Wor.Pk.	
KT4	197 G3
Elmstead Glade, Chis.	
BR7	174 C6
Elmstead La, Chis. BR7	174 C5
Elmstead Rd, Ilf. IG3	99 H2
Elm St, WC1	10 D6
Elmsworth Av, Houns.	
TW3	143 H2
Elm Ter, NW2	90 D3
NW3	
off Constantine Rd	91 H4
SE9	156 D6
Harrow HA3	52 A7
Elmton Way, E5	
off Rendlesham Rd	94 D3
Elm Tree Av, Esher KT10	180 A7
Elm Tree Cl, NW8	7 E3
Northolt UB5	103 F2
Elm Tree Rd, NW8	7 E3
Elmtree Rd, Tedd. TW11	162 B4
Elm Wk, NW3	90 D2
SW20	183 J4
Orpington BR6	206 C3
Elm Way, N11	58 A6
NW10	88 D3
Epsom KT19	196 D5
Worcester Park KT4	197 J3
Elmwood Av, N13	59 E5
Borehamwood WD6	38 B4
Feltham TW13	160 A2
Harrow HA3	68 D5
Elmwood Cl, Epsom	
KT17	197 G2
Wallington SM6	200 A2
Elmwood Ct, SW11	150 B1
Wembley HA0	86 D3
Elmwood Cres, NW9	70 C4
Elmwood Dr, Bex. DA5	158 E7
Epsom KT17	197 G6
Elmwood Gdns, W7	104 B6
Elmwood Rd, SE24	152 A5
W4	126 C6
Croydon CR0	187 H7
Mitcham CR4	185 J3
Elmworth Gro, SE21	170 A2
Elnathan Ms, W9	6 B6
Elphinstone Rd, E17	77 J2
Elphinstone St, N5	
off Avenell Rd	93 H4
Elrington Rd, E8	94 D6
Woodford Green IG8	63 G5
Elruge Cl, West Dr. UB7	120 A3
Elsa Rd, Well. DA16	158 B2
Elsa St, E1	113 H5
Elsdale St, E9	95 F6
Elsden Ms, E2	
off Old Ford Rd	113 F2
Elsden Rd, N17	76 C1
Elsenham Rd, E12	98 D5
Elsenham St, SW18	166 C1
Elsham Rd, E11	96 E3
W14	128 B2
Elsham Ter, W14	128 B2
Elsiedene Rd, N21	43 J7
Elsiemaud Rd, SE4	153 J5
Elsie Rd, SE22	152 C4
Elsinore Av, Stai. TW19	140 B7
Elsinore Gdns, NW2	90 B3
Elsinore Rd, SE23	171 H1
Elsinore Way, Rich. TW9	
off Lower Richmond	
Rd	146 B3
Elsley Rd, SW11	149 J3
Elspeth Rd, SW11	149 J4
Wembley HA0	87 H5
Elsrick Av, Mord. SM4	
off Chalgrove Av	184 D5
Elstan Way, Croy. CR0	189 H7
Elstead Ct, Sutt. SM3	
off Stonecot Hill	198 B1
Elsted St, SE17	36 C2
Elstow Cl, SE9	156 D5
Ruislip HA4	66 D7
Elstow Gdns, Dag. RM9	118 E1
Elstow Rd, Dag. RM9	100 E7
Elstree Gdns, N9	61 E1
Belvedere DA17	139 E4
Ilford IG1	99 F5
Elstree Hill, Brom. BR1	172 E7
Elstree Pk, Borwd. WD6	38 D6
Elstree Way, Borwd. WD6	38 B3
Elswick Rd, SE13	154 B2
Elswick St, SW6	149 F2
Elsworthy, T.Ditt. KT7	180 B6
Elsworthy Ri, NW3	91 H7
Elsworthy Rd, NW3	109 H1
Elsworthy Ter, NW3	91 H7
Elsynge Rd, SW18	149 G5

ELTHAM, SE9	156 A6
Eltham Grn, SE9	155 J5
Eltham Grn Rd, SE9	155 J4
Eltham High St, SE9	156 C6
Eltham Hill, SE9	156 A5
★ Eltham Palace, SE9	156 B7
Eltham Pk Gdns, SE9	156 D4
Eltham Rd, SE9	155 J5
SE12	155 F5
Elthiron Rd, SW6	148 D1
Elthorne Av, W7	124 C2
Elthorne Ct, Felt. TW13	160 C1
Elthorne Pk Rd, W7	124 C2
Elthorne Rd, N19	92 D2
NW9	70 D7
Elthorne Way, NW9	70 D6
Elthruda Rd, SE13	154 D6
Eltisley Rd, Ilf. IG1	98 E4
Elton Av, Barn. EN5	40 C5
Greenford UB6	86 C6
Wembley HA0	87 E5
Elton Cl, Kings.T. KT1	163 F7
Elton Ho, E3	113 J1
Elton Pl, N16	94 B5
Elton Rd, Kings.T. KT2	181 J1
Eltringham St, SW18	149 F4
Elvaston Ms, SW7	22 D5
Elvaston Pl, SW7	22 C6
Elveden Pl, NW10	106 A2
Elveden Rd, NW10	106 A2
Elvendon Rd, N13	58 E6
Elver Gdns, E2	13 J3
Elverson Rd, SE8	154 B2
Elverton St, SW1	33 H1
Elvington Grn, Brom.	
BR2	191 F5
Elvington La, NW9	70 E1
Elvino Rd, SE26	171 H5
Elvis Rd, NW2	89 J6
Elwill Way, Beck. BR3	190 C4
Elwin St, E2	13 H3
Elwood St, N5	93 H3
Elwyn Gdns, SE12	155 G7
Ely Cl, N.Mal. KT3	183 F2
Ely Ct, EC1	19 F2
Ely Gdns, Borwd. WD6	38 D5
Dagenham RM10	101 J3
Ilford IG1	
off Canterbury Av	80 B7
Elyne Rd, N4	75 G6
Ely Pl, EC1	19 F2
Woodford Green IG8	64 D6
Ely Rd, E10	78 C6
Croydon CR0	188 A5
Hounslow (Hthrw.Air.) TW6	
off Eastern Perimeter	
Rd	141 J2
Hounslow (Houns.W.)	
TW4	142 C3
Elysian Av, Orp. BR5	193 J6
Elysium Pl, SW6	
off Fulham Pk Gdns	148 C2
Elysium St, SW6	
off Fulham Pk Gdns	148 C2
Elystan Business Cen,	
Hayes UB4	102 C7
Elystan Pl, SW3	31 H3
Elystan St, SW3	31 G2
Elystan Wk, N1	
off Cloudesley Rd	111 G1
Emanuel Av, W3	106 C6
Emanuel Dr, Hmptn.	
TW12	161 F5
Embankment, SW15	148 A2
Embankment, The, Twick.	
TW1	162 D1
Embankment Gdns, SW3	32 A5
Embankment Pl, WC2	26 B6
Embassy Ct, Sid. DA14	176 B3
Welling DA16	
off Welling High St	158 B3
Embassy Gdns, Beck. BR3	
off Blakeney Rd	189 J1
Emba St, SE16	29 J4
Ember Cl, Orp. BR5	193 F7
Embercourt Rd, T.Ditt.	
KT7	180 B6
Ember Fm Av, E.Mol.	
KT8	180 A6
Ember Fm Way, E.Mol.	
KT8	180 A6
Ember Gdns, T.Ditt.	180 A7
Ember La, E.Mol. KT8	180 A7
Esher KT10	180 A7
Emberton, SE5	36 C5
Embleton Rd, SE13	154 B3
Watford WD19	50 A3
Embleton Wk, Hmptn. TW12	
off Fearnley Cres	161 F6

Embry Cl, Stan. HA7	52 D4
Embry Dr, Stan. HA7	52 D6
Embry Way, Stan. HA7	52 D5
Emden Cl, West Dr. UB7	120 D2
Emden St, SW6	149 E1
Emerald Cl, E16	116 B6
Emerald Gdns, Dag.	
RM8	101 G1
Emerald Sq, Sthl. UB2	122 D3
Emerald St, WC1	18 C1
Emerson Gdns, Har. HA3	69 J6
Emerson Rd, Ilf. IG1	80 D7
Emerson St, SE1	27 J1
Emerton Cl, Bexh. DA6	159 E4
Emery Hill St, SW1	25 G6
Emery St, SE1	27 F5
Emes Rd, Erith DA8	139 J7
Emilia Cl, Enf. EN3	45 E5
Emily Pl, N7	93 G4
Emlyn Gdns, W12	127 E2
Emlyn Rd, W12	127 E2
Emmanuel Rd, SW12	168 C1
Emma Rd, E13	115 F2
Emma St, E2	112 E2
Emmaus Way, Chig. IG7	64 D5
Emmott Av, Ilf. IG6	81 F5
Emmott Cl, E1	113 H4
NW11	73 F6
Emms Pas, Kings.T. KT1	
off High St	181 G2
Emperor's Gate, SW7	22 B6
Empire Av, N18	59 J5
Empire Ct, Wem. HA9	88 B3
Empire Rd, Grnf. UB6	105 F1
Empire Sq, N7	93 E3
SE20 off High St	171 G7
Empire Way, Wem. HA9	87 J4
Empire Wf Rd, E14	134 D4
Empress Av, E4	62 A7
E12	97 J2
Ilford IG1	
Woodford Green IG8	63 F7
Empress Dr, Chis. BR7	174 E6
Empress Pl, SW6	128 D5
Empress St, SE17	36 A5
Empson St, E3	114 B4
Emsworth Cl, N9	61 F1
Emsworth Rd, Ilf. IG6	81 E2
Emsworth St, SW2	169 F2
Emu Rd, SW8	150 B2
Ena Rd, SW16	186 E3
Enbrook St, W10	108 B3
Endale Cl, Cars. SM5	199 J2
Endeavour Ho, Barn.	
EN5	41 F4
Endeavour Way, SW19	166 E4
Barking IG11	118 A2
Croydon CR0	186 D7
Endell St, WC2	18 A3
Enderby St, SE10	134 E5
Enderley Cl, Har. HA3	
off Enderley Rd	68 B1
Enderley Rd, Har. HA3	68 B1
Endersby Rd, Barn. EN5	39 J5
Endersleigh Gdns, NW4	71 G4
Endlebury Rd, E4	62 B2
Endlesham Rd, SW12	150 A7
Endsleigh Gdns, WC1	9 H5
Ilford IG1	98 C2
Surbiton KT6	181 F6
Endsleigh Pl, WC1	9 J5
Endsleigh Rd, W13	104 D7
Southall UB2	123 E4
Endsleigh St, WC1	9 H5
Endway, Surb. KT5	182 A7
Endwell Rd, SE4	153 H2
Endymion Rd, N4	75 G7
SW2	151 F6
Energen Cl, NW10	88 E6
ENFIELD	44 C3
ENFIELD HIGHWAY, Enf.	45 F3
Enfield Retail Pk, Enf.	
EN1	44 E3
Enfield Rd, N1	94 B7
W3	126 B2
Brentford TW8	125 G5
Enfield EN2	42 G2
Hounslow (Hthrw.Air.) TW6	
off Eastern Perimeter	
Rd	141 H2
ENFIELD TOWN, Enf.	44 A2
Enfield Wk, Brent. TW8	125 G5
Enford St, W1	15 J1
Engadine Cl, Croy. CR0	202 C3
Engadine St, SW18	166 C1
Engate St, SE13	154 C4
Engel Pk, NW7	55 J6
Engineer Cl, SE18	136 D6
Engineers Way, Wem.	
HA9	88 A4

Englands La, NW3 .....91 J6
Loughton IG10 .....48 D2
England Way, N.Mal.
KT3 ....182 B4
Englefield Cl, Croy. CR0
..........187 J2
Enfield EN2 ......43 G2
Englefield Ct, Orp.
BR5 ....193 J4
Englefield Cres, Orp.
BR5 ....193 J4
Englefield Path, Orp.
BR5 ....193 J4
Englefield Rd, N1 .....94 A6
Engleheart Dr, Felt.
TW14 ....141 J6
Engleheart Rd, SE6 ....154 B7
Englewood Rd, SW12 ....150 B6
English Gdns, SE1 .....28 D2
English St, E3 ....113 J4
Enid St, SE16 ......29 G5
Enmore Av, SE25 ....188 D5
Enmore Gdns, SW14 ....146 D5
Enmore Rd, SE25 ....188 D5
SW15 ....147 J4
Southall UB1 .....103 G4
Ennerdale Av, Stan. HA7 ..69 F3
Ennerdale Cl, Sutt. (Cheam)
SM1 ....198 C4
Ennerdale Dr, NW9 ....70 E5
Ennerdale Gdns, Wem.
HA9 ....87 G1
Ennerdale Ho, E3 .....113 J4
Ennerdale Rd, Bexh.
DA7 ....159 G1
Richmond TW9 .....145 J2
Ennersdale Rd, SE13 ....154 D5
Ennismore Av, W4 ....127 F4
Greenford UB6 .....86 B6
Ennismore Gdns, SW7 ..23 G4
Thames Ditton KT7 ....180 B6
Ennismore Gdns Ms,
SW7 ....23 G5
Ennismore Ms, SW7 ....23 G4
Ennismore St, SW7 ....23 G5
Ennis Rd, N4 ....93 G1
SE18 ....137 F6
Ensign Dr, N13 ......59 J3
Ensign St, E1 ....21 H5
Enslin Rd, SE9 ......156 D6
Ensor Ms, SW7 ......30 E3
Enstone Rd, Enf. EN3 ....45 H3
Enterprise Cl, Croy. CR0 ..201 G1
Enterprise Way, NW10 ..107 G3
SW18 ....148 D4
Teddington TW11 ....162 C5
Enterprise Way, SE8 ....133 J4
Epirus Ms, SW6 .....128 D7
Epirus Rd, SW6 .....128 C7
Epping Cl, E14 ......134 A4
Romford RM7 .....83 H3
★ Epping Forest,
Epp. & Loug. 47 J1
Epping Glade, E4 .....46 C6
Epping New Rd, Buck.H.
IG9 ....63 H2
Loughton IG10 .....47 H5
Epping Pl, N1
off Liverpool Rd 93 G6
Epping Way, E4 ......46 B6
Epple Rd, SW6 ......148 C1
Epsom Cl, Bexh. DA7 ....159 H4
Northolt UB5 ......85 F5
Epsom Rd, E10 ......78 C6
Croydon CR0 .....201 G4
Ilford IG3 ....81 J6
Morden SM4 .....184 C7
Sutton SM3 .....184 C7
Epsom Sq, Houns. (Hthrw.Air.)
TW6 off Eastern
Perimeter Rd 141 J2
Epstein Rd, SE28 ....138 A1
Epworth Rd, Islw. TW7 ..124 E7
Epworth St, EC2 ......12 C6
Equity Sq, E2
off Shacklewell St 112 C3
Erasmus St, SW1 .....33 J2
Erconwald St, W12 ....107 F6
Eresby Dr, Beck. BR3 ....204 A1
Eresby Pl, NW6 ......90 D7
Erica Gdns, Croy. CR0 ..204 B4
Erica St, W12 ......107 G7
Eric Clarke La, Bark. IG11 ..117 E4
Eric Cl, E7 ....97 G5
Ericcson Cl, SW18 ....148 D5
Eric Rd, E7 ....97 G4
NW10 off Church Rd 89 F6
Romford RM6 .....82 D7
Eric St, E3 ....113 J4
Eridge Rd, W4 ......126 D3

Erin Cl, Brom. BR1 ....172 E7
Ilford IG3 ....82 A6
Erindale, SE18 ......137 G6
Erindale Ter, SE18 ....137 G6
Erith Cres, Rom. RM5 ....83 J1
Erith Rd, Belv. DA17 ....139 G5
Bexleyheath DA7 ....159 H4
Erith Rd, Erith DA8 ....159 H4
Erlanger Rd, SE14 ....153 G1
Erlesmere Gdns, W13 ..124 D3
Ermine Cl, Houns. TW4 ..142 C2
Ermine Ho, N17
off Moselle St 60 C7
Ermine Rd, N15 ......76 C6
SE13 ....154 B3
Ermine Side, Enf. EN1 ....44 D5
Ermington Rd, SE9 ....175 F2
Ernald Av, E6 ....116 B2
Erncroft Way, Twick. TW1 ..144 C6
Ernest Av, SE27 ....169 H4
Ernest Cl, Beck. BR3 ....190 A5
Ernest Gdns, W4 ....126 B6
Ernest Gro, Beck. BR3 ....189 J5
Ernest Rd, Kings.T. KT1 ..182 B2
Ernest Sq, Kings.T. KT1 ..182 B2
Ernest St, E1 ....113 G4
Ernle Rd, SW20 ....165 H7
Ernshaw Pl, SW15
off Carlton Dr 148 B5
Erpingham Rd, SW15 ....147 J3
Erridge Rd, SW19 ....184 D2
Errington Rd, W9 ....108 C4
Errol Gdns, Hayes UB4 ..102 B4
New Malden KT3 ....183 G4
Errol St, EC1 ....12 A6
Erskine Cl, Sutt. SM1 ....199 H3
Erskine Cres, N17 ....76 E4
Erskine Hill, NW11 ....72 D5
Erskine Ms, NW3
off Erskine Rd 91 J7
Erskine Rd, E17 ......77 J4
NW3 ....91 J7
Sutton SM1 ......199 G4
Watford WD19 .....50 C3
Erwood Rd, SE7 ....136 B5
Esam Way, SW16 ....169 G5
Escot Gdns, SE9 ....174 B4
Escot Way, Barn. EN5 ....39 J5
Escreet Gro, SE18 ....136 D4
Esher Av, Rom. RM7 ....83 J6
Sutton SM3 ......198 A3
Walton-on-Thames
KT12 ....178 A7
Esher Bypass, Chess.
KT9 ....195 E7
Esher KT10 ......195 E7
Esher Cl, Bex. DA5 ....176 E1
Esher Cres, Houns. (Hthrw.Air.)
TW6 off Eastern
Perimeter Rd 141 H2
Esher Gdns, SW19 ....166 A2
Esher Ms, Mitch. CR4 ....185 J3
Esher Rd, E.Mol. KT8 ..180 A6
Ilford IG3 ....99 H3
Eskdale Av, Nthlt. UB5 ..103 F1
Eskdale Cl, Wem. HA9 ....87 G2
Eskdale Rd, Bexh. DA7 ..159 G2
Eskmont Ridge, SE19 ....170 B7
Esk Rd, E13 ....115 G4
Esmar Cres, NW9 ....71 G7
Esme Ho, SW15 ....147 F4
Esmeralda Rd, SE1 ....37 J2
Esmond Rd, NW6 ....108 C1
W4 ....126 D4
Esmond St, SW15 ....148 B4
Esparto St, SW18 ....149 E7
Essenden Rd, Belv.
DA17 ....139 G5
South Croydon CR2 ..202 B7
Essendine Rd, W9 ....108 D4
Essex Av, Islw. TW7 ....144 B3
Essex Cl, E17 ....77 H4
Morden SM4 .....184 A7
Romford RM7 .....83 H4
Ruislip HA4 ......84 D1
Essex Ct, EC4 ......18 E4
SW13 ....147 F2
Essex Gdns, N4 ....75 H6
Essex Gro, SE19 ....170 A6
Essex Ho, E14
off Giraud St 114 B6
Essex Pk, N3 ......56 E6
Essex Pk Ms, W3 ....126 E1
Essex Pl, W4 ......126 C4
Essex Pl Sq, W4
off Chiswick High Rd ..126 D4
Essex Rd, E4 ....62 E1
E10 ....78 C6
E12 ....98 B5

Essex Rd, E17 ......77 H6
E18 ....79 H2
N1 ....111 H1
NW10 ....89 E7
W3 ....106 C7
W4 off Belmont Rd 126 D4
Barking IG11 ......99 G7
Borehamwood WD6 ..38 A3
Dagenham RM10 ....101 J5
Enfield EN2 ......44 A4
Romford RM7 .....83 H4
Romford (Chad.Hth.)
RM6 ....82 C7
Essex Rd S, E11 ....78 D7
Essex St, E7 ....97 G5
WC2 ....18 E5
Essex Twr, SE20 ....189 E1
Essex Vil, W8 ......128 D2
Essex Wf, E5 ....95 F2
Essian St, E1 ....113 H5
Essoldo Way, Edg. HA8 ..69 J3
Estate Way, E10 ....95 J1
Estcourt Rd, SE25 ....189 E6
SW6 ....128 C7
Estella Av, N.Mal. KT3 ..183 H4
Estelle Rd, NW3 ....91 J4
Esterbrooke St, SW1 ....33 H2
Este Rd, SW11 ....149 H3
Esther Cl, N21 ......43 G7
Esther Rd, E11 ......78 E7
Estoria Cl, SW2 ....151 G7
★ Estorick Collection of
Modern Italian Art, N1 ..93 H6
Estreham Rd, SW16 ....168 D6
Estridge Cl, Houns. TW3 ..143 G4
Estuary Cl, Bark. IG11 ..118 B3
Eswyn Rd, SW17 ....167 J4
Etchingham Pk Rd, N3 ..57 E7
Etchingham Rd, E15 ....96 C4
Eternit Wk, SW6 ....147 J1
Etfield Gro, Sid. DA14 ..176 B5
Ethelbert Cl, Brom. BR1 ..191 G3
Ethelbert Gdns, Ilf. IG2 ..80 C5
Ethelbert Rd, SW20 ....184 A1
Bromley BR1 ......191 G3
Erith DA8 ....139 J7
Ethelbert St, SW12
off Fernlea Rd 168 B1
Ethelburga St, SW11 ..149 H1
Etheldene Av, N10 ....74 C4
Ethelden Rd, W12 ....127 H1
Ethel Rd, E16 ......115 H6
Ethel St, SE17 ......35 J2
Etheridge Grn, Loug. IG10
off Etheridge Rd 49 F3
Etheridge Rd, NW2 ....71 J7
Loughton IG10 .....49 E2
Etherley Rd, N15 ....75 J5
Etherow St, SE22 ....152 D6
Etherstone Grn, SW16 ..169 G4
Etherstone Rd, SW16 ..169 G4
Ethnard Rd, SE15 ....132 E6
Ethronvi Rd, Bexh. DA7 ..159 E3
Etloe Rd, E10 ......96 A2
Eton Av, N12 ....57 F7
NW3 ....91 G7
Barnet EN4 ......41 H6
Hounslow TW5 ....123 F6
New Malden KT3 ....182 D5
Wembley HA0 .....87 E4
Eton Cl, SW18 ....149 E7
Eton Coll Rd, NW3 ....91 J6
Eton Ct, NW3
off Eton Av 91 G7
Wembley HA0 .....87 F4
Eton Garages, NW3
off Lambolle Pl 91 H6
Eton Gro, NW9 ....70 A3
SE13 ....154 E3
Eton Hall, NW3
off Eton Coll Rd 91 J6
Eton Pl, NW3
off Haverstock Hill ..92 A7
Eton Ri, NW3
off Eton Coll Rd 91 J6
Eton Rd, NW3 ......91 J7
Hayes UB3 ......121 J7
Ilford IG1 ....99 F5
Eton St, Rich. TW9 ....145 H5
Eton Vil, NW3 ......91 J6
Etta St, SE8 ....133 H6
Ettrick St, E14 ....114 C6
Etwell Pl, Surb. KT5 ....181 J6
Euesden Cl, N9
off Plevna Rd 60 E3
Eugenia Rd, SE16 ....133 F4
Eureka Rd, Kings.T. KT1
off Washington Rd ..182 A2
Europa Pl, EC1 ....11 J4

Europe Rd, SE18 ....136 C3
Eustace Rd, E6 ....116 B3
SW6 ....128 D7
Romford RM6 .....82 D7
Euston Cen, NW1
off Triton Sq 110 C4
Euston Gro, NW1 .....9 H4
Euston Rd, N1 ......10 A3
NW1 ....9 E6
Croydon CR0 .....201 G1
Euston Sq, NW1 .....9 H4
Euston Sta Colonnade,
NW1 ....9 H4
Euston St, NW1 .....9 G5
Euston Twr, NW1 ....110 C4
Evandale Rd, SW9 ....151 G2
Evangelist Rd, NW5 ....92 B4
Evans Cl, E8
off Buttermere Wk 94 C6
Evans Gro, Felt. TW13 ..161 G2
Evans Rd, SE6 ......173 E2
Evanston Av, E4 ....62 C7
Evanston Gdns, Ilf. IG4 ..80 B6
Eva Rd, Rom. RM6 ....82 C7
Evelina Rd, SE15 ....153 F3
SE20 ....171 G7
Eveline Lowe Est, SE16 ..29 H6
Eveline Rd, Mitch. CR4 ..185 J1
Evelyn Av, NW9 ....70 D4
Evelyn Cl, Twick. TW2 ..143 H7
Evelyn Ct, N1 ....12 B2
Evelyn Denington Rd,
E6 ....116 B4
Evelyn Dr, Pnr. HA5 ....50 D7
Evelyn Fox Ct, W10 ....107 J5
Evelyn Gdns, SW7 ....30 C3
Richmond TW9
off Kew Rd 145 H4
Evelyn Gro, W5 ....125 J1
Southall UB1 .....103 F6
Evelyn Rd, E16 ....135 H1
E17 ....78 C4
SW19 ....166 E5
W4 ....126 D3
Barnet EN4 ......41 J4
Richmond TW9 ....145 H3
Richmond (Ham)
TW10 ....163 F3
Evelyn St, SE8 ....133 H5
Evelyn Ter, Rich. TW9 ..145 H3
Evelyn Wk, N1 ......12 B2
Evelyn Way, Wall. SM6 ..200 D4
Evelyn Yd, W1 ......17 H3
Evening Hill, Beck. BR3 ..172 C7
Evenwood Cl, SW15 ....148 B5
Everard Av, Brom. BR2 ..205 G1
Everard Way, Wem. HA9 ..87 H3
Everatt Cl, SW18
off Amerland Rd 148 C6
Everdon Rd, SW13 ....127 G6
Everest Pl, E14 ....114 C5
Everest Rd, SE9 ....156 C5
Staines (Stanw.) TW19 ..140 A7
Everett Cl, Bushey
(Bushey Hth.) WD23 ..52 B1
Everett Wk, Belv. DA17
off Osborne Rd 139 F5
Everglade Strand, NW9 ..71 F1
Evergreen Ct, Stai. (Stanw.)
TW19 off Evergreen
Way 140 A7
Evergreen Sq, E8 ....94 C7
Evergreen Way, Stai. (Stanw.)
TW19 ....140 A7
Everilda St, N1 ....111 F1
Evering Rd, E5 ......94 C3
N16 ....94 C3
Everington Rd, N10 ....73 J2
Everington St, W6 ....128 A6
Everitt Rd, NW10 ....106 D3
Everleigh St, N4 ....93 F1
Eversfield Gdns, NW7 ..54 E7
Eversfield Rd, Rich. TW9 ..145 J2
Evershed Wk, W4 ....126 D4
Eversholt St, NW1 ....9 G1
Evershot Rd, N4 ....93 F1
Eversleigh Rd, E6 ....116 A1
N3 ....56 C7
SW11 ....149 J3
Barnet EN5 ......41 F5
Eversley Av, Wem. HA9 ..88 A2
Eversley Cl, N21 ....43 F6
Loughton IG10
off The Broadway 49 F3
Eversley Cres, N21 ....43 F6
Isleworth TW7 ....144 A1

Eversley Mt, N21 . . . . . . .43 F6
Eversley Pk, SW19 . . . .165 H5
Eversley Pk Rd, N21 . . . . .43 F6
Eversley Rd, SE7 . . . . . .135 H6
SE19 . . . . .170 A7
Surbiton KT5 . . . . .181 J4
Eversley Way, Croy. CR0 .204 A4
Everthorpe Rd, SE15 . . . .152 C3
Everton Bldgs, NW1 . . . . . .9 F4
Everton Dr, Stan. HA7 . . . .69 J3
Everton Rd, Croy. CR0 . .202 D1
Evesham Av, E17 . . . . . . .78 A2
Evesham Cl, Grnf. UB6 . .103 H2
Sutton SM2 . . . . .198 D7
Evesham Grn, Mord.
SM4 . . . . .184 E6
Evesham Rd, E15 . . . . . .115 F1
N11 . . . . .58 C5
Morden SM4 . . . . .185 E6
Evesham St, W11 . . . . . .108 A7
Evesham Wk, SE5
off Love Wk 152 A2
SW9 . . . . .151 G2
Evesham Way, SW11 . . . .150 A3
Ilford IG5 . . . . .80 D3
Evry Rd, Sid. DA14 . . . . .176 C6
Ewald Rd, SW6 . . . . .148 C2
Ewanrigg Ter, Wdf.Grn.
IG8 . . . . .63 J5
Ewart Pl, E3
off Roman Rd 113 J2
Ewart Rd, SE23 . . . . . . .153 G7
Ewe Cl, N7 . . . . .93 E6
Ewell Bypass, Epsom
KT17 . . . . .197 G7
Ewell Ct Av, Epsom
KT19 . . . . .197 E5
Ewellhurst Rd, Ilf. IG5 . . . .80 B2
Ewell Pk Gdns, Epsom
KT17 . . . . .197 G7
Ewell Pk Way, Epsom (Ewell)
KT17 . . . . .197 G6
Ewell Rd, Surb. KT6 . . . .181 H6
Surbiton (Long Dit.)
KT6 . . . . .180 E7
Sutton SM3 . . . . .198 B6
Ewelme Rd, SE23 . . . . . .171 F1
Ewen Cres, SW2 . . . . . .151 G7
Ewer St, SE1 . . . . .27 J2
Ewhurst Cl, E1 . . . . .113 F6
Ewhurst Rd, SE4 . . . . . .153 J6
Exbury Rd, SE6 . . . . .172 A2
★ ExCeL, E16 . . . . .115 H7
Excel Ct, WC2 . . . . .17 J6
Excelsior Cl, Kings.T. KT1
off Washington Rd . . .182 A2
Excelsior Gdns, SE13 . . .154 C2
Exchange Arc, EC2 . . . . .20 E1
Exchange Bldgs, E1
off Cutler St 112 B6
Exchange Cl, N11
off Benfleet Way 58 A2
Exchange Ct, WC2 . . . . . .18 B6
Exchange Pl, EC2 . . . . . .20 D1
Exchange Sq, EC2 . . . . . .20 D1
Exchange III Shop Cen, The, Ilf.
IG1 . . . . .99 E2
Exeter Cl, E6
off Harper Rd 116 C6
Exeter Gdns, Ilf. IG1 . . . . .98 B1
Exeter Ho, SW15
off Putney Heath 147 J6
Exeter Ms, NW6
off West Hampstead
Ms 90/91 E6
SW6 off Farm La 128 D7
Exeter Rd, E16 . . . . .115 G6
E17 . . . . .78 A5
N9 . . . . .61 F2
N14 . . . . .58 B1
NW2 . . . . .90 B5
Croydon CR0 . . . . .188 B7
Dagenham RM10 . . . . .101 H6
Enfield EN3 . . . . .45 G3
Feltham TW13 . . . . . . .161 F3
Harrow HA2 . . . . .85 E2
Hounslow (Hthrw.Air.)
TW6 . . . . .141 H4
Welling DA16 . . . . .157 J2
Exeter St, WC2 . . . . .18 B5
Exeter Way, SE14 . . . . . .133 J7
Hounslow (Hthrw.Air.)
TW6 . . . . .141 H3
Exford Gdns, SE12 . . . . .173 H1
Exford Rd, SE12 . . . . . . .173 H2
Exhibition Cl, W12 . . . . .107 J7
Exhibition Rd, SW7 . . . . .23 F4
Exmoor Cl, Ilf. IG6 . . . . . .81 F1
Exmoor St, W10 . . . . . . .108 A4

Exmouth Mkt, EC1 . . . . . .11 E5
Exmouth Ms, NW1 . . . . . .9 G4
Exmouth Pl, E8 . . . . .94 E7
Exmouth Rd, E17 . . . . . . .77 J5
Bromley BR2 . . . . .191 H3
Ruislip HA4 . . . . .84 C3
Welling DA16 . . . . .158 C1
Exmouth St, E1
off Commercial Rd . . .113 F6
Exning Rd, E16 . . . . .115 F4
Exon St, SE17 . . . . .36 D3
Express Dr, Ilf. IG3 . . . . .100 B1
Exton Cres, NW10 . . . . . .88 C7
Exton Gdns, Dag. RM8 . .100 C5
Exton St, SE1 . . . . .27 E2
Eyebright Cl, Croy. CR0
off Primrose La 203 G1
Eyhurst Cl, NW2 . . . . . . .89 G2
Eylewood Rd, SE27 . . . . .169 J5
Eynella Rd, SE22 . . . . . .152 C7
Eynham Rd, W12 . . . . . .107 J6
Eynsford Cl, Orp. BR5 . . .193 F7
Eynsford Cres, Bex. DA5 .176 C1
Eynsford Rd, Ilf. IG3 . . . . .99 H2
Eynsham Dr, SE2 . . . . . .138 A4
Eynswood Dr, Sid. DA14 .176 B5
Eyot Gdns, W6 . . . . .127 F5
Eyot Grn, W4
off Chiswick Mall 127 F6
Eyre Ct, NW8 . . . . .6 E1
Eyre St Hill, EC1 . . . . .11 E6
Eythorne Rd, SW9 . . . . . .151 G1
Ezra St, E2 . . . . .13 G3

F

Faber Gdns, NW4 . . . . . . .71 G5
Fabian Rd, SW6 . . . . .128 C7
Fabian St, E6 . . . . .116 C4
Factory La, N17 . . . . .76 C2
Croydon CR0 . . . . .201 G1
Factory Rd, E16 . . . . .136 B1
Factory Sq, SW16 . . . . . .168 E6
Factory Yd, W7
off Uxbridge Rd 124 B1
Faggs Rd, Felt. TW14 . . .142 A5
Fairacre, N.Mal. KT3 . . . .182 E3
Fairacres, SW15 . . . . . . .147 G4
Fair Acres, Brom. BR2 . . .191 G5
Fairbairn Grn, SW9 . . . . .151 G1
Fairbank Av, Orp. BR6 . . .206 E2
Fairbank Est, N1
off East Rd 112 A2
Fairbanks Rd, N17 . . . . . .76 C3
Fairbourne Rd, N17 . . . . .76 B3
Fairbridge Rd, N19 . . . . . .92 D2
Fairbrook Cl, N13 . . . . . . .59 G5
Fairbrook Rd, N13 . . . . . .59 G6
Fairburn Cl, Borwd.
WD6 . . . . .38 A1
Fairburn Ct, SW15
off Mercier Rd 148 B5
Fairby Rd, SE12 . . . . . . .155 H5
Faircharm Trd Est, SE8 . .134 B7
Fairchild Cl, SW11
off Wye St 149 G2
Fairchild Pl, EC2 . . . . .12 E6
Fairchild St, EC2 . . . . .13 E6
Fairclough St, E1 . . . . .21 J4
Faircross Av, Bark. IG11 . . .99 F6
Fairdale Gdns, SW15 . . . .147 H4
Hayes UB3 . . . . .122 A1
Fairey Av, Hayes UB3 . . .121 J4
Fairfax Gdns, SE3 . . . . . .156 A1
Fairfax Ms, E16
off Wesley Av 135 H1
SW15 . . . . .147 J4
Fairfax Pl, NW6 . . . . .91 F7
W14 off Holland Rd . . .128 B3
Fairfax Rd, N8 . . . . .75 G4
NW6 . . . . .91 F7
W4 . . . . .127 E3
Teddington TW11 . . . . .162 D6
Fairfax Way, N10
off Cromwell Rd 58 A7
Fairfield Av, NW4 . . . . . . .71 H6
Edgware HA8 . . . . .54 B6
Twickenham TW2 . . . . .161 H1
Watford WD19 . . . . .50 C3
Fairfield Cl, N12 . . . . .57 F4
Enfield EN3
off Scotland Grn Rd N .45 H4
Epsom (Ewell) KT19 . . .196 E5
Mitcham CR4 . . . . .167 H7
Sidcup DA15 . . . . .157 J6
Fairfield Ct, NW10 . . . . . .107 G1
Northwood HA6
off Windsor Cl 66 A2
Fairfield Cres, Edg. HA8 . . .54 B6

Fairfield Dr, SW18 . . . . . .149 E5
Greenford UB6 . . . . . . .105 F1
Harrow HA2 . . . . .67 J3
Fairfield E, Kings.T. KT1 .181 H2
Fairfield Gdns, N8
off Elder Av 74/75 E5
Fairfield Gro, SE7 . . . . . .136 A5
★ Fairfield Halls, Croy.
CR0 . . . . .202 A3
Fairfield Ind Est, Kings.T.
KT1 . . . . .181 J3
Fairfield N, Kings.T. KT1 .181 H2
Fairfield Path, Croy. CR0 .202 A3
Fairfield Pl, Kings.T. KT1 .181 H3
Fairfield Rd, E3 . . . . .114 A2
E17 . . . . .77 H2
N8 . . . . .75 E5
N18 . . . . .60 D4
W7 . . . . .124 D3
Beckenham BR3 . . . . . .190 A2
Bexleyheath DA7 . . . . .159 F2
Bromley BR1 . . . . .173 G7
Croydon CR0 . . . . .202 B3
Ilford IG1 . . . . .99 E6
Kingston upon Thames
KT1 . . . . .181 H2
Orpington BR5 . . . . . . .193 G6
Southall UB1 . . . . .103 F6
West Drayton UB7 . . . .120 B1
Woodford Green IG8 . . . .63 G6
Fairfields, SW9 . . . . .70 C5
Fairfields Cres, NW9 . . . . .70 C4
Fairfield S, Kings.T. KT1 .181 H2
Fairfields, Houns.
TW3 . . . . .143 J3
Fairfield St, SW18 . . . . . .149 E5
Fairfield Way, Barn. EN5 . .40 D5
Epsom KT19 . . . . .196 E5
Fairfield W, Kings.T. KT1 .181 H2
Fairfoot Rd, E3 . . . . .114 A4
Fairford Av, Croy. CR0 . . .189 G5
Fairford Cl, Croy. CR0 . . .189 H5
Fairford Ct, Sutt. SM2
off Grange Rd 198/199 E7
Fairford Gdns, Wor.Pk.
KT4 . . . . .197 F3
Fairford Ho, SE11 . . . . . . .35 F2
Fairgreen, Barn. EN4 . . . . .41 J3
Fairgreen E, Barn. EN4 . . .41 J3
Fairgreen Par, Mitch. CR4
off London Rd 185 J3
Fairgreen Rd, Th.Hth.
CR7 . . . . .187 H5
Fairhaven Av, Croy. CR0 .189 G6
Fairhaven Cres, Wat.
WD19 . . . . .50 A3
Fairhazel Gdns, NW6 . . . .91 E6
Fairholme, Felt. TW14 . . .141 G7
Fairholme Cl, N3 . . . . .72 B4
Fairholme Gdns, N3 . . . . .72 B3
Fairholme Rd, W14 . . . . .128 B5
Croydon CR0 . . . . .187 G7
Harrow HA1 . . . . .68 C5
Ilford IG1 . . . . .80 C7
Sutton SM1 . . . . .198 C6
Fairholt Cl, N16 . . . . .94 B1
Fairholt Rd, N16 . . . . .94 A1
Fairholt St, SW7 . . . . .23 H5
Fairland Rd, E15 . . . . .97 F6
Fairlands Av, Buck.H. IG9 . .63 G2
Sutton SM1 . . . . .198 D2
Thornton Heath CR7 . .187 F4
Fairlands Ct, SE9
off North Pk 156 D6
Fairlawn, SE7 . . . . .135 J6
Fairlawn Av, N2 . . . . .73 H4
W4 . . . . .126 C4
Bexleyheath DA7 . . . . .158 D2
Fairlawn Cl, N14 . . . . .42 C6
Esher (Clay.) KT10 . . . .194 C6
Feltham TW13 . . . . . . .161 F4
Kingston upon Thames
KT2 . . . . .164 C6
Fairlawn Dr, Wdf.Grn. IG8 .63 G7
Fairlawnes, Wall. SM6
off Maldon Rd 200 B5
Fairlawn Gdns, Sthl.
UB1 . . . . .103 F7
Fairlawn Gro, W4 . . . . . .126 C4
Fairlawn Pk, SE26 . . . . . .171 H5
Fairlawn Rd, SW19 . . . . .166 C7
Fairlawns, Pnr. HA5 . . . . .66 C2
Sunbury-on-Thames
TW16 . . . . .178 A3
Twickenham TW1 . . . . .145 F6
Fairlea Pl, W5 . . . . .105 G4
Fairlie Gdns, SE23 . . . . . .153 F7
Fairlight Av, E4 . . . . .62 D2
NW10 . . . . .107 E2
Woodford Green IG8 . . . .63 G6

Fairlight Cl, E4 . . . . .62 D2
Worcester Park KT4 . . .197 J4
Fairlight Rd, SW17 . . . . . .167 G4
Fairlop Gdns, Ilf. IG6 . . . . .65 F7
Fairlop Rd, E11 . . . . .78 D7
Ilford IG6 . . . . .81 F2
Fairmead, Brom. BR1 . . .192 C4
Surbiton KT5 . . . . .196 B1
Fairmead Cl, Brom. BR1 .192 C4
Hounslow TW5 . . . . . . .122 D7
New Malden KT3 . . . . .182 D3
Fairmead Cres, Edg.
HA8 . . . . .54 C3
Fairmead Gdns, Ilf. IG4 . . .80 B5
Fairmead Rd, N19 . . . . . . .92 D3
Croydon CR0 . . . . .201 F1
Loughton IG10 . . . . .47 H4
Fairmeads, Loug. IG10 . . . .48 E2
Fairmead Side, Loug.
IG10 . . . . .47 J5
Fairmile Av, SW16 . . . . . .168 D5
Fairmile Ho, Tedd. TW11
off Twickenham Rd . . .162 D4
Fairmont Cl, Belv. DA17
off Lullingstone Rd . . .139 F5
Fairmount Rd, SW2 . . . . .151 F6
Fairoak Cl, Orp. BR5 . . . .193 E7
Fairoak Dr, SE9 . . . . .157 G5
Fairseat Cl, Bushey
(Bushey Hth.) WD23
off Hive Rd 52 B2
Fairstead Wk, N1
off Popham Rd 111 J1
Fair St, SE1 . . . . .29 E3
Hounslow TW3
off High St 143 J3
Fairthorn Rd, SE7 . . . . . .135 G5
Fairview Av, Wem. HA0 . . .87 G6
Fairview Cl, E17 . . . . .77 H1
Chigwell IG7 . . . . .65 H4
Fairview Cres, Har. HA2 . . .85 G1
Fairview Dr, Chig. IG7 . . . .65 H4
Orpington BR6 . . . . . . .207 G4
Fairview Gdns, Wdf.Grn.
IG8 . . . . .79 H1
Fairview Pl, SW2 . . . . . . .151 F7
Fairview Rd, N15 . . . . .76 C5
SW16 . . . . .187 F1
Chigwell IG7 . . . . .65 H4
Enfield EN2 . . . . .43 G1
Sutton SM1 . . . . .199 G5
Fairview Way, Edg. HA8 . . .54 A4
Fairwater Av, Well.
DA16 . . . . .158 A4
Fairway, SW20 . . . . .183 J3
Bexleyheath DA6 . . . . .159 E5
Orpington BR5 . . . . . . .193 G6
Woodford Green IG8 . . . .63 J5
Fairway, The, N13 . . . . . . .59 J3
N14 . . . . .42 B6
NW7 . . . . .54 D3
W3 . . . . .106 E6
Barnet EN5 . . . . .41 E6
Bromley BR1 . . . . .192 C5
New Malden KT3 . . . . .182 D1
Northolt UB5 . . . . .85 J6
Ruislip HA4 . . . . .84 D3
Wembley HA0 . . . . .87 E3
West Molesey KT8 . . . .179 H3
Fairway Av, NW9 . . . . .70 B3
Borehamwood WD6 . . . .38 B2
Fairway Cl, NW11 . . . . . . .73 F7
Croydon CR0 . . . . .189 H5
Epsom KT19 . . . . .196 C4
Hounslow TW4 . . . . . . .142 C5
Fairway Ct, NW7
off The Fairway 54 D3
Fairway Dr, SE28 . . . . . . .118 D6
Greenford UB6 . . . . . . .85 H7
Fairway Gdns, Beck.
BR3 . . . . .190 D6
Ilford IG1 . . . . .99 F5
Fairways, Stan. HA7 . . . . .69 H2
Teddington TW11 . . . . .163 G7
Fairweather Cl, N15 . . . . . .76 B4
Fairweather Rd, N16 . . . . .76 D6
Fairwyn Rd, SE26 . . . . . .171 H4
Fakenham Cl, NW7 . . . . . .55 G7
Northolt UB5
off Goodwood Dr 85 G6
Fakruddin St, E1 . . . . .13 J4
Falcon Av, Brom. BR1 . . .192 B4
Falconberg Ct, W1 . . . . . .17 J3
Falconberg Ms, W1 . . . . . .17 H3
Falcon Cl, SE1 . . . . .27 H1
W4 off Sutton La S . . .126 C6
Falcon Ct, EC4 . . . . .19 E4
Falcon Cres, Enf. EN3 . . . .45 G5
Falcon Dr, Stai. (Stanw.)
TW19 . . . . .140 A6

Falconer Wk, N7
off Newington Barrow
Way 93 F2
Falcon Gro, SW11 . . . . . .149 H3
Falcon Ho, W13 . . . . . . .104 C4
Falcon La, SW11 . . . . . .149 H3
Falcon Pk Ind Est, NW10 . .89 F5
Falcon Rd, SW11 . . . . . .149 H2
Enfield EN3 . . . . .45 G5
Hampton TW12 . . . . . . .161 F7
Falcon St, E13 . . . . . . .115 G4
Falcon Ter, SW11 . . . . . .149 H3
Falcon Way, E11 . . . . . . .79 G4
E14 . . . . .134 B4
Falcon Way, NW9 . . . . . .71 E2
Feltham TW14 . . . . . . .142 B5
Harrow HA3 . . . . .69 H5
FALCONWOOD, Well. 157 G3
Falconwood Av, Well.
DA16 . . . . .157 G2
Falconwood Par, Well.
DA16 . . . . .157 H4
Falconwood Rd, Croy.
CR0 . . . . .204 A7
Falcourt Cl, Sutt. SM1 . . .198 E5
Falkirk Gdns, Wat. WD19
off Blackford Rd 50 D5
Falkirk Ho, W9 . . . . .6 B3
Falkirk St, N1 . . . . .12 E2
Falkland Av, N3 . . . . . . .56 D7
N11 . . . . .58 A4
Falkland Pk Av, SE25 . . .188 B3
Falkland Pl, NW5
off Falkland Rd 92 C5
Falkland Rd, N8 . . . . . . .75 G4
NW5 . . . . .92 C5
Barnet EN5 . . . . .40 B2
Fallaize Av, Ilf. IG1
off Riverdene Rd . .98/99 E4
Fallodon Way, NW11 . . . .72 D4
Fallow Cl, Chig. IG7 . . . . .65 J5
Fallow Ct, SE16 . . . . . . .37 J4
Fallow Ct Av, N12 . . . . . .57 F7
Fallowfield, Stan. HA7 . . .52 D3
Fallowfield Ct, Stan. HA7 .52 D3
Fallow Flds, Loug. IG10 . .47 J7
Fallowfields Dr, N12 . . . .57 H6
Fallows Cl, N2 . . . . .73 F2
Fallsbrook Rd, SW16 . . . .168 C7
Falman Cl, N9
off Croyland Rd 60 D1
Falmer Rd, E17 . . . . . . .78 B3
N15 . . . . .75 J5
Enfield EN1 . . . . .44 B4
Falmouth Av, E4 . . . . . . .62 D5
Falmouth Cl, N22
off Truro Rd 59 F7
SE12 . . . . .155 F5
Falmouth Gdns, Ilf. IG4 . .80 B5
Falmouth Rd, SE1 . . . . . .28 A5
Falmouth St, E15 . . . . . .96 D5
Falmouth Way, E17
off Gosport Rd 77 J5
Falstaff Ms, Hmptn. (Hmptn.H.)
TW12
off Hampton Rd 162 A5
Fambridge Cl, SE26 . . . .171 J4
Fambridge Rd, Dag.
RM8 . . . . .101 G1
★ Family Records Cen, Public
Record Office, EC1 . . . .11 F4
Fane St, W14
off North Ford Rd 128 C6
★ Fan Mus, SE10 . . . . . .134 C7
Fann St, EC1 . . . . .11 J6
EC2 . . . . .11 J6
Fanshawe Av, Bark. IG11 .99 F6
Fanshawe Cres, Dag.
RM9 . . . . .101 E5
Fanshawe Rd, Rich.
TW10 . . . . .163 F4
Fanshaw St, N1 . . . . . . .12 D3
Fanthorpe St, SW15 . . . .147 J3
Faraday Av, Sid. DA14 . . .176 A2
Faraday Cl, N7
off Bride St 93 F6
★ Faraday Mus, W1
off Albermarle St 17 F6
Faraday Rd, E15 . . . . . . .97 F6
SW19 . . . . .166 D6
W3 . . . . .106 C7
W10 . . . . .108 B5
Southall UB1 . . . . . . .103 H7
Welling DA16 . . . . . . .158 A3
West Molesey KT8 . . . .179 G4
Faraday Way, SE18 . . . .136 A3
Croydon CR0
off Ampere Way 201 F1
Fareham Rd, Felt. TW14 .142 C7
Fareham St, W1 . . . . . . .17 H3

Farewell Pl, Mitch. CR4 . .185 H1
Faringdon Av, Brom.
BR2 . . . . .192 E6
Faringford Rd, E15 . . . . . .96 E7
Farjeon Rd, SE3 . . . . . . .156 A1
Farleigh Av, Brom. BR2 . .191 F6
Farleigh Pl, N16
off Farleigh Rd 94 C4
Farleigh Rd, N16 . . . . . . .94 C4
Farley Dr, Ilf. IG3 . . . . . . .99 H1
Farley Ms, SE6 . . . . . . .154 C7
Farley Pl, SE25 . . . . . . .188 D4
Farley Rd, SE6 . . . . . . .154 B7
South Croydon CR2 . . .202 E7
Farlington Pl, SW15
off Roehampton La . .147 H7
Farlow Rd, SW15 . . . . . .148 A3
Farlton Rd, SW18 . . . . . .149 E7
Farman Gro, Nthlt. UB5
off Wayfarer Rd 102 D3
Farm Av, NW2 . . . . .90 B3
SW16 . . . . .169 E4
Harrow HA2 . . . . .67 F7
Wembley HA0 . . . . .87 F6
Farmborough Cl, Har. HA1
off Pool Rd 68 A7
Farm Cl, SW6
off Farm La 128 D7
Barnet EN5 . . . . .39 J5
Buckhurst Hill IG9 . . . .63 J3
Dagenham RM10 . . . . .101 J7
Southall UB1 . . . . . . .103 H7
Sutton SM2 . . . . .199 G7
West Wickham BR4 . . .205 E3
Farmcote Rd, SE12 . . . . .173 G1
Farm Ct, NW4 . . . . .71 G3
Farmdale Rd, SE10 . . . . .135 G5
Carshalton SM5 . . . . .199 H7
Farm Dr, Croy. CR0 . . . . .203 J2
Farm End, E4 . . . . .46 E5
Farmer Rd, E10 . . . . .96 B1
Farmers Rd, SE5 . . . . . . .35 H7
Farmer St, W8
off Uxbridge St 128 D1
Farmfield Rd, Brom.
BR1 . . . . .172 E5
Farmhouse Rd, SW16 . . .168 C7
Farmilo Rd, E17 . . . . . . .77 J7
Farmington Av, Sutt.
SM1 . . . . .199 G3
Farmlands, Enf. EN2 . . . . .43 G1
Pinner HA5 . . . . .66 A4
Farmlands, The, Nthlt.
UB5 . . . . .85 F6
Farmland Wk, Chis. BR7 .174 E5
Farm La, N14 . . . . .42 A6
SW6 . . . . .128 D6
Croydon CR0 . . . . . . .203 J2
Farmleigh, N14 . . . . .42 C7
Farm Pl, W8
off Uxbridge St 128 D1
Farm Rd, N21 . . . . .59 H1
NW10
off Mordaunt Rd 106 D1
Edgware HA8 . . . . .54 B6
Hounslow TW4 . . . . . .161 E1
Morden SM4 . . . . . . .185 E5
Sutton SM2 . . . . .199 G7
Farmstead Rd, SE6 . . . . .172 B4
Harrow HA3 . . . . .68 A1
Farm St, W1 . . . . .16 D6
Farm Vale, Bex. DA5 . . . .159 H6
Farm Wk, NW11 . . . . . . .72 C5
Farm Way, Buck.H. IG9 . . .63 J4
Farmway, Dag. RM8 . . . .100 C4
Farm Way, Wor.Pk. KT4 . .197 J3
Farnaby Rd, SE9 . . . . . . .155 J4
Bromley BR1, BR2 . . . .172 D7
Farnan Av, E17 . . . . .78 A2
Farnan Rd, SW16 . . . . . .169 E5
FARNBOROUGH, Orp. . . .206 E5
Farnborough Av, E17 . . . .77 H3
South Croydon CR2 . . .203 G7
Farnborough Cl, Wem. HA9
off Chalkhill Rd 88 B2
Farnborough Common, Orp.
BR6 . . . . .206 C3
Farnborough Cres, Brom. BR2
off Saville Row 205 F1
Farnborough Hill, Orp.
BR6 . . . . .207 G5
Farnborough Ho, SW15
off Fontley Way 165 G1
Farnborough Way, SE15 . .37 E7
Orpington BR6 . . . . . .207 F4
Farncombe St, SE16 . . . . .29 J4
Farndale Av, N13 . . . . . . .59 H3
Farndale Cres, Grnf. UB6 .103 J3
Farnell Ms, SW5 . . . . . . .30 A3
Farnell Rd, Islw. TW7 . . .144 A3

Farnham Cl, N20 . . . . . . .41 F7
Farnham Gdns, SW20 . . .183 H2
Farnham Pl, SE1 . . . . . . .27 H2
Farnham Rd, Ilf. IG3 . . . . .81 J7
Welling DA16 . . . . . . .158 C2
Farningham Rd, N17 . . . . .60 D7
Farnley Rd, E4 . . . . .46 E7
SE25 . . . . .188 A4
Faro Cl, Brom. BR1 . . . . .192 D2
Faroe Rd, W14 . . . . .128 A3
Farorna Wk, Enf. EN2 . . . .43 G1
Farquhar Rd, SE19 . . . . .170 C5
SW19 . . . . .166 D3
Farquharson Rd, Croy.
CR0 . . . . .201 J1
Farrance Rd, Rom. RM6 . .83 E6
Farrance St, E14 . . . . . . .113 J6
Farrans Ct, Har. HA3 . . . .69 E7
Farrant Av, N22 . . . . .75 G2
Farr Av, Bark. IG11 . . . . .118 A2
Farrell Ho, E1 . . . . .113 F6
Farren Rd, SE23 . . . . . . .171 H2
Farrer Ms, N8
off Farrer Rd 74 C4
Farrer Rd, N8 . . . . .74 C4
Harrow HA3 . . . . .69 H5
Farrer's Pl, Croy. CR0 . . .203 G4
Farrier Cl, Sun. TW16 . . .178 A4
Farrier Rd, Nthlt. UB5 . . .103 G2
Farriers Ct, Sutt. SM3
off Forge La 198 B7
Farrier St, NW1 . . . . . . .92 B7
Farriers Way, Borwd. WD6 .38 C6
Farrier Wk, SW10 . . . . . . .30 C5
Farringdon La, EC1 . . . . .11 F6
Farringdon Rd, EC1 . . . . .10 E5
Farringdon St, EC4 . . . . .19 G3
Farrington Pl, Chis. BR7 .175 G7
Farrins Rents, SE16 . . . .133 H1
Farrow La, SE14 . . . . . . .133 F7
Farrow Pl, SE16
off Ropemaker Rd . . .133 H3
Farr Rd, Enf. EN2 . . . . . .44 A1
Farthingale Wk, E15 . . . . .96 D7
Farthing All, SE1 . . . . . . .29 H4
Farthing Flds, E1
off Raine St 132/133 E1
Farthings, The, Kings.T. KT2
off Brunswick Rd 182 A1
Farthings Cl, E4 . . . . .63 E3
Pinner HA5 . . . . .66 B6
Farthing St, Orp. BR6 . . .206 C7
Farwell Rd, Sid. DA14 . . .176 B3
Farwig La, Brom. BR1 . . .191 F1
Fashion St, E1 . . . . .21 F2
Fashoda Rd, Brom. BR2 . .192 A4
Fassett Rd, E8 . . . . .94 D6
Kingston upon Thames
KT1 . . . . .181 H4
Fassett Sq, E8 . . . . .94 D6
Fauconberg Rd, W4 . . . .126 C6
Faulkner Cl, Dag. RM8 . . .82 D7
Faulkner St, SE14 . . . . . .153 F1
Fauna Cl, Rom. RM6 . . . . .82 C7
Faunce St, SE17 . . . . . . .35 G5
Favart Rd, SW6 . . . . . . .148 D1
Faversham Av, E4 . . . . . . .63 E1
Enfield EN1 . . . . .44 A6
Faversham Rd, SE6 . . . . .153 J7
Beckenham BR3 . . . . .189 J2
Morden SM4 . . . . . . .185 E6
Fawcett Cl, SW11 . . . . . .149 G2
SW16 . . . . .169 G4
Fawcett Est, E5 . . . . .94 D1
Fawcett Rd, NW10 . . . . .107 F1
Croydon CR0 . . . . . . .201 J3
Fawcett St, SW10 . . . . . .30 C5
Fawcus Cl, Esher (Clay.)
KT10 off Dalmore Av .194 C6
Fawe Pk Rd, SW15 . . . . .148 C4
Fawe St, E14 . . . . .114 B5
Fawley Rd, NW6 . . . . . . .90 E5
Fawnbrake Av, SE24 . . . .151 H5
Fawn Rd, E13 . . . . .115 J2
Chigwell IG7 . . . . .65 J5
Fawood Av, NW10 . . . . . .88 D7
Faygate Cres, Bexh. DA6 .159 G5
Faygate Rd, SW2 . . . . . .169 F2
Fayland Av, SW16 . . . . . .168 C5
Fearnley Cres, Hmptn.
TW12 . . . . .161 E5
Fearon St, SE10 . . . . . . .135 G5
Featherbed La, Croy.
CR0 . . . . .203 J7
Feathers Pl, SE10 . . . . . .134 D6
Featherstone Av, SE23 . .171 E2
Featherstone Gdns, Borwd.
WD6 . . . . .38 C4

Featherstone Ind Est, Sthl.
UB2 . . . . .123 E2
Featherstone Rd, NW7 . . .55 H6
Southall UB2 . . . . . . .122 E3
Featherstone St, EC1 . . . .12 B5
Featherstone Ter, Sthl.
UB2 . . . . .123 E3
Featley Rd, SW9 . . . . . . .151 H3
Federal Rd, Grnf. UB6 . . .105 F2
Federation Rd, SE2 . . . . .138 B4
Fee Fm Rd, Esher (Clay.)
KT10 . . . . .194 C7
Felbridge Av, Stan. HA7 . .68 D1
Felbridge Cl, SW16 . . . . .169 G4
Felbridge Rd, Ilf. IG3 . . . . .99 J2
Felday Rd, SE13 . . . . . . .154 B6
Felden Cl, Pnr. HA5 . . . . .51 E7
Felden St, SW6 . . . . . . .148 C1
Feldman Cl, N16 . . . . . . .94 D1
Felgate Ms, W6 . . . . . . .127 H4
Felhampton Rd, SE9 . . . .174 E2
Felhurst Cres, Dag.
RM10 . . . . .101 H4
Felix Av, N8 . . . . .74 E6
Felix Rd, W13 . . . . .104 D7
Walton-on-Thames
KT12 . . . . .178 A6
Felixstowe Ct, E16
off Fishguard
Way 136/137 E2
Felixstowe Rd, N9 . . . . . .60 D4
N17 . . . . .76 C3
NW10 . . . . .107 H3
SE2 . . . . .138 B3
Fellbrigg Rd, SE22 . . . . .152 C5
Fellbrigg St, E1
off Headlam St . .112/113 E4
Fellbrook, Rich. TW10 . . .163 E3
Fellmongers Path, Sel1 . .29 E4
off Surrey St 201 J2
Fellmongers Yd, Croy. CR0
off Paddington Cl 201 J2
Fellowes Cl, Hayes UB4
off Paddington Cl 102 D4
Fellowes Rd, Cars. SM5 .199 H3
Fellows Ct, E2 . . . . .13 F2
Fellows Rd, NW3 . . . . . . .91 G7
Fell Rd, Croy. CR0 . . . . . .201 J3
Felltram Way, SE7
off Woolwich Rd 135 G5
Fell Wk, Edg. HA8
off East Rd 70 B1
Felmersham Cl, SW4
off Haslerigge Rd . . .150 D4
Felmingham Rd, SE20 . .189 F2
Felnex Trd Est, Wall.
SM6 . . . . .200 A2
Felsberg Rd, SW2 . . . . . .151 E6
Fels Cl, Dag. RM10 . . . . .101 H3
Fels Fm Av, Dag. RM10 . .101 J3
Felsham Rd, SW15 . . . . .148 A3
Felspar Cl, SE18 . . . . . . .137 J5
Felstead Av, Ilf. IG5 . . . . .80 D1
Felstead Gdns, E14
off Ferry St 134 C5
Felstead Rd, E11 . . . . . . .79 G7
Loughton IG10 . . . . . . .48 B7
Felstead St, E9 . . . . .95 J6
Felsted Rd, E16 . . . . . . .116 A6
FELTHAM 160 A3
Feltham Av, E.Mol. KT8 . .180 B4
Felthambrook Way, Felt.
TW13 . . . . .160 B3
Feltham Business Complex,
Felt. TW13 . . . . .160 B2
Feltham Hill Rd, Felt.
TW13 . . . . .160 A4
Feltham Rd, Mitch. CR4 . .185 J2
Felton Cl, Orp. BR5 . . . . .192 E6
Felton Gdns, Bark. IG11
off Sutton Rd 117 H1
Felton Ho, SE3
off Ryan Cl 155 H4
Felton Lea, Sid. DA14 . . .175 J5
Felton Rd, W13
off Camborne Av 125 F2
Barking IG11
off Sutton Rd 117 H2
Felton St, N1 . . . . .112 A1
Fencepiece Rd, Chig. IG7 .65 F5
Ilford IG6 . . . . .65 F5
Fenchurch Av, EC3 . . . . . .20 D4
Fenchurch Bldgs, EC3 . . .20 E4
Fenchurch Pl, EC3 . . . . . .20 E5
Fenchurch St, EC3 . . . . . .20 D5
Fen Ct, EC3 . . . . .20 D5
Fendall Rd, Epsom KT19 .196 C5
Fendall St, SE1 . . . . .29 E6
Fendt Cl, E16
off Bowman Av 115 F7
Fendyke Rd, Belv. DA17 .138 D3

Fenelon Pl, W14 . . . . . . 128 C4
Fen Gro, Sid. DA15 . . . . . 157 J6
Fenham Rd, SE15 . . . . . 132 D7
Fenman Ct, N17
  off Shelbourne Rd .76/77 E1
Fenman Gdns, Ilf. IG3 . . . 100 B1
Fenn Cl, Brom. BR1 . . . . 173 G6
Fennel Cl, E16
  off Cranberry La .114/115 E4
  Croydon CR0
  off Primrose La 203 G1
Fennel St, SE18 . . . . . . 136 D6
Fenner Cl, SE16
  off Layard Rd 132/133 E4
Fenner Sq, SW11
  off Thomas Baines
  Rd 149 G3
Fenning St, SE1 . . . . . . 28 D3
Fenn St, E9 . . . . 95 F5
Fenstanton Av, N12 . . . . 57 G5
Fen St, E16
  off Victoria Dock Rd .115 F7
Fenswood Cl, Bex. DA5 .159 G5
Fentiman Rd, SW8 . . . . 34 B6
Fenton Cl, E8
  off Laurel St 94 C6
  SW9 . . . . 151 F2
  Chislehurst BR7 . . . . 174 C5
★ Fenton Ho, NW3
  (Hampstead) 91 F3
Fenton Rd, N17 . . . . 59 J7
Fentons Av, E13 . . . . . . 115 H2
Fenwick Cl, SE18
  off Ritter St 136 D6
Fenwick Gro, SE15 . . . . 152 D3
Fenwick Pl, SW9 . . . . . 150 E3
  South Croydon CR2
  off Columbine Av 201 H7
Fenwick Rd, SE15 . . . . 152 D3
Ferdinand Pl, NW1
  off Ferdinand St 92 A7
Ferdinand St, NW1 . . . . 92 A6
Ferguson Av, Surb. KT5 .181 J5
Ferguson Cl, E14 . . . . . 134 A4
  Bromley BR2 . . . . . . 190 C3
Ferguson Dr, W3 . . . . . 106 D6
Fergus Rd, N5
  off Calabria Rd 93 H5
Ferme Pk Rd, N4 . . . . . 75 E5
  N8 . . . . 75 E5
Fermor Rd, SE23 . . . . . 171 H1
Fermoy Rd, W9 . . . . . . 108 C4
  Greenford UB6 . . . . . 103 H4
Fern Av, Mitch. CR4 . . . 186 D4
Fernbank, Buck.H. IG9 . . 63 H1
Fernbank Av, Walt. KT12 .179 E4
  Wembley HA0 . . . . . . 86 C4
Fernbank Ms, SW12 . . . 150 C6
Fernbrook Av, Sid. DA15
  off Blackfen Rd 157 H5
Fernbrook Cres, SE13 . . .154 E6
Fernbrook Dr, Har. HA2 . .67 H7
Fernbrook Rd, SE13 . . . 154 E6
Ferncliff Rd, E8 . . . . . . 94 D5
Ferncroft Av, N12 . . . . . 57 H6
  NW3 . . . . 90 D3
  Ruislip HA4 . . . . 84 C2
Ferndale, Brom. BR1 . . . 191 J2
Ferndale Av, E17 . . . . . 78 D5
  Hounslow TW4 . . . . . 143 E3
Ferndale Cl, Bexh. DA7 . .158 E1
Ferndale Ct, SE3 . . . . . 135 F7
Ferndale Rd, E7 . . . . . . 97 H7
  E11 . . . . 97 E2
  N15 . . . . 76 C6
  SE25 . . . . 188 E5
  SW4 . . . . 150 E4
  SW9 . . . . 151 F3
  Romford RM5 . . . . . . 83 J2
Ferndale St, E6 . . . . . . 116 E7
Ferndale Ter, Har. HA1 . .68 C4
Ferndale Way, Orp. BR6 .207 G5
Fern Dene, W13
  off Templewood .104/105 E5
Ferndene Rd, SE24 . . . . 151 J4
Fernden Way, Rom. RM7 .83 H6
Ferndown, Nthwd. HA6 . .66 A2
Ferndown Av, Orp. BR6 .207 G1
Ferndown Cl, Pnr. HA5 . .50 E7
  Sutton SM2 . . . . 199 G6
Ferndown Rd, SE9 . . . . 156 A7
  Watford WD19 . . . . . . 50 C3
Ferney Meade Way, Islw.
  TW7 . . . . 144 D2
Ferney Rd, Barn. EN4 . . .42 A7
Fern Gro, Felt. TW14 . . . 142 B7
Fernhall Dr, Ilf. IG4 . . . . 80 A5
Fernham Rd, Th.Hth. CR7 .187 J3
Fernhead Rd, W9 . . . . . 108 C4
Fernhill Ct, E17 . . . . . . 78 D2

Fernhill Gdns, Kings.T.
  KT2 . . . . 163 G5
Fernhill St, E16 . . . . . . 136 C1
Fernholme Rd, SE15 . . . 153 G5
Fernhurst Gdns, Edg.
  HA8 . . . . 54 A6
Fernhurst Rd, SW6 . . . . 148 B1
  Croydon CR0 . . . . . . 188 D7
Fern La, Houns. TW5 . . . 123 F5
Fernlea Rd, SW12 . . . . 168 B1
  Mitcham CR4 . . . . . . 186 A2
Fernleigh Cl, W9 . . . . . 108 C3
  Croydon CR0
  off Stafford Rd 201 G4
Fernleigh Ct, Har. HA2 . .67 H2
  Wembley HA9 . . . . . . 87 H2
Fernleigh Rd, N21 . . . . .59 G2
Fernsbury St, WC1 . . . . .10 E4
Fernshaw Rd, SW10 . . . .30 C6
Fernside, NW11
  off Finchley Rd 90 D2
  Buckhurst Hill IG9 . . . .63 H1
Fernside Av, NW7 . . . . .54 D3
  Feltham TW13 . . . . . 160 B4
Fernside Rd, SW12 . . . 167 J1
Ferns Rd, E15 . . . . 97 F6
Fern St, E3 . . . . 114 A4
Fernthorpe Rd, SW16 . . 168 C6
Ferntower Rd, N5 . . . . . 94 A5
Fern Wk, SE16 . . . . 37 J4
Fernways, Ilf. IG1
  off Cecil Rd 98/99 E4
Fernwood Av, SW16 . . . 168 D4
  Wembley HA0
  off Bridgewater Rd . . . 87 F5
Fernwood Cl, Brom. BR1 .191 J2
Fernwood Cres, N20 . . . .57 J3
Ferranti Cl, SE18 . . . . . 136 A3
Ferraro Cl, Houns. TW5 . 123 G6
Ferrers Av, Wall. SM6 . . 200 D4
  West Drayton UB7 . . . 120 A2
Ferrers Rd, SW16 . . . . 168 D5
Ferrestone Rd, N8 . . . . .75 F4
Ferrey Ms, SW9 . . . . . . 151 G2
Ferriby Cl, N1
  off Bewdley St 93 G7
Ferrier Pt, E16
  off Forty Acre La 115 H5
Ferrier St, SW18 . . . . . 149 E4
Ferring Cl, Har. HA2 . . . .85 J1
Ferrings, SE21 . . . . . . 170 B2
Ferris Av, Croy. CR0 . . . 203 J3
Ferris Rd, SE22 . . . . . . 152 D4
Ferron Rd, E5 . . . . 94 E3
Ferrour Ct, N2 . . . . 73 G3
Ferryhills Cl, Wat. WD19 .50 C3
Ferry La, N17 . . . . .76 D4
  SW13 . . . . 127 F6
  Brentford TW8 . . . . . 125 H6
  Richmond TW9 . . . . . 125 J6
Ferryman's Quay, SW6 . 149 F2
Ferrymead Av, Grnf.
  UB6 . . . . 103 G3
Ferrymead Dr, Grnf.
  UB6 . . . . 103 G2
Ferrymead Gdns, Grnf.
  UB6 . . . . 103 J2
Ferrymoor, Rich. TW10 . 163 E3
Ferry Pl, SE18
  off Woolwich High St .136 D3
Ferry Rd, SW13 . . . . . . 127 G7
  Teddington TW11 . . . . 162 E5
  Thames Ditton KT7 . . 180 E6
  Twickenham TW1 . . . 162 E1
  West Molesey KT8 . . . 179 G3
Ferry Sq, Brent. TW8 . . 125 H6
Ferry St, E14 . . . . 134 C5
Festing Rd, SW15 . . . . 148 A3
Festival Cl, Bex. DA5 . . 176 D1
Festival Wk, Cars. SM5 . 199 J5
Fetter La, EC4 . . . . .19 F4
Ffinch St, SE8 . . . . 134 A7
Field Cl, E4 . . . . 62 B6
  NW2 . . . . 89 G2
  Bromley BR1 . . . . . . 191 J2
  Buckhurst Hill IG9 . . . .63 J3
  Chessington KT9 . . . . 195 F5
  Hayes UB3 . . . . 121 F7
  Hounslow TW4 . . . . . 142 B1
  West Molesey KT8 . . . 179 H5
Fieldcommon La, Walt.
  KT12 . . . . 179 F7
Field Ct, WC1 . . . . .18 D2
Field End, Barn. EN5 . . . .39 H4
  Northolt UB5 . . . . . . .84 D6
  Ruislip HA4 . . . . .84 C6
  Twickenham TW1 . . . 162 C4
Fieldend Rd, SW16 . . . 186 C1
Field End Rd, Pnr. HA5 . .66 B6
  Ruislip HA4 . . . . .85 E4

Fielders Cl, Enf. EN1
  off Woodfield Cl 44 B4
  Harrow HA2 . . . . .85 J1
Fieldfare Rd, SE28 . . . . 118 C7
Fieldgate La, Mitch. CR4 .185 H3
Fieldgate St, E1 . . . . . . .21 J2
Fieldhouse Cl, E18 . . . . .79 G1
Fieldhouse Rd, SW12 . . 168 C1
Fielding Av, Twick. TW2 .161 J2
Fielding Ho, NW6 . . . . . 108 D3
Fielding Ms, SW13
  off Castelnau 127 H6
Fielding Rd, W4 . . . . . . 126 D3
  W14 . . . . 128 A3
Fieldings, The, SE23 . . . 171 F1
Fielding St, SE17 . . . . . .35 J5
Fielding Wk, W13 . . . . . 124 E3
Field La, Brent. TW8 . . . 125 F7
  Teddington TW11 . . . . 162 D5
Field Mead, NW7 . . . . . .55 E7
  NW9 . . . . .55 E7
Field Pl, N.Mal. KT3 . . . 183 F6
Field Rd, E7 . . . . .97 F4
  N17 . . . . .76 A3
  W6 . . . . 128 B5
  Feltham TW14 . . . . . 142 B6
Fieldsend Rd, Sutt. SM3 .198 B5
Fields Est, E8 . . . . .94 D7
Fieldside Cl, Orp. BR6
  off State Fm Av 207 F4
Fieldside Rd, Brom. BR1 .172 D5
Fields Pk Cres, Rom.
  RM6 . . . . .82 D5
Field St, WC1 . . . . .10 C3
Fieldview, SW18 . . . . . 167 G1
Field Way, NW10
  off Twybridge Way 88 C7
  Croydon CR0 . . . . . . 204 B6
Fieldway, Dag. RM8 . . . 100 B4
Field Way, Grnf. UB6 . . . 103 H1
Fieldway, Orp. BR5 . . . . 193 G6
Fieldway Cres, N5 . . . . .93 G5
Fiennes Cl, Dag. RM8 . . 100 C1
Fiesta Dr, Dag. RM9 . . . 119 J4
Fife Rd, E16 . . . . 115 G5
  N22 . . . . .59 H7
  SW14 . . . . 146 C5
  Kingston upon Thames
  KT1 . . . . 181 H2
Fife Ter, N1 . . . . .10 D1
Fifield Path, SE23
  off Bampton Rd 171 G3
Fifth Av, E12 . . . . .98 C4
  W10 . . . . 108 B3
  Hayes UB3 . . . . 121 J1
Fifth Cross Rd, Twick.
  TW2 . . . . 162 A2
Fifth Way, Wem. HA9 . . .88 B4
Figges Rd, Mitch. CR4 . . 168 A7
Fig Tree Cl, NW10
  off Craven Pk . . . 106/107 E1
Filby Rd, Chess. KT9 . . . 195 J6
Filey Av, N16 . . . . .94 D1
Filey Cl, Sutt. SM2 . . . . 199 F7
Filey Waye, Ruis. HA4 . . .84 A2
Filigree Ct, SE16
  off Silver Wk 133 J1
Fillebrook Av, Enf. EN1 . .44 B2
Fillebrook Rd, E11 . . . . .96 D1
Filmer Rd, SW6 . . . . . . 148 B1
Filston Rd, Erith DA8
  off Riverdale Rd 139 H5
Finborough Rd, SW10 . . .30 A5
  SW17 . . . . 167 J6
Finchale Rd, SE2 . . . . . 138 A3
Finch Av, SE27 . . . . 170 A4
Finch Cl, NW10 . . . . . . .88 D5
  Barnet EN5 . . . . .40 D5
Finchdean Ho, SW15
  off Tangley Gro 147 F7
Finch Dr, Felt. TW14 . . . 142 D7
Finch Gdns, E4 . . . . . . .62 A5
Finchingfield Av, Wdf.Grn.
  IG8 . . . . .63 J7
Finch La, EC3 . . . . .20 C4
FINCHLEY, N3 . . . . .72 E1
Finchley Ct, N3 . . . . . . .57 E6
Finchley La, NW4 . . . . . .71 J4
Finchley Pk, N12 . . . . . .57 F4
Finchley Pl, NW8 . . . . . . .6 E1
Finchley Rd, NW2 . . . . . .90 D3
  NW3 . . . . .91 F6
  NW8 . . . . 109 G1
  NW11 . . . . .72 C6
Finchley Way, N3 . . . . . .56 D7
Finch Ms, SE15 . . . . . . 132 C7
Finck St, SE1 . . . . .26 D4
Finden Rd, E7 . . . . .97 H5
Findhorn Av, Hayes UB4 .102 B5
Findhorn St, E14 . . . . . 114 C6

Findon Cl, SW18
  off Wimbledon Pk Rd .148 D6
  Harrow HA2 . . . . .85 H3
Findon Rd, N9 . . . . .60 E1
  W12 . . . . 127 G2
Fingal St, SE10 . . . . . . 135 F5
Finland Quay, SE16
  off Finland St 133 H3
Finland Rd, SE4 . . . . . . 153 H3
Finland St, SE16 . . . . . 133 H3
Finlays Cl, Chess. KT9 . . 196 A5
Finlay St, SW6 . . . . . . 148 A1
Finney La, Islw. TW7 . . . 144 D1
Finnis St, E2 . . . . 113 E3
Finnymore Rd, Dag.
  RM9 . . . . 101 E7
FINSBURY, EC1 . . . . . . .11 F3
Finsbury Av, EC2 . . . . . .20 C2
Finsbury Circ, EC2 . . . . .20 C2
Finsbury Cotts, N22
  off Clarence Rd 58/59 E7
Finsbury Est, EC1 . . . . . .11 G4
Finsbury Ho, N22 . . . . . .75 E1
Finsbury Mkt, EC2 . . . . .12 D6
FINSBURY PARK, N4 . . . .93 G1
★ Finsbury Park, N4 . . . .75 H7
Finsbury Pk Av, N4 . . . . .75 J6
Finsbury Pk Rd, N4 . . . . .93 H2
Finsbury Pavement, EC2 .20 C1
Finsbury Rd, N22 . . . . . .75 F1
Finsbury Sq, EC2 . . . . . .20 C1
Finsbury St, EC2 . . . . . .20 B1
Finsbury Twr, EC1 . . . . . .12 B6
Finsbury Way, Bex. DA5 .159 F6
Finsen Rd, SE5 . . . . . . 151 J3
Finstock Rd, W10 . . . . . 108 A6
Finucane Ri, Bushey
  (Bushey Hth.) WD23 . . .51 J2
Firbank Cl, E16 . . . . . . 116 A5
  Enfield EN2
  off Gladbeck Way 43 J4
Firbank Rd, SE15 . . . . . 153 E2
Fir Cl, Walt. KT12 . . . . . 178 A7
Fircroft Gdns, Har. HA1 . .86 B3
Fircroft Rd, SW17 . . . . . 167 J2
  Chessington KT9 . . . . 195 J4
Fir Dene, Orp. BR6 . . . . 206 C3
Firdene, Surb. KT5 . . . . 196 C1
Fire Bell All, Surb. KT6 . .181 H6
Firecrest Dr, NW3 . . . . . .91 E3
Firefly Cl, Wall. SM6 . . . 200 E7
Firefly Gdns, E6
  off Jack Dash Way . . . 116 B4
★ Firepower, SE18 . . . . 137 E3
Fire Sta All, Barn. EN5
  off Christchurch La 40 C2
Firethorn Cl, Edg. HA8
  off Larkspur Gro 54 C4
Fir Gro, N.Mal. KT3 . . . . 183 F6
Firhill Rd, SE6 . . . . 172 A4
Fir Rd, Felt. TW13 . . . . . 160 D5
  Sutton SM3 . . . . 198 C1
Firs, The, E17
  off Leucha Rd 77 H5
  N20 . . . . .57 G1
  W5 . . . . 105 G5
Firs Av, N10 . . . . .74 A3
  N11 . . . . .58 A6
  SW14 . . . . 146 C4
Firsby Av, Croy. CR0 . . . 203 G1
Firsby Rd, N16 . . . . .94 C1
Firs Cl, N10
  off Firs Av 74 A3
  SE23 . . . . 153 G7
  Esher (Clay.) KT10 . . . 194 B6
  Mitcham CR4 . . . . . . 186 B2
Firscroft, N13 . . . . .59 J3
Firs Dr, Houns. TW5 . . . 122 B7
  Loughton IG10 . . . . . .48 D1
Firside Gro, Sid. DA15 . . 175 J1
Firs La, N13 . . . . .59 J3
  N21 . . . . .59 J2
Firs Pk Av, N21 . . . . . . .60 A1
Firs Pk Gdns, N21 . . . . .59 J1
First Av, E12 . . . . .98 B4
  E13 . . . . 115 G3
  E17 . . . . .78 A5
  N18 . . . . .61 F4
  NW4 . . . . .71 J4
  SW14 . . . . 146 E3
  W3 . . . . 127 F1
  W10 . . . . 108 C4
  Bexleyheath DA7 . . . . 138 C7
  Dagenham RM10 . . . . 119 H2
  Enfield EN1 . . . . .44 C6
  Greenford UB6 . . . . . .86 A7
  Hayes UB3 . . . . 121 J1
  Romford RM6 . . . . . . .82 C5
  Walton-on-Thames
  KT12 . . . . 178 B6

First Av, Wembley HA9 . . .87 G2
West Molesey KT8 . . . .179 F4
First Cl, W.Mol. KT8 . . . . .179 J3
First Cross Rd, Twick.
   TW2 . . . . .162 B2
First Dr, NW10 . . . . .88 C7
First St, SW3 . . . . .31 H1
Firstway, SW20 . . . . .183 J2
First Way, Wem. HA9 . . . . .88 B4
Firs Wk, Wdf.Grn. IG8 . . . .63 G5
Firswood Av, Epsom
   KT19 . . . . .197 F5
Firth Gdns, SW6 . . . . . . .148 B1
Fir Tree Av, Mitch. CR4 . . .186 A2
   West Drayton UB7 . . . .120 D3
Fir Tree Cl, SW16 . . . . . . .168 C5
   W5 . . . . .105 H6
   Epsom (Ewell) KT19 . . .197 F4
   Orpington BR6
      off Highfield Av 207 J5
Fir Tree Gdns, Croy.
   CR0 . . . . .204 A4
Fir Tree Gro, Cars. SM5 . .199 J7
Fir Tree Rd, Houns.TW4 . .143 E4
Fir Trees Cl, SE16 . . . . . .133 H1
Fir Tree Wk, Dag. RM10
   off Wheel Fm Dr 101 J3
Enfield EN1 . . . . .44 A3
Fisher Cl, Croy. CR0
   off Grant Rd 202 C1
Greenford UB6
   off Gosling Cl 103 G3
Fisherman Cl, Rich. TW10
   off Locksmeade Rd . . .163 F4
Fishermans Dr, SE16 . . . .133 G2
Fisherman's Wk, E14 . . . .134 A1
Fishermans Wk, SE28
   off Tugboat St 137 H2
Fisher Rd, Har. HA3 . . . . . .68 C2
Fishers Cl, SW16
   off Garrad's Rd 168 D3
Fishers Ct, SE14
   off Besson St 153 G1
Fishersdene, Esher (Clay.)
   KT10 . . . . .194 D7
Fishers La, W4 . . . . .126 D4
Fisher St, E16 . . . . .115 G5
   WC1 . . . . .18 B2
Fishers Way, Belv. DA17 . .139 J1
Fisherton St, NW8 . . . . .7 E6
Fishguard Way, E16 . . . . .137 E2
Fishponds Rd, SW17 . . . .167 H4
   Keston BR2 . . . . .206 A5
Fish St Hill, EC3 . . . . .20 C5
Fitzalan Rd, N3 . . . . .72 B3
   Esher (Clay.) KT10 . . . .194 B7
Fitzalan St, SE11 . . . . .34 D1
Fitzgeorge Av, W14 . . . . .128 B4
   New Malden KT3 . . . . .182 D1
Fitzgerald Av, SW14 . . . . .147 E3
Fitzgerald Cl, E11
   off Fitzgerald Rd 79 G5
Fitzgerald Ho, E14 . . . . . .114 B6
   Hayes UB3 . . . . .122 B1
Fitzgerald Rd, E11 . . . . . . .79 G5
   SW14 . . . . .146 D3
   Thames Ditton KT7 . . .180 D6
Fitzhardinge St, W1 . . . . . .16 B3
Fitzherbert Rd, Rich. TW10
   off Kingsmead 145 J6
Fitzhugh Gro, SW18 . . . . .149 G6
Fitzjames Av, W14 . . . . . .128 B4
   Croydon CR0 . . . . .202 D2
Fitzjohn Av, Barn. EN5 . . . .40 B5
Fitzjohn's Av, NW3 . . . . . . .91 G5
Fitzmaurice Pl, W1 . . . . . . .24 E1
Fitzneal St, W12 . . . . .107 F6
Fitzroy Cl, N6 . . . . .91 J1
Fitzroy Ct, W1 . . . . .9 G6
Fitzroy Cres, W4 . . . . .126 D7
Fitzroy Gdns, SE19 . . . . . .170 B7
Fitzroy Ms, W1 . . . . .9 F6
Fitzroy Pk, N6 . . . . .91 J1
Fitzroy Rd, NW1 . . . . .110 A1
Fitzroy Sq, W1 . . . . .9 F6
Fitzroy St, W1 . . . . .9 F6
Fitzroy Yd, NW1
   off Fitzroy Rd 110 A1
Fitzstephen Rd, Dag.
   RM8 . . . . .100 B5
Fitzwarren Gdns, N19 . . . .92 C1
Fitzwilliam Av, Rich.
   TW9 . . . . .145 J2
Fitzwilliam Ms, E16
   off Hanover Av 135 G1
Fitzwilliam Rd, SW4 . . . . .150 C3
Fitzwygram Cl, Hmptn.
   (Hmptn.H.) TW12 . . . .161 J5
Five Acre, NW9 . . . . .71 F1
Fiveacre Cl, Th.Hth. CR7 . .187 G6

Five Bell All, E14
   off Three Colt St 113 J7
Five Elms Rd, Brom.
   BR2 . . . . .205 H3
   Dagenham RM9 . . . . . .101 F3
Five Flds Cl, Wat. WD19 . . .51 F3
Fives Ct, SE11 . . . . .35 G1
Fiveways Rd, SW9 . . . . . .151 G2
Fladbury Rd, N15 . . . . .76 A6
Fladgate Rd, E11 . . . . .79 E6
Flag Cl, Croy. CR0 . . . . . .203 G1
Flag Wk, Pnr. HA5
   off Eastcote Rd 66 A6
Flamback Rd, Har. HA1 . . .68 D6
Flamborough Rd, Ruis.
   HA4 . . . . .84 A3
Flamborough St, E14 . . . .113 H6
Flamborough Wk, E14
   off Flamborough St . . .113 H6
Flamingo Gdns, Nthlt. UB5
   off Jetstar Way . . .102/103 E3
Flamstead Gdns, Dag. RM9
   off Flamstead Rd 100 C7
Flamstead Rd, Dag.
   RM9 . . . . .100 C7
Flamsted Av, Wem. HA9 . . .88 A4
★ Flamsteed House Mus,
   SE10 . . . . .134 D7
Flamsteed Rd, SE7 . . . . . .136 B5
Flanchford Rd, W12 . . . . .127 F3
Flanders Cres, SW17 . . . .167 J7
Flanders Rd, E6 . . . . .116 C2
   W4 . . . . .127 E4
Flanders Way, E9 . . . . .95 G6
Flank St, E1 . . . . .21 H5
Flask Cotts, NW3
   off New End Sq 91 G4
Flask Wk, NW3 . . . . .91 G4
Flat Iron Sq, SE1
   off Union St 131 J1
Flavell Ms, SE10 . . . . .135 E5
Flaxen Cl, E4
   off Flaxen Rd 62 B3
Flaxen Rd, E4 . . . . .62 B3
Flaxley Rd, Mord. SM4 . . .184 E6
Flaxman Ct, W1 . . . . .17 H4
Flaxman Rd, SE5 . . . . . . .151 H2
Flaxman Ter, WC1 . . . . .9 J4
Flaxton Rd, SE18 . . . . . . .157 G1
Flecker Cl, Stan. HA7 . . . . .52 C5
Fleece Dr, N9 . . . . .60 D4
Fleece Rd, Surb. KT6 . . . .195 F1
Fleece Wk, N7
   off Manger Rd 92/93 E6
Fleeming Cl, E17
   off Pennant Ter 77 J2
Fleeming Rd, E17 . . . . .77 J2
Fleet Cl, W.Mol. KT8 . . . . .179 F5
Fleet La, W.Mol. KT8 . . . . .179 F6
Fleet Pl, EC4
   off Farringdon St 111 G6
Fleet Rd, NW3 . . . . .91 H5
Fleetside, W.Mol. KT8 . . . .179 H6
Fleet Sq, WC1 . . . . .10 C4
Fleet St, EC4 . . . . .19 E4
Fleet St Hill, E1 . . . . .13 H6
Fleetway Business Pk, Grnf.
   UB6 . . . . .105 E2
Fleetwood Cl, E16 . . . . . . .116 A5
   Chessington KT9 . . . . .195 G7
   Croydon CR0 . . . . .202 C3
Fleetwood Ct, E6
   off Evelyn Denington
   Rd 116 C5
Fleetwood Gro, W3
   off East Acton La .106/107 E7
Fleetwood Rd, NW10 . . . . .89 G5
   Kingston upon Thames
   KT1 . . . . .182 B3
Fleetwood Sq, Kings.T.
   KT1 . . . . .182 B3
Fleetwood St, N16
   off Stoke Newington
   Ch St 94 B2
Fleetwood Way, Wat.
   WD19 . . . . .50 C4
Fleming Cl, W9
   off Chippenham Rd . . .108 D4
Fleming Ct, W2 . . . . .14 E1
   Croydon CR0 . . . . .201 G5
Fleming Dr, N21 . . . . .43 F5
Fleming Mead, Mitch.
   CR4 . . . . .167 H7
Fleming Rd, SE17 . . . . .35 H5
   Southall UB1 . . . . .103 H6
Fleming Wk, NW9
   off Pasteur Cl 70/71 E2
Fleming Way, SE28 . . . . . .118 D7
   Isleworth TW7 . . . . . . .144 C3

Flemming Av, Ruis. HA4 . .84 B1
Flempton Rd, E10 . . . . .95 H1
Fletcher Cl, E6
   off Trader Rd 116/117 E6
Fletcher La, E10 . . . . .78 C7
Fletcher Path, SE8
   off New Butt La 134 A7
Fletcher Rd, W4 . . . . .126 C3
   Chigwell IG7 . . . . .65 J5
Fletchers Cl, Brom. BR2 . .191 H4
Fletcher St, E1 . . . . .21 J5
Fletching Rd, E5 . . . . .95 F3
   SE7 . . . . .135 J6
Fletton Rd, N11 . . . . .58 E7
Fleur de Lis St, E1 . . . . . . .13 E6
Fleur Gates, SW19
   off Princes Way 148 A7
Flexmere Gdns, N17
   off Flexmere Rd 76 A1
Flexmere Rd, N17 . . . . .76 A1
Flight App, NW9 . . . . .71 F2
Flimwell Cl, Brom. BR1 . . .172 E5
Flintmill Cres, SE3 . . . . . .156 B2
Flinton St, SE17 . . . . .36 E3
Flint St, SE17 . . . . .36 C2
Flitcroft St, WC2 . . . . .17 J3
Flock Mill Pl, SW18 . . . . . .166 E1
Flockton St, SE16 . . . . .29 H4
Flodden Rd, SE5 . . . . .151 J1
Flood La, Twick. TW1
   off Church La 162 D1
Flood Pas, SE18
   off Samuel St 136 C4
Flood St, SW3 . . . . .31 H4
Flood Wk, SW3 . . . . .31 H5
Flora Cl, E14 . . . . .114 B6
Flora Gdns, W6
   off Ravenscourt Rd . . .127 H4
   Romford RM6 . . . . .82 C6
Floral St, WC2 . . . . .18 A5
Flora St, Belv. DA17
   off Victoria St 139 F5
Florence Av, Enf. EN2 . . . . .43 J3
   Morden SM4 . . . . .185 F5
Florence Cantwell Wk, N19
   off Hillrise Rd 74/75 E7
Florence Cl, Walt. KT12
   off Florence Rd 178 B7
Florence Dr, Enf. EN2 . . . . .43 J3
Florence Elson Cl, E12
   off Grantham Rd 98 D4
Florence Gdns, W4 . . . . . .126 C6
   Romford RM6
   off Roxy Av 82 C7
Florence Nightingale Ho, N1
   off Clephane Rd 94 A6
★ Florence Nightingale Mus,
   SE1 . . . . .26 C4
Florence Rd, E6 . . . . .115 J1
   E13 . . . . .115 F2
   N4 . . . . .93 G1
   SE2 . . . . .138 C3
   SE14 . . . . .153 J1
   SW19 . . . . .166 E6
   W4 . . . . .126 D3
   W5 . . . . .105 H7
   Beckenham BR3 . . . . .189 G2
   Bromley BR1 . . . . .191 G1
   Feltham TW13 . . . . . . .160 B1
   Kingston upon Thames
   KT2 . . . . .163 J7
   Southall UB2 . . . . .122 D4
   Walton-on-Thames
   KT12 . . . . .178 B7
Florence St, E16 . . . . .115 F4
   N1 . . . . .93 H7
   NW4 . . . . .71 J4
Florence Ter, SE14 . . . . . .153 J1
Florence Way, SW12 . . . . .167 J1
Florfield Pas, E8
   off Reading La 94/95 E6
Florfield Rd, E8
   off Reading La 94/95 E6
Florian Av, Sutt. SM1 . . . .199 G4
Florian Rd, SW15 . . . . . . .148 B4
Florida Cl, Bushey
   (Bushey Hth.) WD23 . . .52 A2
Florida Rd, Th.Hth. CR7 . .187 H1
Florida St, E2 . . . . .13 H4
Florin Ct, SE1
   off Tanner St 132 C2
Floris Pl, SW4
   off Fitzwilliam Rd 150 C3
Floriston Cl, Stan. HA7 . . . .69 E1
Floriston Ct, Nthlt. UB5 . . .85 H5
Floriston Gdns, Stan.
   HA7 . . . . .69 E1
Floss St, SW15 . . . . .147 J2
Flower & Dean Wk, E1 . . . .21 G2
Flower La, NW7 . . . . .55 F5

★ Flower Mkt, New Covent
   Garden Mkt, SW8 . . . .34 A6
Flower Ms, NW11 . . . . .72 B6
Flower Pot Cl, N15
   off St. Ann's Rd 76 C6
Flowers Cl, NW2 . . . . .89 G3
Flowersmead, SW17 . . . . .168 A2
Flowers Ms, N19
   off Archway Rd 92 C2
Floyd Rd, SE7 . . . . .135 J5
Fludyer St, SE13 . . . . .154 E4
Foley La, Esher (Clay.)
   KT10 . . . . .194 B7
Foley Rd, Esher (Clay.)
   KT10 . . . . .194 B7
Foley St, W1 . . . . .17 F2
Folgate St, E1 . . . . .21 E1
Foliot St, W12 . . . . .107 F6
Folkestone Rd, E6 . . . . . . .116 D2
   E17 . . . . .78 B4
   N18 . . . . .60 D4
Folkingham La, NW9 . . . . . .70 D1
Folkington Cor, N12 . . . . . .56 C5
Follett St, E14 . . . . .114 C6
Folly La, E4 . . . . .61 J7
   E17 . . . . .77 H1
Folly Ms, W11
   off Portobello Rd 108 C6
Folly Wall, E14 . . . . .134 C2
Fontaine Rd, SW16 . . . . . .169 F7
Fontarabia Rd, SW11 . . . .150 A4
Fontayne Av, Chig. IG7 . . . .65 F4
Fontenoy Rd, SW12 . . . . .168 B2
Fonteyne Gdns, Wdf.Grn. IG8
   off Lechmere Av 80 A2
Fonthill Cl, SE20
   off Selby Rd 188 D2
Fonthill Ms, N4
   off Lennox Rd 93 G2
Fonthill Rd, N4 . . . . .93 F1
Font Hills, N2 . . . . .73 F2
Fontley Way, SW15 . . . . . .147 G7
Fontwell Cl, Har. HA3 . . . . .52 B7
   Northolt UB5 . . . . .85 G6
Fontwell Dr, Brom.
   BR2 . . . . .192 D5
Football La, Har. HA1 . . . . .86 B1
Footpath, The, SW15 . . . .147 G5
FOOTS CRAY, Sid. 176 B6
Foots Cray High St, Sid.
   DA14 . . . . .176 C6
Foots Cray La, Sid.
   DA14 . . . . .176 C1
Footscray Rd, SE9 . . . . . .156 D6
Footway, The, SE9 . . . . . .157 F7
Forbes Cl, NW2 . . . . .89 G3
Forbes Ct, SE19 . . . . .170 B5
Forbes St, E1 . . . . .21 J4
Forbes Way, Ruis. HA4 . . . .84 B2
Forburg Rd, N16 . . . . .94 D1
Ford Cl, E3
   off Roman Rd 113 H2
   Harrow HA1 . . . . .68 A7
   Thornton Heath CR7 . .187 H6
Forde Av, Brom. BR1 . . . .191 J3
Fordel Rd, SE6 . . . . .172 D1
Ford End, Wdf.Grn. IG8 . . .63 H6
Fordham Cl, Barn. EN4 . . .41 H3
Fordham Rd, Barn. EN4 . . .41 G3
Fordham St, E1 . . . . .21 J3
Fordhook Av, W5 . . . . .105 J7
Fordingley Rd, W9 . . . . . . .108 C3
Fordington Rd, N6 . . . . . . .73 J5
Fordmill Rd, SE6 . . . . .172 A2
Ford Rd, E3 . . . . .113 H1
   Dagenham RM9,
   RM10 . . . . .101 F7
Fords Gro, N21 . . . . .59 J1
Fords Pk Rd, E16 . . . . .115 G6
Ford Sq, E1 . . . . .113 E5
Ford St, E3 . . . . .113 H1
   E16 . . . . .115 F6
Fordwich Cl, Orp. BR6 . . . .193 J7
Fordwych Rd, NW2 . . . . . . .90 B5
Fordyce Ho, SW16
   off Colson Way 168 C4
Fordyce Rd, SE13 . . . . . . .154 C6
Fordyke Rd, Dag. RM8 . . . .101 F2
★ Foreign & Commonwealth
   Office, SW1 . . . . .26 A3
Foreland Ct, NW4 . . . . .72 B1
Foreland St, SE18
   off Plumstead Rd 137 G4
Foreman Ct, W6
   off Hammersmith
   Bdy 127 J4
Foremark Cl, Ilf. IG6 . . . . . .65 J5
Foreshore, SE8 . . . . .133 J4
Forest, The, E11 . . . . .79 E4

Forest App, E4 . . . . .47 E7
  Woodford Green IG8 . .63 F7
Forest Av, E4 . . . . .47 E7
  Chigwell IG7 . . . . .64 D5
Forest Business Pk, E17 . .77 G7
Forest Cl, E11 . . . . .79 F5
  Chislehurst BR7 . . . . .192 D1
  Woodford Green IG8 . .63 H3
Forest Ct, E4 . . . . .63 F1
  E11 . . . . .79 E4
Forestdale, N14 . . . . .58 D4
Forest Dr, E12 . . . . .98 A3
  Keston BR2 . . . . .206 B4
  Woodford Green IG8 . .62 D7
Forest Dr E, E11 . . . . .78 D7
Forest Dr W, E11 . . . . .78 C7
Forest Edge, Buck.H. IG9 .63 J4
Forester Rd, SE15 . . . . . .153 E4
Foresters Cl, Wall. SM6 . .200 D7
Foresters Cres, Bexh.
  DA7 . . . . .159 H4
Foresters Dr, E17 . . . . . . .78 D4
  Wallington SM6 . . . . .200 D7
Forest Gdns, N17 . . . . . . .76 C2
FOREST GATE, E7 . . . . . .97 G5
Forest Gate, NW9 . . . . . . .70 E5
Forest Glade, E4 . . . . .62 E4
  E11 . . . . .79 E6
Forest Gro, E8 . . . . .94 C7
Forest Hts, Buck.H. IG9 . .63 G2
FOREST HILL, SE23 . . . .171 G1
Forest Hill Business Cen,
  SE23 . . . . .171 F2
Forest Hill Ind Est, SE23
  off Perry Vale 171 F2
Forest Hill Rd, SE22 . . . .152 E5
  SE23 . . . . .152 E5
Forestholme Cl, SE23 . . .171 F2
Forest Ind Pk, Ilf. IG6 . . . .81 H1
Forest La, E7 . . . . .97 E5
  E15 . . . . .97 E5
  Chigwell IG7 . . . . .64 D5
Forest Mt Rd, Wdf.Grn.
  IG8 . . . . .62 D7
Fore St, EC2 . . . . .20 A2
  N9 . . . . .60 D5
  N18 . . . . .60 C6
  Pinner HA5 . . . . .66 A5
Fore St Av, EC2 . . . . .20 B2
Forest Ridge, Beck.
  BR3 . . . . .190 A3
  Keston BR2 . . . . .206 B4
Forest Ri, E17 . . . . .78 D5
Forest Rd, E7 . . . . .97 G4
  E8 . . . . .94 C6
  E11 . . . . .78 D7
  E17 . . . . .77 F4
  N9 . . . . .61 E1
  N17 . . . . .77 F4
  Feltham TW13 . . . . . .160 C2
  Ilford IG6 . . . . .81 H1
  Loughton IG10 . . . . . .48 A3
  Richmond TW9 . . . . .126 A7
  Romford RM7 . . . . . . .83 H3
  Sutton SM3 . . . . .198 D1
  Woodford Green IG8 . .63 G3
Forest Side, E4 . . . . .47 F7
  E7 off Capel Rd 97 H4
  Buckhurst Hill IG9 . . . .63 J1
  Worcester Park KT4 . .197 F1
Forest St, E7 . . . . .97 G5
Forest Vw, E4 . . . . .46 D7
  E11 off High Rd
  Leytonstone 79 F7
Forest Vw Av, E10 . . . . . .78 D5
Forest Vw Rd, E12 . . . . . .98 B4
  E17 . . . . .78 C1
  Loughton IG10 . . . . . .48 A4
Forest Way, N19
  off Hargrave Pk 92 C2
  Loughton IG10 . . . . . .48 B3
  Orpington BR5 . . . . . .193 J5
  Sidcup DA15 . . . . . . .157 G7
  Woodford Green IG8 . .63 H4
Forfar Rd, N22 . . . . .75 H1
  SW11 . . . . .150 A1
Forge Cl, Brom. BR2 . . . .205 G1
  Hayes UB3
  off High St 121 G6
Forge Cotts, W5
  off Ealing Grn 125 G1
Forge Dr, Esher (Clay.)
  KT10 . . . . .194 D7
Forge La, Felt. TW13 . . . .160 E6
  Sunbury-on-Thames
  TW16 . . . . .178 A3
  Sutton SM3 . . . . .198 B7
Forge Ms, Sun. TW16
  off Forge La 178 A3

Forge Pl, NW1
  off Malden Cres 92 A6
Forlong Path, Nthlt. UB5
  off Arnold Rd 84/85 E6
Forman Pl, N16
  off Farleigh Rd 94 C4
Formation, The, E16
  off Woolwich Manor
  Way 136/137 E2
Formby Av, Stan. HA7 . . . .69 F3
Formosa St, W9 . . . . .6 C6
Formunt Cl, E16
  off Vincent St 115 F5
Forres Gdns, NW11 . . . . . .72 D6
Forrester Path, SE26 . . . .171 G4
Forrest Gdns, SW16 . . . .187 F3
Forris Av, Hayes UB3 . . . .121 J1
Forset St, W1 . . . . .15 H3
Forstal Cl, Brom. BR2
  off Ridley Rd 191 G3
Forster Cl, E17 . . . . .62 D7
Forster Rd, E17 . . . . .77 H6
  N17 . . . . .76 C3
  SW2 . . . . .150 E7
  Beckenham BR3 . . . .189 H3
  Croydon CR0
  off Windmill Rd 187 J7
Forsters Cl, Rom. RM6 . . .83 F6
Forster's Way, SW18 . . . .166 E1
Forsters Way, Hayes
  UB4 . . . . .102 B6
Forston St, N1 . . . . .12 B1
Forsyte Cres, SE19 . . . . .188 B1
Forsyth Gdns, SE17 . . . . .35 H5
Forsythia Cl, Ilf. IG1 . . . . .98 E5
Forsyth Pl, Enf. EN1 . . . . .44 B5
Forterie Gdns, Ilf. IG3 . . .100 A3
Fortescue Av, E8
  off Mentmore Ter . .94/95 E7
  Twickenham TW2 . . . .161 J3
Fortescue Rd, SW19 . . . .167 G7
  Edgware HA8 . . . . . . .70 D1
Fortess Gro, NW5
  off Fortess Rd 92 B5
Fortess Rd, NW5 . . . . .92 B5
Fortess Wk, NW5
  off Fortess Rd 92 B5
Forthbridge Rd, SW11 . . .150 A4
Fortis Cl, E16 . . . . .115 J6
FORTIS GREEN, N2 . . . . .73 J4
Fortis Grn, N2 . . . . .73 H4
  N10 . . . . .73 H4
Fortis Grn Av, N2 . . . . . . .73 J3
Fortis Grn Rd, N10 . . . . . .74 A3
Fortismere Av, N10 . . . . . .74 A3
Fortnam Rd, N19 . . . . .92 D2
★ Fortnum & Mason,
  W1 . . . . .25 F1
Fortnums Acre, Stan.
  HA7 . . . . .52 C6
Fort Rd, SE1 . . . . .37 G2
  Northolt UB5 . . . . .85 G7
Fortrose Gdns, SW2
  off New Pk Rd 168 D1
Fort St, E1 . . . . .21 E2
  E16 . . . . .135 H1
Fortuna Cl, N7 . . . . .93 F6
  off Vulcan Way
Fortune Gate Rd,
  NW10 . . . . .107 E1
Fortune Grn Rd, NW6 . . . .90 D4
Fortunes Mead, Nthlt.
  UB5 . . . . .85 E6
Fortune St, EC1 . . . . .12 A6
Fortune Wk, SE28
  off Broadwater Rd . . .137 G3
Fortune Way, NW10 . . . . .107 G3
Forty Acre La, E16 . . . . . .115 G5
Forty Av, Wem. HA9 . . . . .87 J3
Forty Cl, Wem. HA9 . . . . .87 J2
Forty Footpath, SW14 . . .146 C3
Forty La, Wem. HA9 . . . . .88 B2
Forum, The, W.Mol. KT8 .179 H4
Forum Magnum Sq, SE1 .26 C3
Forumside, Edg. HA8
  off High St 54 A6
Forum Way, Edg. HA8
  off High St 54 A6
Forval Cl, Mitch. CR4 . . . .185 J5
Forward Dr, Har. HA3 . . . .68 C4
Fosbury Ms, W2 . . . . .14 B6
Foscote Ms, W9
  off Amberley Rd 108 D5
Foscote Rd, NW4 . . . . . . .71 H6
Foskett Rd, SW6 . . . . . . .148 C2
Foss Av, Croy. CR0 . . . . .201 G5
Fossdene Rd, SE7 . . . . . .135 H5
Fossdyke Cl, Hayes UB4 .103 E5
Fosse Way, W13 . . . . .104 D5

Fossil Rd, SE13 . . . . .154 A3
Fossington Rd, Belv.
  DA17 . . . . .138 D4
Foss Rd, SW17 . . . . .167 G4
Fossway, Dag. RM8 . . . . .100 C2
Foster La, EC2 . . . . .19 J3
Foster Rd, E13 . . . . .115 G4
  W3 . . . . .106 E7
  W4 . . . . .126 D5
Fosters Cl, E18 . . . . .79 H1
  Chislehurst BR7 . . . .174 C5
Foster St, NW4 . . . . .71 J4
Foster Wk, NW4
  off New Brent St 71 J4
Fothergill Cl, E13 . . . . . . .115 G2
Fothergill Dr, N21 . . . . . . .43 E5
Fotheringham Rd, Enf.
  EN1 . . . . .44 C4
Foubert's Pl, W1 . . . . .17 F4
Foulden Rd, N16 . . . . .94 C4
Foulden Ter, N16
  off Foulden Rd 94 C4
Foulis Ter, SW7 . . . . .31 F3
Foulser Rd, SW17 . . . . . .167 J3
Foulsham Rd, Th.Hth.
  CR7 . . . . .187 J3
Founder Cl, E6
  off Trader Rd 116/117 E6
Founders Ct, EC2 . . . . . . .20 B3
Founders Gdns, SE19 . . .169 J7
Foundry Cl, SE16 . . . . . . .133 H1
Foundry Ms, NW1 . . . . .9 G5
Fountain Ct, EC4 . . . . .19 E5
Fountain Dr, SE19 . . . . . .170 C4
Fountain Grn Sq, SE16 . . .29 J3
Fountain Ms, N5
  off Kelross Rd 93 J4
  NW3
  off Haverstock Hill 91 J6
Fountain Pl, SW9 . . . . . . .151 G1
Fountain Rd, SW17 . . . . .167 G5
  Thornton Heath CR7 . .187 J2
Fountains, The, Loug. IG10
  off Fallow Flds 48 A7
Fountains Av, Felt. TW13 .161 F3
Fountains Cl, Felt. TW13 .161 F2
Fountains Cres, N14 . . . . .42 E7
Fountain Sq, SW1 . . . . . . .32 D1
Fountain St, E2
  off Columbia Rd 112 C3
Fountayne Rd, N15 . . . . . .76 D4
  N16 . . . . .94 D2
Fount St, SW8 . . . . .130 D7
Fouracres, SW12
  off Little Dimocks 168 B2
  Enfield EN3 . . . . .45 H1
Fourland Wk, Edg. HA8 . .54 C6
Fournier St, E1 . . . . .21 F1
Four Seasons Cl, E3 . . . .114 A2
Fourth Av, E12 . . . . .98 C4
  W10 . . . . .108 B4
  Hayes UB3 . . . . .121 J1
Fourth Cross Rd, Twick.
  TW2 . . . . .162 A2
Fourth Way, Wem. HA9 . . .88 C4
Four Wents, The, E4
  off Kings Rd 62 D2
Fowey Av, Ilf. IG4 . . . . . . .80 A5
Fowey Cl, E1
  off Kennet St 132/133 E1
Fowler Cl, SW11 . . . . .149 G3
Fowler Rd, E7 . . . . .97 G4
  N1 off Halton Rd 93 H7
  Mitcham CR4 . . . . . . .186 A2
Fowlers Cl, Sid. DA14
  off Thursland Rd .176/177 E5
Fowlers Wk, W5 . . . . .105 G4
Fownes St, SW11 . . . . . . .149 H3
Fox & Knot St, EC1 . . . . . .19 H1
Foxberry Rd, SE4 . . . . . . .153 H3
Foxborough Gdns, SE4 . .154 A6
Foxbourne Rd, SW17 . . . .168 A2
Foxbury Av, Chis. BR7 . . .175 G6
Foxbury Cl, Brom. BR1 . .173 H6
Foxbury Rd, Brom. BR1 . .173 G6
Fox Cl, E1 . . . . .113 F4
  E16 . . . . .115 G5
Foxcombe, Croy. (New Adgtn.)
  CR0 . . . . .204 B6
Foxcombe Cl, E6
  off Boleyn Rd 116 A2
Foxcombe Rd, SW15
  off Alton Rd 165 G1
Foxcote, SE5 . . . . .36 E4
Foxcroft Rd, SE18 . . . . . .157 E1
Foxes Dale, SE3 . . . . .155 G3
  Bromley BR2 . . . . . . .190 D3
Foxfield Rd, Orp. BR6 . . .207 G2
Foxglove Cl, Sthl. UB1 . . .103 E7
Foxglove Gdns, E11 . . . . .79 J4

Foxglove La, Chess.
  KT9 . . . . .196 A4
Foxglove St, W12 . . . . . . .107 F7
Foxglove Way, Wall.
  SM6 . . . . .200 B1
Foxgrove, N14 . . . . .58 E3
Fox Gro, Walt. KT12 . . . . .178 B7
Foxgrove Av, Beck. BR3 .172 B7
Foxgrove Path, Wat.
  WD19 . . . . .50 D5
Foxgrove Rd, Beck. BR3 .172 B7
Foxham Rd, N19 . . . . .92 D3
Fox Hill, SE19 . . . . .170 C7
  Keston BR2 . . . . .205 J5
Fox Hill Gdns, SE19 . . . . .170 C7
Foxhole Rd, SE9 . . . . .156 B5
Fox Hollow Cl, SE18 . . . .137 H5
Fox Hollow Dr, Bexh.
  DA7 . . . . .158 D3
Foxholt Gdns, NW10 . . . . .88 C7
Foxhome Cl, Chis. BR7 . .174 D6
Fox Ho Rd, Belv. DA17 . .139 H4
Foxlands Cres, Dag.
  RM10 . . . . .101 J5
Foxlands La, Dag. RM10 .101 J5
Foxlands Rd, Dag. RM10 .101 J5
Fox La, N13 . . . . .59 F3
  W5 . . . . .105 H4
  Keston BR2 . . . . .205 H5
Foxlees, Wem. HA0 . . . . . .86 D4
Foxley Cl, E8
  off Ferncliff Rd 94 D5
  Loughton IG10 . . . . . .49 E2
Foxley Ct, Sutt. SM2 . . . .199 F7
Foxley Rd, SW9 . . . . .35 F7
  Thornton Heath CR7 . .187 H4
Foxleys, Wat. WD19 . . . . . .51 E3
Foxley Sq, SW9
  off Cancell Rd 131 H7
Foxmead Cl, Enf. EN2 . . . .43 F3
Foxmore St, SW11 . . . . . .149 J1
Fox Rd, E16 . . . . .115 F5
Fox's Path, Mitch. CR4 . .185 H2
Foxton Gro, Mitch. CR4 . .185 G2
Foxwell Ms, SE4
  off Foxwell St 153 H3
Foxwell St, SE4 . . . . .153 H3
Foxwood Cl, NW7 . . . . . . .54 E4
  Feltham TW13 . . . . . .160 B3
Foxwood Grn Cl, Enf.
  EN1 . . . . .44 B6
Foxwood Rd, SE3 . . . . . . .155 F4
Foyle Rd, N17 . . . . .76 D1
  SE3 . . . . .135 F6
Framfield Cl, N12 . . . . .56 D3
Framfield Ct, Enf. EN1 . . . .44 B6
Framfield Rd, N5 . . . . .93 H5
  W7 . . . . .104 B6
  Mitcham CR4 . . . . . . .168 A7
Framlingham Cl, E5
  off Detmold Rd 95 F2
Framlingham Cres, SE9 . .174 B4
Frampton Cl, Sutt. SM2 .198 D7
Frampton Pk Rd, E9 . . . . . .95 F6
Frampton Rd, Houns.
  TW4 . . . . .142 E5
Frampton St, NW8 . . . . . . .7 E6
Francemary Rd, SE4 . . . .154 A5
Frances Rd, E4 . . . . .62 A6
Frances St, SE18 . . . . . . .136 C4
Franche Ct Rd, SW17 . . .167 F3
Francis Av, Bexh. DA7 . . .159 G2
  Feltham TW13 . . . . . .160 A3
  Ilford IG1 . . . . .99 G2
Francis Barber Cl, SW16
  off Well Cl 169 F4
Franciscan Rd, SW17 . . .167 J5
Francis Chichester Way,
  SW11 . . . . .150 A1
Francis Cl, E14
  off Saunders Ness
  Rd 134 D4
  Epsom KT19 . . . . . . .196 D4
Francis Gro, SW19 . . . . . .166 C6
Francis Rd, E10 . . . . .96 C1
  N2 off Lynmouth Rd . . .73 J4
  Croydon CR0 . . . . . . .187 H7
  Greenford UB6 . . . . . .105 F1
  Harrow HA1 . . . . .68 D5
  Hounslow TW4 . . . . . .142 D2
  Ilford IG1 . . . . .99 G2
  Pinner HA5 . . . . .66 C5
  Wallington SM6 . . . . .200 C6
Francis St, E15 . . . . .96 E5
  SW1 . . . . .33 F1
  Ilford IG1 . . . . .99 G2
Francis Ter, N19
  off Junction Rd 92 C3
Francis Wk, N1
  off Bingfield St 111 F1

Francklyn Gdns, Edg. HA8 **54** A3
Franconia Rd, SW4 **150** C5
Frank Bailey Wk, E12 *off Gainsborough Av* **98** D5
Frank Burton Cl, SE7 *off Victoria Way* **135** H5
Frank Dixon Cl, SE21 **170** B1
Frank Dixon Way, SE21 **170** B1
Frankfurt Rd, SE24 **151** J5
Frankham St, SE8 **134** A7
Frankland Cl, SE16 **133** E3
Woodford Green IG8 **63** J5
Frankland Rd, E4 **62** A5
SW7 **23** E6
Franklin Cl, N20 **41** F7
SE13 **154** B1
Franklin Cl, SE27 **169** H3
Kingston upon Thames KT1 **182** A3
Franklin Cres, Mitch. CR4 **186** C4
Franklin Ho, NW9 **71** F7
Franklin Pas, SE9 **156** B3
Franklin Rd, SE20 **171** F7
Bexleyheath DA7 **159** E1
Franklins Ms, Har. HA2 **85** J2
Franklin Sq, W14 *off Marchbank Rd* **128** C5
Franklin's Row, SW3 **32** A3
Franklin St, E3 *off St. Leonards St* **114** B3
N15 **76** B6
Franklin Way, Croy. CR0 **187** E7
Franklyn Gdns, Ilf. IG6 **65** G6
Franklyn Rd, NW10 **89** F7
Walton-on-Thames KT12 **178** A6
Franks Av, N.Mal. KT3 **182** C4
Frank St, E13 **115** G4
Frankswood Av, Orp. BR5 **193** E5
Frank Towell Ct, Felt. TW14 **160** A1
Franlaw Cres, N13 **59** J4
Fransfield Gro, SE26 **171** E3
Frant Cl, SE20 **171** F7
Franthorne Way, SE6 **172** B2
Frant Rd, Th.Hth. CR7 **187** H5
Fraser Cl, E6 *off Linton Gdns* **116** B6
Bexley DA5 *off Dartford Rd* **177** J1
Fraser Ho, Brent. TW8 *off Green Dragon La* **125** J5
Fraser Rd, E17 **78** B5
N9 **60** E3
Erith DA8 **139** J5
Greenford UB6 **105** E1
Fraser St, W4 **126** E5
Frating Cres, Wdf.Grn. IG8 **63** G6
Frays Av, West Dr. UB7 **120** A2
Frays Cl, West Dr. UB7 **120** A3
Frazer Av, Ruis. HA4 **84** C5
Frazier St, SE1 **26** E4
Frean St, SE16 **29** H5
Freda Corbett Cl, SE15 **37** H7
Frederica Rd, E4 **46** D7
Frederica St, N7 *off Caledonian Rd* **93** F7
Frederick Cl, W2 **15** J5
Sutton SM1 **198** C4
Frederick Ct, NW2 *off Douglas Ms* **90** B3
Frederick Cres, SW9 **131** H7
Enfield EN3 **45** F2
Frederick Gdns, Sutt. SM1 **198** C5
Frederick Pl, SE18 **137** E5
Frederick Rd, SE17 **35** H5
Sutton SM1 **198** C5
Frederick's Pl, EC2 **20** B4
Fredericks Pl, N12 **57** F4
Frederick Sq, SE16 *off Rotherhithe St* **113** H7
Frederick's Row, EC1 **11** G3
Frederick St, WC1 **10** C4
Frederick Ter, E8 *off Haggerston Rd* **112** C1
Frederick Vil, W7 *off Lower Boston Rd* **124** B1
Frederic Ms, SW1 **24** A4
Frederic St, E17 **77** H5
Fred White Wk, N7 *off Market Rd* **92/93** E6
Fred Wigg Twr, E11 **97** F2
Freedom Cl, E17 **77** H4
Freedom Rd, N17 **76** A2
Freedom St, SW11 **149** J2
Freegrove Rd, N7 **93** E5
Freeland Pk, NW4 **72** B2
Freeland Rd, W5 **105** J7
Freelands Gro, Brom. BR1 **191** H1
Freelands Rd, Brom. BR1 **191** H1
Freeling St, N1 *off Caledonian Rd* **93** F7
Freeman Cl, Nthlt. UB5 **85** E7
Freeman Ct, N7 *off Tollington Way* **92/93** E3
Freeman Dr, W.Mol. KT8 **179** F3
Freeman Rd, Mord. SM4 **185** G5
Freemantle Av, Enf. EN3 **45** G5
Freemantle St, SE17 **36** D3
★ **Freemason's Hall (United Grand Lodge of England)**, WC2 **18** B3
Freemasons Rd, E16 **115** H5
Croydon CR0 **202** B1
Freesia Cl, Orp. BR6 *off Briarswood Way* **207** J5
Freethorpe Cl, SE19 **188** A1
Free Trade Wf, E1 *off The Highway* **115** F7
★ **Freightliners City Fm**, N7 **93** F6
Freke Rd, SW11 **150** A3
Fremantle Rd, Belv. DA17 **139** G4
Ilford IG6 **81** F2
Fremont St, E9 **113** F1
French Ordinary Ct, EC3 **21** E5
French Pl, E1 **13** E4
French St, Sun. TW16 **178** C2
Frendsbury Rd, SE4 **153** H4
Frensham Cl, Sthl. UB1 **103** F4
Frensham Ct, Mitch. CR4 *off Phipps Br Rd* **185** G3
Frensham Dr, SW15 **165** G2
Croydon (New Adgtn.) CR0 **204** C7
Frensham Rd, SE9 **175** G2
Frensham St, SE15 **37** J6
Frere St, SW11 **149** H2
Freshfield Av, E8 **94** C7
Freshfield Cl, SE13 *off Marischal Rd* **154** D4
Freshfield Dr, N14 **42** B7
Freshfields, Croy. CR0 **189** J7
Freshford St, SW18 **167** F3
Freshwater Cl, SW17 **168** A6
Freshwater Rd, SW17 **168** A6
Dagenham RM8 **100** D1
Freshwell Av, Rom. RM6 **82** C4
Fresh Wf Rd, Bark. IG11 **117** E1
Freshwood Cl, Beck. BR3 **190** B1
Freston Gdns, Barn. EN4 **42** A5
Freston Pk, N3 **72** C2
Freston Rd, W10 **108** A7
W11 **108** A7
Freta Rd, Bexh. DA6 **159** F5
★ **Freud Mus**, NW3 **91** F6
Frewin Rd, SW18 **167** G1
Friar Ms, SE27 *off Prioress Rd* **169** H3
Friar Rd, Hayes UB4 **102** D4
Friars, The, Chig. IG7 **65** H4
Friars Av, N20 **57** H3
SW15 **165** F3
Friars Cl, E4 **62** C3
N2 **73** G4
SE1 *off Bear La* **131** H1
Ilford IG1 *off Leeds Rd* **99** G1
Northolt UB5 *off Broomcroft Av* **102** D3
Friars Gdns, W3 *off St. Dunstans Av* **106** D6
Friars Gate Cl, Wdf.Grn. IG8 **63** G4
Friars La, Rich. TW9 **145** G5
Friars Mead, E14 **134** C3
Friars Ms, SE9 **156** D5
Friars Pl La, W3 **106** D7
Friars Rd, E6 **116** A1
Friars Stile Pl, Rich. TW10 *off Friars Stile Rd* **145** H6
Friars Stile Rd, Rich. TW10 **145** H6
Friar St, EC4 **19** H4
Friars Wk, N14 **58** B1
SE2 **138** D5
Friars Way, W3 **106** D6
Friary Cl, N12 **57** H5
Friary Ct, SW1 **25** G2
Friary Est, SE15 **37** J6
Friary La, Wdf.Grn. IG8 **63** G4
Friary Rd, N12 **57** G4
SE15 **37** J6
W3 **106** D6
Friary Way, N12 **57** H4
FRIDAY HILL, E4 **62** D2
Friday Hill, E4 **62** E2
Friday Hill E, E4 **62** E3
Friday Hill W, E4 **62** E2
Friday Rd, Mitch. CR4 **167** J7
Friday St, EC4 **19** J4
Frideswide Pl, NW5 *off Islip St* **92** C5
Friendly Pl, SE13 *off Lewisham Rd* **154** B1
Friendly St, SE8 **154** A1
Friendly St Ms, SE8 *off Friendly St* **154** A2
Friendship Wk, Nthlt. UB5 *off Wayfarer Rd* **102** D3
Friends Rd, Croy. CR0 **202** A3
Friend St, EC1 **11** G3
FRIERN BARNET, N11 **57** H4
Friern Barnet La, N11 **57** H4
N20 **57** H4
Friern Barnet Rd, N11 **57** J5
Friern Br Retail Pk, N11 **58** B6
Friern Ct, N20 **57** G3
Friern Mt Dr, N20 **41** F7
Friern Pk, N12 **57** F5
Friern Rd, SE22 **152** D6
Friern Watch Av, N12 **57** F4
Frigate Ms, SE8 *off Watergate St* **134** A6
Frimley Av, Wall. SM6 **201** E5
Frimley Cl, SW19 **166** B2
Croydon (New Adgtn.) CR0 **204** C7
Frimley Ct, Sid. DA14 **176** B5
Frimley Cres, Croy. (New Adgtn.) CR0 **204** C7
Frimley Gdns, Mitch. CR4 **185** H3
Frimley Rd, Chess. KT9 **195** H5
Ilford IG3 **99** H3
Frimley Way, E1 **113** G4
Frinstead Ho, W10 **108** A7
Frinton Cl, Wat. WD19 **50** B2
Frinton Dr, Wdf.Grn. IG8 **62** D7
Frinton Ms, Ilf. IG2 *off Bramley Cres* **80** D6
Frinton Rd, E6 **116** A3
N15 **76** B6
SW17 **168** A6
Sidcup DA14 **176** E2
Friston Path, Chig. IG7 **65** H5
Friston St, SW6 **148** E2
Friswell Pl, Bexh. DA6 **159** G4
Fritham Cl, N.Mal. KT3 **182** E6
Frith Ct, NW7 **56** B7
Frith La, NW7 **56** B7
Frith Rd, E11 **96** C4
Croydon CR0 **201** J2
Frith St, W1 **17** H4
Frithville Gdns, W12 **127** J1
Frizlands La, Dag. RM10 **101** H4
Frobisher Cl, Pnr. HA5 **66** D7
Frobisher Cres, EC2 *off Beech St* **111** J5
Staines TW19 **140** B7
Frobisher Gdns, Stai. TW19 **140** B7
Frobisher Pas, E14 *off North Colonnade* **133** J1
Frobisher Rd, E6 **116** C6
N8 **75** G4
Frobisher St, SE10 **135** E6
Froghall La, Chig. IG7 **65** G4
Frogley Rd, SE22 **152** C4
Frogmore, SW18 **148** D5
Frogmore Cl, Sutt. SM3 **198** A3
Frogmore Est, Ruis. HA4 **84** D5
Frogmore Gdns, Sutt. SM3 **198** B4
Frogmore Ind Est, NW10 **106** C3
Frognal, NW3 **91** F5
Frognal Av, Har. HA1 **68** C4
Sidcup DA14 **176** A5
Frognal Cl, NW3 **91** F5
Frognal Ct, NW3 **91** F6
Frognal Gdns, NW3 **91** F4
Frognal La, NW3 **90** E5
Frognal Par, NW3 *off Frognal Ct* **91** F6
Frognal Pl, Sid. DA14 **176** A6
Frognal Ri, NW3 **91** F4
Frognal Way, NW3 **91** F4
Froissart Rd, SE9 **156** A5
Frome Rd, N22 *off Westbury Av* **75** H3
Frome St, N1 **11** J1
Fromondes Rd, Sutt. SM3 **198** B5
Frostic Wk, E1 **21** G2
Froude St, SW8 **150** B2
Fruen Rd, Felt. TW14 **141** J7
Fruiterers Pas, EC4 *off Southwark Br* **111** J7
Fryatt Rd, N17 **60** A7
Fryent Cl, NW9 **70** A6
Fryent Cres, NW9 **70** E6
Fryent Flds, NW9 **71** E6
Fryent Gro, NW9 **70** E6
Fryent Way, NW9 **70** A5
Frye's Bldgs, N1 **11** F1
Frying Pan All, E1 **21** F2
Fry Rd, E6 **98** A7
NW10 **107** F1
Fryston Av, Croy. CR0 **202** D2
Fuchsia St, SE2 **138** B5
Fulbeck Dr, NW9 **70** E1
Fulbeck Wk, Edg. HA8 *off Knightswood Cl* **54** B2
Fulbeck Way, Har. HA2 **67** J2
Fulbourne Rd, E17 **78** C1
Fulbourne St, E1 *off Durward St* **112/113** E5
Fulbrook Rd, N19 *off Junction Rd* **92** C4
Fulford Gro, Wat. WD19 **50** B2
Fulford Rd, Epsom KT19 **196** D7
Fulford St, SE16 **133** E2
FULHAM, SW6 **148** B2
Fulham Bdy, SW6 **128** D7
Fulham Ct, SW6 *off Shottendane Rd* **128** D7
★ **Fulham FC (share Loftus Rd Stadium with QPR FC)**, SW6 **148** A1
Fulham High St, SW6 **148** B2
★ **Fulham Palace Mus**, SW6 **148** A2
Fulham Palace Rd, SW6 **128** A7
W6 **127** J5
Fulham Pk Gdns, SW6 **148** C2
Fulham Pk Rd, SW6 **148** C2
Fulham Rd, SW3 **30** E4
SW6 **30** B7
SW10 **30** E4
Fullbrooks Av, Wor.Pk. KT4 **197** F1
Fuller Cl, E2 **13** H5
Orpington BR6 **207** J5
Fuller Rd, Dag. RM8 **100** B3
Fullers Av, Surb. KT6 **195** J2
Woodford Green IG8 **63** F7
★ **Fuller's Griffin Brewery**, W4 **127** F6
Fullers Rd, E18 **79** F1
Fuller St, NW4 **71** J4
Fullers Way N, Surb. KT6 **195** J3
Fullers Way S, Chess. KT9 **195** H4
Fullers Wd, Croy. CR0 **204** A5
Fuller Ter, Ilf. IG1 *off Oaktree Gro* **99** F5
Fullerton Rd, SW18 **149** F5
Croydon CR0 **188** C7
Fuller Way, Hayes UB3 **121** J5
Fullwell Av, Ilf. IG5, IG6 **80** C1
FULLWELL CROSS, Ilf. **81** G1
Fullwell Cross Roundabout, Ilf. IG6 *off Fencepiece Rd* **81** G2
Fullwoods Ms, N1 **12** C3
Fulmar Cl, Surb. KT5 **181** J6
Fulmead St, SW6 **149** E1
Fulmer Cl, Hmptn. TW12 **161** E5
Fulmer Rd, E16 **116** A5
Fulmer Way, W13 **124** E3
Fulready Rd, E10 **78** D5
Fulstone Cl, Houns. TW4 **143** F4
Fulthorp Rd, SE3 **155** F2
Fulton Ms, W2 **14** C5
Fulton Rd, Wem. HA9 **88** A3
Fulwell Pk Av, Twick. TW2 **161** H2
Fulwell Rd, Tedd. TW11 **162** A4
Fulwood Av, Wem. HA0 **105** J1
Fulwood Gdns, Twick. TW1 **144** C6
Fulwood Pl, WC1 **18** D2
Fulwood Wk, SW19 **166** B1
Furber St, W6 **127** H3
Furham Feild, Pnr. HA5 **51** G7
Furley Rd, SE15 **132** D7
Furlong Cl, Wall. SM6 **200** A1
Furlong Rd, N7 **93** G6
Furmage St, SW18 **149** E7
Furneaux Av, SE27 **169** H5

Furness Rd, NW10 . . . . .**107** G2
SW6 . . . .**149** E2
Harrow HA2 . . . .**67** H7
Morden SM4 . . . .**185** E7
Furnival St, EC4 . . . .**19** E3
Furrow La, E9 . . . .**95** F5
Fursby Av, N3 . . . .**56** D6
Further Acre, NW9 . . . . .**71** F2
Furtherfield Cl, Croy.
  CRO **187** G2
Further Grn Rd, SE6 . . . .**155** E7
FURZEDOWN, SW17 . . . .**168** A5
Furzedown Dr, SW17 . . .**168** B5
Furzedown Rd, SW17 . . .**168** B5
Furze Fm Cl, Rom. RM6 . .**83** E2
Furzefield Cl, Chis. BR7 . .**174** E6
Furzefield Rd, SE3 . . . . .**135** H6
Furzeground Way, Uxb.
  UB11 . . . .**121** H7
Furzeham Rd, West Dr.
  UB7 . . . .**120** B2
Furzehill Rd, Borwd. WD6 .**38** A4
Furze Rd, Th.Hth. CR7 . . .**187** J3
Furze St, E3 . . . .**114** A5
Furzewood, Sun. TW16 . .**178** A1
Fuschia Cl, Wdf.Grn. IG8
  off The Bridle Path .**62/63** E7
Fyfe Way, Brom. BR1
  off Widmore Rd **191** G2
Fyfield Cl, Brom. BR2 . . .**190** D4
Fyfield Ct, E7 . . . .**97** G6
Fyfield Rd, E17 . . . .**78** D3
  SW9 . . . .**151** G3
  Enfield EN1 . . . .**44** B3
  Woodford Green IG8 . .**63** J7
Fynes St, SW1 . . . .**33** H1

G

Gable Cl, Pnr. HA5 . . . . . .**51** G7
Gable Ct, SE26
  off Lawrie Pk Av .**170/171** E5
Gables, The, Wem. HA9 . .**87** J3
Gables Cl, SE5 . . . .**152** B1
  SE12 . . . .**173** G1
Gabriel Cl, Felt. TW13 . . .**160** D4
Gabrielle Cl, Wem. HA9 . .**87** J3
Gabrielle Ct, NW3 . . . . . .**91** G6
Gabriel St, SE23 . . . .**153** G7
Gabriel's Wf, SE1 . . . .**27** E1
Gad Cl, E13 . . . .**115** H3
Gaddesden Av, Wem.
  HA9 . . . .**87** J6
Gade Cl, Hayes UB3 . . . .**122** B1
Gadesden Rd, Epsom
  KT19 . . . .**196** C6
Gadsbury Cl, NW9 . . . . . .**71** F6
Gadwall Cl, E16
  off Freemasons Rd . .**115** H6
Gadwall Way, SE28 . . . .**137** G2
Gage Rd, E16
  off Malmesbury
  Rd **114/115** E5
Gage St, WC1 . . . .**18** B1
Gainford St, N1
  off Richmond Av **111** G1
Gainsboro Gdns, Grnf.
  UB6 . . . .**86** B5
Gainsborough Av, E12 . . .**98** D5
Gainsborough Cl, Beck.
  BR3 . . . .**172** A7
  Esher KT10
    off Lime Tree Av . . .**194** B1
Gainsborough Ct, N12 . . .**57** E5
  W12 off Lime Gro **127** J2
Gainsborough Gdns,
  NW3 . . . .**91** G3
  NW11 . . . .**72** C7
  Edgware HA8 . . . .**69** J2
  Isleworth TW7 . . . . . .**144** A5
Gainsborough Ho, Enf. EN1
  off Ayley Cft **44** D5
Gainsborough Ms, SE26
  off Panmure Rd .**170/171** E3
Gainsborough Pl, Chig.
  IG7 . . . .**65** J3
Gainsborough Rd, E11 . . .**79** E7
  E15 . . . .**114** E3
  N12 . . . .**57** E5
  W4 . . . .**127** F4
  Dagenham RM8 . . . . .**100** B4
  New Malden KT3 . . . .**182** D7
  Richmond TW9 . . . . .**145** J3
  Woodford Green IG8 . .**64** B6
Gainsborough Sq, Bexh. DA6
  off Regency Way **158** D3
Gainsford Rd, E17 . . . . . .**77** J4
Gainsford St, SE1 . . . . . .**29** F3

Gairloch Rd, SE5 . . . . . .**152** B2
Gaisford St, NW5 . . . .**92** C6
Gaitskell Ct, SW11 . . . . .**149** H2
Gaitskell Rd, SE9 . . . . . .**175** F1
Galahad Rd, Brom. BR1 .**173** G3
Galata Rd, SW13 . . . . . .**127** G7
Galatea Sq, SE15
  off Scylla Rd **152/153** E3
Galbraith St, E14 . . . . . .**134** C3
Galdana Av, Barn. EN5 . . .**41** F3
Galeborough Av, Wdf.Grn.
  IG8 . . . .**62** D7
Gale Cl, Hmptn. TW12
  off Stewart Cl . . .**160/161** E6
  Mitcham CR4 . . . . . .**185** G3
Galena Ho, SE18
  off Grosmont Rd **137** J5
Galena Rd, W6 . . . .**127** H4
Galen Pl, WC1 . . . .**18** B2
Galesbury Rd, SW18 . . .**149** F6
Gales Gdns, E2 . . . .**113** E3
Gale St, E3 . . . .**114** A5
  Dagenham RM9 . . . . .**118** D1
Gales Way, Wdf.Grn. IG8 . .**64** B7
Galgate Cl, SW19 . . . . . .**166** B1
Gallants Fm Rd, Barn.
  EN4 . . . .**41** H7
Galleon Cl, SE16
  off Kinburn St **133** G2
Galleons Dr, Bark. IG11 . .**118** A3
Gallery Gdns, Nthlt.
  UB5 . . . .**102** D2
Gallery Rd, SE21 . . . . . .**170** A1
Galley La, Barn. EN5 . . . .**39** H3
Galleywall Rd, SE16 . . . .**132** E4
Galliard Cl, N9 . . . .**45** F6
Galliard Rd, N9 . . . .**60** D1
Gallia Rd, N5 . . . .**93** H5
Gallions Cl, Bark. IG11 . . .**118** A3
Gallions Rd, SE7 . . . . . .**135** H4
Gallions Roundabout,
  E16 . . . .**116** E7
Gallions Vw Rd, SE28
  off Goldfinch Rd **137** H2
Gallon Cl, SE7 . . . .**135** J4
Gallop, The, S.Croy. CR2 .**203** E7
  Sutton SM2 . . . .**199** F7
Gallosson Rd, SE18 . . . .**137** H4
Galloway Path, Croy.
  CRO **202** A4
Galloway Rd, W12 . . . . .**127** G1
Gallus Cl, N21 . . . .**43** F6
Gallus Sq, SE3 . . . .**155** H3
Galpins Rd, Th.Hth. CR7 .**187** F4
Galsworthy Av, E14 . . . .**113** H5
  Romford RM6 . . . .**82** B7
Galsworthy Cl, SE28 . . . .**138** B1
Galsworthy Cres, SE3
  off Merriman Rd **155** J1
Galsworthy Rd, NW2 . . . .**90** B4
  Kingston upon Thames
    KT2 . . . .**164** B7
Galsworthy Ter, N16
  off Hawksley Rd **94** B3
Galton St, W10 . . . .**108** B4
Galva Cl, Barn. EN4 . . . . .**42** A4
Galvani Way, Croy. CR0
  off Ampere Way **201** F1
Galveston Rd, SW15 . . . .**148** C5
Galway Cl, SE16
  off Masters Dr . .**132/133** E5
Galway St, EC1 . . . .**12** A4
Gambetta St, SW8 . . . . .**150** B2
Gambia St, SE1 . . . .**27** H2
Gambole Rd, SW17 . . . .**167** H4
Games Rd, Barn. EN4 . . . .**41** J3
Gamlen Rd, SW15 . . . . .**148** A4
Gamuel Cl, E17 . . . .**78** A6
Gander Grn Cres, Hmptn.
  TW12 . . . .**179** G1
Gander Grn La, Sutt. SM1,
  SM3 . . . .**198** B2
Gandhi Cl, E17 . . . .**78** A6
Gandolfi St, SE15 . . . . . .**36** D6
Ganton St, W1 . . . .**17** F5
Ganton Wk, Wat. WD19
  off Woodhall La . . .**50/51** E4
GANTS HILL, Ilf. **80** D5
Gants Hill, Ilf. IG2
  off Eastern Av **80** D6
Gantshill Cres, Ilf. IG2 . . .**80** D5
Gap Rd, SW19 . . . .**166** D5
Garage Rd, W3 . . . .**106** A6
Garbutt Pl, W1 . . . .**16** C1
Garden Av, Bexh. DA7 . . .**159** G3
  Mitcham CR4 . . . . . .**168** B7
Garden City, Edg. HA8 . . .**54** A6
Garden Cl, E4 . . . .**62** A5
  SE12 . . . .**173** H3
  SW15 . . . .**147** H7

Garden Cl, Barn. EN5 . . . .**39** J4
  Hampton TW12 . . . . .**161** F5
  Northolt UB5 . . . .**103** E1
  Wallington SM6 . . . . .**200** E5
Garden Ct, EC4 . . . .**18** E5
  N12 off Holden Rd . .**56/57** E5
  Richmond TW9
    off Lichfield Rd **145** J1
  Stanmore HA7
    off Marsh La **53** F5
  West Molesey KT8
    off Avern Rd **179** H4
Gardeners Cl, N11 . . . . . .**58** A2
Gardeners Rd, Croy.
  CR0 . . . .**201** H1
Gardenia Rd, Enf. EN1 . . .**44** B6
Gardenia Way, Wdf.Grn.
  IG8 . . . .**63** G5
Garden La, SW2
  off Christchurch Rd . .**169** F1
  Bromley BR1 . . . .**173** H6
Garden Ms, W2
  off Linden Gdns **108** D7
Garden Rd, NW8 . . . .**6** D3
  SE20 . . . .**189** F1
  Bromley BR1 . . . .**173** H1
  Richmond TW9 . . . . .**146** A3
  Walton-on-Thames
    KT12 . . . .**178** B6
Garden Row, SE1 . . . .**27** G6
Gardens, The, SE22 . . . .**152** D4
  Beckenham BR3 . . . .**190** C2
  Feltham TW14 . . . . . .**141** G5
  Harrow HA1 . . . .**67** J6
  Pinner HA5 . . . .**67** F6
Garden St, E1 . . . .**113** G5
Garden Ter, SW1 . . . .**33** H3
Garden Wk, EC2 . . . .**12** D4
  Beckenham BR3
    off Hayne Rd **189** J1
Garden Way, NW10 . . . . .**88** C6
Gardiner Av, NW2 . . . . . .**89** J5
Gardiner Cl, Dag. RM8 . .**100** D4
  Enfield EN3 . . . .**45** G6
Gardner Cl, E11 . . . .**79** H6
Gardner Gro, Felt. TW13 .**161** F2
Gardner Pl, Felt. TW14 . .**142** B6
Gardner Rd, E13 . . . .**115** H4
Gardners La, EC4 . . . .**19** J5
Gardnor Rd, NW3
  off Flask Wk **91** G4
Gard St, EC1 . . . .**11** H3
Garendon Gdns, Mord.
  SM4 . . . .**184** E7
Garendon Rd, Mord.
  SM4 . . . .**184** E7
Gareth Cl, Wor.Pk. KT4
  off Burnham Dr **198** A2
Gareth Gro, Brom. BR1 . .**173** G4
Garfield Ms, SW11
  off Garfield Rd **150** A3
Garfield Rd, E4 . . . .**62** D1
  E13 . . . .**115** F4
  SW11 . . . .**150** A3
  SW19 . . . .**167** F5
  Enfield EN3 . . . .**45** F4
  Twickenham TW1 . . . .**162** D1
Garford St, E14 . . . .**114** A7
Garganey Wk, SE28 . . . .**118** D7
Garibaldi St, SE18 . . . . .**137** H4
Garland Rd, SE18 . . . . . .**137** G7
  Stanmore HA7 . . . . . .**69** H1
Garlands Ct, Croy. CR0
  off Chatsworth Rd . . .**202** A4
Garlick Hill, EC4 . . . .**20** A5
Garlies Rd, SE23 . . . . . .**171** H3
Garlinge Rd, NW2 . . . . . .**90** C6
Garman Cl, N18 . . . .**60** A5
Garman Rd, N17 . . . .**61** F7
Garnault Ms, EC1 . . . . . .**11** F4
Garnault Pl, EC1 . . . .**11** F4
Garner Cl, Dag. RM8 . . .**100** D1
Garner Rd, E17 . . . .**78** C1
Garner St, E2 . . . .**13** J2
Garnet Rd, NW10 . . . .**89** E6
  Thornton Heath CR7 .**188** A4
Garnet St, E1 . . . .**113** F7
Garnett Cl, SE9 . . . .**156** C3
Garnett Rd, NW3 . . . .**91** J5
Garnett Way, E17
  off McEntee Av **77** H1
Garnet Wk, E6 . . . .**116** B5
Garnham Cl, N16
  off Garnham St **94** C2
Garnham St, N16 . . . .**94** C2
Garnies Cl, SE15 . . . .**37** F7
Garrad's Rd, SW16 . . . . .**168** D3
Garrard Cl, Bexh. DA7 . . .**159** G3
  Chislehurst BR7 . . . . .**175** E5

Garrard Wk, NW10
  off Garnet Rd **88/89** E6
Garratt Cl, Croy. CR0 . . .**200** E4
Garratt La, SW17 . . . . . .**167** G4
  SW18 . . . .**148** E5
Garratt Rd, Edg. HA8 . . . .**54** A7
Garratt Ter, SW17 . . . . .**167** H4
Garrett Cl, W3
  off Jenner Av **106** D5
Garrett St, EC1 . . . .**12** A5
Garrick Av, NW11 . . . .**72** B6
Garrick Cl, SW18 . . . . . .**149** F4
  W5 . . . .**105** H4
  Richmond TW9
    off The Green **145** G5
Garrick Cres, Croy. CR0 .**202** B2
Garrick Dr, NW4 . . . .**71** J2
  SE28
    off Broadwater Rd . .**137** G3
Garrick Gdns, W.Mol.
  KT8 . . . .**179** G3
Garrick Pk, NW4 . . . .**72** A2
Garrick Rd, NW9 . . . .**71** F6
  Greenford UB6 . . . . .**103** H4
  Richmond TW9 . . . . .**146** A2
Garrick St, WC2 . . . .**18** A5
Garrick Way, NW4 . . . . . .**72** A4
Garrison Cl, SE18
  off Red Lion La **136** D7
  Hounslow TW4 . . . . .**143** F5
Garrison La, Chess. KT9 .**195** G7
Garsdale Cl, N11 . . . .**58** A6
Garside Cl, SE28
  off Goosander Way . .**137** G3
  Hampton TW12 . . . . .**161** H6
Garsington Ms, SE4 . . . .**153** J3
Garter Way, SE16
  off Poolmans St **133** G2
Garth, The, N12
  off Holden Rd **56/57** E5
  Hampton (Hmptn.H.) TW12
    off Uxbridge Rd . . .**161** H6
  Harrow HA3 . . . .**69** J6
Garth Cl, W4 . . . .**126** D5
  Kingston upon Thames
    KT2 . . . .**163** J5
  Morden SM4 . . . .**184** A7
  Ruislip HA4 . . . .**84** D1
Garth Ct, W4
  off Garth Rd **126** D5
Garthland Dr, Barn. EN5 . .**39** H5
Garth Ms, W5
  off Greystoke Gdns . .**105** H4
Garthorne Rd, SE23 . . . .**153** G7
Garth Rd, NW2 . . . .**90** C2
  W4 . . . .**126** D6
  Kingston upon Thames
    KT2 . . . .**163** J5
  Morden SM4 . . . .**183** J6
Garth Rd Ind Cen, Mord.
  SM4 . . . .**184** A7
Garthside, Rich. TW10 . .**163** H5
Garthway, N12 . . . .**57** H6
Gartmoor Gdns, SW19 . .**166** C1
Gartmore Rd, Ilf. IG3 . . . .**99** J1
Garton Pl, SW18 . . . .**149** F6
Gartons Cl, Enf. EN3 . . . .**45** F5
Gartons Way, SW11 . . . .**149** F3
Garvary Rd, E16 . . . .**115** H6
Garway Rd, W2 . . . .**14** A4
Gascoigne Gdns, Wdf.Grn.
  IG8 . . . .**63** E7
Gascoigne Pl, E2 . . . .**13** F4
Gascoigne Rd, Bark.
  IG11 . . . .**117** F1
Gascony Av, NW6 . . . .**90** D7
Gascoyne Rd, E9 . . . .**95** G7
Gaselee St, E14 . . . .**114** C7
Gasholder Pl, SE11 . . . . .**34** D4
Gaskarth Rd, SW12 . . . .**150** B6
Gaskell Rd, N6 . . . .**73** J6
Gaskell St, SW4 . . . .**150** E2
Gaskin St, N1 . . . .**111** H1
Gaspar Cl, SW5 . . . .**30** B1
Gaspar Ms, SW5 . . . .**30** B1
Gassiot Rd, SW17 . . . . .**167** J4
Gassiot Way, Sutt. SM1 .**199** G3
Gastein Rd, W6 . . . .**128** A6
Gatcombe Ms, W5 . . . . .**105** J7
Gatcombe Rd, E16 . . . . .**135** G1
  N19 . . . .**92** D3
Gatcombe Way, Barn.
  EN4 . . . .**41** J3
Gate Cl, Borwd. WD6 . . . .**38** C1
Gate End, Nthwd. HA6 . . .**50** A7

Gateforth St, NW8 . . . . .7 G6
Gatehouse Cl, Kings.T.
  KT2 . . . . .164 C7
Gatehouse Sq, SE1
  off Southwark Br Rd . .131 J1
Gateley Rd, SW9 . . . . .151 F3
Gate Ms, SW7 . . . . .23 H4
Gater Dr, Enf. EN2 . . . . .44 A1
Gatesborough St, EC2 . . . .12 D5
Gates Grn Rd, Kes. BR2 .205 G4
  West Wickham BR4 . . . .205 F3
Gateside Rd, SW17 . . . . . .167 J3
Gatestone Rd, SE19 . . . . . .170 B6
Gate St, WC2 . . . . .18 C3
Gateway, SE17 . . . . .36 A5
Gateway Arc, N1
  off Islington High St . .111 H2
Gateway Ho, Bark. IG11
  off St. Ann's 117 F1
Gateway Ind Est, NW10 .107 F3
Gateway Ms, E8
  off Shacklewell La 94 C5
Gateway Retail Pk, E6 . . .117 E4
Gateway Rd, E10 . . . . .96 B3
Gateways, The, SW3 . . . . . .31 H2
Gatfield Gro, Felt. TW13 .161 G2
Gathorne Rd, N22 . . . . .75 G2
Gathorne St, E2
  off Mace St 113 G2
Gatley Av, Epsom KT19 .196 B5
Gatliff Rd, SW1 . . . . .32 D4
Gatling Rd, SE2 . . . . .138 A5
Gatonby St, SE15
  off Kelly Av 132 C7
Gatting Cl, Edg. HA8
  off Pavilion Way 54 C7
Gatton Rd, SW17 . . . . .167 H4
Gattons Way, Sid. DA14 .177 F4
Gatward Cl, N21 . . . . .43 H6
Gatward Grn, N9 . . . . .60 B2
Gatwick Rd, SW18 . . . . . . .148 C7
Gauden Cl, SW4 . . . . .150 D3
Gauden Rd, SW4 . . . . .150 D2
Gaumont Ter, W12
  off Lime Gro 127 J2
Gauntlet Cl, Nthlt. UB5 . . .84 E7
Gauntlett Ct, Wem. HA0 . .86 E5
Gauntlett Rd, Sutt. SM1 .199 G5
Gaunt St, SE1 . . . . .27 H5
Gautrey Rd, SE15 . . . . .153 F2
Gautrey Sq, E6 . . . . .116 C6
Gavel St, SE17 . . . . .36 C1
Gavestone Cres, SE12 . . . .155 H7
Gavestone Rd, SE12 . . . . . .155 H7
Gaviller Pl, E5
  off Clarence Rd 94/95 H4
Gavina Cl, Mord. SM4 . . . .185 H5
Gavin St, SE18 . . . . .137 H4
Gawber St, E2 . . . . .113 F3
Gawsworth Cl, E15
  off Ash Rd 96/97 E5
Gawthorne Av, NW7
  off Lane App 56 B5
Gawthorne Ct, E3
  off Mostyn Gro 114 A2
Gay Cl, NW2 . . . . .89 H5
Gaydon Ho, W2 . . . . .14 B1
Gaydon La, NW9 . . . . .70 E1
Gayfere Rd, Epsom
  KT17 . . . . .197 G5
  Ilford IG5 . . . . .80 C3
Gayfere St, SW1 . . . . .26 A6
Gayford Rd, W12 . . . . .127 F2
Gay Gdns, Dag. RM10 . . .101 J4
Gayhurst, SE17 . . . . .36 C5
Gayhurst Rd, E8 . . . . .94 D7
Gaylor Rd, Nthlt. UB5 . . . .85 F5
Gaynesford Rd, SE23 . . . .171 G2
  Carshalton SM5 . . . . . .199 J7
Gaynes Hill Rd, Wdf.Grn.
  IG8 . . . . .64 B6
Gay Rd, E15 . . . . .114 D2
Gaysham Av, Ilf. IG2 . . . . . .80 D5
Gaysham Hall, Ilf. IG5 . . . .80 E3
Gay St, SW15 . . . . .148 A3
Gayton Cl, Har. HA1 . . . . . .68 C6
Gayton Cres, NW3 . . . . .91 G4
Gayton Rd, NW3 . . . . .91 G4
  SE2 off Florence Rd . . .138 C3
  Harrow HA1 . . . . .68 C6
Gayville Rd, SW11 . . . . . . .149 J6
Gaywood Cl, SW2 . . . . .169 F1
Gaywood Est, SE1 . . . . .27 H6
Gaywood Rd, E17 . . . . .78 A3
Gaywood St, SE1 . . . . .27 H6
Gaza St, SE17 . . . . .35 G4
Geariesville Gdns, Ilf. IG6 .81 E4
Geary Rd, NW10 . . . . .89 G5
Geary St, N7 . . . . .93 F5
G.E.C. Est, Wem. HA9 . . . .87 G3

Geddes Pl, Bexh. DA6
  off Market Pl 159 G4
Gedeney Rd, N17 . . . . .75 J1
Gedling Pl, SE1 . . . . .29 G5
Gee Rd, E15 . . . . .115 F1
Gees Ct, W1 . . . . .16 C4
Gee St, EC1 . . . . .11 J5
Geffrye Ct, N1 . . . . .12 E2
Geffrye Est, N1
  off Stanway St 112 B2
★ Geffrye Mus, E2 . . . . . . .13 E2
Geffrye St, E2 . . . . .13 F1
Geldart Rd, SE15 . . . . .132 E7
Geldeston Rd, E5 . . . . .94 D2
Gellatly Rd, SE14 . . . . .153 F2
  off Javelin Way . .102/103 E3
Geldart Rd, SE15 . . . . .132 E7
General Gordon Pl,
  SE18 . . . . .136 E4
General Wolfe Rd, SE10 .154 D1
Genesta Rd, SE18 . . . . .137 E6
Geneva Dr, SW9 . . . . .151 G4
Geneva Gdns, Rom. RM6 .82 E5
Geneva Rd, Kings.T. KT1 .181 H4
  Thornton Heath CR7 . .187 J5
Genever Cl, E4 . . . . .62 A5
Genista Rd, N18 . . . . .61 E5
Genoa Av, SW15 . . . . .147 J5
Genoa Rd, SE20 . . . . .189 F1
Genotin Rd, Enf. EN1 . . . . .44 A3
Genotin Ter, Enf. EN1
  off Genotin Rd 44 A3
Gentian Row, SE13
  off Sparta St 154 C1
Gentlemans Row, Enf.
  EN2 . . . . .43 J3
Gentry Gdns, E13 . . . . .115 G4
Geoffrey Cl, SE5 . . . . .151 J2
Geoffrey Gdns, E6 . . . . . . .116 B2
Geoffrey Rd, SE4 . . . . .153 J3
George Comberton Wk, E12
  off Gainsborough Av . .98 D5
George Ct, WC2 . . . . .18 B6
George Cres, N10 . . . . .58 A7
George Downing Est, N16
  off Cazenove Rd 94 C2
George V Av, Pnr. HA5 . . . .67 G3
George V Cl, Pnr. HA5
  off George V Av 67 G3
George V Way, Grnf.
  UB6 . . . . .105 E1
George Gange Way, Har.
  (Wldste.) HA3 . . . . . . .68 B3
George Gro Rd, SE20 . . . .188 D1
★ George Inn, SE1
  off Borough High St . .28 B2
George Inn Yd, SE1 . . . . . .28 B2
George La, E18 . . . . .79 G2
  SE13 . . . . .154 C6
  Bromley BR2 . . . . .205 H4
George Lansbury Ho, N22
  off Progress Way 75 G1
George Loveless Ho, E2 . .13 G3
George Lowe Ct, W2 . . . . . .14 A1
George Mathers Rd, SE11 .35 G1
George Ms, NW1 . . . . .9 F4
  Enfield EN2
  off Sydney Rd 44 A3
George Pl, N17 . . . . .76 B3
  off Dongola Rd 76 B3
George Rd, E4 . . . . .62 A6
  Kingston upon Thames
  KT2 . . . . .164 B7
  New Malden KT3 . . . . .183 F4
George Row, SE16 . . . . .29 H4
George Sq, SW19
  off Mostyn Rd 184 C3
George's Rd, N7 . . . . .93 F5
Georges Sq, SW6
  off North End Rd 128 C6
George St, E16 . . . . .115 F6
  W1 . . . . .16 A3
  W7 off The Broadway . .124 B1
  Barking IG11 . . . . .99 F7
  Croydon CR0 . . . . .202 A2
  Hounslow TW3 . . . . . .143 F2
  Richmond TW9 . . . . . .145 G5
  Southall UB2 . . . . .122 E4
Georgetown Cl, SE19
  off St. Kitts Ter 170 A5
Georgette Pl, SE10
  off King George St . . .134 C7
Georgeville Gdns, Ilf. IG6 .81 E4
George Wyver Cl, SW19 . .166 A1
  off Beaumont Rd 148 B7
George Yd, EC3 . . . . .20 C4
  W1 . . . . .16 C5
Georgiana St, NW1 . . . . . .110 C1

Georgian Cl, Brom. BR2 .191 H7
  Stanmore HA7 . . . . . . .52 D7
Georgian Ct,
  off Gleneldon Rd .168/169 E4
  Wembley HA9 . . . . .88 A6
Georgian Way, Har. HA1 . .86 A2
Georgia Rd, N.Mal. KT3 .182 C4
  Thornton Heath CR7 . .187 H1
Georgina Gdns, E2 . . . . . . .13 G3
Geraint Rd, Brom. BR1 . . .173 G4
Geraldine Rd, SW18 . . . . .149 F5
  W4 . . . . .126 A6
Geraldine St, SE11 . . . . . . .27 G6
Gerald Ms, SW1 . . . . .32 C1
Gerald Rd, E16 . . . . .115 F4
  SW1 . . . . .32 C1
  Dagenham RM8 . . . . . .101 F2
Gerard Av, Houns. TW4
  off Redfern Av 143 G7
Gerard Rd, SW13 . . . . .147 F1
  Harrow HA1 . . . . .68 D6
Gerards Cl, SE16 . . . . .133 F5
Gerda Rd, SE9 . . . . .175 F2
Germander Way, E15 . . . . .115 E3
Gernigan Ho, SW18
  off Fitzhugh Gro 149 G6
Gernon Rd, E3 . . . . .113 H2
Geron Way, NW2 . . . . .89 H1
Gerrard Gdns, Pnr. HA5 . .66 A5
Gerrard Pl, W1 . . . . .17 J5
Gerrard Rd, N1 . . . . .11 H1
Gerrards Cl, N14 . . . . .42 C5
Gerrard St, W1 . . . . .17 H5
Gerridge St, SE1 . . . . .27 F4
Gerry Raffles Sq, E15
  off Great Eastern Rd . .96 D6
Gertrude Rd, Belv. DA17 .139 G4
Gertrude St, SW10 . . . . .30 D6
Gervase Cl, Wem. HA9 . . . .88 C3
Gervase Rd, Edg. HA8 . . . .70 C1
Gervase St, SE15 . . . . .133 E7
Ghent St, SE6 . . . . .172 A2
Ghent Way, E8
  off Tyssen St 94 C6
Giant Arches Rd, SE24 . . .151 J7
Giant Tree Hill, Bushey
  (Bushey Hth.) WD23 . .52 A1
Gibbard Ms, SW19 . . . . . . .166 A5
Gibbfield Cl, Rom. RM6 . .82 E3
Gibbins Rd, E15 . . . . .96 C7
Gibbon Rd, SE15 . . . . .153 F2
  W3 . . . . .106 E7
  Kingston upon Thames
  KT2 . . . . .181 H1
Gibbons Rents, SE1
  off Magdalen St 132 B1
Gibbons Rd, NW10 . . . . . . .88 D6
Gibbon Wk, SW15
  off Swinburne Rd 147 G4
Gibbs Av, SE19 . . . . .170 A5
Gibbs Cl, SE19 . . . . .170 A5
Gibbs Couch, Wat. WD19 .50 D3
Gibbs Grn, W14 . . . . .128 C5
  Edgware HA8 . . . . .54 C5
Gibbs Rd, N18 . . . . .61 F4
Gibbs Sq, SE19 . . . . .170 A5
Gibraltar Wk, E2 . . . . .13 G4
Gibson Cl, E1
  off Colebert Av 113 F4
  N21 . . . . .43 G6
  Chessington KT9 . . . . .195 F6
  Isleworth TW7 . . . . . . .144 A3
Gibson Gdns, N16
  off Northwold Rd 94 C2
Gibson Rd, SE11 . . . . .34 D2
  Dagenham RM8 . . . . . .100 C1
  Sutton SM1 . . . . .198 E5
Gibson's Hill, SW16 . . . . . .169 G6
Gibson Sq, N1 . . . . .111 G1
Gibson St, SE10 . . . . .134 E5
Gideon Cl, Belv. DA17 . . .139 H4
Gideon Ms, W5 . . . . .125 G2
Gideon Rd, SW11 . . . . .150 A3
Giesbach Rd, N19 . . . . .92 C2
Giffard Rd, N18 . . . . .60 B5
Giffin St, SE8 . . . . .134 A7
Gifford Gdns, W7 . . . . .104 A5
Gifford St, N1 . . . . .93 E7
Gift La, E15 . . . . .115 E1
Giggs Hill Gdns, T.Ditt.
  KT7 . . . . .194 D1
Giggs Hill Rd, T.Ditt. KT7 .180 D1
Gilbert Cl, SE18 . . . . .156 C1
Gilbert Gro, Edg. HA8 . . . .70 D1
Gilbert Ho, EC2
  off The Barbican 111 J5
  SE8 off McMillan St . .134 A6
Gilbert Pl, WC1 . . . . .18 A2
Gilbert Rd, SE11 . . . . .35 F2
  SW19 . . . . .167 F7

Gilbert Rd, Belv. DA17 . . .139 G3
  Bromley BR1 . . . . .173 G7
  Pinner HA5 . . . . .66 D4
Gilbert St, E15 . . . . .96 E4
  W1 . . . . .16 C4
  Hounslow TW3
  off High St 143 J3
Gilbert Way, Croy. CR0
  off Beddington Fm
  Rd 200/201 E1
Gilbey Rd, SW17 . . . . .167 H4
Gilbeys Yd, NW1 . . . . .92 A7
Gilbourne Rd, SE18 . . . . . .137 J6
Gilda Av, Enf. EN3 . . . . .45 H5
Gilda Cres, N16 . . . . .94 D1
Gildea Cl, Pnr. HA5 . . . . . . .51 G7
Gildea St, W1 . . . . .17 E2
Gilden Cres, NW5 . . . . .92 A5
Gildersome St, SE18
  off Nightingale Vale . .136 D6
Gilders Rd, Chess. KT9 . . .195 J6
Giles Coppice, SE19 . . . . .170 C4
Gilkes Cres, SE21 . . . . .152 B6
Gilkes Pl, SE21 . . . . .152 B6
Gillan Grn, Bushey
  (Bushey Hth.) WD23 . .51 J2
Gillards Ms, E17
  off Gillards Way 78 A4
Gillards Way, E17 . . . . .78 A4
Gill Av, E16 . . . . .115 G6
Gillender St, E3 . . . . .114 C4
  E14 . . . . .114 C4
Gillespie Rd, N5 . . . . .93 G3
Gillett Av, E6 . . . . .116 B2
Gillette Cor, Islw. TW7 . . .124 D7
Gillett Pl, N16
  off Gillett St 94 B5
Gillett Rd, Th.Hth. CR7 . . .188 A4
Gillett St, N16 . . . . .94 B5
Gillfoot, NW1 . . . . .9 G2
Gillham Ter, N17 . . . . .60 D6
Gillian Pk Rd, Sutt. SM3 .198 C1
Gillian St, SE13 . . . . .154 B5
Gillies St, NW5 . . . . .92 A5
Gilling Ct, NW3 . . . . .91 H6
Gillingham Ms, SW1 . . . . . .33 F1
Gillingham Rd, NW2 . . . . . .90 B3
Gillingham Row, SW1 . . . . .33 F1
Gillingham St, SW1 . . . . . . .33 F1
Gillison Wk, SE16 . . . . .29 J5
Gillman Dr, E15 . . . . .115 F1
Gill St, E14 . . . . .113 J6
Gillum Cl, Barn. EN4 . . . . . .57 J1
Gilmore Rd, SE13 . . . . .154 D4
Gilpin Av, SW14 . . . . .146 D4
Gilpin Cl, W2 . . . . .14 E1
  Mitcham CR4 . . . . .185 H2
Gilpin Cres, N18 . . . . .60 C5
  Twickenham TW2 . . . . .143 H7
Gilpin Rd, E5 . . . . .95 H4
Gilpin Way, Hayes UB3 . . .121 G7
Gilsland Rd, Th.Hth. CR7 .188 A4
Gilstead Ho, Bark. IG11 . .118 B2
Gilstead Rd, SW6 . . . . .149 E2
Gilston Rd, SW10 . . . . .30 D4
Gilton Rd, SE6 . . . . .173 E3
Giltspur St, EC1 . . . . .19 H3
Gilwell Cl, E4
  off Antlers Hill 46 B4
Gilwell La, E4 . . . . .46 C4
Gilwell Pk, E4 . . . . .46 C3
Gippeswyck Cl, Pnr. HA5
  off Uxbridge Rd 66 D1
Gipsy Hill, SE19 . . . . .170 B4
Gipsy La, SW15 . . . . .147 G3
★ Gipsy Moth IV, SE10 .134 C6
Gipsy Rd, SE27 . . . . .169 J4
  Welling DA16 . . . . .158 D1
Gipsy Rd Gdns, SE27 . . . .169 J4
Giralda Cl, E16
  off Fulmer Rd 116 A5
Giraud St, E14 . . . . .114 B6
Girdlers Rd, W14 . . . . .128 A4
Girdlestone Wk, N19 . . . . . .92 C2
Girdwood Rd, SW18 . . . . . .148 B7
Girling Way, Felt. TW14 . .142 A3
Gironde Rd, SW6 . . . . .128 C7
Girton Av, NW9 . . . . .70 A3
Girton Cl, Nthlt. UB5 . . . . .85 J6
Girton Gdns, Croy. CR0 .204 A3
Girton Rd, SE26 . . . . .171 G5
  Northolt UB5 . . . . .85 J6
Girton Vil, W10 . . . . .108 A6
Gisbourne Cl, Wall. SM6 .200 D3
Gisburn Rd, N8 . . . . .75 F4
Gissing Wk, N1
  off Lofting Rd 93 G7
Gittens Cl, Brom. BR1 . . .173 F4
Given Wilson Wk, E13 . . . .115 F2
Glacier Way, Wem. HA0 . .105 G2

Gladbeck Way, Enf. EN2 . .43 H4
Gladding Rd, E12 . . . . . . .98 A4
Glade, The, N21 . . . . .43 F6
SE7 . . . . .135 J7
Bromley BR1 . . . . .192 A2
Croydon CR0 . . . . .189 G5
Enfield EN2 . . . . .43 G3
Epsom KT17 . . . . .197 G5
Ilford IG5 . . . . .80 C1
West Wickham BR4 . . .204 B3
Woodford Green IG8 . . .63 H3
Glade Cl, Surb. KT6 . . . .195 G2
Glade Ct, Ilf. IG5
off The Glade 80 C1
Glade Gdns, Croy. CR0 . .189 H7
Glade La, Sthl. UB2 . . . .123 H2
Gladeside, N21 . . . . .43 F6
Croydon CR0 . . . . .189 G6
Glademore Rd, N15 . . . . .76 C6
Glades Shop Cen, The, Brom.
BR1 . . . . .191 G2
Gladeswood Rd, Belv.
DA17 . . . . .139 H4
Gladiator St, SE23 . . . . .153 H6
Glading Ter, N16 . . . . . . .94 C3
Gladioli Cl, Hmptn. TW12
off Gresham Rd 161 G6
Gladsdale Dr, Pnr. HA5 . . .66 A4
Gladsmuir Rd, N19 . . . . . .92 C1
Barnet EN5 . . . . .40 B2
Gladstone Av, E12 . . . . . .98 B7
N22 . . . . .75 G2
Feltham TW14 . . . . . . .142 A6
Twickenham TW2 . . . . .144 A7
Gladstone Ct, SW19
off Gladstone Rd 166 D7
Gladstone Gdns, Houns. TW3
off Palmerston Rd . . .143 J1
Gladstone Ms, N22
off Pelham Rd 75 G2
NW6 off Cavendish Rd .90 C7
SE20 . . . . .171 F7
Gladstone Par, NW2
off Edgware Rd 89 H1
Gladstone Pk Gdns, NW2 .89 H3
Gladstone Pl, E3
off Roman Rd 113 J2
Barnet EN5 . . . . .40 A4
Gladstone Rd, SW19 . . . .166 D7
W4 off Acton La 126 D3
Buckhurst Hill IG9 . . . .63 H1
Croydon CR0 . . . . .188 A7
Kingston upon Thames
KT1 . . . . .182 A3
Orpington BR6 . . . . . . .207 F6
Southall UB2 . . . . .122 E3
Surbiton KT6 . . . . .195 G2
Gladstone St, SE1 . . . . . .27 G5
Gladstone Ter, SE27 . . . .169 J4
SW8 . . . . .150 B1
Gladstone Way, Har. (Widste.)
HA3 . . . . .68 B3
Gladwell Rd, N8 . . . . .75 F6
Bromley BR1 . . . . .173 G6
Gladwyn Rd, SW15 . . . .148 A3
Gladys Rd, NW6 . . . . .90 D7
Glaisher St, SE8 . . . . . . .134 B6
Glamis Cres, Hayes UB3 .121 F3
Glamis Pl, E1 . . . . .113 F7
Glamis Rd, E1 . . . . .113 F7
Glamis Way, Nthlt. UB5 . .85 J6
Glamorgan Rd, Mitch.
CR4 . . . . .186 E3
Glamorgan Rd, Kings.T.
KT1 . . . . .163 F7
Glanfield Rd, Beck. BR3 .189 J4
Glanleam Rd, Stan. HA7 . .53 G4
Glanville Rd, SW2 . . . . . .151 E5
Bromley BR2 . . . . .191 H3
Glasbrook Av, Twick.
TW2 . . . . .161 F1
Glasbrook Rd, SE9 . . . . .156 A7
Glaserton Rd, N16 . . . . . .76 B7
Glasford St, SW17 . . . . .167 J6
Glasgow Ho, W9 . . . . .6 B3
Glasgow Rd, E13 . . . . . .115 H2
N18 off Aberdeen
Rd 60/61 E5
Glasgow Ter, SW1 . . . . . .33 F4
Glasse Cl, W13 . . . . .104 D7
Glasshill St, SE1 . . . . . . .27 H3
Glasshouse Flds, E1 . . . .113 G7
Glasshouse St, W1 . . . . . .17 G6
Glasshouse Wk, SE11 . . . .34 B3
Glasshouse Yd, EC1 . . . . .19 J1
Glasslyn Rd, N8 . . . . .74 D5
Glassmill La, Brom.
BR2 . . . . .191 F2
Glass St, E2
off Coventry Rd . .112/113 E4

Glass Yd, SE18
off Woolwich High St .136 D3
Glastonbury Av, Wdf.Grn.
IG8 . . . . .64 A7
Glastonbury Pl, E1
off Sutton St 113 F6
Glastonbury Rd, N9 . . . . .60 D1
Morden SM4 . . . . .184 D7
Glastonbury St, NW6 . . . .90 C5
Glaucus St, E3 . . . . .114 B5
Glazbury Rd, W14 . . . . . .128 B4
Glazebrook Cl, SE21 . . . .170 A2
Glazebrook Rd, Tedd.
TW11 . . . . .162 C7
Glebe, The, SE3 . . . . . . .154 E3
SW16 . . . . .168 D4
Chislehurst BR7 . . . . . .193 F1
West Drayton UB7 . . . .120 C4
Worcester Park KT4 . . .197 F1
Glebe Av, Enf. EN2 . . . . . .43 H3
Harrow HA3 . . . . .69 H3
Mitcham CR4 . . . . .185 H2
Ruislip HA4 . . . . .84 B6
Woodford Green IG8 . . .63 G6
Glebe Cl, W4
off Glebe St 126/127 E5
Glebe Cotts, Sutt. SM1
off Vale Rd 198/199 E4
Glebe Ct, W7 . . . . .104 A7
Mitcham CR4 . . . . .185 J3
Stanmore HA7
off Glebe Rd 53 F5
Glebe Cres, NW4 . . . . . . .71 J4
Harrow HA3 . . . . .69 H3
Glebe Gdns, N.Mal. KT3 .183 E7
Glebe Ho Dr, Brom. BR2 .205 H1
Glebe Hyrst, SE19
off Giles Coppice 170 C4
Glebelands, W.Mol. KT8 .179 H5
Glebelands Av, E18 . . . . . .79 G2
Ilford IG2 . . . . .81 G7
Glebelands Cl, SE5
off Grove Hill Rd 152 B3
Glebelands Rd, Felt.
TW14 . . . . .142 A7
Glebe La, Barn. EN5 . . . . .39 G5
Harrow HA3 . . . . .69 H4
Glebe Path, Mitch. CR4 . .185 H3
Glebe Pl, SW3 . . . . .31 G5
Glebe Rd, E8
off Middleton Rd 94 C7
N3 . . . . .73 F1
N8 . . . . .75 F4
NW10 . . . . .89 F6
SW13 . . . . .147 G2
Bromley BR1 . . . . .191 G1
Carshalton SM5 . . . . . .199 J6
Dagenham RM10 . . . . .101 H6
Hayes UB3 . . . . .121 J1
Stanmore HA7 . . . . .53 F5
Glebe Side, Twick. TW1 . .144 C6
Glebe St, W4 . . . . .126 E5
Glebe Ter, E3
off Bow Rd 114 A3
Glebe Way, Felt. TW13 . .161 G3
West Wickham BR4 . . .204 C2
Glebeway, Wdf.Grn. IG8 . .63 J5
Gledhow Gdns, SW5 . . . . .30 C2
Gledstanes Rd, W14 . . . .128 B5
Gleed Av, Bushey
(Bushey Hth.) WD23 . .52 A2
Gleeson Dr, Orp. BR6 . . .207 J5
Glegg Pl, SW15 . . . . .148 A4
Glen, The, Brom. BR2 . . .190 E2
Croydon CR0 . . . . .203 G2
Enfield EN2 . . . . .43 H4
Orpington BR6 . . . . . . .206 C3
Pinner HA5 . . . . .67 E7
Pinner (Eastcote) HA5 . .66 B5
Southall UB2 . . . . .123 F5
Wembley HA9 . . . . .87 G4
Glenaffric Av, E14 . . . . . .134 D4
Glen Albyn Rd, SW19 . . .166 A2
Glenalmond Rd, Har.
HA3 . . . . .69 H4
Glenalvon Way, SE18 . . .136 B4
Glena Mt, Sutt. SM1 . . . .199 F4
Glenarm Rd, E5 . . . . .95 F5
Glenavon Cl, Esher (Clay.)
KT10 . . . . .194 D7
Glenavon Rd, E15 . . . . . . .97 E7
Glenbarr Cl, SE9
off Dumbreck Rd .156/157 E3
Glenbow Rd, Brom. BR1 .172 E6
Glenbrook N, Enf. EN2 . . .43 F4
Glenbrook Rd, NW6 . . . . .90 D5
Glenbrook S, Enf. EN2 . . .43 F4
Glenbuck Ct, Surb. KT6
off Glenbuck Rd 181 G6
Glenbuck Rd, Surb. KT6 .181 G6

Glenburnie Rd, SW17 . . .167 J3
Glencairn Dr, W5 . . . . . . .105 E4
Glencairne Cl, E16 . . . . . .116 A5
Glencairn Rd, SW16 . . . .186 E1
Glencoe Av, Ilf. IG2 . . . . . .81 G7
Glencoe Dr, Dag. RM10 . .101 G4
Glencoe Rd, Hayes UB4 .102 D5
Glencorse Grn, Wat. WD19
off Caldwell Rd 50 D4
Glen Cres, Wdf.Grn. IG8 . .63 H6
Glendale Av, N22 . . . . . . .59 G7
Edgware HA8 . . . . .53 J4
Romford RM6 . . . . .82 C7
Glendale Cl, SE9
off Dumbreck Rd 156 D3
Glendale Dr, SW19 . . . . .166 C5
Glendale Gdns, Wem.
HA9 . . . . .87 G1
Glendale Ms, Beck. BR3 .190 B1
Glendale Rd, Erith DA8 . .139 J4
Glendale Way, SE28 . . . .118 C7
Glendall St, SW9 . . . . . . .151 F4
Glendarvon St, SW15 . . .148 A3
Glendevon Cl, Edg. HA8
off Tayside Dr 54 B3
Glendish Rd, N17 . . . . . . .76 D1
Glendor Gdns, NW7 . . . . .54 D4
Glendower Gdns, SW14
off Glendower Rd 146 D3
Glendower Pl, SW7 . . . . . .31 E1
Glendower Rd, E4 . . . . . . .62 D1
SW14 . . . . .146 D3
Glendown Rd, SE2 . . . . .138 A5
Glendun Rd, W3 . . . . . . .107 E7
Gleneagle Ms, SW16
off Ambleside Av 168 D5
Gleneagle Rd, SW16 . . . .168 D5
Gleneagles, Stan. HA7 . . .52 E6
Gleneagles Cl, SE16
off Ryder Dr 132/133 E5
Orpington BR6 . . . . . . .207 G2
Staines (Stanw.) TW19 .140 A6
Watford WD19 . . . . . . .50 D4
Gleneagles Grn, Orp. BR6
off Tandridge Dr 207 G1
Gleneagles Twr, Sthl.
UB1 . . . . .103 J6
Gleneldon Ms, SW16 . . . .168 E4
Gleneldon Rd, SW16 . . . .168 E4
Glenelg Rd, SW2 . . . . . . .151 E5
Glenesk Rd, SE9 . . . . . . .156 D3
Glenfarg Rd, SE6 . . . . . .172 D1
Glenfield Rd, SW12 . . . . .168 C1
W13 . . . . .125 E2
Glenfield Ter, W13 . . . . .124 E2
Glenfinlas Way, SE5 . . . . .35 H7
Glengall Causeway, E14 .134 A3
Glengall Gro, E14 . . . . . .134 B3
Glengall Rd, NW6 . . . . . .108 C1
SE15 . . . . .37 G5
Bexleyheath DA7 . . . . .159 E3
Edgware HA8 . . . . .54 B2
Woodford Green IG8 . . .63 G6
Glengall Ter, SE15 . . . . . .37 G5
Glen Gdns, Croy. CR0 . . .201 G3
Glengarnock Av, E14 . . . .134 C4
Glengarry Rd, SE22 . . . . .152 B5
Glenham Dr, Ilf. IG2 . . . . .80 E5
Glenhaven Av, Borwd.
WD6 . . . . .38 A3
Glenhead Cl, SE9
off Dumbreck Rd .156/157 E3
Glenhouse Rd, SE9 . . . . .156 D5
Glenhurst Av, NW5 . . . . . .92 A4
Bexley DA5 . . . . .177 F1
Glenhurst Ct, SE19 . . . . .170 C5
Glenhurst Ri, SE19 . . . . .169 J7
Glenhurst Rd, N12 . . . . . .57 G5
Brentford TW8 . . . . . . .125 F6
Glenilla Rd, NW3 . . . . . . .91 H6
Glenister Ho, Hayes
UB3 . . . . .122 B1
Glenister Pk Rd, SW16 .168 D7
Glenister Rd, SE10 . . . . .135 F5
Glenister St, E16 . . . . . . .136 D1
Glenkerry Ho, E14
off Burcham St 114 C6
Glenlea Rd, SE9 . . . . . . .156 C5
Glenloch Rd, NW3 . . . . . .91 H6
Enfield EN3 . . . . .45 F2
Glenluce Rd, SE3 . . . . . .135 G7
Glenlyon Rd, SE9 . . . . . .156 D5
Glenmere Av, NW7 . . . . . .55 G7
Glen Ms, E17
off Glen Rd 77 J5
Glenmill, Hmptn. TW12 . .161 F5
Glenmore Rd, NW3 . . . . . .91 H6
Welling DA16 . . . . .157 J1

Glenmore Way, Bark.
IG11 . . . . .118 A3
Glenmount Path, SE18
off Raglan Rd 137 F5
Glennie Rd, SE27 . . . . . .169 G3
Glenny Rd, Bark. IG11 . . .99 F6
Glenorchy Cl, Hayes
UB4 . . . . .103 E5
Glenparke Rd, E7 . . . . . . .97 H6
Glen Ri, Wdf.Grn. IG8 . . .63 H6
Glen Rd, E13 . . . . .115 J4
E17 . . . . .77 J5
Chessington KT9 . . . . .195 H3
Glenrosa St, SW6 . . . . . .149 F2
Glenrose Ct, Sid. DA14 . .176 B5
Glenroy St, W12 . . . . . . .107 J6
Glensdale Rd, SE4 . . . . .153 J3
Glenshiel Rd, SE9 . . . . . .156 D5
Glenside, Chig. IG7 . . . . . .65 E6
Glentanner Way, SW17
off Aboyne Rd 167 G3
Glen Ter, E14
off Manchester Rd . . .134 C2
Glentham Gdns, SW13
off Glentham Rd 127 H6
Glentham Rd, SW13 . . . .127 G6
Glenthorne Av, Croy.
CR0 . . . . .203 E1
Glenthorne Cl, Sutt.
SM3 . . . . .198 D1
Glenthorne Gdns, Ilf.
IG6 . . . . .80 D3
Sutton SM3 . . . . .198 D1
Glenthorne Ms, W6
off Glenthorne Rd . . .127 H4
Glenthorne Rd, E17 . . . . .77 H5
N11 . . . . .57 J5
W6 . . . . .127 J4
Kingston upon Thames
KT1 . . . . .181 J4
Glenthorpe Rd, Mord.
SM4 . . . . .184 A5
Glenton Rd, SE13 . . . . . .154 E4
Glentrammon Av, Orp.
BR6 . . . . .207 J6
Glentrammon Cl, Orp.
BR6 . . . . .207 J6
Glentrammon Gdns, Orp.
BR6 . . . . .207 J6
Glentrammon Rd, Orp.
BR6 . . . . .207 J6
Glentworth St, NW1 . . . . .8 A6
Glenure Rd, SE9 . . . . . . .156 D5
Glenview, SE2 . . . . .138 D6
Glenview Rd, Brom.
BR1 . . . . .192 A2
Glenville Ct, SE19
off Lymer Av 170 C5
Glenville Gro, SE8 . . . . . .133 J7
Glenville Ms, SW18 . . . .148 E7
Glenville Rd, Kings.T.
KT2 . . . . .182 A1
Glen Wk, Islw. TW7 . . . .144 A5
Glenwood Av, NW9 . . . . . .88 E1
Glenwood Cl, Har. HA1 . . .68 C5
Glenwood Ct, E18
off Clarendon Rd 79 G3
Glenwood Gdns, Ilf. IG2 . .80 D5
Glenwood Gro, NW9 . . . . .88 C1
Glenwood Rd, N15 . . . . . .75 H5
NW7 . . . . .55 E3
SE6 . . . . .171 J1
Epsom KT17 . . . . .197 G6
Hounslow TW3 . . . . . .144 A3
Glenwood Way, Croy.
CR0 . . . . .189 G6
Glenworth Av, E14 . . . . . .134 D4
Gliddon Rd, W14 . . . . . . .128 B4
Glimpsing Grn, Erith
DA18 . . . . .139 E3
Global App, E3
off Hancock Rd 114 B2
Globe Pond Rd, SE16 . . .133 H1
Globe Rd, E1 . . . . .113 F3
E2 . . . . .113 F3
E15 . . . . .97 F5
Woodford Green IG8 . . .63 J6
Globe Rope Wk, E14 . . . .134 C4
Globe St, SE1 . . . . .28 A5
Globe Ter, E2
off Globe Rd 113 F3
Globe Yd, W1 . . . . .16 D4
Gloster Rd, N.Mal. KT3 . .182 E4
Gloucester Arc, SW7 . . . . .30 C1
Gloucester Av, NW1 . . . . .92 A7
Sidcup DA15 . . . . .175 H2
Welling DA16 . . . . .157 J4
Gloucester Circ, SE10 . . .134 C7
Gloucester Cl, NW10 . . . . .88 D7
Thames Ditton KT7 . . .194 D1

Gloucester Ct, EC3 . . . . . .21 E6
 Richmond TW9 . . . . .126 A7
Gloucester Cres, NW1 . . .110 B1
Gloucester Dr, N4 . . . . . . .93 H2
 NW11 . . . . .72 D4
Gloucester Gdns, NW11 . .72 C7
 W2 . . . . .14 B3
 Barnet EN4 . . . . .42 A4
 Ilford IG1 . . . . .80 B7
 Sutton SM1 . . . . .199 E2
Gloucester Gate, NW1 . . . .8 D1
Gloucester Gate Ms, NW1 . .8 D1
Gloucester Gro, Edg.
 HA8 . . . . .70 D1
Gloucester Gro Est, SE15 .37 E6
Gloucester Ho, NW6 . . . .108 D2
Gloucester Ms, E10
 off Gloucester Rd 78 A7
 W2 . . . . .14 D4
Gloucester Ms W, W2 . . . .14 C4
Gloucester Par, Sid.
 DA15 . . . . .158 A5
Gloucester Pk, SW7
 off Courtfield Rd 129 F4
Gloucester Pl, NW1 . . . . . .7 J5
 W1 . . . . .16 A1
 Enfield EN2
 off Chase Side 43 J2
Gloucester Pl Ms, W1 . . . .16 A2
Gloucester Rd, E10 . . . . . .78 A7
 E11 . . . . .79 H5
 E12 . . . . .98 C3
 E17 . . . . .77 G2
 N17 . . . . .76 A2
 N18 . . . . .60 C5
 SW7 . . . . .22 C5
 W3 . . . . .126 C2
 W5 . . . . .125 F2
 Barnet EN5 . . . . .41 F5
 Belvedere DA17 . . . . . .139 F5
 Croydon CR0 . . . . .188 A6
 Feltham TW13 . . . . .160 C1
 Hampton TW12 . . . . . . .161 H7
 Harrow HA1 . . . . .67 H5
 Hounslow TW4 . . . . . . .142 E4
 Kingston upon Thames
 KT1 . . . . .182 B2
 Richmond TW9 . . . . . . .126 A7
 Teddington TW11 . . . . .162 B5
 Twickenham TW2 . . . . .161 J1
Gloucester Sq, E2
 off Whiston Rd 112 D1
 W2 . . . . .15 F4
Gloucester St, SW1 . . . . . .33 F4
Gloucester Ter, W2 . . . . . .14 C3
Gloucester Wk, W8 . . . . .128 D2
Gloucester Way, EC1 . . . .11 F4
Gloxinia Wk, Hmptn.
 TW12 . . . . .161 G6
Glycena Rd, SW11 . . . . . .149 J3
Glyn Av, Barn. EN4 . . . . . .41 G4
Glyn Cl, SE25 . . . . .188 B2
Glyn Ct, SW16 . . . . .169 G3
Glyndebourne Pk, Orp.
 BR6 . . . . .207 E2
Glynde Ms, SW3 . . . . .23 H6
Glynde Rd, Bexh. DA7 . . .158 D3
Glynde St, SE4 . . . . .153 J6
Glyndon Rd, SE18 . . . . . .137 F4
Glyn Dr, Sid. DA14 . . . . .176 B4
Glynfield Rd, NW10 . . . . . .89 E7
Glynne Rd, N22 . . . . .75 G2
Glyn Rd, E5 . . . . .95 G3
 Enfield EN3 . . . . .45 F4
 Worcester Park KT4 . . .198 A2
Glyn St, SE11 . . . . .34 C4
Glynwood Ct, SE23 . . . . .171 F2
Goaters All, SW6 . . . . . . .128 C7
Goat La, Surb. KT6 . . . . . .195 F2
Goat Rd, Mitch. CR4 . . . .186 A7
Goat St, SE1 . . . . .29 F3
Goat Wf, Brent. TW8 . . . .125 H6
Godalming Av, Wall.
 SM6 . . . . .201 E5
Godalming Rd, E14 . . . . .114 B5
Godbold Rd, E15 . . . . . . .114 E3
Goddard Pl, N19 . . . . .92 C3
Goddard Rd, Beck. BR3 . .189 G4
Goddards Way, Ilf. IG1 . . . .99 G1
Godfrey Av, Nthlt. UB5 . .102 E1
 Twickenham TW2 . . . . .144 A7
Godfrey Hill, SE18 . . . . . .136 B4
Godfrey Rd, SE18 . . . . . .136 C4
Godfrey St, E15 . . . . .114 C2
 SW3 . . . . .31 H3
Godfrey Way, Houns.
 TW4 . . . . .143 F7

Goding St, SE11 . . . . .34 B4
Godley Rd, SW18 . . . . . .167 G1
Godliman St, EC4 . . . . . . .19 J4
Godman Rd, SE15 . . . . . .152 E2
Godolphin Cl, N13 . . . . . . .59 H6
Godolphin Pl, W3
 off Vyner Rd 106 D7
Godolphin Rd, W12 . . . . .127 H2
Godson Rd, Croy. CR0 . . .201 G3
Godson St, N1 . . . . .11 E1
Godstone Rd, Sutt. SM1 .199 F4
 Twickenham TW1 . . . . .144 D6
Godstow Rd, SE2 . . . . . . .138 C2
Godwin Cl, N1 . . . . .12 A1
 Epsom KT19 . . . . .196 C6
Godwin Ct, NW1 . . . . .9 G1
Godwin Rd, E7 . . . . .97 H4
 Bromley BR2 . . . . .191 J3
Goffers Rd, SE3 . . . . .154 D1
Goidel Cl, Wall. SM6 . . . .200 D4
Golborne Gdns, W10
 off Golborne Rd 108 C4
Golborne Ms, W10
 off Portobello Rd 108 B5
Golborne Rd, W10 . . . . . .108 B5
Golda Cl, Barn. EN5 . . . . .40 A6
Goldbeaters Gro, Edg.
 HA8 . . . . .54 E6
Goldcliff Cl, Mord. SM4 .184 D6
Goldcrest Cl, E16
 off Sheerwater Rd 116 A5
 SE28 . . . . .118 C7
Goldcrest Ms, W5
 off Montpelier Av 105 G5
Goldcrest Way, Bushey
 WD23 . . . . .51 J1
Golden Ct, Rich.TW9
 off George St 145 G5
Golden Cres, Hayes UB3 .121 J1
Golden Cross Ms, W11
 off Basing St 108 C6
★ Golden Hinde, SE1
 off Cathedral St 28 B1
Golden La, EC1 . . . . .11 J6
Golden La Est, EC1 . . . . . .11 J6
Golden Manor, W7 . . . . . .104 B7
Golden Plover Cl, E16
 off Maplin Rd 115 H6
Golden Sq, W1 . . . . .17 G5
Golden Yd, NW3
 off Heath St 91 F4
Golders Cl, Edg. HA8 . . . . .54 B5
Golders Gdns, NW11 . . . .72 B7
GOLDERS GREEN, NW11 .72 D7
Golders Grn Cres, NW11 . .72 C7
Golders Grn Rd, NW11 . . .72 B6
Golders Manor Dr, NW11 .72 A6
Golders Pk Cl, NW11 . . . . .90 E1
Golders Ri, NW4 . . . . .72 A5
Golders Way, NW11 . . . . . .72 C7
Goldfinch Rd, SE28 . . . . .137 G3
Goldfinch Way, Borwd.
 WD6 . . . . .38 A4
Goldhawk Ms, W12
 off Devonport Rd 127 H2
Goldhawk Rd, W6 . . . . . .127 F4
 W12 . . . . .127 G3
Goldhaze Cl, Wdf.Grn.
 IG8 . . . . .64 A7
Gold Hill, Edg. HA8 . . . . . .54 D6
Goldhurst Ter, NW6 . . . . . .90 E7
Golding Cl, Chess. KT9
 off Coppard Gdns 195 F6
Goldingham Av, Loug.
 IG10 . . . . .49 F2
Goldings Hill, Loug.IG10 .48 D1
Goldings Ri, Loug. IG10 . .48 D1
Goldings Rd, Loug. IG10 .48 D1
Golding St, E1 . . . . .21 J4
Golding Ter, SW11
 off Longhedge St 150 A2
Goldington Cres, NW1 . . . .9 H1
Goldington St, NW1 . . . . . .9 H1
Gold La, Edg. HA8 . . . . . . .54 D6
Goldman Cl, E2 . . . . .13 H5
Goldmark Ho, SE3
 off Lebrun Sq 155 H3
Goldney Rd, W9 . . . . .108 D4
Goldrill Dr, N11 . . . . .58 A2
Goldsboro Rd, SW8 . . . . .150 D1
Goldsborough Cres, E4 . . .62 C2
Goldsdown Cl, Enf. EN3 . .45 H2
Goldsdown Rd, Enf.
 EN3 . . . . .45 G2
Goldsmid St, SE18
 off Sladedale Rd 137 H5
Goldsmith Av, E12 . . . . . . .98 B6
 NW9 . . . . .71 F6
 W3 . . . . .106 D7
 Romford RM7 . . . . .83 G7

Goldsmith Cl, W3
 off East Acton La .126/127 E1
 Harrow HA2 . . . . .85 H1
Goldsmith Rd, E10 . . . . . . .96 A1
 E17 . . . . .77 G2
 N11 . . . . .57 J5
 SE15 . . . . .152 D1
 W3 . . . . .126 D1
Goldsmith's Row, E2 . . . . .13 H2
Goldsmith's Sq, E2 . . . . . .13 J1
★ Goldsmiths' Hall, EC2 .20 A3
Goldsmith St, EC2 . . . . . .20 A3
Goldsworthy Gdns,
 SE16 . . . . .133 F4
Goldwell Rd, Th.Hth.
 CR7 . . . . .187 F4
Goldwin Cl, SE14 . . . . . . .153 F1
Goldwing Cl, E16 . . . . . . .115 G6
Golf Cl, Stan. HA7 . . . . . . .53 F7
 Thornton Heath CR7
 off Kensington Av 187 G1
Golf Club Dr, Kings.T.
 KT2 . . . . .164 D7
Golfe Rd, Ilf. IG1 . . . . .99 G3
Golf Rd, W5 . . . . .105 J6
 Bromley BR1 . . . . .192 D3
Golf Side, Twick. TW2 . . .162 A3
Golfside Cl, N20 . . . . .57 H3
 New Malden KT3 . . . . . .183 E2
Goliath Cl, Wall. SM6 . . . .200 E7
Gollogly Ter, SE7 . . . . . . .135 J5
Gomer Gdns, Tedd. TW11 .162 D6
Gomer Pl, Tedd. TW11 . . .162 D6
Gomm Rd, SE16 . . . . . . .133 F3
Gomshall Av, Wall. SM6 .200 E5
Gondar Gdns, NW6 . . . . . .90 C5
Gonson Pl, SE8 . . . . .134 A6
Gonson St, SE8 . . . . .134 B6
Gonston Cl, SW19
 off Boddicott Cl 166 B2
Gonville Cres, Nthlt. UB5 .85 H6
Gonville Rd, Th.Hth. CR7 .187 F5
Gonville St, SW6
 off Putney Br App 148 B3
Goodall Rd, E11 . . . . .96 C3
Gooden Ct, Har. HA1 . . . . .86 B3
Goodenough Rd, SW19 .166 C7
Goodge Pl, W1 . . . . .17 G2
Goodge St, W1 . . . . .17 G2
Goodhall St, NW10 . . . . .107 E3
Goodhart Pl, E14 . . . . . . .113 H7
Goodhart Way, W.Wick.
 BR4 . . . . .190 E7
Goodhew Rd, Croy. CR0 .188 D6
Gooding Cl, N.Mal. KT3 .182 C4
Gooding Cl, N7 . . . . .92 E6
Goodman Cres, SW2 . . . .168 D2
Goodman Rd, E10 . . . . . . .78 C7
Goodmans Ct, E1 . . . . . . .21 F5
 Wembley HA0 . . . . .87 G4
Goodman's Stile, E1 . . . . .21 H4
Goodmans Yd, E1 . . . . . . .21 F5
GOODMAYES, Ilf. 100 B2
Goodmayes Av, Ilf. IG3 . .100 A1
Goodmayes La, Ilf. IG3 . .100 A4
Goodmayes Rd, Ilf. IG3 . .100 A1
Goodrich Rd, SE22 . . . . .152 C6
Goodson Rd, NW10 . . . . . .89 E7
Goods Way, NW1 . . . . .10 A1
Goodway Gdns, E14 . . . . .114 D6
Goodwin Cl, SE16 . . . . . . .29 G6
 Mitcham CR4 . . . . .185 G3
Goodwin Ct, Barn. EN4 . . .41 H6
Goodwin Dr, Sid. DA14 . .176 D3
Goodwin Gdns, Croy.
 CR0 . . . . .201 H6
Goodwin Rd, N9 . . . . .61 F1
 W12 . . . . .127 G2
 Croydon CR0 . . . . .201 H5
Goodwins Ct, WC2 . . . . . .18 A5
Goodwin St, N4
 off Fonthill Rd 93 G2
Goodwood Cl, Mord.
 SM4 . . . . .184 D4
 Stanmore HA7 . . . . .53 F5
Goodwood Dr, Nthlt.
 UB5 . . . . .85 G6
Goodwood Path, Borwd.WD6
 off Stratfield Rd 38 A3
Goodwood Rd, SE14 . . . .133 H7
Goodwyn Av, NW7 . . . . . . .55 E5
Goodwyns Vale, N10 . . . . .74 A1
Goodyers Gdns, NW4 . . . .72 A5
Goosander Way, SE28 . . .137 G3
Gooseacre La, Har. HA3 . .69 G5
Gooseley La, E6 . . . . .116 D3
Goosens Cl, Sutt. SM1
 off Turnpike La 199 F5

Goose Sq, E6
 off Harper Rd 116 C6
Gophir La, EC4 . . . . .20 B5
Gopsall St, N1 . . . . .112 A1
Gordon Av, E4 . . . . .62 E6
 SW14 . . . . .146 E4
 Stanmore HA7 . . . . .52 E6
 Twickenham TW1 . . . . .144 D5
Gordonbrock Rd, SE4 . . .154 A5
Gordon Cl, E17 . . . . .78 A6
 N19
 off Highgate Hill 92 C1
Gordon Ct, W12 . . . . .107 J6
Gordon Cres, Croy. CR0 .202 B1
 Hayes UB3 . . . . .122 A2
Gordondale Rd, SW19 . .166 D2
Gordon Gdns, Edg. HA8 . .70 B2
Gordon Gro, SE5 . . . . . . .151 H2
Gordon Hill, Enf. EN2 . . . .43 J1
Gordon Ho, E1
 off Glamis Rd 113 F7
Gordon Ho Rd, NW5 . . . . .92 A4
Gordon Pl, W8 . . . . .128 D2
Gordon Rd, E4 . . . . .47 E7
 E11 . . . . .79 G6
 E15 . . . . .96 C4
 E18 . . . . .79 H1
 N3 . . . . .56 C7
 N9 . . . . .61 E2
 N11 . . . . .58 D7
 SE15 . . . . .152 E2
 W4 . . . . .126 B6
 W5 . . . . .105 F7
 W13 . . . . .104 E7
 Barking IG11 . . . . .117 H1
 Beckenham BR3 . . . . . .189 J3
 Belvedere DA17 . . . . . .139 J4
 Carshalton SM5 . . . . . .199 J6
 Enfield EN2 . . . . .43 J1
 Esher (Clay.) KT10 . . . .194 B6
 Harrow HA3 . . . . .68 B3
 Hounslow TW3 . . . . . . .143 J4
 Ilford IG1 . . . . .99 G3
 Kingston upon Thames
 KT2 . . . . .181 J1
 Richmond TW9 . . . . . . .145 J2
 Romford RM6 . . . . .83 F6
 Sidcup DA15 . . . . .157 H5
 Southall UB2 . . . . .123 E4
 Surbiton KT5 . . . . .181 J7
Gordon Sq, WC1 . . . . .9 J6
Gordon St, E13
 off Grange Rd 115 G3
 WC1 . . . . .9 H5
Gordon Way, Barn. EN5 . .40 C4
 Bromley BR1 . . . . .191 G1
Gore Ct, NW9 . . . . .70 A5
Gorefield Pl, NW6 . . . . . .108 D2
Gore Rd, E9 . . . . .113 F1
 SW20 . . . . .183 J2
Goresbrook Rd, Dag.
 RM9 . . . . .118 B1
Goresbrook Village, Dag. RM9
 off Goresbrook Rd 118 B1
Gore St, SW7 . . . . .22 D5
Gorham Pl, W11
 off Mary Pl 108 B7
Goring Cl, Rom. RM5 . . . . .83 J1
Goring Gdns, Dag. RM8 .100 C4
Goring Rd, N11 . . . . .58 E6
Goring St, EC3 . . . . .21 E3
Goring Way, Grnf. UB6 . .103 J2
Gorleston Rd, N15 . . . . . . .76 A5
Gorleston St, W14 . . . . . .128 B4
Gorman Rd, SE18 . . . . . .136 C4
Gorringe Pk Av, Mitch.
 CR4 . . . . .167 J7
Gorse Cl, E16 . . . . .115 G6
Gorse Ri, SW17 . . . . .168 A5
Gorse Rd, Croy. CR0 . . . .204 A4
Gorst Rd, NW10 . . . . .106 C4
 SW11 . . . . .149 J6
Gorsuch Pl, E2 . . . . .13 F3
Gorsuch St, E2 . . . . .13 F3
Gosberton Rd, SW12 . . .168 A1
Gosbury Hill, Chess.
 KT9 . . . . .195 H4
Gosfield Rd, Dag. RM8 . .101 G2
Gosfield St, W1 . . . . .17 F1
Gosford Gdns, Ilf. IG4 . . . .80 C5
Gosforth La, Wat. WD19 . .50 C3
Gosforth Path, Wat.
 WD19 . . . . .50 A3
Goslett Yd, WC2 . . . . .17 J4
Gosling Cl, Grnf. UB6 . . .103 G3
Gosling Way, SW9 . . . . . .151 G1
Gospatrick Rd, N17 . . . . . .59 J7
GOSPEL OAK, NW5 . . . . . .92 A4
Gospel Oak Est, NW5 . . . .91 J5
Gosport Rd, E17 . . . . .77 J5

Gosport Wk, N17
off Yarmouth Cres . .**76/77** E5
Gosport Way, SE15 . . . . . .**37** F7
Gossage Rd, SE18
off Ancona Rd **137** G5
Gosset St, E2 . . . .**13** G3
Gosshill Rd, Chis. BR7 . .**192** D2
Gossington Cl, Chis. BR7
off Beechwood Ri **174/175** E4
Gosterwood St, SE8 . . . .**133** H6
Gostling Rd, Twick. TW2 .**161** G1
Goston Gdns, Th.Hth. CR7 . . . .**187** G3
Goswell Rd, EC1 . . . .**11** J6
Gothic Ct, Hayes UB3
off Sipson La **121** G6
Gothic Rd, Twick. TW2 . . .**162** A2
Gottfried Ms, NW5
off Fortess Rd **92** C4
Gouch Ho, E5 . . . .**95** E3
Goudhurst Rd, Brom. BR1 . . . .**173** E5
Gough Rd, E15 . . . .**97** F4
Enfield EN1 . . . .**44** E2
Gough Sq, EC4 . . . .**19** F3
Gough St, WC1 . . . .**10** D5
Gough Wk, E14
off Saracen St **114** A6
Gould Ct, SE19 . . . .**170** C5
Goulden Ho App, SW11 .**149** H2
Goulding Gdns, Th.Hth. CR7 . . . .**187** H2
Gould Rd, Felt. TW14 . . . .**141** H7
Twickenham TW2 . . . . .**162** B1
Gould Ter, E8
off Kenmure Rd . . .**94/95** E5
Goulston St, E1 . . . .**21** F3
Goulton Rd, E5 . . . .**95** E4
Gourley Pl, N15
off Gourley St **76** B5
Gourley St, N15 . . . .**76** B5
Gourock Rd, SE9 . . . .**156** D5
Govan St, E2
off Whiston Rd **112** D1
Govier Cl, E15 . . . .**97** E7
Gowan Av, SW6 . . . .**148** B1
Gowan Rd, NW10 . . . .**89** H6
Gower Cl, SW4 . . . .**150** C6
Gower Ct, WC1 . . . .**9** H5
Gower Ms, WC1 . . . .**17** H2
Gower Pl, WC1 . . . .**9** G5
Gower Rd, E7 . . . .**97** G6
Isleworth TW7 . . . .**124** C6
Gower St, WC1 . . . .**9** H6
Gower's Wk, E1 . . . .**21** H3
Gowland Pl, Beck. BR3 . . .**189** J2
Gowlett Rd, SE15 . . . . . .**152** D3
Gowrie Rd, SW11 . . . . . .**150** A3
Graburn Way, E.Mol. KT8 . . . .**180** A3
Grace Av, Bexh. DA7 . . . .**159** F2
Grace Business Cen, Mitch. CR4 . . . .**185** J5
Gracechurch St, EC3 . . . . .**20** C5
Grace Cl, SE9 . . . .**174** A3
Borehamwood WD6 . . . .**38** D1
Edgware HA8
off Pavilion Way **54** C7
Ilford IG6 . . . .**65** J6
Gracedale Rd, SW16 . . . .**168** B5
Gracefield Gdns, SW16 . .**169** E3
Grace Jones Cl, E8
off Parkholme Rd **94** D6
Grace Path, SE26 . . . . . .**171** F4
Grace Pl, E3
off St. Leonards St . . .**114** B3
Grace Rd, Croy. CR0 . . . .**187** J6
Grace's All, E1 . . . .**21** H5
Graces Ms, SE5 . . . .**152** B2
Graces Rd, SE5 . . . .**152** B2
Grace St, E3 . . . .**114** B3
Gradient, The, SE26 . . . . .**170** D4
Graduate Pl, SE1
off Long La **132** B3
Graeme Rd, Enf. EN1 . . . .**44** A2
Graemesdyke Av, SW14 .**146** B3
Grafton Cl, W13 . . . .**104** D6
Hounslow TW4 . . . .**161** E1
Worcester Park KT4 . . .**197** E3
Grafton Cres, NW1 . . . . . .**92** B6
Grafton Gdns, N4 . . . .**75** J6
Dagenham RM8 . . . . . .**101** E2
Grafton Ho, E3 . . . .**114** A3
Grafton Ms, W1 . . . .**9** F6
Grafton Pk Rd, Wor.Pk. KT4 . . . .**196** E2
Grafton Pl, NW1 . . . .**9** H4
Grafton Rd, NW5 . . . .**92** A5
W3 . . . .**106** C7
Grafton Rd, Croy. CR0 . . .**201** G1
Dagenham RM8 . . . . . .**101** E2
Enfield EN2 . . . .**43** F3
Harrow HA1 . . . .**67** J5
New Malden KT3 . . . . .**182** E3
Worcester Park KT4 . . .**196** D3
Graftons, The, NW2
off Hermitage La **90** D3
Grafton Sq, SW4 . . . .**150** C3
Grafton St, W1 . . . .**17** E6
Grafton Ter, NW5 . . . .**91** J5
Grafton Way, W1 . . . .**9** F6
WC1 . . . .**9** F6
West Molesey KT8 . . . .**179** F4
Grafton Yd, NW5
off Prince of Wales Rd .**92** B6
Graham Av, W13 . . . .**124** E2
Mitcham CR4 . . . .**186** A1
Graham Cl, Croy. CR0 . . .**204** A2
Grahame Pk Est, NW9 . . .**71** E1
Grahame Pk Way, NW7 . . .**55** F7
NW9 . . . .**71** F2
Graham Gdns, Surb. KT6 . . . .**195** H1
Graham Rd, E8 . . . .**94** D6
E13 . . . .**115** G4
N15 . . . .**75** H3
NW4 . . . .**71** H6
SW19 . . . .**166** C7
W4 . . . .**126** D3
Bexleyheath DA6 . . . . .**159** G4
Hampton TW12 . . . .**161** G4
Harrow HA3 . . . .**68** B3
Mitcham CR4 . . . .**186** A1
Graham St, N1 . . . .**11** H2
Graham Ter, SW1 . . . .**32** B2
Grainger Cl, Nthlt. UB5
off Lancaster Rd **85** J5
Grainger Rd, N22 . . . .**75** J1
Isleworth TW7 . . . .**144** C2
Gramer Cl, E11
off Norman Rd **96** D2
Grampian Cl, Hayes UB3 . . . .**121** G7
Orpington BR6
off Cotswold Ri **193** J6
Sutton SM2
off Devonshire Rd . . .**199** F7
Grampian Gdns, NW2 . . . .**90** B1
Grampian Ho, N9
off Plevna Rd **60/61** E2
Granard Av, SW15 . . . . . .**147** H5
Granard Rd, SW12 . . . . .**149** J7
Granary Cl, N9
off Turin Rd **45** F7
Granary Rd, E1 . . . .**112** E4
Granary St, NW1 . . . .**110** D1
Granby Pl, SE1 . . . .**26** E4
Granby Rd, SE9 . . . .**156** C2
Granby St, E2 . . . .**13** G5
Granby Ter, NW1 . . . .**9** F2
Grand Arc, N12
off Ballards La **57** F5
Grand Av, EC1 . . . .**19** H1
N10 . . . .**74** A4
Surbiton KT5 . . . .**182** B5
Wembley HA9 . . . .**88** A5
Grand Av E, Wem. HA9 . . .**88** B5
Grand Depot Rd, SE18 . .**136** D5
Grand Dr, SW20 . . . .**183** J2
Southall UB2 . . . .**123** J2
Granden Rd, SW16 . . . . .**187** E2
Grandison Rd, SW11 . . . .**149** J5
Worcester Park KT4 . . .**197** J2
Grand Junct Wf, N1 . . . . . .**11** J2
Grand Par Ms, SW15
off Upper Richmond Rd **148** B5
Grand Union Canal Wk, W7 . . . .**124** B3
Grand Union Cl, W9
off Woodfield Rd **108** C5
Grand Union Cres, E8 . . . .**94** D7
Grand Union Ind Est, NW10 . . . .**106** B2
Grand Union Wk, NW1 . . .**92** B7
Grand Wk, E1
off Solebay St **113** H4
Granfield St, SW11 . . . . .**149** G1
Grange, The, N2
off Central Av **73** G2
N20 . . . .**57** F1
SE1 . . . .**29** F5
SW19 . . . .**166** A6
Croydon CR0 . . . .**203** J2
Wembley HA0 . . . .**88** A7
Worcester Park KT4 . . .**196** D3
Grange Av, N12 . . . .**57** F5
N20 . . . .**40** B7
SE25 . . . .**188** B2
Grange Av, Barn. EN4 . . . .**57** H1
Stanmore HA7 . . . .**69** E2
Twickenham TW2 . . . . .**162** B2
Woodford Green IG8 . . .**63** G6
Grangecliffe Gdns, SE25 .**188** B2
Grange Cl, Edg. HA8 . . . . .**54** C5
Hounslow TW5 . . . .**123** F6
Sidcup DA15 . . . .**176** A3
West Molesey KT8 . . . .**179** H4
Woodford Green IG8 . . .**63** G7
Grange Ct, WC2 . . . .**18** D4
Chigwell IG7 . . . .**65** F2
Loughton IG10 . . . .**48** A5
Northolt UB5 . . . .**102** C2
Grangecourt Rd, N16 . . . . .**94** B1
Grange Cres, SE28 . . . . . .**118** C6
Chigwell IG7 . . . .**65** G5
Grange Dr, Chis. BR7 . . .**174** B6
Grange Fm Cl, Har. HA2 . .**85** J2
Grange Gdns, N14 . . . . . .**58** D1
NW3 . . . .**91** E3
SE25 . . . .**188** B2
Pinner HA5 . . . .**67** F4
Grange Gro, N1 . . . .**93** H6
GRANGE HILL, Chig. **65** G6
Grange Hill, SE25 . . . . . .**188** B2
Edgware HA8 . . . .**54** C5
Grangehill Pl, SE9
off Westmount Rd . . .**156** C3
Grangehill Rd, SE9 . . . . .**156** C3
Grange Ho, Bark. IG11
off St. Margarets **117** G1
Grange La, SE21 . . . .**170** C2
Grange Mans, Epsom KT17 . . . .**197** F7
Grange Ms, SE10
off Crooms Hill **134** D7
Grangemill Rd, SE6 . . . . .**172** A3
Grangemill Way, SE6 . . . .**172** A2
★ **Grange Mus of Comm History**, NW10
off Neasden La **89** E4
GRANGE PARK, N21 . . . . .**43** H5
Grange Pk, W5 . . . .**125** H1
Grange Pk Av, N21 . . . . . .**43** H6
Grange Pk Pl, SW20 . . . . .**165** H7
Grange Pk Rd, E10 . . . . . .**96** B1
Thornton Heath CR7 . .**188** A4
Grange Pl, NW6 . . . .**90** D7
Grange Rd, E10 . . . .**96** A1
E13 . . . .**115** F3
E17 . . . .**77** H5
N6 . . . .**74** A6
N17 . . . .**60** D6
N18 . . . .**60** D6
NW10 . . . .**89** H6
SE1 . . . .**28** E5
SE19 . . . .**188** A4
SE25 . . . .**188** A4
SW13 . . . .**147** G1
W4 . . . .**126** B5
W5 . . . .**125** G1
Chessington KT9 . . . . .**195** H4
Edgware HA8 . . . .**54** D6
Harrow HA1 . . . .**68** D6
Harrow (S.Har.) HA2 . . .**86** A2
Ilford IG1 . . . .**99** E4
Kingston upon Thames KT1 . . . .**181** H3
Orpington BR6 . . . .**207** F2
Southall UB1 . . . .**122** E2
Sutton SM2 . . . .**198** D7
Thornton Heath CR7 . .**188** A4
West Molesey KT8 . . . .**179** H4
Grange St, N1 . . . .**112** A1
Grange Vale, Sutt. SM2 . .**199** E7
Grange Vw Rd, N20 . . . . .**57** F1
Grange Wk, SE1 . . . .**28** E5
Grangeway, N12 . . . .**57** E4
NW6 *off Messina Av* . . .**90** D7
Woodford Green IG8 . . .**63** J4
Grangeway, The, N21 . . . .**43** H6
Grangeway Gdns, Ilf. IG4 .**80** B5
Grangewood, Bex. DA5
off Hurst Rd **177** F1
Grangewood Cl, Pnr. HA5 . . . .**66** A5
Grangewood La, Beck. BR3 . . . .**171** J6
Grangewood St, E6 . . . . .**115** J1
Grangewood Ter, SE25
off Grange Rd **188** A3
Grange Yd, SE1 . . . .**29** F6
Granham Gdns, N9 . . . . . .**60** C2
Granite St, SE18 . . . .**137** J5
Granleigh Rd, E11 . . . .**96** E2
Gransden Av, E8 . . . .**95** E7
Gransden Rd, W12
off Wendell Rd **127** F2
Grantbridge St, N1 . . . . . .**11** H1
Grantchester Cl, Har. HA1 . . . .**86** C3
Grant Cl, N14 . . . .**42** C7
Grantham Cl, Edg. HA8 . .**53** H3
Grantham Gdns, Rom. RM6 . . . .**83** F6
Grantham Grn, Borwd. WD6 . . . .**38** C5
Grantham Pl, W1 . . . .**24** D2
Grantham Rd, E12 . . . .**98** D4
SW9 . . . .**151** E2
W4 . . . .**126** E7
Grantley Rd, Houns. TW4 . . . .**142** C2
Grantley St, E1 . . . .**113** G3
Grantock Rd, E17 . . . .**78** D1
Granton Rd, SW16 . . . . .**186** C1
Ilford IG3 . . . .**100** A1
Sidcup DA14 . . . .**176** C6
Grant Pl, Croy. CR0 . . . . .**202** C1
Grant Rd, SW11 . . . .**149** G4
Croydon CR0 . . . .**202** C1
Harrow HA3 . . . .**68** B3
Grants Cl, NW7 . . . .**55** J7
Grant's Quay Wf, EC3 . . . .**20** C6
Grant St, E13 . . . .**115** G3
N1 . . . .**11** E1
Grantully Rd, W9 . . . .**6** A4
Grant Way, Islw. TW7 . . .**124** D6
Granville Av, N9 . . . .**61** F3
Feltham TW13 . . . .**160** A2
Hounslow TW3 . . . .**143** G5
Granville Cl, Croy. CR0 . .**202** B2
Granville Ct, N1 . . . .**112** A1
Granville Gdns, SW16 . . .**187** F1
W5 . . . .**125** J1
Granville Gro, SE13 . . . . .**154** C3
Granville Ms, Sid. DA14 .**176** A4
Granville Pk, SE13 . . . . .**154** C3
Granville Pl, N12 (N.Finchley)
off High Rd **57** F7
SW6 *off Maxwell Rd* **128/129** E7
W1 . . . .**16** B4
Pinner HA5 . . . .**66** D3
Granville Rd, E17 . . . .**78** B6
E18 . . . .**79** H2
N4 . . . .**75** F6
N12 . . . .**57** E7
N13 *off Russell Rd* **59** F6
N22 . . . .**75** H1
NW2 . . . .**90** C2
NW6 . . . .**108** D2
SW18 . . . .**148** D7
SW19 *off Russell Rd* . . .**166** D7
Barnet EN5 . . . .**39** J4
Hayes UB3 . . . .**121** J4
Ilford IG1 . . . .**98** E1
Sidcup DA14 . . . .**176** A4
Welling DA16 . . . .**158** C3
Granville Sq, SE15 . . . . .**132** B7
WC1 . . . .**10** D4
Granville St, WC1 . . . .**10** D4
Grape St, WC2 . . . .**18** A3
Graphite Sq, SE11 . . . .**34** C3
Grapsome Cl, Chess. KT9
off Nigel Fisher Way . .**195** F7
Grasdene Rd, SE18 . . . . .**138** A7
Grasmere Av, SW15 . . . .**164** D4
SW19 . . . .**184** D3
W3 . . . .**106** C7
Hounslow TW3 . . . .**143** H6
Orpington BR6 . . . .**206** E3
Wembley HA9 . . . .**69** G7
Grasmere Cl, Loug. IG10 . .**48** C2
Grasmere Ct, N22
off Palmerston Rd **59** F6
Grasmere Gdns, Har. HA3 . . . .**68** D2
Ilford IG4 . . . .**80** C5
Orpington BR6 . . . .**206** E3
Grasmere Pt, SE15
off Ilderton Rd **133** F7
Grasmere Rd, E13 . . . . . .**115** G2
N10 . . . .**74** B1
N17 . . . .**60** D6
SE25 . . . .**189** E6
SW16 . . . .**169** F5
Bexleyheath DA7 . . . . .**159** J1
Bromley BR1 . . . .**191** F1
Orpington BR6 . . . .**206** E3
Grasshaven Way, SE28 . .**137** J1
Grassington Cl, N11
off Ribblesdale Av **58** A6
Grassington Rd, Sid. DA14 . . . .**176** A4
Grassmount, SE23 . . . . . .**171** E2
Grass Pk, N3 . . . .**72** C1
Grassway, Wall. SM6 . . .**200** C4
Grasvenor Av, Barn. EN5 .**40** D6

Grately Way, SE15 . . . . . . .37 F7
Gratton Rd, W14 . . . . .128 B3
Gratton Ter, NW2 . . . . .90 A3
Graveley, Kings.T. KT1
  off Willingham Way . .182 A2
Graveley Av, Borwd.
  WD6 . . . . .38 C4
Gravel Hill, N3 . . . . .72 C2
  Bexleyheath DA6 . . . .159 H5
  Croydon CR0 . . . . . . .203 G6
Gravel Hill Cl, Bexh.
  DA6 . . . . .159 H5
Gravel La, E1 . . . . .21 F3
Gravelly Ride, SW19 . . . . .165 H4
Gravel Pit La, SE9 . . . . . . .157 F5
Gravel Rd, Brom. BR2 . . . .206 B2
  Twickenham TW2 . . . .162 B1
Gravelwood Cl, Chis.
  BR7 . . . . .175 F3
Graveney Gro, SE20 . . . . .171 F7
Graveney Rd, SW17 . . . . .167 H4
Gravesend Rd, W12 . . . . .107 G7
Gray Av, Dag. RM8 . . . . . .101 F1
Grayham Cres, N.Mal.
  KT3 . . . . .182 D4
Grayham Rd, N.Mal.
  KT3 . . . . .182 D4
Grayland Cl, Brom. BR1 . .192 A1
Grayling Cl, E16
  off Cranberry La .114/115 E4
Grayling Rd, N16 . . . . .94 A2
Grayling Sq, E2 . . . . .13 J3
Grayscroft Rd, SW16 . . . .168 D7
Grayshott Rd, SW11 . . . . .150 A2
★ Gray's Inn, WC1 . . . . . . .18 D1
Gray's Inn Rd, WC1 . . . . . .18 D1
Gray's Inn Pl, WC1 . . . . . . .18 D2
Gray's Inn Rd, WC1 . . . . . .10 C4
Gray's Inn Sq, WC1 . . . . . .18 E1
Gray St, SE1 . . . . .27 F4
Grayswood Gdns, SW20
  off Farnham Gdns . . .183 H2
Grayswood Pt, SW15
  off Norley Vale 165 G1
Gray's Yd, W1 . . . . .16 C4
Graywood Ct, N12 . . . . . . .57 F7
Grazebrook Rd, N16 . . . . . .94 A2
Grazeley Cl, Bexh. DA6 . .159 J5
Grazeley Ct, SE19
  off Gipsy Hill 170 B4
Great Acre Ct, SW4
  off St. Alphonsus Rd .150 D4
Great Bell All, EC2 . . . . . . .20 B3
Great Benty, West Dr.
  UB7 . . . . .120 B4
Great Brownings, SE21 . .170 C4
Great Bushey Dr, N20 . . . .57 E1
Great Cambridge Rd, N9 . .60 B1
  N17 . . . . .60 A5
  N18 . . . . .60 A5
  Enfield EN1 . . . . .44 D4
Great Castle St, W1 . . . . . .17 E3
Great Cen Av, Ruis. HA4 . .84 C5
Great Cen St, NW1 . . . . . .15 J1
Great Cen Way, NW10 . . . .88 E5
  Wembley HA9 . . . . . . .88 C4
Great Chapel St, W1 . . . . .17 H3
Great Chertsey Rd, W4 . .146 C2
  Feltham TW13 . . . . . .161 G3
Great Ch La, W6 . . . . .128 A5
Great Coll St, SW1 . . . . . . .26 A5
Great Cross Av, SE10 . . . .134 E7
Great Cumberland Ms,
  W1 . . . . .15 J4
Great Cumberland Pl, W1 .15 J3
Great Dover St, SE1 . . . . . .28 A4
Greatdown Rd, W7 . . . . . .104 C4
Great Eastern Rd, E15 . . . .96 D7
Great Eastern St, EC2 . . . .12 D4
Great Eastern Wk, EC2 . . .20 E2
Great Elms Rd, Brom.
  BR2 . . . . .191 J4
Great Fld, NW9 . . . . .71 E1
Greatfield Av, E6 . . . . .116 C4
Greatfield Cl, N19
  off Warrender Rd 92 C4
  SE4 . . . . .154 A4
Greatfields Rd, Bark.
  IG11 . . . . .117 G1
Great Fleete Way, Bark. IG11
  off Choats Rd 118 C2
Great Galley Cl, Bark.
  IG11 . . . . .118 B3
Great Gatton Cl, Croy.
  CR0 . . . . .189 H7
Great George St, SW1 . . . .25 J4
Great Guildford St, SE1 . . .27 J1
Greatham Wk, SW15 . . . .165 G1
Great Harry Dr, SE9 . . . . .174 D3
Great James St, WC1 . . . .10 C6

Great Marlborough St,
  W1 . . . . .17 F4
Great Maze Pond, SE1 . . . .28 C3
Great Newport St, WC2
  off Cranbourn St 110 D7
Great New St, EC4 . . . . . . .19 F3
Great N Leisure Pk, N12
  off Chaplin Sq 57 G7
Great N Rd, N2 . . . . .73 H4
  N6 . . . . .73 H4
  Barnet (New Barn.)
  EN5 . . . . .40 D5
Great N Way, NW4 . . . . . . .71 J2
Great Oaks, Chig. IG7 . . . .65 F4
Greatorex St, E1 . . . . .21 H1
Great Ormond St, WC1 . . .18 B1
Great Owl Rd, Chig. IG7 . .64 D3
Great Percy St, WC1 . . . . .10 D3
Great Peter St, SW1 . . . . . .25 H6
Great Portland St, W1 . . . .17 E1
Great Pulteney St, W1 . . . .17 G5
Great Queen St, WC2 . . . . .18 B4
Great Russell St, WC1 . . . .17 J3
Great St. Helens, EC3 . . . .20 D3
Great St. Thomas Apostle,
  EC4 . . . . .20 A5
Great Scotland Yd, SW1 . .26 A2
Great Smith St, SW1 . . . . .25 J5
Great South-West Rd, Felt.
  TW14 . . . . .141 F7
  Hounslow TW4 . . . . .141 J4
Great Spilmans, SE22 . . . .152 B5
Great Strand, NW9 . . . . . . .71 F1
Great Suffolk St, SE1 . . . . .27 H2
Great Sutton St, EC1 . . . . .11 H6
Great Swan All, EC2 . . . . . .20 B3
Great Thrift, Orp. BR5 . . . .193 F4
Great Titchfield St, W1 . . .17 F3
Great Twr St, EC3 . . . . .20 D5
Great Trinity La, EC4 . . . . .20 A5
Great Turnstile, WC1 . . . . .18 D2
Great Western Rd, W2 . . .108 C5
  W9 . . . . .108 C5
  W11 . . . . .108 C5
Great W Rd, W4 . . . . .126 B5
  W6 . . . . .127 F5
  Brentford TW8 . . . . . .126 B5
  Hounslow TW5 . . . . .142 D2
  Isleworth TW7 . . . . . .124 B7
Great Wf Rd, E14
  off Churchill Pl 134 B1
Great Winchester St, EC2 .20 C3
Great Windmill St, W1 . . . .17 H5
Greatwood, Chis. BR7 . . . .174 D7
Greaves Yd, SE1 . . . . .28 E3
Greaves Cl, Bark. IG11
  off Norfolk Rd 99 H7
Greaves Pl, SW17 . . . . . . .167 H4
Grebe Av, Hayes UB4
  off Cygnet Way 102 D6
Grebe Cl, E7
  off Cormorant Rd 97 F5
  E17 . . . . .61 H7
  Barking IG11 . . . . . . .118 A4
Grebe Ct, Sutt. SM1 . . . . .198 C5
Grecian Cres, SE19 . . . . . .169 H6
Gredo Ho, Bark. IG11 . . . .118 B3
Greek Ct, W1 . . . . .17 J4
Greek St, W1 . . . . .17 J4
Greek Yd, WC2 . . . . .18 A5
Green, The, E4 . . . . .62 C1
  E11 . . . . .79 H6
  E15 . . . . .97 E6
  N9 . . . . .60 D2
  N14 . . . . .58 D3
  N21 . . . . .43 G7
  SW14 . . . . .146 C3
  SW19 . . . . .166 A5
  W3 . . . . .107 E6
  W5 off High St 125 G1
  Bexleyheath DA7 . . . .159 G1
  Bromley BR1
  off Downham Way . . .173 G3
  Bromley (Hayes) BR2 .191 G7
  Carshalton SM5 . . . . .200 A4
  Esher (Clay.) KT10 . . .194 C6
  Feltham TW13 . . . . . .160 B2
  Hounslow TW5
  off Heston Rd 123 G6
  Morden SM4 . . . . . . .184 B4
  New Malden KT3 . . . .182 C3
  Orpington (St.P.Cray) BR5
  off The Avenue 176 B7
  Richmond TW9 . . . . .145 G5
  Sidcup DA14 . . . . . . .176 A4
  Southall UB2 . . . . . . .123 E3
  Sutton SM1 . . . . .198 E3
  Twickenham TW2 . . . .162 B1
  Welling DA16 . . . . . . .157 H4
  Wembley HA0 . . . . . . .86 D2

Green, The, West Dr.
  UB7 . . . . .120 A3
  Woodford Green IG8 . . .63 G5
Greenacre Cl, Nthlt. UB5 . .85 F5
Greenacre Gdns, E17 . . . . .78 C4
  off Fishermans Dr . . .133 G2
Greenacre Wk, N14 . . . . . .58 E3
Greenacres, N3 . . . . .72 B2
  SE9 . . . . .156 D6
  Bushey (Bushey Hth.)
  WD23 . . . . .52 A2
Green Acres, Croy. CR0 . .202 C3
Greenacres Cl, Orp. BR6 .207 F4
Greenacres Dr, Stan. HA7 .52 E7
Greenacre Sq, SE16
  off Fishermans Dr . . .133 G2
Greenacre Wk, N14 . . . . . .58 E3
Green Arbour Ct, EC1 . . . .19 G3
Green Av, NW7 . . . . .54 D4
  W13 . . . . .125 E3
Greenaway Gdns, NW3 . . .90 E4
Green Bk, E1 . . . . .132 E1
  N12 . . . . .57 E4
Greenbank Av, Wem. HA0 .86 D5
Greenbank Cl, E4 . . . . .62 C2
Greenbank Cres, NW4 . . . .72 B4
Greenbay Rd, SE7 . . . . . . .136 A7
Greenberry St, NW8 . . . . . .7 G2
Greenbrook Av, Barn.
  EN4 . . . . .41 F1
Green Cl, NW9 . . . . .70 C6
  NW11 . . . . .73 F7
  Bromley BR2 . . . . . . .190 E3
  Carshalton SM5 . . . . .199 J2
  Feltham TW13 . . . . . .160 E5
Greencoat Pl, SW1 . . . . . . .33 G1
Greencoat Row, SW1 . . . . .25 G6
Greencourt Av, Croy.
  CR0 . . . . .203 E2
  Edgware HA8 . . . . . . .70 B1
Greencourt Gdns, Croy.
  CR0 . . . . .203 E1
Greencourt Rd, Orp.
  BR5 . . . . .193 G5
Greencrest Pl, NW2
  off Dollis Hill La 89 G3
Green Cft, Edg. HA8
  off Deans La 54 C5
Greencroft Av, Ruis. HA4 . .84 C2
Greencroft Cl, E6 . . . . .116 B5
  off Neatscourt Rd . . .116 B5
Greencroft Gdns, NW6 . . .91 E7
  Enfield EN1 . . . . .44 B3
Greencroft Rd, Houns.
  TW5 . . . . .143 F1
Green Dale, SE5 . . . . .152 A4
  SE22 . . . . .152 B5
Green Dale Cl, SE22
  off Green Dale 152 A5
Green Dragon Ct, SE1 . . . .28 B1
Green Dragon La, N21 . . . .43 H6
  Brentford TW8 . . . . . .125 H5
Green Dragon Yd, E1 . . . . .21 H2
Green Dr, Sthl. UB1 . . . . . .123 G1
Green End, N21 . . . . .59 H2
  Chessington KT9 . . . .195 H4
Greenend Rd, W4 . . . . . . .126 E2
Greenfarm Cl, Orp. BR6 .207 J5
Greenfield Av, Surb. KT5 .182 B7
  Watford WD19 . . . . . .50 D2
Greenfield Gdns, NW2 . . . .90 B2
  Dagenham RM9 . . . . .118 D1
  Orpington BR5 . . . . . .193 G7
Greenfield Rd, E1 . . . . .21 J2
  N15 . . . . .76 B5
  Dagenham RM9 . . . . .118 C1
Greenfields, Loug. IG10 . .48 D4
Greenfields Cl, Loug.
  IG10 . . . . .48 D4
Greenfield Way, Har.
  HA2 . . . . .67 H3
GREENFORD 103 H3
Greenford Av, W7 . . . . . . .104 B4
  Southall UB1 . . . . . . .103 F7
Greenford Gdns, Grnf.
  UB6 . . . . .103 H3
Greenford Rd, Grnf.
  UB6 . . . . .103 J5
  Harrow HA1 . . . . .86 B5
  Southall UB1 . . . . . . .123 J1
  Sutton SM1 . . . . .198 E4
Green Gdns, Orp. BR6 . . .207 F5
Greengate, Grnf. UB6 . . . .86 E6
Greengate St, E13 . . . . . . .115 H2
Greenhalgh Wk, N2 . . . . . .73 F4
Greenham Cl, SE1 . . . . . . .27 E4
Greenham Cres, E4 . . . . . .61 J6
Greenham Rd, N10 . . . . . .74 A2
Greenhaven Dr, SE28 . . . .118 B6
Greenheys Dr, E18 . . . . . . .79 F3

Greenhill, NW3
  off Hampstead High
  St 91 G4
  SE18 . . . . .136 C5
Green Hill, Buck.H. IG9 . . .63 J1
Greenhill, Sutt. SM1 . . . . .199 F2
  Wembley HA9 . . . . . . .88 B2
Greenhill Gdns, Nthlt.
  UB5 . . . . .103 F2
Greenhill Gro, E12 . . . . . . .98 B4
Greenhill Pk, NW10 . . . . .106 E1
  Barnet EN5 . . . . .40 E5
Greenhill Rd, NW10 . . . . .106 E1
  Harrow HA1 . . . . .68 B6
Greenhill's Rents, EC1 . . . .19 H1
Greenhills Ter, N1
  off Baxter Rd 94 A6
Greenhill Ter, SE18 . . . . . .136 C5
  Northolt UB5 . . . . . . .103 F2
Greenhill Way, Har. HA1 . .68 B6
  Wembley HA9 . . . . . . .88 B2
Greenhithe Cl, Sid.
  DA15 . . . . .157 H7
Greenholm Rd, SE9 . . . . .156 E5
Green Hundred Rd, SE15 .37 J6
Greenhurst Rd, SE27 . . . .169 G5
Greening St, SE2 . . . . .138 C4
Greenland Cres, Sthl.
  UB2 . . . . .122 C3
Greenland Ms, SE8
  off Trundleys Rd 133 G5
Greenland Pl, NW1
  off Greenland Rd 110 B1
Greenland Quay, SE16 . . .133 G4
Greenland Rd, NW1 . . . . .110 C1
  Barnet EN5 . . . . .39 J6
Greenland St, NW1
  off Camden High St . .110 B1
Green La, E4 . . . . .46 E3
  NW4 . . . . .72 A5
  SE9 . . . . .174 D2
  SE20 . . . . .171 G7
  SW16 . . . . .169 F7
  W7 . . . . .124 B2
  Chigwell IG7 . . . . .65 G2
  Chislehurst BR7 . . . . .174 E4
  Dagenham RM8 . . . . .100 A1
  Edgware HA8 . . . . . . .54 A5
  Feltham TW13 . . . . . .160 E5
  Harrow HA1 . . . . .86 B3
  Hounslow TW4 . . . . .142 B3
  Ilford IG1, IG3 . . . . . . .99 F2
  Morden SM4 . . . . . . .184 E6
  New Malden KT3 . . . .182 C5
  Stanmore HA7 . . . . . .53 F4
  Thornton Heath CR7 .187 G1
  Watford WD19 . . . . . .50 C1
  West Molesey KT8 . . .179 H5
  Worcester Park KT4 . .197 G1
Green La Gdns, Th.Hth.
  CR7 . . . . .187 J2
Green Las, N4 . . . . .93 J1
  N8 . . . . .75 H3
  N13 . . . . .59 F6
  N15 . . . . .75 H3
  N16 . . . . .93 J3
  N21 . . . . .59 H1
Greenlaw Gdns, N.Mal.
  KT3 . . . . .183 F7
Green Lawns, Ruis. HA4 . .84 C1
Greenlaw St, SE18 . . . . . .136 D3
Green Leaf Av, Wall.
  SM6 . . . . .200 D4
Greenleaf Cl, SW2
  off Tulse Hill 151 G7
Greenleafe Dr, Ilf. IG6 . . . .81 E4
Greenleaf Rd, E6
  off Redclyffe Rd 115 J1
  E17 . . . . .77 J3
Greenlea Pk, SW19 . . . . . .185 G1
Green Man Gdns, W13 . . .104 D7
Green Man La, W13 . . . . . .124 D1
  Feltham TW14 . . . . . .142 A4
Green Man Pas, W13 . . . .104 D7
Green Man Roundabout,
  E11 . . . . .79 F7
Greenman St, N1 . . . . .93 J7
Greenmead Cl, SE25 . . . .188 D5
Green Moor Link, N21 . . . .43 H7
Greenmoor Rd, Enf. EN3 . .45 F2
Greenoak Pl, Barn. EN4 . .41 J2
Greenoak Way, SW19 . . . .166 A4
Greenock Rd, SW16 . . . . .186 D1
  W3 . . . . .126 B3
★ Green Park, SW1 . . . . . .24 E2
Greenpark Ct, Wem. HA0 .87 F7
Green Pk Way, Grnf.
  UB6 . . . . .104 B1
Green Pt, E15 . . . . .97 E6
Green Pond Cl, E17 . . . . . .77 J3

Green Pond Rd, E17 ... **77** H3
Green Ride, Loug. IG10 ... **47** G5
Green Rd, N14 ... **42** B6
N20 ... **57** F3
Greenroof Way, SE10 ... **135** F3
Greens Cl, The, Loug. IG10 ... **48** D2
Green's Ct, W1 ... **17** H5
Green's End, SE18 ... **136** E4
Greenshank Cl, E17
off Banbury Rd ... **61** H7
Greenshields Ind Est, E16 ... **135** H1
Greenside, Bex. DA5 ... **177** E1
Dagenham RM8 ... **100** C1
Greenside Cl, N20 ... **57** G2
SE6 ... **172** D2
Greenside Rd, W12 ... **127** G3
Croydon CR0 ... **187** G7
Greenslade Rd, Bark. IG11 ... **99** G7
Green Slip Rd, Barn. EN5 .**40** C2
Greenstead Av, Wdf.Grn. IG8 ... **63** J7
Greenstead Cl, Wdf.Grn. IG8
off Greenstead Gdns .. **63** J6
Greenstead Gdns, SW15 .**147** G5
Woodford Green IG8 ... **63** J6
Greensted Rd, Loug. IG10 .**48** B7
Greenstone Ms, E11 ... **79** G6
Green St, E7 ... **97** H6
E13 ... **115** J1
W1 ... **16** A5
Enfield EN3 ... **45** F2
Sunbury-on-Thames TW16 ... **178** A1
GREEN STREET GREEN, Orp. ... **207** H6
Green Ter, EC1 ... **11** F4
Green Vale, W5 ... **105** J6
Bexleyheath DA6 ... **158** D5
Greenvale Rd, SE9 ... **156** C4
Green Verges, Stan. HA7 .. **53** G7
Green Vw, Chess. KT9 .. **195** J7
Greenview Av, Beck. BR3 ... **189** H6
Croydon CR0 ... **189** H6
Greenview Cl, W3 ... **126** E1
Green Wk, NW4 ... **72** A5
SE1 ... **28** D6
Buckhurst Hill IG9 ... **48** B7
Hampton TW12
off Orpwood Cl ... **161** F6
Southall UB2 ... **123** G5
Woodford Green IG8 ... **64** B6
Green Wk, The, E4 ... **62** C1
Greenway, N14 ... **58** E2
N20 ... **56** D2
Green Way, SE9 ... **156** A5
Greenway, SW20 ... **183** J4
Green Way, Brom. BR2 .. **192** B6
Greenway, Chis. BR7 ... **174** D5
Dagenham RM8 ... **100** C2
Harrow HA3 ... **69** H5
Hayes UB4 ... **102** B4
Pinner HA5 ... **66** B2
Green Way, Sun. TW16 .. **178** A4
Greenway, Wall. SM6 .. **200** C4
Woodford Green IG8 ... **63** J5
Greenway, The, NW9 ... **70** D2
Harrow HA3 ... **68** B1
Hounslow TW4 ... **143** F4
Pinner HA5 ... **67** F6
Greenway Av, E17 ... **78** D4
Greenway Cl, N4 ... **93** J2
N11 ... **58** A6
N15 *off Copperfield Dr* .. **76** C4
N20 ... **56** D2
NW9 ... **70** D2
Greenway Gdns, NW9 .. **70** D2
Croydon CR0 ... **203** J3
Greenford UB6 ... **103** G3
Harrow HA3 ... **68** B2
Greenways, Beck. BR3 ... **190** A2
Esher KT10 ... **194** B4
Greenways, The, Twick. TW1
off South Western Rd .**144** D6
Greenwell St, W1 ... **9** E6
GREENWICH, SE10 ... **134** D6
★ **Greenwich Borough Mus**, SE18 *off Plumstead High St* ... **137** J5
Greenwich Ch St, SE10 .. **134** C6
Greenwich Cres, E6
off Swan App ... **116** B5
Greenwich Foot Tunnel, E14 ... **134** C5
SE10 ... **134** C5
Greenwich High Rd, SE10 ... **154** B1
Greenwich Ind Est, SE7 .**135** H4
Greenwich Mkt, SE10
off King William Wk .. **134** C6
★ **Greenwich Park**, SE10 ... **134** D7
Greenwich Pk, SE10 ... **134** E7
Greenwich Pk St, SE10 .. **134** D5
★ **Greenwich Pier**, SE10 ... **134** C6
Greenwich S St, SE10 ... **154** B1
Greenwich Vw Pl, E14 ... **134** B3
Greenwood Av, Dag. RM10 ... **101** H4
Enfield EN3 ... **45** H2
Greenwood Cl, Mord. SM4 ... **184** B4
Orpington BR5 ... **193** H6
Sidcup DA15
off Hurst Rd ... **176** A2
Thames Ditton KT7 ... **194** D1
Greenwood Ct, SW1 ... **33** F3
Greenwood Dr, E4
off Avril Way ... **62** C5
Greenwood Gdns, N13 ... **59** H3
Ilford IG6 ... **65** F7
Greenwood La, Hmptn. (Hmptn.H.) TW12 ... **161** H5
Greenwood Pk, Kings.T. KT2 ... **165** E7
Greenwood Pl, NW5
off Highgate Rd ... **92** B5
Greenwood Rd, E8 ... **94** D6
E13 *off Maud Rd* ... **115** F2
Croydon CR0 ... **187** H7
Isleworth TW7 ... **144** B3
Mitcham CR4 ... **186** D3
Thames Ditton KT7 ... **194** D1
Greenwoods, The, Har. (S.Har.) HA2 ... **85** J2
Greenwood Ter, NW10 .. **106** D1
Green Wrythe Cres, Cars. SM5 ... **199** H1
Green Wrythe La, Cars. SM5 ... **185** G6
Greer Rd, Har. HA3 ... **67** J1
Greet St, SE1 ... **27** F2
Greg Cl, E10 ... **78** C6
Gregor Ms, SE3 ... **135** G7
Gregory Cres, SE9 ... **156** A7
Gregory Pl, W8 ... **22** A3
Gregory Rd, Rom. RM6 ... **82** D4
Southall UB2 ... **123** G3
Gregson Cl, Borwd. WD6 .**38** C1
Greig Cl, N8 ... **74** E5
Greig Ter, SE17 ... **35** H5
Grenaby Av, Croy. CR0 .. **188** A7
Grenaby Rd, Croy. CR0 .. **188** A7
Grenada Rd, SE7 ... **135** J7
Grenade St, E14 ... **113** J7
Grenadier St, E16 ... **136** D1
Grena Gdns, Rich. TW9 .. **145** J4
Grena Rd, Rich. TW9 ... **145** J4
Grendon Gdns, Wem. HA9 ... **88** A2
Grendon St, NW8 ... **7** G5
Grenfell Cl, Borwd. WD6 .. **38** C1
Grenfell Gdns, Har. HA3 .. **69** H7
Grenfell Rd, W11 ... **108** A7
Mitcham CR4 ... **167** J6
Grenfell Twr, W11 ... **108** A7
Grenfell Wk, W11 ... **108** A7
Grennell Cl, Sutt. SM1 .. **199** G2
Grennell Rd, Sutt. SM1 .. **199** F2
Grenoble Gdns, N13 ... **59** G6
Grenville Cl, N3 ... **72** C1
Surbiton KT5 ... **196** C1
Grenville Gdns, Wdf.Grn. IG8 ... **79** J1
Grenville Ms, SW7 ... **30** D1
Hampton TW12 ... **161** H5
Grenville Pl, NW7 ... **54** D5
SW7 ... **22** C6
Grenville Rd, N19 ... **92** E1
Grenville St, WC1 ... **10** B6
Gresham Av, N20 ... **57** J4
Gresham Cl, Bex. DA5 .. **159** E6
Enfield EN2 ... **43** J3
Gresham Dr, Rom. RM6 .. **82** B5
Gresham Gdns, NW11 ... **90** B1
Gresham Rd, E6 ... **116** C2
E16 ... **115** H6
NW10 ... **88** D5
SE25 ... **188** D4
SW9 ... **151** G3
Beckenham BR3 ... **189** H2
Edgware HA8 ... **53** J6
Hampton TW12 ... **161** G6
Hounslow TW3 ... **143** J1
Gresham St, EC2 ... **19** J3
Gresham Way, SW19 ... **166** D3
Gresley Cl, E17 ... **77** H6
N15 *off Clinton Rd* ... **76** A4
Gresley Rd, N19 ... **92** C1
Gressenhall Rd, SW18 .. **148** C6
Gresse St, W1 ... **17** H2
Gresswell Cl, Sid. DA14 .**176** A3
Greswell St, SW6 ... **148** A1
Gretton Rd, N17 ... **60** B7
Greville Cl, Twick. TW1 ... **144** E7
Greville Hall, NW6 ... **6** A1
Greville Ms, NW6
off Greville Rd ... **108/109** E2
Greville Pl, NW6 ... **6** B1
Greville Rd, E17 ... **78** C4
NW6 ... **6** A1
Richmond TW10 ... **145** J6
Greville St, EC1 ... **19** F2
Grey Cl, NW11 ... **73** F6
Greycoat Pl, SW1 ... **25** H6
Greycoat St, SW1 ... **25** H6
Greycot Rd, Beck. BR3 .. **172** A5
Grey Eagle St, E1 ... **21** F1
Greyfell Cl, Stan. HA7
off Coverdale Cl ... **52/53** E5
Greyfriars Pas, EC1 ... **19** H3
Greyhound Hill, NW4 ... **71** G3
Greyhound La, SW16 ... **168** D6
Greyhound Rd, N17 ... **76** B3
NW10 ... **107** H3
W6 ... **128** A6
W14 ... **128** B6
Sutton SM1 ... **199** F5
Greyhound Ter, SW16 ... **186** C1
Greys Pk Cl, Kes. BR2 .. **205** J5
Greystead Rd, SE23 ... **153** F7
Greystoke Av, Pnr. HA5 ... **67** G3
Greystoke Gdns, W5 ... **105** H4
Enfield EN2 ... **42** D4
Greystoke Pk Ter, W5 ... **105** G3
Greystoke Pl, EC4 ... **19** E3
Greystone Gdns, Har. HA3 ... **69** F6
Ilford IG6 ... **81** F2
Greystone Path, E11
off Grove Rd ... **79** F7
Greyswood St, SW16 ... **168** B6
Grierson Rd, SE23 ... **153** G7
Griffin Cen, The, Felt. TW14 ... **142** B5
Griffin Cl, NW10 ... **89** H5
Griffin Manor Way, SE28 .**137** G3
Griffin Rd, N17 ... **76** B2
SE18 ... **137** G5
Griffin Way, Sun. TW16 .. **178** A2
Griffith Cl, Dag. RM8
off Gibson Rd ... **100** C1
Griffiths Cl, Wor.Pk. KT4 .**197** H2
Griffiths Rd, SW19 ... **166** D7
Griggs App, Ilf. IG1 ... **99** F2
Griggs Pl, SE1 ... **28** E6
Griggs Rd, E10 ... **78** C6
Grilse Cl, N9 ... **61** E4
Grimsby Gro, E16 ... **137** E1
Grimsby St, E2 ... **13** G6
Grimsdyke Cres, Barn. EN5 ... **39** J3
Grimsdyke Rd, Pnr. HA5 .. **51** E7
Grimsel Path, SE5 ... **35** H7
Grimshaw Cl, N6 ... **74** A7
Grimston Rd, SW6 ... **148** C2
Grimwade Av, Croy. CR0 .**202** D3
Grimwade Cl, SE15 ... **153** F3
Grimwood Rd, Twick. TW1 ... **144** C7
Grindall Cl, Croy. CR0
off Hillside Rd ... **201** H4
Grindal St, SE1 ... **26** E4
Grindleford Av, N11 ... **58** A2
Grindley Gdns, Croy. CR0 ... **188** C6
Grinling Pl, SE8 ... **134** A6
Grinstead Rd, SE8 ... **133** H5
Grittleton Av, Wem. HA9 .. **88** B6
Grittleton Rd, W9 ... **108** D4
Grizedale Ter, SE23 ... **171** E2
Grocer's Hall Ct, EC2 ... **20** B4
Grogan Cl, Hmptn. TW12 ... **161** F6
Groombridge Cl, Well. DA16 ... **158** A5
Groombridge Rd, E9 ... **95** G7
Groom Cl, Brom. BR2 ... **191** H4
Groom Cres, SW18 ... **149** G7
Groomfield Cl, SW17 ... **168** A4
Groom Pl, SW1 ... **24** C5
Grooms Dr, Pnr. HA5 ... **66** A5
Grosmont Rd, SE18 ... **137** J5
Grosse Way, SW15 ... **147** H6
Grosvenor Av, N5 ... **93** J5
SW14 ... **146** E3
Grosvenor Av, Cars. SM5 .**199** J6
Harrow HA2 ... **67** H6
Richmond TW10
off Grosvenor Rd ... **145** H5
Grosvenor Cl, Loug. IG10 .**48** E1
Grosvenor Cotts, SW1 ... **32** B1
Grosvenor Ct, N14 ... **42** C7
NW6 ... **108** A1
Grosvenor Cres, NW9 ... **70** A4
SW1 ... **24** C4
Grosvenor Cres Ms, SW1 .**24** B4
Grosvenor Dr, Loug. IG10 .**49** E1
Grosvenor Est, SW1 ... **33** J1
Grosvenor Gdns, E6 ... **116** A3
N10 ... **74** C3
N14 ... **42** D5
NW2 ... **89** J5
NW11 ... **72** C6
SW1 ... **24** D5
SW14 ... **146** E3
Kingston upon Thames KT2 ... **163** G6
Wallington SM6 ... **200** C7
Woodford Green IG8 ... **63** G6
Grosvenor Gdns Ms E, SW1 ... **24** E5
Grosvenor Gdns Ms N, SW1 ... **24** D6
Grosvenor Gdns Ms S, SW1 ... **24** E6
Grosvenor Gate, W1 ... **16** A6
Grosvenor Hill, SW19 ... **166** B6
W1 ... **16** D5
Grosvenor Pk, SE5 ... **35** J6
Grosvenor Pk Rd, E17 ... **78** A5
Grosvenor Path, Loug. IG10 ... **49** E1
Grosvenor Pl, SW1 ... **24** C4
Grosvenor Ri E, E17 ... **78** B5
Grosvenor Rd, E6 ... **116** A1
E7 ... **97** H6
E10 ... **96** C1
E11 ... **79** G5
N3 ... **56** C7
N9 ... **60** E1
N10 ... **74** B1
SE25 ... **188** D4
SW1 ... **32** D5
W4 ... **126** B5
W7 ... **124** D1
Belvedere DA17 ... **139** G6
Bexleyheath DA6 ... **158** D5
Borehamwood WD6 ... **38** A3
Brentford TW8 ... **125** G6
Dagenham RM8 ... **101** F1
Hounslow TW3 ... **143** F3
Ilford IG1 ... **99** F3
Orpington BR5 ... **193** H6
Richmond TW10 ... **145** H5
Southall UB2 ... **123** F3
Twickenham TW1 ... **144** D7
Wallington SM6 ... **200** B6
West Wickham BR4 ... **204** B1
Grosvenor Sq, W1 ... **16** C5
Grosvenor St, W1 ... **16** D5
Grosvenor Ter, SE5 ... **35** H7
Grosvenor Way, E5 ... **95** F2
Grosvenor Wf Rd, E14 ... **134** D4
Grote's Bldgs, SE3 ... **155** E2
Grote's Pl, SE3 ... **154** E2
Groton Rd, SW18 ... **167** E2
Grotto Pas, W1 ... **16** C1
Grotto Rd, Twick. TW1 ... **162** C2
Grove, The, E15 ... **96** E6
N3 ... **72** D1
N4 ... **75** F7
N6 ... **92** A1
N8 ... **74** D5
N13 ... **59** G5
N14 ... **42** C5
NW9 ... **70** D5
NW11 ... **72** B7
W5 ... **125** G1
Bexleyheath DA6 ... **158** D4
Edgware HA8 ... **54** B4
Enfield EN2 ... **43** G2
Greenford UB6 ... **103** J6
Isleworth TW7 ... **144** B1
Sidcup DA14 ... **177** E4
Stanmore HA7 ... **52** D2
Teddington TW11 ... **162** D4
Twickenham TW1
off Bridge Rd ... **144/145** E6
Walton-on-Thames KT12 ... **178** B7
West Wickham BR4 ... **204** B3
Grove Av, N3 ... **56** D7
N10 ... **74** C2
W7 ... **104** B6
Pinner HA5 ... **67** E4

Grove Av, Sutt. SM1 . . . . .198 D6
Twickenham TW1 . . . . .162 C1
Grove Bk, Wat. WD19 . . . .50 D1
Grovebury Rd, SE2 . . . . . .138 B2
Grove Cl, N14
off Avenue Rd 42 B7
SE23 . . . . .171 G1
Bromley BR2 . . . . .205 G2
Feltham TW13 . . . . .160 E4
Kingston upon Thames
KT1 . . . . .181 J4
Grove Cotts, SW3 . . . . . . .31 H5
Grove Ct, SE3 . . . . .155 G1
Barnet EN5
off High St 40 C3
East Molesey KT8
off Walton Rd 180 A5
Grove Cres, E18 . . . . .79 F2
NW9 . . . . .70 C4
SE5 . . . . .152 B2
Feltham TW13 . . . . .160 E4
Kingston upon Thames
KT1 . . . . .181 H3
Walton-on-Thames
KT12 . . . . .178 B7
Grove Cres Rd, E15 . . . . .96 D6
Grovedale Rd, N19 . . . . . .92 D2
Grove End, E18
off Grove Hill 79 F2
NW5 off Chetwynd Rd . .92 B4
Grove End Gdns, NW8
off Grove End Rd 109 G2
Grove End La, Esher
KT10 . . . . .194 A1
Grove End Rd, NW8 . . . . . .6 E3
Grove Fm Ct, Mitch. CR4
off Brookfields Av 185 J4
Grove Footpath, Surb.
KT5 . . . . .181 H4
Grove Gdns, NW4 . . . . . . .71 G4
NW8 . . . . .7 H4
Dagenham RM10 . . . . . .101 J3
Enfield EN3 . . . . .45 G1
Teddington TW11 . . . . .162 D4
Grove Grn Rd, E11 . . . . . .96 C3
Grove Hall Ct, NW8 . . . . . .6 D3
Grove Hill, E18 . . . . .79 F2
Harrow HA1 . . . . .68 B7
Grove Hill Rd, SE5 . . . . .152 B3
Harrow HA1 . . . . .68 B7
Grove Ho Rd, N8 . . . . .74 E4
Groveland Av, SW16 . . . .169 F7
Groveland Ct, EC4 . . . . . .20 A4
Groveland Rd, Beck.
BR3 . . . . .189 J3
Grovelands, W.Mol. KT8 .179 G4
Grovelands Cl, SE5 . . . . .152 B2
Harrow HA2 . . . . .85 H3
Grovelands Ct, N14 . . . . .42 D7
Grovelands Rd, N13 . . . . .59 F4
N15 . . . . .76 D6
Orpington BR5 . . . . . . .176 A7
Groveland Way, N.Mal.
KT3 . . . . .182 C5
Grove La, SE5 . . . . .152 A1
Chigwell IG7 . . . . .65 J3
Kingston upon Thames
KT1 . . . . .181 H4
Grove La Ter, SE5
off Grove La 152 B3
Grove Mkt Pl, SE9 . . . . . .156 C6
Grove Ms, W6 . . . . .127 J3
W11
off Portobello Rd 108 C6
Grove Mill Pl, Cars. SM5 .200 A3
GROVE PARK, SE12 . . . .173 G2
GROVE PARK, W4 . . . . . .126 B7
Grove Pk, E11 . . . . .79 H6
NW9 . . . . .70 C4
SE5 . . . . .152 B2
Grove Pk Av, E4 . . . . .62 B7
Grove Pk Br, W4 . . . . . . .126 C7
Grove Pk Gdns, W4 . . . . .126 B6
Grove Pk Ms, W4 . . . . . .126 C7
Grove Pk Rd, N15 . . . . . . .76 B4
SE9 . . . . .173 J3
W4 . . . . .126 B7
Grove Pk Ter, W4 . . . . . . .126 B6
Grove Pas, E2 . . . . .113 E2
Teddington TW11 . . . . .162 D5
Grove Pl, NW3
off Christchurch Hill . .91 G4
SW12 off Cathles Rd . .150 B6
W3 . . . . .126 C1
W5 off The Grove 125 G1
Barking IG11
off Clockhouse Av 117 F1
Grove Rd, E3 . . . . .113 G1
E4 . . . . .62 B4
E11 . . . . .79 F7

Grove Rd, E17 . . . . .78 B6
E18 . . . . .79 F2
N11 . . . . .58 B5
N12 . . . . .57 G5
N15 . . . . .76 B5
NW2 . . . . .89 J6
SW13 . . . . .147 F2
SW19 . . . . .167 F7
W3 . . . . .126 C1
W5 . . . . .105 G7
Barnet EN4 . . . . .41 H3
Belvedere DA17 . . . . . .139 F6
Bexleyheath DA7 . . . . .159 J4
Borehamwood WD6 . . . .38 A1
Brentford TW8 . . . . . . .125 F5
East Molesey KT8 . . . . .180 A4
Edgware HA8 . . . . .54 A6
Hounslow TW3 . . . . . . .143 H4
Isleworth TW7 . . . . . . .144 B1
Mitcham CR4 . . . . .186 B2
Pinner HA5 . . . . .67 F5
Richmond TW10 . . . . . .145 J6
Romford RM6 . . . . .82 B7
Surbiton KT6 . . . . .181 G5
Sutton SM1 . . . . .199 E6
Thornton Heath CR7 . . .187 G4
Twickenham TW2 . . . . .162 A3
Groveside Cl, W3 . . . . . . .106 A6
Carshalton SM5 . . . . . .199 H2
Groveside Rd, E4 . . . . . . .62 E2
Grovestile Waye, Felt.
TW14 . . . . .141 G7
Grove St, N18 . . . . .60 C6
SE8 . . . . .133 J4
Grove Ter, NW5 . . . . .92 B3
Teddington TW11 . . . . .162 D4
Grove Ter Ms, NW5
off Grove Ter 92 B3
Grove Vale, SE22 . . . . . . .152 B4
Chislehurst BR7 . . . . . .174 D6
Grove Vil, E14 . . . . .114 B7
Groveway, SW9 . . . . .151 F1
Dagenham RM8 . . . . . .100 D4
Grove Way, Esher KT10 . .179 J7
Wembley HA9 . . . . .88 B5
Grovewood, Rich. TW9
off Sandycombe Rd . .146 A1
Grovewood Pl, Wdf.Grn.
IG8 . . . . .64 C6
Grummant Rd, SE15 . . . .152 C1
Grundy St, E14 . . . . .114 B6
Gruneisen Rd, N3 . . . . . . .56 E7
Guardian Mus, SW1 . . . . .25 G4
Gubyon Av, SE24 . . . . . . .151 H5
Guerin Sq, E3 . . . . .113 J3
Guernsey Cl, Houns.
TW5 . . . . .143 G1
Guernsey Gro, SE24 . . . .151 J7
Guernsey Rd, E11 . . . . . . .96 D1
Guibal Rd, SE12 . . . . . . .155 H7
Guildersfield Rd, SW16 .168 E7
Guildford Gro, SE10 . . . .154 B1
Guildford Rd, E6 . . . . . . .116 B6
E17 . . . . .78 C1
SW8 . . . . .151 E1
Croydon CR0 . . . . .188 A6
Ilford IG3 . . . . .99 H2
Guildford Way, Wall.
SM6 . . . . .201 E5
★ Guildhall, The, EC2 . . .20 B3
★ Guildhall Art Gall, Guildhall
Lib, EC2 . . . . .20 A3
Guildhall Bldgs, EC2
off Basinghall St 112 A6
Guildhall Yd, EC2 . . . . . . .20 B3
Guildhouse St, SW1 . . . . .33 F1
Guildown Av, N12 . . . . . . .56 E4
Guild Rd, SE7 . . . . .136 A5
Guildsway, E17 . . . . .77 J1
Guilford Av, Surb. KT5 . .181 J5
Guilford Pl, WC1 . . . . . . .10 C6
Guilford St, WC1 . . . . . . .10 A6
Guilford Vil, Surb. KT5
off Alpha Rd 181 J6
Guilsborough Cl, NW10 . .88 E7
Guinness Cl, E9 . . . . .95 H7
Hayes UB3 . . . . .121 G3
Guinness Sq, SE1 . . . . . . .36 D1
Guinness Trust Bldgs, SE1
off Snowsfields 132 B2
SE11 . . . . .35 H3
SW3 . . . . .31 J2
SW9 . . . . .151 H4
Guinness Trust Est, N16
off Holmleigh Rd 94 B1
Guion Rd, SW6 . . . . .148 C2
Gulland Wk, N1
off Clephane Rd 93 J6
Gull Cl, Wall. SM6 . . . . . .200 E7
Gulliver Cl, Nthlt. UB5 . .103 F1

Gulliver Rd, Sid. DA15 . .175 H2
Gulliver St, SE16 . . . . . . .133 J3
Gulston Wk, SW3 . . . . . . .32 A2
Gumleigh Rd, W5 . . . . . . .125 F4
Gumley Gdns, Islw.
TW7 . . . . .144 D3
Gumping Rd, Orp. BR5 . .207 F2
Gundulph Rd, Brom.
BR2 . . . . .191 J3
Gunmakers La, E3 . . . . . .113 H1
Gunnell Cl, SE26 . . . . . . .170 D5
Croydon CR0 . . . . .188 D6
Gunner La, SE18 . . . . . . .136 D5
GUNNERSBURY, W4 . . . .126 B4
Gunnersbury Av, W3 . . . .126 A3
W4 . . . . .126 A3
W5 . . . . .125 J1
Gunnersbury Cl, W4
off Grange Rd 126 B5
Gunnersbury Ct, W3
off Bollo La 126 B2
Gunnersbury Cres, W3 . .126 A4
Gunnersbury Dr, W5 . . . .125 J2
Gunnersbury Gdns, W3 .126 A2
Gunnersbury La, W3 . . . .126 A3
Gunnersbury Ms, W4
off Chiswick High Rd .126 B5
★ Gunnersbury Park, W3
(Ealing) 125 J4
Gunnersbury Pk, W3 . . . .125 J4
W5 . . . . .125 J4
★ Gunnersbury Park Mus
& Art Cen, W3 . . . . . .125 J4
Gunners Gro, E4 . . . . .62 C3
Gunners Rd, SW18 . . . . . .167 G2
Gunning St, SE18 . . . . . . .137 H4
Gunpowder Sq, EC4 . . . . .19 F3
Gunstor Rd, N16 . . . . .94 B4
Gun St, E1 . . . . .21 F2
Gunter Gro, SW10 . . . . . .30 C6
Edgware HA8 . . . . .70 D1
Gunterstone Rd, W14 . . .128 B4
Gunthorpe St, E1 . . . . . . .21 G2
Gunton Rd, E5 . . . . .95 E3
SW17 . . . . .168 A6
Gunwhale Cl, SE16 . . . . .133 G1
Gurdon Rd, SE7 . . . . .135 G5
Gurnell Gro, W13 . . . . . . .104 C4
Gurney Cl, E15
off Gurney Rd 96/97 E5
E17 . . . . .77 G1
Barking IG11 . . . . .98 E6
Gurney Cres, Croy. CR0 .201 F1
Gurney Dr, N2 . . . . .73 F5
Gurney Rd, E15 . . . . .96 E5
Carshalton SM5 . . . . . .200 A4
Northolt UB5 . . . . .102 B3
Guthrie St, SW3 . . . . .31 G3
Gutter La, EC2 . . . . .20 A3
Guyatt Gdns, Mitch. CR4
off Ormerod Gdns . . .186 A2
Guy Barnett Gro, SE3
off Casterbridge Rd . .155 G3
Guy Rd, Wall. SM6 . . . . .200 D3
Guyscliff Rd, SE13 . . . . .154 C5
Guy St, SE1 . . . . .28 C3
Gwalior Rd, SW15
off Felsham Rd 148 A3
Gwendolen Av, SW15 . . .148 A5
Gwendolen Cl, SW15 . . . .148 A5
Gwendoline Av, E13 . . . .115 H1
Gwendwr Rd, W14 . . . . . .128 B5
Gwillim Cl, Sid. DA15 . . .158 A5
Gwydor Rd, Beck. BR3 . .189 G4
Gwydyr Rd, Brom. BR2 . .191 F3
Gwyn Cl, SW6 . . . . .129 F7
Gwynne Av, Croy. CR0 . .189 G7
Gwynne Cl, W4
off Pumping Sta Rd . .127 F6
Gwynne Pk Av, Wdf.Grn.
IG8 . . . . .64 C6
Gwynne Pl, WC1 . . . . . . .10 D4
Gwynne Rd, SW11 . . . . . .149 G2
Gylcote Cl, SE5 . . . . .152 A4
Gyles Pk, Stan. HA7 . . . . .69 F1
Gyllyngdune Gdns, Ilf.
IG3 . . . . .99 J2

H

Haarlem Rd, W14 . . . . . . .128 A3
Haberdasher Est, N1
off Haberdasher St . .112 A3
Haberdasher Pl, N1 . . . . .12 C3
Haberdasher St, N1 . . . . .12 C3
Habgood Rd, Loug. IG10 . .48 B3
Haccombe Rd, SW19
off Haydons Rd 167 F6
HACKBRIDGE, Wall. 200 B2

Hackbridge Grn, Wall.
SM6 . . . . .200 A2
Hackbridge Pk Gdns, Cars.
SM5 . . . . .200 A2
Hackbridge Rd, Wall.
SM6 . . . . .200 A2
Hackford Rd, SW9 . . . . . .151 F1
Hackforth Cl, Barn. EN5 . .39 H5
Hackington Cres, Beck.
BR3 . . . . .172 A6
HACKNEY, E8 . . . . .94 E6
★ Hackney City Fm, E2 . .13 H2
Hackney Cl, Borwd. WD6 .38 D5
Hackney Gro, E8
off Reading La 94/95 E6
★ Hackney Marsh, E9 . . .95 H3
★ Hackney Mus, E8 . . . . .95 E6
Hackney Rd, E2 . . . . .13 F4
HACKNEY WICK, E9 . . . . .96 A5
Hackworth Pt, E3
off Rainhill Way 114 B3
Hadden Rd, SE28 . . . . . . .137 H3
Hadden Way, Grnf. UB6 . .86 A6
Haddington Rd, Brom.
BR1 . . . . .172 D3
Haddon Cl, Borwd. WD6 . .38 A3
Enfield EN1 . . . . .44 D6
New Malden KT3 . . . . .183 F5
Haddonfield, SE8 . . . . . . .133 G4
Haddon Gro, Sid. DA15 . .158 A7
Haddon Rd, Sutt. SM1 . .198 E4
Haddo St, SE10 . . . . .134 B6
Hadfield Cl, Sthl. UB1
off Adrienne Av 103 F3
Hadfield Rd, Stai. (Stanw.)
TW19 . . . . .140 A6
Hadleigh Cl, E1
off Mantus Rd 113 F4
E17 . . . . .78 D4
SW20 . . . . .184 C2
Hadleigh Rd, N9 . . . . .44 E7
Hadleigh St, E2 . . . . .113 F4
Hadleigh Wk, E6 . . . . . . .116 B6
HADLEY, Barn. 40 C2
Hadley Cl, N21 . . . . .43 G6
Hadley Common, Barn.
EN5 . . . . .40 D2
Hadley Gdns, W4 . . . . . . .126 D5
Southall UB2 . . . . .123 F5
Hadley Grn, Barn. EN5 . . .40 C2
Hadley Grn Rd, Barn.
EN5 . . . . .40 C2
Hadley Grn W, Barn. EN5 .40 C2
Hadley Gro, Barn. EN5 . . .40 B2
Hadley Highstone, Barn.
EN5 . . . . .40 C1
Hadley Ridge, Barn. EN5 .40 C3
Hadley Rd, Barn. (New Barn.)
EN5 . . . . .41 E4
Belvedere DA17 . . . . . .139 F4
Mitcham CR4 . . . . .186 D4
Hadley St, NW1 . . . . .92 B6
Hadley Way, N21 . . . . .43 G6
Hadlow Pl, SE19 . . . . . . .170 D7
Hadlow Rd, Sid. DA14 . .176 A4
Welling DA16 . . . . .138 C7
Hadrian Cl, Wall. SM6 . .201 E7
Hadrian Ct, Sutt. SM2
off Stanley Rd . . .198/199 E7
Hadrian Est, E2 . . . . .13 J2
Hadrian Ms, N7
off Roman Way 93 F7
Hadrians Ride, Enf. EN1 . .44 C5
Hadrian St, SE10 . . . . . . .134 E5
Hadrian Way, Stai. (Stanw.)
TW19 . . . . .140 B7
Hadyn Pk Rd, W12 . . . . . .127 G2
Hafer Rd, SW11 . . . . .149 J4
Hafton Rd, SE6 . . . . .173 E1
Haggard Rd, Twick. TW1 .144 E7
HAGGERSTON, E2 . . . . . .13 G1
Haggerston Rd, E8 . . . . . .94 C7
Hague St, E2 . . . . .13 J4
Ha-Ha Rd, SE18 . . . . .136 C6
Haig Pl, Mord. SM4
off Green La 184 D6
Haig Rd, Stan. HA7 . . . . . .53 F5
Haig Rd E, E13 . . . . .115 J3
Haig Rd W, E13 . . . . .115 J3
Haigville Gdns, Ilf. IG6 . .81 E4
Hailes Cl, SW19
off North Rd 167 F6
Haileybury Av, Enf. EN1 . .44 C6
Hailey Rd, Erith DA18 . . .139 G2
Hailsham Av, SW2 . . . . . .169 F2
Hailsham Cl, Surb. KT6 . .181 G7
Hailsham Dr, Har. HA1 . . .68 A3
Hailsham Rd, SW17 . . . .168 A6
Hailsham Ter, N18 . . . . . .59 J5
Haimo Rd, SE9 . . . . .156 A5
HAINAULT, Ilf. 65 H7

Hainault Ct, E17 . . . . .78 D4
Hainault Gore, Rom.
    RM6 . . . . .83 E5
Hainault Gro, Chig. IG7 . . .65 F4
Hainault Rd, E11 . . . . .96 C1
    Chigwell IG7 . . . . .65 E3
    Romford RM5 . . . . .83 J2
    Romford (Chad.Hth.)
    RM6 . . . . .82 B3
    Romford (Lt.Hth.) RM6 . .82 B3
Hainault St, SE9 . . . . . . .175 E1
    Ilford IG1 . . . . .99 E2
Haines Wk, Mord. SM4
    off Dorchester
    Rd 184/185 E7
Hainford Cl, SE4 . . . . . . .153 G4
Haining Cl, W4
    off Wellesley Rd 126 A5
Hainthorpe Rd, SE27 . . . .169 H3
Hainton Cl, E1 . . . . .113 E6
Halberd Ms, E5
    off Knightland Rd . .94/95 E2
Halbutt Gdns, Dag. RM9 .101 F3
Halbutt St, Dag. RM9 . . . .101 F4
Halcomb St, N1 . . . . .112 B1
Halcot Av, Bexh. DA6 . . . .159 H5
Halcrow St, E1
    off Newark St 112/113 F5
Haldane Cl, N10 . . . . .58 B7
Haldane Pl, SW18 . . . . . .166 E1
Haldane Rd, E6 . . . . .116 A3
    SE28 . . . . .118 D7
    SW6 . . . . .128 C7
    Southall UB1 . . . . .103 J6
Haldan Rd, E4 . . . . .62 C6
Haldon Cl, Chig. IG7
    off Arrowsmith Rd 65 H5
Haldon Rd, SW18 . . . . . .148 C5
Hale, The, E4 . . . . .62 D7
    N17 . . . . .76 D4
Hale Cl, E4 . . . . .62 C3
    Edgware HA8 . . . . .54 C5
    Orpington BR6 . . . . . . .207 F4
Hale Dr, NW7 . . . . .54 C6
HALE END, E4 . . . . .62 D6
Hale End Cl, Ruis. HA4 . . . .66 A6
Hale End Rd, E4 . . . . .62 D6
    E17 . . . . .78 D1
    Woodford Green IG8 . . .62 D7
Halefield Rd, N17 . . . . . . .76 D1
Hale Gdns, N17 . . . . .76 D3
    W3 . . . . .126 A1
Hale Gro Gdns, NW7 . . . . .54 D5
Hale La, NW7 . . . . .54 D5
    Edgware HA8 . . . . .54 B5
Hale Path, SE27 . . . . .169 H4
Hale Rd, E6 . . . . .116 B4
    N17 . . . . .76 D3
Halesowen Rd, Mord.
    SM4 . . . . .184 E7
Hales St, SE8
    off Deptford High St . .134 A7
Hale St, E14 . . . . .114 B7
Halesworth Cl, E5
    off Theydon Rd 95 F2
Halesworth Rd, SE13 . . . .154 B3
Hale Wk, W7 . . . . .104 B5
Haley Rd, NW4 . . . . .71 J6
Half Acre, Brent. TW8 . . .125 G6
Half Acre Rd, W7 . . . . . . .124 B1
Half Moon Ct, EC1 . . . . . . .19 J2
Half Moon Cres, N1 . . . . . .10 D1
Half Moon La, SE24 . . . . .151 J6
Half Moon Pas, E1 . . . . . . .21 G4
Half Moon St, W1 . . . . . . .24 E1
Halford Cl, Edg. HA8 . . . . .70 B2
Halford Rd, E10 . . . . .78 D5
    SW6 . . . . .128 D6
    Richmond TW10 . . . . . .145 H5
Halfway St, Sid. DA15 . . . .157 G7
Haliburton Rd, Twick.
    TW1 . . . . .144 D5
Haliday Wk, N1
    off Balls Pond Rd 94 A6
Halidon Cl, E9
    off Urswick Rd 95 F5
Halifax Rd, Enf. EN2 . . . . .43 J2
    Greenford UB6 . . . . . . .103 H1
Halifax St, SE26 . . . . . . .171 E4
Halifield Dr, Belv. DA17 . .138 E3
Haling Gro, S.Croy. CR2 . .201 J7
Haling Pk, S.Croy. CR2 . . .201 J6
Haling Pk Gdns, S.Croy.
    CR2 . . . . .201 H6
Haling Pk Rd, S.Croy.
    CR2 . . . . .201 H5
Haling Rd, S.Croy. CR2 . . .202 A6
Halkin Arc, SW1 . . . . .24 B5
Halkin Ms, SW1 . . . . .24 B5
Halkin Pl, SW1 . . . . .24 B5

Halkin St, SW1 . . . . .24 C4
Hall, The, SE3 . . . . .155 G3
Hallam Cl, Chis. BR7 . . . .174 C5
Hallam Gdns, Pnr. HA5 . . .51 E7
Hallam Ms, W1 . . . . .16 E1
Hallam Rd, N15 . . . . .75 H4
    SW13 . . . . .147 H3
Hallam St, W1 . . . . .8 E6
Hall Av, N18
    off Weir Hall Av 60 A6
Hall Cl, W5 . . . . .105 H5
Hall Ct, Tedd. TW11
    off Teddington Pk 162 C5
Hall Dr, SE26 . . . . .171 F5
    W7 . . . . .104 B6
Halley Gdns, SE13 . . . . . .154 D4
Halley Rd, E7 . . . . .97 J6
    E12 . . . . .98 A6
Halley St, E14 . . . . .113 H5
Hall Fm Cl, Stan. HA7 . . . .52 E4
Hall Fm Dr, Twick. TW2 . .144 A7
Hallfield Est, W2 . . . . .14 C4
Hall Gdns, E4 . . . . .61 J4
Hall Gate, NW8 . . . . .6 D3
Halliards, The, Walt. KT12
    off Felix Rd 178 A6
Halliday Sq, Sthl. UB2 . . .124 A1
Halliford St, N1 . . . . .93 J7
Hallingbury Ct, E17 . . . . . .78 B3
Halliwell Rd, SW2 . . . . . .151 F6
Halliwick Rd, N10 . . . . . . .74 A1
Hall La, E4 . . . . .61 H5
    NW4 . . . . .71 G1
    Hayes UB3 . . . . .121 G7
Hallmark Trd Est, NW10
    off Great Cen Way 88 C4
Hallmead Rd, Sutt. SM1 . .198 E3
Hall Oak Wk, NW6
    off Barlow Rd 90 C6
Hallowell Av, Croy. CR0 . .200 E4
Hallowell Cl, Mitch. CR4 .186 A3
Hallowes Cres, Wat. WD19
    off Hayling Rd 50 A3
Hallowfield Way, Mitch.
    CR4 . . . . .185 G4
★ Hall Pl, Bex. DA5 . . . . .159 J6
Hall Pl, W2 . . . . .6 E6
Hall Pl Cres, Bex. DA5 . . .159 J5
Hall Rd, E6 . . . . .116 C1
    E15 . . . . .96 D4
    NW8 . . . . .6 D4
    Isleworth TW7 . . . . . . .144 A5
    Romford (Chad.Hth.)
    RM6 . . . . .82 C6
Hall St, EC1 . . . . .11 H3
    N12 . . . . .57 F5
Hallsville Rd, E16 . . . . . . .115 F6
Hallswelle Rd, NW11 . . . .72 C5
Hall Twr, W2 . . . . .15 F1
Hall Vw, SE9 . . . . .174 A2
Hallywell Cres, E6 . . . . . .116 C5
Halons Rd, SE9 . . . . .156 D7
Halpin Pl, SE17 . . . . .36 C2
Halsbrook Rd, SE3 . . . . . .156 A3
Halsbury Cl, Stan. HA7 . . .52 E4
Halsbury Rd, W12 . . . . . .127 H1
Halsbury Rd E, Nthlt.
    UB5 . . . . .85 J4
Halsbury Rd W, Nthlt.
    UB5 . . . . .85 H5
Halsend, Hayes UB3 . . . .122 B1
Halsey Ms, SW3 . . . . .31 J1
Halsey St, SW3 . . . . .31 J1
Halsham Cres, Bark. IG11 .99 J6
Halsmere Rd, SE5 . . . . . .151 H1
Halstead Cl, Croy. CR0
    off Charles St 201 J3
Halstead Ct, N1 . . . . .12 C2
Halstead Gdns, N21 . . . . .60 A1
Halstead Rd, E11 . . . . . . .79 G5
    N21 . . . . .59 J1
    Enfield EN1 . . . . .44 B4
Halston Cl, SW11 . . . . . . .149 J6
Halstow Rd, NW10 . . . . . .108 A3
    SE10 . . . . .135 G5
Halsway, Hayes UB3 . . . .122 A1
Halter Cl, Borwd. WD6
    off Clydesdale Cl 38 D5
Halton Cl, N11
    off Colney Hatch La . . .57 J6
Halton Cross St, N1 . . . . .111 H1
Halton Pl, N1
    off Dibden St 111 J1
Halton Rd, N1 . . . . .93 H7
Halt Robin La, Belv. DA17
    off Halt Robin Rd 139 H4
Halt Robin Rd, Belv.
    DA17 . . . . .139 G4
HAM, Rich. 163 G3
Ham, The, Brent. TW8 . . .125 F7

Hambalt Rd, SW4 . . . . . .150 C5
Hamble Ct, Kings.T. KT1 .163 G7
Hambledon Gdns, SE25 . .188 C3
Hambledon Pl, SE21 . . . .170 B1
Hambledon Rd, SW18 . . .148 C7
Hambledown Rd, Sid.
    DA15 . . . . .157 G7
Hamble St, SW6 . . . . . . .149 E3
Hambleton Cl, Wor.Pk. KT4
    off Cotswold Way 197 J2
Hamble Wk, Nthlt. UB5
    off Brabazon Rd 103 G2
Hambridge Way, SW2 . . .151 G7
Hambro Av, Brom. BR2 . .205 G1
Hambrook Rd, SE25 . . . .188 E3
Hambro Rd, SW16 . . . . . .168 D6
Hambrough Rd, Sthl.
    UB1 . . . . .122 E1
Ham Cl, Rich. TW10 . . . . .163 F3
Ham Common, Rich.
    TW10 . . . . .163 J4
Hamden Cres, Dag.
    RM10 . . . . .101 H3
Hamel Cl, Har. HA3 . . . . . .69 G3
Hamelin St, E14
    off St. Leonards Rd . . .114 C6
Hameway, E6 . . . . .116 D4
Ham Fm Rd, Rich. TW10 .163 G4
Hamfrith Rd, E15 . . . . .97 F6
Ham Gate Av, Rich.
    TW10 . . . . .163 G3
★ Ham Ho, Rich. TW10 . .163 F1
Hamilton Av, N9 . . . . .44 D7
    Ilford IG6 . . . . .81 E4
    Surbiton KT6 . . . . .196 B1
    Sutton SM3 . . . . .198 B2
Hamilton Cl, N17 . . . . .76 C3
    NW8 . . . . .6 E4
    SE16
    off Somerford Way . . .133 H2
    Barnet EN4 . . . . .41 H4
    Stanmore HA7 . . . . . . .52 C2
Hamilton Ct, W5 . . . . .105 J7
    W9 . . . . .6 C3
Hamilton Cres, N13 . . . . . .59 G4
    Harrow HA2 . . . . .85 F3
    Hounslow TW3 . . . . . . .143 H5
Hamilton Gdns, NW8 . . . . .6 D3
Hamilton La, N5
    off Hamilton Pk 93 H4
Hamilton Ms, SW18
    off Merton Rd 166 D1
    W1 . . . . .24 D3
Hamilton Pk, N5 . . . . .93 H4
Hamilton Pk W, N5 . . . . . .93 H4
Hamilton Pl, N19
    off Wedmore St 92 D3
    W1 . . . . .24 C2
    Sunbury-on-Thames
    TW16 . . . . .160 B7
Hamilton Rd, E15 . . . . . . .115 E3
    E17 . . . . .77 H2
    N2 . . . . .73 F3
    N9 . . . . .44 D7
    NW10 . . . . .89 G5
    NW11 . . . . .72 A7
    SE27 . . . . .170 A4
    SW19 . . . . .167 E7
    W4 . . . . .126 E2
    W5 . . . . .105 H7
    Barnet EN4 . . . . .41 H4
    Bexleyheath DA7 . . . . .159 E2
    Brentford TW8 . . . . . . .125 G6
    Harrow HA1 . . . . .68 B5
    Hayes UB3 . . . . .102 B7
    Ilford IG1 . . . . .98 E4
    Sidcup DA15 . . . . .176 A4
    Southall UB1 . . . . .123 F1
    Thornton Heath CR7 . .188 A3
    Twickenham TW2 . . . . .162 B1
    Watford WD19 . . . . . . .50 B3
Hamilton Rd Ind Est,
    SE27 . . . . .170 A4
Hamilton Sq, N12
    off Sandringham
    Gdns 57 G6
    SE1 . . . . .28 C3
Hamilton St, SE8
    off Deptford High St . .134 A6
Hamilton Ter, NW8 . . . . . .6 A3
Hamilton Way, N3 . . . . . . .56 D6
    N13 . . . . .59 H4
Hamlea Cl, SE12 . . . . . . .155 F5
Hamlet, The, SE5 . . . . . . .152 A3
Hamlet Cl, SE13
    off Old Rd 154/155 E4
Hamlet Gdns, W6 . . . . . . .127 G4
Hamlet Rd, SE19 . . . . . . .170 C7
Hamlet Sq, NW2 . . . . .90 B3
Hamlets Way, E3 . . . . . . .113 J4

Hamlet Way, SE1 . . . . .28 C3
★ Hamleys, W1 . . . . .17 F5
Hamlin Cres, Pnr. HA5 . . . .66 C5
Hamlyn Cl, Edg. HA8 . . . . .53 H3
Hamlyn Gdns, SE19 . . . . .170 B7
Hammelton Grn, SW9
    off Cromwell Rd 151 H1
Hammelton Rd, Brom.
    BR1 . . . . .191 F1
Hammers La, NW7 . . . . . . .55 G5
HAMMERSMITH, W6 . . . .127 J4
Hammersmith Br, SW13 .127 H5
    W6 . . . . .127 H5
Hammersmith Br Rd,
    W6 . . . . .127 J5
Hammersmith Bdy, W6 . .127 J4
Hammersmith Flyover,
    W6 . . . . .127 J5
Hammersmith Gro, W6 . .127 J3
Hammersmith Rd, W6 . . .128 A3
    W14 . . . . .128 A4
Hammersmith Ter, W6 . . .127 G5
Hammet Cl, Hayes UB4
    off Willow Tree La 102 D5
Hammett St, EC3 . . . . .21 F5
Hammond Av, Mitch.
    CR4 . . . . .186 B2
Hammond Cl, Barn. EN5 . .40 B5
    Greenford UB6
    off Lilian Board Way . . .86 A5
    Hampton TW12 . . . . . .179 G1
Hammond Rd, Enf. EN1 . . .45 E2
    Southall UB2 . . . . .123 E3
Hammonds Cl, Dag.
    RM8 . . . . .100 C3
Hammond St, NW5 . . . . . .92 C6
Hammond Way, SE28
    off Oriole Way 118 B7
Hamonde Cl, Edg. HA8 . . .54 B2
Ham Pk Rd, E7 . . . . .97 F7
    E15 . . . . .97 F7
Hampden Av, Beck. BR3 . .189 H2
Hampden Cl, NW1 . . . . . . .9 J2
Hampden Gurney St, W1 .15 J4
Hampden La, N17 . . . . . . .76 C1
Hampden Rd, N8 . . . . .75 G4
    N10 . . . . .58 A7
    N17 . . . . .76 D1
    N19 off Holloway Rd . . .92 D2
    Beckenham BR3 . . . . . .189 H2
    Harrow HA3 . . . . .67 J1
    Kingston upon Thames
    KT1 . . . . .182 A3
Hampden Sq, N14
    off Osidge La 58 B1
Hampden Way, N14 . . . . . .58 B2
Hampshire Cl, N18
    off Berkshire Gdns .60/61 E5
Hampshire Hog La, W6
    off King St 127 H4
Hampshire Rd, N22 . . . . . .59 F7
Hampshire St, NW5
    off Torriano Av 92 D6
Hampson Way, SW8 . . . . .151 F1
HAMPSTEAD, NW3 . . . . . .91 G4
Hampstead Cl, SE28 . . . .138 B1
Hampstead Gdns, NW11 .72 D6
    Romford (Chad.Hth.)
    RM6 . . . . .82 B5
HAMPSTEAD GARDEN
SUBURB, N2 . . . . .73 F5
Hampstead Grn, NW3 . . . .91 H5
Hampstead Gro, NW3 . . . .91 F3
★ Hampstead Heath,
    NW3 . . . . .91 G2
Hampstead Hts, N2 . . . . . .73 F4
Hampstead High St,
    NW3 . . . . .91 G4
Hampstead Hill Gdns,
    NW3 . . . . .91 H4
Hampstead La, N6 . . . . . . .73 G7
    NW3 . . . . .73 G7
Hampstead Rd, NW1 . . . . .9 F2
Hampstead Sq, NW3 . . . . .91 F3
Hampstead Wk, E3
    off Parnell Rd 113 J1
Hampstead Way, NW11 . . .91 F1
HAMPTON 179 H1
Hampton Cl, N11 . . . . .58 B5
    off Balmoral Av 58 B5
    NW6 . . . . .108 D3
    SW20 . . . . .165 J7
Hampton Ct, N1
    off Upper St 93 H6
Hampton Ct Av, E.Mol.
    KT8 . . . . .180 A5
Hampton Ct Cres, E.Mol.
    KT8 . . . . .180 A3
★ Hampton Ct Palace, E.Mol.
    KT8 . . . . .180 C3

★ Hampton Court Palace
& Pk, E.Mol. KT8 . . . . . . .180 B3
Hampton Ct Par, E.Mol. KT8
off Creek Rd 180 B4
Hampton Ct Rd, E.Mol.
KT8 . . . . .180 C3
Hampton TW12 . . . . .179 J2
Kingston upon Thames
KT1 . . . . .180 C3
Hampton Ct Way, E.Mol.
KT8 . . . . .180 B6
Thames Ditton KT7 . . . .194 B2
Hampton Fm Ind Est, Felt.
TW13 . . . . .161 F3
HAMPTON HILL, Hmptn. .161 J6
Hampton Hill Business Pk,
Hmptn. TW12
off Wellington Rd 161 J5
Hampton La, Felt. TW13 .161 E4
Hampton Mead, Loug.
IG10 . . . . .48 E3
Hampton Ms, NW10
off Minerva Rd 106 D3
Hampton Ri, Har. HA3 . . .69 H6
Hampton Rd, E4 . . . . .61 J5
E7 . . . . .97 H5
E11 . . . . .96 D1
Croydon CR0 . . . . .187 J6
Hampton (Hmptn.H.)
TW12 . . . . .162 A5
Ilford IG1 . . . . .99 E4
Teddington TW11 . . . . .162 A6
Twickenham TW2 . . . . .162 A3
Worcester Park KT4 . . .197 G2
Hampton Rd E, Felt.
TW13 . . . . .161 F3
Hampton Rd W, Felt.
TW13 . . . . .160 E2
Hampton St, SE1 . . . . . . .35 H2
SE17 . . . . .35 H2
HAMPTON WICK,
Kings.T. 181 E1
Ham Ridings, Rich.
TW10 . . . . .163 J5
Hamshades CI, Sid.
DA15 . . . . .175 J3
Ham St, Rich. TW10 . . . .163 F2
Ham Vw, Croy. CR0 . . . .189 H6
Ham Yd, W1 . . . . .17 H5
Hanah Ct, SW19 . . . . . . .166 A7
Hanameel St, E16 . . . . . .135 G1
Hanbury CI, NW4 . . . . . . .71 J3
Hanbury Dr, N21 . . . . . . .43 F5
Hanbury Ms, N1
off Mary St 111 J1
Hanbury Rd, N17 . . . . . . .76 E2
W3 . . . . .126 B2
Hanbury St, E1 . . . . .21 F1
Hancock Ct, Borwd. WD6 .38 C1
Hancock Rd, E3 . . . . .114 C3
SE19 . . . . .170 A6
Handa Wk, N1
off Clephane Rd 94 A6
Hand Ct, WC1 . . . . .18 D2
Handcroft Rd, Croy. CR0 .187 H7
Handel CI, Edg. HA8 . . . . .53 J6
Handel PI, NW10
off Mitchellbrook Way .88 D6
Handel St, WC1 . . . . .10 A5
Handel Way, Edg. HA8 . . .54 A7
Handen Rd, SE12 . . . . . . .155 E6
Handforth Rd, SW9 . . . . . .34 E7
Ilford IG1
off Winston Way 98/99 E3
Handley Gro, NW2
off Clephane Rd 90 A3
Handley Page Rd, Wall.
SM6 . . . . .201 F7
Handley Rd, E9 . . . . .95 F7
Handowe CI, NW4 . . . . . . .71 G4
Handside CI, Wor.Pk. KT4
off Carters CI 198 A1
Hands Wk, E16 . . . . .115 G6
Handsworth Av, E4 . . . . . .62 D6
Handsworth Rd, N17 . . . .76 A3
Handsworth Way, Wat. WD19
off Hayling Rd 50 A3
Handtrough Way, Bark. IG11
off Fresh Wf Rd . . .116/117 E2
Hanford CI, SW18 . . . . . .166 D1
Hanford Row, SW19 . . . . .165 J6
Hangar Ruding, Wat.
WD19 . . . . .51 F3
Hanger Grn, W5 . . . . .106 A4
Hanger La, W5 . . . . .105 J4
Hanger Vale La, W5 . . . . .105 J6
Hanger Vw Way, W3 . . . .106 A6
Hanging Sword All, EC4
off Salisbury Ct 111 G6
Hankey PI, SE1 . . . . .28 C4
Hankins La, NW7 . . . . . . .54 E3

Hanley PI, Beck. BR3 . . . .172 A7
Hanley Rd, N4 . . . . .93 E1
Hanmer Wk, N7
off Newington Barrow
Way 93 F3
Hannah CI, NW10 . . . . . . .88 C4
Beckenham BR3 . . . . . .190 C3
Hannah Mary Way, SE1 . .37 J2
Hannah Ms, Wall. SM6 . .200 C7
Hannay La, N8 . . . . .74 D7
Hannay Wk, SW16 . . . . . .168 D2
Hannell Rd, SW6 . . . . . . .128 B7
Hannen Rd, SE27
off Norwood High St .169 H3
Hannibal Rd, E1 . . . . .113 F5
Staines (Stanw.) TW19 .140 A7
Hannibal Way, Croy. CR0 .201 F5
Hannington Rd, SW4 . . . .150 B3
Hanover Av, E16 . . . . .135 G1
Feltham TW13 . . . . .160 A1
Hanover CI, Rich. TW9 . . .126 A7
Sutton SM3 . . . . .198 C4
Hanover Ct, SE19
off Anerley Rd 170 D7
W12 off Uxbridge Rd .127 G1
Hanover Dr, Chis. BR7 . . .175 F4
Hanover Gdns, SE11 . . . . .34 E6
Ilford IG6 . . . . .65 F3
Hanover Gate, NW1 . . . . . .7 H4
Hanover Gate Mans, NW1 . .7 H5
Hanover Ho, Surb. KT6
off Lenelby Rd 196 A1
Hanover Pk, SE15 . . . . . . .152 D1
Hanover PI, E3
off Brokesley St 113 J3
WC2 . . . . .18 B4
Hanover Rd, N15 . . . . . . .76 C4
NW10 . . . . .89 J7
SW19 . . . . .167 F7
Hanover Sq, W1 . . . . .17 E4
Hanover St, W1 . . . . .17 E4
Croydon CR0
off Abbey Rd 201 H3
Hanover Ter, NW1 . . . . . . .7 H3
Hanover Ter Ms, NW1 . . . .7 H4
Hanover Way, Bexh.
DA6 . . . . .158 D3
Hanover W Ind Est,
NW10 . . . . .106 D2
Hanover Yd, N1 . . . . .11 H1
Hansard Ms, W14
off Holland Rd 128 A2
Hansart Way, Enf. EN2
off The Ridgeway 43 G1
Hans Cres, SW1 . . . . .23 J5
Hanselin CI, Stan. HA7
off Chenduit Way 52 C5
Hansen Dr, N21 . . . . .43 F5
Hansha Dr, Edg. HA8 . . . .70 D1
Hansler Gro, E.Mol. KT8 .180 A4
Hansler Rd, SE22 . . . . . . .152 C5
Hansol Rd, Bexh. DA6 . . .158 E5
Hanson CI, SW12 . . . . . . .150 B7
SW14 . . . . .146 C3
Beckenham BR3 . . . . . .172 B6
Loughton IG10
off Hanson Dr 49 F2
West Drayton UB7 . . . . .120 C3
Hanson Dr, Loug. IG10 . . .49 F2
Hanson Gdns, Sthl. UB1 .123 E2
Hanson Grn, Loug. IG10
off Hanson Dr 49 F2
Hanson St, W1 . . . . .17 F1
Hans PI, SW1 . . . . .24 A5
Hans Rd, SW3 . . . . .23 J5
Hans St, SW1 . . . . .24 A6
Hanway PI, W1 . . . . .17 H3
Hanway Rd, W7 . . . . .104 A6
Hanway St, W1 . . . . .17 H3
HANWELL, W7 . . . . .124 C1
HANWORTH, Felt. 160 D4
Hanworth Rd, Felt.
TW13 . . . . .160 B1
Hampton TW12 . . . . . . .161 H4
Hounslow TW3, TW4 . .143 H3
Sunbury-on-Thames
TW16 . . . . .160 A2
Hanworth Ter, Houns.
TW3 . . . . .143 H4
Hanworth Trd Est, Felt.
TW13 . . . . .161 E3
Hapgood CI, Grnf. UB6 . .86 A5
Harads PI, E1 . . . . .21 H6
Harben Rd, NW6 . . . . .91 F7
Harberson Rd, E15 . . . . . .115 F1
SW12 . . . . .168 B1
Harberton Rd, N19 . . . . . .92 C1
Harbet Rd, E4 . . . . .61 G5
N18 . . . . .61 G5
W2 . . . . .15 F2

Harbex CI, Bex. DA5 . . . .159 H7
Harbinger Rd, E14 . . . . . .134 B4
Harbledown Rd, SW6 . . .148 D1
Harbord CI, SE5
off De Crespigny Pk . .152 A2
Harbord St, SW6 . . . . . . .148 A1
Harborne CI, Wat. WD19 . .50 C5
Harborough Av, Sid.
DA15 . . . . .157 H7
Harborough Rd, SW16 . .169 F4
Harbour Av, SW10 . . . . . .149 F1
Harbour Ex Sq, E14 . . . . .134 B2
Harbour Rd, SE5 . . . . . . .151 J3
Harbour Yd, SW10
off Harbour Av 149 F1
Harbridge Av, SW15 . . . .147 F7
Harbut Rd, SW11 . . . . . . .149 G4
Harcombe Rd, N16 . . . . . .94 B3
Harcourt Av, E12 . . . . .98 C4
Edgware HA8 . . . . .54 C3
Sidcup DA15 . . . . .158 C6
Wallington SM6 . . . . . .200 B4
Harcourt CI, Islw. TW7 . .144 D3
Harcourt Fld, Wall. SM6 .200 B4
Harcourt Lo, Wall. SM6
off Croydon Rd 200 B4
Harcourt Rd, E15 . . . . . . .115 F2
N22 . . . . .74 D1
SE4 . . . . .153 H4
SW19 off Russell Rd . .166 D7
Bexleyheath DA6 . . . . .159 E4
Thornton Heath CR7 . .187 F6
Wallington SM6 . . . . . .200 B4
Harcourt St, W1 . . . . .15 H2
Harcourt Ter, SW10 . . . . . .30 B4
Hardcastle CI, Croy. CR0 .188 D6
Hardcourts CI, W.Wick.
BR4 . . . . .204 B3
Hardel Ri, SW2 . . . . .169 H2
Hardel Wk, SW2
off Papworth Way 151 G2
Hardens Manorway,
SE7 . . . . .136 A3
Harders Rd, SE15 . . . . . . .152 E2
Hardess St, SE24
off Herne Hill Rd 151 J4
Hardie CI, NW10 . . . . .88 D5
Hardie Rd, Dag. RM10 . . .101 J3
Harding CI, SE17 . . . . .35 J5
Croydon CR0 . . . . .202 C3
Hardinge Rd, N18 . . . . . . .60 B5
NW10 . . . . .107 H1
Hardinge St, E1 . . . . .113 F6
Harding Ho, Hayes UB3 .102 B6
Harding Rd, Bexh. DA7 . .159 F2
Harding's CI, Kings.T.
KT2 . . . . .181 J1
Hardings La, SE20 . . . . . .171 G6
Hardman Rd, SE7 . . . . . . .135 H5
Kingston upon Thames
KT2 . . . . .181 H2
Hardwick CI, Stan. HA7 . .53 F5
Hardwicke Av, Houns.
TW5 . . . . .143 G1
Hardwicke Ms, WC1 . . . . .10 D4
Hardwicke Rd, N13 . . . . . .58 E6
W4 . . . . .126 D4
Richmond TW10 . . . . . .163 F4
Hardwicke St, Bark. IG11 .117 F1
Hardwick Grn, W13 . . . . .105 E5
Hardwick St, EC1 . . . . .11 F4
Hardwicks Way, SW18
off Buckhold Rd 148 D5
Hardwidge St, SE1 . . . . . .28 D3
Hardy Av, E16 . . . . .135 G1
off Wesley Av 135 G1
Ruislip HA4 . . . . .84 B5
Hardy CI, SE16
off Middleton Dr 133 G2
Barnet EN5 . . . . .40 B6
Pinner HA5 . . . . .66 D7
Hardy Rd, E4 . . . . .61 J6
SE3 . . . . .135 F7
SW19 . . . . .167 E7
Hardy Way, Enf. EN2 . . . . .43 G1
Hare & Billet Rd, SE3 . . . .154 D1
Harebell Dr, E6 . . . . .116 D5
Harecastle CI, Hayes UB4
off Braunston Dr .102/103 E4
Hare Ct, EC4 . . . . .19 E4
Harecourt Rd, N1 . . . . . . .93 J6
Haredale Rd, SE24 . . . . . .151 J4
Haredon CI, SE23 . . . . . . .153 F7
Harefield, Esher KT10 . . .194 B4
Harefield CI, Enf. EN2 . . . .43 G1
Harefield Ms, SE4 . . . . . .153 J3
Harefield Rd, N8 . . . . .74 D5
SE4 . . . . .153 J3
SW16 . . . . .169 F7
Sidcup DA14 . . . . .176 D2

Hare La, Esher (Clay.)
KT10 . . . . .194 B6
Hare Marsh, E2 . . . . .13 H5
Hare PI, EC4 . . . . .19 F4
Hare Row, E2 . . . . .113 E2
Haresfield Rd, Dag.
RM10 . . . . .101 G6
Hare St, SE18 . . . . .136 D3
Hare Wk, N1 . . . . .12 E2
Harewood Av, NW1 . . . . . . .7 H6
Northolt UB5 . . . . .85 E7
Harewood CI, Nthlt. UB5 .85 F7
Harewood Dr, Ilf. IG5 . . . .80 C2
Harewood PI, W1 . . . . .16 E4
Harewood Rd, SW19 . . . .167 H6
Isleworth TW7 . . . . . . .124 C7
South Croydon CR2 . . .202 B6
Watford WD19 . . . . .50 B3
Harewood Row, NW1 . . . .15 H1
Harewood Ter, Sthl.
UB2 . . . . .123 F4
Harfield Gdns, SE5 . . . . .152 B3
Harfield Rd, Sun. TW16 . .178 D2
Harford CI, E4 . . . . .46 B7
Harford Ms, N19
off Wedmore St 92 D3
Harford Rd, E4 . . . . .46 B7
Harford St, E1 . . . . .113 H4
Harford Wk, N2 . . . . .73 G5
Hargood CI, Har. HA3 . . . .69 H6
Hargood Rd, SE3 . . . . . . .155 J1
Hargrave Pk, N19 . . . . . . .92 C2
Hargrave PI, N7 . . . . .92 D5
off Brecknock Rd 92 D5
Hargrave Rd, N19 . . . . . . .92 C2
Hargwyne St, SW9 . . . . . .151 F3
Haringey Pk, N8 . . . . .74 E6
Haringey Pas, N4 . . . . . . .75 H6
N8 . . . . .75 G4
Haringey Rd, N8 . . . . .74 E4
Harington Ter, N9 . . . . . . .60 A3
N18 . . . . .60 A3
Harkett CI, Har. HA3
off Byron Rd 68 C2
Harkett Ct, Har. HA3 . . . .68 C2
Harland Av, Croy. CR0 . . .202 C3
Sidcup DA15 . . . . .175 G3
Harland CI, SW19 . . . . . .184 E3
Harland Rd, SE12 . . . . . . .173 G1
Harlands Gro, Orp. BR6
off Pinecrest
Gdns 206/207 E4
Harlech Gdns, Houns.
TW5 . . . . .122 C6
Pinner HA5 . . . . .66 D7
Harlech Rd, N14 . . . . .59 E3
Harlech Twr, W3 . . . . . . .126 B2
Harlequin Av, Brent.
TW8 . . . . .124 D6
Harlequin CI, Hayes UB4
off Cygnet Way 102 D5
Isleworth TW7 . . . . . . .144 B5
Harlequin Ho, Erith DA18
off Kale Rd 138/139 E3
Harlequin Rd, Tedd.
TW11 . . . . .162 E7
★ Harlequins FC (Rugby),
Twick. TW2 . . . . .144 B7
Harlescott Rd, SE15 . . . . .153 G4
HARLESDEN, NW10 . . . . .107 E2
Harlesden Gdns, NW10 .107 F1
Harlesden La, NW10 . . . .107 G1
Harlesden Rd, NW10 . . . .107 G1
Harleston CI, E5
off Theydon Rd 95 F2
Harley CI, Wem. HA0 . . . .87 G6
Harley Ct, E11 . . . . .79 G7
off Blake Hall Rd 79 G7
Harley Cres, Har. HA1 . . .68 A4
Harleyford, Brom. BR1 . .191 H1
Harleyford Rd, SE11 . . . . .34 C5
Harleyford St, SE11 . . . . . .34 E6
Harley Gdns, SW10 . . . . . .30 D4
Orpington BR6 . . . . . . .207 H4
Harley Gro, E3 . . . . .113 J3
Harley PI, W1 . . . . .16 D2
Harley Rd, NW3 . . . . .91 G7
NW10 . . . . .106 E2
Harrow HA1 . . . . .68 A4
Harley St, W1 . . . . .16 D2
Harling Ct, SW11
off Latchmere Rd 149 J2
Harlinger St, SE18 . . . . . .136 B3
HARLINGTON, Hayes . . .121 F6
Harlington CI, Hayes UB3
off New Rd 121 F7
Harlington Rd, Bexh.
DA7 . . . . .159 E3
Hounslow (Hthrw.Air.)
TW6 . . . . .141 J4

Harlington Rd E, Felt.
TW13, TW14 . . . . .142 B7
Harlington Rd W, Felt.
TW14 . . . . .142 B6
Harlow Rd, N13 . . . . . . .60 A3
Harlyn Dr, Pnr. HA5 . . . . .66 B3
Harman Av, Wdf.Grn. IG8 .63 F7
Harman Cl, E4 . . . . .62 D4
NW2 . . . . .90 B3
Harman Dr, NW2 . . . . . . .90 B3
Sidcup DA15 . . . . .157 J6
Harman Rd, Enf. EN1 . . . .44 C5
HARMONDSWORTH,
West Dr. 120 A6
Harmondsworth La,
West Dr. UB7 . . . . . . .120 B6
Harmondsworth Rd,
West Dr. UB7 . . . . . . .120 B5
Harmony Cl, NW11 . . . . .72 B5
Harmony Way, NW4
off Victoria Rd 71 J4
Harmood Gro, NW1
off Clarence Way 92 B7
Harmood Pl, NW1
off Harmood St 92 B7
Harmood St, NW1 . . . . . .92 B7
Harmsworth Ms, SE11 . . .27 G6
Harmsworth St, SE17 . . . .35 G4
Harmsworth Way, N20 . . .56 C1
Harness Rd, SE28 . . . . .138 A2
Harold Av, Belv. DA17 . .139 F5
Hayes UB3 . . . . .121 J3
Harold Est, SE1 . . . . .28 E6
Harold Gibbons Ct, SE7
off Victoria Way 135 J6
Harold Pl, SE11 . . . . .34 E4
Harold Rd, E4 . . . . .62 C4
E11 . . . . .96 E1
E13 . . . . .115 H1
N8 . . . . .75 F5
N15 . . . . .76 C5
NW10 . . . . .106 D3
SE19 . . . . .170 B6
Sutton SM1 . . . . .199 G4
Woodford Green IG8 . . .79 G1
Haroldstone Rd, E17 . . . .77 G5
Harp All, EC4 . . . . .19 G3
Harpenden Rd, E12 . . . . .97 J2
SE27 . . . . .169 H3
Harpenmead Pt, NW2
off Granville Rd 90 C2
Harper Cl, N14
off Alexandra Ct 42 C5
Harper Ms, SW17 . . . . .167 F3
Harper Rd, E6 . . . . .116 C6
SE1 . . . . .27 J5
Harpers Yd, N17
off Ruskin Rd 76 C1
Harp Island Cl, NW10 . . .88 D2
Harp La, EC3 . . . . .20 D6
Harpley Sq, E1 . . . . .113 F3
Harpour Rd, Bark. IG11 . . .99 F6
Harp Rd, W7 . . . . .104 C4
Harpsden St, SW11 . . . .150 A1
Harpur Ms, WC1 . . . . . . .18 C1
Harpur St, WC1 . . . . .18 C1
Harraden Rd, SE3 . . . . .155 J1
Harrap St, E14 . . . . .114 C7
Harrier Av, E11
off Eastern Av 79 H6
Harrier Ms, SE28 . . . . . .137 G3
Harrier Rd, NW9 . . . . . . .71 E2
Harriers Cl, W5 . . . . . . .105 H7
Harrier Way, E6 . . . . . . .116 C5
Harries Rd, Hayes UB4 . .102 C4
Harriet Cl, E8 . . . . .112 D1
Harriet Gdns, Croy. CR0 .202 D2
Harriet St, SW1 . . . . .24 A4
Harriet Tubman Cl, SW2 .151 G7
Harriet Wk, SW1 . . . . . . .24 A4
HARRINGAY, N8 . . . . . . .75 G5
Harringay Gdns, N8 . . . .75 H4
Harringay Rd, N15 . . . . . .75 H5
Harrington Cl, NW10 . . . .88 D3
Croydon CR0 . . . . . . .200 E2
Harrington Ct, W10
off Dart St 108 C3
Harrington Gdns, SW7 . . .30 B2
Harrington Hill, E5 . . . . . .95 E1
Harrington Rd, E11 . . . . . .97 E1
SE25 . . . . .188 D4
SW7 . . . . .30 E1
Harrington Sq, NW1 . . . . .9 F2
Harrington St, NW1 . . . . . .9 F3
Harrington Way, SE18 . .136 A3
Harriott Cl, SE10 . . . . . .135 F4
Harris Cl, Enf. EN2 . . . . . .43 H1
Hounslow TW3 . . . . .143 G1
Harrison Cl, N20 . . . . . . .57 H1

Harrison Rd, Dag. RM10 .101 H6
Harrisons Ri, Croy. CR0 . .201 H3
Harrison St, WC1 . . . . . . .10 B4
Harris Rd, Bexh. DA7 . . .159 E1
Dagenham RM9 . . . . .101 F5
Harris St, E17 . . . . .77 J7
SE5 . . . . .132 A7
★ Harrods, SW1 . . . . . . .23 J5
Harrogate Ct, N11
off Coverdale Rd 58 A6
Harrogate Rd, Wat.
WD19 . . . . .50 C3
Harrold Rd, Dag. RM8 . . .100 B5
HARROW 68 A7
★ Harrow Arts Cen, Pnr.
HA5 . . . . .51 H7
Harrow Av, Enf. EN1 . . . .44 C6
Harroway Rd, SW11 . . . .149 G2
Harrowby St, W1 . . . . . . .15 H3
Harrow Cl, Chess. KT9 . .195 G7
Harrowdene Cl, Wem.
HA0 . . . . .87 G4
Harrowdene Gdns, Tedd.
TW11 . . . . .162 D6
Harrowdene Rd, Wem.
HA0 . . . . .87 G3
Harrow Dr, N9 . . . . .60 C1
Harrowes Meade, Edg.
HA8 . . . . .54 A3
Harrow Flds Gdns, Har.
HA1 . . . . .86 B3
Harrowgate Rd, E9 . . . . .95 H6
Harrow Grn, E11
off Harrow Rd 96/97 E3
Harrow La, E14 . . . . . . .114 C7
Harrow Manorway, SE2 .138 C1
★ Harrow Mus & Heritage Cen,
Har. HA2 . . . . .67 J3
HARROW ON THE HILL,
Har. 86 B2
Harrow Pk, Har. HA1 . . . .86 B2
Harrow Pl, E1 . . . . .21 E3
Harrow Rd, E6 . . . . .116 B1
E11 . . . . .97 E3
NW10 . . . . .107 H3
W2 . . . . .14 A2
W9 . . . . .108 C4
W10 . . . . .108 A4
Barking IG11 . . . . . . .117 H1
Carshalton SM5 . . . . .199 H5
Ilford IG1 . . . . .99 F4
Wembley HA0 . . . . . . .87 F5
Wembley (Tkgtn.) HA9 . .87 J5
★ Harrow Sch, Har. HA1 . .86 B1
Harrow Vw, Har. HA1,
HA2 . . . . .68 A4
Hayes UB3 . . . . .102 A6
Harrow Vw Rd, W5 . . . . .105 E4
Harrow Way, Wat. WD19 . .50 C3
HARROW WEALD, Har. . . .68 A1
Harrow Weald Pk, Har.
HA3 . . . . .52 A6
Hart Cres, Chig. IG7 . . . . .65 J5
Harte Rd, Houns. TW3 . .143 F2
Hartfield Av, Borwd. (Elstree)
WD6 . . . . .38 A5
Northolt UB5 . . . . . . .102 B2
Hartfield Cl, Borwd. (Elstree)
WD6 . . . . .38 A5
Hartfield Cres, SW19 . . .166 C2
West Wickham BR4 . . .205 G3
Hartfield Gro, SE20 . . . .189 E1
Hartfield Rd, SW19 . . . .166 C7
Chessington KT9 . . . .195 G5
West Wickham BR4 . . .205 G4
Hartfield Ter, E3 . . . . . . .114 A2
Hartford Av, Har. HA3 . . .68 D3
Hartforde Rd, Borwd.
WD6 . . . . .38 A2
Hartford Rd, Bex. DA5 . .159 G6
Epsom KT19 . . . . .196 A6
Hart Gro, W5 . . . . .126 A1
Southall UB1 . . . . .103 G5
Hartham Cl, N7 . . . . .93 E5
Isleworth TW7 . . . . . .144 D1
Hartham Rd, N7 . . . . .92 E5
N17 . . . . .76 C2
Isleworth TW7 . . . . . .144 C1
Harting Rd, SE9 . . . . . . .174 B4
Hartington Cl, Har. HA1 . .86 B4
Hartington Ct, W4 . . . . . .126 B7
Hartington Rd, E16 . . . . .115 H6
E17 . . . . .77 H6
SW8 . . . . .150 E1
W4 . . . . .126 B7
W13 . . . . .105 E7
Southall UB2 . . . . . . .122 E2
Twickenham TW1 . . . .144 E7

Hartismere Rd, SW6 . . . .128 C7
Hartlake Rd, E9 . . . . .95 G6
Hartland Cl, N21
off Elmscott Gdns . . .43 J6
Edgware HA8 . . . . .54 A2
Hartland Dr, Edg. HA8 . . .54 A2
Ruislip HA4 . . . . .84 B3
Hartland Rd, E15 . . . . . . .97 F7
N11 . . . . .57 J5
NW1 . . . . .92 B7
NW6 . . . . .108 C2
Hampton (Hmptn.H.)
TW12 . . . . .161 H4
Isleworth TW7 . . . . . .144 D3
Morden SM4 . . . . . . .184 D4
Hartlands Cl, Bex. DA5 . .159 F6
Hartland Way, Croy. CR0 .203 H2
Morden SM4 . . . . . . .184 C3
Hartlepool Ct, E16
off Fishguard
Way 136/137 E2
Hartley Av, E6 . . . . .116 B1
NW7 . . . . .55 F5
Hartley Cl, NW7 . . . . .55 F5
Bromley BR1 . . . . . . .192 C2
Hartley Rd, E11 . . . . .97 F1
Croydon CR0 . . . . . . .187 H7
Welling DA16 . . . . . . .138 C7
Hartley St, E2 . . . . .113 F3
Hartmann Rd, E16 . . . . .136 A1
Hartnoll St, N7
off Eden Gro 93 F5
Harton Cl, Brom. BR1 . . .192 A1
Harton Rd, N9 . . . . .61 E2
Harton St, SE8 . . . . .154 A1
Hartsbourne Av, Bushey
(Bushey Hth.) WD23 . . .51 J2
Hartsbourne Cl, Bushey
(Bushey Hth.) WD23 . . .52 A2
Hartsbourne Rd, Bushey
(Bushey Hth.) WD23 . . .52 A2
Harts Gro, Wdf.Grn. IG8 . .63 G5
Hartshorn All, EC3 . . . . . .21 E4
Hartshorn Gdns, E6 . . . .116 D4
Harts La, SE14 . . . . .133 H7
Barking IG11 . . . . .98 E6
Hartslock Dr, SE2 . . . . . .138 D2
Hartsmead Rd, SE9 . . . .174 C2
Hart St, EC3 . . . . .20 E5
Hartsway, Enf. EN3 . . . . .45 F4
Hartswood Gdns, W12 . .127 F3
Hartswood Grn, Bushey
(Bushey Hth.) WD23 . . .52 A2
Hartswood Rd, W12 . . . .127 F2
Hartsworth Cl, E13 . . . . .115 F2
Hartville Rd, SE18 . . . . .137 H4
Hartwell Dr, E4 . . . . .62 C6
Hartwell St, E8
off Dalston La 94 C6
Harvard Hill, W4 . . . . . . .126 B6
Harvard La, W4 . . . . .126 B5
Harvard Rd, SE13 . . . . . .154 C5
W4 . . . . .126 B5
Isleworth TW7 . . . . . .144 B1
Harvel Cres, SE2 . . . . . .138 D5
Harvest Bk Rd, W.Wick.
BR4 . . . . .205 F3
Harvesters Cl, Islw. TW7 .144 A5
Harvest La, Loug. IG10 . . .48 A7
Thames Ditton KT7 . . .180 D6
Harvest Rd, Felt. TW13 . .160 A4
Harvey Dr, Hmptn. TW12 .179 H1
Harvey Gdns, E11
off Harvey Rd 97 F1
SE7 . . . . .136 A4
Loughton IG10 . . . . . .49 E3
Harvey Ho, Brent. TW8
off Green Dragon La .125 H5
Harvey Pt, E16
off Fife Rd 115 H5
Harvey Rd, E11 . . . . .97 E1
N8 . . . . .75 F5
SE5 . . . . .152 A1
Hounslow TW4 . . . . . .143 F7
Ilford IG1 . . . . .99 E5
Northolt UB5 . . . . .84 D7
Walton-on-Thames
KT12 . . . . .178 A7
Harvey St, N1 . . . . .112 A1
Harvill Rd, Sid. DA14 . . .176 D5
Harvington Wk, E8
off Wilman Gro 94 D7
Harvist Est, N7 . . . . .93 G4
Harvist Rd, NW6 . . . . . .108 A2
Harwater Dr, Loug. IG10 . .48 C2
Harwell Pas, N2 . . . . .73 J4
Harwich La, EC2 . . . . . . .20 E1
Harwood Av, Brom.
BR1 . . . . .191 H2
Mitcham CR4 . . . . . . .185 H3

Harwood Cl, N12
off Summerfields Av . .57 H6
Wembley HA0
off Harrowdene Rd 87 G4
Harwood Rd, SW6 . . . . .128 D7
Harwoods Yd, N21
off Wades Hill 43 G7
Harwood Ter, SW6 . . . . .148 E1
Hascombe Ter, SE5
off Love Wk 152 A2
Haselbury Rd, N9 . . . . . . .60 B4
N18 . . . . .60 B4
Haseley End, SE23
off Tyson Rd 153 F7
Haselrigge Rd, SW4 . . . .150 D4
Haseltine Rd, SE26 . . . . .171 J4
Haselwood Dr, Enf. EN2 . .43 H4
Haskard Rd, Dag. RM9 . .100 D4
Haskell Ho, NW10 . . . . .106 D1
Hasker St, SW3 . . . . .31 H1
Haslam Av, Sutt. SM3 . . .198 B1
Haslam Cl, N1 . . . . .93 G7
Haslam St, SE15 . . . . . .132 C7
Haslemere Av, NW4 . . . . .72 A6
SW18 . . . . .166 E2
W7 . . . . .124 D3
W13 . . . . .124 D3
Barnet EN4 . . . . .57 J1
Hounslow TW5 . . . . . .142 C2
Mitcham CR4 . . . . . . .185 G2
Haslemere Cl, Hmptn.
TW12 . . . . .161 F5
Wallington SM6
off Stafford Rd . . .200/201 E5
Haslemere Gdns, N3 . . . .72 C3
Haslemere Heathrow Est,
Houns. TW4 . . . . . . .142 B1
Haslemere Rd, N8 . . . . . .74 D7
N21 . . . . .59 H2
Bexleyheath DA7 . . . .159 F2
Ilford IG3 . . . . .99 J2
Thornton Heath CR7 . .187 H5
Hasler Cl, SE28 . . . . . . .118 B7
Hasluck Gdns, Barn. EN5 .41 F5
Hassard St, E2 . . . . .13 G2
Hassendean Rd, SE3 . . .135 H6
Hassett Rd, E9 . . . . .95 G6
Hassocks Cl, SE26 . . . . .171 E3
Hassocks Rd, SW16 . . . .186 D1
Hassock Wd, Kes. BR2 . .206 A4
Hassop Rd, NW2 . . . . . . .90 A4
Hassop Wk, SE9 . . . . . . .174 B4
Hasted Rd, SE7 . . . . . . .136 A5
Hastings Av, Ilf. IG6 . . . . .81 F4
Hastings Cl, SE15 . . . . . .132 D7
Barnet EN5
off Leicester Rd 41 F4
Hastings Ho, SE18 . . . . .136 C4
Hastings Rd, N11 . . . . . . .58 C5
N17 . . . . .76 A3
W13 . . . . .104 E7
Bromley BR2 . . . . . . .206 B1
Croydon CR0 . . . . . . .202 C1
Hastings St, WC1 . . . . . . .10 A4
Hastingwood Trd Est,
N18 . . . . .61 G6
Hastoe Cl, Hayes UB4
off Kingsash Dr . .102/103 E4
Hat & Mitre Ct, EC1 . . . . .11 H6
Hatch, The, Enf. EN3 . . . .45 G1
Hatcham Pk Ms, SE14
off Hatcham Pk Rd . .153 G1
Hatcham Pk Rd, SE14 . .153 G1
Hatcham Rd, SE15 . . . . .133 F6
Hatchard Rd, N19 . . . . . .92 D2
Hatchcroft, NW4 . . . . . . .71 H3
HATCH END, Pnr. 50 E7
Hatchers Ms, SE1 . . . . . .28 E4
Hatch Gro, Rom. RM6 . . .83 E4
Hatch La, E4 . . . . .62 D4
West Drayton UB7 . . .120 A7
Hatch Pl, Kings.T. KT2 . .163 J5
Hatch Rd, SW16 . . . . . . .187 E2
Hatch Side, Chig. IG7 . . . .64 D5
Hatchwood Cl, Wdf.Grn. IG8
off Sunset Av 63 F4
Hatcliffe Cl, SE3 . . . . . . .155 F3
Hatcliffe St, SE10
off Woolwich Rd 135 F5
Hatfield Cl, SE14
off Reaston St 133 G7
Ilford IG6 . . . . .81 E3
Mitcham CR4 . . . . . . .185 G4
Hatfield Mead, Mord. SM4
off Central Rd 184 D5
Hatfield Rd, E15 . . . . . . .97 E5
W4 . . . . .126 D2
W13 . . . . .124 D1
Dagenham RM9 . . . . .101 E6

Hatfields, SE1 . . . . .27 F1
Loughton IG10 . . . . .48 E3
Hathaway Cl, Brom.
    BR2 . . . . .206 C1
    Stanmore HA7 . . . . . . .52 D5
Hathaway Cres, E12 . . . . .98 C6
Hathaway Gdns, W13 . . .104 C5
    Romford RM6 . . . . .82 D5
Hathaway Rd, Croy. CR0 .187 H7
Hatherleigh Cl, NW7
    off Bittacy Hill 56 B7
    Chessington KT9 . . . . .195 G5
    Morden SM4 . . . . .184 D4
Hatherleigh Rd, Ruis.
    HA4 . . . . .84 A2
Hatherley Cres, Sid.
    DA14 . . . . .176 A2
Hatherley Gdns, E6 . . . . .116 A2
    N8 . . . . .74 E6
Hatherley Gro, W2 . . . . . .14 A3
Hatherley Ms, E17 . . . . . .78 A4
Hatherley Rd, E17 . . . . . . .77 J4
    Richmond TW9 . . . . . .145 J2
    Sidcup DA14 . . . . .176 A4
Hatherley St, SW1 . . . . . .33 G1
Hathern Gdns, SE9 . . . . .174 D4
Hatherop Rd, Hmptn.
    TW12 . . . . .161 F7
Hathorne Cl, SE15 . . . . . .153 E2
Hathway St, SE15
    off Gibbon Rd 153 F2
Hathway Ter, SE14
    off Kitto Rd 153 F2
Hatley Av, Ilf. IG6 . . . . . . .81 F4
Hatley Cl, N11 . . . . .57 J5
Hatley Rd, N4 . . . . .93 F2
Hatteraick St, SE16
    off Brunel Rd 133 F2
Hattersfield Cl, Belv.
    DA17 . . . . .139 F4
HATTON, Felt. 141 J4
Hatton Cl, SE18 . . . . .137 G7
Hatton Ct, E5
    off Gilpin Rd 95 H4
Hatton Gdn, EC1 . . . . .19 F1
Hatton Gdns, Mitch.
    CR4 . . . . .185 J5
Hatton Grn, Felt. TW14 . .142 B4
Hatton Gro, West Dr.
    UB7 . . . . .120 A2
Hatton Ho, E1 . . . . .21 J5
Hatton Pl, EC1 . . . . .11 F6
Hatton Rd, Croy. CR0 . . .201 G1
    Feltham TW14 . . . . . . .141 H5
Hatton Row, NW8 . . . . .7 F6
Hatton St, NW8 . . . . .7 F6
Hatton Wall, EC1 . . . . .19 E1
Haunch of Venison Yd,
    W1 . . . . .16 D4
Havana Rd, SW19 . . . . . .166 D2
Havannah St, E14 . . . . . .134 A2
Havant Rd, E17 . . . . .78 C3
Havant Way, SE15 . . . . . . .37 F7
Havelock Pl, Har. HA1 . . . .68 B6
Havelock Rd, N17 . . . . . . .76 D2
    SW19 . . . . .167 F5
    Belvedere DA17 . . . . . .139 F4
    Bromley BR2 . . . . .191 J4
    Croydon CR0 . . . . .202 C1
    Harrow HA3 . . . . .68 B3
    Southall UB2 . . . . .123 F3
Havelock St, N1 . . . . .111 E1
    Ilford IG1 . . . . .98 E2
Havelock Ter, SW8 . . . . . .130 B7
Havelock Wk, SE23 . . . . .171 F1
Haven, The, SE26
    off Springfield
    Rd 170/171 E5
    Richmond TW9 . . . . . .146 A3
    Sunbury-on-Thames
    TW16 . . . . .160 A4
Haven Cl, SE9 . . . . .174 C3
    SW19 . . . . .166 A3
    Sidcup DA14 . . . . .176 C6
Haven Grn, W5 . . . . .105 G6
Haven Grn Ct, W5
    off Haven Grn 105 G6
Haven La, W5 . . . . .105 H6
Haven Ms, E3
    off St. Pauls Way 113 J5
Haven Pl, W5
    off The Broadway 105 G7
Haven St, NW1
    off Castlehaven Rd 92 B7
Haven Ter, W5
    off The Broadway 105 G7
Havenwood, Wem. HA9 . . .88 B3
Haverfield Gdns, Rich.
    TW9 . . . . .126 A7

Haverfield Rd, E3 . . . . . . .113 H3
Haverford Way, Edg. HA8 .69 J1
Haverhill Rd, E4 . . . . .62 C1
    SW12 . . . . .168 C1
Havering Gdns, Rom.
    RM6 . . . . .82 C5
Havering St, E1
    off Devonport St 113 G6
Havering Way, Bark. IG11 .118 B3
Haversfield Est, Brent.
    TW8 . . . . .125 H5
Haversham Cl, Twick.
    TW1 . . . . .145 G6
Haversham Pl, N6 . . . . . . .91 J2
Haverstock Hill, NW3 . . . .91 H5
Haverstock Pl, N1
    off Haverstock St 111 H2
Haverstock Rd, NW5 . . . . .92 A5
Haverstock St, N1 . . . . . . .11 H2
Haverthwaite Rd, Orp.
    BR6 . . . . .207 G2
Havil St, SE5 . . . . .132 B7
Havisham Pl, SE19 . . . . . .169 H6
Hawarden Gro, SE24 . . . .151 J7
Hawarden Hill, NW2 . . . . .89 G3
Hawarden Rd, E17 . . . . . . .77 G4
Hawbridge Rd, E11 . . . . . .96 D1
Hawes La, W.Wick. BR4 . .204 D1
Hawes Rd, N18 . . . . .60 E6
    Bromley BR1 . . . . .191 H1
Hawes St, N1 . . . . .93 H7
Haweswater Ho, Islw. TW7
    off Summerwood Rd .144 C5
Hawgood St, E3 . . . . .114 A5
Hawkdene, E4 . . . . .46 B6
Hawke Pk Rd, N22 . . . . . . .75 H3
Hawke Pl, SE16
    off Middleton Dr 133 G2
Hawker Cl, Wall. SM6 . . . .201 E7
Hawke Rd, SE19 . . . . .170 B6
Hawkesbury Rd, SW15 . .147 H5
Hawkesfield Rd, SE23 . . .171 H2
Hawkesley Cl, Twick.
    TW1 . . . . .162 D4
Hawkes Rd, Felt. TW14 . .142 A7
    Mitcham CR4 . . . . .185 H1
Hawke Twr, SE14
    off Nynehead St 133 H6
Hawkewood Rd, Sun.
    TW16 . . . . .178 A3
Hawkhurst Gdns, Chess.
    KT9 . . . . .195 H4
Hawkhurst Rd, SW16 . . . .186 D1
Hawkhurst Way, N.Mal.
    KT3 . . . . .182 D5
    West Wickham BR4 . . .204 B2
Hawkins Cl, NW7
    off Hale La 54 D5
    Borehamwood WD6
    off Banks Rd 38 C2
    Harrow HA1 . . . . .68 A7
Hawkins Rd, Tedd. TW11 .163 E6
Hawkins Way, SE6 . . . . . .172 A5
Hawkley Gdns, SE27 . . . .169 H2
Hawkridge Cl, Rom. RM6 .82 C7
Hawksbrook La, Beck.
    BR3 . . . . .190 B6
Hawkshaw Cl, SW2
    off Tierney Rd 150/151 E7
Hawkshead Cl, Brom.
    BR1 . . . . .173 E7
Hawkshead Rd, NW10 . . . .89 F7
    W4 . . . . .126 E2
Hawkslade Rd, SE15 . . . .153 G5
Hawksley Rd, N16 . . . . . . .94 B3
Hawks Ms, SE10
    off Luton Pl 134 C7
Hawksmoor Cl, E6 . . . . . .116 B6
    SE18 . . . . .137 H5
Hawksmoor Ms, E1
    off Cable St 112/113 E7
Hawksmoor St, W6 . . . . . .128 A6
Hawksmouth, E4 . . . . .46 B7
Hawks Rd, Kings.T. KT1 .181 J2
Hawkstone Rd, SE16 . . . .133 F4
Hawk Ter, Ilf. IG5
    off Tiptree Cres 80 D3
Hawkwell Ct, E4
    off Colvin Gdns 62 C3
Hawkwell Ho, Dag. RM8 .101 G1
Hawkwell Wk, N1
    off Basire St 111 J1
Hawkwood Cres, E4 . . . . .46 B6
Hawkwood La, Chis.
    BR7 . . . . .193 F1
Hawkwood Mt, E5 . . . . . . .95 E1
Hawlands Dr, Pnr. HA5 . . .66 E7
Hawley Cl, Hmptn.
    TW12 . . . . .161 F6

Hawley Cres, NW1 . . . . . .92 B7
Hawley Ms, NW1
    off Hawley St 92 B7
Hawley Rd, N18 . . . . .61 G5
    NW1 . . . . .92 B7
Hawley St, NW1 . . . . .92 B7
Hawstead Rd, SE6 . . . . . .154 B6
Hawsted, Buck.H. IG9 . . . .47 H1
Hawthorn Av, E3 . . . . .113 J1
    N13 . . . . .59 E6
    Carshalton SM5 . . . . . .200 A7
    Richmond TW9
    off Kew Rd 145 H2
    Thornton Heath CR7 . .187 H1
Hawthorn Cen, Har. HA1 . .68 C4
Hawthorn Cl, Hmptn.
    TW12 . . . . .161 G5
    Hounslow TW5 . . . . . .122 B7
    Orpington BR5 . . . . . . .193 G6
Hawthorn Cotts, Well. DA16
    off Hook La 158 A3
Hawthorn Ct, Rich. TW9
    off West Hall Rd 146 B1
Hawthorn Cres, SW17 . . .168 A5
Hawthornden Cl, N12
    off Fallowfields Dr 57 H6
Hawthornden Gdns, Brom.
    BR2 . . . . .205 F2
Hawthornden Rd, Brom.
    BR2 . . . . .205 F2
Hawthorn Dr, Har. HA2 . . .67 F6
    West Wickham BR4 . . .205 E4
Hawthorne Av, Har. HA3 . .68 D6
    Mitcham CR4 . . . . .185 G2
    Ruislip HA4 . . . . .66 B6
Hawthorne Cl, N1 . . . . . . .94 B6
    Bromley BR1 . . . . .192 C3
    Sutton SM1
    off Aultone Way . . .198/199 E2
Hawthorne Ct, Nthwd. HA6
    off Ryefield Cres 66 A2
Hawthorne Cres, West Dr.
    UB7 . . . . .120 C2
Hawthorne Fm Av, Nthlt.
    UB5 . . . . .103 E1
Hawthorne Gro, NW9 . . . .70 C7
Hawthorne Ms, Grnf. UB6
    off Greenford Rd 103 J6
Hawthorne Rd, E17 . . . . . .78 A3
    Bromley BR1 . . . . .192 B3
Hawthorn Gdns, W5 . . . . .125 G3
Hawthorn Gro, SE20 . . . .171 E7
    Barnet EN5 . . . . .39 F6
Hawthorn Hatch, Brent.
    TW8 . . . . .125 E7
Hawthorn Ms, NW7
    off Holders Hill Rd 72 B1
Hawthorn Pl, Erith DA8 . .139 J5
Hawthorn Rd, N8 . . . . .74 D3
    N18 . . . . .60 C5
    NW10 . . . . .89 G7
    Bexleyheath DA6 . . . . .159 F4
    Brentford TW8 . . . . . . .125 E7
    Buckhurst Hill IG9 . . . . .64 A4
    Sutton SM1 . . . . .199 H6
    Wallington SM6 . . . . . .200 B7
Hawthorns, Wdf.Grn. IG8 .63 G3
    Loughton IG10 . . . . . . .48 D4
Hawthorn Wk, W10
    off Droop St 108 B4
Hawtrey Av, Nthlt. UB5 . .102 D2
Hawtrey Dr, Ruis. HA4 . . .66 A7
Hawtrey Rd, NW3 . . . . . . .91 H7
Haxted Rd, Brom. BR1
    off North Rd 191 H1
Hay Cl, E15 . . . . .97 E7
    Borehamwood WD6 . . .38 C2
Haycroft Gdns, NW10 . . .107 G1
Haycroft Rd, SW2 . . . . . . .151 E5
    Surbiton KT6 . . . . .195 H3
Hay Currie St, E14 . . . . . .114 B6
Hayday Rd, E16 . . . . .115 G5
Haydens Pl, W11
    off Portobello Rd 108 C6
Hayden Way, Rom. RM5 . .83 J2
Haydns Ms, W3 . . . . .106 B5
    off Emanuel Av 106 C6
Haydock Av, Nthlt. UB5 . . .85 G6
Haydock Grn, Nthlt. UB5
    off Haydock Av 85 G6
Haydon Cl, NW9 . . . . .70 C4
    Enfield EN1
    off Mortimer Dr 44 B6
Haydon Pk Rd, SW19 . . . .166 E5
Haydon Rd, Dag. RM8 . . .100 C2

Haydons Rd, SW19 . . . . . .167 G5
Haydon St, EC3 . . . . .21 F5
Haydon Wk, E1 . . . . .21 G4
Haydon Way, SW11 . . . . .149 G4
HAYES, Brom. 205 G2
Hayes Bypass, Hayes UB3,
    UB4 . . . . .102 D4
Hayes Chase, W.Wick.
    BR4 . . . . .190 E5
Hayes Cl, Brom. BR2 . . . .205 G2
Hayes Ct, SW2 . . . . .168 E1
Hayes Cres, NW11 . . . . . . .72 C5
    Sutton SM3 . . . . .198 A4
Hayesford Pk Dr, Brom.
    BR2 . . . . .191 F5
Hayes Gdn, Brom. BR2 . .205 G2
Hayes Hill, Brom. BR2 . . .204 E1
Hayes Hill Rd, Brom.
    BR2 . . . . .205 F1
Hayes La, Beck. BR3 . . . .190 C3
    Bromley BR2 . . . . .191 G5
Hayes Mead Rd, Brom.
    BR2 . . . . .205 E1
Hayes Metro Cen, Hayes
    UB4 . . . . .102 C7
Hayes Pl, NW1 . . . . .7 H6
    Southall UB2 . . . . .122 B4
Hayes St, Brom. BR2 . . . .205 H1
HAYES TOWN, Hayes . . .121 H2
Hayes Wd Av, Brom.
    BR2 . . . . .205 H1
Hayfield Pas, E1
    off Stepney Grn 113 F4
Hayfield Yd, E1
    off Mile End Rd 113 F4
Haygarth Pl, SW19 . . . . . .166 A5
Haygreen Cl, Kings.T.
    KT2 . . . . .164 B6
Hay Hill, W1 . . . . .17 E6
Hayland Cl, NW9 . . . . .70 D4
Hay La, NW9 . . . . .70 D4
Hayles St, SE11 . . . . .35 G1
Haylett Gdns, Kings.T. KT1
    off Anglesea Rd 181 G4
Hayling Av, Felt. TW13 . . .160 A3
Hayling Cl, N16
    off Pellerin Rd 94 B5
Hayling Rd, Wat. WD19 . . .50 B2
Hayman St, N1
    off Cross St 93 H7
Haymarket, SW1 . . . . .17 H6
Haymarket Arc, SW1 . . . . .17 H6
Haymer Gdns, Wor.Pk.
    KT4 . . . . .197 G3
Haymerle Rd, SE15 . . . . . .37 H6
Haymill Cl, Grnf. UB6 . . . .104 C3
Hayne Rd, Beck. BR3 . . . .189 J2
Haynes Cl, N11 . . . . .58 A3
    N17 . . . . .60 E7
    SE3 . . . . .155 E3
Haynes Dr, N9
    off Plevna Rd 60 E3
Haynes La, SE19 . . . . .170 B6
Haynes Rd, Wem. HA0 . . .87 H7
Hayne St, EC1 . . . . .19 H1
Haynt Wk, SW20 . . . . .184 B3
★ Hay's Galleria, SE1 . . .28 D1
Hay's Galleria, SE1 . . . . . .28 D1
Hay's La, SE1 . . . . .28 D2
Haysleigh Gdns, SE20 . . .188 D2
Hay's Ms, W1 . . . . .16 D6
Hay St, E2 . . . . .112 D1
Hayter Ct, E11 . . . . .97 H2
Hayter Rd, SW2 . . . . .151 E5
Hayton Cl, E8
    off Buttermere Wk 94 C6
Hayward Cl, SW19 . . . . . .185 E1
★ Hayward Gall, SE1 . . . .26 D1
Hayward Gdns, SW15 . . .147 J6
Hayward Rd, N20 . . . . .57 F2
    Thames Ditton KT7 . . .194 D1
Haywards Cl, Rom. (Chad.Hth.)
    RM6 . . . . .82 B5
Hayward's Pl, EC1 . . . . . . .11 G6
Haywood Cl, Pnr. HA5 . . . .66 D2
Haywood Ri, Orp. BR6 . . .207 H4
Haywood Rd, Brom.
    BR2 . . . . .192 A4
Hayworth Cl, Enf. EN3
    off Green St 45 H2
Hazel Av, West Dr. UB7 . .120 D3
Hazelbank, Surb. KT5 . . . .196 C1
Hazelbank Rd, SE6 . . . . . .172 D2
Hazelbourne Rd, SW12 . .150 B6
Hazelbrouck Gdns, Ilf.
    IG6 . . . . .65 G7
Hazelbury Cl, SW19 . . . . .184 D2
Hazelbury Grn, N9 . . . . . . .60 B3

Hazelbury La, N9 . . . . .60 B3
Hazel Cl, N13 . . . . .60 A3
    N19 off Hargrave Pk 92 C2
    SE15 . . . . .152 D2
    Brentford TW8 . . . . .125 E7
    Croydon CR0 . . . . .189 G7
    Mitcham CR4 . . . . .186 D4
    Twickenham TW2 . . . . . .143 J7
Hazelcroft, Pnr. HA5 . . . . .51 G6
Hazeldean Rd, NW10 . . . . . .88 D7
Hazeldene Dr, Pnr. HA5 . . .66 C3
Hazeldene Rd, Ilf. IG3 . . . .100 B2
    Welling DA16 . . . . .158 C2
Hazeldon Rd, SE4 . . . . . . .153 H5
Hazeleigh Gdns, Wdf.Grn.
    IG8 . . . . .64 B5
Hazel Gdns, Edg. HA8 . . . .54 B4
Hazelgreen Cl, N21 . . . . . . .59 H1
Hazel Gro, SE26 . . . . .171 G4
    Enfield EN1
        off Dimsdale Dr 44 D6
    Orpington BR6 . . . . .206 E2
    Romford RM6 . . . . .82 E3
    Wembley HA0
        off Carlyon Rd 105 H1
Hazel Gro Est, SE26 . . . . .171 G4
Hazelhurst, Beck. BR3 . . .190 D1
Hazelhurst Rd, SW17 . . . .167 F4
Hazel La, Rich. TW10 . . . .163 H2
Hazell Cres, Rom. RM5 . . .83 H1
Hazellville Rd, N19 . . . . . . .74 D7
Hazel Mead, Barn. EN5 . . .39 H5
Hazelmere Cl, Felt.
    TW14 . . . . .141 G6
    Northolt UB5 . . . . .103 F2
Hazelmere Dr, Nthlt.
    UB5 . . . . .103 F2
Hazelmere Rd, NW6 . . . . .108 D1
    Northolt UB5 . . . . .103 F2
    Orpington BR5 . . . . .193 H4
Hazelmere Wk, Nthlt.
    UB5 . . . . .103 F2
Hazelmere Way, Brom.
    BR2 . . . . .191 G6
Hazel Ms, N22
    off Alexandra Rd 75 G3
Hazel Rd, E15
    off Wingfield Rd . . .96/97 E5
    NW10 . . . . .107 J3
Hazeltree La, Nthlt. UB5 .103 E3
Hazel Wk, Brom. BR2 . . . .192 D6
Hazel Way, E4 . . . . .61 J6
    SE1 . . . . .37 F1
Hazelwood, Loug. IG10 . . .48 A5
Hazelwood Av, Mord.
    SM4 . . . . .185 E4
Hazelwood Cl, W5 . . . . . . .125 H2
    Harrow HA2 . . . . .67 H4
Hazelwood Ct, NW10
    off Neasden La N . .88/89 E3
Hazelwood Cres, Nthlt. . . .59 G4
Hazelwood Cft, Surb.
    KT6 . . . . .181 H6
Hazelwood Dr, Pnr. HA5 . .66 B2
Hazelwood La, N13 . . . . . . .59 G4
Hazelwood Pk Cl, Chig.
    IG7 . . . . .65 H5
Hazelwood Rd, E17 . . . . . . .77 H5
    Enfield EN1 . . . . .44 C6
Hazlebury Rd, SW6 . . . . . .148 E2
Hazledean Rd, Croy.
    CR0 . . . . .202 A2
Hazledene Rd, W4 . . . . . . .126 C6
Hazlemere Gdns, Wor.Pk.
    KT4 . . . . .197 H1
Hazlewell Rd, SW15 . . . . .147 H5
Hazlewood Cl, E5
    off Mandeville St 95 H3
Hazlewood Cres, W10 . . . .108 B4
Hazlitt Cl, Felt. TW13 . . . .161 E4
Hazlitt Ms, W14
    off Hazlitt Rd 128 B3
Hazlitt Rd, W14 . . . . .128 B3
Headcorn Pl, Th.Hth. CR7
    off Headcorn Rd 187 F4
Headcorn Rd, N17 . . . . .60 C7
    Bromley BR1 . . . . .173 F5
    Thornton Heath CR7 . . .187 F4
Headfort Pl, SW1 . . . . .24 C4
Headingley Cl, Ilf. IG6 . . . .65 J6
Headington Rd, SW18 . . . .167 F2
Headlam Rd, SW4 . . . . . . .150 D6
Headlam St, E1 . . . . .113 E4
Headley App, Ilf. IG2 . . . . .80 D5
Headley Av, Wall. SM6 . . .201 F5
Headley Cl, Epsom KT19 .196 A6
Headley Ct, SE26 . . . . .171 E5
Headley Dr, Croy. (New Adgtn.)
    CR0 . . . . .204 B7
    Ilford IG2 . . . . .80 E6

Head's Ms, W11
    off Artesian Rd 108 D6
HEADSTONE, Har. 67 J4
Headstone Dr, Har. HA1,
    HA3 . . . . .68 B3
Headstone Gdns, Har.
    HA2 . . . . .67 J4
Headstone La, Har. HA2,
    HA3 . . . . .67 H4
Headstone Rd, Har. HA1 . .68 B5
Head St, E1 . . . . .113 G6
Headway Cl, Rich. TW10
    off Locksmeade Rd . . .163 F4
Heald St, SE14 . . . . .153 J1
Healey Dr, Orp. BR6 . . . . .207 J4
Healey St, NW1 . . . . .92 B6
Heanor Ct, E5
    off Pedro St 95 G3
Hearne Rd, W4 . . . . .126 A6
Hearn Ri, Nthlt. UB5 . . . . .102 D1
Hearn's Bldgs, SE17 . . . . .36 C2
Hearn St, EC2 . . . . .12 E6
Hearnville Rd, SW12 . . . . .168 A1
Heath, The, W7
    off Lower Boston Rd .124 B1
Heatham Pk, Twick.
    TW2 . . . . .144 C7
Heath Av, Bexh. DA7 . . . . .138 D6
Heathbourne Rd, Bushey
    (Bushey Hth.) WD23 . .52 B2
    Stanmore HA7 . . . . .52 B2
Heath Brow, NW3
    off North End Way 91 F3
Heath Cl, NW11 . . . . .72 E7
    W5 . . . . .105 J4
    Hayes UB3 . . . . .121 G7
Heathcock Ct, WC2
    off Strand 110/111 E7
Heathcote Av, Ilf. IG5 . . . .80 C2
Heathcote Ct, Ilf. IG5
    off Heathcote Av 80 C2
Heathcote Gro, E4 . . . . .62 C3
Heathcote Pt, E9
    off Wick Rd 95 G6
Heathcote Rd, Twick.
    TW1 . . . . .145 E6
Heathcote St, WC1 . . . . . . .10 C5
Heathcote Way, West Dr. UB7
    off Tavistock Rd 120 A1
Heath Ct, Houns. TW4 . . .143 F4
Heathcroft, NW11 . . . . .91 E1
    W5 . . . . .105 J4
Heathcroft Gdns, E17 . . . .78 D1
Heathdale Av, Houns.
    TW4 . . . . .143 E3
Heathdene Dr, Belv.
    DA17 . . . . .139 H4
Heathdene Rd, SW16 . . . .169 F7
    Wallington SM6 . . . . . .200 B7
Heath Dr, NW3 . . . . .90 E4
    SW20 . . . . .183 J4
Heathedge, SE26 . . . . .170 E2
Heatherbank, SE9 . . . . . . .156 C2
    Chislehurst BR7 . . . . . .192 D2
Heather Cl, E6 . . . . .116 E6
    N7 off Newington
        Barrow Way 93 F3
    SE13 . . . . .154 D7
    SW8 . . . . .150 B3
    Hampton TW12 . . . . . . .179 F1
    Isleworth TW7
        off Harvesters Cl . . .144 A5
Heatherdale Cl, Kings.T.
    KT2 . . . . .164 A6
Heatherdene Cl, N12
    off Bow La 73 F1
    Mitcham CR4 . . . . .185 H4
Heather Dr, Enf. EN2
    off Chasewood Av 43 H2
Heather Gdns, NW11 . . . . .72 B6
    Sutton SM2 . . . . .198 D6
Heatherlands, Sun.
    TW16 . . . . .160 A6
Heatherley Dr, Ilf. IG5 . . . .80 B3
Heather Pk Dr, Wem.
    HA0 . . . . .88 A7
Heather Rd, E4 . . . . .61 J6
    NW2 . . . . .89 F2
    SE12 . . . . .173 G2
Heathers, The, Stai.
    TW19 . . . . .140 C7
Heatherset Gdns, SW16 . .169 F7
Heatherside Rd, Epsom
    KT19 . . . . .196 D7
    Sidcup DA14
        off Wren Rd 176 D3
Heatherton Ter, N3 . . . . . . .73 E2
Heather Wk, W10
    off Droop St 108 B4
    Edgware HA8 . . . . .54 B5

Heather Wk, Twick. TW2
    off Stephenson Rd . . .143 G7
Heather Way, Stan. HA7 . .52 C5
Heatherwood Cl, E12 . . . . .97 J2
Heathfield, E4 . . . . .62 C3
    Chislehurst BR7 . . . . . .175 F6
Heathfield Av, SW18
    off Heathfield Rd 149 G7
Heathfield Cl, E16 . . . . . . .116 A5
    Keston BR2 . . . . .205 J5
Heathfield Dr, Mitch.
    CR4 . . . . .185 H1
Heathfield Gdns, NW11 . . .72 A6
    SE3 . . . . .154 E2
    SW18
        off Heathfield Rd . . .149 G6
    W4 . . . . .126 C5
    Croydon CR0
        off Coombe Rd 202 A4
Heathfield La, Chis. BR7 . .175 E6
Heathfield N, Twick. TW2 .144 C7
Heathfield Pk, NW2 . . . . . . .89 J6
Heathfield Pk Dr, Rom.
    (Chad.Hth.) RM6 . . . . .82 B5
Heathfield Rd, SW18 . . . . .149 F6
    W3 . . . . .126 B2
    Bexleyheath DA6 . . . . .159 F4
    Bromley BR1 . . . . .173 F7
    Croydon CR0 . . . . .202 A4
    Keston BR2 . . . . .205 J5
Heathfields Ct, Houns. TW4
    off Frampton Rd . .142/143 E5
Heathfield S, Twick. TW2 .144 C7
Heathfield Sq, SW18 . . . . .149 G7
Heathfield St, W11
    off Portland Rd 108 B7
Heathfield Ter, SE18 . . . . .137 J6
    W4 . . . . .126 C5
Heath Gdns, Twick. TW1 . .162 C1
Heathgate, NW11 . . . . .72 E6
Heathgate Pl, NW3
    off Agincourt Rd 91 J5
Heath Gro, SE20
    off Maple Rd 171 F7
Heath Hurst Rd, NW3 . . . . .91 H4
Heathland Rd, N16 . . . . . . .94 B1
Heathlands Cl, Sun.
    TW16 . . . . .178 A2
    Twickenham TW1 . . . . .162 C2
Heathlands Way, Houns.
    TW4 . . . . .143 E5
Heath La, SE3 . . . . .154 D2
Heathlee Rd, SE3 . . . . .155 F4
Heathley End, Chis. BR7 . .175 F6
Heathmans Rd, SW6 . . . . .148 C1
Heath Mead, SW19 . . . . . .166 A3
Heath Pk Dr, Brom. BR1 . .192 B3
Heath Pas, NW3 . . . . .91 E2
    Bromley BR2 . . . . .191 F6
Heath Ri, SW15 . . . . .148 A6
Heath Rd, SW8 . . . . .150 B2
    Bexley DA5 . . . . .177 J1
    Harrow HA1 . . . . .67 J7
    Hounslow TW3 . . . . . . .143 H4
    Romford RM6 . . . . .82 D7
    Thornton Heath CR7 . . .187 J3
    Twickenham TW1, TW2 .162 C1
★ Heathrow Airport (London),
    Houns. TW6 . . . . .140 E1
Heathrow Interchange, Hayes
    UB4 . . . . .122 C1
Heathrow Int Trd Est, Houns.
    TW4 . . . . .142 B3
Heathrow Tunnel App, Houns.
    (Hthrw.Air.) TW6 . . . . .140 E1
Heathrow Vehicle Tunnel, Houns.
    (Hthrw.Air.) TW6 . . . . .140 E1
Heaths Cl, Enf. EN1 . . . . . .44 B3
Heath Side, NW3 . . . . .91 G4
Heathside, Esher KT10 . . .194 B3
    Hounslow TW4 . . . . . . .143 F7
    Orpington BR5 . . . . .207 F1
Heathside Av, Bexh.
    DA7 . . . . .159 E1
Heathside Cl, Esher
    KT10 . . . . .194 B3
    Ilford IG2 . . . . .81 G5
Heathstan Rd, W12 . . . . . .107 G6
Heath St, NW3 . . . . .91 F4
Heath Vw, N2 . . . . .73 F4
Heath Vw Cl, N2 . . . . .73 F4
Heathview Ct, SW19 . . . . .166 A2
Heathview Dr, SE2 . . . . . . .138 D6
Heathview Gdns, SW15 . . .147 J7
Heathview Rd, Th.Hth.
    CR7 . . . . .187 G4
Heath Vil, SE18 . . . . .137 J5
    SW18 off Cargill Rd . . .167 F1
Heathville Rd, N19 . . . . . . .74 E7
Heathwall St, SW11 . . . . . .149 J3

Heathway, SE3 . . . . .135 F7
    Croydon CR0 . . . . .203 J3
    Dagenham RM9,
        RM10 . . . . .101 G7
Heath Way, Erith DA8 . . . .159 J1
Heathway, Wdf.Grn. IG8 . .63 J4
Heathway Ind Est, Dag. RM10
    off Manchester Way . .101 H4
Heathwood Gdns, SE7 . . .136 B4
Heathwood Pt, SE23
    off Dacres Rd 171 G3
Heaton Cl, E4 . . . . .62 C3
Heaton Rd, SE15 . . . . .152 D3
    Mitcham CR4 . . . . .168 A7
Heaver Rd, SW11
    off Wye St 149 G3
Heavitree Cl, SE18 . . . . . . .137 G5
Heavitree Rd, SE18 . . . . . .137 G5
Hebden Ct, E2
    off Laburnum St 112 C1
Hebden Ter, N17
    off Commercial Rd 60 B6
Hebdon Rd, SW17 . . . . . . .167 H3
Heber Rd, NW2 . . . . .90 A5
    SE22 . . . . .152 C6
Hebron Rd, W6 . . . . .127 H3
Hecham Cl, E17 . . . . .77 H2
Heckfield Pl, SW6
    off Fulham Rd 128 D7
Heckford St, E1
    off The Highway 113 G7
Hector St, SE18 . . . . .137 H4
Heddington Gro, N7 . . . . . .93 F5
Heddon Cl, Islw. TW7 . . . .144 D4
Heddon Ct Av, Barn. EN4 . .41 J5
Heddon Rd, Barn. EN4 . . . .41 J5
Heddon St, W1 . . . . .17 F5
Hedge Hill, Enf. EN2 . . . . . .43 H1
Hedge La, N13 . . . . .59 H3
Hedgeley, Ilf. IG4 . . . . .80 C4
Hedgemans Rd, Dag.
    RM9 . . . . .100 D6
Hedgemans Way, Dag.
    RM9 . . . . .100 E6
Hedgerley Gdns, Grnf.
    UB6 . . . . .103 J2
Hedgerow La, Barn. EN5 . .39 H5
Hedgers Cl, Loug. IG10
    off Newmans La 48 D4
Hedgers Gro, E9 . . . . .95 H6
Hedger St, SE11 . . . . .35 G1
Hedge Wk, SE6 . . . . .172 B4
Hedgewood Gdns, Ilf.
    IG5 . . . . .80 D5
Hedgley St, SE12 . . . . .155 F5
Hedingham Cl, N1
    off Popham Rd 93 J7
Hedingham Rd, Dag.
    RM8 . . . . .100 B5
Hedley Rd, Twick. TW2 . . .143 G7
Hedley Row, N5
    off Poets Rd 94 A5
Heenan Cl, Bark. IG11
    off Glenny Rd 99 F6
Heene Rd, Enf. EN2 . . . . . . .44 A1
Heidegger Cres, SW13
    off Trinity Ch Rd 127 H6
Heigham Rd, E6 . . . . .98 A7
Heighton Gdns, Croy.
    CR0 . . . . .201 H5
Heights, The, SE7 . . . . . . .135 J5
    Beckenham BR3 . . . . . .172 C7
    Loughton IG10 . . . . .48 C2
    Northolt UB5 . . . . .85 F5
Heights Cl, SW20 . . . . .165 H7
★ Heinz Gall, RIBA, W1 . .16 B3
Heiron St, SE17 . . . . .35 H6
Helby Rd, SW4 . . . . .150 D6
Helder Gro, SE12 . . . . .155 F7
Helder St, S.Croy. CR2 . . .202 A6
Heldmann Cl, Houns.
    TW3 . . . . .144 A4
Helegon Cl, Orp. BR6 . . . .207 J4
Helena Cl, Wall. SM6
    off Kingsford Av .200/201 F7
Helena Pl, E9
    off Fremont St 113 F1
Helena Rd, E13 . . . . .115 F2
    E17 . . . . .78 A5
    NW10 . . . . .89 H5
    W5 . . . . .105 G5
Helena Sq, SE16
    off Rotherhithe St 113 H7
Helen Av, Felt. TW14 . . . . .142 B7
Helen Cl, N2
    off Thomas More Way .73 F3
    West Molesey KT8 . . . .179 H4
Helenslea Av, NW11 . . . . . .90 C1
Helen's Pl, E2
    off Roman Rd 113 F3

Helen St, SE18
off Wilmount St . .136/137 E4
Helios Rd, Wall. SM6
off London Rd 200 A1
Helix Gdns, SW2
off Helix Rd 151 F6
Helix Rd, SW2 . . . . .151 F6
Hellings St, E1 . . . . .29 J2
Helme Cl, SW19 . . . . . . .166 C5
Helmet Row, EC1 . . . . . . .12 A5
Helmore Rd, Bark. IG11 . . .99 J7
Helmsdale Cl, Hayes
UB4 . . . . .102 E4
Helmsdale Rd, SW16 . . . .186 C1
Helmsley Pl, E8 . . . . .94 E7
Helsinki Sq, SE16 . . . . . .133 H3
Helston Cl, Pnr. HA5 . . . . .51 F7
Helvetia St, SE6 . . . . .171 J2
Hemans St, SW8 . . . . .33 J7
Hemberton Rd, SW9 . . . .150 E3
Hemery Rd, Grnf. UB6 . . . .86 A5
Hemingford Cl, N12 . . . . . .57 G5
Hemingford Rd, N1 . . . . .111 F1
Sutton SM3 . . . . .197 J4
Heming Rd, Edg. HA8 . . . .54 B7
Hemington Av, N11 . . . . . .57 J5
Hemlock Rd, W12 . . . . . .107 F7
Hemming Cl, Hmptn. TW12
off Chandler Cl 179 G1
Hemmings Cl, Sid. DA14 .176 B2
Hemming St, E1 . . . . .13 J6
Hempstead Cl, Buck.H.
IG9 . . . . .63 G2
Hempstead Rd, E17 . . . . . .78 D2
Hemp Wk, SE17 . . . . .36 C1
Hemsby Rd, Chess. KT9 .195 J6
Hemstal Rd, NW6 . . . . . . .90 D7
Hemswell Dr, NW9 . . . . . .70 E1
Hemsworth Ct, N1
off Hemsworth St 112 B2
Hemsworth St, N1 . . . . . .12 D1
Hemus Pl, SW3 . . . . .31 H4
Hen & Chicken Ct, EC4
off Fleet St 111 G6
Henbury Way, Wat. WD19 .50 D3
Henchman St, W12 . . . . .107 F6
Hendale Av, NW4 . . . . . . .71 G3
Henderson Cl, NW10 . . . . .88 C6
Henderson Dr, NW8 . . . . . .7 E5
Henderson Rd, E7 . . . . . . .97 J6
N9 . . . . .60 E1
SW18 . . . . .149 H7
Croydon CR0 . . . . .188 A6
Hayes UB4 . . . . .102 A3
Hendham Rd, SW17 . . . .167 H2
HENDON, NW4 . . . . .71 H4
Hendon Av, N3 . . . . .72 B1
Hendon Hall Ct, NW4
off Parson St 72 A3
Hendon La, N3 . . . . .72 B3
Hendon Pk Row, NW11 . . .72 C6
Hendon Rd, N9 . . . . .60 D2
Hendon Way, NW2 . . . . . .90 C3
NW4 . . . . .71 H6
Staines (Stanw.) TW19 .140 A6
Hendon Wd La, NW7 . . . . .39 F6
Hendren Cl, Grnf. UB6
off Dimmock Dr 86 A5
Hendre Rd, SE1 . . . . .36 E2
Hendrick Av, SW12 . . . . .149 J6
Heneage La, EC3 . . . . .21 E4
Heneage St, E1 . . . . .21 G1
Henfield Cl, N19 . . . . .92 C1
Bexley DA5 . . . . .159 G6
Henfield Rd, SW19 . . . . .184 C1
Hengelo Gdns, Mitch.
CR4 . . . . .185 G4
Hengist Rd, SE12 . . . . . .155 H7
Erith DA8 . . . . .139 H7
Hengist Way, Brom.
BR2 . . . . .190 E4
Hengrave Rd, SE23 . . . . .153 G2
Hengrove Ct, Bex. DA5
off Hurst Rd 176/177 E1
Henley Av, Sutt. SM3 . . . .198 B3
Henley Cl, Grnf. UB6 . . . .103 J2
Isleworth TW7 . . . . . . .144 C1
Henley Ct, N14 . . . . .42 C7
Henley Cross, SE3 . . . . . .155 H3
Henley Dr, SE1 . . . . .37 G1
Kingston upon Thames
KT2 . . . . .165 G2
Henley Gdns, Pnr. HA5 . . .66 B3
Romford RM6 . . . . .82 E5
Henley Rd, E16 . . . . .136 C2
N18 . . . . .60 B4
NW10 . . . . .107 J1
Ilford IG1 . . . . .99 F4
Henley St, SW11 . . . . . . .150 A2
Henley Way, Felt. TW13 .160 D5

Henlow Pl, Rich. TW10
off Sandpits Rd 163 G2
Hennel Cl, SE23 . . . . . . .171 F3
Henniker Gdns, E6 . . . . . .116 A3
Henniker Ms, SW3 . . . . . .30 E5
Henniker Pt, E15 . . . . .96 E5
Henniker Rd, E15 . . . . . . .96 D5
Henningham Rd, N17 . . . .76 A1
Henning St, SW11 . . . . . .149 H1
Henrietta Cl, SE8 . . . . . . .134 A6
Henrietta Ms, WC1 . . . . . .10 B5
Henrietta Pl, W1 . . . . .16 D4
Henrietta St, E15 . . . . . . .96 C5
WC2 . . . . .18 B5
Henriques St, E1 . . . . .21 J3
Henry Addlington Cl,
E6 . . . . .116 E5
Henry Cooper Way, SE9 .174 A3
Henry Darlot Dr, NW7 . . . .56 A5
Henry Dickens Ct, W11 . .128 A1
Henry Doulton Dr,
SW17 . . . . .168 B4
Henry Jackson Rd,
SW15 . . . . .148 A3
Henry Macaulay Av, Kings.T.
KT2 . . . . .181 G1
Henry Rd, E6 . . . . .116 B2
N4 . . . . .93 J1
Barnet EN4 . . . . .41 G5
Henry's Av, Wdf.Grn. IG8 .63 F5
Henryson Rd, SE4 . . . . . .154 A5
Henry St, Brom. BR1 . . . .191 H1
Henry's Wk, Ilf. IG6 . . . . . .65 G7
Hensford Gdns, SE26
off Wells Pk Rd . .170/171 E4
Henshall St, N1 . . . . .94 A6
Henshawe Rd, Dag.
RM8 . . . . .100 D3
Henshaw St, SE17 . . . . . . .36 B1
Henshill Pt, E3
off Bromley High St . .114 B3
Hensley Pt, E9
off Wick Rd 95 G6
Henslowe Rd, SE22 . . . . .152 D5
Henson Av, NW2 . . . . .89 J5
Henson Cl, Orp. BR6 . . . .207 E2
Henson Path, Har. HA3 . . .69 G3
Henson Pl, Nthlt. UB5 . . . .102 C1
Henstridge Pl, NW8 . . . . . .7 G1
Henty Cl, SW11 . . . . .129 H7
Henty Wk, SW15 . . . . . . .147 H5
Henville Rd, Brom. BR1 . .191 H1
Henwick Rd, SE9 . . . . . . .156 A3
Henwood Side, Wdf.Grn. IG8
off Love La 64 C6
Hepburn Gdns, Brom.
BR2 . . . . .205 E1
Hepburn Ms, SW11
off Webbs Rd 149 J5
Hepple Cl, Islw. TW7 . . . .144 E2
Hepplestone Cl, SW15
off Dover Pk Dr 147 H6
Hepscott Rd, E9 . . . . .96 A7
Hepworth Ct, Bark. IG11 .100 A5
Hepworth Gdns, Bark.
IG11 . . . . .100 A5
Hepworth Rd, SW16 . . . .169 E7
Hepworth Wk, NW3
off Haverstock Hill 91 H5
Heracles Cl, Wall. SM6 . . .200 E7
Herald Gdns, Wall. SM6 .200 B3
Herald's Ct, SE11 . . . . . . .35 G2
Herald's Pl, SE11 . . . . .35 F1
Herald St, E2
off Three Colts La .112/113 E4
Herbal Hill, EC1 . . . . .11 F6
Herbert Cres, SW1 . . . . . . .24 A5
Herbert Gdns, NW10 . . . .107 H2
W4 off Magnolia Rd . . .126 B6
Romford RM6 . . . . .82 D7
Herbert Ms, SW2
off Bascombe St 151 G6
Herbert Morrison Ho, SW6
off Clem Attlee Ct 128 C6
Herbert Pl, SE18
off Plumstead Common
Rd 136/137 E6
Herbert Rd, E12 . . . . .98 B4
E17 . . . . .77 J7
N11 . . . . .58 E7
N15 . . . . .76 C5
NW9 . . . . .71 G6
SE18 . . . . .136 D7
SW19 . . . . .166 C7
Bexleyheath DA7 . . . . .159 E2
Bromley BR2 . . . . .192 A5
Ilford IG3 . . . . .99 H2
Kingston upon Thames
KT1 . . . . .181 J3
Southall UB1 . . . . .123 F1

Herbert St, E13 . . . . .115 G2
NW5 . . . . .92 A6
Herbert Ter, SE18
off Herbert Rd 136/137 E6
Herbrand St, WC1 . . . . . . .10 A5
Hercules Pl, N7
off Hercules St 92/93 E3
Hercules Rd, SE1 . . . . .26 D5
Hercules St, N7 . . . . .93 E3
Hereford Av, Barn. EN4 . . .57 J1
Hereford Ct, Sutt. SM2
off Worcester Rd 198 D7
Hereford Gdns, SE13
off Longhurst Rd .154/155 E5
Ilford IG1 . . . . .80 B7
Pinner HA5 . . . . .66 E5
Twickenham TW2 . . . . .161 J1
Hereford Ho, NW6 . . . . . .108 D2
Hereford Ms, W2
off Hereford Rd 108 D6
Hereford Pl, SE14 . . . . . . .133 J7
Hereford Retreat, SE15 . . .37 H6
Hereford Rd, E11 . . . . .79 H5
W2 . . . . .108 D6
W3 . . . . .106 B7
W5 . . . . .125 F3
Feltham TW13 . . . . . . .160 C1
Hereford Sq, SW7 . . . . . . .30 D2
Hereford St, E2 . . . . .13 H5
Hereford Way, Chess.
KT9 . . . . .195 F5
Herent Dr, Ilf. IG5 . . . . . . .80 C3
Hereward Gdns, N13 . . . . .59 G5
Hereward Grn, Loug.
IG10 . . . . .49 F1
Hereward Rd, SW17 . . . . .167 J4
Herga Ct, Har. HA1 . . . . . .86 B3
Herga Rd, Har. HA3 . . . . . .68 C4
Heriot Av, E4 . . . . .62 A2
Heriot Rd, NW4 . . . . .71 J5
Heriots Cl, Stan. HA7 . . . . .52 D4
Heritage Cl, SW9 . . . . . . .151 H3
Heritage Hill, Kes. BR2 . . .205 J5
Heritage Pl, SW18
off Earlsfield Rd 167 F1
Heritage Vw, Har. HA1 . . . .86 C3
Herlwyn Gdns, SW17 . . . .167 J4
Hermes Cl, W9
off Chippenham Rd . . .108 D4
Hermes St, N1 . . . . .10 E2
Hermes Wk, Nthlt. UB5
off Hotspur Rd 103 G2
Hermes Way, Wall. SM6 .200 D7
Hermiston Av, N8 . . . . . . .75 E5
Hermitage, The, SE23 . . . .171 F1
SW13 . . . . .147 F1
Richmond TW10 . . . . . .145 G5
Hermitage Cl, E18 . . . . . . .79 F4
Enfield EN2 . . . . .43 H2
Esher (Clay.) KT10 . . . .194 D6
Hermitage Ct, E18 . . . . . . .79 G4
NW2 off Hermitage La . .90 D3
Hermitage Gdns, NW2 . . . .90 D3
SE19 . . . . .169 J6
Hermitage La, N18 . . . . . . .60 A5
NW2 . . . . .90 D3
SE25 . . . . .188 D6
SW16 . . . . .169 F7
Croydon CR0 . . . . .188 D6
Hermitage Path, SW16 . .187 E1
Hermitage Rd, N4 . . . . . . .75 H7
N15 . . . . .75 H7
SE19 . . . . .169 J7
Hermitage Row, E8 . . . . . .94 D5
Hermitage St, W2 . . . . . . .15 E2
Hermitage Wk, E18 . . . . . .79 F4
Hermitage Wall, E1 . . . . . .29 J2
Hermitage Waterside, E1 .29 H1
Hermitage Way, Stan.
HA7 . . . . .68 D1
Hermit Pl, NW6
off Belsize Rd 108/109 E1
Hermit Rd, E16 . . . . .115 F5
Hermit St, EC1 . . . . .11 G3
Hermon Gro, Hayes
UB3 . . . . .122 A1
Hermon Hill, E11 . . . . .79 G5
E18 . . . . .79 G5
Herndon Rd, SW18 . . . . .149 F5
Herne Cl, NW10
off North Circular Rd . .88 D5
HERNE HILL, SE24 . . . . . .151 J5
Herne Hill, SE24 . . . . .151 J6
Herne Hill Ho, SE24
off Railton Rd 151 H6
Herne Hill Rd, SE24 . . . . .151 J3
Herne Ms, N18 . . . . .60 D4
Herne Pl, SE24 . . . . .151 H5
Herne Rd, Surb. KT6 . . . .195 G2

Heron Cl, E17 . . . . .77 J2
NW10 . . . . .89 E6
Buckhurst Hill IG9 . . . . .63 G1
Sutton SM1
off Sandpiper Rd 198 C5
Heron Ct, Brom. BR2 . . . .191 J4
Heron Cres, Sid. DA14 . . .175 H3
Herondale Av, SW18 . . . .167 G1
Heron Dr, N4 . . . . .93 J2
Herongate Rd, E12 . . . . . .97 J2
Heron Hill, Belv. DA17 . . .139 F4
Heron Ms, Ilf. IG1
off Balfour Rd 98/99 E2
Heron Pl, SE16 . . . . .133 H1
Heron Quay, E14 . . . . . . .134 A1
Heron Rd, SE24 . . . . .151 J4
Croydon CR0
off Tunstall Rd 202 B2
Twickenham TW1 . . . . .144 D4
Herons, The, E11 . . . . .79 F6
Heronsforde, W13 . . . . . .105 F6
Heronsgate, Edg. HA8 . . . .54 A5
Heronslea Dr, Stan. HA7 . .53 H5
Heron's Pl, Islw. TW7 . . . .144 E3
Heron Sq, Rich. TW9
off Bridge St 145 G5
Herons Ri, Barn. EN4 . . . . .41 H4
Heron Trd Est, W3
off Alliance Rd 106 A4
Heron Way, Felt. TW14
off The Causeway 142 A4
Heronway, Wdf.Grn. IG8 . .63 J4
Herrick Rd, N5 . . . . .93 J3
Herrick St, SW1 . . . . .33 J1
Herries St, W10 . . . . .108 B2
Herringham Rd, SE7 . . . . .135 J3
Herrongate Cl, Enf. EN1 . . .44 C2
Hersant Cl, NW10 . . . . . .107 G1
Herschell Rd, SE23 . . . . . .153 H7
Hersham Cl, SW15 . . . . . .147 G7
Hertford Av, SW14 . . . . . .146 E5
Hertford Cl, Barn. EN4 . . . .41 G3
Hertford Pl, W1 . . . . .9 F6
Hertford Rd, N1 . . . . .112 B1
N2 . . . . .73 H3
N9 . . . . .60 E2
Barking IG11 . . . . .98 E7
Barnet EN4 . . . . .41 F3
Enfield EN3 . . . . .45 F3
Ilford IG2 . . . . .81 H6
Hertford Sq, Mitch. CR4
off Hertford Way . .186/187 E4
Hertford St, W1 . . . . .24 D1
Hertford Wk, Belv. DA17
off Hoddesdon Rd 139 G5
Hertford Way, Mitch.
CR4 . . . . .186 E4
Hertslet Rd, N7 . . . . .93 F3
Hertsmere Rd, E14 . . . . . .114 A7
Hervey Cl, N3 . . . . .72 D1
Hervey Pk Rd, E17 . . . . . . .77 H4
Hervey Rd, SE3 . . . . .155 H1
Hesa Rd, Hayes UB3 . . . .102 A6
Hesewall Cl, SW4
off Brayburne Av 150 C2
Hesketh Pl, W11 . . . . .108 B7
Hesketh Rd, E7 . . . . .97 G3
Heslop Rd, SW12 . . . . . . .167 J1
Hesper Ms, SW5 . . . . .30 A3
Hesperus Cres, E14 . . . . .134 B4
Hessel Rd, W13 . . . . .124 D2
Hessel St, E1 . . . . .112 E6
Hestercombe Av, SW6 . . .148 B2
Hesterman Way, Croy.
CR0 . . . . .201 E1
Hester Rd, N18 . . . . .60 D5
SW11 . . . . .129 H7
Hester Ter, Rich. TW9
off Chilton Rd 146 A3
HESTON, Houns. 123 F7
Heston Av, Houns. TW5 . .123 E7
Heston Gra La, Houns.
TW5 . . . . .123 F6
Heston Ind Mall, Houns.
TW5 . . . . .123 G7
Heston Rd, Houns. TW5 . .123 G7
Heston St, SE14 . . . . .153 J1
Heswall Grn, Wat. WD19
off Fairhaven Cres 50 A3
Hetherington Rd, SW4 . . .150 E4
Hetley Gdns, SE19
off Fox Hill 170 C7
Hetley Rd, W12 . . . . .127 H1
Heton Gdns, NW4 . . . . . . .71 G4
Hevelius Cl, SE10 . . . . . . .135 F5
Hever Cft, SE9 . . . . .174 D4
Hever Gdns, Brom. BR1 .192 D3
Heverham Rd, SE18 . . . . .137 H4
Heversham Rd, Bexh.
DA7 . . . . .159 G2

Hewer St, W10 . . . .**108** A5
Hewett Cl, Stan. HA7 . . . .**53** E4
Hewett Rd, Dag. RM8 . . .**100** D5
Hewett St, EC2 . . . .**12** E6
Hewish Rd, N18 . . . .**60** B4
Hewison St, E3 . . . .**113** J2
Hewitt Av, N22 . . . .**75** H2
Hewitt Cl, Croy. CR0 . . .**204** A3
Hewitt Rd, N8 . . . .**75** G5
Hewlett Rd, E3 . . . .**113** H2
Hexagon, The, N6 . . . .**91** J1
Hexal Rd, SE6 . . . .**172** E3
Hexham Gdns, Islw.
   TW7 . . . .**124** D7
Hexham Rd, SE27 . . . . . .**169** J2
  Barnet EN5 . . . .**41** E4
  Morden SM4 . . . .**198** E1
Heybourne Rd, N17 . . . . . .**61** E7
Heybridge Av, SW16 . . . .**169** E7
Heybridge Dr, Ilf. IG6 . . . .**81** G3
Heybridge Way, E10 . . . . .**77** H7
Heyford Av, SW8 . . . .**34** B7
  SW20 . . . .**184** C3
Heyford Rd, Mitch. CR4 . .**185** H2
Heyford Ter, SW8
   off Heyford Av . . .**130/131** E7
Heygate St, SE17 . . . .**35** J2
Heylyn Sq, E3
   off Malmesbury Rd . . .**113** J3
Heynes Rd, Dag. RM8 . . .**100** C4
Heysham Dr, Wat. WD19 . .**50** C5
Heysham La, NW3 . . . .**91** E3
Heysham Rd, N15 . . . .**76** A6
Heythorp St, SW18 . . . . .**166** C1
Heywood Av, NW9 . . . .**70** E1
Heyworth Rd, E5 . . . .**94** E4
  E15 . . . .**97** F5
Hibbert Rd, E17 . . . .**77** J7
  Harrow HA3 . . . .**68** C2
Hibbert St, SW11 . . . . . .**149** F3
Hibernia Gdns, Houns.
   TW3 . . . .**143** G4
Hibernia Pt, SE2
   off Wolvercote Rd **138** D2
Hibernia Rd, Houns.
   TW3 . . . .**143** G4
Hibiscus Cl, Edg. HA8
   off Campion Way **54** C4
Hichisson Rd, SE15 . . . .**153** F5
Hickin Cl, SE7 . . . .**136** A4
Hickin St, E14
   off Plevna St **134** C3
Hickling Rd, Ilf. IG1 . . . . .**99** E5
Hickman Av, E4 . . . .**62** C6
Hickman Cl, E16 . . . .**116** A5
Hickman Rd, Rom. RM6 . .**82** C7
Hickmore Wk, SW4 . . . . .**150** C3
Hickory Cl, N9 . . . .**44** D7
Hicks Av, Grnf. UB6 . . . .**104** A2
Hicks Cl, SW11 . . . .**149** H3
Hicks St, SE8 . . . .**133** H5
Hidcote Gdns, SW20 . . . .**183** H3
Hide, E6
   off Downings **116** D6
Hide Pl, SW1 . . . .**33** H2
Hide Rd, Har. HA1 . . . .**68** A4
Hides St, N7
   off Sheringham Rd . . .**93** F6
Hide Twr, SW1 . . . .**33** H2
Higgins Wk, Hmptn. TW12
   off Abbott Cl . . .**160/161** B6
High Acres, Enf. EN2
   off Old Pk Vw **43** H3
HIGHAM HILL, E17 . . . . . .**77** H1
Higham Hill Rd, E17 . . . . .**77** H2
Higham Pl, E17 . . . .**77** H3
Higham Rd, N17 . . . .**76** A3
  Woodford Green IG8 . . .**63** G6
Highams Ct, E4
   off Friars Cl **62** D3
Highams Lo Business Cen,
   E17 . . . .**77** H3
HIGHAMS PARK, E4 . . . . .**62** D5
Highams Pk Ind Est, E4 . .**62** C6
Higham Sta Av, E4 . . . . . .**62** B6
Higham St, E17 . . . .**77** H3
Highbanks Cl, Well.
   DA16 . . . .**138** B7
Highbanks Rd, Pnr. HA5 . .**51** H5
Highbank Way, N8 . . . .**75** G6
HIGH BARNET, Barn. **40** A2
Highbarrow Rd, Croy.
   CR0 . . . .**188** D7
HIGH BEACH, Loug. **47** G1
High Beech, S.Croy. CR2 .**202** B7
High Beeches, Sid.
   DA14 . . . .**176** E5
High Beech Rd, Loug.
   IG10 . . . .**48** A4
High Br, SE10 . . . .**134** D5

Highbridge Rd, Bark.
   IG11 . . . .**116** E1
High Br Wf, SE10 . . . .**134** D5
Highbrook Rd, SE3 . . . . .**156** A3
High Broom Cres, W.Wick.
   BR4 . . . .**190** B7
HIGHBURY, N5 . . . .**93** H5
Highbury Av, Th.Hth.
   CR7 . . . .**187** G2
Highbury Cl, N.Mal. KT3 .**182** C4
  West Wickham BR4 . . .**204** B2
Highbury Cor, N5 . . . .**93** G6
Highbury Cres, N5 . . . . . .**93** G5
Highbury Est, N5 . . . .**93** J5
Highbury Gdns, Ilf. IG3 . .**99** H2
Highbury Gra, N5 . . . .**93** H4
Highbury Gro, N5 . . . .**93** H6
Highbury Hill, N5 . . . .**93** G3
Highbury Ms, N7
   off Holloway Rd **93** G6
Highbury New Pk, N5 . . . .**93** J5
Highbury Pk, N5 . . . .**93** H3
Highbury Pk Ms, N5
   off Highbury Gra **93** J4
Highbury Pl, N5 . . . .**93** H6
Highbury Quad, N5 . . . . . .**93** J3
Highbury Rd, SW19 . . . .**166** B5
Highbury Sta Rd, N1 . . . . .**93** G6
Highbury Ter, N5 . . . .**93** H5
Highbury Ter Ms, N5 . . . . .**93** H5
High Cedar Dr, SW20 . . .**165** H7
Highclere Rd, N.Mal.
   KT3 . . . .**182** D3
Highclere St, SE26 . . . . .**171** H4
Highcliffe Dr, SW15 . . . .**147** F6
Highcliffe Gdns, Ilf. IG4 . .**80** B5
Highcombe, SE7 . . . .**135** H6
Highcombe Cl, SE9 . . . . .**174** A1
High Coombe Pl, Kings.T.
   KT2 . . . .**164** D7
Highcroft, NW9 . . . .**70** D5
Highcroft Av, Wem. HA0 .**106** A1
Highcroft Gdns, NW11 . . .**72** C6
Highcroft Rd, N19 . . . .**74** E7
High Cross Cen, N15 . . . . .**76** D4
High Cross Rd, N17 . . . . . .**76** D3
Highcross Way, SW15 . . .**165** G1
Highdaun Dr, SW16 . . . . .**187** F4
Highdown, Wor.Pk. KT4 . .**197** E2
Highdown Rd, SW15 . . . .**147** H6
High Dr, N.Mal. KT3 . . . . .**182** C1
High Elms, Chig. IG7 . . . . .**65** H4
  Woodford Green IG8 . . .**63** G5
Highfield, Bushey (Bushey Hth.)
   WD23 off High Rd **52** B2
  Feltham TW13 . . . .**160** A1
  Watford WD19 . . . .**51** F3
Highfield Av, NW9 . . . .**70** C5
  NW11 . . . .**72** A7
  Erith DA8 . . . .**139** H6
  Greenford UB6 . . . .**86** B5
  Orpington BR6 . . . . . .**207** J5
  Pinner HA5 . . . .**67** F5
  Wembley HA9 . . . .**87** J3
Highfield Cl, N22 . . . .**75** G1
  NW9 . . . .**70** C5
  SE13 . . . .**154** D7
  Surbiton KT6 . . . .**195** F1
Highfield Ct, N14 . . . .**42** C6
Highfield Dr, Brom. BR2 .**191** E4
  Epsom KT19 . . . .**197** F7
  West Wickham BR4 . . .**204** B2
Highfield Gdns, NW11 . . .**72** B6
Highfield Hill, SE19 . . . . .**170** A7
Highfield Ms, NW6
   off Compayne Gdns . . .**90** E7
Highfield Rd, N21 . . . .**59** H2
  NW11 . . . .**72** B6
  W3 . . . .**106** B5
  Bexleyheath DA6 . . . . .**159** F5
  Bromley BR1 . . . .**192** C4
  Chislehurst BR7 . . . . .**193** J3
  Feltham TW13 . . . .**160** A2
  Isleworth TW7 . . . .**144** C1
  Surbiton KT5 . . . .**182** C7
  Sutton SM1 . . . .**199** H5
  Woodford Green IG8 . . .**64** B7
Highfields Gro, N6 . . . .**91** J1
High Foleys, Esher (Clay.)
   KT10 . . . .**194** E7
High Gables, Loug. IG10 . .**48** A5
HIGHGATE, N6 . . . .**92** A2
Highgate Av, N6 . . . .**74** B6
Highgate Cl, N6 . . . .**74** A7
Highgate High St, N6 . . . . .**92** A1
Highgate Hill, N6 . . . .**92** B1
  N19 . . . .**92** B1
Highgate Rd, NW5 . . . .**92** B4
Highgate Wk, SE23 . . . . .**171** F2

Highgate W Hill, N6 . . . . . .**92** A2
High Gro, SE18 . . . .**137** G7
  Bromley BR1 . . . .**191** J1
Highgrove Cl, N11
   off Balmoral Av **58** A5
  Chislehurst BR7 . . . . .**192** B1
Highgrove Ms, Cars.
   SM5 . . . .**199** J3
Highgrove Rd, Dag.
   RM8 . . . .**100** C5
Highgrove Way, Ruis. **66** A6
High Hill, Est, E5
   off Mount Pleasant
   La **94/95** E1
High Hill Ferry, E5 . . . .**95** E1
High Holborn, WC1 . . . . . .**18** B3
Highland Av, W7 . . . .**104** B6
  Dagenham RM10 . . . . .**101** J3
  Loughton IG10 . . . .**48** B6
Highland Cotts, Wall.
   SM6 . . . .**200** B4
Highland Cft, Beck. BR3 .**172** B5
Highland Rd, SE19 . . . . . .**170** B6
  Bexleyheath DA6 . . . . .**159** G5
  Bromley BR1, BR2 . . . .**191** F1
Highlands, Wat. WD19 . . . .**50** C1
Highlands, The, Edg. HA8 .**70** B2
  Potters Bar EN6 . . . . . .**40** E5
Highlands Av, N21 . . . .**43** F5
  W3 . . . .**106** C7
Highlands Cl, N4
   off Mount Vw Rd . . .**74/75** E7
  Hounslow TW3 . . . . . .**143** H1
Highlands Gdns, Ilf. IG1 . .**98** C1
Highlands Heath, SW15 .**147** J7
Highlands Rd, Barn. EN5 . .**40** D5
  Orpington BR6 . . . . . .**207** J1
High Lawns, Har. HA1 . . . .**86** B3
Highlea Cl, NW9 . . . .**71** E1
High Level Dr, SE26 . . . . .**170** D4
Highlever Rd, W10 . . . . . .**107** J5
Highmead, SE18 . . . .**137** J7
High Mead, Chig. IG7 . . . .**65** F2
  Harrow HA1 . . . .**68** B5
  West Wickham BR4 . . .**204** D2
Highmead Cres, Wem.
   HA0 . . . .**87** J7
High Meadow Cl, Pnr. HA5
   off Daymer Gdns **66** B4
High Meadow Cres, NW9 .**70** D5
High Meadows, Chig. IG7 .**65** G5
High Meads Rd, E16 . . . .**116** A6
Highmore Rd, SE3 . . . . . .**135** E7
High Mt, NW4 . . . .**71** G6
High Pk Av, Rich. TW9 . . .**146** A1
High Pk Rd, Rich. TW9 . .**146** A1
High Path, SW19 . . . .**185** E1
High Pt, N6 . . . .**74** A7
  SE9 . . . .**175** E3
High Rd, N2 . . . .**73** G1
  N11 . . . .**58** B5
  N12 . . . .**57** F6
  N15 . . . .**76** C6
  N17 . . . .**76** C1
  N20 . . . .**41** F7
  N22 . . . .**75** G3
  NW10 (Willesden) **89** H6
  Buckhurst Hill IG9 . . . . .**63** H2
  Bushey (Bushey Hth.)
   WD23 . . . .**52** A1
  Chigwell IG7 . . . .**64** C5
  Harrow (Har.Wld.) HA3 . .**52** B7
  Ilford IG1 . . . .**98** E3
  Ilford (Seven Kings) IG3 .**99** J1
  Loughton IG10 . . . .**47** J7
  Pinner HA5 . . . .**66** B4
  Romford (Chad.Hth.)
   RM6 . . . .**100** B1
  Wembley HA0, HA9 . . . .**87** G5
High Rd Leyton, E10 . . . . .**96** B1
  E15 . . . .**96** D2
High Rd Leytonstone, E11 .**96** E4
  E15 . . . .**96** E4
High Rd Woodford Grn,
   E18 . . . .**63** F7
  Woodford Green IG8 . . .**63** F7
Highshore Rd, SE15 . . . .**152** C2
High Silver, Loug. IG10 . . .**48** A4
Highstone Av, E11 . . . .**79** G6
High St, E11 . . . .**79** G5
  E13 . . . .**115** G2
  E15 . . . .**114** C2
  E17 . . . .**77** J5
  N8 . . . .**74** E4
  N14 . . . .**58** D1
  NW7 . . . .**55** H4
  NW10 (Harlesden) **107** F2
  SE20 . . . .**171** E6

High St, SE25
   (S.Norwood) **188** C4
  W3 . . . .**126** B1
  W5 . . . .**105** G7
  Barnet EN5 . . . .**40** B3
  Beckenham BR3 . . . . .**190** A2
  Brentford TW8 . . . .**125** G6
  Bromley BR1 . . . .**191** G2
  Carshalton SM5 . . . . .**200** A4
  Chislehurst BR7 . . . . .**174** E6
  Croydon CR0 . . . .**201** J2
  Edgware HA8 . . . .**54** A6
  Enfield (Pond.End) EN3 .**45** F4
  Esher (Clay.) KT10 . . . .**194** C6
  Feltham TW13 . . . .**160** A3
  Hampton TW12 . . . . . .**161** J6
  Harrow HA1, HA2 . . . . .**86** B1
  Harrow (Wldste.) HA3 . .**68** B3
  Hayes UB3 . . . .**121** H5
  Hounslow TW3 . . . . . .**143** J3
  Hounslow (Cran.) TW5 .**122** B7
  Ilford (Barkingside) IG6 .**81** F2
  Kingston upon Thames
   KT1 . . . .**181** G2
  Kingston upon Thames
   (Hmptn.W.) KT1 . . . . .**181** F1
  New Malden KT3 . . . . .**183** E3
  Orpington (Farnboro.)
   BR6 . . . .**207** E5
  Orpington (Grn.St.Grn.)
   BR6 . . . .**207** J7
  Pinner HA5 . . . .**66** E3
  Southall UB1 . . . .**123** F1
  Staines (Stanw.) TW19 .**140** A6
  Sutton SM1 . . . .**198** E4
  Sutton (Cheam) SM3 . .**198** B6
  Teddington TW11 . . . . .**162** D5
  Thames Ditton KT7 . . .**180** D7
  Thornton Heath CR7 . .**187** J4
  Twickenham (Whitton)
   TW2 . . . .**143** J7
  Wembley HA9 . . . .**87** J4
  West Drayton (Harm.)
   UB7 . . . .**120** A6
  West Drayton (Yiew.)
   UB7 . . . .**120** A1
  West Molesey KT8 . . . .**179** G4
  West Wickham BR4 . . .**204** B1
High St Colliers Wd,
   SW19 . . . .**167** G7
High St Ms, SW19 . . . . . .**166** B5
High St N, E6 . . . .**116** B1
  E12 . . . .**98** B5
High St S, E6 . . . .**116** C2
High St Wimbledon,
   SW19 . . . .**166** A5
High Timber St, EC4 . . . . .**19** J5
High Tor Cl, Brom. BR1
   off Babbacombe Rd . .**173** H7
High Tree Ct, W7 . . . .**104** B7
High Trees, SW2 . . . .**169** G1
  Barnet EN4 . . . .**41** H5
  Croydon CR0 . . . .**203** H1
Highview, Nthlt. UB5 . . . .**103** E3
High Vw, Pnr. HA5 . . . .**66** C4
Highview Av, Edg. HA8 . . .**54** C4
  Wallington SM6 . . . . . .**201** F5
Highview Cl, SE19 . . . . . .**188** C2
  Loughton IG10 . . . .**47** J5
Highview Gdns, N3 . . . . . .**72** B3
  N11 . . . .**58** C5
  Edgware HA8 . . . .**54** C4
Highview Ho, Rom. RM6 .**83** E4
High Vw Rd, E18 . . . .**79** F3
Highview Rd, SE19 . . . . .**170** A6
  W13 . . . .**104** D5
  Sidcup DA14 . . . .**176** B4
Highway, The, E1 . . . .**21** J6
  E14 . . . .**21** J6
  Stanmore HA7 . . . .**68** C1
Highwood, Brom. BR2 . . .**190** E3
Highwood Av, N12 . . . .**57** F4
Highwood Cl, Orp. BR6 . .**207** F2
Highwood Dr, Orp. BR6 . .**207** F2
Highwood Gdns, Ilf. IG5 . .**80** C5
Highwood Gro, NW7 . . . . .**54** D5
HIGHWOOD HILL, NW7 . . .**55** G2
Highwood Hill, NW7 . . . . .**55** F2
Highwood La, Loug.
   IG10 . . . .**48** D5
Highwood Rd, N19 . . . .**92** E3
High Worple, Har. HA2 . . . .**67** F7
Highworth Rd, N11 . . . .**58** D6
Hilary Av, Mitch. CR4 . . .**186** A3
Hilary Cl, SW6 . . . .**30** A7
  Erith DA8 . . . .**159** J1
Hilary Rd, W12 . . . .**107** F6
Hilbert Rd, Sutt. SM3 . . .**198** A4
Hilborough Way, Orp.
   BR6 . . . .**207** G5

Hilda Rd, E6 . . . . .98 A7
E16 . . . . .115 E4
Hilda Ter, SW9 . . . . .151 G2
Hilda Vale Cl, Orp. BR6 .206 E4
Hilda Vale Rd, Orp. BR6 .206 D4
Hildenborough Gdns,
  Brom. BR1 . . . . .173 E6
Hildenlea Pl, Brom. BR2 .190 E4
Hildreth St, SW12 . . . . . . .168 B3
Hildyard Rd, SW6 . . . . . . .128 D6
Hiley Rd, NW10 . . . . .107 J3
Hilgrove Rd, NW6 . . . . .91 F7
Hiliary Gdns, Stan. HA7 . . .69 F2
Hilary Dr, Islw. TW7 . . . . .144 C4
Hillary Ri, Barn. EN5 . . . . .40 D4
Hillary Rd, Sthl. UB2 . . . .123 G3
Hillbeck Cl, SE15 . . . . . . .133 F7
Hillbeck Way, Grnf. UB6 .104 A1
Hillborne Cl, Hayes UB3 .122 A5
Hillborough Cl, SW19 . . . .167 F7
Hillbrook Rd, SW17 . . . . . .167 J3
Hill Brow, Brom. BR1 . . . .192 A1
Hillbrow, N.Mal. KT3 . . . .183 F3
Hillbrow Rd, Brom. BR1 . .172 E7
Hillbury Av, Har. HA3 . . . . .69 E5
Hillbury Rd, SW17 . . . . . .168 B3
Hill Cl, NW2 . . . . .89 H3
NW11 . . . . .72 D6
Barnet EN5 . . . . .39 J5
Chislehurst BR7 . . . . . .174 E5
Harrow HA1 . . . . .86 B3
Stanmore HA7 . . . . .52 E4
Hillcote Av, SW16 . . . . . .169 G7
Hill Ct, Nthlt. UB5 . . . . . . .85 G5
Hillcourt Av, N12 . . . . .56 E6
Hillcourt Est, N16 . . . . . . .94 A1
Hillcourt Rd, SE22 . . . . . .152 E6
Hill Cres, N20 . . . . .56 E2
Bexley DA5 . . . . .177 J1
Harrow HA1 . . . . .68 D5
Surbiton KT5 . . . . .181 J5
Worcester Park KT4 . . . .197 J2
Hillcrest, N6 . . . . .74 A7
N21 . . . . .43 H7
Hill Crest, Sid. DA15 . . . .158 A7
Hillcrest Av, NW11 . . . . . . .72 B5
Edgware HA8 . . . . .54 B4
Pinner HA5 . . . . .66 D4
Hillcrest Cl, SE26 . . . . . .170 D4
Beckenham BR3 . . . . . . .189 J5
Hillcrest Ct, Sutt. SM2
  off Eaton Rd 199 G6
Hillcrest Gdns, N3 . . . . . . .72 B4
NW2 . . . . .89 G3
Esher KT10 . . . . .194 C3
Hillcrest Rd, E17 . . . . .78 D2
E18 . . . . .79 F2
W3 . . . . .126 A1
W5 . . . . .105 H5
Bromley BR1 . . . . .173 G5
Loughton IG10 . . . . .48 A6
Hillcrest Vw, Beck. BR3 . .189 J6
Hillcroft, Loug. IG10 . . . . . .48 D2
Hillcroft Av, Pnr. HA5 . . . .67 F6
Hillcroft Cres, W5 . . . . . .105 H6
Ruislip HA4 . . . . .84 D3
Watford WD19 . . . . .50 B1
Wembley HA9 . . . . .87 J4
Hillcroft Rd, E6 . . . . .116 E5
Hillcroome Rd, Sutt.
  SM2 . . . . .199 G6
Hillcross Av, Mord. SM4 .184 C5
Hilldale Rd, Sutt. SM1 . . .198 C4
Hilldown Rd, SW16 . . . . . .169 E7
Bromley BR2 . . . . .205 E1
Hill Dr, NW9 . . . . .88 C1
SW16 . . . . .187 F3
Hilldrop Cres, N7 . . . . .92 D5
Hilldrop Est, N7 . . . . .92 D5
Hilldrop La, N7 . . . . .92 D5
Hilldrop Rd, N7 . . . . .92 D5
Bromley BR1 . . . . .173 G6
Hillend, SE18 . . . . .156 D1
Hill End, Orp. BR6
  off The Approach 207 J2
Hillersdon Av, SW13 . . . .147 G2
Edgware HA8 . . . . .53 J5
Hillery Cl, SE17 . . . . .36 C2
Hill Fm Rd, W10 . . . . .107 J5
Hillfield Av, N8 . . . . .75 E5
NW9 . . . . .71 E5
Wembley HA0 . . . . .87 H7
Hillfield Cl, Har. HA2 . . . . .67 J4
Hillfield Ct, NW3 . . . . .91 H5
Hillfield Par, Mord. SM4 .185 H6
Hillfield Pk, N10 . . . . .74 B4
N21 . . . . .59 G2
Hillfield Pk Ms, N10 . . . . . .74 B4
Hillfield Rd, NW6 . . . . .90 C5
Hampton TW12 . . . . . . .161 F7

Hillfoot Av, Rom. RM5 . . . .83 J1
Hillfoot Rd, Rom. RM5 . . .83 J1
Hillgate Pl, SW12 . . . . . . .150 B7
W8 . . . . .128 D1
Hillgate St, W8 . . . . .128 D1
Hill Gro, Felt. TW13
  off Watermill Way 161 F2
Hill Ho Av, Stan. HA7 . . . .52 C7
Hill Ho Cl, N21 . . . . .43 G7
Hill Ho Dr, Hmptn. TW12 .179 G1
Hill Ho Rd, SW16 . . . . . . .169 F5
Hilliards Ct, E1
  off Wapping High
  St 132/133 E1
Hillier Cl, Barn. EN5 . . . . .40 E6
Hillier Gdns, Croy. CR0
  off Crowley Cres 201 G5
Hillier Pl, Chess. KT9 . . . .195 F6
Hillier Rd, SW11 . . . . .149 J6
Hilliers La, Croy. CR0 . . . .200 E3
Hillingdon Rd, Bexh.
  DA7 . . . . .159 J2
Hillingdon St, SE5 . . . . . . .35 H6
SE17 . . . . .35 H6
Hillington Gdns, Wdf.Grn.
  IG8 . . . . .80 A2
Hillman Dr, W10 . . . . .107 J4
Hillman St, E8 . . . . .95 E6
Hillmarton Rd, N7 . . . . . . .93 E5
Hillmead Dr, SW9 . . . . . . .151 H4
Hillmont Rd, Esher KT10 .194 B3
Hillmore Gro, SE26 . . . . .171 G5
Hill Path, SW16
  off Valley Rd 169 F5
Hillreach, SE18 . . . . .136 C5
Hill Ri, N9 . . . . .45 E6
NW11 . . . . .73 E4
SE23
  off London Rd . . .170/171 E1
Esher KT10 . . . . .194 E2
Greenford UB6 . . . . .85 J7
Richmond TW10 . . . . . .145 G5
Hillrise Rd, N19 . . . . .74 E7
Hill Rd, N10 . . . . .73 J1
NW8 . . . . .6 D2
Carshalton SM5 . . . . . .199 H6
Harrow HA1 . . . . .68 D5
Mitcham CR4 . . . . .186 B1
Pinner HA5 . . . . .66 E5
Sutton SM1 . . . . .199 E5
Wembley HA0 . . . . .86 E3
Hillsborough Grn, Wat. WD19
  off Ashburnham Dr 50 A3
Hillsborough Rd, SE22 . . .152 B5
Hillsgrove, Well. DA16 . . .138 C7
Hillside, NW9 . . . . .70 D4
NW10 . . . . .106 C1
SW19 . . . . .166 A6
Barnet EN5 . . . . .41 F5
Hillside Av, N11 . . . . .57 J6
Borehamwood WD6 . . . .38 B4
Wembley HA9 . . . . .87 J4
Woodford Green IG8 . . . .63 J5
Hillside Cl, NW8 . . . . .6 B1
Morden SM4 . . . . .184 B4
Woodford Green IG8 . . . .63 J5
Hillside Cres, Har. HA2 . . .85 J1
Northwood HA6 . . . . .66 A1
Hillside Dr, Edg. HA8 . . . . .54 A6
Hillside Est, N15 . . . . .76 C6
Hillside Gdns, E17 . . . . . . .78 D3
N6 . . . . .74 A6
SW2 . . . . .169 G2
Barnet EN5 . . . . .40 B4
Edgware HA8 . . . . .53 J4
Harrow HA3 . . . . .69 H1
Northwood HA6 . . . . .50 A7
Wallington SM6 . . . . . . .200 C7
Hillside Gro, N14 . . . . .42 D7
NW7 . . . . .55 G7
Hillside La, Brom. BR2 . . .205 G2
Hillside Pas, SW2 . . . . . . .169 F2
Hillside Ri, Nthwd. HA6 . . .50 A7
Hillside Rd, N15 . . . . .76 B7
SW2 . . . . .169 G2
W5 . . . . .105 H5
Bromley BR2 . . . . .191 F3
Croydon CR0 . . . . .201 H5
Northwood HA6 . . . . .50 A7
Pinner HA5 . . . . .50 A7
Southall UB1 . . . . .103 G4
Surbiton KT5 . . . . .181 J5
Sutton SM2 . . . . .198 C7
Hillsleigh Rd, W8 . . . . . . .128 C1
Hills Ms, W5 . . . . .105 H7
Hills Pl, W1 . . . . .17 F4
Hills Rd, Buck.H. IG9 . . . . .63 H1
Hillstowe St, E5 . . . . .95 F2
Hill St, W1 . . . . .24 C1
Richmond TW9 . . . . . . .145 G5

Hill Top, NW11 . . . . .73 E4
Loughton IG10 . . . . .48 D2
Morden SM4 . . . . .184 D6
Sutton SM3 . . . . .184 C7
Hill Top Cl, Loug. IG10 . . . .48 D3
Hilltop Gdns, NW4 . . . . . . .71 H2
Orpington BR6 . . . . .207 H2
Hill Top Pl, Loug. IG10 . . . .48 D3
Hilltop Rd, NW6 . . . . .90 D7
Hill Top Vw, Wdf.Grn. IG8 .64 C6
Hilltop Way, Stan. HA7 . . .52 D3
Hillview, SW20 . . . . .165 H7
Mitcham CR4 . . . . .186 E4
Hillview Av, Har. HA3 . . . . .69 H5
Hillview Cl, Pnr. HA5 . . . . .51 F6
Wembley HA9 . . . . .87 J2
Hillview Cres, Ilf. IG1 . . . . .80 C6
Hill Vw Cres, Orp. BR6 . .207 J1
Hill Vw Dr, Well. DA16 . . .157 H2
Hillview Gdns, NW4 . . . . . .72 A4
Hill Vw Gdns, NW9 . . . . . . .70 D5
Hillview Gdns, Har. HA2 . .67 G3
Hillview Rd, NW7 . . . . .56 A4
Chislehurst BR7 . . . . . .174 D5
Hill Vw Rd, Esher (Clay.)
  KT10 . . . . .194 D7
Orpington BR6 . . . . .207 J1
Hillview Rd, Pnr. HA5 . . . . .51 F7
Sutton SM1 . . . . .199 F3
Hill Vw Rd, Twick. TW1 . . .144 D6
Hillway, N6 . . . . .92 A2
NW9 . . . . .88 E1
Hillworth Rd, SW2 . . . . . .151 G7
Hillyard Rd, W7 . . . . .104 B5
Hillyard St, SW9 . . . . .151 G1
Hillyfield, E17 . . . . .77 H2
Hillyfields, Loug. IG10 . . . .48 D2
Hilly Flds Cres, SE4 . . . . .154 A3
Hilsea Pt, SW15
  off Wanborough Dr . .165 H1
Hilsea St, E5 . . . . .95 F4
Hilton Av, N12 . . . . .57 G5
Hilversum Cres, SE22
  off East Dulwich Gro .152 B5
Himley Rd, SW17 . . . . . . .167 H5
Hinchcliffe Cl, Wall. SM6 .201 F7
Hinchley Cl, Esher KT10 .194 C3
Hinchley Dr, Esher KT10 .194 C3
Hinchley Way, Esher
  KT10 . . . . .194 D3
HINCHLEY WOOD,
  Esher 194 C3
Hinckley Rd, SE15 . . . . . .152 D4
Hind Cl, Chig. IG7 . . . . . . .65 J5
Hind Ct, EC4 . . . . .19 F4
Hinde Ms, W1
  off Marylebone La 110 A6
Hindes Rd, Har. HA1 . . . . .68 A5
Hinde St, W1 . . . . .16 C3
Hind Gro, E14 . . . . .114 A6
Hindhead Cl, N16 . . . . .94 B1
Hindhead Gdns, Nthlt.
  UB5 . . . . .102 E1
Hindhead Grn, Wat. WD19 .50 C5
Hindhead Pt, SW15
  off Wanborough Dr . .165 H1
Hindhead Way, Wall.
  SM6 . . . . .200 E5
Hind Ho, N7
  off Harvist Est 93 G4
Hindmans Rd, SE22 . . . . .152 D5
Hindmans Way, Dag.
  RM9 . . . . .119 F4
Hindmarsh Cl, E1 . . . . . . .21 J5
Hindrey Rd, E5 . . . . .95 E5
Hindsley's Pl, SE23 . . . . .171 F2
Hinkler Cl, Wall. SM6 . . . .201 E7
Hinkler Rd, Har. HA3 . . . . .69 G3
Hinksey Path, SE2 . . . . . .138 D3
Hinstock Rd, SE18 . . . . . .137 F6
Hinton Av, Houns. TW4 . .142 D4
Hinton Cl, SE9 . . . . .174 B1
Hinton Rd, N18 . . . . .60 B4
SE24 . . . . .151 H3
Wallington SM6 . . . . . . .200 C6
Hippodrome Ms, W11
  off Portland Rd 108 B7
Hippodrome Pl, W11 . . . .108 B7
Hiscocks Ho, NW10 . . . . . .88 C7
Hitcham Rd, E17 . . . . .77 J7
Hitchin Sq, E3 . . . . .113 H2
Hitherbroom Rd, Hayes
  UB3 . . . . .122 A1
Hither Fm Rd, SE3 . . . . . .155 J3
Hitherfield Rd, SW16 . . . .169 F2
Dagenham RM8 . . . . . . .101 E2
HITHER GREEN, SE13 . .154 E6
Hither Grn La, SE13 . . . . .154 C5
Hitherlands, SW12 . . . . . .168 B2
Hitherwell Dr, Har. HA3 . . .68 A1

Hitherwood Dr, SE19 . . .170 C4
Hive Cl, Bushey
  (Bushey Hth.) WD23 . .52 A2
Hive Rd, Bushey
  (Bushey Hth.) WD23 . .52 A2
★ HMS Belfast, SE1 . . . . .28 E1
★ HMS President, EC4 . . .19 F5
★ HM Treasury, SW1 . . . .26 A3
Hoadly Rd, SW16 . . . . . . .168 D3
Hobart Cl, N20
  off Oakleigh Rd N 57 H2
Hayes UB4 . . . . .102 C4
Hobart Dr, Hayes UB4 . . .102 C4
Hobart Gdns, Th.Hth.
  CR7 . . . . .188 A3
Hobart La, Hayes UB4 . . .102 C4
Hobart Pl, SW1 . . . . .24 D5
Richmond TW10
  off Chisholm Rd 145 J6
Hobart Rd, Dag. RM9 . . . .100 D4
Hayes UB4 . . . . .102 D4
Ilford IG6 . . . . .81 F2
Worcester Park KT4 . . . .197 H3
Hobbayne Rd, W7 . . . . . .104 A6
Hobbes Wk, SW15 . . . . . .147 H5
Hobbs Grn, N2 . . . . .73 F3
Hobbs Ms, Ilf. IG3
  off Ripley Rd 99 J2
Hobbs Pl Est, N1 . . . . . . .112 B1
Hobbs Rd, SE27 . . . . .169 J4
Hobday St, E14 . . . . .114 B5
Hobill Wk, Surb. KT5 . . . .181 J6
Hoblands End, Chis.
  BR7 . . . . .175 H6
Hobsons Pl, E1 . . . . .21 H1
Hobury St, SW10 . . . . .30 D6
Hocker St, E2 . . . . .13 F4
Hockett Cl, SE8
  off Grove St 133 J4
Hockley Av, E6 . . . . .116 B2
Hockley Ct, E18
  off Churchfields 79 G1
Hockley Ms, Bark. IG11 . .117 H2
Hocroft Av, NW2 . . . . .90 C4
Hocroft Rd, NW2 . . . . .90 C4
Hocroft Wk, NW2 . . . . .90 C4
Hodder Dr, Grnf. UB6 . . . .104 C2
Hoddesdon Rd, Belv.
  DA17 . . . . .139 G5
Hodford Rd, NW11 . . . . . . .90 C2
Hodgkin Cl, SE28
  off Fleming Way 118 D7
Hodister Cl, SE5
  off Badsworth Rd 131 J7
Hodnet Gro, SE16 . . . . . .133 G4
Hodson Cl, Har. HA2 . . . . .85 F3
Hoe, The, Wat. WD19 . . . .50 D2
Hoechst, Houns. TW4 . . .142 C3
Hoe St, E17 . . . . .78 A4
Hofland Rd, W14 . . . . .128 A3
Hogan Ms, W2 . . . . .14 E1
Hogan Way, E5
  off Geldeston Rd 94 D2
Hogarth Business Pk,
  W4 . . . . .127 E6
Hogarth Cl, E16 . . . . .116 A5
W5 . . . . .105 H5
Hogarth Ct, EC3 . . . . .20 E5
SE19 off Fountain Dr . .170 C4
Hogarth Cres, SW19 . . . .185 G1
Croydon CR0 . . . . .187 J7
Hogarth Gdns, Houns.
  TW5 . . . . .123 G7
Hogarth Hill, NW11 . . . . . .72 C4
Hogarth La, W4 . . . . .126 E6
Hogarth Pl, SW5 . . . . .30 A2
Hogarth Reach, Loug.
  IG10 . . . . .48 C5
Hogarth Rd, SW5 . . . . .30 A2
Dagenham RM8 . . . . . . .100 B5
Edgware HA8 . . . . .70 A2
Hogarth Roundabout,
  W4 . . . . .127 E6
Hogarth Roundabout Flyover,
  W4 off Burlington
  La 126/127 E6
★ Hogarth's Ho, W4
  off Hogarth La 127 E6
Hogarth Way, Hmptn.
  TW12 . . . . .179 J1
Hogshead Pas, E1
  off Pennington St .112/113 E7
Hogsmill Way, Epsom
  KT19 . . . . .196 C5
Holbeach Gdns, Sid.
  DA15 . . . . .157 H6
Holbeach Ms, SW12
  off Harberson Rd 168 B1
Holbeach Rd, SE6 . . . . . .154 A7

Holbeck Row, SE15 . . . . .**132** D7
Holbein Ms, SW1 . . . .**32** B3
Holbein Pl, SW1 . . . .**32** B2
Holbein Ter, Dag. RM8
    off Marlborough Rd . . .**100** B4
Holberton Gdns, NW10 . .**107** H3
HOLBORN, WC2 . . . .**18** C3
Holborn, EC1 . . . .**18** E2
Holborn Circ, EC1 . . . .**19** F2
Holborn Pl, WC1 . . . .**18** C2
Holborn Rd, E13 . . . .**115** H4
Holborn Viaduct, EC1 . . . .**19** F2
Holborn Way, Mitch.
    CR4 . . . .**185** J2
Holbrook Cl, N19
    off Dartmouth Pk Hill . .**92** B1
Enfield EN1 . . . .**44** C1
Holbrooke Ct, N7 . . . .**93** E4
Holbrooke Pl, Rich. TW10
    off Hill Ri **145** G5
Holbrook La, Chis. BR7 . .**175** G7
Holbrook Rd, E15 . . . .**115** F2
Holbrook Way, Brom.
    BR2 . . . .**192** C6
Holburne Cl, SE3 . . . .**155** J1
Holburne Gdns, SE3 . . . . .**156** A1
Holburne Rd, SE3 . . . .**155** J1
Holcombe Hill, NW7 . . . . . .**55** G3
Holcombe Rd, N17 . . . .**76** C3
Ilford IG1 . . . .**80** D7
Holcombe St, W6 . . . .**127** H5
Holcote Cl, Belv. DA17
    off Blakemore
    Way **138/139** E3
Holcroft Rd, E9 . . . .**95** F7
Holden Av, N12 . . . .**57** E5
NW9 . . . .**88** C1
Holdenby Rd, SE4 . . . .**153** H5
Holden Cl, Dag. RM8 . . . .**100** B3
Holdenhurst Av, N12 . . . . .**57** E7
Holden Pt, E15
    off Waddington Rd **96** D6
Holden Rd, N12 . . . .**56** E5
Holden St, SW11 . . . .**150** A2
Holder Cl, N3 . . . .**57** E7
Holdernesse Cl, Islw.
    TW7 . . . .**144** D1
Holdernesse Rd, SW17 . .**167** J3
Holderness Way, SE27 . .**169** H5
HOLDERS HILL, NW4 . . . . .**72** A2
Holders Hill Av, NW4 . . . . .**72** A2
Holders Hill Circ, NW7
    off Dollis Rd **56** B7
Holders Hill Cres, NW4 . .**72** A2
Holders Hill Dr, NW4 . . . . .**72** A3
Holders Hill Gdns, NW4 . .**72** B2
Holders Hill Rd, NW4 . . . . .**72** A2
NW7 . . . .**72** A2
Holdgate St, SE7
    off Westmoor St **136** A3
Holford Ms, WC1
    off Cruikshank St **111** G3
Holford Pl, WC1 . . . .**10** D3
Holford Rd, NW3 . . . .**91** F3
Holford St, WC1 . . . .**10** E3
Holford Yd, WC1
    off Cruikshank St **111** G3
Holgate Av, SW11 . . . .**149** G3
Holgate Gdns, Dag.
    RM10 . . . .**101** G5
Holgate Rd, Dag. RM10 . .**101** G5
Holland Av, SW20 . . . .**183** F1
Holland Cl, Barn. EN5 . . . .**41** G7
Bromley BR2 . . . .**205** F2
Romford RM7 . . . .**83** J5
Stanmore HA7 . . . .**52** E5
Holland Ct, E17
    off Evelyn Rd **78** C4
NW7 off Page St **55** G6
Holland Dr, SE23 . . . .**171** H3
Holland Gdns, W14 . . . . .**128** B3
Holland Gro, SW9 . . . .**131** G7
★ Holland Ho & Pk,
    W8 . . . .**128** C2
Holland Pk, W8 . . . .**128** C2
W11 . . . .**128** B2
Holland Pk Av, W11 . . . . .**128** B2
Ilford IG3 . . . .**81** H6
Holland Pk Gdns, W14 . . .**128** B1
Holland Pk Ms, W11 . . . . .**128** B1
Holland Pk Rd, W14 . . . . .**128** C3
Holland Pas, N1
    off Basire St **111** J1
Holland Pl, W8 . . . .**22** A3
Holland Rd, E6 . . . .**116** C1
E15 . . . .**115** E3
NW10 . . . .**107** G1
SE25 . . . .**188** D5
W14 . . . .**128** A2
Wembley HA0 . . . .**87** G6

Hollands, The, Felt.
    TW13 . . . .**160** D4
Worcester Park KT4 . . .**197** F1
Holland St, SE1 . . . .**27** H1
W8 . . . .**128** D2
Holland Vil Rd, W14 . . . . .**128** B2
Holland Wk, N19
    off Duncombe Rd **92** D1
W8 . . . .**128** D2
Stanmore HA7 . . . .**52** D5
Holland Way, Brom. BR2 .**205** F2
Hollar Rd, N16
    off Stoke Newington
    High St **94** C3
Hollen St, W1 . . . .**17** H3
Holles Cl, Hmptn. TW12 .**161** G6
Holles St, W1 . . . .**16** E3
Holley Rd, W3 . . . .**127** E2
Hollickwood Av, N12 . . . . .**57** J6
Holliday Sq, SW11
    off Fowler Cl **149** G3
Hollidge Way, Dag.
    RM10 . . . .**101** H6
Hollies, The, E11 . . . .**79** G5
N20
    off Oakleigh Pk N **57** G1
Harrow HA3 . . . .**68** D4
Hollies Av, Sid. DA15 . . . .**175** J2
Hollies Cl, SW16 . . . .**169** G6
Twickenham TW1 . . . . .**162** C2
Hollies End, NW7 . . . .**55** H5
Hollies Rd, W5 . . . .**125** F4
Hollies Way, SW12
    off Bracken Av **150** A7
Holligrave Rd, Brom.
    BR1 . . . .**191** G1
Hollingbourne Av, Bexh.
    DA7 . . . .**139** F7
Hollingbourne Gdns,
    W13 . . . .**104** E5
Hollingbourne Rd, SE24 .**151** J5
Hollingsworth Rd, Croy.
    CR0 . . . .**203** E6
Hollington Cres, N.Mal.
    KT3 . . . .**183** F6
Hollington Rd, E6 . . . .**116** C3
N17 . . . .**76** D2
Hollingworth Cl, W.Mol.
    KT8 . . . .**179** F4
Hollingworth Rd, Orp.
    BR5 . . . .**192** E6
Hollman Gdns, SW16 . . .**169** H6
Hollow, The, Wdf.Grn. IG8 .**63** F4
HOLLOWAY, N7 . . . .**92** E4
Holloway Cl, West Dr.
    UB7 . . . .**120** B5
Holloway La, West Dr.
    UB7 . . . .**120** B6
Holloway Rd, E6 . . . .**116** C3
E11 . . . .**96** E3
N7 . . . .**93** F4
N19 . . . .**92** D2
Holloway St, Houns.
    TW3 . . . .**143** H3
Hollowfield Wk, Nthlt.
    UB5 . . . .**84** E6
Hollows, The, Brent. TW8
    off Kew Br Rd **125** J6
Hollow Wk, Rich. TW9
    off Kew Rd **125** H7
Hollybank Cl, Hmptn.
    TW12 . . . .**161** G5
Hollyberry La, NW3
    off Holly Wk **91** F4
Hollybrake Cl, Chis.
    BR7 . . . .**175** G7
Hollybush Cl, E11 . . . .**79** G5
Harrow HA3 . . . .**68** B1
Hollybush Gdns, E2 . . . . .**113** E3
Hollybush Hill, E11 . . . .**79** F6
Hollybush La, Hmptn.
    TW12 . . . .**161** F7
Hollybush Pl, E2
    off Bethnal Grn
    Rd **112/113** E3
Hollybush Rd, Kings.T.
    KT2 . . . .**163** H5
Holly Bush Steps, NW3
    off Heath St **91** F4
Hollybush St, E13 . . . .**115** H3
Holly Bush Vale, NW3
    off Heath St **91** F4
Hollybush Wk, SW9 . . . . .**151** H4
Holly Cl, NW10 . . . .**88** E7
Beckenham BR3 . . . . . .**190** C4
Buckhurst Hill IG9 . . . . .**64** A3
Feltham TW13 . . . .**160** E5
Wallington SM6 . . . .**200** B7

Holly Ct, Sutt. SM2
    off Worcester Rd **198** D7
Holly Cres, Beck. BR3 . . .**189** J5
Woodford Green IG8 . . .**62** D7
Hollycroft Av, NW3 . . . .**90** D3
Wembley HA9 . . . .**87** J2
Hollycroft Cl, S.Croy.
    CR2 . . . .**202** B5
West Drayton UB7 . . . .**120** D6
Hollycroft Gdns, West Dr.
    UB7 . . . .**120** D6
Hollydale Cl, Nthlt. UB5
    off Dorchester Rd **85** H4
Hollydale Dr, Brom. BR2 .**206** C3
Hollydale Rd, SE15 . . . . .**153** F1
Hollydene, SE15 . . . .**152** E1
Hollydown Way, E11 . . . . .**96** D3
Holly Dr, E4 . . . .**46** B7
Brentford TW8 . . . .**124** D6
Holly Fm Rd, Sthl. UB2 . .**122** E5
Hollyfield Av, N11 . . . .**57** J5
Hollyfield Rd, Surb. KT5 .**181** J7
Holly Gdns, West Dr.
    UB7 . . . .**120** C2
Holly Gro, NW9 . . . .**70** C7
SE15 . . . .**152** C2
Pinner HA5 . . . .**67** E1
Holly Hedge Ter, SE13 . .**154** D5
Holly Hill, N21 . . . .**43** F6
NW3 . . . .**91** F4
Holly Hill Rd, Belv. DA17 .**139** H5
Erith DA8 . . . .**139** H5
Holly Lo Gdns, N6 . . . .**92** A2
Hollymead, Cars. SM5 . .**199** J3
Holly Ms, SW10 . . . .**30** D4
Holly Mt, NW3
    off Holly Bush Hill **91** F4
Hollymount Cl, SE10 . . . .**154** C1
Holly Pk, N3 . . . .**72** C3
N4 . . . .**75** F7
Holly Pk Est, N4
    off Blythwood Rd **75** F7
Holly Pk Gdns, N3 . . . .**72** D3
Holly Pk Rd, N11 . . . .**58** A5
W7 . . . .**124** C1
Holly Pl, NW3
    off Holly Wk **91** F4
Holly Rd, E11 . . . .**79** F7
W4 off Dolman Rd **126** D4
Hampton (Hmptn.H.)
    TW12 . . . .**161** J6
Hounslow TW3 . . . .**143** H4
Twickenham TW1 . . . . .**162** D1
Holly St, E8 . . . .**94** C6
Holly Ter, N6
    off Highgate W Hill . . .**92** A1
N20 off Swan La **57** F2
Hollytree Cl, SW19 . . . . . .**166** A1
Holly Vw Cl, NW4 . . . .**71** G6
Holly Village, N6
    off Swains La **92** B2
Holly Wk, NW3 . . . .**91** F4
Enfield EN2 . . . .**43** J3
Richmond TW9 . . . .**145** H2
Holly Way, Mitch. CR4 . .**186** D4
Hollywood Gdns, Hayes
    UB4 . . . .**102** B6
Hollywood Ms, SW10 . . . .**30** C5
Hollywood Rd, E4 . . . .**61** H5
SW10 . . . .**30** C4
Hollywood Way, Wdf.Grn.
    IG8 . . . .**62** D7
Holman Rd, SW11 . . . . . .**149** G2
Epsom KT19 . . . .**196** C5
Holmbridge Gdns, Enf.
    EN3 . . . .**45** G4
Holmbrook Dr, NW4 . . . . .**72** A5
Holmbury Cl, SW17 . . . . .**167** J3
SW19 off Cavendish
    Rd **167** H7
Holmbury Gdns, Hayes UB3
    off Church Rd **121** J1
Holmbury Gro, Croy.
    CR0 . . . .**203** J7
Holmbury Pk, Brom.
    BR1 . . . .**174** B7
Holmbury Vw, E5 . . . .**95** E1
Holmbush Rd, SW15 . . . .**148** B6
Holmcote Gdns, N5 . . . . . .**93** J5
Holmcroft Way, Brom.
    BR2 . . . .**192** C6
Holmdale Gdns, NW4 . . . .**72** A5
Holmdale Rd, NW6 . . . .**90** D5
Chislehurst BR7 . . . . . .**175** F5
Holmdale Ter, N15 . . . .**76** B7
Holmdene Av, NW7 . . . . . .**55** G6
SE24 . . . .**151** J5
Harrow HA2 . . . .**67** H3
Holmdene Cl, Beck. BR3 .**190** C2
Holmead Rd, SW6 . . . . . .**129** E7

Holmebury Cl, Bushey
    (Bushey Hth.) WD23 . . .**52** B2
Holmefield Ct, NW3 . . . . . .**91** H6
Holme Lacey Rd, SE12 . .**155** F6
Holme Rd, E6 . . . .**116** B1
Holmes Av, E17 . . . .**77** J3
NW7 . . . .**56** B5
Holmesdale Av, SW14 . .**146** B3
Holmesdale Cl, SE25 . . .**188** C3
Holmesdale Rd, N6 . . . . . .**74** B7
SE25 . . . .**188** A5
Bexleyheath DA7 . . . . .**158** D2
Croydon CR0 . . . .**188** A5
Richmond TW9 . . . .**145** J1
Teddington TW11 . . . . .**163** F6
Holmesley Rd, SE23 . . . .**153** H6
Holmes Pl, SW10 . . . .**30** D5
Holmes Rd, NW5 . . . .**92** B5
SW19 . . . .**167** F7
Twickenham TW1 . . . . .**162** C2
Holmes Ter, SE1 . . . .**27** E3
Holme Way, Stan. HA7 . . .**52** C6
Holmewood Gdns, SW2 .**151** F7
Holmewood Rd, SE25 . . .**188** B3
SW2 . . . .**151** E7
Holmfield Av, NW4 . . . .**72** A5
Holmhurst Rd, Belv.
    DA17 . . . .**139** H5
Holmleigh Rd, N16 . . . .**94** B1
Holmleigh Rd Est, N16
    off Holmleigh Rd **94** C1
Holm Oak Cl, SW15
    off West Hill **148** C6
Holm Oak Ms, SW4
    off King's Av **150/151** E5
Holmshaw Cl, SE26 . . . . .**171** H4
Holmside Ri, Wat. WD19 . .**50** B3
Holmside Rd, SW12 . . . . .**150** A6
Holmsley Cl, N.Mal. KT3 .**183** F6
Holmsley Ho,
    SW15 off Tangley Gro . .**147** F7
Holms St, E2 . . . .**13** H1
Holmstall Av, Edg. HA8 . .**70** C3
Holm Wk, SE3
    off Blackheath Pk **155** G2
Holmwood Cl, Har. HA2 . .**67** J3
Northolt UB5 . . . .**85** H6
Sutton SM2 . . . .**198** A7
Holmwood Gdns, N3 . . . .**72** D2
Wallington SM6 . . . . . .**200** B6
Holmwood Gro, NW7 . . . .**54** D5
Holmwood Rd, Chess.
    KT9 . . . .**195** G5
Ilford IG3 . . . .**99** H2
Holmwood Vil, SE7
    off Woolwich Rd **135** G5
Holne Chase, N2 . . . .**73** F6
Morden SM4 . . . .**184** C6
Holness Rd, E15 . . . .**97** F6
Holroyd Rd, SW15 . . . . . .**147** J4
Holstein Way, Erith
    DA18 . . . .**138** E3
Holstock Rd, Ilf. IG1 . . . . . .**99** F3
Holsworth Cl, Har. HA2 . . .**67** J5
Holsworthy Sq, WC1 . . . . .**10** D6
Holsworthy Way, Chess.
    KT9 . . . .**195** F5
Holt, The, Ilf. IG6 . . . .**65** F6
Wallington SM6 . . . . . .**200** C4
Holt Cl, N10 . . . .**74** A4
SE28 . . . .**118** B7
Chigwell IG7 . . . .**65** J5
Holt Ct, E15
    off Clays La **96** C5
Holton St, E1 . . . .**113** G4
Holt Rd, E16 . . . .**136** B1
Wembley HA0 . . . .**87** E3
Holt Way, Chig. IG7 . . . . . .**65** J5
Holtwhite Av, Enf. EN2 . . .**43** J2
Holtwhites Hill, Enf. EN2 .**43** H1
Holwell Pl, Pnr. HA5 . . . . . .**66** E4
Holwood Pk Av, Orp.
    BR6 . . . .**206** C4
Holwood Pl, SW4 . . . .**150** D4
Holybourne Av, SW15 . . .**147** G7
Holyhead Cl, E3 . . . .**114** A3
E6 off Valiant Way **116** C5
Holyoake Ct, SE16
    off Bryan Rd **133** J2
Holyoake Wk, N2 . . . .**73** F3
W5 . . . .**105** F4
Holyoak Rd, SE11 . . . .**35** G1
Holyport Rd, SW6 . . . . . .**127** J7
Holyrood Av, Har. HA2 . . .**85** E4
Holyrood Gdns, Edg.
    HA8 . . . .**70** B3
Holyrood Ms, E16
    off Wesley Av **135** G2
Holyrood Rd, Barn. EN5 . .**41** F6
Holyrood St, SE1 . . . .**28** D2

Holywell Cl, SE3 . . . . .135 G6
SE16 off Masters
Dr 132/133 E5
Holywell La, EC2 . . . . .12 E5
Holywell Row, EC2 . . . . . . .12 D6
Home Cl, Cars. SM5 . . . . . .199 J2
Northolt UB5 . . . . .103 F3
Home Ct, Felt. TW13 . . . . .160 A1
Homecroft Gdns, Loug.
IG10 . . . . .48 E4
Homecroft Rd, N22 . . . . .75 J1
SE26 . . . . .171 F5
Home Fm Cl, T.Ditt. KT7 .160 C7
Homefarm Rd, W7 . . . . . .104 B6
Homefield Av, Ilf. IG2 . . . .81 H5
Homefield Cl, NW10 . . . . . .88 C5
Hayes UB4 . . . . .102 C4
Homefield Gdns, N2 . . . . .73 G3
Mitcham CR4 . . . . .185 F2
Homefield Ms, Beck.
BR3 . . . . .190 A1
Homefield Pk, Sutt.
SM1 . . . . .198 E6
Homefield Rd, SW19 . . . .166 A6
W4 . . . . .127 F4
Bromley BR1 . . . . .191 J1
Edgware HA8 . . . . .54 D6
Walton-on-Thames
KT12 . . . . .179 J2
Wembley HA0 . . . . .86 D4
Homefield St, N1 . . . . .12 D2
Home Gdns, Dag. RM10 .101 J3
Homelands Dr, SE19 . . . .170 B7
Home Lea, Orp. BR6 . . . . .207 J5
Homeleigh Rd, SE15 . . . .153 G5
Homemead, SW12 . . . . . .168 C2
Home Mead, Stan. HA7 . .69 F1
Homemead Rd, Brom.
BR2 . . . . .192 C5
Croydon CR0 . . . . .186 C6
★ Home Office, SW1 . . .25 H4
Home Pk Rd, SW19 . . . . . .166 D3
Home Pk Wk, Kings.T.
KT1 . . . . .181 G4
Homer Cl, Bexh. DA7 . . . .159 J1
Homer Dr, E14 . . . . .134 A4
Home Rd, SW11 . . . . .149 H2
Homer Rd, E9 . . . . .95 H6
Croydon CR0 . . . . .189 G6
Homer Row, W1 . . . . .15 H2
Homersham Rd, Kings.T.
KT1 . . . . .182 A2
Homer St, W1 . . . . .15 H2
HOMERTON, E9 . . . . .95 H5
Homerton Gro, E9 . . . . . . .95 G5
Homerton High St, E9 . .95 H5
Homerton Rd, E9 . . . . .95 H5
Homerton Row, E9 . . . . . . .95 F5
Homerton Ter, E9
off Morning La 95 F6
Homesdale Cl, E11 . . . . . . .79 G5
Homesdale Rd, Brom. BR1,
BR2 . . . . .191 J4
Orpington BR5 . . . . . . .193 H7
Homesfield, NW11 . . . . . . .72 D5
Homestall Rd, SE22 . . . . .153 F5
Homestead, The, N11 . . . .58 B4
Homestead Gdns, Esher
(Clay.) KT10 . . . . .194 B5
Homestead Paddock, N14 .42 B5
Homestead Pk, NW2 . . . . .89 F3
Homestead Rd, SW6 . . . .128 C7
Dagenham RM8 . . . . . .101 F2
Homewillow Cl, N21 . . . . . .43 H6
Homewood Cl, Hmptn. TW12
off Fearnley Cres 161 F6
Homewood Cres, Chis.
BR7 . . . . .175 H6
Honduras St, EC1 . . . . . . .11 J5
Honeybourne Rd, NW6 . . . .90 E5
Honeybourne Way, Orp.
BR5 . . . . .207 G1
Honeybrook Rd, SW12 .150 C7
Honey Cl, Dag. RM10 . . .101 H6
Honeycroft, Loug. IG10 . .48 D4
Honeyden Rd, Sid. DA14 .177 E6
Honey La, EC2 . . . . .20 A4
Honeyman Cl, NW6 . . . . . .90 A7
Honeypot Cl, NW9 . . . . . . .69 J4
Honeypot La, NW9 . . . . . . .69 J3
Stanmore HA7 . . . . .69 J3
Honeysett Rd, N17
off Reform Row 76 C2
Honeysuckle Cl, Sthl.
UB1 . . . . .102 E7
Honeysuckle Gdns, Croy. CR0
off Primrose La 203 G1
Honeywell Rd, SW11 . . . .149 J6
Honeywood Rd, NW10 . . .107 F2
Isleworth TW7 . . . . . . .144 D4

Honeywood Wk, Cars.
SM5 . . . . .199 J4
Honister Cl, Stan. HA7 . . . .69 E1
Honister Gdns, Stan. HA7 .53 E7
Honister Pl, Stan. HA7 . . . .69 E1
Honiton Gdns, NW7
off Bittacy Hill 56 B7
Honiton Rd, NW6 . . . . . . .108 C2
Welling DA16 . . . . .157 J2
Honley Rd, SE6 . . . . .154 B7
Honnor Gdns, Islw. TW7 .144 A2
HONOR OAK, SE23 . . . . . .153 F6
HONOR OAK PARK, SE4 .153 H6
Honor Oak Pk, SE23 . . . .153 F6
Honor Oak Ri, SE23 . . . . .153 F6
Honor Oak Rd, SE23 . . . .171 F1
Hood Av, N14 . . . . .42 B6
SW14 . . . . .146 C5
Hood Cl, Croy. CR0
off Parson's Mead 201 H1
Hoodcote Gdns, N21 . . . . .43 H7
Hood Ct, EC4 . . . . .19 F4
Hood Rd, SW20 . . . . .165 F7
Hood Wk, Rom. RM7 . . . . .83 H1
HOOK, Chess. 195 H4
Hook, The, Barn. EN5 . . . .41 G6
Hookers Rd, E17 . . . . .77 G3
Hook Fm Rd, Brom. BR2 .192 A5
Hooking Grn, Har. HA2 . . .67 H5
Hook La, Well. DA16 . . . . .157 J5
Hook Ri N, Surb. KT6 . . . .196 A3
Hook Ri S, Surb. KT6 . . . .196 A3
Hook Ri S Ind Pk, Surb.
KT6 . . . . .196 A3
Hook Rd, Chess. KT9 . . . .195 G5
Epsom KT19 . . . . .196 C7
Surbiton KT6 . . . . .195 H3
Hooks Cl, SE15
off Woods Rd . . .152/153 E1
Hooks Hall Dr, Dag.
RM10 . . . . .101 J3
Hookstone Way, Wdf.Grn.
IG8 . . . . .64 A7
Hooks Way, SE22
off Dulwich Common .170 D1
Hook Wk, Edg. HA8 . . . . . .54 C6
Hooper Rd, E16 . . . . .115 G6
Hooper's Ct, SW3 . . . . . . .23 J4
Hooper Sq, E1
off Hooper St 112 D7
Hooper St, E1 . . . . .21 H5
Hoop La, NW11 . . . . .72 C7
Hope Cl, N1
off Wallace Rd 93 J6
SE12 . . . . .173 H3
Brentford TW8
off Burford Rd 125 H5
Romford (Chad.Hth.)
RM6 . . . . .82 C4
Sutton SM1 . . . . .199 F5
Woodford Green IG8
off West Gro 63 J6
Hopedale Rd, SE7 . . . . . .135 H6
Hopefield Av, NW6 . . . . . .108 B2
Hope Pk, Brom. BR1 . . . .173 F7
Hopes Cl, Houns. TW5
off Old Cote Dr 123 G6
Hope St, SW11 . . . . .149 G3
Hopetown St, E1 . . . . .21 G2
Hopewell St, SE5 . . . . . . .132 A7
Hopewell Yd, SE5
off Hopewell St 132 A7
Hope Wf, SE16
off St. Marychurch St .133 F2
Hop Gdns, WC2 . . . . .18 A6
Hopgood St, W12
off Macfarlane Rd 127 J1
Hopkins Cl, N10 . . . . .58 A7
Hopkins Ms, E15
off West Rd 115 F1
Hopkinsons Pl, NW1
off Fitzroy Rd 110 A1
Hopkins St, W1 . . . . .17 G4
Hoppers Rd, N13 . . . . .59 G2
N21 . . . . .59 G2
Hoppett Rd, E4 . . . . .62 E3
Hopping La, N1
off St. Mary's Gro 93 H6
Hoppingwood Av, N.Mal.
KT3 . . . . .183 E3
Hop St, SE10 . . . . .135 F4
Hopton Gdns, SE1 . . . . . . .27 H1
New Malden KT3 . . . . .183 G6
Hopton Rd, SW16 . . . . . .168 E5
Hopton St, SE1 . . . . .27 H1
Hopwood Cl, SW17 . . . . . .167 F3
Hopwood Rd, SE17 . . . . . .36 C5
Hopwood Wk, E8
off Wilman Gro 94 D7
Horace Av, Rom. RM7 . . .101 J1

Horace Rd, E7 . . . . .97 H4
Ilford IG6 . . . . .81 F3
Kingston upon Thames
KT1 . . . . .181 J3
Horatio Cl, SE16
off Rotherhithe St . . .133 F1
Horatio Pl, E14
off Cold Harbour 134 C2
SW19 off Kingston Rd .166 D7
Horatio St, E2 . . . . .13 H2
Horatius Way, Croy. CR0 .201 F5
Horbury Cres, W11 . . . . . .108 D7
Horbury Ms, W11
off Ladbroke Rd 108 C7
Horder Rd, SW6 . . . . .148 B1
Hordle Prom E, SE15 . . . .37 G7
Hordle Prom N, SE15 . . . .37 E7
Hordle Prom S, SE15 . . . .37 E7
Hordle Prom W, SE15 . . . .37 E7
Horizon Way, SE7 . . . . . .135 H4
Horle Wk, SE5
off Lilford Rd 151 H2
Horley Cl, Bexh. DA6 . . . .159 G5
Horley Rd, SE9 . . . . .174 B4
Hormead Rd, W9 . . . . . . .108 C4
Hornbeam Cl, NW7 . . . . . .55 F3
SE11 . . . . .34 E1
Borehamwood WD6 . . .38 A1
Buckhurst Hill IG9
off Hornbeam Rd 64 A3
Ilford IG1 . . . . .99 G5
Northolt UB5 . . . . .85 F5
Hornbeam Cres, Brent.
TW8 . . . . .125 E7
Hornbeam Gro, E4 . . . . . .63 E3
Hornbeam La, E4 . . . . . . .47 E5
Bexleyheath DA7 . . . . .159 J2
Hornbeam Rd, Buck.H.
IG9 . . . . .64 A3
Hayes UB4 . . . . .102 C5
Hornbeams Ri, N11 . . . . . .58 A6
Hornbeam Ter, Cars.
SM5 . . . . .199 H1
Hornbeam Wk, Rich.
TW10 . . . . .163 J3
Hornbeam Way, Brom.
BR2 . . . . .192 D6
Hornblower Cl, SE16
off Greenland Quay . .133 H4
Hornbuckle Cl, Har. HA2 .86 A2
Hornby Cl, NW3 . . . . .91 G7
Horncastle Cl, SE12 . . . . .155 G7
Horncastle Rd, SE12 . . . .155 G7
Hornchurch Cl, Kings.T.
KT2 . . . . .163 G4
Horndean Cl, SW15
off Bessborough Rd . .165 G1
Horndon Cl, Rom. RM5 . . .83 J1
Horndon Grn, Rom. RM5 .83 J1
Horndon Rd, Rom. RM5 . .83 J1
Horne Way, SW15 . . . . . . .147 J2
Hornfair Rd, SE7 . . . . .135 J6
Horniman Dr, SE23 . . . . . .171 E1
★ Horniman Mus, SE23 .170 E1
Horning Cl, SE9 . . . . .174 B4
Horn La, SE10 . . . . .135 G4
W3 . . . . .106 C7
Woodford Green IG8 . .63 G6
Horn Link Way, SE10 . . . .135 G4
Horn Pk Cl, SE12 . . . . . . .155 H5
Horn Pk La, SE12 . . . . . . .155 H5
Horns End Pl, Pnr. HA5 . .66 C4
HORNSEY, N8 . . . . .75 F3
Hornsey La, N6 . . . . .92 B1
N19 . . . . .92 C1
Hornsey La Est, N19
off Hornsey La 74 D7
Hornsey La Gdns, N6 . . . .74 C7
Hornsey Pk Rd, N8 . . . . . .75 F3
Hornsey Ri, N19 . . . . .74 D7
Hornsey Ri Gdns, N19 . . .74 D7
Hornsey Rd, N7 . . . . .93 E2
N19 . . . . .93 E2
Hornsey St, N7 . . . . .93 F5
Hornshay St, SE15 . . . . . .133 F6
Horns Rd, Ilf. IG2, IG6 . . .81 F5
Hornton Pl, W8 . . . . .22 A4
Hornton St, W8 . . . . .128 D2
Horsa Rd, E7 . . . . .97 J6
SE12 . . . . .155 J7
Erith DA8 . . . . .139 J7
Horse & Dolphin Yd, W1 .17 J5
Horsebridge Cl, Dag.
RM9 . . . . .119 E1
Horsecroft Rd, Edg. HA8 . .54 D7
Horse Fair, Kings.T. KT1 .181 G2
Horseferry Pl, SE10 . . . . .134 C6
Horseferry Rd, E14 . . . . . .113 H7
SW1 . . . . .25 H6

Horse Guards Av, SW1 . . .26 A2
★ Horse Guards Par,
SW1 . . . . .25 J2
Horse Guards Rd, SW1 . . .25 J2
Horse Leaze, E6 . . . . .116 D6
Horsell Rd, N5 . . . . .93 G5
Horselydown La, SE1 . . . .29 F3
Horselydown Old Stairs,
SE1 . . . . .29 F2
Horsemongers Ms, SE1 . .28 A4
Horsenden Av, Grnf. UB6 .86 B5
Horsenden Cres, Grnf.
UB6 . . . . .86 C5
Horsenden La N, Grnf.
UB6 . . . . .86 C6
Horsenden La S, Grnf.
UB6 . . . . .104 D1
Horse Ride, SW1 . . . . .25 H2
Horse Rd, E7
off Centre Rd 97 H3
Horseshoe Cl, E14 . . . . . .134 C5
NW2 . . . . .89 H2
Horse Shoe Cres, Nthlt.
UB5 . . . . .103 G2
Horse Shoe Grn, Sutt. SM1
off Aultone Way . . .198/199 E2
Horseshoe La, N20 . . . . . .56 A1
Enfield EN2
off Chase Side 43 J3
Horse Yd, N1
off Essex Rd 111 H1
Horsfeld Gdns, SE9 . . . . .156 B5
Horsfeld Rd, SE9 . . . . . . .156 A5
Horsford Rd, SW2 . . . . . .151 F5
Horsham Av, N12 . . . . .57 H5
Horsham Rd, Bexh. DA6 .159 G5
Feltham TW14 . . . . . . .141 F6
Horsley Dr, Croy.
(New Adgtn.) CR0 . . . .204 C7
Kingston upon Thames
KT2 . . . . .163 G5
Horsley Rd, E4 . . . . .62 C2
Bromley BR1
off Palace Rd 191 H1
Horsley St, SE17 . . . . .36 B5
Horsmonden Cl, Orp.
BR6 . . . . .193 H7
Horsmonden Rd, SE4 . . . .153 J5
Hortensia Rd, SW10 . . . . . .30 C7
Horticultural Pl, W4
off Heathfield Ter 126 D5
Horton Av, NW2 . . . . .90 B4
Horton Br Rd, West Dr.
UB7 . . . . .120 C1
Horton Cl, West Dr. UB7 .120 C1
Horton Ind Pk, West Dr.
UB7 . . . . .120 C1
Horton Rd, E8 . . . . .94 E6
West Drayton UB7 . . . .120 D1
Horton St, SE13 . . . . .154 B3
Horton Way, Croy. CR0 . .189 G5
Hortus Rd, E4 . . . . .62 C2
Southall UB2 . . . . .123 F2
Hosack Rd, SW17 . . . . . . .167 J2
Hoser Av, SE12 . . . . .173 G2
Hosier La, EC1 . . . . .19 G2
Hoskins Cl, E16 . . . . .115 J6
Hayes UB3
off Cranford Dr 121 J5
Hoskins St, SE10 . . . . . . .134 D5
Hospital Br Rd, Twick.
TW2 . . . . .143 H7
Hospital Rd, E9
off Homerton Row 95 G5
Hounslow TW3 . . . . . . .143 G3
Hotham Cl, W.Mol. KT8
off Garrick Gdns 179 G3
Hotham Rd, SW15 . . . . . .147 J3
SW19 . . . . .167 F7
Hotham Rd Ms, SW19
off Haydons Rd 167 F7
Hotham St, E15 . . . . .114 E1
Hothfield Pl, SE16
off Lower Rd 133 F3
Hotspur Rd, Nthlt. UB5 . .103 G2
Hotspur St, SE11 . . . . .34 E3
Houblon Rd, Rich. TW10 .145 H5
Houghton Cl, E8
off Buttermere Wk . . .94 C6
Hampton TW12 . . . . . .161 E6
Houghton Rd, N15
off West Grn Rd 76 C5
Houghton St, WC2 . . . . . . .18 D4
Houlder Cres, Croy. CR0 .201 H6
Houndsden Rd, N21 . . . . . .43 F6
Houndsditch, EC3 . . . . . . .20 E3
Houndsfield Rd, N9 . . . . . .44 E7
HOUNSLOW 143 F4
Hounslow Av, Houns.
TW3 . . . . .143 H5

Hounslow Business Pk,
Houns. TW3 . . . . **143** G4
Hounslow Gdns, Houns.
TW3 . . . . **143** H5
★ Hounslow Heath, Houns.
TW4 . . . . **142** E6
Hounslow Rd, Felt. (Feltham)
TW14 . . . . **160** B1
Feltham (Han.) TW13 . . **160** B4
Twickenham TW2 . . . . . **143** J6
HOUNSLOW WEST,
Houns. **142** D3
Houseman Way, SE5
off Hopewell St **132** A7
★ Houses of Parliament,
SW1 . . . .**26** B4
Houston Pl, Esher KT10
off Lime Tree Av **194** B1
Houston Rd, SE23 . . . . . **171** H2
Surbiton KT6 . . . . **181** E6
Hove Av, E17 . . . .**77** J5
Hoveden Rd, NW2 . . . .**90** B5
Hove Gdns, Sutt. SM1 . . **199** E1
Hoveton Rd, SE28 . . . . . . **118** C6
Howard Av, Bex. DA5 . . **176** C1
Howard Cl, N11 . . . .**58** A2
NW2 . . . .**90** B4
W3 . . . .**106** B6
Hampton TW12 . . . . . . **161** J6
Loughton IG10 . . . .**48** B6
Howard Dr, Borwd. WD6 . .**38** D4
Howard Ms, N5
off Hamilton Pk **93** H4
Howard Pl, SW1 . . . .**25** F6
Howard Rd, E6 . . . . **116** C2
E11 . . . .**97** E3
E17 . . . .**78** A3
N15 . . . .**76** B6
N16 . . . .**94** A4
NW2 . . . .**90** A4
SE20 . . . . **189** F1
SE25 . . . . **188** D4
Barking IG11 . . . . **117** G1
Bromley BR1 . . . . **173** G7
Ilford IG1 . . . .**99** E4
Isleworth TW7 . . . . **144** C3
New Malden KT3 . . . . . **183** E3
Southall UB1 . . . . **103** H6
Surbiton KT5 . . . . **181** J6
Howards Cl, Pnr. HA5 . . . .**66** B2
Howards Crest Cl, Beck.
BR3 . . . . **190** C2
Howards La, SW15 . . . . . **147** H4
Howards Rd, E13 . . . . . . **115** G3
Howard St, T.Ditt. KT7 . . **181** E7
Howard Wk, N2 . . . .**73** F4
Howard Way, Barn. EN5 . .**40** A5
Howarth Ct, E15
off Clays La **96** C5
Howarth Rd, SE2 . . . . . . **138** A5
Howberry Cl, Edg. HA8 . . .**53** G6
Howberry Rd, Edg. HA8 . .**53** G6
Stanmore HA7 . . . .**53** G6
Thornton Heath CR7 . . **188** A1
Howbury Rd, SE15 . . . . . **153** F3
Howcroft Cres, N3 . . . .**56** D7
Howcroft La, Grnf. UB6
off Cowgate Rd **104** A3
Howden Cl, SE28 . . . . . . **118** D7
Howden Rd, SE25 . . . . . . **188** C2
Howden St, SE15 . . . . . . **152** D3
Howe Cl, Rom. RM7 . . . . . .**83** G1
Howell Cl, Rom. RM6 . . . . .**82** D5
Howell Wk, SE1 . . . .**35** H2
Howes Cl, N3 . . . .**72** D3
Howfield Pl, N17 . . . .**76** C3
Howgate Rd, SW14 . . . . . **146** D3
Howick Pl, SW1 . . . .**25** G6
Howie St, SW11 . . . . **129** H7
Howitt Cl, N16
off Allen Rd **94** B4
NW3 off Howitt Rd **91** H6
Howitt Rd, NW3 . . . .**91** H6
Howland Est, SE16 . . . . . **133** F3
Howland Ms E, W1 . . . .**17** G1
Howland St, W1 . . . .**17** F1
Howland Way, SE16 . . . . . **133** H2
Howletts Rd, SE24 . . . . . **151** J6
Howley Pl, W2 . . . .**14** D1
Howley Rd, Croy. CR0 . . **201** H3
Howsman Rd, SW13 . . . . **127** G6
Howson Rd, SE4 . . . . **153** H4
Howson Ter, Rich. TW10 **145** H6
Hows St, E2 . . . .**13** F1
Howton Pl, Bushey
(Bushey Hth.) WD23 . . .**52** A1
HOXTON, N1 . . . .**12** D2
Hoxton Mkt, N1 . . . .**12** D4
Hoxton Sq, N1 . . . .**12** D4
Hoxton St, N1 . . . .**12** E4

Hoylake Gdns, Mitch.
CR4 . . . . **186** C3
Ruislip HA4 . . . .**84** B1
Watford WD19 . . . .**50** D4
Hoylake Rd, W3 . . . . **107** E6
Hoyland Cl, SE15
off Commercial
Way **132/133** E7
Hoyle Rd, SW17 . . . . **167** H5
Hoy St, E16 . . . . **115** F6
★ HQS Wellington, Master .
Mariners' Hall, WC2 . . .**19** E5
Hubbard Dr, Chess. KT9 . **195** F6
Hubbard Rd, SE27 . . . . . . **169** J4
Hubbard St, E15 . . . . **114** E1
Hubbinet Ind Est, Rom.
RM7 . . . .**83** J3
Hubert Gro, SW9 . . . . **151** E3
Hubert Rd, E6 . . . . **116** A3
Huddart St, E3 . . . . **113** J5
Huddleston Cl, E2 . . . . . . **113** F2
Huddlestone Rd, E7 . . . . . .**97** F4
NW2 . . . .**89** H6
Huddleston Rd, N7 . . . .**92** D4
Hudson Ct, E14
off Maritime Quay **134** A5
SW19 . . . . **167** E7
Hudson Gdns, Orp. BR6
off Superior Dr **207** J6
Hudson Pl, SE18 . . . . **137** F5
Hudson Rd, Bexh. DA7 . . **159** F2
Hayes UB3 . . . . **121** G6
Hudson's Pl, SW1 . . . .**33** E1
Hudson Way, NW2
off Gratton Ter **90** A3
Huggin Ct, EC4 . . . .**20** A5
Huggin Hill, EC4 . . . .**20** A5
Huggins Pl, SW2
off Roupell Rd **169** F1
Hughan Rd, E15 . . . .**96** D5
Hugh Dalton Av, SW6 . . . **128** C6
Hughenden Av, Har. HA3 . .**69** E5
Hughenden Gdns, Nthlt.
UB5 . . . . **102** C3
Hughenden Rd, Wor.Pk.
KT4 . . . . **183** G7
Hughendon Ter, E15
off Westdown Rd **96** C4
Hughes Cl, N12
off Coleridge Rd **57** F5
Hughes Rd, Hayes UB3 . **102** B7
off St. Saviours Rd **187** J7
Hugh Gaitskell Cl, SW6 . **128** C6
Hugh Ms, SW1 . . . .**32** E2
Hugh Pl, SW1 . . . .**33** H1
Hugh St, SW1 . . . .**32** E2
Hugon Rd, SW6 . . . . **148** E3
Hugo Rd, N19 . . . .**92** C4
Huguenot Pl, E1 . . . .**21** G1
SW18 . . . . **149** F5
Huguenot Sq, SE15
off Scylla Rd **152/153** E3
Hullbridge Ms, N1
off Sherborne St **112** A1
Hull Cl, SE16 . . . . **133** G2
Hull Pl, E16
off Fishguard
Way **136/137** E2
Hull St, EC1 . . . .**11** J4
Hulme Pl, SE1 . . . .**28** A4
Hulse Av, Bark. IG11 . . . . . .**99** G6
Romford RM7 . . . .**83** H1
Hulse Ter, Ilf. IG1
off Buttsbury Rd **99** F5
Humber Cl, West Dr.
UB7 . . . . **120** A1
Humber Dr, W10 . . . . **108** A4
Humber Rd, NW2 . . . .**89** H2
SE3 . . . . **135** F6
Humberstone Rd, E13 . . **115** J3
Humberton Cl, E9
off Marsh Hill **95** H5
Humbolt Rd, W6 . . . . **128** B6
Humes Av, W7 . . . . **124** B3
Hume Ter, E16
off Prince Regent La . . **115** J6
Hume Way, Ruis. HA4 . . . . .**66** A6
Humphrey Cl, Ilf. IG5 . . . . .**80** C1
Humphrey St, SE1 . . . .**37** F3
Humphries Cl, Dag. RM9 **101** F4
Hundred Acre, NW9 . . . . . .**71** F2
Hungerdown, E4 . . . .**62** C1
Hungerford La, WC2 . . . . . .**26** A1
Hungerford Rd, N7 . . . .**92** D5
Hungerford St, E1
off Commercial
Rd **112/113** E6

Hunsdon Cl, Dag. RM9 . .**101** E6
Hunsdon Rd, SE14 . . . . **133** G6
Hunslett St, E2
off Royston St **113** F2
Hunston Rd, Mord. SM4 **198** E1
Hunter Cl, SE1 . . . .**28** C6
SW12 off Balham Pk
Rd **168** A1
Borehamwood WD6 . . . .**38** C5
Huntercombe Gdns, Wat.
WD19 . . . .**50** C5
Hunter Ho, Felt. TW13 . . **160** A1
Hunter Rd, SW20 . . . . . . **183** J1
Ilford IG1 . . . .**99** E5
Thornton Heath CR7 . . **188** A3
Hunters, The, Beck. BR3 **190** C1
Hunters Ct, Rich. TW9
off Friars La **145** G5
Hunters Gro, Har. HA3 . . . .**69** F4
Hayes UB3 . . . . **122** A1
Orpington BR6 . . . . **207** E4
Hunters Hall Rd, Dag.
RM10 . . . . **101** G4
Hunters Hill, Ruis. HA4 . . . .**84** C3
Hunters Meadow, SE19
off Dulwich Wd Av **170** B4
Hunters Rd, Chess. KT9 . **195** H3
Hunters Sq, Dag. RM10 . **101** G4
Hunter St, WC1 . . . .**10** B5
Hunters Way, Croy. CR0
off Brownlow Rd **202** B4
Enfield EN2 . . . .**43** G1
Hunter Wk, E13 . . . . **115** G2
Borehamwood WD6
off Hunter Cl **38** C5
Huntingdon Cl, Mitch.
CR4 . . . . **187** E3
Huntingdon Gdns, W4 . . **126** C7
Worcester Park KT4 . . . **197** J3
Huntingdon Rd, N2 . . . .**73** H3
N9 . . . .**61** F1
Huntingdon St, E16 . . . . . **115** F6
N1 . . . .**93** F7
Huntingfield, Croy. CR0 .**203** J7
Huntingfield Rd, SW15 . . **147** G4
Hunting Gate Cl, Enf.
EN2 . . . .**43** G3
Hunting Gate Dr, Chess.
KT9 . . . . **195** H7
Hunting Gate Ms, Sutt.
SM1 . . . . **199** E3
Twickenham TW2
off Colne Rd **162** B1
Huntings Rd, Dag. RM10 **101** G6
Huntley Cl, Stai. (Stanw.) TW19
off Cambria Gdns **140** B7
Huntley Dr, N3 . . . .**56** D6
Huntley St, WC1 . . . .**9** G6
Huntley Way, SW20 . . . . **183** G2
Huntly Rd, SE25 . . . . **188** B4
Hunton St, E1 . . . .**13** H6
Hunt Rd, Sthl. UB2 . . . . . **123** G3
Hunt's Cl, SE3 . . . . **155** G2
Hunt's Ct, WC2 . . . .**17** J6
Hunts La, E15 . . . . **114** C2
Huntsmans Cl, Felt.
TW13 . . . . **160** B4
Huntsman St, SE17 . . . . . .**36** C2
Hunts Mead, Enf. EN3 . . . .**45** G3
Hunts Mead Cl, Chis.
BR7 . . . . **174** C7
Huntsmoor Rd, Epsom
KT19 . . . . **196** D5
Huntspill St, SW17 . . . . . **167** F3
Hunts Slip Rd, SE21 . . . . **170** B3
Huntsworth Ms, NW1 . . . . . .**7** J6
Hunt Way, SE22
off Dulwich Common . **170** D1
Hurdwick Pl, NW1
off Harrington Sq **110** C2
Hurley Cres, SE16
off Marlow Way **133** G2
Hurley Ho, SE11 . . . .**35** F2
Hurley Rd, Grnf. UB6 . . . . **103** H6
Hurlingham Business Pk,
SW6 . . . . **148** D3
Hurlingham Ct, SW6 . . . . **148** C3
Hurlingham Gdns, SW6 . **148** C3
★ Hurlingham Ho, SW6 .**148** D3
★ Hurlingham Park,
SW6 . . . . **148** C3
Hurlingham Retail Pk, SW6
off Carnwath Rd **148/149** E3
Hurlingham Rd, SW6 . . . **148** C2
Bexleyheath DA7 . . . . . **139** F7
Hurlingham Sq, SW6 . . . **148** D3
Hurlock St, N5 . . . .**93** H3
Hurlstone Rd, SE25 . . . . . **188** A5
Hurn Ct Rd, Houns. TW4
off Renfrew Rd **142** D2

Huron, Orp. BR6
off Winnipeg Dr **207** J6
Huron Rd, SW17 . . . . . . **168** A2
Hurren Cl, SE3 . . . . **154** E3
Hurricane Rd, Wall. SM6 **201** F7
Hurry Cl, E15 . . . .**97** E7
Hursley Rd, Chig. IG7
off Tufter Rd **65** J5
Hurst Av, E4 . . . .**62** A4
N6 . . . .**74** C6
Hurstbourne, Esher (Clay.)
KT10 . . . . **194** C6
Hurstbourne Gdns, Bark.
IG11 . . . .**99** H6
Hurstbourne Ho, SW15
off Tangley Gro **147** F6
Hurstbourne Rd, SE23 . . **171** H1
Hurst Cl, E4 . . . .**62** A3
NW11 . . . .**72** E6
Bromley BR2 . . . . **205** F1
Chessington KT9 . . . . . **196** A5
Northolt UB5 . . . .**85** F6
Hurstcourt Rd, Sutt.
SM1 . . . . **198** E2
Hurstdene Av, Brom.
BR2 . . . . **205** F1
Hurstdene Gdns, N15 . . . .**76** B7
Hurst Est, SE2 . . . . **138** D5
Hurstfield, Brom. BR2 . . **191** G5
Hurstfield Rd, W.Mol.
KT8 . . . . **179** G3
Hurst La, SE2 . . . . **138** D5
East Molesey KT8 . . . . **179** J4
Hurstleigh Gdns, Ilf. IG5 . .**80** C1
Hurstmead Ct, Edg. HA8 . .**54** B4
Hurst Ri, Barn. EN5 . . . .**40** D3
Hurst Rd, E17 . . . .**78** B3
N21 . . . .**59** G1
Bexley DA5 . . . . **176** D1
Buckhurst Hill IG9 . . . . .**64** A1
Croydon CR0 . . . . **202** A5
East Molesey KT8 . . . . **179** G3
Erith DA8 . . . . **139** J7
Sidcup DA15 . . . . **176** A2
Walton-on-Thames
KT12 . . . . **178** C5
West Molesey KT8 . . . **179** E3
Hurst Springs, Bex. DA5 **177** E1
Hurst St, SE24 . . . . **151** H6
Hurst Vw Rd, S.Croy.
CR2 . . . . **202** B7
Hurst Way, S.Croy. CR2 . **202** B6
Hurstway Wk, W11 . . . . . **108** A7
Hurstwood Av, E18 . . . .**79** H4
Bexley DA5 . . . . **176** E1
Hurstwood Dr, Brom.
BR1 . . . . **192** C3
Hurstwood Rd, NW11 . . . .**72** B4
Hurtwood Rd, Walt.
KT12 . . . . **179** F7
Huson Cl, NW3 . . . .**91** H7
Hussars Cl, Houns. TW4 . **142** E3
Husseywell Cres, Brom.
BR2 . . . . **205** G1
Hutchings St, E14 . . . . . . **134** A2
Hutchings Wk, NW11 . . . . .**73** E4
Hutchins Cl, E15
off Gibbins Rd **96** C7
Hutchinson Ter, Wem.
HA9 . . . .**87** G3
Hutchins Rd, SE28 . . . . . **118** A7
Hutton Cl, Grnf. UB6
off Mary Peters Dr **86** A5
Woodford Green IG8 . . . .**63** H6
Hutton Gdns, Har. HA3 . . . .**51** J7
Hutton Gro, N12 . . . .**57** E5
Hutton La, Har. HA3 . . . . . .**51** J7
Hutton Row, Edg. HA8
off Pavilion Way **54** C7
Hutton St, EC4 . . . .**19** F4
Hutton Wk, Har. HA3 . . . . . .**51** J7
Huxbear St, SE4 . . . . **153** J5
Huxley Cl, Nthlt. UB5 . . . **103** E1
Huxley Dr, Rom. RM6 . . . . .**82** B7
Huxley Gdns, NW10 . . . . **105** J3
Huxley Par, N18 . . . .**60** A5
Huxley Pl, N13 . . . .**59** H4
Huxley Rd, E10 . . . .**96** C2
N18 . . . .**60** A4
Welling DA16 . . . . **157** J3
Huxley Sayze, N18 . . . .**60** A5
Huxley St, W10 . . . . **108** B3
Hyacinth Cl, Hmptn. TW12
off Gresham Rd **161** G6
Ilford IG1 . . . .**98** E6
Hyacinth Ct, Pnr. HA5
off Tulip Ct **66** C3
Hyacinth Rd, SW15 . . . . . **165** G1
Hycliffe Gdns, Chig. IG7 . .**65** F4
HYDE, THE, NW9 . . . .**71** F4

Hyde, The, NW9 ....71 E5
Hyde Cl, E13 ....115 G2
Barnet EN5 ....40 C3
Hyde Ct, N20 ....57 G3
Hyde Cres, NW9 ....71 E5
Hyde Est Rd, NW9 ....71 F5
Hyde Fm Ms, SW12
  off Telferscot Rd 168 D1
Hydefield Cl, N21 ....60 A1
Hydefield Ct, N9 ....60 B2
Hyde Ho, NW9 ....71 E5
Hyde La, SW11
  off Battersea Br Rd ...149 H1
★ Hyde Park, W2 ....23 G1
Hyde Pk, SW7 ....23 G1
  W1 ....23 G1
  W2 ....23 G1
Hyde Pk Av, N21 ....59 J2
Hyde Pk Cor, W1 ....24 C3
Hyde Pk Cres, W2 ....15 G4
Hyde Pk Gdns, N21 ....59 J1
  W2 ....15 F5
Hyde Pk Gdns Ms, W2 ...15 F5
Hyde Pk Gate, SW7 ....22 D4
Hyde Pk Gate Ms, SW7 ..22 D4
Hyde Pk Pl, W2 ....15 H5
Hyde Pk Sq, W2 ....15 G4
Hyde Pk Sq Ms, W2 ....15 G4
Hyde Pk St, W2 ....15 G4
Hyderabad Way, E15 ....96 E7
Hyde Rd, N1 ....112 A1
  Bexleyheath DA7 ....159 F2
  Richmond TW10
  off Albert Rd 145 J3
Hydeside Gdns, N9 ....60 C2
Hydes Pl, N1
  off Compton Av 93 H7
Hyde St, SE8
  off Deptford High St ..134 A6
Hydethorpe Av, N9 ....60 C2
Hydethorpe Rd, SW12 ..168 C1
Hyde Vale, SE10 ....134 C7
Hyde Wk, Mord. SM4 ...184 D7
Hyde Way, N9 ....60 C2
  Hayes UB3 ....121 J4
Hylands Rd, E17 ....78 D2
Hylton St, SE18 ....137 J4
Hyndewood, SE23 ....171 G3
Hyndman St, SE15 ....132 E6
Hynton Rd, Dag. RM8 ...100 C2
Hyrstdene, S.Croy. CR2 ..201 H4
Hyson Rd, SE16 off Galleywall
  Rd 132/133 E4
Hythe Av, Bexh. DA7 ...139 F7
Hythe Cl, N18 ....60 D4
Hythe Path, Th.Hth. CR7 .188 A3
Hythe Rd, NW10 ....107 G4
  Thornton Heath CR7 ...188 A2
Hythe Rd Ind Est, NW10 .107 G3
Hyver Hill, NW7 ....38 D6

I

Ian Sq, Enf. EN3
  off Lansbury Rd 45 G1
Ibbetson Path, Loug.
  IG10 ....49 E3
Ibbotson Av, E16 ....115 F6
Ibbott St, E1
  off Mantus Rd 113 F4
Iberian Av, Wall. SM6 ...200 D4
Ibis La, W4 ....126 C1
Ibis Way, Hayes UB4
  off Cygnet Way 102 D6
Ibscott Cl, Dag. RM10 ...101 J6
Ibsley Gdns, SW15 ....165 G1
Ibsley Way, Barn. EN4 ...41 H5
Iceland Rd, E3 ....114 A1
Iceni Ct, E3
  off Roman Rd 113 J1
Ice Wf, N1
  off New Wf Rd 110 E2
Ice Wf Marina, N1
  off New Wf Rd ...110/111 E2
Ickburgh Est, E5
  off Ickburgh Rd ...94/95 E3
Ickburgh Rd, E5 ....94 E3
Ickleton Rd, SE9 ....174 B4
Icknield Dr, Ilf. IG2 ....81 E5
Ickworth Pk Rd, E17 ....77 H4
Ida Rd, N15 ....76 A5
Ida St, E14 ....114 C6
Iden Cl, Brom. BR2 ....191 E3
Idlecombe Rd, SW17 ...168 A6
Idmiston Rd, E15 ....97 F5
  SE27 ....169 J3
  Worcester Park KT4 ...183 F7
Idmiston Sq, Wor.Pk.
  KT4 ....183 F7

Idol La, EC3 ....20 D6
Idonia St, SE8 ....133 J7
Iffley Rd, W6 ....127 H3
Ifield Rd, SW10 ....30 B5
Ifor Evans Pl, E1
  off Mile End Rd 113 G4
Ightham Rd, Erith DA8 ..139 G7
Ikea Twr, NW10 ....88 D5
Ilbert St, W10 ....108 A3
Ilchester Gdns, W2 ....14 A5
Ilchester Pl, W14 ....128 C3
Ilchester Rd, Dag.
  RM8 ....100 B5
Ildersly Gro, SE21 ....170 A2
Ilderton Rd, SE15 ....133 F7
  SE16 ....133 E5
Ilex Cl, Sun. TW16
  off Oakington Dr 178 C2
Ilex Ho, N4 ....75 F7
Ilex Rd, NW10 ....89 F6
Ilex Way, SW16 ....169 G5
ILFORD 99 F3
Ilford Hill, Ilf. IG1 ....98 D3
Ilford La, Ilf. IG1 ....98 E3
Ilfracombe Gdns, Rom.
  RM6 ....82 B7
Ilfracombe Rd, Brom.
  BR1 ....173 F3
Iliffe St, SE17 ....35 H3
Iliffe Yd, SE17 ....35 H3
Ilkeston Ct, E5
  off Overbury St 95 G4
Ilkley Cl, SE19 ....170 A6
Ilkley Rd, E16 ....115 J5
  Watford WD19 ....50 D5
Illingworth Cl, Mitch.
  CR4 ....185 G3
Illingworth Way, Enf. EN1 .44 B4
Ilmington Rd, Har. HA3 ...69 G6
Ilminster Gdns, SW11 ...149 H4
Imber Cl, N14 ....42 C7
  Esher KT10
  off Ember La 194 A1
Imber Ct Trd Est, E.Mol.
  KT8 ....180 A6
Imber Gro, Esher KT10 .180 A7
Imber Pk Rd, Esher
  KT10 ....194 A1
Imber St, N1 ....112 A1
Imer Pl, T.Ditt. KT7 ....180 C7
Imperial Av, N16
  off Victorian Rd 94 C3
Imperial Cl, Har. HA2 ...67 G6
★ Imperial Coll,
  Uni of London, SW7 ..22 E5
Imperial Coll Rd, SW7 ...22 E6
Imperial Dr, Har. HA2 ...67 G7
Imperial Gdns, Mitch.
  CR4 ....186 B3
Imperial Ms, E6
  off Central Pk Rd 115 J2
Imperial Rd, N22 ....74 E1
  SW6 ....149 E1
  Feltham TW14 ....141 H7
Imperial Sq, SW6 ....149 E1
Imperial St, E3 ....114 C3
★ Imperial War Mus,
  SE1 ....27 F6
Imperial Way, Chis. BR7 .175 F3
  Croydon CR0 ....201 F6
  Harrow HA3 ....69 H6
Imprimo Pk, Loug. IG10
  off Lenthall Rd 49 G4
Imre Cl, W12
  off Ellerslie Rd 127 H1
Inca Dr, SE9 ....156 E7
Inchmery Rd, SE6 ....172 B2
Inchwood, Croy. CR0 ...204 B4
Independent Pl, E8
  off Downs Pk Rd 94 C5
Independents Rd, SE3
  off Blackheath Village .155 F3
Inderwick Rd, N8 ....75 F5
Indescon Ct, E14 ....134 B2
India Pl, WC2 ....18 C5
India St, EC3 ....21 F4
India Way, W12 ....107 H7
Indigo Ms, E14
  off Ashton St 114 C7
  N16 ....94 A3
Indus Rd, SE7 ....135 J7
Industry Ter, SW9
  off Canterbury Cres ..151 G3
Ingal Rd, E13 ....115 G4
Ingate Pl, SW8 ....150 B1
Ingatestone Rd, E12 ....97 J1
  SE25 ....188 E4
  Woodford Green IG8 ...63 G7
Ingelow Rd, SW8 ....150 B2
Ingersoll Rd, W12 ....127 H1

Ingestre Pl, W1 ....17 G4
Ingestre Rd, E7 ....97 G4
  NW5 ....92 B4
Ingham Rd, NW6 ....90 D4
Inglebert St, EC1 ....11 E3
Ingleborough St, SW9 ..151 G2
Ingleby Dr, Har. HA1 ...86 A3
Ingleby Rd, N7
  off Bryett Rd 92/93 E3
  Dagenham RM10 ....101 H6
  Ilford IG1 ....98 E1
Ingleby Way, Chis. BR7 .174 D5
Ingle Cl, Pnr. HA5 ....67 E3
Ingledew Rd, SE18 ....137 G5
Inglehurst Gdns, Ilf. IG4 .80 C5
Inglemere Rd, SE23 .....171 G3
  Mitcham CR4 ....167 J7
Inglesham Wk, E9 ....95 J6
Ingleside Cl, Beck. BR3 .172 A7
Ingleside Gro, SE3 ....135 F6
Inglethorpe St, SW6 ...148 A1
Ingleton Av, Well. DA16 .158 A5
Ingleton Rd, N18 ....60 D6
  Carshalton SM5 ....199 H7
Ingleway, N12 ....57 G6
Inglewood Cl, E14 ....134 A4
  Ilford IG6 ....65 J6
Inglewood Copse, Brom.
  BR1 ....192 B2
Inglewood Rd, NW6 ....90 D5
  Bexleyheath DA7 ....159 J4
Inglis Barracks, NW7 .....56 A5
Inglis Rd, W5 ....105 J7
  Croydon CR0 ....202 C1
Inglis St, SE5 ....151 H1
Ingram Av, NW11 ....73 F7
Ingram Cl, SE11 ....34 D1
  Stanmore HA7 ....53 F5
Ingram Rd, N2 ....73 H4
  Thornton Heath CR7 ...187 J1
Ingram Way, Grnf. UB6 .104 A1
Ingrave Ho, Dag. RM9 ...118 B1
Ingrave St, SW11 ....149 G3
Ingress St, W4 off Devonshire
  Rd 126/127 E5
Inigo Jones Rd, SE7 ...136 B7
Inigo Pl, WC2 ....18 A5
Inkerman Rd, NW5 ....92 B6
Inkerman Ter, W8
  off Allen St 128 D3
Inks Grn, E4 ....62 C5
Inman Rd, NW10 ....106 E1
  SW18 ....149 F7
Inmans Row, Wdf.Grn.
  IG8 ....63 G4
Inner Circle, NW1 ....8 A3
Inner Pk Rd, SW19 ....166 A1
Inner Ring E, Houns.
  (Hthrw.Air.) TW6 ....140 E3
Inner Ring W, Houns.
  (Hthrw.Air.) TW6 ....140 D3
Inner Temple La, EC4 ....19 E4
Innes Cl, SW20 ....184 B2
Innes Gdns, SW15 ....147 H6
Innes Yd, Croy. CR0
  off Whitgift St 201 J3
Inniskilling Rd, E13 ....115 J2
Innovation Cl, Wem.
  HA0 ....105 H1
Inskip Cl, E10 ....96 B2
Inskip Rd, Dag. RM8 ...100 D1
★ Institute of Contemporary
  Arts (ICA), SW1 ....25 J1
Institute Pl, E8
  off Amhurst Rd ...94/95 E5
Instone Cl, Wall. SM6 ...201 E7
Integer Gdns, E11
  off Forest Rd 78 D7
Interchange E Ind Est, E5
  off Theydon Rd 95 F1
International Av, Houns.
  TW5 ....122 C5
International Trd Est, Sthl.
  UB2 ....122 B3
Inveraray Pl, SE18
  off Old Mill Rd 137 G6
Inver Cl, E5
  off Theydon Rd 95 F2
Inverclyde Gdns, Rom.
  RM6 ....82 C4
Inver Ct, W2 ....14 B4
Inveresk Gdns, Wor.Pk.
  KT4 ....197 F3
Inverforth Cl, NW3
  off North End Way 91 F2
Inverforth Rd, N11 ....58 B5
Inverine Rd, SE7 ....135 H5
Invermore Pl, SE18 ....137 F4
Inverness Av, Enf. EN1 ...44 B1
Inverness Dr, Ilf. IG6 .....65 H6
Inverness Gdns, W8 ....22 A2

Inverness Ms, E16 ....137 F1
  W2 ....14 B5
Inverness Pl, W2 ....14 B5
Inverness Rd, N18
  off Aberdeen Rd 60/61 E5
  Hounslow TW3 ....143 F4
  Southall UB2 ....123 E4
  Worcester Park KT4 ...198 A1
Inverness St, NW1 ....110 B1
Inverness Ter, W2 ....14 B5
Inverton Rd, SE15 ....153 G4
Invicta Cl, Chis. BR7 ...174 D5
Invicta Gro, Nthlt. UB5 ..103 F3
Invicta Plaza, SE1 ....27 G1
Invicta Rd, SE3 ....135 G7
Inville Rd, SE17 ....36 C4
Inwen Ct, SE8 ....133 H5
Inwood Av, Houns. TW3 .143 J3
Inwood Cl, Croy. CR0 ...203 H2
Inwood Rd, Houns. TW3 .143 H4
Inworth St, SW11 ....149 H2
Inworth Wk, N1
  off Popham St 111 J1
Iona Cl, SE6 ....154 A7
  Morden SM4 ....184 E7
Ion Sq, E2 ....13 H2
Ipswich Rd, SW17 ....168 A6
Ireland Cl, E6
  off Bradley Stone Rd .116 C5
Ireland Pl, N22
  off Whittington Rd .58/59 E7
Ireland Yd, EC4 ....19 H4
Irene Rd, SW6 ....148 D1
  Orpington BR6 ....193 J7
Ireton Cl, N10 ....58 A7
Ireton St, E3
  off Tidworth Rd 114 A4
Iris Av, Bex. DA5 ....159 E5
Iris Cl, E6 ....116 B4
  Croydon CR0 ....203 G1
  Surbiton KT6 ....181 J7
Iris Ct, Pnr. HA5 ....66 C3
Iris Cres, Bexh. DA7 ...139 F6
Iris Rd, Epsom (W.Ewell)
  KT19 ....196 B5
Iris Wk, Edg. HA8
  off Ash Cl 54 C4
Iris Way, E4 ....61 J6
Irkdale Av, Enf. EN1 ....44 C1
Iron Br Cl, NW10 ....88 E5
  Southall UB2 ....123 J1
Iron Br Rd, Uxb. UB11 ...120 D2
  West Drayton UB7 ....120 D2
Iron Mill Pl, SW18
  off Garratt La ...148/149 E6
Iron Mill Rd, SW18 ....149 E6
Ironmonger La, EC2 ....20 B4
Ironmonger Pas, EC1 ....12 A5
Ironmonger Row, EC1 ...12 A5
Ironmongers Pl, E14
  off Spindrift Av 134 A4
Ironside Cl, SE16 ....133 G2
  off Kinburn St 133 G2
Irvine Av, Har. HA3 ....68 D3
Irvine Cl, N20 ....57 H2
Irvine Way, Orp. BR6 ...193 J7
Irving Av, Nthlt. UB5 ...102 D1
Irving Gro, SW9 ....151 F2
Irving Ms, N1
  off Alwyne Rd 93 J6
Irving Rd, W14 ....128 A3
Irving St, WC2 ....17 J5
Irving Way, NW9 ....71 F5
Irwin Av, SE18 ....137 H7
Irwin Gdns, NW10 ....107 H1
Isabel Hill Cl, Hmptn. TW12
  off Upper Sunbury Rd.179 H1
Isabella Cl, N14 ....42 C7
Isabella Ct, Rich. TW10
  off Grove Rd 145 J6
Isabella Dr, Orp. BR6 ...207 F4
Isabella Rd, E9 ....95 F5
Isabella St, SE1 ....27 G2
Isabel St, SW9 ....151 F1
Isambard Ms, E14 ....134 C3
Isambard Pl, SE16
  off Rotherhithe St .133 F1
Isel Way, SE22
  off East Dulwich Gro .152 B5
Isham Rd, SW16 ....186 E2
Isis Cl, SW15 ....147 J4
Isis St, SW18 ....167 F2
Island Fm Av, W.Mol.
  KT8 ....179 F5
Island Fm Rd, W.Mol.
  KT8 ....179 F5
Island Rd, Mitch. CR4 ...167 J7
Island Row, E14 ....113 J6
Isla Rd, SE18 ....137 F6
Islay Gdns, Houns. TW4 .142 D5

Islay Wk, N1
off Douglas Rd **93** J7
Isledon Rd, N7 . . . .**93** G3
Islehurst Cl, Chis. BR7 . . .**192** D1
ISLEWORTH **144** C3
Isleworth Business Complex,
Islw. TW7
off St. John's Rd **144** C2
Isleworth Prom, Twick.
TW1 . . . .**144** E4
ISLINGTON, N1 . . . .**111** F1
Islington Grn, N1 . . . . . .**111** H1
Islington High St, N1 . . .**11** F2
Islington Pk Ms, N1
off Islington Pk St **93** G7
Islington Pk St, N1 . . . .**93** G7
Islip Gdns, Edg. HA8 . . . .**54** D7
Northolt UB5 . . . .**85** E7
Islip Manor Rd, Nthlt.
UB5 . . . .**85** E7
Islip St, NW5 . . . .**92** C5
Ismailia Rd, E7 . . . .**97** H7
★ Ismaili Cen & Zamana
Gall, SW7 . . . .**31** F1
Isom Cl, E13
off Belgrave Rd **115** J4
Ivanhoe Dr, Har. HA3 . . . .**68** D3
Ivanhoe Rd, SE5 . . . . . .**152** C3
Hounslow TW4 . . . . . .**142** D3
Ivatt Pl, W14 . . . .**128** C5
Ivatt Way, N17 . . . .**75** H3
Iveagh Av, NW10 . . . . . .**106** A2
Iveagh Cl, E9 . . . .**113** G1
NW10 . . . .**106** A2
Iveagh Ter, NW10
off Iveagh Av **106** A2
Ivedon Rd, Well. DA16 . .**158** C2
Ive Fm Cl, E10 . . . .**96** A2
Ive Fm La, E10 . . . .**96** A2
Iveley Rd, SW4 . . . .**150** C2
Ivere Dr, Barn. EN5 . . . . .**40** E6
Iverhurst Cl, Bexh. DA6 . .**158** D5
Iverna Ct, W8 . . . .**128** D3
Iverna Gdns, W8 . . . . . .**128** D3
Feltham TW14 . . . . . .**141** G5
Iverson Rd, NW6 . . . .**90** C6
Ivers Way, Croy. (New Adgtn.)
CR0 . . . .**204** B7
Ives Rd, E16 . . . .**114** E5
Ives St, SW3 . . . .**31** H1
Ivestor Ter, SE23 . . . . . .**153** F7
Ivimey St, E2 . . . .**13** J3
Ivinghoe Cl, Enf. EN1 . . . .**44** B2
Ivinghoe Rd, Dag. RM8 . .**100** B5
Ivor Gro, SE9 . . . .**175** E1
Ivor Pl, NW1 . . . .**7** J6
Ivor St, NW1 . . . .**92** C7
Ivorydown, Brom. BR1 . .**173** G4
Ivory Sq, SW11
off Gartons Way **149** F3
Ivybridge Cl, Twick.
TW1 . . . .**144** D6
Ivybridge Est, Islw.
TW7 . . . .**144** C5
Ivybridge La, WC2 . . . . . .**18** B6
Ivychurch Cl, SE20 . . . . .**171** F7
Ivychurch La, SE17 . . . . .**37** F3
Ivy Cl, Har. HA2 . . . .**85** F4
Pinner HA5 . . . .**66** C7
Sunbury-on-Thames
TW16 . . . .**178** C2
Ivy Cotts, E14
off Grove Vil **114** B7
Ivy Ct, SE16 . . . .**37** J4
Ivy Cres, W4 . . . .**126** C4
Carshalton SM5 . . . . .**199** J2
Ivyday Gro, SW16 . . . . .**169** F3
Ivydene, W.Mol. KT8 . . .**179** F5
Ivydene Cl, Sutt. SM1 . .**199** F4
Ivy Gdns, N8 . . . .**74** E6
Mitcham CR4 . . . . . .**186** D3
Ivyhouse Rd, Dag.
RM9 . . . .**100** D6
Ivy La, Houns. TW4 . . . .**143** F4
Ivymount Rd, SE27 . . . .**169** G3
Ivy Pl, Surb. KT5
off Alpha Rd **181** J6
Ivy Rd, E16
off Pacific Rd **115** G6
E17 . . . .**78** A6
N14 . . . .**42** C7
NW2 . . . .**89** J4
SE4 . . . .**153** J4
SW17
off Tooting High St . .**167** H5
Hounslow TW3 . . . . .**143** H4
Surbiton KT6 . . . . . .**196** A1
Ivy St, N1 . . . .**12** D1
Ivy Wk, Dag. RM9 . . . . .**100** E6

Ixworth Pl, SW3 . . . .**31** G3
Izane Rd, Bexh. DA6 . . . .**159** F4

J

Jacaranda Cl, N.Mal.
KT3 . . . .**182** E3
Jacaranda Gro, E8 . . . . . .**94** C7
Jackass La, Kes. BR2 . . . .**205** H6
Jack Barnett Way, N22 . . .**75** F2
Jack Clow Rd, E15 . . . . .**115** E2
Jack Cornwell St, E12 . . . .**98** D4
Jack Dash Way, E6 . . . . .**116** B4
Jack Goodchild Way, Kings.T.
KT1 off Kingston Rd .**182** B3
Jacklin Grn, Wdf.Grn. IG8 .**63** G4
Jackman Ms, NW10 . . . . .**88** E3
Jackman St, E8 . . . .**112** E1
Jackson Cl, E9 . . . .**95** F7
Jackson Ct, E11
off Brading Cres **97** H1
Jackson Rd, N7 . . . .**93** F4
Barnet EN4 . . . .**41** H6
Barking IG11 . . . .**117** G1
Bromley BR2 . . . .**206** B2
Jacksons La, N6 . . . .**74** A7
off Cross Rd **202** A1
Jackson St, SE18 . . . . . .**136** D6
Jacksons Way, Croy.
CR0 . . . .**204** A3
Jackson Way, Sthl. UB2 .**123** H2
Jack Walker Ct, N5 . . . . . .**93** H4
Jacob Ho, Erith DA18
off Kale Rd **138** D2
Jacobs Cl, Dag. RM10 . .**101** H4
Jacobs Ho, E13 . . . .**115** J3
Jacob St, SE1 . . . .**29** G3
Jacob's Well Ms, W1 . . . .**16** C3
Jacqueline Cl, Nthlt. UB5
off Canford Av **103** F1
Jade Cl, E16 . . . .**116** A6
NW2 off Marble Dr **72** A7
Dagenham RM8 . . . . .**100** C1
Jaffe Rd, Ilf. IG1 . . . .**99** F1
Jaffray Pl, SE27
off Chapel Rd **169** H4
Jaffray Rd, Brom. BR2 . .**192** A4
Jaggard Way, SW12 . . . .**149** J7
Jago Cl, SE18 . . . .**137** F6
Jago Wk, SE5 . . . .**132** A7
Jamaica Rd, SE1 . . . .**29** G4
SE16 . . . .**132** C2
Thornton Heath CR7 . .**187** H6
Jamaica St, E1 . . . .**113** F6
James Av, NW2 . . . .**89** J5
Dagenham RM8 . . . . .**101** F1
James Bedford Cl, Pnr.
HA5 . . . .**66** C2
James Boswell Cl, SW16
off Curtis Fld Rd **169** G4
James Cl, E13
off Richmond St **115** G2
NW11 off Woodlands . .**72** B6
James Collins Cl, W9
off Fermoy Rd **108** C4
James Ct, N1
off Morton Rd **93** J7
James Dudson Ct, NW10 .**88** C7
James Gdns, N22 . . . . . .**59** H7
James Hammett Ho, E2 . .**13** G2
James Joyce Wk, SE24
off Shakespeare Rd .**151** H4
James La, E10 . . . .**78** D7
E11 . . . .**78** D6
James Newman Ct, SE9
off Great Harry Dr . . .**174** D3
Jameson Cl, W3
off Acton La **126** C2
Jameson Ct, E2 . . . .**113** F2
Jameson St, W8 . . . .**128** D1
Jameson Wk, Wdf.Grn. IG8
off Baddow Cl **64** A6
James Pl, N17 . . . .**76** C1
James's Cotts, Rich. TW9
off Kew Rd **126** A7
James Sinclair Pt, E13 . . .**115** J1
James St, W1 . . . .**16** C3
WC2 . . . .**18** B5
Barking IG11 . . . .**99** F7
Enfield EN1 . . . .**44** C5
Hounslow TW3 . . . . . .**144** A3
James Ter, SW14
off Mullins Path **146** D3
Jamestown Rd, NW1 . . . .**110** B1
Jamestown Way, E14 . . .**114** D7
James Yd, E4 . . . .**62** D6
Jamieson Ho, Houns.
TW4 . . . .**143** F7

Jamuna Cl, E14 . . . .**113** H5
Jane St, E1 off Commercial
Rd **112/113** E6
Janet St, E14 . . . .**134** A3
Janeway Pl, SE16
off Janeway St . . .**132/133** E2
Janeway St, SE16 . . . . . .**29** J4
Janice Ms, Ilf. IG1
off Oakfield Rd **98/99** E3
Jansen Wk, SW11
off Hope St **149** G4
Janson Cl, E15
off Janson Rd **96/97** E5
NW10 . . . .**88** D3
Janson Rd, E15 . . . .**96** E5
Jansons Rd, N15 . . . .**76** B3
Japan Cres, N4 . . . .**75** F7
Japan Rd, Rom. RM6 . . . .**82** D6
Jardine Rd, E1 . . . .**113** G7
Jarrett Cl, SW2 . . . .**169** H1
Jarrow Cl, Mord. SM4 . .**184** E5
Jarrow Rd, N17 . . . .**76** E4
SE16 . . . .**133** F4
Romford RM6 . . . .**82** C6
Jarrow Way, E9 . . . .**95** H4
Jarvis Cl, Bark. IG11
off Westbury Rd **117** G1
Barnet EN5 . . . .**40** A5
Jarvis Rd, SE22
off Melbourne Gro . .**152** B4
South Croydon CR2 . .**202** A6
Jasmine Cl, Ilf. IG1 . . . . . .**99** E5
Orpington BR6 . . . . .**206** E2
Southall UB1 . . . .**103** E7
Jasmine Gdns, Croy.
CR0 . . . .**204** B3
Harrow HA2 . . . .**85** G2
Jasmine Gro, SE20 . . . . .**189** E1
Jasmine Ter, West Dr.
UB7 . . . .**120** D2
Jasmine Way, E.Mol. KT8
off Hampton Ct Way .**180** B4
Jasmin Rd, Epsom KT19 .**196** B5
Jason Ct, W1
off Marylebone La . . .**110** A6
Jason Wk, SE9 . . . .**174** D4
Jasper Pas, SE19 . . . . . .**170** C6
Jasper Rd, E16 . . . .**116** A6
SE19 . . . .**170** C5
Jasper Wk, N1 . . . .**12** B3
Javelin Way, Nthlt. UB5 .**102** D3
Jaycroft, Enf. EN2
off The Ridgeway **43** G1
Jay Gdns, Chis. BR7 . . . .**174** C4
Jay Ms, SW7 . . . .**22** D4
Jean Batten Cl, Wall. SM6
off Lancastrian Rd . . .**201** F7
Jebb Av, SW2 . . . .**151** E6
Jebb St, E3 . . . .**114** A2
Jedburgh Rd, E13 . . . . . .**115** J3
Jedburgh St, SW11 . . . . .**150** A4
Jeddo Rd, W12 . . . .**127** F2
Jefferson Cl, W13 . . . . . .**125** E3
Ilford IG2 . . . .**81** E5
Jefferson Wk, SE18
off Kempt St **136** D6
Jeffreys Pl, NW1
off Jeffreys St **92** C7
Jeffreys Rd, SW4 . . . . . .**150** E2
Enfield EN3 . . . .**45** J3
Jeffreys St, NW1 . . . .**92** B7
Jeffreys Wk, SW4 . . . . . .**150** E2
Jeffries Ho, NW10 . . . . .**106** D1
Jeffs Cl, Hmptn. TW12
off Uxbridge Rd **161** H6
Jeffs Rd, Sutt. SM1 . . . .**198** C4
Jeger Av, E2 . . . .**112** C1
Jeken Rd, SE9 . . . .**155** J4
Jelf Rd, SW2 . . . .**151** G5
Jellicoe Gdns, Stan. HA7 .**52** C6
Jellicoe Rd, E13
off Jutland Rd **115** G4
N17 . . . .**60** A7
Jemmett Cl, Kings.T.
KT2 . . . .**182** B1
Jengar Cl, Sutt. SM1 . . . .**199** E4
Jenkins La, E6 . . . .**116** D2
Barking IG11 . . . .**117** E2
Jenkins Rd, E13 . . . .**115** H4
Jenner Av, W3 . . . .**106** D5
Jenner Ho, SE3 . . . .**135** E6
Jenner Pl, SW13 . . . .**127** H6
Jenner Rd, N16 . . . .**94** C2
Jennett Rd, Croy. CR0 . . .**201** G3
Jennifer Rd, Brom. BR1 .**173** F3
Jennings Cl, Surb. KT6 . .**181** F7
Jennings Rd, SE22 . . . . .**152** C6
Jennings Way, Barn. EN5 .**39** J3
Jenningtree Way, Belv.
DA17 . . . .**139** J2

Jenny Hammond Cl, E11
off Newcomen Rd **97** F3
Jenson Way, SE19 . . . . .**170** C7
Jenton Av, Bexh. DA7 . . .**158** E1
Jephson Rd, E7 . . . .**97** J7
Jephson St, SE5
off Grove La **152** A1
Jephtha Rd, SW18 . . . . .**148** D6
Jeppos La, Mitch. CR4 . .**185** J4
Jerdan Pl, SW6 . . . .**128** D7
Jeremiah St, E14 . . . . . .**114** B6
Jeremys Grn, N18 . . . . . .**61** E4
Jermyn St, SW1 . . . .**25** F1
Jerningham Av, Ilf. IG5 . . .**80** E2
Jerningham Rd, SE14 . . .**153** H2
Jerome Cres, NW8 . . . . . .**7** G5
Jerome Pl, Kings.T. KT1
off Wadbrook St **181** G2
Jerome St, E1 . . . .**21** F1
Jerrard St, N1 . . . .**12** E2
SE13 . . . .**154** B3
Jersey Av, Stan. HA7 . . . .**69** E2
Jersey Dr, Orp. BR5 . . . .**193** G6
Jersey Par, Houns. TW5 .**143** H1
Jersey Rd, E11 . . . .**96** D1
E16
off Prince Regent La .**115** J6
SW17 . . . .**168** B6
W7 . . . .**124** D2
Hounslow TW3, TW5 .**143** H1
Ilford IG1 . . . .**99** E4
Isleworth TW7 . . . . . .**124** B6
Jersey St, E2 off Bethnal Grn
Rd **112/113** E3
Jerusalem Pas, EC1 . . . . .**11** G6
Jervis Ct, W1 . . . .**17** E4
Jerviston Gdns, SW16 . .**169** G6
Jesmond Av, Wem. HA9 . .**87** J6
Jesmond Cl, Mitch. CR4 .**186** B3
Jesmond Rd, Croy. CR0 .**188** C7
Jesmond Way, Stan. HA7 .**53** H5
Jessam Av, E5 . . . .**94** E1
Jessamine Rd, W7 . . . . .**124** B1
Jessel Dr, Loug. IG10 . . . .**49** F1
Jesse Rd, E10 . . . .**96** C1
Jessica Rd, SW18 . . . . . .**149** F6
Jessie Blythe La, N19 . . .**74** E7
Jessop Av, Sthl. UB2 . . . .**123** F4
Jessop Rd, SE24
off Milkwood Rd **151** H4
Jessop Sq, E14
off Heron Quay **134** A1
Jessops Way, Croy. CR0 .**186** C6
Jessup Cl, SE18 . . . .**137** F4
Jetstar Way, Nthlt. UB5 .**102** E3
Jevington Way, SE12 . . .**173** H1
Jewel Rd, E17 . . . .**78** A3
★ Jewel Twr, Houses of
Parliament, SW1 . . . . .**26** A5
★ Jewish Mus, NW1 . . .**110** B1
Jewry St, EC3 . . . .**21** F4
Jew's Row, SW18 . . . . . .**149** E4
Jews Wk, SE26 . . . .**171** E4
Jeymer Av, NW2 . . . .**89** H5
Jeymer Dr, Grnf. UB6 . . .**103** J1
Jeypore Pas, SW18
off Jeypore Rd **149** F6
Jeypore Rd, SW18 . . . . .**149** F7
Jillian Cl, Hmptn. TW12 .**161** G7
Jim Bradley Cl, SE18
off John Wilson St . .**136** D4
Jim Griffiths Ho, SW6
off Clem Attlee Ct . . .**128** C6
Joan Cres, SE9 . . . .**156** A7
Joan Gdns, Dag. RM8 . . .**100** E2
Joan Rd, Dag. RM8 . . . . .**100** E2
Joan St, SE1 . . . .**27** G2
Jocelyn Rd, Rich. TW9 . .**145** H3
Jocelyn St, SE15 . . . . . .**152** D1
Jockey's Flds, WC1 . . . . .**18** D1
Jodane St, SE8 . . . .**133** J4
Jodrell Cl, Islw. TW7 . . . .**144** D1
Jodrell Rd, E3 . . . .**113** J1
Joel St, Nthwd. HA6 . . . . .**66** A3
Pinner HA5 . . . .**66** A3
Johanna St, SE1 . . . .**27** E4
John Adam St, WC2 . . . . .**18** B6
John Aird Ct, W2 . . . .**14** D1
John Archer Way, SW18 .**149** G6
John Ashby Cl, SW2 . . . .**151** E6
John Austin Cl, Kings.T. KT2
off Queen Elizabeth
Rd **181** J1
John Barnes Wk, E15 . . . .**97** F6
John Bradshaw Rd, N14
off High St **58** D1
John Burns Dr, Bark.
IG11 . . . .**99** H7
John Campbell Rd, N16 . .**94** B5
John Carpenter St, EC4 . .**19** G5

John Cornwell VC Ho,
E12 . . . . .98 D4
John Drinkwater Cl, E11
off Browning Rd 79 F7
John Felton Rd, SE16 . . . .29 H4
John Fisher St, E1 . . . . . .21 H5
John Gooch Dr, Enf. EN2 .43 H1
John Harrison Way,
SE10 . . . . .135 F3
off Frome St 111 J2
John Islip St, SW1 . . . . . .34 A2
John Keats Ho, N22 . . . . .59 F7
John Maurice Cl, SE17 . . .36 B1
John McKenna Wk, SE16 .29 J5
John Newton Ct, Well. DA16
off Danson La 158 B3
John Parker Cl, Dag.
RM10 . . . . .101 H7
John Parker Sq, SW11
off Thomas Baines
Rd 149 G3
John Perrin Pl, SE13 . . . .154 B1
John Perrin Pl, Har. HA3 . .69 H7
John Princes St, W1 . . . . .17 E3
John Rennie Wk, E1
off Wine Cl 132/133 E1
John Roll Way, SE16 . . . . .29 J5
John Ruskin St, SE5 . . . . .35 G7
Johns Av, NW4 . . . . .71 J4
Johns Ct, Sutt. SM2
off Mulgrave Rd .198/199 E6
John Silkin La, SE8 . . . . .133 G5
Johns La, Mord. SM4 . . . .185 F5
John's Ms, WC1 . . . . .10 D6
John Smith Av, SW6 . . . .128 C7
Johnson Cl, E8 . . . . .112 D1
Johnson Rd, NW10
off Milton Av 106 D1
Bromley BR2 . . . . .192 A5
Croydon CR0 . . . . .188 A7
Hounslow TW5 . . . . . . .122 C7
Johnsons Cl, Cars. SM5 .199 J3
Johnson's Ct, EC4
off Fleet St 111 G6
Johnsons Dr, Hmptn.
TW12 . . . . .179 J1
Johnson's Pl, SW1 . . . . . .33 F4
Johnson St, E1
off Cable St 113 F7
Southall UB2 . . . . .122 C3
Johnsons Way, NW10 . . .106 B4
John Spencer Sq, N1 . . . .93 H6
John's Pl, E1
off Damien St 112/113 E6
John's Ter, Croy. CR0 . . .202 A1
Johnston Cl, SW9
off Hackford Rd 151 F1
Johnstone Rd, E6 . . . . . .116 C3
Johnston Rd, Wdf.Grn.
IG8 . . . . .63 G5
Johnston Ter, NW2
off Kara Way 90 A3
John St, E15 . . . . .115 F1
SE25 . . . . .188 D4
WC1 . . . . .10 D6
Enfield EN1 . . . . .44 C5
Hounslow TW3 . . . . . . .143 E2
John Trundle Ct, EC2
off The Barbican 111 J5
John Walsh Twr, E11 . . . . .97 F2
John Williams Cl, SE14 . .133 G6
Kingston upon Thames KT2
off Henry Macaulay
Av 181 G1
John Wilson St, SE18 . . .136 D3
John Woolley Cl, SE13 . .154 E4
Joiner's Arms Yd, SE5
off Denmark Hill 152 A1
Joiners Pl, N5
off Leconfield Rd 94 A4
Joiner St, SE1 . . . . .28 C2
Jollys La, Har. HA2 . . . . . .86 A1
Hayes UB4 . . . . .102 D5
Jonathan Ct, W4
off Windmill Rd . .126/127 E4
Jonathan St, SE11 . . . . . .34 C3
Jones Rd, E13
off Holborn Rd 115 H4
Jones St, W1 . . . . .16 D6
Jones Wk, Rich. TW10
off Pyrland Rd 145 J6
Jonquil Gdns, Hmptn. TW12
off Partridge Rd 161 F6
Jonson Cl, Hayes UB4 . .102 A5
Mitcham CR4 . . . . .186 B4
Jordan Cl, Dag. RM10
off Muggeridge Rd . . .101 H4
Harrow HA2
off Hamilton Cres 85 F3

Jordan Ct, SW15
off Charlwood Rd 148 A4
Jordan Rd, Grnf. UB6 . . .105 E1
Jordans Cl, Islw. TW7 . . .144 B1
Joseph Av, W3 . . . . .106 D6
Josephine Av, SW2 . . . . .151 F5
Joseph Powell Cl, SW12
off Hazelbourne Rd . . .150 B6
Joseph Ray Rd, E11 . . . . .97 E2
Joseph St, E3 . . . . .113 J4
Joseph Trotter Cl, EC1
off Myddelton St 111 G3
Joshua Cl, N10
off Roman Rd 58 B7
Joshua St, E14
off St. Leonards Rd . . .114 C6
Joubert St, SW11 . . . . . .149 J2
Jowett St, SE15 . . . . . . .132 C7
Joyce Av, N18 . . . . .60 C5
Joyce Dawson Way, SE28
off Thamesmere Dr . . .118 A7
Joyce Page Cl, SE7
off Lansdowne La 136 A6
Joyce Wk, SW2 . . . . .151 G6
JOYDENS WOOD, Bex. . .177 J5
Joydon Dr, Rom. RM6 . . . .82 B6
Joyners Cl, Dag. RM9 . . .101 F4
Jubb Powell Ho, N15 . . . .76 B6
Jubilee Av, E4 . . . . .62 C6
Romford RM7 . . . . .83 H5
Twickenham TW2 . . . . .161 J1
Jubilee Cl, NW9 . . . . .70 D6
Pinner HA5 . . . . .66 C2
Romford RM7 . . . . .83 H5
Jubilee Cres, E14 . . . . . .134 C3
N9 . . . . .60 D1
Jubilee Dr, Ruis. HA4 . . . .84 D4
★ Jubilee Gdns, SE1 . . .26 C2
Jubilee Gdns, Sthl. UB1 .103 G6
Jubilee Pl, SW3 . . . . .31 H3
Jubilee Rd, Grnf. UB6 . . .104 E1
Sutton SM3 . . . . .198 A7
Jubilee St, E1 . . . . .113 F6
Jubilee Wk, Wat. WD19 . .50 B4
Jubilee Way, SW19 . . . . .185 E1
Chessington KT9 . . . . .196 A4
Sidcup DA14 . . . . .176 A2
Judd St, WC1 . . . . .10 A4
Jude St, E16 . . . . .115 F6
Judge Wk, Esher (Clay.)
KT10 . . . . .194 B6
Juer St, SW11 . . . . .129 H7
Jules Thorn Av, Enf. EN1 . .44 C3
Julia Gdns, Bark. IG11 . . .118 D2
Julia Garfield Ms, E16
off Wesley Av 135 H1
Juliana Cl, N2 . . . . .73 F3
Julian Av, W3 . . . . .106 B7
Julian Cl, Barn. EN5 . . . . .40 E3
Julian Hill, Har. HA1 . . . . .86 B2
Julian Pl, E14 . . . . .134 B5
Julia St, NW5
off Oak Village 92 A4
Julien Rd, W5 . . . . .125 F3
Juliette Rd, E13 . . . . .115 F2
Julius Nyerere Cl, N1
off Copenhagen St . . .111 G4
Junction App, SE13 . . . . .154 C3
SW11 . . . . .149 H3
Junction Av, W10 . . . .
off Harrow Rd 107 J3
Junction Ms, W2 . . . . . . .15 G3
Junction Pl, W2 . . . . .15 G3
Junction Rd, E13 . . . . . . .115 H2
N9 . . . . .60 D1
N17 . . . . .76 D3
N19 . . . . .92 C4
W5 . . . . .125 G4
Brentford TW8 . . . . . . .125 G4
Harrow HA1 . . . . .68 B6
South Croydon CR2 . . .202 A5
Junction Rd E, Rom. RM6
off Kenneth Rd 82/83 E7
Junction Rd W, Rom.
RM6 . . . . .82 E7
Junction Shop Cen, The, SW11
off St. John's Hill 149 H4
Juniper Cl, Barn. EN5 . . . .40 A5
Chessington KT9 . . . . .195 J6
Wembley HA9 . . . . .87 J5
Juniper Cres, NW1 . . . . . .92 A7
Juniper Gdns, SW16
off Leonard Rd 186 C1
Juniper La, E6 . . . . .116 B5
Juniper Rd, Ilf. IG1 . . . . . .98 D4
Juniper St, E1 . . . . .113 F7
Juno Way, SE14 . . . . . . .133 G6
Jupiter Way, N7 . . . . .93 F6
Jupp Rd, E15 . . . . .96 D7
Jupp Rd W, E15 . . . . .114 C1

Justice Wk, SW3 . . . . . . .31 G6
Justin Cl, Brent. TW8 . . .125 G7
Justin Rd, E4 . . . . .61 J6
Jute La, Enf. EN3 . . . . . . .45 H2
Jutland Cl, N19
off Sussex Way 92/93 E1
Jutland Rd, E13 . . . . .115 G4
SE6 . . . . .154 C7
Jutsums Av, Rom. RM7 . .83 H6
Jutsums La, Rom. RM7 . .83 H6
Juxon Cl, Har. HA3
off Augustine Rd 67 H1
Juxon St, SE11 . . . . .34 D1

K

Kaduna Cl, Pnr. HA5 . . . . .66 A5
Kale Rd, Erith DA18 . . . .138 E2
Kambala Rd, SW11 . . . . .149 G3
Kangley Br Rd, SE26 . . . .171 J5
Kaplan Dr, N21 . . . . .43 E5
Kara Way, NW2 . . . . .90 A4
Karen Ct, SE4
off Wickham Rd 153 J2
Bromley BR1
off Blyth Rd 191 F1
Karen Ter, E11
off Montague Rd 97 F2
Karenza Ct, Wem. HA9
off Lulworth Av 69 F7
Karina Cl, Chig. IG7 . . . . .65 H5
Karoline Gdns, Grnf. UB6
off Oldfield La N 104 A2
Kashgar Rd, SE18 . . . . . .137 J5
Kashmir Rd, SE7 . . . . . . .136 A7
Kassala Rd, SW11 . . . . . .149 J1
Katella Trd Est, Bark.
IG11 . . . . .117 H3
Kates Cl, Barn. EN5 . . . . .39 G5
Katharine St, Croy.
CR0 . . . . .201 J3
Katherine Cl, SE16
off Rotherhithe St 133 G1
Katherine Gdns, SE9 . . .156 A4
Ilford IG6 . . . . .65 F7
Katherine Rd, E6 . . . . . . .98 A7
E7 . . . . .97 J5
Twickenham TW1
off London Rd 162 D1
Katherine Sq, W11
off Wilsham St 128 B1
Kathleen Av, W3 . . . . . . .106 C5
Wembley HA0 . . . . .87 H7
Kathleen Rd, SW11 . . . . .149 J3
Kayemoor Rd, Sutt.
SM2 . . . . .199 H7
Kay Rd, SW9 . . . . .151 E2
Kays Ter, E18
off Walpole Rd 79 F1
Kay St, E2 . . . . .13 J1
Welling DA16 . . . . .158 B1
Kay Way, SE10 off Greenwich
High Rd 134 B7
Kean St, WC2 . . . . .18 C4
Keatley Grn, E4 . . . . .61 J6
Keats Av, E16
off Wesley Av 135 H1
Keats Cl, E11
off Nightingale La 79 H5
NW3 off Keats Gro 91 H4
SE1 . . . . .37 F2
SW19 off North Rd . . .167 G6
Chigwell IG7 . . . . .65 H6
Enfield EN3 . . . . .45 G5
Hayes UB4 . . . . .102 A5
Keats Gro, NW3 . . . . .91 G4
★ Keats Ho, Beck. BR3 . .91 H4
Keats Ho, Beck. BR3 . . .172 A6
Keats Pl, EC2 . . . . .20 B2
Keats Rd, Belv. DA17 . . .139 J3
Welling DA16 . . . . .157 H1
Keats Way, Croy. CR0 . . .189 F6
Greenford UB6 . . . . . . .103 H5
West Drayton UB7 . . . .120 C4
Keble Cl, Nthlt. UB5 . . . . .85 J5
Worcester Park KT4 . . .197 F1
Keble Pl, SW13
off Somerville Av 127 H6
Keble St, SW17 . . . . .167 F4
Kechill Gdns, Brom. BR2 .191 G7
Kedeston Ct, Sutt. SM1
off Hurstcourt Rd .198/199 E1
Kedleston Dr, Orp. BR5 . .193 J6
Kedleston Wk, E2
off Middleton St .112/113 E3
Keedonwood Rd, Brom.
BR1 . . . . .172 E5

Keel Cl, SE16 . . . . .133 G1
Barking IG11 . . . . .118 C2
Keeley Rd, Croy. CR0 . . .201 J2
Keeley St, WC2 . . . . .18 C4
Keeling Rd, SE9 . . . . . . .156 A5
Keely Cl, Barn. EN4 . . . . .41 H5
Keemor Cl, SE18
off Llanover Rd 136 D7
Keens Cl, SW16 . . . . . . .168 D5
Keens Rd, Croy. CR0 . . .201 J4
Keens Yd, N1
off St. Paul's Rd 93 H6
Keep, The, SE3 . . . . .155 G2
Kingston upon Thames
KT2 . . . . .163 J6
Keepers Ms, Tedd. TW11 .163 F6
Keep La, N11
off Gardeners Cl 58 A2
Keesey St, SE17 . . . . . . .36 B5
Keetons Rd, SE16 . . . . . .132 E3
Keevil Dr, SW19 . . . . . . .148 A7
Keighley Cl, N7
off Penn Rd 92/93 E5
Keightley Dr, SE9 . . . . . .175 F1
Keildon Rd, SW11 . . . . . .149 J4
Keir, The, SW19 off West Side
Common 165 J5
Keir Hardie Est, E5
off Springfield 94/95 E1
Keir Hardie Ho, W6
off Lochaline St 127 J6
Keir Hardie Way, Bark.
IG11 . . . . .100 A7
Hayes UB4 . . . . .102 A3
Keith Connor Cl, SW8
off Daley Thompson
Way 150 B3
Keith Gro, W12 . . . . .127 G2
Keith Rd, E17 . . . . .77 J1
Barking IG11 . . . . .117 G2
Hayes UB3 . . . . .121 H3
Kelbrook Rd, SE3 . . . . . .156 B3
Kelby Path, SE9 . . . . . . .175 E3
Kelceda Cl, NW2 . . . . . . .89 G2
Kelfield Gdns, W10 . . . . .107 J6
Kelfield Ms, W10
off Kelfield Gdns 108 A6
Kelland Cl, N8
off Palace Rd 74 D5
Kelland Rd, E13 . . . . . . .115 G4
Kellaway Rd, SE3 . . . . . .155 J2
Keller Cres, E12 . . . . .98 A4
Kellerton Rd, SE13 . . . . .154 E5
Kellett Rd, SW2 . . . . .151 G4
Kelling Gdns, Croy. CR0 .187 H7
Kellino St, SW17 . . . . . . .167 J4
Kellner Rd, SE28 . . . . . . .137 J3
Kell St, SE1 . . . . .27 H5
Kelly Av, SE15 . . . . .132 C7
Kelly Cl, NW10 . . . . .88 D3
Kelly Ct, Borwd. WD6 . . . .38 C2
Kelly Ms, W9
off Woodfield Rd 108 C5
Kelly Rd, NW7 . . . . .56 B6
Kelly St, NW1 . . . . .92 B6
Kelly Way, Rom. RM6 . . . .82 E5
Kelman Cl, SW4 . . . . . . .150 D2
Kelmore Gro, SE22 . . . . .152 D4
Kelmscott Cl, E17 . . . . . . .77 J2
Kelmscott Gdns, W12 . . .127 G3
Kelmscott Rd, SW11 . . . .149 H5
Kelross Pas, N5
off Kelross Rd 93 J4
Kelross Rd, N5 . . . . .93 H4
Kelsall Cl, SE3 . . . . .155 H2
Kelsey Gate, Beck. BR3 .190 B2
Kelsey La, Beck. BR3 . . .190 A2
Kelsey Pk Av, Beck. BR3 .190 B2
Kelsey Pk Rd, Beck. BR3 .190 A2
Kelsey Sq, Beck. BR3 . . .190 A2
Kelsey St, E2 . . . . .13 J5
Kelsey Way, Beck. BR3 . .190 A3
Kelshall Ct, N4
off Brownswood Rd . . .93 J2
Kelsie Way, Ilf. IG6 . . . . . .65 H7
Kelson Ho, E14 . . . . .134 C3
Kelso Pl, W8 . . . . .22 B6
Kelso Rd, Cars. SM5 . . . .185 F7
Kelston Rd, Ilf. IG6 . . . . . .81 E2
Kelvedon Cl, Kings.T.
KT2 . . . . .163 J6
Kelvedon Ho, SW8 . . . . .150 E1
Kelvedon Rd, SW6 . . . . .128 C7
Kelvedon Way, Wdf.Grn.
IG8 . . . . .64 C6
Kelvin Av, N13 . . . . .59 F6
Teddington TW11 . . . . .162 B6
Kelvinbrook, W.Mol. KT8 .179 H3
Kelvin Cl, Epsom KT19 . .196 A6
Kelvin Cres, Har. HA3 . . . .52 B7

Kelvin Dr, Twick. TW1 . . .145 E6
Kelvin Gdns, Croy. CR0 . .187 E7
 Southall UB1 . . . . .103 G6
Kelvin Gro, SE26 . . . . . . .170 E3
 Chessington KT9 . . . . .195 H3
Kelvington Cl, Croy. CR0 .189 H7
Kelvington Rd, SE15 . . . .153 G5
Kelvin Ind Est, Grnf.
 UB6 . . . . .85 H7
Kelvin Par, Orp. BR6 . . . .207 H1
Kelvin Rd, N5 . . . . .93 H4
 Welling DA16 . . . . .158 A3
Kember St, N1
 off Carnoustie Dr 93 F7
Kemble Dr, Brom. BR2 . .206 B3
Kemble Rd, N17 . . . . .76 D1
 SE23 . . . . .171 G1
 Croydon CR0 . . . . .201 G3
Kemble St, WC2 . . . . .18 C4
Kemerton Rd, SE5 . . . . .151 J3
 Beckenham BR3 . . . . . .190 B2
 Croydon CR0 . . . . .188 C7
Kemeys St, E9 . . . . .95 H5
Kemnal Rd, Chis. BR7 . . .175 G4
Kempe Rd, NW6 . . . . . . .108 A2
Kemp Gdns, Croy. CR0
 off St. Saviours Rd . . .187 J6
Kempis Way, SE22
 off East Dulwich Gro .152 B5
Kemplay Rd, NW3 . . . . . .91 G4
Kemp Rd, Dag. RM8 . . . .100 D1
Kemp's Ct, W1 . . . . .17 G4
Kemps Dr, E14
 off Morant St 114 A7
Kempsford Gdns, SW5 . .128 D5
Kempsford Rd, SE11 . . . .35 G1
Kemps Gdns, SE13
 off Thornford Rd 154 C5
Kempshott Rd, SW16 . . .168 D7
Kempson Rd, SW6 . . . . .148 D1
Kempthorne Rd, SE8 . . .133 H4
Kempton Av, Nthlt. UB5 . .85 G6
 Sunbury-on-Thames
 TW16 . . . . .178 B1
Kempton Cl, Erith DA8 . .139 J6
Kempton Ct, E1
 off Durward St 112/113 E5
 Sunbury-on-Thames
 TW16 . . . . .178 B1
★ Kempton Park Racecourse,
 Sun. TW16 . . . . .160 C7
Kempton Rd, E6 . . . . . . .116 C1
 Hampton TW12 . . . . . .179 F2
Kempton Wk, Croy. CR0 .189 H6
Kempt St, SE18 . . . . .136 D6
Kemsing Cl, Bex. DA5 . . .159 E7
 Bromley BR2 . . . . .205 F2
 Thornton Heath CR7 . .187 J4
Kemsing Rd, SE10 . . . . .135 G5
Kemsley, SE13 . . . . .154 C5
Kenbury Gdns, SE5
 off Kenbury St 151 J2
Kenbury St, SE5 . . . . . . .151 J2
Kenchester Cl, SW8 . . . .131 E7
Kencot Cl, Erith DA18 . . .139 F2
Kendal Av, N18 . . . . .60 A4
 W3 . . . . .106 A4
 Barking IG11 . . . . .99 H7
Kendal Cl, SW9 . . . . .35 G7
 Woodford Green IG8 . . .63 F2
Kendale Rd, Brom. BR1 . .172 E5
Kendal Gdns, N18 . . . . . .60 A4
 Sutton SM1 . . . . .199 F2
Kendal Par, N18
 off Great Cambridge
 Rd 60 A4
Kendal Pl, SW15 . . . . . . .148 C5
Kendal Rd, NW10 . . . . . . .89 G4
Kendal St, W2 . . . . .15 H4
Kender St, SE14 . . . . . . .133 F7
Kendoa Rd, SW4 . . . . . . .150 D4
Kendon Cl, E11
 off The Avenue 79 H5
Kendra Hall Rd, S.Croy.
 CR2 . . . . .201 H7
Kendrey Gdns, Twick.
 TW2 . . . . .144 B6
Kendrick Ms, SW7 . . . . . .31 E1
Kendrick Pl, SW7 . . . . . . .31 E2
Kenelm Cl, Har. HA1 . . . . .86 D3

Kenerne Dr, Barn. EN5 . . . .40 B5
Kenilford Rd, SW12 . . . . .150 B7
Kenilworth Av, E17 . . . . . .78 A2
 SW19 . . . . .166 D5
 Harrow HA2 . . . . .85 F4
Kenilworth Cl, Borwd.
 WD6 . . . . .38 C3
Kenilworth Ct, SW15
 off Lower Richmond
 Rd 148 A3
Kenilworth Cres, Enf.
 EN1 . . . . .44 B1
Kenilworth Dr, Borwd.
 WD6 . . . . .38 C3
Kenilworth Gdns, SE18 . .156 E2
 Ilford IG3 . . . . .99 J2
 Loughton IG10 . . . . . . .48 C6
 Southall UB1 . . . . .103 F3
 Watford WD19 . . . . .50 C5
Kenilworth Rd, E3 . . . . . .113 H2
 NW6 . . . . .108 C1
 SE20 . . . . .189 G1
 W5 . . . . .125 H1
 Edgware HA8 . . . . .54 C3
 Epsom KT17 . . . . .197 G6
 Orpington BR5 . . . . . . .193 F6
Kenley Av, NW9 . . . . .70 E1
Kenley Cl, Barn. EN4 . . . . .41 H4
 Bexley DA5 . . . . .159 G2
 Chislehurst BR7 . . . . . .193 H3
Kenley Gdns, Th.Hth.
 CR7 . . . . .187 H4
Kenley Rd, SW19 . . . . . .184 C2
 Kingston upon Thames
 KT1 . . . . .182 B2
 Twickenham TW1 . . . . .144 D6
Kenley Wk, W11 . . . . . . .108 B7
 Sutton SM3 . . . . .198 A4
Kenlor Rd, SW17 . . . . . . .167 G5
Kenmare Dr, Mitch.
 CR4 . . . . .167 J1
Kenmare Gdns, N13 . . . . .59 H4
Kenmare Rd, Th.Hth.
 CR7 . . . . .187 G6
Kenmere Gdns, Wem.
 HA0 . . . . .106 A1
Kenmere Rd, Well. DA16 .158 C2
Kenmont Gdns, NW10 . .107 H3
Kenmore Av, Har. HA3 . . .68 D4
Kenmore Cl, Rich. TW9
 off Kent Rd 126 A7
Kenmore Gdns, Edg. HA8 .70 B2
Kenmore Rd, Har. HA3 . . .69 G3
 Kenley CR8 . . . . .95 E5
Kenmure Yd, E8
 off Kenmure Rd 94/95 E5
Kennacraig Cl, E16
 off Hanameel St 135 G1
Kennard Rd, E15 . . . . .96 D7
 N11 . . . . .57 J5
Kennard St, E16 . . . . . . .136 C1
 SW11 . . . . .150 A2
Kennedy Av, Enf. EN3 . . . .45 F6
Kennedy Cl, E13 . . . . . . .115 G2
 Mitcham CR4 . . . . .186 A2
 Orpington BR5 . . . . . . .207 G1
 Pinner HA5 . . . . .51 F6
Kennedy Path, W7
 off Harp Rd 104 C4
Kennedy Rd, W7 . . . . . . .104 B5
 Barking IG11 . . . . .117 H1
Kennedy Wk, SE17
 off Flint St 132 A4
Kennet Cl, SW11
 off Maysoule Rd 149 G4
Kenneth Av, Ilf. IG1 . . . . . .98 E4
Kenneth Cres, NW2 . . . . .89 H5
Kenneth Gdns, Stan. HA7 .52 D6
Kenneth More Rd, Ilf. IG1
 off Oakfield Rd 98/99 E3
Kenneth Rd, Rom. RM6 . .82 D7
Kenneth Robbins Ho,
 N17 . . . . .60 E7
Kennet Rd, W9 . . . . .108 C4
 Isleworth TW7 . . . . . . .144 C3
Kennet Sq, Mitch. CR4 . .185 H1
Kennet St, E1 . . . . .29 J1
Kennett Dr, Hayes UB4 . .102 E5
Kennet Wf La, EC4 . . . . . .20 A5
Kenninghall Rd, E5 . . . . . .94 D3
 N18 . . . . .61 F5
Kenning St, SE16
 off Railway Av 133 F2
Kennings Way, SE11 . . . . .35 G3
Kenning Ter, N1 . . . . .112 B1
KENNINGTON, SE11 . . . . .35 E5
Kennington Grn, SE11 . . . .35 E4
Kennington Gro, SE11 . . . .34 D5
Kennington La, SE11 . . . . .35 F3
Kennington Oval, SE11 . . .34 D5

Kennington Pk Est, SE11 .35 E6
Kennington Pk Gdns,
 SE11 . . . . .35 F5
Kennington Pk Pl, SE11 . .35 F4
Kennington Pk Rd, SE11 . .35 F5
Kennington Rd, SE1 . . . . .27 E5
 SE11 . . . . .27 E6
Kenny Rd, NW7 . . . . .56 B5
Kenrick Pl, W1 . . . . .16 B1
KENSAL GREEN, NW10 .107 J3
★ Kensal Green Cem,
 W10 . . . . .107 J3
KENSAL RISE, NW6 . . . .108 A2
Kensal Rd, W10 . . . . .108 B4
KENSAL TOWN, W10 . . .108 A4
KENSINGTON, W8 . . . . . .128 C2
Kensington Av, E12 . . . . . .98 B6
 Thornton Heath CR7 . .187 G1
Kensington Ch Ct, W8 . . .22 A4
Kensington Ch St, W8 . . .128 D1
Kensington Ch Wk, W8 . . .22 A4
Kensington Cl, N11 . . . . . .58 A6
Kensington Ct, NW7
 off Grenville Pl 54 D5
 W8 . . . . .22 B4
Kensington Ct Gdns, W8
 off Kensington Ct
 Pl 128/129 E3
Kensington Ct Ms, W8 . . .22 B4
Kensington Ct Pl, W8 . . . .22 B5
Kensington Dr, Wdf.Grn.
 IG8 . . . . .80 A1
★ Kensington Gdns, W2 .22 D2
Kensington Gdns, W2 . . . .22 E2
 Ilford IG1 . . . . .98 C2
 Kingston upon Thames KT1
 off Portsmouth Rd . . .181 G3
Kensington Gdns Sq, W2 .14 A4
Kensington Gate, W8 . . . .22 C5
Kensington Gore, SW7 . . .23 E4
Kensington Hall Gdns, W14
 off Beaumont Av 128 C5
Kensington High St, W8 .128 D3
 W14 . . . . .128 B4
Kensington Mall, W8 . . .128 D1
★ Kensington Palace,
 W8 . . . . .22 B2
Kensington Palace Gdns,
 W8 . . . . .22 A1
Kensington Pk Gdns,
 W11 . . . . .108 C7
 off Kensington Pk Rd .108 C6
Kensington Pk Ms, W11
 off Kensington Pk Rd .108 C6
Kensington Pk Rd, W11 .108 C7
Kensington Pl, W8 . . . . . .128 D1
Kensington Rd, SW7 . . . . .23 F4
 W8 . . . . .22 C4
 Northolt UB5 . . . . .103 G3
 Romford RM7 . . . . .83 J6
Kensington Sq, W8 . . . . . .22 A4
Kensington Ter, S.Croy. CR2
 off Sanderstead Rd .202 A7
Kensington Way, Borwd.
 WD6 . . . . .38 D3
Kent Av, W13 . . . . .104 E5
 Dagenham RM9 . . . . . .119 G4
 Welling DA16 . . . . .157 J5
Kent Cl, Mitch. CR4 . . . . .187 E4
 Orpington BR6 . . . . . . .207 H6
Kent Dr, Barn. EN4 . . . . . .42 A4
 Teddington TW11 . . . . .162 B5
Kentford Way, Nthlt.
 UB5 . . . . .102 E1
Kent Gdns, W13 . . . . .105 E5
 Ruislip HA4 . . . . .66 B6
Kent Gate Way, Croy.
 CR0 . . . . .204 A5
Kent Ho La, Beck. BR3 . .171 H5
Kent Ho Rd, SE26 . . . . . .189 F2
 Beckenham BR3 . . . . . .171 H5
Kentish Bldgs, SE1 . . . . . .28 B2
Kentish Rd, Belv. DA17 . .139 G4
KENTISH TOWN, NW5 . . .92 C6
Kentish Town Rd, NW1 . . .92 B7
 NW5 . . . . .92 B7
Kentish Way, Brom. BR1 .191 G2
Kentmere Rd, SE18 . . . . .137 H4
KENTON, Har. 68 E5
Kenton Av, Har. HA1 . . . . .68 C7
 Southall UB1 . . . . .103 G7
 Sunbury-on-Thames
 TW16 . . . . .178 E2
Kenton Ct, W14
 off Kensington High
 St 128 C3
Kenton Gdns, Har. HA3 . . .69 F5
Kenton La, Har. HA3 . . . . .69 F3
Kenton Pk Av, Har. HA3 . . .69 G4
Kenton Pk Cl, Har. HA3 . . .69 F4

Kenton Pk Cres, Har. HA3 .69 G4
Kenton Pk Rd, Har. HA3 . .69 F4
Kenton Rd, E9 . . . . .95 G6
 Harrow HA1, HA3 . . . . . .69 G5
Kenton St, WC1 . . . . .10 A5
Kent Pas, NW1 . . . . .7 J5
 W4 . . . . .126 C3
 Dagenham RM10 . . . . .101 H5
 East Molesey KT8 . . . .179 J4
 Kingston upon Thames KT1
 off The Bittoms 181 G3
 Richmond TW9 . . . . . . .126 A7
 West Wickham BR4 . . .204 B1
Kents Pas, Hmptn. TW12 .179 F1
Kent St, E2 . . . . .13 G1
 E13 . . . . .115 J3
Kent Ter, NW1 . . . . .7 H4
Kent Twr, SE20 . . . . .170 E7
Kent Vw Gdns, Ilf. IG3 . . .99 H2
Kent Wk, SW9
 off Moorland Rd 151 H4
Kent Way, Surb. KT6 . . . .195 H3
Kentwode Grn, SW13 . . .127 G7
Kent Yd, SW7 . . . . .23 H4
Kenver Av, N12 . . . . .57 G6
Kenward Rd, SE9 . . . . . . .155 J5
Kenway, Rom. RM5 . . . . . .83 J2
Ken Way, Wem. HA9 . . . . .88 C2
Kenway Rd, SW5 . . . . .30 A2
Kenwood Av, N14 . . . . . . .42 D5
 SE14 off Besson St . . .153 G1
Kenwood Cl, NW3 . . . . . . .91 G1
 West Drayton UB7 . . . .120 D6
Kenwood Dr, Beck.
 BR3 . . . . .190 C3
Kenwood Gdns, E18 . . . . .79 H3
 Ilford IG2 . . . . .80 D4
★ Kenwood Ho (The Iveagh
 Bequest), NW3 . . . . . . .91 H1
Kenwood Rd, N6 . . . . .73 J6
 N9 . . . . .60 D1
Kenworthy Rd, E9 . . . . . . .95 H5
Kenwyn Dr, NW2 . . . . .89 E3
Kenwyn Rd, SW4 . . . . . . .150 D4
 SW20 . . . . .183 J1
Kenya Rd, SE7 . . . . .136 A7
Kenyngton Dr, Sun.
 TW16 . . . . .160 A5
Kenyngton Pl, Har. HA3 . . .69 F5
Kenyon St, SW6 . . . . .148 A1
Keogh Rd, E15 . . . . .97 E6
Kepler Rd, SW4 . . . . .150 E4
Keppel Rd, E6 . . . . .98 C7
 Dagenham RM9 . . . . . .100 E4
Keppel Row, SE1 . . . . .27 J2
Keppel St, WC1 . . . . .17 J1
Kerbela St, E2 . . . . .13 H5
Kerbey St, E14 . . . . .114 B6
Kerfield Cres, SE5 . . . . . .152 A1
Kerfield Pl, SE5 . . . . .152 A1
Kerri Cl, Barn. EN5 . . . . . .39 J4
Kerridge Ct, N1 . . . . .94 B6
Kerrison Pl, W5 . . . . .125 G1
Kerrison Rd, E15 . . . . . . .114 D1
 SW11 . . . . .149 H3
 W5 . . . . .125 G1
Kerrison Vil, W5
 off Kerrison Pl 125 G1
Kerry Av, Stan. HA7 . . . . . .53 G4
Kerry Cl, E16 . . . . .115 H6
 N13 . . . . .59 F2
Kerry Ct, Stan. HA7 . . . . . .53 G4
Kerry Path, SE14
 off Kerry Rd 133 J6
Kerry Rd, SE14 . . . . .133 J6
Kersey Gdns, SE9 . . . . . .174 B4
Kersfield Rd, SW15 . . . . .148 A6
Kershaw Cl, SW18
 off Westover Rd 149 G6
Kershaw Rd, Dag.
 RM10 . . . . .101 G3
Kersley Ms, SW11 . . . . . .149 J2
Kersley Rd, N16 . . . . .94 B3
Kersley St, SW11 . . . . . . .149 J2
Kerswell Cl, N15 . . . . .76 B5
Kerwick Cl, N7
 off Sutterton St 93 F7
Keslake Rd, NW6 . . . . . . .108 A2
Kessock Cl, N17 . . . . .76 E5
Kesteven Cl, Ilf. IG6 . . . . .65 J6
Kestlake Rd, Bex. DA5
 off East Rochester
 Way 158 C6
KESTON 205 J5
Keston Av, Kes. BR2 . . . .205 J5
Keston Cl, N18 . . . . .60 A3
 Welling DA16 . . . . .138 C7
Keston Gdns, Kes. BR2 . .205 J4
Keston Pk Cl, Kes. BR2 . .206 C3

Keston Rd, N17 . . . . .76 A3
    SE15 . . . . .152 D3
    Thornton Heath CR7 . .187 G6
Kestral Ct, Wall. SM6
    off Carew Rd 200 C5
Kestrel Av, E6
    off Swan App 116 B5
    SE24 . . . . .151 H5
Kestrel Cl, NW9 . . . . .71 E2
    NW10 . . . . .88 D5
Kingston upon Thames
    KT2 . . . . .163 G4
Kestrel Ho, EC1 . . . . .11 J3
    W13 . . . . .104 C4
Enfield EN3
    off Alma Rd 45 G5
Kestrel Pl, SE14
    off Milton Ct Rd 133 H6
Kestrel Way, Hayes UB3 . .121 G2
Keswick Av, SW15 . . . . . . .164 E5
    SW19 . . . . .184 D2
Keswick Bdy, SW15
    off Upper Richmond
    Rd 148 B5
Keswick Cl, Sutt. SM1 . . . .199 F4
Keswick Gdns, Ilf. IG4 . . . .80 B5
Wembley HA9 . . . . .87 H4
Keswick Ms, SW1 . . . . . . .125 H1
Keswick Rd, SW15 . . . . . . .148 B5
Bexleyheath DA7 . . . . . .159 G2
Orpington BR6 . . . . .207 J1
Twickenham TW2 . . . . . .143 J6
West Wickham BR4 . . . .204 E2
Kettering St, SW16 . . . . . .168 C6
Kett Gdns, SW2 . . . . .151 F5
Kettlebaston Rd, E10 . . . .95 J1
Kettlewell Cl, N11 . . . . . . .58 A6
Kevan Ho, SE5 . . . . .131 J7
Kevelioc Rd, N17 . . . . .75 J1
Kevin Cl, Houns. TW4 . . . .142 D2
Kevington Cl, Orp. BR5 . .193 J4
Kevington Dr, Chis. BR7 .193 J4
    Orpington BR5 . . . . . . .193 J4
KEW, Rich. 126 A6
Kew Br, Brent. TW8 . . . . . .125 J6
    Richmond TW9 . . . . . . .125 J6
Kew Br Arches, Rich. TW9
    off Kew Br 125 J6
Kew Br Ct, W4 . . . . .126 A5
Kew Br Rd, Brent. TW8 . . .125 J6
★ Kew Bridge Steam Mus, .
    Brent. TW8 . . . . .125 J5
Kew Cres, Sutt. SM3 . . . . .198 B3
Kew Foot Rd, Rich. TW9 .145 H4
Kew Gdns Rd, Rich. TW9 125 J7
Kew Grn, Rich. TW9 . . . . .126 A6
★ Kew Meadow Path, Rich.
    TW9 . . . . .146 A1
★ Kew Observatory, Rich.
    TW9 . . . . .145 E3
★ Kew Palace, Royal Botanic
    Gdns, Rich. TW9 . . . . .125 H7
Kew Palace, Rich. TW9 . . .125 H7
Kew Rd, Rich. TW9 . . . . . .126 A6
Keybridge Ho, SW8 . . . . . .34 B6
Key Cl, E1 . . . . .113 E4
Keyes Rd, NW2 . . . . .90 A5
Keymer Rd, SW2 . . . . .169 F2
Keynes Cl, N2 . . . . .73 J3
Keynsham Av, Wdf.Grn.
    IG8 . . . . .63 E4
Keynsham Gdns, SE9 . . . .156 B5
Keynsham Rd, SE9 . . . . . .156 A5
    Morden SM4 . . . . .198 E1
Keynsham Wk, Mord.
    SM4 . . . . .198 E1
Keyse Rd, SE1 . . . . .29 F6
Keysham Av, Houns. TW5
    off The Avenue 142 A4
Keystone Cres, N1 . . . . . . .10 B2
Keywood Dr, Sun. TW16 .160 A6
Keyworth Cl, E5 . . . . .95 H4
Keyworth St, SE1 . . . . .27 H5
Kezia St, SE8
    off Trundleys Rd 133 H5
Khalsa Ct, N22
    off Acacia Rd 75 H1
Khama Rd, SW17 . . . . . . .167 H4
Khartoum Rd, E13 . . . . . .115 H3
    SW17 . . . . .167 G4
    Ilford IG1 . . . . .99 E5
Khyber Rd, SW11 . . . . . . .149 H2
Kibworth St, SW8 . . . . . . .131 F7
KIDBROOKE, SE3 . . . . . . .155 H3
Kidbrooke Gdns, SE3 . . . .155 H2
Kidbrooke Gro, SE3 . . . . .155 G1
Kidbrooke La, SE9 . . . . . .156 B4
Kidbrooke Pk Cl, SE3 . . . .155 H1
Kidbrooke Pk Rd, SE3 . . .155 H1

Kidbrooke Way, SE3 . . . .155 H2
Kidderminster Pl, Croy. CR0
    off Kidderminster Rd .201 H1
Kidderminster Rd, Croy.
    CR0 . . . . .201 H1
Kidderpore Av, NW3 . . . . .90 D4
Kidderpore Gdns, NW3 . .90 D4
Kidd Pl, SE7 . . . . .136 B5
Kidlington Way, NW9 . . . .70 E2
Kielder Cl, Ilf. IG6 . . . . . . .65 J6
Kiffen St, EC2 . . . . .12 C5
Kilberry Cl, Islw. TW7 . . .144 A1
KILBURN, NW6 . . . . .108 D2
Kilburn Br, NW6
    off Kilburn High Rd . . .90 C7
Kilburn Gate, NW6 . . . . . . .6 A1
Kilburn High Rd, NW6 . . .90 C7
Kilburn La, W9 . . . . .108 A3
    W10 . . . . .108 A3
Kilburn Pk Rd, NW6 . . . . .108 D3
Kilburn Pl, NW6 . . . . .108 D1
Kilburn Priory, NW6 . . . . .108 E1
Kilburn Sq, NW6
    off Kilburn High Rd . . .108 D1
Kilburn Vale, NW6
    off Belsize Rd 108/109 E1
Kilby Ter, Wdf.Grn. IG8
    off Baddow Cl 64 A6
Kildare Cl, Ruis. HA4 . . . .84 C1
Kildare Gdns, W2 . . . . . . .108 D6
Kildare Rd, E16 . . . . .115 G5
Kildare Ter, W2 . . . . .108 D6
Kildare Wk, E14
    off Farrance St 114 A6
Kildoran Rd, SW2 . . . . . . .150 E5
Kildowan Rd, Ilf. IG3 . . . .100 A1
Kilgour Rd, SE23 . . . . . . .153 H6
Kilkie St, SW6 . . . . .149 F2
Killarney Rd, SW18 . . . . .149 F6
Killburns Mill Cl, Wall. SM6
    off London Rd 200 B4
Killearn Rd, SE6 . . . . .172 D1
Killester Gdns, Wor.Pk.
    KT4 . . . . .197 H4
Killick St, N1 . . . . .10 C1
Killieser Av, SW2 . . . . . . .168 E2
Killip Cl, E16 . . . . .115 F6
Killowen Av, Nthlt. UB5 . .85 J5
Killowen Rd, E9 . . . . .95 G6
Killyon Rd, SW8 . . . . .150 C2
Killyon Ter, SW8 . . . . .150 C2
Kilmaine Rd, SW6 . . . . . .128 B7
Kilmarnock Gdns, Dag. RM8
    off Lindsey Rd 100 C3
Kilmarnock Rd, Wat.
    WD19 . . . . .50 D4
Kilmarsh Rd, W6 . . . . . . .127 J4
Kilmartin Av, SW16 . . . . .187 F3
Kilmartin Rd, Ilf. IG3 . . . .100 A2
Kilmeston Way, SE15 . . . .37 F7
Kilmington Rd, SW13 . . .127 G6
Kilmorey Gdns, Twick.
    TW1 . . . . .144 E5
Kilmorey Rd, Twick.
    TW1 . . . . .144 E4
Kilmorie Rd, SE23 . . . . . .171 H1
Kiln Cl, Hayes UB3
    off Brickfield La 121 G6
Kilner St, E14 . . . . .114 A5
Kiln Ms, SW17 . . . . .167 G5
Kiln Pl, NW5 . . . . .92 A5
Kilnside, Esher (Clay.)
    KT10 . . . . .194 D7
Kilpatrick Way, Hayes
    UB4 . . . . .103 E5
Kilravock St, W10 . . . . . . .108 B3
Kilsby Wk, Dag. RM9
    off Rugby Rd 100 B6
Kilsha Rd, Walt. KT12 . . .178 B6
Kimbell Gdns, SW6 . . . . .148 B1
Kimbell Pl, SE3
    off Tudway Rd 155 J4
Kimberley Av, E6 . . . . . . .116 B2
    SE15 . . . . .153 E2
    Ilford IG2 . . . . .81 G7
    Romford RM7 . . . . .83 J4
Kimberley Dr, Sid. DA14 .176 D2
Kimberley Gdns, N4 . . . . .75 H5
    Enfield EN1 . . . . .44 C3
Kimberley Gate, Brom. BR1
    off Oaklands Rd 173 F7
Kimberley Ind Est, E17 . .77 J1
Kimberley Rd, E4 . . . . .62 E1
    E11 . . . . .96 D2
    E16 . . . . .115 F4
    E17 . . . . .77 J1
    N17 . . . . .76 D2
    N18 . . . . .61 E6
    NW6 . . . . .108 B1
    SW9 . . . . .151 E2

Kimberley Rd, Beck. BR3 .189 G2
    Croydon CR0 . . . . .187 H6
Kimberley Way, E4 . . . . . .63 E1
Kimber Rd, SW18 . . . . . . .148 D7
Kimble Rd, SW19 . . . . . . .167 G6
Kimbolton Cl, SE12 . . . . .155 F6
Kimbolton Grn, Borwd.
    WD6 . . . . .38 C4
Kimbolton Row, SW3 . . . .31 G2
Kimmeridge Gdns, SE9 .174 B4
Kimmeridge Rd, SE9 . . . .174 B4
Kimpton Ho, SW15
    off Fontley Way 147 G7
Kimpton Rd, SE5 . . . . .152 A1
    Sutton SM3 . . . . .198 C2
Kimpton Trade Business Cen,
    Sutt. SM3 . . . . .198 C2
Kinburn St, SE16 . . . . . . .133 G2
Kincaid Rd, SE15 . . . . . . .132 E7
Kincardine Gdns, W9
    off Harrow Rd 108 C4
Kinch Gro, Wem. HA9 . . . .69 J7
Kinder Cl, SE28 . . . . .118 D7
Kinder St, E1
    off Cannon St Rd .112/113 E6
Kinfauns Rd, SW2 . . . . . .169 G2
    Ilford IG3 . . . . .100 A1
King Alfred Av, SE6 . . . . .172 A3
King & Queen Cl, SE9
    off St. Keverne Rd 174 B4
King & Queen St, SE17 . .36 A2
King Arthur Cl, SE15 . . . .133 F7
King Charles Cres, Surb.
    KT5 . . . . .181 J7
King Charles Rd, Surb.
    KT5 . . . . .181 J5
King Charles St, SW1 . . . .25 J3
King Charles Ter, E1
    off Sovereign Cl .112/113 E7
King Charles Wk, SW19
    off Princes Way 166 B1
Kingcup Cl, Croy. CR0
    off Primrose La 203 G1
King David La, E1 . . . . . . .113 F7
Kingdon Rd, NW6 . . . . . . .90 D6
King Edward Dr, Chess. KT9
    off Kelvin Gro 195 H3
King Edward Ms, SW13 .147 G1
King Edward Rd, E10 . . . .96 C1
    E17 . . . . .77 H3
    Barnet EN5 . . . . .40 D4
King Edward's Gdns,
    W3 . . . . .126 A1
King Edwards Gro, Tedd.
    TW11 . . . . .163 E6
King Edward's Pl, W3
    off King Edward's
    Gdns 126 A1
King Edwards Rd, E9 . . . .113 E1
    N9 . . . . .44 E7
    Barking IG11 . . . . .117 G1
King Edward's Rd, Enf.
    EN3 . . . . .45 G4
King Edward St, EC1 . . . . .19 J3
King Edward III Ms, SE16
    off Paradise St .132/133 E2
King Edward Wk, SE1 . . . .27 F5
Kingfield Rd, W5 . . . . .105 G4
Kingfield St, E14 . . . . .134 C4
Kingfisher Av, E11
    off Eastern Av 79 H6
Kingfisher Cl, SE28 . . . . .118 C7
Harrow (Har.Wld.) HA3 .52 C7
Kingfisher Ct, SW19
    off Queensmere Rd . .166 B2
Surbiton KT6
    off Ewell Rd 181 J7
Sutton SM1
    off Sandpiper Rd 198 C5
Kingfisher Dr, Rich.
    TW10 . . . . .163 E4
Kingfisher Sq, SE8 . . . . . .133 J6
Kingfisher St, E6 . . . . . . .116 B5
Kingfisher Wk, NW9
    off Eagle Dr 70/71 E2
Kingfisher Way, NW10 . . .88 D5
    Beckenham BR3 . . . . .189 G5
King Frederik IX Twr,
    SE16 . . . . .133 J3
King Gdns, Croy. CR0 . . .201 H5
King George Av, E16 . . . .116 A6
    Ilford IG2 . . . . .81 G5
King George Cl, Rom.
    RM7 . . . . .83 J3
King Georges Dr, Sthl.
    UB1 . . . . .103 F5
King George VI Av, Mitch.
    CR4 . . . . .185 J4
King George Sq, Rich.
    TW10 . . . . .145 J6

King George's Trd Est, Chess.
    KT9 . . . . .196 A4
King George St, SE10 . . . .134 C7
Kingham Cl, SW18 . . . . . .149 F7
    W11 . . . . .128 B2
King Harolds Way, Bexh.
    DA7 . . . . .138 D7
King Henry Ms, Orp. BR6
    off Osgood Av 207 J5
King Henry's Reach, W6 .127 J6
King Henry's Rd, NW3 . . .91 H7
Kingston upon Thames
    KT1 . . . . .182 B3
King Henry St, N16 . . . . . .94 B4
King Henry's Wk, N1 . . . . .94 B6
King Henry Ter, E1
    off Sovereign Cl . .112/113 E7
Kinghorn St, EC1 . . . . .19 J2
King James Ct, SE1
    off Borough Rd 131 H2
King James St, SE1 . . . . . .27 H4
King John Ct, EC2 . . . . . . .12 E5
King John St, E1 . . . . .113 G5
King Johns Wk, SE9 . . . . .174 A1
Kinglake Est, SE17 . . . . . .37 E3
Kinglake St, SE17 . . . . . . .36 D4
Kingly Ct, W1 . . . . .17 F5
Kingly St, W1 . . . . .17 F4
Kingsand Rd, SE12 . . . . . .173 G2
Kings Arbour, Sthl. UB2 .122 E5
Kings Arms Ct, E1 . . . . . . .21 H2
Kings Arms Yd, EC2 . . . . .20 B3
Kingsash Dr, Hayes UB4 .102 E4
Kings Av, N10 . . . . .74 A3
    N21 . . . . .59 H1
King's Av, SW4 . . . . .150 D7
    SW12 . . . . .168 D1
Kings Av, W5 . . . . .105 G6
    Bromley BR1 . . . . .173 F6
    Buckhurst Hill IG9 . . . .64 A2
    Carshalton SM5 . . . . . .199 H7
    Greenford UB6 . . . . . . .103 H6
    Hounslow TW3 . . . . . . .143 H1
    New Malden KT3 . . . . .183 E4
    Romford RM6 . . . . .83 F6
    Woodford Green IG8 . .63 H6
Kings Bench St, SE1 . . . . .27 H3
Kings Bench Wk, EC4 . . . .19 F4
Kingsbridge Av, W3 . . . . .125 J2
Kingsbridge Ct, E14
    off Dockers Tanner
    Rd 134 A4
Kingsbridge Cres, Sthl.
    UB1 . . . . .103 F5
Kingsbridge Dr, NW7
    off Bittacy Hill 56 B7
Kingsbridge Rd, W10 . . . .107 J6
    Barking IG11 . . . . .117 G2
    Morden SM4 . . . . .184 A7
    Southall UB2 . . . . .123 F4
    Walton-on-Thames
    KT12 . . . . .178 B7
KINGSBURY, NW9 . . . . . . .70 B6
Kingsbury Circle, NW9 . . .70 A5
Kingsbury Rd, N1 . . . . .94 B6
    NW9 . . . . .70 B5
Kingsbury Ter, N1 . . . . . . .94 B6
Kingsbury Trd Est, NW9 . .70 D6
Kings Chace Vw, Enf. EN2
    off Crofton Way 43 G2
Kings Chase, E.Mol.
    KT8 . . . . .179 J3
Kingsclere Cl, SW15 . . . .147 G7
Kingsclere Ct, Barn. EN5
    off Gloucester Rd 41 F5
Kingsclere Pl, Enf. EN2
    off Chase Side 43 J2
Kingscliffe Gdns, SW19 .166 C1
Kings Cl, E10 . . . . .78 B7
    NW4 . . . . .72 A4
Thames Ditton KT7 . . . .180 D6
Kings Coll Rd, NW3 . . . . . .91 H7
Kingscote Rd, W4 . . . . . . .126 D3
    Croydon CR0 . . . . .188 E7
    New Malden KT3 . . . . .182 D3
Kingscote St, EC4 . . . . . . .19 G5
Kings Ct, E13 . . . . .115 H1
    W6 off King St 127 G4
    Wembley HA9 . . . . .88 B2
Kingscourt Rd, SW16 . . . .168 D3
Kings Ct S, SW3
    off Chelsea Manor
    Gdns 129 H5
Kings Cres, N4 . . . . .93 J3
Kings Cres Est, N4 . . . . . . .93 J2
Kingscroft Rd, NW2 . . . . .90 C6
KING'S CROSS, N1 . . . . .110 D1
King's Cross Br, N1 . . . . . .10 B1
King's Cross Rd, WC1 . . . .10 D3
Kingsdale Gdns, W11 . . . .128 A1

Kin–Kir 295

Kingsdale Rd, SE18 . . . . . **137** J7
SE20 . . . . **171** G7
Kingsdown Av, W3 . . . . . **107** E7
W13 . . . . **125** E2
Kingsdown Cl, SE16
off Masters Dr . . . **132/133** E5
W10 . . . . **108** A6
Kingsdowne Rd, Surb.
KT6 . . . . **181** H7
Kingsdown Rd, E11 . . . . . . **97** E3
N19 . . . . **92** E2
Sutton SM3 . . . . **198** B5
Kingsdown Way, Brom.
BR2 . . . . **191** G7
Kings Dr, Edg. HA8 . . . . . . **53** J4
Surbiton KT5 . . . . **182** A7
Teddington TW11 . . . . . **162** A5
Thames Ditton KT7 . . . **180** E6
Wembley HA9 . . . . **88** B2
Kings Fm Av, Rich. TW10 . **146** A4
Kingsfield Av, Har. HA2 . . . **67** H4
Kingsfield Ho, SE9 . . . . . . **174** A3
Kingsfield Rd, Har. HA1 . . **68** A7
Kingsford Av, Wall. SM6 . **201** E7
Kingsford St, NW5 . . . . . . **91** J5
Kingsford Way, E6 . . . . . . **116** C5
Kings Gdns, NW6
off West End La **90** D7
Ilford IG1 . . . . **99** G1
King's Garth Ms, SE23
off London Rd **171** F2
Kingsgate, Wem. HA9 . . . . **88** C3
Kingsgate Av, N3 . . . . **72** D3
Kingsgate Cl, Bexh. DA7 . **158** E1
Kingsgate Pl, NW6 . . . . . . **90** D7
Kingsgate Rd, NW6 . . . . . . **90** D7
Kingston upon Thames
KT2 . . . . **181** H1
Kings Grn, Loug. IG10 . . . **48** B3
Kingsground, SE9 . . . . . . **156** B7
Kings Gro, SE15 . . . . **133** E7
Kingshall Ms, SE13
off Lewisham Rd **154** C3
Kings Hall Rd, Beck. BR3 . **171** H7
Kings Head Hill, E4 . . . . . . **46** B7
Kings Head Yd, SE1 . . . . . **28** B2
Kings Highway, SE18 . . . **137** H6
Kings Hill, Loug. IG10 . . . . **48** B2
Kingshill Av, Har. HA3 . . . . **69** E4
Northolt UB5 . . . . **102** A3
Worcester Park KT4 . . . **183** G7
Kingshill Dr, Har. HA3 . . . . **68** E3
Kingshold Est, E9
off Victoria Pk Rd **113** F1
Kingshold Rd, E9 . . . . **95** F7
Kingsholm Gdns, SE9 . . . **156** A4
Kingshurst Rd, SE12 . . . . **155** G7
Kingside Business Pk, SE18
off Woolwich Ch St . . . **136** B3
Kings Keep, Kings.T. KT1
off Beaufort Rd **181** H4
KINGSLAND, N1 . . . . **94** B6
Kingsland, NW8
off Broxwood Way . . . **109** H1
Kingsland Grn, E8 . . . . **94** B6
Kingsland High St, E8 . . . . **94** C5
Kingsland Pas, E8
off Kingsland Grn **94** B6
Kingsland Rd, E2 . . . . **13** E3
E8 . . . . **112** B2
E13 . . . . **115** J3
Kings La, Sutt. SM1 . . . . **199** G6
Kingslawn Cl, SW15
off Howards La **147** H5
Kingsleigh Pl, Mitch. CR4
off Chatsworth Pl **185** J3
Kingsleigh Wk, Brom. BR2
off Stamford Dr **191** F4
Kingsley Av, W13 . . . . **104** D6
Hounslow TW3 . . . . **143** J2
Southall UB1 . . . . **103** G7
Sutton SM1 . . . . **199** G4
Kingsley Cl, N2 . . . . **73** F5
Dagenham RM10 . . . . . **101** H4
Kingsley Ct, Edg. HA8 . . . . **54** B2
Kingsley Dr, Wor.Pk. KT4
off Badgers Copse . . . **197** F2
Kingsley Flats, SE1
off Old Kent Rd **132** B4
Kingsley Gdns, E4 . . . . **62** A5
Kingsley Ms, E1
off Wapping La . . **112/113** E7
W8 . . . . **22** B6
Chislehurst BR7 . . . . . . **175** E6
Kingsley Pl, N6 . . . . **74** A7
Kingsley Rd, E7 . . . . **97** G7
E17 . . . . **78** C2
N13 . . . . **59** G4
NW6 . . . . **108** C1
SW19 . . . . **167** E5
Kingsley Rd, Croy. CR0 . . **201** G1
Harrow HA2 . . . . **85** J4
Hounslow TW3 . . . . **143** J2
Ilford IG6 . . . . **81** F1
Loughton IG10 . . . . **49** G3
Orpington BR6 . . . . **207** J7
Pinner HA5 . . . . **67** F4
Kingsley St, SW11 . . . . . . **149** J3
Kingsley Way, N2 . . . . **73** F6
Kingsley Wd Dr, SE9 . . . . **174** C3
Kingslyn Cres, SE19 . . . . **188** B1
Kings Mall, W6 . . . . **127** J4
Kingsman Par, SE18
off Woolwich Ch St . . . **136** C3
Kingsman St, SE18 . . . . . **136** C3
Kingsmead, Barn. EN5 . . . **40** D4
Richmond TW10 . . . . . . **145** J6
Kingsmead Av, N9 . . . . . . **60** E1
NW9 . . . . **70** D7
Mitcham CR4 . . . . **186** C3
Sunbury-on-Thames
TW16 . . . . **178** C3
Surbiton KT6 . . . . **196** A2
Worcester Park KT4 . . . **197** H3
Kingsmead Cl, Epsom
KT19 . . . . **196** D7
Sidcup DA15 . . . . **176** A2
Teddington TW11 . . . . . **162** D6
Kingsmead Dr, Nthlt.
UB5 . . . . **85** F7
Kingsmead Est, E9
off Kingsmead Way . . . **95** H4
Kings Mead Pk, Esher (Clay.)
KT10 . . . . **194** B7
Kingsmead Rd, SW2 . . . . **169** G2
Kingsmead Way, E9 . . . . . **95** H4
Kingsmere Cl, SW15
off Felsham Rd **148** B3
Kingsmere Pk, NW9 . . . . . **88** B1
Kingsmere Pl, N16 . . . . . . **94** A1
Kingsmere Rd, SW19 . . . . **166** A2
Kings Ms, SW4
off King's Av **150/151** E5
King's Ms, WC1 . . . . **10** D6
Kings Ms, Chig. IG7 . . . . . **65** F2
Kingsmill Gdns, Dag.
RM9 . . . . **101** F5
Kingsmill Rd, Dag. RM9 . **101** F5
Kingsmill Ter, NW8 . . . . **7** F1
Kingsnympton Pk, Kings.T.
KT2 . . . . **164** B6
Kings Oak, Rom. RM7 . . . . **83** G3
King's Orchard, SE9 . . . . **156** B6
Kings Paddock, Hmptn.
TW12 . . . . **179** J1
Kings Par, Cars. SM5
off Wrythe La **199** H3
Kingspark Ct, E18 . . . . **79** G3
King's Pas, E11 . . . . **78** E7
Kings Pas, Kings.T. KT1 . . **181** G2
Kings Pl, SE1 . . . . **27** J4
W4 . . . . **126** C5
Buckhurst Hill IG9 . . . . . **63** J2
Loughton IG10 . . . . **48** A7
King Sq, EC1 . . . . **11** J4
King's Reach Twr, SE1 . . . . **27** F1
Kings Ride Gate, Rich.
TW10 . . . . **146** A4
Kingsridge, SW19 . . . . . . **166** B2
Kings Rd, E4 . . . . **62** D1
E6 . . . . **115** J1
E11 . . . . **78** E7
King's Rd, N17 . . . . **76** C1
Kings Rd, N18 . . . . **60** D5
N22 . . . . **75** F1
NW10 . . . . **89** H7
SE25 . . . . **188** D3
King's Rd, SW1 . . . . **31** H3
SW3 . . . . **31** H3
SW6 . . . . **148** E1
SW10 . . . . **148** E1
Kings Rd, SW14 . . . . **146** D3
SW19 . . . . **166** D6
W5 . . . . **105** G5
Barking IG11
off North St **99** F7
Barnet EN5 . . . . **39** J3
Feltham TW13 . . . . **160** C1
Harrow HA2 . . . . **85** F2
Kingston upon Thames
KT2 . . . . **163** H7
Mitcham CR4 . . . . **186** A3
Orpington BR6 . . . . **207** J4
Richmond TW10 . . . . . . **145** J5
Surbiton KT6 . . . . **195** F1
Teddington TW11 . . . . . **162** A5
Twickenham TW1 . . . . . **145** E6
West Drayton UB7 . . . . **120** C2
Kings Rd Bungalows, Har. HA2
off Kings Rd **85** F3
King's Scholars' Pas,
SW1 . . . . **33** F1
King Stairs Cl, SE16
off Elephant La . . **132/133** E2
King's Ter, NW1
off Plender St **110** C1
Kings Ter, Islw. TW7
off Worple Rd **144** D3
Kingsthorpe Rd, SE26 . . . **171** G4
Kingston Av, Felt. TW14 . **141** H6
Sutton SM3 . . . . **198** B3
Kingston Br, Kings.T.
KT1 . . . . **181** G2
Kingston Bypass, SW15 . **165** E4
SW20 . . . . **165** E4
Esher KT10 . . . . **194** D3
New Malden KT3 . . . . . **183** F1
Surbiton KT5, KT6 . . . . **195** H3
Kingston Cl, Nthlt. UB5 . . **103** F1
Romford RM6 . . . . **82** E3
Teddington TW11 . . . . . **162** E6
Kingston Ct, N4
off Wiltshire Gdns **75** J6
Kingston Cres, Beck.
BR3 . . . . **189** J1
Kingston Gdns, Croy. CR0
off Wandle Rd . . . **200/201** E3
Kingston Hall Rd, Kings.T.
KT1 . . . . **181** G3
Kingston Hill, Kings.T.
KT2 . . . . **164** C6
Kingston Hill Av, Rom.
RM6 . . . . **83** E3
Kingston Hill Pl, Kings.T.
KT2 . . . . **164** C4
Kingston La, Tedd. TW11 . **162** D5
West Drayton UB7 . . . . **120** C2
★ **Kingston Mus & Heritage Cen**, Kings.T. KT1 . . . . **181** H2
Kingston Pk Est, Kings.T.
KT2 . . . . **164** B6
Kingston Pl, Har. HA3
off Richmond Gdns . . . **52** C7
Kingston Rd, N9 . . . . **60** D2
SW15 . . . . **165** G1
SW19 . . . . **184** C1
SW20 . . . . **183** J2
Barnet EN4 . . . . **41** G5
Epsom KT17, KT19 . . . . **196** E5
Ilford IG1 . . . . **99** E4
Kingston upon Thames
KT1 . . . . **182** B3
New Malden KT3 . . . . . **182** D4
Southall UB2 . . . . **123** F2
Surbiton KT5 . . . . **196** B2
Teddington TW11 . . . . . **162** E5
Worcester Park KT4 . . . **196** B2
Kingston Sq, SE19 . . . . . **170** A5
KINGSTON UPON THAMES **181** H2
KINGSTON VALE, SW15 . **165** E4
Kingston Vale, SW15 . . . . **164** D4
Kingstown St, NW1 . . . . . **110** A1
King St, E13 . . . . **115** G4
EC2 . . . . **20** A4
N2 . . . . **73** G3
N17 . . . . **76** C1
SW1 . . . . **25** G2
W3 . . . . **126** B1
W6 . . . . **127** G4
WC2 . . . . **18** A5
Richmond TW9 . . . . **145** G5
Southall UB2 . . . . **123** E3
Twickenham TW1 . . . . . **162** D1
King's Wk, Kings.T. KT2 . . **181** G1
Kings Wk Shop Mall, SW3
off King's Rd **129** J5
Kingswater Pl, SW11
off Battersea Ch Rd . . **129** H7
Kingsway, N12 . . . . **57** F6
SW14 . . . . **146** B3
WC2 . . . . **18** C3
Croydon CR0 . . . . **201** F5
Enfield EN3 . . . . **45** E5
Kings Way, Har. HA1 . . . . . **68** B4
Kingsway, N.Mal. KT3 . . . **183** J4
Orpington BR5 . . . . **193** H5
Wembley HA9 . . . . **87** H4
West Wickham BR4 . . . **205** E3
Woodford Green IG8 . . . **63** J5
Kingsway Business Pk,
Hmptn. TW12 . . . . **179** F1
Kingsway Cres, Har. HA2 . **67** J4
Kingsway Pl, EC1 . . . . **11** F5
Kingsway Rd, Sutt. SM3 . **198** B7
Kingsway Shop Cen, NW3
off Hampstead High St . **91** F4
Kingswear Rd, NW5 . . . . . **92** B3
Ruislip HA4 . . . . **84** A2
Kingswood Av, NW6 . . . . **108** B1
Kingswood Av, Belv.
DA17 . . . . **139** F4
Bromley BR2 . . . . **190** E3
Hampton TW12 . . . . **161** H6
Hounslow TW3 . . . . **143** F1
Thornton Heath CR7 . . **187** G5
Kingswood Cl, N20 . . . . . . **41** F6
SW8 . . . . **131** E7
Enfield EN1 . . . . **44** B5
New Malden KT3
off Motspur Pk **183** F6
Orpington BR6 . . . . **193** G7
Surbiton KT6 . . . . **181** H7
Kingswood Dr, SE19 . . . . **170** B4
Carshalton SM5 . . . . . . **199** J1
Kingswood Est, SE21
off Bowen Dr **170** B4
Kingswood Ms, N15
off Harringay Rd **75** H5
Kingswood Pk, N3 . . . . . . **72** C2
Kingswood Pl, SE13 . . . . **155** E4
Kingswood Rd, E11
off Grove Grn Rd **96** D2
SE20 . . . . **171** F6
SW2 . . . . **150** E6
SW19 . . . . **166** C7
W4 . . . . **126** C3
Bromley BR2 . . . . **190** D4
Ilford IG3 . . . . **100** A1
Wembley HA9 . . . . **88** A3
Kingswood Ter, W4
off Kingswood Rd . . . **126** C3
Kingswood Way, Wall.
SM6 . . . . **201** E5
Kingsworth Cl, Beck.
BR3 . . . . **189** H5
Kingsworthy Cl, Kings.T.
KT1 . . . . **181** J3
King's Yd, SW15
off Stanbridge Rd **147** J3
Kingthorpe Rd, NW10 . . . . **88** D7
Kingthorpe Ter, NW10 . . . . **88** D6
Kingweston Cl, NW2
off Windmill Dr **90** B3
King William IV Gdns, SE20
off St. John's Rd **171** F6
King William La, SE10
off Orlop St **134/135** E5
King William St, EC4 . . . . **20** C6
King William Wk, SE10 . . **134** C6
Kingwood Rd, SW6 . . . . . **148** A1
Kinlet Rd, SE18 . . . . **157** F1
Kinloch Dr, NW9 . . . . **70** E7
Kinloch St, N7
off Hornsey Rd **93** F3
Kinloss Ct, N3
off Haslemere Gdns . . . **72** C4
Kinloss Gdns, N3 . . . . **72** C4
Kinloss Rd, Cars. SM5 . . . **185** F7
Kinnaird Av, W4 . . . . **126** C7
Bromley BR1 . . . . **173** F6
Kinnaird Cl, Brom. BR1 . . **173** F6
Kinnaird Way, Wdf.Grn.
IG8 . . . . **64** C6
Kinnear Rd, W12 . . . . **127** F2
Kinnerton Pl N, SW1 . . . . . **24** A4
Kinnerton Pl S, SW1 . . . . . **24** A4
Kinnerton St, SW1 . . . . . . **24** B4
Kinnerton Yd, SW1 . . . . . . **24** A4
Kinnoul Rd, W6 . . . . **128** B6
Kinross Av, Wor.Pk. KT4 . **197** G2
Kinross Cl, Edg. HA8
off Tayside Dr **54** B2
Harrow HA3 . . . . **69** J5
Kinross Ter, E17 . . . . **77** J2
Kinsale Rd, SE15 . . . . **152** D3
Kintore Way, SE1 . . . . **37** F1
Kintyre Cl, SW16 . . . . **187** F3
Kinveachy Gdns, SE7 . . . **136** B5
Kinver Rd, SE26 . . . . **171** F4
Kipling Dr, SW19 . . . . **167** G6
Kipling Est, SE1 . . . . **28** C4
Kipling Pl, Stan. HA7
off Uxbridge Rd **52** C6
Kipling Rd, Bexh. DA7 . . . **159** E1
Kipling St, SE1 . . . . **28** C4
Kipling Ter, N9 . . . . **60** A3
Kippington Dr, SE9 . . . . . **174** A1
Kirby Cl, Epsom KT19 . . . **197** F5
Ilford IG6 . . . . **65** H6
Loughton IG10 . . . . **48** B7
Kirby Est, SE16 . . . . **132** E3
Kirby Gro, SE1 . . . . **28** D3
Kirby St, EC1 . . . . **19** F1
Kirby Way, Walt. KT12 . . . **178** C6
Kirchen Rd, W13 . . . . **104** E7
Kirkby Cl, N11
off Coverdale Rd **58** A6
Kirkcaldy Grn, Wat. WD19
off Trevose Way **50** C3

Kirkdale, SE26 . . . .**170** E2
Kirkdale Rd, E11 . . . .**97** E1
Kirkfield Cl, W13
　off Broomfield
　Rd **124/125** E1
Kirkham Rd, E6 . . . .**116** B6
Kirkham St, SE18 . . . .**137** H6
Kirkland Av, Ilf. IG5 . . . . .**80** D2
Kirkland Cl, Sid. DA15 . . .**157** H6
Kirkland Dr, Enf. EN2 . . . .**43** H1
Kirkland Wk, E8 . . . .**94** C6
Kirk La, SE18 . . . .**137** F6
Kirkleas Rd, Surb. KT6 .**195** H1
Kirklees Rd, Dag. RM8 . .**100** C5
　Thornton Heath CR7 . .**187** G5
Kirkley Rd, SW19 . . . . . .**184** D1
Kirkman Pl, W1 . . . .**17** H2
Kirkmichael Rd, E14
　off Dee St **114** C6
Kirk Ri, Sutt. SM1 . . . . . .**199** E3
Kirk Rd, E17 . . . .**77** J6
Kirkside Rd, SE3 . . . .**135** G6
Kirks Pl, E14
　off Rhodeswell Rd . . .**113** J5
Kirkstall Av, N17 . . . .**76** A4
Kirkstall Gdns, SW2 . . . .**168** D1
Kirkstall Rd, SW2 . . . . . .**168** D1
Kirkstead Ct, E5
　off Mandeville St **95** H3
Kirksted Rd, Mord. SM4 .**198** E1
Kirkstone Way, Brom.
　BR1 . . . .**173** E7
Kirk St, WC1
　off Northington St . . .**111** F4
Kirkton Rd, N15 . . . .**76** B4
Kirkwall Pl, E2 . . . .**113** F3
Kirkwood Rd, SE15 . . . . .**153** E2
Kirn Rd, W13
　off Kirchen Rd . . .**104/105** E7
Kirrane Cl, N.Mal. KT3 . .**183** F5
Kirtley Rd, SE26 . . . .**171** H4
Kirtling St, SW8 . . . .**33** F7
Kirton Cl, W4
　off Dolman Rd **126** D4
Kirton Gdns, E2 . . . .**13** G4
Kirton Rd, E13 . . . .**115** J2
Kirton Wk, Edg. HA8 . . . . .**54** C7
Kirwyn Way, SE5 . . . .**35** H7
Kitcat Ter, E3 . . . .**114** A3
Kitchener Rd, E7 . . . .**97** H6
　E17 . . . .**78** B1
　N2 . . . .**73** H3
　N17 . . . .**76** A3
　Dagenham RM10 . . . .**101** H6
　Thornton Heath CR7 . .**188** A3
Kite Pl, E2 . . . .**13** J3
Kite Yd, SW11
　off Cambridge Rd **149** J1
Kitley Gdns, SE19 . . . . . .**188** C1
Kitson Rd, SE5 . . . .**36** A7
　SW13 . . . .**147** G1
Kittiwake Pl, Sutt. SM1
　off Sandpiper Rd **198** C5
Kittiwake Way, Hayes
　UB4 . . . .**102** D5
Kitto Rd, SE14 . . . .**153** G2
Kiver Rd, N19 . . . .**92** D2
Kiwi Cl, Twick. TW1
　off Crown Rd **144/145** E6
Klea Av, SW4 . . . .**150** C6
Knapdale Cl, SE23 . . . . . .**171** E2
Knapmill Rd, SE6 . . . . . .**172** A2
Knapmill Way, SE6 . . . . .**172** B2
Knapp Cl, NW10 . . . .**89** E6
Knapp Rd, E3 . . . .**114** A4
Knapton Ms, SW17
　off Seely Rd **168** A6
Knaresborough Dr,
　SW18 . . . .**166** E1
Knaresborough Pl, SW5 . .**30** A1
Knatchbull Rd, NW10 . . .**106** D1
　SE5 . . . .**151** J1
Knebworth Av, E17 . . . . . .**78** A1
Knebworth Path, Borwd.
　WD6 . . . .**38** D4
Knebworth Rd, N16
　off Nevill Rd **94** B4
Knee Hill, SE2 . . . .**138** C4
Knee Hill Cres, SE2 . . . . .**138** C4
Kneller Gdns, Islw. TW7 .**144** A5
Kneller Rd, SE4 . . . .**153** H4
　New Malden KT3 . . . .**182** E7
　Twickenham TW2 . . . .**143** J6
Knighten St, E1 . . . .**29** J2
Knighthead Pt, E14 . . . . .**134** A3
Knightland Rd, E5 . . . .**94** E2
Knighton Cl, S.Croy.
　CR2 . . . .**201** H7
　Woodford Green IG8 . .**63** H4

Knighton Dr, Wdf.Grn.
　IG8 . . . .**63** G4
Knighton Grn, Buck.H. IG9
　off High Rd **63** H2
Knighton La, Buck.H. IG9 .**63** H2
Knighton Pk Rd, SE26 . . .**171** G5
Knighton Rd, E7 . . . .**97** G3
　Romford RM7 . . . .**83** J6
Knightrider Ct, EC4 . . . . . .**19** J5
Knightrider St, EC4
　off Godliman St **111** J7
Knights Arc, SW1 . . . .**23** J4
Knights Av, W5 . . . .**125** H2
Knightsbridge, SW1 . . . . .**24** A4
　SW7 . . . .**23** H4
Knightsbridge Grn, SW1 . .**23** J4
Knights Cl, E9
　off Churchill Wk **95** F5
Knights Ct, Kings.T. KT1 .**181** H3
　Romford RM6 . . . .**83** E6
Knights Hill, SE27 . . . . . .**169** H5
Knights Hill Sq, SE27
　off Knights Hill **169** H4
Knights La, N9 . . . .**60** D3
Knights Ms, Sutt. SM2
　off York Rd **198** D7
Knights Pk, Kings.T. KT1 .**181** H3
Knights Rd, E16 . . . .**135** G2
　Stanmore HA7 . . . .**53** F4
Knights Wk, SE11 . . . .**35** G2
Knights Way, Ilf. IG6 . . . . .**65** F6
Knightswood Cl, Edg.
　HA8 . . . .**54** C2
Knightwood Cres, N.Mal.
　KT3 . . . .**182** E6
Knivet Rd, SW6 . . . .**128** D6
Knobs Hill Rd, E15 . . . . . .**114** B1
Knockholt Rd, SE9 . . . . . .**156** A5
Knole, The, SE9 . . . .**174** D4
Knole Cl, Croy. CR0
　off Stockbury Rd **189** F6
Knole Gate, Sid. DA15
　off Woodside Cres . . .**175** H3
Knoll, The, W13 . . . .**105** F5
　Beckenham BR3 . . . . .**190** B1
　Bromley BR2 . . . .**205** G2
Knoll Ct, SE19 . . . .**170** C5
Knoll Dr, N14 . . . .**42** A7
Knollmead, Surb. KT5 . . .**196** C1
Knoll Ri, Orp. BR6 . . . . . .**207** J1
Knoll Rd, SW18 . . . .**149** F5
　Bexley DA5 . . . .**159** G7
　Sidcup DA14 . . . .**176** B5
Knolls Cl, Wor.Pk. KT4 . .**197** H3
Knollys Cl, SW16 . . . .**169** G3
Knollys Rd, SW16 . . . . . .**169** G3
Knottisford St, E2 . . . . . .**113** F3
Knotts Grn Ms, E10 . . . . . .**78** B6
Knotts Grn Rd, E10 . . . . . .**78** B6
Knowle Av, Bexh. DA7 . . .**139** E7
Knowle Cl, SW9 . . . .**151** G3
Knowle Rd, Brom. BR2 . .**206** B2
　Twickenham TW2 . . . .**162** B1
Knowles Cl, West Dr.
　UB7 . . . .**120** B1
Knowles Hill Cres, SE13 .**154** D5
Knowles Wk, SW4 . . . . . .**150** C3
Knowlton Grn, Brom.
　BR2 . . . .**191** F5
Knowsley Av, Sthl. UB1 .**123** G1
Knowsley Rd, SW11 . . . .**149** J2
Knox Rd, E7 . . . .**97** F6
Knox St, W1 . . . .**15** J1
Knoyle St, SE14
　off Chubworthy St . . .**133** H6
Kohat Rd, SW19 . . . .**167** E5
Kossuth St, SE10 . . . . . .**134** E5
Kotree Way, SE1 . . . .**37** J2
Kramer Ms, SW5
　off Kempsford Gdns . .**128** D5
Kreedman Wk, E8 . . . .**94** D5
Kreisel Wk, Rich.TW9 . . .**125** J6
Kuala Gdns, SW16 . . . . .**187** F1
Kuhn Way, E7
　off Forest La **97** G5
Kydbrook Cl, Orp. BR5 . .**193** G7
Kylemore Cl, E6
　off Parr Rd **116** A2
Kylemore Rd, NW6 . . . . . .**90** D7
Kymberley Rd, Har. HA1 . .**68** B6
Kynance Gdns, Stan. HA7 .**69** F1
Kynance Ms, SW7 . . . .**22** C6
Kynance Pl, SW7 . . . .**22** C6
Kynaston Av, N16
　off Dynevor Rd **94** C3
　Thornton Heath CR7 . .**187** J5
Kynaston Cl, Har. HA3 . . . .**52** A7
Kynaston Cres, Th.Hth.
　CR7 . . . .**187** J5
Kynaston Rd, N16 . . . .**94** B3

Kynaston Rd,Brom. BR1 .**173** G5
　Enfield EN2 . . . .**44** A1
　Thornton Heath CR7 . .**187** J5
Kynaston Wd, Har. HA3 . .**52** A7
Kynersley Cl, Cars. SM5
　off William St **199** J3
Kynock Rd, N18 . . . .**61** F4
Kyrle Rd, SW11 . . . .**150** A5
Kyverdale Rd, N16 . . . .**94** C2

L

Laburnham Cl, Wem. HA0
　off Highcroft Av **106** A1
Laburnum Av, N9 . . . .**60** B2
　N17 . . . .**60** A7
　Sutton SM1 . . . .**199** H3
Laburnum Cl, E4 . . . .**61** J6
　N11 . . . .**58** A6
　SE15 off Clifton Way .**133** F7
Laburnum Ct, E2
　off Laburnum St **112** C1
Stanmore HA7 . . . .**53** F4
Laburnum Cres, Sun. TW16
　off Batavia Rd **178** B1
Laburnum Gdns, N21 . . . .**59** J2
　Croydon CR0 . . . .**189** G7
Laburnum Gro, N21 . . . . . .**59** J2
　NW9 . . . .**70** C7
　Hounslow TW3 . . . . . .**143** F4
　New Malden KT3 . . . .**182** D2
　Southall UB1 . . . .**103** F4
Laburnum Ho, Dag. RM10
　off Bradwell Av **101** G2
Laburnum Rd, SW19 . . . .**167** F7
　Hayes UB3 . . . .**121** J4
　Mitcham CR4 . . . .**186** A2
Laburnum St, E2 . . . .**112** C1
Laburnum Way, Brom.
　BR2 . . . .**192** D7
Lacebark Cl, Sid. DA15 . .**157** J7
Lacey Cl, N9 . . . .**60** D2
Lacey Dr, Dag. RM8 . . . .**100** B4
　Edgware HA8 . . . .**53** H4
　Hampton TW12 . . . . .**179** F1
Lacey Wk, E3 . . . .**114** A2
Lackington St, EC2 . . . . . .**20** C1
Lacock Cl, SW19 . . . .**167** F6
Lacon Rd, SE22 . . . .**152** D4
Lacy Rd, SW15 . . . .**148** A4
Ladas Rd, SE27 . . . .**169** J4
Ladbroke Cres, W11
　off Ladbroke Gro **108** B6
Ladbroke Gdns, W11 . . . .**108** C7
Ladbroke Gro, W10 . . . . .**108** A4
　W11 . . . .**108** B6
Ladbroke Ms, W11
　off Ladbroke Rd **128** B1
Ladbroke Rd, W11 . . . . . .**128** C1
　Enfield EN1 . . . .**44** C6
Ladbroke Sq, W11 . . . . . .**108** C7
Ladbroke Ter, W11 . . . . . .**108** C7
Ladbroke Wk, W11 . . . . . .**128** C1
Ladbrook Cl, Pnr. HA5 . . .**67** F5
Ladbrooke Cres, Sid.
　DA14 . . . .**176** D3
Ladbrook Rd, SE25 . . . . .**188** A3
Ladderstile Ride, Kings.T.
　KT2 . . . .**164** B5
Ladderswood Way, N11 . .**58** C5
Lady Booth Rd, Kings.T.
　KT1 . . . .**181** H2
Ladybower Ct, E5
　off Gilpin Rd **95** H4
Ladycroft Gdns, Orp.
　BR6 . . . .**207** F5
Ladycroft Rd, SE13 . . . . .**154** B3
Ladycroft Wk, Stan. HA7 . .**69** G1
Ladycroft Way, Orp. BR6 .**207** F5
Lady Dock Path, SE16
　off Salter Rd **133** H2
Ladyfield Cl, Loug. IG10 . .**49** E4
Ladyfields, Loug. IG10 . . .**49** E4
Lady Hay, Wor.Pk. KT4 . .**197** F2
Lady Margaret Rd, N19 . .**92** D4
　NW5 . . . .**92** C5
　Southall UB1 . . . .**103** F5
Ladysmith Av, E6 . . . .**116** B2
　Ilford IG2 . . . .**81** G7
Ladysmith Cl, NW7
　off Colenso Dr **55** G7
Ladysmith Rd, E16 . . . . . .**115** F3
　N17 . . . .**76** D2
　N18 . . . .**61** E5
　SE9 . . . .**156** D6
　Enfield EN1 . . . .**44** B3
　Harrow HA3 . . . .**68** B2
Lady Somerset Rd, NW5 .**92** B4
LADYWELL, SE13 . . . . . .**154** A5

Ladywell Cl, SE4
　off Adelaide Av **153** J4
Ladywell Hts, SE4 . . . . . .**153** J6
Ladywell Rd, SE13 . . . . . .**154** A5
Ladywell St, E15
　off Plaistow Gro **115** F1
Ladywood Av, Orp. BR5 .**193** H5
Ladywood Rd, Surb. KT6.**196** A2
Lafone Av, Felt. TW13
　off Alfred Rd **160** C1
Lafone St, SE1 . . . .**29** F3
Lagado Ms, SE16 . . . . . .**133** G1
Lagonda Av, Ilf. IG6 . . . . . .**65** J6
Laidlaw Dr, N21 . . . .**43** F4
Laing Cl, Ilf. IG6 . . . .**65** G6
Laing Dean, Nthlt. UB5 . .**102** C1
Laings Av, Mitch. CR4 . . .**185** J2
Lainlock Pl, Houns. TW3
　off Spring Gro Rd **143** H1
Lainson St, SW18 . . . . . .**148** D7
Lairdale Cl, SE21 . . . .**169** J1
Laird Ho, SE5 . . . .**131** J7
Lairs Cl, N7
　off Manger Rd **92/93** E6
Laitwood Rd, SW12 . . . . .**168** B1
Lake, The, Bushey
　(Bushey Hth.) WD23 . .**51** J1
Lake Av, Brom. BR1 . . . .**173** G6
Lake Cl, SW19
　off Lake Rd **166** C5
Lakedale Rd, SE18 . . . . .**137** H6
Lake Dr, Bushey
　(Bushey Hth.) WD23 . .**51** J2
Lakefield Cl, SE20
　off Limes Av **170/171** E7
Lakefield Rd, N22 . . . .**75** H2
Lake Gdns, Dag. RM10 . .**101** G5
　Richmond TW10 . . . . .**163** E2
　Wallington SM6 . . . . .**200** B3
Lakehall Gdns, Th.Hth.
　CR7 . . . .**187** H5
Lakehall Rd, Th.Hth. CR7 .**187** H5
Lake Ho Rd, E11 . . . .**97** G3
Lakehurst Rd, Epsom
　KT19 . . . .**196** E5
Lakeland Cl, Har. HA3 . . . .**52** A6
Lakenheath, N14 . . . .**42** D6
Lake Rd, SW19 . . . .**166** C5
　Croydon CR0 . . . .**203** J2
　Romford RM6 . . . .**82** D4
Laker Pl, SW15 . . . .**148** C6
Lakeside, N3 . . . .**73** E2
　W13 off Edgehill Rd . .**105** F6
　Beckenham BR3 . . . . .**190** B3
　Enfield EN2 . . . .**42** D4
　Wallington SM6
　　off Derek Av **200** B3
Lakeside Av, SE28 . . . . . .**138** A1
　Ilford IG4 . . . .**80** A4
Lakeside Cl, SE25 . . . . . .**188** D2
　Chigwell IG7 . . . .**65** J4
　Sidcup DA15 . . . .**158** C5
Lakeside Ct, N4 . . . .**93** H2
　Borehamwood (Elstree) WD6
　　off Cavendish Cres . .**38** A5
Lakeside Dr, Barn. EN4 .**41** J5
Lakeside Dr, Brom. BR2 .**206** B3
Lakeside Rd, N13 . . . .**59** F4
　W14 . . . .**128** A3
Lakeside Way, Wem. HA9 .**88** A4
Lakes Rd, Kes. BR2 . . . . .**205** J5
Lakeswood Rd, Orp. BR5.**193** E6
Lake Vw, Edg. HA8 . . . . . .**53** J5
Lakeview Ct, SW19
　off Victoria Dr **166** B2
Lakeview Rd, SE27 . . . . .**169** G5
　Welling DA16 . . . .**158** B4
Lakis Cl, NW3
　off Flask Wk **91** F4
Laleham Av, NW7 . . . .**54** D3
Laleham Rd, SE6 . . . .**154** C6
Lalor St, SW6 . . . .**148** B2
Lambarde Av, SE9 . . . . . .**174** D4
Lamberhurst Rd, SE27 . .**169** G4
　Dagenham RM8 . . . . .**101** F1
Lambert Av, Rich.TW9 . . .**146** B3
Lambert Jones Ms, EC2
　off The Barbican **111** J5
Lambert Rd, E16 . . . .**115** H6
　N12 . . . .**57** G5
　SW2 . . . .**151** E5
Lamberts Pl, Croy. CR0 . .**202** A1
Lamberts Rd, Surb. KT5 .**181** H5
Lambert St, N1 . . . .**93** G7
Lambert Wk, Wem. HA9 . .**87** G3
Lambert Way, N12
　off Woodhouse Rd **57** F5
LAMBETH, SE1 . . . .**26** C5
Lambeth Br, SE1 . . . .**34** B1
　SW1 . . . .**34** B1

Lambeth High St, SE1 . .34 C2
Lambeth Hill, EC4 . . . . . .19 J5
★ Lambeth Palace, SE1 . .26 C6
Lambeth Palace Rd, SE1 . .26 C6
Lambeth Rd, SE1 . . . . . . .26 D6
SE11 . . . . .26 D6
Croydon CR0 . . . . .187 G7
Lambeth Wk, SE11 . . . . . .34 D1
Lamb La, E8 . . . . .94 E7
Lamble St, NW5 . . . . .92 A5
Lambley Rd, Dag. RM9 . .100 B6
Lambolle Pl, NW3 . . . . . .91 H6
Lambolle Rd, NW3 . . . . . .91 H6
Lambourn Cl, W7 . . . . . .124 C2
Lambourne Av, SW19 . . .166 C4
Lambourne Ct, Wdf.Grn. IG8
    off Navestock Cres 63 J7
Lambourne Gdns, E4 . . . .62 A2
    Barking IG11
    off Lambourne Rd 99 J7
    Enfield EN1 . . . . .44 C2
Lambourne Gro, Kings.T. KT1
    off Kenley Rd 182 B2
Lambourne Pl, SE3
    off Shooter's Hill Rd . .155 H1
Lambourne Rd, E11 . . . . .78 C7
    Barking IG11 . . . . .99 H7
    Chigwell IG7 . . . . .65 H4
    Ilford IG3 . . . . .99 H2
Lambourn Rd, SW4 . . . . .150 B3
Lambrook Ter, SW6 . . . . .148 B1
Lamb's Bldgs, EC1 . . . . . .12 B6
Lambs Conduit Pas, WC1 .18 C1
Lamb's Conduit St, WC1 . .10 C6
Lambscroft Av, SE9 . . . . .173 J3
Lambs Meadow, Wdf.Grn.
    IG8 . . . . .80 A2
Lambs Ms, N1
    off Colebrooke Row . .111 H1
Lamb's Pas, EC1 . . . . . . .12 B6
Lambs Ter, N9 . . . . .60 A2
Lamb St, E1 . . . . .21 F1
Lambs Wk, Enf. EN2 . . . . .43 J2
Lambton Pl, W11
    off Westbourne Gro . .108 C6
Lambton Rd, N19 . . . . . . .92 E1
SW20 . . . . .183 J1
Lamb Wk, SE1 . . . . .28 D4
Lamerock Rd, Brom. BR1 .173 F4
Lamerton Rd, Ilf. IG6 . . . .81 E2
Lamerton St, SE8 . . . . . .134 A6
Lamford Cl, N17 . . . . .60 A7
Lamington St, W6 . . . . . .127 H4
Lamlash St, SE11 . . . . . . .35 G1
Lammas Av, Mitch. CR4 . .186 A2
Lammas Grn, SE26 . . . . . .170 E3
Lammas Pk, W5 . . . . . . .125 F2
Lammas Pk Gdns, W5 . . .125 F2
Lammas Pk Rd, W5 . . . . .125 F1
Lammas Rd, E9 . . . . .95 G7
E10 . . . . .95 H2
Richmond TW10 . . . . . .163 F4
Lammermoor Rd, SW12 .150 B7
Lamont Rd, SW10 . . . . . . .30 D6
Lamont Rd Pas, SW10
    off Lamont Rd 129 G6
LAMORBEY, Sid. 175 J1
Lamorbey Cl, Sid. DA15 .175 J1
Lamorna Cl, E17 . . . . .78 C1
Lamorna Gro, Stan. HA7 . .69 G1
Lampard Gro, N16 . . . . . .94 C1
Lampern Sq, E2 . . . . .13 J3
Lampeter Cl, NW9 . . . . . .70 E6
Lampeter Sq, W6
    off Humbolt Rd 128 B6
Lamplighter Cl, E1
    off Cleveland Way 113 F4
Lampmead Rd, SE12 . . . .155 E5
Lamp Office Ct, WC1 . . . . .10 C6
Lamport Cl, SE18 . . . . . .136 C4
LAMPTON, Houns. 143 H1
Lampton Av, Houns.
    TW3 . . . . .143 H1
Lampton Ho Cl, SW19 . .166 A4
Lampton Pk Rd, Houns.
    TW3 . . . . .143 H2
Lampton Rd, Houns.
    TW3 . . . . .143 H2
Lanacre Av, NW9 . . . . . . .71 F1
Lanark Cl, W5 . . . . .105 F5
Lanark Ms, W9 . . . . .6 C4
Lanark Pl, W9 . . . . .6 D5
Lanark Rd, W9 . . . . .6 C4
Lanark Sq, E14 . . . . .134 B3
Lanata Wk, Hayes UB4
    off Ramulus Dr 102 D4
Lanbury Rd, SE15 . . . . . .153 G4
Lancashire Ct, W1 . . . . . . .16 E5
Lancaster Av, E18 . . . . . . .79 H4
SE27 . . . . .169 H2

Lancaster Av, SW19 . . . .166 A5
Barking IG11 . . . . .99 H7
Mitcham CR4 . . . . .186 E5
Lancaster Cl, N1
    off Hertford Rd 94 B7
    N17 off Park La 60 D7
    NW9 . . . . .55 F7
    Bromley BR2 . . . . .191 F4
    Kingston upon Thames
    KT2 . . . . .163 G5
    Staines (Stanw.) TW19 .140 B6
Lancaster Cotts, Rich. TW10
    off Lancaster Pk 145 H6
Lancaster Ct, SE27 . . . . .169 H2
SW6 . . . . .128 C7
W2 . . . . .14 D6
    Walton-on-Thames
    KT12 . . . . .178 A7
Lancaster Dr, E14
    off Prestons Rd 134 C1
    NW3 . . . . .91 H6
    Loughton IG10 . . . . .48 B6
Lancaster Gdns, SW19 . .166 B5
    W13 . . . . .125 E2
    Bromley BR1
    off Southborough Rd .192 B5
    Kingston upon Thames
    KT2 . . . . .163 G5
Lancaster Gro, NW3 . . . . .91 G6
★ Lancaster Ho, SW1 . . .25 F3
Lancaster Ms, SW18
    off East Hill 148/149 E5
    W2 . . . . .14 D5
    Richmond TW10
    off Richmond Hill 145 H6
Lancaster Pk, Rich.
    TW10 . . . . .145 H5
Lancaster Pl, SW19
    off Lancaster Rd 166 A5
    WC2 . . . . .18 C5
    Hounslow TW4 . . . . . .142 C2
    Ilford IG1
    off Staines Rd 99 F5
    Twickenham TW1 . . . .144 D6
Lancaster Rd, E7 . . . . . . .97 G7
    E11 . . . . .97 E2
    E17 . . . . .77 G2
    N4 . . . . .75 G7
    N11 . . . . .58 D6
    N18 . . . . .60 C5
    NW10 . . . . .89 G5
    SE25 . . . . .188 C2
    SW19 . . . . .166 A5
    W11 . . . . .108 B6
    Barnet EN4 . . . . .41 G5
    Enfield EN2 . . . . .44 A1
    Harrow HA2 . . . . .67 G5
    Northolt UB5 . . . . .85 J6
    Southall UB1 . . . . .103 E7
Lancaster St, SE1 . . . . . . .27 H4
Lancaster Ter, W2 . . . . . . .15 E5
Lancaster Wk, W2 . . . . . . .22 E3
Lancaster W, W11
    off Grenfell Rd 108 A7
Lancastrian Rd, Wall.
    SM6 . . . . .201 E7
Lancefield St, W10 . . . . .108 C3
Lancell St, N16
    off Stoke Newington Ch
    St 94 B2
Lancelot Av, Wem. HA0 . .87 G4
Lancelot Cres, Wem. HA0 .87 G4
Lancelot Gdns, Barn.
    EN4 . . . . .42 A7
Lancelot Ho, N9
    off Barbot Cl 60 D3
Lancelot Pl, SW7 . . . . .23 J4
Lancelot Rd, Ilf. IG6 . . . . .65 H6
    Welling DA16 . . . . . . .158 A4
    Wembley HA0 . . . . .87 G5
Lance Rd, Har. HA1 . . . . . .67 J7
Lancer Sq, W8 . . . . .22 A3
Lancey Cl, SE7
    off Cleveley Cl 136 A4
Lanchester Rd, N6 . . . . . .73 J5
Lancing Gdns, N9 . . . . . . .60 C1
Lancing Rd, W13
    off Drayton Grn
    Rd 104/105 E7
    Croydon CR0 . . . . .187 F6
    Ilford IG2 . . . . .81 G6
Lancing St, NW1 . . . . .9 H4
Lancresse Ct, N1 . . . . . . .112 B1
Landcroft Rd, SE22 . . . . .152 C6
Landells Rd, SE22 . . . . . .152 C6
Landford Rd, SW15 . . . . .147 J3
Landgrove Rd, SW19 . . . .166 D5
Landmann Way, SE14 . . .133 G6
Landon Pl, SW1 . . . . .23 J5

Landons Cl, E14 . . . . .134 C1
Landon Wk, E14
    off Cottage St 114 B7
Landor Rd, SW9 . . . . . . .150 E3
Landor Wk, W12 . . . . . . .127 G2
Landport Way, SE15 . . . . .37 G7
Landra Gdns, N21 . . . . . . .43 H6
Landridge Rd, SW6 . . . . .148 C2
Landrock Rd, N8 . . . . .75 E6
Landscape Rd, Wdf.Grn.
    IG8 . . . . .63 H7
Landseer Av, E12 . . . . . . .98 D5
Landseer Cl, SW19
    off Brangwyn Cres . . .185 F1
    Edgware HA8 . . . . .70 A2
Landseer Rd, N19 . . . . . . .92 E3
    Enfield EN1 . . . . .44 D5
    New Malden KT3 . . . . .182 D7
    Sutton SM1 . . . . .198 D6
Landstead Rd, SE18 . . . .137 G7
Lane, The, NW8 . . . . .6 C1
    SE3 . . . . .155 G3
Lane App, NW7 . . . . .56 B5
Lane Cl, NW2 . . . . .89 H3
Lane End, Bexh. DA7 . . . .159 H3
Lane Ms, E12
    off Colchester Av 98 C3
Lanercost Cl, SW2 . . . . . .169 G2
Lanercost Gdns, N14 . . . .42 E7
Lanercost Rd, SW2 . . . . .169 G2
Lanesborough Pl, SW1 . .24 B3
Laneside, Chis. BR7 . . . . .175 E5
    Edgware HA8 . . . . .54 C5
Laneside Av, Dag. RM8 . .83 F7
Laneway, SW15 . . . . .147 H5
Lanfranc Rd, E3 . . . . .113 H2
Lanfrey Pl, W14
    off North End Rd 128 C5
Langbourne Av, N6 . . . . . .92 A2
Langbourne Pl, E14 . . . . .134 B5
Langbourne Way, Esher
    (Clay.) KT10 . . . . .194 D6
Langbrook Rd, SE3 . . . . .156 A3
Langcroft Cl, Cars. SM5 . .199 J3
Langdale Av, Mitch. CR4 .185 J3
Langdale Cl, SE17 . . . . . . .35 J5
    SW14 . . . . .146 B4
    Dagenham RM8 . . . . .100 C1
    Orpington BR6
    off Grasmere Rd .206/207 E3
Langdale Cres, Bexh.
    DA7 . . . . .139 G7
Langdale Gdns, Grnf.
    UB6 . . . . .105 E3
Langdale Rd, SE10 . . . . .134 C7
    Thornton Heath CR7 . .187 G4
Langdale St, E1
    off Burslem St 112/113 E6
Langdon Ct, NW10 . . . . .106 E1
Langdon Cres, E6 . . . . . .116 D2
Langdon Dr, NW9 . . . . . . .88 C1
Langdon Pk Rd, N6 . . . . . .74 C7
Langdon Pl, SW14
    off Rosemary La 146 C3
Langdon Rd, E6 . . . . .116 D1
    Bromley BR2 . . . . .191 H3
    Morden SM4 . . . . .185 F5
Langdons Ct, Sthl. UB2 .123 G3
Langdon Shaw, Sid.
    DA14 . . . . .175 J5
Langdon Wk, Mord.
    SM4 . . . . .185 F5
Langdon Way, SE1 . . . . . .37 J2
Langford Cl, E8 . . . . .94 D5
    N15 . . . . .76 B6
    NW8 . . . . .6 D1
    W3 . . . . .126 B2
Langford Ct, NW8 . . . . . . .6 C2
Langford Cres, Barn. EN4 .41 J4
Langford Grn, SE5 . . . . . .152 B3
Langford Pl, NW8 . . . . . . .6 D1
    Sidcup DA14 . . . . .176 A3
Langford Rd, SW6 . . . . . .149 E2
    Barnet EN4 . . . . .41 H4
    Woodford Green IG8 . . .64 A2
Langfords, Buck.H. IG9 . . .64 A2
Langham Cl, N15
    off Langham Rd 75 H3
Langham Dr, Rom. RM6 . .82 B6
Langham Gdns, N21 . . . . .43 G5
    W13 . . . . .105 E7
    Edgware HA8 . . . . .54 C7
    Richmond TW10 . . . . .163 F4
    Wembley HA0 . . . . .87 F2
Langham Ho Cl, Rich.
    TW10 . . . . .163 G4
Langham Pk Pl, Brom.
    BR2 . . . . .191 F4
Langham Pl, N15 . . . . .75 H3
    W1 . . . . .16 E2

Langham Pl, W4
    off Hogarth
    Roundabout 126/127 E6
Langham Rd, N15 . . . . . . .75 H3
    SW20 . . . . .183 J1
    Edgware HA8 . . . . .54 C6
    Teddington TW11 . . . .162 E5
Langham St, W1 . . . . .17 E2
Langhedge Cl, N18
    off Langhedge La 60 C6
Langhedge La, N18 . . . . . .60 C5
Langhedge La Ind Est,
    N18 . . . . .60 C6
Langholm Cl, SW12
    off King's Av 150 D7
Langhorne, Bushey
    WD23 . . . . .51 J1
Langhorn Dr, Twick. TW2 .144 B7
Langhorne Rd, Dag.
    RM10 . . . . .101 G7
Langland Cres, Stan. HA7 .69 H3
Langland Dr, Pnr. HA5 . . .50 E7
Langland Gdns, NW3 . . . .91 E5
    Croydon CR0 . . . . .203 J2
Langler Rd, NW10 . . . . . .107 J2
Langley Av, Ruis. HA4 . . . .84 B1
    Surbiton KT6 . . . . .195 G1
    Worcester Park KT4 . .198 A2
Langley Ct, SE9 . . . . .156 D6
    WC2 . . . . .18 A5
    Beckenham BR3 . . . . .190 B5
Langley Cres, E11 . . . . . . .79 J7
    Dagenham RM9 . . . . .100 C7
    Edgware HA8 . . . . .54 C3
    Hayes UB3 . . . . .121 J7
Langley Dr, E11 . . . . .79 H7
    W3 . . . . .126 B2
Langley Gdns, Brom.BR2 .191 J4
    Dagenham RM9 . . . . .100 C7
    Orpington BR5 . . . . . .193 E6
Langley Gro, N.Mal. KT3 .182 E2
Langley La, SW8 . . . . .34 B5
Langley Meadow, Loug.
    IG10 . . . . .49 G2
Langley Pk, NW7 . . . . .54 E6
Langley Pk Rd, Sutt. SM1,
    SM2 . . . . .199 F5
Langley Rd, SW19 . . . . . .184 C1
    Beckenham BR3 . . . . .189 H4
    Isleworth TW7 . . . . . . .144 C2
    Surbiton KT6 . . . . .181 H7
    Welling DA16 . . . . . . .138 C6
Langley Row, Barn. EN5 . .40 C1
Langley St, WC2 . . . . .18 A4
Langley Way, W.Wick.
    BR4 . . . . .204 D1
Langmead Dr, Bushey
    (Bushey Hth.) WD23 . .52 A1
Langmead St, SE27
    off Beadman St 169 H4
Langmore Ct, Bexh. DA6
    off Regency Way 158 D3
Langridge Ms, Hmptn. TW12
    off Oak Av 161 F6
Langroyd Rd, SW17 . . . . .167 J2
Langside Av, SW15 . . . . .147 G4
Langside Cres, N14 . . . . . .58 D3
Langston Hughes Cl, SE24
    off Shakespeare Rd .151 H4
Langston Rd, Loug. IG10 .49 F5
Lang St, E1 . . . . .113 F4
Langthorn Ct, EC2 . . . . . .20 B3
Langthorne Rd, E11 . . . . .96 D3
Langthorne St, SW6 . . . .128 A7
Langton Av, E6 . . . . .116 D3
    N20 . . . . .41 F7
Langton Cl, WC1 . . . . .10 D4
Langton Ho, SW16
    off Colson Way 168 C4
Langton Pl, SW18
    off Merton Rd 166 D1
Langton Ri, SE23 . . . . . . .152 E7
Langton Rd, NW2 . . . . . . .89 J3
    SW9 . . . . .131 H7
    Harrow HA3 . . . . .51 J7
    West Molesey KT8 . . . .179 J4
Langton St, SW10 . . . . . . .30 D6
Langton Way, SE3 . . . . . .155 F1
    Croydon CR0 . . . . .202 B4
Langtry Pl, SW6
    off Seagrave Rd 128 D6
Langtry Rd, NW8 . . . . . . .108 E1
    Northolt UB5 . . . . .102 D2
Langtry Wk, NW8
    off Alexandra Pl 91 F7
Langwood Chase, Tedd.
    TW11 . . . . .163 F6
Langworth Dr, Hayes
    UB4 . . . . .102 A6
Lanhill Rd, W9 . . . . .108 D4

Lanier Rd, SE13 ....154 C6
Lanigan Dr, Houns. TW3 .143 H5
Lankaster Gdns, N2 ....73 G1
Lankers Dr, Har. HA2 ....67 F6
Lankton Cl, Beck. BR3 ..190 C1
Lannoy Rd, SE9 ....175 F1
Lanrick Rd, E14 ....114 D6
Lanridge Rd, SE2 ......138 D3
Lansbury Av, N18 ......60 A5
  Barking IG11 ....100 A7
  Feltham TW14 ......142 B6
  Romford RM6 ....83 E5
Lansbury Cl, NW10 .....88 C5
Lansbury Est, E14 ......114 B6
Lansbury Gdns, E14 ....114 D6
Lansbury Rd, Enf. EN3 ..45 G1
Lansbury Way, N18 .....60 B5
Lanscombe Wk, SW8 ..150 E1
Lansdell Rd, Mitch. CR4 .186 A2
Lansdown Av, Bexh.
  DA7 ....138 D7
  Orpington BR6 ....207 E1
Lansdowne Cl, SW20 ..166 A7
  Surbiton KT5
  off Kingston Rd 196 B2
  Twickenham TW1
  off Lion Rd 162 C1
Lansdowne Copse, Wor.Pk.
  KT4 off The Avenue ..197 G2
Lansdowne Ct, Wor.Pk. KT4
  off The Avenue 197 G2
Lansdowne Cres, W11 ..108 B7
Lansdowne Dr, E8 ......94 D6
Lansdowne Gdns, SW8 .150 E1
Lansdowne Grn, SW8
  off Hartington Rd.150/151 E1
Lansdowne Gro, NW10 ..89 E4
Lansdowne Hill, SE27 ..169 H3
Lansdowne La, SE7 ....136 A6
Lansdowne Ms, SE7 ....136 A5
  W11 off Lansdowne Rd.128 C1
Lansdowne Pl, SE1 .....28 C6
  SE19 ....170 C7
Lansdowne Ri, W11 ....108 B7
Lansdowne Rd, E4 .....62 A2
  E11 ....97 F2
  E17 ....78 A5
  E18 ....79 G3
  N3 ....56 C7
  N10 ....74 C2
  N17 ....76 C1
  SW20 ....165 J7
  W11 ....108 B7
  Bromley BR1 ....173 G7
  Croydon CR0 ....202 A2
  Epsom KT19 ....196 C7
  Harrow HA1 ....68 B7
  Hounslow TW3 ......143 H3
  Ilford IG3 ....99 J1
  Stanmore HA7 ....53 F6
Lansdowne Row, W1 ...24 E1
Lansdowne Ter, WC1 ...10 B6
Lansdowne Wk, W11 ...128 B1
Lansdowne Way, SW8 .150 E1
Lansdowne Wd Cl, SE27 .169 H3
Lansdown Rd, E7 ......97 J7
  Sidcup DA14 ....176 B3
Lansfield Av, N18 ......60 D4
Lantern Cl, SW15 ......147 G4
  Wembley HA0 ....87 G5
Lanterns Ct, E14 ......134 A2
Lantern Way, West Dr.
  UB7 ....120 B2
Lant St, SE1 ....27 J3
Lanvanor Rd, SE15 ....153 F2
Lapford Cl, W9 ....108 C4
Lapponum Wk, Hayes UB4
  off Lochan Cl 102 D5
Lapse Wd Wk, SE23 ...170 E1
Lapstone Gdns, Har. HA3 .69 F6
Lapwing Ct, Surb. KT6
  off Chaffinch Cl 196 A3
Lapwing Twr, SE8
  off Abinger Gro 133 J6
Lapwing Way, Hayes
  UB4 ....102 D6
Lara Cl, SE13 ....154 C6
  Chessington KT9 ....195 H7
Larbert Rd, SW16 .....186 C1
Larch Av, W3 ....126 E1
Larch Cl, E13 ....115 H4
  N11 ....58 A7
  N19 off Bredgar Rd ..92 C2
  SE8 off Clyde St 133 J6
  SW12 ....168 B2
Larch Cres, Epsom
  KT19 ....196 B6
  Hayes UB4 ....102 C4
Larchdene, Orp. BR6 ..206 D2

Larch Dr, W4
  off Gunnersbury Av ..126 A5
Larches, The, N13 .....59 J3
Larches Av, SW14 .....146 D4
Larch Grn, NW9
  off Clayton Fld 70/71 E1
Larch Gro, Sid. DA15 ..175 J1
Larch Rd, E10
  off Walnut Rd 96 A2
  NW2 ....89 J4
Larch Tree Way, Croy.
  CR0 ....204 A3
Larch Way, Brom. BR2 .192 D7
Larchwood Rd, SE9 ...175 E2
Larcombe Cl, Croy. CR0 .202 C4
Larcom St, SE17 ......36 A2
Larden Rd, W3 ....127 E1
Largewood Av, Surb.
  KT6 ....196 A2
Larissa St, SE17 ......36 C3
Larkbere Rd, SE26 ....171 H4
Larken Cl, Bushey WD23
  off Larken Dr 51 J1
Larken Dr, Bushey WD23 .51 J1
Larkfield Av, Har. HA3 ..69 E3
Larkfield Cl, Brom. BR2 .205 F2
Larkfield Rd, Rich. TW9 .145 H4
  Sidcup DA14 ....175 J3
Larkhall La, SW4 ......150 D2
Larkhall Ri, SW4 ......150 C3
Larkhill Ter, SE18 .....156 D1
Lark Row, E2 ....113 F1
Larksfield Gro, Enf. EN1 .45 E1
Larks Gro, Bark. IG11 ..99 H7
Larkshall Ct, Rom. RM7 .83 J2
Larkshall Cres, E4 .....62 C4
Larkshall Rd, E4 ......62 C5
Larkspur Cl, E6 ....116 B5
  N17 off Fryatt Rd 60 A7
  NW9 ....70 B5
Larkspur Gro, Edg. HA8 .54 C4
Larkspur Way, Epsom
  KT19 ....196 C5
Larkswood Ct, E4 .....62 D5
Larkswood Ri, Pnr. HA5 .66 C4
Larkswood Rd, E4 .....62 A4
Lark Way, Cars. SM5 ..185 H7
Larkway Cl, NW9 .....70 D4
Larnach Rd, W6 ....128 A6
Larpent Av, SW15 ....147 J5
Larwood Cl, Grnf. UB6 .86 A5
Lascelles Av, Har. HA1 ..68 A7
Lascelles Cl, E11 .....96 D2
Lascotts Rd, N22 .....59 F6
Lassa Rd, SE9 ....156 B5
Lassell St, SE10 ......134 D5
Lasseter Pl, SE3
  off Vanbrugh Hill ...135 F6
Latchett Rd, E18 ......79 H1
Latchingdon Ct, E17 ...77 G4
Latchingdon Gdns, Wdf.Grn.
  IG8 ....64 B6
Latchmere Cl, Rich.
  TW10 ....163 H5
Latchmere La, Kings.T.
  KT2 ....163 J6
Latchmere Pas, SW11
  off Cabul Rd 149 H2
Latchmere Rd, SW11 ..149 J2
  Kingston upon Thames
  KT2 ....163 H7
Latchmere St, SW11 ..149 J2
Lateward Rd, Brent.
  TW8 ....125 G6
Latham Cl, E6
  off Oliver Gdns 116 B6
  Twickenham TW1 ....144 D7
Latham Ho, E1 ....113 G6
Latham Rd, Bexh. DA6 .159 G5
  Twickenham TW1 ....144 C7
Lathams Way, Croy. CR0 .201 F1
Lathkill Cl, Enf. EN1 ...44 D7
Lathom Rd, E6 ....98 C7
Latimer, SE17 ....36 D4
Latimer Av, E6 ....116 C1
Latimer Cl, Pnr. HA5 ...66 C1
  Worcester Park KT4 ..197 H4
Latimer Gdns, Pnr. HA5 .66 C1
Latimer Pl, W10 ......107 J6
Latimer Rd, E7 ....97 H4
  N15 ....76 B6
  SW19 ....166 E6
  W10 ....107 J6
  Barnet EN5 ....40 E3
  Croydon CR0
  off Abbey Rd 201 H3
  Teddington TW11 ....162 C5
Latona Rd, SE15 ......37 H6
La Tourne Gdns, Orp.
  BR6 ....207 F3

Lattimer Pl, W4 ....127 E6
Latton Cl, Walt. KT12 ..179 E7
Latymer Ct, W6 ....128 A4
Latymer Rd, N9 ....60 C1
Latymer Way, N9 .....60 A2
Lauder Cl, Nthlt. UB5 ..102 D2
Lauderdale Dr, Rich.
  TW10 ....163 G3
Lauderdale Pl, EC2
  off Beech St 111 J5
Lauderdale Rd, W9 ....6 A4
Lauderdale Twr, EC2 ...19 J1
Laud St, SE11 ....34 C3
  Croydon CR0 ....201 J3
Laughton Ct, Borwd. WD6
  off Banks Rd 38 D2
Laughton Rd, Nthlt. UB5 .102 D1
Launcelot Rd, Brom.
  BR1 ....173 G4
Launcelot St, SE1 .....26 E4
Launceston Gdns, Grnf.
  UB6 ....105 F1
Launceston Pl, W8 ....22 C5
Launceston Rd, Grnf.
  UB6 ....105 F1
Launch St, E14 ....134 C3
Laundress La, N16 ....94 D3
Laundry La, N1
  off Greenman St 111 J1
Laundry Rd, W6 ......128 B6
Laura Cl, E11 ....79 J5
  Enfield EN1 ....44 B5
Lauradale Rd, N2 .....73 J4
Laura Pl, E5 ....95 F4
Laurel Av, Twick. TW1 ..162 C1
Laurel Bk Gdns, SW6
  off New Kings Rd ...148 C2
Laurel Bk Rd, Enf. EN2 .43 J1
Laurel Bk Vil, W7
  off Lower Boston Rd .124 B1
Laurel Cl, N19
  off Hargrave Pk 92 C2
  SW17 ....167 H5
  Ilford IG6 ....65 F6
  Sidcup DA14 ....176 A3
Laurel Cres, Croy. CR0 .204 A3
Laurel Dr, N21 ....43 G7
Laurel Gdns, E4 ......46 B7
  NW7 ....54 D3
  W7 ....124 B1
  Bromley BR1
  off Southborough Rd .192 B4
  Hounslow TW4 ......142 E4
Laurel Gro, SE20 ....171 E7
  SE26 ....171 G4
Laurel La, West Dr. UB7 .120 B4
Laurel Manor, Sutt. SM2
  off Devonshire Rd ...199 F7
Laurel Pk, Har. HA3 ...52 C7
Laurel Rd, SW13 .....147 G2
  SW20 ....183 H1
  Hampton (Hmptn.H.)
  TW12 ....162 A5
Laurel St, E8 ....94 C6
  Walton-on-Thames KT12 .56 E3
Laurel Way, E18 ......79 F4
  N20 ....56 D3
Laurence Ms, W12
  off Askew Rd 127 G2
Laurence Pountney Hill,
  EC4 ....20 B5
Laurence Pountney La,
  EC4 ....20 B5
Laurie Gro, SE14 .....153 H1
Laurie Rd, W7 ....104 B5
Laurier Rd, NW5 ......92 B3
  Croydon CR0 ....188 C7
Laurimel Cl, Stan. HA7
  off September Way .52/53 E6
Laurino Pl, Bushey
  (Bushey Hth.) WD23 ..51 J2
Lauriston Rd, E9 ......113 G1
  SW19 ....166 A6
Lausanne Rd, N8 .....75 G4
  SE15 ....153 F1
Lavell St, N16 ....94 A4
Lavender Av, NW9 ....88 C1
  Mitcham CR4 ....185 H1
  Worcester Park KT4 ..197 J2
Lavender Cl, SW3 .....31 F6
  Bromley BR2 ....192 B6
  Carshalton SM5 ....200 A4
Lavender Ct, W.Mol. KT8
  off Molesham Way ...179 H3
Lavender Gdns, SW11 .149 J4
  Enfield EN2 ....43 H1
  Harrow HA3
  off Uxbridge Rd 52 B6
Lavender Gro, E8 .....94 C7
  Mitcham CR4 ....185 H1

Lavender Hill, SW11 ..149 H4
  Enfield EN2 ....43 G1
Lavender Pl, Ilf. IG1 ...98 E5
Lavender Ri, West Dr.
  UB7 ....120 D2
Lavender Rd, SE16 ...133 H1
  SW11 ....149 G3
  Carshalton SM5 ....200 A4
  Croydon CR0 ....187 F6
  Enfield EN2 ....44 A1
  Epsom KT19 ....196 B5
  Sutton SM1 ....199 G4
Lavender Sq, E11
  off Anglian Rd 96 D3
Lavender St, E15
  off Manbey Gro ..96/97 E6
Lavender Sweep, SW11 .149 J4
Lavender Ter, SW11
  off Falcon Rd 149 H3
Lavender Vale, Wall.
  SM6 ....200 D6
Lavender Wk, SW11 ..149 J4
  Mitcham CR4 ....186 A3
Lavender Way, Croy.
  CR0 ....189 G6
Lavengro Rd, SE27 ...169 J2
Lavenham Rd, SW18 ..166 C2
Lavernock Rd, Bexh.
  DA7 ....159 G2
Lavers Rd, N16 ....94 B3
Laverstoke Gdns, SW15 .147 G7
Laverton Ms, SW5 ....30 B2
Laverton Pl, SW5 .....30 B2
Lavidge Rd, SE9 ......174 B2
Lavina Gro, N1 ....10 C1
Lavington Cl, E9 ......95 J6
Lavington Rd, W13 ...125 E1
  Croydon CR0 ....201 F3
Lavington St, SE1 ....27 H2
Lawdons Gdns, Croy.
  CR0 ....201 H4
Lawford Rd, N1 ....94 B7
  NW5 ....92 C6
  W4 ....126 C7
Law Ho, Bark. IG11 ...118 A2
Lawless St, E14 ......114 B7
Lawley Rd, N14 ....42 B7
Lawley St, E5 ....95 F4
Lawn, The, Sthl. UB2 ..123 G5
Lawn Cl, N9 ....44 C7
  Bromley BR1 ....173 H6
  New Malden KT3 ...182 E2
Lawn Cres, Rich. TW9 ..146 A2
Lawn Fm Gro, Rom. RM6 .82 E4
Lawnfield, NW2
  off Coverdale Rd 90 A7
Lawn Gdns, W7 ......124 B1
Lawn Ho Cl, E14 .....134 C2
Lawn La, SW8 ....34 B6
Lawn Rd, NW3 ....91 J5
  Beckenham BR3 ....171 J7
Lawns, The, E4 ....62 A5
  SE3 off Lee Ter ..154/155 E3
  SE19 ....188 A1
  Pinner HA5 ....51 H7
  Sidcup DA14 ....176 B4
  Sutton SM2 ....198 B7
Lawns Ct, Wem. HA9
  off The Avenue 87 J2
Lawnside, SE3 ....155 F4
Lawn Ter, SE3 ....155 E3
Lawn Vale, Pnr. HA5 ...66 D2
Lawrence Av, E12 .....98 D4
  E17 ....77 G1
  N13 ....59 H4
  NW7 ....55 F4
  New Malden KT3 ...182 D6
Lawrence Bldgs, N16 ..94 C3
Lawrence Campe Cl, N20
  off Friern Barnet La ..57 G3
Lawrence Cl, E3 ......114 A2
  N15 off Lawrence Rd ..76 B3
Lawrence Ct, NW7 ....55 E5
  Woodford Green IG8
  off Baddow Cl 63 J6
Lawrence Cres, Dag.
  RM10 ....101 H3
  Edgware HA8 ....70 A2
Lawrence Gdns, NW7 ..55 F3
Lawrence Hill, E4 .....62 A2
Lawrence La, EC2 .....20 A4
Lawrence Pl, N1
  off Outram Pl ...110/111 E1
Lawrence Rd, E6 .....116 A1
  E13 ....115 H1
  N15 ....76 B4
  N18 ....60 E4
  SE25 ....188 C4
  W5 ....125 G4
  Erith DA8 ....139 H7

Lawrence Rd, Hmptn.
  TW12 . . . . .161 F7
Hounslow TW4 . . . . . . .142 C4
Pinner HA5 . . . . .66 D5
Richmond TW10 . . . . . . .163 F4
West Wickham BR4 . . .205 G4
Lawrence St, E16 . . . . . .115 F5
NW7 . . . . .55 F4
SW3 . . . . .31 G6
Lawrence Way, NW10 . . .88 C3
Lawrence Weaver Cl, Mord.
SM4
  off Green La 184/185 K6
Lawrie Pk Av, SE26 . . . .171 E5
Lawrie Pk Cres, SE26 . . .171 E5
Lawrie Pk Gdns, SE26 . .171 E4
Lawrie Pk Rd, SE26 . . . .171 E6
Lawson Cl, E16 . . . . .115 J5
SW19 . . . . .166 A3
Lawson Est, SE1 . . . . . . .28 B6
Lawson Gdns, Pnr. HA5 . .66 B3
Lawson Rd, Enf. EN3 . . . .45 F1
Southall UB1 . . . . .103 F4
Law St, SE1 . . . . .28 C5
Lawton Rd, E3 . . . . .113 H3
E10 . . . . .96 C1
Barnet EN4 . . . . .41 G3
Loughton IG10 . . . . .48 E3
Laxcon Cl, NW10 . . . . . . .88 C5
Laxey Rd, Orp. BR6 . . . .207 J6
Laxley Cl, SE5 . . . . .35 H7
Laxton Pl, NW1 . . . . .9 E5
Layard Rd, SE16 . . . . . . .133 E4
Enfield EN1 . . . . .44 C1
Thornton Heath CR7 . . .188 A2
Layard Sq, SE16 . . . . . . .133 E4
Laycock St, N1 . . . . .93 G6
Layer Gdns, W3 . . . . . . .106 A7
Layfield Cl, NW4 . . . . . . .71 H7
Layfield Cres, NW4 . . . . .71 H7
Layfield Rd, NW4 . . . . . . .71 H7
Layhams Rd, Kes. BR2 . .205 F5
West Wickham BR4 . . .204 D3
Laymarsh Cl, Belv.
DA17 . . . . .139 F3
Laymead Cl, Nthlt. UB5 . .84 E6
Laystall St, EC1 . . . . .10 E6
Layton Cres, Croy. CR0 . .201 G5
Layton Pl, Rich. TW9
  off Station Av 146 A1
Layton Rd, Brent. TW8 . .125 G5
Hounslow TW3 . . . . . . .143 H4
Laytons Bldgs, SE1 . . . . .28 A3
Layzell Wk, SE9
  off Mottingham La . . .174 A1
Lazar Wk, N7
  off Briset Way 93 F2
Leabank Cl, Har. HA1 . . . .86 B3
Leabank Sq, E9 . . . . .96 A6
Leabourne Rd, N16 . . . . .76 D6
LEA BRIDGE, E5 . . . . . . .95 G3
Lea Br Business Cen, E10
  off Burwell Rd 95 H1
Lea Br Rd, E5 . . . . .95 F3
E10 . . . . .95 H1
E17 . . . . .78 D4
Lea Cl, Twick. TW2 . . . . .143 F7
Leacroft Av, SW12 . . . . .149 J7
Leadale Av, E4 . . . . .62 A2
Leadale Rd, N15 . . . . . . .76 D6
N16 . . . . .76 D6
Leadbeaters Cl, N11
  off Goldsmith Rd 57 J5
★ Leadenhall Mkt, EC3 . .20 D4
Leadenhall Mkt, EC3 . . . .20 D4
Leadenhall Pl, EC3 . . . . . .20 D4
Leadenhall St, EC3 . . . . .20 D4
Leader Av, E12 . . . . .98 D5
Leadings, The, Wem.
HA9 . . . . .88 C3
Leaf Cl, T.Ditt. KT7 . . . . .180 B5
Leaf Gro, SE27 . . . . .169 G5
Leafield Cl, SW16 . . . . . .169 H6
Leafield La, Sid. DA14 . . .177 F4
Leafield Rd, SW20 . . . . .184 C3
Sutton SM1 . . . . .198 D2
Leafy Gro, Kes. BR2 . . . .205 J5
Leafy Oak Rd, SE12 . . . .173 J3
Leafy Way, Croy. CR0 . . .202 C2
Lea Gdns, Wem. HA9 . . . .87 H4
Leagrave St, E5 . . . . .95 F3
Lea Hall Rd, E10 . . . . .96 A1
Leahurst Rd, SE13 . . . . .154 D5
Leake St, SE1 . . . . .26 D3
Lealand Rd, N15 . . . . . . .76 C6
Leamington Av, E17 . . . . .78 A5
Bromley BR1 . . . . .173 J5
Morden SM4 . . . . .184 C4
Orpington BR6 . . . . . . .207 H4

Leamington Cl, E12 . . . . .98 B5
Bromley BR1 . . . . .173 J5
Hounslow TW3 . . . . . . .143 J5
Leamington Cres, Har.
HA2 . . . . .85 E3
Leamington Gdns, Ilf. IG3 .99 J2
Leamington Pk, W3 . . . .106 D5
Leamington Rd, Sthl.
UB2 . . . . .122 D4
Leamington Rd Vil, W11 .108 C5
Leamore St, W6 . . . . . . .127 H4
Leamouth Rd, E6
  off Remington Rd 116 B6
E14 . . . . .114 D6
Leander Ct, SE8 . . . . . . .154 A1
Leander Rd, SW2 . . . . . .151 F6
Northolt UB5 . . . . .103 G2
Thornton Heath CR7 . .187 F4
Learner Dr, Har. HA2 . . . .85 G2
Lea Rd, Beck. BR3
  off Fairfield Rd 190 A2
Enfield EN2 . . . . .44 A1
Southall UB2 . . . . .122 E4
Learoyd Gdns, E6 . . . . . .116 D7
Leas Cl, Chess. KT9 . . . .195 J7
Leas Dale, SE9 . . . . .174 D3
Leas Grn, Chis. BR7 . . . .175 J6
Leaside Av, N10 . . . . .74 A3
Leaside Rd, E5 . . . . .95 F1
Leasowes Rd, E10 . . . . . .96 A1
Leatherbottle Grn, Erith
DA18 . . . . .139 F3
Leather Bottle La, Belv.
DA17 . . . . .139 E4
Leather Cl, Mitch. CR4 . .186 A2
Leatherdale St, E1
  off Portelet Rd 113 G4
Leather Gdns, E15
  off Abbey Rd 114/115 E1
Leatherhead Cl, N16 . . . .94 C1
Leather La, EC1 . . . . .19 F2
Leathermarket Ct, SE1 . .28 D4
Leathermarket St, SE1 . .28 D4
Leathersellers Cl, Barn. EN5
  off The Avenue 40 B4
Leathsail Rd, Har. HA2 . . .85 H3
Leathwaite Rd, SW11 . . .149 J4
Leathwell Rd, SE8 . . . . .154 B2
Lea Valley Rd, E4 . . . . . . .45 G5
Enfield EN3 . . . . .45 G5
Lea Valley Viaduct, E4 . . .61 G5
N18 . . . . .61 G5
Lea Valley Wk, E3 . . . . . .114 C4
E5 . . . . .95 H3
E9 . . . . .95 H3
E10 . . . . .95 H3
E14 . . . . .114 B5
E15 . . . . .114 C3
E17 . . . . .77 F1
N9 . . . . .61 H1
N15 . . . . .76 D6
N16 . . . . .76 D6
N17 . . . . .77 F1
N18 . . . . .77 F1
Enfield EN3 . . . . .45 J3
Leaveland Cl, Beck. BR3 .190 A4
Leaver Gdns, Grnf. UB6 .104 A2
Leavesden Rd, Stan. HA7 .52 D6
Lea Vw Hos, E5
  off Springfield 94/95 E1
Leaway, E10 . . . . .95 G1
Lebanon Av, Felt. TW13 .160 D5
Lebanon Ct, Twick. TW1 .144 E7
Lebanon Gdns, SW18 . . .148 D6
Lebanon Pk, Twick. TW1 .144 E7
Lebanon Rd, SW18 . . . . .148 D5
Croydon CR0 . . . . .202 B1
Lebrun Sq, SE3 . . . . .155 H3
Lechmere App, Wdf.Grn.
IG8 . . . . .79 J2
Lechmere Av, Chig. IG7 . .65 F4
Woodford Green IG8 . . .80 A2
Lechmere Rd, NW2 . . . . . .89 H6
Leckford Rd, SW18 . . . . .167 F2
Leckwith Av, Bexh. DA7 .138 E6
Lecky St, SW7 . . . . .31 E3
Leclair Ho, SE3
  off Gallus Sq 155 H3
Leconfield Av, SW13 . . . .147 F3
Leconfield Rd, N5 . . . . . .94 A4
Leda Av, Enf. EN3 . . . . . .45 G1
Leda Rd, SE18 . . . . .136 C3
Ledbury Est, SE15 . . . . . .132 E7
Ledbury Ms N, W11
  off Ledbury Rd 108 D7
Ledbury Ms W, W11
  off Ledbury Rd 108 D7
Ledbury Pl, Croy. CR0
  off Ledbury Rd 201 J4

Ledbury Rd, W11 . . . . . .108 C6
Croydon CR0 . . . . .201 J4
Ledbury St, SE15 . . . . . . .37 J7
Ledrington Rd, SE19
  off Anerley Hill 170 D6
Ledway Dr, Wem. HA9 . . .69 J7
LEE, SE12 . . . . .154 E4
Lee Av, Rom. RM6 . . . . . .82 E6
Lee Br, SE13 . . . . .154 C3
Leechcroft Av, Sid. DA15 .157 J5
Leechcroft Rd, Wall.
SM6 . . . . .200 A3
Lee Ch St, SE13 . . . . . . .155 E4
Lee Cl, E17 . . . . .77 G1
Barnet EN5 . . . . .41 F4
Lee Conservancy Rd, E9 . .95 J5
Leecroft Rd, Barn. EN5 . .40 B5
Leeds Pl, N4
  off Tollington Pk 93 F2
Leeds Rd, Ilf. IG1 . . . . . . .99 G1
Leeds St, N18 . . . . .60 D5
Leefern Rd, W12 . . . . . . .127 G2
Leegate, SE12 . . . . .155 F5
Lee Grn, SE12
  off Lee High Rd 155 F5
Lee Gro, Chig. IG7 . . . . . .64 D2
Lee High Rd, SE12 . . . . .154 D3
SE13 . . . . .154 D3
Leeke St, WC1 . . . . .10 C3
Leeland Rd, W13 . . . . . .124 D1
Leeland Ter, W13 . . . . . .124 D1
Leeland Way, NW10 . . . . .89 F4
Lee Pk, SE3 . . . . .155 F4
Lee Pk Way, N9 . . . . .61 G4
N18 . . . . .61 G4
Leerdam Dr, E14 . . . . . . .134 C3
Lee Rd, NW7 . . . . .56 A7
SE3 . . . . .155 F3
SW19 . . . . .185 E1
Enfield EN1 . . . . .44 D6
Greenford UB6 . . . . . .105 F1
Lees, The, Croy. CR0 . . . .203 J2
Leeside, Barn. EN5 . . . . . .40 B5
Leeside Ct, SE16
  off Rotherhithe St . . .133 G1
Leeside Cres, NW11 . . . . .72 C6
Leeside Rd, N17 . . . . .61 E6
Leeson Rd, SE24 . . . . . .151 G4
Leesons Hill, Chis. BR7 . .193 H3
Leesons Way, Orp. BR5 . .193 J2
Lees Pl, W1 . . . . .16 B5
Lee St, E8 . . . . .112 C1
Lee Ter, SE3 . . . . .154 E3
SE13 . . . . .154 E3
Lee Valley Pathway, E9 . . .95 J3
E10 . . . . .77 F7
E17 . . . . .77 F7
Lee Valley Technopark,
N17 . . . . .76 D3
Lee Vw, Enf. EN2 . . . . . . .43 H1
Leeward Gdns, SW19 . . .166 C6
Leeway, SE8 . . . . .133 J5
Leeway Cl, Pnr. HA5 . . . .51 F7
Leewood Cl, SE12
  off Upwood Rd 155 F6
Lefevre Wk, E3 . . . . .114 A1
Lefroy Rd, W12 . . . . .127 F2
Legard Rd, N5 . . . . .93 H3
Legatt Rd, SE9 . . . . .156 A5
Leggatt Rd, E15 . . . . . . .114 C2
Legge St, SE13 . . . . .154 C5
Leghorn Rd, NW10 . . . . .107 F2
SE18 . . . . .137 G5
Legion Cl, N1 . . . . .93 G6
Legion Ct, Mord. SM4 . . .184 D6
Legion Rd, Grnf. UB6 . . .103 J1
Legion Ter, E3
  off Lefevre Wk 113 J1
Legion Way, N12 . . . . . . .57 H7
Legrace Av, Houns. TW4 .142 D2
Leicester Av, Mitch. CR4 .187 E4
Leicester Cl, Wor.Pk.
KT4 . . . . .197 J4
Leicester Ct, WC2 . . . . . .17 J5
Leicester Gdns, Ilf. IG3 . .81 H7
Leicester Ms, N2
  off Leicester Rd 73 H3
Leicester Pl, WC2 . . . . . .17 J5
Leicester Rd, E11 . . . . . . .79 H5
N2 . . . . .73 H3
Barnet EN5 . . . . .40 E5
Croydon CR0 . . . . .188 B7
Leicester Sq, WC2 . . . . . .17 J6
Leicester St, WC2 . . . . . .17 J5
Leigham Av, SW16 . . . . .169 E3
Leigham Ct, Wall. SM6
  off Stafford Rd 200 C6
Leigham Ct Rd, SW16 . . .169 E2
Leigham Dr, Islw. TW7 . .124 B7

Leigham Vale, SW2 . . . . .169 F3
SW16 . . . . .169 F3
Leigh Av, Ilf. IG4 . . . . .80 A4
Leigh Cl, N.Mal. KT3 . . . .182 D4
Leigh Ct, SE4
  off Lewisham Way . . .154 A2
Borehamwood WD6
  off Banks Rd 38 D2
Harrow HA2 . . . . .86 B1
Leigh Cres, Croy.
  (New Adgtn.) CR0 . . .204 B7
Leigh Gdns, NW10 . . . . .107 J2
Leigh Hunt Dr, N14 . . . . . .58 D1
Leigh Hunt St, SE1 . . . . . .27 J3
Leigh Orchard Cl, SW16 .169 F3
Leigh Pl, EC1 . . . . .19 E1
Welling DA16 . . . . .158 A2
Leigh Rd, E6 . . . . .98 D6
E10 . . . . .78 C7
N5 . . . . .93 H4
Hounslow TW3 . . . . . . .144 A4
Leigh Rodd, Wat. WD19 . .51 F3
Leigh St, WC1 . . . . .10 A5
Leighton Av, E12 . . . . . . .98 D5
Pinner HA5 . . . . .66 E3
Leighton Cl, Edg. HA8 . . .70 A2
Leighton Cres, NW5
  off Leighton Gro 92 C5
Leighton Gdns, NW10 . . .107 H2
Leighton Gro, NW5 . . . . .92 C5
★ Leighton Ho Mus,
  W14 . . . . .128 C3
Leighton Pl, NW5 . . . . . .92 C5
Leighton Rd, NW5 . . . . . .92 D5
W13 . . . . .124 D2
Enfield EN1 . . . . .44 C5
Harrow (Har.Wld.) HA3 .68 A2
Leighton St, Croy. CR0 . .201 H1
Leila Parnell Pl, SE7 . . . .135 J6
Leinster Av, SW14 . . . . .146 C3
Leinster Gdns, W2 . . . . . .14 C4
Leinster Ms, W2 . . . . .14 C5
Leinster Pl, W2 . . . . .14 C4
Leinster Rd, N10 . . . . . . .74 B4
Leinster Sq, W2 . . . . . . .108 D6
Leinster Ter, W2 . . . . . . .14 C5
Leisure Way, N12 . . . . . . .57 G7
Leith Cl, NW9 . . . . .88 D1
Leithcote Gdns, SW16 . .169 F4
Leithcote Path, SW16 . . .169 F3
Leith Rd, N22 . . . . .75 H1
Leith Yd, NW6
  off Quex Rd 108 D1
Lela Av, Houns. TW4 . . . .142 C2
Lelitia Cl, E8
  off Pownall Rd 112 D1
Leman St, E1 . . . . .21 G4
Lemark Cl, Stan. HA7 . . . .53 F5
Le May Av, SE12 . . . . . . .173 H3
Lemmon Rd, SE10 . . . . .134 E6
Lemna Rd, E11 . . . . .79 E7
Lemonwell Ct, SE9
  off Lemonwell Dr 157 F5
Lemonwell Dr, SE9 . . . . .157 F5
Lemsford Cl, N15 . . . . . . .76 D5
Lemsford Ct, N4
  off Brownswood Rd . . .93 J2
Borehamwood WD6 . . .38 C4
Lemuel St, SW18 . . . . . .149 E6
Lena Gdns, W6 . . . . .127 J3
Lena Kennedy Cl, E4 . . . .62 B6
Lenanton Steps, E14
  off Manilla St 134 A2
Lendal Ter, SW4 . . . . . . .150 D3
Lenelby Rd, Surb. KT6 . .196 A1
Len Freeman Pl, SW6
  off John Smith Av 128 C7
Lenham Rd, SE12 . . . . . .155 F4
Bexleyheath DA7 . . . . .139 F6
Sutton SM1 . . . . .199 E4
Thornton Heath CR7 . .188 A2
Lennard Av, W.Wick.
BR4 . . . . .205 E2
Lennard Cl, W.Wick.
BR4 . . . . .205 E2
Lennard Rd, SE20 . . . . . .171 F6
Beckenham BR3 . . . . . .171 G6
Bromley BR2 . . . . .206 C1
Croydon CR0 . . . . .201 J1
Lennon Rd, NW2 . . . . . . .89 J5
Lennox Gdns, NW10 . . . . .89 F4
SW1 . . . . .23 J6
Croydon CR0 . . . . .201 H4
Ilford IG1 . . . . .98 C1
Lennox Gdns Ms, SW1 . . .23 J6
Lennox Rd, E17 . . . . .77 J6
N4 . . . . .93 F2
Lenor Cl, Bexh. DA6 . . . .159 E4
Lensbury Way, SE2 . . . . .138 C3
Lens Rd, E7 . . . . .97 J7

Lenthall Rd, E8 . . . . . .94 D7
Loughton IG10 . . . . . .49 G4
Lenthorp Rd, SE10 . . . .135 F4
Lentmead Rd, Brom.
  BR1 . . . . .173 F3
Lenton Path, SE18 . . . .137 G6
Lenton Ri, Rich. TW9
  off Evelyn Ter 145 H3
Lenton St, SE18 . . . . . .137 G4
Leof Cres, SE6 . . . . . .172 B5
Leominster Rd, Mord.
  SM4 . . . . .185 F6
Leominster Wk, Mord.
  SM4 . . . . .185 F6
Leonard Av, Mord. SM4 .185 F5
Leonard Pl, N16
  off Allen Rd 94 B4
Leonard Rd, E4 . . . . . . .62 A6
  E7 . . . . .97 G4
  N9 . . . . .60 C3
  SW16 . . . . .186 C1
  Southall UB2 . . . . . .122 D3
Leonard Robbins Path, SE28
  off Tawney Rd 118 B7
Leonard St, E16 . . . . . .136 B1
  EC2 . . . . .12 C5
Leontine Cl, SE15 . . . . .132 D7
Leopards Ct, EC1 . . . . . .19 E1
Leopold Av, SW19 . . . . .166 C5
Leopold Ms, E9
  off Fremont St 113 F1
Leopold Rd, E17 . . . . . . .78 A5
  N2 . . . . .73 G3
  N18 . . . . .61 E5
  NW10 . . . . .89 E7
  SW19 . . . . .166 C4
  W5 . . . . .125 J1
Leopold St, E3 . . . . . . .113 J5
Leopold Ter, SW19
  off Dora Rd 166 D5
Leo St, SE15 . . . . .133 E7
Leo Yd, EC1 . . . . .11 H6
Leppoc Rd, SW4 . . . . . .150 D5
Leroy St, SE1 . . . . .36 D1
Lescombe Cl, SE23 . . . .171 H3
Lescombe Rd, SE23 . . . .171 H3
Lesley Cl, Bex. DA5 . . . .159 H7
Leslie Gdns, Sutt. SM2 .198 D7
Leslie Gro, Croy. CR0 . .202 B1
Leslie Gro Pl, Croy. CR0
  off Leslie Gro 202 A1
Leslie Pk Rd, Croy. CR0 .202 B1
Leslie Rd, E11 . . . . .96 C4
  E16 . . . . .115 H6
  N2 . . . . .73 G3
Leslie Smith Sq, SE18
  off Nightingale Vale .136 D6
★ Lesnes Abbey (ruins),
  Erith DA18 . . . . . . .138 D4
Lessar Av, SW4 . . . . . .150 C5
Lessingham Av, SW17 .167 J4
  Ilford IG5 . . . . .80 D3
Lessing St, SE23 . . . . . .153 H7
Lessington Av, Rom.
  RM7 . . . . .83 J6
Lessness Av, Bexh. DA7 .138 D7
LESSNESS HEATH,
  Belv. 139 H5
Lessness Pk, Belv. DA17 .139 F5
Lessness Rd, Belv. DA17
  off Stapley Rd 139 G5
  Morden SM4 . . . . . .185 F6
Lester Av, E15 . . . . . . .115 E3
Leswin Pl, N16
  off Leswin Rd 94 C3
Leswin Rd, N16 . . . . . . .94 C3
Letchford Gdns, NW10 .107 G3
Letchford Ms, NW10
  off Letchford Gdns . . .107 G3
Letchford Ter, Har. HA3 . .67 H1
Letchworth Av, Felt.
  TW14 . . . . .141 J7
Letchworth Cl, Brom.
  BR2 . . . . .191 G5
  Watford WD19 . . . . . .50 D5
Letchworth Dr, Brom.
  BR2 . . . . .191 G5
Letchworth St, SW17 . .167 J4
Lethbridge Cl, SE13 . . . .154 C1
Letterstone Rd, SW6
  off Varna Rd 128 C7
Lettice St, SW6 . . . . . . .148 C1
Lett Rd, E15 . . . . .96 D7
Lettsom St, SE5 . . . . . .152 B2
Lettsom Wk, E13 . . . . . .115 G2
Leucha Rd, E17 . . . . . . .77 H5
Levana Cl, SW19 . . . . . .166 B1
Levehurst Way, SW4 . . .151 E2
Leven Cl, Wat. WD19 . . .50 D5
Levendale Rd, SE23 . . . .171 H2

Leven Rd, E14 . . . . .114 C5
Leverett St, SW3 . . . . . .31 H1
Leverholme Gdns, SE9 . .174 D3
Leverson St, SW16 . . . .168 C6
Leverton Pl, NW5
  off Leverton St 92 C5
Leverton St, NW5 . . . . . .92 C5
Levett Gdns, Ilf. IG3 . . . .99 J4
Levett Rd, Bark. IG11 . . .99 H6
Levine Gdns, Bark. IG11 .118 D2
Levison Way, N19
  off Grovedale Rd 92 D2
Lewes Cl, Nthlt. UB5 . . . .85 G6
Lewesdon Cl, SW19 . . . .166 A1
Lewes Rd, N12 . . . . .57 H5
  Bromley BR1 . . . . . .192 A2
Leweston Pl, N16 . . . . . .76 C7
Lewey Ho, E3 . . . . .113 J4
Lewgars Av, NW9 . . . . . .70 C6
Lewin Rd, SW14 . . . . . .146 D3
  SW16 . . . . .168 D6
  Bexleyheath DA6 . . . .159 E4
Lewis Av, E17 . . . . .78 A1
Lewis Cl, N14
  off Orchid Rd 42 C7
Lewis Cres, NW10 . . . . . .88 C5
Lewis Gdns, N2 . . . . . . .73 G2
Lewis Gro, SE13 . . . . . .154 C3
LEWISHAM, SE13 . . . . . .154 B4
Lewisham Cen, SE13 . . . .154 C3
Lewisham High St,
  SE13 . . . . .154 C3
Lewisham Hill, SE13 . . . .154 C2
Lewisham Pk, SE13 . . . . .154 B6
Lewisham Rd, SE13 . . . . .154 B1
Lewisham St, SW1 . . . . . .25 J4
Lewisham Way, SE4 . . . .153 J1
  SE14 . . . . .153 J1
Lewis Pl, E8 . . . . .94 D5
Lewis Rd, Mitch. CR4 . . .185 G2
  Richmond TW10
    off Red Lion St 145 G5
  Sidcup DA14 . . . . . . .176 C3
  Southall UB1 . . . . . . .123 E2
  Sutton SM1 . . . . . . .199 E4
  Welling DA16 . . . . . .158 C3
Lewis St, NW1 . . . . .92 B6
Lewis Way, Dag. RM10 . .101 H6
Lexden Dr, Rom. RM6 . . .82 B6
Lexden Rd, W3 . . . . . . .106 B7
  Mitcham CR4 . . . . . .186 D4
Lexham Ct, Grnf. UB6 . . .104 A1
Lexham Gdns, W8 . . . . . .30 A1
Lexham Gdns Ms, W8 . . .22 B6
Lexham Ho, Bark. IG11
  off St. Margarets . . .117 G1
Lexham Ms, W8 . . . . . . .128 D4
Lexham Wk, W8 . . . . . . .22 B6
Lexington, The, EC1 . . . .12 B5
Lexington St, W1 . . . . . . .17 G4
Lexington Way, Barn.
  EN5 . . . . .40 A4
Leybourne Gdns, SW12 . . .168 D1
Leyborne Av, W13 . . . . .125 E2
Leyborne Pk, Rich. TW9 .146 A1
Leybourne Cl, Brom.
  BR2 . . . . .191 G6
Leybourne Rd, E11 . . . . .97 F1
  NW1 . . . . .92 B7
  NW9 . . . . .70 A5
Leybourne St, NW1
  off Hawley St 92 B7
Leybridge Ct, SE12 . . . .155 G5
Leyburn Cl, E17
  off Church La 78 B4
Leyburn Gdns, Croy.
  CR0 . . . . .202 B2
Leyburn Gro, N18 . . . . . .60 D6
Leyburn Rd, N18 . . . . . . .60 D6
Leycroft Cl, Loug. IG10 . .48 D5
Leyden St, E1 . . . . .21 F2
Leydon Cl, SE16
  off Lagado Ms 133 G1
Leyfield, Wor.Pk. KT4 . . .197 E1
Leyland Av, Enf. EN3 . . . .45 H2
Leyland Gdns, Wdf.Grn.
  IG8 . . . . .63 J5
Leyland Rd, SE12 . . . . . .155 G5
Leylang Rd, SE14 . . . . . .133 G7
Leys, The, N2 . . . . .73 F4
  Harrow HA3 . . . . . . .69 J6
Leys Av, Dag. RM10 . . . .101 J7
Leys Cl, Dag. RM10 . . . .101 J7
  Harrow HA1 . . . . .68 A5
Leysdown Av, Bexh.
  DA7 . . . . .159 J4
Leysdown Rd, SE9 . . . . .174 B2
Leysfield Rd, W12 . . . . .127 G2
Leys Gdns, Barn. EN4 . . .42 A5

Leyspring Rd, E11 . . . . . .97 F1
Leys Rd E, Enf. EN3 . . . . .45 H1
Leys Rd W, Enf. EN3 . . . .45 H1
Ley St, Ilf. IG1, IG2 . . . . .99 E2
Leyswood Dr, Ilf. IG2 . . . .81 H5
Leythe Rd, W3 . . . . .126 C2
LEYTON, E11 . . . . .96 B1
  Leyton Business Cen,
    E10 . . . . .96 A2
Leyton Gra, E10 . . . . .96 B1
  off Goldsmith Rd 96 B1
Leyton Gra Est, E10 . . . . .96 B1
Leyton Grn Rd, E10 . . . . .78 C6
Leyton Ind Village, E10 . .96 B2
★ Leyton Orient FC, E10 .96 B3
Leyton Pk Rd, E10 . . . . . .96 C3
Leyton Rd, E15 . . . . .96 D5
  SW19 . . . . .167 F2
LEYTONSTONE, E11 . . . . .78 D7
Leytonstone Rd, E15 . . . .96 E5
Leyton Way, E11 . . . . . . .79 E7
Leywick St, E15 . . . . . . .114 E2
Liardet St, SE14 . . . . . .133 H6
Liberia Rd, N5 . . . . .93 H6
★ Liberty, W1 . . . . .17 F4
Liberty Av, SW19 . . . . . .185 G1
Liberty Ms, SW12 . . . . .150 B6
Liberty St, SW9 . . . . . . .151 F1
Libra Rd, E3 . . . . .113 J1
  E13 . . . . .115 G2
Library Pl, E1
  off Cable St 112/113 E7
Library St, SE1 . . . . .27 G4
Library Way, Twick. TW2
  off Nelson Rd 143 J7
Lichfield Cl, Barn. EN4 . . .41 J3
Lichfield Ct, Rich. TW9
  off Sheen Rd 145 H4
Lichfield Gdns, Rich.
  TW9 . . . . .145 H4
Lichfield Gro, N3 . . . . . . .72 D1
Lichfield Rd, E3 . . . . . . .113 H3
  E6 . . . . .116 A3
  N9 off Winchester Rd . .60 D2
  NW2 . . . . .90 B4
  Dagenham RM8 . . . .100 B4
  Hounslow TW4 . . . . .142 C3
  Northwood HA6 . . . . .66 A3
  Richmond TW9 . . . . .145 J1
  Woodford Green IG8 . .63 E4
Lichlade Cl, Orp. BR6 . . .207 J4
Lidbury Rd, NW7 . . . . . . .56 B6
Lidcote Gdns, SW9 . . . .151 G2
Liddall Way, West Dr.
  UB7 . . . . .120 C1
Liddell Cl, Har. HA3 . . . . .69 G3
Liddell Gdns, NW10 . . . .107 J2
Liddell Rd, NW6 . . . . . . .90 D6
Lidding Rd, Har. HA3 . . . .69 G5
Liddington Rd, E15 . . . .115 F1
Liddon Rd, E13 . . . . . . .115 H3
  Bromley BR1 . . . . . .191 J3
Liden Cl, E17
  off Hitcham Rd 95 J1
Lidfield Rd, N16 . . . . .94 A4
Lidgate Rd, SE15
  off Chandler Way . . .132 C7
Lidiard Rd, SW18 . . . . . .167 F2
Lidlington Pl, NW1 . . . . . .9 F2
Lido Sq, N17 . . . . .76 A2
Lidyard Rd, N19 . . . . .92 C1
★ Lifetimes Mus, Croy.
  CR0 . . . . .201 J3
Liffler Rd, SE18 . . . . . . .137 H5
Liffords Pl, SW13 . . . . . .147 F2
Lifford St, SW15 . . . . . .148 A4
Lightcliffe Rd, N13 . . . . . .59 G4
Lighter Cl, SE16 . . . . . . .133 H4
Lighterman Ms, E1 . . . .113 G6
Lightermans Rd, E14 . . .134 A2
Lightfoot Rd, N8 . . . . . . .74 E5
Lightley Cl, Wem. HA0
  off Stanley Av 87 J7
Ligonier St, E2 . . . . .13 F5
Lilac Cl, E4 . . . . .61 J6
Lilac Gdns, W5 . . . . .125 G3
  Croydon CR0 . . . . . .204 A3
Lilac Ms, N8
  off Courcy Rd 75 G3
Lilac St, W12 . . . . .107 G7
Liburne Gdns, SE9 . . . . .156 B5
Lilburne Rd, SE9 . . . . . .156 B5
Lilburne Wk, NW10 . . . . .88 C6
Lile Cres, W7 . . . . .104 B5
Lilestone Est, NW8 . . . . . .7 E6
Lilestone St, NW8 . . . . . .7 G5
Lilford Rd, SE5 . . . . .151 H2
Lilian Barker Cl, SE12 . .155 G5

Lilian Board Way, Grnf.
  UB6 . . . . .86 A5
Lilian Cl, N16
  off Barbauld Rd 94 B3
Lilian Gdns, Wdf.Grn. IG8 .79 H1
Lilian Rd, SW16 . . . . . . .186 C1
Lillechurch Rd, Dag.
  RM8 . . . . .100 B6
Lilleshall Rd, Mord. SM4 .185 G6
Lilley Cl, E1 . . . . .29 J2
Lilley La, NW7 . . . . .54 D5
Lillian Av, W3 . . . . .126 A2
Lillian Rd, SW13 . . . . . .127 G6
Lillie Rd, SW6 . . . . .128 B7
Lillieshall Rd, SW4 . . . . .150 B3
Lillie Yd, SW6 . . . . .128 D6
Lillington Gdns Est, SW1 .33 G2
Lillington Ho, N7
  off Harvist Est 93 G4
Lilliput Av, Nthlt. UB5 . . .103 F1
Lily Cl, W14 . . . . .128 B4
Lily Dr, West Dr. UB7 . . .120 A4
Lily Gdns, Wem. HA0 . . .105 F2
Lily Pl, EC1 . . . . .19 F1
Lily Rd, E17 . . . . .78 A6
Lilyville Rd, SW6 . . . . . .148 C1
Limbourne Av, Dag.
  RM8 . . . . .83 F7
Limburg Rd, SW11 . . . . .149 J4
Limeburner La, EC4 . . . . .19 G4
Lime Cl, E1 . . . . .29 J1
  Bromley BR1 . . . . . .192 B4
  Buckhurst Hill IG9 . . .64 A3
  Carshalton SM5 . . . .199 J2
  Harrow HA3 . . . . . . .68 C2
  Romford RM7 . . . . . .83 J4
Lime Ct, Mitch. CR4
  off Lewis Rd 185 G2
Lime Cres, Sun. TW16 . .178 C2
Limecroft Cl, Epsom
  KT19 . . . . .196 D7
Limedene Cl, Pnr. HA5 . . .66 D1
Lime Gro, E4
  off Burnside Av 61 J6
  N20 . . . . .56 C1
  W12 . . . . .127 J2
  Ilford IG6 . . . . .65 J6
  New Malden KT3 . . . .182 D3
  Orpington BR6 . . . . .207 E2
  Ruislip HA4 . . . . .66 B7
  Sidcup DA15 . . . . . .157 J6
  Twickenham TW1 . . .144 C6
Limeharbour, E14 . . . . .134 B3
LIMEHOUSE, E14 . . . . . .113 H7
Limehouse Causeway,
  E14 . . . . .113 J7
Limehouse Flds Est, E14 .113 H5
Limehouse Link, E14 . . .113 H7
Limekiln Dr, SE7 . . . . . .135 H6
Limekiln Pl, SE19 . . . . . .170 C7
Limerick Cl, SW12 . . . . .150 C7
Lime Rd, Rich. TW9
  off St. Mary's Gro . . .145 J4
Lime Row, Erith DA18
  off Northwood Pl . . .139 F3
Limerston St, SW10 . . . . .30 D5
Limes, The, W2
  off Linden Gdns 108 D7
  Bromley BR2 . . . . . .206 B2
Limes Av, E11 . . . . .79 H4
  N12 . . . . .57 F4
  NW7 . . . . .54 E6
  NW11 . . . . .72 B7
  SE20 . . . . .171 E7
  SW13 . . . . .147 F2
  Carshalton SM5 . . . .199 J1
  Chigwell IG7 . . . . . . .65 G6
  Croydon CR0 . . . . . .201 G3
Limes Av, The, N11 . . . . .58 B5
Limesdale Gdns, Edg.
  HA8 . . . . .70 C2
Limes Fld Rd, SW14
  off White Hart La .146/147 E3
Limesford Rd, SE15 . . . .153 G4
Limes Gdns, SW18 . . . . .148 D6
Limes Gro, SE13 . . . . . .154 C4
Limes Pl, Croy. CR0 . . . .188 A7
Limes Rd, Beck. BR3 . . . .190 B2
  Croydon CR0 . . . . . .188 A6
Limes Row, Orp. BR6
  off Orchard Rd . .206/207 E5
Limestone Wk, Erith
  DA18 . . . . .138 D3
Lime St, E17 . . . . .77 H4
  EC3 . . . . .20 D5
Lime St Pas, EC3 . . . . . . .20 D4
Limes Wk, SE15 . . . . . . .153 E4
  W5 off Chestnut Gro .125 G2
Lime Ter, W7
  off Manor Ct Rd 104 B7

Lime Tree Av, Esher
  KT10 . . . . .194 A1
  Thames Ditton KT7 . . .194 A1
Limetree Cl, SW2 . . . . . .169 F1
Lime Tree Gro, Croy.
  CR0 . . . . .203 J3
Lime Tree Pl, Mitch. CR4 .186 B1
Lime Tree Rd, Houns.
  TW5 . . . . .143 H1
Lime Tree Ter, SE6
  off Winterstoke Rd . . .171 J1
Lime Tree Wk, SW17
  off Church La 168 A5
Lime Tree Wk, Bushey
  (Bushey Hth.) WD23 . .52 B1
  West Wickham BR4 . .205 F4
Lime Wk, E15
  off Church St N . .114/115 E1
Limewood Cl, E17 . . . . . .77 J4
  W13 off St. Stephens
  Rd 104/105 D6
  Beckenham BR3 . . . . .190 C5
Limewood Ct, Ilf. IG4 . . . .80 C5
Limewood Rd, Erith
  DA8 . . . . .139 J7
Limpsfield Av, SW19 . . . .166 A2
  Thornton Heath CR7 .187 F5
Linacre Ct, W6 . . . . .128 A5
Linacre Rd, NW2 . . . . . . .89 H6
Linberry Wk, SE8 . . . . . .133 J4
Linchmere Rd, SE12 . . . .155 F7
Lincoln Av, N14 . . . . .58 C3
  SW19 . . . . .166 A3
  Twickenham TW2 . . . .161 H2
Lincoln Cl, SE25
  off Woodside Grn 188 D6
  Greenford UB6 . . . . . .103 J1
  Harrow HA2 . . . . .67 F5
Lincoln Ct, N16 . . . . .76 A7
  Borehamwood WD6 . . .38 D5
Lincoln Cres, Enf. EN1 . . .44 B5
Lincoln Dr, Wat. WD19 . . .50 C3
Lincoln Gdns, Ilf. IG1 . . . .80 B7
Lincoln Grn Rd, Orp.
  BR5 . . . . .193 J5
Lincoln Ms, NW6
  off Willesden La 108 C1
  SE21 . . . . .170 A1
Lincoln Rd, E7 . . . . .98 A6
  E13 . . . . .115 H4
  E18 off Grove Rd 79 G1
  N2 . . . . .73 H3
  SE25 . . . . .188 E3
  Enfield EN1, EN3 . . . . .44 D5
  Feltham TW13 . . . . . .161 F3
  Harrow HA2 . . . . .67 F5
  Mitcham CR4 . . . . . . .186 E5
  New Malden KT3 . . . .182 C3
  Sidcup DA14 . . . . . . .176 B5
  Wembley HA0 . . . . . . .87 G6
  Worcester Park KT4 . .197 H1
Lincolns, The, NW7 . . . . .55 F3
★ Lincoln's Inn, WC2 . . .18 D3
Lincoln's Inn Flds, WC2 . .18 D3
Lincoln St, E11 . . . . .96 E2
  SW3 . . . . .31 J2
Lincoln Way, Enf. EN1 . . .44 E5
Lincombe Rd, Brom.
  BR1 . . . . .173 F3
Lindal Cres, Enf. EN2 . . . .43 E4
Lindales, The, N17
  off Brantwood Rd 60 C6
Lindal Rd, SE4 . . . . .153 J5
Lindbergh Rd, Wall.
  SM6 . . . . .200 E7
Linden Av, NW10 . . . . . .108 A2
  Enfield EN1 . . . . .44 D1
  Hounslow TW3 . . . . . .143 H5
  Ruislip HA4 . . . . .84 A1
  Thornton Heath CR7 .187 H4
  Wembley HA9 . . . . . . .87 J5
Linden Cl, N14 . . . . .42 C6
  Ruislip HA4 . . . . .84 A1
  Stanmore HA7 . . . . . .52 E5
  Thames Ditton KT7 . .180 C7
Linden Ct, W12 . . . . .127 J1
Linden Cres, Grnf. UB6 . . .86 C6
  Kingston upon Thames
  KT1 . . . . .181 J2
  Woodford Green IG8 . . .63 H6
Lindenfield, Chis. BR7 . . .192 E2
Linden Gdns, W2 . . . . . .108 D7
  W4 . . . . .126 D5
  Enfield EN1 . . . . .44 D1
Linden Gro, SE15 . . . . . .153 E3
  SE26 . . . . .171 F6
  New Malden KT3 . . . .182 E3

Linden Gro, Tedd. TW11
  off Waldegrave Rd . . .162 C5
Linden Lawns, Wem.
  HA9 . . . . .87 J4
Linden Lea, N2 . . . . .73 F5
Linden Leas, W.Wick.
  BR4 . . . . .204 D2
Linden Ms, N1
  off Mildmay Gro N . . .94 A5
  W2 off Linden Gdns . .108 D7
Linden Pas, W4
  off Linden Gdns 126 D5
Linden Pl, Mitch. CR4 . . .185 H4
Linden Rd, E17
  off High St 77 J5
  N10 . . . . .74 B4
  N11 . . . . .57 J2
  N15 . . . . .75 J4
  Hampton TW12 . . . . .161 G7
Lindens, The, N12 . . . . . .57 G5
  W4 off Hartington Rd .146 C1
  Croydon (New Adgtn.)
  CR0 . . . . .204 C6
  Loughton IG10 . . . . . .48 C5
Linden Wk, N19
  off Hargrave Pk 92 C2
Linden Way, N14 . . . . . . .42 C6
Lindeth Cl, Stan. HA7
  off Old Ch La 53 F6
Lindfield Gdns, NW3 . . . .91 E5
Lindfield Rd, W5 . . . . . . .105 F4
  Croydon CR0 . . . . . . .188 C6
Lindfield St, E14 . . . . . . .114 A6
Lindhill Cl, Enf. EN3 . . . . .45 G1
Lindisfarne Rd, SW20 . . .165 G7
  Dagenham RM8 . . . . .100 C3
Lindisfarne Way, E9 . . . . .95 H4
Lindley Est, SE15 . . . . . . .37 H7
Lindley Pl, Rich. TW9 . . . .146 A1
Lindley Rd, E10 . . . . .96 B2
Lindley St, E1 . . . . .113 F5
Lindore Rd, SW11 . . . . . .149 J4
Lindores Rd, Cars. SM5 . .185 F7
Lindo St, SE15
  off Selden Rd 153 F2
Lind Rd, Sutt. SM1 . . . . .199 F5
Lindrop St, SW6 . . . . . . .149 F2
Lindsay Cl, Chess. KT9 . .195 H7
  Staines (Stanw.) TW19 .140 A5
Lindsay Dr, Har. HA3 . . . .69 H6
Lindsay Rd, Hmptn.
  (Hmptn.H.) TW12 . . . .161 H4
  Worcester Park KT4 . .197 H2
Lindsay Sq, SW1 . . . . . . .33 J3
Lindsell St, SE10 . . . . . .154 C1
Lindsey Cl, Brom. BR1 . .192 A3
  Mitcham CR4 . . . . . . .187 E4
Lindsey Gdns, Felt. TW14 .141 G7
Lindsey Ms, N1 . . . . .93 J7
Lindsey Rd, Dag. RM8 . . .100 C4
Lindsey St, EC1 . . . . .19 H1
Lind St, SE8 . . . . .154 B2
Lindum Rd, Tedd. TW11 . .163 F7
Lindway, SE27 . . . . .169 H5
Lindwood Cl, E6
  off Northumberland
  Rd 116 B5
Linfield Cl, NW4 . . . . .71 J3
Linford Rd, E17 . . . . .78 C3
Linford St, SW8 . . . . . . .150 C1
Lingards Rd, SE13 . . . . . .154 C4
Lingey Cl, Sid. DA15 . . . .175 J2
Lingfield Av, Kings.T.
  KT1 . . . . .181 H4
Lingfield Cl, Enf. EN1 . . . .44 B6
Lingfield Cres, SE9 . . . . .157 G4
Lingfield Gdns, N9 . . . . . .45 E7
Lingfield Rd, SW19 . . . . .166 A5
  Worcester Park KT4 . .197 J3
Lingham St, SW9 . . . . . .151 E2
Lingholm Way, Barn. EN5 .40 A5
Lingmere Cl, Chig. IG7 . . .65 F2
Ling Rd, E16 . . . . .115 G5
  Erith DA8 . . . . .139 J6
Lingrove Gdns, Buck.H. IG9
  off Beech La 63 H2
Lings Coppice, SE21 . . . .170 A2
Lingwell Rd, SW17 . . . . .167 H3
Lingwood Gdns, Islw.
  TW7 . . . . .124 B7
Lingwood Rd, E5 . . . . . . .76 D7
Linhope St, NW1 . . . . . . .7 J5
Link, The, SE9 . . . . .174 D3
  W3 . . . . .106 B6
  Enfield EN3 . . . . .45 H1
  Northolt UB5
  off Eastcote La 85 F5
  Pinner HA5 . . . . .66 C7
  Wembley HA0
  off Nathans Rd 87 F1

Linkfield, Brom. BR2 . . . .191 G6
  West Molesey KT8 . . .179 G3
Linkfield Rd, Islw. TW7 . .144 C2
Link La, Wall. SM6 . . . . . .200 D6
Linklea Cl, NW9 . . . . .55 E7
Link Rd, N11 . . . . .58 A4
  Dagenham RM9 . . . . .119 H2
  Feltham TW14 . . . . . .141 J7
  Wallington SM6 . . . . .200 A1
Links, The, E17 . . . . .77 H4
Links Av, Mord. SM4 . . . .184 D4
Links Dr, N20 . . . . .56 D1
Links Gdns, SW16 . . . . . .169 G7
Linkside, N12 . . . . .56 C6
  Chigwell IG7 . . . . .65 F5
  New Malden KT3 . . . .183 E2
Linkside Cl, Enf. EN2 . . . .43 F3
Linkside Gdns, Enf. EN2 . .43 F3
Links Rd, NW2 . . . . .89 F2
  SW17 . . . . .167 J6
  W3 . . . . .106 A6
  West Wickham BR4 . .204 C1
  Woodford Green IG8 . . .63 G5
Links Side, Enf. EN2 . . . . .43 G3
Link St, E9 . . . . .95 F6
Links Vw, N3 . . . . .56 C7
Links Vw Cl, Stan. HA7 . . .52 D6
Links Vw Rd, Croy. CR0 . .204 A3
  Hampton (Hmptn.H.)
  TW12 . . . . .161 J5
Linksway, NW4 . . . . .72 A2
Links Way, Beck. BR3 . . .190 A6
Links Yd, E1 . . . . .21 H1
Linkway, N4 . . . . .75 J7
  SW20 . . . . .183 H3
Link Way, Brom. BR2 . . .192 B7
Linkway, Dag. RM8 . . . . .100 C4
Link Way, Pnr. HA5 . . . . . .66 D1
Linkway, Rich. TW10 . . . .163 E2
Linkway, The, Barn. EN5 . .40 E6
Linkwood Wk, NW1
  off Maiden La 92 D7
Linley Cres, Rom. RM7 . . .83 H3
Linley Rd, N17 . . . . .76 B2
★ Linley Sambourne Ho,
  W8 . . . . .128 D2
Linnell Cl, NW11 . . . . . . .72 E6
Linnell Dr, NW11 . . . . . . .72 E6
Linnell Rd, N18
  off Fairfield Rd 60 D5
  SE5 . . . . .152 B2
Linnet Cl, N9 . . . . .61 G1
  SE28 . . . . .118 C7
Linnet Ms, SW12 . . . . . .150 A7
Linnett Cl, E4 . . . . .62 C4
Linnet Ter, Ilf. IG5
  off Tiptree Cres 80 D3
Linom Rd, SW4 . . . . .150 E4
Linscott Rd, E5 . . . . .95 F4
Linsdell Rd, Bark. IG11 . .117 F1
Linsey St, SE16 . . . . .37 H1
Linslade Cl, Houns. TW4
  off Frampton Rd .142/143 E5
Pinner HA5 . . . . .66 B3
Linstead St, NW6 . . . . . . .90 D7
Linstead Way, SW18 . . . .148 B7
Linster Gro, Borwd. WD6 . .38 C5
Lintaine Cl, W6
  off Moylan Rd 128 B6
Linthorpe Av, Wem. HA0 . .87 F6
Linthorpe Rd, N16 . . . . . .76 B7
  Barnet EN4 . . . . .41 H3
Linton Cl, Mitch. CR4 . . .185 J7
  Welling DA16
  off Anthony Rd 158 B1
Linton Gdns, E6 . . . . . . .116 B6
Linton Gro, SE27 . . . . . . .169 H5
Linton Rd, Bark. IG11 . . . .99 F7
Lintons, The, Bark. IG11 . .99 F7
Linton St, N1 . . . . .111 J1
Lintott Ct, Stai. (Stanw.)
  TW19 . . . . .140 A6
Linver Rd, SW6 . . . . .148 D2
Linwood Cl, SE5 . . . . . . .152 C2
Linwood Cres, Enf. EN1 . .44 D1
Linwood Way, SE15 . . . . .37 F7
Linzee Rd, N8 . . . . .74 E4
Lion Av, Twick. TW1
  off Lion Rd 162 C1
Lion Cl, SE4 . . . . .154 A6
Lion Ct, Borwd. WD6 . . . .38 C1
Lionel Gdns, SE9 . . . . . . .156 A5
Lionel Ms, W10
  off Telford Rd 108 B5
Lionel Rd, SE9 . . . . .156 A5
Lionel Rd N, Brent. TW8 .125 H4
Lionel Rd S, Brent. TW8 .125 J5
Lion Gate Gdns, Rich.
  TW9 . . . . .145 J3

Lion Pk Av, Chess. KT9 . .196 A4
Lion Plaza, EC2
  off Threadneedle St . . .112 A6
Lion Rd, E6 . . . . .116 C5
  N9 . . . . .60 D2
  Bexleyheath DA6 . . . .159 F4
  Croydon CR0 . . . . . . .187 J5
  Twickenham TW1 . . . .162 C1
Lions Cl, SE9 . . . . .173 J3
Lion Way, Brent. TW8 . . .125 G7
Lion Wf Rd, Islw. TW7 . . .144 E3
Lion Yd, SW4
  off Tremadoc Rd 150 D4
Liphook Cres, SE23 . . . .153 F7
Liphook Rd, Wat. WD19 . .50 D4
Lippitts Hill, Loug.
  (High Beach) IG10 . . . .47 E1
Lipton Cl, SE28
  off Aisher Rd 118 C7
Lipton Rd, E1
  off Bower St 113 G6
Lisbon Av, Twick. TW2 . . .161 J2
Lisbon Cl, E17 . . . . .77 J2
Lisburne Rd, NW3 . . . . . . .91 J4
Lisford St, SE15 . . . . . . .152 C1
Lisgar Ter, W14 . . . . . . .128 C4
Liskeard Cl, Chis. BR7 . . .175 F6
Liskeard Gdns, SE3 . . . .155 G1
Lisle Cl, SW17 . . . . .168 B4
Lisle St, WC2 . . . . .17 J5
Lismore Circ, NW5 . . . . . .92 A5
Lismore Cl, Islw. TW7 . . .144 D2
Lismore Rd, N17 . . . . . . .76 A3
  South Croydon CR2 . .202 B6
Lismore Wk, N1
  off Clephane Rd 93 J6
Lissenden Gdns, NW5 . . .92 A4
Lisson Grn Est, NW8 . . . . .7 G4
LISSON GROVE, NW8 . . . .7 F6
Lisson Gro, NW1 . . . . .7 G5
  NW8 . . . . .7 F4
Lisson St, NW1 . . . . .15 G1
Liss Way, SE15 . . . . .37 G7
Lister Cl, W3 . . . . .106 D5
  Mitcham CR4 . . . . . .185 H1
Lister Ct, NW9
  off Pasteur Cl 70/71 E2
Lister Gdns, N18 . . . . . . .59 J5
Lister Ho, SE3 . . . . .135 E6
Lister Rd, E11 . . . . .97 E1
Lister Wk, SE28
  off Haldane Rd 118 D7
Liston Ct, Wdf.Grn. IG8
  off Navestock Cres . . .63 J7
Liston Rd, N17 . . . . .76 D1
  SW4 . . . . .150 C3
Liston Way, Wdf.Grn. IG8 .63 J7
Listowel Cl, SW9 . . . . . . .35 F7
Listowel Rd, Dag. RM10 .101 G3
Listria Pk, N16 . . . . .94 B2
Litchfield Av, E15 . . . . . . .96 E6
  Morden SM4 . . . . . . .184 C7
Litchfield Gdns, NW10 . . .89 G6
Litchfield Rd, Sutt. SM1 .199 F4
Litchfield St, WC2 . . . . . .17 J5
Litchfield Way, NW11 . . . .73 E5
Lithos Rd, NW3 . . . . .91 E6
Little Acre, Beck. BR3 . . .190 A3
Little Albany St, NW1 . . . .8 E5
Little Argyll St, W1 . . . . . .17 F4
Little Benty, West Dr.
  UB7 . . . . .120 A5
Little Birches, Sid. DA15 .175 H2
Little Boltons, The, SW5 . .30 B3
  SW10 . . . . .30 B3
Little Bornes, SE21 . . . . .170 B4
Little Britain, EC1 . . . . . . .19 J3
Littlebrook Cl, Croy.
  CR0 . . . . .189 G6
Little Brownings, SE23 . .170 E2
Littlebury Rd, SW4 . . . . .150 D3
Little Bury St, N9 . . . . . . .60 A1
Little Cedars, N12
  off Woodside Av 57 F4
Little Chester St, SW1 . . .24 C5
Little Cloisters, SW1
  off Tufton St 130 D3
Little Coll La, EC4
  off Garlick Hill 112 A7
Little Coll St, SW1 . . . . . .26 A5
Littlecombe, SE7 . . . . . . .135 H6
Littlecombe Cl, SW15 . . .148 A6
Little Common, Stan.
  HA7 . . . . .52 D3
Littlecote Cl, SW19 . . . . .148 A6
Littlecote Pl, Pnr. HA5 . . .67 E1
Little Ct, W.Wick. BR4 . . .204 E2
Littlecroft, SE9 . . . . .156 D3
Littledale, SE2 . . . . .138 A6
Little Dean's Yd, SW1 . . .26 A5

Little Dimocks, SW12 . . .168 B2
Little Dorrit Ct, SE1 . . . . .28 A3
Little Dragons, Loug.
  IG10 . . . . .48 A4
LITTLE EALING, W5 . . . . .125 F4
Little Ealing La, W5 . . . . .125 F4
Little Edward St, NW1 . . . . .8 E3
Little Elms, Hayes UB3 . .121 C6
Little Essex St, WC2 . . . . .18 E5
Little Ferry Rd, Twick. TW1
  off Ferry Rd 162/163 E1
Littlefield Cl, N19
  off Tufnell Pk Rd 92 C4
Kingston upon Thames KT1
  off Fairfield W 181 H2
Littlefield Rd, Edg. HA8 . .54 C7
Little Friday Rd, E4 . . . . .62 E2
Little Gearies, Ilf. IG6 . . . .80 E4
Little George St, SW1 . . . .26 A4
Little Gra, Grnf. UB6
  off Perivale La 104 D3
Little Grn, Rich. TW9 . . .145 G4
Little Grn St, NW5
  off College La 92 B4
Littlegrove, Barn. EN4 . . . .41 H6
Little Halliards, Walt. KT12
  off Felix Rd 178 A6
Little Heath, SE7 . . . . . .136 B6
Romford (Chad.Hth.)
  RM6 . . . . .82 B4
Little Heath Rd, Bexh.
  DA7 . . . . .159 F1
Littleheath Rd, S.Croy.
  CR2 . . . . .202 E7
★ Little Holland Ho, Cars.
  SM5 . . . . .199 H7
LITTLE ILFORD, E12 . . . .98 B5
Little Ilford La, E12 . . . . .98 C4
Littlejohn Rd, W7 . . . . . .104 C6
Little Marlborough St,
  W1 . . . . .17 F4
Littlemead, Esher KT10 . .194 A4
Littlemede, SE9 . . . . . . .174 C3
Littlemoor Rd, Ilf. IG1 . . .99 G3
Littlemore Rd, SE2 . . . . .138 A2
Little Moss La, Pnr. HA5 . .67 E2
Little Newport St, WC2 . . .17 J5
Little New St, EC4 . . . . . .19 F3
Little Orchard Cl, Pnr. HA5
  off Barrow Pt La . . .66/67 E2
Little Oxhey La, Wat.
  WD19 . . . . .50 D5
Little Pk Dr, Felt. TW13 . .160 D2
Little Pk Gdns, Enf. EN2 . .43 J3
Little Plucketts Way, Buck.H.
  IG9 . . . . .63 J1
Little Portland St, W1 . . . .17 F3
Little Queens Rd, Tedd.
  TW11 . . . . .162 C6
Little Redlands, Brom.
  BR1 . . . . .192 B2
Little Rd, Croy. CR0
  off Lower Addiscombe
  Rd 202 B1
Hayes UB3 . . . . .121 C4
Littlers Cl, SW19
  off Runnymede 185 G1
Little Russell St, WC1 . . . .18 A2
Little St. James's St,
  SW1 . . . . .25 F2
Little St. Leonards,
  SW14 . . . . .146 C3
Little Sanctuary, SW1 . . . .25 J4
Little Smith St, SW1 . . . . .25 J5
Little Somerset St, E1 . . . .21 F4
Littlestone Cl, Beck. BR3
  off Abbey La 172 A6
Little Strand, NW9 . . . . . .71 F2
Little Thrift, Orp. BR5 . . .193 F4
Little Titchfield St, W1 . . .17 F2
Littleton Av, E4 . . . . .63 F1
Littleton Cres, Har. HA1 . .86 C2
Littleton Rd, Har. HA1 . . .86 C2
Littleton St, SW18 . . . . . .167 F2
Little Trinity La, EC4 . . . . .20 A5
Little Turnstile, WC1 . . . . .18 C3
★ Little Venice (Waterbuses),
  W2 . . . . .14 C1
Littlewood, SE13 . . . . . .154 C5
Littlewood Cl, W13 . . . . .125 E3
Littleworth Av, Esher
  KT10 . . . . .194 A5
Littleworth Common Rd,
  Esher KT10 . . . . .194 A3
Littleworth La, Esher
  KT10 . . . . .194 A4
Littleworth Pl, Esher
  KT10 . . . . .194 A4
Littleworth Rd, Esher
  KT10 . . . . .194 B4

Livermere Rd, E8 . . . . . . .112 C1
Liverpool Gro, SE17 . . . . .36 A4
Liverpool Rd, E10 . . . . . .78 C6
  E16 . . . . .115 E5
  N1 . . . . .111 G2
  N7 . . . . .93 G5
  W5 . . . . .125 G2
Kingston upon Thames
  KT2 . . . . .164 A7
Thornton Heath CR7 . . .187 J3
Liverpool St, EC2 . . . . . .20 D2
Livesey Cl, Kings.T. KT1 .181 J3
★ Livesey Mus, SE15 . . .132 E6
Livesey Pl, SE15 . . . . . . .37 J5
Livingstone Ct, E10
  off Matlock Rd 78 C6
Barnet EN5
  off Christchurch La . . .40 B2
Livingstone Pl, E14
  off Ferry St 134 C5
Livingstone Rd, E15 . . . .114 C1
  E17 . . . . .78 B6
  N13 . . . . .59 E6
  SW11
  off Winstanley Rd 149 G3
Hounslow TW3 . . . . . . .143 J4
Southall UB1 . . . . .102 D7
Thornton Heath CR7 . . .187 J2
Livingstone Wk, SW11 . .149 G3
Livonia St, W1 . . . . .17 G4
Lizard St, EC1 . . . . .12 A4
Lizban St, SE3 . . . . .135 H7
Llanelly Rd, NW2 . . . . . . .90 C2
Llanover Rd, SE18 . . . . .136 D6
Wembley HA9 . . . . .87 G3
Llanthony Rd, Mord.
  SM4 . . . . .185 G6
Llanvanor Rd, NW2 . . . . .90 C2
Llewellyn St, SE16 . . . . . .29 J4
Lloyd Av, SW16 . . . . . . .187 E1
Lloyd Baker St, WC1 . . . .10 D4
Lloyd Ct, Pnr. HA5 . . . . . .66 D5
Lloyd Pk Av, Croy. CR0 . .202 C4
Lloyd Rd, E6 . . . . .116 C1
  E17 . . . . .77 G4
Dagenham RM9 . . . . . .101 F6
Worcester Park KT4 . . .197 J3
Lloyd's Av, EC3 . . . . .21 E4
★ Lloyds of London, EC3 .20 D4
Lloyds Pl, SE3 . . . . .155 E2
Lloyd Sq, WC1 . . . . .10 E3
Lloyd's Row, EC1 . . . . . . .11 F4
Lloyd St, WC1 . . . . .10 E3
Lloyds Way, Beck. BR3 . .189 H5
Loampit Hill, SE13 . . . . .154 A2
Loampit Vale, SE13 . . . . .154 B3
Loanda Cl, E8
  off Clarissa St 112 C1
Loats Rd, SW2 . . . . .150 E6
Lobelia Cl, E6
  off Sorrel Gdns 116 B5
Locarno Rd, W3
  off High St 126 C1
Greenford UB6 . . . . . . .103 J4
Lochaber Rd, SE13 . . . . .154 E4
Lochaline St, W6 . . . . . . .127 J6
Lochan Cl, Hayes UB4 . .102 E4
Lochinvar St, SW12 . . . .150 B7
Lochmere Cl, Erith DA8 . .139 H6
Lochnagar St, E14 . . . . .114 C5
Lock Chase, SE3 . . . . . .155 E3
Lock Cl, Sthl. UB2
  off Navigator Dr 123 J2
Lockesfield Pl, E14 . . . . .134 B5
Lockesley Dr, Orp. BR5 . .193 J6
Lockesley Sq, Surb. KT6 .181 G6
Locket Rd, Har. HA3 . . . . .68 B3
Lockfield Av, Enf. EN3 . . . .45 H2
Lockgate Cl, E9
  off Lee Conservancy
  Rd 95 J5
Lockhart Cl, N7 . . . . .93 F6
Enfield EN3
  off Derby Rd 44/45 E5
Lockhart St, E3 . . . . .113 J4
Lockhurst St, E5 . . . . . . .95 G4
Lockie Pl, SE25 . . . . . . .188 D3
Lockier Wk, Wem. HA9 . . .87 G3
Lockington Rd, SW8 . . . .150 B1
Lockmead Rd, N15 . . . . . .76 D6
  SE13 . . . . .154 C3
Lock Rd, Rich. TW10 . . . .163 F4
Locks La, Mitch. CR4 . . .185 J1
Locksley Est, E14 . . . . . .113 J6
Locksley St, E14 . . . . . . .113 J5
Locksmeade Rd, Rich.
  TW10 . . . . .163 F4
Lockwood Cl, Barn. EN4 .41 J4
Lockwood Cl, SE26 . . . . .171 G4
Lockwood Ind Pk, N17 . . .76 E3

Lockwood Sq, SE16 . . . .132 E3
Lockwood Way, E17 . . . . .77 G2
Chessington KT9 . . . . .196 A5
Lockyer Est, SE1 . . . . . . .28 C3
Lockyer St, SE1 . . . . .28 C4
Loddiges Rd, E9 . . . . . . .95 F7
Loder St, SE15 . . . . .153 F1
Lodge Av, SW14 . . . . . .146 E3
Croydon CR0 . . . . .201 G3
Dagenham RM8, RM9 .118 A1
Harrow HA3 . . . . .69 H4
Lodge Cl, N18 . . . . .59 J5
Edgware HA8 . . . . .53 J6
Isleworth TW7 . . . . . . .144 E1
Wallington SM6 . . . . . .200 A1
Lodge Ct, Wem. HA0 . . . .87 H5
Lodge Dr, N13 . . . . .59 G4
Lodge Gdns, Beck. BR3 .189 J5
Lodge Hill, SE2 . . . . .138 B7
Ilford IG4 . . . . .80 B4
Welling DA16 . . . . .138 B7
Lodgehill Pk Cl, Har. HA2 .85 H2
Lodge La, N12 . . . . .57 F5
Bexley DA5 . . . . .158 D6
Croydon (New Adgtn.)
  CR0 . . . . .204 A6
Lodge Pl, Sutt. SM1 . . . .199 E5
Lodge Rd, NW4 . . . . .71 J4
  NW8 . . . . .7 F4
Bromley BR1 . . . . .173 H7
Croydon CR0 . . . . .187 H6
Sutton SM1
  off Throwley Way .198/199 E5
Wallington SM6 . . . . . .200 B5
Lodge Vil, Wdf.Grn. IG8 . .63 F7
Lodore Gdns, NW9 . . . . . .70 E5
Lodore St, E14 . . . . .114 C6
Lofthouse Pl, Chess.
  KT9 . . . . .195 F6
Loftie St, SE16 . . . . .29 J4
Lofting Rd, N1 . . . . .93 F7
Loftus Rd, W12 . . . . .127 H1
Logan Cl, Enf. EN3 . . . . . .45 G1
Hounslow TW4 . . . . . . .143 F3
Logan Ms, W8 . . . . .128 D4
Logan Pl, W8 . . . . .128 D4
Logan Rd, N9 . . . . .61 E2
Wembley HA9 . . . . .87 H2
Loggetts, The, SE21 . . . .170 B2
Logs Hill, Brom. BR1 . . .174 B7
Chislehurst BR7 . . . . . .174 B7
Logs Hill Cl, Chis. BR7 . .192 B1
Lolesworth Cl, E1 . . . . . . .21 G2
Lollard St, SE11 . . . . .34 D1
Loman St, SE1 . . . . .27 H3
Lomas Cl, Croy. CR0 . . . .204 C7
Lomas Dr, E8 . . . . .94 C7
Lomas St, E1 . . . . .21 J1
Lombard Av, Enf. EN3 . . . .45 F1
Ilford IG3 . . . . .99 H1
Lombard Business Pk,
  SW19 . . . . .185 F2
Lombard Ct, EC3 . . . . . . .20 C5
W3 off Crown St 126 B1
Lombard La, EC4 . . . . . . .19 F4
Lombard Rd, N11 . . . . . . .58 B5
  SW11 . . . . .149 G2
  SW19 . . . . .185 E2
Lombard St, EC3 . . . . . . .20 C4
Lombard Wall, SE7 . . . . .135 H3
Lombardy Pl, W2 . . . . . . .14 A6
Lombardy Retail Pk, Hayes
  UB3 . . . . .102 B7
Lomond Cl, N15 . . . . .76 B4
Wembley HA0 . . . . .87 J7
Lomond Gdns, S.Croy.
  CR2 . . . . .203 H7
Lomond Gro, SE5 . . . . . . .36 B7
Loncroft Rd, SE5 . . . . . . .37 E5
Londesborough Rd, N16 .94 B4
★ London Aquarium,
  SE1 . . . . .26 D3
★ London Arena, E14 . . .134 B3
★ London Brass Rubbing Cen,
  St. Martin-in-the-Fields
  Church, WC2 . . . . .18 A6
London Br, EC4 . . . . .28 C1
  SE1 . . . . .28 C1
London Br St, SE1 . . . . . .28 B2
London Br Wk, SE1 . . . . .28 C1
★ London Broncos RLC
  (share Griffin Pk with
  Brentford FC), Brent.
  TW8 . . . . .125 G6
★ London Butterfly Ho, Syon
  Pk, Brent. TW8 . . . . . .145 E1
★ London Canal Mus, The,
  N1 . . . . .10 B1
★ London Cen Mosque,
  NW8 . . . . .7 H4

★ London City Airport,
  E16 . . . . .136 B1
London City Airport,
  E16 . . . . .136 C1
★ London Commodity
  Exchange, E1 . . . . .21 G6
★ London Dungeon, SE1 .28 C2
★ London Eye, SE1 . . . . .26 C3
London Flds, E8 . . . . .94 E7
London Flds E Side, E8 . .94 E7
London Flds W Side, E8 . .94 D7
★ London Fire Brigade Mus,
  SE1 . . . . .27 J3
★ London Heathrow Airport,
  Houns. TW6 . . . . .140 E1
London La, E8 . . . . .95 E7
Bromley BR1 . . . . .173 F7
★ London Metropolitan
  Archives, EC1 . . . . . . .11 F5
London Ms, W2 . . . . .15 F4
★ London Palladium, W1 .17 F4
★ London Peace Pagoda,
  SW11 . . . . .32 A6
★ London Regatta Cen,
  E16 . . . . .116 A7
London Rd, E13 . . . . . . .115 G2
  SE1 . . . . .27 G5
  SE23 . . . . .170 D1
  SW16 . . . . .187 F1
  SW17 . . . . .185 J2
Barking IG11 . . . . .98 E7
Brentford TW8 . . . . . . .125 F7
Bromley BR1 . . . . .173 F7
Croydon CR0 . . . . .187 H7
Enfield EN2 . . . . .44 A3
Harrow HA1 . . . . .86 B2
Hounslow TW3 . . . . . . .143 J3
Isleworth TW7 . . . . . . .144 C2
Kingston upon Thames
  KT2 . . . . .181 J2
Mitcham CR4 . . . . .185 J2
Mitcham (Bedd.Cor.)
  CR4 . . . . .186 A7
Morden SM4 . . . . .184 D5
Romford (Abridge)
  RM4 . . . . .49 J4
Romford (Chad.Hth.)
  RM6, RM7 . . . . .83 G6
Stanmore HA7 . . . . . . .53 F5
Sutton SM3 . . . . .198 B4
Thornton Heath CR7 . . .187 G5
Twickenham TW1 . . . . .144 D5
Wallington SM6 . . . . . .200 B4
Wembley HA9 . . . . .87 H6
London Shop Pavilion,
  W1 . . . . .17 H6
★ London Silver Vaults,
  WC2 . . . . .18 E2
London Silver Vaults,
  WC2 . . . . .18 E2
London Stile, W4
  off Wellesley Rd 126 A5
★ London Stone, EC4 . . .20 B5
London St, EC3 . . . . .20 E5
  W2 . . . . .15 E4
★ London Transport Mus, WC2
  off Covent Gdn 18 B5
London Wall, EC2 . . . . . . .20 A2
London Wall Bldgs, EC2 . .20 C2
★ London Wildlife Trust,
  NW1 . . . . .110 D1
★ London Zoo, NW1 . . . . .8 B1
Lonesome Way, SW16 . .186 B1
Long Acre, WC2 . . . . .18 A5
Longacre Pl, Cars. SM5
  off Beddington Gdns .200 A6
Longacre Rd, E17 . . . . . . .78 D1
Longbeach Rd, SW11 . . .149 J3
Longberrys, NW2 . . . . . . .90 C3
Longboat Row, Sthl.
  UB1 . . . . .103 F6
Longbridge Rd, Bark.
  IG11 . . . . .99 F7
Dagenham RM8 . . . . . .100 A4
Longbridge Way, SE13 . .154 C5
Longcliffe Path, Wat. WD19
  off Gosforth La 50 A3
Longcroft, SE9 . . . . .174 D3
Longcrofte Rd, Edg. HA8 .53 G7
Longcroft Ri, Loug. IG10 . .48 D5
Long Deacon Rd, E4 . . . . .62 E1
LONG DITTON, Surb. 195 F1
Longdon Wd, Kes. BR2 . .206 B4
Longdown Rd, SE6 . . . . .172 A4
Long Dr, W3 . . . . .106 E6
Greenford UB6 . . . . . . .103 H1
Ruislip HA4 . . . . .84 D4
Long Elmes, Har. HA3 . . . .67 H1
Longfellow Rd, E17 . . . . . .77 J6
Worcester Park KT4 . . .197 G2

Longfellow Way, SE1 . . .37 G2
Long Fld, NW9 . . . . .55 E7
Longfield, Brom. BR1 . .191 F1
  Loughton IG10 . . . . . . .47 J5
Longfield Av, E17 . . . . . .77 H4
  NW7 . . . . .55 G7
  W5 . . . . .105 F7
  Wallington SM6 . . . . . .200 A1
  Wembley HA9 . . . . .87 H1
Longfield Cres, SE26 . . .171 F3
Longfield Dr, SW14 . . . .146 B5
  Mitcham CR4 . . . . .167 H7
Longfield Est, SE1 . . . . . .37 G2
Longfield Rd, W5 . . . . . .105 F7
Longfield St, SW18 . . . .148 D7
Longfield Wk, W5 . . . . . .105 F6
Longford Av, Felt.TW14 .141 H6
  Southall UB1 . . . . .103 G7
Longford Cl, Hmptn.
  (Hmptn.H.)TW12 . . .161 G4
  Hayes UB4
   off Longford Gdns . . .102 D7
Longford Ct, E5
   off Pedro St 95 G4
  NW4 . . . . .72 A4
  Epsom KT19 . . . . .196 C4
Longford Gdns, Hayes
  UB4 . . . . .102 D7
  Sutton SM1 . . . . .199 F3
Longford Rd, Twick.TW2 .161 G1
Longford St, NW1 . . . . . . .8 E5
Longford Wk, SW2
   off Papworth Way . . .151 G7
Long Grn, Chig. IG7 . . . .65 H4
Longhayes Av, Rom. RM6 .82 D4
Longhayes Ct, Rom. RM6
   off Longhayes Av 82 D4
Longheath Gdns, Croy.
  CR0 . . . . .189 F5
Longhedge Ho, SE26 . . .170 C4
Long Hedges, Houns.
  TW3 . . . . .143 G1
Longhedge St, SW11 . . .150 A2
Longhill Rd, SE6 . . . . . .172 D2
Longhook Gdns, Nthlt.
  UB5 . . . . .102 A2
Longhope Cl, SE15 . . . . .37 E6
Longhurst Rd, SE13 . . . .154 D5
  Croydon CR0 . . . . .189 E6
Longland Ct, SE1 . . . . . .37 H3
Longland Dr, N20 . . . . . .56 E3
LONGLANDS, Chis. 175 F3
Longlands Ct, W11
   off Portobello Rd 108 C7
  Mitcham CR4
   off Summerhill Way .186 A1
Longlands Pk Cres, Sid.
  DA15 . . . . .175 H3
Longlands Rd, Sid.
  DA15 . . . . .175 H3
Long La, EC1 . . . . .19 H1
  N2 . . . . .73 F2
  N3 . . . . .73 F2
  SE1 . . . . .28 B4
  Bexleyheath DA7 . . . . .138 D7
  Croydon CR0 . . . . .189 F5
  Staines (Stanw.)TW19 .140 C7
Longleat Rd, Enf. EN1 . . .44 B5
Longleat Way, Felt.
  TW14 . . . . .141 G2
Longleigh La, SE2 . . . . .138 C6
  Bexleyheath DA7 . . . . .138 C6
Longlents Ho, NW10 . . .106 D1
Longley Av, Wem. HA0 . .105 J1
Longley Rd, SW17 . . . . .167 H6
  Harrow HA1 . . . . .67 J5
  Croydon CR0 . . . . .187 H7
Long Leys, E4 . . . . .62 B6
Longley St, SE1 . . . . .37 H2
Longley Way, NW2 . . . . .89 J3
Long Mark Rd, E16
   off Fulmer Rd 116 A5
Long Mead, NW9 . . . . . . .71 F1
Longmead, Chis. BR7 . . .192 D2
Longmead Dr, Sid.
  DA14 . . . . .176 D2
Long Meadow, NW5
   off Torriano Av 92 D5
Long Meadow Cl, W.Wick.
  BR4 . . . . .190 C7
Longmeadow Rd, Sid.
  DA15 . . . . .175 H1
Longmead Rd, SW17 . . .167 J5
  Thames Ditton KT7 . . .180 B7
Longmoore St, SW1 . . . .33 F2
Longmoor Pt, SW15
   off Norley Vale 165 H4
Longmore Av, Barn. EN4,
  EN5 . . . . .41 F6
Longnor Rd, E1 . . . . . . .113 G3

Long Pond Rd, SE3 . . . . .155 E1
Long Reach Ct, Bark.
  IG11 . . . . .117 G2
Longreach Rd, Bark.
  IG11 . . . . .117 J4
Longridge La, Sthl. UB1 .103 H7
Longridge Rd, SW5 . . . .128 D4
Long Rd, SW4 . . . . .150 B4
Long's Ct, WC2 . . . . .17 H5
Longs Ct, Rich.TW9
   off Crown Ter 145 J4
Longshaw Rd, E4 . . . . . .62 D3
Longshore, SE8 . . . . . . .133 J4
Longstaff Cres, SW18 . .148 D6
Longstaff Rd, SW18 . . . .148 D6
Longstone Av, NW10 . . . .89 F7
Longstone Rd, SW17 . . .168 B5
Long St, E2 . . . . .13 F3
Longthornton Rd, SW16 .186 C2
Longton Av, SE26 . . . . . .170 D4
Longton Gro, SE26 . . . . .170 E4
Longville Rd, SE11 . . . . . .35 G1
Long Wk, SE1 . . . . .28 E5
  SE18 . . . . .136 E6
  SW13 . . . . .147 E2
  New Malden KT3 . . . . .182 C3
Longwalk Rd, Uxb.
  UB11 . . . . .121 E1
Longwood Dr, SW15 . . .147 G6
Longwood Gdns, Ilf. IG5,
  IG6 . . . . .80 C4
Longworth Cl, SE28 . . . .118 D6
Long Yd, WC1 . . . . .10 C6
Loning, The, NW9 . . . . . .71 E4
Lonsdale Av, E6 . . . . . . .116 A3
  Romford RM7 . . . . .83 J6
  Wembley HA9 . . . . .87 H5
Lonsdale Cl, E6
   off Lonsdale Av 116 B4
  SE9 . . . . .174 A3
  Edgware HA8
   off Orchard Dr 53 J5
  Pinner HA5 . . . . .51 E7
Lonsdale Cres, Ilf. IG2 . . .80 E6
Lonsdale Dr, Enf. EN2 . . . .43 E5
Lonsdale Gdns, Th.Hth.
  CR7 . . . . .187 F4
Lonsdale Ms, Rich.TW9
   off Elizabeth Cotts . .146 A1
Lonsdale Pl, N1
   off Barnsbury St 93 G7
Lonsdale Rd, E11 . . . . . . .79 F7
  NW6 . . . . .108 C2
  SE25 . . . . .188 E4
  SW13 . . . . .127 G6
  W4 . . . . .127 F4
  W11 . . . . .108 C6
  Bexleyheath DA7 . . . . .159 F2
  Southall UB2 . . . . .122 D3
Lonsdale Sq, N1 . . . . .93 G7
Loobert Rd, N15 . . . . . . .76 B3
Looe Gdns, Ilf. IG6 . . . . . .81 E3
Loom Ct, E1 . . . . .13 E6
Loop Rd, Chis. BR7 . . . . .175 F6
Lopen Rd, N18 . . . . .60 B4
Loraine Cl, Enf. EN3 . . . . .45 F5
Loraine Rd, N7 . . . . .93 F4
  W4 . . . . .126 B6
Lord Amory Way, E14 . .134 C2
Lord Av, Ilf. IG5 . . . . .80 C4
Lord Chancellor Wk, Kings.T.
  KT2 . . . . .182 C1
Lord Cl, SE21 . . . . .169 J2
Lord Gdns, Ilf. IG5 . . . . . .80 B4
Lord Hills Br, W2 . . . . . . .14 B2
Lord Hills Rd, W2 . . . . . . .14 B1
Lord Holland La, SW9
   off St. Lawrence Way .151 G1
Lord Knyvett Cl, Stai. (Stanw.)
  TW19 . . . . .140 A6
Lord Napier Pl, W6
   off Upper Mall 127 G5
Lord N St, SW1 . . . . .26 A6
Lord Roberts Ms, SW6
   off Moore Pk Rd .128/129 E7
Lord Roberts Ter, SE18 . .136 D5
★ Lord's, Middlesex County
  Cricket Club & Mus,
  NW8 . . . . .7 F3
Lord's Cl, SE21 . . . . .169 J2
Lords Cl, Felt.TW13 . . . .161 E2
Lordship Gro, N16 . . . . . .94 A2
Lordship La, N17 . . . . . . .75 J1
  N22 . . . . .75 G2
  SE22 . . . . .152 C6
Lordship La Est, SE22 . . .170 D1
Lordship Pk, N16 . . . . . . .93 J2
Lordship Pk Ms, N16
   off Allerton Rd 93 J2

Lordship Pl, SW3 . . . . . . .31 G5
Lordship Rd, N16 . . . . . . .94 A2
  Northolt UB5 . . . . .84 E7
Lordship Ter, N16 . . . . . . .94 A2
Lordsmead Rd, N17 . . . . .76 B1
Lord St, E16 . . . . .136 B1
Lord's Vw, NW8 . . . . .7 F4
Lord Warwick St, SE18 . .136 C3
Lorenzo St, WC1 . . . . . . .10 C3
Loretto Gdns, Har. HA3 . .69 H4
Lorian Cl, N12 . . . . .56 E4
Loring Rd, N20 . . . . .57 H2
  Isleworth TW7 . . . . . . .144 C2
Loris Rd, W6 . . . . .127 J3
Lorn Ct, SW9 . . . . .151 G2
Lorne Av, Croy. CR0 . . . .189 G7
Lorne Cl, NW8 . . . . .7 H4
Lorne Gdns, E11 . . . . .79 J4
  W11 . . . . .128 A2
  Croydon CR0 . . . . .189 G7
Lorne Rd, E7 . . . . .97 H4
  E17 . . . . .78 A5
  Harrow HA3 . . . . .68 C2
  Richmond TW10
   off Albert Rd 145 J5
Lorn Rd, SW9 . . . . .151 F2
Lorraine Pk, Har. HA3 . . .52 B7
Lorrimore Rd, SE17 . . . . .35 H5
Lorrimore Sq, SE17 . . . . .35 H5
Loseberry Rd, Esher (Clay.)
  KT10 . . . . .194 A5
Lothair Rd, W5 . . . . .125 G2
Lothair Rd N, N4 . . . . . . .75 H6
Lothair Rd S, N4 . . . . . . .75 G7
Lothbury, EC2 . . . . .20 B3
Lothian Av, Hayes UB4 .102 B5
Lothian Cl, Wem. HA0 . . .86 D4
Lothian Rd, SW9 . . . . . . .151 H1
Lothrop St, W10 . . . . . . .108 B3
Lots Rd, SW10 . . . . .129 F7
Lotus Cl, SE21 . . . . .169 J3
Loubet St, SW17 . . . . . . .167 J6
Loudoun Av, Ilf. IG6 . . . . .81 E5
Loudoun Rd, NW8 . . . . . . .6 D1
Loudoun Rd Ms, NW8
   off Loudoun Rd 109 F1
Loudwater Cl, Sun.
  TW16 . . . . .178 A4
Loudwater Rd, Sun.
  TW16 . . . . .178 A4
Loughborough Est, SW9
   off Loughborough Rd .151 H2
Loughborough Pk, SW9 .151 H4
Loughborough Rd, SW9 .151 G2
Loughborough St, SE11 . .34 D3
Lough Rd, N7 . . . . .93 F6
LOUGHTON 48 C5
Loughton Way, Buck.H.
  IG9 . . . . .64 A1
Louisa Gdns, E1 . . . . . . .113 G4
   off Louisa St 113 G4
Louisa Ho, SW15 . . . . . .147 E4
Louisa St, E1 . . . . .113 G4
Louise Aumonier Wk, N19
   off Hillrise Rd 74/75 E7
Louise Bennett Cl, SE24
   off Shakespeare Rd .151 H4
Louise Ct, E11
   off Grosvenor Rd 79 H5
Louise Rd, E15 . . . . .97 E6
Louis Ms, N10 . . . . .74 B1
Louisville Rd, SW17 . . . .168 A3
Louvaine Rd, SW11 . . . .149 G4
Lovage App, E6 . . . . . . .116 B5
Lovat Cl, NW2 . . . . .89 F3
Lovat La, EC3 . . . . .20 D6
Lovatt Cl, Edg. HA8 . . . . .54 B6
Lovatt Dr, Ruis. HA4 . . . . .66 A5
Lovatt Wk, Houns.TW5
   off Cranford La . .122/123 E7
Loveday Rd, W13 . . . . . .125 E1
Lovegrove St, SE1 . . . . . .37 J4
Lovegrove Wk, E14 . . . . .134 C1
Lovekyn Cl, Kings.T. KT2
   off Queen Elizabeth
  Rd 181 J2
Lovelace Av, Brom. BR2 .192 D6
Lovelace Gdns, Bark.
  IG11 . . . . .100 A4
  Surbiton KT6 . . . . .181 G7
Lovelace Grn, SE9 . . . . .156 C3
Lovelace Rd, SE21 . . . . .169 J2
  Barnet EN4 . . . . .41 H7
  Surbiton KT6 . . . . .181 F7
Love La, EC2 . . . . .20 A3
  N17 . . . . .60 C7
  SE18 . . . . .136 E4
  SE25 . . . . .189 E3
  Bexley DA5 . . . . .159 F6

Love La, Mitch. CR4 . . . .185 H3
  Morden SM4 . . . . .184 D7
  Pinner HA5 . . . . .66 E3
  Surbiton KT6 . . . . .195 G2
  Sutton SM3 . . . . .198 B5
  Woodford Green IG8 . . .64 C6
Lovel Av, Well. DA16 . . . .158 A2
Lovelinch Cl, SE15 . . . . .133 F6
Lovell Ho, E8 . . . . .112 D1
Lovell Pl, SE16
   off Ropemaker Rd . . .133 H3
Lovell Rd, Rich.TW10 . . .163 F3
  Southall UB1 . . . . .103 H6
Loveridge Ms, NW6
   off Loveridge Rd 90 C6
Loveridge Rd, NW6 . . . . .90 C6
Lovers Wk, N3 . . . . .56 D7
  NW7 . . . . .56 C6
  SE10 . . . . .134 E6
Lover's Wk, W1 . . . . .24 B1
Lovett Dr, Cars. SM5 . . .185 F7
Lovett's Pl, SW18
   off Old York Rd . .148/149 E4
Lovett Way, NW10 . . . . . .88 C5
Love Wk, SE5 . . . . .152 A2
Lovibonds Av, Orp.
  BR6 . . . . .207 E4
Lowbrook Rd, Ilf. IG1 . . . .99 E5
Low Cross Wd La, SE21 .170 C3
Lowden Rd, N9 . . . . .61 E1
  SE24 . . . . .151 H4
  Southall UB1 . . . . .102 E7
Lowe Av, E16 . . . . .115 G5
Lowell St, E14 . . . . .113 H6
Lower Addiscombe Rd,
  Croy. CR0 . . . . .202 B1
Lower Addison Gdns,
  W14 . . . . .128 B2
Lower Alderton Hall La, Loug.
  IG10 . . . . .48 D5
Lower Belgrave St, SW1 . .24 D6
Lower Boston Rd, W7 . . .124 B1
Lower Broad St, Dag.
  RM10 . . . . .119 G1
Lower Camden, Chis. . . .174 C7
Lower Ch St, Croy. CR0
   off Waddon New Rd . .201 H2
LOWER CLAPTON, E5 . . .95 G4
Lower Clapton Rd, E5 . . . .95 F5
Lower Clarendon Wk, W11
   off Lancaster Rd 108 B6
Lower Common S,
  SW15 . . . . .147 H3
Lower Coombe St, Croy.
  CR0 . . . . .201 J4
Lower Downs Rd, SW20 .184 A1
Lower Drayton Pl, Croy. CR0
   off Drayton Rd 201 H2
LOWER EDMONTON, N9 .60 C1
Lower George St, Rich.TW9
   off George St 145 G5
Lower Gravel Rd, Brom.
  BR2 . . . . .206 B1
Lower Grn W, Mitch. 185 H3
Lower Grosvenor Pl,
  SW1 . . . . .24 D5
Lower Gro Rd, Rich. 145 J6
Lower Hall La, E4 . . . . . . .61 H1
Lower Hampton Rd, Sun.
  TW16 . . . . .178 C3
Lower Ham Rd, Kings.T.
  KT2 . . . . .181 G1
LOWER HOLLOWAY, N7 . .93 F5
Lower James St, W1 . . . . .17 G5
Lower John St, W1 . . . . . .17 G5
Lower Kenwood Av, Enf.
  EN2 . . . . .42 D5
Lower Lea Crossing, E14 .114 E7
  E16 . . . . .114 E7
Lower Maidstone Rd, N11
   off Telford Rd 58 C6
Lower Mall, W6 . . . . .127 H5
Lower Mardyke Av, Rain.
  RM13 . . . . .119 J2
Lower Marsh, SE1 . . . . . .26 E4
Lower Marsh La, Kings.T.
  KT1 . . . . .181 J4
Lower Merton Ri, NW3 . . .91 H7
Lower Morden La, Mord.
  SM4 . . . . .183 J6
Lower Mortlake Rd, Rich.
  TW9 . . . . .145 H4
Lower Pk Rd, N11 . . . . . . .58 C5
  Belvedere DA17 . . . . . .139 G3
  Loughton IG10 . . . . . . .48 A5
Lower Queens Rd, Buck.H.
  IG9 . . . . .64 A2

Lower Richmond Rd,
  SW14 . . . . .146 B3
  SW15 . . . . .147 J3
  Richmond TW9 . . . . . .146 A3
Lower Rd, SE8 . . . . . . .133 F3
  SE16 . . . . .133 F3
  Belvedere DA17 . . . . .139 G3
  Harrow HA2 . . . . .86 A2
  Loughton IG10 . . . . . . .48 D2
  Sutton SM1 . . . . .199 F4
Lower Robert St, WC2
  off John Adam St .110/111 E7
Lower Sand Hills, T.Ditt.
  KT7 . . . . .181 F7
Lower Sloane St, SW1 . .32 B2
Lower Strand, NW9 . . . . .71 F2
Lower Sunbury Rd, Hmptn.
  TW12 . . . . .179 F2
LOWER SYDENHAM,
  SE26 . . . . .171 G4
Lower Sydenham Ind Est,
  SE26 . . . . .171 J5
Lower Tail, Wat. WD19 . . .51 E3
Lower Talbot Wk, W11
  off Lancaster Rd 108 B6
Lower Teddington Rd,
  Kings.T. KT1 . . . . .181 G1
Lower Ter, NW3 . . . . .91 F3
Lower Thames St, EC3 . . .20 C6
Lower Wd Rd, Esher (Clay.)
  KT10 . . . . .194 D6
Lowestoft CI, E5
  off Theydon Rd 95 F2
Lowestoft Ms, E16 . . . .137 E2
Loweswater CI, Wem.
  HA9 . . . . .87 G2
Lowfield Rd, NW6 . . . . . .90 D7
  W3 . . . . .106 C6
Low Hall CI, E4 . . . . .46 A7
Low Hall La, E17 . . . . . . .77 H6
Lowick Rd, Har. HA1 . . . .68 B4
Lowlands Dr, Stai. (Stanw.)
  TW19 . . . . .140 A5
Lowlands Gdns, Rom.
  RM7 . . . . .83 H6
Lowlands Rd, Har. HA1 . .68 B7
  Pinner HA5 . . . . .66 C7
Lowman Rd, N7 . . . . .93 F4
Lowndes CI, SW1 . . . . . .24 C6
Lowndes Ct, W1 . . . . . . .17 F4
  Bromley BR1
  off Queens Rd 191 G2
Lowndes PI, SW1 . . . . . .24 B6
Lowndes Sq, SW1 . . . . . .24 A4
Lowndes St, SW1 . . . . . .24 A5
Lowood Ct, SE19 . . . . . .170 C5
Lowood St, E1
  off Dellow St 112/113 E7
Lowry Cres, Mitch. CR4 .185 H2
Lowry Rd, Dag. RM8 . . . .100 B4
Lowshoe La, Rom. RM5 . .83 H1
Lowther Dr, Enf. EN2 . . . .42 A4
Lowther Gdns, SW7 . . . . .23 F4
Lowther Hill, SE23 . . . . .153 H7
Lowther Rd, E17 . . . . . . .77 H2
  N7 off Mackenzie Rd . .93 G5
  SW13 . . . . .147 F1
  Kingston upon Thames
  KT2 . . . . .181 J1
  Stanmore HA7 . . . . . . .69 J3
Lowth Rd, SE5 . . . . .151 J2
LOXFORD, IIf. 99 F5
Loxford Av, E6 . . . . .116 A2
Loxford La, IIf. IG1, IG3 . . .99 F5
Loxford Rd, Bark. IG11 . . .99 E6
Loxford Ter, Bark. IG11
  off Fanshawe Av 99 E6
Loxham Rd, E4 . . . . .62 A7
Loxham St, WC1 . . . . . . .10 B4
Loxley CI, SE26 . . . . . . .171 G5
Loxley Rd, SW18 . . . . . .167 G1
  Hampton TW12 . . . . . .161 F4
Loxton Rd, SE23 . . . . . .171 G1
Loxwood Rd, N17 . . . . . . .76 B3
Lubbock Rd, Chis. BR7 . .174 C7
Lubbock St, SE14 . . . . . .133 F7
Lucan PI, SW3 . . . . .31 G2
Lucan Rd, Barn. EN5 . . . .40 B3
Lucas Av, E13 . . . . .115 H1
  Harrow HA2 . . . . .85 G2
Lucas CI, NW10
  off Pound La 89 G7
Lucas Ct, Har. HA2 . . . . . .85 G1
Lucas Gdns, N2 . . . . .73 F2
Lucas Rd, SE20 . . . . . . .171 F6
Lucas Sq, NW11
  off Hampstead Way . . .72 D6
Lucas St, SE8 . . . . .154 A1
Lucerne Ct, N13 . . . . .58 E4

Lucerne Ct, Erith DA18
  off Middle Way . .138/139 E3
Lucerne Gro, E17 . . . . . . .78 D4
Lucerne Ms, W8
  off Kensington Mall . .128 D1
Lucerne Rd, N5 . . . . .93 H4
  Orpington BR6 . . . . . . .207 J1
  Thornton Heath CR7 . .187 H5
Lucey CI, SE16 . . . . .29 H6
Lucey Way, SE16 . . . . . . .29 J6
Lucien Rd, SW17 . . . . . .168 A4
  SW19 . . . . .166 E2
Lucknow St, SE18 . . . . . .137 H7
Lucorn CI, SE12 . . . . . . .155 F6
Lucton Ms, Loug. IG10 . . .48 E4
Luctons Av, Buck.H. IG9 . .63 J1
Lucy Cres, W3 . . . . .106 C5
Lucy Gdns, Dag. RM8
  off Grafton Rd . . .100/101 E3
Luddesdon Rd, Erith
  DA8 . . . . .139 G7
Ludford CI, NW9 . . . . .70 E2
  Croydon CR0
  off Warrington Rd 201 H4
Ludgate Bdy, EC4 . . . . . . .19 G4
Ludgate Circ, EC4 . . . . . . .19 G4
Ludgate Hill, EC4 . . . . . . .19 G4
Ludgate Sq, EC4 . . . . .19 H4
Ludham, CI, SE28
  off Rollesby Way 118 C6
Ludlow CI, Brom. BR2
  off Aylesbury Rd 191 G3
  Harrow HA2 . . . . .85 F4
Ludlow Mead, Wat.
  WD19 . . . . .50 B3
Ludlow Rd, W5 . . . . .105 F4
  Feltham TW13 . . . . . . .160 A4
Ludlow St, EC1 . . . . .11 J5
Ludlow Way, N2 . . . . .73 F4
Ludovick Wk, SW15 . . . . .147 E4
Ludwick Ms, SE14 . . . . . .133 H7
Luffield Rd, SE2 . . . . . . .138 B3
Luffman Rd, SE12 . . . . . .173 H3
Lugard Rd, SE15 . . . . . . .153 E2
Lugg App, E12 . . . . .98 D3
Luke Ho, E1 . . . . .113 E6
Luke St, EC2 . . . . .12 D5
Lukin Cres, E4 . . . . .62 D3
Lukin St, E1 . . . . .113 F6
Lukintone CI, Loug. IG10 . .48 B4
Lullingstone CI, Orp. BR5
  off Lullingstone Cres .176 B7
Lullingstone Cres, Orp.
  BR5 . . . . .176 A7
Lullingstone La, SE13 . . .154 D7
Lullingstone Rd, Belv.
  DA17 . . . . .139 F6
Lullington Garth, N12 . . . .56 C5
  Borehamwood WD6 . . . .38 B5
  Bromley BR1 . . . . .173 E7
Lullington Rd, SE20 . . . .170 D7
  Dagenham RM9 . . . . . .100 E7
Lulot Gdns, N19 . . . . .92 B2
Lulworth, SE17 . . . . .36 B3
Lulworth Av, Houns.
  TW5 . . . . .123 H7
  Wembley HA9 . . . . .69 F7
Lulworth CI, Har. HA2 . . . .85 F3
Lulworth Cres, Mitch.
  CR4 . . . . .185 H2
Lulworth Dr, Pnr. HA5 . . . .66 D7
Lulworth Gdns, Har. HA2 .85 E2
Lulworth Rd, SE9 . . . . . .174 B2
  SE15 . . . . .153 E2
  Welling DA16 . . . . .157 J2
Lulworth Waye, Hayes
  UB4 . . . . .102 C6
Lumen Rd, Wem. HA9 . . . .87 G2
Lumley CI, Belv. DA17 . . .139 G6
Lumley Ct, WC2 . . . . .18 B6
Lumley Gdns, Sutt. SM3 .198 B5
Lumley Rd, Sutt. SM3 . . .198 B6
Lumley St, W1 . . . . .16 C4
Luna Rd, Th.Hth. CR7 . . .187 J3
Lundin Wk, Wat. WD19
  off Woodhall La 50 D4
Lundy Dr, Hayes UB3 . . .121 H4
Lundy Wk, N1
  off Clephane Rd 93 J6
Lunham Rd, SE19 . . . . . .170 B6
Lupin CI, SW2
  off Palace Rd 169 H2
  Croydon CR0
  off Primrose La 203 G1
  West Drayton UB7
  off Magnolia St 120 A5
Lupin Cres, IIf. IG1
  off Bluebell Way . . .98/99 E5
Lupton CI, SE12 . . . . . . .173 H3
Lupton St, NW5 . . . . .92 C4

Lupus St, SW1 . . . . .33 G4
Luralda Gdns, E14
  off Saunders Ness
  Rd 134 C5
Lurgan Av, W6 . . . . .128 A6
Lurline Gdns, SW11 . . . .150 A1
Luscombe Ct, Brom.
  BR2 . . . . .190 E2
Luscombe Way, SW8 . . . .34 A7
Lushes Ct, Loug. IG10
  off Lushes Rd 48/49 E5
Lushes Rd, Loug. IG10 . . .49 E5
Lushington Rd, NW10 . . .107 H2
  SE6 . . . . .172 B5
Lushington Ter, E8
  off Wayland Av 94 D5
Luther CI, Edg. HA8 . . . . .54 C2
Luther King CI, E17 . . . . . .77 H6
Luther Rd, Tedd. TW11 . .162 C5
Luton PI, SE10 . . . . .134 C7
Luton Rd, E17 . . . . .77 J3
  Sidcup DA14 . . . . .176 C3
Luton St, NW8 . . . . .7 F6
Lutton Ter, NW3
  off Flask Wk 91 G4
Luttrell Av, SW15 . . . . . .147 H5
Lutwyche Rd, SE6 . . . . . .171 J2
Luxborough La, Chig.
  IG7 . . . . .64 B3
Luxborough St, W1 . . . . . .16 B1
Luxemburg Gdns, W6 . . .128 A4
Luxfield Rd, SE9 . . . . . . .174 B1
Luxford St, SE16 . . . . . . .133 G4
Luxmore St, SE4 . . . . . . .153 J1
Luxor St, SE5 . . . . .151 J3
Lyall Av, SE21 . . . . .170 B3
Lyall Ms, SW1 . . . . .24 B6
Lyall Ms W, SW1 . . . . . . .24 B6
Lyall St, SW1 . . . . .24 B6
Lyal Rd, E3 . . . . .113 H2
Lycett PI, W12
  off Becklow Rd 127 G2
Lyconby Gdns, Croy.
  CR0 . . . . .189 H7
Lydd CI, Sid. DA14 . . . . .175 H3
Lydden Ct, SE9 . . . . .157 H6
Lydden Gro, SW18 . . . . .148 E7
Lydden Rd, SW18 . . . . . .148 E7
Lydd Rd, Bexh. DA7 . . . .139 F7
Lydeard Rd, E6 . . . . .98 C7
Lydford CI, N16
  off Pellerin Rd 94 B5
Lydford Rd, N15 . . . . .76 A5
  NW2 . . . . .90 A6
  W9 . . . . .108 C4
Lydhurst Av, SW2 . . . . . .169 F2
Lydney CI, SE15 . . . . .36 E7
  SW19 off Princes Way .166 B2
Lydon Rd, SW4 . . . . .150 C3
Lydstep Rd, Chis. BR7 . .174 D4
Lyford Rd, SW18 . . . . . . .149 G7
Lygon PI, SW1 . . . . .24 D6
Lyham CI, SW2 . . . . .151 E6
Lyham Rd, SW2 . . . . .150 E5
Lyle CI, Mitch. CR4 . . . . .186 A7
Lyme Fm Rd, SE12 . . . . .155 G4
Lyme Gro, E9
  off St. Thomas's Sq . . .95 F7
Lymer Av, SE19 . . . . .170 C5
Lyme Rd, Well. DA16 . . . .158 B1
Lymescote Gdns, Sutt.
  SM1 . . . . .198 D2
Lyme St, NW1 . . . . .92 C7
Lyme Ter, NW1
  off Royal Coll St 92 C7
Lyminge CI, Sid. DA14 . .175 J4
Lyminge Gdns, SW18 . . .167 H1
Lymington Av, N22 . . . . . .75 G2
Lymington CI, E6
  off Valiant Way 116 C5
  SW16 . . . . .186 D2
Lymington Gdns, Epsom
  KT19 . . . . .197 F5
Lymington Rd, NW6 . . . . .90 E6
  Dagenham RM8 . . . . . .100 D1
Lympstone Gdns, SE15 . .37 J7
Lynbridge Gdns, N13 . . . .59 H4
Lynbrook CI, SE15 . . . . . .36 E7
Lynchen CI, Houns. TW5
  off The Avenue 142 A1
Lynch Wk, SE8
  off Prince St 133 J6
Lyncott Cres, SW4 . . . . .150 B4
Lyncroft Av, Pnr. HA5 . . . .66 E5
Lyncroft Gdns, NW6 . . . . .90 D5
  W13 . . . . .125 F2
  Hounslow TW3 . . . . . .143 J4
Lyndale, NW2 . . . . .90 C4
Lyndale Av, NW2 . . . . .90 C3
Lyndale CI, SE3 . . . . .135 F6

Lyndhurst Av, N12 . . . . . .57 J6
  NW7 . . . . .54 E6
  SW16 . . . . .186 D2
  Pinner HA5 . . . . .66 B1
  Southall UB1 . . . . .123 H1
  Sunbury-on-Thames
  TW16 . . . . .178 A3
  Surbiton KT5 . . . . .196 B1
  Twickenham TW2 . . . .161 F1
Lyndhurst CI, NW10 . . . . .88 D3
  Bexleyheath DA7 . . . . .159 H3
  Croydon CR0 . . . . .202 C3
  Orpington BR6 . . . . . . .207 E4
Lyndhurst Ct, E18
  off Churchfields 79 G1
  Sutton SM2
  off Overton Rd 198 D7
Lyndhurst Dr, E10 . . . . . . .78 C7
  New Malden KT3 . . . . .183 E6
Lyndhurst Gdns, N3 . . . . .72 B1
  NW3 . . . . .91 G5
  Barking IG11 . . . . .99 H6
  Enfield EN1 . . . . .44 B4
  Ilford IG2 . . . . .81 G6
  Pinner HA5 . . . . .66 B1
Lyndhurst Gro, SE15 . . . .152 B2
Lyndhurst Ho, SW15
  off Ellisfield Dr 147 G7
Lyndhurst Ri, Chig. IG7 . . .64 D4
Lyndhurst Rd, E4 . . . . . . .62 C7
  N18 . . . . .60 D4
  N22 . . . . .59 F6
  NW3 . . . . .91 G5
  Bexleyheath DA7 . . . . .159 H3
  Greenford UB6 . . . . . . .103 H4
  Thornton Heath CR7 . .187 G4
Lyndhurst Sq, SE15 . . . .152 C1
Lyndhurst Ter, NW3 . . . . .91 G5
Lyndhurst Way, SE15 . . .152 C1
  Sutton SM2 . . . . .198 D7
Lyndon Av, Pnr. HA5 . . . . .51 E6
  Sidcup DA15 . . . . .157 J5
  Wallington SM6 . . . . . .200 A3
Lyndon Rd, Belv. DA17 . .139 G4
Lyne Cres, E17 . . . . .77 J1
Lyneham Wk, E5 . . . . . . .95 H5
Lynette Av, SW4 . . . . . . .150 B6
Lynett Rd, Dag. RM8 . . . .100 D3
Lynford CI, Barn. EN5
  off Rowley La 39 F5
  Edgware HA8 . . . . .54 E7
Lynford Gdns, Edg. HA8 . .54 B3
  Ilford IG3 . . . . .99 J2
Lynmere Rd, Well. DA16 .158 B2
Lyn Ms, E3
  off Tredegar Sq 113 J3
  N16 . . . . .94 B4
Lynmouth Av, Enf. EN1 . . .44 C6
  Morden SM4 . . . . .184 A7
Lynmouth Dr, Ruis. HA4 . .84 B2
Lynmouth Gdns, Grnf.
  UB6 . . . . .105 E1
  Hounslow TW5 . . . . . .142 D1
Lynmouth Rd, E17 . . . . . .77 H6
  N2 . . . . .73 J3
  N16 . . . . .94 C1
  Greenford UB6 . . . . . . .105 E1
Lynn CI, Har. HA3 . . . . . . .68 A2
Lynne CI, Orp. BR6 . . . . .207 J6
Lynne Way, NW10 . . . . . . .88 E6
  Northolt UB5 . . . . .102 D2
Lynn Ms, E11
  off Lynn Rd 96/97 E2
Lynn Rd, E11 . . . . .96 E2
  SW12 . . . . .150 B7
  Ilford IG2 . . . . .81 G2
Lynn St, Enf. EN2 . . . . . . .44 A1
Lynsted CI, Bexh. DA6 . .159 H5
  Bromley BR1 . . . . .191 J2
Lynsted Ct, Beck. BR3
  off Churchfields Rd . .189 H2
Lynsted Gdns, SE9 . . . . .156 A3
Lynton Av, N12 . . . . .57 G4
  NW9 . . . . .71 F4
  W13 . . . . .104 D6
  Romford RM7 . . . . .83 G1
Lynton CI, NW10 . . . . .88 E5
  Chessington KT9 . . . . .195 H4
  Isleworth TW7 . . . . . . .144 C4
Lynton Cres, Ilf. IG2 . . . . .80 E6
Lynton Est, SE1 . . . . .37 H2
Lynton Gdns, N11 . . . . . . .58 D6
  Enfield EN1 . . . . .44 B7
Lynton Mead, N20 . . . . . .56 D3
Lynton Rd, E4 . . . . .62 B5
  N8 . . . . .74 D5
  NW6 . . . . .108 C1
  SE1 . . . . .37 G2
  W3 . . . . .106 A7
  Croydon CR0 . . . . .187 G6

Lyn–Mal 305

Lynton Rd, Har. HA2 ... 85 E2
New Malden KT3 ... 182 D5
Lynton Ter, W3
off Lynton Rd ... 106 C6
Lynwood Cl, E18 ... 79 J1
Harrow HA2 ... 85 E3
Lynwood Dr, Wor.Pk.
KT4 ... 197 G2
Lynwood Gdns, Croy.
CR0 ... 201 F4
Southall UB1 ... 103 F6
Lynwood Gro, N21 ... 59 G1
Orpington BR6 ... 193 H7
Lynwood Rd, SW17 ... 167 J3
W5 ... 105 H4
Thames Ditton KT7 ... 194 C2
Lyon Business Pk, Bark.
IG11 ... 117 H2
Lyon Meade, Stan. HA7 ... 69 F1
Lyon Pk Av, Wem. HA0 ... 87 H6
Lyon Rd, SW19 ... 185 F1
Harrow HA1 ... 68 C6
Lyonsdown Av, Barn.
EN5 ... 41 F6
Lyonsdown Rd, Barn.
EN5 ... 41 F6
Lyons Pl, NW8 ... 7 E5
Lyon St, N1
off Caledonian Rd ... 93 F7
Lyons Wk, W14 ... 128 B4
Lyon Way, Grnf. UB6 ... 104 B1
Lyoth Rd, Orp. BR5 ... 207 F2
Lyric Dr, Grnf. UB6 ... 103 H4
Lyric Ms, SE26 ... 171 F4
Lyric Rd, SW13 ... 147 F1
Lysander Gdns, Surb. KT6
off Ewell Rd ... 181 J6
Lysander Gro, N19 ... 92 D1
Lysander Ms, N19
off Lysander Gro ... 92 C1
Lysander Rd, Croy. CR0 ... 201 F6
Lysander Way, Orp. BR6 ... 207 F3
Lysias Rd, SW12 ... 150 A6
Lysia St, SW6 ... 128 A7
Lysons Wk, SW15
off Swinburne Rd ... 147 G5
Lytchet Rd, Brom. BR1 ... 173 H7
Lytchet Way, Enf. EN3 ... 45 F1
Lytchgate Cl, S.Croy.
CR2 ... 202 B7
Lytcott Dr, W.Mol. KT8
off Freeman Dr ... 179 F3
Lytcott Gro, SE22 ... 152 C5
Lyte St, E2
off Bishops Way ... 113 F2
Lytham Av, Wat. WD19 ... 50 D5
Lytham Cl, SE28 ... 118 E6
Lytham Gro, W5 ... 105 H3
Lytham St, SE17 ... 36 B4
Lyttelton Cl, NW3 ... 91 H7
Lyttelton Rd, E10 ... 96 B3
N2 ... 73 F5
Lyttleton Rd, N8 ... 75 G3
Lytton Av, N13 ... 59 G2
Lytton Cl, N2 ... 73 G5
Loughton IG10 ... 49 G3
Northolt UB5 ... 85 F7
Lytton Gdns, Wall.
SM6 ... 200 D4
Lytton Gro, SW15 ... 148 A5
Lytton Rd, E11 ... 78 E7
Barnet EN5 ... 41 F4
Pinner HA5 ... 50 E7
Lytton Strachey Path, SE28
off Titmuss Av ... 118 B7
Lyveden Rd, SE3 ... 135 H7
SW17 ... 167 H6

M

Maberley Cres, SE19 ... 170 D7
Maberley Rd, SE19 ... 188 C1
Beckenham BR3 ... 189 G3
Mabledon Pl, WC1 ... 9 J4
Mablethorpe Rd, SW6 ... 128 B7
Mabley St, E9 ... 95 H6
McAdam Dr, Enf. EN2
off Rowantree Rd ... 43 H2
Macaret Cl, N20 ... 41 E7
MacArthur Cl, E7 ... 97 G6
MacArthur Ter, SE7 ... 136 B6
Macaulay Av, Esher
KT10 ... 194 B2
Macaulay Ct, SW4 ... 150 B3
Macaulay Rd, E6 ... 116 A2
SW4 ... 150 B3
Macaulay Sq, SW4 ... 150 B4
Macaulay Way, SE28
off Booth Cl ... 118 B7
McAuley Cl, SE1 ... 26 E5
SE9 ... 156 E5
Macauley Ms, SE13 ... 154 C2
Macbean St, SE18 ... 136 D3
Macbeth St, W6 ... 127 H5
McCall Cl, SW4
off Jeffreys Rd ... 150/151 E2
McCall Cres, SE7 ... 136 B5
McCarthy Rd, Felt.
TW13 ... 160 D5
Macclesfield Br, NW1 ... 7 H1
Macclesfield Rd, EC1 ... 11 J3
SE25 ... 189 E5
Macclesfield St, W1 ... 17 J5
McCoid Way, SE1 ... 27 J4
McCrone Ms, NW3
off Belsize La ... 91 G6
McCullum Rd, E3 ... 113 J1
McDermott Cl, SW11 ... 149 H3
McDermott Rd, SE15 ... 152 D3
Macdonald Av, Dag.
RM10 ... 101 H3
Macdonald Rd, E7 ... 97 G4
E17 ... 78 C2
N11 ... 57 J5
N19 ... 92 C2
McDonough Cl, Chess.
KT9 ... 195 H4
McDowall Cl, E16 ... 115 F5
McDowall Rd, SE5 ... 151 J1
Macduff Rd, SW11 ... 150 A1
Mace Cl, E1
off Kennet St ... 132/133 E1
Mace Gateway, E16 ... 115 G7
McEntee Av, E17 ... 77 H1
Mace St, E2 ... 113 G2
McEwen Way, E15 ... 114 D1
MacFarlane La, Islw.
TW7 ... 124 C6
Macfarlane Rd, W12 ... 127 J1
Macfarren Pl, NW1 ... 8 C6
McGrath Rd, E15 ... 97 F5
Macgregor Rd, E16 ... 115 J5
McGregor Rd, W11 ... 108 C6
Machell Rd, SE15 ... 153 F3
McIntosh Cl, Wall.
SM6 ... 200 E7
Mackay Rd, SW4 ... 150 B3
McKay Rd, SW20 ... 165 H7
McKellar Cl, Bushey
(Bushey Hth.) WD23 ... 51 J2
Mackennal St, NW8 ... 7 H2
Mackenzie Rd, N7 ... 93 F6
Beckenham BR3 ... 189 F2
Mackenzie Wk, E14 ... 134 A1
McKerrell Rd, SE15 ... 152 D1
Mackeson Rd, NW3 ... 91 J4
Mackie Rd, SW2 ... 151 G7
Mackintosh La, E9
off Homerton High St ... 95 G5
Macklin St, WC2 ... 18 B3
Mackrow Wk, E14
off Robin Hood La ... 114 C7
Macks Rd, SE16 ... 37 J1
Mackworth St, NW1 ... 9 F3
Maclaren Ms, SW15
off Clarendon Dr ... 147 J4
Maclean Rd, SE23 ... 153 H6
Macleod Rd, N21 ... 43 E5
McLeod Rd, SE2 ... 138 B4
McLeod's Ms, SW7 ... 22 B6
Macleod St, SE17 ... 36 A4
Maclise Rd, W14 ... 128 B3
McMillan St, SE8 ... 134 A6
Macmillan Way, SW17
off Church La ... 168 B4
McNair Rd, Sthl. UB2 ... 123 H2
McNeil Rd, SE5 ... 152 B2
McNicol Dr, NW10 ... 106 C2
Macoma Rd, SE18 ... 137 G6
Macoma Ter, SE18 ... 137 G6
Maconochies Rd, E14 ... 134 B5
Macquarie Way, E14 ... 134 B4
McRae La, Mitch. CR4 ... 185 J7
Macroom Rd, W9 ... 108 C3
Mac's Pl, EC4
off Norwich St ... 111 G6
★ Madame Tussaud's,
NW1 ... 8 B6
Mada Rd, Orp. BR6 ... 206 E3
Maddams St, E3 ... 114 B4
Maddison Cl, Tedd.
TW11 ... 162 C6
Maddocks Cl, Sid.
DA14 ... 176 E5
Maddock Way, SE17 ... 35 H6
Maddox St, W1 ... 16 E5
Madeira Av, Brom. BR1 ... 172 E7
Madeira Gro, Wdf.Grn.
IG8 ... 63 J6
Madeira Rd, E11 ... 96 D1
N13 ... 59 H4
SW16 ... 169 E5
Mitcham CR4 ... 185 J4
Madeley Rd, W5 ... 105 H6
Madeline Gro, Ilf. IG1 ... 99 G5
Madeline Rd, SE20 ... 188 D1
Madge Gill Way, E6
off Ron Leighton Way ... 116 B1
Madinah Rd, E8 ... 94 D6
Madingley, Kings.T. KT1
off St. Peters Rd ... 182 A2
Madison Cres, Bexh.
DA7 ... 138 C7
Madison Gdns, Bexh.
DA7 ... 138 C7
Bromley BR2 ... 191 F3
Madras Pl, N7 ... 93 G6
Madras Rd, Ilf. IG1 ... 99 E4
Madrid Rd, SW13 ... 147 G1
Madrigal La, SE5 ... 131 H7
Madron St, SE17 ... 36 E3
Mafeking Av, E6 ... 116 A2
Brentford TW8 ... 125 H6
Ilford IG2 ... 81 G7
Mafeking Rd, E16 ... 115 F4
N17 ... 76 D2
Enfield EN1 ... 44 C3
Magdala Av, N19 ... 92 B2
Magdala Rd, Islw. TW7 ... 144 D3
South Croydon CR2
off Napier Rd ... 202 A7
Magdalene Cl, SE15
off Heaton Rd ... 152/153 E2
Magdalene Gdns, E6 ... 116 D4
Magdalen Pas, E1 ... 21 G5
Magdalen Rd, SW18 ... 167 F1
Magdalen St, SE1 ... 28 D2
Magee St, SE11 ... 35 E5
Magellan Pl, E14
off Maritime Quay ... 134 A5
Magnet Rd, Wem. HA9 ... 87 G2
Magnin Cl, E8
off Wilde Cl ... 112 D1
Magnolia Cl, E10 ... 96 A2
Kingston upon Thames
KT2 ... 164 C6
Magnolia Ct, Har. HA3 ... 69 J7
Richmond TW9
off West Hall Rd ... 146 B1
Wallington SM6
off Parkgate Rd ... 200 B5
Magnolia Gdns, Edg.
HA8 ... 54 C4
Magnolia Pl, SW4 ... 150 E5
W5
off Montpelier Rd ... 105 H5
Magnolia Rd, W4 ... 126 B6
Magnolia St, West Dr.
UB7 ... 120 A4
Magnolia Way, Epsom
KT19 ... 196 C5
Magpie All, EC4 ... 19 F4
Magpie Cl, E7 ... 97 F5
NW9 off Eagle Dr ... 70/71 E2
Enfield EN1 ... 44 D1
Magpie Hall Cl, Brom.
BR2 ... 192 B6
Magpie Hall La, Brom.
BR2 ... 192 C5
Magpie Hall Rd, Bushey
(Bushey Hth.) WD23 ... 52 B2
Magpie Pl, SE14
off Milton Ct Rd ... 133 H6
Magri Wk, E1
off Ashfield St ... 113 F5
Maguire Dr, Rich. TW10 ... 163 F4
Maguire St, SE1 ... 29 G3
Mahatma Gandhi Ho, Wem.
HA9 ... 88 A5
Mahlon Av, Ruis. HA4 ... 84 B5
Mahogany Cl, SE16 ... 133 H1
Mahon Cl, Enf. EN1 ... 44 C1
Maida Av, E4 ... 46 B7
W2 ... 14 D1
MAIDA HILL, W9 ... 108 C4
Maida Rd, Belv. DA17 ... 139 G3
MAIDA VALE, W9 ... 6 B5
Maida Vale, W9 ... 6 C4
Maida Way, E4 ... 46 B7
Maiden Erlegh Av, Bex.
DA5 ... 176 E1
Maiden La, NW1 ... 92 D7
SE1 ... 28 A1
WC2 ... 18 B6
Maiden Rd, E15 ... 97 E7
Maidenstone Hill, SE10 ... 154 C1
Maids of Honour Row, Rich.
TW9 off The Green ... 145 G5
Maidstone Av, Rom. RM5 ... 83 J2
Maidstone Bldgs, SE1 ... 28 A2
Maidstone Ho, E14
off Carmen St ... 114 B6
Maidstone Rd, N11 ... 58 C6
Sidcup DA14 ... 176 D6
Maidstone St, E2 ... 13 J1
Main Av, Enf. EN1 ... 44 C5
Main Dr, Wem. HA9 ... 87 G3
Mainridge Rd, Chis. BR7 ... 174 D4
Main Rd, Sid. DA14 ... 175 H3
Main St, Felt. TW13 ... 160 D5
Maisemore St, SE15 ... 37 J7
Maitland Cl, SE10 ... 134 B7
Hounslow TW4 ... 143 F3
Maitland Pk Est, NW3 ... 91 J6
Maitland Pk Rd, NW3 ... 91 J6
Maitland Pk Vil, NW3 ... 91 J6
Maitland Pl, E5
off Clarence Rd ... 94/95 E4
Maitland Rd, E15 ... 97 F6
SE26 ... 171 G6
Majendie Rd, SE18 ... 137 G5
Majestic Way, Mitch.
CR4 ... 185 J2
Major Rd, E15 ... 96 C5
SE16 ... 29 J5
Makepeace Av, N6 ... 92 A2
Makepeace Rd, E11 ... 79 G4
Northolt UB5 ... 102 E2
Makins St, SW3 ... 31 H2
Malabar St, E14 ... 134 A2
Malam Gdns, E14
off Wades Pl ... 114 B7
Malbrook Rd, SW15 ... 147 H4
Malcolm Ct, Stan. HA7 ... 53 F5
Malcolm Cres, NW4 ... 71 G6
Malcolm Dr, Surb. KT6 ... 195 H1
Malcolm Pl, E2 ... 113 F4
Malcolm Rd, E1 ... 113 F4
SE20 ... 171 F7
SE25 ... 188 D6
SW19 ... 166 B6
Malcolms Way, N14 ... 42 C5
Malcolm Way, E11 ... 79 G5
Malden Av, SE25 ... 188 E4
Greenford UB6 ... 86 B5
Malden Cres, NW1 ... 92 A6
Malden Grn Av, Wor.Pk.
KT4 ... 197 F1
Malden Hill, N.Mal. KT3 ... 183 F3
Malden Hill Gdns, N.Mal.
KT3 ... 183 F3
Malden Pk, N.Mal. KT3 ... 183 F6
Malden Pl, NW5
off Grafton Ter ... 92 A5
Malden Rd, NW5 ... 92 A5
Borehamwood WD6 ... 38 A3
New Malden KT3 ... 183 E5
Sutton SM3 ... 198 A4
Worcester Park KT4 ... 183 F7
Malden Way, N.Mal. KT3 ... 183 F5
Maldon Cl, E15
off David St ... 96 D5
N1 off Popham Rd ... 111 J1
SE5 ... 152 B3
Maldon Ct, Wall. SM6
off Maldon Rd ... 200 C5
Maldon Rd, N9 ... 60 C3
W3 ... 106 C7
Romford RM7 ... 83 J7
Wallington SM6 ... 200 B5
Maldon Wk, Wdf.Grn. IG8 ... 63 J6
Malet Pl, WC1 ... 9 H6
Malet St, WC1 ... 9 H6
Maley Av, SE27 ... 169 H2
Malford Ct, E18 ... 79 G2
Malford Gro, E18 ... 79 F4
Malfort Rd, SE5 ... 152 B3
Malham Cl, N11
off Catterick Cl ... 58 A6
Malham Rd, SE23 ... 171 G1
Malins Cl, Barn. EN5 ... 39 H5
Mall, The, E15 ... 96 D7
N14 ... 58 E3
SW1 ... 25 G3
SW14 ... 146 C5
W5 ... 105 H7
Croydon CR0 ... 201 J2
Harrow HA3 ... 69 J6
Surbiton KT6 ... 181 G5
Mallams Ms, SW9
off St. James's Cres ... 151 H3
Mallard Cl, E9
off Berkshire Rd ... 95 J6
NW6 ... 108 D2
W7 ... 124 B2
Barnet EN5
off The Hook ... 41 G6
Twickenham TW2
off Stephenson Rd ... 143 G7

Mallard Path, SE28 . . . . .137 G3
Mallard Pl, Twick. TW1 . .162 D3
Mallard Pt, E3
  off Rainhill Way 114 B3
Mallards Rd, Bark. IG11 . .118 A4
  Woodford Green IG8 . .63 H7
Mallard Wk, Beck. BR3 . .189 G5
  Sidcup DA14 . . . . .176 C5
Mallet Dr, Nthlt. UB5 . . . .85 F5
Mallet Rd, SE13 . . . . .154 D6
★ Mall Galleries, SW1 . .25 J1
Malling, SE13 . . . . .154 C5
Malling Cl, Croy. CR0 . . .189 F6
Malling Gdns, Mord.
  SM4 . . . . .185 F6
Malling Way, Brom. BR2 .191 F7
Mallinson Rd, SW11 . . . .149 H5
  Croydon CR0 . . . . .200 D3
Mallord St, SW3 . . . . .31 F5
Mallory Cl, SE4 . . . . .153 H4
Mallory Gdns, Barn. EN4 .42 A7
Mallory St, NW8 . . . . .7 H5
Mallow Cl, Croy. CR0
  off Marigold Way 203 G1
Mallow Mead, NW7 . . . . .56 B7
Mallow St, EC1 . . . . .12 B5
Mall Rd, W6 . . . . .127 H5
Malmains Cl, Beck. BR3 .190 D5
Malmains Way, Beck.
  BR3 . . . . .190 C4
Malmesbury Rd, E3 . . . . .113 J3
  E16 . . . . .115 E5
  E18 . . . . .79 F1
  Morden SM4 . . . . .185 F7
Malmesbury Ter, E16 . . .115 F5
Malpas Dr, Pnr. HA5 . . . . .66 D5
Malpas Rd, E8 . . . . .94 E6
  SE4 . . . . .153 J2
  Dagenham RM9 . . . . .100 D6
Malta Rd, E10 . . . . .96 A1
Malta St, EC1 . . . . .11 H5
Maltby Rd, Chess. KT9 . .196 A6
Maltby St, SE1 . . . . .29 F4
Malthouse Dr, W4 . . . . . .127 E6
  Feltham TW13 . . . . . . .160 D5
Malthouse Pas, SW13
  off The Terrace 146/147 E2
Malthus Path, SE28
  off Owen Cl 138 C1
Malting Ho, E14 . . . . . . .113 J7
Maltings, The, Orp. BR6 .207 J1
Maltings Cl, SW13
  off Cleveland
  Gdns 146/147 E2
Maltings Ms, Sid. DA15
  off Station Rd 176 A3
Maltings Pl, SW6 . . . . . . .149 E1
Malting Way, Islw. TW7 .144 C3
Malton Ms, SE18
  off Malton St 137 H6
  W10
  off Cambridge Gdns . .108 B6
Malton Rd, W10
  off St. Marks Rd 108 B6
Malton St, SE18 . . . . . . .137 H6
Maltravers St, WC2 . . . . .18 D5
Malt St, SE1 . . . . .37 H5
Malva Cl, SW18
  off St. Ann's
  Hill 148/149 E5
Malvern Av, E4 . . . . .62 D7
  Bexleyheath DA7 . . . .138 E7
  Harrow HA2 . . . . .85 E3
Malvern Cl, SE20
  off Derwent Rd 188 D2
  W10 . . . . .108 C5
  Mitcham CR4 . . . . . . .186 C3
  Surbiton KT6 . . . . . . .195 H1
Malvern Ct, SE14
  off Avonley Rd 133 F7
  SW7 . . . . .31 F2
  Sutton SM2
  off Overton Rd 198 D7
  Ilford IG3 . . . . .99 J4
  Woodford Green IG8 . .63 J5
Malvern Gdns, NW2 . . . . .90 B2
  NW6 off Carlton Vale . .108 C2
  Harrow HA3 . . . . .69 H3
  Loughton IG10 . . . . . . .48 C6
Malvern Ms, NW6
  off Malvern Rd 108 D3
Malvern Pl, NW6 . . . . . . .108 C3
Malvern Rd, E6 . . . . .116 B1
  E8 . . . . .94 D7
  E11 . . . . .97 E2
  N8 . . . . .75 F3
  N17 . . . . .76 D3
  NW6 . . . . .108 D3

Malvern Rd, Hmptn.
  TW12 . . . . .161 G7
  Hayes UB3 . . . . .121 H7
  Surbiton KT6 . . . . . . .195 H2
  Thornton Heath CR7 .187 G4
Malvern Ter, N1 . . . . .111 G1
  N9 off Latymer Rd 60 C1
Malvern Way, W13
  off Templewood . .104/105 E5
Malwood Rd, SW12 . . . . .150 B6
Malyons Rd, SE13 . . . . . .154 B5
Malyons Ter, SE13 . . . . . .154 B5
Managers St, E14
  off Prestons Rd 134 C1
Manatee Pl, Wall. SM6
  off Croydon Rd 200 D3
Manaton Cl, SE15 . . . . . .152 E3
Manaton Cres, Sthl.
  UB1 . . . . .103 G6
Manbey Gro, E15 . . . . . . .96 E6
Manbey Pk Rd, E15 . . . . .96 E6
Manbey Rd, E15 . . . . .96 E6
Manbey St, E15 . . . . .96 E6
Manbre Rd, W6 . . . . .127 J6
Manbrough Av, E6 . . . . .116 C3
Manchester Ct, E16 . . . . .115 H6
Manchester Dr, W10 . . . .108 B4
Manchester Gro, E14 . . .134 C5
Manchester Ms, W1 . . . . .16 B2
Manchester Rd, E14 . . . .134 C5
  N15 . . . . .76 A6
  Thornton Heath CR7 .187 J3
Manchester Sq, W1 . . . . . .16 B3
Manchester St, W1 . . . . . .16 B2
Manchester Way, Dag.
  RM10 . . . . .101 H4
Manchuria Rd, SW11 . . .150 A6
Manciple St, SE1 . . . . . . .28 B4
Mandalay Rd, SW4 . . . . .150 C5
Mandarin St, E14
  off Salter St 114 A7
Mandarin Way, Hayes
  UB4 . . . . .102 D5
Mandela Cl, NW10 . . . . . .88 C7
Mandela Rd, E16 . . . . . . .115 G6
Mandela St, NW1 . . . . . .110 C1
  SW9 . . . . .131 G7
Mandela Way, SE1 . . . . . .36 E1
Mandeville Cl, SE3
  off Vanbrugh Pk 135 F7
  SW20 . . . . .184 B1
Mandeville Ct, E4 . . . . . . .61 H4
Mandeville Dr, Surb.
  KT6 . . . . .195 G1
Mandeville Ms, SW4
  off Clapham Pk
  Rd 150/151 E4
Mandeville Pl, W1 . . . . . . .16 C3
Mandeville Rd, N14 . . . . .58 B2
  Isleworth TW7 . . . . . .144 D2
  Northolt UB5 . . . . .85 G7
Mandeville St, E5 . . . . . . .95 H3
Mandrake Rd, SW17 . . . .167 J3
Mandrake Way, E15 . . . . .96 E7
Mandrell Rd, SW2 . . . . . .150 E5
Manette St, W1 . . . . .17 J4
Manford Way, Chig. IG7 . .65 H4
Manfred Rd, SW15 . . . . .148 C5
Manger Rd, N7 . . . . .93 E6
Mangold Way, Erith
  DA18 . . . . .138 E3
Manhattan Wf, E16 . . . . .135 G2
Manilla St, E14 . . . . .134 A2
Manister Rd, SE2 . . . . . . .138 A3
Manitoba Ct, SE16
  off Renforth St 133 F2
Manitoba Gdns, Orp. BR6
  off Superior Dr 207 J6
Manley Ct, N16
  off Stoke Newington
  High St 94 C3
Manley St, NW1 . . . . .110 A1
Mann Cl, Croy. CR0
  off Salem Pl 201 J3
Manningford Cl, EC1 . . . .11 G3
Manning Gdns, Har. HA3 .69 G7
Manning Pl, Rich. TW10
  off Grove Rd 145 J6
Manning Rd, E17
  off Southcote Rd 77 H5
  Dagenham RM10 . . . .101 G6
Manningtree Cl, SW19 . .166 B1
Manningtree Rd, Ruis.
  HA4 . . . . .84 B4
Manningtree St, E1 . . . . . .21 H3
Mannin Rd, Rom. RM6 . . .82 B7
Mannock Dr, Loug. IG10 .49 F2
Mannock Rd, N22 . . . . . . .75 H3
Manns Cl, Islw. TW7 . . . .144 C5
Manns Rd, Edg. HA8 . . . . .54 A6

Manoel Rd, Twick. TW2 . .161 J2
Manor Av, SE4 . . . . .153 J2
  Hounslow TW4 . . . . . .142 D3
  Northolt UB5 . . . . .85 F7
Manorbrook, SE3 . . . . . .155 G4
Manor Cl, E17
  off Manor Rd 77 H2
  NW7 off Manor Dr 54 D5
  NW9 . . . . .70 B5
  SE28 . . . . .118 C6
  Barnet EN5 . . . . .40 B4
  Worcester Park KT4 . .197 E1
Manor Cotts App, N2 . . . .73 F2
Manor Ct, E10
  off Grange Pk Rd 96 B1
  N2 . . . . .73 J5
  SW6
  off Bagley's La . .148/149 E1
  Twickenham TW2 . . . .161 J2
  Wembley HA9 . . . . .87 H5
Manor Ct Rd, W7 . . . . . . .104 B7
Manor Cres, Surb. KT5 . .182 A6
Manordene Cl, T.Ditt.
  KT7 . . . . .194 D1
Manordene Rd, SE28 . . .118 C6
Manor Dr, N14 . . . . .42 B7
  N20 . . . . .57 H3
  NW7 . . . . .54 D5
  Epsom KT19 . . . . .196 E6
  Esher KT10 . . . . .194 C2
  Feltham TW13
  off Lebanon Av 160 D5
  Sunbury-on-Thames
  TW16 . . . . .178 A2
  Surbiton KT5 . . . . .181 J6
  Wembley HA9 . . . . .87 J4
Manor Dr, The, Wor.Pk.
  KT4 . . . . .197 E1
Manor Dr N, N.Mal. KT3 .182 D7
  Worcester Park KT4 . .196 E1
Manor Est, SE16 . . . . . . .132 E4
Manor Fm Cl, Wor.Pk.
  KT4 . . . . .196 E1
Manor Fm Dr, E4 . . . . . . .63 E3
Manor Fm Rd, Th.Hth.
  CR7 . . . . .187 G2
  Wembley HA0 . . . . . . .105 G2
Manorfield Cl, N19
  off Junction Rd 92 C4
Manor Flds, SW15 . . . . . .148 A6
Manorfields Cl, Chis.
  BR7 . . . . .193 J3
  SW20 . . . . .184 C2
  W3 . . . . .126 A4
  W4 off Devonshire
  Rd 126/127 E5
  Hampton TW12 . . . . . .161 H7
  Richmond TW9 . . . . . .145 J4
  Ruislip HA4 . . . . .84 C5
  South Croydon CR2 . .202 C6
  Sunbury-on-Thames
  TW16 . . . . .178 A2
Manor Gate, Nthlt. UB5 . .84 E7
Manorgate Rd, Kings.T.
  KT2 . . . . .182 A1
Manor Gro, SE15 . . . . . . .133 F6
  Beckenham BR3 . . . . .190 B2
  Richmond TW9 . . . . . .146 A4
Manor Hall Av, NW4 . . . . .71 J2
Manor Hall Dr, NW4 . . . . .72 A2
Manorhall Gdns, E10 . . . .96 A1
Manor Ho Dr, NW6 . . . . . .90 A7
Manor Ho Est, Stan. HA7
  off Old Ch La 52/53 E6
Manor Ho Way, Islw.
  TW7 . . . . .144 E3
Manor La, SE12 . . . . .155 E6
  SE13 . . . . .154 E4
  Feltham TW13 . . . . . . .160 A2
  Hayes UB3 . . . . .121 G6
  Sunbury-on-Thames
  TW16 . . . . .178 A2
  Sutton SM1 . . . . .199 F5
Manor La Ter, SE13 . . . . .154 E4
Manor Ms, NW6
  off Cambridge Av 108 D2
  SE4 . . . . .153 J2
Manor Mt, SE23 . . . . .171 F1
Manor Par, NW10
  off Station Rd 107 F2
MANOR PARK, E12 . . . . . .98 B4
Manor Pk, SE13 . . . . .154 D4
  Chislehurst BR7 . . . . .193 G2
  Richmond TW9 . . . . . .145 J4
Manor Pk Cl, W.Wick.
  BR4 . . . . .204 B1
Manor Pk Cres, Edg.
  HA8 . . . . .54 A6
Manor Pk Dr, Har. HA2 . . .67 H3

Manor Pk Gdns, Edg.
  HA8 . . . . .54 A5
Manor Pk Par, SE13
  off Lee High Rd 154 D4
Manor Pk Rd, E12 . . . . . . .98 A4
  N2 . . . . .73 G3
  NW10 . . . . .107 F1
  Chislehurst BR7 . . . . .193 F1
  Sutton SM1 . . . . .199 F5
  West Wickham BR4 . . .204 B1
Manor Pl, SE17 . . . . .35 H4
  Chislehurst BR7 . . . . .193 G1
  Feltham TW14 . . . . . . .160 A1
  Mitcham CR4 . . . . . . .186 C3
  Sutton SM1 . . . . .199 E4
Manor Rd, E10 . . . . .78 A7
  E15 . . . . .114 E3
  E16 . . . . .114 E3
  E17 . . . . .77 H2
  N16 . . . . .94 A2
  N17 . . . . .76 D1
  N22 . . . . .59 E6
  SE25 . . . . .188 D4
  SW20 . . . . .184 C2
  W13 . . . . .104 D7
  Barking IG11 . . . . .99 J6
  Barnet EN5 . . . . .40 B5
  Beckenham BR3 . . . . .190 B2
  Bexley DA5 . . . . .177 H1
  Chigwell IG7 . . . . .64 E5
  Dagenham RM10 . . . .101 J6
  East Molesey KT8 . . . .180 A4
  Enfield EN2 . . . . .44 A2
  Harrow HA1 . . . . .68 D6
  Hayes UB3 . . . . .102 A6
  Loughton IG10 . . . . . . .47 H6
  Loughton (High Beach)
  IG10 . . . . .47 H1
  Mitcham CR4 . . . . . . .186 C4
  Richmond TW9 . . . . . .145 J3
  Romford (Chad.Hth.)
  RM6 . . . . .82 D6
  Sidcup DA15 . . . . .175 J3
  Sutton SM2 . . . . .198 C7
  Teddington TW11 . . . .162 E5
  Twickenham TW2 . . . .161 J2
  Wallington SM6 . . . . . .200 B4
  West Wickham BR4 . . .204 B2
  Woodford Green IG8 . .64 C6
Manor Rd N, Esher
  KT10 . . . . .194 C3
  Thames Ditton KT7 . . .194 D2
  Wallington SM6 . . . . . .200 B4
Manor Rd S, Esher KT10 .194 B4
Manorside, Barn. EN5 . . . .40 B4
Manorside Cl, SE2 . . . . . .138 C4
Manor Sq, Dag. RM8 . . . .100 D2
Manor Vale, Brent. TW8 . .125 F5
Manor Vw, N3 . . . . .72 E2
Manor Way, E4 . . . . .62 D4
  NW9 . . . . .70 E3
  SE3 . . . . .155 F4
  SE28 . . . . .138 C1
  Beckenham BR3 . . . . .190 A2
  Bexley DA5 . . . . .177 G1
  Borehamwood WD6 . . .38 C4
  Bromley BR2 . . . . .192 B6
  Enfield EN1 . . . . .44 B7
  Harrow HA2 . . . . .67 H4
  Mitcham CR4 . . . . . . .186 C3
  Orpington BR5 . . . . . .193 F4
  South Croydon CR2 . .202 B6
  Southall UB2 . . . . .122 D4
Manorway, Wdf.Grn.
  IG8 . . . . .63 J5
Manor Way, Wor.Pk. KT4 .197 E1
Manor Way, The, Wall.
  SM6 . . . . .200 B4
Manpreet Ct, E12
  off Morris Av 98 C5
Manresa Rd, SW3 . . . . . . .31 G4
Mansard Beeches,
  SW17 . . . . .168 A5
Mansard Ct, Pnr. HA5 . . . .66 D3
Mansbridge Way, NW7
  off Bittacy Hill 56 B7
Manse Cl, Hayes UB3 . . .121 G6
Mansel Gro, E17 . . . . .78 A1
Mansell Rd, W3 . . . . .126 D2
  Greenford UB6 . . . . . .103 H5
Mansell St, E1 . . . . .21 G6
Mansel Rd, SW19 . . . . . .166 B6
Mansergh Cl, SE18 . . . . .136 B7
Manse Rd, N16 . . . . .94 C3
Mansfield Av, N15 . . . . . . .76 A4
  Barnet EN4 . . . . .41 J6
  Ruislip HA4 . . . . .84 B1
Mansfield Cl, N9 . . . . .44 D6
Mansfield Hill, E4 . . . . . . .62 B1
Mansfield Ms, W1 . . . . . . .16 D2

Mansfield Pl, NW3
  off New End 91 F4
Mansfield Rd, E11 . . . . .79 H6
  E17 . . . . .77 J4
  NW3 . . . . .91 J5
  W3 . . . . .106 B4
  Chessington KT9 . . . . .195 F5
  Ilford IG1 . . . . .98 D2
  South Croydon CR2 . . .202 A6
Mansfield St, W1 . . . . . .16 D2
Mansford St, E2 . . . . . . .13 J2
Manship Rd, Mitch. CR4 .168 A7
Mansion Cl, SW9
  off Cowley Rd 151 G1
Mansion Gdns, NW3 . . . .91 E3
★ Mansion Ho, EC4 . . . . .20 B4
Mansion Ho, EC4 . . . . . .20 B4
Mansion Ho Pl, EC4 . . . .20 B4
Mansion Ho St, EC4 . . . .20 B4
Manson Ms, SW7 . . . . . .30 D2
Manson Pl, SW7 . . . . . . .30 D2
Mansted Gdns, Rom.
  RM6 . . . . .82 C7
Manston Av, Sthl. UB2 . .123 G4
Manston Cl, SE20
  off Garden Rd 189 F1
Manstone Rd, NW2 . . . . .90 B5
Manston Gro, Kings.T.
  KT2 . . . . .163 G5
Manthorp Rd, SE18 . . . .137 F5
Mantilla Rd, SW17 . . . . .168 A4
Mantle Rd, SE4 . . . . . . .153 H3
Mantlet Cl, SW16 . . . . . .168 C7
Mantle Way, E15
  off Romford Rd 96/97 E7
Manton Av, W7 . . . . . . .124 C2
Manton Rd, SE2 . . . . . . .138 A4
Mantua St, SW11 . . . . . .149 G3
Mantus Cl, E1
  off Mantus Rd 113 F4
Mantus Rd, E1 . . . . .113 F4
Manus Way, N20
  off Blakeney Cl 57 F2
Manville Gdns, SW17 . . .168 B2
Manville Rd, SW17 . . . . .168 A2
Manwood Rd, SE4 . . . . .153 J5
Manwood St, E16 . . . . .136 C1
Manygates, SW12 . . . . .168 B2
Mapesbury Rd, NW2 . . . .90 B6
Mapeshill Pl, NW2 . . . . .89 J6
Mape St, E2 . . . . .112 E4
Maple Av, E4 . . . . .61 J5
  W3 . . . . .127 E1
  Harrow HA2 . . . . .85 H2
Maple Cl, N3 . . . . .56 D6
  N16 . . . . .76 D6
  SW4 . . . . .150 D6
  Buckhurst Hill IG9 . . . . .64 A3
  Hampton TW12 . . . . . .161 F6
  Hayes UB4 . . . . .102 D3
  Ilford IG6 . . . . .65 H5
  Mitcham CR4 . . . . .186 B1
  Orpington BR5 . . . . . . .193 G5
  Ruislip HA4 . . . . .66 B6
Maple Ct, N.Mal. KT3 . . .182 E3
Maple Cres, Sid. DA15 . .158 A6
Maplecroft Cl, E6
  off Allhallows Rd 116 B6
Mapledale Av, Croy. CR0 .202 D2
Mapledene, Chis. BR7
  off Kemnal Rd 175 F5
Mapledene Rd, E8 . . . . . .94 C7
Maple Gdns, Edg. HA8 . . .54 E7
Maple Gate, Loug. IG10 . .48 D2
Maple Gro, NW9 . . . . . . .70 C7
  W5 . . . . .125 G3
  Brentford TW8 . . . . . .124 E7
  Southall UB1 . . . . .103 F5
Maplehurst Cl, Kings.T.
  KT1 . . . . .181 H4
Maple Ind Est, Felt. TW13
  off Maple Way 160 A3
Maple Leaf Dr, Sid.
  DA15 . . . . .175 J1
Mapleleafe Gdns, Ilf. IG6 .80 E3
Maple Leaf Sq, SE16
  off St. Elmos Rd 133 G2
Maple Ms, NW6 . . . . .6 A1
  SW16 . . . . .169 F5
Maple Pl, W1 . . . . .9 G6
Maple Rd, E11 . . . . .79 E6
  SE20 . . . . .189 E1
  Hayes UB4 . . . . .102 C3
  Surbiton KT6 . . . . .181 H5
Maples, The, Esher (Clay.)
  KT10 . . . . .194 D7
Maples Pl, E1
  off Raven Row . . .112/113 E5
Maplestead Rd, SW2 . . .151 F7
  Dagenham RM9 . . . . . .118 B1

Maple St, W1 . . . . .17 F1
  Romford RM7 . . . . .83 J4
Maplethorpe Rd, Th.Hth.
  CR7 . . . . .187 H4
Mapleton Cl, Brom. BR2 .191 G6
Mapleton Cres, SW18 . . .148 E6
Mapleton Rd, E4 . . . . . . .62 C3
  SW18 . . . . .148 E6
  Enfield EN1 . . . . .45 E2
Maple Wk, W10
  off Droop St 108 A4
Maple Way, Felt. TW13 . .160 A3
Maplin Cl, N21 . . . . .43 F6
Maplin Ho, SE2
  off Wolvercote Rd 138 D2
Maplin Rd, E16 . . . . .115 G6
Maplin St, E3 . . . . .113 J3
Mapperley Dr, Wdf.Grn. IG8
  off Forest Dr 62/63 E7
Maran Way, Erith DA18 . .138 D2
Marban Rd, W9 . . . . . . .108 C3
★ Marble Arch, W1 . . . . . .16 A5
Marble Arch, W1 . . . . . . .16 A5
Marble Cl, W3 . . . . .126 B1
Marble Dr, NW2 . . . . . . .90 A1
Marble Hill Cl, Twick.
  TW1 . . . . .144 E7
Marble Hill Gdns, Twick.
  TW1 . . . . .144 E7
★ Marble Hill Ho, Twick.
  TW1 . . . . .145 F7
Marble Ho, SE18
  off Felspar Cl 137 J5
Marble Quay, E1 . . . . . . .29 H1
Marbrook Ct, SE12 . . . . .173 J3
Marcella Rd, SW9 . . . . . .151 G2
Marcellina Way, Orp.
  BR6 . . . . .207 H3
Marchant Rd, E11 . . . . . .96 D2
Marchant St, SE14
  off Sanford St 133 H6
Marchbank Rd, W14 . . . .128 C6
Marchmont Gdns, Rich. TW10
  off Marchmont Rd 145 J5
Marchmont Rd, Rich.
  TW10 . . . . .145 J5
  Wallington SM6 . . . . . .200 C7
Marchmont St, WC1 . . . .10 A5
March Rd, Twick. TW1 . . .144 D7
Marchside Cl, Houns. TW5
  off Springwell Rd 142 D1
Marchwood Cl, SE5 . . . .132 B7
Marchwood Cres, W5 . . .105 F6
Marcia Rd, SE1 . . . . .37 E2
Marcilly Rd, SW18 . . . . .149 G5
Marconi Rd, E10 . . . . . . .96 A1
Marconi Way, Sthl. UB1 .103 H6
Marcon Pl, E8 . . . . .94 E6
Marco Rd, W6 . . . . .127 J3
Marcourt Lawns, W5 . . .105 H4
Marcus Ct, E15 . . . . .115 E1
Marcus Garvey Ms, SE22
  off St. Aidan's Rd.152/153 E5
Marcus Garvey Way,
  SE24 . . . . .151 G4
Marcus St, E15 . . . . .115 F1
  SW18 . . . . .149 E6
Marcus Ter, SW18 . . . . .149 E6
Mardale Dr, NW9 . . . . . . .70 D5
Mardell Rd, Croy. CR0 . . .189 G5
Marden Av, Brom. BR2 . .191 G6
Marden Cres, Bex. DA5 . .159 J5
  Croydon CR0 . . . . .187 F6
Marden Rd, N17 . . . . .76 B3
  Croydon CR0 . . . . .187 F6
Marden Sq, SE16 . . . . . .132 E3
Marder Rd, W13 . . . . . . .124 D2
Mardyke Cl, Rain. RM13
  off Lower Mardyke Av.119 J2
Marechal Niel Av, Sid.
  DA15 . . . . .175 G3
Maresfield, Croy. CR0 . . .202 B3
Maresfield Gdns, NW3 . . .91 F5
Mare St, E8 . . . . .113 E1
Marfleet Cl, Cars. SM5 . .199 H2
Margaret Av, E4 . . . . .46 B6
Margaret Bondfield Av,
  Bark. IG11 . . . . .100 A7
Margaret Bldgs, N16
  off Margaret Rd 94 C1
Margaret Ct, W1 . . . . . . .17 F3
Margaret Gardner Dr,
  SE9 . . . . .174 C2
Margaret Ingram Cl, SW6
  off John Smith Av 128 C7
Margaret Lockwood Cl,
  Kings.T. KT1 . . . . .181 J4
Margaret Rd, N16 . . . . . .94 C1
  Barnet EN4 . . . . .41 G4
  Bexley DA5 . . . . .158 D6

Margaret St, W1 . . . . . . .17 E3
Margaretta Ter, SW3 . . . .31 G5
Margaretting Rd, E12 . . . .97 J2
Margaret Way, Ilf. IG4 . . .80 B6
Margate Rd, SW2 . . . . . .150 E5
Margeholes, Wat. WD19 . .50 E2
Margery Pk Rd, E7 . . . . . .97 G6
Margery Rd, Dag. RM8 . .100 D3
Margery St, WC1 . . . . . . .10 E4
Margin Dr, SW19 . . . . . .166 A5
Margravine Gdns, W6 . . .128 A5
Margravine Rd, W6 . . . . .128 A5
Marham Gdns, SW18 . . .167 H1
  Morden SM4 . . . . .185 F6
Maria Cl, SE1
  off Beatrice Rd 132 D4
Marian Cl, Hayes UB4 . . .102 D4
Marian Ct, Sutt. SM1 . . .198 E5
Marian Pl, E2 . . . . .112 E2
Marian Rd, SW16 . . . . . .186 C1
Marian Sq, E2 . . . . .13 J1
Marian St, E2
  off Hackney Rd . .112/113 E2
Marian Way, NW10 . . . . . .89 F7
Maria Ter, E1 . . . . .113 G4
Maria Theresa Cl, N.Mal.
  KT3 . . . . .182 D5
Maricas Av, Har. HA3 . . . .68 A1
Marie Lloyd Gdns, N19
  off Hornsey Ri
  Gdns 74/75 E7
Marie Lloyd Wk, E8
  off Forest Rd 94 D6
Marigold All, SE1 . . . . . . .19 G6
Marigold Cl, Sthl. UB1
  off Lancaster Rd .102/103 E7
Marigold Rd, N17 . . . . . . .61 F7
Marigold St, SE16 . . . . . .132 E2
Marigold Way, E4
  off Silver Birch Av 61 J6
  Croydon CR0 . . . . .203 G1
Marina App, Hayes
  UB4 . . . . .103 E5
Marina Av, N.Mal. KT3 . .183 H5
Marina Cl, Brom. BR2 . . .191 G3
Marina Dr, Well. DA16 . . .157 H2
Marina Gdns, Rom. RM7 . .83 J6
Marina Way, Tedd. TW11
  off Fairways 163 G7
Marine Dr, SE18 . . . . . . .136 C4
  Barking IG11 . . . . .118 B4
Marinefield Rd, SW6 . . . .149 E2
Mariner Gdns, Rich.
  TW10 . . . . .163 F3
Mariner Rd, E12
  off Dersingham Av 98 C4
Mariners Ms, E14 . . . . . .134 D4
Marine St, SE16 . . . . .29 H5
Marine Twr, SE8
  off Abinger Gro 133 J6
Marion Cl, Ilf. IG6 . . . . . . .65 G7
Marion Gro, Wdf.Grn. IG8 .63 E5
Marion Rd, NW7 . . . . .55 G5
  Thornton Heath CR7 . . .187 J5
Marischal Rd, SE13 . . . . .154 D3
Maritime Ho, Bark. IG11
  off Linton Rd 99 F7
Maritime Quay, E14 . . . .134 A5
Maritime St, E3 . . . . .113 J4
Marius Pas, SW17
  off Marius Rd 168 A2
Marius Rd, SW17 . . . . . .168 A2
Marjorams Av, Loug.
  IG10 . . . . .48 C2
Marjorie Gro, SW11 . . . .149 J4
Marjorie Ms, E1
  off Arbour Sq 113 G6
Mark Av, E4 . . . . .46 B6
Mark Cl, Bexh. DA7 . . . . .158 E1
  Southall UB1
  off Longford Av 123 H1
Marke Cl, Kes. BR2 . . . . .206 B4
Markeston Grn, Wat.
  WD19 . . . . .50 D4
Market Ct, W1 . . . . .17 F3
Market Est, N7 . . . . .92 E6
Market Hill, SE18 . . . . . .136 D3
Market La, Edg. HA8 . . . .70 C1
Market Ms, W1 . . . . .24 D2
Market Pl, N2 . . . . .73 H3
  NW11 . . . . .73 F4
  SE16 . . . . .37 J1
  W1 . . . . .17 F3
  W3 . . . . .126 C1
  Bexleyheath DA6 . . . . .159 G4
  Brentford TW8 . . . . . .125 F7
  Enfield EN2
  off The Town 44 A3
  Kingston upon Thames
  KT1 . . . . .181 G2

Market Rd, N7 . . . . .92 E6
  Richmond TW9 . . . . . .146 A3
Market Row, SW9
  off Atlantic Rd 151 G4
Market Sq, E2 . . . . .13 F3
  E14 off Chrisp St 114 B6
  N9 off New Rd 60 D2
  Bromley BR1 . . . . .191 G2
Market St, E6 . . . . .116 C2
  SE18 . . . . .136 D4
Market Way, E14
  off Kerbey St 114 B6
  Wembley HA0
  off Turton Rd 87 H5
Markfield Gdns, E4 . . . . .46 B7
Markfield Rd, N15 . . . . . .76 D4
Markham Pl, SW3 . . . . . .31 J3
Markham Sq, SW3 . . . . . .31 J3
Markham St, SW3 . . . . . .31 H3
Markhole Cl, Hmptn. TW12
  off Priory Rd 161 F7
Markhouse Av, E17 . . . . .77 H6
Markhouse Rd, E17 . . . . .77 J5
Markland Ho, W10 . . . . .108 A4
Mark La, EC3 . . . . .20 E6
Markmanor Av, E17 . . . . .77 H7
Mark Rd, N22 . . . . .75 H2
Marksbury Av, Rich.
  TW9 . . . . .146 A3
MARK'S GATE, Rom. 82 E2
Mark Sq, EC2 . . . . .12 D5
Marks Rd, Rom. RM7 . . . .83 J5
Mark St, E15 . . . . .96 E7
  EC2 . . . . .12 D5
Markway, Sun. TW16 . . .178 C2
Markwell Cl, SE26
  off Longton Gro .170/171 E4
Markyate Rd, Dag. RM8 .100 B5
Marlands Rd, Ilf. IG5 . . . .80 B3
Marlborough, SW3 . . . . . .31 J1
Marlborough Av, E8 . . . .112 D1
  N14 . . . . .58 C3
  Edgware HA8 . . . . .54 B3
Marlborough Cl, N20
  off Marlborough Gdns .57 J3
  SE17 . . . . .35 H2
  SW19 . . . . .167 H6
  Orpington BR6
  off Aylesham Rd 193 J7
Marlborough Ct, W1 . . . .17 F4
  W8 . . . . .128 D4
  Wallington SM6
  off Cranley Gdns 200 C7
Marlborough Cres, W4 . .126 D3
Marlborough Dr, Ilf. IG5 . .80 B3
Marlborough Gdns, N20 . .57 J3
Marlborough Gate Ho,
  W2 . . . . .14 E5
Marlborough Gro, SE1 . . .37 H4
Marlborough Hill, NW8 . .109 F1
  Harrow HA1 . . . . .68 C4
★ Marlborough Ho,
  SW1 . . . . .25 G2
Marlborough La, SE7 . . .135 J6
Marlborough Pk Av, Sid.
  DA15 . . . . .158 A7
Marlborough Pl, NW8 . . . .6 C2
Marlborough Rd, E4 . . . . .62 A6
  E7 . . . . .97 J4
  E15 off Borthwick Rd .96/97 F4
  E18 . . . . .79 G3
  N9 . . . . .60 C1
  N19 . . . . .92 D2
  N22 . . . . .59 E7
  SW1 . . . . .25 G2
  SW19 . . . . .167 G6
  W4 . . . . .126 C5
  W5 . . . . .125 G2
  Bexleyheath DA7 . . . . .158 D3
  Bromley BR2 . . . . .191 J4
  Dagenham RM8 . . . . . .100 B4
  Feltham TW13 . . . . . . .160 D2
  Hampton TW12 . . . . . .161 G6
  Isleworth TW7 . . . . . . .144 E1
  Richmond TW10 . . . . .145 H6
  Romford RM7 . . . . .83 G4
  South Croydon CR2 . . .201 J7
  Southall UB2 . . . . .122 C3
  Sutton SM1 . . . . .198 D3
Marlborough St, SW3 . . . .31 G2
Marlborough Yd, N19 . . . .92 D2
Marler Rd, SE23 . . . . . . .171 H1
Marlescroft Way, Loug.
  IG10 . . . . .48 E5
Marley Av, Bexh. DA7 . . .138 D6
Marley Cl, N15
  off Stanmore Rd 75 H4
  Greenford UB6 . . . . . .103 G3
Marley Wk, NW2
  off Lennon Rd 89 J5

Marlingdene Cl, Hmptn.
TW12 . . . .**161** G6
Marlings Cl, Chis. BR7 . .**193** H4
Marlings Pk Av, Chis.
BR7 . . . .**193** H4
Marlins Cl, Sutt. SM1
off Turnpike La **199** F5
Marloes Cl, Wem. HA0 . . .**87** G4
Marloes Rd, W8 . . . .**22** A6
Marlow Cl, SE20 . . . .**189** E3
Marlow Ct, NW6 . . . .**90** A7
NW9 . . . .**71** F3
Marlow Cres, Twick. TW1 .**144** C6
Marlow Dr, Sutt. SM3 . . .**198** A2
Marlowe Cl, Chis. BR7 . .**175** G6
Ilford IG6 . . . .**81** F1
Marlowe Ct, SE19
off Lymer Av **170** C5
Marlowe Gdns, SE9 . . . .**156** D6
Marlowe Rd, E17 . . . .**78** C4
Marlowes, The, NW8 . . . .**109** G1
Marlowe Sq, Mitch. CR4 .**186** C4
Marlowe Way, Croy. CR0 .**201** E2
Marlow Gdns, Hayes
UB3 . . . .**121** G3
Marlow Rd, E6 . . . .**116** C3
SE20 . . . .**189** E3
Southall UB2 . . . .**123** F3
Marlow Way, SE16 . . . . .**133** G2
Marl Rd, SW18 . . . .**149** E4
Marl St, SW18
off Marl Rd **149** F4
Marlton St, SE10
off Woolwich Rd **135** F5
Marlwood Cl, Sid. DA15 .**175** H2
Marmadon Rd, SE18 . . . .**137** J4
Marmion App, E4 . . . .**62** A4
Marmion Av, E4 . . . .**61** J4
Marmion Cl, E4 . . . .**61** J4
Marmion Ms, SW11
off Taybridge Rd **150** A3
Marmion Rd, SW11 . . . . .**150** A4
Marmont Rd, SE15 . . . . .**152** D1
Marmora Rd, SE22 . . . . .**153** F6
Marmot Rd, Houns. TW4 .**142** D3
Marne Av, N11 . . . .**58** B4
Welling DA16 . . . .**158** A3
Marnell Way, Houns.
TW4 . . . .**142** D3
Marne St, W10 . . . .**108** B3
Marney Rd, SW11 . . . . . .**150** A4
Marnfield Cres, SW2 . . . .**169** F1
Marnham Av, NW2 . . . . . .**90** B4
Marnham Cres, Grnf.
UB6 . . . .**103** H3
Marnock Rd, SE4 . . . . . .**153** H5
Maroon St, E14 . . . .**113** H5
Maroons Way, SE6 . . . . .**172** A5
Marquess Rd, N1 . . . .**94** A6
Marquis Cl, Wem. HA0 . . .**87** J7
Marquis Rd, N4 . . . .**93** F1
N22 . . . .**59** F6
NW1 . . . .**92** D6
Marrabon Cl, Sid. DA15 .**176** A1
Marrick Cl, SW15 . . . . . .**147** G4
Marriots Cl, NW9 . . . .**71** F6
Marriott Cl, Felt. TW14 . .**141** G6
Marriott Rd, E15 . . . .**114** E1
N4 . . . .**93** F1
N10 . . . .**73** J1
Barnet EN5 . . . .**40** A3
Marryat Pl, SW19 . . . . . .**166** B4
Marryat Rd, SW19 . . . . . .**166** A5
Marryat Sq, SW6 . . . . . .**148** B1
Marsala Rd, SE13 . . . . . .**154** B4
Marsden Rd, N9 . . . .**60** E2
SE15 . . . .**152** C3
Marsden St, NW5 . . . .**92** A6
Marsden Way, Orp. BR6 .**207** J4
Marshall Cl, SW18
off Allfarthing La **149** F6
Harrow HA1
off Bowen Rd **68** A7
Hounslow TW4 . . . .**143** F5
Marshall Path, SE28
off Attlee Rd **118** B7
Marshall Rd, E10 . . . .**96** B3
N17 . . . .**76** A1
Marshalls Cl, N11 . . . .**58** B4
Marshall's Gro, SE18 . . . .**136** B4
Marshalls Pl, SE16 . . . . . .**29** G6
Marshall's Rd, Sutt.
SM1 . . . .**198** E4
Marshall St, W1 . . . .**17** G4
Marshalsea Rd, SE1 . . . . .**28** A3
Marsham Cl, Chis. BR7 . .**174** E5
Marsham St, SW1 . . . .**25** J6
Marsh Av, Mitch. CR4 . . .**186** A2
Marshbrook Cl, SE3 . . . .**156** A3
Marsh Cl, NW7 . . . .**55** F3

Marsh Ct, SW19 . . . .**185** F1
Marsh Dr, NW9 . . . .**71** F6
Marsh Fm Rd, Twick.
TW2 . . . .**162** C1
Marshfield St, E14 . . . . . .**134** C3
Marshgate La, E15 . . . . . .**114** B1
Marshgate Path, SE28
off Tom Cribb Rd **137** F4
Marshgate Sidings, E15
off Marshgate La **96** B7
Marsh Grn Rd, Dag.
RM10 . . . .**119** G1
Marsh Hill, E9 . . . .**95** H5
Marsh La, E10 . . . .**96** A2
N17 . . . .**61** E7
NW7 . . . .**54** E4
Stanmore HA7 . . . .**53** F5
Marsh Rd, Pnr. HA5 . . . . . .**66** E4
Wembley HA0 . . . .**105** G2
Marshside Cl, N9 . . . .**61** F1
Marsh St, E14
off Harbinger Rd **134** B4
Marsh Wall, E14 . . . .**134** A1
Marsland Cl, SE17 . . . .**35** H4
Marston Av, Chess. KT9 .**195** H6
Dagenham RM10 . . . . .**101** G2
Marston Cl, NW6
off Fairfax Rd **91** F7
Dagenham RM10 . . . . .**101** G3
Marston Rd, Ilf. IG5 . . . . . .**80** B1
Teddington TW11 . . . . .**162** E5
Marston Way, SE19 . . . . .**169** H7
Marsworth Av, Pnr. HA5 . .**66** D1
Marsworth Cl, Hayes
UB4 . . . .**103** E5
Martaban Rd, N16 . . . .**94** B2
Martello St, E8 . . . .**94** E7
Martello Ter, E8 . . . .**94** E7
Martell Rd, SE21 . . . .**170** A3
Martel Pl, E8
off Dalston La **94** C6
Marten Rd, E17 . . . .**78** A2
Martens Av, Bexh. DA7 . .**159** J4
Martens Cl, Bexh. DA7 . .**159** J4
Martha Ct, E2 . . . .**113** E2
Martham Cl, SE28 . . . . . .**118** D7
Martha Rd, E4 . . . .**61** J6
E15 . . . .**97** E6
Martha's Bldgs, EC1 . . . . .**12** B5
Martha St, E1 . . . .**113** E6
Marthorne Cres, Har. HA3 .**68** A2
Martina Ter, Chig. IG7
off Manford Way **65** J5
Martin Bowes Rd, SE9 . .**156** C3
Martinbridge Trd Est, Enf.
EN1 . . . .**44** D5
Martin Cl, N9 . . . .**61** G1
Martin Cres, Croy. CR0 . .**201** G1
Martindale, SW14 . . . . . .**146** C5
Martindale Av, E16 . . . . . .**115** G7
Martindale Rd, SW12 . . . .**150** B7
Hounslow TW4 . . . .**142** E3
Martin Dene, Bexh. DA6 .**159** F5
Martin Dr, Nthlt. UB5 . . . .**85** F5
Martineau Cl, Esher
KT10 . . . .**194** A4
Martineau Ms, N5
off Martineau Rd **93** H4
Martineau Rd, N5 . . . .**93** H4
Martineau St, E1 . . . .**113** F7
Martingale Cl, Sun.
TW16 . . . .**178** A4
Martingales Cl, Rich.
TW10 . . . .**163** G3
Martin Gdns, Dag. RM8 .**100** C4
Martin Gro, Mord. SM4 . .**184** D3
Martin La, EC4 . . . .**20** C5
Martin Ri, Bexh. DA6 . . . .**159** F5
Martin Rd, Dag. RM8 . . . .**100** C4
Martins Cl, W.Wick. BR4 .**204** D1
Martinsfield Cl, Chig. IG7 .**65** H4
Martins Mt, Barn. EN5 . . . .**40** D4
Martins Rd, Brom. BR2 . .**191** E2
Martin St, SE28 . . . .**137** H1
Martins Wk, N10 . . . .**74** A1
Borehamwood WD6
off Siskin Cl **38** A4
Martin Way, SW20 . . . . . .**184** B3
Morden SM4 . . . .**184** B3
Martlet Gro, Nthlt. UB5
off Javelin Way **102** D3
Martlett Ct, WC2 . . . .**18** B4
Martley Dr, Ilf. IG2 . . . .**80** E5
Martock Ct, Har. HA3 . . . .**68** D4
Martock Gdns, N11 . . . . . .**57** J5
Marton Cl, SE6 . . . .**172** A3
Marton Rd, N16 . . . .**94** B2
Martys Yd, NW3
off Hampstead
High St **91** G4

Marvell Av, Hayes UB4 . .**102** A5
Marvels Cl, SE12 . . . .**173** H2
Marvels La, SE12 . . . .**173** H2
Marville Rd, SW6 . . . .**128** C7
Marvin St, E8
off Sylvester Rd . . .**94/95** E6
Marwell Cl, W.Wick. BR4
off Deer Pk Way **205** F2
Marwood Cl, Well. DA16 .**158** B3
Marwood Dr, NW7
off Bittacy Hill **56** B7
Mary Adelaide Cl, SW15 .**164** E4
Mary Ann Gdns, SE8 . . . .**134** A6
Maryatt Av, Har. HA2 . . . .**85** H2
Marybank, SE18 . . . .**136** C4
Mary Cl, Stan. HA7 . . . . . .**69** J4
Mary Datchelor Cl, SE5 . .**152** A1
Mary Grn, NW8 . . . .**109** E1
Maryland Ind Est, E15
off Maryland Rd **96** D5
Maryland Pk, E15 . . . .**96** E5
Maryland Pt, E15
off Leytonstone Rd .**96/97** E6
Maryland Rd, E15 . . . .**96** D5
N22 . . . .**59** F6
Thornton Heath CR7 . .**187** H1
Maryland Sq, E15 . . . .**96** E5
Marylands Rd, W9 . . . . . .**108** D4
Maryland St, E15 . . . .**96** D5
Maryland Wk, N1
off Popham St **111** J1
Maryland Way, Sun.
TW16 . . . .**178** A2
Mary Lawrenson Pl, SE3 .**135** F7
MARYLEBONE, NW1 . . . .**15** J3
Marylebone Flyover,
NW1 . . . .**15** F2
W2 . . . .**15** F2
Marylebone High St, W1 . .**16** C1
Marylebone La, W1 . . . . . .**16** D4
Marylebone Ms, W1 . . . . .**16** D2
Marylebone Pas, W1 . . . . .**17** G3
Marylebone Rd, NW1 . . . .**15** H1
Marylebone St, W1 . . . . . .**16** C2
Marylee Way, SE11 . . . . . .**34** D3
Mary Macarthur Ho, W6
off Field Rd **128** B6
Maryon Gro, SE7 . . . .**136** B4
Maryon Ms, NW3
off South End Rd **91** H4
Maryon Rd, SE7 . . . .**136** B4
SE18 . . . .**136** B4
Mary Peters Dr, Grnf.
UB6 . . . .**86** A5
Mary Pl, W11 . . . .**108** B7
Mary Rose Cl, Hmptn. TW12
off Ashley Rd **179** G1
Mary Rose Mall, E6
off Frobisher Rd **116** D5
Maryrose Way, N20 . . . . . .**57** G1
Mary Seacole Cl, E8
off Clarissa St **112** C1
Mary's Ter, Twick. TW1 . .**144** D7
Mary St, E16
off Barking Rd **115** F5
N1 . . . .**111** J1
Mary Ter, NW1 . . . .**110** B1
Masbro' Rd, W14 . . . .**128** A3
Mascalls Cl, SE7
off Victoria Way **135** J6
Mascalls Rd, SE7 . . . .**135** J6
Mascotte Rd, SW15 . . . . .**148** A4
Mascotts Cl, NW2 . . . .**89** H3
Masefield Av, Borwd.
WD6 . . . .**38** B5
Southall UB1 . . . .**103** G7
Stanmore HA7 . . . .**52** C5
Masefield Cres, N14 . . . . .**42** C6
Masefield Gdns, E6 . . . . .**116** D4
Masefield La, Hayes
UB4 . . . .**102** B4
Masefield Rd, Hmptn. TW12
off Wordsworth Rd **161** F4
Masefield Vw, Orp. BR6 .**207** F3
Masham Ho, Erith DA18
off Kale Rd **138** D2
Mashie Rd, W3 . . . .**106** E6
Maskall Cl, SW2 . . . .**169** G1
Maskani Wk, SW16
off Bates Cres **168** C7
Maskell Rd, SW17 . . . . . .**167** F3
Maskelyne Cl, SW11 . . . .**149** H1
Mason Bradbear Ct, N1
off St. Paul's Rd **94** A6
Mason Cl, E16 . . . .**115** G7
SE16 . . . .**37** J3
SW20 . . . .**184** A1
Bexleyheath DA7 . . . . .**159** H3
Borehamwood WD6 . . . .**38** C2
Hampton TW12 . . . . . .**179** F1

Mason Rd, Sutt. SM1
off Manor Pl **198/199** E5
Woodford Green IG8 . . .**63** E4
Masons Arms Ms, W1 . . . .**17** E4
Masons Av, EC2 . . . .**20** B3
Croydon CR0 . . . .**201** J3
Harrow HA3 . . . .**68** C4
Masons Ct, Wem. HA9
off Mayfields **88** A2
Masons Grn La, W3 . . . . .**106** A5
Masons Hill, SE18 . . . . . .**137** E4
Bromley BR1, BR2 . . . .**191** G3
Mason's Pl, EC1 . . . .**11** H3
Masons Pl, Mitch. CR4 . . .**185** J1
Mason St, SE17 . . . .**36** C1
Mason's Yd, SW1 . . . .**25** G1
SW19 off High St
Wimbledon **166** A5
Massey Cl, N11
off Grove Rd **58** B5
Massey Ct, E6 . . . .**115** J1
Massie Rd, E8
off Graham Rd **94** D6
Massingberd Way,
SW17 . . . .**168** B4
Massinger St, SE17 . . . . . .**36** D2
Massingham St, E1 . . . . .**113** G4
Masson Av, Ruis. HA4 . . . .**84** C6
Master Gunner Pl, SE18 .**136** B7
Masterman Ho, SE5 . . . . . .**36** B7
Masterman Rd, E6 . . . . . .**116** B3
Masters Cl, SW16
off Blegborough Rd . .**168** C6
Masters Dr, SE16 . . . .**132** E5
Masters St, E1 . . . .**113** G5
Mast Ho Ter, E14 . . . .**134** A4
Mast Leisure Pk, SE16 . .**133** G3
Mastmaker Rd, E14 . . . . .**134** A2
Maswell Pk Cres, Houns.
TW3 . . . .**143** J5
Maswell Pk Rd, Houns.
TW3 . . . .**143** H5
Matcham Rd, E11 . . . .**97** E3
Matchless Dr, SE18 . . . . .**136** D7
Matfield Cl, Brom. BR2 . .**191** G5
Matfield Rd, Belv. DA17 .**139** G6
Matham Gro, SE22 . . . . . .**152** C4
Matham Rd, E.Mol. KT8 .**180** A5
Matheson Rd, W14 . . . . . .**128** C4
Mathews Av, E6 . . . .**116** D2
Mathews Pk Av, E15 . . . . .**97** F6
Matilda Cl, SE19
off Elizabeth Way **170** A7
Matilda St, N1 . . . .**111** F1
Matlock Cl, SE24 . . . .**151** J4
Barnet EN5 . . . .**40** A5
Matlock Ct, SE5
off Denmark Hill Est . .**152** A4
Matlock Cres, Sutt. SM3 .**198** B4
Watford WD19 . . . .**50** C3
Matlock Gdns, Sutt.
SM3 . . . .**198** B4
Matlock Pl, Sutt. SM3 . . .**198** B4
Matlock Rd, E10 . . . .**78** C6
Matlock St, E14 . . . .**113** H6
Matlock Way, N.Mal.
KT3 . . . .**182** D1
Matrimony Pl, SW8 . . . . .**150** C2
Matson Ct, Wdf.Grn. IG8
off The Bridle Path . .**62/63** E7
Matthew Cl, W10 . . . .**108** A4
Matthew Ct, Mitch.
CR4 . . . .**186** D5
Matthew Parker St, SW1 . .**25** J4
Matthews Rd, Grnf. UB6 . .**86** A5
Matthews St, SW11 . . . . .**149** J2
Matthews Yd, WC2 . . . . . .**18** A4
Matthias Rd, N16 . . . .**94** A5
Mattingley Way, SE15 . . . .**37** F7
Mattison Rd, N4 . . . .**75** G6
Mattock La, W5 . . . .**125** E1
W13 . . . .**125** E1
Maud Cashmore Way,
SE18 . . . .**136** C3
Maude Rd, E17 . . . .**77** H5
SE5 . . . .**152** B1
Maudesville Cotts, W7
off The Broadway **124** B1
Maude Ter, E17 . . . .**77** H4
Maud Gdns, E13 . . . .**115** F1
Barking IG11 . . . .**117** J2
Maudlin's Grn, E1 . . . .**29** H1
Maud Rd, E10 . . . .**96** C3
E13 . . . .**115** F2
Maudslay Rd, SE9 . . . . . .**156** C3
Maudsley Ho, Brent. TW8
off Green Dragon La .**125** H5
Maud St, E16 . . . .**115** F5
Maud Wilkes Cl, NW5 . . . .**92** C5
Mauleverer Rd, SW2 . . . .**150** E5

Maundeby Wk, NW10
  off Neasden La 88/89 E6
Maunder Rd, W7 . . . . . . .124 C1
Maunsel St, SW1 . . . . . . .33 H1
Maurice Av, N22 . . . . .75 H2
Maurice Brown Cl, NW7 . .56 A5
Maurice St, W12 . . . . . . .107 H6
Maurice Wk, NW11 . . . . . .73 F4
Maurier Cl, Nthlt. UB5 . . .102 C1
Mauritius Rd, SE10 . . . .135 E4
Maury Rd, N16 . . . . .94 D2
Mavelstone Cl, Brom.
  BR1 . . . . .192 B1
Mavelstone Rd, Brom.
  BR1 . . . . .192 B1
Maverton Rd, E3 . . . . . . .114 A1
Mavis Av, Epsom KT19 . .197 E5
Mavis Cl, Epsom KT19 . .197 E5
Mavis Wk, E6 . . . . .116 B5
Mawbey Est, SE1 . . . . . . .37 H4
Mawbey Pl, SE1 . . . . .37 G4
Mawbey Rd, SE1 . . . . . . .37 G4
Mawbey St, SW8 . . . . . .130 E7
Mawney Cl, Rom. RM7 . . .83 H2
Mawney Rd, Rom. RM7 . . .83 J4
Mawson, SW20 . . . . . . .184 B2
Mawson La, W4
  off Great W Rd 127 F6
Maxey Gdns, Dag. RM9 . .101 E4
Maxey Rd, SE18 . . . . . . .137 F4
  Dagenham RM9 . . . . .100 E4
Maxfield Cl, N20 . . . . .41 F7
Maxilla Gdns, W10
  off Cambridge Gdns . .108 A6
Maxilla Wk, W10
  off Kingsdown Cl 108 A6
Maxim Rd, N21 . . . . .43 G6
Maxted Pk, Har. HA1 . . . .68 B7
Maxted Rd, SE15 . . . . . .152 C3
Maxwell Cl, Croy. CR0 . . .201 E1
  Hayes UB3 . . . . .102 A7
Maxwell Gdns, Orp.
  BR6 . . . . .207 J3
Maxwell Rd, SW6 . . . . . .128 E7
  Borehamwood WD6 . . .38 B3
  Welling DA16 . . . . . . .158 A3
  West Drayton UB7 . . .120 C4
Maxwelton Av, NW7 . . . . .54 D5
Maxwelton Cl, NW7 . . . . .54 D5
Maya Angelou Ct, E4
  off Bailey Cl 62 C4
Maya Cl, SE15
  off Gordon Rd 152 E2
Mayall Rd, SE24 . . . . . . .151 H5
Maya Rd, N2 . . . . .73 F4
Maybank Av, E18 . . . . . . .79 H2
  Wembley HA0 . . . . . . .86 C5
Maybank Gdns, Pnr. HA5 .66 A5
Maybank Rd, E18 . . . . . . .79 H1
May Bate Av, Kings.T.
  KT2 . . . . .181 G1
Maybells Commercial Est,
  Bark. IG11 . . . . .118 D2
Mayberry Pl, Surb. KT5 . .181 J7
Maybourne Cl, SE26 . . . .171 E5
Maybrook Meadow Est, Bark.
  IG11 . . . . .100 A7
Maybury Cl, Loug. IG10 . .48 E4
  Orpington BR5 . . . . . .193 E5
Maybury Gdns, NW10 . . .89 H6
Maybury Ms, N6 . . . . .74 C7
Maybury Rd, E13 . . . . . .115 J4
  Barking IG11 . . . . . . .117 J2
Maybury St, SW17 . . . . .167 H5
Maychurch Cl, Stan. HA7 .53 G7
May Cl, Chess. KT9 . . . . .195 J6
May Ct, SW19 . . . . .185 F1
Maycroft, Pnr. HA5 . . . . . .66 B2
Maycross Av, Mord.
  SM4 . . . . .184 C3
Mayday Gdns, SE3 . . . . .156 B2
Mayday Rd, Th.Hth. CR7 .187 H6
Mayerne Rd, SE9 . . . . . .156 A5
Mayesbrook Rd, Bark.
  IG11 . . . . .117 J1
  Dagenham RM8 . . . . .100 A3
  Ilford IG3 . . . . .100 A3
Mayesford Rd, Rom. RM6 .82 C7
Mayes Rd, N22 . . . . .75 G2
Mayeswood Rd, SE12 . . .173 J3
MAYFAIR, W1 . . . . .16 D6
Mayfair Av, Bexh. DA7 . .158 D1
  Ilford IG1 . . . . .98 C2
  Romford RM6 . . . . . . .82 D6
  Twickenham TW2 . . . .143 J7
  Worcester Park KT4 . .197 G1
Mayfair Cl, Beck. BR3 . . .190 B1
  Surbiton KT6 . . . . . . .195 H1
Mayfair Gdns, N17 . . . . . .60 A6
  Woodford Green IG8 . .63 G7

Mayfair Ms, NW1
  off Regents Pk Rd 91 J7
Mayfair Pl, W1 . . . . .25 E1
Mayfair Ter, N14 . . . . .42 D7
Mayfield, Bexh. DA7 . . . .159 F3
Mayfield Av, N12 . . . . . . .57 F4
  N14 . . . . .58 D2
  W4 . . . . .127 E4
  W13 . . . . .124 E3
  Harrow HA3 . . . . .68 E5
  Orpington BR6 . . . . . .207 J1
  Woodford Green IG8 . .63 G7
Mayfield Cl, E8
  off Forest Rd 94 C6
  SW4 . . . . .150 D5
  Thames Ditton KT7 . .194 E1
Mayfield Cres, N9 . . . . . . .44 E6
  Thornton Heath CR7 .187 F4
Mayfield Dr, Pnr. HA5 . . . .67 F4
Mayfield Gdns, NW4 . . . .72 A6
  W7 . . . . .104 A6
Mayfield Mans, SW15
  off West Hill 148 A7
Mayfield Rd, E4 . . . . .62 C2
  E8 . . . . .94 C7
  E13 . . . . .115 F4
  E17 . . . . .77 H2
  N8 . . . . .75 F6
  SW19 . . . . .184 C1
  W3 . . . . .106 B7
  W12 . . . . .127 E2
  Belvedere DA17 . . . . .139 J4
  Bromley BR1 . . . . . . .192 B5
  Dagenham RM8 . . . . .100 C1
  Enfield EN3 . . . . .45 G2
  Sutton SM2 . . . . .199 G6
  Thornton Heath CR7 .187 F4
Mayfields, Wem. HA9 . . . .88 A2
Mayfields Cl, Wem. HA9 . .88 A2
Mayflower Cl, SE16
  off Greenland Quay . .133 G4
Mayflower Ct, SE16
  off St. Marychurch St .133 F2
Mayflower Rd, SW9 . . . .150 E3
Mayflower St, SE16 . . . .133 F2
Mayfly Cl, Pnr. HA5 . . . . .66 C7
Mayfly Gdns, Nthlt. UB5
  off Ruislip Rd 102 D3
Mayford Cl, SW12 . . . . . .149 J7
  Beckenham BR3 . . . . .189 G3
Mayford Rd, SW12 . . . . .149 J7
May Gdns, Wem. HA0 . . .105 F2
Maygood St, N1 . . . . .10 E1
Maygrove Rd, NW6 . . . . . .90 C6
Mayhew Cl, E4 . . . . .62 A3
Mayhill Rd, SE7 . . . . .135 H6
  Barnet EN5 . . . . .40 B6
Maylands Dr, Sid. DA14 .176 D3
Maylands Rd, Wat. WD19 .50 C4
Maynard Cl, N15
  off Brunswick Rd 76 B4
  SW6 off Cambria
    St 128/129 E7
Maynard Path, E17 . . . . . .78 C5
Maynard Rd, E17 . . . . . . .78 C5
Maynards Quay, E1
  off Garnet St 113 F7
Maynooth Gdns, Cars.
  SM5 . . . . .185 J7
Mayola Rd, E5 . . . . .95 F4
Mayo Rd, NW10 . . . . .88 E6
  Croydon CR0 . . . . . . .188 A5
Mayow Rd, SE23 . . . . . . .171 G3
  SE26 . . . . .171 G4
Mayplace Cl, Bexh. DA7 .159 H3
Mayplace La, SE18 . . . . .137 E7
Mayplace Rd E, Bexh.
  DA7 . . . . .159 H3
Mayplace Rd W, Bexh.
  DA7 . . . . .159 G4
Maypole Cres, Ilf. IG6 . . . .65 G7
May Rd, E4 . . . . .62 A6
  E13 . . . . .115 G2
  Twickenham TW2 . . . .162 B1
Mayroyd Av, Surb. KT6 . .196 A2
Mays Ct, WC2 . . . . .18 A6
Mays Hill Rd, Brom.
  BR2 . . . . .191 E2
Mays La, E4 . . . . .62 D2
  Barnet EN5 . . . . .40 B5
Maysoule Rd, SW11 . . . .149 G4
Mays Rd, Tedd. TW11 . . .162 A5
Mayston Ms, SE10
  off Westcombe Hill . . .135 G5
May St, W14
  off North End Rd 128 C5
Mayswood Gdns, Dag.
  RM10 . . . . .101 J6
Mayton St, N7 . . . . .93 F3

Maytree Cl, Edg. HA8 . . . .54 C3
Maytree Gdns, W5
  off South Ealing Rd . .125 G2
May Tree La, Stan. HA7 . . .52 C7
Maytree Wk, SW2 . . . . . .169 G2
Mayville Est, N16
  off King Henry St 94 B5
Mayville Rd, E11 . . . . .96 E2
  Ilford IG1 . . . . .98 E5
May Wk, E13 . . . . .115 H2
Maywood Cl, Beck. BR3 .172 B7
Maze Hill, SE3 . . . . .134 E6
  SE10 . . . . .134 E6
Mazenod Av, NW6 . . . . . .90 D7
Maze Rd, Rich. TW9 . . . .126 A7
Mead, The, N2 . . . . .73 F2
  W13 . . . . .104 E5
  Beckenham BR3 . . . . .190 C1
  Wallington SM6 . . . . .200 D6
  Watford WD19 . . . . . . .50 E3
  West Wickham BR4 . .204 D1
Mead Cl, Har. HA3 . . . . . .68 A1
  Loughton IG10 . . . . . . .48 E2
Mead Ct, NW9 . . . . .70 C5
Mead Cres, E4 . . . . .62 C4
  Sutton SM1 . . . . .199 H4
Meadcroft Rd, SE11 . . . . .35 G6
Meade Cl, W4 . . . . .126 A6
Meadfield, Edg. HA8 . . . . .54 B2
Mead Fld, Har. HA2
  off Kings Rd 85 F3
Meadfield Grn, Edg. HA8 .54 B2
Meadfoot Rd, SW16 . . . .168 C7
Meadgate Av, Wdf.Grn.
  IG8 . . . . .64 B5
Mead Gro, Rom. RM6 . . . .82 E3
Meadlands Dr, Rich.
  TW10 . . . . .163 G2
Meadow, The, Chis.
  BR7 . . . . .175 F6
Meadow Av, Croy. CR0 . .189 G6
Meadow Bk, N21 . . . . .43 F6
Meadowbank, NW3 . . . . . .91 J7
  SE3 . . . . .155 F3
  Surbiton KT5 . . . . . . .181 J6
Meadowbank Cl, SW6 . . .127 J7
Meadowbank Gdns, Houns.
  TW5 . . . . .142 A2
Meadowbank Rd, NW9 . . .70 D7
Meadowbanks, Barn.
  EN5 . . . . .39 F5
Meadow Cl, E4
  off Mount Echo Av 62 B1
  E9 . . . . .95 J5
  SE6 . . . . .172 A5
  SW20 . . . . .183 J4
  Barnet EN5 . . . . .40 C6
  Bexleyheath DA6 . . . .159 F5
  Chislehurst BR7 . . . . .174 E5
  Esher KT10 . . . . .194 C3
  Hounslow TW4 . . . . . .143 G6
  Northolt UB5 . . . . . . .103 G2
  Richmond TW10 . . . . .163 H1
  Sutton SM1
    off Aultone Way . .198/199 G2
Meadowcourt Rd, SE3 . .155 F4
Meadowcroft, Brom.
  BR1 . . . . .192 C3
Meadowcroft Rd, N13 . . . .59 G2
Meadow Dr, N10 . . . . .74 B3
  NW4 . . . . .71 J2
Meadow Gdns, Edg.
  HA8 . . . . .54 C6
Meadow Garth, NW10 . . . .88 C6
Meadow Hill, N.Mal.
  KT3 . . . . .182 E6
Meadow La, SE12 . . . . . .173 H3
Meadowlea Cl, West Dr.
  UB7 . . . . .120 A6
Meadow Ms, SW8 . . . . . .34 C6
Meadow Pl, SW8 . . . . . . .34 B7
  W4 off Edensor
    Rd 126/127 E7
Meadow Rd, SW8 . . . . . .34 C7
  SW19 . . . . .167 F7
  Barking IG11 . . . . .99 J7
  Borehamwood WD6 . . .38 B2
  Bromley BR2 . . . . . . .191 E1
  Dagenham RM9 . . . . .101 F6
  Esher (Clay.) KT10 . . .194 B6
  Feltham TW13 . . . . . .160 E2
  Loughton IG10 . . . . . . .48 B5
  Pinner HA5 . . . . .66 D5
  Romford RM7 . . . . . . .101 J1
  Southall UB1 . . . . . . .103 F7
  Sutton SM1 . . . . .199 H5
Meadow Row, SE1 . . . . . .27 J6
Meadows Cl, E10 . . . . . . .96 A2
Meadows End, Sun.
  TW16 . . . . .178 A1

Meadowside, SE9 . . . . . .155 J4
Meadow Stile, Croy. CR0
  off High St 201 J3
Meadowsweet Cl, E16
  off Monarch Dr 116 A5
Meadow Vw, Har. HA1 . . .86 B1
  Sidcup DA15 . . . . . . .158 B7
Meadowview Rd, SE6 . . .171 J5
  Bexley DA5 . . . . .159 E6
Meadow Vw Rd, Th.Hth.
  CR7 . . . . .187 H5
Meadow Wk, E18 . . . . . . .79 G4
  Dagenham RM9 . . . . .101 F6
  Epsom KT17, KT19 . . .197 E6
  Wallington SM6 . . . . .200 B3
Meadow Way, NW9 . . . . . .70 D5
  Chessington KT9 . . . .195 H5
  Chigwell IG7 . . . . .65 F3
  Orpington BR6 . . . . . .206 D3
  Ruislip HA4 . . . . .66 B6
  Wembley HA9 . . . . . . .87 G4
Meadow Way, The, Har.
  HA3 . . . . .68 B1
Meadow Waye, Houns.
  TW5 . . . . .123 G6
Mead Path, SW17 . . . . . .167 F5
Mead Pl, E9 . . . . .95 F6
  Croydon CR0 . . . . . . .201 H1
Mead Plat, NW10 . . . . . . .88 C6
Mead Rd, Chis. BR7 . . . .175 F6
  Edgware HA8 . . . . .54 A6
  Richmond TW10 . . . . .163 F3
Mead Row, SE1 . . . . .27 E5
Meads, The, Edg. HA8 . . .54 D6
  Sutton SM3 . . . . .198 B3
Meads La, Ilf. IG3 . . . . . . .81 H7
Meads Rd, N22 . . . . .75 H2
  Enfield EN3 . . . . .45 H1
Mead Ter, Wem. HA9
  off Meadow Way 87 G4
Meadvale Rd, W5 . . . . . .105 E4
  Croydon CR0 . . . . . . .188 C7
Meadway, N14 . . . . .58 D2
  NW11 . . . . .72 E6
  SW20 . . . . .183 J4
  Barnet EN5 . . . . .40 D4
  Beckenham BR3 . . . . .190 C1
Mead Way, Brom. BR2 . .191 F6
  Croydon CR0 . . . . . . .203 H2
Meadway, Ilf. IG3 . . . . . . .99 H4
  Surbiton KT5 . . . . . . .196 C1
  Twickenham TW2 . . . .162 A1
  Woodford Green IG8 . .63 J5
Meadway, The, SE3
  off Heath La 154 D2
  Buckhurst Hill IG9 . . . .64 A1
  Loughton IG10 . . . . . . .48 C6
Meadway Cl, NW11 . . . . . .73 E6
  Barnet EN5 . . . . .40 D4
  Pinner HA5
    off Highbanks Rd 51 H6
Meadway Ct, NW11 . . . . .73 E6
Meadway Gate, NW11 . . .72 D6
Meaford Way, SE20 . . . . .171 E7
Meakin Est, SE1 . . . . .28 D5
Meanley Rd, E12 . . . . .98 B4
Meard St, W1 . . . . .17 H4
Meath Rd, E15 . . . . .115 F2
  Ilford IG1 . . . . .99 F3
Meath St, SW11 . . . . . . .150 B1
Mecklenburgh Pl, WC1 . . .10 C5
Mecklenburgh Sq, WC1 . .10 C5
Mecklenburgh St, WC1 . .10 C5
Medburn St, NW1 . . . . .9 H1
Medcroft Gdns, SW14 . .146 C4
Medebourne Cl, SE3 . . . .155 G3
Medesenge Way, N13 . . . .59 H6
Medfield St, SW15 . . . . .147 H7
Medhurst Cl, E3
  off Arbery Rd 113 H2
Medhurst Rd, E3
  off Arbery Rd 113 H2
Median Rd, E5 . . . . .95 F5
★ Medici Gall, W1
  off Grafton St 16 E6
Medina Av, Esher KT10 . .194 B3
Medina Gro, N7
  off Medina Rd 93 G3
Medina Rd, N7 . . . . .93 G3
Medland Cl, Wall. SM6 . .200 A1
Medland Ho, E14
  off Branch Rd 113 H7
Medlar Cl, Nthlt. UB5
  off Parkfield Av . .102/103 E2
Medlar St, SE5 . . . . .151 J1
Medley Rd, NW6 . . . . .90 D6
Medora Rd, SW2 . . . . . . .151 F7
Medusa Rd, SE6 . . . . . . .154 B6
Medway Bldgs, E3
  off Medway Rd 113 H2

Medway Cl, Croy. CR0 ...189 F6
Ilford IG1 ....99 F5
Medway Dr, Grnf. UB6 ..104 C2
Medway Gdns, Wem.
HA0 ....86 D4
Medway Ms, E3
off Medway Rd 113 H2
Medway Par, Grnf. UB6 .104 C2
Medway Rd, E3 ....113 H2
Medway St, SW1 ....25 J6
Medwin St, SW4 ......151 F4
Meerbrook Rd, SE3 ....155 J3
Meeson Rd, E15 ......115 F1
Meeson St, E5 ....95 H4
Meeting Flds Path, E9
off Morning La 95 F6
Meeting Ho All, E1
off Wapping La ..132/133 E1
Meeting Ho La, SE15 ..152 E1
Mehetabel Rd, E9 .....95 F6
Meister Cl, Ilf. IG1 .....99 G1
Melancholy Wk, Rich.
TW10 ....163 F2
Melanda Cl, Chis. BR7 ..174 C5
Melanie Cl, Bexh. DA7 .158 E1
Melba Way, SE13 ......154 B1
Melbourne Av, N13 .....59 F6
W13 ....124 D1
Pinner HA5 ....67 H3
Melbourne Cl, Orp. BR6 .193 H7
Wallington SM6
off Melbourne Rd ...200 C5
Melbourne Ct, E5
off Daubeney Rd 95 H4
N10 off Sydney Rd 58 B7
SE20 ....170 D7
Melbourne Gdns, Rom.
RM6 ....82 E5
Melbourne Gro, SE22 ..152 B4
Melbourne Ho, Hayes
UB4 ....102 C4
Melbourne Ms, SE6 ...154 C7
SW9 ....151 G1
Melbourne Pl, WC2 .....18 D5
Melbourne Rd, E6 .....116 C1
E10 ....78 B7
E17 ....77 H4
SW19 ....184 D1
Ilford IG1 ....99 E1
Teddington TW11 .....163 F6
Wallington SM6 .....200 B5
Melbourne Sq, SW9
off Melbourne Ms ...151 G1
Melbourne Ter, SW6
off Waterford Rd .128/129 E7
Melbourne Way, Enf. EN1 .44 C6
Melbury Av, Sthl. UB2 ..123 H3
Melbury Cl, Chis. BR7 ..174 C6
Esher (Clay.) KT10 ....194 E6
Melbury Ct, W8 ....128 C3
Melbury Dr, SE5
off Sedgmoor Pl 132 B7
Melbury Gdns, SW20 ..183 H1
Melbury Rd, W14 .....128 C3
Harrow HA3 ....69 J5
Melcombe Gdns, Har.
HA3 ....69 J6
Melcombe Pl, NW1 .....15 J1
Melcombe St, NW1 .....8 A6
Meldex Cl, NW7 ....55 J6
Meldon Cl, SW6
off Bagley's La ..148/149 E1
Meldone Cl, Surb. KT5 .182 B6
Meldrum Rd, Ilf. IG3 ...100 A2
Melfield Gdns, SE6 ....172 B4
Melford Av, Bark. IG11 ...99 H6
Melford Cl, Chess. KT9 .195 J5
Melford Rd, E6 ....116 C4
E11 ....96 E2
E17 ....77 H4
SE22 ....152 D7
Ilford IG1 ....99 G2
Melfort Av, Th.Hth. CR7 .187 H3
Melfort Rd, Th.Hth. CR7 .187 H3
Melgund Rd, N5 ....93 G5
Melina Pl, NW8 ....6 E4
Melina Rd, W12 ......127 H2
Melior Pl, SE1 ....28 D3
Melior St, SE1 ....28 C3
Meliot Rd, SE6 ....172 D2
Meller Cl, Croy. CR0 ...200 E3
Melling Dr, Enf. EN1 ....44 D1
Melling St, SE18 .....137 H6
Mellish Cl, Bark. IG11 ..117 J1
Mellish Gdns, Wdf.Grn.
IG8 ....63 G5
Mellish Ind Est, SE18 ..136 B3
Mellish St, E14 ......134 A3
Mellison Rd, SW17 ....167 H5
Melliss Av, Rich. TW9 ..146 B1

Mellitus St, W12 ......107 F6
Mellor Cl, Walt. KT12 ..179 F7
Mellows Rd, Ilf. IG5 .....80 C3
Wallington SM6 .....200 D5
Mells Cres, SE9 ......174 C4
Mell St, SE10
off Trafalgar Rd .134/135 E5
Melody La, N5 ....93 H5
Melody Rd, SW18 ....149 F5
Melon Pl, W8 ....22 A3
Melon Rd, E11 ....96 E3
SE15 ....152 D1
Melrose Av, N22 ......75 H1
NW2 ....89 H5
SW16 ....187 F3
SW19 ....166 D2
Borehamwood WD6 ...38 B5
Greenford UB6 ......103 H2
Mitcham CR4 ....168 B7
Twickenham TW2 ....143 H7
Melrose Cl, SE12 .....173 G1
Greenford UB6 ......103 H2
Hayes UB4 ....102 A5
Melrose Cres, Orp. BR6 .207 G4
Melrose Dr, Sthl. UB1 ..123 G1
Melrose Gdns, W6 .....127 J3
Edgware HA8 ....70 B2
New Malden KT3 ....182 D3
Melrose Rd, SW13 ....147 F2
SW18 ....148 C6
SW19 ....184 D2
W3 off Stanley Rd ...126 C3
Pinner HA5 ....67 F4
Melrose Ter, W6 ......127 J2
Melsa Rd, Mord. SM4 ..185 F6
Melthorne Dr, Ruis. HA4 ..84 C3
Melthorpe Gdns, SE3 ..156 B1
Melton Cl, Ruis. HA4 ...84 C1
Melton Ct, SW7 ....31 F2
Sutton SM2 ....199 F7
Melton St, NW1 ....9 G4
Melville Av, SW20 ....165 G7
Greenford UB6 ......86 C5
South Croydon CR2 ..202 C5
Melville Gdns, N13 ....59 H5
Melville Pl, N1
off Essex Rd 111 H1
Melville Rd, E17 ....77 J3
NW10 ....88 D7
SW13 ....147 G1
Sidcup DA14 ....176 C2
Melville Vil Rd, W3
off High St 126 D1
Melvin Rd, SE20 .....189 F1
Melyn Cl, N7
off Anson Rd 92 C4
Memel Ct, EC1 ....11 J6
Memel St, EC1 ....11 J6
Memess Path, SE18 ...136 D6
Memorial Av, E15 .....114 E3
Memorial Cl, Houns.
TW5 ....123 F6
Mendip Cl, SE26 .....171 F4
Hayes UB3 ....121 G7
Worcester Park KT4 ..197 J1
Mendip Dr, NW2 ....90 A2
Mendip Ho, N9
off New Rd 60 D3
Mendip Rd, SW11 ....149 F3
Ilford IG2 ....81 H5
Mendora Rd, SW6 ....128 B7
Menelik Rd, NW2 ......90 B4
Menlo Gdns, SE19 ....170 A7
Menon Dr, N9
off Plevna Rd 60 E3
Menotti St, E2 ....13 J5
Mentmore Cl, Har. HA3 ..69 F6
Mentmore Ter, E8 ......95 E7
Meon Ct, Islw. TW7 ...144 B2
Meon Rd, W3 ....126 C2
Meopham Rd, Mitch.
CR4 ....186 C1
Mepham Cres, Har. HA3 ..51 J7
Mepham Gdns, Har. HA3 ..51 J7
Mepham St, SE1 ....26 D2
Mera Dr, Bexh. DA7 ...159 G4
Merantun Way, SW19 ..185 F1
Merbury Cl, SE13 .....154 C5
Merbury Rd, SE28 ....137 H2
Mercator Pl, E14
off Napier Av 134 A5
Mercator Rd, SE13 ....154 D4
Mercer Cl, T.Ditt. KT7 ..180 C7
Merceron St, E1 ....112 E4
Mercer Pl, Pnr. HA5
off Crossway 66 C2
Mercers Cl, SE10 .....135 F4
Mercers Pl, W6 ......127 J4
Mercers Rd, N19 ....92 D3
Mercer St, WC2 ....18 A4

Merchant St, E3 ......113 J3
Merchiston Rd, SE6 ...172 D2
Merchland Rd, SE9 ...175 F1
Mercia Gro, SE13 ....154 C4
Mercier Rd, SW15 ....148 B5
Mercury Cen, Felt. TW14 .142 B5
Mercury Way, SE14 ...133 G6
Merebank La, Croy. CR0 .201 F5
Mercy Ter, SE13 .....154 B4
Mere Cl, SW15 ....148 A7
Orpington BR6 .....206 E2
Meredith Av, NW2 .....89 J5
Meredith Cl, Pnr. HA5 ...50 D7
Meredith St, E13 .....115 G3
EC1 ....11 G4
Meredyth Rd, SW13 ..147 G2
Mere End, Croy. CR0 ..189 G7
Mere Side, Orp. BR6 ..206 D2
Meretone Cl, SE4 ....153 H4
Merevale Cres, Mord.
SM4 ....185 F6
Mereway Rd, Twick. TW2 .162 A1
Merewood Cl, Brom.
BR1 ....192 D2
Merewood Rd, Bexh.
DA7 ....159 J2
Mereworth Cl, Brom.
BR2 ....191 F5
Mereworth Dr, SE18 ..137 E7
Merganser Gdns, SE28
off Avocet Ms 137 G3
Meriden Cl, Brom. BR1 .174 A7
Ilford IG6 ....81 F1
Meridian Gate, E14 ...134 C2
Meridian Pl, E14 .....134 B2
Meridian Rd, SE7 ....136 A7
Meridian Sq, E15 ......96 D7
Meridian Trd Est, SE7 .135 H4
Meridian Wk, N17
off Commercial Rd ...60 B6
Meridian Way, N9 .....61 F5
N18 ....61 F6
Enfield EN3 ....45 G6
Merifield Rd, SE9 ....155 J4
Merino Cl, E11 ....79 J4
Merino Pl, Sid. DA15
off Blackfen Rd 158 A6
Merivale Rd, SW15 ...148 B4
Harrow HA1 ....67 J7
Merlewood Dr, Chis.
BR7 ....192 C1
Merley Ct, NW9 ....88 C1
Merlin Cl, Croy. CR0
off Minster Dr 202 B4
Mitcham CR4 ......185 H3
Northolt UB5 ....102 C3
Wallington SM6 .....201 F6
Merlin Cres, Edg. HA8 ...69 J1
Merlin Gdns, Brom. BR1 .173 G3
Merling Cl, Chess. KT9
off Coppard Gdns ...195 G5
Merlin Gro, Beck. BR3 .189 J4
Ilford IG6 ....65 E7
Merlin Ho, Enf. EN3
off Allington Ct 45 G5
Merlin Rd, E12 ....97 J2
Welling DA16 ......158 A4
Merlin Rd N, Well. DA16 .158 A4
Merlins Av, Har. HA2 ...85 F3
Merlin St, WC1 ....11 E4
Mermaid Ct, SE1 ......28 B3
SE16 ....133 J1
Mermaid Twr, SE8
off Abinger Gro 133 J6
Merredene St, SW2 ...151 F6
Merriam Cl, E4 ....62 C5
E9 ....95 J6
Merrick Rd, Sthl. UB2 ..123 F2
Merrick Sq, SE1 ......28 B6
Merridale, SE12 .....155 G5
Merridene, N21 ....43 H6
Merrielands Cres, Dag.
RM9 ....119 F1
Merrilands Rd, Wor.Pk.
KT4 ....197 J1
Merrilees Rd, Sid. DA15 .175 H1
Merrilyn Cl, Esher (Clay.)
KT10 ....194 D6
Merriman Rd, SE3 ....155 J1
Merrington Rd, SW6 ..128 D6
Merrion Av, Stan. HA7 ..53 G5
Merrion Wk, SE17
off Dawes St 132 A5
Merritt Gdns, Chess.
KT9 ....195 F6
Merritt Rd, SE4 ......153 J5
Merrivale, N14 ....42 D6
Merrivale Av, Ilf. IG4 ....80 A4
Merrow St, SE17 ......36 B5
Merrow Wk, SE17 .....36 C3

Merrow Way, Croy.
(New Adgtn.) CR0 ..204 C6
Merrydown Way, Chis.
BR7 ....192 B1
Merryfield, SE3 ......155 F2
Merryfield Gdns, Stan.
HA7 ....53 F5
Merryfield Ho, SE9
off Grove Pk Rd 173 J3
Merryfields Way, SE6 ..154 B7
MERRY HILL, Bushey ...51 G1
Merryhill Cl, E4 ....46 B7
Merry Hill Mt, Bushey
WD23 ....51 H1
Merry Hill Rd, Bushey
WD23 ....51 H1
Merryhills Ct, N14 .....42 C5
Merryhills Dr, Enf. EN2 ..42 D4
Mersea Ho, Bark. IG11 ..98 E6
Mersey Rd, E17 ......77 J3
Mersey Wk, Nthlt. UB5
off Brabazon Rd 103 G2
Mersham Dr, NW9 .....70 A5
Mersham Pl, SE20 ...189 E1
Mersham Rd, Th.Hth.
CR7 ....188 A3
Merten Rd, Rom. RM6 ...83 E7
Merthyr Ter, SW13 ...127 H6
MERTON, SW19 ......184 D1
Merton Av, W4 ....127 F4
Northolt UB5 ....85 J5
Merton Gdns, Orp. BR5 .193 E5
Merton Hall Gdns,
SW20 ....184 B1
Merton Hall Rd, SW19 .184 B1
Merton High St, SW19 .167 E7
Merton Ind Pk, SW19 .185 F1
Merton La, N6 ....91 J2
Merton Mans, SW20 ..184 A2
MERTON PARK, SW19 .184 D2
Merton Pk Par, SW19
off Kingston Rd 184 C1
Merton Ri, NW3 ....91 H7
Merton Rd, E17 ....78 C5
SE25 ....188 D5
SW18 ....148 D5
SW19 ....166 E7
Barking IG11 ....99 J7
Harrow HA2 ....85 J1
Ilford IG3 ....81 J7
Merton Way, W.Mol. KT8 .179 H4
Merttins Rd, SE15 ....153 G5
Meru Cl, NW5 ....92 A4
Mervan Rd, SW2 .....151 G4
Mervyn Av, SE9 ......175 F3
Mervyn Rd, W13 .....124 D3
Messaline Av, W3 ....106 C6
Messent Rd, SE9 .....155 J5
Messeter Pl, SE9 ....156 D6
Messina Av, NW6 .....90 D7
Metcalf Wk, Felt. TW13
off Gabriel Cl ...160/161 E4
Meteor St, SW11 .....150 A4
Meteor Way, Wall. SM6 .200 E7
Metheringham Way, NW9 .70 E1
Methley St, SE11 ......35 F4
★ Methodist Cen Hall,
SW1 ....25 J4
Methuen Cl, Edg. HA8 ...54 A7
Methuen Pk, N10 ......74 B2
Methuen Rd, Bexh. DA17 .139 H4
Bexleyheath DA6 ....159 F4
Edgware HA8 ....54 A7
Methwold Rd, W10 ...108 A5
Metro Cen, The, Islw.
TW7 ....144 B2
Metropolis Cen, Borwd.
WD6 ....38 A3
Metropolitan Cen, The, Grnf.
UB6 ....103 H1
Metropolitan Cl, E14
off Broomfield St ...114 A5
Mews, The, N1
off St. Paul St 111 J1
Ilford IG4 ....80 A5
Twickenham TW1
off Bridge Rd ..144/145 E6
Mews Deck, E1 ....113 E7
Mews Pl, Wdf.Grn. IG8 ..63 G4
Mews St, E1 ....29 H1
Mexfield Rd, SW15 ...148 C5
Meyer Rd, Erith DA8 ..139 J6
Meymott St, SE1 ......27 G2
Meynell Cres, E9 ......95 G7
Meynell Gdns, E9 .....95 G7
Meynell Rd, E9 ....95 G7
Meyrick Rd, NW10 .....89 G6
SW11 ....149 G3
Miah Ter, E1
off Wapping High St ..132 D1

Miall Wk, SE26 . . . . .171 H4
Micawber St, N1 . . . . .12 A3
Michael Faraday Ho,
  SE17 . . . . .36 C4
Michael Gaynor Cl, W7 . .124 C1
Michaelmas Cl, SW20 . . .183 J3
Michael Rd, E11 . . . . .97 E1
  SE25 . . . . .188 B3
  SW6 . . . . .149 E1
Michaels Cl, SE13 . . . . . .154 E4
Micheldever Rd, SE12 . . .155 E6
Michelham Gdns, Twick.
  TW1 . . . . .162 C3
Michels Row, Rich. TW9
  off Kew Foot Rd 145 H4
Michigan Av, E12 . . . . . . .98 B4
Michleham Down, N12 . . .56 C4
Mickleham Cl, Orp.
  BR5 . . . . .193 J2
Mickleham Gdns, Sutt.
  SM3 . . . . .198 B6
Mickleham Rd, Orp. BR5 .193 J1
Mickleham Way, Croy.
  (New Adgtn.) CR0 . . .204 D7
Micklethwaite Rd, SW6 .128 D6
Midas Metropolitan
  Ind Est, The, Mord. SM4
  off Garth Rd 198 A1
Middle Dene, NW7 . . . . . .54 D3
Middle Fld, NW8 . . . . . . .109 G1
Middlefielde, W13 . . . . . .104 E5
Middlefield Gdns, Ilf. IG2 .81 E6
Middle Grn Cl, Surb. KT5
  off Alpha Rd 181 J6
Middleham Gdns, N18 . . .60 D6
Middleham Rd, N18 . . . . .60 D6
Middle La, N8 . . . . .74 E5
  Teddington TW11 . . . .162 C6
Middle La Ms, N8
  off Middle La 74/75 E5
Middle Pk Av, SE9 . . . . .156 A6
Middle Path, Har. HA2
  off Middle Rd 86 A1
Middle Rd, E13
  off London Rd 115 G2
  SW16 . . . . .186 D2
  Barnet EN4 . . . . .41 H6
  Harrow HA2 . . . . .86 A2
Middle Row, W10 . . . . . .108 B4
Middlesborough Rd, N18 .60 D6
Middlesex Business Cen, Sthl.
  UB2 . . . . .123 G2
Middlesex Ct, W4
  off British Gro 127 F4
★ Middlesex Guildhall,
  SW1 . . . . .26 A4
Middlesex Ho, Wem.
  HA0 . . . . .105 G1
Middlesex Pas, EC1 . . . . .19 H2
Middlesex St, E1 . . . . . . .20 E2
Middlesex Wf, E5 . . . . . . .95 F2
Middle St, EC1 . . . . .19 J4
  Croydon CR0
  off Surrey St 201 J3
Middle Temple, EC4 . . . . .19 E5
Middle Temple La, EC4 . .18 E4
Middleton Av, E4 . . . . . . .61 J4
  Greenford UB6 . . . . . .104 A2
  Sidcup DA14 . . . . . . .176 C6
Middleton Cl, E4 . . . . . . .61 J3
Middleton Dr, SE16 . . . . .133 G2
  Pinner HA5 . . . . .66 A3
Middleton Gdns, Ilf. IG2 .80 E6
Middleton Gro, N7 . . . . . .92 E5
Middleton Ms, N7
  off Middleton Gro . .92/93 E5
Middleton Pl, W1 . . . . . . .17 F2
Middleton Rd, E8 . . . . . . .94 C7
  NW11 . . . . .72 D7
  Carshalton SM5 . . . . .185 H7
  Morden SM4 . . . . . . .185 F6
Middleton St, E2 . . . . . . .112 E3
Middleton Way, SE13 . . .154 D4
Middleway, NW11 . . . . . . .73 E5
Middle Way, SW16 . . . . .186 D2
  Erith DA18 . . . . .138 E3
  Hayes UB4 . . . . .102 C4
Middle Way, The, Har.
  HA3 . . . . .68 C2
Middle Yd, SE1 . . . . .28 C1
Midfield Av, Bexh. DA7 .159 J3
Midfield Par, Bexh. DA7 .159 J3
Midford Pl, W1 . . . . .9 G6
Midholm, NW11 . . . . .72 E4
  Wembley HA9 . . . . .88 A1
Midholm Cl, NW11 . . . . . .72 E4
Midholm Rd, Croy. CR0 .203 H2
Midhope St, WC1 . . . . . . .10 B4

Midhurst Av, N10 . . . . . . .74 A3
  Croydon CR0 . . . . . . .187 G7
Midhurst Hill, Bexh.
  DA6 . . . . .159 G6
Midhurst Rd, W13 . . . . . .124 D2
Midland Cres, NW3
  off Finchley Rd 91 F6
Midland Pl, E14
  off Ferry St 134 C5
Midland Rd, E10 . . . . .78 C7
  NW1 . . . . .9 J2
Midland Ter, NW2 . . . . . . .90 A3
  NW10 . . . . .107 E4
Midleton Rd, N.Mal.
  KT3 . . . . .182 C3
Midlothian Rd, E3 . . . . . .113 J5
Midmoor Rd, SW12 . . . . .168 C1
  SW19 . . . . .184 A1
Midship Cl, SE16
  off Surrey Water Rd . .133 G1
Midship Pt, E14 . . . . .134 A2
Midstrath Rd, NW10 . . . . .89 E4
Midsummer Av, Houns.
  TW4 . . . . .143 F4
Midway, Sutt. SM3 . . . . .184 C7
Midwinter Cl, Well. DA16
  off Hook La 158 A3
Midwood Cl, NW2 . . . . . . .89 H3
Miers Cl, E6 . . . . .116 D1
Mighell Av, Ilf. IG4 . . . . . .80 A5
Milan Rd, Sthl. UB1 . . . .123 F2
Milborne Gro, SW10 . . . . .30 D4
Milborne St, E9 . . . . .95 F6
Milborough Cres, SE12 . .155 E6
Milcote St, SE1 . . . . .27 G4
Mildenhall Rd, E5 . . . . . . .95 F4
Mildmay Av, N1 . . . . .94 A6
Mildmay Gro N, N1 . . . . . .94 A5
Mildmay Gro S, N1 . . . . . .94 A5
Mildmay Pk, N1 . . . . .94 A5
Mildmay Pl, N16
  off Boleyn Rd 94 B5
Mildmay Rd, N1 . . . . .94 A5
  Ilford IG1
  off Winston Way . . .98/99 E3
  Romford RM7 . . . . .83 J5
Mildmay St, N1 . . . . .94 A6
Mildred Av, Borwd. WD6 . .38 A4
  Hayes UB3 . . . . .121 G4
  Northolt UB5 . . . . .85 H5
MILE END, E1 . . . . .113 G3
Mile End Pl, E1 . . . . .113 G4
Mile End Rd, E1 . . . . . . .113 G4
Mile End, The, E17 . . . . . .77 G1
Mile Rd, Wall. SM6 . . . . .200 C1
Miles Dr, SE28 . . . . .137 G1
Milespit Hill, NW7 . . . . . . .55 H5
Miles Pl, NW1 . . . . .15 F1
  Surbiton KT5
  off Villiers Av 181 J4
Miles Rd, N8 . . . . .75 E3
  Mitcham CR4 . . . . . . .185 H3
Miles St, SW8 . . . . .34 A6
Milestone Cl, N9
  off Chichester Rd 60 D2
  Sutton SM2 . . . . .199 G6
Milestone Rd, SE19 . . . .170 C6
Miles Way, N20 . . . . .57 H2
Milfoil St, W12 . . . . .107 G7
Milford Cl, SE2 . . . . .139 E6
Milford Gdns, Croy. CR0
  off Tannery Cl 189 G5
  Edgware HA8 . . . . .54 A7
  Wembley HA0 . . . . .87 G5
Milford Gro, Sutt. SM1 . .199 F4
Milford La, WC2 . . . . .18 D5
Milford Ms, SW16 . . . . . .169 F3
Milford Rd, W13 . . . . . . .124 E1
  Southall UB1 . . . . . . .103 G7
Milk St, E16 . . . . .136 E1
  EC2 . . . . .20 A4
  Bromley BR1 . . . . . . .173 H6
Milkwell Gdns, Wdf.Grn.
  IG8 . . . . .63 H7
Milkwell Yd, SE5 . . . . . . .151 J1
Milkwood Rd, SE24 . . . . .151 H5
Milk Yd, E1 . . . . .113 F7
Millais Av, E12 . . . . .98 D5
Millais Gdns, Edg. HA8 . .70 A2
Millais Rd, E11 . . . . .96 C4
  Enfield EN1 . . . . .44 C5
  New Malden KT3 . . . . .182 E6
Millais Way, Epsom
  KT19 . . . . .196 C4
Milland Ct, Borwd. WD6 . .38 D1
Millard Cl, N16
  off Boleyn Rd 94 B5
Millard Ter, Dag. RM10
  off Church Elm La 101 G6

Millbank, SW1 . . . . .26 A6
Millbank Twr, SW1 . . . . . .34 A2
Millbank Way, SE12 . . . .155 G5
Millbourne Rd, Felt.
  TW13 . . . . .161 E4
Millbrook Av, Well.
  DA16 . . . . .157 G4
Millbrook Gdns, Rom.
  (Chad.Hth.) RM6 . . . . .83 F6
Millbrook Pl, NW1
  off Hampstead Rd 110 C2
Millbrook Rd, N9 . . . . . . .60 E1
  SW9 . . . . .151 H3
Mill Cl, Cars. SM5 . . . . . .200 A2
  West Drayton UB7 . . . .120 A3
Mill Cor, Barn. EN5 . . . . .40 C1
Mill Ct, E10 . . . . .96 C3
Millcroft Ho, SE6 . . . . . .172 C4
Millender Wk, SE16 . . . . .133 F4
Millennium Br, EC4 . . . . .111 J7
  SE1 . . . . .111 J7
Millennium Cl, E16
  off Russell Rd 115 G6
Millennium Dr, E14 . . . . .134 D4
Millennium Harbour,
  E14 . . . . .133 J2
Millennium Pl, E2 . . . . . .113 E2
Millennium Sq, SE1 . . . . .29 G3
Millennium Way, SE10 . .134 E2
Miller Cl, Mitch. CR4 . . . .185 J1
  Pinner HA5 . . . . .66 C2
Miller Rd, SW19 . . . . . . .167 G6
  Croydon CR0 . . . . . . .201 F1
Miller's Av, E8 . . . . .94 C5
Millers Cl, NW7 . . . . .55 G4
Millers Ct, W4
  off Chiswick Mall 127 F5
Millers Grn Cl, Enf. EN2 . .43 H3
Millers Meadow Cl, SE3
  off Meadowcourt Rd .155 F5
Miller's Ter, E8 . . . . .94 C5
Miller St, NW1 . . . . .9 F1
Millers Way, W6 . . . . . . .127 J2
Miller Wk, SE1 . . . . .27 F2
Millet Rd, Grnf. UB6 . . . .103 H3
Mill Fm Cl, Pnr. HA5 . . . . .66 C2
Mill Fm Cres, Houns.
  TW4 . . . . .161 E1
Millfield Av, E17 . . . . .77 H1
Millfield La, N6 . . . . .91 J2
Millfield Pl, N6 . . . . .92 A2
Millfield Rd, Edg. HA8 . . .70 C2
  Hounslow TW4 . . . . . .161 E1
Millfields Est, E5
  off Denton Way 95 G3
Millfields Rd, E5 . . . . .95 F4
Mill Gdns, SE26 . . . . . . .171 E4
Mill Grn, Mitch. CR4
  off London Rd 186 A7
Mill Grn Business Pk, Mitch.
  CR4 off Mill Grn Rd . .186 A7
Mill Grn Rd, Mitch.
  CR4 . . . . .185 J7
Millgrove St, SW11 . . . . .150 A2
Millharbour, E14 . . . . . . .134 B3
Millhaven Cl, Rom. RM6 . .82 B6
MILL HILL, NW7 . . . . .55 G5
Mill Hill, SW13
  off Mill Hill Rd 147 G2
Mill Hill Circ, NW7
  off Watford Way 55 F5
Mill Hill Gro, W3
  off Mill Hill Rd 126 B1
Mill Hill Rd, SW13 . . . . . .147 G2
  W3 . . . . .126 B2
Millhouse Pl, SE27 . . . . .169 H4
Millicent Rd, E10 . . . . . . .95 J1
Milligan St, E14 . . . . . . .113 J7
Milliners Ct, Loug. IG10
  off The Croft 48 D2
Milling Rd, Edg. HA8 . . . .54 D7
Millington Rd, Hayes
  UB3 . . . . .121 H3
Mill La, E4 . . . . .46 B3
  NW6 . . . . .90 C5
  SE18 . . . . .136 D5
  Carshalton SM5 . . . . .199 J4
  Croydon CR0 . . . . . . .201 F3
  Romford (Chad.Hth.)
  RM6 . . . . .82 E6
  Woodford Green IG8 . .63 F5
Mill La Trd Est, Croy.
  CR0 . . . . .201 F3
Millman Ms, WC1 . . . . . . .10 C6
Millman Pl, WC1
  off Millman St 111 F4
Millman St, WC1 . . . . . . .10 C6
Millmark Gro, SE14 . . . .153 H2
Millmarsh La, Enf. EN3 . .45 H2
Mill Mead Rd, N17 . . . . . .76 E4

Mill Pl,
  E14 off East India
  Dock Rd 113 J6
  Chislehurst BR7 . . . . .192 E1
  Kingston upon Thames
  KT1 . . . . .181 J3
Mill Plat, Islw. TW7 . . . .144 D2
Mill Plat Av, Islw. TW7 . .144 D2
Mill Pond Cl, SW8
  off Crimscott Rd 130 D7
Millpond Est, SE16
  off West La 132/133 E2
Mill Ridge, Edg. HA8 . . . .53 J5
Mill Rd, E16 . . . . .135 H1
  SW19 . . . . .167 F7
  Erith DA8 . . . . .139 J7
  Ilford IG1 . . . . .98 D3
  Twickenham TW2 . . . .161 J2
Mill Row, N1 . . . . .112 B1
Mills Ct, EC2 . . . . .12 E4
Mills Gro, E14
  off Dewberry St 114 C5
  NW4 . . . . .72 A3
Mill Shot Cl, SW6 . . . . . .127 J7
Millside, Cars. SM5 . . . . .199 J2
Millside Pl, Islw. TW7 . . .144 E2
Millsmead Way, Loug.
  IG10 . . . . .48 C2
Millson Cl, N20 . . . . .57 G2
Mills Row, W4 . . . . .126 D4
Millstream Cl, N13 . . . . . .59 G5
Millstream Rd, SE1 . . . . .29 F4
Mill St, SE1 . . . . .29 G4
  W1 . . . . .17 E5
  Kingston upon Thames
  KT1 . . . . .181 H3
Mill Vale, Brom. BR2 . . . .191 F2
Mill Vw Cl, Epsom (Ewell)
  KT17 . . . . .197 F7
Mill Vw Gdns, Croy. CR0 .203 G3
MILLWALL, E14 . . . . .134 B3
Millwall Dock Rd, E14 . . .134 A3
★ Millwall FC, SE16 . . . .133 F5
Millway, NW7 . . . . .54 E5
Mill Way, Felt. TW14 . . . .142 B5
Millway Gdns, Nthlt. UB5 .85 F6
Millwell Cres, Chig. IG7 . .65 G5
Millwood Rd, Houns.
  TW3 . . . . .143 J5
Millwood St, W10
  off St. Charles Sq 108 B5
Milman Cl, Pnr. HA5 . . . . .66 D3
Milman Rd, NW6 . . . . . . .108 B2
Milman's St, SW10 . . . . . .31 E6
Milmead Ind Cen, N17 . . .76 E2
Milne Ct, E18
  off Churchfields 79 G1
Milne Feild, Pnr. HA5 . . . .51 G7
Milne Gdns, SE9 . . . . . . .156 B5
Milner Dr, Twick. TW2 . . .144 A7
Milner Pl, N1 . . . . .111 G1
  Carshalton SM5
  off High St 200 A4
Milner Rd, E15 . . . . .114 E3
  SW19 . . . . .184 E1
  Dagenham RM8 . . . . .100 C2
  Kingston upon Thames
  KT1 . . . . .181 G3
  Morden SM4 . . . . . . .185 G5
  Thornton Heath CR7 . .188 A3
Milner Sq, N1 . . . . .93 H7
Milner St, SW3 . . . . .31 J1
Milner Wk, SE9 . . . . .175 G2
Milnthorpe Rd, W4 . . . . .126 D6
Milo Rd, SE22 . . . . .152 C6
Milroy Wk, SE1 . . . . .27 G1
Milson Rd, W14 . . . . .128 B3
Milton Av, E6 . . . . .98 A7
  N6 . . . . .74 C7
  NW9 . . . . .70 C3
  NW10 . . . . .106 C1
  Barnet EN5 . . . . .40 C5
  Croydon CR0 . . . . . . .188 A1
  Sutton SM1 . . . . .199 G3
Milton Cl, N2 . . . . .73 F7
  SE1 . . . . .37 F2
  Hayes UB4 . . . . .102 A6
  Sutton SM1 . . . . .199 G3
Milton Ct, EC2 . . . . .20 B1
  Romford (Chad.Hth.) RM6
  off Cross Rd 82 C7
Milton Ct Rd, SE14 . . . . .133 H6
Milton Cres, Ilf. IG2 . . . . .81 F7
Milton Dr, Borwd. WD6 . . .38 B5
Milton Gdn Est, N16
  off Milton Gro 94 B4
Milton Gro, N11 . . . . .58 C5
  N16 . . . . .94 A4
Milton Pk, N6 . . . . .74 C7

Milton PI, N7
off George's Rd 93 G5
Milton Rd, E17 . . . . .78 A4
N6 . . . . .74 C7
N15 . . . . .75 H4
NW7 . . . . .55 G5
NW9
off West Hendon Bdy . .71 G7
SE24 . . . . .151 H6
SW14 . . . . .146 D3
SW19 . . . . .167 F6
W3 . . . . .126 D1
W7 . . . . .104 C7
Belvedere DA17 . . . . . .139 G4
Croydon CR0 . . . . .202 A1
Hampton TW12 . . . . . .161 G7
Harrow HA1 . . . . .68 B4
Mitcham CR4 . . . . .168 A7
Sutton SM1 . . . . .198 D3
Wallington SM6 . . . . . .200 C6
Welling DA16 . . . . .157 J1
Milton St, EC2 . . . . .20 B1
Milton Way, West Dr.
UB7 . . . . .120 C4
Milverton Gdns, Ilf. IG3 . .99 J2
Milverton Ho, SE23 . . . .171 H3
Milverton Rd, NW6 . . . . .89 J7
Milverton St, SE11 . . . . . .35 F4
Milverton Way, SE9 . . . .174 D4
Milward St, E1
off Stepney Way .112/113 E5
Milward Wk, SE18
off Spearman St 136 D6
Mimosa Rd, Hayes
UB4 . . . . .102 C5
Mimosa St, SW6 . . . . . .148 C1
Minard Rd, SE6 . . . . . . .154 E7
Mina Rd, SE17 . . . . .36 E4
SW19 . . . . .184 D1
Minchenden Cres, N14 . .58 C3
Mincing La, EC3 . . . . .20 D5
Minden Rd, SE20 . . . . . .188 E1
Sutton SM3 . . . . .198 C2
Minehead Rd, SW16 . . . .169 F5
Harrow HA2 . . . . .85 G3
Mineral St, SE18 . . . . . .137 H4
Minera Ms, SW1 . . . . .32 C1
Minerva CI, SW9 . . . . . .131 G7
Sidcup DA14 . . . . .175 H3
Minerva Rd, E4 . . . . .62 B7
NW10 . . . . .106 C4
Kingston upon Thames
KT1 . . . . .181 J2
Minerva St, E2 . . . . .112 E2
Minet Av, NW10 . . . . . . .106 E2
Minet Dr, Hayes UB3 . . .122 A1
Minet Gdns, NW10 . . . . .106 E2
Hayes UB3 . . . . .122 A1
Minet Rd, SW9 . . . . .151 H2
Minford Gdns, W14 . . . .128 A2
Mingard Wk, N7
off Hornsey Rd 93 F2
Ming St, E14 . . . . .114 A7
★ Ministry of Defence,
SW1 . . . . .26 A2
Ministry Way, SE9 . . . . .174 C2
Miniver PI, EC4
off Garlick Hill 111 J7
Mink Ct, Houns. TW4 . . .142 C3
Minniedale, Surb. KT5 . .181 J5
Minnow St, SE17
off East St 132 B4
Minnow Wk, SE17 . . . . . .36 E2
Minories, EC3 . . . . .21 F5
Minshull PI, Beck. BR3 . .172 A7
Minshull St, SW8
off Wandsworth Rd . .150 D1
Minson Rd, E9 . . . . .113 G1
Minstead Gdns, SW15 . .147 F7
Minstead Way, N.Mal.
KT3 . . . . .182 E6
Minster Av, Sutt. SM1
off Leafield Rd 198 D2
Minster Ct, EC3
off Mincing La 112 A7
Minster Dr, Croy. CR0 . .202 B4
Minster Gdns, W.Mol. KT8
off Molesey Av 179 F5
Minster Pavement, EC3
off Mincing La 112 A7
Minster Rd, NW2 . . . . . . .90 B5
Bromley BR1 . . . . .173 H7
Minster Wk, N8
off Lightfoot Rd 74/75 E4
Minstrel Gdns, Surb.
KT5 . . . . .181 J4
Mint Business Pk, E16 . .115 G5
Mintern CI, N13 . . . . .59 H3
Minterne Av, Sthl. UB2 . .123 G4
Minterne Rd, Har. HA3 . . .69 J5

Minterne Waye, Hayes
UB4 . . . . .102 C6
Mintern St, N1 . . . . .12 C1
Minton Ms, NW6
off Lymington Rd . .90/91 E6
Mint Rd, Wall. SM6 . . . . .200 B4
Mint St, SE1 . . . . .27 J3
Mint Wk, Croy. CR0
off High St 201 J3
Mirabel Rd, SW6 . . . . . .128 C7
Miranda CI, E1
off Sidney St 113 F5
Miranda Ct, W3
off Queens Dr 105 J6
Miranda Rd, N19 . . . . . . .92 C1
Mirfield St, SE7 . . . . . . .136 A4
Miriam Rd, SE18 . . . . . .137 H5
Mirravale Trd Est, Dag.
RM8 . . . . .83 F7
Mirren CI, Har. HA2 . . . . .85 F4
Mirror Path, SE9
off Lambscroft Av 173 J3
Missenden Gdns, Mord.
SM4 . . . . .185 F6
Mission Gro, E17 . . . . . . .77 H5
Mission PI, SE15 . . . . . .152 D1
Mission Sq, Brent. TW8 .125 H6
Mistletoe CI, Croy. CR0
off Marigold Way 203 G1
Mitali Pas, E1 . . . . .21 H4
MITCHAM 186 A3
Mitcham Gdn Village, Mitch.
CR4 . . . . .186 A5
Mitcham Ind Est, Mitch.
CR4 . . . . .186 A1
Mitcham La, SW16 . . . . .168 C6
Mitcham Pk, Mitch. CR4 .185 J4
Mitcham Rd, E6 . . . . . . .116 B3
SW17 . . . . .167 J5
Croydon CR0 . . . . .186 E6
Ilford IG3 . . . . .81 J7
Mitchellbrook Way,
NW10 . . . . .88 D6
Mitchell CI, SE2 . . . . . . .138 C4
Belvedere DA17 . . . . . .139 J3
Mitchell Rd, N13 . . . . . . .59 H5
Orpington BR6 . . . . . .207 J4
Mitchell's PI, SE21
off Dulwich Village . . .152 B7
Mitchell St, EC1 . . . . .11 J5
Mitchell Wk, E6 . . . . . . .116 B5
Mitchell Way, NW10 . . . . .88 C6
Bromley BR1 . . . . .191 G1
Mitchison Rd, N1 . . . . . . .94 A6
Mitchley Rd, N17 . . . . . . .76 D3
Mitford CI, Chess. KT9
off Merritt Gdns 195 F6
Mitford Rd, N19 . . . . .93 E2
Mitre, The, E14
off Three Colt St 113 J7
Mitre Av, E17
off Greenleaf Rd 77 J3
Mitre CI, Brom. BR2
off Beckenham La . . .191 F2
Sutton SM2 . . . . .199 F7
Mitre Ct, EC2 . . . . .20 A3
EC4 . . . . .19 F4
Mitre Rd, E15 . . . . .114 E2
SE1 . . . . .27 F3
Mitre Sq, EC3 . . . . .21 E4
Mitre St, EC3 . . . . .21 E4
Mitre Way, W10 . . . . . . .107 H4
Moat, The, N.Mal. KT3 . .182 E1
Moat CI, Orp. BR6 . . . . . .207 J6
Moat Cres, N3 . . . . .72 E3
Moat Cft, Well. DA16 . . . .158 C3
Moat Dr, E13
off Boundary Rd 115 J2
Harrow HA1 . . . . .67 J4
Moat Fm Rd, Nthlt. UB5 . .85 F6
Moat PI, SW9 . . . . .151 F3
W3 . . . . .106 B6
Moatside, Enf. EN3 . . . . .45 G4
Feltham TW13 . . . . . . .160 C4
Moberley Rd, SW4 . . . . .150 D7
Modbury Gdns, NW5
off Queen's Cres 92 A6
Modder PI, SW15 . . . . . .148 A4
Model Cotts, SW14
off Upper Richmond
Rd W 146 C4
Model Fm CI, SE9 . . . . . .174 B3
Modling Ho, E2 . . . . .113 G2
Moelwyn Hughes Ct, N7
off Hilldrop Cres 92 D5
Moelyn Ms, Har. HA1 . . . .68 D5
Moffat Rd, N13 . . . . .59 E6
SW17 . . . . .167 H4
Thornton Heath CR7 . .187 J2
Mogden La, Islw. TW7 . .144 B5

Mohmmad Khan Rd, E11
off Harvey Rd 97 F1
Moira CI, N17 . . . . .76 B2
Moira Rd, SE9 . . . . .156 C4
Moland Mead, SE16
off Crane Mead 133 G3
Molasses Row, SW11
off Cinnamon Row . . .149 F3
Mole Abbey Gdns, W.Mol.
KT8 off New Rd 179 G3
Mole Ct, Epsom KT19 . .196 C4
Molember Ct, E.Mol.
KT8 . . . . .180 B5
Molember Rd, E.Mol.
KT8 . . . . .180 B5
Molescroft, SE9 . . . . . . .175 F3
Molesey Av, W.Mol. KT8 .179 F4
Molesey Dr, Sutt. SM3 . .198 B2
Molesey Pk Av, W.Mol.
KT8 . . . . .179 H5
Molesey Pk CI, E.Mol.
KT8 . . . . .179 J5
Molesey Pk Rd, E.Mol.
KT8 . . . . .180 A5
West Molesey KT8 . . . .179 H5
Molesey Rd, W.Mol. KT8 .179 E5
Molesford Rd, SW6 . . . .148 D1
Molesham CI, W.Mol.
KT8 . . . . .179 H3
Molesham Way, W.Mol.
KT8 . . . . .179 H3
Molesworth St, SE13 . . .154 C3
Mollison Av, Enf. EN3 . . .45 H5
Mollison Dr, Wall. SM6 . .201 E6
Mollison Way, Edg. HA8 . .70 A2
Molly Huggins CI, SW12 .150 C7
Molyneux Dr, SW17 . . . .168 B4
Molyneux St, W1 . . . . . . .15 H2
Monarch CI, Felt. TW14 .141 H7
West Wickham BR4 . . .205 F4
Monarch Dr, E16 . . . . . . .116 A5
Monarch Ms, E17 . . . . . . .78 B5
SW16 . . . . .169 G5
Monarch Par, Mitch. CR4
off London Rd 185 J2
Monarch PI, Buck.H. IG9 . .63 J2
Monarch Rd, Belv. DA17 .139 G3
Monarchs Ct, NW7
off Grenville PI 54 D5
Mona Rd, SE15 . . . . . . .153 F2
Monastery Gdns, Enf.
EN2 . . . . .44 A2
Mona St, E16 . . . . .115 F5
Monaveen Gdns, W.Mol.
KT8 . . . . .179 G3
Monck St, SW1 . . . . .25 J6
Monclar Rd, SE5 . . . . . . .152 A4
Moncorvo CI, SW7 . . . . . .23 G4
Moncrieff CI, E6
off Linton Gdns 116 B6
Moncrieff PI, SE15
off Rye La 152 D2
Moncrieff St, SE15 . . . . .152 D2
Mondial Way, Hayes
UB3 . . . . .121 F7
Monega Rd, E7 . . . . .97 J6
Monier Rd, E3 . . . . .96 A7
Monivea Rd, Beck. BR3 . .171 J7
Monkchester CI, Loug.
IG10 . . . . .48 D1
Monk Dr, E16 . . . . .115 G6
MONKEN HADLEY, Barn. .40 C1
Monkfrith Av, N14 . . . . . .42 B6
Monkfrith CI, N14 . . . . . .42 B7
Monkfrith Way, N14 . . . . .42 A7
Monkhams Av, Wdf.Grn.
IG8 . . . . .63 G5
Monkhams Dr, Wdf.Grn.
IG8 . . . . .63 H4
Monkhams La, Buck.H.
IG9 . . . . .63 G4
Woodford Green IG8 . . .63 G5
Monkleigh Rd, Mord.
SM4 . . . . .184 B3
Monk Pas, E16
off Monk Dr 115 G7
Monks Av, Barn. EN5 . . . .41 F6
West Molesey KT8 . . . .179 F5
Monks CI, SE2 . . . . .138 D4
Enfield EN2 . . . . .43 J2
Harrow HA2 . . . . .85 H2
Ruislip HA4 . . . . .84 D4
Monksdene Gdns, Sutt.
SM1 . . . . .199 E3
Monks Dr, W3 . . . . .106 A5
Monksgrove, Loug. IG10 . .48 D5
Monksmead, Borwd.
WD6 . . . . .38 C4

Monks Orchard,
Croy. 189 J7
Monks Orchard Rd, Beck.
BR3 . . . . .204 A1
Monks Pk, Wem. HA9 . . . .88 C6
Monks Pk Gdns, Wem.
HA9 . . . . .88 B6
Monk's Ridge, N20 . . . . . .55 H1
Monks Rd, Enf. EN2 . . . . .43 J2
Monk St, SE18 . . . . .136 D4
Monks Way, NW11
off Hurstwood Rd 72 C4
Beckenham BR3 . . . . .190 A5
Orpington BR5 . . . . . .207 F1
West Drayton UB7
off Harmondsworth
La 120 B6
Monkswell Ct, N10
off Pembroke Rd 74 A1
Monkswood Gdns, Borwd.
WD6 . . . . .38 D4
Ilford IG5 . . . . .80 D3
Monkton Rd, Well. DA16 .157 J2
Monkton St, SE11 . . . . . .35 F1
Monkville Av, NW11 . . . . .72 C4
Monkwell Sq, EC2 . . . . . .20 A2
Monmouth Av, E18 . . . . . .79 H4
Kingston upon Thames
KT1 . . . . .163 F7
Monmouth CI, W4
off Beaumont Rd 126 D3
Mitcham CR4
off Recreation
Way 186/187 E4
Welling DA16 . . . . .158 A4
Monmouth Gro, Brent. TW8
off Sterling PI 125 H4
Monmouth PI, W2
off Monmouth Rd 108 D6
Monmouth Rd, E6 . . . . . .116 C3
N9 . . . . .60 E2
W2 . . . . .108 D6
Dagenham RM9 . . . . .101 F5
Hayes UB3 . . . . .121 H4
Monmouth St, WC2 . . . . .18 A4
Monnery Rd, N19 . . . . . . .92 C3
Monnow Rd, SE1 . . . . . . .37 H3
Mono La, Felt. TW13 . . . .160 B2
Monoux Gro, E17 . . . . . . .78 A1
Monroe Cres, Enf. EN1 . . .44 E1
Monroe Dr, SW14 . . . . . .146 B5
Monro Gdns, Har. HA3 . . .52 B7
Monro Way, E5
off Downs Rd 94 D3
Monsal Ct, E5
off Redwald Rd 95 G4
Monsell Ct, N4
off Monsell Rd 93 H3
Monsell Rd, N4 . . . . .93 H3
Monson Rd, NW10 . . . . .107 G2
SE14 . . . . .133 G7
Mons Way, Brom. BR2 . .192 B6
Montacute Rd, SE6 . . . . .153 J7
Morden SM4 . . . . .185 G6
Montagu Cres, N18 . . . . .61 E4
Montague Av, SE4 . . . . . .153 J4
W7 . . . . .124 C1
Montague CI, SE1 . . . . . .28 B1
Walton-on-Thames
KT12 . . . . .178 A7
Montague Gdns, W3 . . . .106 A7
Montague PI, WC1 . . . . . .17 J1
Montague Rd, E8 . . . . . . .94 D5
E11 . . . . .97 F2
N8 . . . . .75 F5
N15 . . . . .76 D4
SW19 . . . . .166 E7
W7 . . . . .124 C1
W13 . . . . .105 E6
Croydon CR0 . . . . .201 H1
Hounslow TW3 . . . . . .143 H3
Richmond TW10 . . . . .145 H6
Southall UB2 . . . . .122 E4
Montague Sq, SE15
off Clifton Way 133 F7
Montague St, EC1 . . . . . .19 J2
WC1 . . . . .18 A1
Montague Waye, Sthl.
UB2 . . . . .122 E3
Montagu Gdns, N18 . . . . .61 E4
Wallington SM6 . . . . . .200 C4
Montagu Mans, W1 . . . . .16 A1
Montagu Ms N, W1 . . . . .16 A2
Montagu Ms S, W1 . . . . .16 A3
Montagu Ms W, W1 . . . . .16 A3
Montagu PI, W1 . . . . .15 J2
Montagu Rd, N9 . . . . .61 F4
N18 . . . . .61 E5
NW4 . . . . .71 G6
Montagu Rd Ind Est, N18 .61 F4

Montagu Row, W1 ......16 A2
Montagu Sq, W1 ....16 A3
Montagu St, W1 ....16 A3
Montalt Rd, Wdf.Grn. IG8 .63 F5
Montana Gdns, SE26 ...171 J5
  Sutton SM1
    off Lind Rd 199 F5
Montana Rd, SW17 ....168 A4
  SW20 ....183 J1
Montbelle Rd, SE9 ....174 E3
Montcalm Cl, Brom.
  BR2 ....191 G6
  Hayes UB4
    off Ayles Rd 102 B3
Montcalm Rd, SE7 ....136 A7
Montclare St, E2 ....13 F4
Monteagle Av, Bark. IG11 .99 F6
Monteagle Way, E5
  off Rendlesham Rd ...94 D3
  SE15 ....153 E3
Montefiore St, SW8 ...150 B2
Montego Cl, SE24
  off Railton Rd 151 G4
Montem Rd, SE23 .....153 J7
  New Malden KT3 ....182 E4
Montem St, N4
  off Thorpedale Rd 93 F1
Montenotte Rd, N8 ....74 C5
Monterey Cl, Bex. DA5 ..177 J2
Montesole Ct, Pnr. HA5 ..66 C2
Montevetro, SW11 ....149 G1
Montford Pl, SE11 .....34 E4
Montford Rd, Sun. TW16 .178 A4
Montfort Gdns, Ilf. IG6 ..65 F6
Montfort Pl, SW19 ....166 A1
Montgolfier Wk, Nthlt. UB5
  off Jetstar Way ..102/103 E3
Montgomery Av, Esher
  KT10 ....194 B3
Montgomery Cl, Mitch.
  CR4 ....187 E4
  Sidcup DA15 ....157 J6
Montgomery Rd, W4 ...126 C4
  Edgware HA8 ....53 J6
Montgomery St, E14 ...134 B1
Montholme Rd, SW11 .149 J6
Monthope Rd, E1 ......21 H2
Montolieu Gdns, SW15 .147 H5
Montpelier Av, W5 ....105 F5
  Bexley DA5 ....158 D7
Montpelier Gdns, E6 ...116 A3
  Romford RM6 ....82 C7
Montpelier Gro, NW5 ...92 C5
Montpelier Ms, SW7 ....23 H5
Montpelier Pl, E1 ......113 F6
  SW7 ....23 H5
Montpelier Ri, NW11 ...72 B7
  Wembley HA9 ....87 G1
Montpelier Rd, N3 .....73 E1
  SE15 ....153 E1
  W5 ....105 G5
  Sutton SM1 ....199 F4
Montpelier Row, SE3 ..155 F2
  Twickenham TW1 ....145 E7
Montpelier Sq, SW7 ....23 H4
Montpelier St, SW7 ....23 H4
Montpelier Ter, SW7 ...23 H4
Montpelier Vale, SE3 ..155 F2
Montpelier Wk, SW7 ...23 H5
Montpelier Way, NW11 .72 B7
Montrave Rd, SE20 ...171 F6
Montreal Pl, WC2 ......18 C5
Montreal Rd, Ilf. IG1 ...81 F7
Montrell Rd, SW2 .....169 E1
Montrose Av, NW6 ....108 B2
  Edgware HA8 ....70 C2
  Sidcup DA15 ....158 A7
  Twickenham TW2 ....143 H7
  Welling DA16 ....157 J4
Montrose Cl, Well. DA16 .157 J3
  Woodford Green IG8 ..63 G4
Montrose Ct, SW7 .....23 F4
Montrose Cres, N12 ....57 F6
  Wembley HA0 ....87 H6
Montrose Gdns, Mitch.
  CR4 ....185 J3
  Sutton SM1 ....199 E2
Montrose Pl, SW1 ......24 C4
Montrose Rd, Felt. TW14 .141 G6
  Harrow HA3 ....68 B2
Montrose Way, SE23 ...171 G1
Montserrat Av, Wdf.Grn.
  IG8 ....62 D7
Montserrat Cl, SE19 ..170 A5
Montserrat Rd, SW15 .148 B4
★ Monument, The, EC3 .20 C6
Monument Gdns, SE13 .154 C5
Monument St, EC3 .....20 C5
Monument Way, N17 ...76 C3
Monza St, E1 ....113 F7

Moodkee St, SE16 .....133 F3
Moody Rd, SE15 ......132 C7
Moody St, E1 ....113 G3
Moon La, Barn. EN5 ...40 C3
Moon St, N1 ....111 H1
Moorcroft Gdns, Brom. BR2
  off Southborough Rd .192 B5
Moorcroft Rd, SW16 ..168 E3
Moorcroft Way, Pnr. HA5 .66 E5
Moordown, SE18 ......156 D1
Moore Cl, SW14
  off Little St. Leonards .146 C3
  Mitcham CR4 ....186 B2
Moore Cres, Dag. RM9 .118 B1
Moorefield Rd, N17 ....76 C2
Moorehead Way, SE3 ..155 H3
Mooreland Rd, Brom.
  BR1 ....173 F7
Moore Pk Rd, SW6 ...128 E7
Moore Rd, SE19 ......169 J6
Moore St, SW3 ....31 J1
Moore Wk, E7
  off Stracey Rd 97 G4
Moore Way, SE22
  off Lordship La 170 D1
Moorey Cl, E15
  off Stephen's Rd 115 F1
Moorfield Av, W5 .....105 G4
Moorfield Rd, Chess.
  KT9 ....195 H5
  Enfield EN3 ....45 F1
Moorfields, EC2 ....20 B2
Moorfields Highwalk, EC2
  off Fore St 112 A5
Moorgate, EC2 ....20 B3
Moorgate Pl, EC2 .....20 B3
Moorhouse Rd, W2 ...108 D6
  Harrow HA3 ....69 G3
Moorings, SE28 ....118 B7
Moorland Cl, Twick. TW2
  off Telford Rd 143 G7
Moorland Rd, SW9 ...151 H4
Moorlands Av, NW7 ...55 H6
Moorlands Est, SW9 ..151 G4
Moor La, EC2 ....20 B2
  Chessington KT9 ....195 H4
Moormead Dr, Epsom
  KT19 ....197 E5
Moor Mead Rd, Twick.
  TW1 ....144 D6
Moor Pk Gdns, Kings.T.
  KT2 ....165 E7
Moor Pl, EC2 ....20 B2
Moorside Rd, Brom.
  BR1 ....173 E3
Moor St, W1 ....17 J4
Moortown Rd, Wat.
  WD19 ....50 C4
Moot Ct, NW9 ....70 A5
Morant Pl, N22
  off Commerce Rd 75 F1
Morant St, E14 ....114 A7
Mora Rd, NW2 ....89 J4
Mora St, EC1 ....12 A4
Morat St, SW9 ....151 F1
Moravian Pl, SW10 ...31 F6
Moravian St, E2 ......113 F3
Moray Av, Hayes UB3 .121 J1
Moray Cl, Edg. HA8
  off Pentland Av 54 B2
Moray Ms, N7
  off Durham Rd 93 F2
Moray Rd, N4 ....93 F2
Mordaunt Gdns, Dag.
  RM9 ....100 E7
Mordaunt Ho, NW10 ..106 D1
Mordaunt Rd, NW10 ..106 D1
Mordaunt St, SW9 ...151 F3
MORDEN 184 D3
Morden Cl, SE13 .....154 C2
Morden Ct, Mord. SM4 .184 E4
Morden Gdns, Grnf. UB6 .86 C5
  Mitcham CR4 ....185 G4
★ Morden Hall Park NT,
  Mord. SM4 ....185 E3
Morden Hall Rd, Mord.
  SM4 ....185 E3
Morden Hill, SE13 ....154 C2
Morden La, SE13 .....154 C1
MORDEN PARK, Mord. .184 B5
Morden Rd, SE3 ......155 G2
  SW19 ....185 E1
  Mitcham CR4 ....185 F4
  Romford RM6 ....83 E7
Morden Rd Ms, SE3 ...155 G2
Morden St, SE13 .....154 B1
Morden Way, Sutt. SM3 .184 D7
Morden Wf Rd, SE10 ..134 E3
Mordon Rd, Ilf. IG3 ...81 J7
Mordred Rd, SE6 ....172 E2

Morecambe Cl, E1 ....113 G5
Morecambe Gdns, Stan.
  HA7 ....53 G4
Morecambe St, SE17 ..36 A2
Morecambe Ter, N18 ..60 A4
More Cl, E16 ....115 F6
  W14 ....128 B4
Morecoombe Cl, Kings.T.
  KT2 ....164 B7
Moree Way, N18 ......60 D4
Moreland St, EC1 .....11 H3
Moreland Way, E4 .....62 B3
Morella Rd, SW12 ...149 J7
Morell Cl, Barn. EN5
  off Galdana Av 41 F3
Moremead Rd, SE6 ...171 J4
Morena St, SE6 ......154 B7
Moresby Av, Surb. KT5 .182 B7
Moresby Rd, E5 ....94 E1
Moresby Wk, SW8 ...150 C2
Moreton Av, Islw. TW7 .144 B1
Moreton Cl, E5 ....95 F2
  N15 ....76 A6
  NW7 ....55 J6
  SW1 ....33 G3
Moreton Gdns, Wdf.Grn.
  IG8 ....64 B5
Moreton Pl, SW1 ......33 G3
Moreton Rd, N15 ......76 A6
  South Croydon CR2 .202 A5
  Worcester Park KT4 .197 G2
Moreton St, SW1 ......33 G3
Moreton Ter, SW1 .....33 G3
Moreton Ter Ms N, SW1 .33 G3
Moreton Ter Ms S, SW1 .33 G3
Moreton Twr, W3 .....126 B1
Morford Cl, Ruis. HA4 ..66 B7
Morford Way, Ruis. HA4 .66 B7
Morgan Av, E17 ....78 D4
Morgan Rd, N7 ....93 G5
  W10 ....108 C5
  Bromley BR1 ....173 G7
Morgans La, SE1 ......28 D2
Morgan St, E3 ....113 H3
  E16 ....115 F5
Morgan Way, Wdf.Grn.
  IG8 ....64 B6
Moriatry Cl, N7 ....92 E4
Morie St, SW18 ......149 E5
Morieux Rd, E10 ......95 J1
Moring Rd, SW17 ....168 A4
Morkyns Wk, SE21 ...170 B3
Morland Av, Croy. CR0 .202 B1
Morland Cl, NW11 ....91 E1
  Hampton TW12 .....161 F5
  Mitcham CR4 ....185 H3
Morland Gdns, NW10 ..88 D7
  Southall UB1 ....123 H1
Morland Ms, N1
  off Lofting Rd 93 G2
Morland Rd, E17 ......77 G5
  SE20 ....171 G6
  Croydon CR0 ....202 B1
  Dagenham RM10 ....101 G2
  Harrow HA3 ....69 H5
  Ilford IG1 ....98 E2
  Sutton SM1 ....199 F5
Morley Av, E4 ....62 D7
  N18 ....60 D4
  N22 ....75 G2
Morley Cl, Orp. BR6 ...207 E2
Morley Cres, Edg. HA8 ..54 C2
  Ruislip HA4 ....84 C2
Morley Cres E, Stan. HA7 .69 F2
Morley Cres W, Stan. HA7 .69 F2
Morley Rd, E10 ....96 C1
  E15 ....115 F2
  SE13 ....154 C4
  Barking IG11 ....117 G1
  Chislehurst BR7 .....193 F1
  Romford RM6 ....82 E5
  Sutton SM3 ....198 C1
  Twickenham TW1 ....145 G6
Morley St, SE1 ....27 F5
Morna Rd, SE5 ....151 J2
Morning La, E9 ....95 F6
Morningside Rd, Wor.Pk.
  KT4 ....197 H2
Mornington Av, W14 ..128 C4
  Bromley BR1 ....191 J3
  Ilford IG1 ....80 D7
Mornington Cl, Wdf.Grn.
  IG8 ....63 G4
Mornington Ct, Bex.
  DA5 ....177 J1
Mornington Cres, NW1 ..9 F1
  Hounslow TW5 ......142 B1
Mornington Gro, E3 ..114 A3
Mornington Ms, SE5 ..151 J1

Mornington Pl, NW1 ....9 F1
Mornington Rd, E4 .....46 D7
  E11 ....97 F1
  SE8 ....133 J7
  Greenford UB6 .....103 H5
  Loughton IG10 ....49 F3
  Woodford Green IG8 ..63 F4
Mornington St, NW1 ....8 E1
Mornington Ter, NW1 ..110 B1
Mornington Wk, Rich.
  TW10 ....163 G4
Morocco St, SE1 ......28 D4
Morpeth Gro, E9 .....113 G1
Morpeth Rd, E9 ......113 F1
Morpeth St, E2 ....113 G3
Morpeth Ter, SW1 .....25 F6
Morpeth Wk, N17
  off West Rd 60/61 E7
Morrab Gdns, Ilf. IG3 ..99 J3
Morris Av, E12 ....98 C5
Morris Cl, Croy. CR0 ..189 H6
  Orpington BR6 ......207 H3
Morris Ct, E4
  off Flaxen Rd 62 B3
Morris Gdns, SW18 ...148 D7
Morrish Rd, SW2 .....151 E7
Morrison Av, N17 .....76 B3
Morrison Rd, Bark. IG11 .118 E2
  Hayes UB4 ....102 B3
Morrison St, SW11 ...150 A3
Morris Pl, N4 ....93 G2
Morris Rd, E14 ......114 B5
  E15 ....96 E4
  Dagenham RM8 ....101 F2
  Isleworth TW7 ......144 C3
Morris St, E1 ....113 E6
Morriston Cl, Wat. WD19 .50 C5
Morse Cl, E13 ....115 G3
Morshead Rd, W9 .....108 D3
Morson Rd, Enf. EN3 ..45 H6
Morston Gdns, SE9 ...174 C4
Morten Cl, SW4 ......150 D6
Morteyne Rd, N17 .....76 A1
Mortgramit Sq, SE18
  off Powis St 136 D3
Mortham St, E15 .....114 D1
Mortimer Cl, NW2 .....90 C3
  SW16 ....168 D2
Mortimer Cres, NW6 ..108 E1
  Worcester Park KT4 .196 E3
Mortimer Dr, Enf. EN1 ..44 A5
Mortimer Est, NW6 ...108 E1
Mortimer Ho, W11
  off St. Anns Rd 128 A1
Mortimer Mkt, WC1 ....9 G6
Mortimer Pl, NW6 ....108 E1
Mortimer Rd, E6 .....116 C3
  N1 ....94 B7
  NW10 ....107 J3
  W13 ....105 F6
  Mitcham CR4 ....185 J1
Mortimer Sq, W11
  off St. Anns Rd 108 A7
Mortimer St, W1 ......17 F2
Mortimer Ter, NW5
  off Gordon Ho Rd 92 B4
MORTLAKE, SW14 ...146 C3
Mortlake Cl, Croy. CR0
  off Richmond Rd .200/201 E3
Mortlake Dr, Mitch. CR4 .185 H1
Mortlake High St, SW14 .146 D3
Mortlake Rd, E16 ....115 H6
  Ilford IG1 ....99 F4
  Richmond TW9 .....126 A7
Mortlake Ter, Rich. TW9
  off Kew Rd 126 A7
Mortlock Cl, SE15
  off Cossall Wk ..152/153 E1
Morton, Wall. SM6
  off Lancastrian Rd ..201 F7
Morton Cr, Nthlt. UB5 ..85 J5
Morton Cres, N14 .....58 D4
Morton Gdns, Wall.
  SM6 ....200 C5
Morton Ms, SW5 ......30 A2
Morton Pl, SE1 ....26 E6
Morton Rd, E15 ....97 F7
  N1 ....93 J7
  Morden SM4 ....185 G5
Morton Way, N14 .....58 C2
Morvale Cl, Belv. DA17 .139 F4
Morval Rd, SW2 .....151 G5
Morven Rd, SW17 ....167 J3
Morville Ho, SW18
  off Fitzhugh Gro ...149 G6
Morville St, E3 ....114 A2
Morwell St, WC1 ......17 J2
Moscow Pl, W2 ....14 A5
Moscow Rd, W2 ....14 A5
Moseley Row, SE10 ..135 F4

Moselle Av, N22 . . . . .75 G2
Moselle Cl, N8
  off Miles Rd 75 F3
Moselle Ho, N17
  off William St 60 C7
Moselle Pl, N17
  off High Rd 60 C7
Moselle St, N17 . . . . .60 C7
Mossborough Cl, N12 . . .57 E6
Mossbury Rd, SW11 . . . .149 H3
Moss Cl, E1 . . . . .21 J1
  Pinner HA5 . . . . .67 F2
Mossdown Cl, Belv.
  DA17 . . . . .139 G4
Mossford Ct, Ilf. IG6 . . . .81 E3
Mossford Grn, Ilf. IG6 . . .81 E3
Mossford La, Ilf. IG6 . . . .81 E2
Mossford St, E3 . . . . . . .113 J4
Moss Gdns, Felt. TW13 . .160 A2
  South Croydon CR2
  off Warren Av 203 G7
Moss Hall Ct, N12 . . . . . .57 E6
Moss Hall Cres, N12 . . . .57 E6
Moss Hall Gro, N12 . . . . .56 E6
Mossington Gdns, SE16
  off Abbeyfield Rd 133 F4
Moss La, Pnr. HA5 . . . . . .67 F3
Mosslea Rd, SE20 . . . . .171 F6
  Bromley BR2 . . . . . . .192 A5
  Orpington BR6 . . . . . .207 F3
Mossop St, SW3 . . . . . . .31 H1
Moss Rd, Dag. RM10 . . . .101 G7
Mossville Gdns, Mord.
  SM4 . . . . .184 C3
Moston Cl, Hayes UB3
  off Fuller Way 121 J5
Mostyn Av, Wem. HA9 . . .87 J5
Mostyn Gdns, NW10 . . . .108 A2
Mostyn Gro, E3 . . . . . . .113 J2
Mostyn Rd, SW9 . . . . . .151 G1
  SW19 . . . . .184 C1
  Edgware HA8 . . . . . . .54 D7
Mosul Way, Brom. BR2 . .192 B6
Motcomb St, SW1 . . . . . .24 A5
Moth Cl, Wall. SM6
  off Lancastrian
  Rd 200/201 E7
Mothers' Sq, E5 . . . . .95 E4
Motley Av, EC2
  off Scrutton St 112 B4
Motley St, SW8
  off St. Rule St 150 C2
MOTSPUR PARK, N.Mal. .183 G6
Motspur Pk, N.Mal. KT3 .183 F6
MOTTINGHAM, SE9 . . . .173 J2
Mottingham La, SE9 . . . .173 J1
  SE12 . . . . .173 J1
Mottingham Rd, N9 . . . . .45 G6
  SE9 . . . . .174 B2
Mottisfont Rd, SE2 . . . . .138 A3
Mott St, Loug. (High Beach)
  IG10 . . . . .47 F1
Moulins Rd, E9 . . . . .113 F1
Moulsford Ho, N7 . . . . . . .92 D5
Moulton Av, Houns.
  TW3 . . . . .143 E2
Mound, The, SE9 . . . . . .174 D3
Moundfield Rd, N16 . . . . .76 D6
Mount, The, N20 . . . . . . .57 F2
  NW3 off Heath St 91 F4
  W3 . . . . .126 B1
  New Malden KT3 . . . .183 F3
  Wembley HA9 . . . . . . .88 B2
  Worcester Park KT4 . .197 H4
Mountacre Cl, SE26 . . . .170 C4
Mount Adon Pk, SE22 . . .152 D7
Mountague Pl, E14 . . . . .114 C7
Mount Angelus Rd,
  SW15 . . . . .147 F7
Mount Ararat Rd, Rich.
  TW10 . . . . .145 H5
Mount Ash Rd, SE26 . . . .170 E3
Mount Av, E4 . . . . .62 A3
  W5 . . . . .105 G5
  Southall UB1 . . . . . . .103 G6
Mountbatten Cl, SE18 . . .137 H6
  SE19 . . . . .170 B5
Mountbatten Ct, SE16
  off Rotherhithe St 133 F1
  Buckhurst Hill IG9 . . . .64 A2
Mountbatten Gdns, Beck. BR3
  off Balmoral Av 189 H4
Mountbatten Ms, SW18
  off Inman Rd 167 F1
Mountbel Rd, Stan.
  HA7 . . . . .68 D1
Mount Cl, W5 . . . . .105 F5
  Barnet EN4 . . . . .42 A4
  Bromley BR1 . . . . . . .192 B1

Mountcombe Cl, Surb.
  KT6 . . . . .181 H7
Mount Cor, Felt. TW13 . .160 D2
Mount Ct, SW15
  off Weimar St 148 B3
  West Wickham BR4 . . .204 E2
Mount Culver Av, Sid.
  DA14 . . . . .176 D6
Mount Dr, Bexh. DA6 . . .158 E5
  Harrow HA2 . . . . .67 F5
  Wembley HA9 . . . . . . .88 C2
Mountearl Gdns, SW16 . .169 F3
Mount Echo Av, E4 . . . . .62 B2
Mount Echo Dr, E4 . . . . .62 B1
Mount Ephraim La,
  SW16 . . . . .168 D3
Mount Ephraim Rd,
  SW16 . . . . .168 D3
Mount Est, The, E5
  off Mount Pleasant
  La 94/95 E2
Mountfield Cl, SE6 . . . . .154 D7
Mountfield Rd, E6 . . . . . .116 D2
  N3 . . . . .72 D3
  W5 . . . . .105 G6
Mountford St, E1 . . . . . . .21 H3
Mountfort Cres, N1
  off Barnsbury Sq 93 G7
Mountfort Ter, N1
  off Barnsbury Sq 93 G7
Mount Gdns, SE26 . . . . .170 E3
Mount Gro, Edg. HA8 . . . .54 C3
Mountgrove Rd, N5 . . . . .93 H3
Mounthurst Rd, Brom.
  BR2 . . . . .191 F7
Mountington Pk Cl, Har.
  HA3 . . . . .69 G6
Mountjoy Cl, SE2 . . . . . .138 B2
Mountjoy Ho, EC2
  off The Barbican 111 J5
Mount Ms, Hmptn.
  TW12 . . . . .179 H1
Mount Mills, EC1 . . . . . . .11 H4
Mount Nod Rd, SW16 . . .169 F3
Mount Pk Av, Har. HA1 . . .86 A2
Mount Pk Cres, W5 . . . . .105 G6
Mount Pk Rd, W5 . . . . . .105 G5
  Harrow HA1 . . . . .86 A5
  Pinner HA5 . . . . .66 A5
Mount Pl, W3
  off High St 126 B1
Mount Pleasant, SE27 . . .169 J4
  WC1 . . . . .10 D6
  Barnet EN4 . . . . .41 H4
  Ruislip HA4 . . . . .84 C2
  Wembley HA0 . . . . . .105 H1
Mount Pleasant Cres,
  N4 . . . . .75 F7
Mount Pleasant Hill, E5 . .95 E2
Mount Pleasant La, E5 . . .94 E2
Mount Pleasant Pl, SE18
  off Orchard St 137 G4
Mount Pleasant Rd, E17 . .77 H2
  N17 . . . . .76 B2
  NW10 . . . . .89 J7
  SE13 . . . . .154 B6
  W5 . . . . .105 F4
  Chigwell IG7 . . . . .65 G4
  New Malden KT3 . . . .182 C3
Mount Pleasant Vil, N4 . .75 F7
Mount Pleasant Wk, Bex.
  DA5 . . . . .159 J5
Mount Rd, NW2 . . . . .89 H3
  NW4 . . . . .71 G6
  SE19 . . . . .170 A6
  SW19 . . . . .166 D2
  Barnet EN4 . . . . .41 H5
  Bexleyheath DA6 . . . .158 D5
  Chessington KT9 . . . .195 J5
  Dagenham RM8 . . . . .101 F1
  Feltham TW13 . . . . . .160 E3
  Hayes UB3 . . . . .121 J2
  Ilford IG1 . . . . .98 E5
  Mitcham CR4 . . . . . . .185 H2
  New Malden KT3 . . . .182 D3
Mount Row, W1 . . . . .16 D6
Mountside, Felt. TW13 . .154 D6
Mountside, Felt. TW13 . .161 E3
  Stanmore HA7 . . . . . .68 C1
Mounts Pond Rd, SE3 . . .154 C3
Mount Sq, The, NW3
  off Heath St 91 F3
Mount Stewart Av, Har.
  HA3 . . . . .69 G6
Mount St, W1 . . . . .16 C6
Mount Ter, E1
  off New Rd 112/113 E5
Mount Vernon, NW3 . . . . .91 F4
Mount Vw, NW7 . . . . .54 D3
  W5 . . . . .105 G4

Mountview Ct, N8
  off Green Las 75 H4
Mount Vw Rd, E4 . . . . . . .46 C7
  N4 . . . . .75 E7
  NW9 . . . . .70 D4
Mountview Rd, Esher (Clay.)
  KT10 . . . . .194 E7
Mount Vil, SE27 . . . . . . .169 H3
Mountwood, W.Mol.
  KT8 . . . . .179 G3
Movers La, Bark. IG11 . . .117 H2
Mowatt Cl, N19 . . . . .92 D1
Mowbray Rd, NW6 . . . . . .90 B7
  SE19 . . . . .188 C1
  Barnet EN5 . . . . .41 F4
  Edgware HA8 . . . . . . .54 A4
  Richmond TW10 . . . . .163 F3
Mowbrays Cl, Rom. RM5 .83 J1
Mowbrays Rd, Rom. RM5 .83 J2
Mowbrey Gdns, Loug.
  IG10 . . . . .49 F2
Mowlem St, E2 . . . . .113 E2
Mowlem Trd Est, N17 . . . .61 F7
Mowll St, SW9 . . . . .131 G7
Moxon Cl, E13
  off Whitelegg Rd 115 F2
Moxon St, W1 . . . . .16 B2
  Barnet EN5 . . . . .40 C3
Moye Cl, E2 . . . . .13 J1
Moyers Rd, E10 . . . . .78 C7
Moylan Rd, W6 . . . . .128 B6
Moyne Pl, NW10 . . . . . . .106 A2
Moynihan Dr, N21 . . . . . .43 E5
Moys Cl, Croy. CR0 . . . . .186 E6
Moyser Rd, SW16 . . . . . .168 B5
Mozart St, W10 . . . . .108 C3
Mozart Ter, SW1 . . . . . . .32 C2
Muchelney Rd, Mord.
  SM4 . . . . .185 F6
Mud La, W5 . . . . .105 G5
Muggeridge Cl, S.Croy.
  CR2 . . . . .202 A5
Muggeridge Rd, Dag.
  RM10 . . . . .101 H4
Muirdown Av, SW14 . . . .146 C4
Muir Dr, SW18 . . . . .149 G6
Muirfield, W3 . . . . .107 E6
Muirfield Cl, SE16
  off Ryder Dr . . .132/133 E5
  Watford WD19 . . . . . .50 C4
Muirfield Cres, E14
  off Millharbour 134 B3
Muirfield Grn, Wat. WD19 .50 C4
Muirfield Rd, Wat. WD19 . .50 D4
Muirkirk Rd, SE6 . . . . . . .172 C1
Muir Rd, E5 . . . . .94 D4
Muir St, E16
  off Newland St 136 C1
Mulberry Business Cen, SE16
  off Quebec Way 133 G2
Mulberry Cl, E4 . . . . .62 A2
  N8 . . . . .74 E5
  NW3
  off Hampstead High St .91 G4
  NW4 . . . . .71 J3
  SE7
  off Charlton Pk Rd . . .136 A6
  SE22 . . . . .152 E5
  SW3 off Beaufort St . .129 G6
  SW16 . . . . .168 C4
  Barnet EN4 . . . . .41 G4
  Northolt UB5
  off Parkfield Av . .102/103 E2
Mulberry Cres, Bark. IG11
  off Westrow Dr 99 J7
Mulberry Cres, Brent.
  TW8 . . . . .125 E7
  West Drayton UB7 . . . .120 D2
Mulberry La, Croy. CR0 . .202 C1
Mulberry Ms, SE14
  off Lewisham Way . . .153 J1
  Wallington SM6
  off Ross Rd 200 C6
Mulberry Par, West Dr.
  UB7 . . . . .120 D3
Mulberry Pl, W6
  off Chiswick Mall 127 G5
Mulberry Rd, E8 . . . . .94 C7
Mulberry St, E1 . . . . .21 H3
Mulberry Wk, SW3 . . . . . .31 F5
Mulberry Way, E18 . . . . . .79 H2
  Belvedere DA17 . . . . .139 J2
  Ilford IG6 . . . . .81 F4
Mulgrave Rd, NW10 . . . . .89 F4
  SE18 . . . . .136 C4
  SW6 . . . . .128 C6
  W5 . . . . .105 G3
  Croydon CR0 . . . . . . .202 A3
  Harrow HA1 . . . . .86 D2
  Sutton SM2 . . . . .198 D6

Mulholland Cl, Mitch.
  CR4 . . . . .186 B2
Mulkern Rd, N19 . . . . . . .92 D1
Mullards Cl, Mitch. CR4 . .199 J1
Muller Rd, SW4 . . . . .150 D6
Mullet Gdns, E2 . . . . .13 J3
Mullins Path, SW14 . . . . .146 D3
Mullion Cl, Har. HA3 . . . . .67 H1
Mullion Wk, Wat. WD19
  off Ormskirk Rd 50 D4
Mull Wk, N1
  off Clephane Rd 93 J6
Mulready St, NW8 . . . . . . .7 G6
Multi-way, W3
  off Valetta Rd 126/127 J2
Multon Rd, SW18 . . . . . .149 G7
Mulvaney Way, SE1 . . . . .28 C4
Mumford Ct, EC2 . . . . . . .20 A3
Mumford Rd, SE24
  off Railton Rd 151 H5
Muncaster Rd, SW11 . . .149 J5
Muncies Ms, SE6 . . . . . .172 C2
Mundania Rd, SE22 . . . .153 E6
Munday Rd, E16 . . . . . . .115 G6
Munden St, W14 . . . . . . .128 B4
Mundesley Cl, Wat. WD19 .50 C4
Mundford Rd, E5 . . . . . . .95 F2
Mundon Gdns, Ilf. IG1 . . .99 G1
Mund St, W14 . . . . .128 C5
Mundy St, N1 . . . . .12 D3
Mungo Pk Cl, Bushey
  (Bushey Hth.) WD23 . .51 J2
Munnery Way, Orp. BR6 .206 D3
Munnings Gdns, Islw.
  TW7 . . . . .144 A5
Munro Dr, N11 . . . . .58 C6
Munro Ms, W10 . . . . .108 B5
Munro Ter, SW10 . . . . . . .31 E7
Munslow Gdns, Sutt.
  SM1 . . . . .199 G4
Munster Av, Houns.
  TW4 . . . . .143 F4
Munster Ct, Tedd. TW11 .163 F6
Munster Gdns, N13 . . . . .59 H4
Munster Ms, SW6
  off Munster Rd 128 B7
Munster Rd, SW6 . . . . . .148 C1
  Teddington TW11 . . . .163 E6
Munster Sq, NW1 . . . . . . .9 E4
Munton Rd, SE17 . . . . . . .36 A1
Murchison Av, Bex.
  DA5 . . . . .176 D1
Murchison Rd, E10 . . . . . .96 C2
Murdock Cl, E16
  off Rogers Rd 115 F6
Murdock St, SE15 . . . . . .132 E6
Murfett Cl, SW19 . . . . . .166 B2
Muriel St, N1 . . . . .10 D1
Murillo Rd, SE13 . . . . . . .154 D4
Murphy St, SE1 . . . . .27 E4
Murray Av, Brom. BR1 . . .191 H2
  Hounslow TW3 . . . . . .143 H5
Murray Cres, Pnr. HA5 . . .66 D7
Murray Gro, N1 . . . . .12 A2
Murray Ms, NW1 . . . . . . .92 D7
Murray Rd, SW19 . . . . . .166 A6
  W5 . . . . .125 F4
  Richmond TW10 . . . . .163 E2
Murray Sq, E16 . . . . .115 G6
Murray St, NW1 . . . . .92 D7
Murray Ter, NW3
  off Flask Wk 91 G4
  W5 off Murray Rd 125 G4
Mursell Est, SW8 . . . . . .151 F1
Murtwell Dr, Chig. IG7 . . .65 F6
Musard Rd, W6 . . . . .128 B6
  W14 . . . . .128 B6
Musbury St, E1 . . . . .113 F6
Muscal, W6 . . . . .128 B6
Muscatel Pl, SE5
  off Dalwood St 152 B1
Muschamp Rd, SE15 . . .152 C3
  Carshalton SM5 . . . . .199 H2
Muscovy Ho, Erith DA18
  off Kale Rd 138/139 E2
Muscovy St, EC3 . . . . . . .21 E6
★ Museum Interpretative Cen,
  E6 off Norman Rd 116 C4
Museum La, SW7 . . . . . . .23 E6
★ Museum of Artillery, The
  Rotunda, SE18 . . . . . .136 C5
★ Museum of Docklands,
  E14 . . . . .114 A7
★ Museum of Garden History,
  SE1 . . . . .26 C6
★ Museum of Instruments,
  Royal Coll of Music,
  SW7 . . . . .22 E5
★ Museum of London,
  EC2 . . . . .19 J2

★ Museum of Richmond,
Rich. TW9 . . . . .145 G5
Museum Pas, E2
off Victoria Pk Sq .112/113 E3
Museum St, WC1 . . . . . .18 A2
Musgrave Cl, Barn. EN4 . .41 F1
Musgrave Cres, SW6 . . . .148 D1
Musgrave Rd, Islw. TW7 .144 C1
Musgrove Rd, SE14 . . . .153 G1
★ Musical Mus, Brent. TW8
off High St 125 H6
Musjid Rd, SW11
off Kambala Rd 149 G2
Musket Cl, Barn. EN4
off East Barnet Rd 41 G5
Musquash Way, Hounс.
TW4 . . . . .142 C2
Muston Rd, E5 . . . . .94 E2
Mustow Pl, SW6
off Munster Rd 148 C2
Muswell Av, N10 . . . . . . .74 B2
MUSWELL HILL, N10 . . . .74 B3
Muswell Hill, N10 . . . . . .74 B3
Muswell Hill Bdy, N10 . . .74 B3
Muswell Hill Pl, N10 . . . .74 B4
Muswell Hill Pl, N6 . . . . .74 A6
N10 . . . . .74 A4
Muswell Ms, N10
off Muswell Rd 74 B3
Muswell Rd, N10 . . . . . .74 B3
Mutrix Rd, NW6 . . . . . .108 D1
Mutton Pl, NW1
off Harmood St 92 B6
Muybridge Rd, N.Mal.
KT3 . . . . .182 C2
Myatt Rd, SW9 . . . . . . .151 H1
Myatt's Flds N, SW9
off Eythorne Rd 151 G1
Myatt's Flds S, SW9
off Loughborough
Rd 151 G2
Mycenae Rd, SE3 . . . . .135 G3
Myddelton Cl, Enf. EN1 . .44 C1
Myddelton Gdns, N21 . . .43 H7
Myddelton Pk, N20 . . . . .57 G3
Myddelton Pas, EC1 . . . .11 F3
Myddelton Rd, N8 . . . . .75 E4
Myddelton Sq, EC1 . . . . .11 F3
Myddelton St, EC1 . . . . .11 F4
Myddleton Av, N4 . . . . . .93 J2
Myddleton Ms, N22 . . . . .59 E7
Myddleton Rd, N22 . . . . .59 E7
Myers La, SE14 . . . . . .133 G6
Mylis Cl, SE26 . . . . . . .171 E4
Mylius Cl, SE14
off Kender St 153 F1
Mylne St, EC1 . . . . .11 E2
Mynterne Ct, SW19
off Swanton Gdns . . .166 A1
Myra St, SE2 . . . . .138 A5
Myrdle St, E1 . . . . .21 J2
Myrna Cl, SW19 . . . . . .167 H7
Myron Pl, SE13 . . . . . . .154 C3
Myrtle Av, Felt. TW14 . . .141 H4
Ruislip HA4 . . . . .66 A4
Myrtleberry Cl, E8
off Beechwood Rd 94 C6
Myrtle Cl, Barn. EN4 . . . .57 J1
West Drayton UB7 . . .120 C3
Myrtledene Rd, SE2 . . . .138 A5
Myrtle Gdns, W7 . . . . . .124 B1
Myrtle Gro, N.Mal. KT3 . .182 C2
Myrtle Rd, E6 . . . . .116 B1
E17 . . . . .77 H6
N13 . . . . .59 J3
W3 . . . . .126 C1
Croydon CR0 . . . . . . .204 A3
Hampton (Hmptn.H.)
TW12 . . . . .161 J6
Hounslow TW3 . . . . . .143 J2
Ilford IG1 . . . . .99 E2
Sutton SM1 . . . . .199 F5
Myrtle Wk, N1 . . . . .12 D2
Mysore Rd, SW11 . . . . .149 J3
Myton Rd, SE21 . . . . . .170 A3

N

N1 Shop Cen, N1 . . . . . .11 F1
Nadine St, SE7 . . . . . . .135 J5
Nafferton Ri, Loug. IG10 . .48 A5
Nagle Cl, E17 . . . . .78 D2
Nag's Head Ct, EC1 . . . .11 J6
Nags Head La, Well.
DA16 . . . . .158 B3
Nags Head Rd, Enf. EN3 . .45 F4
Nags Head Shop Cen, N7 .93 F4
Nairne Gro, SE24 . . . . .152 A5
Nairn Grn, Wat. WD19 . . .50 A3
Nairn Rd, Ruis. HA4 . . . .84 C6
Nairn St, E14 . . . . .114 C5
Naish Ct, N1 . . . . .111 E1
Nallhead Rd, Felt. TW13 .160 C5
Namba Roy Cl, SW16 . . .169 F4
Namton Dr, Th.Hth.
CR7 . . . . .187 F4
Nan Clark's La, NW7 . . . .55 F2
Nankin St, E14 . . . . . . .114 A6
Nansen Rd, SW11 . . . . .150 A4
Nansen Village, N12 . . . .57 E4
Nantes Cl, SW18 . . . . . .149 F4
Nantes Pas, E1 . . . . . . .21 F1
Nant Rd, NW2 . . . . .90 C2
Nant St, E2 off Cambridge
Heath Rd 112/113 E3
Naoroji St, WC1 . . . . . . .11 E4
Napier Av, E14 . . . . . . .134 A5
SW6 . . . . .148 C3
Napier Cl, SE8
off Amersham Vale . . .133 J7
W14 off Napier Rd . . .128 C3
West Drayton UB7 . . .120 C3
Napier Ct, SW6
off Ranelagh Gdns . . .148 C3
Napier Gro, N1 . . . . .12 A2
Napier Pl, W14 . . . . . . .128 C3
Napier Rd, E6 . . . . .116 D1
E11 . . . . .96 E4
E15 . . . . .115 E2
N17 . . . . .76 B3
NW10 . . . . .107 H3
SE25 . . . . .188 E4
W14 . . . . .128 B3
Belvedere DA17 . . . . .139 F4
Bromley BR2 . . . . . . .191 H4
Enfield EN3 . . . . .45 G5
Hounslow (Hthrw.Air.)
TW6 . . . . .140 A1
Isleworth TW7 . . . . . .144 D4
South Croydon CR2 . .202 A7
Wembley HA0 . . . . . . .87 G5
Napier Ter, N1 . . . . .93 H7
Napoleon Rd, E5 . . . . . .94 E3
Twickenham TW1 . . . .145 E7
Napton Cl, Hayes UB4
off Kingsash Dr .102/103 E4
Narbonne Av, SW4 . . . .150 C5
Narborough St, SW6 . . .148 E2
Narcissus Rd, NW6 . . . . .90 D5
Naresby Fold, Stan. HA7
off Bernays Cl 53 F6
Narford Rd, E5 . . . . .94 D3
Narrow Boat Cl, SE28
off Ridge Cl 137 G2
Narrow St, E14 . . . . . . .113 H7
Narrow Way, Brom.
BR2 . . . . .192 B6
Nascot St, W12 . . . . . . .107 J6
Naseberry Ct, E4
off Merriam Cl 62 C5
Naseby Cl, NW6
off Fairfax Rd 91 F7
Isleworth TW7 . . . . . .144 B1
Naseby Rd, SE19 . . . . . .170 A6
Dagenham RM10 . . . .101 G3
Ilford IG5 . . . . .80 C1
Nash Cl, Sutt. SM1 . . . . .199 G3
Nash Ct, E14
off South Colonnade .134 B1
Nash Grn, Brom. BR1 . . .173 G6
Nash La, Kes. BR2 . . . . .205 G5
Nash Rd, N9 . . . . .61 F2
SE4 . . . . .153 H4
Romford RM6 . . . . . . .82 D4
Nash St, NW1 . . . . .8 E4
Nash Way, Har. HA3 . . . .69 E6
Nasmyth St, W6 . . . . . .127 H3
Nassau Path, SE28
off Disraeli Cl 138 C1
Nassau Rd, SW13 . . . . .147 F1
Nassau St, W1 . . . . .17 F2
Nassington Rd, NW3 . . . .91 H4
Natalie Cl, Felt. TW14 . . .141 G7
Natalie Ms, Twick. TW2
off Sixth Cross Rd . . .162 A3
Natal Rd, N11 . . . . .58 E6
SW16 . . . . .168 D6
Ilford IG1 . . . . .99 E4
Thornton Heath CR7 . .188 A3
Nathaniel Cl, E1 . . . . . . .21 G2
Nathans Rd, Wem. HA0 . .87 F1
Nathan Way, SE28 . . . . .137 H4
National Ter, SE16
off Bermondsey
Wall E 132/133 E2
Nation Way, E4 . . . . . . .62 C1
★ Natural History Mus,
SW7 . . . . .22 E6
Naval Row, E14 . . . . . . .114 C7
Naval Wk, Brom. BR1
off High St 191 G3
Navarino Gro, E8 . . . . . .94 D6
Navarino Rd, E8 . . . . . . .94 D6
Navarre Rd, E6 . . . . . . .116 B2
Navarre St, E2 . . . . .13 F5
Navenby Wk, E3
off Rounton Rd 114 A4
Navestock Cl, E4
off Mapleton Rd 62 C3
Navestock Cres, Wdf.Grn.
IG8 . . . . .79 J1
Navestock Ho, Bark.
IG11 . . . . .118 B2
Navigator Dr, Sthl. UB2 .123 J2
Navy St, SW4 . . . . .150 D3
Naylor Gro, Enf. EN3
off South St 45 G5
Naylor Rd, N20 . . . . . . .57 F2
SE15 . . . . .132 E7
Nazareth Gdns, SE15 . . .152 E2
Nazrul St, E2 . . . . .13 F3
Neagle Cl, Borwd. WD6
off Balcon Way 38 C1
Neal Av, Sthl. UB1 . . . . .103 F4
Neal Cl, Nthwd. HA6 . . . .66 A1
Nealden St, SW9 . . . . . .151 F3
Neale Cl, N2 . . . . .73 F3
Neal St, WC2 . . . . .18 A4
Neal's Yd, WC2 . . . . .18 A4
Near Acre, NW9 . . . . . . .71 F1
NEASDEN, NW2 . . . . . . .89 E3
Neasden Cl, NW10 . . . . .89 E5
Neasden La, NW10 . . . . .89 E4
Neasden La N, NW10 . . .88 D3
Neasham Rd, Dag. RM8 .100 B5
Neate St, SE5 . . . . .37 H5
SM4 . . . . .185 F6
Neathouse Pl, SW1 . . . . .33 F1
Neatscourt Rd, E6 . . . . .116 A5
Nebraska St, SE1 . . . . . .28 B4
Neckinger, SE16 . . . . . . .29 G5
Neckinger Est, SE16 . . . .29 G5
Neckinger St, SE1 . . . . . .29 G4
Nectarine Way, SE13 . . .154 B2
Needham Rd, W11
off Westbourne Gro . .108 D6
Needham Ter, NW2
off Kara Way 90 A3
Needleman St, SE16 . . . .133 G2
Neeld Cres, NW4 . . . . . .71 H5
Wembley HA9 . . . . . . .88 A5
Neeld Par, Wem. HA9
off Harrow Rd 88 A5
Neil Wates Cres, SW2 . . .169 G1
Nelgarde Rd, SE6 . . . . .154 A7
Nella Rd, W6 . . . . .128 A6
Nelldale Rd, SE16 . . . . .133 F4
Nello James Gdns,
SE27 . . . . .170 A4
Nelson Cl, NW6 . . . . . . .108 D2
Croydon CR0 . . . . . . .201 H1
Romford RM7 . . . . . . .83 H1
Nelson Ct, SE16
off Brunel Rd 133 F1
Nelson Gdns, E2 . . . . . . .13 J3
Hounslow TW3 . . . . . .143 G6
Nelson Gro Rd, SW19 . . .185 E1
Nelson Mandela Cl, N10 .74 A2
Nelson Mandela Rd,
SE3 . . . . .155 J3
Nelson Pas, EC1 . . . . . . .12 A4
Nelson Pl, N1 . . . . .11 H2
Sidcup DA14 . . . . . . .176 A4
Nelson Rd, E4 . . . . .62 B6
E11 . . . . .79 G4
N8 . . . . .75 F5
N9 . . . . .61 E2
N15 . . . . .76 B4
SE10 . . . . .134 C6
SW19 . . . . .167 E7
Belvedere DA17 . . . . .139 F5
Bromley BR2 . . . . . . .191 J4
Enfield EN3 . . . . .45 G5
Harrow HA1 . . . . .86 A1
Hounslow TW3 . . . . . .143 J7
Hounslow (Hthrw.Air.)
TW6 . . . . .140 C1
New Malden KT3 . . . .182 D5
Sidcup DA14 . . . . . . .176 A4
Stanmore HA7 . . . . . .53 F6
Twickenham TW2 . . . .143 J6
★ Nelson's Column,
WC2 . . . . .26 A1
Nelson Sq, SE1 . . . . .27 G3
Nelson's Row, SW4 . . . .150 D4
Nelson St, E1 . . . . .112 E6
E6 . . . . .116 C2
E16 off Huntingdon St .115 F7
Nelsons Yd, NW1 . . . . . . .9 F1
Nelson Ter, N1 . . . . .11 H2
Nelson Trd Est, SW19 . . .184 E1
Nelson Wk, SE16
off Rotherhithe St . . .133 H1
Nemoure Rd, W3 . . . . . .106 C7
Nene Gdns, Felt. TW13 . .161 F2
Nene Rd, Hounс. (Hthrw.Air.)
TW6 . . . . .141 E1
Nepaul Rd, SW11 . . . . . .149 H2
Nepean St, SW15 . . . . . .147 G6
Neptune Ct, Borwd. WD6
off Clarendon Rd 38 A3
Neptune Rd, Har. HA1 . . .68 A6
Hounslow (Hthrw.Air.)
TW6 . . . . .141 G1
Neptune St, SE16 . . . . . .133 F3
Nesbit Rd, SE9 . . . . . . .156 A4
Nesbitt Cl, SE3
off Hurren Cl 154/155 E3
Nesbitts All, Barn. EN5
off Bath Pl 40 C3
Nesbitt Sq, SE19
off Coxwell Rd 170 B7
Nesham St, E1 . . . . .29 H1
Ness St, SE16 . . . . .29 H5
Nesta Rd, Wdf.Grn. IG8 . .63 E6
Nestles Av, Hayes UB3 . .121 J3
Nestor Av, N21 . . . . .43 H6
Netheravon Rd, W4 . . . .127 F4
W7 . . . . .124 C1
Netheravon Rd S, W4 . . .127 F5
Netherbury Rd, W5 . . . .125 G3
Netherby Gdns, Enf. EN2 .42 E4
Netherby Rd, SE23 . . . . .153 F7
Nether Cl, N3 . . . . .56 D7
Nethercourt Av, N3 . . . . .56 D6
Netherfield Gdns, Bark.
IG11 . . . . .99 G6
Netherfield Rd, N12 . . . .57 E5
SW17 . . . . .168 A3
Netherford Rd, SW4 . . . .150 C2
Netherhall Gdns, NW3 . .91 F6
Netherhall Way, NW3
off Netherhall Gdns . .91 F5
Netherlands Rd, Barn.
EN5 . . . . .41 G6
Netherleigh Cl, N6 . . . . .92 B1
Nether St, N3 . . . . .72 D1
N12 . . . . .56 D7
Netherton Gro, SW10 . . .30 D6
Netherton Rd, N15 . . . . .76 A6
Twickenham TW1 . . . .144 E5
Netherwood, N2 . . . . . . .73 G2
Netherwood Pl, W14
off Netherwood Rd . . .128 A3
Netherwood Rd, W14 . . .128 A3
Netherwood St, NW6 . . . .90 C7
Netherwood St Est, NW6 .90 C7
Netley Cl, Croy. (New Adgtn.)
CR0 . . . . .204 C7
Sutton SM3 . . . . .198 A5
Netley Dr, Walt. KT12 . . .179 F7
Netley Gdns, Mord.
SM4 . . . . .185 F7
Netley Rd, E17 . . . . .77 J5
Brentford TW8 . . . . . .125 H6
Hounslow (Hthrw.Air.)
TW6 . . . . .141 G1
Ilford IG2 . . . . .81 G5
Morden SM4 . . . . . . .185 F7
Netley St, NW1 . . . . .9 F4
Nettleden Av, Wem. HA9 .88 A6
Nettlefold Pl, SE27 . . . . .169 H3
Nettlestead Cl, Beck. BR3
off Copers Cope Rd . .171 J7
Nettleton Rd, SE14 . . . .153 G1
Hounslow (Hthrw.Air.)
TW6 . . . . .141 G1
Nettlewood Rd, SW16 . . .168 D7
Neuchatel Rd, SE6 . . . . .171 J2
Nevada Cl, N.Mal. KT3
off Georgia Rd 182 C4
Nevada St, SE10 . . . . . .134 C6
Nevern Pl, SW5 . . . . . . .128 D4
Nevern Rd, SW5 . . . . . .128 D4
Nevern Sq, SW5 . . . . . .128 D4
Neville Av, N.Mal. KT3 . .182 D1
Neville Cl, E11 . . . . .97 F3
NW1 . . . . .9 J2
NW6 . . . . .108 C2
SE15 . . . . .132 D7
W3 off Acton La 126 C2

Neville Cl, Houns. TW3 . .143 H2
  Sidcup DA15 . . . . .175 J4
Neville Dr, N2 . . . . .73 F6
Neville Gdns, Dag.
  RM8 . . . . .100 D3
Neville Gill Cl, SW18 . . .148 D6
Neville Pl, N22 . . . . .75 F1
Neville Rd, E7 . . . . .97 G7
  NW6 . . . . .108 C2
  W5 . . . . .105 G4
  Croydon CR0 . . . . .188 A7
  Dagenham RM8 . . . . . . .100 D2
  Ilford IG6 . . . . .81 F1
  Kingston upon Thames
    KT1 . . . . .182 A2
  Richmond TW10 . . . . . .163 F3
Nevilles Ct, NW2 . . . . . . .89 G3
Neville St, SW7 . . . . .31 G3
Neville Ter, SW7 . . . . . . .31 G3
Neville Wk, Cars. SM5
  off Green Wrythe La . .185 H7
Nevill Rd, N16 . . . . .94 B4
Nevill Way, Loug. IG10
  off Valley Hill 48 B7
Nevin Dr, E4 . . . . .62 B1
Nevinson Cl, SW18 . . . . .149 G6
Nevis Rd, SW17 . . . . . . .168 A2
Newacres Rd, SE28 . . . . .137 H1
Newall Rd, Houns. (Hthrw.Air.)
  TW6 . . . . .141 F1
Newark Cres, NW10 . . . .106 D3
Newark Grn, Borwd. WD6 .38 D3
Newark Knok, E6 . . . . . .116 D6
Newark Par, NW4
  off Greyhound Hill 71 G3
Newark Rd, S.Croy. CR2 .202 A6
Newark St, E1 . . . . .112 E5
Newark Way, NW4 . . . . . .71 G4
New Ash Cl, N2
  off Oakridge Dr 73 G3
New Atlas Wf, E14
  off Arnhem Pl 133 J3
New Barn Cl, Wall. SM6
  off Merlin Cl 201 F6
NEW BARNET, Barn. 41 E4
New Barns Av, Mitch.
  CR4 . . . . .186 D4
New Barn St, E13 . . . . . .115 G4
New Barns Way, Chig.
  IG7 . . . . .64 E3
NEW BECKENHAM,
  Beck. 171 J6
Newbiggin Path, Wat.
  WD19 . . . . .50 C4
Newbolt Av, Sutt. SM3 . .197 J5
Newbolt Rd, Stan. HA7 . .52 C6
New Bond St, W1 . . . . . . .16 D4
Newborough Grn, N.Mal.
  KT3 . . . . .182 D4
New Brent St, NW4 . . . . .71 J5
Newbridge Pt, SE23
  off Windrush La 171 G3
New Br St, EC4 . . . . .19 G4
New Broad St, EC2 . . . . . .20 D2
New Bdy, W5 . . . . .105 F7
  Hampton (Hmptn.H.) TW12
    off Hampton Rd 162 A5
Newburgh Rd, W3 . . . . . .126 C1
Newburgh St, W1 . . . . . . .17 F4
New Burlington Ms, W1 . .17 F5
New Burlington Pl, W1 . . .17 F5
New Burlington St, W1 . . .17 F5
Newburn St, SE11 . . . . . .34 D3
Newbury Cl, Nthlt. UB5 . .85 F6
Newbury Gdns, Epsom
  KT19 . . . . .197 F4
Newbury Ho, N22 . . . . . . .75 E1
Newbury Ms, NW5
  off Malden Rd 92 A6
NEWBURY PARK, Ilf. 81 G5
Newbury Rd, E4 . . . . .62 C6
  Bromley BR2 . . . . . . .191 G3
  Hounslow (Hthrw.Air.)
    TW6 . . . . .140 C1
  Ilford IG2 . . . . .81 G6
Newbury St, EC1 . . . . . . .19 J2
Newbury Way, Nthlt. UB5 .85 E6
New Butt La, SE8 . . . . . .134 A7
New Butt La N, SE8
  off Reginald Rd 134 A7
Newby Cl, Enf. EN1 . . . . .44 B2
Newby Pl, E14 . . . . .114 C7
Newby St, SW8 . . . . .150 B3
New Caledonian Wf,
  SE16 . . . . .133 J3
Newcastle Cl, EC4 . . . . . .19 G3
Newcastle Pl, W2 . . . . . . .15 F2
Newcastle Row, EC1 . . . . .11 F5
New Cavendish St, W1 . . .17 E1
New Change, EC4 . . . . . . .19 J4

New Chapel Sq, Felt.
  TW13 . . . . .160 B1
New Charles St, EC1 . . . .11 H3
NEW CHARLTON, SE7 . .135 J4
New Ch Ct, SE19
  off Waldegrave Rd . . .170 D7
New Ch Rd, SE5 . . . . .36 A7
New City Rd, E13 . . . . . .115 J3
New Cl, SW19 . . . . .185 F3
  Feltham TW13 . . . . . .160 E5
New Coll Ct, NW3
  off College Cres 91 F7
New Coll Ms, N1
  off Islington Pk St . . .93 G7
New Coll Par, NW3
  off College Cres 91 G6
Newcombe Gdns, SW16 .169 E4
Newcombe Pk, NW7 . . . . .55 E5
  Wembley HA0 . . . . . . .105 J1
Newcombe St, W8
  off Kensington Pl 128 D1
Newcomen Rd, E11 . . . . . .97 F3
  SW11 . . . . .149 G3
Newcomen St, SE1 . . . . . .28 B3
New Compton St, WC2 . . .17 J4
New Concordia Wf, SE1 . .29 H3
New Ct, EC4 . . . . .18 E5
Newcourt St, NW8 . . . . . . .7 G2
  off Garnet St 133 F1
NEW CROSS, SE14 . . . . .153 H1
NEW CROSS GATE,
  SE14 . . . . .153 G1
New Cross Rd, SE14 . . . .133 F7
Newdales Cl, N9
  off Balham Rd 60 D2
Newdene Av, Nthlt. UB5 .102 D2
Newell St, E14 . . . . .113 J6
NEW ELTHAM, SE9 . . . . .174 D2
New End, NW3 . . . . .91 F4
New End Sq, NW3 . . . . . . .91 G4
Newent Cl, SE15 . . . . .36 D7
  Carshalton SM5 . . . . .199 J1
New Era Est, N1
  off Phillipp St 112 B1
New Fm Av, Brom. BR2 .191 G4
New Ferry App, SE18 . . . .136 D3
New Fetter La, EC4 . . . . . .19 F3
Newfield Cl, Hmptn. TW12
  off Percy Rd 179 G1
Newfield Ri, NW2 . . . . . . .89 H3
New Forest La, Chig. IG7 .64 D6
Newgale Gdns, Edg. HA8 .69 J1
New Gdn Dr, West Dr. UB7
  off Drayton Gdns 120 B2
Newgate, Croy. CR0 . . . .201 J1
Newgate Cl, Felt. TW13 . .161 E2
Newgate St, E4 . . . . .63 F3
  EC1 . . . . .19 H3
New Globe Wk, SE1 . . . . .27 J1
New Goulston St, E1 . . . . .21 F3
New Grn Pl, SE19
  off Hawke Rd 170 B6
Newhams Row, SE1 . . . . .28 E4
Newham Way, E6 . . . . . .115 J5
  E16 . . . . .115 F5
Newhaven Cl, Hayes
  UB3 . . . . .121 J4
Newhaven Gdns, SE9 . . .156 A4
Newhaven La, E16 . . . . . .115 F4
Newhaven Rd, SE25 . . . .188 A5
New Heston Rd, Houns.
  TW5 . . . . .123 F7
New Horizons Ct, Brent. TW8
  off Shield Dr 124 D6
Newhouse Av, Rom.
  RM6 . . . . .82 D3
Newhouse Cl, N.Mal.
  KT3 . . . . .183 E7
Newhouse Wk, Mord.
  SM4 . . . . .185 F7
Newick Cl, Bex. DA5 . . . .159 H6
Newick Rd, E5 . . . . .95 E3
Newing Grn, Brom.
  BR1 . . . . .174 A7
NEWINGTON, SE1 . . . . . .35 J1
Newington Barrow Way,
  N7 . . . . .93 F3
Newington Butts, SE1 . . .35 H2
  SE11 . . . . .35 H2
Newington Causeway,
  SE1 . . . . .27 H6
Newington Grn, N1 . . . . . .94 A5
  N16 . . . . .94 A5
Newington Grn Rd, N1 . . .94 A6
New Inn Bdy, EC2 . . . . . .12 E5

New Inn Pas, WC2 . . . . . .18 D4
New Inn St, EC2 . . . . .12 E5
New Inn Yd, EC2 . . . . . . .12 E5
New James Ct, SE15
  off Nunhead La . .152/153 E3
New Jersey St, SE15
  off Nunhead La . .152/153 E3
New Jubilee Ct, Wdf.Grn. IG8
  off Grange Av 63 G7
New Kent Rd, SE1 . . . . . . .27 J6
New Kings Rd, SW6 . . . .148 C2
New King St, SE8 . . . . . .134 A6
Newland Cl, Pnr. HA5 . . . .51 E6
Newland Ct, Wem. HA9
  off Forty Av 88 A2
Newland Dr, Enf. EN1 . . . .44 E1
Newland Gdns, W13 . . . .124 D2
Newland Rd, N8 . . . . .74 E3
Newlands, The, Wall.
  SM6 . . . . .200 C7
Newlands Av, T.Ditt.
  KT7 . . . . .194 B1
Newlands Cl, Edg. HA8 . .53 H3
  Southall UB2 . . . . . . .122 C6
  Wembley HA0 . . . . . . .87 F6
Newlands Ct, SE9 . . . . . .156 D6
Newlands Pk, SE26 . . . . .171 G5
Newlands Pl, Barn. EN5 . .40 A5
Newlands Quay, E1 . . . . .113 F7
Newlands Rd, SW16 . . . .187 E2
  Woodford Green IG8 . . .63 F2
Newlands Ter, E16 . . . . . .136 B1
Newlands Way, Chess.
  KT9 . . . . .195 F5
Newling Cl, E6
  off Porter Rd 116 C6
New London St, EC3 . . . . .21 E5
New Lydenburg St, SE7 .135 J3
Newlyn Cl, Orp. BR6 . . . .207 J4
Newlyn Gdns, Har. HA2 . .67 F7
Newlyn Rd, N17 . . . . .76 C1
  NW2 off Tilling Rd 89 J1
  Barnet EN5 . . . . .40 C4
  Welling DA16 . . . . . . .157 J2
NEW MALDEN 182 D3
Newman Pas, W1 . . . . . . .17 G2
Newman Rd, E13 . . . . . . .115 H3
  E17 off Southcote Rd . . .77 G5
  Bromley BR1 . . . . . . .191 G1
  Croydon CR0 . . . . . . .201 F1
  Hayes UB3 . . . . .102 B7
Newmans Cl, Loug. IG10 . .48 E3
Newman's Ct, EC3 . . . . . .20 C4
Newmans La, Loug. IG10 .48 D3
  Surbiton KT6 . . . . . . .181 G6
Newman's Row, WC2 . . . .18 D2
Newman St, W1 . . . . .17 G2
Newmans Way, Barn.
  EN4 . . . . .41 F1
Newman Yd, W1 . . . . .17 H3
Newmarket Av, Nthlt.
  UB5 . . . . .85 G5
Newmarket Grn, SE9
  off Middle Pk Av 156 A7
Newmarsh Rd, SE28 . . . .137 J1
Newminster Rd, Mord.
  SM4 . . . . .185 F6
New Mt St, E15 . . . . .96 D7
Newnes Path, SW15
  off Putney Pk La 147 H4
Newnham Av, Ruis. HA4 . .84 C1
Newnham Cl, Loug. IG10 .48 A6
  Northolt UB5 . . . . .85 J5
  Thornton Heath CR7 . .187 J2
Newnham Gdns, Nthlt.
  UB5 . . . . .85 J5
Newnham Ms, N22
  off Newnham Rd 75 F1
Newnham Rd, N22 . . . . . .75 F1
Newnhams Cl, Brom.
  BR1 . . . . .192 C3
Newnham Ter, SE1 . . . . . .26 E5
Newnham Way, Har.
  HA3 . . . . .69 H5
New N Pl, EC2 . . . . .12 D6
New N Rd, N1 . . . . .12 C2
  Ilford IG6 . . . . .65 G7
New N St, WC1 . . . . .18 C1
Newnton Cl, N4 . . . . .76 A7
New Oak Rd, N2 . . . . .73 F2
New Orleans Wk, N19 . . . .74 D7
New Oxford St, WC1 . . . . .17 J3
New Pk Av, N13 . . . . .59 J3
New Pk Cl, Nthlt. UB5 . . .84 E6
New Pk Ct, SW2 . . . . . . .151 E7
New Pk Par, SW2
  off Doverfield Rd .150/151 E6
New Pk Rd, SW2 . . . . . . .168 D1
Newpiece, Loug. IG10 . . . .48 E3
New Pl Sq, SE16 . . . . . . .132 E3

New Plaistow Rd, E15 . . .115 E1
Newport Av, E13 . . . . . . .115 H4
  E14 . . . . .114 D7
Newport Ct, WC2 . . . . . . .17 J5
Newport Mead, Wat. WD19
  off Kilmarnock Rd 50 D4
Newport Pl, WC2 . . . . . . .17 J5
Newport Rd, E10 . . . . .96 C2
  E17 . . . . .77 H4
  SW13 . . . . .147 G1
  Hounslow (Hthrw.Air.)
    TW6 . . . . .140 D1
Newport St, SE11 . . . . . . .34 C2
New Printing Ho Sq, WC1
  off Gray's Inn Rd 111 F4
New Priory Ct, NW6
  off Mazenod Av 90 D7
Newquay Cres, Har. HA2 .85 E2
Newquay Gdns, Wat. WD19
  off Fulford Gro 50 B2
Newquay Rd, SE6 . . . . . .172 B2
New Quebec St, W1 . . . . .16 A4
New Ride, SW7 . . . . .23 J3
New River Cres, N13 . . . .59 H4
New River Head, EC1 . . . .11 F3
New River Wk, N1 . . . . . . .93 J6
New River Way, N4 . . . . . .76 A7
New Rd, E1 . . . . .112 E5
  E4 . . . . .62 B4
  N8 . . . . .74 E5
  N9 . . . . .60 D3
  N17 . . . . .76 C1
  N22 . . . . .75 J1
  NW7 . . . . .56 B7
  NW7 (Barnet Gate) 39 F7
  SE2 . . . . .138 D4
  Brentford TW8 . . . . . .125 G6
  Dagenham RM9,
    RM10 . . . . .119 G1
  Feltham TW14 . . . . . .141 G6
  Feltham (E.Bed.) TW14 .160 B3
  Feltham (Han.) TW13 . .160 E5
  Harrow HA1 . . . . .86 C4
  Hayes UB3 . . . . .121 F7
  Hounslow TW3
    off Station Rd 143 H4
  Ilford IG3 . . . . .99 H2
  Kingston upon Thames
    KT2 . . . . .164 A7
  Mitcham CR4 . . . . . . .199 J1
  Richmond TW10 . . . . .163 F4
  Welling DA16 . . . . . . .158 B2
  West Molesey KT8 . . . .179 G3
New Row, WC2 . . . . .18 A5
Newry Rd, Twick. TW1 . . .144 D4
Newsam Av, N15 . . . . . . .76 A5
★ New Scotland Yd,
  SW1 . . . . .25 H5
Newsholme Dr, N21 . . . . .43 F5
NEW SOUTHGATE, N11 . .58 D4
New Spring Gdns Wk,
  SE11 . . . . .34 B4
New Sq, WC2 . . . . .18 D3
New Sq Pas, WC2
  off New Sq 111 F6
Newstead Av, Orp. BR6 .207 G3
Newstead Rd, SE12 . . . . .155 E7
Newstead Wk, Cars.
  SM5 . . . . .185 F7
Newstead Way, SW19 . . .166 A4
New St, EC2 . . . . .20 E2
New St Hill, Brom. BR1 . .173 H5
New St Sq, EC4 . . . . .19 F3
Newton Av, N10 . . . . .74 A1
  W3 . . . . .126 C2
Newton Cl, E17 . . . . .77 H6
  Harrow HA2 . . . . .85 G2
Newton Cres, Borwd.
  WD6 . . . . .38 C4
Newton Gro, W4 . . . . . . .126 E4
Newton Pl, E14 . . . . .134 A4
Newton Rd, E15 . . . . .96 D5
  N15 . . . . .76 C5
  NW2 . . . . .89 J3
  SW19 . . . . .166 B6
  W2 . . . . .108 D6
  Harrow HA3 . . . . .68 B2
  Isleworth TW7 . . . . . .144 C2
  Welling DA16 . . . . . . .158 A3
  Wembley HA0 . . . . . . .87 J7
Newton St, WC2 . . . . .18 B3
Newtons Yd, SW18
  off Wandsworth
    High St 148/149 E5
Newton Wk, Edg. HA8
  off North Rd 70 B1
Newton Way, N18 . . . . . . .59 J5
Newtown St, SW11
  off Strasburg Rd 150 B1
New Trinity Rd, N2 . . . . . .73 G3

New Turnstile, WC1 . . . . . .18 C2
New Union Cl, E14 . . . . . .134 C3
New Union St, EC2 . . . . . .20 B2
New Wanstead, E11 . . . . . .79 F6
New Way Rd, NW9 . . . . . .71 E4
New Wf Rd, N1 . . . . .10 B1
New Zealand Way W12 . .107 H7
Niagara Av, W5 . . . . . . .125 H4
Niagara Cl, N1
  off Cropley St 112 A2
Nibthwaite Rd, Har. HA1 .68 B5
Nicholas Cl, Grnf. UB6 . .103 H2
Nicholas Cl, E13 . . . . . . .115 H3
  off Tunmarsh La 115 H3
Nicholas Gdns, W5 . . . . .125 G2
Nicholas La, EC4 . . . . . . .20 C5
Nicholas Ms, W4
  off Short Rd 126/127 E6
Nicholas Pas, EC4 . . . . . .20 C5
Nicholas Rd, E1 . . . . . . .113 F4
  Croydon CR0 . . . . . . .201 E4
  Dagenham RM8 . . . . .101 F2
Nicholay Rd, N19 . . . . . .92 D1
Nichol Cl, N14 . . . . .58 D1
Nicholes Rd, Houns.
  TW3 . . . . .143 G4
Nichol La, Brom. BR1 . .173 G7
Nichollsfield Wk, N7
  off Hillmarton Rd 93 F5
Nicholls Pt, E15
  off Park Gro 115 G1
Nicholl St, E2 . . . . .112 D1
Nichols Cl, N4
  off Osborne Rd 93 G1
  Chessington KT9
  off Merritt Gdns 195 F6
Nichols Grn, W5
  off Montpelier Rd 105 H5
Nicholson Rd, Croy.
  CR0 . . . . .202 C1
Nicholson St, SE1 . . . . . . .27 G2
Nickelby Cl, SE28 . . . . . .118 C6
Nicola Cl, Har. HA3 . . . . .68 A2
  South Croydon CR2 . .201 J6
Nicola Ms, IIf. IG6 . . . . . . .65 E7
Nicol Cl, Twick. TW1
  off Cassilis Rd . . .144/145 E6
Nicoll Pl, NW4 . . . . .71 H6
Nicoll Rd, NW10 . . . . . . .107 E1
Nicoll Way, Borwd. WD6 .38 D5
Nicolson Dr, Bushey
  (Bushey Hth.) WD23 . .51 J1
Nicosia Rd, SW18 . . . . . .149 H7
Niederwald Rd, SE26 . . .171 H4
Nield Rd, Hayes UB3 . . . .121 J2
Nigel Cl, Nthlt. UB5
  off Church Rd . . .102/103 E1
Nigel Fisher Way, Chess.
  KT9 . . . . .195 F7
Nigel Ms, IIf. IG1 . . . . . . .98 E4
Nigel Playfair Av, W6
  off King St 127 H4
Nigel Rd, E7 . . . . .97 J5
  SE15 . . . . .152 D3
Nigeria Rd, SE7 . . . . . . .135 J7
Nightingale Av, E4 . . . . . .62 E5
  Harrow HA1 . . . . .68 E7
Nightingale Cl, E4 . . . . . . .62 E4
  W4 off Grove Pk Ter . .126 C6
  Carshalton SM5 . . . . .200 A2
  Pinner HA5 . . . . .66 C5
Nightingale Ct, E11
  off Nightingale La 79 H5
Nightingale Dr, Epsom
  KT19 . . . . .196 B6
Nightingale Est, E5 . . . . . .94 D3
Nightingale Gro, SE13 . .154 D5
Nightingale La, E11 . . . . . .79 G5
  N6 . . . . .91 H1
  N8 . . . . .74 E4
  SW4 . . . . .149 J7
  SW12 . . . . .149 J7
  Bromley BR1 . . . . . . .191 J2
  Richmond TW10 . . . . .145 H7
Nightingale Ms, E3
  off Chisenhale Rd . . .113 H2
  E11 . . . . .79 G5
  SE11 . . . . .35 F1
  Kingston upon Thames
  KT1 off South La 181 G3
Nightingale Pl, SE18 . . . .136 D6
  SW10 . . . . .30 D5
Nightingale Rd, E5 . . . . . .94 E3
  N9 . . . . .45 F6
  N22 . . . . .75 E1
  NW10 . . . . .107 F2
  W7 . . . . .124 C1
  Carshalton SM5 . . . . .199 J3
  Hampton TW12 . . . . .161 G5
  Orpington BR5 . . . . . .193 F6

Nightingale Rd, Walt.
  KT12 . . . . .178 B7
  West Molesey KT8 . . .179 H5
Nightingales, The, Stai.
  TW19 . . . . .140 C7
Nightingale Sq, SW12 . . .150 A7
Nightingale Vale, SE18 . .136 D6
Nightingale Wk, SW4 . . .150 B6
Nightingale Way, E6 . . . .116 B5
Nile Path, SE18
  off Jackson St 136 D6
Nile Rd, E13 . . . . .115 J2
Nile St, N1 . . . . .12 A3
Nile Ter, SE15 . . . . .37 F4
Nimegen Way, SE22 . . . .152 B5
Nimrod Cl, Nthlt. UB5
  off Britannia Cl 102 D3
Nimrod Pas, N1
  off Tottenham Rd 94 B6
Nimrod Rd, SW16 . . . . . .168 B6
Nina Mackay Cl, E15
  off Arthingworth
  St 114/115 E1
Nine Acres Cl, E12 . . . . . .98 B5
NINE ELMS, SW8 . . . . . . .33 G7
Nine Elms La, SW8 . . . . . .33 G7
Nineteenth Rd, Mitch.
  CR4 . . . . .186 E4
Ninhams Wd, Orp.
  BR6 . . . . .206 D4
Ninth Av, Hayes UB3 . . . .102 A7
Nisbet Ho, E9
  off Homerton High St .95 G5
Nithdale Rd, SE18 . . . . . .137 E7
Niton Cl, Barn. EN5 . . . . . .40 A6
Niton Rd, Rich. TW9 . . . .146 A3
Niton St, SW6 . . . . .128 A7
Niven Cl, Borwd. WD6 . . .38 C1
N.L.A. Twr, Croy. CR0 . . .202 A2
Nobel Dr, Hayes UB3 . . . .121 G7
Nobel Rd, N18 . . . . .61 F5
Noble St, EC2 . . . . .19 J3
NOEL PARK, N22 . . . . . . .75 G2
Noel Pk Rd, N22 . . . . .75 G2
Noel Rd, E6 . . . . .116 B4
  N1 . . . . .11 G1
  W3 . . . . .106 B6
Noel Sq, Dag. RM8 . . . . .100 C4
Noel St, W1 . . . . .17 G4
Noel Ter, SE23
  off Dartmouth Rd 171 F2
Nolan Way, E5 . . . . .94 D4
Nolton Pl, Edg. HA8 . . . . .69 J1
Nonsuch Cl, IIf. IG6 . . . . .65 E6
★ Nonsuch Mansion Ho, Sutt.
  SM3 . . . . .197 J6
Nora Gdns, NW4 . . . . .72 A4
NORBITON, Kings.T. 182 B2
Norbiton Av, Kings.T. KT1 .182 A2
Norbiton Common Rd,
  Kings.T. KT1 . . . . . . .182 B3
Norbiton Rd, E14 . . . . . . .113 J6
Norbreck Gdns, NW10
  off Lytham Gro 105 J3
Norbreck Par, NW10
  off Lytham Gro 105 J3
Norbroke St, W12 . . . . . .107 F7
Norburn St, W10
  off Chesterton Rd . . .108 B5
NORBURY, SW16 . . . . . .187 G1
Norbury Av, SW16 . . . . . .187 F1
  Hounslow TW3 . . . . .144 A5
  Thornton Heath CR7 . .187 G2
Norbury Cl, SW16 . . . . . .187 G1
Norbury Ct Rd, SW16 . . .186 E3
Norbury Cres, SW16 . . . .187 F1
Norbury Cross, SW16 . . .186 E3
Norbury Gdns, Rom.
  RM6 . . . . .82 D5
Norbury Gro, NW7 . . . . . .54 E3
Norbury Hill, SW16 . . . . .169 G7
Norbury Ri, SW16 . . . . . .186 E3
Norbury Rd, E4 . . . . .62 A5
  Thornton Heath CR7 . .187 J2
Norcombe Gdns, Har.
  HA3 . . . . .69 F6
Norcott Cl, Hayes UB4
  off Willow Tree La . . .102 C4
Norcott Rd, N16 . . . . .94 D2
Norcroft Gdns, SE22 . . . .152 D7
Norcutt Rd, Twick. TW2 . .162 B1
Norfield Rd, Dart. DA2 . .177 J4
Norfolk Av, N13 . . . . .59 H6
  N15 . . . . .76 C6
Norfolk Cl, N2
  off Park Rd 73 H3
  N13 . . . . .59 H6
  Barnet EN4 . . . . .42 A4
  Twickenham TW1
  off Cassilis Rd . . .144/145 E6

Norfolk Cres, W2 . . . . .15 H3
  Sidcup DA15 . . . . . . .157 H7
Norfolk Gdns, Bexh.
  DA7 . . . . .159 F1
  Borehamwood WD6 . . .38 D4
Norfolk Ho, SE3 . . . . .135 E6
Norfolk Ho Rd, SW16 . . . .168 D3
Norfolk Ms, W10
  off Blagrove Rd 108 C5
Norfolk Pl, W2 . . . . .15 F3
  Welling DA16 . . . . . . .158 A2
Norfolk Rd, E6 . . . . .116 C1
  E17 . . . . .77 G2
  NW8 . . . . .109 G1
  NW10 . . . . .88 E7
  SW19 . . . . .167 H7
  Barking IG11 . . . . .99 H7
  Barnet EN5 . . . . .40 D3
  Dagenham RM10 . . . .101 H5
  Enfield EN3 . . . . .45 E6
  Esher (Clay.) KT10 . . .194 B5
  Feltham TW13 . . . . . .160 C1
  Harrow HA1 . . . . .67 H5
  Ilford IG3 . . . . .99 H1
  Romford RM7 . . . . . . .83 J6
  Thornton Heath CR7 . .187 J3
Norfolk Row, SE1 . . . . . . .34 C1
Norfolk Sq, W2 . . . . .15 F4
Norfolk Sq Ms, W2 . . . . . .15 F4
Norfolk St, E7 . . . . .97 G4
Norfolk Ter, W6
  off Field Rd 128 B5
Norgrove St, SW12 . . . . .150 A7
Norhyrst Av, SE25 . . . . . .188 C3
Norland Ho, W11 . . . . . . .128 A1
Norland Pl, W11 . . . . .128 B1
Norland Rd, W11 . . . . . . .128 A1
Norlands Cres, Chis.
  BR7 . . . . .192 E1
Norlands Gate, Chis.
  BR7 . . . . .193 E1
Norland Sq, W11 . . . . . . .128 B1
Norley Vale, SW15 . . . . . .165 G1
Norlington Rd, E10 . . . . . .96 C1
  E11 . . . . .96 C1
Norman Av, N22 . . . . .75 H1
  Feltham TW13 . . . . . .161 E2
  Southall UB1 . . . . . . .103 E7
  Twickenham TW1 . . . .145 E7
Normanby Cl, SW15
  off Manfred Rd 148 C5
Normanby Rd, NW10 . . . . .89 F4
Norman Cl, Orp. BR6 . . . .207 F3
  Romford RM5 . . . . . . .83 H2
Norman Ct, IIf. IG2 . . . . . .81 G7
  Woodford Green IG8
  off Monkhams Av 63 H5
Norman Cres, Houns.
  TW5 . . . . .142 D1
  Pinner HA5 . . . . .66 C1
Normand Gdns, W14
  off Greyhound Rd . . .128 B6
Normand Ms, W14
  off Normand Rd 128 B6
Normand Rd, W14 . . . . . .128 C6
Normandy Av, Barn.
  EN5 . . . . .40 C5
Normandy Cl, SE26 . . . . .171 H3
Normandy Rd, SW9 . . . . .151 G1
Normandy Ter, E16 . . . . . .115 H6
Norman Gro, E3 . . . . .113 H2
Normanhurst Av, Bexh.
  DA7 . . . . .158 E1
Normanhurst Dr, Twick. TW1
  off St. Margarets
  Rd 144/145 E5
Normanhurst Rd, SW2 . .169 F2
Norman Rd, E6 . . . . .116 C4
  E11 . . . . .96 D2
  N15 . . . . .76 C5
  SE10 . . . . .134 B7
  SW19 . . . . .167 F7
  Belvedere DA17 . . . . .139 H3
  Ilford IG1 . . . . .99 E5
  Sutton SM1 . . . . .198 D5
  Thornton Heath CR7 . .187 H5
Norman's Bldgs, EC1
  off Ironmonger Row . .111 J3
Normans Cl, NW10 . . . . . .88 D6
Normansfield Av, Tedd.
  TW11 . . . . .163 F7
Normanshire Av, E4 . . . . .62 C4
Normanshire Dr, E4 . . . . .62 A4
Normans Mead, NW10 . . .88 D6
Norman St, EC1 . . . . .11 J4
Normanton Av, SW19 . . .166 D2
Normanton Pk, E4 . . . . . .62 E3
Normanton Rd, S.Croy.
  CR2 . . . . .202 B6
Normanton St, SE23 . . . .171 G2

Norman Way, N14 . . . . . . .58 E2
  W3 . . . . .106 B5
Normington Cl, SW16 . . .169 G5
Norrice Lea, N2 . . . . .73 G5
Norris St, SW1 . . . . .17 H6
Norroy Rd, SW15 . . . . . . .148 A4
Norrys Cl, Barn. EN4 . . . . .41 J5
Norrys Rd, Barn. EN4 . . . .41 J4
Norseman Cl, IIf. IG3 . . . .100 B1
Norseman Way, Grnf. UB6
  off Olympic Way 103 H1
Norstead Pl, SW15 . . . . . .165 G2
North Access Rd, E17 . . . .77 G6
North Acre, NW9 . . . . .71 E1
NORTH ACTON, W3 . . . . .106 D4
North Acton Rd, NW10 . . .106 D3
Northall Rd, Bexh. DA7 . .159 J2
Northampton Gro, N1 . . . .94 A5
Northampton Pk, N1 . . . . .93 J6
Northampton Rd, EC1 . . . .11 F5
  Croydon CR0 . . . . . . .202 D2
  Enfield EN3 . . . . .45 H4
Northampton Sq, EC1 . . . .11 G4
Northampton St, N1 . . . . .93 J7
Northanger Rd, SW16 . . .168 E6
North Arc, Croy. CR0
  off North End 201 J2
North Audley St, W1 . . . . .16 B4
North Av, N18 . . . . .60 D4
  W13 . . . . .104 E6
  Carshalton SM5 . . . . .199 J7
  Harrow HA2 . . . . .67 H6
  Hayes UB3 . . . . .102 A7
  Richmond TW9
  off Sandycombe Rd . .146 A1
  Southall UB1 . . . . . . .103 F7
North Bk, NW8 . . . . .7 F4
Northbank Rd, E17 . . . . . .78 C2
NORTH BECKTON, E6 . . .116 B4
North Birkbeck Rd, E11 . . .96 D3
Northborough Rd,
  SW16 . . . . .186 D3
Northbourne, Brom.
  BR2 . . . . .191 G7
Northbourne Rd,
  SW4 . . . . .150 D4
North Branch Av, W10
  off Harrow Rd 107 J3
Northbrook Rd, N22 . . . . .59 E7
  SE13 . . . . .154 D5
  Barnet EN5 . . . . .40 B6
  Croydon CR0 . . . . . . .188 A5
  Ilford IG1 . . . . .98 D2
Northburgh St, EC1 . . . . .11 H5
North Carriage Dr, W2 . . .15 G5
NORTH CHEAM, Sutt. . . .197 J3
Northchurch, SE17 . . . . . .36 C3
Northchurch Rd, N1 . . . . . .94 A7
  Wembley HA9 . . . . . . .87 J6
Northchurch Ter, N1 . . . . .94 B7
North Circular Rd, E4 . . . .61 J7
  E18 . . . . .79 J2
  N3 . . . . .72 E3
  N12 . . . . .73 G1
  N13 . . . . .59 G5
  NW2 . . . . .88 B3
  NW10 . . . . .88 B7
  NW11 . . . . .72 B4
Northcliffe Cl, Wor.Pk.
  KT4 . . . . .197 E3
Northcliffe Dr, N20 . . . . . .56 C1
North Cl, Barn. EN5 . . . . . .39 J5
  Bexleyheath DA6 . . . .158 D4
  Dagenham RM10 . . . .119 G3
  Feltham TW14
  off North Rd 141 G6
  Morden SM4 . . . . . . .184 B4
North Colonnade, E14 . . .134 A1
North Common Rd, W5 . .105 H7
Northcote, Pnr. HA5 . . . . .66 C2
Northcote Av, W5 . . . . . . .105 H7
  Isleworth TW7 . . . . . .144 D5
  Southall UB1 . . . . . . .103 E7
  Surbiton KT5 . . . . . . .182 A7
Northcote Ms, SW11
  off Northcote Rd 149 H4
Northcote Rd, E17 . . . . . .77 H4
  NW10 . . . . .89 E7
  SW11 . . . . .149 H4
  Croydon CR0 . . . . . . .188 A6
  New Malden KT3 . . . .182 C3
  Sidcup DA14 . . . . . . .175 H4
  Twickenham TW1 . . . .144 D5
Northcott Av, N22 . . . . . . .75 E1
North Countess Rd, E17 . .77 J2
North Ct, W1 . . . . .17 G1
NORTH CRAY, Sid. 177 G3
North Cray Rd, Bex.
  DA5 . . . . .177 F3
  Sidcup DA14 . . . . . . .176 E6

North Cres, E16 .... **114** D4
N3 .... **72** C2
WC1 .... **17** H1
Northcroft Rd, W13 .... **124** E2
Epsom KT19 .... **196** D7
Northcroft Ter, W13
off Northcroft Rd **124/125** E2
North Cross Rd, SE22 .... **152** C5
Ilford IG6 .... **81** F4
North Dene, NW7 .... **54** D3
Northdene, Chig. IG7 .... **65** G5
North Dene, Houns. TW3 .... **143** H1
Northdene Gdns, N15 .... **76** C6
Northdown Gdns, Ilf. IG2 .... **81** H5
Northdown Rd, Well. DA16 .... **158** B2
Northdown St, N1 .... **10** B1
North Dr, SW16 .... **168** C4
Hounslow TW3 .... **143** J2
Orpington BR6 .... **207** H4
North End, NW3 .... **91** F2
Buckhurst Hill IG9 .... **47** J7
Croydon CR0 .... **201** J2
North End Av, NW3 .... **91** F2
North End Cres, W14 .... **128** C4
North End Ho, W14 .... **128** B4
North End Par, W14
off North End Rd **128** B4
North End Rd, NW11 .... **90** D1
SW6 .... **128** C6
W14 .... **128** B4
Wembley HA9 .... **88** A3
North End Way, NW3 .... **91** F2
Northern Av, N9 .... **60** C2
Northernhay Wk, Mord. SM4 .... **184** B4
Northern Perimeter Rd, Houns. (Hthrw.Air.) TW6 .... **141** F1
Northern Perimeter Rd W, Houns. (Hthrw.Air.) TW6 .... **140** A1
Northern Relief Rd, Bark. IG11 .... **99** E7
Northern Rd, E13 .... **115** H1
Northern Service Rd, Barn. EN5 .... **40** B3
North Eyot Gdns, W6 .... **127** G5
Northey St, E14 .... **113** H7
Northfield, Loug. IG10 .... **48** A4
Northfield Av, W5 .... **125** E2
W13 .... **125** E2
Pinner HA5 .... **66** D4
Northfield Cl, Brom. BR1 .... **192** B1
Hayes UB3 .... **121** J3
Northfield Cres, Sutt. SM3 .... **198** B4
Northfield Gdns, Dag. RM9
off Northfield Rd **101** F4
Northfield Ind Est, NW10 .... **106** A3
Northfield Pk, Hayes UB3 .... **121** J3
Northfield Path, Dag. RM9 .... **101** F3
Northfield Rd, E6 .... **98** C7
N16 .... **76** B7
W13 .... **124** E2
Barnet EN4 .... **41** H3
Borehamwood WD6 .... **38** B1
Dagenham RM9 .... **101** F4
Enfield EN3 .... **44** E5
Hounslow TW5 .... **122** D6
Northfields, SW18 .... **148** D4
Northfields Ind Est, Wem. HA0 .... **106** A1
Northfields Rd, W3 .... **106** B5
NORTH FINCHLEY, N12 .... **57** G5
North Flockton St, SE16 .... **29** H3
North Gdn, E14
off Westferry Circ **133** J1
North Gdns, SW19 .... **167** G7
Northgate Dr, NW9 .... **70** E6
Northgate Ind Pk, Rom. RM5 .... **83** F2
North Glade, The, Bex. DA5 .... **159** F7
North Gower St, NW1 .... **9** G4
North Grn, NW9
off Clayton Fld **54/55** E7
North Gro, N6 .... **74** A7
N15 .... **76** A5
NORTH HARROW, Har. **67** G6
North Hatton Rd, Houns. (Hthrw.Air.) TW6 .... **141** G1
North Hill, N6 .... **73** J6
North Hill Av, N6 .... **74** A6
NORTH HYDE, Sthl. **123** E4
North Hyde Gdns, Hayes UB3 .... **122** A4
North Hyde La, Houns. TW5 .... **123** E5
Southall UB2 .... **123** E5
North Hyde Rd, Hayes UB3 .... **121** J3
Northiam, N12 .... **56** D3
Northiam St, E9 .... **113** E1
Northington St, WC1 .... **10** D6
NORTH KENSINGTON, W10 .... **107** J6
Northlands Av, Orp. BR6 .... **207** H4
Northlands St, SE5 .... **151** J2
North La, Tedd. TW11 .... **162** C6
North Lo Cl, SW15
off Westleigh Av **148** A5
North Mall, N9
off St. Martins Rd **60/61** E2
North Ms, WC1 .... **10** D6
Northolm, Edg. HA8 .... **54** D4
Northolme Gdns, Edg. HA8 .... **70** A1
Northolme Ri, Orp. BR6 .... **207** H2
Northolme Rd, N5 .... **93** J4
NORTHOLT **85** F7
Northolt Av, Ruis. HA4 .... **84** B5
Northolt Gdns, Grnf. UB6 .... **86** C5
Northolt Rd, Har. HA2 .... **85** H4
Hounslow (Hthrw.Air.) TW6 .... **140** A1
Northover, Brom. BR1 .... **173** F3
North Par, Chess. KT9 .... **195** H5
North Pk, SE9 .... **156** C6
North Pas, SW18 .... **148** D4
North Peckham Est, SE15 .... **37** E7
North Pl, Mitch. CR4 .... **167** J7
Teddington TW11 .... **162** C6
North Pole La, Kes. BR2 .... **205** F6
North Pole Rd, W10 .... **107** J5
Northport St, N1 .... **112** A1
North Ride, W2 .... **15** G6
North Rd, N6 .... **74** A7
N7 .... **92** E6
N9 .... **60** E1
SE18 .... **137** H4
SW19 .... **167** F6
W5 .... **125** G3
Belvedere DA17 .... **139** H3
Brentford TW8 .... **125** H6
Bromley BR1 .... **191** H1
Edgware HA8 .... **70** B1
Feltham TW14 .... **141** G6
Ilford IG3 .... **99** H2
Richmond TW9 .... **146** A3
Romford (Chad.Hth.) RM6 .... **82** E5
Southall UB1 .... **103** G7
Surbiton KT6 .... **181** G6
West Drayton UB7 .... **120** C3
West Wickham BR4 .... **204** B1
Northrop Rd, Houns. (Hthrw.Air.) TW6 .... **141** H1
North Row, W1 .... **16** A5
North Several, SE3
off Orchard Rd **154** D2
NORTH SHEEN, Rich. **146** A2
Northside Rd, Brom. BR1
off Mitchell Way **191** G1
North Side Wandsworth Common, SW18 .... **149** G5
Northspur Rd, Sutt. SM1 .... **198** D3
North Sq, N9
off St. Martins Rd **60/61** E2
NW11 .... **72** D5
Northstead Rd, SW2 .... **169** G2
North St, E13 .... **115** G2
NW4 .... **71** J5
SW4 .... **150** C3
Barking IG11 .... **99** E6
Bexleyheath DA7 .... **159** G4
Bromley BR1 .... **191** G1
Carshalton SM5 .... **199** J3
Isleworth TW7 .... **144** D3
North St Pas, E13 .... **115** H2
North Tenter St, E1 .... **21** G4
North Ter, SW3 .... **23** G6
Northumberland All, EC3 .... **21** E4
Northumberland Av, E12 .... **97** J1
WC2 .... **26** A1
Enfield EN1 .... **45** E1
Isleworth TW7 .... **144** C1
Welling DA16 .... **157** G4
Northumberland Cl, Erith DA8 .... **139** J7
Staines (Stanw.) TW19 .... **140** B6
Northumberland Cres, Felt. TW14 .... **141** H6
Northumberland Gdns, N9 .... **60** C3
Bromley BR1 .... **192** D4
Isleworth TW7 .... **124** D7
Mitcham CR4 .... **186** D5
Northumberland Gro, N17 .... **60** E7
NORTHUMBERLAND HEATH, Erith **139** J7
Northumberland Pk, N17 .... **60** C7
Erith DA8 .... **139** J7
Northumberland Pl, W2 .... **108** D6
Richmond TW10 .... **145** G5
Northumberland Rd, E6 .... **116** B6
E17 .... **78** A7
Barnet EN5 .... **41** F6
Harrow HA2 .... **67** F5
Northumberland Row, Twick. TW2 *off Colne Rd* **162** B1
Northumberland St, WC2 .... **26** A1
Northumberland Way, Erith DA8 .... **159** J1
Northumbria St, E14 .... **114** A6
North Verbena Gdns, W6
off St. Peter's Sq **127** G5
Northview, N7 .... **93** E3
North Vw, SW19 .... **165** H5
W5 .... **105** F4
Pinner HA5 .... **66** C7
Northview Cres, NW10 .... **89** F4
North Vw Dr, Wdf.Grn. IG8 .... **80** A2
North Vw Rd, N8 .... **74** D3
North Vil, NW1 .... **92** D6
North Wk, W2 .... **14** C6
Croydon (New Adgtn.) CR0 .... **204** B5
North Way, N9 .... **61** F2
N11 .... **58** C6
NW9 .... **70** B3
Northway, NW11 .... **72** E5
Morden SM4 .... **184** B3
North Way, Pnr. HA5 .... **66** C3
Northway, Wall. SM6 .... **200** C4
Northway Circ, NW7 .... **54** D4
Northway Cres, NW7 .... **54** D4
Northway Ho, N20 .... **57** F1
Northway Rd, SE5 .... **151** J3
Croydon CR0 .... **188** C6
Northways Par, NW3
off College Cres **91** G7
Northweald La, Kings.T. KT2 .... **163** G5
NORTH WEMBLEY, Wem. **87** E2
Northwest Pl, N1 .... **11** F1
North Wf Rd, W2 .... **14** E2
Northwick Av, Har. HA3 .... **68** D6
Northwick Circle, Har. HA3 .... **69** F6
Northwick Cl, NW8 .... **6** E5
Harrow HA1
off Nightingale Av **68/69** E7
Northwick Pk Rd, Har. HA1 .... **68** C6
Northwick Rd, Wat. WD19 .... **50** C4
Wembley HA0 .... **105** G1
Northwick Ter, NW8 .... **6** E5
Northwick Wk, Har. HA1 .... **68** C7
Northwold Dr, Pnr. HA5
off Cuckoo Hill **66** C3
Northwold Est, E5 .... **94** D2
Northwold Rd, E5 .... **94** C2
N16 .... **94** C2
North Wd Ct, SE25
off Regina Rd **188** D3
Northwood Gdns, N12 .... **57** G5
Greenford UB6 .... **86** C5
Ilford IG5 .... **80** D4
Northwood Hall, N6 .... **74** C7
Northwood Ho, SE27 .... **170** A4
Northwood Pl, Erith DA18 .... **139** F3
Northwood Rd, N6 .... **74** B7
SE23 .... **171** J1
Carshalton SM5 .... **200** A6
Hounslow (Hthrw.Air.) TW6 .... **140** A1
Thornton Heath CR7 .... **187** H2
Northwood Twr, E17 .... **78** C4
Northwood Way, SE19
off Roman Ri **170** A6
Northwood HA6 .... **50** A7
NORTH WOOLWICH, E16 .... **136** B2
North Woolwich Rd, E16 .... **135** G1
North Woolwich Roundabout, E16 *off North Woolwich Rd* **136** A1
★ **North Woolwich Station Mus**, E16 .... **136** D2
North Worple Way, SW14 .... **146** D3
Norton Av, Surb. KT5 .... **182** B7
Norton Cl, E4 .... **62** A5
Borehamwood WD6 .... **38** A1
Enfield EN1
off Brick La **44/45** E2
Norton Folgate, E1 .... **21** E1
Norton Gdns, SW16 .... **186** E2
Norton Rd, E10 .... **95** J1
Wembley HA0 .... **87** G6
Norval Rd, Wem. HA0 .... **86** E2
Norway Gate, SE16 .... **133** H3
Norway Pl, E14
off East India Dock Rd **113** J6
Norway St, SE10 .... **134** B6
Norwich Ho, E14
off Cordelia St **114** B6
Norwich Ms, Ilf. IG3
off Ashgrove Rd **100** A1
Norwich Pl, Bexh. DA6 .... **159** G4
Norwich Rd, E7 .... **97** G5
Dagenham RM9 .... **119** G2
Greenford UB6 .... **103** H1
Thornton Heath CR7 .... **187** J3
Norwich St, EC4 .... **19** E3
Norwich Wk, Edg. HA8 .... **54** C7
NORWOOD, SE19 .... **170** B6
Norwood Av, Wem. HA0 .... **105** J1
Norwood Cl, NW2 .... **90** B3
Southall UB2 .... **123** G4
Twickenham TW2
off Fourth Cross Rd **162** A2
Norwood Cres, Houns. (Hthrw.Air.) TW6 .... **141** F1
Norwood Dr, Har. HA2 .... **67** F6
Norwood Gdns, Hayes UB4 .... **102** C4
Southall UB2 .... **123** F4
NORWOOD GREEN, Sthl. **123** G4
Norwood Grn Rd, Sthl. UB2 .... **123** G4
Norwood High St, SE27 .... **169** H3
NORWOOD NEW TOWN, SE19 .... **169** J6
Norwood Pk Rd, SE27 .... **169** J5
Norwood Rd, SE24 .... **169** H1
SE27 .... **169** H2
Southall UB2 .... **123** F4
Norwood Ter, Sthl. UB2
off Tentelow La **123** H4
Notley St, SE5 .... **36** B7
Notre Dame Est, SW4 .... **150** C4
Notson Rd, SE25 .... **188** E4
Notting Barn Rd, W10 .... **108** A4
Nottingdale Sq, W11
off Wilsham St **128** B1
Nottingham Av, E16 .... **115** J5
Nottingham Ct, WC2 .... **18** A4
Nottingham Pl, W1 .... **8** B6
Nottingham Rd, E10 .... **78** C6
SW17 .... **167** J1
Isleworth TW7 .... **144** C2
South Croydon CR2 .... **201** J4
Nottingham St, W1 .... **16** B1
Nottingham Ter, NW1 .... **8** B6
NOTTING HILL, W11 .... **108** B7
Notting Hill Gate, W11 .... **128** D1
Nova Ms, Sutt. SM3 .... **198** B1
Novar Cl, Orp. BR6 .... **193** J7
Nova Rd, Croy. CR0 .... **187** H7
Novar Rd, SE9 .... **175** F1
Novello St, SW6 .... **148** D1
Novello Way, Borwd. WD6 .... **38** D1
Nowell Rd, SW13 .... **127** G6
Nower Hill, Pnr. HA5 .... **67** F4
Noyna Rd, SW17 .... **167** J3
Nuding Cl, SE13 .... **154** A3
Nugent Rd, N19 .... **93** E1
SE25 .... **188** C3
Nugents Ct, Pnr. HA5
off St. Thomas' Dr **66/67** E1
Nugents Pk, Pnr. HA5 .... **67** E1
Nugent Ter, NW8 .... **6** D2
★ **No. 2 Willow Rd**, NW3 .... **91** H4
Nun Ct, EC2 .... **20** B3
Nuneaton Rd, Dag. RM9 .... **100** D7
NUNHEAD, SE15 .... **153** F3
Nunhead Cres, SE15 .... **152** E3
Nunhead Est, SE15 .... **152** E4
Nunhead Grn, SE15 .... **153** E3
Nunhead Gro, SE15 .... **153** E3

Nunhead La, SE15 . . . . . .**152** E3
Nunhead Pas, SE15
  off Peckham Rye **152** D3
Nunnington Cl, SE9 . . . . .**174** B3
Nunns Rd, Enf. EN2 . . . . .**43** J2
Nupton Dr, Barn. EN5 . . . .**39** J6
Nursery Av, N3 . . . .**73** F2
  Bexleyheath DA7 . . . .**159** F3
  Croydon CR0 . . . .**203** G2
Nursery Cl, SE4 . . . .**153** J2
  SW15 . . . .**148** A4
  Croydon CR0 . . . .**203** G2
  Enfield EN3 . . . .**45** G1
  Feltham TW14 . . . . . .**142** B7
  Romford RM6 . . . .**82** D6
  Woodford Green IG8 . . .**63** H5
Nursery Ct, N17
  off Nursery St **60** C7
Nursery Gdns, Chis.
  BR7 . . . .**174** E6
  Enfield EN3 . . . .**45** G1
  Hounslow TW4 . . . . . .**143** F5
Nursery La, E2 . . . .**112** C1
  E7 . . . .**97** G6
  W10 . . . .**107** J5
Nurserymans Rd, N11 . . . .**58** A2
Nursery Rd, E9
  off Morning La **95** F6
  N2 . . . .**73** G1
  N14 . . . .**42** C7
  SW9 . . . .**151** F4
  Loughton IG10 . . . .**47** J5
  Loughton (High Beach)
  IG10 . . . .**47** H1
  Pinner HA5 . . . .**66** C3
  Sutton SM1 . . . .**199** F4
  Thornton Heath CR7 . .**188** A4
Nursery Rd Merton,
  SW19 . . . .**185** E2
Nursery Rd Mitcham, Mitch.
  CR4 . . . .**185** H3
Nursery Rd Wimbledon, SW19
  off Worple Rd **166** B7
Nursery Row, SE17 . . . . . .**36** B2
  Barnet EN5
  off St. Albans Rd **40** B3
Nursery St, N17 . . . .**60** C7
Nursery Wk, NW4 . . . .**71** H3
Nurstead Rd, Erith DA8 .**139** G7
Nutbourne St, W10 . . . . .**108** B3
Nutbrook St, SE15 . . . . . .**152** D3
Nutbrowne Rd, Dag.
  RM9 . . . .**119** F1
Nutcroft Rd, SE15 . . . . . .**132** E7
Nutfield Cl, N18 . . . .**60** D6
  Carshalton SM5 . . . . .**199** H3
Nutfield Gdns, Ilf. IG3 . . . .**99** J2
  Northolt UB5 . . . .**102** C2
Nutfield Rd, E15 . . . .**96** C4
  NW2 . . . .**89** G2
  SE22 . . . .**152** C5
  Thornton Heath CR7 . .**187** H4
Nutfield Way, Orp. BR6 .**206** D2
Nutford Pl, W1 . . . .**15** H3
Nuthatch Gdns, SE28 . . .**137** G2
Nuthurst Av, SW2 . . . . . .**169** F2
Nutley Ter, NW3 . . . .**91** F6
Nutmead Cl, Bex. DA5 . .**177** J1
Nutmeg Cl, E16
  off Cranberry La .**114/115** E4
Nutmeg La, E14 . . . .**114** D6
Nuttall St, N1 . . . .**12** E1
Nutter La, E11 . . . .**79** J6
Nutt Gro, Edg. HA8 . . . . .**53** G2
Nutt St, SE15 . . . .**37** G7
Nutwell St, SW17 . . . . . .**167** H5
Nuxley Rd, Belv. DA17 . .**139** F6
Nyanza St, SE18 . . . .**137** G6
Nye Bevan Est, E5 . . . . . .**95** G3
Nylands Av, Rich. TW9 . .**146** A1
Nymans Gdns, SW20
  off Hidcote Gdns **183** H3
Nynehead St, SE14 . . . .**133** H7
Nyon Gro, SE6 . . . .**171** J2
Nyssa Cl, Wdf.Grn. IG8
  off Gwynne Pk Av **64** C6
Nyton Cl, N19
  off Courtauld Rd . .**92/93** E1

O

Oak Apple Ct, SE12 . . . .**173** G2
Oak Av, N8 . . . .**74** E4
  N10 . . . .**58** B7
  N17 . . . .**60** A7
  Croydon CR0 . . . .**204** A2
  Hampton TW12 . . . . .**161** E5
  Hounslow TW5 . . . . . .**122** D7
  West Drayton UB7 . . .**120** D3

Oak Bk, Croy. (New Adgtn.)
  CR0 . . . .**204** C6
Oakbank Av, Walt. KT12 .**179** F7
Oakbank Gro, SE24 . . . .**151** J4
Oakbrook Cl, Brom. BR1 .**173** H4
Oakbury Rd, SW6 . . . . . .**149** E2
Oak Cl, N14 . . . .**42** B7
  Sutton SM1 . . . .**199** F2
Oakcombe Cl, N.Mal. KT3
  off Traps La **182/183** E1
Oak Cottage Cl, SE6 . . .**173** F1
Oak Cres, E16 . . . .**115** E5
Oakcroft Cl, Pnr. HA5 . . . .**66** B2
Oakcroft Rd, SE13 . . . . .**154** D2
  Chessington KT9 . . . .**195** J4
Oakcroft Vil, Chess. KT9 .**195** J4
Oakdale, N14 . . . .**58** B1
Oakdale Av, Har. HA3 . . . .**69** H5
  Northwood HA6 . . . . . .**66** A2
Oakdale Cl, Wat. WD19 . . .**50** C4
Oakdale Gdns, E4 . . . .**62** C5
Oakdale Rd, E7 . . . .**97** H7
  E11 . . . .**96** D2
  E18 . . . .**79** H2
  N4 . . . .**75** J6
  SE15 . . . .**153** F3
  SW16 . . . .**169** E5
  Watford WD19 . . . .**50** C3
Oakdale Way, Mitch. CR4
  off Wolseley Rd **186** A7
Oakdene, SE15
  off Carlton Gro .**152/153** E1
Oak Dene, W13
  off The Dene **104/105** E5
Oakdene Av, Chis. BR7 . .**174** D5
  Erith DA8 . . . .**139** J6
  Thames Ditton KT7 . .**194** D1
Oakdene Cl, Pnr. HA5 . . . .**51** F7
Oakdene Dr, Surb. KT5 . .**182** C7
Oakdene Ms, Sutt. SM3 .**198** C1
Oakdene Pk, N3 . . . .**56** C7
Oakdene Rd, Orp. BR5 . .**193** J5
Oakden St, SE11 . . . .**35** F1
Oake Ct, SW15 . . . .**148** B5
Oaken Dr, Esher (Clay.)
  KT10 . . . .**194** C6
Oakenholt Ho, SE2
  off Hartslock Dr **138** D2
Oaken La, Esher (Clay.)
  KT10 . . . .**194** B5
Oakenshaw Cl, Surb.
  KT6 . . . .**181** H7
Oakes Cl, E6
  off Savage Gdns **116** C6
Oakeshott Av, N6 . . . .**92** A2
Oakey La, SE1 . . . .**27** E5
Oak Fm, Borwd. WD6 . . . .**38** C5
Oakfield, E4 . . . .**62** B5
Oakfield Av, Har. HA3 . . . .**69** E3
Oakfield Cl, N.Mal. KT3
  off Blakes La **183** F5
Oakfield Ct, N8 . . . .**74** E7
  NW2 off Hendon Way . .**72** A7
  Borehamwood WD6 . . .**38** B3
Oakfield Gdns, N18 . . . . . .**60** B4
  SE19 . . . .**170** B5
  Beckenham BR3 . . . .**190** A5
  Carshalton SM5 . . . .**199** H1
  Greenford UB6 . . . . .**104** A4
Oakfield La, Kes. BR2 . .**205** J4
Oakfield Rd, E6 . . . .**116** B1
  E17 . . . .**77** H2
  N3 . . . .**72** E1
  N4 . . . .**75** G6
  N14 . . . .**58** E3
  SE20 . . . .**171** E7
  SW19 . . . .**166** A3
  Croydon CR0 . . . .**201** J1
  Ilford IG1 . . . .**99** E2
Oakfields Rd, NW11 . . . . .**72** B6
Oakfield St, SW10 . . . . . .**30** C5
Oakford Rd, NW5 . . . .**92** C4
Oak Gdns, Croy. CR0 . . .**204** A2
  Edgware HA8 . . . .**70** C2
Oak Gro, NW2 . . . .**90** B4
  Ruislip HA4 . . . .**66** B7
  Sunbury-on-Thames
  TW16 . . . .**160** B7
  West Wickham BR4 . .**204** C2
Oak Gro Rd, SE20 . . . . .**189** F1
Oakhall Ct, E11 . . . .**79** H6
Oak Hall Rd, E11 . . . .**79** H6
Oakham Cl, SE6
  off Rutland Wk **171** J2
  Barnet EN4 . . . .**41** J3
Oakham Dr, Brom.
  BR2 . . . .**191** F4
Oakhampton Rd, NW7 . . .**56** A7
Oakhill, Esher (Clay.)
  KT10 . . . .**194** D6

Oak Hill, Surb. KT6 . . . . .**181** H7
  Woodford Green IG8 . .**62** D7
Oakhill Av, NW3 . . . .**90** E4
  Pinner HA5 . . . .**66** E2
Oak Hill Cl, Wdf.Grn. IG8 .**62** D7
Oakhill Ct, SW19 . . . . . .**166** A7
Oak Hill Cres, Surb. KT6 .**181** H7
  Woodford Green IG8 . .**62** D7
Oakhill Dr, Surb. KT6 . . .**181** H7
Oak Hill Gdns, Wdf.Grn.
  IG8 . . . .**79** E1
Oak Hill Gro, Surb. KT6 .**181** H6
Oak Hill Pk, NW3 . . . .**91** E4
Oak Hill Pk Ms, NW3 . . . .**91** F4
Oakhill Path, Surb. KT6 .**181** H6
Oak Hill Rd, Surb. KT6 . .**181** H6
Oakhill Rd, SW15 . . . . . .**148** C5
  SW16 . . . .**187** E1
  Beckenham BR3 . . . .**190** C2
  Orpington BR6 . . . . .**207** J1
Oak Hill Rd, Surb. KT6 . .**181** H6
Oakhill Rd, Sutt. SM1 . . .**199** E3
Oak Hill Way, NW3 . . . . . .**91** F4
Oakhouse Rd, Bexh.
  DA6 . . . .**159** G5
Oakhurst Av, Barn. EN4 . .**41** H7
  Bexleyheath DA7 . . . .**138** E7
Oakhurst Cl, E17 . . . .**78** E4
  Chislehurst BR7 . . . . .**192** C1
  Ilford IG6 . . . .**81** F1
  Teddington TW11 . . . .**162** B5
Oakhurst Gdns, E4 . . . . . .**63** F1
  E17 . . . .**78** E4
  Bexleyheath DA7 . . . .**139** E7
Oakhurst Gro, SE22 . . . .**152** D4
Oakhurst Rd, Epsom
  KT19 . . . .**196** C6
Oakington Av, Har. HA2 . .**67** G7
  Hayes UB3 . . . .**121** G4
  Wembley HA9 . . . .**87** J3
Oakington Dr, Sun.
  TW16 . . . .**178** C2
Oakington Manor Dr, Wem.
  HA9 . . . .**88** A5
Oakington Rd, W9 . . . . . .**108** D4
Oakington Way, N8 . . . . . .**75** E6
Oakland Pl, Buck.H. IG9 . .**63** G2
Oakland Rd, E15 . . . .**96** D4
Oaklands, N21 . . . .**59** F2
  Twickenham TW2 . . . .**143** J7
Oaklands Av, N9 . . . .**44** E6
  Esher KT10 . . . .**194** A1
  Isleworth TW7 . . . . . .**124** C6
  Sidcup DA15 . . . .**157** J7
  Thornton Heath CR7 . .**187** G4
  Watford WD19 . . . .**50** B1
  West Wickham BR4 . .**204** B3
Oaklands Cl, Bexh. DA6 .**159** F5
  Chessington KT9 . . . .**195** F4
  Orpington BR5 . . . . .**193** H6
Oaklands Ct, Wem. HA0 . .**87** G5
Oaklands Est, SW4 . . . . .**150** C6
Oaklands Gro, W12 . . . . .**127** G1
Oaklands La, Barn. EN5 . .**39** H4
Oaklands Pk Av, Ilf. IG1
  off High Rd **99** G2
Oaklands Pl, SW4
  off St. Alphonsus Rd .**150** C4
Oaklands Rd, N20 . . . .**40** C4
  NW2 . . . .**90** A4
  SW14 . . . .**146** D3
  W7 . . . .**124** C2
  Bexleyheath DA6 . . . .**159** F4
  Bromley BR1 . . . .**173** E7
Oaklands Way, Wall.
  SM6 . . . .**200** D7
Oakland Way, Epsom
  KT19 . . . .**196** D6
Oak La, E14 . . . .**113** J7
  N2 . . . .**73** G2
  N11 . . . .**58** D6
  Isleworth TW7 . . . . . .**144** B4
  Twickenham TW1 . . . .**144** D7
  Woodford Green IG8 . .**63** F3
Oakleafe Gdns, Ilf. IG6 . . .**80** E3
Oaklea Pas, Kings.T. KT1 .**181** G3
Oakleigh Av, N20 . . . .**57** G2
  Edgware HA8 . . . .**70** B2
  Surbiton KT6 . . . .**196** A1
Oakleigh Cl, N20 . . . .**57** J3
Oakleigh Ct, Barn. EN4
  off Church Hill Rd **41** H6
  Edgware HA8 . . . .**70** C2
Oakleigh Cres, N20 . . . . . .**57** H2
Oakleigh Gdns, N20 . . . . .**57** F1
  Edgware HA8 . . . .**53** J5
  Orpington BR6 . . . . .**207** H4
Oakleigh Ms, N20
  off Oakleigh Rd N **57** F2

OAKLEIGH PARK, N20 . . . .**57** G1
Oakleigh Pk Av, Chis.
  BR7 . . . .**192** D1
Oakleigh Pk N, N20 . . . . . .**57** G1
Oakleigh Pk S, N20 . . . . . .**57** H2
Oakleigh Rd, Pnr. HA5 . . .**51** F6
Oakleigh Rd N, N20 . . . . . .**57** G2
Oakleigh Rd S, N11 . . . . . .**58** A3
Oakleigh Way, Mitch.
  CR4 . . . .**186** B1
  Surbiton KT6 . . . .**196** A1
Oakley Av, W5 . . . .**106** A7
  Barking IG11 . . . .**99** J7
  Croydon CR0 . . . .**201** E4
Oakley Cl, E4 . . . .**62** C3
  E6 off Northumberland
  Rd **116** B6
  W7 . . . .**104** B7
  Isleworth TW7 . . . . . .**144** A1
Oakley Ct, Loug. IG10
  off Hillyfields **48** D2
  Mitcham CR4
  off London Rd **200** A1
Oakley Cres, EC1 . . . .**11** H2
Oakley Dr, SE9 . . . .**175** G1
  SE13 off Hither Grn La .**154** C5
  Bromley BR2 . . . .**206** B3
Oakley Gdns, N8 . . . .**75** F5
  SW3 . . . .**31** H5
Oakley Pk, Bex. DA5 . . .**158** C7
Oakley Pl, SE1 . . . .**37** F4
Oakley Rd, N1 . . . .**94** A7
  SE25 . . . .**188** E5
  Bromley BR2 . . . .**206** B3
  Harrow HA1 . . . .**68** B6
Oakley Sq, NW1 . . . .**9** G1
Oakley St, SW3 . . . .**31** G5
Oakley Wk, W6 . . . .**128** A6
Oakley Yd, E2 . . . .**13** G5
Oak Lo Av, Chig. IG7 . . . .**65** G5
Oak Lo Cl, Stan. HA7
  off Dennis La **53** F5
Oak Lo Dr, W.Wick. BR4 .**190** B7
Oak Manor Dr, Wem. HA9
  off Oakington
  Manor Dr **87** J5
Oakmead Av, Brom. BR2 .**191** G6
Oakmeade, Pnr. HA5 . . . .**51** G6
Oakmead Gdns, Edg.
  HA8 . . . .**54** D4
Oakmead Pl, Mitch. CR4 .**185** H1
Oakmead Rd, SW12 . . . .**168** A1
  Croydon CR0 . . . .**186** D6
Oakmere Rd, SE2 . . . . . .**138** A6
Oakmoor Way, Chig. IG7 . .**65** H5
Oakmount Pl, Orp. BR6 .**207** G1
Oak Pk Gdns, SW19 . . . .**148** A7
Oak Pl, SW18
  off East Hill **148/149** E5
Oakridge Dr, N2 . . . .**73** G3
Oakridge La, Brom. BR1
  off Downham Way . . .**172** D5
Oakridge Rd, Brom. BR1 .**172** D4
Oak Ri, Buck.H. IG9 . . . . .**64** A3
Oak Rd, W5
  off The Broadway . . .**105** G7
  Erith (Northumb.Hth.)
  DA8 . . . .**139** J7
  New Malden KT3 . . . .**182** D2
Oak Row, SW16 . . . .**186** C2
Oaks, The, N12 . . . .**57** E4
  SE18 . . . .**137** F5
  Watford WD19 . . . .**50** B1
  Woodford Green IG8 . .**63** E6
Oaks Av, SE19 . . . .**170** B5
  Feltham TW13 . . . . . .**160** E2
  Romford RM5 . . . .**83** J2
  Worcester Park KT4 . .**197** H3
Oaksford Av, SE26 . . . . .**170** E3
Oaks Gro, E4 . . . .**62** E2
Oakshade Rd, Brom.
  BR1 . . . .**172** D4
Oakshaw Rd, SW18 . . . .**149** E7
Oaks La, Croy. CR0 . . . .**203** F3
  Ilford IG2 . . . .**81** H5
Oaks Rd, Croy. CR0 . . . .**202** E5
  Staines (Stanw.) TW19 .**140** A6
Oak St, Rom. RM7 . . . . . .**83** J5
Oaks Way, Cars. SM5 . . .**199** J7
  Surbiton KT6 . . . .**195** G2
Oakthorpe Rd, N13 . . . . . .**59** G5
Oaktree Av, N13 . . . .**59** H3
Oak Tree Cl, W5
  off Pinewood Gro . . .**105** F6
  Loughton IG10 . . . .**49** F1
  Stanmore HA7 . . . .**53** F7
Oak Tree Dell, NW9 . . . . .**70** C5
Oak Tree Dr, N20 . . . .**57** E1
Oak Tree Gdns, Brom.
  BR1 . . . .**173** H5

Oaktree Gro, Ilf. IG1 . . . . . .99 G5
Oak Tree Rd, NW8 . . . . . . .7 F4
Oakview Gdns, N2 . . . . . .73 G4
Oakview Gro, Croy. CR0 .203 H1
Oakview Rd, SE6 . . . . . .172 B5
Oak Village, NW5 . . . . . . .92 A4
Oak Wlk, Wall. SM6
  off London Rd 200 A1
Oak Way, N14 . . . . .42 B7
Oakway, SW20 . . . . .183 J4
Oak Way, W3 . . . . .126 E1
Oakway, Brom. BR2 . . . . .190 D2
Oak Way, Croy. CR0 . . . .189 G6
Oakway Cl, Bex. DA5 . . . .159 E6
Oakways, SE9 . . . . .156 E6
OAKWOOD, N14 . . . . .42 D6
Oakwood Av, N14 . . . . . . .42 D7
  Beckenham BR3 . . . . . .190 C2
  Borehamwood WD6 . . .38 B4
  Bromley BR2 . . . . .191 H3
  Mitcham CR4 . . . . .185 G2
  Southall UB1 . . . . .103 G7
Oakwood Cl, N14 . . . . . . .42 C6
  Chislehurst BR7 . . . . . .174 C6
  Woodford Green IG8
    off Green Wk 64 B6
Oakwood Ct, N14 . . . . . .128 C3
Oakwood Cres, N21 . . . . .43 E6
  Greenford UB6 . . . . . . .86 D6
Oakwood Dr, SE19 . . . . .170 A6
  Edgware HA8 . . . . .54 C6
Oakwood Gdns, Ilf. IG3 . .99 J2
  Orpington BR6 . . . . . . .207 F2
  Sutton SM1 . . . . .198 D2
Oakwood Hill, Loug. IG10 .48 C6
Oakwood Hill Ind Est, Loug.
  IG10 . . . . .49 F5
Oakwood La, W14 . . . . . .128 C3
Oakwood Pk Rd, N14 . . . .42 D7
Oakwood Pl, Croy. CR0 . .187 G6
Oakwood Rd, NW11 . . . . .72 E5
  SW20 . . . . .183 G1
  Croydon CR0 . . . . .187 G6
  Orpington BR6 . . . . . . .207 F2
  Pinner HA5 . . . . .66 B2
Oakwood Vw, N14 . . . . . .42 D6
Oakworth Rd, W10 . . . . .107 J5
Oarsman Pl, E.Mol. KT8 .180 B4
Oates Cl, Brom. BR2 . . . .190 D3
Oatfield Ho, N15
  off Bushey Rd 76 B6
Oatfield Rd, Orp. BR6 . . .207 J1
Oatland Ri, E17 . . . . .77 H2
Oatlands Rd, Enf. EN3 . . .45 F1
Oat La, EC2 . . . . .19 J3
Oban Cl, E13 . . . . .115 J4
Oban Ho, Bark. IG11
  off Wheelers Cross 117 G2
Oban Rd, E13 . . . . .115 J3
  SE25 . . . . .188 A4
Oban St, E14 . . . . .114 D6
Oberon Cl, Borwd. WD6 . .38 C1
Oberstein Rd, SW11 . . . .149 G4
Oborne Cl, SE24 . . . . . . .151 H5
Observatory Gdns, W8 . .128 D2
Observatory Ms, E14
  off Storers Quay 134 D4
Observatory Rd, SW14 . .146 C4
Occupation La, SE18 . . . .156 E1
  W5 . . . . .125 G4
Occupation Rd, SE17 . . . .35 J3
  W13 . . . . .124 E2
Ocean Est, E1 . . . . .113 G4
Ocean St, E1 . . . . .113 G5
Ocean Wf, E14 . . . . .134 A2
Ockendon Ms, N1
  off Ockendon Rd 94 A6
Ockendon Rd, N1 . . . . . . .94 A6
Ockham Dr, Orp. BR5 . . .176 A7
Ockley Ct, Sutt. SM1
  off Oakhill Rd 199 F4
Ockley Rd, SW16 . . . . . .168 E3
  Croydon CR0 . . . . .187 F7
Octagon Arc, EC2 . . . . . .20 D2
Octavia Cl, Mitch. CR4 . .185 H5
Octavia Rd, Islw. TW7 . . .144 C2
Octavia St, SW11 . . . . . .149 H1
Octavia Way, SE28
  off Booth Cl 118 B7
Octavius St, SE8 . . . . . . .134 A7
Odard Rd, W.Mol. KT8
  off Down St 179 G4
Oddesey Rd, Borwd.
  WD6 . . . . .38 B1
Odell Cl, Bark. IG11 . . . . .99 J7
Odessa Rd, E7 . . . . .97 F3
  NW10 . . . . .107 G2
Odessa St, SE16 . . . . . . .133 J2
Odger St, SW11 . . . . . . .149 J2
Odhams Wk, WC2 . . . . . .18 A4

Odyssey Business Pk, Ruis.
  HA4 . . . . .84 B5
Offa's Mead, E9
  off Lindisfarne Way . . .95 H4
Offenbach Ho, E2 . . . . . .113 G2
Offenham Rd, SE9 . . . . . .174 C4
Offers Ct, Kings.T. KT1
  off Winery La 181 J3
Offerton Rd, SW4 . . . . . .150 C3
Offham Slope, N12 . . . . . .56 C5
Offley Pl, Islw. TW7 . . . . .144 A2
Offley Rd, SW9 . . . . .35 E7
Offord Cl, N17 . . . . .60 D7
Offord Rd, N1 . . . . .93 F7
Offord St, N1 . . . . .93 F7
Ogilby St, SE18 . . . . .136 C4
Oglander Rd, SE15 . . . . .152 C4
Ogle St, W1 . . . . .17 F1
Oglethorpe Rd, Dag.
  RM10 . . . . .101 F3
Ohio Rd, E13 . . . . .115 F4
Oil Mill La, W6 . . . . .127 G5
Okeburn Rd, SW17 . . . . .168 A5
Okehampton Cl, N12 . . . .57 G5
Okehampton Cres, Well.
  DA16 . . . . .158 B1
Okehampton Rd, NW10 .107 J1
Olaf St, W11 . . . . .108 A7
Oldacre Ms, SW12
  off Balham Gro 150 B7
★ Old Admiralty Bldgs (MoD),
  SW1 . . . . .25 J2
Old Bailey, EC4 . . . . .19 H4
Old Barge Ho All, SE1
  off Upper Grd 131 G1
Old Barn Cl, Sutt. SM2 . .198 B7
Old Barrack Yd, SW1 . . . .24 B4
Old Barrowfield, E15
  off New Plaistow
    Rd 114/115 E1
Old Bellgate Pl, E14 . . . .134 A3
Oldberry Rd, Edg. HA8 . . .54 D6
Old Bethnal Grn Rd, E2 . .13 H3
OLD BEXLEY, Bex. 159 H7
Old Billingsgate Wk, EC3
  off Lower Thames St .112 B6
Old Bond St, W1 . . . . .17 F6
Oldborough Rd, Wem.
  HA0 . . . . .87 F2
Old Brewers Yd, WC2 . . . .18 A4
Old Brewery Ms, NW3
  off Hampstead High St .91 G4
Old Br Cl, Nthlt. UB5 . . . .103 G2
Old Br St, Kings.T. KT1 . .181 G2
Old Broad St, EC2 . . . . . .20 C4
Old Bromley Rd, Brom.
  BR1 . . . . .172 D5
Old Brompton Rd, SW5 . .128 D5
  SW7 . . . . .30 C3
Old Bldgs, WC2 . . . . .18 E3
Old Burlington St, W1 . . .17 F5
Oldbury Pl, W1 . . . . .16 C1
Oldbury Rd, Enf. EN1 . . . .44 D2
Old Canal Ms, SE15 . . . . .37 G4
Old Castle St, E1 . . . . . . .21 F3
Old Cavendish St, W1 . . .16 D3
Old Change Ct, EC4
  off Carter La 111 J6
Old Chelsea Ms, SW3 . . .31 F6
Old Ch La, NW9 . . . . .88 C2
  Greenford UB6
    off Perivale La 104 D3
  Stanmore HA7 . . . . . . .53 F7
Old Ch Rd, E1 . . . . .113 G6
  E4 . . . . .62 A4
Old Ch St, SW3 . . . . .31 F4
Old Claygate La, Esher (Clay.)
  KT10 . . . . .194 D6
Old Clem Sq, SE18
  off Kempt St 136 D6
Old Coal Yd, SE28
  off Pettman Cres 137 G4
Old Compton St, W1 . . . .17 H5
Old Cote Dr, Hounds.
  TW5 . . . . .123 G6
Old Ct Pl, W8 . . . . .22 A3
★ Old Curiosity Shop,
  WC2 . . . . .18 C3
Old Dairy Ms, SW12
  off Chestnut Gro 150 A7
Old Deer Pk Gdns, Rich.
  TW9 . . . . .145 H3
Old Devonshire Rd,
  SW12 . . . . .150 B7
Old Dock Cl, Rich. TW9
  off Watcombe Cotts . .126 A6
Old Dover Rd, SE3 . . . . .135 G7
Old Fm Av, N14 . . . . .42 C7
  Sidcup DA15 . . . . .175 G1
Old Fm Cl, Hounds. TW4 .143 F4

Old Fm Pas, Hmptn.
  TW12 . . . . .179 J1
Old Fm Rd, N2 . . . . .73 G1
  Hampton TW12 . . . . . .161 F6
  West Drayton UB7 . . . .120 A2
Old Fm Rd E, Sid. DA15 .176 A2
Old Fm Rd W, Sid. DA15 .175 J2
Oldfield Cl, Brom. BR1 . .192 C4
  Greenford UB6 . . . . . . .86 B5
  Stanmore HA7 . . . . . . .52 D5
Oldfield Fm Gdns, Grnf.
  UB6 . . . . .104 A1
Oldfield Gro, SE16 . . . . .133 G4
Oldfield La N, Grnf. UB6 . .86 B6
Oldfield La S, Grnf. UB6 .103 J4
Oldfield Ms, N6 . . . . .74 C7
Oldfield Rd, N16 . . . . .94 B3
  NW10 . . . . .89 F7
  SW19 . . . . .166 B6
  W3 off Valetta Rd 127 F2
  Bexleyheath DA7 . . . . .159 E2
  Bromley BR1 . . . . .192 C4
  Hampton TW12 . . . . . .179 F1
Oldfields Circ, Nthlt. UB5 .85 J6
Oldfields Rd, Sutt. SM1 . .198 C3
Oldfields Trd Est, Sutt.
  SM1 . . . . .198 D3
Old Fish St Hill, EC4 . . . .19 J5
Old Fleet La, EC4 . . . . . . .19 G3
Old Fold Cl, Barn. EN5
  off Old Fold La 40 C1
Old Fold La, Barn. EN5 . . .40 C1
Old Fold Vw, Barn. EN5 . .39 J3
OLD FORD, E3 . . . . .95 J7
Old Ford Rd, E2 . . . . .113 F2
  E3 . . . . .113 H2
Old Forge Cl, Stan. HA7 . .52 D4
Old Forge Ms, W12
  off Goodwin Rd 127 H2
Old Forge Way, Sid.
  DA14 . . . . .176 B4
Old Fox Footpath, S.Croy. CR2
  off Essenden Rd 202 B7
Old Gloucester St, WC1 . .18 B1
Old Hall Cl, Pnr. HA5 . . . .67 E1
Old Hall Dr, Pnr. HA5 . . . .66 E1
Oldham Ter, W3 . . . . . . .126 C1
Old Hill, Chis. BR7 . . . . .192 D1
  Orpington BR6 . . . . . . .207 G6
Oldhill St, N16 . . . . .94 D1
Old Homesdale Rd, Brom.
  BR2 . . . . .191 J4
Old Hosp Cl, SW12 . . . . .167 J1
Old Ho Cl, SW19 . . . . . . .166 B5
Old Ho Gdns, Twick.
  TW1 . . . . .145 F5
Old Jamaica Rd, SE16 . . .29 H5
Old James St, SE15 . . . .152 E3
Old Jewry, EC2 . . . . .20 B4
Old Kenton La, NW9 . . . . .70 B5
Old Kent Rd, SE1 . . . . . . .36 D1
  SE15 . . . . .37 J5
Old Kingston Rd, Wor.Pk.
  KT4 . . . . .196 C3
Old Lo Pl, Twick. TW1
  off St. Margarets
    Rd 144/145 E6
Old Lo Way, Stan. HA7 . . .52 D5
Old Maidstone Rd, Sid.
  DA14 . . . . .177 F7
OLD MALDEN, Wor.Pk. . .196 D1
Old Malden La, Wor.Pk.
  KT4 . . . . .196 D2
Old Manor Dr, Islw.
  TW7 . . . . .143 J6
Old Manor Rd, Sthl.
  UB2 . . . . .122 D4
Old Manor Way, Chis.
  BR7 . . . . .174 C5
Old Manor Yd, SW5
  off Earls Ct Rd . . .128/129 E4
Old Marylebone Rd,
  NW1 . . . . .15 H2
Old Ms, Har. HA1
  off Hindes Rd 68 B5
Old Mill Ct, E18 . . . . .79 J3
Old Mill Rd, SE18 . . . . . .137 G6
Old Mitre Ct, EC4
  off Fleet St 111 G6
Old Montague St, E1 . . . .21 H2
Old Nichol St, E2 . . . . . . .13 F5
Old N St, WC1 . . . . .18 C1
Old Oak Cl, Chess. KT9 . .195 J4
OLD OAK COMMON,
  NW10 . . . . .107 F5
Old Oak Common La,
  NW10 . . . . .107 E4
  W3 . . . . .107 E5
Old Oak La, NW10 . . . . .107 E3
Old Oak Rd, W3 . . . . . . .107 F7

★ Old Operating Thea Mus
  & Herb Garret, SE1 . . .28 C2
Old Orchard, Sun. TW16 .178 C2
Old Orchard, The, NW3
  off Nassington Rd 91 J4
Old Palace La, Rich. TW9 .145 F5
Old Palace Rd, Croy.
  CR0 . . . . .201 H3
Old Palace Ter, Rich. TW9
  off King St 145 G5
Old Palace Yd, SW1 . . . . .26 A5
  Richmond TW9 . . . . . .145 F5
Old Paradise St, SE11 . . .34 C1
Old Pk Av, SW12 . . . . . .150 A6
  Enfield EN2 . . . . .43 J4
Old Pk Gro, Enf. EN2 . . . .43 J4
Old Pk La, W1 . . . . .24 C2
Old Pk Ms, Houns. TW5 .123 F7
Old Pk Ridings, N21 . . . . .43 H6
Old Pk Rd, N13 . . . . .59 F4
  SE2 . . . . .138 A5
  Enfield EN2 . . . . .43 H3
Old Pk Rd S, Enf. EN2 . . .43 H4
Old Pk Vw, Enf. EN2 . . . .43 G3
Old Perry St, Chis. BR7 . .175 H7
Old Pound Cl, Islw. TW7 .144 D1
Old Pye St, SW1 . . . . .25 H5
Old Quebec St, W1 . . . . . .16 A4
Old Queen St, SW1 . . . . . .25 J4
Old Rectory Gdns, Edg.
  HA8 . . . . .54 A6
Old Redding, Har. HA3 . . .51 J4
Oldridge Rd, SW12 . . . . .150 A7
Old Rd, SE13 . . . . .155 E4
  Enfield EN3 . . . . .45 F1
Old Rope Wk, Sun. TW16
  off The Avenue 178 B3
Old Royal Free Pl, N1
  off Liverpool Rd 111 G1
Old Royal Free Sq, N1 . .111 G1
Old Ruislip Rd, Nthlt.
  UB5 . . . . .102 D2
Old Savill's Cotts, Chig. IG7
  off The Chase 65 F4
Old Sch Cl, SE10 . . . . . .135 E3
  SW19 . . . . .184 D2
  Beckenham BR3 . . . . . .189 G2
Old Sch Cres, E7 . . . . . . .97 F6
Old Sch Sq, E14
  off Pelling St 114 A6
  Thames Ditton KT7 . . .180 C6
Old Seacoal La, EC4 . . . . .19 G3
Old S Cl, Pnr. HA5 . . . . . .66 D1
Old S Lambeth Rd, SW8 . .34 B7
★ Old Spitalfields Mkt,
  E1 . . . . .21 F1
Old Spitalfields Mkt, E1 . .21 F1
Old Sq, WC2 . . . . .18 D3
Old Sta Rd, Hayes UB3 . .121 J3
  Loughton IG10 . . . . . . .48 B5
Old Sta Yd, Brom. BR2
  off Bourne Way 205 F1
Oldstead Rd, Brom. BR1 .172 D4
Old Stockley Rd, West Dr.
  UB7 . . . . .120 E2
Old St, E13 . . . . .115 H2
  EC1 . . . . .11 J5
Old Swan Yd, Cars. SM5 .199 J4
Old Town, SW4 . . . . .150 C3
  Croydon CR0 . . . . .201 H3
Old Tram Yd, SE18
  off Lakedale Rd 137 H4
Old Woolwich Rd, SE10 .134 D6
Old York Rd, SW18 . . . . .149 E5
Oleander Cl, Orp. BR6 . . .207 G5
O'Leary Sq, E1 . . . . .113 F5
Olga St, E3 . . . . .113 H2
Olinda Rd, N16 . . . . .76 C6
Oliphant St, W10 . . . . . . .108 A3
Oliver Av, SE25 . . . . .188 C3
Oliver Cl, W4 . . . . .126 B6
Oliver Gdns, E6 . . . . .116 B6
Oliver-Goldsmith Est,
  SE15 . . . . .152 D1
Oliver Gro, SE25 . . . . . . .188 C4
Olive Rd, E13 . . . . .115 J3
  NW2 . . . . .89 J4
  SW19 off Norman Rd . .167 F7
  W5 . . . . .125 G3
Oliver Rd, E10 . . . . .96 B2
  E17 . . . . .78 C5
  NW10 . . . . .106 C2
  New Malden KT3 . . . . .182 C2
  Sutton SM1 . . . . .199 G4
Olivers Yd, EC1 . . . . .12 C5
Olivette St, SW15 . . . . . .148 A3
Ollards Gro, Loug. IG10 . .48 A4
Ollerton Grn, E3 . . . . . . .113 J1
Ollerton Rd, N11 . . . . . . .58 D5
Olley Cl, Wall. SM6 . . . . .200 E7

Ollgar Cl, W12 . . . .**127** F1
Olliffe St, E14 . . . .**134** C3
Olmar St, SE1 . . . .**37** H5
Olney Rd, SE17 . . . .**35** J5
Olron Cres, Bexh. DA6 . .**158** D5
Olven Rd, SE18 . . . .**137** F7
Olveston Wk, Cars. SM5 .**185** G6
Olwen Ms, Pnr. HA5 . . . . .**66** D2
Olyffe Av, Well. DA16 . . .**158** A2
Olyffe Dr, Beck. BR3 . . . .**190** C1
★ Olympia, W14 . . . .**128** B3
Olympia Ms, W2 . . . .**14** B6
Olympia Way, W14 . . . . . .**128** B3
Olympic Way, Grnf. UB6 .**103** H1
  Wembley HA9 . . . .**88** A4
Olympus Sq, E5
  off Nolan Way **94** D4
Oman Av, NW2 . . . .**89** J4
O'Meara St, SE1 . . . .**28** A2
Omega Cl, E14
  off Tiller Rd **134** B3
Omega Pl, N1 . . . .**10** B2
Omega St, SE14 . . . .**154** A1
Ommaney Rd, SE14 . . . . .**153** G1
Omnibus Way, E17 . . . . . .**78** A2
Ondine Rd, SE15 . . . .**152** C4
Onega Gate, SE16 . . . . . .**133** H3
O'Neill Path, SE18
  off Kempt St **136** D6
One Tree Cl, SE23 . . . . . .**153** F6
Ongar Cl, Rom. RM6 . . . . .**82** C5
Ongar Rd, SW6 . . . .**128** D6
Onra Rd, E17 . . . .**78** A7
Onslow Av, Rich. TW10 . .**145** H5
Onslow Cl, E4 . . . .**62** C2
  Thames Ditton KT7 . . .**194** B1
Onslow Cres, Chis. BR7 .**192** E1
Onslow Dr, Sid. DA14 . . .**176** D2
Onslow Gdns, E18 . . . . . .**79** H3
  N10 . . . .**74** B5
  N21 . . . .**43** G5
  SW7 . . . .**30** E2
  Thames Ditton KT7 . . .**194** B1
  Wallington SM6 . . . . . .**200** C6
Onslow Ms E, SW7 . . . . . .**31** E2
Onslow Ms W, SW7 . . . . . .**30** E2
Onslow Rd, Croy. CR0 . . .**187** F7
  New Malden KT3 . . . . .**183** G4
  Richmond TW10 . . . . . .**145** H5
Onslow Sq, SW7 . . . .**31** F1
Onslow St, EC1 . . . .**11** F6
Onslow Way, T.Ditt. KT7 .**194** B1
Ontario St, SE1 . . . .**27** H6
Ontario Way, E14 . . . . . .**114** A7
On The Hill, Wat. WD19 . .**50** E2
Opal Cl, E16 . . . .**116** A6
Opal Ms, NW6
  off Priory Pk Rd **108** C1
  Ilford IG1 off Ley St .**98/99** E2
Opal St, SE11 . . . .**35** G2
Openshaw Rd, SE2 . . . . .**138** B4
Openview, SW18 . . . .**167** F1
Ophelia Gdns, NW2
  off Hamlet Sq **90** B3
Ophir Ter, SE15 . . . .**152** D1
Opossum Way, Houns.
  TW4 . . . .**142** C2
Oppenheim Rd, SE13 . . .**154** C2
Oppidans Ms, NW3
  off Meadowbank **91** J7
Oppidans Rd, NW3 . . . . . .**91** J7
Orange Ct, E1 . . . .**29** J2
Orange Gro, E11 . . . .**96** E3
  Chigwell IG7 . . . .**65** F6
Orange Hill Rd, Edg. HA8 .**54** C7
Orange Pl, SE16
  off Lower Rd **133** F3
Orangery, The, Rich.
  TW10 . . . .**163** F2
Orangery La, SE9 . . . . . .**156** C5
Orange Sq, SW1
  off Ebury St **130** A5
Orange St, WC2 . . . .**17** H6
Orange Yd, W1 . . . .**17** J4
Oratory La, SW3 . . . .**31** F3
Orbain Rd, SW6 . . . .**128** B7
Orbel St, SW11 . . . .**149** H1
Orb St, SE17 . . . .**36** B2
Orchard, The, N14 . . . . . .**42** B5
  N21 . . . .**44** A6
  NW11 . . . .**72** D5
  SE3 . . . .**154** D2
  W4 . . . .**126** D4
  W5 . . . .**105** G5
  Epsom KT17 . . . .**197** F7
  Hounslow TW3 . . . . . .**143** J2
Orchard Av, N3 . . . .**72** D3
  N14 . . . .**42** C6
  N20 . . . .**57** G2
  Belvedere DA17 . . . . . .**139** E6

Orchard Av, Croy. CR0 . .**189** H7
  Feltham TW14 . . . .**141** G5
  Hounslow TW5 . . . . . .**123** E7
  Mitcham CR4 . . . .**200** A1
  New Malden KT3 . . . . .**183** E2
  Southall UB1 . . . .**123** E1
  Thames Ditton KT7 . . .**194** D1
Orchard Cl, E4
  off Chingford Mt Rd . . .**62** A4
  E11 . . . .**79** H4
  N1 off Morton Rd **93** J7
  NW2 . . . .**89** G3
  SE23
  off Brenchley Gdns . .**153** F6
  SW20 off Grand Dr . . .**183** J4
  W10 . . . .**108** B5
  Bexleyheath DA7 . . . .**158** E1
  Bushey (Bushey Hth.)
  WD23 . . . .**52** A1
  Edgware HA8 . . . .**53** H6
  Epsom (W.Ewell) KT19 .**196** B6
  Northolt UB5 . . . .**85** J5
  Surbiton KT6 . . . .**181** E7
  Walton-on-Thames KT12
  off Garden Rd **178** B7
  Wembley HA0 . . . .**105** H1
Orchard Ct, Islw. TW7
  off Thornbury Av **144** A1
  Twickenham TW2 . . . . .**162** A2
  Wallington SM6
  off Parkgate Rd **200** B5
  Worcester Park KT4
  off The Avenue **197** G1
Orchard Cres, Edg. HA8 . .**54** C5
  Enfield EN1 . . . .**44** C1
Orchard Dr, SE3
  off Orchard Rd **154/155** E2
  Edgware HA8 . . . .**53** J5
Orchard Gdns, Chess.
  KT9 . . . .**195** H4
  Sutton SM1 . . . .**198** D5
Orchard Gate, NW9 . . . . . .**70** E4
  Esher KT10 . . . .**194** A1
  Greenford UB6 . . . .**86** E6
Orchard Grn, Orp. BR6 . .**207** H2
Orchard Gro, SE20 . . . . .**170** D7
  Croydon CR0 . . . .**189** H7
  Edgware HA8 . . . .**70** A1
  Harrow HA3 . . . .**69** H6
  Orpington BR6 . . . . . .**207** J2
Orchard Hill, SE13
  off Coldbath St **154** B2
  Carshalton SM5 . . . . .**199** J5
Orchard La, SW20 . . . . . .**183** H1
  East Molesey KT8 . . . .**180** A6
  Woodford Green IG8 . . .**63** J4
Orchardleigh Av, Enf.
  EN3 . . . .**45** F2
Orchardmede, N21 . . . . . .**44** A6
Orchard Ms, N1
  off Southgate Gro **94** A7
Orchard Pl, E14 . . . .**114** E7
  N17 . . . .**60** C7
Orchard Ri, Croy. CR0 . .**203** H1
  Kingston upon Thames
  KT2 . . . .**182** C1
  Richmond TW10 . . . . .**146** B4
Orchard Ri E, Sid. DA15 .**157** J5
Orchard Ri W, Sid. DA15 .**157** H5
Orchard Rd, N6 . . . .**74** B7
  SE3 . . . .**155** E2
  SE18 . . . .**137** G4
  Barnet EN5 . . . .**40** C4
  Belvedere DA17 . . . . .**139** G4
  Brentford TW8 . . . .**125** F6
  Bromley BR1 . . . .**191** J1
  Chessington KT9 . . . . .**195** H4
  Dagenham RM10 . . . . .**119** G1
  Enfield EN3 . . . .**45** F5
  Hampton TW12 . . . . . .**161** F7
  Hayes UB3 . . . .**102** A7
  Hounslow TW4 . . . . . .**143** F5
  Kingston upon Thames
  KT1 . . . .**181** H2
  Mitcham CR4 . . . .**200** A1
  Orpington (Farnboro.)
  BR6 . . . .**207** E5
  Richmond TW9 . . . . . .**146** A3
  Romford RM7 . . . .**83** H1
  Sidcup DA14 . . . .**175** H4
  Sunbury-on-Thames TW16
  off Hanworth Rd **160** B7
  Sutton SM1 . . . .**198** D5
  Twickenham TW1 . . . .**144** D5
  Welling DA16 . . . .**158** B3
Orchardson St, NW8 . . . . . .**7** E6
Orchard Sq, W14
  off Sun Rd **128** C5
Orchard St, E17 . . . .**77** H4
  W1 . . . .**16** B4

Orchard Ter, Enf. EN1
  off Great Cambridge
  Rd **44** D6
Orchard Vil, Sid. DA14
  off Haven Cl **176** C6
Orchard Way, Beck. BR3 .**189** H5
  Croydon CR0 . . . .**203** H1
  Enfield EN1 . . . .**44** B3
  Sutton SM1 . . . .**199** G4
Orchid Cl, E6 . . . .**116** B5
  Chessington KT9 . . . . .**195** F7
  Southall UB1 . . . .**103** E6
Orchid Rd, N14 . . . .**42** C7
Orchid St, W12 . . . .**107** G7
Orde Hall St, WC1 . . . .**10** C6
Ordell Rd, E3 . . . .**113** J2
Ordnance Cl, Felt. TW13 .**160** A3
Ordnance Cres, SE10 . . .**134** D2
Ordnance Hill, NW8 . . . .**109** G1
Ordnance Ms, NW8 . . . .**7** F1
Ordnance Rd, E16 . . . . . .**115** F5
  SE18 . . . .**136** D6
Oregano Dr, E14 . . . .**114** D6
Oregon Av, E12 . . . .**98** C4
Oregon Cl, N.Mal. KT3
  off Georgia Rd **182** C4
Oregon Sq, Orp. BR6 . . .**207** G1
Orestes Ms, NW6
  off Aldred Rd **90** D5
Orford Ct, SE27 . . . .**169** H2
Orford Gdns, Twick. TW1 .**162** C2
Orford Rd, E17 . . . .**78** A5
  E18 . . . .**79** H3
  SE6 . . . .**172** B3
Organ La, E4 . . . .**62** C2
Oriel Cl, Mitch. CR4 . . . .**186** D4
Oriel Ct, NW3
  off Heath St **91** F4
Oriel Dr, SW13 . . . .**127** H6
Oriel Gdns, Ilf. IG5 . . . . . .**80** C3
Oriel Pl, NW3
  off Heath St **91** F4
Oriel Rd, E9 . . . .**95** G6
Oriel Way, Nthlt. UB5 . . . .**85** H7
Oriental Rd, E16 . . . .**136** A1
Oriental St, E14
  off Morant St **114** A7
Orient Ind Pk, E10 . . . .**96** A2
Orient St, SE11 . . . .**35** G1
Orient Way, E5 . . . .**95** G3
  E10 . . . .**95** H2
Oriole Way, SE28 . . . .**118** B7
Orion Rd, N11 . . . .**58** B6
Orissa Rd, SE18 . . . .**137** H5
Orkney St, SW11 . . . .**150** A2
Orlando Rd, SW4 . . . .**150** C3
Orleans Cl, Esher KT10 . .**194** A2
★ Orleans Ho Gall, Twick.
  TW1 . . . .**163** E1
Orleans Rd, SE19 . . . . . .**170** A6
  Twickenham TW1 . . . .**145** E7
Orleston Ms, N7 . . . .**93** G6
Orleston Rd, N7 . . . .**93** G6
Orley Fm Rd, Har. HA1 . . .**86** B3
Orlop St, SE10 . . . .**134** E5
Ormanton Rd, SE26 . . . . .**170** D4
Orme Ct, W2 . . . .**14** A6
Orme Ct Ms, W2 . . . .**14** B6
Orme La, W2 . . . .**14** A6
Ormeley Rd, SW12 . . . . . .**168** B1
Orme Rd, Kings.T. KT1 . .**182** B2
  Sutton SM1
  off Grove Rd **198/199** E6
Ormerod Gdns, Mitch.
  CR4 . . . .**186** A2
Ormesby Cl, SE28
  off Wroxham Rd **118** D7
Ormesby Way, Har. HA3 . .**69** J6
Orme Sq, W2 . . . .**14** A6
Ormiston Gro, W12 . . . . .**127** H1
Ormiston Rd, SE10 . . . . .**135** G5
Ormond Av, Hmptn.
  TW12 . . . .**179** H1
  Richmond TW10
  off Ormond Rd **145** G5
Ormond Cl, WC1 . . . .**18** B1
Ormond Cres, Hmptn.
  TW12 . . . .**179** H1
Ormond Dr, Hmptn.
  TW12 . . . .**161** H7
Ormonde Av, Orp. BR6 . .**207** F3
Ormonde Gate, SW3 . . . .**32** A4
Ormonde Pl, SW1 . . . .**32** B2
Ormonde Ri, Buck.H. IG9 .**63** J1
Ormonde Rd, SW14 . . . . .**146** B3
Ormonde Ter, NW8 . . . . .**109** J1
Ormond Ms, WC1 . . . .**10** B6
Ormond Rd, N19 . . . .**93** E1
  Richmond TW10 . . . . .**145** G5
Ormond Yd, SW1 . . . .**25** G1

Ormsby, Sutt. SM2
  off Grange Rd . . .**198/199** E7
Ormsby Gdns, Grnf.
  UB6 . . . .**103** J2
Ormsby Pl, N16
  off Victorian Gro **94** C3
Ormsby Pt, SE18
  off Troy Ct **136/137** E4
Ormsby St, E2 . . . .**13** F1
Ormside St, SE15 . . . . . .**133** F6
Ormskirk Rd, Wat. WD19 . .**50** D4
Ornan Rd, NW3 . . . .**91** H5
Oronsay Wk, N1
  off Clephane Rd **93** J6
Orpen Wk, N16 . . . .**94** B3
Orpheus St, SE5 . . . .**152** A1
ORPINGTON **207** H1
Orpington Gdns, N18 . . . .**60** B3
Orpington Rd, N21 . . . . . .**59** H1
  Chislehurst BR7 . . . . .**193** H3
Orpwood Cl, Hmptn.
  TW12 . . . .**161** F5
Orsett St, SE11 . . . .**34** D3
Orsett Ter, W2 . . . .**14** B3
  Woodford Green IG8 . . .**79** J1
Orsman Rd, N1 . . . .**112** B1
Orton St, E1 . . . .**29** H2
Orville Rd, SW11 . . . .**149** G2
Orwell Cl, N5 . . . .**93** J4
Orwell Rd, E13 . . . .**115** J2
Osbaldeston Rd, N16 . . . .**94** D2
Osberton Rd, SE12 . . . . .**155** G5
Osbert St, SW1 . . . .**33** H2
Osborn Cl, E8 . . . .**112** D1
Osborne Cl, Barn. EN4 . . .**41** J3
  Beckenham BR3 . . . . .**189** H4
  Feltham TW13 . . . .**160** D5
Osborne Gdns, Th.Hth.
  CR7 . . . .**187** J2
Osborne Gro, E17 . . . .**77** J4
  N4 . . . .**93** G1
Osborne Ms, E17
  off Osborne Gro **77** J4
Osborne Pl, Sutt. SM1 . .**199** G5
Osborne Rd, E7 . . . .**97** H5
  E9 . . . .**95** J6
  E10 . . . .**96** B3
  N4 . . . .**93** G1
  N13 . . . .**59** G3
  NW2 . . . .**89** H6
  W3 . . . .**126** B3
  Belvedere DA17 . . . . .**139** F5
  Buckhurst Hill IG9 . . . .**63** H1
  Dagenham RM9 . . . . .**101** F5
  Enfield EN3 . . . .**45** H2
  Hounslow TW3 . . . . . .**143** F3
  Kingston upon Thames
  KT2 . . . .**163** H7
  Southall UB1 . . . .**103** J6
  Thornton Heath CR7 . .**187** J2
Osborne Sq, Dag. RM9 . .**101** F4
Osborne Ter, SW17
  off Church La **168** A5
Osborn Gdns, NW7 . . . . . .**56** A7
Osborn La, SE23 . . . . . .**153** H7
Osborn St, E1 . . . .**21** G2
Osborn Ter, SE3
  off Lee Rd **155** F4
Osbourne Av, NW7
  off Bittacy Hill **56** B7
Oscar St, SE8 . . . .**154** A1
Oseney Cres, NW5 . . . . . .**92** C6
Osgood Av, Orp. BR6 . . .**207** J5
Osgood Gdns, Orp.
  BR6 . . . .**207** J5
OSIDGE, N14 . . . .**58** B1
Osidge La, N14 . . . .**58** A1
Osier Cres, N10 . . . .**73** J1
Osier La, SE10 . . . .**135** F3
Osier Ms, W4 . . . .**127** F6
Osiers Rd, SW18 . . . .**148** D4
Osier St, E1 . . . .**113** F4
Osier Way, E10 . . . .**96** B3
  Mitcham CR4 . . . .**185** H5
Oslac Rd, SE6 . . . .**172** B5
Oslo Ct, NW8 . . . .**7** G2
Oslo Sq, SE16 . . . .**133** H3
Osman Cl, N15
  off Tewkesbury Rd **76** A6
Osman Rd, N9 . . . .**60** D3
  W6 off Batoum Gdns .**127** J3
Osmond Cl, Har. HA2 . . . .**85** J2
Osmond Gdns, Wall.
  SM6 . . . .**200** C5
Osmund St, W12
  off Braybrook St **107** F6
Osnaburgh St, NW1 . . . . . .**9** E6
  NW1 (north section)
  off Robert St **110** B3
Osnaburgh Ter, NW1 . . . . . .**8** E5

Osney Ho, SE2
  off Hartslock Dr **138** D2
Osney Wk, Cars. SM5 . .**185** G6
Osprey Cl, E6
  off Dove App **116** B5
E11 ... .**79** G4
E17 ... .**61** H7
Sutton SM1
  off Sandpiper Rd **198** C5
West Drayton UB7 ... .**120** A2
Osprey Ms, Enf. EN3 ... .**45** E5
Ospringe Cl, SE20 ... . .**171** F7
Ospringe Ct, SE9
  off Alderwood Rd **157** G6
Ospringe Rd, NW5 ... .**92** C4
Osram Ct, W6
  off Lena Gdns **127** J3
Osram Rd, Wem. HA9 ... .**87** G3
Osric Path, N1 ... .**12** D2
Ossian Ms, N4 ... .**75** F7
Ossian Rd, N4 ... .**75** F7
Ossington Bldgs, W1 ... .**16** B1
Ossington Cl, W2
  off Ossington St .**108/109** E7
Ossington St, W2 ... . . .**14** A6
Ossory Rd, SE1 ... .**37** H4
Ossulston St, NW1 ... . .**9** H2
Ossulton Pl, N2
  off East End Rd **73** F3
Ossulton Way, N2 ... . . .**73** F4
Ostade Rd, SW2 ... . . .**151** F7
Osten Ms, SW7 ... .**22** B6
OSTERLEY, Islw. **123** J7
Osterley Av, Islw. TW7 . .**124** A7
Osterley Ct, Islw. TW7 . .**144** A1
Osterley Cres, Islw. TW7 .**144** B1
Osterley Gdns, Th.Hth.
  CR7 ... .**187** J2
Osterley Ho, E14
  off Giraud St **114** B6
Osterley La, Islw. TW7 . .**124** B5
Southall UB2 ... .**123** G5
Osterley Pk, Islw. TW7 . .**124** A5
★ Osterley Park Ho, Islw.
  TW7 ... .**123** J5
Osterley Pk Rd, Sthl.
  UB2 ... .**123** F3
Osterley Pk Vw Rd, W7 .**124** B2
Osterley Rd, N16 ... . . .**94** B4
Isleworth TW7 ... .**124** B7
Osterley Views, Sthl. UB2
  off West Pk Rd **123** J1
Oster Ter, E17
  off Southcote Rd **77** G5
Ostliffe Rd, N13 ... .**59** J5
Oswald Rd, Sthl. UB1 . .**123** E1
Oswald's Mead, E9
  off Lindisfarne Way **95** H4
Oswald St, E5 ... .**95** G3
Oswald Ter, NW2
  off Temple Rd **89** J3
Osward Pl, N9 ... .**60** E2
Osward Rd, SW17 ... . .**167** J2
Oswell Ho, E1 ... .**133** E1
Oswin St, SE11 ... .**35** H1
Oswyth Rd, SE5 ... . . .**152** B2
Otford Cl, SE20 ... .**189** F1
Bexley DA5
  off Southwold Rd **159** H6
Bromley BR1 ... .**192** D3
Otford Cres, SE4 ... . . .**153** J6
Othello Cl, SE11 ... . . .**35** G3
Otis St, E3 ... .**114** C3
Otley App, Ilf. IG2 ... . . .**81** E6
Otley Dr, Ilf. IG2 ... .**80** E5
Otley Rd, E16 ... .**115** J6
Otley Ter, E5 ... .**95** G2
Otley Way, Wat. WD19 . .**50** C3
Ottaway St, E5
  off Stellman Cl **94** D3
Ottenden Cl, Orp. BR6
  off Southfleet Rd **207** H4
Otterbourne Rd, E4 ... . .**62** D3
Croydon CR0 ... .**201** J2
Otterburn Gdns, Islw.
  TW7 ... .**124** D7
Otterburn Ho, SE5 ... . .**35** J7
Otterburn St, SW17 ... .**167** J6
Otter Cl, E15 ... .**114** C1
Otterden St, SE6 ... . . .**172** A4
Otter Rd, Grnf. UB6 ... .**103** J4
Otto Cl, SE26 ... .**170** E3
Otto St, SE17 ... .**35** G6
Oulton Cl, E5
  off Mundford Rd **95** F2
SE28 off Rollesby Way .**118** C6
Oulton Cres, Bark. IG11 . .**99** J6
Oulton Rd, N15 ... .**76** A5
Oulton Way, Wat. WD19 .**51** E4
Ouseley Rd, SW12 ... .**167** J1

Outer Circle, NW1 ... .**8** B6
Outgate Rd, NW10 ... . .**89** F7
Outram Pl, N1 ... .**111** E1
Outram Rd, E6 ... .**116** B1
N22 ... .**74** D1
Croydon CR0 ... .**202** C1
Outwich St, EC3 ... .**20** E3
★ Oval, The, Surrey County
  Cricket Club, SE11 ... .**34** D5
Oval, The, E2 ... .**112** E2
Sidcup DA15 ... .**158** A7
Oval Pl, SW8 ... .**34** C7
Oval Rd, NW1 ... .**110** B1
Croydon CR0 ... .**202** B1
Oval Rd N, Dag. RM10 . .**119** H1
Oval Rd S, Dag. RM10 . .**119** H2
Oval Way, SE11 ... .**34** D4
Overbrae, Beck. BR3 ... .**172** A6
Overbrook Wk, Edg. HA8 .**54** A7
Overbury Av, Beck. BR3 .**190** B3
Overbury Rd, N15 ... . . .**76** A6
Overbury St, E5 ... .**95** G4
Overcliff Rd, SE13 ... . .**154** A3
Overcourt Cl, Sid. DA15 .**158** B6
Overdale Av, N.Mal. KT3 .**182** C2
Overdale Rd, W5 ... . . .**125** F3
Overdown Rd, SE6 ... . .**172** A4
Overhill Rd, SE22 ... . .**152** D7
Overhill Way, Beck. BR3 .**190** D5
Overlea Rd, E5 ... .**76** D7
Overmead, Sid. DA15 . .**157** G7
Oversley Ho, W2 ... . . .**108** D5
Overstand Cl, Beck. BR3 .**190** A5
Overstone Gdns, Croy.
  CR0 ... .**189** J7
Overstone Rd, W6 ... . .**127** J3
Overton Cl, NW10 ... . . .**88** C6
Isleworth TW7
  off Avenue Rd **144** C1
Overton Ct, E11 ... .**79** G1
Overton Dr, E11 ... .**79** H7
Romford RM6 ... .**82** C7
Overton Ho, SW15
  off Tangley Gro **147** F7
Overton Rd, E10 ... .**95** H1
N14 ... .**42** E5
SE2 ... .**138** C3
SW9 ... .**151** G2
Sutton SM2 ... .**198** D6
Overton Rd E, SE2 ... .**138** D3
Overtons Yd, Croy. CR0 .**201** J3
Ovesdon Av, Har. HA2 ... .**85** F1
Ovett Cl, SE19 ... .**170** B6
Ovex Cl, E14 ... .**134** C2
Ovington Gdns, SW3 ... .**23** H6
Ovington Ms, SW3 ... . .**23** H6
Ovington Sq, SW3 ... . .**23** H6
Ovington St, SW3 ... . . .**23** H6
Owen Cl, SE28 ... .**138** C1
Croydon CR0 ... .**188** A6
Hayes UB4 ... .**102** B3
Owen Gdns, Wdf.Grn.
  IG8 ... .**64** B6
Owenite St, SE2 ... . . .**138** B4
Owen Rd, N13 ... .**59** J5
Hayes UB4 ... .**102** B3
Owen's Ct, EC1 ... .**11** G3
Owen's Row, EC1 ... . . .**11** G3
Owen St, EC1 ... .**11** G2
Owens Way, SE23 ... . .**153** H7
Owen Wk, SE20
  off Sycamore Gro **170** D7
Owen Waters Ho, Ilf. IG5 . .**80** C1
Owen Way, NW10 ... . . .**88** C6
Owgan Cl, SE5
  off Benhill Rd **132** A7
Owl Pk, Loug. (High Beach)
  IG10 ... .**47** F2
Oxberry Av, SW6 ... . . .**148** B2
Oxendon St, SW1 ... . . .**17** H6
Oxenford St, SE15 ... . .**152** C3
Oxenholme, NW1 ... .**9** G2
Oxenpark Av, Wem. HA9 . .**69** H7
Oxestalls Rd, SE8 ... . .**133** H5
Oxford Av, SW20 ... . . .**184** B2
Hayes UB3 ... .**121** J7
Hounslow TW5 ... . . .**123** G5
★ Oxford Circus, W1 ... . .**17** F3
Oxford Circ Av, W1 ... . .**17** F4
Oxford Cl, N9 ... .**60** E2
Mitcham CR4 ... .**186** C3
Oxford Ct, EC4 ... .**20** B5
W3 ... .**106** A6
Feltham TW13
  off Oxford Way **160** D4
Oxford Cres, N.Mal. KT3 .**182** D6
Oxford Dr, SE1 ... .**28** D2
Ruislip HA4 ... .**84** C2
Oxford Gdns, N20 ... . . .**57** G1
N21 ... .**43** J7

Oxford Gdns, W4 ... . .**126** A5
W10 ... .**108** B6
Oxford Gate, W6 ... . .**128** A4
Oxford Ms, Bex. DA5
  off Bexley High St **159** G7
Oxford Pl, NW10
  off Neasden La N **88** D3
Oxford Rd, E15 ... .**96** D6
N4 ... .**93** G1
N9 ... .**61** E2
NW6 ... .**108** D2
SE19 ... .**170** A6
SW15 ... .**148** B4
W5 ... .**105** G7
Carshalton SM5 ... . .**199** H6
Enfield EN3 ... .**45** E5
Harrow HA1 ... .**67** J6
Harrow (Wldste.) HA3 . .**68** C3
Ilford IG1 ... .**99** F4
Sidcup DA14 ... .**176** B5
Teddington TW11 ... . .**162** A5
Wallington SM6 ... . . .**200** C5
Woodford Green IG8 . . .**63** J5
Oxford Rd N, W4 ... . . .**126** B5
Oxford Rd S, W4 ... . . .**126** A5
Oxford Sq, W2 ... .**15** H4
Oxford St, W1 ... .**16** B4
Oxford Wk, Sthl. UB1 . .**123** F1
Oxford Way, Felt. TW13 .**160** D4
Oxgate Gdns, NW2 ... . .**89** H3
Oxgate La, NW2 ... .**89** H2
Oxhawth Cres, Brom.
  BR2 ... .**192** D5
Oxhey Dr, Nthwd. HA6 . . .**50** B5
Watford WD19 ... .**50** C3
Oxhey Dr S, Nthwd.
  HA6 ... .**50** A5
Oxhey La, Har. HA3 ... . .**51** G5
Pinner HA5 ... .**51** G5
Watford WD19 ... .**51** F2
Oxhey Ridge Cl, Nthwd.
  HA6 ... .**50** A5
Oxleas, E6 ... .**116** E6
Oxleas Cl, Well. DA16 . .**157** G2
Oxleay Ct, Har. HA2 ... . .**85** G1
Oxleay Rd, Har. HA2 ... . .**85** G1
Oxleigh Cl, N.Mal.
  KT3 ... .**183** E5
Oxley Cl, SE1 ... .**37** G3
Oxleys Rd, NW2 ... .**89** H3
Oxlip Cl, Croy. CR0
  off Marigold Way **203** G1
Oxlow La, Dag. RM9,
  RM10 ... .**101** G4
Oxonian St, SE22 ... . .**152** C4
Oxo Twr Wf, SE1 ... .**19** F6
Oxted Cl, Mitch. CR4 . .**185** G3
Oxtoby Way, SW16 ... .**186** D2
Oyster Catchers Cl, E16
  off Freemasons Rd . .**115** H6
Oyster Catcher Ter, Ilf. IG5
  off Tiptree Cres **80** D3
Oyster Row, E1
  off Lukin St **113** F6
Ozolins Way, E16 ... . .**115** G6

P

Pablo Neruda Cl, SE24
  off Shakespeare Rd .**151** H4
Pace Pl, E1
  off Bigland St **112/113** E6
Pacific Rd, E16 ... .**115** G6
Packham Ct, Wor.Pk. KT4
  off Lavender Av **197** J3
Packington Rd, W3 ... .**126** C3
Packington Sq, N1 ... . .**111** J1
Packington St, N1 ... . .**111** H1
Packmores Rd, SE9 ... .**157** G5
Padbury, SE17 ... .**36** D4
Padbury Ct, E2 ... .**13** G4
Padcroft Rd, West Dr.
  UB7 ... .**120** A1
Padden Ct, NW7
  off Bittacy Hill **56** B7
Paddenswick Rd, W6 ... .**127** G3
PADDINGTON, W2 ... . .**14** C2
Paddington Cl, Hayes
  UB4 ... .**102** D4
Paddington Grn, W2 ... .**15** F1
Paddington St, W1 ... . .**16** B1
Paddock Cl, SE3 ... . . .**155** G2
SE26 ... .**171** G4
Northolt UB5 ... .**103** G2
Orpington BR6
  off State Fm Av .**206/207** E1
Worcester Park KT4 ... .**196** E1
Paddock Gdns, SE19
  off Westow St **170** B6

Paddock Rd, NW2 ... . . .**89** G3
Bexleyheath DA6 ... . .**159** E4
Ruislip HA4 ... .**84** D3
Paddocks, The, NW7 ... .**56** B6
Barnet EN4 ... .**41** J3
Wembley HA9 ... .**88** B2
Paddocks Cl, Har. HA2 . .**85** H4
Paddock Way, Chis.
  BR7 ... .**175** G7
Padfield Rd, SE5 ... . . .**151** J3
Padley Cl, Chess. KT9
  off Moor La **195** J5
Padnall Ct, Rom. RM6
  off Padnall Rd **82** D3
Padnall Rd, Rom. RM6 . .**82** D4
Padstow Cl, Orp. BR6 . .**207** J4
Padstow Rd, Enf. EN2 ... .**43** H1
Padua Rd, SE20 ... . . .**189** F1
Pagden St, SW8 ... . . .**150** B1
Pageant Av, NW9 ... . . .**70** D1
Pageant Cres, SE16
  off Rotherhithe St **133** H1
Pageantmaster Ct, EC4 . .**19** G4
Pageant Wk, Croy. CR0 .**202** B3
Page Av, Wem. HA9 ... . .**88** C3
Page Cl, Dag. RM9 ... . .**101** E5
Hampton TW12 ... . . .**161** E6
Harrow HA3 ... .**69** J6
Page Cres, Croy. CR0 . .**201** G5
Page Grn Rd, N15 ... . . .**76** D5
Page Grn Ter, N15 ... . . .**76** C5
Page Heath La, Brom.
  BR1 ... .**192** A3
Page Heath Vil, Brom.
  BR1 ... .**192** A3
Pagehurst Rd, Croy. CR0 .**188** E7
Page Meadow, NW7 ... . .**55** G7
Page Rd, Felt. TW14 ... .**141** G6
Pages Hill, N10 ... .**74** A2
Pages La, N10 ... .**74** A2
Page St, NW7 ... .**71** G1
SW1 ... .**33** J1
Pages Wk, SE1 ... .**36** D1
Pages Yd, W4
  off Church St **126/127** E6
Paget Av, Sutt. SM1 ... .**199** G3
Paget Cl, Hmptn. TW12 .**162** A4
Paget Gdns, Chis. BR7 . .**192** E1
Paget La, Islw. TW7 ... .**144** A3
Paget Pl, Kings.T. KT2 . .**164** C6
Thames Ditton KT7
  off Brooklands Rd **194** D1
Paget Ri, SE18 ... .**136** D7
Paget Rd, N16 ... .**94** A1
Ilford IG1 ... .**98** E4
Paget St, EC1 ... .**11** G3
Paget Ter, SE18 ... . . .**136** D6
Pagitts Gro, Barn. EN4 . .**40** E1
Pagnell St, SE14 ... . . .**133** J7
Pagoda Av, Rich.TW9 ... .**145** J3
Pagoda Gdns, SE3 ... . .**154** D2
Pagoda Vista, Rich.TW9 .**145** J2
Paignton Rd, N15 ... . . .**76** B6
Ruislip HA4 ... .**84** A3
Paines Cl, Pnr. HA5 ... . .**67** E3
Paines La, Pnr. HA5 ... . .**66** E1
Pains Cl, Mitch. CR4 ... .**186** B2
Painsthorpe Rd, N16
  off Oldfield Rd **94** B3
Painters Ms, SE16
  off Macks Rd **132** D4
Painters Rd, Ilf. IG2 ... . .**81** J3
Paisley Rd, N22 ... .**75** H1
Carshalton SM5 ... . .**199** G1
Pakeman St, N7 ... .**93** F3
Pakenham Cl, SW12
  off Balham Pk Rd **168** A1
Pakenham St, WC1 ... . .**10** D5
Palace Av, W8 ... .**22** B2
Palace Ct, NW3 ... .**91** E5
W2 ... .**14** A5
Bromley BR1
  off Palace Gro **191** H1
Harrow HA3 ... .**69** H6
Palace Ct Gdns, N10 . . .**74** C3
Palace Gdns, Buck.H. IG9 .**64** A1
Palace Gdns Ms, W8 ... .**128** D1
Palace Gdns Prec, Enf. EN2
  off Sydney Rd **44** A3
Palace Gdns Ter, W8 ... .**128** D1
Palace Gate, W8 ... .**22** C4
Palace Gates Rd, N22 . . .**74** E1
Palace Grn, W8 ... .**22** B3
Croydon CR0 ... .**203** J7
Palace Gro, SE19 ... . .**170** C7
Bromley BR1 ... .**191** H1
Palace Ms, E17 ... .**77** J4
SW1 ... .**32** C2
SW6
  off Hartismere Rd **128** C7

Palace of Industry, Wem.
HA9 . . . . .88 A4
Palace Par, E17 . . . . .78 A4
Palace Pl, SW1 . . . . .25 F5
Palace Rd, N8 . . . . .74 D5
N11 . . . . .58 E7
SE19 . . . . .170 C7
SW2 . . . . .169 F1
Bromley BR1 . . . . .191 H1
East Molesey KT8 . . . .180 A3
Kingston upon Thames
KT1 . . . . .181 G4
Ruislip HA4 . . . . .84 E4
Palace Rd Est, SW2 . . . .169 F1
Palace Sq, SE19 . . . . . . .170 C7
Palace St, SW1 . . . . .25 F5
Palace Vw, SE12 . . . . . .173 G2
Bromley BR1 . . . . .191 G3
Croydon CR0 . . . . .203 J4
Palace Vw Rd, E4 . . . . . .62 B5
Palamos Rd, E10 . . . . . . .96 A1
Palatine Av, N16
off Stoke Newington
Rd 94 C4
Palatine Rd, N16 . . . . . . .94 B4
Palermo Rd, NW10 . . . . .107 G2
Palestine Gro, SW19 . . . .185 G1
Palewell Common Dr,
SW14 . . . . .146 C5
Palewell Pk, SW14 . . . . .146 D5
Paley Gdns, Loug. IG10 . .49 E3
Palfrey Pl, SW8 . . . . .34 D7
Palgrave Av, Sthl. UB1 . .103 G7
Palgrave Gdns, NW1 . . . . .7 H5
Palgrave Rd, W12 . . . . . .127 F3
Palissy St, E2 . . . . .13 F4
Palladino Ho, SW17
off Laurel Cl 167 H5
Pallant Way, Orp. BR6 . .206 D3
Pallet Way, SE18 . . . . . .156 B1
Palliser Rd, W14 . . . . . . .128 B5
Pall Mall, SW1 . . . . .25 G2
Pall Mall E, SW1 . . . . . . .25 J1
Palmar Cres, Bexh. DA7 .159 G3
Palmar Rd, Bexh. DA7 . .159 G2
Palm Av, Sid. DA14 . . . .176 D6
Palm Cl, E10 . . . . .96 B3
Palmeira Rd, Bexh. DA7 .158 D3
Palmer Av, Sutt. SM3 . . .197 J4
West Wickham BR4 . . .204 D3
Palmer Cres, Kings.T.
KT1 . . . . .181 H3
Palmer Gdns, Barn. EN5 .40 A5
Palmer Pl, N7 . . . . .93 G5
Palmer Rd, E13 . . . . . . .115 H4
Dagenham RM8 . . . . . .100 D1
PALMERS GREEN, N13 . .59 G3
Palmers Gro, W.Mol.
KT8 . . . . .179 G4
Palmers La, Enf. EN1,
EN3 . . . . .45 E1
Palmers Pas, SW14
off Palmers Rd 146 C3
Palmers Rd, E2 . . . . . . .113 G2
N11 . . . . .58 C5
SW14 . . . . .146 C3
SW16 . . . . .187 F2
Borehamwood WD6 . . .38 B1
Palmerston Cres, N13 . . .59 F5
SE18 . . . . .137 F6
Palmerston Gro, SW19 . .166 D7
Palmerston Rd, E7 . . . . . .97 H5
E17 . . . . .77 J4
N22 . . . . .59 F7
NW6 . . . . .90 D7
SW14 . . . . .146 C4
SW19 . . . . .166 D7
W3 . . . . .126 C3
Buckhurst Hill IG9 . . . . .63 H2
Carshalton SM5 . . . . . .199 J4
Croydon CR0 . . . . .188 A5
Harrow HA3 . . . . .68 C3
Hounslow TW3 . . . . . .143 J1
Orpington BR6 . . . . . . .207 F4
Sutton SM1
off Vernon Rd 199 F5
Twickenham TW2 . . . . .144 C6
Palmerston Way, SW8
off Bradmead 130 A7
Palmer St, SW1 . . . . .25 H4
Palm Gro, W5 . . . . .125 H3
Palm Rd, Rom. RM7 . . . . .83 J5
Pamela Gdns, Pnr. HA5 . .66 B5
Pamela Wk, E8
off Marlborough Av . . .112 D1
Pampisford Rd, S.Croy.
CR2 . . . . .201 H7
Pams Way, Epsom KT19 .196 D5
Pancras La, EC4 . . . . .20 A4

Pancras Rd, NW1 . . . . .9 H1
Pandora Rd, NW6 . . . . . .90 D6
Panfield Ms, Ilf. IG2
off Cranbrook Rd 80 D6
Pangbourne Av, W10 . . . .107 J5
Pangbourne Dr, Stan.
HA7 . . . . .53 G5
Pangbourne Ho, N7 . . . . .92 E5
Panhard Pl, Sthl. UB1 . .103 H7
Pank Av, Barn. EN5 . . . . .41 F5
Pankhurst Cl, SE14
off Briant St 133 G7
Isleworth TW7 . . . . . . .144 C3
Pankhurst Rd, Walt.
KT12 . . . . .178 C7
Panmuir Rd, SW20 . . . . .183 H1
Panmure Cl, N5 . . . . .93 H4
Panmure Rd, SE26 . . . . .170 E3
Pansy Gdns, W12 . . . . . .107 G7
Panther Dr, NW10 . . . . . .88 D5
Pantiles, The, NW11
off Willifield Way 72 C5
Bexleyheath DA7 . . . . .139 F7
Bromley BR1 . . . . .192 B3
Pantiles Cl, N13 . . . . .59 H5
Panton St, SW1 . . . . .17 H6
Panyer All, EC4 . . . . .19 J3
Papermill Cl, Cars. SM5 .200 A4
Papillons Wk, SE3 . . . . .155 G2
Papworth Gdns, N7
off Liverpool Rd 93 F5
Papworth Way, SW2 . . . .151 G7
Parade, The, SW11 . . . . . .32 A7
Esher (Clay.) KT10 . . . .194 B6
Hampton TW12
off Hampton Rd 162 A5
Watford (Carp.Pk.)
WD19 . . . . .50 E3
Watford (S.Oxhey) WD19
off Prestwick Rd 50 D3
Parade Ms, SE27
off Norwood Rd 169 H2
Paradise Pas, N7 . . . . . . .93 G5
Paradise Pl, SE18
off Woodhill 136 B4
Paradise Rd, SW4 . . . . . .150 E2
Richmond TW9 . . . . . . .145 G5
Paradise Row, E2
off Bethnal Grn
Rd 112/113 E3
Paradise St, SE16 . . . . . .132 E2
Paradise Wk, SW3 . . . . . .31 J5
Paragon, The, SE3 . . . . . .155 F2
Paragon Cl, E16 . . . . . . .115 G6
Paragon Gro, Surb. KT5 .181 J6
Paragon Ms, SE1 . . . . . . .36 C1
Paragon Pl, SE3 . . . . . . .155 F2
Surbiton KT5
off Berrylands Rd 181 J6
Paragon Rd, E9 . . . . .95 F6
Parbury Rd, Chess. KT9 .195 H6
Parbury Rd, SE23 . . . . . .153 H6
Parchmore Rd, Th.Hth.
CR7 . . . . .187 H2
Parchmore Way, Th.Hth.
CR7 . . . . .187 H2
Pardoner St, SE1 . . . . . . .28 C5
Pardon St, EC1 . . . . .11 H5
Parfett St, E1 . . . . .21 J2
Parfitt Cl, NW3
off North End 91 F2
Parfrey St, W6 . . . . .127 J6
Parham Dr, Ilf. IG2 . . . . . .80 E6
Parham Way, N10 . . . . . .74 C2
Paris Gdn, SE1 . . . . .27 G1
Parish Gate Dr, Sid.
DA15 . . . . .157 H6
Parish La, SE20 . . . . .171 G6
Parish Ms, SE20 . . . . . . .171 G7
Parish Wf Pl, SE18
off Woodhill 136 B4
Park, The, N6 . . . . .74 A6
NW11 . . . . .90 E1
SE19 . . . . .170 B7
SE23 off Park Hill .170/171 E1
W5 . . . . .125 G1
Carshalton SM5 . . . . . .199 J5
Sidcup DA14 . . . . .175 J5
Park App, Well. DA16 . . .158 B4
Park Av, E6 . . . . .116 D1
E15 . . . . .96 E6
N3 . . . . .73 E1
N13 . . . . .59 G3
N18 . . . . .60 D4
N22 . . . . .75 E2
NW2 . . . . .89 H6
NW10 . . . . .105 J3
NW11 . . . . .90 E1
SW14 . . . . .146 D4

Park Av, Bark. IG11 . . . . . .99 F6
Bromley BR1 . . . . .173 F6
Carshalton SM5 . . . . . .200 A6
Enfield EN1 . . . . .44 B6
Hounslow TW3 . . . . . .143 H6
Ilford IG1 . . . . .98 D2
Mitcham CR4 . . . . .168 B7
Orpington (Farnboro.)
BR6 . . . . .206 C3
Southall UB1 . . . . .123 G1
West Wickham BR4 . . .204 C2
Woodford Green IG8 . . .63 H5
Park Av E, Epsom KT17 .197 G6
Park Av Ms, Mitch. CR4
off Park Av 168 B7
Park Av N, N8 . . . . .74 D3
NW10 . . . . .89 H5
Park Av Rd, N17 . . . . .61 E7
Park Av S, N8 . . . . .74 C4
Park Av W, Epsom KT17 .197 G6
Park Chase, Wem. HA9 . . .87 J4
Park Cl, E9 . . . . .113 F1
NW2 . . . . .89 H3
NW10 . . . . .105 J3
SW1 . . . . .23 J4
W4 . . . . .126 D5
W14 . . . . .128 C3
Carshalton SM5 . . . . . .199 J6
Hampton TW12 . . . . . .179 J1
Harrow HA3 . . . . .68 B1
Hounslow TW3 . . . . . .143 J5
Kingston upon Thames
KT2 . . . . .182 A1
New Malden KT3 . . . . .182 D4
Wembley HA9 . . . . .87 H5
Park Cres, N3 . . . . .57 E7
W1 . . . . .8 D6
Enfield EN2 . . . . .44 A4
Erith DA8 . . . . .139 J6
Harrow HA3 . . . . .68 B1
Twickenham TW2 . . . . .162 A1
Park Cres Ms E, W1 . . . . . .8 E6
Park Cres Ms W, W1 . . . .16 D1
Park Cft, Edg. HA8 . . . . . .70 C1
Parkcroft Rd, SE12 . . . . .155 F7
Park Dale, N11 . . . . .58 D6
Parkdale Cres, Wor.Pk.
KT4 . . . . .196 D3
Parkdale Rd, SE18 . . . . . .137 H5
Park Dr, N21 . . . . .43 J6
NW11 . . . . .90 E1
SE7 . . . . .136 B6
SW14 . . . . .146 D4
W3 . . . . .126 A3
Dagenham RM10 . . . . .101 J3
Harrow (Har.Wld.) HA3 .52 B6
Harrow (N.Har.) HA2 . . .67 G7
Park Dr Cl, SE7 . . . . .136 B5
Park End, NW3
off South Hill Pk 91 H4
Bromley BR1 . . . . .191 F1
Parker Cl, E16 . . . . .136 B1
Parker Ms, WC2 . . . . .18 B3
Parke Rd, SW13 . . . . . . .147 G1
Sunbury-on-Thames
TW16 . . . . .178 A4
Parker Rd, Croy. CR0 . . .201 J4
Parkers Row, SE1 . . . . . . .29 G4
Parker St, E16 . . . . .136 B1
WC2 . . . . .18 B3
Parkes Rd, Chig. IG7 . . . . .65 H5
Park Fm Cl, N2 . . . . .73 F3
Pinner HA5
off Field End Rd 66 B5
Park Fm Rd, Brom. BR1 .192 A1
Kingston upon Thames
KT2 . . . . .163 H7
Parkfield Av, SW14 . . . . .146 E4
Feltham TW13 . . . . . . .160 A3
Harrow HA2 . . . . .67 J2
Northolt UB5 . . . . .102 D2
Parkfield Cl, Edg. HA8 . . .54 B6
Northolt UB5 . . . . .102 E2
Parkfield Cres, Felt.
TW13 . . . . .160 A3
Harrow HA2 . . . . .67 J2
Ruislip HA4 . . . . .84 E3
Parkfield Dr, Nthlt. UB5 .102 D2
Parkfield Gdns, Har.
HA2 . . . . .67 H3
Parkfield Rd, NW10 . . . . .89 G7
SE14 . . . . .153 J1
Feltham TW13 . . . . . . .160 A3
Harrow HA2 . . . . .85 J3
Northolt UB5 . . . . .102 E2
Parkfields, SW15 . . . . . . .147 J4
Croydon CR0 . . . . .203 J1

Parkfields Av, NW9 . . . . . .88 D1
SW20 . . . . .183 H1
Parkfields Cl, Cars. SM5
off Devonshire Rd 200 A4
Parkfields Rd, Kings.T.
KT2 . . . . .163 J5
Parkfield St, N1 . . . . .11 F1
Parkfield Way, Brom.
BR2 . . . . .192 C6
Park Gdns, NW9 . . . . .70 B3
Kingston upon Thames
KT2 . . . . .163 J5
Park Gate, N2 . . . . .73 G3
N21 . . . . .43 F7
Parkgate, SE3 . . . . .155 F3
Park Gate, W5
off Mount Av 105 G5
Parkgate Av, Barn. EN4 . .41 F1
Parkgate Cl, Kings.T. KT2
off Warboys App 164 B6
Parkgate Cres, Barn. EN4 .41 F2
Parkgate Gdns, SW14 . . .146 D5
Parkgate Ms, N6
off Stanhope Rd 74 C7
Parkgate Rd, SW11 . . . . .129 H7
Wallington SM6 . . . . . .200 A5
Park Gates, Har. HA2 . . . .85 G4
Park Gro, E15 . . . . .115 G1
N11 . . . . .58 D7
Bexleyheath DA7 . . . . .159 J4
Bromley BR1 . . . . .191 H1
Edgware HA8 . . . . .53 J5
Park Gro Rd, E11 . . . . . . .96 E2
Park Hall Rd, N2 . . . . .73 H4
SE21 . . . . .169 J3
Parkham Ct, Brom. BR2 .191 E2
Parkham St, SW11 . . . . . .149 H1
Park Hill, SE23 . . . . .171 E2
SW4 . . . . .150 D5
W5 . . . . .105 G5
Bromley BR1 . . . . .192 B4
Carshalton SM5 . . . . . .199 H6
Loughton IG10 . . . . . . .48 A5
Richmond TW10 . . . . . .145 J6
Park Hill Cl, Cars. SM5 . .199 H5
Park Hill Ct, SW17
off Beeches Rd 167 J3
Park Hill Ri, Croy. CR0 . .202 B2
Parkhill Rd, E4 . . . . .62 C1
NW3 . . . . .91 J5
Bexley DA5 . . . . .159 F7
Park Hill Rd, Brom. BR2 .190 E2
Croydon CR0 . . . . .202 B2
Parkhill Rd, Sid. DA15 . .175 G3
Park Hill Rd, Wall. SM6 .200 B7
Parkhill Wk, NW3 . . . . . . .91 J5
Parkholme Rd, E8 . . . . . . .94 C6
Park Ho, N21 . . . . .43 F7
Park Ho Gdns, Twick.
TW1 . . . . .145 F6
Parkhouse St, SE5 . . . . . .36 C7
Parkhurst Av, E16
off Wesley Av 135 H1
Parkhurst Gdns, Bex.
DA5 . . . . .159 G3
Parkhurst Rd, E12 . . . . . . .98 D4
E17 . . . . .77 H4
N7 . . . . .92 E4
N11 . . . . .58 A4
N17 . . . . .76 D2
N22 . . . . .59 F7
Bexley DA5 . . . . .159 G3
Sutton SM1 . . . . .199 G4
Parkland Cl, Chig. IG7 . . .65 F3
Parkland Gdns, SW19 . . .166 A1
Parkland Rd, N22 . . . . . . .75 F2
Woodford Green IG8 . . .63 G7
Parklands, N6 . . . . .74 B7
Chigwell IG7 . . . . .65 F3
Surbiton KT5 . . . . .181 J5
Parklands Cl, SW14 . . . . .146 C5
Ilford IG2 . . . . .81 F7
Parklands Ct, Houns.
TW5 . . . . .142 D2
Parklands Dr, N3 . . . . . . .72 B3
Parklands Rd, SW16 . . . .168 B5
Parklands Way, Wor.Pk.
KT4 . . . . .197 E3
Parkland Wk, N4 . . . . .75 F7
N6 . . . . .74 D7
N10 . . . . .74 A8
Park La, E15
off High St 114 D1
N9 . . . . .60 C3
N17 . . . . .60 D7
W1 . . . . .24 C2
Carshalton SM5 . . . . . .200 A4
Croydon CR0 . . . . .202 A3
Harrow HA2 . . . . .85 H3
Hounslow TW5 . . . . . .122 A7

Park La, Rich. TW9 . . . . .**145** G4
Romford (Chad.Hth.)
RM6 . . . .**82** D6
Stanmore HA7 . . . .**52** D3
Sutton SM3 . . . .**198** B6
Teddington TW11 . . . . .**162** C6
Wallington SM6 . . . . . .**200** A4
Wembley HA9 . . . .**87** H5
Park La Cl, N17 . . . .**60** D7
PARK LANGLEY, Beck. .**190** C5
Park Lawns, Wem. HA9 . . .**87** J4
Parklea Cl, NW9 . . . .**71** E1
Parkleigh Rd, SW19 . . . . .**184** E2
Parkleys, Rich. TW10 . . . .**163** G4
Parkmead, SW15 . . . .**147** H6
Park Mead, Har. HA2 . . . .**85** H3
Parkmead, Loug. IG10 . . . .**48** D5
Park Mead, Sid. DA15 . . .**158** B5
Parkmead Gdns, NW7 . . . .**55** F6
Park Ms, SE24
off Croxted Rd **151** J4
Chislehurst BR7 . . . . . .**175** E6
East Molesey KT8 . . . .**179** J4
Hampton (Hmptn.H.) TW12
off Park Rd **161** J5
Parkmore Cl, Wdf.Grn.
IG8 . . . .**63** G4
Park Par, NW10 . . . .**107** F2
Park Pl, E14 . . . .**134** A1
SW1 . . . .**25** F2
W3 . . . .**126** A4
W5 . . . .**125** G1
Hampton (Hmptn.H.)
TW12 . . . .**161** J6
Wembley HA9 . . . .**87** J4
Park Pl Vil, W2 . . . .**14** D1
Park Ridings, N8 . . . .**75** G3
Park Ri, SE23 . . . .**171** H1
Harrow HA3 . . . .**68** B1
Park Ri Rd, SE23 . . . .**171** H1
Park Rd, E6 . . . .**115** J1
E10 . . . .**96** A1
E12 . . . .**97** H1
E15 . . . .**115** G1
E17 . . . .**77** J5
N2 . . . .**73** G3
N8 . . . .**74** C4
N11 . . . .**58** D7
N14 . . . .**42** D7
N15 . . . .**75** H4
N18 . . . .**60** C4
NW1 . . . .**7** G3
NW4 . . . .**71** G7
NW8 . . . .**7** G3
NW9 . . . .**70** D7
NW10 . . . .**106** E1
SE25 . . . .**188** B4
SW19 . . . .**167** G6
W4 . . . .**126** C7
W7 . . . .**104** C7
Barnet EN5 . . . .**40** C4
Barnet (New Barn.)
EN4 . . . .**41** H4
Beckenham BR3 . . . . .**171** J7
Bromley BR1 . . . .**191** H1
Chislehurst BR7 . . . . .**175** E6
East Molesey KT8 . . . .**179** J4
Feltham TW13 . . . . . .**160** D4
Hampton (Hmptn.H.)
TW12 . . . .**161** H4
Hounslow TW3 . . . . . .**143** J4
Ilford IG1 . . . .**99** G3
Isleworth TW7 . . . . . .**144** E1
Kingston upon Thames
KT2 . . . .**163** J5
Kingston upon Thames
(Hmptn.W.) KT1 . . . . .**162** C6
New Malden KT3 . . . .**182** D4
Richmond TW10 . . . . .**145** J6
Sunbury-on-Thames
TW16 . . . .**160** B7
Surbiton KT5 . . . .**181** J5
Sutton SM3 . . . .**198** B6
Teddington TW11 . . . .**181** F1
Twickenham TW1 . . . .**145** H6
Wallington SM6 . . . . .**200** B5
Wallington (Hackbr.)
SM6 . . . .**200** B2
Wembley HA0 . . . .**87** H6
Park Rd E, W3 . . . .**126** B2
Park Rd N, W3 . . . .**126** B2
W4 . . . .**126** D5
Park Row, SE10 . . . .**134** D6
PARK ROYAL, NW10 . . .**106** A3
Park Royal Rd, NW10 . . .**106** C3
W3 . . . .**106** C3
Parkshot, Rich. TW9 . . . .**145** H4
Parkside, N3 . . . .**72** E1
NW2 . . . .**89** G3
NW7 . . . .**55** G6

Parkside, SE3 . . . .**135** F7
SW19 . . . .**166** A4
Buckhurst Hill IG9 . . . .**63** H2
Hampton (Hmptn.H.)
TW12 . . . .**162** A5
Sidcup DA14 . . . .**176** B2
Sutton SM3 . . . .**198** B6
Parkside Av, SW19 . . . . .**166** A5
Bromley BR1 . . . .**192** B4
Parkside Business Est, SE8
off Rolt St **133** H6
Parkside Cl, SE20 . . . . . .**171** F7
Parkside Cres, N7 . . . . . .**93** G3
Surbiton KT5 . . . .**182** C6
Parkside Dr, Edg. HA8 . . .**54** A3
Parkside Est, E9
off Rutland Rd **113** F1
Parkside Gdns, SW19 . . .**166** A4
Barnet EN4 . . . .**41** J1
Parkside Ho, Dag. RM10 .**101** J3
Parkside Rd, SW11 . . . . .**150** A1
Belvedere DA17 . . . . .**139** J4
Hounslow TW3 . . . . . .**143** H5
Parkside Ter, N18
off Great Cambridge
Rd **60** A4
Parkside Wk, SE10 . . . . .**134** C5
Parkside Way, Har. HA2 . .**67** H4
Park S, SW11
off Austin Rd **150** A1
Park Sq E, NW1 . . . .**8** D5
Park Sq Ms, NW1 . . . .**8** D6
Park Sq W, NW1 . . . .**8** D5
Parkstead Rd, SW15 . . . .**147** G5
Parkstone Av, N18 . . . . . .**60** C5
Parkstone Rd, E17 . . . . . .**78** C3
SE15 off Rye La **152** D2
Park St, SE1 . . . .**27** J1
W1 . . . .**16** B5
Croydon CR0 . . . .**201** J2
Teddington TW11 . . . .**162** B6
Park Ter, Wor.Pk. KT4 . . .**197** G1
Parkthorne Cl, Har. HA2 . .**67** H6
Parkthorne Dr, Har. HA2 . .**67** G6
Parkthorne Rd, SW12 . . .**150** D7
Park Vw, N21 . . . .**43** F7
W3 . . . .**106** C5
New Malden KT3 . . . .**183** F3
Pinner HA5 . . . .**67** F1
Wembley HA9 . . . .**88** B5
Parkview Ct, SW18
off Broomhill Rd **148** D6
Park Vw Ct, Ilf. IG2
off Brancaster Rd **81** H6
Park Vw Cres, N11 . . . . . .**58** B4
Parkview Dr, Mitch. CR4 .**185** G2
Park Vw Est, E2 . . . .**113** G2
Park Vw Gdns, NW4 . . . . .**71** J5
Ilford IG4 . . . .**80** C4
Park Vw Ho, SE24
off Hurst St **151** H6
Park Vw Rd, N3 . . . .**73** E1
N17 . . . .**76** D3
NW10 . . . .**89** F4
Parkview Rd, SE9 . . . . . .**174** E2
Park Vw Rd, W5 . . . .**105** H5
Parkview Rd, Croy. CR0 . .**202** D1
Park Vw Rd, Pnr. HA5 . . . .**50** B7
Southall UB1 . . . .**123** G1
Welling DA16 . . . .**158** C3
Park Village E, NW1 . . . . .**110** B2
Park Village W, NW1 . . . . . .**8** D1
Parkville Rd, SW6 . . . . . .**128** C7
Park Vista, SE10 . . . .**134** D6
Park Wk, N6
off North Rd **74** A7
SE10 off Crooms Hill .**134** D7
SW10 . . . .**30** D5
Parkway, N14 . . . .**58** D2
Park Way, N20 . . . .**57** J4
Parkway, NW1 . . . .**110** B1
Park Way, NW11 . . . .**72** B5
Parkway, SW20 . . . .**184** A4
Park Way, Edg. HA8 . . . . .**70** B1
Enfield EN2 . . . .**43** G2
Parkway, Erith DA18 . . . .**139** E3
Park Way, Felt. TW14 . . . .**142** B7
Parkway, Ilf. IG3 . . . .**99** J3
Park Way, Ruis. HA4 . . . . .**84** A1
West Molesey KT8 . . .**179** H3
Parkway, Wdf.Grn. IG8 . . .**63** J5
Parkway, The, Hayes UB3,
UB4 . . . .**102** C6
Hounslow (Cran.) TW4,
TW5 . . . .**142** B2
Northolt UB5 . . . .**102** D3
Southall UB2 . . . .**122** A5
Parkway Trd Est, Houns.
TW5 . . . .**122** C6

Park W, W2 . . . .**15** H4
Park W Pl, W2 . . . .**15** H3
Parkwood, N20 . . . .**57** J3
Beckenham BR3 . . . . .**190** A1
Parkwood Gro, Sun.
TW16 . . . .**178** A3
Parkwood Ms, N6 . . . .**74** B6
Parkwood Rd, SW19 . . . .**166** C5
Bexley DA5 . . . .**159** F7
Isleworth TW7 . . . . . .**144** C1
Parliament Ct, E1
off Sandy's Row **112** B5
Parliament Hill, NW3 . . . .**91** H4
Parliament Ms, SW14
off Thames Bk **146** C2
Parliament Sq, SW1 . . . . .**26** A4
Parliament St, SW1 . . . . .**26** A4
Parliament Vw Apartments,
SE1 . . . .**34** C1
Parma Cres, SW11 . . . . .**149** J4
Parmiter St, E2 . . . .**113** E2
Parmoor Ct, EC1 . . . .**11** J5
Parnell Cl, Edg. HA8 . . . . .**54** B4
Parnell Rd, E3 . . . .**113** J1
Parnham St, E14
off Blount St **113** H6
Parolles Rd, N19 . . . .**92** C1
Paroma Rd, Belv. DA17 . .**139** G3
Parr Cl, N9 . . . .**60** E4
N18 . . . .**60** E4
Parr Ct, N1 . . . .**12** B1
Feltham TW13 . . . . . .**160** C4
Parr Pl, W4
off Chiswick High Rd .**127** F4
Parr Rd, E6 . . . .**116** A1
Stanmore HA7 . . . . . .**69** G1
Parrs Pl, Hmptn. TW12 . .**161** G7
Parr St, N1 . . . .**12** B1
Parry Av, E6 . . . .**116** C6
Parry Cl, Epsom KT17 . . .**197** G7
Parry Pl, SE18 . . . .**137** E4
Parry Rd, SE25 . . . .**188** B3
W10 . . . .**108** B3
Parry St, SW8 . . . .**34** A5
Parsifal Rd, NW6 . . . .**90** D5
Parsley Gdns, Croy. CR0
off Primrose La **203** G1
Parsloes Av, Dag. RM9 . .**100** D4
Parsonage Gdns, Enf.
EN2 . . . .**43** J2
Parsonage La, Enf. EN1,
EN2 . . . .**44** A2
Sidcup DA14 . . . .**177** F4
Parsonage Manorway, Belv.
DA17 . . . .**139** G6
Parsonage St, E14 . . . . . .**134** C4
Parsons Cres, Edg. HA8 . .**54** A3
PARSONS GREEN, SW6 .**148** D1
Parsons Grn, SW6 . . . . . .**148** D1
Parsons Grn La, SW6 . . . .**148** D1
Parsons Gro, Edg. HA8 . . .**54** A3
Parsons Hill, SE18
off Powis St **136** D3
Parsons Ho, SW2
off New Pk Rd **150/151** E7
Parson's Ho, W2 . . . .**7** E6
Parson's Mead, Croy.
CR0 . . . .**201** H1
Parsons Mead, E.Mol.
KT8 . . . .**179** J3
Parsons Rd, E13
off Old St **115** J2
Parson St, NW4 . . . .**71** J4
Parthenia Rd, SW6 . . . . .**148** D1
Partingdale La, NW7 . . . . .**56** A5
Partington Cl, N19 . . . . . .**92** D1
Partridge Cl, E16 . . . .
off Fulmer Rd **116** A5
E16 . . . .**39** J6
Bushey WD23 . . . .**51** H1
Stanmore HA7 . . . . . .**53** H4
Partridge Ct, EC1
off Percival St **111** H4
Partridge Dr, Orp. BR6 . .**207** F3
Partridge Grn, SE9 . . . . .**174** D3
Partridge Rd, Hmptn.
TW12 . . . .**161** F6
Sidcup DA14 . . . .**175** H3
Partridge Sq, E6
off Nightingale Way . .**116** B5
Partridge Way, N22 . . . . . .**75** E1
Parvin St, SW8 . . . .**150** D1
Pasadena Cl, Hayes UB3 .**122** B2
Pasadena Cl Trd Est, Hayes UB3
off Pasadena Cl **122** B2
Pascal St, SW8 . . . .**33** J7
Pascoe Rd, SE13 . . . .**154** D5
Pasley Cl, SE17 . . . .**35** J4
Pasquier Rd, E17 . . . .**77** H3
Passey Pl, SE9 . . . .**156** C6

Passfield Dr, E14 . . . .
off Uamvar St **114** B5
Passfield Path, SE28
off Booth Cl **118** B7
Passing All, EC1 . . . .**11** H6
Passmore Gdns, N11 . . . . .**58** D6
Passmore St, SW1 . . . .**32** B2
★ **Passport Office**, SW1 . .**25** G5
Pasteur Cl, NW9 . . . .**71** E2
Pasteur Gdns, N18 . . . . . .**59** H5
Paston Cl, E5
off Caldecott Way **95** G3
Wallington SM6 . . . . .**200** C3
Paston Cres, SE12 . . . . . .**155** H7
Pastor St, SE11 . . . .**35** H1
Pasture Cl, Wem. HA0 . . . .**86** E3
Pasture Rd, SE6 . . . .**173** F1
Dagenham RM9 . . . . .**101** F4
Wembley HA0 . . . .**86** E2
Pastures, The, N20 . . . . . .**56** C1
Patcham Ter, SW8 . . . . . .**150** B1
Paternoster Row, EC4 . . . .**19** J4
Paternoster Sq, EC4 . . . . .**19** H3
Pater St, W8 . . . .**128** D3
Pates Manor Dr, Felt.
TW14 . . . .**141** G7
Path, The, SW19 . . . .**184** E1
Pathfield Rd, SW16 . . . . .**168** D6
Pathway, The, Wat. WD19
off Anthony Cl **50** D1
Patience Rd, SW11 . . . . .**149** H2
Patio Cl, SW4 . . . .**150** D6
Patmore Est, SW8 . . . . . .**150** C1
Patmore St, SW8 . . . .**150** C1
Patmos Rd, SW9 . . . .**131** H7
Paton Cl, E3 . . . .**114** A3
Paton St, EC1 . . . .**11** J4
Patricia Ct, Chis. BR7
off Manor Pk Rd **193** G1
Welling DA16 . . . .**138** B7
Patrick Connolly Gdns, E3
off Talwin St **114** B3
Patrick Rd, E13 . . . .**115** J3
Patriot Sq, E2 . . . .**113** E2
Patrol Pl, SE6 . . . .**154** B6
Patshull Pl, NW5
off Patshull Rd **92** C6
Patshull Rd, NW5 . . . .**92** C6
Patten All, Rich. TW10
off The Hermitage . . .**145** G5
Pattenden Rd, SE6 . . . . . .**171** J1
Patten Rd, SW18 . . . .**149** H7
Patterdale Cl, Brom.
BR1 . . . .**173** F6
Patterdale Rd, SE15 . . . .**133** F7
Patterson Ct, SE19 . . . . . .**170** C7
Patterson Rd, SE19 . . . . . .**170** C6
Pattina Wk, SE16 . . . .**133** J1
Pattison Pl, E16
off Fife Rd **115** G5
Pattison Rd, NW2 . . . .**90** D3
Pattison Wk, SE18 . . . . . .**137** F5
Paul Cl, E15 . . . .**96** E7
EC2 . . . .**12** C6
Paulet Rd, SE5 . . . .**151** H2
Paul Gdns, Croy. CR0 . . . .**202** C2
Paulhan Rd, Har. HA3 . . . .**69** G4
Paulin Dr, N21 . . . .**43** G7
Pauline Cres, Twick. TW2 .**161** J1
Paul Julius Cl, E14 . . . . . .**114** D7
Paul Robeson Cl, E6
off Eastbourne Rd . . .**116** D3
Paul St, E15 . . . .**114** D1
EC2 . . . .**12** C6
Paul's Wk, EC4 . . . .**19** H5
Paultons Sq, SW3 . . . .**31** F5
Paultons St, SW3 . . . .**31** F6
Pauntley St, N19 . . . .**92** C1
Paved Ct, Rich. TW9 . . . .**145** G5
Paveley Dr, SW11 . . . . . .**129** H7
Paveley St, NW8 . . . .**7** H5
Pavement, The, SW4 . . . .**150** C4
W5 off Popes La **125** H3
Pavement, Rom. RM6
off Clarissa Rd **82** D7
Pavement Sq, Croy.
CR0 . . . .**202** D1
Pavet Cl, Dag. RM10 . . . .**101** H6
Pavilion La, Beck. BR3
off Lennard Rd **171** J6
Pavilion Ms, N3
off Windermere Av . . .**72** D2
Pavilion Rd, SW1 . . . .**24** A6
Ilford IG1 . . . .**80** C7
Pavilion St, SW1 . . . .**24** A6
Pavilion Ter, E.Mol. KT8 . .**180** C4
Ilford IG2
off Southdown Cres . .**81** H5
Pavilion Way, Edg. HA8 . . .**54** B7
Ruislip HA4 . . . .**84** C2
Pawleyne Cl, SE20 . . . . . .**171** F7

Pawsey Cl, E13
off Plashet Rd 115 G1
Pawson's Rd, Croy. CR0 .187 J6
Paxford Rd, Wem. HA0 . .86 E2
Paxton Cl, Rich.TW9 . . . .145 J2
Walton-on-Thames
KT12 . . . . .178 C7
Paxton Pl, SE27 . . . . . . .170 B4
Paxton Rd, N17 . . . . .60 C7
SE23 . . . . .171 H3
W4 . . . . .126 E6
Bromley BR1 . . . . . . .173 G7
Paxton Ter, SW1 . . . . . . .33 E5
Payne Cl, Bark. IG11 . . . .99 H7
Paynell Ct, SE3
off Lawn Ter 154/155 E3
Payne Rd, E3 . . . . .114 B2
Paynesfield Av, SW14 . . .146 D3
Payne St, SE8 . . . . .133 J6
Paynes Wk, W6 . . . . .128 B6
Peabody Av, SW1 . . . . . . .32 D3
Peabody Cl, SE10
off Devonshire Dr 154 B1
SW1 off Lupus St 130 B6
Croydon CR0
off Shirley Rd 203 F1
Peabody Dws, WC1 . . . . . .10 A5
Peabody Est, EC1 . . . . . . .12 A6
N17 . . . . .76 B1
SE1 . . . . .27 F2
SE24 . . . . .151 J7
SW3 . . . . .31 H5
W6 off The Square 127 J5
W10 . . . . .107 J5
Peabody Hill, SE21 . . . . .169 H1
Peabody Hill Est, SE21 . .151 H7
Peabody Sq, N1
off Essex Rd 111 H1
SE1 . . . . .27 G4
Peabody Twr, EC1
off Golden La 111 J4
Peabody Trust, SE1 . . . . . .27 J2
Peabody Yd, N1
off Greenman St 111 J1
Peace Cl, N14 . . . . .42 B5
SE25 . . . . .188 B4
Peace Gro, Wem. HA9 . . . .88 B3
Peace St, SE18
off Nightingale
Vale 136/137 E6
Peaches Cl, Sutt. SM2 . . .198 B7
Peach Rd, W10 . . . . .108 A3
Peachum Rd, SE3 . . . . . .135 F6
Peachwalk Ms, E3
off Grove Rd 113 G2
Peacock St, SE17 . . . . . . .35 H2
Peacock Wk, E16 . . . . . . .115 H6
Peacock Yd, SE17 . . . . . . .35 H2
Peak, The, SE26 . . . . . . .171 F3
Peaketon Av, IIf. IG4 . . . .80 A4
Peak Hill, SE26 . . . . .171 F4
Peak Hill Av, SE26 . . . . . .171 F4
Peak Hill Gdns, SE26 . . . .171 F4
Peal Gdns, W13
off Ruislip Rd E 104 D4
Peall Rd, Croy. CR0 . . . . .187 F6
Pearce Cl, Mitch. CR4 . . .186 A2
Pearcefield Av, SE23 . . . .171 F1
Pearce Rd, W.Mol. KT8 . .179 H3
Pear Cl, NW9 . . . . .70 D4
SE14 off Southerngate
Way 133 H7
Pearcroft Rd, E11 . . . . . . .96 D2
Peardon St, SW8 . . . . . . .150 B2
Peareswood Gdns, Stan.
HA7 . . . . .69 G1
Pearfield Rd, SE23 . . . . . .171 H3
Pearl Cl, E6 . . . . .116 D6
NW2 off Marble Dr 72 A7
Pearl Rd, E17 . . . . .78 A3
Pearl St, E1
off Penang St . . .132/133 E1
Pearman St, SE1 . . . . .27 F5
Pear Pl, SE1 . . . . .27 E3
Pear Rd, E11 . . . . .96 D3
Pearscroft Ct, SW6 . . . . .149 E1
Pearscroft Rd, SW6 . . . . .149 E1
Pearse St, SE15 . . . . .36 E6
Pearson Ms, SW4
off Edgeley Rd 150 D3
Pearsons Av, SE14
off Tanners Hill 154 A1
Pearson St, E2 . . . . .13 E1
Pears Rd, Houns.TW3 . . .143 J3
Peartree Av, SW17 . . . . . .167 F3
Pear Tree Cl, E2 . . . . .112 C1
Chessington KT9 . . . . .196 A6
Mitcham CR4 . . . . . . .185 H2
Peartree Ct, E18 . . . . .79 H1

Pear Tree Ct, EC1 . . . . . . .11 F6
Peartree Gdns, Dag.
RM8 . . . . .100 B4
Romford RM7 . . . . .83 H2
Peartree La, E1
off Glamis Rd 113 F7
Peartree Rd, Enf. EN1 . . . .44 B3
Pear Tree St, EC1 . . . . . . .11 H5
Peartree Way, SE10 . . . . .135 G4
Peary Pl, E2
off Kirkwall Pl 113 F3
Peatfield Cl, Sid. DA15
off Woodside Rd 175 H3
Pebble Way, W3 . . . . . . .126 B1
Pebworth Rd, Har. HA1 . . .86 D2
Peckarmans Wd, SE26 . . .170 D3
Peckett Sq, N5
off Highbury Gra 93 J4
Peckford Pl, SW9 . . . . . . .151 G2
PECKHAM, SE15 . . . . . . .152 D1
Peckham Gro, SE15 . . . . . .36 E7
Peckham High St, SE15 . .152 D1
Peckham Hill St, SE15 . . . .37 H7
Peckham Pk Rd, SE15 . . . .37 H7
Peckham Rd, SE5 . . . . . . .152 B1
SE15 . . . . .152 B1
Peckham Rye, SE15 . . . . .152 D3
SE22 . . . . .152 D4
Pecks Yd, E1 . . . . .21 F1
Peckwater St, NW5 . . . . . .92 C5
Pedlars Wk, N7 . . . . .93 E6
Pedley Rd, Dag. RM8 . . . .100 C1
Pedley St, E1 . . . . .13 G6
Pedro St, E5 . . . . .95 G3
Pedworth Gdns, SE16
off Rotherhithe
New Rd 133 F4
Peek Cres, SW19 . . . . . . .166 A5
Peel Cl, E4 . . . . .62 B2
N9 off Plevna Rd 60 D3
Peel Dr, NW9 . . . . .71 F3
Ilford IG5 . . . . .80 B3
Peel Gro, E2 . . . . .113 F2
Peel Pas, W8
off Peel St 128 D1
Peel Pl, Ilf. IG5 . . . . .80 B2
Peel Prec, NW6 . . . . .108 D2
Peel Rd, E18 . . . . .79 F1
NW6 . . . . .108 C3
Harrow (Wldste.) HA3 . .68 C3
Orpington BR6 . . . . . . .207 F5
Wembley HA9 . . . . .87 G3
Peel St, W8 . . . . .128 D1
Peerless St, EC1 . . . . .12 B4
Pegamoid Rd, N18 . . . . . . .61 F3
Pegasus Cl, N16
off Green Las 94 A4
Pegasus Pl, SE11 . . . . .35 E5
SW6 off Ackmar Rd . . .148 D1
Pegasus Rd, Croy. CR0 . .201 G6
Pegasus Way, N11 . . . . . . .58 B6
Pegg Rd, Houns.TW5 . . . .122 D7
Pegley Gdns, SE12 . . . . .173 G2
Pegwell St, SE18 . . . . . . .137 H7
Pekin Cl, E14
off Pekin St 114 A6
Pekin St, E14 . . . . .114 A6
Peldon Ct, Rich.TW9 . . . .145 J4
Peldon Pas, Rich.TW10
off Worple Way 145 J4
Peldon Wk, N1
off Britannia Row 111 H1
Pelham Av, Bark. IG11 . . .117 J1
Pelham Cl, SE5 . . . . .152 B2
Pelham Cres, SW7 . . . . . . .31 G2
W13 off Ruislip Rd E . . .104 C4
Pelham Rd, E18 . . . . .79 H3
N15 . . . . .76 C4
N22 . . . . .75 G2
SW19 . . . . .166 D7
Beckenham BR3 . . . . . .189 F2
Bexleyheath DA7 . . . . .159 G3
Ilford IG1 . . . . .99 G2
Pelham St, SW7 . . . . .31 F1
Pelican Est, SE15 . . . . . . .152 C1
Pelican Pas, E1
off Cambridge Heath
Rd 113 F4
Pelican Wk, SW9
off Loughborough Pk .151 H4
Pelier St, SE17 . . . . .36 A5
Pelinore Rd, SE6 . . . . . . .172 E2
Pellant Rd, SW6 . . . . . . .128 B7
Pellatt Gro, N22 . . . . .75 G1
Pellatt Rd, SE22 . . . . . . .152 C5
Wembley HA9 . . . . .87 G2
Pellerin Rd, N16 . . . . .94 B5
Pelling St, E14 . . . . .114 A6
Pellipar Cl, N13 . . . . .59 G3

Pellipar Gdns, SE18 . . . . .136 C5
Pelly Rd, E13 . . . . .115 G2
Pelter St, E2 . . . . .13 F3
Pelton Rd, SE10 . . . . .134 E5
Pembar Av, E17 . . . . .77 H3
Pemberley Chase, Epsom
(W.Ewell) KT19 . . . . . .196 B5
Pemberley Cl, Epsom
(W.Ewell) KT19 . . . . . .196 B5
Pember Rd, NW10 . . . . . .108 A3
Pemberton Gdns, N19 . . . .92 C2
Romford RM6 . . . . .82 E5
Pemberton Ho, SE26
off High Level Dr 170 D4
Pemberton Pl, E8
off Mare St 94/95 E7
Pemberton Rd, N4 . . . . . . .75 G5
East Molesey KT8 . . . . .179 J4
Pemberton Row, EC4 . . . . .19 F3
Pemberton Ter, N19 . . . . . .92 C3
Pembridge Av, Twick.
TW2 . . . . .161 F1
Pembridge Cres, W11 . . . .108 D7
Pembridge Gdns, W2 . . . .108 D7
Pembridge Ms, W11 . . . . .108 D7
Pembridge Pl, SW15 . . . .148 D5
W2 . . . . .108 D7
Pembridge Rd, W11 . . . . .108 D7
Pembridge Sq, W2 . . . . . .108 D7
Pembridge Vil, W2 . . . . . .108 D7
W11 . . . . .108 D7
Pembroke Av, N1
off Bingfield St 110 E1
Harrow HA3 . . . . .68 D3
Pinner HA5 . . . . .84 D1
Surbiton KT5 . . . . .182 B5
Pembroke Cl, SW1 . . . . . . .24 C4
Pembroke Cotts, W8
off Pembroke Sq 128 D3
Pembroke Gdns, W8 . . . . .128 C4
Dagenham RM10 . . . . .101 H3
Pembroke Gdns Cl, W8 . .128 D3
Pembroke Ms, E3
off Morgan St 113 H3
N10 off Pembroke Rd . . .74 A1
W8 off Earls Wk 128 D3
Pembroke Pl, W8 . . . . . . .128 D3
Edgware HA8 . . . . .54 A7
Isleworth TW7
off Thornbury Rd 144 B2
Pembroke Rd, E6 . . . . . . .116 C5
E17 . . . . .78 B5
N8 . . . . .74 E4
N10 . . . . .74 A1
N13 . . . . .59 J3
N15 . . . . .76 C5
SE25 . . . . .188 B4
W8 . . . . .128 D4
Bromley BR1 . . . . .191 J2
Erith DA8 . . . . .139 J5
Greenford UB6 . . . . . .103 H4
Ilford IG3 . . . . .99 J1
Mitcham CR4 . . . . . . .186 A2
Wembley HA9 . . . . .87 G3
Pembroke Sq, W8 . . . . . .128 D3
Pembroke St, N1 . . . . .93 E7
Pembroke Studios, W8 . .128 C3
Pembroke Vil, W8 . . . . . .128 D4
Richmond TW9 . . . . . .145 G4
Pembroke Wk, W8 . . . . . .128 D4
Pembroke Way, Hayes
UB3 . . . . .121 F3
Pembry Cl, SW9 . . . . . . .151 G1
Pembury Av, Wor.Pk.
KT4 . . . . .183 G7
Pembury Cl, Brom. BR2 .191 F7
Pembury Ct, Hayes UB3 .121 G6
Pembury Cres, Sid.
DA14 . . . . .176 E2
Pembury Pl, E5 . . . . .94 E5
Pembury Rd, E5 . . . . .94 E5
N17 . . . . .76 C2
SE25 . . . . .188 D4
Bexleyheath DA7 . . . . .139 E7
Pemdevon Rd, Croy.
CR0 . . . . .187 G7
Pemell Cl, E1 . . . . .113 F4
off Colebert Av 113 F4
Pemerich Cl, Hayes UB3 .121 J5
Pempath Pl, Wem. HA9 . .87 G2
Penally Pl, N1
off Shepperton Rd 112 A1
Penang St, E1 . . . . .133 E1
Penard Rd, Sthl. UB2 . . . .123 G3
Penarth St, SE15 . . . . . . .133 F6
Penates, Esher KT10 . . . .194 A4
Penberth Rd, SE6 . . . . . .172 C2
Penbury Rd, Sthl. UB2 . . .123 F4
Pencombe Ms, W11
off Denbigh Rd 108 C7

Pencraig Way, SE15 . . . . .132 E6
Pendall Cl, Barn. EN4 . . . .41 H4
Penda Rd, Erith DA8 . . . .139 H7
Pendarves Rd, SW20 . . . .183 J1
Penda's Mead, E9
off Lindisfarne Way . . .95 H4
Pendell Av, Hayes UB3 . .121 J7
Pendennis Rd, N17 . . . . . .76 A3
SW16 . . . . .168 E4
Penderel Rd, Houns.
TW3 . . . . .143 G5
Penderry Ri, SE6 . . . . . . .172 D2
Penderyn Way, N7 . . . . . . .92 D4
Pendle Rd, SW16 . . . . . . .168 B6
Pendlestone Rd, E17 . . . . .78 A5
Pendragon Ho, N9
off Salisbury Rd 60 D3
Pendragon Rd, Brom.
BR1 . . . . .173 F3
Pendrell Rd, SE4 . . . . . . .153 H2
Pendrell St, SE18 . . . . . . .137 G7
Pendula Dr, Hayes UB4 . .102 D4
Pendulum Ms, E8
off Birkbeck Rd 94 C5
Penerley Rd, SE6 . . . . . . .172 B1
Penfold Cl, Croy. CR0
off Epsom Rd 201 G3
Penfold La, Bex. DA5 . . . .176 D2
Penfold Pl, NW1 . . . . .15 G1
Penfold Rd, N9 . . . . .61 G1
Penfold St, NW1 . . . . .7 F6
NW8 . . . . .7 F6
Penford Gdns, SE9 . . . . . .156 A3
Penford St, SE5 . . . . .151 H2
Pengarth Rd, Bex. DA5 . .158 D5
PENGE, SE20 . . . . .171 F7
Penge Ho, SW11
off Wye St 149 G3
Penge La, SE20 . . . . .171 F7
Penge Rd, E13 . . . . .97 J7
SE20 . . . . .188 D3
SE25 . . . . .188 D3
Penhall Rd, SE7 . . . . .136 A4
Penhill Rd, Bex. DA5 . . . .158 C7
Penhurst Rd, Ilf. IG6 . . . . .65 E7
Penifather La, Grnf. UB6 .104 A3
Peninsular Cl, Felt.TW14 .141 G6
Peninsular Pk Rd, SE7 . . .135 G4
Penistone Rd, SW16 . . . . .168 E7
Penketh Dr, Har. HA1 . . . .86 A3
Penmon Rd, SE2 . . . . . . .138 A3
Pennack Rd, SE15 . . . . . . .37 G6
Pennant Ms, W8 . . . . .30 A1
Pennant Ter, E17 . . . . .77 J2
Pennard Rd, W12 . . . . . . .127 J2
Pennards, The, Sun.
TW16 . . . . .178 C2
Penn Cl, Grnf. UB6 . . . . . .103 H2
Harrow HA3 . . . . .69 F4
Penner Cl, SW19
off Victoria Dr 166 B2
Penners Gdns, Surb.
KT6 . . . . .181 H7
Pennethorne Cl, E9
off Victoria Pk Rd 113 F1
Pennethorne Rd, SE15 . . .132 E7
Penn Gdns, Chis. BR7 . . .192 E2
Pennine Dr, NW2 . . . . .90 B2
Pennine Ho, N9
off Plevna Rd 60 D3
Pennine La, NW2
off Pennine Dr 90 B2
Pennine Way, Hayes
UB3 . . . . .121 G7
Pennington Cl, SE27
off Hamilton Rd 170 A4
Pennington Dr, N21 . . . . . .43 E5
Pennington St, E1 . . . . . . .21 J6
Pennington Way, SE12 . . .173 H2
Penniston Cl, N17 . . . . . . .75 J2
Penn La, Bex. DA5 . . . . . .158 D5
Penn Rd, N7 . . . . .93 E5
Penn St, N1 . . . . .112 A1
Pennyfather La, Enf. EN2 . .43 J2
Pennyfields, E14 . . . . . . .114 A7
Penny Ms, SW12
off Caistor Rd 150 B7
Pennymoor Wk, W9
off Ashmore Rd 108 C3
Penny Rd, NW10 . . . . . . .106 B3
Pennyroyal Av, E6 . . . . . .116 D6
Penpoll Rd, E8 . . . . .94 E6
Penpool La, Well. DA16 . .158 B3
Penrhyn Av, E17 . . . . .77 J1
Penrhyn Cres, E17 . . . . . . .78 A1
SW14 . . . . .146 C4
Penrhyn Gdns, Kings.T. KT1
off Surbiton Rd 181 G4
Penrhyn Gro, E17 . . . . . . .78 A1

Penrhyn Rd, Kings.T.
KT1 . . . .**181** H3
Penrith Cl, SW15 . . . .**148** B5
Beckenham BR3
off Albemarle Rd **190** B1
Penrith Pl, SE27
off Harpenden Rd **169** H2
Penrith Rd, N15 . . . .**76** A5
Ilford IG6 . . . .**65** J6
New Malden KT3 . . . . . .**182** D4
Thornton Heath CR7 . .**187** J2
Penrith St, SW16 . . . .**168** C6
Penrose Av, Wat.WD19 . . .**50** D2
Penrose Gro, SE17 . . . .**35** J4
Penrose Ho, SE17 . . . .**35** J4
Penrose St, SE17 . . . .**35** J4
Penryn St, NW1 . . . .**9** H1
Penry St, SE1 . . . .**37** E2
Pensbury Pl, SW8 . . . .**150** C2
Pensbury St, SW8 . . . .**150** C2
Penscroft Gdns, Borwd.
WD6 . . . .**38** D4
Pensford Av, Rich.TW9 . .**146** A2
Penshurst Av, Sid. DA15 .**158** A6
Penshurst Gdns, Edg.
HA8 . . . .**54** B5
Penshurst Grn, Brom.
BR2 . . . .**191** F5
Penshurst Rd, E9 . . . .**95** G2
N17 . . . .**60** C7
Bexleyheath DA7 . . . . .**159** F1
Thornton Heath CR7 . .**187** H5
Penshurst Wk, Brom. BR2
off Hayesford Pk Dr . .**191** F5
Penshurst Way, Sutt.
SM2 . . . .**198** D7
Pensilver Cl, Barn. EN4 . . .**41** H4
Penstemon Cl, N3 . . . .**56** D7
Penstock Footpath, N22 . .**75** E3
Pentavia Retail Pk, NW7
off Bunns La **55** F7
Pentelow Gdns, Felt.
TW14 . . . .**142** A6
Pentire Rd, E17 . . . .**78** D1
Pentland Av, Edg. HA8 . . . .**54** B2
Pentland Cl, NW11 . . . .**90** B2
Pentland Gdns, SW18
off St. Ann's Hill **149** F6
Pentland Pl, Nthlt. UB5 . .**102** E1
Pentlands Cl, Mitch. CR4 .**186** B3
Pentland St, SW18 . . . . . .**149** F6
Pentlow St, SW15 . . . .**147** J3
Pentlow Way, Buck.H. IG9 .**48** B7
Pentney Rd, E4 . . . .**62** D1
SW12 . . . .**168** C1
SW19 off Midmoor Rd .**184** B1
Penton Gro, N1 . . . .**11** E2
Penton Ho, SE2
off Hartslock Dr **138** D2
Penton Pl, SE17 . . . .**35** H3
Penton Ri, WC1 . . . .**10** D3
Penton St, N1 . . . .**10** E1
PENTONVILLE, N1 . . . .**10** E2
Pentonville Rd, N1 . . . .**10** C2
Pentridge St, SE15 . . . . . .**132** C7
Pentyre Av, N18 . . . .**60** A5
Penwerris Av, Islw.TW7 . .**123** J7
Penwith Rd, SW18 . . . . . .**166** E2
Penwood Ho, SW15
off Tunworth Cres **147** F6
Penwortham Rd, SW16 . .**168** B6
Penylan Pl, Edg. HA8 . . . . .**54** A7
Penywern Rd, SW5 . . . . . .**128** D5
Penzance Pl, W11 . . . .**128** B1
Penzance St, W11 . . . .**128** B1
Peony Ct, Wdf.Grn. IG8
off The Bridle Path .**62/63** E7
Peony Gdns, W12 . . . .**107** G7
Pepler Ms, SE5 . . . .**37** F5
Peploe Rd, NW6 . . . .**108** A2
Peplow Cl, West Dr. UB7
off Tavistock Rd **120** A1
Pepper All, Loug. (High Beach)
IG10 . . . .**47** G1
Pepper Cl, E6 . . . .**116** C5
Peppercorn Cl, Th.Hth.
CR7 . . . .**188** A2
Peppermead Sq, SE13 . . .**154** A5
Peppermint Cl, Croy.
CR0 . . . .**186** E7
Peppermint Pl, E11
off Birch Gro **96/97** E3
Pepper St, E14 . . . .**134** B3
SE1 . . . .**27** J3
Peppie Cl, N16
off Bouverie Rd **94** B2
Pepys Cres, E16
off Britannia Gate **135** G2
Barnet EN5 . . . .**39** J5
Pepys Ri, Orp. BR6 . . . . . .**207** J1

Pepys Rd, SE14 . . . .**153** G1
SW20 . . . .**183** J1
Pepys St, EC3 . . . .**21** E5
Perceval Av, NW3 . . . .**91** H5
Percheron Cl, Islw.TW7 . .**144** D3
Percheron Rd, Borwd.
WD6 . . . .**38** D6
Perch St, E8 . . . .**94** C4
Percival Ct, N17
off High Rd **60** C7
Northolt UB5 . . . .**85** G5
★ **Percival David Foundation
of Chinese Art**, WC1
off Gordon Sqaure **9** J5
Percival Gdns, Rom. RM6 .**82** C6
Percival Rd, SW14 . . . . . .**146** C4
Enfield EN1 . . . .**44** C4
Orpington BR6 . . . .**207** E2
Percival St, EC1 . . . .**11** G5
Percival Way, Epsom
KT19 . . . .**196** C4
Percy Bush Rd, West Dr.
UB7 . . . .**120** C3
Percy Circ, WC1 . . . .**10** D3
Percy Gdns, Enf. EN3 . . . . .**45** G5
Isleworth TW7 . . . .**144** D2
Worcester Park KT4 . . .**196** D1
Percy Ms, W1 . . . .**17** H2
Percy Pas, W1 . . . .**17** G2
Percy Rd, E11 . . . .**78** E7
E16 . . . .**115** E5
N12 . . . .**57** F5
N21 . . . .**43** J7
SE20 . . . .**189** G1
SE25 . . . .**188** D5
W12 . . . .**127** G2
Bexleyheath DA7 . . . . .**159** E2
Hampton TW12 . . . . . .**161** G7
Ilford IG3 . . . .**82** A7
Isleworth TW7 . . . .**144** D4
Mitcham CR4 . . . .**186** A7
Romford RM7 . . . .**83** H3
Twickenham TW2 . . . . .**161** H1
Percy St, W1 . . . .**17** H2
Percy Way, Twick.TW2 . .**161** J1
Percy Yd, WC1 . . . .**10** D3
Peregrine Cl, NW10 . . . . . .**88** D5
SW16
off Leithcote Gdns . . .**169** F4
Welling DA16 . . . .**157** J1
Peregrine Gdns, Croy.
CR0 . . . .**203** H2
Peregrine Ho, EC1 . . . .**11** H3
Peregrine Way, SW19 . . .**165** J7
Perham Rd, W14 . . . .**128** B5
Peridot St, E6 . . . .**116** B5
Perifield, SE21 . . . .**169** J1
Perimeade Rd, Grnf.
UB6 . . . .**105** F2
Periton Rd, SE9 . . . .**156** A4
PERIVALE, Grnf. **105** F1
Perivale Gdns, W13
off Bellevue Rd . .**104/105** E4
Perivale Gra, Grnf. UB6 . .**104** D3
Perivale Ind Pk, Grnf.
UB6 . . . .**104** E2
Perivale La, Grnf. UB6 . . .**104** D3
Perivale New Business Cen,
Grnf. UB6 . . . .**105** E2
Perkin Cl, Wem. HA0 . . . . .**86** E5
Perkin's Rents, SW1 . . . . .**25** H5
Perkins Rd, Ilf. IG2 . . . .**81** G5
Perkins Sq, SE1 . . . .**28** A1
Perks Cl, SE3
off Hurren Cl **154/155** E3
Perpins Rd, SE9 . . . .**157** H6
Perran Rd, SW2
off Christchurch Rd . .**169** H2
Perran Wk, Brent.TW8 . . .**125** H5
Perren St, NW5
off Ryland Rd **92** B6
Perrers Rd, W6 . . . .**127** H4
Perrin Rd, Wem. HA0 . . . . .**86** D4
Perrins Ct, NW3
off Hampstead High
St **91** F4
Perrins La, NW3 . . . .**91** F4
Perrin's Wk, NW3 . . . .**91** F4
Perrott St, SE18 . . . .**137** F4
Perry Av, W3 . . . .**106** D6
Perry Ct, E14
off Napier Av **134** A5
N15 off Albert Rd **76** B6
Perryfield Way, NW9 . . . . .**71** F6
Richmond TW10 . . . . . .**163** E2
Perry Gdns, N9
off Deansway **60** B3
Perry Garth, Nthlt. UB5 . .**102** C1
Perry Hall Rd, Orp. BR6 . .**193** J6
Perry Hill, SE6 . . . .**171** J3

Perry Ho, SW2
off Tierney Rd **150/151** E7
Perry How, Wor.Pk. KT4 . .**197** F1
Perryman Ho, Bark. IG11 .**117** F1
Perrymans Fm Rd, Ilf. IG2 .**81** G6
Perry Mead, Enf. EN2 . . . .**43** H2
Perrymead St, SW6 . . . . .**148** D1
Perryn Rd, SE16
off Drummond
Rd **132/133** E3
W3 . . . .**106** D7
Perry Ri, SE23 . . . .**171** H3
Perry Rd, Dag. RM9 . . . . .**119** F4
Perrys Pl, W1 . . . .**17** H3
Perry St, Chis. BR7 . . . . . .**175** G6
Perry St Gdns, Chis. BR7
off Old Perry St **175** H6
Perry Vale, SE23 . . . .**171** F2
Persant Rd, SE6 . . . .**172** E2
Perseverance Pl, SW9 . . .**131** G7
Richmond TW9
off Shaftesbury Rd . . .**145** H3
Pershore Gro, Cars.
SM5 . . . .**185** G6
Pert Cl, N10 . . . .**58** B7
Perth Av, NW9 . . . .**70** D7
Hayes UB4 . . . .**102** C4
Perth Cl, SW20
off Huntley Way **183** G2
Perth Rd, E10 . . . .**95** H1
E13 . . . .**115** H2
N4 . . . .**93** G1
N22 . . . .**75** H1
Barking IG11 . . . .**117** G2
Beckenham BR3 . . . . . .**190** C2
Ilford IG2 . . . .**80** D6
Perth Ter, Ilf. IG2 . . . .**81** F7
Perwell Av, Har. HA2 . . . . .**85** F1
Perwell Ct, Har. HA2 . . . . .**85** F1
Peter Av, NW10 . . . .**89** H7
Peterboat Cl, SE10
off Tunnel Av **134/135** E4
Peterborough Gdns, Ilf. .**80** B7
Peterborough Ms, SW6 . .**148** D2
Peterborough Rd, E10 . . . .**78** C5
SW6 . . . .**148** D2
Carshalton SM5 . . . . . .**185** H6
Harrow HA1 . . . .**86** B1
Peterborough Vil, SW6 . .**148** E1
Peterchurch Ho, SE15
off Commercial
Way **132/133** E6
Petergate, SW11 . . . .**149** F4
Peterhouse Gdns, SW6
off Bagley's La . .**148/149** E1
Peter James Business Cen,
Hayes UB3 . . . .**122** A2
Peterley Business Cen, E2
off Hackney Rd . . .**112/113** E2
★ **Peter Pan Statue**, W2 . .**23** E1
Peters Cl, Dag. RM8 . . . . .**100** D1
Stanmore HA7 . . . .**53** G6
Welling DA16 . . . .**157** H2
Petersfield Cl, N18 . . . .**59** J5
Petersfield Ri, SW15 . . . .**165** H1
Petersfield Rd, W3 . . . . . .**126** C2
PETERSHAM, Rich. **163** H1
Petersham Cl, Rich.
TW10 . . . .**163** G2
Sutton SM1 . . . .**198** D5
Petersham Dr, Orp. BR5 .**193** J2
Petersham Gdns, Orp.
BR5 . . . .**193** J2
Petersham La, SW7 . . . . . .**22** C5
Petersham Ms, SW7 . . . . .**22** C6
Petersham Pl, SW7 . . . . . .**22** C6
Petersham Rd, Rich.
TW10 . . . .**145** H6
Petersham Ter, Croy. CR0
off Richmond
Grn **200/201** E3
Peters Hill, EC4 . . . .**19** J5
Peter's La, EC1 . . . .**19** H1
Peters Path, SE26 . . . .**170** E4
Peterstone Rd, SE2 . . . . .**138** B3
Peterstow Cl, SW19 . . . . .**166** B2
Peter St, W1 . . . .**17** G5
Peterwood Way, Croy.
CR0 . . . .**201** F2
Petherton Rd, N5 . . . .**93** J5
Petley Rd, W6 . . . .**127** J6
Peto Pl, NW1 . . . .**8** E5
Peto St N, E16
off Victoria Dock Rd . .**115** F7
Petrie Cl, NW2 . . . .**90** B6
★ **Petrie Mus of Egyptian
Archaeology**, WC1
off Malet Pl **9** H6

Petticoat La, E1 . . . .**21** E2
★ **Petticoat La (Mkt)**,
E1 . . . .**21** E2
Petticoat Sq, E1 . . . .**21** F3
Pettits Pl, Dag. RM10 . . . .**101** G5
Pettits Rd, Dag. RM10 . . .**101** G5
Pettiward Cl, SW15 . . . . . .**147** J4
Pettman Cres, SE28 . . . . .**137** G3
Pettsgrove Av, Wem.
HA0 . . . .**87** F5
Petts Hill, Nthlt. UB5 . . . . .**85** H5
Pett St, SE18 . . . .**136** B4
PETTS WOOD, Orp. **193** G5
Petts Wd Rd, Orp. BR5 . . .**193** F5
Petty France, SW1 . . . .**25** G5
Petworth Cl, Nthlt. UB5 . .**85** F7
Petworth Gdns, SW20
off Hidcote Gdns **183** H3
Petworth Rd, N12 . . . .**57** H5
Bexleyheath DA6 . . . . .**159** G5
Petworth St, SW11 . . . . . .**149** H1
Petyt Pl, SW3 . . . .**31** G6
Petyward, SW3 . . . .**31** H2
Pevensey Av, N11 . . . .**58** D5
Enfield EN1 . . . .**44** A2
Pevensey Cl, Islw.TW7 . .**123** J7
Pevensey Rd, E7 . . . .**97** F4
SW17 . . . .**167** G4
Feltham TW13 . . . .**160** E1
Peverel, E6
off Downings **116** D6
Peverel Ho, Dag. RM10 . .**101** G2
Peveret Cl, N11
off Woodland Rd **58** B5
Peveril Dr, Tedd. TW11 . .**162** A5
Pewsey Cl, E4 . . . .**62** A5
Peyton Pl, SE10 . . . .**134** C7
Pharaoh Cl, Mitch. CR4 . .**185** J7
Pheasant Cl, E16
off Maplin Rd **115** G6
Phelp St, SE17 . . . .**36** B5
Phelps Way, Hayes UB3 .**121** J4
Phene St, SW3 . . . .**31** H5
Philbeach Gdns, SW5 . . .**128** D5
Phil Brown Pl, SW8
off Heath Rd **150** B2
Philchurch Pl, E1 . . . .**21** J4
Philimore Cl, SE18 . . . . . .**137** H5
Philip Gdns, Croy. CR0 . .**203** J2
Philip La, N15 . . . .**76** A4
Philpot Path, SE9 . . . .**156** C6
Philippa Gdns, SE9 . . . . .**156** A5
Philips Cl, Cars. SM5 . . . .**200** A1
Philip St, E13 . . . .**115** G4
Philip Wk, SE15 . . . .**152** D3
Phillimore Gdns, NW10 . .**107** J1
W8 . . . .**128** D2
Phillimore Gdns Cl, W8
off Phillimore Gdns . .**128** D3
Phillimore Pl, W8 . . . .**128** D2
Phillimore Wk, W8 . . . . . .**128** D3
Phillipp St, N1 . . . .**112** B1
Philpot La, EC3 . . . .**20** D5
Philpot Path, Ilf. IG1
off Sunnyside Rd **99** F3
Philpot Sq, SW6
off Peterborough
Rd **148/149** E3
Philpot St, E1 . . . .**113** E6
Phineas Pett Rd, SE9 . . . .**156** B3
Phipps Br Rd, SW19 . . . . .**185** F2
Mitcham CR4 . . . .**185** F2
Phipp's Ms, SW1 . . . .**24** D6
Phipp St, EC2 . . . .**12** D5
Phoebeth Rd, SE4 . . . .**154** A5
Phoenix Cl, E8
off Stean St **112** C1
E17 . . . .**77** J2
West Wickham BR4 . . .**204** E2
Phoenix Dr, Kes. BR2 . . .**206** A3
Phoenix Pk, Brent.
TW8 . . . .**125** G5
Phoenix Pl, WC1 . . . .**10** D5
Phoenix Rd, NW1 . . . .**9** H3
SE20 . . . .**171** F6
Phoenix St, WC2 . . . .**17** J4
Phoenix Way, Houns.
TW5 . . . .**122** C6
Phoenix Wf, SE10 . . . .**135** F2
Phoenix Wf Rd, SE1 . . . . .**29** G4
Phoenix Yd, WC1
off King's Cross Rd . . .**111** F3
★ **Photographers' Gall**, WC2
off Great Newport St . .**17** J5
Phyllis Av, N.Mal. KT3 . . .**183** H5
★ **Physical Energy Statue**,
W2 . . . .**22** D2
Physic Pl, SW3 . . . .**31** J5
Piazza, The, WC2
off Covent Gdn . . .**110/111** E7

Picardy Manorway, Belv.
DA17 . . . . .139 H3
Picardy Rd, Belv. DA17 . .139 G4
Picardy St, Belv. DA17 . .139 G3
Piccadilly, W1 . . . . .24 E2
Piccadilly Arc, SW1 . . . . . .25 F1
Piccadilly Circ, W1 . . . . . .17 H6
Pickard St, EC1 . . . . .11 H3
Pickering Av, E6 . . . . . . .116 D2
Pickering CI, E9
off Cassland Rd 95 G7
Pickering Gdns, N11 . . . . .58 A6
Croydon CR0 . . . . .188 C6
Pickering Ms, W2 . . . . . . .14 B3
Pickering PI, SW1 . . . . . . .25 G2
Pickering St, N1
off Essex Rd 111 H1
Pickets CI, Bushey
(Bushey Hth.) WD23 . . .52 A1
Pickets St, SW12 . . . . . .150 B7
Pickett Cft, Stan. HA7 . . . .69 G1
Picketts Lock La, N9 . . . . .61 F2
Pickford CI, Bexh. DA7 . .158 E2
Pickford La, Bexh. DA7 . .159 E2
Pickford Rd, Bexh. DA7 . .158 E3
Pickfords Wf, N1 . . . . . . .11 J2
Pickhurst Grn, Brom.
BR2 . . . . .191 F7
Pickhurst La, Brom. BR2 .205 F1
West Wickham BR4 . .191 E6
Pickhurst Mead, Brom.
BR2 . . . . .191 F7
Pickhurst Pk, Brom. BR2 .191 E5
Pickhurst Ri, W.Wick.
BR4 . . . . .190 C7
Pickle Herring St, SE1
off Tooley St 132 B1
Pickwick CI, Houns. TW4
off Dorney Way . .142/143 E3
Pickwick Ct, SE9
off West Pk 174 B1
Pickwick Ms, N18 . . . . . . .60 B5
Pickwick PI, Har. HA1 . . . .68 B7
Pickwick Rd, SE21 . . . . .152 A7
Pickwick St, SE1 . . . . . . .27 J4
Pickwick Way, Chis. BR7 .175 F6
Pickworth CI, SW8
off Kenchester CI .130/131 E7
Picton PI, W1 . . . . .16 C4
Surbiton KT6 . . . . . . .196 A1
Picton St, SE5 . . . . .132 A7
Piedmont Rd, SE18 . . . .137 G5
Pier Head, E1
off Wapping High
St 132/133 E1
Piermont CI, SE22 . . . . .152 E5
Piermont PI, Brom. BR1 .192 B2
Piermont Rd, SE22 . . . . .152 E5
Pier Par, E16
off Pier Rd 136 D2
Pierrepoint Arc, N1
off Islington High St . .111 H2
Pierrepoint Rd, W3 . . . . .106 B7
Pierrepoint Row, N1 . . . .11 G1
Pier Rd, E16 . . . . .136 C2
Feltham TW14 . . . . . . .142 B5
Pier St, E14 . . . . .134 C4
Pier Ter, SW18
off Jew's Row 149 F4
Pier Way, SE28 . . . . . . .137 G3
Pigeon La, Hmptn.
TW12 . . . . .161 G4
Pigott St, E14 . . . . .114 A6
Pike CI, Brom. BR1 . . . . .173 H5
Pike Rd, NW7
off Ellesmere Av 54 D4
Pikes End, Pnr. HA5 . . . . .66 B4
Pikestone CI, Hayes UB4
off Berrydale Rd .102/103 E4
Pilgrimage St, SE1 . . . . . .28 B4
Pilgrim CI, Mord. SM4 . . .185 E7
Pilgrim Hill, SE27 . . . . . .169 J4
Pilgrims CI, N13 . . . . .59 F4
Northolt UB5 . . . . .85 J5
Pilgrims Ct, SE3 . . . . . . .155 G1
Pilgrim's La, NW3 . . . . . . .91 G4
Pilgrims Ms, E14
off Blackwall Way . . .114 C7
Pilgrims PI, NW3
off Hampstead High
St 91 G4
Pilgrims Ri, Barn. EN4 . . .41 H5
Pilgrim St, EC4 . . . . .19 G4
Pilgrims Way, E6
off High St N 116 B1
N19 . . . . .92 D1
South Croydon CR2 . . .202 C5
Pilgrim's Way, Wem.
HA9 . . . . .88 B1

Pilkington Rd, SE15 . . . .152 E2
Orpington BR6 . . . . . .207 F2
Pilot CI, SE8 . . . . .133 J6
Pilsdon CI, SW19
off Inner Pk Rd 166 A1
Piltdown Rd, Wat. WD19 . .50 D4
Pilton Est, The, Croy. (Pitlake)
CR0 off Pitlake 201 H2
Pilton PI, SE17 . . . . .36 A3
Pimento Ct, W5
off Olive Rd 125 G3
PIMLICO, SW1 . . . . .33 F3
Pimlico Rd, SW1 . . . . .32 B3
Pimlico Wk, N1 . . . . .12 D3
Pinchbeck Rd, Orp. BR6 .207 J6
Pinchin St, E1 . . . . .21 J5
Pincott CI, SE4 . . . . .153 G4
Pincott Rd, SW19 . . . . . .167 F7
Bexleyheath DA6 . . . . .159 G5
Pindar St, EC2 . . . . .20 D1
Pindock Ms, W9 . . . . .6 B6
Pineapple Ct, SW1 . . . . . .25 F5
Pine Av, E15 . . . . .96 D5
West Wickham BR4 . .204 B1
Pine CI, E10
off Walnut Rd 96 B2
N14 . . . . .42 C7
N19 off Hargrave Pk . . .92 C2
SE20 . . . . .189 F1
Stanmore HA7 . . . . . . .52 E4
Pine Coombe, Croy. CR0 .203 G4
Pinecrest Gdns, Orp.
BR6 . . . . .207 E4
Pinecroft Cres, Barn. EN5
off Hillside Gdns 40 B4
Pinedene, SE15
off Meeting Ho
La 152/153 E1
Pinefield CI, E14 . . . . . . .114 A7
Pine Gdns, Ruis. HA4 . . . .84 B1
Surbiton KT5 . . . . . . .182 A6
Pine Glade, Orp. BR6 . . .206 C4
Pine Gro, N4 . . . . .93 E2
N20 . . . . .56 C1
SW19 . . . . .166 C5
Pinehurst Wk, Orp. BR6 .207 H1
Pinelands CI, SE3
off St. John's Pk 135 F7
Pinemartin CI, NW2 . . . . .89 J3
Pine Ms, NW10
off Clifford Gdns 108 A2
Pine Rd, N11 . . . . .58 A2
NW2 . . . . .89 J4
Pines, The, N14 . . . . .42 C5
Sunbury-on-Thames
TW16 . . . . .178 A3
Woodford Green IG8 . . .63 G3
Pines Rd, Brom. BR1 . . . .192 B2
Pine St, EC1 . . . . .11 E5
Pine Tree CI, Houns. TW5 .142 B1
Pine Wk, Brom. BR1 . . . . .191 J1
Surbiton KT5 . . . . . . .182 A6
Pine Wd, Sun. TW16 . . . .178 A1
Pinewood Av, Pnr. HA5 . . .51 H6
Sidcup DA15 . . . . . . .175 H1
Pinewood CI, Borwd.
WD6 . . . . .38 D1
Croydon CR0 . . . . . . .203 H3
Northwood HA6 . . . . . .50 B5
Orpington BR6 . . . . . .207 G1
Pinner HA5 . . . . .51 H6
Pinewood Dr, Orp. BR6 .207 H5
Pinewood Gro, W5 . . . . .105 F6
Pinewood Ms, Stai. (Stanw.)
TW19 off Oaks Rd . . .140 A6
Pinewood Rd, SE2 . . . . .138 D6
Bromley BR2 . . . . .191 G4
Feltham TW13 . . . . . . .160 B3
Pinfold Rd, SW16 . . . . . .168 E4
Pinglestone CI, West Dr.
UB7 . . . . .120 B7
Pinkcoat CI, Felt. TW13
off Tanglewood Way . .160 B3
Pinkerton PI, SW16
off Riggindale Rd 168 D4
Pinkham Way, N11 . . . . . .58 A7
Pinkwell Av, Hayes UB3 .121 G4
Pinkwell La, Hayes UB3 .121 F4
Pinley Gdns, Dag. RM9
off Stamford Rd 118 B1
Pinnacle Hill, Bexh. DA7 .159 H4
Pinnacle Hill N, Bexh.
DA7 . . . . .159 H3
Pinnell Rd, SE9 . . . . .156 A4
PINNER 67 E4
Pinner Ct, Pnr. HA5 . . . . .67 G4
PINNER GREEN, Pnr. 66 C1
Pinner Grn, Pnr. HA5 . . . . .66 C2
Pinner Gro, Pnr. HA5 . . . . .67 E4
Pinner Hill, Pnr. HA5 . . . . .66 C1

Pinner Hill Rd, Pnr. HA5 . .66 C2
Pinner Pk, Pnr. HA5 . . . . . .67 G1
Pinner Pk Av, Har. HA2 . . .67 H3
Pinner Pk Gdns, Har. HA2 .67 J2
Pinner Rd, Har. HA1, HA2 .67 H5
Pinner HA5 . . . . .67 F4
Pinner Vw, Har. HA1,
HA2 . . . . .67 J6
PINNERWOOD PARK,
Pnr. 50 C7
Pintail CI, E6
off Swan App 116 B5
Pintail Rd, Wdf.Grn. IG8 . .63 H7
Pintail Way, Hayes UB4 .102 D5
Pinter Ho, SW9
off Grantham Rd .150/151 E2
Pinto CI, Borwd. WD6
off Percheron Rd 38 D6
Pinto Way, SE3 . . . . .155 H4
Pioneers Ind Pk, Croy.
CR0 . . . . .200 D1
Pioneer St, SE15 . . . . . .152 D1
Pioneer Way, W12
off Du Cane Rd 107 H6
Piper CI, N7 . . . . .93 F5
Piper Rd, Kings.T. KT1 . .182 A3
Piper's Gdns, Croy. CR0 .189 H7
Pipers Grn, NW9 . . . . . . .70 C5
Pipers Grn La, Edg. HA8 . .53 H3
Pipewell Rd, Cars. SM5 .185 H6
Pippin CI, NW2 . . . . .89 H3
Croydon CR0 . . . . . . .203 J1
Pippins CI, West Dr. UB7 .120 A3
Piquet Rd, SE20 . . . . . . .189 F2
Pirbright Cres, Croy.
(New Adgtn.) CR0 . . .204 C6
Pirbright Rd, SW18 . . . . .166 C1
Pirie CI, SE5
off Denmark Hill 152 A3
Pirie St, E16 . . . . .135 H1
Pitcairn CI, Rom. RM7 . . .83 G4
Pitcairn Rd, Mitch. CR4 .167 J7
Pitcairn's Path, Har. HA2
off Eastcote Rd 85 J3
Pitchford St, E15 . . . . . . .96 D7
Pitfield Cres, SE28 . . . . .138 A1
Pitfield Est, N1 . . . . .12 C3
Pitfield St, N1 . . . . .12 D4
Pitfield Way, NW10 . . . . . .88 C6
Enfield EN3 . . . . .45 F1
Pitfold CI, SE12 . . . . .155 G6
Pitfold Rd, SE12 . . . . . . .155 G6
Pitlake, Croy. CR0 . . . . . .201 H2
Pitman St, SE5 . . . . .35 J7
Pitmaston Ho, SE13
off Lewisham Rd 154 C2
Pitsea PI, E1 . . . . .113 G6
Pitsea St, E1 . . . . .113 G6
Pitshanger La, W5 . . . . . .105 E4
★ Pitshanger Manor & Gall,
W5 (Ealing) 125 F1
Pitt Cres, SW19 . . . . .166 E4
Pittman Gdns, IIf. IG1 . . . .99 F5
Pitt Rd, Croy. CR0 . . . . . .187 J5
Orpington BR6 . . . . . .207 F4
Thornton Heath CR7 . .187 J5
Pitt's Head Ms, W1 . . . . . .24 C2
Pittsmead Av, Brom.
BR2 . . . . .191 G7
Pitt St, W8 . . . . .128 D2
Pittville Gdns, SE25 . . . .188 D3
Pixfield Ct, Brom. BR2
off Beckenham La . . .191 F2
Pixley St, E14 . . . . .113 J6
Place Fm Av, Orp. BR6 . .207 G1
PLAISTOW, E13 . . . . .115 F3
PLAISTOW, Brom. 173 F6
Plaistow Gro, E15 . . . . . .115 F1
Bromley BR1 . . . . .173 H7
Plaistow La, Brom.
BR1 . . . . .173 H7
Plaistow Pk Rd, E13 . . . .115 H2
Plaistow Rd, E13 . . . . . . .115 F1
E15 . . . . .115 F1
Plane St, SE26 . . . . .170 E3
★ Planetarium, NW1 . . . . .8 A6
Plane Tree Cres, Felt.
TW13 . . . . .160 B3
Plane Tree Wk, N2 . . . . . .73 G3
SE19 off Central Hill . .170 B6
Plantagenet CI, Wor.Pk.
KT4 . . . . .196 D4
Plantagenet Gdns, Rom.
RM6 . . . . .82 D7
Plantagenet PI, Rom. RM6
off Broomfield Rd . . .82 D7
Plantagenet Rd, Barn.
EN5 . . . . .41 F4

Plantain Gdns, E11
off Hollydown Way 96 D3
Plantain PI, SE1 . . . . .28 B3
Plantation, The, SE3 . . . .155 G2
Plantation Wf, SW11 . . . .149 F3
Plasel Ct, E13
off Plashet Rd 115 G1
Plashet Gro, E6 . . . . .115 J1
Plashet Rd, E13 . . . . .115 G1
Plassy Rd, SE6 . . . . .154 B7
Platina St, EC2 . . . . .12 C5
Plato Rd, SW2 . . . . .151 E4
Platt, The, SW15 . . . . . . .148 A3
Platt's Eyot, Hmptn.
TW12 . . . . .179 G2
Platt's La, NW3 . . . . .90 D4
Platts Rd, Enf. EN3 . . . . . .45 F1
Platt St, NW1 . . . . .9 H1
Plawsfield Rd, Beck.
BR3 . . . . .189 G1
Plaxtol CI, Brom. BR1 . . .191 J1
Plaxtol Rd, Erith DA8 . . .139 G7
Plaxton Ct, E11
off Woodhouse Rd 97 F3
Playfair St, W6
off Winslow Rd 127 J5
Playfield Av, Rom. RM5 . .83 J1
Playfield Cres, SE22 . . . .152 C5
Playfield Rd, Edg. HA8 . . .70 C2
Playford Rd, N4 . . . . .93 F2
Playgreen Way, SE6 . . . . .172 A4
Playground CI, Beck. BR3
off Churchfields Rd . .189 G2
Playhouse Yd, EC4 . . . . .19 G4
Plaza Par, NW6
off Kilburn High
Rd 108/109 E2
Plaza Shop Cen, The, W1 .110 C6
Plaza W, Houns. TW3 . . .143 H1
Pleasance, The, SW15 . . .147 H4
Pleasance Rd, SW15 . . . .147 H5
Pleasant Gro, Croy. CR0 .203 J3
Pleasant PI, N1 . . . . .93 H7
Pleasant Row, NW1 . . . . .110 B1
Pleasant Vw PI, Orp. BR6
off High St 206/207 E5
Pleasant Way, Wem.
HA0 . . . . .105 F2
Plender St, NW1 . . . . . . .110 C1
Pleshey Rd, N7 . . . . .92 D4
Plevna Cres, N15 . . . . . . .76 B6
Plevna Rd, N9 . . . . .60 D3
Hampton TW12 . . . . . .179 H1
Plevna Rd Shop Cen, N9
off Plevna Rd 60/61 E2
Plevna St, E14 . . . . .134 C3
Pleydell Av, SE19 . . . . . .170 C7
W6 . . . . .127 F4
Pleydell Ct, EC4 . . . . .19 F4
Pleydell Est, EC1
off Radnor St 111 J3
Pleydell St, EC4 . . . . .19 F4
Plimsoll CI, E14
off Grundy St 114 B6
Plimsoll Rd, N4 . . . . .93 G3
Plough CI, EC3 . . . . .20 C5
Plough La, SE22 . . . . . . .152 C6
SW17 . . . . .167 E5
SW19 . . . . .167 E5
Teddington TW11 . . . .162 D5
Wallington SM6 . . . . .200 E4
Plough La CI, Wall.
SM6 . . . . .200 E5
Ploughmans CI, NW1
off Crofters Way 110 D1
Ploughmans End, Islw.
TW7 . . . . .144 A5
Ploughmans Wk, N2
off Long La 73 F2
Plough PI, EC4 . . . . .19 F3
Plough Rd, SW11 . . . . . .149 G3
Plough St, E1 . . . . .21 H3
Plough Ter, SW11 . . . . . .149 G4
Plough Way, SE16 . . . . . .133 G4
Plough Yd, EC2 . . . . .12 E6
Plover Way, SE16 . . . . . .133 H3
Hayes UB4 . . . . .102 D6
Plowden Bldgs, EC4
off Middle Temple La .111 G6
Plowman CI, N18 . . . . . . .60 A5
Plowman Way, Dag.
RM8 . . . . .100 C1
Plumbers Row, E1 . . . . . .21 H2
Plumbridge St, SE10
off Blackheath Hill . . .154 C1
Plum CI, Felt. TW13
off Highfield Rd 160 A1
Plum Garth, Brent. TW8 .125 G4

Plum La, SE18 . . . . .137 E7
Plummer La, Mitch. CR4 .185 J2
Plummer Rd, SW4 . . . . . .150 D7
Plumpton Cl, Nthlt. UB5 . .85 G6
Plumpton Way, Cars.
  SM5 . . . . .199 H3
PLUMSTEAD, SE18 . . . . .137 H5
Plumstead Common Rd,
  SE18 . . . . .136 E6
Plumstead High St,
  SE18 . . . . .137 H4
Plumstead Rd, SE18 . . . .137 G4
Plumtree Cl, Dag. RM10 .101 H6
  Wallington SM6 . . . . . .200 D7
Plumtree Ct, EC4 . . . . . .19 F3
Plumtree Mead, Loug.
  IG10 . . . . .48 D3
Plymouth Rd, E16 . . . . . .115 G5
  Bromley BR1 . . . . .191 H1
Plymouth Wf, E14 . . . . . .134 D4
Plympton Av, NW6 . . . . . .90 C7
Plympton Cl, Belv. DA17
  off Halifield Dr . . .138/139 E3
Plympton Pl, NW8 . . . . . . .7 G6
Plympton Rd, NW6 . . . . . .90 C7
Plympton St, NW8 . . . . . . .7 G6
Plymstock Rd, Well.
  DA16 . . . . .138 C7
Pocklington Cl, NW9 . . . . .70 E2
Pocock Av, West Dr.
  UB7 . . . . .120 C3
Pocock St, SE1 . . . . .27 G3
Podmore Rd, SW18 . . . . .149 F4
Poets Rd, N5 . . . . .94 A5
Poets Way, Har. HA1
  off Blawith Rd 68 B4
Pointalls Cl, N3 . . . . .73 F2
Point Cl, SE10
  off Point Hill 154 C1
Pointer Cl, SE28 . . . . . . .118 D6
Pointers Cl, E14 . . . . . . .134 B5
Point Hill, SE10 . . . . .134 C7
Point of Thomas Path, E1
  off Glamis Rd 113 F7
Point Pl, Wem. HA9 . . . . . .88 B7
Point Pleasant, SW18 . . .148 D4
Poland Ho, E15 . . . . .114 D1
Poland St, W1 . . . . .17 G4
Polebrook Rd, SE3 . . . . .155 J3
Pole Cat All, Brom. BR2 .205 F2
Polecroft La, SE6 . . . . . .171 J2
Polehamptons, The, Hmptn.
  TW12 off High St 161 J7
Pole Hill Rd, E4 . . . . .46 C7
Polesden Gdns, SW20 . . .183 H2
Polesworth Ho, W2 . . . . .108 D5
Polesworth Rd, Dag.
  RM9 . . . . .100 D2
★ Polish Institute & Sikorski
  Mus, SW7
  off Princes Gate 23 H4
Pollard Cl, E16 . . . . .115 G4
  N7 . . . . .93 F4
Pollard Rd, N20 . . . . .57 H2
  Morden SM4 . . . . .185 G5
Pollard Row, E2 . . . . .13 J3
Pollards Cl, Loug. IG10 . . .47 J5
Pollards Cres, SW16 . . . .187 E3
Pollards Hill E, SW16 . . .187 F3
Pollards Hill N, SW16 . . .187 E3
Pollards Hill S, SW16 . . .187 E3
Pollards Hill W, SW16 . . .187 E3
Pollard St, E2 . . . . .13 J3
Pollards Wd Rd, SW16 . .187 E2
Pollard Wk, Sid. DA14 . . .176 C6
Pollen St, W1 . . . . .17 E4
Pollitt Dr, NW8 . . . . .7 E5
★ Pollock's Toy Mus, W1
  off Scala St 17 G1
Polperro Cl, Orp. BR6
  off Cotswold Ri 193 J6
Polperro Ms, SE11 . . . . . .35 F1
Polsted Rd, SE6 . . . . . . .153 J7
Polthorne Est, SE18 . . . .137 G4
Polthorne Gro, SE18 . . . .137 F4
Polworth Rd, SW16 . . . . .168 E5
Polygon, The, SW4
  off Old Town 150 C4
Polygon Rd, NW1 . . . . . . .9 H2
Polytechnic St, SE18 . . . .136 D4
Pomell Way, E1 . . . . .21 G3
Pomeroy St, SE14 . . . . . .153 F1
Pomfret Rd, SE5
  off Flaxman Rd 151 H3
Pomoja La, N19 . . . . .92 E2
Pond Cl, N12
  off Summerfields Av . . .57 H6
  SE3 . . . . .155 F2
Pond Cottage La, W.Wick.
  BR4 . . . . .204 A1

Pond Cotts, SE21 . . . . . .170 B1
PONDERS END, Enf. 45 F5
Ponders End Ind Est, Enf.
  EN3 . . . . .45 J4
Ponder St, N7 . . . . .93 F7
Pond Fld End, Loug.
  IG10 . . . . .47 J7
Pondfield Rd, Brom.
  BR2 . . . . .205 E1
  Dagenham RM10 . . . . .101 H5
  Orpington BR6 . . . . . . .207 E3
Pond Hill Gdns, Sutt.
  SM3 . . . . .198 B6
Pond Mead, SE21 . . . . . .152 A6
Pond Path, Chis. BR7
  off Heathfield La .174/175 E6
Pond Pl, SW3 . . . . .31 G2
Pond Rd, E15 . . . . .114 E2
  SE3 . . . . .155 F2
Pondside Cl, Hayes UB3
  off Providence La 121 G7
Pond Sq, N6
  off South Gro 92 A1
Pond St, NW3 . . . . .91 H5
Pond Way, Tedd. TW11
  off Holmesdale Rd 163 F6
Pondwood Ri, Orp. BR6 .193 H7
Ponler St, E1 . . . . .112 E6
Ponsard Rd, NW10 . . . . .107 H3
Ponsford St, E9 . . . . .95 F6
Ponsonby Pl, SW1 . . . . . .33 J3
Ponsonby Rd, SW15 . . . .147 H7
Ponsonby Ter, SW1 . . . . .33 J3
Pontefract Rd, Brom.
  BR1 . . . . .173 F5
Ponton Rd, SW8 . . . . .33 J6
Pont St, SW1 . . . . .23 J6
Pont St Ms, SW1 . . . . . . .23 J6
Pontypool Pl, SE1 . . . . . .27 G3
Pool Cl, Beck. BR3 . . . . .172 A5
  West Molesey KT8 . . . .179 F5
Pool Ct, SE6 . . . . .172 A2
Poole Ct Rd, Houns. TW4
  off Vicarage Fm
  Rd 142/143 E2
Poole Rd, E9 . . . . .95 G6
  Epsom KT19 . . . . .196 D6
Pooles Bldgs, EC1 . . . . . .10 E6
Pooles La, SW10
  off Lots Rd 129 F7
  Dagenham RM9 . . . . . .119 E2
Pooles Pk, N4
  off Seven Sisters Rd . .93 G2
Poole St, N1 . . . . .112 A1
Poolmans St, SE16 . . . . .133 G2
Pool Rd, Har. HA1 . . . . . .68 A7
  West Molesey KT8 . . . .179 F6
Poolsford Rd, NW9 . . . . . .71 E4
Poonah St, E1 . . . . .113 F6
  off Hardinge St 113 F6
Pope Cl, SW19 . . . . .167 G6
Pope Rd, Brom. BR2 . . . .192 A5
Popes Av, Twick. TW2 . . .162 B2
Popes Dr, N3 . . . . .72 D1
Popes Gro, Croy. CR0 . . .203 J3
  Twickenham TW1,
  TW2 . . . . .162 C2
Pope's Head All, EC3
  off Cornhill 112 A6
Popes La, W5 . . . . .125 G3
Popes Rd, SW9 . . . . .151 G3
Pope St, SE1 . . . . .29 E4
Popham Cl, Felt. TW13 . .161 F3
Popham Gdns, Rich. TW9
  off Lower Richmond
  Rd 146 A3
Popham Rd, N1 . . . . .111 J1
Popham St, N1 . . . . .111 H1
POPLAR, E14 . . . . .114 B7
Poplar Av, Mitch. CR4 . . .185 J1
  Orpington BR6 . . . . . . .207 E2
  Southall UB2 . . . . .123 H3
Poplar Bath St, E14
  off Lawless St 114 B7
Poplar Business Pk, E14 .114 C7
Poplar Cl, E9
  off Lee Conservancy
  Rd 95 J5
  Pinner HA5 . . . . .66 D1
Poplar Ct, SW19 . . . . . . .166 D5
Poplar Cres, Epsom
  KT19 . . . . .196 C6
Poplar Fm Cl, Epsom
  KT19 . . . . .196 C6
Poplar Gdns, N.Mal.
  KT3 . . . . .182 D2
Poplar Gro, N11 . . . . .58 A6
  W6 . . . . .127 J2
  New Malden KT3 . . . . .182 D3
  Wembley HA9 . . . . .88 C3

Poplar High St, E14 . . . . .114 A7
  SE9 . . . . .174 B2
  SE25 . . . . .188 D4
  W11 . . . . .108 B7
  Bromley BR1 . . . . .173 J4
Kingston upon Thames
  KT1 . . . . .181 H3
  Mitcham CR4 . . . . .185 H2
  Southall UB2 . . . . .123 F3
Portland Sq, E1
  off Watts St 132/133 E1
Portland St, SE17 . . . . . . .36 B3
Portland Ter, Rich. TW9 . .145 G4
Portland Wk, SE17 . . . . . .36 C5
Portman Av, SW14 . . . . . .146 D3
Portman Cl, W1 . . . . .16 A3
  Bexleyheath DA7
  off Queen Anne's
  Gate 158 D3
Portman Dr, Wdf.Grn.
  IG8 . . . . .80 A2
Portman Gdns, NW9 . . . . .70 D2
Portman Gate, NW1 . . . . .7 H6
Portman Ms S, W1 . . . . . .16 B4
Portman Pl, E2 . . . . .113 F3
Portman Rd, Kings.T.
  KT1 . . . . .181 J2
Portman Sq, W1 . . . . .16 A3
Portman St, W1 . . . . .16 B4
Portmeadow Wk, SE2 . . .138 D2
Portmeers Cl, E17
  off Lennox Rd 77 J6
Portnall Rd, W9 . . . . .108 C2
Portobello Ct, W11
  off Westbourne Gro . . .108 C7
Portobello Ms, W11
  off Portobello Rd 108 D7
Portobello Rd, W10 . . . . .108 C6
  W11 . . . . .108 C6
Porton Ct, Surb. KT6 . . . .181 F6
Portpool La, EC1 . . . . . . .18 E1
Portree Cl, N22
  off Nightingale Rd 59 F7
Portree St, E14 . . . . .114 D6
Portsdown, Edg. HA8
  off Rectory La 54 A5
Portsdown Av, NW11 . . . .72 C6
Portsdown Ms, NW11 . . . .72 C6
Portsea Ms, W2 . . . . .15 H4
Portsea Pl, W2 . . . . .15 H4
Portslade Rd, SW8 . . . . .150 C2
Portsmouth Av, T.Ditt.
  KT7 . . . . .180 D7
Portsmouth Ms, E16
  off Wesley Av 135 H1
Portsmouth Rd, SW15 . . .147 H7
Kingston upon Thames
  KT1 . . . . .181 F5
  Surbiton KT6 . . . . .181 F5
  Thames Ditton KT7 . . .194 B2
Portsmouth St, WC2 . . . . .18 C4
Portsoken St, E1 . . . . .21 F5
Portugal Gdns, Twick. TW2
  off Fulwell Pk Av 161 J2
Portugal St, WC2 . . . . . . .18 C4
Portway, E15 . . . . .115 F1
Portway Gdns, SE18
  off Shooter's Hill Rd . .136 A7
Postern Grn, Enf. EN2 . . . .43 G2
Post La, Twick. TW2 . . . .162 A1
Postmill Cl, Croy. CR0 . . .203 G3
Post Office App, E7 . . . . . .97 H5
Post Office Ct, EC3 . . . . . .20 C4
Post Office Way, SW8 . . . .33 H7
Post Rd, Sthl. UB2 . . . . . .123 H3
Postway Ms, Ilf. IG1
  off Clements Rd . . .98/99 E3
Potier St, SE1 . . . . .28 C6
Potter Cl, Mitch. CR4 . . . .186 B2
Potterne Cl, SW19 . . . . . .148 A7
Potters Cl, Croy. CR0 . . . .203 H1
  Loughton IG10 . . . . .48 B2
Potters Flds, SE1
  off Tooley St 132 B1
Potters Gro, N.Mal. KT3 .182 C4
Potters Hts Cl, Pnr. HA5 . .50 B7
Potters La, SW16 . . . . . . .168 D6
  Barnet EN5 . . . . .40 D4
  Borehamwood WD6 . . .38 C1
Potters Rd, SW6 . . . . . . .149 F2
  Barnet EN5 . . . . .40 E4
Potter St, Nthwd. HA6 . . . .66 A1
  Pinner HA5 . . . . .66 B1
Potter St Hill, Pnr. HA5 . . .50 B6
Pottery La, W11
  off Portland Rd 108 B7
Pottery Rd, Bex. DA5 . . . .177 J2
  Brentford TW8 . . . . . . .125 H6
Pottery St, SE16 . . . . . . .132 E2
Pott St, E2 . . . . .113 E3

Portland Rd, N15 . . . . .76 C4
Poplar Mt, Belv. DA17 . . .139 H4
Poplar Pl, SE28 . . . . .118 C2
  W2 . . . . .14 A5
  Hayes UB3
  off Central Av 102 A7
Poplar Rd, SE24 . . . . . . .151 J4
  SW19 . . . . .184 D2
  Sutton SM3 . . . . .198 C1
Poplar Rd S, SW19 . . . . .184 D3
Poplars, The, N14 . . . . . . .42 B5
Poplars Av, NW10 . . . . . . .89 J6
Poplar St, Rom. RM7 . . . .83 J4
Poplar Vw, Wem. HA9
  off Magnet Rd 87 G2
Poplar Wk, SE24 . . . . . . .151 J4
  Croydon CR0 . . . . .201 J2
Poplar Way, Felt. TW13 . .160 A3
  Ilford IG6 . . . . .81 F4
Poppins Ct, EC4 . . . . .19 G4
Poppleton Rd, E11 . . . . . .79 E6
Poppy Cl, Wall. SM6 . . . .200 A1
★ Poppy Factory Mus, The,
  Rich. TW10 . . . . .145 G6
Poppy La, Croy. CR0 . . . .189 F7
Porchester Cl, SE5 . . . . . .151 J4
Porchester Gdns, W2 . . . .14 A5
Porchester Gdns Ms, W2 .14 B4
Porchester Mead, Beck.
  BR3 . . . . .172 B6
Porchester Ms, W2 . . . . . .14 B3
Porchester Pl, W2 . . . . . . .15 H4
Porchester Rd, W2 . . . . . .14 A3
Kingston upon Thames
  KT1 . . . . .182 B2
Porchester Sq, W2 . . . . . .14 A3
Porchester Ter, W2 . . . . . .14 C4
Porchester Ter N, W2 . . . .14 B3
Porch Way, N20 . . . . .57 J3
Porcupine Cl, SE9 . . . . . .174 B2
Porden Rd, SW2 . . . . . . .151 F4
Porlock Av, Har. HA2 . . . .85 J1
Porlock Rd, W10
  off Ladbroke Gro 108 A4
  Enfield EN1 . . . . .44 C7
Porlock St, SE1 . . . . .28 B3
Porrington Cl, Chis.
  BR7 . . . . .192 C1
Portal Cl, SE27 . . . . .169 G3
  Ruislip HA4 . . . . .84 A4
Portbury Cl, SE15
  off Clayton Rd 152 D1
Port Cres, E13
  off Jenkins Rd 115 H4
★ Portcullis House - New
  Parliamentary Building,
  SW1 . . . . .26 A3
Portcullis Lo Rd, Enf.
  EN2 . . . . .44 A3
Portelet Ct, N1 . . . . .112 B1
  off De Beauvoir Est . . .112 B1
Portelet Rd, E1 . . . . .113 G3
Porten Rd, W14 . . . . .128 B3
Porter Rd, E6 . . . . .116 C6
Porters Av, Dag. RM8,
  RM9 . . . . .100 B6
Portersfield Rd, Enf. EN1 .44 B4
Porter Sq, N19
  off Hornsey Rd 92/93 E1
Porter St, SE1 . . . . .28 A1
  W1 . . . . .16 A1
Porters Wk, E1
  off Pennington
  St 112/113 E7
Porters Way, West Dr.
  UB7 . . . . .120 C3
Porteus Rd, W2 . . . . .14 D2
Portgate Cl, W9 . . . . .108 C4
Porthallow Cl, Orp. BR6
  off Sevenoaks Rd 207 J4
Porthcawe Rd, SE26 . . . .171 H4
Porthkerry Av, Well.
  DA16 . . . . .158 A4
Portia Way, E3 . . . . .113 J4
Portinscale Rd, SW15 . . .148 B5
Portland Av, N16 . . . . .76 C7
  New Malden KT3 . . . . .183 F7
  Sidcup DA15 . . . . .158 A6
Portland Cl, Rom. RM6 . . .82 E5
Portland Cres, SE9 . . . . . .174 B2
  Greenford UB6 . . . . . . .103 H4
  Stanmore HA7 . . . . .69 G2
Portland Gdns, N4 . . . . . . .75 H6
  Romford RM6 . . . . .82 D5
Portland Gro, SW8 . . . . . .151 F1
Portland Ms, W1 . . . . .17 G4
Portland Pl, W1 . . . . .16 E2
Portland Ri, N4 . . . . .93 H1
Portland Ri Est, N4 . . . . . .93 J1

Poulett Gdns, Twick.
  TW1 . . . .**162** D1
Poulett Rd, E6 . . . .**116** C2
Poulner Way, SE15
  off Daniel Gdns **132** C7
Poulton Av, Sutt. SM1 . . .**199** G3
Poulton Cl, Orp.
  off Spurstowe Ter . .**94/95** E5
Poultry, EC2 . . . .**20** B4
Pound Cl, Orp. BR6 . . . . .**207** G2
  Surbiton KT6 . . . .**195** F1
Pound Ct Dr, Orp. BR6 . .**207** G2
Pound Fm Cl, Esher KT10
  off Ember La **194** A1
Poundfield Rd, Loug.
  IG10 . . . .**48** D5
Pound La, NW10 . . . .**89** G6
Pound Pk Rd, SE7 . . . . . .**136** A4
Pound Pl, SE9 . . . .**156** D6
Pound St, Cars. SM5 . . . .**199** J5
Pound Way, Chis. BR7
  off Royal Par **175** F7
Pountney Rd, SW11 . . . . .**150** A3
POVEREST, Orp. **193** J5
Poverest Rd, Orp. BR5 . .**193** J5
Powder Mill La, Twick.
  TW2 . . . .**161** F1
Powell Cl, Chess. KT9
  off Coppard Gdns **195** G5
  Edgware HA8 . . . .**53** J6
  Wallington SM6 . . . . . .**200** D7
Powell Gdns, Dag. RM10 .**101** G4
Powell Rd, E5 . . . .**95** J5
  Buckhurst Hill IG9 . . . . .**47** J7
Powell's Wk, W4 . . . .**127** E6
Powergate Business Pk,
  NW10 . . . .**106** D3
Power Rd, W4 . . . .**126** A4
Powers Ct, Twick. TW1 . . .**145** F4
Powerscroft Rd, E5 . . . . . .**95** F4
  Sidcup DA14 . . . .**176** C6
Powis Gdns, NW11 . . . .**72** C7
  W11 . . . .**108** C6
Powis Ms, W11
  off Westbourne Pk Rd .**108** C6
Powis Pl, WC1 . . . .**10** B6
Powis Rd, E3 . . . .**114** B3
Powis Sq, W11 . . . .**108** C6
Powis St, SE18 . . . .**136** D3
Powis Ter, W11 . . . .**108** C6
Powle Ter, Ilf. IG1
  off Oaktree Gro **99** F5
Powlett Pl, NW1
  off Harmood St **92** B6
Pownall Gdns, Houns.
  TW3 . . . .**143** H4
Pownall Rd, E8 . . . .**112** C1
  Hounslow TW3 . . . .**143** H4
Pownsett Ter, Ilf. IG1
  off Buttsbury Rd **99** F5
Powster Rd, Brom. BR1 .**173** H5
Powys Cl, Bexh. DA7 . . .**138** D6
Powys Ct, Borwd. WD6
  off Kensington Way . . .**38** D3
Powys La, N13 . . . .**58** E5
  N14 . . . .**58** E4
Poynders Ct, SW4
  off Poynders Rd **150** C6
Poynders Gdns, SW4 . . . .**150** C7
Poynders Rd, SW4 . . . . . .**150** C6
Poynings Rd, N19 . . . .**92** C3
Poynings Way, N12 . . . . . .**56** D5
Poyntell Cres, Chis. BR7 .**193** G1
Poynter Ho, W11 . . . .**128** A1
Poynter Rd, Enf. EN1 . . . . .**44** D5
Poynton Rd, N17 . . . .**76** D2
Poyntz Rd, SW11 . . . .**149** J2
Poyser St, E2 . . . .**113** E2
Praed Ms, W2 . . . .**15** F3
Praed St, W2 . . . .**15** G2
Pragel St, E13 . . . .**115** H2
Pragnell Rd, SE12 . . . . . .**173** H2
Prague Pl, SW2 . . . .**150** E5
Prah Rd, N4 . . . .**93** G2
Prairie St, SW8 . . . .**150** A2
Pratt Ms, NW1
  off Pratt St **110** C1
Pratt St, NW1 . . . .**110** C1
Pratt Wk, SE11 . . . .**34** D1
Prayle Gro, NW2 . . . .**90** A1
Prebend Gdns, W4 . . . . . .**127** F3
  W6 . . . .**127** F3
Prebend St, N1 . . . .**111** J1
Precinct, The, W.Mol. KT8
  off Victoria Av **179** H3
Precinct Rd, Hayes
  UB3 . . . .**102** A7

Precincts, The, Mord. SM4
  off Green La **184/185** E6
Premier Cor, W9
  off Kilburn La **108** C2
Premiere Pl, E14
  off Garford St **114** A7
Premier Pk, NW10 . . . . . .**106** B1
Premier Pk Rd, NW10 . . .**106** B2
Premier Pl, SW15
  off Putney High St . . .**148** B4
Prendergast Rd, SE3 . . . .**155** E3
Prentis Rd, SW16 . . . .**168** D4
Prentiss Ct, SE7 . . . .**136** A4
Presburg Rd, N.Mal.
  KT3 . . . .**183** E5
Presburg St, E5
  off Glyn Rd **95** G3
Prescelly Pl, Edg. HA8 . . . .**69** J1
Prescot St, E1 . . . .**21** G5
Prescott Av, Orp. BR5 . . .**192** E6
Prescott Cl, SW16 . . . . . .**168** E7
Prescott Grn, Loug. IG10 . .**49** F3
Prescott Ho, SE17 . . . .**35** H6
Prescott Pl, SW4 . . . .**150** D3
Presentation Ms, SW2
  off Palace Rd **169** F1
President Dr, E1
  off Waterman
  Way **132/133** E1
President St, EC1 . . . .**11** J3
Press Rd, NW10 . . . .**88** D3
Prestage Way, E14 . . . . . .**114** C7
Prestbury Rd, E7 . . . .**97** J7
Prestbury Sq, SE9 . . . . . .**174** C4
Prested Rd, SW11
  off St. John's Hill **149** H4
Prestige Way, NW4
  off Heriot Rd **71** J5
PRESTON, Wem. **69** G7
Preston Av, E4 . . . .**62** D6
Preston Cl, SE1 . . . .**36** D1
  Twickenham TW2 . . . . .**162** B3
Preston Dr, E11 . . . .**79** J5
  Bexleyheath DA7 . . . . .**158** D1
  Epsom KT19 . . . .**197** E6
Preston Gdns, NW10
  off Church Rd **88/89** E6
  Ilford IG1 . . . .**80** B6
Preston Hill, Har. HA3 . . . .**69** J6
Preston Pl, NW2 . . . .**89** G6
  Richmond TW10 . . . . . .**145** H5
Preston Rd, E11 . . . .**79** E6
  SE19 . . . .**169** H6
  SW20 . . . .**165** F7
  Harrow HA3 . . . .**69** H7
  Wembley HA9 . . . .**87** H2
Prestons Rd, E14 . . . .**134** C2
  Bromley BR2 . . . .**205** G3
Preston Waye, Har. HA3 . . .**87** H1
Prestwick Cl, Sthl. UB2
  off Ringway **122/123** E5
Prestwick Rd, Wat. WD19 .**50** D5
Prestwood Av, Har. HA3 . .**69** E4
Prestwood Cl, SE18 . . . . .**138** A7
  Harrow HA3 . . . .**69** F4
Prestwood Gdns, Croy.
  CR0 . . . .**187** J7
Prestwood St, N1 . . . .**12** A2
Pretoria Av, E17 . . . .**77** H4
Pretoria Cl, N17
  off Pretoria Rd **60** C7
Pretoria Cres, E4 . . . .**62** C1
Pretoria Rd, E4 . . . .**62** C1
  E11 . . . .**96** D3
  E16 . . . .**115** F3
  N17 . . . .**60** C7
  SW16 . . . .**168** B6
  Ilford IG1 . . . .**98** E5
  Romford RM7 . . . .**83** J4
Pretoria Rd N, N18 . . . .**60** C6
Prevost Rd, N11 . . . .**58** A2
Price Cl, NW7 . . . .**56** B6
  SW17 . . . .**167** J3
Price Rd, Croy. CR0 . . . . .**201** H5
Price's Ct, SW11 . . . .**149** G3
Price's St, SE1
  off Bear La **131** H1
Price's Yd, N1 . . . .**111** F1
Price Way, Hmptn. TW12
  off Victors Dr **160/161** E6
Pricklers Hill, Barn. EN5 . .**41** E6
Prickley Wd, Brom. BR2 .**205** F1
Priddy's Yd, Croy. CR0
  off Church St **201** J2
Prideaux Pl, W3
  off Friars Pl La **106** D7
  WC1 . . . .**10** D3
Prideaux Rd, SW9 . . . . . .**151** E3
Pridham Rd, Th.Hth. CR7 .**188** A4
Priest Ct, EC2 . . . .**19** J3

Priestfield Rd, SE23 . . . . .**171** H3
Priestlands Pk Rd, Sid.
  DA15 . . . .**175** J3
Priestley Cl, N16
  off Ravensdale Rd **76** C7
Priestley Gdns, Rom.
  RM6 . . . .**82** B6
Priestley Rd, Mitch.
  CR4 . . . .**186** A2
Priestley Way, E17 . . . .**77** G3
  NW2 . . . .**89** G1
Priestman Pt, E3
  off Rainhill Way **114** B3
Priest Pk Av, Har. HA2 . . . .**85** G2
Priests Br, SW14 . . . .**147** E3
  SW15 . . . .**147** E3
Prima Rd, SW9 . . . .**35** E7
Primrose Av, Enf. EN2 . . . .**44** A1
  Romford RM6 . . . .**82** B7
Primrose Cl, SE6 . . . .**172** C5
  Harrow HA2 . . . .**85** F4
  Wallington SM6 . . . . . .**200** B1
Primrose Dr, West Dr.
  UB7 . . . .**120** A4
Primrose Gdns, NW3 . . . . .**91** H6
  Ruislip HA4 . . . .**84** C5
PRIMROSE HILL, NW8 . . .**109** J1
Primrose Hill, EC4 . . . .**19** F4
Primrose Hill Ct, NW3 . . . .**91** J7
Primrose Hill Rd, NW3 . . . .**91** H7
Primrose Hill Studios, NW1
  off Fitzroy Rd **110** A1
Primrose La, Croy. CR0 . .**203** G1
Primrose Ms, NW1
  off Sharpleshall St **91** J7
  SE3 . . . .**135** H7
  W5 off St. Mary's Rd . .**125** G2
Primrose Rd, E10 . . . .**96** B1
  E18 . . . .**79** H2
Primrose Sq, E9 . . . .**95** F7
Primrose St, EC2 . . . .**20** D1
Primrose Wk, SE14
  off Alexandra St **133** H7
  Epsom KT17 . . . .**197** F2
Primrose Way, Wem.
  HA0 . . . .**105** G2
Primula St, W12 . . . .**107** G6
Prince Albert Rd, NW1 . . . . .**7** H2
  NW8 . . . .**7** H2
Prince Arthur Ms, NW3
  off Perrins La **91** F4
Prince Arthur Rd, NW3 . . . .**91** F5
Prince Charles Dr, NW4 . . .**71** J7
Prince Charles Rd, SE3 . .**155** F1
Prince Charles Way, Wall.
  SM6 . . . .**200** B3
Prince Consort Dr, Chis. .**193** G1
Prince Consort Rd, SW7 . .**22** E5
Princedale Rd, W11 . . . . .**128** B1
Prince Edward Rd, E9 . . . . .**95** J6
Prince George Av, N14 . . . .**42** C4
Prince George Duke of Kent Ct,
  Chis. BR7
  off Holbrook La **175** G7
Prince George Rd, N16 . . . .**94** B4
Prince George's Av,
  SW20 . . . .**183** J2
Prince George's Rd,
  SW19 . . . .**185** G1
Prince Henry Rd, SE7 . . . .**136** A7
★ Prince Henry's Room,
  EC4 . . . .**19** E4
Prince Imperial Rd, SE18 .**156** C1
  Chislehurst BR7 . . . . . .**175** E7
Prince John Rd, SE9 . . . . .**156** B5
Princelet St, E1 . . . .**21** G1
Prince of Orange La, SE10
  off Greenwich High
  Rd **134** C7
Prince of Wales Cl, NW4
  off Church Ter **71** H4
Prince of Wales Dr, SW8 .**130** B7
  SW11 . . . .**149** J1
Prince of Wales Gate,
  SW7 . . . .**23** G3
Prince of Wales Pas, NW1 . .**9** F4
Prince of Wales Rd, NW5 . .**92** A6
  SE3 . . . .**155** F1
  Sutton SM1 . . . .**199** G2
Prince of Wales Ter, W4 . .**126** E5
  W8 . . . .**22** B4
Prince Regent La, E13 . . .**115** H3
  E16 . . . .**115** J5
Prince Regent Ms, NW1
  off Hampstead Rd **110** C3
Prince Regent Rd, Houns.
  TW3 . . . .**143** J3
Prince Rd, SE25 . . . .**188** B5
Prince Rupert Rd, SE9 . . .**156** C4

Prince's Arc, SW1 . . . .**25** G1
Princes Av, N3 . . . .**72** D1
  N10 . . . .**74** A3
  N13 . . . .**59** G5
  N22 . . . .**74** D1
  NW9 . . . .**70** B4
  W3 . . . .**126** A3
  Carshalton SM5 . . . . . .**199** J7
  Greenford UB6 . . . .**103** H6
  Orpington BR5 . . . .**193** H5
  Surbiton KT6 . . . .**196** A1
  Woodford Green IG8 . . .**63** H4
Princes Cl, N4 . . . .**93** H1
  NW9 . . . .**70** A4
  SW4 off Old Town **150** C3
  Edgware HA8 . . . .**54** A5
  Sidcup DA14 . . . .**176** D3
  Teddington TW11 . . . . .**162** A4
Princes Ct, E1 . . . .**113** E7
  SE16 . . . .**133** J3
  Wembley HA9 . . . .**87** H5
Princes Dr, Har. HA1 . . . . .**68** B3
Princes Gdns, SW7 . . . . . .**23** F5
  W3 . . . .**106** A5
  W5 . . . .**105** F4
Princes Gate, SW7 . . . . . .**23** G4
Princes Gate Ct, SW7 . . . .**23** F4
Princes Gate Ms, SW7 . . .**23** F5
Princes La, N10 . . . .**74** B3
Princes Ms, W2 . . . .**14** A5
Princes Pk Av, NW11 . . . . .**72** B6
Princes Pl, SW1 . . . .**25** G1
  W11 . . . .**128** B1
Princes Plain, Brom.
  BR2 . . . .**192** B7
Princes Ri, SE13 . . . .**154** C2
Princes Riverside Rd,
  SE16 . . . .**133** G1
Princes Rd, N18 . . . .**61** F4
  SE20 . . . .**171** G6
  SW14 . . . .**146** D3
  SW19 . . . .**166** D6
  W13
  off Broomfield
  Rd **124/125** E1
  Buckhurst Hill IG9 . . . . .**63** J2
  Ilford IG6 . . . .**81** G4
  Kingston upon Thames
  KT2 . . . .**164** A7
  Richmond TW10 . . . . . .**145** J5
  Richmond (Kew) TW9 . .**125** J7
  Teddington TW11 . . . . .**162** A4
Princess Alice Way,
  SE28 . . . .**137** G2
Princess Av, Wem. HA9 . . .**87** H2
Princess Cres, N4 . . . .**93** H2
Princesses Wk, Rich. TW9
  off Kew Rd **125** H7
Princess Louise Cl, W2 . . .**15** F1
Princess May Rd, N16 . . . .**94** B4
Princess Ms, NW3
  off Belsize Cres **91** G6
Princess Par, Orp. BR6
  off Crofton Rd **206** D3
Princess Pk Manor, N11 . .**58** A5
Princes Sq, W2 . . . .**14** A5
Princess Rd, NW1 . . . .**110** A1
  NW6 . . . .**108** D2
  Croydon CR0 . . . .**187** J6
Princess St, SE1 . . . .**27** H6
  EC2 . . . .**20** B4
  N17 off Queen St **60** B6
  W1 . . . .**17** E4
  Bexleyheath DA7 . . . . .**159** F4
  Richmond TW9
  off Sheen Rd **145** H5
  Sutton SM1 . . . .**199** G4
Princes Ter, E13 . . . .**115** H1
Prince St, SE8 . . . .**133** J6
Princes Way, SW19 . . . . .**148** A7
  Buckhurst Hill IG9 . . . . .**63** J2
  Croydon CR0 . . . .**201** F5
  Ruislip HA4 . . . .**84** E4
  West Wickham BR4 . . .**205** F4
Princes Yd, W11
  off Princedale Rd **128** B1
Princethorpe Ho, W2 . . . . .**14** A1
Princethorpe Rd, SE26 . . .**171** G4
Princeton Ct, SW15
  off Felsham Rd **148** A3
Princeton St, WC1 . . . .**18** C1
Pringle Gdns, SW16 . . . . .**168** C4
Printers Inn Ct, EC4 . . . . . .**19** E3
Printers Ms, E3 . . . .**113** H1
Printer St, EC4 . . . .**19** F3
Printing Ho La, Hayes
  UB3 . . . .**121** H2
Printing Ho Yd, E2 . . . .**13** E3
Print Village, SE15
  off Chadwick Rd **152** C2

Priolo Rd, SE7 . . . .**135** J5
Prior Av, Sutt. SM2 . . . . .**199** H7
Prior Bolton St, N1 . . . . . .**93** H6
Prioress Rd, SE27 . . . . . .**169** H3
Prioress St, SE1 . . . .**28** C6
Prior Rd, Ilf. IG1 . . . .**98** D3
Priors Cft, E17 . . . .**77** H2
off Arnold Rd **84/85** E6
Priors Gdns, Ruis. HA4 . . .**84** C5
Priors Mead, Enf. EN1 . . . .**44** B1
Priors Shop Cen, The, N12
off High Rd **57** F5
Prior St, SE10 . . . .**134** C7
Priory, The, SE3 . . . .**155** F4
Priory Av, E4 . . . .**61** J3
E17 . . . .**78** A5
N8 . . . .**74** D4
W4 . . . .**127** E4
Orpington BR5 . . . .**193** G6
Sutton SM3 . . . .**198** A4
Wembley HA0 . . . .**86** C4
Priory Cl, E4 . . . .**61** J3
E18 . . . .**79** G1
N3 *off Church Cres* . . .**72** C1
N14 . . . .**42** B5
N20 . . . .**40** C6
SW19 *off High*
Path **184/185** E1
Beckenham BR3 . . . . . .**189** H3
Chislehurst BR7 . . . . . .**192** C1
Hampton TW12
off Priory Gdns **179** F1
Hayes UB3 . . . .**102** B7
Stanmore HA7 . . . .**52** C3
Sunbury-on-Thames TW16
off Staines Rd E **160** A7
Wembley (Sudbury)
HA0 . . . .**86** C4
Priory Ct, E17 . . . .**77** J3
EC4 *off Ludgate Hill* . .**111** H6
SW8 . . . .**150** D1
Priory Ct Est, E17
off Priory Ct **77** J2
Priory Cres, SE19 . . . . . .**169** J7
Sutton SM3 . . . .**198** A4
Wembley HA0 . . . .**86** D3
Priory Dr, SE2 . . . .**138** D5
Stanmore HA7 . . . .**52** C3
Priory Fld Dr, Edg. HA8 . . .**54** B4
Priory Gdns, N6 . . . .**74** B6
SE25 . . . .**188** C4
SW13 . . . .**147** F3
W4 . . . .**127** E4
W5 *off Hanger La* **105** H3
Hampton TW12 . . . .**161** F7
Wembley HA0 . . . .**86** D4
Priory Grn Est, N1 . . . .**10** D1
Priory Gro, SW8 . . . .**150** E1
Barnet EN5 . . . .**40** D5
Priory Hill, Wem. HA0 . . . .**86** D4
Priory La, SW15 . . . .**147** E6
Richmond TW9
off Forest Rd **126** A7
West Molesey KT8 . . . .**179** G4
Priory Ms, SW8 . . . .**150** D1
Priory Pk, SE3 . . . .**155** F3
Priory Pk Rd, NW6 . . . . . .**108** C1
Wembley HA0 . . . .**86** D4
Priory Rd, E6 . . . .**116** A1
N8 . . . .**74** D4
NW6 . . . .**108** E1
SW19 . . . .**167** G7
W4 . . . .**126** D3
Barking IG11 . . . .**99** G7
Chessington KT9 . . . . .**195** H3
Croydon CR0 . . . .**187** G7
Hampton TW12 . . . .**161** F7
Hounslow TW3 . . . .**143** J5
Loughton IG10 . . . .**48** H4
Richmond TW9 . . . .**126** A6
Sutton SM3 . . . .**198** A4
Priory St, E3 . . . .**114** B3
off St. Leonards St . . .**114** B3
Priory Ter, NW6 . . . .**108** E1
Sunbury-on-Thames TW16
off Staines Rd E **160** A7
Priory Wk, SW10 . . . .**30** D4
Priory Way, Har. HA2 . . . . .**67** H4
Southall UB2 . . . .**122** D3
West Drayton UB7 . . . .**120** B6
Pritchard's Rd, E2 . . . . . .**112** D1
Priter Rd, SE16 . . . .**29** J6
Priter Way, SE16
off Dockley Rd **132** D3
Private Rd, Enf. EN1 . . . . . .**44** B5
Probert Rd, SW2 . . . .**151** G5
Probyn Rd, SW2 . . . .**169** H2
Procter St, WC1 . . . .**18** C2
Proctor Cl, Mitch. CR4 . . .**186** A1

Proctors Cl, Felt. TW14 . .**160** A1
Progress Business Pk, Croy.
CR0 . . . .**201** F2
Progress Way, N22 . . . . . .**75** G1
Croydon CR0 . . . .**201** F2
Enfield EN1 . . . .**44** D5
Promenade, The, W4 . . . .**147** E1
Promenade App Rd, W4 .**126** E7
Promenade Mans, Edg. HA8.
off Hale La **54** B5
Prospect Business Pk, Loug.
IG10 . . . .**49** F4
Prospect Cl, SE26 . . . . . .**170** E4
Belvedere DA17 . . . . . .**139** G4
Hounslow TW3 . . . .**143** F1
Ruislip HA4 . . . .**66** D7
Prospect Cotts, SW18
off Point Pleasant . . .**148** D4
Prospect Cres, Twick.
TW2 . . . .**143** J6
Prospect Hill, E17 . . . .**78** B4
Prospect Pl, E1 . . . .**133** F1
N2 . . . .**73** G3
N7 *off Parkhurst Rd* .**92/93** A4
N17 . . . .**76** B1
NW2 *off Ridge Rd* **90** C3
NW3 *off Holly Wk* **91** F4
Bromley BR2 . . . .**191** H3
Romford RM5 . . . .**83** J2
Prospect Quay, SW18 . . .**148** D4
Prospect Ring, N2 . . . .**73** G3
Prospect Rd, NW2 . . . .**90** C3
Barnet EN5 . . . .**40** D5
Surbiton KT6 . . . .**181** F6
Woodford Green IG8 . . .**63** J5
Prospect St, SE16
off Jamaica Rd . . .**132/133** E2
Prospect Vale, SE18 . . . .**136** B4
Prospero Rd, N19 . . . .**92** C1
Protea Cl, E16
off Hermit Rd **115** F4
Prothero Gdns, NW4 . . . . .**71** H5
Prothero Ho, NW10 . . . . . .**88** D7
Prothero Rd, SW6 . . . . . .**128** B7
Prout Gro, NW10 . . . .**89** E4
Prout Rd, E5 . . . .**95** E3
Provence St, N1
off St. Peters St **111** J2
Providence Ct, W1 . . . .**16** C5
Providence La, Hayes
UB3 . . . .**121** G7
Providence Pl, N1
off Upper St **111** H1
Romford RM5 . . . .**83** F2
Providence Rd, West Dr.
UB7 . . . .**120** B1
Providence Row, N1
off Pentonville Rd . . .**111** F2
Providence Row Cl, E2
off Ainsley St **112/113** E3
Providence Sq, SE1
off Jacob St **132** C2
Providence St, N1
off St. Peters St **111** J2
Providence Yd, E2 . . . .**13** H3
Provident Ind Est, Hayes
UB3 . . . .**122** A2
Provost Est, N1 . . . .**12** B3
Provost Rd, NW3 . . . .**91** J7
Provost St, N1 . . . .**12** B4
Prowse Av, Bushey
(Bushey Hth.) WD23 . . .**51** J2
Prowse Pl, NW1
off Bonny St **92** B7
Pruden Cl, N14 . . . .**58** C2
Prudent Pas, EC2 . . . .**20** A3
Prusom St, E1 . . . .**133** E1
Pryors, The, NW3 . . . .**91** G3
★ **PS Tattershall Castle,**
SW1 . . . .**26** B2
★ **Public Record Office,** Rich.
TW9 . . . .**126** B7
Pudding La, EC3 . . . .**20** C6
Chigwell IG7 . . . .**65** J1
Pudding Mill La, E15 . . . .**114** B1
Puddle Dock, EC4 . . . .**19** H5
Puffin Cl, Bark. IG11 . . . .**118** B3
Beckenham BR3 . . . . . .**189** G5
Puffin Ter, Ilf. IG5
off Tiptree Cres **80** D3
Pulborough Rd, SW18 . . .**148** C7
Pulborough Way, Houns.
TW4 . . . .**142** C4
Pulford Rd, N15 . . . .**76** A6
Pulham Av, N2 . . . .**73** F4
Puller Rd, Barn. EN5 . . . . .**40** B2
Pulleyns Av, E6 . . . .**116** B3
Pullman Cl, SW2 . . . .**169** E1
Pullman Gdns, SW15 . . . .**147** J6
Pullman Pl, SE9 . . . .**156** B5

Pulross Rd, SW9 . . . .**151** F3
Pulteney Cl, E3 . . . .**113** J1
Pulteney Gdns, E18
off Pulteney Rd **79** H3
Pulteney Rd, E18 . . . .**79** H3
Pulteney Ter, N1 . . . .**111** F1
Pulton Pl, SW6 . . . .**128** D7
Puma Ct, E1 . . . .**21** F1
Pump All, Brent. TW8 . . . .**125** G7
Pump Cl, Nthlt. UB5
off Union Rd **103** G2
Pump Ct, EC4 . . . .**19** E4
Pumphandle Path, N2
off Tarling Rd **73** F2
Pump Hill, Loug. IG10 . . . .**48** C2
Pump Ho Cl, SE16
off Renforth St **133** F2
Bromley BR2 . . . .**191** F2
Pumping Sta Rd, W4 . . . .**127** E7
Pump La, SE14 . . . .**133** F7
Hayes UB3 . . . .**122** B2
Pump Pail N, Croy. CR0
off Old Town **201** J3
Pump Pail S, Croy. CR0
off Southbridge Rd . . .**201** J3
Pundersons Gdns, E2 . . .**113** E3
Punjab La, Sthl. UB1
off Herbert Rd **123** F1
Purbeck Av, N.Mal. KT3 .**183** F6
Purbeck Dr, NW2 . . . .**90** B2
Purbrook Est, SE1 . . . .**29** E4
Purbrook St, SE1 . . . .**29** E5
Purcell Cres, SW6 . . . . . .**128** B7
Purcell Ms, NW10
off Suffolk Rd **88/89** E7
Purcell Rd, Grnf. UB6 . . . .**103** H5
Purcells Av, Edg. HA8 . . . .**54** A5
Purcell St, N1 . . . .**12** D1
Purchese St, NW1 . . . .**9** J1
Purdy St, E3 . . . .**114** B4
Purelake Ms, SE13 . . . . .**154** D3
Purland Cl, Dag. RM8 . . .**101** F1
Purland Rd, SE28 . . . . . .**137** J2
Purleigh Av, Wdf.Grn.
IG8 . . . .**64** B6
Purley Av, NW2 . . . .**90** B3
Purley Cl, Ilf. IG5 . . . .**80** D2
Purley Pl, N1
off Islington Pk St **93** H7
Purley Rd, N9 . . . .**60** A3
South Croydon CR2 . . .**202** A7
Purley Way, Croy. CR0 . . .**187** F7
Purley Way, Croy. CR0 . . .**201** G7
Purley Way Cres, Croy. CR0
off Purley Way **187** F7
Purneys Rd, SE9 . . . .**156** A4
Purrett Rd, SE18 . . . .**137** J5
Purser's Cross Rd, SW6 .**148** C1
Pursewardens Cl, W13 . .**125** F1
Pursley Rd, NW7 . . . .**55** H7
Purves Rd, NW10 . . . . . .**107** J2
Puteaux Ho, E2 . . . .**113** G2
PUTNEY, SW15 . . . .**148** B4
Putney Br, SW6 . . . .**148** B3
SW15 . . . .**148** B3
Putney Br App, SW6 . . . .**148** B3
Putney Br Rd, SW15 . . . .**148** B4
SW18 . . . .**148** D5
Putney Common, SW15 .**147** J3
Putney Ex Shop Cen,
SW15 . . . .**148** A4
Putney Gdns, Rom.
(Chad.Hth.) RM6
off Heathfield Pk Dr . . .**82** B6
PUTNEY HEATH, SW15 . .**147** J6
Putney Heath, SW15 . . . .**147** J6
Putney Heath La, SW15 .**148** A6
Putney High St, SW15 . . .**148** A4
Putney Hill, SW15 . . . . . .**148** A6
Putney Pk Av, SW15 . . . .**147** G4
Putney Pk La, SW15 . . . .**147** H4
PUTNEY VALE, SW15 . . .**165** F3
Puttenham Cl, Wat. WD19 .**50** C3
Pycroft Way, N9 . . . .**60** D4
Pyecombe Cor, N12 . . . . .**56** C4
Pylbrook Rd, Sutt. SM1 . .**198** D3
Pylon Way, Croy. CR0 . . .**201** E1
Pymers Mead, SE21 . . . .**169** J1
Pymmes Cl, N13 . . . .**59** F5
N17 . . . .**60** E1
Pymmes Gdns N, N9 . . . .**60** C3
Pymmes Gdns S, N9 . . . .**60** C3
Pymmes Grn Rd, N11 . . . .**58** B4
Pymmes Rd, N13 . . . .**59** E6
Pymms Brook Dr, Barn.
EN4 . . . .**41** H4
Pyne Rd, Surb. KT6 . . . . .**196** A1
Pyne Ter, SW19
off Windlesham Gro . .**166** A1

Pynfolds, SE16
off Paradise St . . .**132/133** E2
Pynham Cl, SE2 . . . .**138** A3
Pynnacles Cl, Stan. HA7 . .**52** E5
Pyrland Rd, N5 . . . .**94** A5
Richmond TW10 . . . . . .**145** J6
Pyrles Grn, Loug. IG10 . . .**48** E1
Pyrles La, Loug. IG10 . . . .**48** E2
Pyrmont Gro, SE27 . . . . .**169** H3
Pyrmont Rd, W4 . . . .**126** A6
Ilford IG1
off High Rd **99** F2
Pytchley Cres, SE19 . . . .**169** J6
Pytchley Rd, SE22 . . . . . .**152** B3

Q

Quadrangle, The, W2 . . . . .**15** G3
Quadrangle Ms, Stan.
HA7 . . . .**53** F7
Quadrant, The, SE24
off Herne Hill **151** J5
SW20 . . . .**184** B1
Bexleyheath DA7 . . . . .**138** D7
Richmond TW9 . . . .**145** H4
Sutton SM2 . . . .**199** F6
Quadrant Arc, W1 . . . .**17** G6
Quadrant Cl, NW4
off The Burroughs **71** H5
Quadrant Gro, NW5 . . . . . .**91** J5
Quadrant Ho, Sutt. SM2 .**199** F6
Quadrant Rd, Rich. TW9 .**145** G4
Thornton Heath CR7 . .**187** H4
Quad Rd, Wem. HA9
off Courtenay Rd **87** G3
Quaggy Wk, SE3 . . . .**155** G4
Quainton St, NW10 . . . . . .**88** D3
Quaker Ct, E1 . . . .**13** F6
Quaker La, Sthl. UB2 . . . .**123** G3
Quakers Course, NW9 . . . .**71** F1
Quakers La, Islw. TW7 . . .**144** D1
Quaker's Pl, E7 . . . .**98** A5
Quaker St, E1 . . . .**13** F6
Quakers Wk, N21 . . . .**44** A6
Quality Ct, WC2 . . . .**18** E3
Quantock Cl, Hayes UB3 .**121** G7
Quantock Dr, Wor.Pk.
KT4 . . . .**197** J2
Quantock Gdns, NW2 . . . .**90** A2
Quarley Way, SE15 . . . . . .**37** F7
Quarrendon St, SW6 . . . .**148** D2
Quarr Rd, Cars. SM5 . . . .**185** G6
Quarry Pk Rd, Sutt. SM1 .**198** C6
Quarry Ri, Sutt. SM1 . . . .**198** C6
Quarry Rd, SW18 . . . .**149** F6
Quarterdeck, The, E14 . . .**134** A2
Quarter Mile La, E10 . . . . .**96** B4
Quayside Wk, Kings.T. KT1
off Bishop's Hall **181** G2
Quay W, Tedd. TW11 . . . .**162** E5
Quebec Ms, W1 . . . .**16** A4
Quebec Rd, Hayes UB4 . .**102** C7
Ilford IG1, IG2 . . . .**81** E7
Quebec Way, SE16 . . . . .**133** G2
Queen Adelaide Rd,
SE20 . . . .**171** F6
Queen Alexandra's Ct,
SW19 . . . .**166** C5
off Suffield Rd **76** C5
Bromley BR2 . . . .**191** F3
Queen Anne Dr, Esher (Clay.)
KT10 . . . .**194** B7
Queen Anne Ms, W1 . . . . .**16** E2
Queen Anne Rd, E9 . . . . . .**95** G6
Queen Anne's Cl, Twick.
TW2 . . . .**162** A3
Queen Anne's Gdns, W4 .**127** E3
Queen Annes Gdns, W5 .**125** H2
Enfield EN1 . . . .**44** B6
Queen Anne's Gdns, Mitch.
CR4 . . . .**185** J3
Queen Anne's Gate,
SW1 . . . .**25** H4
Bexleyheath DA7 . . . . .**158** G3
Queen Anne's Gro, W4 . .**126** E3
Queen Annes Gro, W5 . . .**125** H2
Enfield EN1 . . . .**44** A7
Queen Annes Pl, Enf.
EN1 . . . .**44** B6
Queen Anne St, W1 . . . . . .**16** D3
Queen Anne's Wk, WC1
off Guilford St **110/111** E4
Queen Anne Ter, E1
off Sovereign Cl . . .**112/113** E7
Queenborough Gdns, Chis.
BR7 . . . .**175** G6
Ilford IG2 . . . .**80** D4
Queen Caroline Est, W6 .**127** J5

Queen Caroline St, W6 . .127 J4
Queen Elizabeth Gdns, Mord.
SM4 . . . . .184 D4
★ Queen Elizabeth Hall &
Purcell Room, SE1 . . . .26 C1
Queen Elizabeth Rd, E17 .77 H3
Kingston upon Thames
KT2 . . . . .181 J1
Queen Elizabeths Cl, N16 .94 A2
Queen Elizabeths Dr, N14 .58 E1
★ Queen Elizabeth II Conf Cen,
SW1 . . . . .25 J4
★ Queen Elizabeth's Hunting
Lodge, Epping Forest, E4 .47 F7
Queen Elizabeths St, SE1 . .29 E3
Queen Elizabeths Wk,
N16 . . . . .94 A2
Queen Elizabeth's Wk, Wall.
SM6 . . . . .200 D4
Queen Elizabeth Wk,
SW13 . . . . .147 H1
Queenhithe, EC4 . . . . .20 A5
Queen Margaret's Gro,
N1 . . . . .94 B5
Queen Mary Av, Mord.
SM4 . . . . .184 A5
Queen Mary Cl, Surb.
KT6 . . . . .196 A3
Queen Mary Rd, SE19 . .169 H6
Queen Mary's Av, Cars.
SM5 . . . . .199 J7
★ Queen Mary's Gdns, NW1
off Regent's Pk 8 B4
Queen of Denmark Ct,
SE16 . . . . .133 J3
Queens Acre, Sutt. SM3 .198 A7
Queens Av, N3 . . . . .57 F7
N10 . . . . .74 A3
N20 . . . . .57 G2
Queen's Av, N21 . . . . .59 H1
Queens Av, Felt. TW13 . .160 C4
Greenford UB6 . . . . . . .103 H6
Stanmore HA7 . . . . .69 F3
Woodford Green IG8 . . .63 H5
Queensberry Ms W, SW7 .30 E1
Queensberry Pl, E12 . . . .98 A5
SW7 . . . . .30 E1
Richmond TW9
off Friars La 145 G5
Queensberry Way, SW7 . .31 E1
Queensborough Ms, W2 . .14 C5
Queensborough Pas, W2 .14 C5
Queensborough S Bldgs, W2
off Porchester Ter 109 F7
Queensborough Studios,
W2 . . . . .14 C5
Queensborough Ter, W2 . .14 B5
Queensbridge Pk, Islw.
TW7 . . . . .144 B5
Queensbridge Rd, E2 . . . .112 C1
E8 . . . . .94 C7
QUEENSBURY, Har. 69 G3
Queensbury Circle Par, Har.
HA3 off Streatfield Rd .69 H3
Stanmore HA7
off Streatfield Rd 69 H3
Queensbury Rd, NW9 . . . .70 D7
Wembley HA0 . . . . . . .105 J2
Queensbury Sta Par, Edg.
HA8 . . . . .69 J3
Queensbury St, N1 . . . . . .93 J7
Queen's Circ, SW8
off Queenstown Rd . .130 B7
SW11
off Queenstown Rd . .130 B7
Queens Cl, Edg. HA8 . . . .54 A5
Wallington SM6
off Queens Rd 200 B5
★ Queens Club (Tennis Cen),
W14 . . . . .128 B5
Queens Club Gdns, W14 .128 B6
Queens Ct, SE23 . . . . . . .171 F1
Richmond TW10 . . . . . .145 J6
Queenscourt, Wem.
HA9 . . . . .87 H4
Queen's Cres, NW5 . . . . .92 A6
Queens Cres, Rich.
TW10 . . . . .145 J5
Queenscroft Rd, SE9 . . . .156 A5
Queensdale Cres, W11 . .128 A1
Queensdale Pl, W11 . . . .128 B1
Queensdale Rd, W11 . . . .128 A1
Queensdale Wk, W11 . . .128 B1
Queensdown Rd, E5 . . . . .94 E4
Queens Dr, E10 . . . . .78 A7
N4 . . . . .93 H2
W3 . . . . .105 J6
W5 . . . . .105 J6
Surbiton KT5 . . . . .182 A7
Thames Ditton KT7 . . .180 D7

Queens Elm Par, SW3
off Old Ch St 129 G5
Queen's Elm Sq, SW3 . . .31 F4
Queensferry Wk, N17
off Jarrow Rd 76/77 E4
★ Queen's Gall, The,
SW1 . . . . .25 E4
Queens Gdns, NW4 . . . . .71 J5
W2 . . . . .14 C5
W5 . . . . .105 F4
Queen's Gdns, Hous.
TW5 . . . . .142 E1
Queen's Gate, SW7 . . . . .30 E1
Queen's Gate Gdns, SW7 .22 D6
Queens Gate Gdns, SW15
off Upper Richmond
Rd 147 H4
Queensgate Gdns, Chis.
BR7 . . . . .193 G1
Queen's Gate Ms, SW7 . .22 D4
Queensgate Pl, NW6 . . . .90 D7
Queen's Gate Pl, SW7 . . .22 D6
Queen's Gate Pl Ms, SW7 .22 D6
Queen's Gate Ter, SW7 . .22 C5
Queen's Gro, NW8 . . . . .109 G1
Queen's Gro Ms, NW8 . .109 G1
Queens Gro Rd, E4 . . . . .62 D1
Queen's Head St, N1 . . . .111 H1
Queens Head Yd, SE1 . . .28 B2
Queens Ho, Tedd. TW11 .162 C6
★ Queen's Ice Rink, W2
off Queensway 14 B6
Queensland Av, N18 . . . .59 J6
SW19 . . . . .184 E1
Queensland Cl, E17 . . . . .77 J2
Queensland Ho, E16
off Rymill St 136 D1
Queensland Pl, N7
off Queensland Rd 93 G4
Queensland Rd, N7 . . . . .93 G4
Queens La, N10 . . . . .74 B3
Queens Mkt, E13
off Green St 115 J1
Queensmead, NW8 . . . . .109 G1
Queensmead Rd, Brom.
BR2 . . . . .191 F2
Queensmere Cl, SW19 . .166 A2
Queensmere Rd, SW19 . .166 A2
Queens Ms, W2 . . . . .14 B5
Queensmill Rd, SW6 . . . .128 A7
Queens Par, N11
off Colney Hatch La . . .57 J5
W5 . . . . .105 J6
Queens Par Cl, N11
off Colney Hatch La . . .57 J5
Queens Pk Ct, W10 . . . .108 A3
★ Queens Park Rangers FC,
W12 . . . . .127 H1
Queens Pas, Chis. BR7
off High St 174/175 E6
Queen's Pl, Mord. SM4 . .184 D4
Queen's Prom, Kings.T. KT1
off Portsmouth Rd . . .181 G3
Queen Sq, WC1 . . . . .10 B6
Queen Sq Pl, WC1 . . . . . .10 B6
Queens Reach, E.Mol.
KT8 . . . . .180 B4
Queens Ride, SW13 . . . .147 G3
SW15 . . . . .147 G3
Queen's Ride, Rich.
TW10 . . . . .164 B1
Queens Ri, Rich. TW10 . .145 J6
E13 . . . . .115 H1
Queen's Rd, E17 . . . . .77 J6
Queen's Rd, N3 . . . . .73 F1
N9 . . . . .60 E3
Queen's Rd, N11 . . . . . . .58 E7
SE14 . . . . .152 E1
SE15 . . . . .152 E1
SW14 . . . . .146 D3
SW19 . . . . .166 C6
W5 . . . . .105 H6
Barking IG11 . . . . .99 F7
Barnet EN5 . . . . .40 A3
Beckenham BR3 . . . . . .189 H2
Bromley BR1 . . . . .191 G2
Buckhurst Hill IG9 . . . .63 H2
Chislehurst BR7 . . . . .175 E6
Queen's Rd, Croy. CR0 .187 H6
Feltham TW13 . . . . . . .160 B1
Hampton (Hmptn.H.)
TW12 . . . . .161 H4
Queen's Rd, Houns.
TW3 . . . . .143 H3
Queens Rd, Kings.T.
KT2 . . . . .164 A7
Loughton IG10 . . . . . . .48 B3

Queen's Rd, Mitch. CR4 .185 G3
Morden SM4 . . . . .184 D4
New Malden KT3 . . . . .183 F4
Richmond TW10 . . . . . .145 H7
Southall UB7 . . . . .122 D2
Queen's Rd, Tedd. TW11 .162 B6
Thames Ditton KT7 . . .180 C5
Queen's Rd, Twick. TW1 .162 C1
Wallington SM6 . . . . . .200 B5
Queen's Rd, Well. DA16 .158 B2
Queens Rd, West Dr.
UB7 . . . . .120 C2
Queens Rd W, E13 . . . . .115 G2
Queen's Row, SE17 . . . . .36 B5
Queens Ter, E13 . . . . . . .115 H1
Queen's Ter, NW8 . . . . . . .7 E1
Queens Ter, Islw. TW7 . .144 D4
Queens Ter Cotts, W7
off Boston Rd 124 B2
Queensthorpe Rd, SE26 .171 G4
★ Queen's Twr, SW7 . . . . .23 E5
Queenstown Ms, SW8
off Queenstown Rd . . .150 B2
Queenstown Rd, SW8 . . .32 D6
Queen St, EC4 . . . . .20 A5
N17 . . . . .60 B6
Queen St, W1 . . . . .24 E1
Bexleyheath DA7 . . . . .159 F3
Croydon CR0
off Church Rd 201 J3
Queen St Pl, EC4 . . . . . . .20 A6
Queensville Rd, SW12 . .150 D7
Queens Wk, E4
off The Green Wk 62 D1
NW9 . . . . .88 C2
Queen's Wk, SE1 . . . . . . .26 C2
SW1 . . . . .25 F2
Queens Wk, W5 . . . . . . .105 F4
Queen's Wk, Har. HA1 . . .68 B4
Queens Wk, Ruis. HA4 . . .84 D3
Queensway, NW4 . . . . . . .71 J5
Queensway, W2 . . . . .14 B4
Queensway, Croy. CR0 . .201 F6
Queensway, Enf. EN3 . . . .45 E4
Queensway, Felt. TW13 .160 C4
Queensway, Orp. BR5 . .193 F5
Sunbury-on-Thames
TW16 . . . . .178 B2
West Wickham BR4 . . .205 E3
Queens Well Av, N20 . . . .57 H3
Queenswood Av, E17 . . . .78 C1
Hampton TW12 . . . . . .161 H6
Hounslow TW3 . . . . . .143 F2
Thornton Heath CR7 . .187 G5
Wallington SM6 . . . . . .200 D4
Queenswood Gdns, E11 . .97 G1
Queenswood Pk, N3 . . . .72 B2
Queen's Wd Rd, N10 . . . .74 B6
Queenswood Rd, SE23 . .171 G3
Sidcup DA15 . . . . .157 J5
Queens Yd, WC1 . . . . .9 G6
Queen Victoria Av, Wem.
HA0 . . . . .87 G7
★ Queen Victoria Mem,
SW1 . . . . .25 F3
Queen Victoria St, EC4 . .19 H5
Queen Victoria Ter, E1
off Sovereign Cl . .112/113 E7
Quemerford Rd, N7 . . . . .93 F5
Quentin Pl, SE13 . . . . . .155 E3
Quentin Rd, SE13 . . . . . .155 E3
Quernmore Cl, Brom.
BR1 . . . . .173 G6
Quernmore Rd, N4 . . . . .75 G6
Bromley BR1 . . . . .173 G6
Querrin St, SW6 . . . . . . .149 F2
Quex Ms, NW6
off Quex Rd 108 D1
Quex Rd, NW6 . . . . .108 D1
Quick Pl, N1 . . . . .111 H1
Quick Rd, W4 . . . . .126 E5
Quicks Rd, SW19 . . . . . .167 E7
Quick St, N1 . . . . .11 H2
Quick St Ms, N1 . . . . .11 G2
Quickswood, NW3
off King Henry's Rd . . .91 H7
Quiet Nook, Brom. BR2
off Croydon Rd 206 A3
Quill La, SW15 . . . . .148 A4
Quill St, N4 . . . . .93 G3
W5 . . . . .105 H3
Quilp St, SE1 . . . . .27 J3
Quilter St, E2 . . . . .13 H3
SE18 . . . . .137 J5
Quilting Ct, SE16
off Poolmans St 133 G2
Quinta Dr, Barn. EN5 . . .39 H5
Quintin Av, SW20 . . . . . .184 C1
Quintin Cl, Pnr. HA5
off High Rd 66 B5

Quinton Cl, Beck. BR3 . . .190 C3
Hounslow TW5 . . . . . .122 B7
Wallington SM6 . . . . . .200 B4
Quinton Rd, T.Ditt. KT7 . .194 D1
Quinton St, SW18 . . . . . .167 F2
Quixley St, E14 . . . . .114 D7
Quorn Rd, SE22 . . . . . . .152 B4

R

Rabbit Row, W8
off Kensington Mall . .128 D1
Rabbits Rd, E12 . . . . .98 B4
Rabournmead Dr, Nthlt.
UB5 . . . . .84 E5
Raby Rd, N.Mal. KT3 . . .182 D4
Raby St, E14
off Salmon La 113 H6
Raccoon Way, Houns.
TW4 . . . . .142 C2
Rachel Cl, Ilf. IG6 . . . . . . .81 G3
Rachel Pt, E5
off Muir Rd 94 D4
Rackham Cl, Well.
DA16 . . . . .158 B2
Rackham Ms, SW16 . . . .168 C6
off Westcote Rd
Racton Rd, SW6 . . . . . . .128 D6
Radbourne Av, W5 . . . . .125 F4
Radbourne Cl, E5
off Overbury St 95 G4
Radbourne Cres, E17 . . . .78 D2
Radbourne Rd, SW12 . . .150 C7
Radcliffe Av, NW10 . . . .107 G2
Enfield EN2 . . . . .43 J1
Radcliffe Gdns, Cars.
SM5 . . . . .199 H7
Radcliffe Ms, Hmptn.
(Hmptn.H.) TW12
off Taylor Cl 161 J5
Radcliffe Path, SW8
off St. Rule St 150 C2
Radcliffe Rd, N21 . . . . . . .59 H1
SE1 . . . . .29 E5
Croydon CR0 . . . . .202 C2
Harrow HA3 . . . . .68 D2
Radcliffe Sq, SW15 . . . .148 A6
Radcliffe Way, Nthlt.
UB5 . . . . .102 D3
Radcot Pt, SE23 . . . . . . .171 G3
Radcot St, SE11 . . . . .35 F4
Raddington Rd, W10 . . .108 B5
Radfield Way, Sid. DA15 .157 G7
Radford Rd, SE13 . . . . . .154 C6
Radford Way, Bark. IG11 .117 J3
Radipole Rd, SW6 . . . . . .148 C1
Radius Pk, Felt. TW14 . .141 J4
Radland Rd, E16 . . . . . . .115 F6
Radlet Av, SE26 . . . . . . .171 E3
Radlett Cl, E7 . . . . .97 F6
Radlett Pl, NW8 . . . . . . .109 H1
Radley Av, Ilf. IG3 . . . . . . .99 J4
Radley Ct, SE16
off Thame Rd 133 G2
Radley Gdns, Har. HA3 . .69 H4
Radley Ho, SE2
off Wolvercote Rd 138 D2
Radley Ms, W8 . . . . .128 D3
Radley Rd, N17 . . . . .76 B2
Radley's La, E18 . . . . .79 G2
Radleys Mead, Dag.
RM10 . . . . .101 H6
Radlix Rd, E10 . . . . .96 A1
Radnor Av, Har. HA1 . . . .68 B5
Welling DA16 . . . . .158 B5
Radnor Cl, Chis. BR7
off Homewood Cres . .175 H6
Mitcham CR4 . . . . .187 E4
Radnor Cres, SE18 . . . . .138 A6
Ilford IG4 . . . . .80 C5
Radnor Gdns, Enf. EN1 . .44 B1
Twickenham TW1 . . . . .162 C2
Radnor Ms, W2 . . . . .15 F4
Radnor Pl, W2 . . . . .15 G4
Radnor Rd, NW6 . . . . . .108 B1
SE15 . . . . .37 H7
Harrow HA1 . . . . .68 A5
Twickenham TW1 . . . . .162 C2
Radnor St, EC1 . . . . .12 A4
Radnor Ter, W14 . . . . . . .128 C4
Radnor Wk, E14
off Copeland Dr 134 A4
SW3 . . . . .31 H4
Croydon CR0 . . . . .189 J6
Radnor Way, NW10 . . . .106 B4
Radstock Av, Har. HA3 . .68 D3
Radstock Cl, N11
off Martock Gdns 58 A6
Radstock St, SW11 . . . .129 H1

332   Rae–Rav

Raeburn Gdns, Barn. EN5 .39 H5
Raeburn Av, Surb. KT5 . .182 B6
Raeburn Cl, NW11 . . . . .73 F6
  Kingston upon Thames
  KT1 . . . . .163 G7
Raeburn Rd, Edg. HA8 . . .70 A2
  Sidcup DA15 . . . . .157 H6
Raeburn St, SW2 . . . . . .151 E4
Rafford Way, Brom. BR1 .191 H2
Raft Rd, SW18
  off North Pas 148 D4
★ Ragged Sch Mus, E3
  off Copperfield Rd 113 H5
Raggleswood, Chis. BR7 .192 D1
Raglan Cl, Houns. TW4
  off Vickers Way . .142/143 E5
Raglan Ct, SE12 . . . . . .155 G5
  South Croydon CR2 . .201 H5
  Wembley HA9 . . . . . . .87 J4
Raglan Gdns, Wat.
  WD19 . . . . .50 B1
Raglan Rd, E17 . . . . . . .78 C5
  SE18 . . . . .137 F5
  Belvedere DA17 . . . . .139 F4
  Bromley BR2 . . . . . . .191 J4
  Enfield EN1 . . . . .44 B7
Raglan St, NW5 . . . . . . .92 B6
Raglan Ter, Har. HA2 . . . .85 H4
Raglan Way, Nthlt. UB5 . . .85 J6
Ragley Cl, W3
  off Church Rd 126 C2
Ragwort Ct, SE26
  off Lawrie Pk Gdns . . .170 E5
Raider Cl, Rom. RM7 . . . .83 G1
Railey Ms, NW5 . . . . . . .92 C5
Railshead Rd, Islw.
  TW7 . . . . .144 E4
Railton Rd, SE24 . . . . . .151 E4
Railway App, N4
  off Wightman Rd 75 G6
  SE1 . . . . .28 C1
  Harrow HA3 . . . . .68 C4
  Twickenham TW1 . . . .144 D7
  Wallington SM6 . . . . .200 B6
Railway Av, SE16 . . . . . .133 F2
Railway Ms, E3
  off Wellington Way 114 A3
  W10 off Ladbroke Gro .108 B6
Railway Pas, Tedd. TW11
  off Victoria Rd 162 D6
Railway Pl, SW19
  off Hartfield Rd 166 C6
  Belvedere DA17 . . . . .139 G3
Railway Ri, SE22
  off Grove Vale 152 B4
Railway Rd, Tedd. TW11 .162 C4
Railway Side, SW13 . . . .147 E3
Railway St, N1 . . . . .10 B2
  Romford RM6 . . . . . . .100 C1
Railway Ter, SE13
  off Ladywell Rd 154 B5
  Feltham TW13 . . . . . .160 A1
Rainborough Cl, NW10 . .88 C6
Rainbow Av, E14 . . . . . .134 B5
Rainbow Quay, SE16 . . .133 H3
Rainbow St, SE5 . . . . . .132 B7
Raine St, E1 . . . . .133 E1
Rainham Cl, SE9 . . . . . .157 G6
  SW11 . . . . .149 H6
Rainham Rd, NW10 . . . .107 J3
Rainham Rd N, Dag.
  RM10 . . . . .101 H2
Rainham Rd S, Dag.
  RM10 . . . . .101 H4
Rainhill Way, E3 . . . . . .114 A3
Rainsborough Av, SE8 .133 H4
Rainsford Cl, Stan. HA7
  off Coverdale Cl 53 F5
Rainsford Rd, NW10 . . .106 B3
Rainsford St, W2 . . . . . .15 G3
Rainton Rd, SE7 . . . . . .135 G5
Rainville Rd, W6 . . . . . .127 J6
Raisins Hill, Pnr. HA5 . . .66 C3
Raith Av, N14 . . . . .58 D3
Raleana Rd, E14 . . . . . .134 C1
Raleigh Av, Hayes UB4 .102 B5
  Wallington SM6 . . . . .200 D4
Raleigh Cl, NW4 . . . . . . .71 J5
  Pinner HA5 . . . . .66 D7
Raleigh Ct, SE16
  off Rotherhithe St 133 G1
  SE19 off Lymer Av . . .170 C5
  Beckenham BR3 . . . . .190 B1
  Wallington SM6 . . . . .200 B6
Raleigh Dr, N20 . . . . . . .57 H3
  Esher (Clay.) KT10 . . .194 A5
  Surbiton KT5 . . . . . . .196 C1
Raleigh Gdns, SW2
  off Brixton Hill 151 F6
  Mitcham CR4 . . . . . . .185 J2

Raleigh Ms, N1
  off Queen's Head St . .111 H1
  Orpington BR6
  off Osgood Av 207 J5
Raleigh Rd, N8 . . . . .75 G4
  SE20 . . . . .171 G7
  Enfield EN2 . . . . .44 A4
  Richmond TW9 . . . . . .145 J3
  Southall UB2 . . . . . . .122 E5
Raleigh St, N1 . . . . .111 H1
Raleigh Way, N14 . . . . . .58 D1
  Feltham TW13 . . . . . .160 C5
Ralph Ct, W2 . . . . .14 B3
Ralph Perring Ct, Beck.
  BR3 . . . . .190 A4
Ralston St, SW3 . . . . . . .31 J4
Ralston Way, Wat. WD19 .50 D2
Rama Cl, SW16 . . . . . . .168 D7
Rama Ct, Har. HA1 . . . . .86 B2
Ramac Way, SE7 . . . . . .135 H4
Rama La, SE19 . . . . . . .170 C7
Rambler Cl, SW16 . . . . .168 C4
Rame Cl, SW17 . . . . . . .168 A5
Ramillies Pl, W1 . . . . . . .17 F4
Ramillies Rd, NW7 . . . . .54 E2
  W4 . . . . .126 D4
  Sidcup DA15 . . . . . . .158 B6
Ramillies St, W1 . . . . . . .17 F4
Rampart St, E1
  off Commercial
  Rd 112/113 E6
Ram Pas, Kings.T. KT1
  off High St 181 G2
Rampayne St, SW1 . . . . .33 H3
Ram Pl, E9
  off Chatham Pl 95 F6
Rampton Cl, E4 . . . . .62 A3
Ramsay Ms, SW3 . . . . . .31 G5
Ramsay Pl, Har. HA1 . . . .86 B1
Ramsay Rd, E7 . . . . .97 E4
  W3 . . . . .126 C3
Ramscroft Cl, N9 . . . . . . .44 B7
Ramsdale Rd, SW17 . . .168 A5
Ramsden Rd, N11 . . . . . .57 J5
  SW12 . . . . .150 A6
Ramsey Cl, NW9 . . . . . . .71 F6
  Greenford UB6 . . . . . . .85 J5
Ramsey Ho, Wem. HA9 . .87 H6
Ramsey Ms, N4
  off Monsell Rd 93 H3
Ramsey Rd, Th.Hth. CR7 .187 F6
Ramsey St, E2 . . . . .13 J5
Ramsey Wk, N1
  off Clephane Rd 94 A6
Ramsey Way, N14 . . . . . .42 C7
Ramsgate Cl, E16
  off Hanameel St 135 H1
Ramsgate St, E8
  off Dalston La 94 C6
Ramsgill App, Ilf. IG2 . . .81 J4
Ramsgill Dr, Ilf. IG2 . . . .81 J5
Rams Gro, Rom. RM6 . . .83 E4
Ram St, SW18 . . . . .148 E5
Ramulis Dr, Hayes UB4 .102 D4
Ramus Wd Av, Orp. BR6 .207 H5
Rancliffe Gdns, SE9 . . . .156 B4
Rancliffe Rd, E6 . . . . . . .116 B2
Randall Av, NW2 . . . . . . .89 F3
Randall Cl, SW11 . . . . . .149 H1
  Erith DA8 . . . . .139 J6
Randall Ct, NW7
  off Page St 55 G7
Randall Pl, SE10 . . . . . .134 C7
Randall Rd, SE11 . . . . . .34 C3
Randall Row, SE11 . . . . .34 C2
Randell's Rd, N1 . . . . . .111 E1
Randle Rd, Rich. TW10 .163 F4
Randlesdown Rd, SE6 . .172 A4
Randolph App, E16 . . . .116 A6
Randolph Av, W9 . . . . . . .6 D5
Randolph Cl, Bexh.
  DA7 . . . . .159 J3
  Kingston upon Thames
  KT2 . . . . .164 C5
Randolph Cres, W9 . . . . .6 C6
Randolph Gdns, NW6 . . . .6 A2
Randolph Gro, Rom. RM6
  off Donald Dr 82 C5
Randolph Ho, Croy.
  CR0 . . . . .201 J1
Randolph Ms, W9 . . . . . .6 D6
Randolph Rd, E17 . . . . . .78 B5
  W9 . . . . .6 C6
  Bromley BR2 . . . . . . .206 C1
  Southall UB1 . . . . . . .123 F2
Randolph St, NW1 . . . . . .92 C7
Randon Cl, Har. HA2 . . . .67 H2
Ranelagh Av, SW6 . . . . .148 C3
  SW13 . . . . .147 G2

Ranelagh Br, W2
  off Gloucester
  Ter 108/109 E5
Ranelagh Cl, Edg. HA8 . .54 A4
Ranelagh Dr, Edg. HA8 . .54 A4
  Twickenham TW1 . . . .145 E5
★ Ranelagh Gdns, SW3 . .32 B4
Ranelagh Gdns, E11 . . . .79 J5
  SW6 . . . . .148 B3
  W4 off Grove Pk Gdns .126 C7
  W6 . . . . .127 F3
  Ilford IG1 . . . . .98 D1
Ranelagh Gro, SW1 . . . . .32 C3
Ranelagh Ms, W5
  off Ranelagh Rd 125 G2
Ranelagh Pl, N.Mal. KT3
  off Rodney Rd . . .182/183 E5
Ranelagh Rd, E6 . . . . . .116 D1
  E11 . . . . .96 E4
  E15 . . . . .115 E1
  N17 . . . . .76 B3
  N22 . . . . .75 F1
  NW10 . . . . .107 F2
  SW1 . . . . .33 G4
  W5 . . . . .125 G2
  Southall UB1 . . . . . . .122 D1
  Wembley HA0 . . . . . . .87 G5
Ranfurly Rd, Sutt. SM1 .198 D2
Rangefield Rd, Brom.
  BR1 . . . . .172 E5
Rangemoor Rd, N15 . . . .76 C5
Rangers Rd, E4 . . . . .47 E7
  Loughton IG10 . . . . . . .47 E7
Rangers Sq, SE10 . . . . .154 D1
Rangeworth Pl, Sid. DA15
  off Priestlands Pk Rd .175 J3
Rangoon St, EC3
  off Northumberland
  All 112 C6
Rankin Cl, NW9 . . . . .71 E3
Ranleigh Gdns, Bexh.
  DA7 . . . . .139 F7
Ranmere St, SW12
  off Ormeley Rd 168 B1
Ranmoor Cl, Har. HA1 . . .68 A4
Ranmoor Gdns, Har.
  HA1 . . . . .68 A4
Ranmore Av, Croy. CR0 .202 C3
Rannoch Cl, Edg. HA8 . . .54 B2
Rannoch Rd, W6 . . . . . .127 J6
Rannock Av, NW9 . . . . . .70 E7
Ranskill Rd, Borwd.
  WD6 . . . . .38 A1
Ransom Rd, SE7
  off Harvey Gdns 135 J5
Ransom Wk, SE7
  off Woolwich Rd 135 J5
Ranston St, NW1 . . . . . .15 G1
Ranulf Rd, NW2 . . . . . . .90 C4
Ranwell Cl, E3
  off Beale Rd 113 J1
Ranwell St, E3 . . . . .113 J1
Ranworth Rd, N9 . . . . . . .61 F2
Ranyard Cl, Chess. KT9 .195 J3
Raphael Dr, T.Ditt. KT7 . .180 C7
Raphael St, SW7 . . . . . . .23 J4
Rashleigh St, SW8
  off Peardon St 150 B2
Rasper Rd, N20 . . . . .57 F2
Rastell Av, SW2 . . . . . . .168 D2
Ratcliffe Cl, SE12 . . . . . .155 G7
Ratcliffe Cross St, E1 . . .113 G6
Ratcliffe La, E14 . . . . . . .113 H6
Ratcliffe Orchard, E1 . . .113 G7
Ratcliff Rd, E7 . . . . .97 J5
Rathbone Mkt, E16
  off Barking Rd 115 F5
Rathbone Pl, W1 . . . . . . .17 H3
Rathbone Pt, E5
  off Nolan Way 94 D4
Rathbone St, E16 . . . . . .115 F5
  W1 . . . . .17 G2
Rathcoole Av, N8 . . . . . . .75 F4
Rathcoole Gdns, N8 . . . .75 F5
Rathfern Rd, SE6 . . . . . .171 J1
Rathgar Av, W13 . . . . . .125 E1
Rathgar Cl, N3 . . . . .72 C2
Rathgar Rd, SW9
  off Coldharbour La . . .151 H3
Rathlin Wk, N1
  off Clephane Rd 93 J6
Rathmell Dr, SW4 . . . . .150 D6
Rathmore Rd, SE7 . . . . .135 H5
Rattray Rd, SW2 . . . . . .151 G4
Raul Rd, SE15 . . . . .152 D1
Raveley St, NW5 . . . . . . .92 C4
Raven Cl, NW9
  off Eagle Dr 70/71 E2
Raven Ct, E5
  off Stellman Cl 94 D3

Ravenet St, SW11
  off Strasburg Rd 150 B1
Ravenfield Rd, SW17 . . .167 J3
Ravenhill Rd, E13 . . . . . .115 J2
Ravenna Rd, SW15 . . . .148 A5
Ravenoak Way, Chig.
  IG7 . . . . .65 H5
Ravenor Pk Rd, Grnf.
  UB6 . . . . .103 H3
Raven Rd, E18 . . . . .79 J2
Raven Row, E1 . . . . .113 E5
Ravensbourne Av, Beck.
  BR3 . . . . .172 D7
  Bromley BR2 . . . . . . .172 D7
Ravensbourne Gdns,
  W13 . . . . .104 E5
  Ilford IG5 . . . . .80 D1
Ravensbourne Pk, SE6 .154 A7
Ravensbourne Pk Cres,
  SE6 . . . . .153 J7
Ravensbourne Pl, SE13 .154 B2
Ravensbourne Rd, SE6 .153 J7
  Bromley BR1 . . . . . . .191 G3
  Twickenham TW1 . . . .145 F6
Ravensbury Av, Mord. . .185 F5
Ravensbury Ct, Mitch. CR4
  off Ravensbury Gro . .185 G4
Ravensbury Gro, Mitch.
  CR4 . . . . .185 G4
Ravensbury La, Mitch.
  CR4 . . . . .185 G4
Ravensbury Path, Mitch.
  CR4 . . . . .185 G4
Ravensbury Rd, SW18 . .166 D2
  Orpington BR5 . . . . . .193 J4
Ravensbury Ter, SW18 .166 E2
Ravenscar Rd, Brom.
  BR1 . . . . .172 E4
  Surbiton KT6 . . . . . . .195 J2
Ravens Cl, Brom. BR2 . .191 F2
  Chessington KT9 . . . .181 G6
  Enfield EN1 . . . . .44 B2
Ravenscourt Av, W6 . . . .127 G4
Ravenscourt Gdns, W6 .127 G4
Ravenscourt Pk, W6 . . .127 G3
Ravenscourt Pl, W6 . . . .127 H4
Ravenscourt Rd, W6 . . .127 H4
Ravenscourt Sq, W6 . . .127 G3
Ravenscraig Rd, N11 . . .58 B4
Ravenscroft Av, NW11 . .72 C7
  Wembley HA9 . . . . . . .87 J1
Ravenscroft Cl, E16 . . . .115 G5
Ravenscroft Cres, SE9 .174 C3
Ravenscroft Pk, Barn.
  EN5 . . . . .40 A4
Ravenscroft Pt, E9
  off Kenton Rd 95 G6
Ravenscroft Rd, E16 . . .115 G5
  W4 . . . . .126 C4
  Beckenham BR3 . . . . .189 F2
Ravenscroft St, E2 . . . . .13 G2
Ravensdale Av, N12 . . . .57 F4
Ravensdale Gdns, SE19 .170 A7
  Hounslow TW4 . . . . . .142 E3
Ravensdale Rd, N16 . . . .76 C7
  Hounslow TW4 . . . . . .142 E3
Ravensdon St, SE11 . . . .35 F4
Ravensfield Cl, Dag.
  RM9 . . . . .100 D4
Ravensfield Gdns, Epsom
  KT19 . . . . .197 E5
Ravenshaw St, NW6 . . . .90 C5
Ravenshill, Chis. BR7 . .192 E1
Ravenshurst Av, NW4 . . .71 J4
Ravenside Cl, N18 . . . . . .61 G6
Ravenside Retail Pk, N18 .61 G5
Ravenslea Rd, SW12 . . .149 J7
Ravensmead Rd, Brom.
  BR2 . . . . .172 D7
Ravensmede Way, W4 . .127 F4
Ravens Ms, SE12
  off Ravens Way 155 G5
Ravenstone, SE17 . . . . . .36 E4
Ravenstone Rd, N8 . . . . .75 G3
  NW9
  off West Hendon Bdy . .71 F6
Ravenstone St, SW12 . .168 A1
Ravens Way, SE12 . . . . .155 G5
Ravenswood, Bex. DA5 .177 E1
Ravenswood Av, Surb.
  KT6 . . . . .195 J2
  West Wickham BR4 . .204 C1
Ravenswood Ct, Kings.T.
  KT2 . . . . .164 B6
Ravenswood Cres, Har.
  HA2 . . . . .85 F2
  West Wickham BR4 . .204 C1
Ravenswood Gdns, Islw.
  TW7 . . . . .144 B1

Ravenswood Pk, Nthwd.
HA6 . . . . .50 A6
Ravenswood Rd, E17 . . .78 B4
SW12 . . . . .150 B7
Croydon CR0 . . . . . . .201 H3
Ravensworth Rd, NW10 .107 H3
SE9 . . . . .174 C4
Ravent Rd, SE11 . . . . . . .34 D2
Ravey St, EC2 . . . . .12 D5
Ravine Gro, SE18 . . . . .137 H6
Rawlings Cl, Orp. BR6 . .207 J5
Rawlings Cres, Wem.
HA9 . . . . .88 B3
Rawlings St, SW3 . . . . . .31 J1
Rawlins Cl, N3 . . . . .72 B3
South Croydon CR2 . .203 H7
Rawnsley Av, Mitch.
CR4 . . . . .185 G5
Rawreth Wk, N1
off Basire St 111 J1
Rawson St, SW11
off Strasburg Rd 150 A1
Rawstone Cl, E16 . . . . . .136 C1
Rawstone Wk, E13 . . . . .115 G2
Rawstorne Pl, EC1 . . . . . .11 G3
Rawstorne St, EC1 . . . . . .11 G3
Ray Cl, Chess. KT9
off Merritt Gdns 195 F6
Raydean Rd, Barn. EN5 . .40 E5
Raydons Gdns, Dag.
RM9 . . . . .101 E5
Raydons Rd, Dag. RM9 . .100 E5
Raydon St, N19 . . . . .92 B2
Rayfield Cl, Brom. BR2 . .192 B6
Rayford Av, SE12 . . . . . .155 F7
Ray Gdns, Bark. IG11 . . .118 A2
Stanmore HA7 . . . . .53 E5
Rayleas Cl, SE18 . . . . . .156 E1
Rayleigh Av, Tedd. TW11 .162 B6
Rayleigh Cl, N13
off Rayleigh Rd 60 A3
Rayleigh Ct, Kings.T.
KT1 . . . . .181 J2
Rayleigh Ri, S.Croy.
CR2 . . . . .202 B6
Rayleigh Rd, E16 . . . . . .135 H1
N13 . . . . .59 J3
SW19 . . . . .184 C1
Woodford Green IG8 . . .63 J6
Ray Lo Rd, Wdf.Grn. IG8 . .63 J6
Ray Massey Way, E6
off Ron Leighton Way .116 B1
Raymead, NW4
off Tenterden Gro 71 J4
Raymead Av, Th.Hth.
CR7 . . . . .187 G5
Raymere Gdns, SE18 . . .137 G7
Raymond Av, E18 . . . . . .79 F3
W13 . . . . .124 D3
Raymond Bldgs, WC1 . . .18 D1
Raymond Cl, SE26 . . . . .171 F5
Raymond Ct, N10
off Pembroke Rd 58 A7
Sutton SM2
off Mulgrave Rd .198/199 E6
Raymond Rd, E13 . . . . . .97 J7
SW19 . . . . .166 B6
Beckenham BR3 . . . . .189 H4
Ilford IG2 . . . . .81 G7
Raymond Way, Esher
(Clay.) KT10 . . . . .194 D6
Raymouth Rd, SE16 . . . .133 E4
Rayne Ct, E18 . . . . .79 F4
Rayners Cl, Wem. HA0 . . .87 G5
Rayners Ct, Har. HA2 . . . .85 G1
Rayners Cres, Nthlt.
UB5 . . . . .102 B3
Rayners Gdns, Nthlt.
UB5 . . . . .102 B2
RAYNERS LANE, Har. . . .85 F1
Rayners La, Har. HA2 . . . .85 H2
Pinner HA5 . . . . .67 F6
Rayners Rd, SW15 . . . . .148 B5
Rayner Twr, E10 . . . . .78 A7
Raynes Av, E11 . . . . .79 J7
RAYNES PARK, SW20 . . .183 H3
Raynham Av, N18 . . . . . .60 D6
Raynham Rd, N18 . . . . . .60 D5
W6 . . . . .127 H4
Raynham Ter, N18 . . . . . .60 D5
Raynor Cl, Sthl. UB1 . . .123 F1
Raynor Pl, N1
off Elizabeth Av 111 J1
Raynton Cl, Har. HA2 . . . .85 E1
Ray Rd, W.Mol. KT8 . . . .179 H5
Rays Av, N18 . . . . .61 F4
Rays Rd, N18 . . . . .61 F4
West Wickham BR4 . . .190 C7
Ray St, EC1 . . . . .11 F6

Ray St Br, EC1 . . . . .11 F6
Ray Wk, N7
off Andover Rd 93 F2
Raywood Cl, Hayes
UB3 . . . . .121 F7
Reachview Cl, NW1
off Baynes St 92 C7
Read Cl, T.Ditt. KT7 . . . .180 D7
Reade Wk, NW10
off Denbigh Cl 88/89 E7
Reading La, E8 . . . . .94 E6
Reading Rd, Nthlt. UB5 . .85 H5
Sutton SM1 . . . . .199 F5
Reading Way, NW7 . . . . .56 A5
Reads Cl, Ilf. IG1
off Chapel Rd 98/99 E3
Reapers Cl, NW1
off Crofters Way 110 D1
Reapers Way, Islw. TW7
off Hall Rd 144 A5
Reardon Ct, N21
off Cosgrove Cl 59 J2
Reardon Path, E1 . . . . . .133 E1
Reardon St, E1 . . . . .132 E1
Reaston St, SE14 . . . . . .133 F7
Reckitt Rd, W4 . . . . .126 E5
Record St, SE15 . . . . . . .133 F6
Recovery St, SW17 . . . . .167 H5
Recreation Av, Rom.
RM7 . . . . .83 J5
Recreation Rd, SE26 . . .171 G4
Bromley BR2 . . . . . . .191 F2
Sidcup DA15
off Woodside Rd 175 H3
Southall UB2 . . . . . . .122 E4
Recreation Way, Mitch.
CR4 . . . . .186 D3
Rector St, N1 . . . . .111 J1
Rectory Cl, E4 . . . . .62 A3
N3 . . . . .72 C1
SW20 . . . . .183 J3
Sidcup DA14 . . . . .176 B4
Stanmore HA7 . . . . .53 E6
Surbiton KT6 . . . . .195 F1
Rectory Cres, E11 . . . . . .79 J6
Rectory Fld Cres, SE7 . .135 J7
Rectory Gdns, N8 . . . . . .74 E4
SW4 off Fitzwilliam Rd .150 C3
Northolt UB5 . . . . .103 F1
Rectory Grn, Beck. BR3 .189 J1
Rectory Gro, SW4 . . . . .150 C3
Croydon CR0 . . . . . . .201 H2
Hampton TW12 . . . . . .161 F4
Rectory La, SW17 . . . . . .168 A6
Edgware HA8 . . . . .54 A6
Loughton IG10 . . . . . . .48 D2
Sidcup DA14 . . . . .176 B4
Stanmore HA7 . . . . .52 E5
Surbiton KT6 . . . . .195 E1
Wallington SM6 . . . . . .200 C4
Rectory Orchard,
SW19 . . . . .166 B4
Rectory Pk Av, Nthlt.
UB5 . . . . .103 F3
Rectory Pl, SE18 . . . . . .136 D4
Rectory Rd, E12 . . . . .98 C5
E17 . . . . .78 B3
N16 . . . . .94 C3
SW13 . . . . .147 G2
W3 . . . . .126 B1
Beckenham BR3 . . . . .190 A1
Dagenham RM10 . . . . .101 G7
Hayes UB3 . . . . .102 A6
Hounslow TW4 . . . . . . .142 B1
Keston BR2 . . . . .206 A7
Southall UB2 . . . . . . .123 F3
Sutton SM1 . . . . .198 D3
Rectory Sq, E1 . . . . .113 G5
Reculver Ms, N18
off Lyndhurst Rd 60 D4
Reculver Rd, SE16 . . . . .133 G5
Red Anchor Cl, SW3 . . . .31 G6
Redan Pl, W2 . . . . .14 A4
Redan St, W14 . . . . .128 A3
Redan Ter, SE5
off Flaxman Rd 151 J2
Red Barracks Rd, SE18 .136 C4
Redberry Gro, SE26 . . . .171 F3
Redbourne Av, N3 . . . . . .72 D1
Redbourne Dr, SE28 . . . .118 D6
REDBRIDGE, Ilf. 80 C6
Redbridge Enterprise Cen, Ilf.
IG1 . . . . .99 F2
Redbridge Gdns, SE5 . . .132 B7
Redbridge La E, Ilf. IG4 . .80 A6
Redbridge La W, E11 . . . .79 H6
Redburn St, SW3 . . . . . . .31 J5
Redcar Cl, Nthlt. UB5 . . . .85 H5
Redcar St, SE5 . . . . .131 J7
Redcastle Cl, E1 . . . . . . .113 F7

Red Cedars Rd, Orp.
BR6 . . . . .193 H7
Redchurch St, E2 . . . . . . .13 F5
Redcliffe Cl, SW5
off Warwick Rd .128/129 E5
Redcliffe Gdns, SW5 . . . .30 B4
SW4 . . . . .126 B7
Ilford IG1 . . . . .98 D1
Redcliffe Ms, SW10 . . . . .30 B4
Redcliffe Pl, SW10 . . . . . .30 C6
Redcliffe Rd, SW10 . . . . .30 C4
Redcliffe Sq, SW10 . . . . .30 B4
Redcliffe St, SW10 . . . . . .30 B5
Redclose Av, Mord. SM4
off Chalgrove Av 184 D5
Redclyffe Rd, E6 . . . . . . .115 J1
Redcross Way, SE1 . . . . .28 A3
Reddings, The, NW7 . . . .55 F3
Reddings Cl, NW7 . . . . . .55 F4
Reddins Rd, SE15 . . . . . .37 H6
Reddons Rd, Beck. BR3 . .171 H7
Redenham Ho, SW15
off Tangley Gro 147 F7
Rede Pl, W2
off Chepstow Pl 108 D6
Redesdale St, SW3 . . . . .31 H5
Redfern Av, Houns.
TW4 . . . . .143 G7
Redfern Rd, NW10 . . . . . .89 E7
SE6 . . . . .154 C7
Redfield La, SW5 . . . . . .128 D4
Redfield Ms, SW5
off Redfield La 128 D4
Redford Av, Th.Hth. CR7 .187 F4
Wallington SM6 . . . . . .200 E6
Redford Wk, N1
off Britannia Row 111 H1
Redgate Dr, Brom. BR2 .205 H2
Redgate Ter, SW15
off Lytton Gro 148 A6
Redgrave Cl, Croy. CR0 .188 C6
Redgrave Rd, SW15 . . . .148 A3
Red Hill, Chis. BR7 . . . . .174 D5
Redhill Dr, Edg. HA8 . . . .70 C2
Redhill St, NW1 . . . . .8 E3
Red Ho La, Bexh. DA6 . . .158 D4
Redhouse Rd, Croy. CR0 .186 D6
Red Ho Sq, N1
off Clephane Rd 93 J6
★ Red Ho, The
(William Morris Ho),
Bexh. DA6 . . . . .158 E4
Redington Gdns, NW3 . . .90 E4
Redington Rd, NW3 . . . . .90 E4
Redland Gdns, W.Mol. KT8
off Dunstable Rd 179 F4
Redlands Ct, Brom. BR1 .173 F7
Redlands Rd, Enf. EN3 . . .45 H1
Redlands Way, SW2 . . . .151 F7
Red La, Esher (Clay.)
KT10 . . . . .194 D6
Redleaf Cl, Belv. DA17 . .139 G6
Redlees Cl, Islw. TW7 . . .144 D4
Red Lion Cl, SE17 . . . . . .36 A5
Red Lion Ct, EC4 . . . . . . .19 F3
Red Lion Hill, N2 . . . . . . .73 G2
Red Lion La, SE18 . . . . . .136 D7
Red Lion Pl, SE18
off Shooter's Hill Rd .156 D1
Red Lion Rd, Surb. KT6 . .195 J2
Red Lion Row, SE17 . . . . .36 A5
Red Lion Sq, SW18
off Wandsworth High
St 148 D5
Red Lion Sq, WC1 . . . . . .18 C2
Richmond TW9 . . . . . .145 G5
Red Lion Yd, W1 . . . . .24 C1
Red Lo Rd, W.Wick. BR4 .190 D6
Redman Cl, Nthlt. UB5 . .102 C2
Redman's Rd, E1 . . . . . . .113 F5
Redmead La, E1 . . . . .29 H2
Redmead Rd, Hayes
UB3 . . . . .121 H4
Redmore Rd, W6 . . . . . . .127 H4
Red Oak Cl, Orp. BR6 . . .207 E3
Red Path, E9 . . . . .95 J6
Red Pl, W1 . . . . .16 B5
Redpoll Way, Erith
DA18 . . . . .138 D3
Red Post Hill, SE21 . . . . .152 A4
SE24 . . . . .152 A4
Redriffe Rd, E13 . . . . . . .115 F1
Redriff Est, SE16 . . . . . .133 J3
Redriff Rd, SE16 . . . . . . .133 G4
Romford RM7 . . . . .83 H2

Redroofs Cl, Beck. BR3 .190 B1
Redruth Cl, N22
off Palmerston Rd 59 F7
Redruth Rd, E9 . . . . .113 G1
Redstart Cl, E6
off Columbine Av 116 B5
SE14 off Southengate
Way 133 H7
Redston Rd, N8 . . . . .74 D4
Redvers Rd, N22 . . . . . . .75 G2
Redvers St, N1 . . . . .13 E3
Redwald Rd, E5 . . . . .95 G4
Redway Dr, Twick. TW2 . .143 J7
Redwing Path, SE28 . . . .137 G2
Redwing Rd, Wall. SM6 .201 F7
Redwood Cl, N14
off The Vale 42 D7
SE16 . . . . .133 H1
Buckhurst Hill IG9
off Beech La 63 H2
Sidcup DA15 . . . . .158 A7
Watford WD19 . . . . . . .50 C4
Redwood Ct, NW6
off The Avenue 90 B7
Redwood Est, Houns.
TW5 . . . . .122 B6
Redwood Gdns, E4 . . . . . .46 B6
Redwood Ms, SW4
off Hannington Rd . . .150 B3
Redwoods, SW15 . . . . . .165 G1
Redwood Wk, Surb.
KT6 . . . . .195 G1
Redwood Way, Barn.
EN5 . . . . .40 A5
Reece Ms, SW7 . . . . .30 E1
Reed Av, Orp. BR6 . . . . .207 H3
Reed Cl, E16 . . . . .115 G5
SE12 . . . . .155 G5
Reede Gdns, Dag.
RM10 . . . . .101 H5
Reede Rd, Dag. RM10 . . .101 G6
Reede Way, Dag. RM10 . .101 H6
Reedham Cl, N17 . . . . . . .76 E4
Reedham St, SE15 . . . . .152 D2
Reedholm Vil, N16
off Winston Rd 94 A4
Reed Rd, N17 . . . . .76 C2
Reeds Pl, NW1
off Royal Coll St 92 C7
Reedworth St, SE11 . . . . .35 F2
Ree La Cotts, Loug. IG10
off Englands La 48 D2
Reenglass Rd, Stan.
HA7 . . . . .53 G4
Rees Dr, Stan. HA7 . . . . .53 H4
Rees Gdns, Croy. CR0 . .188 C6
Reesland Cl, E12 . . . . . . .98 D6
Rees St, N1 . . . . .111 J1
Reets Fm Cl, NW9 . . . . . .71 E6
Reeves Av, NW9 . . . . . . .70 D7
Reeves Cor, Croy. CR0
off Roman Way 201 H2
Reeves Ms, W1 . . . . .16 B6
Reeves Rd, E3 . . . . .114 B4
SE18 . . . . .136 E6
Reflection, The, E16
off Woolwich Manor
Way 136/137 E2
Reform Row, N17 . . . . . . .76 C2
Reform St, SW11 . . . . . . .149 J2
Regal Cl, E1 . . . . .21 J1
W5 . . . . .105 G5
Regal Ct, N18
off College Cl 60 C5
Regal Cres, Wall. SM6 . .200 B3
Regal Dr, N11 . . . . .58 B5
Regal La, NW1
off Regents Pk Rd . . .110 A1
Regal Pl, E3
off Coborn St 113 J3
SW6 off Maxwell
Rd 128/129 E7
Regal Row, SE15
off Queens Rd 153 F1
Regal Way, Har. HA3 . . . . .69 H6
Regan Way, N1 . . . . .12 D2
Regatta Ho, Tedd. TW11
off Twickenham Rd . . .162 D4
Regency Cl, W5 . . . . .105 H6
Chigwell IG7 . . . . .65 F5
Hampton TW12 . . . . . .161 F5
Regency Ct, Sutt. SM1
off Brunswick Rd .198/199 E4
Regency Cres, NW4 . . . . .72 A2
Regency Lo, Buck.H. IG9 . .64 A2
Regency Ms, NW10
off High Rd 89 G6
Beckenham BR3 . . . . .190 C1
Isleworth TW7
off Queensbridge Pk .144 B5

Regency Pl, SW1 . . . .**33** J1
  Woodford Green IG8 . . .**64** D7
Regency St, SW1 . . . .**33** J1
Regency Ter, SW7
  off Fulham Rd **129** G5
Regency Wk, Croy. CR0 . .**189** H6
  Richmond TW10
  off Friars Stile Rd **145** H6
Regency Way, Bexh.
  DA6 . . . .**158** D3
Regent Cl, N12
  off Nether St **57** F5
  Harrow HA3 . . . .**69** H6
  Hounslow TW4 . . . .**142** B1
Regent Gdns, Ilf. IG3 . . . .**82** A6
Regent Pl, SW19
  off Haydons Rd . .**166/167** E5
  W1 . . . .**17** G5
  Croydon CR0
  off Grant Rd **202** C1
Regent Rd, SE24 . . . .**151** H6
  Surbiton KT5 . . . .**181** J5
Regents Av, N13 . . . .**59** F5
Regents Br Gdns, SW8 . .**34** B7
Regents Cl, S.Croy. CR2 .**202** B6
Regents Dr, Kes. BR2 . . .**206** A5
Regents Ms, NW8 . . . .**6** D1
REGENT'S PARK, NW1 . . . .**8** C2
  ★ Regent's Park, NW1 . . . .**7** J2
Regent's Pk, NW1 . . . .**8** A2
Regent's Pk Est, NW1 . . . .**9** F4
Regents Pk Rd, N3 . . . . . .**72** C3
  NW1 . . . .**109** J1
Regents Pk Ter, NW1
  off Oval Rd **110** B1
Regent's Pl, NW1 . . . .**9** F5
  SE3 . . . .**155** G2
Regents Pl, Loug. IG10 . .**48** A7
Regent Sq, E3 . . . .**114** B3
  WC1 . . . .**10** B4
  Belvedere DA17 . . . . . .**139** H4
Regents Row, E8 . . . .**112** D1
Regent St, NW10
  off Wellington Rd **108** A3
  SW1 . . . .**17** H6
  W1 . . . .**17** E3
  W4 . . . .**126** A5
Regents Wf, N1
  off All Saints St **111** F2
Regina Rd, Barn. EN5 . . . .**40** A3
Reginald Rd, E7 . . . .**97** G7
  SE8 . . . .**134** A7
Reginald Sq, SE8 . . . .**134** A7
Regina Pt, SE16
  off Renforth St **133** F3
Regina Rd, N4 . . . .**93** F1
  SE25 . . . .**188** D3
  W13 . . . .**124** D1
  Southall UB2 . . . .**122** E4
Regina Ter, W13 . . . .**124** D1
Regis Pl, SW2 . . . .**151** F4
Regis Rd, NW5 . . . .**92** B5
Regnart Bldgs, NW1 . . . . . .**9** G5
Reid Cl, Pnr. HA5 . . . .**66** A4
Reidhaven Rd, SE18 . . . .**137** H4
Reigate Av, Sutt. SM1 . . .**198** D1
Reigate Rd, Brom. BR1 . .**173** F3
  Ilford IG3 . . . .**99** J2
Reigate Way, Wall. SM6 .**201** E5
Reighton Rd, E5 . . . .**94** D3
Relay Rd, W12 . . . .**107** J7
Relf Rd, SE15 . . . .**152** D3
Relko Gdns, Sutt. SM1 . .**199** G5
Relton Ms, SW7 . . . .**23** H5
Rembrandt Cl, E14 . . . . . .**134** D3
  SW1 . . . .**32** B2
Rembrandt Ct, Epsom
  KT19 . . . .**197** F6
Rembrandt Rd, SE13 . . . .**154** E4
  Edgware HA8 . . . .**70** A2
Remington Rd, E6 . . . . . .**116** B6
  N15 . . . .**76** A6
Remington St, N1 . . . .**11** H2
Remnant St, WC2 . . . .**18** C3
Rempstone Ms, N1 . . . . . .**12** C1
Remus Rd, E3
  off Monier Rd **96** A7
Renaissance Wk, SE10
  off John Harrison
  Way **135** F3
Rendle Cl, Croy. CR0 . . . .**188** C5
Rendlesham Rd, E5 . . . . . .**94** D4
  Enfield EN2 . . . .**43** H1
Renforth St, SE16 . . . . . .**133** F2
Renfrew Cl, E6 . . . .**116** D7
Renfrew Rd, SE11 . . . .**35** G1
  Hounslow TW4 . . . .**142** D2
  Kingston upon Thames
  KT2 . . . .**164** B7
Renmuir St, SW17 . . . . . .**167** J6

Rennell St, SE13 . . . .**154** C3
Rennels Way, Islw. TW7
  off St. John's Rd **144** B2
Renness Rd, E17 . . . .**77** H3
Rennets Cl, SE9 . . . .**157** H5
Rennets Wd Rd, SE9 . . . .**157** G5
Rennie Est, SE16 . . . .**133** E4
Rennie St, SE1 . . . .**27** G1
Renovation, The, E16
  off Woolwich Manor
  Way **136/137** E2
Renown Cl, Croy. CR0 . . .**201** H1
  Romford RM7 . . . .**83** G1
Rensburg Rd, E17 . . . .**77** G5
Renshaw Cl, Belv. DA17
  off Grove Rd **139** F6
Renters Av, NW4 . . . .**71** J6
Renwick Ind Est, Bark.
  IG11 . . . .**118** D3
Renwick Rd, Bark. IG11 . .**118** B4
Repens Way, Hayes UB4
  off Stipularis Dr **102** D4
Rephidim St, SE1 . . . .**28** D6
Replingham Rd, SW18 . .**166** C1
Reporton Rd, SW6 . . . . . .**148** B1
Repository Rd, SE18 . . . .**136** C6
Repton Av, Hayes UB3 . .**121** G4
  Wembley HA0 . . . .**87** F4
Repton Cl, Cars. SM5 . . .**199** H5
Repton Ct, Beck. BR3 . . .**190** B1
  Ilford IG5
  off Repton Gro **80** C1
Repton Gro, Ilf. IG5 . . . . . .**80** C1
Repton Rd, Har. HA3 . . . . .**69** J4
Repton St, E14 . . . .**113** H6
Repulse Cl, Rom. RM5 . . .**83** H1
Reservoir Cl, Th.Hth.
  CR7 . . . .**188** A4
Reservoir Rd, N14 . . . .**42** C5
  SE4 . . . .**153** H2
Resolution Wk, SE18 . . . .**136** C3
Resolution Way, SE8
  off Deptford High St . .**134** A7
Restell Cl, SE3 . . . .**135** E6
Restmor Way, Wall. SM6 .**200** A2
Reston Pl, SW7 . . . .**22** C4
Restons Cres, SE9 . . . . . .**157** G6
Restormel Cl, Houns.
  TW3 . . . .**143** G5
Retcar Cl, N19
  off Dartmouth Pk Hill . .**92** B2
Retcar Pl, N19 . . . .**92** B2
Retford St, N1 . . . .**13** E2
Retingham Way, E4 . . . . . .**62** B2
Retreat, The, NW9 . . . .**70** D5
  SW14
  off South Worple
  Way **146/147** E3
  Harrow HA2 . . . .**67** G7
  Surbiton KT5 . . . .**181** J6
  Thornton Heath CR7 . .**188** A4
  Worcester Park KT4 . .**197** H2
Retreat Cl, Har. HA3 . . . . .**69** F5
Retreat Pl, E9 . . . .**95** F6
Retreat Rd, Rich. TW9 . . .**145** G5
Reunion Row, E1
  off Pennington
  St **112/113** E7
Reveley Sq, SE16
  off Howland Way **133** H2
Revell Ri, SE18 . . . .**137** J6
Revell Rd, Kings.T. KT1 . .**182** B1
  Sutton SM1 . . . .**198** C6
Revelon Rd, SE4 . . . .**153** H4
Revelstoke Rd, SW18 . . .**166** C2
Reventlow Rd, SE9 . . . . .**175** F1
Reverdy Rd, SE1 . . . .**37** H2
Reverend Cl, Har. HA2 . . .**85** H3
Revesby Rd, Cars. SM5 . .**185** G6
Review Rd, NW2 . . . .**89** F2
  Dagenham RM10 . . . . .**119** H1
Rewell St, SW6 . . . .**129** F7
Rewley Rd, Cars. SM5 . . .**185** G6
Rex Pl, W1 . . . .**16** C6
Reydon Av, E11 . . . .**79** J6
Reynard Cl, SE4
  off Foxwell St **153** H3
  Bromley BR1 . . . .**192** C3
Reynard Dr, SE19 . . . .**170** C7
Reynard Pl, SE14
  off Milton Ct Rd **133** H6
Reynardson Rd, N17 . . . . .**59** J7
Reynolah Gdns, SE7
  off Rathmore Rd **135** H5
Reynolds Av, E12 . . . .**98** D5
  Chessington KT9 . . . . .**195** H7
  Romford RM6 . . . .**82** C7
Reynolds Cl, NW11 . . . . . .**72** E7
  SW19 . . . .**185** G1
  Carshalton SM5 . . . . . .**199** J1

Reynolds Ct, E11
  off Cobbold Rd **97** F3
  Romford RM6 . . . .**82** D3
Reynolds Dr, Edg. HA8 . . .**69** J3
Reynolds Pl, SE3 . . . .**135** H7
  Richmond TW10
  off Cambrian Rd **145** J6
Reynolds Rd, SE15 . . . . .**153** F5
  W4 . . . .**126** C3
  Hayes UB4 . . . .**102** C4
  New Malden KT3 . . . . .**182** D7
Reynolds Way, Croy.
  CR0 . . . .**202** B4
Rheidol Ms, N1 . . . .**11** J1
Rheidol Ter, N1 . . . .**11** H1
Rheola Cl, N17 . . . .**76** C1
Rhoda St, E2 . . . .**13** G5
Rhodes Av, N22 . . . .**74** C1
Rhodesia Rd, E11 . . . .**96** D2
  SW9 . . . .**151** E2
Rhodes Moorhouse Ct,
  Mord. SM4 . . . .**184** D6
Rhodes St, N7
  off Mackenzie Rd **93** F5
Rhodeswell Rd, E14 . . . .**113** J6
Rhodrons Av, Chess.
  KT9 . . . .**195** H5
Rhondda Gro, E3 . . . .**113** H3
Rhyl Rd, Grnf. UB6 . . . . . .**104** C2
Rhyl St, NW5 . . . .**92** A6
Rhys Av, N11 . . . .**58** D7
Rialto Rd, Mitch. CR4 . . .**186** A2
Ribble Cl, Wdf.Grn. IG8
  off Prospect Rd **63** J6
Ribblesdale Av, N11 . . . . .**58** A6
  Northolt UB5 . . . .**85** H6
Ribblesdale Rd, N8 . . . . . .**75** F4
  SW16 . . . .**168** B6
Ribchester Av, Grnf.
  UB6 . . . .**104** C3
Ribston Cl, Brom. BR2 . .**206** C1
Ricardo Path, SE28
  off Byron Cl **138** C1
Ricardo St, E14 . . . .**114** B6
Ricards Rd, SW19 . . . . . .**166** C5
Richard Cl, SE18 . . . .**136** B4
Richard Fell Ho, E12
  off Walton Rd **98** D4
Richard Foster Cl, E17 . . .**77** J7
Richard Ho Dr, E16 . . . . .**116** A6
Richards Av, Rom. RM7 . .**83** J5
Richards Cl, Har. HA1 . . . .**68** D5
  Hayes UB3 . . . .**121** G6
Richardson Cl, E8
  off Clarissa St **112** C1
Richardson Rd, E15 . . . . .**114** E2
Richardson's Ms, W1 . . . . .**9** F6
Richards Pl, E17 . . . .**78** A3
  SW3 . . . .**31** H1
Richard St, E1 off Commercial
  Rd **112/113** E6
Richbell Pl, WC1 . . . .**18** C1
Richborne Ter, SW8 . . . . .**34** D7
Richborough Rd, NW2 . . .**90** A4
Richens Cl, Houns.TW3 .**144** A2
Riches Rd, Ilf. IG1 . . . .**99** F2
Richford Rd, E15 . . . .**115** F1
Richford St, W6 . . . .**127** J2
Richlands Av, Epsom
  KT17 . . . .**197** G4
Rich La, SW5 . . . .**30** A4
RICHMOND **145** H6
Richmond Av, E4 . . . .**62** D5
  N1 . . . .**111** F1
  NW10 . . . .**89** A6
  SW20 . . . .**184** B1
  Feltham TW14 . . . .**141** H6
Richmond Br, Rich.TW9 .**145** G6
  Twickenham TW1 . . . .**145** G6
Richmond Bldgs, W1 . . . .**17** H4
Richmond Cl, E17 . . . .**77** J6
  Borehamwood WD6 . . .**38** D5
Richmond Cres, E4 . . . . . .**62** D5
  N1 . . . .**111** F1
  N9 . . . .**60** D1
Richmond Gdns, NW4 . . .**71** G5
  Harrow HA3 . . . .**52** C4
Richmond Grn, Croy.
  CR0 . . . .**201** E3
Richmond Gro, N1 . . . .**93** H7
  Surbiton KT5 . . . .**181** J6
Richmond Hill, Rich.
  TW10 . . . .**145** H6
Richmond Hill Ct, Rich.
  TW10 . . . .**145** H6
Richmond Ms, W1 . . . .**17** H4
  Teddington TW11
  off Broad St **162** C6
★ Richmond Palace (remains),
  Rich. TW9 . . . .**145** F5

★ Richmond Park, Rich.
  TW10 . . . .**164** A1
Richmond Pk, Kings.T.
  KT2 . . . .**164** B1
  Loughton IG10
  off Fallow Flds **47** J7
  Richmond TW10 . . . . .**164** B1
Richmond Pk Rd, SW14 .**146** C5
  Kingston upon Thames
  KT2 . . . .**163** H7
Richmond Pl, SE18 . . . . .**137** F4
Richmond Rd, E4 . . . .**62** D1
  E7 . . . .**97** H5
  E8 . . . .**94** C7
  E11 . . . .**96** D2
  N2 . . . .**73** F2
  N11 . . . .**58** E6
  N15 . . . .**76** B6
  SW20 . . . .**183** H1
  W5 . . . .**125** H2
  Barnet EN5 . . . .**41** E5
  Croydon CR0 . . . .**200** E3
  Ilford IG1 . . . .**99** F3
  Isleworth TW7 . . . .**144** D3
  Kingston upon Thames
  KT2 . . . .**163** G5
  Thornton Heath CR7 . .**187** H3
  Twickenham TW1 . . . .**145** F6
Richmond St, E13 . . . . . .**115** G2
Richmond Ter, SW1 . . . . . .**26** A3
Richmond Ter Ms, SW1
  off Parliament St .**130/131** E2
  W12 . . . .**128** A2
  W14 . . . .**128** A3
Richmount Gdns, SE3 . . .**155** G3
Rich St, E14 . . . .**113** J7
Rickard Cl, NW4 . . . .**71** H4
  SW2 . . . .**169** F1
  West Drayton UB7 . . . .**120** A3
Rickards Cl, Surb. KT6 . .**195** H1
Rickett St, SW6 . . . .**128** D6
Rickman St, E1
  off Mantus Rd **113** F3
Rickmansworth Rd, Pnr.
  HA5 . . . .**66** B2
Rick Roberts Way, E15 . .**114** C1
Rickthorne Rd, N19
  off Landseer Rd . . .**92/93** E2
Rickyard Path, SE9 . . . . .**156** B4
Ridding La, Grnf. UB6 . . . .**86** C5
Riddons Rd, SE12 . . . . . .**173** J3
Ride, The, Brent. TW8 . . .**125** E5
  Enfield EN3 . . . .**45** F3
Rideout St, SE18 . . . .**136** C4
Rider Cl, Sid. DA15 . . . . . .**157** H6
Ridgdale St, E3 . . . .**114** B2
Ridge, The, Bex. DA5 . . .**159** F7
  Orpington BR6 . . . .**207** G2
  Surbiton KT5 . . . .**182** A5
  Twickenham TW2 . . . .**144** A7
Ridge Av, N21 . . . .**43** J7
Ridgebrook Rd, SE3 . . . .**155** J3
Ridge Cl, NW4 . . . .**72** A2
  NW9 . . . .**70** D4
  SE28 . . . .**137** G2
Ridge Crest, Enf. EN2 . . . .**43** F1
Ridgecroft Cl, Bex. DA5 .**177** J1
Ridge Hill, NW11 . . . .**90** B1
Ridgemont Gdns, Edg.
  HA8 . . . .**54** C4
Ridgemount Av, Croy.
  CR0 . . . .**203** G1
Ridgemount Cl, SE20
  off Anerley Pk . . .**170/171** E7
Ridgemount Gdns, Enf.
  EN2 . . . .**43** H2
Ridge Rd, N8 . . . .**75** F6
  N21 . . . .**59** J1
  NW2 . . . .**90** C3
  Mitcham CR4 . . . .**168** B7
  Sutton SM3 . . . .**198** B1
Ridgeview Cl, Barn. EN5 .**40** A6
Ridgeview Rd, N20 . . . . . .**57** E3
Ridge Way, SE19
  off Central Hill **170** B6
Ridgeway, SE28 . . . .**137** G4
  Bromley BR2 . . . .**205** G2
Ridge Way, Felt.TW13 . . .**160** E3
Ridgeway, Wdf.Grn. IG8 . .**63** J4
Ridgeway, The, E4 . . . .**62** B2
  N3 . . . .**56** F7
  N11 . . . .**57** J4
  N14 . . . .**59** E2
  NW7 . . . .**55** G4
  NW9 . . . .**70** E4
  NW11 . . . .**90** C1
  W3 . . . .**126** A3
  Croydon CR0 . . . .**201** F3

Ridgeway, The, Enf. EN2 . .43 G1
Harrow (Kenton) HA3 . . .69 F6
Harrow (N.Har.) HA2 . .67 F5
Ruislip HA4 . . . . .67 G6
Stanmore HA7 . . . . . . .53 F6
Ridgeway Av, Barn. EN4 . .41 J6
Ridgeway Cres, Orp.
BR6 . . . . .207 H3
Ridgeway Cres Gdns, Orp.
BR6 . . . . .207 H2
Ridgeway Dr, Brom.
BR1 . . . . .173 H4
Ridgeway E, Sid. DA15 . .157 J5
Ridgeway Gdns, N6 . . . . .74 C7
Ilford IG4 . . . . .80 B5
Ridgeway Rd, SW9 . . . . .151 H3
Isleworth TW7 . . . . .124 B7
Ridgeway Rd N, Islw.
TW7 . . . . .124 B6
Ridgeway Wk, Nthlt. UB5
off Fortunes Mead .84/85 E6
Ridgeway W, Sid. DA15 .157 H5
Ridgewell Cl, N1
off Basire St 111 J1
SE26 . . . . .171 J4
Dagenham RM10 . . . . . .119 H1
Ridgmount Gdns, WC1 . . .9 H6
Ridgmount Pl, WC1 . . . . .17 H1
Ridgmount Rd, SW18 . . .149 E5
Ridgmount St, WC1 . . . . .17 H1
Ridgway, SW19 . . . . . . .166 A6
Ridgway, The, Sutt. SM2 .199 G7
Ridgway Gdns, SW19 . . .166 A7
Ridgway Pl, SW19 . . . . . .166 B6
Ridgwell Rd, E16 . . . . . .115 J5
Riding, The, NW11
off Golders Grn Rd . .72 C7
Riding Ho St, W1 . . . . . . .17 F2
Ridings, The, E11
off Malcolm Way 79 G5
W5 . . . . .105 J4
Sunbury-on-Thames
TW16 . . . . .178 A1
Surbiton KT5 . . . . .182 A5
Ridings Av, N21 . . . . .43 H4
Ridings Cl, N6
off Hornsey La Gdns . .74 C7
Ridley Av, W13 . . . . .124 E3
Ridley Cl, Bark. IG11 . . . . .99 J7
Ridley Rd, E7 . . . . .97 J4
E8 . . . . .94 C5
NW10 . . . . .107 G2
SW19 . . . . .166 E7
Bromley BR2 . . . . .191 F3
Welling DA16 . . . . .158 B1
Ridsdale Rd, SE20 . . . . .188 E1
Riefield Rd, SE9 . . . . . . .157 F4
Riesco Dr, Croy. CR0 . . .203 F6
Riffel Rd, NW2 . . . . .89 J5
Rifle Pl, SE11 . . . . .35 F5
Rifle St, E14 . . . . .114 B5
Rigault Rd, SW6 . . . . . . .148 B2
Rigby Cl, Croy. CR0 . . . .201 G3
Rigby La, Hayes UB3 . . .121 G2
Rigby Ms, Ilf. IG1
off Cranbrook Rd . .98/99 E2
Rigden St, E14 . . . . .114 B6
Rigeley Rd, NW10 . . . . . .107 G3
Rigg App, E10 . . . . .95 G1
Rigge Pl, SW4 . . . . .150 D4
Riggindale Rd, SW16 . . .168 D5
Riley Rd, SE1 . . . . .29 E5
Riley St, SW10 . . . . .31 E7
Rinaldo Rd, SW12 . . . . . .150 B7
Ring, The, W2 . . . . .15 G5
Ring Cl, Brom. BR1
off Garden Rd 173 H7
Ringcroft St, N7 . . . . .93 G5
Ringers Rd, Brom. BR1 . .191 G3
Ringford Rd, SW18 . . . . .148 C5
Ringlet Cl, E16 . . . . .115 H5
Ringlewell Cl, Enf. EN1
off Central Av 44/45 E2
Ringmer Av, SW6 . . . . . .148 B1
Ringmer Gdns, N19
off Sussex Way 92/93 E2
Ringmer Pl, N21 . . . . .44 A5
Ringmer Way, Brom.
BR1 . . . . .192 C5
Ringmore Ri, SE23 . . . . .153 E7
Ring Rd, W12 . . . . .107 J7
Ringslade Rd, N22 . . . . . .75 F2
Ringstead Rd, SE6 . . . . .154 B7
Sutton SM1 . . . . .199 G4
Ringway, N11 . . . . .58 C6
Southall UB2 . . . . .123 E5
Ringwold Cl, Beck.
BR3 . . . . .171 H7
Ringwood Av, N2 . . . . . . .73 J2
Croydon CR0 . . . . .187 E7

Ringwood Cl, Pnr. HA5 . . .66 C3
Ringwood Gdns, E14
off Inglewood Cl 134 A4
SW15 . . . . .165 G2
Ringwood Rd, E17 . . . . . .77 J6
Hampton (Hmptn.H.)
TW12 . . . . .161 G4
Ripley Cl, Brom. BR1
off Ringmer Way 192 C5
Croydon (New Adgtn.)
CR0 . . . . .204 C6
Ripley Gdns, SW14 . . . . .146 D3
Sutton SM1 . . . . .199 F4
Ripley Ms, E11
off Wadley Rd 78/79 E7
Ripley Rd, E16 . . . . .115 J6
Belvedere DA17 . . . . . .139 G4
Enfield EN2 . . . . .43 J1
Hampton TW12 . . . . . .161 G7
Ilford IG3 . . . . .99 J2
Ripley Vil, W5
off Castlebar Rd 105 F6
Riplington Ct, SW15
off Longwood Dr 147 G7
Ripon Cl, Nthlt. UB5 . . . . .85 G5
Ripon Gdns, Chess. KT9 .195 G5
Ilford IG1 . . . . .80 B6
Ripon Rd, N9 . . . . .44 E7
N17 . . . . .76 A3
SE18 . . . . .136 E6
Ripon Way, Borwd. WD6 . .38 C7
Rippersley Rd, Well.
DA16 . . . . .158 A1
Ripple Rd, Bark. IG11 . . . .99 F7
Dagenham RM9 . . . . . .118 B1
Rippleside Commercial Est,
Bark. IG11 . . . . .118 C2
Ripplevale Gro, N1 . . . . . .93 F7
Rippolson Rd, SE18 . . . . .137 J5
Risborough Dr, Wor.Pk.
KT4 . . . . .183 G7
Risborough St, SE1 . . . . .27 H3
Risdon St, SE16
off Renforth St 133 F2
Rise, The, E11 . . . . .79 G5
N13 . . . . .59 G4
NW7 . . . . .55 F6
NW10 . . . . .88 D4
Bexley DA5 . . . . .158 C7
Buckhurst Hill IG9 . . . . .48 A7
Edgware HA8 . . . . .54 B5
Greenford UB6 . . . . .86 D5
Risedale Rd, Bexh. DA7 .159 H3
Riseldine Rd, SE23 . . . . .153 H6
Rishill Sta, N1 . . . . .10 E1
Risinghill St, N1 . . . . .10 E1
Risingholme Cl, Har. HA3 .68 B1
Risingholme Rd, Har.
HA3 . . . . .68 B2
Risings, The, E17 . . . . . . .78 D4
Rising Sun Ct, EC1 . . . . . .19 H2
Risley Av, N17 . . . . .75 J1
Rita Rd, SW8 . . . . .34 B6
Ritches Rd, N15 . . . . .75 J5
Ritchie Rd, Croy. CR0 . . .189 E6
Ritchie St, N1 . . . . .11 F1
Ritchings Av, E17 . . . . . . .77 H4
Ritherdon Rd, SW17 . . . .168 A2
Ritson Rd, E8 . . . . .94 D6
Ritter St, SE18 . . . . .136 D6
Ritz Par, W5
off Connell Cres 105 J4
Rivaz Pl, E9 . . . . .95 F6
Rivenhall Gdns, E18 . . . . .79 F4
River Av, N13 . . . . .59 H3
Thames Ditton KT7 . . . .180 D7
River Bk, N21 . . . . .43 J7
East Molesey KT8 . . . . .180 B3
Thames Ditton KT7 . . . .180 C5
West Molesey KT8 . . . . .179 F3
Riverbank Way, Brent.
TW8 . . . . .125 F6
River Barge Cl, E14
off Stewart St 134 C2
River Brent Business Pk,
W7 . . . . .124 B3
River Cl, E11 . . . . .79 J6
Southall UB2 . . . . .123 J7
Surbiton KT6
off Catherine Rd 181 G5
Rivercourt Rd, W6 . . . . . .127 H4
River Crane Wk, Felt.
TW13 . . . . .160 D1
Hounslow TW4 . . . . . . .160 D1
River Crane Way, Felt. TW13
off Watermill Way 161 F2
Riverdale, SE13
off Lewisham High
St 154 C3
Riverdale Cl, Bark. IG11 . .118 B4

Riverdale Dr, SW18
off Strathville
Rd 166/167 E1
Riverdale Gdns, Twick.
TW1 . . . . .145 F6
Riverdale Rd, SE18 . . . . .137 J5
Bexley DA5 . . . . .159 F7
Erith DA8 . . . . .139 H5
Feltham TW13 . . . . .161 E4
Twickenham TW1 . . . . .145 F6
Riverdene, Edg. HA8 . . . . .54 C3
Riverdene Rd, Ilf. IG1 . . . . .98 D3
River Front, Enf. EN1 . . . . .44 A3
River Gdns, Cars. SM5 . .200 A2
Feltham TW14 . . . . .142 B5
River Gro Pk, Beck. BR3 .189 J1
Riverhead Cl, E17 . . . . . . .77 G2
River La, Rich. TW10 . . . .163 G1
Rivermead, E.Mol. KT8 . .179 J3
Rivermead Cl, Tedd.
TW11 . . . . .163 E5
Rivermead Ct, SW6 . . . . .148 C3
Rivermeads Av, Twick.
TW2 . . . . .161 G3
Rivernook Cl, Walt. KT12 .178 C5
River Pk Gdns, Brom.
BR2 . . . . .172 D7
River Pk Rd, N22 . . . . . . .75 F2
River Pl, N1 . . . . .93 J7
River Reach, Tedd. TW11 .163 F5
River Rd, Bark. IG11 . . . .117 H2
Buckhurst Hill IG9 . . . . . .64 B1
River Rd Business Pk, Bark.
IG11 . . . . .117 J3
Riverside, NW4 . . . . .71 H7
SE7 . . . . .135 H3
Twickenham TW1 . . . . .162 E1
Riverside, The, E.Mol.
KT8 . . . . .180 A3
Riverside Av, E.Mol. KT8 .180 A5
Riverside Business Cen,
SW18 . . . . .167 E1
Riverside Cl, E5 . . . . .95 F1
W7 . . . . .104 B4
Kingston upon Thames
KT1 . . . . .181 G4
Wallington SM6 . . . . . .200 B3
Riverside Ct, E4
off Chelwood Cl 46 B6
SW8 . . . . .33 J5
Riverside Dr, NW11 . . . . . .72 B6
W4 . . . . .126 D7
Mitcham CR4 . . . . .185 H5
Richmond TW10 . . . . . .162 E2
Riverside Gdns, N3 . . . . . .72 B3
W6 . . . . .127 H5
Enfield EN2 . . . . .43 J2
Wembley HA0 . . . . .105 H2
Riverside Ind Est, Bark.
IG11 . . . . .118 A3
Enfield EN3 . . . . .45 H6
Riverside Mans, E1
off Milk Yd 113 F7
Riverside Ms, Croy. CR0
off Wandle Rd . . .200/201 G3
Riverside Pl, Stai. (Stanw.)
TW19 . . . . .140 A6
Riverside Rd, E15 . . . . . .114 C2
N15 . . . . .76 D6
SW17 . . . . .167 E4
Sidcup DA14 . . . . .177 E3
Staines (Stanw.) TW19 .140 A5
Riverside Twr, SW6 . . . . .149 F2
Riverside Wk, Bex. DA5 . .158 C7
Isleworth TW7 . . . . . . .144 B3
Kingston upon Thames KT1
off High St 181 G2
Loughton IG10 . . . . .48 E6
West Wickham BR4
off The Alders 204 B1
Riverside W, SW18
off Smugglers
Way 148/149 E4
River St, EC1 . . . . .11 E3
River Ter, W6
off Crisp Rd 127 J5
Riverton Cl, W9 . . . . .108 C3
River Vw, Enf. EN2
off Chase Side 43 J3
Riverview Gdns, SW13 . .127 H6
Twickenham TW1 . . . . .162 C2
Riverview Gro, W4 . . . . . .126 B6
Riverview Pk, SE6 . . . . . .172 A2
Riverview Rd, W4 . . . . . .126 B6
Epsom KT19 . . . . .196 C4
River Wk, Walt. KT12 . . . .178 A6

Riverway, N13 . . . . .59 G5
River Way, Epsom KT19 .196 D5
Loughton IG10 . . . . .48 D6
Twickenham TW2 . . . . .161 H2
Riverwood La, Chis.
BR7 . . . . .193 G1
Rivington Av, Wdf.Grn.
IG8 . . . . .80 A2
Rivington Ct, NW10 . . . . .107 G1
Rivington Cres, NW7 . . . . .55 F7
Rivington Pl, EC2 . . . . . . .12 E4
Rivington St, EC2 . . . . . . .12 D4
Rivington Wk, E8
off Wilde Cl 112 D1
Rivulet Rd, N17 . . . . .59 J7
Rixon Ho, SE18
off Barnfield Rd . .136/137 E6
Rixon St, N7 . . . . .93 G3
Rixsen Rd, E12 . . . . .98 B5
Roach Rd, E3 . . . . .96 A7
Roads Pl, N19
off Hornsey Rd 92/93 E2
Roan St, SE10 . . . . .134 C6
Robarts Cl, Pnr. HA5
off Field End Rd 66 B5
Robb Rd, Stan. HA7 . . . . .52 D6
Robert Adam St, W1 . . . .16 B3
Roberta St, E2 . . . . .13 H3
Robert Cl, W9 . . . . .6 D6
Chigwell IG7 . . . . .65 J5
Robert Dashwood Way,
SE17 . . . . .35 J2
Robert Keen Cl, SE15
off Cicely Rd 152 D1
Robert Lowe Cl, SE14 . . .133 G7
Roberton Dr, Brom. BR1 .191 J1
Robert Owen Ho, SW6 . .148 A1
Robertsbridge Rd, Cars.
SM5 . . . . .199 F1
Roberts Cl, SE9 . . . . .175 G1
SE16 . . . . .133 G2
Sutton SM3 . . . . .198 A7
Thornton Heath CR7
off Kitchener Rd 188 A3
West Drayton UB7 . . . .120 B1
Roberts Ms, SW1 . . . . . . .24 B6
Robertson Rd, E15 . . . . . .114 C1
Robertson St, SW8 . . . . .150 B3
Robert's Pl, EC1 . . . . .11 F5
Roberts Rd, E17 . . . . .78 B1
NW7 . . . . .56 B6
Belvedere DA17 . . . . . .139 G5
Robert St, E16 . . . . .136 E1
NW1 . . . . .8 E4
SE18 . . . . .137 G4
WC2 . . . . .18 B6
Croydon CR0
off High St 201 J3
Robeson St, E3
off Ackroyd Dr 113 J5
Robeson Way, Borwd.
WD6 . . . . .38 C1
Robina Cl, Bexh. DA6 . . .158 D4
Robin Cl, NW7 . . . . .54 E3
Hampton TW12 . . . . . .161 E5
Robin Ct, SE16 . . . . .37 H1
Wallington SM6
off Carew Rd 200 C6
Robin Cres, E6 . . . . .116 A5
Robin Gro, N6 . . . . .92 A2
Brentford TW8 . . . . . . .125 F6
Harrow HA3 . . . . .69 J6
Robin Hill Dr, Chis. BR7 .174 B6
Robinhood Cl, Mitch.
CR4 . . . . .186 C3
Robin Hood Dr, Har. HA3 .52 C7
Robin Hood Gdns, E14
off Woolmore St 114 C7
Robin Hood La, E14 . . . . .114 C7
SW15 . . . . .164 E4
Bexleyheath DA6 . . . . .159 E5
Robinhood La, Mitch.
CR4 . . . . .186 C3
Robin Hood La, Sutt.
SM1 . . . . .198 D5
Robin Hood Rd, SW19 . .165 H5
Robin Hood Way,
SW15 . . . . .165 E4
SW20 . . . . .165 E4
Greenford UB6 . . . . .86 C6
Robinia Cl, SE20
off Sycamore Gro 188 D1
Ilford IG6 . . . . .65 H6
Robinia Cres, E10 . . . . . . .96 B2
Robins Ct, SE12 . . . . .173 J3
Robinscroft Ms, SE10
off Sparta St 154 B1
Robins Gro, W.Wick.
BR4 . . . . .205 G3
Robinson Cl, E11 . . . . .97 E3

Robinson Cres, Bushey
  (Bushey Hth.) WD23 . . . .51 J1
Robinson Rd, E2 . . . . .113 F2
  SW17 . . . . .167 H6
  Dagenham RM10 . . . . .101 G4
Robinsons Cl, W13 . . . . . .104 D5
Robinson St, SW3 . . . . . . .31 J5
Robinwood Pl, SW15 . . . . .164 D4
Robsart St, SW9 . . . . .151 F2
Robson Av, NW10 . . . . . . .107 G1
Robson Cl, E6
  off Linton Gdns 116 B6
  Enfield EN2 . . . . .43 H2
Robson Rd, SE27 . . . . . . .169 H3
Roch Av, Edg. HA8 . . . . . .69 J2
Rochdale Rd, E17 . . . . . . .78 A7
  SE2 . . . . .138 B5
Rochdale Way, SE8
  off Octavius St 134 A7
Rochelle Cl, SW11 . . . . . .149 G4
Rochelle St, E2 . . . . .13 F4
Rochemont Wk, E8
  off Pownall Rd 112 C1
Roche Rd, SW16 . . . . .187 F1
Rochester Av, E13 . . . . . .115 J1
  Bromley BR1 . . . . .191 H2
Rochester Cl, SW16 . . . . .169 E7
  Enfield EN1 . . . . .44 B1
  Sidcup DA15 . . . . .158 B6
Rochester Dr, Bex. DA5 . .159 F6
  Pinner HA5 . . . . .66 D5
Rochester Gdns, Croy.
  CRO 202 B3
  Ilford IG1 . . . . .80 C7
Rochester Ms, NW1 . . . . . .92 C7
Rochester Pl, NW1 . . . . . . .92 C6
Rochester Rd, NW1 . . . . . .92 C6
  Carshalton SM5 . . . . . .199 J4
Rochester Row, SW1 . . . . .33 G1
Rochester Sq, NW1 . . . . . .92 C7
Rochester St, SW1 . . . . . . .25 H6
Rochester Ter, NW1 . . . . . .92 C6
Rochester Wk, SE1 . . . . . . .28 B1
Rochester Way, SE3 . . . . .155 H1
  SE9 . . . . .156 C3
Rochester Way Relief Rd,
  SE3 . . . . .155 H1
  SE9 . . . . .156 B4
Roche Wk, Cars. SM5 . . .185 G6
Rochford Av, Loug. IG10 . .49 F3
  Romford RM6 . . . . .82 C5
Rochford Cl, E6
  off Boleyn Rd 116 A2
Rochford Grn, Loug.
  IG10 . . . . .49 F3
Rochford St, NW5 . . . . . . .91 J5
Rochford Wk, E8
  off Wilman Gro 94 D7
Rochford Way, Croy.
  CRO 186 E6
Rock Av, SW14
  off South Worple
  Way 146 D3
Rockbourne Rd, SE23 . . .171 G1
★ Rock Circus, W1 . . . . . . .17 H6
Rockells Pl, SE22 . . . . . . .153 E6
Rockford Av, Grnf. UB6 . .104 D2
Rock Gdns, Dag. RM10 . .101 H5
Rock Gro Way, SE16 . . . . .37 J1
Rockhall Rd, NW2 . . . . . . .90 A4
Rockhall Way, NW2
  off Midland Ter 90 A3
Rockhampton Cl, SE27
  off Rockhampton Rd .169 G4
Rockhampton Rd, SE27 .169 G4
  South Croydon CR2 . .202 B6
Rock Hill, SE26 . . . . .170 C4
Rockingham Cl, SW15 . . .147 F4
Rockingham Est, SE1 . . . .27 J6
Rockingham St, SE1 . . . . .27 J6
Rockland Rd, SW15 . . . . .148 B4
Rocklands Dr, Stan. HA7 . .69 E2
Rockley Rd, W14 . . . . . . .128 A2
Rockmount Rd, SE18 . . . .137 J5
  SE19 . . . . .170 A6
Rocks La, SW13 . . . . .147 G1
Rock St, N4 . . . . .93 G2
Rockware Av, Grnf. UB6 . .104 A1
Rockways, Barn. EN5 . . . . .39 F6
Rockwell Gdns, SE19 . . . .170 B5
Rockwell Rd, Dag. RM10 .101 H5
Rockwood Pl, W12 . . . . . .127 J2
Rocliffe St, N1 . . . . .11 H2
Rocombe Cres, SE23 . . . .153 F7
Rocque La, SE3 . . . . .155 F3
Rodborough Rd, NW11 . . .90 D1
Roden Ct, N6
  off Hornsey La 74 D7
Roden Gdns, Croy. CRO .188 B6
Rodenhurst Rd, SW4 . . . .150 C6

Roden St, N7 . . . . .93 F3
  Ilford IG1 . . . . .98 D3
Roderick Rd, NW3 . . . . . . .91 J4
Roding Av, Wdf.Grn. IG8 . .64 B6
Roding Gdns, Loug. IG10 .48 B6
Roding La, Buck.H. IG9 . . .64 B1
  Chigwell IG7 . . . . .64 D1
Roding La N, Wdf.Grn.
  IG8 . . . . .80 A2
Roding La S, Ilf. IG4 . . . . . .80 A4
  Woodford Green IG8 . . .80 A4
Roding Ms, E1 . . . . .29 J1
Roding Rd, E5 . . . . .95 G4
  E6 . . . . .116 E5
  Loughton IG10 . . . . .48 B5
Rodings, The, Wdf.Grn.
  IG8 . . . . .63 J6
Rodings Row, Barn. EN5
  off Leecroft Rd 40 A5
Roding Trd Est, Bark. IG11 .98 E7
Roding Vw, Buck.H. IG9 . . .64 A1
Rodmarton St, W1 . . . . . . .16 A2
Rodmell Cl, Hayes UB4 . .102 E4
Rodmell Slope, N12 . . . . . .56 C5
Rodmere St, SE10
  off Trafalgar Rd . .134/135 E5
Rodmill La, SW2 . . . . .151 E7
Rodney Cl, Croy. CRO 201 H1
  New Malden KT3 . . . . .182 E5
  Pinner HA5 . . . . .66 E7
Rodney Ct, W9 . . . . .6 D5
Rodney Gdns, Pnr. HA5 . . .66 B5
  West Wickham BR4 . . .205 G4
Rodney Pl, E17 . . . . .77 H2
  SE17 . . . . .36 A1
  SW19 . . . . .185 F1
Rodney Rd, E11 . . . . .79 H4
  SE17 . . . . .36 A1
  Mitcham CR4 . . . . .185 H2
  New Malden KT3 . . . . .182 E5
  Twickenham TW2 . . . . .143 G6
Rodney St, N1 . . . . .10 C1
Rodney Way, Rom. RM7 . .83 G1
Rodway Rd, SW15 . . . . . .147 G2
  Bromley BR1 . . . . .191 H1
Rodwell Cl, Ruis. HA4 . . . .84 C1
Rodwell Pl, Edg. HA8
  off Whitchurch La 54 A6
Rodwell Rd, SE22 . . . . . . .152 C6
Roebourne Way, E16 . . . .136 D2
Roebuck Cl, Felt. TW13 . .160 B4
Roebuck La, N17
  off High Rd 60 C6
  Buckhurst Hill IG9 . . . . .47 J3
Roedean Av, Enf. EN3 . . . .45 F1
Roedean Cl, Enf. EN3 . . . .45 F1
Roedean Cres, SW15 . . . .146 E6
Roe End, NW9 . . . . .70 C4
Roe Grn, NW9 . . . . .70 C5
ROEHAMPTON, SW15 . . .147 G5
Roehampton Cl, SW15 . . .147 G4
Roehampton Dr, Chis.
  BR7 . . . . .175 F6
Roehampton Gate,
  SW15 . . . . .146 E6
Roehampton High St,
  SW15 . . . . .147 H7
Roehampton La, SW15 . .147 G4
Roehampton Vale,
  SW15 . . . . .165 G3
Roe La, NW9 . . . . .70 B4
Roe Way, Wall. SM6 . . . . .201 E6
Roffey St, E14 . . . . .134 C2
Rogate Ho, E5
  off Muir Rd 94 D3
Roger Dowley Ct, E2 . . . .113 F2
Rogers Gdns, Dag.
  RM10 . . . . .101 G5
Rogers Rd, E16 . . . . .115 F6
  SW17 . . . . .167 G4
  Dagenham RM10 . . . . .101 G5
Roger St, WC1 . . . . .10 D6
Rogers Wk, N12
  off Brook Meadow .56/57 E3
Rojack Rd, SE23 . . . . .171 G1
Rokeby Gdns, Wdf.Grn.
  IG8 . . . . .79 G1
Rokeby Pl, SW20 . . . . . . .165 H7
Rokeby Rd, SE4 . . . . .153 J2
Rokeby St, E15 . . . . .114 E1
Rokesby Cl, Well.
  DA16 . . . . .157 G2
Rokesby Pl, Wem. HA0 . . .87 G5
Rokesly Av, N8 . . . . .74 E5
Roland Gdns, SW7 . . . . . .30 D3
  Feltham TW13 . . . . . . .161 E3
Roland Ms, E1
  off Stepney Grn 113 G5
Roland Rd, E17 . . . . .78 D4

Roland Way, SE17 . . . . . . .36 C4
  SW7 . . . . .30 D3
  Worcester Park KT4 . . .197 F2
Roles Gro, Rom. RM6 . . . .82 D4
Rolfe Cl, Barn. EN4 . . . . . .41 H4
Rolinsden Way, Kes.
  BR2 . . . . .206 A4
Rollesby Rd, Chess. KT9 .196 A6
Rollesby Way, SE28 . . . . .118 C7
Rolleston Av, Orp. BR5 . . .192 E6
Rolleston Cl, Orp. BR5 . . .193 E7
Rolleston Rd, S.Croy.
  CR2 . . . . .202 A7
Roll Gdns, Ilf. IG2 . . . . . . .80 D5
Rollins St, SE15 . . . . .133 F6
Rollit Cres, Houns. TW3 .143 G5
Rollit St, N7
  off Hornsey Rd 93 F5
Rolls Bldgs, EC4 . . . . .19 E3
Rollscourt Av, SE24 . . . . .151 J5
Rolls Pk Av, E4 . . . . .62 A6
Rolls Pk Rd, E4 . . . . .62 B5
Rolls Pas, EC4 . . . . .18 E3
Rolls Rd, SE1 . . . . .37 G3
Rolt St, SE8 . . . . .133 H6
Rolvenden Gdns, Brom.
  BR1 . . . . .174 A7
Rolvenden Pl, N17
  off Manor Rd 76 D1
★ Roman Bath, WC2
  off Strand La 18 D5
Roman Cl, W3
  off Avenue Gdns 126 B2
  Feltham TW14 . . . . . . .142 C5
Romanfield Rd, SW2 . . . .151 F7
Romanhurst Av, Brom.
  BR2 . . . . .191 E4
Romanhurst Gdns, Brom.
  BR2 . . . . .190 E4
Roman Ind Est, Croy.
  CRO 188 B7
Roman Ri, SE19 . . . . .170 A6
Roman Rd, E2 . . . . .113 F3
  E3 . . . . .113 H2
  E6 . . . . .116 B4
  N10 . . . . .58 B7
  NW2 . . . . .89 J3
  W4 . . . . .127 F4
  Ilford IG1 . . . . .99 E6
Roman Sq, SE28 . . . . . . .138 A1
Roman Way, N7 . . . . .93 F6
  SE15 off Clifton Way .133 F7
  Croydon CRO 201 H2
  Enfield EN1 . . . . .44 C5
Roman Way Ind Est, N1
  off Offord St 93 F7
Romany Gdns, E17
  off McEntee Av 77 H1
  Sutton SM3 . . . . .184 D7
Romany Ri, Orp. BR5 . . . .207 F3
Roma Read Cl, SW15
  off Bessborough Rd . .147 H7
Roma Rd, E17 . . . . .77 H3
Romberg Rd, SW17 . . . . .168 A3
Romborough Gdns,
  SE13 . . . . .154 C5
Romborough Way, SE13 .154 C5
Romero Cl, SW9
  off Stockwell Rd 151 F3
Romero Sq, SE3 . . . . .155 J4
Romeyn Rd, SW16 . . . . . .169 F3
Romford Rd, E7 . . . . .97 H5
  E12 . . . . .98 B4
  E15 . . . . .96 E7
Romford St, E1 . . . . .21 J2
Romilly Dr, Wat. WD19 . . .51 E4
Romilly Rd, N4 . . . . .93 H2
Romilly St, W1 . . . . .17 H5
Rommany Rd, SE27 . . . . .170 A4
Romney Cl, N17 . . . . .76 E1
  NW11 . . . . .91 F1
  SE14 off Kender St . . .133 F7
  Chessington KT9 . . . . .195 H4
  Harrow HA2 . . . . .67 G7
Romney Dr, Brom. BR1 . .174 A7
  Harrow HA2 . . . . .67 G7
Romney Gdns, Bexh.
  DA7 . . . . .159 F1
Romney Ms, W1 . . . . .16 B1
Romney Rd, SE10 . . . . . .134 C6
  New Malden KT3 . . . . .182 D6
Romney Row, NW2
  off Brent Ter 90 A2
Romney St, SW1 . . . . .25 J6
Romola Rd, SE24 . . . . . . .169 H1
Romsey Cl, Orp. BR6 . . . .207 E4
Romsey Gdns, Dag.
  RM9 . . . . .118 D1
Romsey Rd, W13 . . . . . . .104 D7
  Dagenham RM9 . . . . . .118 D1

Ronald Av, E15 . . . . .115 E3
Ronald Cl, Beck. BR3 . . . .189 J4
Ronald Ho, SE3
  off Cambert Way 155 J4
Ronalds Rd, N5 . . . . .93 G5
  Bromley BR1 . . . . .191 G1
Ronaldstone Rd, Sid.
  DA15 . . . . .157 H6
Ronald St, E1
  off Devonport St 113 F6
Rona Rd, NW3 . . . . .92 A4
Ronart St, Har. (Wldste.) HA3
  off Stuart Rd 68 C3
Rona Wk, N1
  off Clephane Rd 94 A6
Rondu Rd, NW2 . . . . .90 B5
Ronelean Rd, Surb. KT6 .195 J3
Ron Leighton Way, E6 . . .116 B1
Ronver Rd, SE12 . . . . . . .155 F7
Rood La, EC3 . . . . .20 D5
Rookby Ct, N21
  off Carpenter Gdns . .59 H2
Rook Cl, Wem. HA9 . . . . . .88 B3
Rookeries Cl, Felt. TW13 .160 B3
Rookery Cl, NW9 . . . . .71 F5
Rookery Cres, Dag.
  RM10 . . . . .101 H7
Rookery Dr, Chis. BR7 . . .192 D1
Rookery La, Brom. BR2 . .192 A4
Rookery Rd, SW4 . . . . . . .150 C4
Rookery Way, NW9 . . . . . .71 F5
Rooke Way, SE10 . . . . . . .135 F5
Rookfield Av, N10 . . . . . . .74 C4
Rookfield Cl, N10
  off Cranmore Way . . .74 C4
Rookstone Rd, SW17 . . . .167 J5
Rook Wk, E6
  off Allhallows Rd 116 B6
Rookwood Av, Loug.
  IG10 . . . . .49 F3
  New Malden KT3 . . . . .183 G4
  Wallington SM6 . . . . . .200 D4
Rookwood Gdns, E4
  off Whitehall Rd 63 F1
  Loughton IG10 . . . . .49 F3
Rookwood Ho, Bark. IG11
  off St. Marys 117 G2
Rookwood Rd, N16 . . . . . .76 C7
★ Roosevelt Mem, W1
  off Grosvenor Sq 16 C5
Rootes Dr, W10 . . . . .108 A4
Ropemaker Rd, SE16 . . . .133 H3
Ropemakers Flds, E14
  off Narrow St 113 J7
Ropemaker St, EC2 . . . . .20 B1
Roper La, SE1 . . . . .29 E4
Ropers Av, E4 . . . . .62 C5
Ropers Orchard, SW3 . . . .31 F6
Roper St, SE9 . . . . .156 C6
Ropers Wk, SW2
  off Brockwell Pk
  Gdns 151 G7
Roper Way, Mitch. CR4 . .186 A2
Ropery St, E3 . . . . .113 J4
Rope St, SE16 . . . . .133 H4
Rope Wk, Sun. TW16 . . . .178 C3
Rope Wk Gdns, E1 . . . . . .21 J4
Ropewalk Ms, E8
  off Middleton Rd 94 C7
Rope Yd Rails, SE18 . . . . .136 E3
Ropley St, E2 . . . . .13 H2
Rosa Alba Ms, N5
  off Kelross Rd 93 J4
Rosaline Rd, SW6 . . . . . .128 B7
Rosamond St, SE26 . . . . .170 E3
Rosamund Cl, S.Croy.
  CR2 . . . . .202 A4
Rosamun St, Sthl. UB2 . .123 D4
Rosary Cl, Houns. TW3 . .142 E2
Rosary Gdns, SW7 . . . . . .30 C2
Rosaville Rd, SW6 . . . . . .128 C7
Roscoe St, EC1 . . . . .12 A6
Roscoff Cl, Edg. HA8 . . . . .70 C1
Roseacre Cl, W13
  off Middlefielde . .104/105 E5
Roseacre Rd, Well. DA16 .158 B3
Rose All, SE1 . . . . .28 A1
Rose & Crown Ct, EC2 . . .19 J3
Rose & Crown Yd, SW1 . .25 G1
Roseary Cl, West Dr.
  UB7 . . . . .120 A4
Rose Av, E18 . . . . .79 H2
  Mitcham CR4 . . . . .185 J1
  Morden SM4 . . . . .185 F5
Rosebank, SE20 . . . . .170 E7
Rosebank Av, Wem. HA0 .86 C4
Rosebank Cl, N12 . . . . . . .57 H5
  Teddington TW11 . . . . .162 D6
Rosebank Gdns, E3 . . . . .113 J2
Rosebank Gro, E17 . . . . . .77 J3

Rosebank Rd, E17 . . . . . . .78 B6
W7 . . . . .124 B2
Rosebank Vil, E17 . . . . . . .78 A4
Rosebank Wk, NW1
  off Maiden La 92 D7
  SE18 off Woodhill 136 B4
Rosebank Way, W3 . . . . . .106 D6
Rose Bates Dr, NW9 . . . . . .70 A4
Roseberry Gdns, N4 . . . . . .75 H6
  Orpington BR6 . . . . . . .207 H3
Roseberry Pl, E8 . . . . . . .94 C6
Roseberry St, SE16 . . . . . .132 E4
Rosebery Av, E12 . . . . . . .98 B6
  EC1 . . . . .10 E6
  N17 . . . . .76 D2
  Harrow HA2 . . . . .85 F4
  New Malden KT3 . . . . .183 F2
  Sidcup DA15 . . . . .157 H7
  Thornton Heath CR7 . .187 J2
Rosebery Cl, Mord. SM4 .184 A6
Rosebery Ct, EC1
  off Rosebery Av 111 G4
Rosebery Gdns, N8 . . . . . .74 E5
  W13 . . . . .104 D6
  Sutton SM1 . . . . .199 E4
Rosebery Ms, N10 . . . . . .74 C2
  SW2 off Rosebery
    Rd 150/151 E6
Rosebery Rd, N9 . . . . . . .60 D3
  N10 . . . . .74 C2
  SW2 . . . . .150 E6
  Hounslow TW3 . . . . . .143 J5
  Kingston upon Thames
    KT1 . . . . .182 B2
  Sutton SM1 . . . . .198 C6
Rosebery Sq, EC1 . . . . . . .10 E6
  Kingston upon Thames
    KT1 . . . . .182 A2
Rosebine Av, Twick. TW2 .144 A7
Rosebury Rd, SW6 . . . . . .149 E2
Rosebury Sq, Wdf.Grn.
  IG8 . . . . .64 D7
Rose Ct, E1
  off Sandy's Row 112 B5
  SE26 . . . . .170 E2
  Pinner HA5
    off Nursery Rd 66 C3
Rosecourt Rd, Croy. CR0 .187 F6
Rosecroft Av, NW3 . . . . . .90 D3
Rosecroft Gdns, NW2 . . . .89 G3
  Twickenham TW2 . . . . .162 A1
Rosecroft Rd, Sthl. UB1 .103 G4
Rosecroft Wk, Pnr. HA5 . . .66 D5
  Wembley HA0 . . . . .87 G5
Rose Dale, Orp. BR6 . . . .207 E2
Rosedale Cl, SE2
  off Finchale Rd 138 B3
  W7 off Boston Rd 124 C2
  Stanmore HA7 . . . . .53 E6
Rosedale Ct, N5 . . . . .93 H4
Rosedale Gdns, Dag.
  RM9 . . . . .100 B7
Rosedale Pl, Croy. CR0 .189 G7
Rosedale Rd, E7 . . . . .97 J5
  Dagenham RM9 . . . . . .100 B7
  Epsom KT17 . . . . .197 G5
  Richmond TW9 . . . . . .145 H4
  Romford RM1 . . . . .83 J2
Rosedale Ter, W6
  off Dalling Rd 127 H3
Rosedene, NW6 . . . . . . .108 A1
Rosedene Av, SW16 . . . .169 F3
  Croydon CR0 . . . . .187 F7
  Greenford UB6 . . . . . . .103 G3
  Morden SM4 . . . . .184 D5
Rosedene Gdns, Ilf. IG2 . .80 D4
Rosedene Ter, E10 . . . . . .96 B2
Rosedew Rd, W6 . . . . . . .128 A6
Rose End, Wor.Pk. KT4 .198 A1
Rosefield Cl, Cars. SM5 .199 H5
Rosefield Gdns, E14 . . . .114 A7
Roseford Ct, W12 . . . . . . .128 A2
Rose Gdn Cl, Edg. HA8 . .53 H6
Rose Gdns, W5 . . . . .125 G3
  Feltham TW13 . . . . . . .160 A2
  Southall UB1 . . . . .103 G4
  Staines (Stanw.) TW19
    off Diamedes Av 140 A7
Rose Glen, NW9 . . . . . . .70 D4
Rosehart Ms, W11
  off Westbourne Gro . .108 D6
Rosehatch Av, Rom. RM6 .82 D3
Rosehead Rd, Houns.
  TW4 . . . . .143 F5
ROSEHILL, Sutt. SM1 . . .198 E1
Rosehill, Esher (Clay.)
  KT10 . . . . .194 D6
  Hampton TW12 . . . . . .179 G1
Rose Hill, Sutt. SM1 . . . .199 E3
Rosehill Av, Sutt. SM1 . .199 F1

Rosehill Gdns, Grnf. UB6 .86 C5
  Sutton SM1 . . . . .199 E2
Rosehill Pk W, Sutt.
  SM1 . . . . .199 F1
Rosehill Rd, SW18 . . . . . .149 F6
Roseland Cl, N17
  off Cavell Rd 60 A7
Rose La, Rom. RM6 . . . . . .82 D3
Rose Lawn, Bushey
  (Bushey Hth.) WD23 . .51 J1
Roseleigh Av, N5 . . . . . . .93 H4
Roseleigh Cl, Twick. TW1 .145 G6
Rosemary Av, N3 . . . . . . .73 E2
  N9 . . . . .60 E1
  Enfield EN2 . . . . .44 A1
  Hounslow TW4 . . . . . .142 D2
  West Molesey KT8 . . . .179 G3
Rosemary Cl, Croy. CR0 .186 E6
Rosemary Dr, E14 . . . . . .114 D6
  Ilford IG4 . . . . .80 A5
Rosemary Gdns, SW14
  off Rosemary La 146 C3
  Chessington KT9 . . . . .195 H4
  Dagenham RM8 . . . . . .101 F1
Rosemary La, SW14 . . . . .146 C3
Rosemary Rd, SE15 . . . . . .37 G7
  SW17 . . . . .167 F3
  Welling DA16 . . . . .157 J1
Rosemary St, N1
  off Shepperton Rd . . .112 A1
Rosemead, NW9 . . . . . . .71 F7
Rosemead Av, Mitch.
  CR4 . . . . .186 C2
  Wembley HA9 . . . . .87 H5
Rosemont Av, N12 . . . . . .57 F6
Rosemont Rd, NW3 . . . . . .91 F6
  W3 . . . . .106 B7
  New Malden KT3 . . . .182 C3
  Richmond TW10 . . . . .145 H6
  Wembley HA0 . . . . . . .105 H1
Rosemoor St, SW3 . . . . . .31 J2
Rosemount Cl, Wdf.Grn. IG8
  off Chapelmount Rd . .64 C6
Rosemount Dr, Brom.
  BR1 . . . . .192 C4
Rosemount Pt, SE23
  off Dacres Rd 171 G3
Rosemount Rd, W13 . . . .104 D6
Rosenau Cres, SW11 . . . .149 H1
Rosenau Rd, SW11 . . . . . .149 H1
Rosendale Rd, SE21 . . . .151 J7
  SE24 . . . . .151 J7
Roseneath Av, N21 . . . . . .59 H1
Roseneath Rd, SW11 . . . .150 A6
Roseneath Wk, Enf. EN1 .44 B4
Rosens Wk, Edg. HA8 . . . .54 B3
Rosenthal Rd, SE6 . . . . . .154 B6
Rosenthorpe Rd, SE15 . .153 G5
Rose Pk Cl, Hayes UB4 .102 C4
Rosepark Ct, Ilf. IG5 . . . . .80 C2
Roserton St, E14 . . . . . . .134 C2
Rosery, The, Croy. CR0 .189 G6
Roses, The, Wdf.Grn. IG8 .63 F7
Rose Sq, SW3 . . . . .31 F3
Rose St, WC2 . . . . .18 A5
  ★ Rose Thea, SE1
    off Park St 28 A1
Rosethorn Cl, SW12 . . . .150 C7
Rosetta Cl, SW8 . . . . .131 E7
Rosetti Ter, Dag. RM8
  off Marlborough Rd . .100 B4
Roseveare Rd, SE12 . . . .173 J4
Roseville Av, Houns.
  TW3 . . . . .143 G5
Roseville Rd, Hayes
  UB3 . . . . .122 A5
Rosevine Rd, SW20 . . . . .183 J1
Rose Wk, Surb. KT5 . . . .182 B5
  West Wickham BR4 . . .204 D2
Rose Way, SE12 . . . . .155 G5
Roseway, SE21 . . . . .152 A6
Rose Way, Edg. HA8 . . . . .54 C4
Rosewell Cl, SE20 . . . . . .170 E7
Rosewood, Esher KT10 .194 D2
Rosewood Av, Grnf. UB6 .86 D5
Rosewood Cl, Sid. DA14 .176 C3
Rosewood Ct, Brom.
  BR1 . . . . .191 J1
  Romford RM6 . . . . .82 C5
Rosewood Gdns, SE13
  off Lewisham Rd 154 C2
Rosewood Gro, Sutt.
  SM1 . . . . .199 F2
Rosewood Sq, W12
  off Primula St 107 G6
Rosewood Ter, SE20
  off Laurel Gro 171 F7
Rosher Cl, E15 . . . . .96 D7
Rosina St, E9 . . . . .95 G5
Roskell Rd, SW15 . . . . . .148 A3

Roslin Rd, W3 . . . . .126 B3
Roslin Way, Brom. BR1 .173 G5
Roslyn Cl, Mitch. CR4 . .185 G2
Roslyn Rd, N15 . . . . .76 A5
Rosmead Rd, W11 . . . . . .108 B7
Rosoman Pl, EC1 . . . . . . .11 F5
Rosoman St, EC1 . . . . . . .11 F4
Rossall Cres, NW10 . . . .105 J3
Ross Av, NW7 . . . . .56 B5
  Dagenham RM8 . . . . . .101 F2
Ross Cl, Har. HA3 . . . . . . .51 J7
  Hayes UB3 . . . . .121 G3
Ross Ct, SW15 . . . . .148 A7
Rossdale, Sutt. SM1 . . . .199 H5
Rossdale Dr, N9 . . . . .45 F6
  NW9 . . . . .88 C1
Rossdale Rd, SW15 . . . . .147 J4
Rosse Ms, SE3 . . . . .155 H1
Rossendale St, E5 . . . . . . .94 E2
Rossendale Way, NW1 . . . .92 C7
Rossetti Rd, SE16 . . . . . .132 E5
Rossignol Gdns, Cars.
  SM5 . . . . .200 A2
Rossindel Rd, Houns.
  TW3 . . . . .143 G5
Rossington St, E5 . . . . . . .94 D2
Rossiter Flds, Barn. EN5 . .40 B6
Rossiter Rd, SW12 . . . . . .168 B1
Rossland Cl, Bexh. DA6 .159 H5
Rosslyn Av, E4 . . . . .63 F2
  SW13 . . . . .147 E3
  Barnet EN4 . . . . .41 H6
  Dagenham RM8 . . . . . . .83 F7
  Feltham TW14 . . . . . . .142 A6
Rosslyn Cl, W.Wick. BR4 .205 F3
Rosslyn Cres, Har. HA1 . .68 C5
  Wembley HA9 . . . . .87 H4
Rosslyn Gdns, Wem. HA9
  off Rosslyn Cres 87 H3
Rosslyn Hill, NW3 . . . . . .91 G4
Rosslyn Ms, NW3
  off Rosslyn Hill 91 G4
Rosslyn Pk Ms, NW3
  off Lyndhurst Rd 91 G5
Rosslyn Rd, E17 . . . . .78 C4
  Barking IG11 . . . . .99 G7
  Twickenham TW1 . . . .145 F6
Rossmore Ct, NW1 . . . . . . .7 J5
Rossmore Rd, NW1 . . . . . .7 H6
Ross Par, Wall. SM6 . . . .200 B6
Ross Rd, SE25 . . . . .188 A3
  Twickenham TW2 . . . .161 H1
  Wallington SM6 . . . . . .200 C5
Ross Way, SE9 . . . . .156 B3
Rosswood Gdns, Wall.
  SM6 . . . . .200 C6
Rostella Rd, SW17 . . . . . .167 G4
Rostrevor Av, N15 . . . . . . .76 C6
Rostrevor Gdns, Hayes
  UB3 . . . . .121 H1
  Southall UB2 . . . . .122 E5
Rostrevor Ms, SW6 . . . . .148 C1
Rostrevor Rd, SW6 . . . . .148 C1
  SW19 . . . . .166 D5
Rotary St, SE1 . . . . .27 G5
Rothbury Gdns, Islw.
  TW7 . . . . .124 D7
Rothbury Rd, E9 . . . . .95 J7
Rothbury Wk, N17 . . . . . . .60 D7
Rotherfield Rd, Cars.
  SM5 . . . . .200 A4
Rotherfield St, N1 . . . . . . .93 J7
Rotherham Wk, SE1 . . . . .27 G2
Rotherhill Av, SW16 . . . .168 D6
ROTHERHITHE, SE16 . . .133 G3
  ★ Rotherhithe Heritage Mus,
    SE16 . . . . .133 H1
Rotherhithe New Rd,
  SE16 . . . . .37 J4
Rotherhithe Old Rd,
  SE16 . . . . .133 G4
Rotherhithe St, SE16 . .133 F2
Rotherhithe Tunnel, E1 .133 F1
Rotherhithe Tunnel App,
  E14 . . . . .113 H7
  SE16 . . . . .133 F2
Rothermere Rd, Croy.
  CR0 . . . . .201 F5
Rotherwick Hill, W5 . . . .105 J4
Rotherwick Rd, NW11 . .72 D7
Rotherwood Cl, SW20 .184 B1
Rotherwood Rd, SW15 .148 A3
Rothery St, N1
  off Gaskin St 111 H1
Rothery Ter, SW9 . . . . . .131 H7
Rothesay Av, SW20 . . . .184 B2
  Greenford UB6 . . . . . . .86 A6
  Richmond TW10 . . . . .146 B4
Rothesay Rd, SE25 . . . . .188 B4
Rothsay Rd, E7 . . . . .97 J6

Rothsay St, SE1 . . . . .28 D5
Rothsay Wk, E14
  off Charnwood Gdns .134 A4
Rothschild Rd, W4 . . . . .126 C4
Rothschild St, SE27 . . . .169 H4
Roth Wk, N7
  off Durham Rd 93 F3
Rothwell Gdns, Dag.
  RM9 . . . . .100 C7
Rothwell Rd, Dag. RM9 .118 C1
Rothwell St, NW1 . . . . . .109 J1
Rotten Row, SW1 . . . . . . .24 B3
  SW7 . . . . .23 G3
Rotterdam Dr, E14 . . . . .134 C3
Rouel Rd, SE16 . . . . .29 H6
Rougemont Av, Mord.
  SM4 . . . . .184 D6
Roundacre, SW19
  off Inner Pk Rd 166 A2
Roundaway Rd, Ilf. IG5 . .80 C2
Roundel Cl, SE4
  off Adelaide Av 153 J4
Round Gro, Croy. CR0 . .189 G7
Roundhay Cl, SE23 . . . . .171 G2
Round Hill, SE26 . . . . . . .171 F2
Roundhill Dr, Enf. EN2 . . .43 F4
Roundmead Av, Loug.
  IG10 . . . . .48 D3
Roundmead Cl, Loug.
  IG10 . . . . .48 D3
Roundshaw Cen, Wall. SM6
  off Meteor Way . . .200/201 E7
Roundtable Rd, Brom.
  BR1 . . . . .173 F3
Roundtree Rd, Wem.
  HA0 . . . . .86 E5
Roundway, The, N17 . . . .75 J1
  Esher (Clay.) KT10 . . .194 C5
Roundwood, Chis. BR7 .192 E2
Roundwood Av, Uxb.
  UB11 . . . . .121 F1
Roundwood Rd, NW10 . .89 F6
Rounton Rd, E3 . . . . .114 A4
Roupell Rd, SW2 . . . . . . .169 F1
Roupell St, SE1 . . . . .27 F2
Rousden St, NW1 . . . . . . .92 C7
Rouse Gdns, SE21 . . . . . .170 B4
Rous Rd, Buck.H. IG9 . . . .64 B1
Routemaster Cl, E13 . . . .115 H3
Routh Rd, SW18 . . . . . . .149 H7
Routh St, E6 . . . . .116 C5
Routledge Cl, N19 . . . . . .92 D1
Rover Av, Ilf. IG6 . . . . . . .65 J6
Rowallan Rd, SW6 . . . . . .128 B7
Rowan Av, E4 . . . . .61 J6
Rowan Cl, SW16 . . . . . . .186 C1
  W5 . . . . .125 H2
  Ilford IG1 . . . . .99 G5
  New Malden KT3 . . . .182 E2
  Stanmore HA7
    off Woodlands Dr . . .52 C6
  Wembley HA0 . . . . .86 B3
Rowan Cres, SW16 . . . . .186 C1
Rowan Dr, NW9 . . . . .71 G4
Rowan Gdns, Croy. CR0
  off Radcliffe Rd 202 C3
Rowan Rd, SW16 . . . . . . .186 C2
  W6 . . . . .128 A4
  Bexleyheath DA7 . . . . .159 E3
  Brentford TW8 . . . . . .125 E7
  West Drayton UB7 . . . .120 A4
Rowans, The, N13 . . . . . .59 H3
Rowans Way, Loug. IG10 .48 C4
Rowan Ter, SE20
  off Sycamore Gro 188 D1
  W6 off Bute Gdns 128 A4
Rowantree Cl, N21 . . . . . .60 A1
Rowantree Rd, N21 . . . . . .60 A1
  Enfield EN2 . . . . .43 H2
Rowan Wk, N2 . . . . .73 F6
  N19 off Bredgar Rd . . .92 C2
  W10 off Droop St 108 B4
  Barnet EN5
    off Station Rd 40/41 E5
  Bromley BR2 . . . . .206 C3
Rowan Way, Rom. RM6 . .82 C3
Rowanwood Av, Sid.
  DA15 . . . . .176 A1
Rowanwood Ms, Enf. EN2
  off Rowantree Rd 43 H2
Rowben Cl, N20 . . . . .56 E1
Rowberry Cl, SW6 . . . . . .127 J7
Rowcross St, SE1 . . . . . . .37 F3
Rowdell Rd, Nthlt. UB5 . .103 G1
Rowden Pk Gdns, E4
  off Rowden Rd 62 A6
Rowden Rd, E4 . . . . .62 A6
  Beckenham BR3 . . . . . .189 H1
  Epsom KT19 . . . . .196 B4
Rowditch La, SW11 . . . . .150 A2

Rowdon Av, NW10 . . . . . .89 H7
Rowdowns Rd, Dag.
  RM9 . . . . .119 F1
Rowe Gdns, Bark. IG11 . .117 J2
Rowe La, E9 . . . . .95 F5
Rowena Cres, SW11 . . . .149 H2
Rowe Wk, Har. HA2 . . . . .85 G3
Rowfant Rd, SW17 . . . . .168 A1
Rowhill Rd, E5 . . . . .95 E4
Rowington Cl, W2 . . . . . . .14 A1
Rowland Av, Har. HA3 . . . .69 F4
Rowland Ct, E16 . . . . . . .115 F4
Rowland Cres, Chig. IG7 . .65 H4
Rowland Gro, SE26
  off Dallas Rd 170/171 E3
Rowland Hill Av, N17 . . . .59 J7
Rowland Hill St, NW3 . . . .91 H5
Rowlands Av, Pnr. HA5 . . .51 G6
Rowlands Cl, N6
  off North Hill 74 A6
NW7 . . . . .55 G7
Rowlands Rd, Dag. RM8 .101 F2
Rowland Way, SW19 . . . .184/185 E1
Rowley Av, Sid. DA15 . . .158 B7
Rowley Cl, Wem. HA0 . . . .87 J7
Rowley Gdns, N4 . . . . . . .75 J7
ROWLEY GREEN, Barn. . .39 F4
Rowley Grn Rd, Barn. EN5 39 F5
Rowley Ind Pk, W3 . . . . .126 B3
Rowley La, Barn. EN5 . . . .39 F5
  Borehamwood WD6 . . . .38 D1
Rowley Rd, N15 . . . . .75 J5
Rowley Way, NW8 . . . . . .109 E1
Rowlheys Pl, West Dr.
  UB7 . . . . .120 B3
Rowlls Rd, Kings.T. KT1 .181 J3
Rowney Gdns, Dag.
  RM9 . . . . .100 C6
Rowney Rd, Dag. RM9 . .100 B6
Rowntree Clifford Cl, E13
  off Liddon Rd 115 H3
Rowntree Path, SE28
  off Booth Cl 118 B7
Rowntree Rd, Twick.
  TW2 . . . . .162 B1
Rowse Cl, E15 . . . . .96 C7
Rowsley Av, NW4 . . . . . . .71 J3
Rowstock Gdns, N7 . . . . .92 D5
Rowton Rd, SE18 . . . . . .137 F7
Roxborough Av, Har. HA1 .68 A7
  Isleworth TW7 . . . . . .124 C7
Roxborough Pk, Har. HA1 .68 B7
Roxborough Rd, Har.
  HA1 . . . . .68 A6
Roxbourne Cl, Nthlt. UB5 .84 D6
Roxburgh Rd, SE27 . . . .169 H5
Roxby Pl, SW6 . . . . .128 D6
ROXETH, Har. 86 A2
Roxeth Grn Av, Har. HA2 .85 H3
Roxeth Gro, Har. HA2 . . . .85 H4
Roxeth Hill, Har. HA2 . . . .86 A2
Roxley Rd, SE13 . . . . . . .154 B6
Roxton Gdns, Croy. CR0 .204 A5
Roxwell Rd, W12 . . . . . .127 G2
  Barking IG11 . . . . . . .118 A2
Roxwell Trd Pk, E10 . . . . .77 H7
Roxwell Way, Wdf.Grn.
  IG8 . . . . .63 J7
Roxy Av, Rom. RM6 . . . . .82 C7
★ Royal Academy of Arts,
  W1 . . . . .17 F6
★ Royal Academy of Dramatic
  Art (RADA), WC1 . . . . .17 H1
★ Royal Academy of Music,
  NW1 . . . . .8 C4
★ Royal Air Force Museums,
  NW9 (Hendon) 71 G2
★ Royal Albert Dock, E16 .116 C7
★ Royal Albert Hall,
  SW7 . . . . .22 E4
Royal Albert Roundabout, E16
  off Royal Albert Way .116 B7
Royal Albert Way, E16 . .116 A7
Royal Arc, W1 . . . . .17 F6
Royal Artillery Barracks, SE18
  off Repository Rd 136 D5
Royal Av, SW3 . . . . .31 J3
  Worcester Park KT4 . .197 G2
★ Royal Botanic Gardens,
  Kew, Rich. TW9 . . . . .125 H7
Royal Circ, SE27 . . . . . .169 G3
Royal Cl, N16
  off Manor Rd 94 B1
SE8 . . . . .133 J6
SW19
  off Queensmere Rd . .166 A2
  Ilford IG3 . . . . .82 A7
  Orpington BR6 . . . . . .206 E4
  Worcester Park KT4 . .196 E2

★ Royal Coll of Art,
  SW7 . . . . .22 D4
★ Royal Coll of Music,
  SW7 . . . . .22 E5
★ Royal Coll of Surgeons,
  WC2 . . . . .18 D3
Royal Ct, EC3
  off Cornhill 112 A6
SE16 . . . . .133 J3
★ Royal Courts of Justice,
  WC2 . . . . .18 D4
Royal Cres, W11 . . . . . .128 A1
  Ruislip HA4 . . . . .84 E4
Royal Cres Ms, W11
  off Queensdale Rd . . .128 A1
Royal Docks Rd, E6 . . . .117 E6
Royal Dr, N11 . . . . .58 A5
Royal Duchess Ms, SW12
  off Dinsmore Rd 150 B7
Royale Leisure Pk, W3 . .106 A4
Royal Ex, EC3 . . . . .20 C4
Royal Ex Av, EC3 . . . . . . .20 C4
Royal Ex Bldgs, EC3 . . . .20 C4
Royal Ex Steps, EC3
  off Cornhill 112 A6
★ Royal Festival Hall,
  SE1 . . . . .26 C1
Royal Gdns, W7 . . . . . . .124 D3
★ Royal Geographical Society,
  SW7 . . . . .23 E4
★ Royal Herbert Pavilions,
  SE18 . . . . .156 C1
Royal Hill, SE10 . . . . . . .134 C7
★ Royal Horticultural Society
  (Lawrence Hall), SW1 .25 H6
★ Royal Horticultural Society
  (Lindley Hall), SW1 . . .33 H1
★ Royal Hosp Chelsea & Mus,
  SW3 . . . . .32 B4
Royal Hosp Rd, SW3 . . . .31 J5
Royal London Est, The,
  N17 . . . . .60 E6
★ Royal Mews, The, SW1 24 E5
Royal Ms, The, SW1 . . . .25 E5
★ Royal Military Academy,
  SE18 . . . . .136 C7
Royal Mint Ct, EC3 . . . . .21 G6
Royal Mint Pl, E1 . . . . . . .21 G5
Royal Mint St, E1 . . . . . . .21 G5
Royal Mt Ct, Twick. TW2 .162 B3
★ Royal National Thea,
  SE1 . . . . .26 D1
Royal Naval Pl, SE14 . . .133 J7
Royal Oak Ct, N1
  off Pitfield St 112 B3
Royal Oak Pl, SE22 . . . .153 E6
Royal Oak Rd, E8 . . . . . .94 E6
  Bexleyheath DA6 . . . .159 F5
Royal Opera Arc, SW1 . . .25 H1
★ Royal Opera Ho, WC2 .18 B4
Royal Orchard Cl, SW18 .148 B7
Royal Par, SE3 . . . . .155 E2
  SW6 off Dawes Rd . . .128 B7
  W5 off Western Av . . .105 H3
  Chislehurst BR7 . . . . .175 F7
  Richmond TW9
    off Station App 146 A1
Royal Par Ms, SE3
  off Royal Par 155 F2
  Chislehurst BR7 . . . . .175 F7
Royal Pl, SE10 . . . . .134 C7
Royal Rd, E16 . . . . .116 A6
  SE17 . . . . .35 G5
  Sidcup DA14 . . . . . . .176 D3
  Teddington TW11 . . . .162 A5
Royal Route, Wem. HA9 . .87 J4
Royal St, SE1 . . . . .26 D5
Royalty Ms, W1 . . . . .17 H4
Royal Victoria Dock, E16 .115 H7
Royal Victoria Patriotic
  Building, SW18
    off Fitzhugh Gro 149 G6
Royal Victoria Pl, E16
  off Wesley Av 135 H1
Royal Victoria Sq, E16
  off Mace Gateway . . .115 H7
Royal Victor Pl, E3 . . . . .113 G2
Royal Wk, Wall. SM6
  off Prince Charles
    Way 200 B3
Roycraft Av, Bark. IG11 . .117 J2
Roycraft Cl, Bark. IG11 . .117 J2
Roycroft Cl, E18 . . . . .79 H1
  SW2 . . . . .169 G1
Roydene Rd, SE18 . . . . .137 H6
Roydon Cl, SW11
  off Reform St 149 J2
  Loughton IG10 . . . . . . .48 B7

Roydon St, SW11
  off Southolm St 150 B1
Roy Gdns, Ilf. IG2 . . . . . . .81 H4
Roy Gro, Hmptn. TW12 . .161 H6
Royle Cres, W13 . . . . . . .104 D4
Roy Sq, E14
  off Narrow St 113 H7
Royston Av, E4 . . . . .62 A5
  Sutton SM1 . . . . .199 G3
  Wallington SM6 . . . . .200 D4
Royston Cl, Houns. TW5 .142 B1
Royston Ct, SE24
  off Burbage Rd 151 J6
  Richmond TW9
    off Lichfield Rd 145 J1
  Surbiton KT6
    off Hook Ri N 196 A3
Royston Gdns, Ilf. IG1 . . . .80 A6
Royston Gro, Pnr. HA5 . . .51 F6
Royston Par, Ilf. IG1 . . . . .80 A6
Royston Pk Rd, Pnr. HA5 .51 F4
Royston Rd, SE20 . . . . . .189 G1
  Richmond TW10 . . . . .145 H5
Roystons, The, Surb.
  KT5 . . . . .182 B5
Royston St, E2 . . . . .113 F2
Rozel Ct, N1 . . . . .112 B1
Rozel Rd, SW4 . . . . .150 C2
Rubastic Rd, Sthl. UB2 . .122 B3
Rubens Rd, Nthlt. UB5 . .102 C2
Rubens St, SE6 . . . . .171 J2
Rubeus Pl, SW4
  off Dolman St . . .150/151 E4
Ruby Ms, E17
  off Ruby Rd 78 A3
Ruby Rd, E17 . . . . .78 A3
Ruby St, NW10
  off Fawood Av 88 D7
SE15 . . . . .132 E6
Ruby Triangle, SE15
  off Sandgate St .132/133 E6
Ruckholt Cl, E10 . . . . . . .96 B3
Ruckholt Rd, E10 . . . . . . .96 A4
Rucklidge Av, NW10 . . . .107 F2
Rudall Cres, NW3
  off Willoughby Rd 91 G4
Ruddington Cl, E5 . . . . . .95 H4
Ruddock Cl, Edg. HA8 . . .54 C7
Ruddstreet Cl, SE18 . . . .137 E4
Rudgwick Ter, NW8
  off St. Stephens Cl . .109 H1
Rudland Rd, Bexh. DA7 . .159 H3
Rudloe Rd, SW12 . . . . . .150 C7
Rudolf Pl, SW8 . . . . .34 B6
Rudolph Ct, SE22 . . . . . .152 D7
Rudolph Rd, E13 . . . . . . .115 F2
  NW6 . . . . .108 D2
Rudyard Gro, NW7 . . . . . .54 C6
Ruffetts, The, S.Croy.
  CR2 . . . . .203 E7
Ruffetts Cl, S.Croy. CR2 .202 E7
Ruffle Cl, West Dr. UB7 . .120 B2
Rufford Cl, Har. HA3 . . . . .68 D6
Rufford St, N1 . . . . .111 E1
Rufford Twr, W3 . . . . . . .126 B1
Rufus Cl, Ruis. HA4 . . . . .84 E3
Rufus St, N1 . . . . .12 D4
Rugby Av, N9 . . . . .60 C1
  Greenford UB6 . . . . . . .86 A6
  Wembley HA0 . . . . . . .87 E5
Rugby Cl, Har. HA1 . . . . . .68 B5
★ Rugby Football Union
  Twickenham, Twick.
  TW2 . . . . .144 B6
Rugby Gdns, Dag. RM9 . .100 C6
Rugby Rd, NW9 . . . . .70 B4
  W4 . . . . .126 E2
  Dagenham RM9 . . . . .100 B7
  Twickenham TW1 . . . .144 B6
Rugby St, WC1 . . . . .10 C6
Rugg St, E14 . . . . .114 A7
Ruislip Cl, Grnf. UB6 . . . .103 H4
RUISLIP MANOR, Ruis. . . .84 A2
Ruislip Rd, Grnf. UB6 . . .103 G3
  Northolt UB5 . . . . . . .102 D2
  Southall UB1 . . . . . . .103 G3
Ruislip Rd E, W7 . . . . . . .104 A4
  W13 . . . . .104 A4
  Greenford UB6 . . . . . .104 A4
Ruislip St, SW17 . . . . . . .167 J4
Rumbold Rd, SW6 . . . . . .129 E7
Rum Cl, E1 . . . . .113 F7
Rumsey Cl, Hmptn.
  TW12 . . . . .161 F6
Rumsey Ms, N4
  off Monsell Rd 93 H3
Rumsey Rd, SW9 . . . . . . .151 F3
Runbury Circle, NW9 . . . .88 D2
Runcorn Cl, N17 . . . . .76 E4
Runcorn Pl, W11 . . . . . . .108 B7

Rundell Cres, NW4 . . . . . .71 H5
Runes Cl, Mitch. CR4 . . .185 G4
Runnel Fld, Har. HA1 . . . .86 B3
Running Horse Yd, Brent.
  TW8
    off Pottery Rd 125 H6
Runnymede, SW19 . . . . .185 G1
Runnymede Cl, Twick.
  TW2 . . . . .143 H6
Runnymede Ct, Croy.
  CR0 . . . . .202 C2
Runnymede Cres, SW16 .186 D1
Runnymede Gdns, Grnf.
  UB6 . . . . .104 A2
  Twickenham TW2 . . . .143 H6
Runnymede Rd, Twick.
  TW2 . . . . .143 H6
Runway, The, Ruis. HA4 . .84 B5
Rupack St, SE16
  off St. Marychurch St .133 F2
Rupert Av, Wem. HA9 . . . .87 H5
Rupert Ct, W1 . . . . .17 H5
  West Molesey KT8
    off St. Peter's Rd . . .179 G4
Rupert Gdns, SW9 . . . . .151 H2
Rupert Rd, N19
  off Holloway Rd 92 D3
  NW6 . . . . .108 C2
  W4 . . . . .127 E3
Rupert St, W1 . . . . .17 H5
Rural Way, SW16 . . . . . .168 B7
Ruscoe Rd, E16 . . . . . . .115 F6
Ruscombe Way, Felt.
  TW14 . . . . .141 J7
Rush, The, SW19
  off Kingston Rd 184 C1
Rusham Rd, SW12 . . . . .149 J6
Rushbrook Cres, E17 . . . .77 J1
Rushbrook Rd, SE9 . . . . .175 F2
Rush Common Ms,
  SW2 . . . . .151 F7
Rushcroft Rd, E4 . . . . . . .62 A7
  SW2 . . . . .151 G4
Rushden Cl, SE19 . . . . . .170 A7
Rushdene, SE2 . . . . .138 D3
Rushdene Av, Barn. EN4 . .41 H7
Rushdene Cl, Nthlt. UB5 .102 C3
Rushdene Cres, Nthlt.
  UB5 . . . . .102 C2
Rushdene Rd, Pnr. HA5 . .66 D6
Rushden Gdns, NW7 . . . .55 J6
  Ilford IG5 . . . . .80 D3
Rushen Wk, Cars. SM5
  off Paisley Rd 199 G1
Rushett Cl, T.Ditt. KT7 . .194 E1
Rushett Rd, T.Ditt. KT7 . .180 E7
Rushey Cl, N.Mal. KT3 . .182 D4
Rushey Grn, SE6 . . . . . . .154 B7
Rushey Hill, Enf. EN2 . . . .43 F4
Rushey Mead, SE4 . . . . .154 A5
Rushford Rd, SE4 . . . . . .153 J6
RUSH GREEN, Rom. 83 J7
Rush Grn Gdns, Rom.
  RM7 . . . . .101 J1
Rush Grn Rd, Rom. RM7 .101 J1
Rushgrove Av, NW9 . . . . .71 F5
Rush Gro St, SE18 . . . . .136 C4
Rush Hill Ms, SW11
  off Rush Hill Rd 150 A3
Rush Hill Rd, SW11 . . . .150 A3
Rushley Cl, Kes. BR2 . . .206 A4
Rushmead, E2
  off Florida St 112/113 E3
  Richmond TW10 . . . . .163 E3
Rushmead Cl, Croy. CR0 .202 C4
Rushmere Ct, Wor.Pk. KT4
  off The Avenue 197 G2
Rushmere Ho, SW15
  off Fontley Way 165 G1
Rushmere Pl, SW19 . . . .166 A5
Rushmoor Cl, Pnr. HA5 . .66 B4
Rushmore Cl, Brom.
  BR1 . . . . .192 B3
Rushmore Cres, E5
  off Rushmore Rd 95 G4
Rushmore Rd, E5 . . . . . . .95 F4
Rusholme Av, Dag.
  RM10 . . . . .101 G3
Rusholme Gro, SE19 . . . .170 B5
Rusholme Rd, SW15 . . . .148 A6
Rushout Av, Har. HA3 . . . .68 E6
Rushton St, N1 . . . . .12 C1
Rushworth Av, NW4
  off Rushworth Gdns . . .71 G3
Rushworth Gdns, NW4 . . .71 G4
Rushworth St, SE1 . . . . . .27 H3
Rushy Meadow La, Cars.
  SM5 . . . . .199 H2
Ruskin Av, E12 . . . . .98 B6
  Feltham TW14 . . . . . .141 J6

Ruskin Av, Rich. TW9 ....126 A7
  Welling DA16 ......158 A3
Ruskin Cl, NW11 ......72 E6
Ruskin Dr, Orp. BR6 ...207 H3
  Welling DA16 ......158 A3
  Worcester Park KT4 ...197 H2
Ruskin Gdns, W5 ......105 G4
  Harrow HA3 ......69 J4
Ruskin Gro, Well. DA16 .158 A2
Ruskin Pk Ho, SE5 ...152 A3
Ruskin Rd, N17 ......76 C1
  Belvedere DA17 ...139 G4
  Carshalton SM5 ......199 J5
  Croydon CR0 ......201 H2
  Isleworth TW7 ......144 C3
  Southall UB1 ......102 E7
Ruskin Wk, N9
  off Durham Rd 60 D2
  SE24 ......151 J5
  Bromley BR2 ......192 C6
Ruskin Way, SW19 ...185 G1
Rusland Av, Orp. BR6 ...207 G3
Rusland Hts, Har. HA1
  off Rusland Pk Rd ...68 B4
Rusland Pk Rd, Har.
  HA1 ......68 B4
Rusper Cl, NW2 ......89 J3
  Stanmore HA7 ......53 F4
Rusper Rd, N22 ......75 J2
  Dagenham RM9 ...100 C6
Russell Av, N22 ......75 H2
Russell Cl, NW10 ......88 C7
  SE7 ......135 J7
  W4 ......127 F6
  Beckenham BR3 ...190 B3
  Bexleyheath DA7 ...159 G4
  Ruislip HA4 ......84 C2
Russell Ct, SW1 ......25 G2
Russell Dr, Stai. (Stanw.)
  TW19 ......140 A6
Russell Gdns, N20 ...57 H2
  NW11 ......72 B6
  W14 ......128 B3
  Richmond TW10 ...163 F2
  West Drayton UB7 ...120 D5
Russell Gdns Ms, W14 .128 B3
Russell Gro, NW7 ......54 E5
  SW9 ......131 G7
Russell Kerr Cl, W4
  off Burlington La ...126 C7
Russell La, N20 ......57 H2
Russell Mead, Har. (Har.Wld.)
  HA3 ......68 C1
Russell Par, NW11
  off Golders Grn Rd ...72 B6
Russell Pl, NW3
  off Aspern Gro 91 H5
  SE16 off Onega Gate .133 H3
Russell Rd, E4 ......61 J4
  E10 ......78 B6
  E16 ......115 G6
  E17 ......77 J3
  N8 ......74 D6
  N13 ......59 F6
  N15 ......76 B5
  N20 ......57 H2
  NW9 ......71 F6
  SW19 ......166 D7
  W14 ......128 B3
  Buckhurst Hill IG9 ...63 H1
  Mitcham CR4 ......185 H3
  Northolt UB5 ......85 J5
  Twickenham TW2 ...144 C6
  Walton-on-Thames
  KT12 ......178 A4
Russell's Footpath,
  SW16 ......169 E5
Russell Sq, WC1 ......10 A6
Russell St, WC2 ......18 B5
Russell Wk, Rich. TW10
  off Park Hill 145 J6
Russell Way, Sutt. SM1 .198 D5
Russet Cres, N7
  off Stock Orchard Cres .93 F5
Russet Dr, Croy. CR0 ...203 H1
Russets Cl, E4
  off Larkshall Rd 62 D4
Russett Way, SE13
  off Conington Rd ...154 B2
Russia Ct, EC2 ......20 A3
Russia Dock Rd, SE16 ..133 H1
Russia La, E2 ......113 F2
Russia Row, EC2 ......20 A4
Russia Wk, SE16 ......133 H2
Rusthall Av, W4 ......126 D4
Rusthall Cl, Croy. CR0 ..189 F6
Rustic Av, SW16 ......168 B7
Rustic Pl, Wem. HA0 ...87 G4
Rustic Wk, E16
  off Lambert Rd 115 H6

Rustington Wk, Mord.
  SM4 ......184 C7
Ruston Av, Surb. KT5 ...182 B7
Ruston Gdns, N14
  off Farm La 42 A6
Ruston Ms, W11
  off St. Marks Rd 108 B6
Ruston Rd, SE18 ......136 B3
Ruston St, E3 ......113 J1
Rust Sq, SE5 ......36 B7
Rutford Rd, SW16 ......168 E5
Ruth Cl, Stan. HA7 ......69 J4
Rutherford Cl, Borwd.
  WD6 ......38 C2
  Sutton SM2 ......199 G6
Rutherford St, SW1 ......33 H1
Rutherford Twr, Sthl.
  UB1 ......103 H6
Rutherford Way, Bushey
  (Bushey Hth.) WD23 ..52 A1
  Wembley HA9 ......88 A4
Rutherglen Rd, SE2 ......138 A6
Rutherwyke Cl, Epsom
  KT17 ......197 G6
Ruthin Cl, NW9 ......70 E6
Ruthin Rd, SE3 ......135 G6
Ruthven St, E9
  off Lauriston Rd 113 G1
Rutland Av, Sid. DA15 ..158 A7
Rutland Cl, SW14 ......146 C3
  SW19 off Rutland Rd ..167 H7
  Bexley DA5 ......176 D1
  Chessington KT9 ......195 J6
Rutland Ct, Enf. EN3 ...45 F5
Rutland Dr, Mord. SM4 .184 C6
  Richmond TW10 ......163 G1
Rutland Gdns, N4 ......75 H6
  SW7 ......23 H4
  W13 ......104 D5
  Croydon CR0 ......202 B4
  Dagenham RM8 ......100 C5
Rutland Gdns Ms, SW7 .23 H4
Rutland Gate, SW7 ......23 H4
  Belvedere DA17 ......139 H5
  Bromley BR2 ......191 F4
Rutland Gate Ms, SW7 .23 G4
Rutland Gro, W6 ......127 H5
Rutland Ms, NW8
  off Boundary Rd .108/109 E1
Rutland Ms E, SW7 ......23 G5
Rutland Ms S, SW7 ......23 G5
Rutland Ms W, SW7
  off Ennismore St 129 H3
Rutland Pk, NW2 ......89 J6
  SE6 ......171 J2
Rutland Pk Gdns, NW2
  off Rutland Pk 89 J6
Rutland Pk Mans, NW2
  off Walm La 89 J6
Rutland Pl, EC1 ......11 J4
  Bushey (Bushey Hth.) WD23
  off The Rutts 52 A1
Rutland Rd, E7 ......98 A7
  E9 ......113 F1
  E11 ......79 H5
  E17 ......78 A6
  SW19 ......167 H7
  Harrow HA1 ......67 J6
  Hayes UB3 ......121 G4
  Ilford IG1 ......99 E4
  Southall UB1 ......103 G5
  Twickenham TW2 ......162 A2
Rutland St, SW7 ......23 H5
Rutland Wk, SE6 ......171 J2
Rutley Cl, SE17 ......35 G5
Rutlish Rd, SW19 ......184 D1
Rutter Gdns, Mitch. CR4 .185 F4
Rutters Cl, West Dr. UB7 .120 D2
Rutts, The,
  (Bushey Hth.) WD23 ..52 A1
Rutts Ter, SE14 ......153 G1
Ruvigny Gdns, SW15 ...148 A3
Ruxley Cl, Epsom KT19 .196 B5
  Sidcup DA14 ......176 D6
Ruxley Cor Ind Est, Sid.
  DA14 ......176 D6
Ruxley Cres, Esher (Clay.)
  KT10 ......194 E6
Ruxley La, Epsom KT19 .196 B5
Ruxley Ms, Epsom KT19 .196 B5
Ruxley Ridge, Esher (Clay.)
  KT10 ......194 D7
Ryalls Ct, N20 ......57 J3
Ryan Cl, SE3 ......155 J4
  Ruislip HA4 ......84 B1
Ryan Dr, Brent. TW8 ...124 D6
Ryarsh Cres, Orp. BR6 .207 H4
Rycott Path, SE22
  off Lordship La 152 D7
Rycroft Way, N17 ......76 C3

Ryculff Sq, SE3 ......155 F2
Rydal Cl, NW4 ......72 B1
Rydal Cres, Grnf. UB6 ..105 E3
Rydal Dr, Bexh. DA7 ...159 G1
  West Wickham BR4 ...205 E2
Rydal Gdns, NW9 ......71 E5
  SW15 ......164 E5
  Hounslow TW3 ......143 H6
  Wembley HA9 ......87 F1
Rydal Rd, SW16 ......168 D4
Rydal Way, Enf. EN3 ...45 F6
  Ruislip HA4 ......84 C4
Ryde Ho, Twick. TW1 ...145 F6
Ryde Cl, SW1 ......25 G1
Ryder Ct, SW1 ......25 G1
Ryder Dr, SE16 ......132 E5
Ryder Ms, E9
  off Homerton High St .95 F5
Ryders Ter, NW8 ......6 C1
Ryder St, SW1 ......25 G1
Ryder Yd, SW1 ......25 G1
Ryde Vale Rd, SW12 ...168 B2
Rydons Cl, SE9 ......156 B3
Rydon St, N1
  off St. Paul St 111 J1
Rydston Cl, N7
  off Sutterton St 93 F7
Rye, The, N14 ......42 C7
Rye Cl, Bex. DA5 ......159 H6
Ryecotes Mead, SE21 ..170 B1
Ryecroft Av, Ilf. IG5 ...80 E2
  Twickenham TW2 ......143 H7
Ryecroft Cres, Barn. EN5 .39 H5
Ryecroft Rd, SE13 ......154 C5
  SW16 ......169 G6
  Orpington BR5 ......193 G6
Ryecroft St, SW6 ......148 E1
Ryedale, SE22 ......152 E6
Ryefield Cl, Nthwd. HA6
  off Ryefield Cres 66 A2
Ryefield Cres, Nthwd.HA6 .66 A2
Ryefield Par, Nthwd. HA6
  off Ryefield Cres 66 A2
Ryefield Path, SW15 ...165 G1
Ryefield Rd, SE19 ......169 J6
Ryegates, SE15
  off Caulfield Rd ..152/153 E2
Rye Hill Pk, SE15 ......153 F4
Ryelands Cres, SE12 ...155 J6
Rye La, SE15 ......152 D1
Rye Pas, SE15 ......152 D3
Rye Rd, SE15 ......153 G4
Rye Wk, SW15 ......148 A5
Rye Way, Edg. HA8
  off Canons Dr 53 J6
Ryfold Rd, SW19 ......166 D3
Ryhope Rd, N11 ......58 B4
Rylandes Rd, NW2 ......89 G3
Ryland Ho, Croy. CR0 ...201 J3
Ryland Rd, NW5 ......92 B6
Rylett Cres, W12 ......127 F3
Rylett Rd, W12 ......127 F2
Rylston Rd, N13 ......60 A3
  SW6 ......128 C6
Rymer Rd, Croy. CR0 ...188 B7
Rymer St, SE24 ......151 H6
Rymill St, E16 ......136 D1
Rysbrack St, SW3 ......23 J5
Rythe, Chess. KT9
  off Nigel Fisher Way .195 F7
Rythe Ct, T.Ditt. KT7 ...180 D7
Rythe Rd, Esher (Clay.)
  KT10 ......194 A5

S

★Saatchi Gall, NW8 ...109 E1
Sabbarton St, E16
  off Victoria Dock Rd ..115 F6
Sabella Ct, E3 ......113 J2
Sabine Rd, SW11 ......149 J3
Sable Cl, Houns. TW4 ..142 C3
Sable St, N1
  off Canonbury Rd 93 H7
Sach Rd, E5 ......95 E2
Sackville Av, Brom. BR2 .205 G1
Sackville Cl, Har. HA2 ..86 A3
Sackville Est, SW16 ...169 E3
Sackville Gdns, Ilf. IG1 ..98 C1
Sackville Rd, Sutt. SM2 .198 D7
Sackville St, W1 ......17 G6
Sackville Way, SE22
  off Dulwich Common .170 D1
Saddlers Cl, Barn. (Arkley)
  EN5 ......39 H5
  Borehamwood WD6
  off Farriers Way 38 D6
  Pinner HA5 ......51 G6

Saddlers Ms, SW8
  off Portland Gro 151 F1
  Kingston upon Thames
  KT1 ......181 F1
  Wembley HA0
  off The Boltons 86 C4
Saddlers Path, Borwd.
  WD6 ......38 D5
Saddlescombe Way, N12 .56 D5
Saddle Yd, W1 ......24 D1
Sadler Cl, Mitch. CR4 ..185 J2
Sadlers Ride, W.Mol.
  KT8 ......179 J2
★Sadler's Wells Thea,
  EC1 ......11 G3
Saffron Av, E14 ......114 D7
Saffron Cl, NW11 ......72 C5
  Croydon CR0 ......186 E6
Saffron Ct, Felt. TW14
  off Staines Rd 141 F7
Saffron Hill, EC1 ......11 F6
Saffron Rd, Rom. RM5 ..83 J2
Saffron St, EC1 ......11 F6
Saffron Way, Surb. KT6 .195 G1
Sage Cl, E6
  off Bradley Stone Rd .116 C5
Sage St, E1
  off Cable St 113 F7
Sage Way, WC1 ......10 C4
Saigasso Cl, E16
  off Royal Rd 116 A6
Sailmakers Ct, SW6
  off William Morris
  Way 149 F3
Sail St, SE11 ......34 D1
Sainfoin Rd, SW17 ......168 A2
Sainsbury Rd, SE19 ...170 B5
St. Agatha's Dr, Kings.T.
  KT2 ......163 J6
St. Agathas Gro, Cars.
  SM5 ......199 J1
St. Agnes Cl, E9
  off Gore Rd 113 F1
St. Agnes Pl, SE11 ......35 G6
St. Agnes Well, EC1
  off Old St 112 A4
St. Aidans Ct, W13
  off St. Aidans Rd .124/125 E2
  Barking IG11
  off Choats Rd 118 B3
St. Aidan's Rd, SE22 ...152 E6
St. Aidans Rd, W13 ...125 E2
St. Albans Av, E6 ......116 C3
St. Albans Av, W4 ......126 D4
St. Albans Av, Felt.
  TW13 ......160 D5
St. Albans Cl, NW11 ...90 D1
St. Albans Cres, N22 ...75 G1
St. Albans Cres, Wdf.Grn.
  IG8 ......63 G7
St. Alban's Gdns, Tedd.
  TW11 ......162 D5
St. Albans Gro, W8 ......22 B5
St. Alban's Gro, Cars.
  SM5 ......185 H7
St. Albans La, NW11
  off West Heath Dr 90 D1
St. Alban's Pl, N1 ......111 H1
St. Albans Rd, NW5 ...92 A3
  NW10 ......106 E1
  Barnet EN5 ......40 A1
  Ilford IG3 ......99 J1
St. Alban's Rd, Kings.T.
  KT2 ......163 H6
  Sutton SM1 ......198 C4
  Woodford Green IG8 ..63 G7
St. Albans St, SW1 ......17 H6
St. Albans Ter, W6
  off Margravine Rd 128 B6
St. Alban's Vil, NW5
  off Highgate Rd 92 A3
St. Alfege Pas, SE10 ...134 C6
St. Alfege Rd, SE7 ......136 A6
St. Alphage Gdns, EC2 ..20 A2
St. Alphage Highwalk, EC2
  off London Wall 112 A5
St. Alphage Wk, Edg.
  HA8 ......70 C2
St. Alphege Rd, N9 ......45 F7
St. Alphonsus Rd, SW4 .150 C4
St. Amunds Cl, SE6 ...172 A4
St. Andrews Av, Wem.
  HA0 ......86 D4
St. Andrew's Cl, N12 ...57 F4
St. Andrews Cl, NW2 ...89 H3
  SE16 off Ryder Dr .132/133 E5
  SE28 ......118 D6
St. Andrew's Cl, Islw.
  TW7 ......144 A1

St. Andrews Cl, Ruis.
HA4 . . . .**84** D2
Stanmore HA7 . . . .**69** F2
St. Andrew's Ct, SW18
off Waynflete St **167** F2
St. Andrews Dr, Stan.
HA7 . . . .**69** F1
St. Andrew's Gro, N16 . . .**94** A1
St. Andrew's Hill, EC4 . . .**19** H5
St. Andrew's Ms, N16 . . .**94** B1
St. Andrews Ms, SE3
off Mycenae Rd **135** G7
St. Andrews Pl, NW1 . . . . .**8** G5
St. Andrews Rd, E11 . . . .**78** E6
E13 . . . .**115** H3
E17 . . . .**77** G2
N9 . . . .**45** F7
NW9 . . . .**88** D1
NW10 . . . .**89** H6
NW11 . . . .**72** C6
W3 . . . .**107** E7
W7 off Church Rd **124** B2
W14 . . . .**128** B6
Carshalton SM5 . . . . .**199** H3
Croydon CR0
off Lower Coombe St .**201** J4
Enfield EN1 . . . .**44** A3
Ilford IG1 . . . .**80** C7
Sidcup DA14 . . . .**176** D3
St. Andrew's Rd, Surb.
KT6 . . . .**181** G6
St. Andrews Rd, Wat.
WD19 . . . .**50** D3
St. Andrews Sq, W11
off St. Marks Rd **108** B6
St. Andrew's Sq, Surb.
KT6 . . . .**181** G6
St. Andrews Twr, Sthl.
UB1 . . . .**103** J7
St. Andrew St, EC4 . . . . .**19** F4
St. Andrews Way, E3 . . .**114** B4
St. Anna Rd, Barn. EN5
off Sampson Av **40** A5
St. Annes Av, Stai. (Stanw.)
TW19 . . . .**140** A7
St. Anne's Cl, N6
off Highgate W Hill . . .**92** A3
Watford WD19 . . . .**50** C4
St. Anne's Ct, W1 . . . . . .**17** H4
St. Annes Gdns, NW10 . .**105** J3
St. Annes Pas, E14
off Newell St **113** J6
St. Annes Rd, E11 . . . . . .**96** D2
St. Anne's Rd, Wem.
HA0 . . . .**87** G5
St. Anne's Row, E14
off Commercial Rd . .**113** J6
St. Anne St, E14
off Commercial Rd . .**113** J6
St. Ann's, Bark. IG11 . . . .**117** F1
St. Ann's Cres, SW18 . . .**149** F6
St. Ann's Gdns, NW5
off Queen's Cres **92** A6
St. Ann's Hill, SW18 . . . .**149** E5
St. Ann's La, SW1 . . . . . .**25** J5
St. Ann's Pk Rd, SW18 . .**149** F6
St. Ann's Pas, SW13 . . . .**147** E3
St. Anns Rd, N9 . . . .**60** C2
St. Ann's Rd, N15 . . . . . .**75** H5
SW13 . . . .**147** F2
St. Anns Rd, W11 . . . . . .**108** A7
St. Ann's Rd, Bark. IG11
off Axe St **117** F1
Harrow HA1 . . . .**68** B6
St. Ann's Shop Cen, Har.
HA1 . . . .**68** B6
St. Ann's St, SW1 . . . . . .**25** J5
St. Ann's Ter, NW8 . . . . . .**7** F1
St. Anns Vil, W11 . . . . . .**128** A1
St. Anns Way, S.Croy.
CR2 . . . .**201** H6
St. Anselm's Pl, W1 . . . . .**16** D4
St. Anselms Rd, Hayes
UB3 . . . .**121** J2
St. Anthonys Av, Wdf.Grn.
IG8 . . . .**63** J6
St. Anthonys Cl, E1 . . . . .**29** H1
SW17 off College
Gdns **167** H2
St. Anthony's Way, Felt.
TW14 . . . .**141** J4
St. Antony's Rd, E7 . . . . .**97** H7
St. Arvans Cl, Croy. CR0 .**202** B3
St. Asaph Rd, SE4 . . . . .**153** G3
St. Aubyn's Av, SW19 . . .**166** C5
St. Aubyns Av, Houns.
TW3 . . . .**143** G5
St. Aubyns Cl, Orp. BR6 .**207** J3
St. Aubyns Gdns, Orp.
BR6 . . . .**207** J2

St. Aubyn's Rd, SE19 . . . .**170** C6
St. Audrey Av, Bexh.
DA7 . . . .**159** G2
St. Augustine's Av, W5 . .**105** H2
St. Augustines Av, Brom.
BR2 . . . .**192** B5
St. Augustine's Av, S.Croy.
CR2 . . . .**201** J6
St. Augustines Av, Wem.
HA9 . . . .**87** H3
St. Augustine's Path, N5 . .**93** H5
St. Augustines Rd, NW1 . .**92** D7
St. Augustine's Rd, Belv.
DA17 . . . .**139** F4
St. Austell Cl, Edg. HA8 . .**69** J2
St. Austell Rd, SE13 . . . .**154** C2
St. Awdry's Rd, Bark.
IG11 . . . .**99** G7
St. Awdry's Wk, Bark. IG11
off Station Rd **99** F7
St. Barnabas Cl, SE22
off East Dulwich Gro .**152** B5
Beckenham BR3 . . . . .**190** C2
St. Barnabas Ct, Har.
HA3 . . . .**67** J1
St. Barnabas Gdns, W.Mol.
KT8 . . . .**179** G5
St. Barnabas Rd, E17 . . . .**78** A6
Mitcham CR4 . . . .**168** A7
Sutton SM1 . . . .**199** G5
Woodford Green IG8 . . .**79** H1
St. Barnabas St, SW1 . . . .**32** C3
St. Barnabas Ter, E9 . . . . .**95** G5
St. Barnabas Vil, SW8 . . .**151** E1
St. Bartholomews Cl,
SE26 . . . .**171** F4
St. Bartholomew's Rd,
E6 . . . .**116** B1
★ St. Bartholomew-the-Great
Church, EC1
off Cloth Fair **19** H2
St. Benedict's Cl, SW17
off Church La **168** A5
St. Benet's Cl, SW17
off College Gdns **167** H2
St. Benet's Gro, Cars.
SM5 . . . .**185** F7
St. Benet's Pl, EC3 . . . . . .**20** C5
St. Bernards, Croy. CR0 .**202** B3
St. Bernard's Cl, SE27
off St. Gothard Rd . . .**170** A4
St. Bernard's Rd, E6 . . . .**116** A1
St. Blaise Av, Brom. BR1 .**191** H2
St. Botolph Row, EC3 . . . .**21** F4
St. Botolph St, EC3 . . . . . .**21** F4
St. Bride's Av, EC4
off New Br St **111** H6
★ St. Bride's Church & Crypt
Mus, EC4 . . . .**19** G4
St. Brides Cl, Erith DA18
off St. Katherines Rd .**138** D2
St. Bride's Pas, EC4 . . . . .**19** G4
★ St. Bride's Printing Lib, EC4
off Bride La **19** G4
St. Bride St, EC4 . . . .**19** G3
St. Catherines Cl, SW17
off College Gdns **167** H2
St. Catherines Dr, SE14
off Kitto Rd **153** G2
St. Catherine's Ms, SW3 . .**31** J1
St. Catherines Rd, E4 . . . .**62** A2
St. Catherines Twr, E10
off Kings Cl **78** B7
St. Cecilia's Cl, Sutt.
SM3 . . . .**198** B1
St. Chads Cl, Surb. KT6 . .**181** F7
St. Chad's Gdns, Rom.
RM6 . . . .**82** E7
St. Chad's Pl, WC1 . . . . . .**10** B3
St. Chad's Rd, Rom. RM6 .**82** E6
St. Chad's St, WC1 . . . . . .**10** B3
St. Charles Pl, W10
off Chesterton Rd . . .**108** B5
St. Charles Sq, W10 . . . .**108** B5
St. Christopher's Cl, Islw.
TW7 . . . .**144** B1
St. Christopher's Dr, Hayes
UB3 . . . .**102** B7
St. Christophers Gdns, Th.Hth.
CR7 . . . .**187** G3
St. Christophers Ms, Wall.
SM6 . . . .**200** C5
St. Christopher's Pl, W1 . .**16** C3
St. Clair Dr, Wor.Pk. KT4 .**197** H3
St. Clair Rd, E13 . . . .**115** H2
St. Clair's Rd, Croy. CR0 .**202** B2
St. Clare Business Pk, Hmptn.
TW12 . . . .**161** J6
St. Clare Cl, Ilf. IG5 . . . . . .**80** C2

St. Clare St, EC3 . . . .**21** F4
★ St. Clement Danes Church,
WC2 off Strand **18** D4
St. Clements Ct, EC4
off Clements La **112** A7
N7 off Arundel Sq **93** G6
St. Clements Hts, SE26 . .**170** D3
St. Clement's La, WC2 . . . .**18** D4
St. Clements St, N7 . . . . . .**93** G6
St. Cloud Rd, SE27 . . . . .**169** J4
St. Crispins Cl, NW3 . . . . .**91** H4
Southall UB1 . . . .**103** F6
St. Cross St, EC1 . . . .**19** F1
St. Cuthberts Gdns, Pnr. HA5
off Westfield Pk **51** F7
St. Cuthberts Rd, N13 . . . .**59** G6
NW2 . . . .**90** C6
St. Cyprian's St, SW17 . .**167** J4
St. Davids Cl, SE16
off Masters Dr . . .**132/133** E5
Wembley HA9 . . . .**88** C3
St. David's Ct, E17 . . . . . .**78** C2
St. Davids Dr, Edg.
HA8 . . . .**69** J1
St. Davids Ms, E3
off Morgan St **113** H3
St. Davids Pl, NW4 . . . . . .**71** H7
St. Davids Sq, E14 . . . . .**134** B5
St. Denis Rd, SE27 . . . . .**170** A4
St. Dionis Rd, SW6 . . . . .**148** C2
St. Donatts Rd, SE14 . . . .**153** J1
St. Dunstan's All, EC3 . . . .**20** D5
St. Dunstans Av, W3 . . . .**106** D7
St. Dunstans Cl, Hayes
UB3 . . . .**121** J4
St. Dunstan's Ct, EC4
off Fleet St **111** G6
St. Dunstans Gdns, W3
off St. Dunstans Av . .**106** D7
St. Dunstan's Hill, EC3 . . .**20** D6
Sutton SM1 . . . .**198** B5
St. Dunstan's La, EC3 . . . .**20** D6
Beckenham BR3 . . . . .**190** C6
St. Dunstan's Rd, E7 . . . . .**97** J6
W6 . . . .**128** A5
W7 . . . .**124** B2
Hounslow TW4 . . . . . .**142** C2
St. Edmunds Cl, NW8
off St. Edmunds Ter . .**109** J1
SW17 off College
Gdns **167** H2
Erith DA18
off St. Katherines Rd .**138** D2
St. Edmunds Dr, Stan.
HA7 . . . .**68** D1
St. Edmund's La, Twick.
TW2 . . . .**143** H7
St. Edmunds Rd, N9 . . . . .**44** D7
Ilford IG1 . . . .**80** C6
St. Edmunds Sq,
SW13 . . . .**127** J6
St. Edmunds Ter, NW8 . . . .**7** H1
St. Edwards Cl, NW11 . . . .**72** D6
St. Egberts Way, E4 . . . . .**62** C1
St. Elmo Rd, W12 . . . . . .**127** F1
St. Elmos Rd, SE16 . . . . .**133** H2
St. Erkenwald Ms, Bark. IG11
off St. Erkenwald Rd .**117** G1
St. Erkenwald Rd, Bark.
IG11 . . . .**117** G1
St. Ermin's Hill, SW1 . . . . .**25** H5
St. Ervans Rd, W10 . . . . .**108** B5
St. Fabian Twr, E4
off Iris Way **61** J6
St. Faiths Cl, Enf. EN2 . . . .**43** J1
St. Faith's Rd, SE21 . . . . .**169** H1
St. Fillans Rd, SE6 . . . . . .**172** C1
St. Francis Cl, Orp. BR5 . .**193** H6
Watford WD19 . . . .**50** B1
St. Francis Rd, SE22 . . . .**152** B4
St. Francis Way, Ilf. IG1 . . .**99** H4
St. Frideswides Ms, E14
off Lodore St **114** C6
St. Gabriel's Cl, E11 . . . . .**97** H2
St. Gabriels Rd, NW2 . . . .**90** A5
St. Georges Av, E7 . . . . . .**97** H7
N7 . . . .**92** D4
NW9 . . . .**70** C4
St. George's Av, W5 . . . .**125** G2
St. Georges Av, Sthl.
UB1 . . . .**103** F7
St. Georges Cen, Har. HA1
off St. Ann's Rd **68** B6
St. Georges Circ, SE1 . . . .**27** G5
St. Georges Cl, NW11 . . . .**72** C6
SE28 off Redbourne
Dr **118** D6

St. George's Cl, SW8
off Patmore Est **150** C1
St. Georges Cl, Wem.
HA0 . . . .**86** D3
St. Georges Ct, E6 . . . . .**116** C4
EC4 . . . .**19** G3
SW7 . . . .**22** C5
St. George's Dr, SW1 . . . .**33** F3
St. Georges Dr, Wat.
WD19 . . . .**50** E3
St. Georges Flds, W2 . . . .**15** H4
St. Georges Gdns, Surb. KT6
off Hamilton Av **196** B2
St. Georges Gro, SW17 . .**167** G3
St. Georges Gro Est,
SW17 . . . .**167** G3
St. Georges Ind Est, Kings.T.
KT2 off Richmond Rd .**163** G5
St. Georges La, EC3 . . . . .**20** D5
St. Georges Ms, NW1
off Regents Pk Rd **91** J7
St. Georges Pl, Twick. TW1
off Church St **162** D1
St. Georges Rd, E7 . . . . . .**97** H6
E10 . . . .**96** C3
N9 . . . .**60** D3
N13 . . . .**59** F3
NW11 . . . .**72** C6
SE1 . . . .**27** F5
St. George's Rd, SW19 . .**166** C6
St. Georges Rd, W4 . . . .**126** E2
W7 . . . .**124** C1
St. George's Rd, Beck.
BR3 . . . .**190** B1
St. Georges Rd, Brom.
BR1 . . . .**192** C2
Dagenham RM9 . . . . .**100** E5
St. George's Rd, Felt.
TW13 . . . .**160** D4
St. Georges Rd, Ilf. IG1 . . .**80** C7
St. George's Rd, Kings.T.
KT2 . . . .**164** A7
Mitcham CR4 . . . .**186** B3
Orpington BR5 . . . . . .**193** G6
St. Georges Rd, Rich.
TW9 . . . .**145** J3
St. George's Rd, Sid.
DA14 . . . .**176** D6
St. Georges Rd, Twick.
TW1 . . . .**145** E5
Wallington SM6 . . . . .**200** B5
St. Georges Rd W, Brom.
BR1 . . . .**192** B1
St. Georges Sq, E7 . . . . . .**97** H7
E14 off Narrow St . . .**113** H7
SE8 . . . .**133** J4
St. George's Sq, SW1 . . . .**33** H4
New Malden KT3
off High St **182/183** E3
St. George's Sq Ms, SW1 .**33** H4
St. Georges Ter, NW1
off Regents Pk Rd **91** J7
St. George St, W1 . . . .**17** E4
St. Georges Wk, Croy.
CR0 . . . .**201** J3
St. Georges Way, SE15 . . .**36** D6
St. George Wf, SW8 . . . . .**34** A4
St. Gerards Cl, SW4 . . . .**150** C5
St. German's Pl, SE3 . . . .**155** G1
St. Germans Rd, SE23 . . .**171** H1
St. Giles Av, Dag. RM10 .**101** H7
St. Giles Cl, Dag. RM10
off St. Giles Av **101** H7
Orpington BR6 . . . . . .**207** G5
St. Giles Ct, WC2
off St. Giles High
St **110/111** E6
St. Giles High St, WC2 . . .**17** J3
St. Giles Pas, WC2 . . . . . .**17** J4
St. Giles Rd, SE5 . . . . . .**132** B7
St. Gilles Ho, E2 . . . .**113** G2
St. Gothard Rd, SE27 . . . .**170** A4
St. Gregory Cl, Ruis. HA4 .**84** C4
St. Helena Rd, SE16 . . . .**133** G4
St. Helena St, WC1 . . . . . .**10** E4
St. Helens Cres, SW16
off St. Helens Rd **187** F1
St. Helens Gdns, W10 . . .**108** A6
St. Helens Pl, EC3 . . . . . .**20** D3
St. Helens Rd, SW16 . . . .**187** F1
St. Helen's Rd, W13
off Dane Rd **124/125** E1
St. Helens Rd, Erith
DA18 . . . .**138** D2
Ilford IG1 . . . .**80** C6
ST. HELIER, Cars. **185** G7
St. Helier Av, Mord.
SM4 . . . .**185** F7
St. Heliers Av, Houns.
TW3 . . . .**143** G5

St. Heliers Rd, E10 ......78 C6
St. Hildas Cl, NW6 ....90 A7
SW17 ....167 H2
St. Hilda's Rd, SW13 ..127 H6
St. Hughe's Cl, SW17
  off College Gdns 167 H2
St. Hughs Rd, SE20
  off Ridsdale Rd ..188/189 E1
St. James Av, N20 ......57 H3
W13 ....124 D1
Sutton SM1 ....198 D5
St. James Cl, N20 ......57 H3
SE18
  off Congleton Gro ...137 F5
Barnet EN4 ....41 G4
New Malden KT3 ....183 F5
Ruislip HA4 ....84 C2
St. James Gdns, Rom.
  (Lt.Hth.) RM6 ....82 B4
Wembley HA0 ....87 G7
St. James Gate, NW1
  off St. Paul's Cres ...92 D7
St. James Gro, SW11
  off Reform St 149 J2
St. James Ms, E14 ....134 C3
E17
  off St. James's Dr ...77 H5
St. James Rd, E15 .....97 F5
N9 off Queens Rd ...60/61 E2
Carshalton SM5 .....199 H3
Kingston upon Thames
KT1 ....181 H2
Mitcham CR4 ....168 A7
Surbiton KT6 ....181 G6
Sutton SM1 ....198 D5
ST. JAMES'S, SW1 .....25 G2
St. James's, SE14 ....153 H1
St. James's Av, E2 ....113 F2
Beckenham BR3 .....189 H3
Hampton (Hmptn.H.)
TW12 ....161 J5
St. James's Cl, SW17
  off St. James's Dr ..167 J2
St. James's Cotts, Rich. TW9
  off Paradise Rd 145 G5
St. James's Ct, SW1 ...25 G5
St. James's Cres, SW9 .151 G3
St. James's Dr, SW12 ..167 J1
SW17 ....167 J1
St. James's Gdns, W11 .128 B1
St. James's La, N10 ....74 B4
St. James's Mkt, SW1 ..17 H6
★ St. James's Palace,
  SW1 ....25 G3
St. James's Palace, SW1 .25 G3
★ St. James's Park, SW1 .25 H3
St. James's Pk, SW1 ...25 H3
Croydon CR0 ....187 J7
St. James's Pas, EC3 ...21 E4
St. James's Pl, SW1 ...25 G3
St. James's Rd, SE1 ....37 J3
SE16 ....29 J5
Croydon CR0 ....187 H7
Hampton (Hmptn.H.)
TW12 ....161 H5
St. James's Row, EC1 ...11 F5
St. James's Sq, SW1 ...25 G1
St. James's St, E17 ....77 H5
SW1 ....25 F1
St. James's Ter, NW8 ....7 J1
St. James's Ter Ms, NW8 .109 J1
St. James St, W6 ......127 J5
St. James's Wk, EC1 ...11 G5
St. James Way, Sid.
  DA14 ....177 J6
St. Joans Rd, N9 ......60 C1
St. John Fisher Rd, Erith
  DA18 ....138 D3
ST. JOHN'S, SE8 ......154 A4
St. John's Av, N11 .....57 J5
St. John's Av, NW10 ...107 F1
SW15 ....148 A5
St. John's Ch Rd, E9 ...95 F5
St. Johns Cl, N14
  off Chase Rd 42 C6
St. John's Cl, SW6
  off Dawes Rd 128 D7
Wembley HA9 ....87 H5
St. John's Cotts, SE20
  off Maple Rd 171 F7
St. Johns Cotts, Rich. TW9
  off Kew Foot Rd 145 H4
St. Johns Ct, Buck.H.
  IG9 ....63 H1
St. John's Ct, Islw. TW7 .144 C2
St. John's Cres, SW9 ..151 G3
St. Johns Dr, SW18 ...166 E1
St. John's Est, N1 .....12 C1
SE1 ....29 F3
St. John's Gdns, W11 ..108 C7

★ St. John's Gate & Mus
  of the Order of St. John,
  EC1 ....11 G6
St. Johns Gro, N19 .....92 C2
SW13 off Terrace Gdns .147 F2
Richmond TW9
  off Kew Foot Rd 145 H4
St. John's Hill, SW11 ..149 G4
St. John's Hill Gro,
  SW11 ....149 G4
St. John's La, EC1 .....11 G6
St. John's Ms, W11
  off Ledbury Rd 108 D6
St. Johns Par, Sid. DA14 .176 A4
St. John's Pk, SE3 ....135 F7
St. John's Pas, SW19
  off Ridgway Pl 166 B6
St. John's Path, EC1 ...11 G6
St. Johns Pathway, SE23
  off Devonshire Rd ..171 F1
St. John's Pl, EC1 .....11 G6
St. John's Rd, E4 ......62 B3
E6 off Ron Leighton
  Way 116 B1
St. Johns Rd, E16 .....115 G6
St. John's Rd, E17 .....78 B2
N15 ....76 B6
St. Johns Rd, NW11 ....72 C6
St. John's Rd, SE20 ...171 F7
SW11 ....149 H4
SW19 ....166 B7
Barking IG11 ....117 H1
Carshalton SM5 .....199 H3
St. Johns Rd, Croy. CR0
  off Sylverdale Rd ...201 H3
East Molesey KT8 ...180 A4
St. John's Rd, Felt.
TW13 ....161 E4
Harrow HA1 ....68 C6
St. Johns Rd, Ilf. IG2 ...81 G7
St. John's Rd, Islw. TW7 .144 B2
Kingston upon Thames
KT1 ....181 F2
St. Johns Rd, Loug. IG10 .48 C2
New Malden KT3 ....182 C3
St. John's Rd, Orp. BR5 .193 G6
Richmond TW9 ......145 H4
St. Johns Rd, Sid. DA14 .176 B4
Southall UB2 ....122 E3
Sutton SM1 ....198 D2
St. John's Rd, Well.
DA16 ....158 B3
Wembley HA9 ....87 G4
St. John's Sq, EC1 .....11 G6
St. Johns Ter, E7 ......97 H6
SE18 ....137 F6
SW15
  off Kingston Vale ..164 D4
W10 off Harrow Rd ..108 A4
St. John St, EC1 ......11 H6
St. Johns Vale, SE8 ...154 A2
St. Johns Vil, N19 .....92 D2
St. John's Vil, W8 .....22 B6
St. Johns Way, N19 ....92 D1
ST. JOHN'S WOOD, NW8 ..6 E3
St. John's Wd Ct, NW8 ...7 F4
St. John's Wd High St,
  NW8 ....7 F2
St. John's Wd Pk, NW8 .109 G1
St. John's Wd Rd, NW8 ...6 E5
St. John's Wd Ter, NW8 ...7 G1
St. Josephs Cl, W10
  off Bevington Rd ...108 B5
St. Joseph's Cl, Orp.
BR6 ....207 J4
St. Joseph's Ct, SE7 ..135 H6
St. Josephs Dr, Sthl.
UB1 ....123 E1
St. Joseph's Gro, NW4 ..71 H4
St. Josephs Rd, N9 ....45 E7
St. Josephs St, SW8
  off Battersea Pk Rd .150 B1
St. Joseph's Vale, SE3 .154 D2
St. Jude's Rd, E2 .....113 E2
St. Jude St, N16 ......94 B5
St. Julian's Cl, SW16 ..169 G4
St. Julian's Fm Rd, SE27 .169 G4
St. Julian's Rd, NW6 ...90 C7
★ St. Katharine's Dock,
  E1 ....21 G6
St. Katharines Prec, NW1 ..8 D1
St. Katharine's Way, E1 ..29 G1
St. Katherines Rd, Erith
  DA18 ....138 D2
St. Katherine's Row, EC3 .21 E4
St. Katherine's Wk, W11
  off Freston Rd 108 A7
St. Keverne Rd, SE9 ...174 B4
★ St. Kilda Rd, W13 ...124 D1
Orpington BR6 ......207 J1

St. Kilda's Rd, N16 ....94 A1
Harrow HA1 ....68 B6
St. Kitts Ter, SE19 ....170 B5
St. Laurence Cl, NW6 ..108 A1
St. Lawrence Cl, Edg.
HA8 ....53 J7
St. Lawrence Dr, Pnr.
HA5 ....66 B6
★ St. Lawrence Jewry Church,
  EC2 off Gresham St ...20 A3
St. Lawrence St, E14 ..134 C1
St. Lawrence Ter, W10 .108 B5
St. Lawrence Way,
  SW9 ....151 G1
St. Leonards Av, E4 ....62 D6
Harrow HA3 ....69 F4
St. Leonard's Cl, Well. DA16
  off Hook La 158 A3
St. Leonards Ct, N1 ....12 A3
St. Leonard's Gdns, Houns.
TW5 ....122 E7
St. Leonards Gdns, Ilf.
IG1 ....99 F5
St. Leonards Ri, Orp.
BR6 ....207 H4
St. Leonards Rd, E14 ..114 B5
NW10 ....106 D4
St. Leonard's Rd, SW14 .146 B3
St. Leonards Rd, W13 ..105 F7
Croydon CR0 ....201 H3
Esher (Clay.) KT10 ...194 C6
St. Leonard's Rd, Surb.
KT6 ....181 G5
St. Leonards Rd, T.Ditt.
KT7 ....180 D6
St. Leonards Sq, NW5 ..92 A6
St. Leonard's Sq, Surb. KT6
  off St. Leonard's Rd .181 G5
St. Leonards St, E3 ...114 B3
St. Leonard's Ter, SW3 ..31 J4
St. Leonards Wk, SW16 .169 F7
St. Loo Av, SW3 ....31 H5
St. Louis Rd, SE27 ....169 J4
St. Loy's Rd, N17 ......76 B2
St. Lucia Dr, E15 .....115 F1
ST. LUKE'S, EC1 ....12 A5
St. Luke's Av, SW4 ...150 D4
Ilford IG1 ....99 E5
St. Lukes Cl, EC1
  off Old St 111 J4
St. Luke's Cl, SE25 ...189 E6
St. Luke's Est, EC1 ....12 B4
St. Lukes Ms, W11
  off Basing St 108 C6
St. Lukes Pas, Kings.T.
KT2 ....181 J1
St. Lukes Rd, W11 ....108 C5
St. Lukes Sq, E16 ....115 F6
St. Luke's St, SW3 .....31 G3
St. Luke's Yd, W9 ....108 C2
St. Malo Av, N9 ....61 F3
ST. MARGARETS, Twick. .144 D5
St. Margarets, Bark. IG11 .117 G1
St. Margarets Av, N15 ...75 H4
N20 ....57 F2
Harrow HA2 ....85 J3
Sidcup DA15 ....175 E3
St. Margaret's Av, Sutt.
SM3 ....198 B3
St. Margaret's Ct, SE1 ..28 A2
St. Margarets Cres,
  SW15 ....147 H5
St. Margaret's Dr, Twick.
TW1 ....144 E5
St. Margarets Gro, E11 ..97 F3
SE18 ....137 F6
St. Margarets Gro, Twick.
TW1 ....144 D6
St. Margarets La, W8 ...22 A6
St. Margarets Pas, SE13
  off Church Ter ..154/155 E3
St. Margarets Path,
  SE18 ....137 F5
St. Margarets Rd, E12 ...97 J2
St. Margaret's Rd, N17 ..76 B3
NW10 ....107 J3
St. Margarets Rd, SE4 ..153 J4
W7 ....124 B2
Edgware HA8 ....54 B5
Isleworth TW7 ......144 E4
Twickenham TW1 ...144 E4
St. Margarets Rd, SE4
  off Adelaide Av 153 J4
St. Margaret's St, SW1 ..26 A4
St. Margaret's Ter, SE18 .137 F5
St. Marks Cl, SE10
  off Ashburnham Rd .134 C7
SW6 off Ackmar Rd .148 D1
W11 off Lancaster Rd .108 B6
St. Mark's Cl, Barn. EN5 .40 E3

St. Marks Cl, Har. HA1
  off Nightingale Av ..68/69 E7
St. Marks Cres, NW1 ...110 A1
St. Mark's Gate, E9
  off Cadogan Ter 95 J7
St. Mark's Gro, SW10 ...30 B7
St. Mark's Hill, Surb.
KT6 ....181 H6
St. Mark's Pl, SW19
  off Wimbledon
  Hill Rd 166 C6
St. Marks Pl, W11 .....108 B6
St. Marks Ri, E8 ......94 C5
St. Marks Rd, SE25
  off Coventry Rd 188 D4
St. Mark's Rd, W5
  off The Common 125 H1
St. Marks Rd, W7 .....124 B2
W10 ....108 A6
W11 ....108 B6
Bromley BR2 ....191 H3
Enfield EN1 ....44 C6
Mitcham CR4 ....185 J2
St. Mark's Rd, Tedd.
TW11 ....163 E7
St. Marks Sq, NW1 ....110 A1
St. Mark St, E1 ....21 G4
★ St. Martin-in-the-Fields
  Church, WC2
  off Trafalgar Sq 18 A6
St. Martins Av, E6 ....116 A2
St. Martins Cl, NW1 ...110 C1
Enfield EN1 ....44 E1
Erith DA18
  off St. Helens Rd ...138 D2
St. Martin's Cl, Wat. WD19
  off Muirfield Rd 50 C4
West Drayton UB7
  off St. Martin's Rd ..120 A3
St. Martin's Ct, WC2
  off St. Martin's La ..110 D7
St. Martins Est, SW2 ..169 G1
St. Martin's La, WC2 ...18 A5
St. Martins La, Beck.
BR3 ....190 B5
St. Martin's-le-Grand,
  EC1 ....19 J3
St. Martins Ms, WC2 ...18 A6
St. Martins Pl, WC2 ...18 A6
St. Martins Rd, N9 ....60 E2
St. Martin's Rd, SW9 ..151 F2
West Drayton UB7 ..120 A3
St. Martin's St, WC2 ...17 J6
St. Martins Way, SW17 .167 F3
St. Mary Abbots Pl, W8 .128 C3
St. Mary Abbots Ter,
  W14 ....128 C3
★ St. Mary at Hill, EC3 ..20 D6
★ St. Mary at Hill Church, EC3
  off Lovat La 20 D6
St. Mary Av, Wall. SM6 .200 A3
St. Mary Axe, EC3 ....20 D4
St. Marychurch St, SE16 .133 F2
★ St. Mary-le-Bow Church,
  EC2 ....20 A4
St. Mary Rd, E17 .....78 A4
St. Marys, Bark. IG11 ..117 G1
St. Marys App, E12 ....98 C5
St. Marys Av, E11 .....79 H6
St. Mary's Av, N3 .....72 B2
Bromley BR2 ....191 E3
Staines (Stanw.) TW19 .140 A7
Teddington TW11 ...162 C6
St. Mary's Av Cen, Sthl.
UB2 ....123 H4
St. Mary's Av N, Sthl.
UB2 ....123 H4
St. Mary's Av S, Sthl.
UB2 ....123 H4
St. Mary's Cl, N17
  off Kemble Rd 76 C1
St. Marys Cl, Chess. KT9 .195 J7
Epsom KT17 ....197 G7
St. Mary's Cl, Stai. (Stanw.)
TW19 ....140 A7
Sunbury-on-Thames TW16
  off Green Way 178 A4
St. Marys Cl, E6 ......116 C4
St. Mary's Cl, SE7 ....136 A7
W5
  off St. Mary's Rd ...125 G2
St. Mary's Cres, NW4 ...71 H3
St. Marys Cres, Islw.
TW7 ....124 A7
St. Mary's Cres, Stai. (Stanw.)
TW19 ....140 A7
St. Marys Dr, Felt.
TW14 ....141 F7
St. Mary's Gdns, SE11 ...35 F1
St. Mary's Gate, W8 ...22 A6

342   St. M–Sal

St. Marys Grn, N2
  off Thomas More Way .73 F3
St. Mary's Gro, N1 . . . . . .93 H6
  SW13 . . . . .147 H3
  W4 . . . . .126 B6
  Richmond TW9 . . . . . .145 J4
St. Marys Mans, W2 . . . . .14 E1
St. Mary's Ms, NW6
  off Priory Rd 90/91 E7
  Richmond TW10 . . . . .163 F2
St. Marys Path, N1 . . . . .111 H1
St. Mary's PI, SE9
  off Eltham High St . . .156 D6
  W5 off St. Mary's Rd . .125 G2
  W8 . . . . .22 B6
St. Marys Rd, E10 . . . . . .96 C3
  E13 . . . . .115 H2
  N8 off High St 74/75 E4
  N9 . . . . .61 F1
St. Mary's Rd, NW10 . . . .107 E1
St. Mary's Rd, NW11 . . . . .72 B7
St. Mary's Rd, SE15 . . . .153 F1
  SE25 . . . . .188 B3
  SW19 (Wimbledon) . . .166 B5
  W5 . . . . .125 G2
  Barnet EN4 . . . . .41 J7
  Bexley DA5 . . . . .177 J1
St. Marys Rd, E.Mol.
  KT8 . . . . .180 A5
  Ilford IG1 . . . . .99 F2
  Surbiton KT6 . . . . . . .181 G6
  Surbiton (Long Dit.)
  KT6 . . . . .181 F7
St. Mary's Rd, Wor.Pk.
  KT4 . . . . .197 E2
St. Marys Sq, W2 . . . . . .14 E1
St. Mary's Sq, W5
  off St. Mary's Rd 125 G2
St. Marys Ter, W2 . . . . . .14 E1
St. Mary's Twr, EC1
  off Fortune St 111 J4
St. Mary St, SE18 . . . . .136 C4
St. Marys Vw, Har. HA3 . .69 F5
St. Mary's Wk, SE11 . . . .35 F1
St. Mary's Way, Chig. IG7 .64 D5
St. Matthew's Av, Surb.
  KT6 . . . . .195 H1
St. Matthew's Dr, Brom.
  BR1 . . . . .192 C3
St. Matthew's Rd, SW2 .151 F4
St. Matthews Rd, W5
  off The Common 125 H1
St. Matthew's Row, E2 . .13 H4
St. Matthias CI, NW9 . . . .71 F5
St. Maur Rd, SW6 . . . . .148 C1
St. Mellion CI, SE28
  off Redbourne Dr 118 D6
St. Merryn CI, SE18 . . . .137 G7
St. Michaels Av, Pnr.
  HA9 . . . . .88 A6
St. Michael's CI, E16
  off Fulmer Rd 116 A5
St. Michael's CI, N3 . . . . .72 C2
St. Michaels CI, N12 . . . .57 H5
  Bromley BR1 . . . . . . .192 B3
  Erith DA18
  off St. Helens Rd 138 D2
  Worcester Park KT4 . . .197 F4
St. Michaels Cres, Pnr.
  HA5 . . . . .67 E6
St. Michaels Gdns, W10
  off St. Lawrence Ter . .108 B5
St. Michaels Rd, NW2 . . .89 J4
St. Michael's Rd, SW9 . .151 F2
St. Michaels Rd, Croy.
  CRO 201 J4
  Wallington SM6 . . . . .200 C6
  Welling DA16 . . . . . . .158 B3
St. Michaels St, W2 . . . . .15 F3
St. Michaels Ter, N22 . . . .75 E2
  off Poultry 112 A6
St. Mildred's Ct, EC2
  off Poultry 112 A6
St. Mildreds Rd, SE12 . .155 E7
St. Nicholas Glebe,
  SW17 . . . . .168 A6
St. Nicholas Rd, SE18 . . .137 J5
  Sutton SM1 . . . . .199 E5
  Thames Ditton KT7 . . .180 C6
St. Nicholas St, SE8
  off Lucas St 154 A1
St. Nicholas Way, Sutt.
  SM1 . . . . .198 E4
St. Nicolas La, Chis. BR7 .192 B1
St. Ninian's Ct, N20 . . . . .57 J3
St. Norbert Grn, SE4 . . .153 H4
St. Norbert Rd, SE4 . . . .153 H4
St. Olaf's Rd, SW6 . . . . .128 B7

St. Olaves Ct, EC2 . . . . . .20 B4
St. Olave's Est, SE1 . . . . .29 E3
St. Olaves Gdns, SE11 . . .34 E1
St. Olaves Rd, E6 . . . . . .116 D1
St. Olave's Wk, SW16 . . .186 C2
St. Olav's Sq, SE16 . . . .133 F3
St. Oswald's PI, SE11 . . . .34 C4
St. Oswald's Rd, SW16 . .187 H1
St. Oswulf St, SW1 . . . . . .33 J2
St. Patrick's Ct, Wdf.Grn.
  IG8 . . . . .63 E7
St. Paul's All, EC4
  off St. Paul's Chyd . . .111 H6
St. Paul's Av, NW2 . . . . . .89 H6
  SE16 . . . . .133 G1
St. Pauls Av, Har. HA3 . . .69 J5
★ St. Paul's Cathedral,
  EC4 . . . . .19 J4
St. Paul's Chyd, EC4 . . . .19 H4
St. Paul's CI, SE7 . . . . . .136 A5
  W5 . . . . .125 J2
  Carshalton SM5 . . . . .199 H1
St. Pauls CI, Chess.
  KT9 . . . . .195 G4
  Hayes UB3 . . . . .121 G5
St. Paul's CI, Houns.
  TW3 . . . . .143 E2
St. Paul's Ct, W14
  off Colet Gdns 128 A4
St. Pauls Ctyd, SE8
  off Deptford High St . .134 A7
St. Pauls Cray Rd, Chis.
  BR7 . . . . .193 G1
St. Paul's Cres, NW1 . . . .92 D7
St. Pauls Dr, E15 . . . . . . .96 D5
St. Paul's Ms, NW1
  off St. Paul's Cres 92 D7
St. Paul's PI, N1 . . . . .94 A6
St. Pauls Ri, N13 . . . . . . .59 H6
St. Paul's Rd, N1 . . . . . . .93 H6
  N17 . . . . .60 D7
  Barking IG11 . . . . . . .117 F1
  Brentford TW8 . . . . . .125 G6
  Erith DA8 . . . . .139 J7
  Richmond TW9 . . . . . .145 J3
  Thornton Heath CR7 . .187 J3
St. Paul's Shrubbery, N1 . .94 A6
St. Pauls Sq, Brom. BR2 .191 G2
St. Paul's Ter, SE17 . . . . .35 H5
St. Pauls Twr, E10 . . . . . .78 B7
St. Paul St, N1 . . . . .111 J1
St. Pauls Wk, Kings.T. KT2
  off Alexandra Rd 164 A7
St. Pauls Way, E3 . . . . . .113 J5
  E14 . . . . .113 J5
St. Paul's Way, N3 . . . . . .56 E7
St. Pauls Wd Hill, Orp.
  BR5 . . . . .193 H2
St. Peter's All, EC3 . . . . .20 C4
St. Peter's Av, E2 . . . . . .13 J2
  E17 . . . . .78 E4
St. Peters Av, N18 . . . . . .60 D4
St. Petersburgh Ms, W2 . .14 A5
St. Petersburgh PI, W2 . . .14 A5
St. Peter's CI, E2 . . . . . . .13 J2
St. Peters CI, SW17
  off College Gdns 167 H2
St. Peter's CI, Barn. EN5 . .39 H5
St. Peters CI, Bushey
  (Bushey Hth.) WD23 . .52 A1
  Chislehurst BR7 . . . . .175 G7
  Ilford IG2 . . . . .81 H4
St. Peter's CI, Ruis. HA4 . .84 D2
St. Peter's Ct, NW4 . . . . .71 J5
St. Peters Ct, SE3
  off Eltham Rd 155 F4
  SE4 off Wickham Rd . .153 J2
  West Molesey KT8 . . . .179 G4
St. Peter's Gdns, SE27 . .169 G3
St. Peter's Gro, W6 . . . .127 G4
St. Peter's PI, W9 . . . . . . .6 A6
St. Peters Rd, N9 . . . . . . .61 F1
St. Peter's Rd, W6 . . . . .127 G5
  Croydon CRO 202 A4
St. Peters Rd, Kings.T.
  KT1 . . . . .182 A2
  Southall UB1 . . . . . . .103 G5
  Twickenham TW1 . . . .145 E5
St. Peter's Rd, W.Mol.
  KT8 . . . . .179 G4
  W6 . . . . .127 G5
St. Peters St, N1 . . . . . . .111 H1
St. Peter's St, S.Croy.
  CR2 . . . . .202 A5
St. Peters Ter, SW6 . . . .128 B7
St. Peter's Vil, W6 . . . . .127 G4
St. Peter's Way, N1 . . . . .94 B7

St. Peters Way, W5 . . . .105 G5
  Hayes UB3 . . . . .121 G5
St. Philip's Av, Wor.Pk.
  KT4 . . . . .197 H2
St. Philips Gate, Wor.Pk.
  KT4 . . . . .197 H2
St. Philip Sq, SW8 . . . . .150 B2
St. Philip's Rd, E8 . . . . . .94 D6
St. Philips Rd, Surb. KT6 .181 G6
St. Philip St, SW8 . . . . .150 B2
St. Philip's Way, N1
  off Linton St 111 J1
St. Quentin Ho, SW18
  off Fitzhugh Gro 149 G6
St. Quentin Rd, Well.
  DA16 . . . . .157 J3
St. Quintin Av, W10 . . . .107 J5
St. Quintin Gdns, W10 . .107 J5
St. Quintin Rd, E13 . . . .115 H2
St. Raphael's Way, NW10 .88 C5
St. Regis CI, N10 . . . . . . .74 B2
St. Ronans Cres, Wdf.Grn.
  IG8 . . . . .63 G7
St. Rule St, SW8 . . . . . .150 C2
St. Saviour's Est, SE1 . . .29 F5
St. Saviour's Rd, SW2 . .151 F5
St. Saviours Rd, Croy.
  CRO 187 J6
Saints CI, SE27
  off Wolfington Rd 169 H4
Saints Dr, E7 . . . . .98 A5
St. Silas PI, NW5 . . . . . .92 A6
St. Silas St Est, NW5 . . . .92 A6
St. Simon's Av, SW15 . . .147 J5
St. Stephens Av, E17 . . . .78 C5
  W12 . . . . .127 H2
  W13 . . . . .104 E6
St. Stephens CI, E17 . . . .78 B5
  NW8 . . . . .109 H1
  Southall UB1 . . . . . . .103 G5
St. Stephens Cres, W2 . .108 D6
  Thornton Heath CR7 . .187 G3
St. Stephens Gdn Est, W2
  off Shrewsbury Rd . . .108 D6
St. Stephens Gdns, SW15
  off Manfred Rd 148 C5
  W2 . . . . .108 D6
  Twickenham TW1 . . . .145 F6
St. Stephens Gro, SE13 .154 C3
St. Stephens Ms, W2
  off Chepstow Rd 108 D5
St. Stephen's Par, E7
  off Green St 97 J7
St. Stephen's Pas, Twick. TW1
  off Richmond Rd 145 F6
St. Stephen's Rd, E3 . . . .113 J2
St. Stephens Rd, E6 . . . . .97 J7
St. Stephen's Rd, E17
  off Grove Rd 78 B5
St. Stephens Rd, W13 . .105 E6
St. Stephens Rd, Barn.
  EN5 . . . . .40 A5
St. Stephens Rd, Houns.
  TW3 . . . . .143 G6
St. Stephen's Rd, West Dr.
  UB7 . . . . .120 A1
St. Stephens Row, EC4 . . .20 B4
St. Stephens Ter, SW8 . .131 F7
St. Stephen's Wk, SW7 . .30 C1
St. Swithin's La, EC4 . . . .20 B5
St. Swithun's Rd, SE13 . .154 D5
St. Theresa's Rd, Felt.
  TW14 . . . . .141 J4
St. Thomas' CI, Surb.
  KT6 . . . . .195 J1
St. Thomas Ct, Bex. DA5 .159 G7
St. Thomas Dr, Orp. BR5 .207 F1
St. Thomas' Dr, Pnr.
  HA5 . . . . .66 E7
St. Thomas Gdns, Ilf. IG1 .99 F6
St. Thomas Ho, NW1
  off Maiden La 92 D7
St. Thomas Rd, E16 . . . .115 G6
  N14 . . . . .42 D7
St. Thomas' Rd, W4 . . . .126 C6
St. Thomas Rd, Belv.
  DA17 . . . . .139 J2
St. Thomas' Gdns, NW5
  off Queen's Cres 92 A6
St. Thomas's PI, E9 . . . . .95 F7
St. Thomas's Rd, N4 . . . .93 G2
  NW10 . . . . .107 E1
St. Thomas's Sq, E9 . . . . .95 F7
St. Thomas's St, SE1 . . . .28 B2
St. Thomas's Way, SW6 .128 C7
St. Timothy's Ms, Brom. BR1
  off Wharton Rd 191 H1
St. Ursula Gro, Pnr. HA5 .66 D5
St. Ursula Rd, Sthl. UB1 .103 G6
St. Vincent CI, SE27 . . . .169 H5

St. Vincent Rd, Twick.
  TW2 . . . . .143 J6
St. Vincent St, W1 . . . . . .16 C2
St. Wilfrids CI, Barn. EN4 .41 H5
St. Wilfrids Rd, Barn. EN4 .41 G5
St. Winefride's Av, E12 . . .98 C5
St. Winifred CI, Chig.
  IG7 . . . . .65 F5
St. Winifred's Rd, Tedd.
  TW11 . . . . .163 E6
Sala Ho, SE3
  off Pinto Way 155 H4
Salamanca PI, SE1 . . . . . .34 C2
Salamanca St, SE1 . . . . . .34 B2
Salamander CI, Kings.T.
  KT2 . . . . .163 F5
Salcombe Dr, Mord.
  SM4 . . . . .198 A1
  Romford RM6 . . . . . . .83 F6
Salcombe Gdns, NW7 . . .55 J6
Salcombe Pk, Loug. IG10 .48 A5
Salcombe Rd, E17 . . . . . .77 J7
  N16 . . . . .94 B5
Salcombe Way, Ruis. HA4 .84 A2
Salcott Rd, SW11 . . . . . .149 H5
  Croydon CRO 201 E3
Salehurst CI, Har. HA3 . . .69 H5
Salehurst Rd, SE4 . . . . .153 J6
Salem PI, Croy. CRO 201 J3
Salem Rd, W2 . . . . .14 B5
Sale PI, W2 . . . . .15 G2
Sale St, E2 . . . . .13 H5
Salford Rd, SW2 . . . . . .168 D1
Salhouse CI, SE28
  off Rollesby Way 118 C6
Salisbury Av, N3 . . . . . . .72 C3
  Barking IG11 . . . . .99 H7
  Sutton SM1 . . . . .198 C6
Salisbury CI, SE17 . . . . . .36 B1
  Worcester Park KT4 . . .197 F3
Salisbury Ct, EC4 . . . . . .19 F4
Salisbury Gdns, SW19 . .166 B7
  Buckhurst Hill IG9 . . . .64 A2
Salisbury Hall Gdns,
  E4 . . . . .62 A6
Salisbury Ho, E14
  off Hobday St 114 B6
Salisbury Ms, SW6
  off Dawes Rd 128 C7
  Bromley BR2
  off Salisbury Rd 192 B5
Salisbury PI, SW9 . . . . . .131 H7
  W1 . . . . .15 J1
Salisbury Rd, E4 . . . . . . .62 A3
  E7 . . . . .97 G6
  E10 . . . . .96 C2
  E12 . . . . .98 A5
  E17 . . . . .78 C5
  N4 . . . . .75 H5
  N9 . . . . .60 D3
  N22 . . . . .75 H1
  SE25 . . . . .188 D6
  SW19 . . . . .166 B7
  W13 . . . . .124 D2
  Barnet EN5 . . . . .40 B3
  Bexley DA5 . . . . .177 G1
  Bromley BR2 . . . . . . .192 B5
  Carshalton SM5 . . . . .199 J6
  Dagenham RM10 . . . .101 H6
  Feltham TW13 . . . . . .160 C1
  Harrow HA1 . . . . .68 A5
  Hounslow TW4 . . . . . .142 C3
  Hounslow (Hthrw.Air.)
  TW6 . . . . .141 F5
  Ilford IG3 . . . . .99 H2
  New Malden KT3 . . . .182 D3
  Pinner HA5 . . . . .66 A4
  Richmond TW9 . . . . . .145 H4
  Southall UB2 . . . . . . .123 E4
  Worcester Park KT4 . . .197 F3
Salisbury Sq, EC4 . . . . . .19 F4
Salisbury St, NW8 . . . . . . .7 G6
  W3 . . . . .126 C2
Salisbury Ter, SE15 . . . .153 F3
Salisbury Wk, N19 . . . . . .92 C1
Salix CI, Sun. TW16
  off Oak Gro 160 B7
Salliesfield, Twick. TW2 . .144 A6
Sally Murrey CI, E12
  off Grantham Rd 98 D4
Salmen Rd, E13 . . . . . . .115 F2
Salmond CI, Stan. HA7
  off Robb Rd 52 D6
Salmon La, E14 . . . . . . .113 H6
Salmon Rd, Belv. DA17 .139 G5
Salmons Rd, N9 . . . . .60 D1
  Chessington KT9 . . . .195 G6
Salmon St, E14
  off Salmon La 113 J6
  NW9 . . . . .88 B1

Salomons Rd, E13
off Chalk Rd 115 J5
Salop Rd, E17 . . . . .77 G6
Saltash Cl, Sutt. SM1 . .198 C4
Saltash Rd, Ilf. IG6 . . . . .65 G7
Welling DA16 . . . . . . .158 C1
Saltcoats Rd, W4 . . . . . .126 E2
Saltcroft Cl, Wem. HA9 . .88 B1
Salter Cl, Har. HA2 . . . . .85 F3
Salterford Rd, SW17 . . .168 A6
Salter Rd, SE16 . . . . . . .133 G1
Salters Hall Ct, EC4 . . . . .20 B5
Salters Hill, SE19 . . . . . .170 A5
Salters Rd, E17 . . . . .78 D4
W10 . . . . .108 A4
Salter St, E14 . . . . .114 A7
NW10 . . . . .107 G3
Salterton Rd, N7 . . . . . . .93 E3
Saltley Cl, E6
off Dunnock Rd 116 B6
Saltoun Rd, SW2 . . . . . .151 G4
Saltram Cl, N15 . . . . .76 C4
Saltram Cres, W9 . . . . . .108 C3
Saltwell St, E14 . . . . . . .114 A7
Saltwood Gro, SE17 . . . . .36 B4
Salusbury Rd, NW6 . . . .108 B1
Salutation Rd, SE10 . . .135 E4
Salvia Gdns, Grnf. UB6
off Selborne Gdns . . .104 D2
Salvin Rd, SW15 . . . . . .148 A3
Salway Cl, Wdf.Grn. IG8 . .63 F7
Salway Pl, E15
off Broadway 96/97 E6
Salway Rd, E15
off Great Eastern Rd . .96 D6
Samantha Cl, E17 . . . . . .77 J7
Sam Bartram Cl, SE7 . .135 J5
Sambruck Ms, SE6 . . . .172 B1
Samels Ct, W6
off South Black Lion
La 127 G5
Samford St, NW8 . . . . . . .7 F6
Samira Cl, E17
off Colchester Rd 78 A4
Samos Rd, SE20 . . . . . .189 E2
Sampson Av, Barn. EN5 . .40 A5
Sampson Cl, Belv. DA17
off Carrill Way 138 D3
Sampson St, E1 . . . . . . .29 J2
Samson St, E13 . . . . . . .115 J2
Samuel Cl, E8
off Pownall Rd 112 C1
SE14 . . . . .133 G6
SE18 . . . . .136 B4
Samuel Gray Gdns, Kings.T.
KT2 . . . . .181 G1
Samuel Johnson Cl, SW16
off Curtis Fld Rd 169 G4
Samuel Lewis Trust Dws, E8
off Amhurst Rd 94 D4
N1 off Liverpool Rd 93 G7
SW3 . . . . .31 G2
SW6 . . . . .128 D7
Samuels Cl, W6
off South Black Lion
La 127 G5
Samuel St, SE15 . . . . . . .37 F7
SE18 . . . . .136 C4
Sancroft Cl, NW2 . . . . . . .89 H3
Sancroft Rd, Har. HA3 . . .68 C2
Sancroft St, SE11 . . . . . .34 D3
Sanctuary, The, SW1 . . . .25 J4
Bexley DA5 . . . . .158 D6
Morden SM4 . . . . . . .184 D6
Sanctuary Rd, Houns.
(Hthrw.Air.) TW6 . . . .140 D6
Sanctuary St, SE1 . . . . . .28 A4
Sandale Cl, N16
off Stoke Newington Ch
St 94 A3
Sandall Cl, W5 . . . . .105 H4
Sandall Rd, NW5 . . . . . . .92 C6
W5 . . . . .105 H4
Sandal Rd, N18 . . . . .60 D5
New Malden KT3 . . . .182 D5
Sandal St, E15 . . . . .114 E1
Sandalwood Cl, E1
off Solebay St 113 H4
Sandalwood Rd, Felt.
TW13 . . . . .160 B3
Sandbach Pl, SE18 . . . .137 F4
Sandbourne Av, SW19 . .184 E3
Sandbourne Rd, SE4 . . .153 H2
Sandbrook Cl, NW7 . . . . .54 D6
Sandbrook Rd, N16 . . . . .94 B3
Sandby Grn, SE9 . . . . . .156 B3
Sandcroft Cl, N13 . . . . . .59 H6
Sandell St, SE1 . . . . .27 E3
Sanders Cl, Hmptn. (Hmptn.H.)
TW12 . . . . .161 J5

Sanders La, NW7 . . . . . . .56 A7
Sanderson Cl, NW5 . . . . .92 B4
Sanderstead Av, NW2 . . .90 B2
Sanderstead Cl, SW12
off Atkins Rd 150 C7
Sanderstead Rd, E10 . . . .95 H1
South Croydon CR2 . .202 A7
Sandfield Gdns, Th.Hth.
CR7 . . . . .187 H3
Sandfield Pas, Th.Hth.
CR7 . . . . .187 J3
Sandfield Rd, Th.Hth.
CR7 . . . . .187 H3
Sandford Av, N22 . . . . . . .59 J7
Loughton IG10 . . . . . . .49 F3
Sandford Cl, E6 . . . . . . .116 C4
Sandford Ct, N16 . . . . . . .94 B1
Sandford Rd, E6 . . . . . .116 B4
Bexleyheath DA7 . . . .159 E4
Bromley BR2 . . . . . . .191 G4
Sandford St, SW6
off King's Rd 128/129 E7
Sandgate La, SW18 . . . .167 H1
Sandgate Rd, Well.
DA16 . . . . .138 C7
Sandgate St, SE15 . . . . .132 E6
Sandham Pt, SE18
off Troy Ct 136/137 E4
Sandhills, Wall. SM6 . . .200 D4
Sandhurst Av, Har. HA2 . .67 H6
Surbiton KT5 . . . . . . .182 B7
Sandhurst Cl, NW9 . . . . .70 A3
Sandhurst Dr, Ilf. IG3 . . . .99 J4
Sandhurst Rd, N9 . . . . . .45 F6
NW9 . . . . .70 A3
SE6 . . . . .172 D1
Bexley DA5 . . . . .158 D5
Sidcup DA15 . . . . . . .175 J3
Sandhurst Way, S.Croy.
CR2 . . . . .202 B7
Sandifer Dr, NW2 . . . . . . .90 A3
Sandiford Rd, Sutt. SM3 .198 C2
Sandiland Cres, Brom.
BR2 . . . . .205 F2
Sandilands, Croy. CR0 . .202 D2
Sandilands Rd, SW6 . . .148 E1
Sandison St, SE15 . . . . .152 C3
Sandland St, WC1 . . . . . .18 D2
Sandling Ri, SE9 . . . . . .174 D3
Sandlings, The, N22 . . . . .75 G2
Sandlings Cl, SE15
off Pilkington Rd .152/153 E2
Sandmartin Way, Wall. SM6
off London Rd 200 A1
Sandmere Rd, SW4 . . . .150 E4
Sandon Cl, Esher KT10 . .180 A7
Sandow Cres, Hayes
UB3 . . . . .121 J3
Sandown Av, Dag. RM10 .101 J6
Sandown Cl, Houns.
TW5 . . . . .142 A1
Sandown Ct, Sutt. SM2
off Grange Rd 198/199 E7
Sandown Gate, Esher
KT10 . . . . .194 A3
Sandown Rd, SE25 . . . .188 E5
Sandown Way, Nthlt.
UB5 . . . . .85 E6
Sandpiper Cl, E17 . . . . . .77 G1
SE16 . . . . .133 J2
Sandpiper Rd, Sutt. SM1 198 C5
Sandpit Pl, SE7 . . . . . . .136 B5
Sandpit Rd, Brom. BR1 . .172 E5
Sandpits Rd, Croy. CR0 . .203 G4
Richmond TW10 . . . . .163 G2
Sandra Cl, N22
off New Rd 75 J1
Hounslow TW3 . . . . . .143 H5
Sandridge Cl, Har. HA1 . .68 B4
Sandridge St, N19 . . . . . .92 C2
Sandringham Av, SW20 .184 B2
Sandringham Cl, SW19 .166 A1
Enfield EN1 . . . . .44 B2
Ilford IG6 . . . . .81 F3
Sandringham Ct, W9 . . . . .6 D4
Sandringham Cres, Har.
HA2 . . . . .85 G2
Sandringham Dr, Well.
DA16 . . . . .157 H2
Sandringham Gdns, N8 . .75 E6
N12 . . . . .57 H6
Hounslow TW5 . . . . . .142 A1
Ilford IG6 . . . . .81 F3
Sandringham Ms, W5
off High St 105 G7
Sandringham Rd, E7 . . . .97 J5
E8 . . . . .94 C5
E10 . . . . .78 D6

Sandringham Rd, N22 . . .75 J3
NW2 . . . . .89 H6
NW11 . . . . .72 B7
Barking IG11 . . . . .99 J6
Bromley BR1 . . . . . . .173 G5
Hounslow (Hthrw.Air.)
TW6 . . . . .140 B5
Northolt UB5 . . . . .85 J7
Thornton Heath CR7 . .187 J5
Worcester Park KT4 . .197 G3
Sandrock Pl, Croy. CR0 . .203 G4
Sandrock Rd, SE13 . . . .154 A3
SANDS END, SW6 . . . . .149 F1
Sand's End La, SW6 . . . .149 E1
Sandstone Pl, N19 . . . . .173 H2
Sandstone Rd, SE12 . . .173 H2
Sands Way, Wdf.Grn. IG8 .64 B6
Sandtoft Rd, SE7 . . . . . .135 H6
Sandwell Cres, NW6 . . . .90 D6
Sandwich St, WC1 . . . . . .10 A4
Sandwick Cl, NW7
off Sebergham Gro 55 G7
Sandy Bury, Orp. BR6 . .207 G3
Sandycombe Rd, Felt.
TW14 . . . . .160 A1
Richmond TW9 . . . . . .146 A3
Sandycoombe Rd, Twick.
TW1 . . . . .145 F6
Sandycroft, SE2 . . . . . . .138 A6
Sandy Hill Av, SE18 . . . .136 E5
Sandy Hill Rd, SE18 . . . .136 E5
Sandyhill Rd, Ilf. IG1 . . . .98 E4
Sandy La, Har. HA3 . . . . .69 J6
Kingston upon Thames
KT1 . . . . .162 D7
Mitcham CR4 . . . . . . .186 A1
Northwood HA6 . . . . . .50 A5
Richmond TW10 . . . . .163 F2
Sidcup DA14 . . . . . . .176 D7
Sutton SM2 . . . . .198 B7
Teddington TW11 . . . .162 D7
Walton-on-Thames
KT12 . . . . .178 B6
Sandy La Est, Rich.
TW10 . . . . .163 G2
Sandy La N, Wall. SM6 . .200 D6
Sandy La S, Wall. SM6 . .200 D2
Sandymount Av, Stan.
HA7 . . . . .53 F5
Sandy Ridge, Chis. BR7 .174 D6
Sandy Rd, NW3 . . . . .90 E3
Sandy's Row, E1 . . . . . . .21 E2
Sandy Way, Croy. CR0 . .203 J3
Sanford La, N16
off Lawrence Bldgs . . .94 C2
Sanford St, SE14 . . . . . .133 H6
Sanford Ter, N16 . . . . . . .94 C3
Sanford Wk, N16
off Sanford Ter 94 C2
SE14 off Cold Blow La . .133 H6
Sanger Av, Chess. KT9 . .195 H5
Sangley Rd, SE6 . . . . . .154 B7
SE25 . . . . .188 B4
Sangora Rd, SW11 . . . . .149 G4
Sansom Rd, E11 . . . . .97 E2
Sansom St, SE5 . . . . . . .132 A7
Sans Wk, EC1 . . . . .11 F5
Santley St, SW4 . . . . . . .151 F4
Santos Rd, SW18 . . . . . .148 D5
Santway, The, Stan. HA7 .52 B5
Sapcote Trd Cen, NW10 . .89 F5
Saperton Wk, SE11 . . . . .34 D1
Saphora Cl, Orp. BR6
off Oleander Cl 207 G5
Sapperton Ct, EC1 . . . . . .11 J5
Sapphire Cl, E6 . . . . . . .116 D6
Dagenham RM8 . . . . .100 C1
Sapphire Rd, SE8 . . . . . .133 H4
Saracen Cl, Croy. CR0 . .188 A4
Saracen's Head Yd, EC3 . .21 F4
Saracen St, E14 . . . . . . .114 A6
Sara Ct, Beck. BR3
off Albemarle Rd 190 B1
Sarah Ho, SW15 . . . . . . .147 F4
Saratoga Rd, E5 . . . . .95 F4
Sardinia St, WC2 . . . . . . .18 C4
Sarita Cl, Har. HA3 . . . . . .68 A2
Sarjant Path, SW19
off Queensmere Rd . .166 A2
Sark Cl, Houns. TW5 . . .123 G7
Sark Wk, E16 . . . . .115 H6
Sarnesfield Ho, SE15
off Pencraig Way .132/133 E6
Sarnesfield Rd, Enf. EN2
off Church St 44 A3
Sarre Rd, NW2 . . . . .90 C5
Sarsen Av, Houns. TW3 . .143 F2
Sarsfield Rd, SW12 . . . .167 J1
Sarsfield Rd, Grnf. UB6 . .105 E2
Sartor Rd, SE15 . . . . . . .153 G4

Sarum Ter, E3 . . . . .113 J4
Satanita Cl, E16
off Fulmer Rd 116 A6
Satchell Mead, NW9 . . . .71 F1
Satchwell Rd, E2 . . . . . . .13 H4
Sattar Ms, N16
off Clissold Rd 94 A3
Sauls Grn, E11
off Napier Rd 96/97 E3
Saunders Cl, E14
off Limehouse
Causeway 113 J7
Saunders Ness Rd, E14 .134 C5
Saunders Rd, SE18 . . . .137 J5
Saunders St, SE11 . . . . . .34 E1
Saunders Way, SE28
off Oriole Way 118 B7
Saunderton Rd, Wem.
HA0 . . . . .86 E5
Saunton Av, Hayes UB3 .121 J7
Savage Gdns, E6 . . . . . .116 C6
EC3 . . . . .21 E5
Savernake Rd, N9 . . . . . .44 D6
NW3 . . . . .91 J4
Savery Dr, Surb. KT6 . . .181 F7
Savile Cl, N.Mal. KT3 . . .183 E5
Thames Ditton KT7 . .194 C1
Savile Gdns, Croy. CR0 . .202 C2
Savile Row, W1 . . . . .17 F5
Saville Rd, E16 . . . . .136 B1
W4 . . . . .126 D3
Romford RM6 . . . . .83 F6
Twickenham TW1 . . . .162 C1
Saville Row, Brom. BR2 .205 F1
Enfield EN3 . . . . .45 G2
Savill Gdns, SW20
off Bodnant Gdns . . .183 G3
Savill Row, Wdf.Grn. IG8 .63 F6
Savona Cl, SW19 . . . . . .166 B7
Savona Est, SW8 . . . . . .130 C7
Savona St, SW8 . . . . . . .130 C7
Savoy Av, Hayes UB3 . . .121 H5
Savoy Bldgs, WC2 . . . . . .18 C5
Savoy Cl, E15
off Arthingworth
St 114/115 E1
Edgware HA8 . . . . . . .54 A5
Savoy Ct, WC2 . . . . .18 B6
Savoy Hill, WC2 . . . . . . .18 C6
Savoy Pl, WC2 . . . . .18 B6
Savoy Row, WC2 . . . . . . .18 C5
Savoy Steps, WC2
off Savoy St 111 F7
Savoy St, WC2 . . . . .18 C5
Savoy Way, WC2 . . . . . . .18 C6
Sawbill Cl, Hayes UB4 . .102 D5
Sawkins Cl, SW19 . . . . .166 B2
Sawley Rd, W12 . . . . . . .127 F1
Sawmill Yd, E3 . . . . .113 H1
Sawtry Cl, Cars. SM5 . . .185 H7
Sawyer Cl, N9
off Lion Rd 60 D2
Sawyers Cl, Dag. RM10 .101 J6
Sawyer's Hill, Rich.
TW10 . . . . .146 B7
Sawyers Lawn, W13 . . . .104 C6
Sawyer St, SE1 . . . . .27 J3
Saxby Rd, SW2 . . . . . . .150 E7
Saxham Rd, Bark. IG11 . .117 H2
Saxlingham Rd, E4 . . . . . .62 D3
Saxon Av, Felt. TW13 . . .161 F2
Saxonbury Av, Sun.
TW16 . . . . .178 B3
Saxonbury Cl, Mitch.
CR4 . . . . .185 G3
Saxonbury Gdns, Surb.
KT6 . . . . .195 F1
Saxon Cl, E17 . . . . .78 A7
Surbiton KT6 . . . . . . .181 G6
Saxon Dr, W3 . . . . .106 B6
Saxonfield Cl, SW2 . . . .151 F7
Saxon Gdns, Sthl. UB1
off Saxon Rd 102/103 E7
Saxon Rd, E3 . . . . .113 J2
E6 . . . . .116 C4
N22 . . . . .75 H1
SE25 . . . . .188 A5
Bromley BR1 . . . . . . .173 F7
Ilford IG1 . . . . .99 E6
Southall UB1 . . . . . . .123 E1
Wembley HA9 . . . . .88 C3
Saxon Wk, Sid. DA14 . . .176 C6
Saxon Way, N14 . . . . .42 D6
Saxton Cl, SE13 . . . . . . .154 D3
Sayers Wk, Rich. TW10
off Stafford Pl 145 J7
Sayesbury La, N18 . . . . . .60 D5
Sayes Ct, SE8
off Sayes Ct St 133 J5
Sayes Ct St, SE8 . . . . . .133 J5

Scadbury Pk, Chis. BR7 .**175** J6
Scads Hill Cl, Orp. BR6 .**193** J6
Scala St, W1 . . . .**17** G1
Scales Rd, N17 . . . .**76** C3
Scampston Ms, W10 . . . . .**108** A6
Scampton Rd, Houns.
  (Hthrw.Air.) TW6
  off Southampton Rd .**140** C6
Scandrett St, E1 . . . .**132** E1
Scarba Wk, N1
  off Marquess Rd **94** A6
Scarborough Rd, E11 . . . .**96** D1
  N4 . . . .**75** G2
  N9 . . . .**45** F7
  Hounslow (Hthrw.Air.)
  TW6 off Southern Perimeter
  Rd **141** F6
Scarborough St, E1 . . . . . .**21** G4
Scarbrook Rd, Croy. CR0 .**201** J3
Scarle Rd, Wem. HA0 . . . .**87** G6
Scarlet Rd, SE6 . . . .**172** E3
Scarlette Manor Way, SW2
  off Papworth Way **151** G2
Scarsbrook Rd, SE3 . . . . .**156** A3
Scarsdale Pl, W8 . . . .**22** A5
Scarsdale Rd, Har. HA2 . . .**85** J3
Scarsdale Vil, W8 . . . . . .**128** D3
Scarth Rd, SW13 . . . .**147** F3
Scawen Cl, Cars. SM5 . . .**200** A4
Scawen Rd, SE8 . . . .**133** H5
Scawfell St, E2 . . . .**13** G2
Scaynes Link, N12 . . . .**56** D5
Sceaux Est, SE5 . . . .**152** B1
Sceptre Rd, E2 . . . .**113** F3
Schofield Wk, SE3
  off Dornberg Cl **135** H7
Scholars Rd, E4 . . . .**62** C1
  SW12 . . . .**168** C1
Scholefield Rd, N19 . . . . . .**92** D1
Schonfeld Sq, N16 . . . .**94** A2
Schoolbank Rd, SE10 . . . .**135** F4
Schoolbell Ms, E3
  off Arbery Rd **113** H2
Schoolhouse Gdns, Loug.
  IG10 . . . .**48** E4
Schoolhouse La, E1 . . . . .**113** G7
School Ho La, Tedd.
  TW11 . . . .**163** E7
School La, SE23 . . . .**170** E2
  Chigwell IG7 . . . .**65** J4
  Kingston upon Thames KT1
  off School Rd **181** F1
  Pinner HA5 . . . .**66** E4
  Surbiton KT6 . . . .**196** A1
  Welling DA16 . . . .**158** B3
School Pas, Kings.T. KT1 .**181** J2
  Southall UB1 . . . .**123** F1
School Rd, E12
  off Sixth Av **98** C4
  NW10 . . . .**106** D4
  Chislehurst BR7 . . . .**193** F1
  Dagenham RM10 . . . . . .**119** G1
  East Molesey KT8 . . . . .**180** A4
  Hampton (Hmptn.H.)
  TW12 . . . .**161** J4
  Hounslow TW3 . . . .**143** J3
  Kingston upon Thames
  KT1 . . . .**181** F1
  West Drayton UB7 . . . . .**120** A6
School Rd Av, Hmptn.
  (Hmptn.H.) TW12 . . . . .**161** J6
Schoolway, N12 . . . .**57** G6
School Way, N12
  off High Rd **57** F4
  Dagenham RM8 . . . . . .**100** C3
Schooner Cl, E14 . . . .**134** D3
  SE16 off Kinburn St . . .**133** G2
  Barking IG11 . . . .**118** B3
Schubert Rd, SW15 . . . . .**148** C5
★ Science Mus, SW7 . . . .**23** F6
Sclater St, E1 . . . .**13** F5
Scoble Pl, N16
  off Amhurst Rd **94** C4
Scoles Cres, SW2 . . . . . .**169** G1
Scope Way, Kings.T. KT1 .**181** H4
Scoresby St, SE1 . . . .**27** G2
Scorton Av, Grnf. UB6 . . .**104** D2
Scotch Common, W13 . . .**104** D5
Scoter Cl, Wdf.Grn. IG8
  off Mallards Rd **63** H7
Scot Gro, Pnr. HA5 . . . . . .**50** D7
Scotia Rd, SW2 . . . .**151** G7
Scotland Grn, N17 . . . .**76** C2
Scotland Grn Rd, Enf.
  EN3 . . . .**45** G5
Scotland Grn Rd N, Enf.
  EN3 . . . .**45** G4
Scotland Pl, SW1 . . . .**26** A1
Scotland Rd, Buck.H. IG9 .**63** J1
Scotney Cl, Orp. BR6 . . . .**206** D4

Scotsdale Cl, Orp. BR5 . .**193** H4
  Sutton SM3 . . . .**198** B7
Scotsdale Rd, SE12 . . . . .**155** H5
Scotswood St, EC1 . . . .**11** F5
Scotswood Wk, N17 . . . . . .**60** D7
Scott Cl, SW16 . . . .**187** F1
  Epsom KT19 . . . .**196** C5
  West Drayton UB7 . . . . .**120** C4
Scott Ct, W3
  off Petersfield Rd **126** C2
Scott Cres, Har. HA2 . . . . .**85** H1
Scott Ellis Gdns, NW8 . . . . .**6** E4
Scottes La, Dag. RM8
  off Valence Av **100** D1
Scott Fm Cl, T.Ditt. KT7 . .**194** E1
Scott Gdns, Houns. TW5 .**122** D7
Scott Ho, N18 . . . .**60** D5
Scott Lidgett Cres, SE16 . .**29** H4
Scott Russell Pl, E14
  off Westferry Rd **134** B5
Scotts Av, Brom. BR2 . . .**190** D2
Scotts Dr, Hmptn. TW12 .**161** H6
Scotts Fm Rd, Epsom
  KT19 . . . .**196** C6
Scotts La, Brom. BR2 . . .**190** D3
Scotts Rd, E10 . . . .**96** C1
  W12 . . . .**127** H2
  Bromley BR1 . . . .**173** G7
  Southall UB2 . . . .**122** C3
Scott St, E1 . . . .**112** E4
Scott's Yd, EC4 . . . .**20** B5
Scott Trimmer Way, Houns.
  TW3 . . . .**143** E2
Scottwell Dr, NW9 . . . .**71** F5
Scoulding Rd, E16 . . . . . .**115** F6
Scouler St, E14
  off Quixley St **114** D7
Scout App, NW10 . . . .**88** E4
Scout La, SW4
  off Old Town **150** C3
Scout Way, NW7 . . . .**54** D4
Scovell Cres, SE1 . . . .**27** J4
Scovell Rd, SE1 . . . .**27** J4
Scrattons Ter, Bark. IG11 .**118** D2
Scriven St, E8 . . . .**112** C1
Scrooby St, SE6 . . . .**154** B6
Scrubs La, NW10 . . . .**107** G3
  W10 . . . .**107** G3
Scrutton Cl, SW12 . . . . . .**150** D7
Scrutton St, EC2 . . . .**12** D6
Scudamore La, NW9 . . . . .**70** C3
Scutari Rd, SE22 . . . .**153** F5
Scylla Cres, Houns. (Hthrw.Air.)
  TW6 . . . .**141** E7
Scylla Rd, SE15 . . . .**153** E3
  Hounslow (Hthrw.Air.)
  TW6 . . . .**141** E6
Seabright St, E2
  off Bethnal Grn
  Rd **112/113** E3
Seabrook Dr, W.Wick.
  BR4 . . . .**204** E2
Seabrook Gdns, Rom.
  RM7 . . . .**83** G7
Seabrook Rd, Dag. RM8 .**100** D3
Seacole Cl, W3 . . . .**106** D5
Seacourt Rd, SE2 . . . .**138** D2
Seacroft Gdns, Wat.
  WD19 . . . .**50** D3
Seafield Rd, N11 . . . .**58** D4
Seaford Rd, E17 . . . .**78** B3
  N15 . . . .**76** A5
  W13 . . . .**124** E1
  Enfield EN1 . . . .**44** B4
  Hounslow (Hthrw.Air.)
  TW6 . . . .**140** A5
Seaford St, WC1 . . . .**10** B4
Seaforth Av, N.Mal. KT3 .**183** H5
Seaforth Cres, N5 . . . .**93** J5
Seaforth Gdns, N21 . . . . . .**43** F7
  Epsom KT19 . . . .**197** F4
  Woodford Green IG8 . . .**63** J5
Seaforth Pl, SW1
  off Buckingham Gate .**130** C3
Seagrave Rd, SW6 . . . . . .**128** D6
Seagry Rd, E11 . . . .**79** G6
Seagull La, Bark. IG11 . . .**118** A3
Sealand Rd, Houns.
  (Hthrw.Air.) TW6 . . . . .**140** D6
Sealand Wk, Nthlt. UB5
  off Wayfarer Rd .**102/103** E3
Seal St, E8 . . . .**94** C4
Searle Pl, N4
  off Evershot Rd **93** F1
Searles Cl, SW11 . . . .**129** H7
Searles Dr, E6 . . . .**116** E5
Searles Rd, SE1 . . . .**36** C1
Sears St, SE5 . . . .**36** B7
Seasprite Cl, Nthlt. UB5 .**102** D3
Seaton Av, Ilf. IG3 . . . .**99** H5

Seaton Cl, E13 . . . .
  off New Barn St **115** H4
  SE11 . . . .**35** F3
  SW15 . . . .**165** H1
  Twickenham TW2 . . . . .**144** A6
Seaton Gdns, Ruis. HA4 . .**84** A3
Seaton Pt, E5 . . . .**94** E4
Seaton Rd, Hayes UB3 . .**121** G4
  Mitcham CR4 . . . .**185** H2
  Twickenham TW2 . . . . .**143** J6
  Welling DA16 . . . .**138** C7
  Wembley HA0 . . . .**105** H2
Seaton Sq, NW7
  off Bittacy Hill **56** B7
Seaton St, N18 . . . .**60** D5
Sebastian St, EC1 . . . .**11** H4
Sebastopol Rd, N9 . . . .**60** D4
Sebbon St, N1 . . . .**93** H7
Sebergham Gro, NW7 . . . .**55** G7
Sebert Rd, E7 . . . .**97** H5
Sebright Pas, E2 . . . .**13** J2
Sebright Rd, Barn. EN5 . . .**40** A2
Secker Cres, Har. HA3 . . . .**67** J1
Secker St, SE1 . . . .**27** E2
Second Av, E12 . . . .**98** B4
  E13 . . . .**115** G3
  E17 . . . .**78** A5
  N18 . . . .**61** F4
  NW4 . . . .**72** A4
  SW14 . . . .**146** E3
  W3 . . . .**127** F1
  W10 . . . .**108** B4
  Dagenham RM10 . . . . .**119** H1
  Enfield EN1 . . . .**44** C5
  Hayes UB3 . . . .**121** J1
  Romford RM6 . . . .**82** C5
  Walton-on-Thames
  KT12 . . . .**178** B6
  Wembley HA9 . . . .**87** G2
Second Cl, W.Mol. KT8 . .**179** J4
Second Cross Rd, Twick.
  TW2 . . . .**162** B2
Second Way, Wem. HA9 . .**88** B4
Sedan Way, SE17 . . . .**36** D3
Sedcombe Cl, Sid. DA14
  off Knoll Rd **176** B4
Sedcote Rd, Enf. EN3 . . . .**45** F5
Sedding St, SW1 . . . .**32** B1
Seddon Highwalk, EC2
  off Beech St **111** J5
Seddon Ho, EC2
  off The Barbican **111** J5
Seddon Rd, Mord. SM4 . .**185** G5
Seddon St, WC1 . . . .**10** D4
Sedgebrook Rd, SE3 . . . .**156** A2
Sedgecombe Av, Har.
  HA3 . . . .**69** F5
Sedgeford Rd, W12 . . . . .**127** F1
Sedgehill Rd, SE6 . . . . . .**172** A4
Sedgemere Av, N2 . . . .**73** F3
Sedgemere Rd, SE2 . . . . .**138** C3
Sedgemoor Dr, Dag.
  RM10 . . . .**101** G4
Sedge Rd, N17 . . . .**61** F7
Sedgeway, SE6 . . . .**173** F1
Sedgewood Cl, Brom.
  BR2 . . . .**191** F7
Sedgmoor Pl, SE5 . . . . . .**132** B7
Sedgwick Rd, E10 . . . .**96** C2
Sedgwick St, E9 . . . .**95** G5
Sedleigh Rd, SW18 . . . . .**148** C6
Sedlescombe Rd, SW6 . .**128** C6
Sedley Pl, W1 . . . .**16** D4
Sedley Ri, Loug. IG10 . . . .**48** C2
Sedum Cl, NW9 . . . .**70** B5
Seeley Dr, SE21 . . . .**170** B4
Seelig Av, NW9 . . . .**71** G7
Seely Rd, SW17 . . . .**168** A6
Seething La, EC3 . . . .**21** E6
Seething Wells La, Surb.
  KT6 . . . .**181** F6
Sefton Av, NW7 . . . .**54** D5
  Harrow HA3 . . . .**68** A1
Sefton Cl, Orp. BR5 . . . . .**193** J4
Sefton Rd, Croy. CR0 . . .**202** D1
  Orpington BR5 . . . .**193** J4
Sefton St, SW15 . . . .**147** J2
Segal Cl, SE23 . . . .**153** H7
Sekforde St, EC1 . . . .**11** G6
Sekhon Ter, Felt. TW13 . .**161** G3
Selan Gdns, Hayes UB4 .**102** B5
Selbie Av, NW10 . . . .**89** F5
Selborne Av, E12
  off Walton Rd **98** D4
  Bexley DA5 . . . .**176** E1
Selborne Gdns, NW4 . . . . .**71** G4
  Greenford UB6 . . . .**104** D1
Selborne Rd, E17 . . . .**77** J5
  N14 . . . .**58** E3
  N22 . . . .**75** F1

Selborne Rd, SE5 . . . .
  off Denmark Hill **152** A2
  Croydon CR0 . . . .**202** B3
  Ilford IG1 . . . .**98** D2
  New Malden KT3 . . . . .**182** E2
  Sidcup DA14 . . . .**176** B4
Selbourne Av, E17 . . . .**77** J4
  Surbiton KT6 . . . .**195** J2
Selbourne Wk, E17
Selbourne Wk, E17
  off Selbourne Wk Shop
  Cen **77** J4
Selbourne Wk Shop Cen,
  E17 . . . .**77** J4
Selby Chase, Ruis. HA4 . . .**84** B2
Selby Cl, E6
  off Linton Gdns **116** B5
  Chessington KT9 . . . . .**195** H7
  Chislehurst BR7 . . . . . .**174** D6
Selby Gdns, Sthl. UB1 . . .**103** G4
Selby Grn, Cars. SM5 . . .**185** H7
Selby Rd, E11 . . . .**96** E3
  E13 . . . .**115** H5
  N17 . . . .**60** B6
  SE20 . . . .**188** D2
  W5 . . . .**105** E4
  Carshalton SM5 . . . . . .**185** H7
Selby St, E1 . . . .**13** J6
Selden Rd, SE15 . . . .**153** F2
Selden Wk, N7
  off Durham Rd **93** F2
★ Selfridges, W1 . . . .**16** C4
SELHURST, SE25 . . . .**188** B6
Selhurst Cl, SW19 . . . . . .**166** A1
Selhurst New Rd, SE25 .**188** B6
Selhurst Pl, SE25 . . . .**188** B6
Selhurst Rd, N9 . . . .**60** A3
  SE25 . . . .**188** B5
Selinas La, Dag. RM8 . . . . .**83** E7
Selkirk Rd, SW17 . . . .**167** H4
  Twickenham TW2 . . . . .**161** J2
Sellers Cl, Borwd. WD6 . . .**38** C1
Sellers Hall Cl, N3 . . . .**56** D7
Sellincourt Rd, SW17 . . . .**167** H6
Sellindge Cl, Beck. BR3 . .**171** J7
Sellon Ms, SE11 . . . .**34** D2
Sellons Av, NW10 . . . .**107** F1
Sellwood Dr, Barn. EN5 . . .**40** A5
Sellwood St, SW2
  off Tulse Hill **151** G7
Selsdon Av, S.Croy. CR2
  off Selsdon Rd **202** A6
Selsdon Cl, Rom. RM5 . . .**83** J1
  Surbiton KT6 . . . .**181** H5
Selsdon Rd, E11 . . . .**79** G7
  E13 . . . .**115** J1
  NW2 . . . .**89** F2
  SE27 . . . .**169** H3
  South Croydon CR2 . . .**202** A5
Selsdon Rd Ind Est, S.Croy. CR2
  off Selsdon Rd **202** A6
Selsdon Way, E14 . . . . . .**134** B3
Selsea Pl, N16
  off Crossway **94** B5
Selsey Cres, Well. DA16 .**158** D1
Selsey St, E14 . . . .**114** A5
Selvage La, NW7 . . . .**54** D5
Selway Cl, Pnr. HA5 . . . . . .**66** B4
Selwood Pl, SW7 . . . .**30** E3
Selwood Rd, Chess. KT9 .**195** G4
  Croydon CR0 . . . .**202** G2
  Sutton SM3 . . . .**198** C1
Selwood Ter, SW7 . . . .**31** E3
Selworthy Cl, E11 . . . .**79** G5
Selworthy Ho, SW11 . . . .**149** G1
Selworthy Rd, SE6 . . . . . .**171** J3
Selwyn Av, E4 . . . .**62** C6
  Ilford IG3 . . . .**81** H6
  Richmond TW9 . . . .**145** H3
Selwyn Cl, Houns. TW4 . .**143** E4
Selwyn Ct, SE3 . . . .**155** E3
  Edgware HA8
  off Camrose Av **54** B7
Selwyn Cres, Well. DA16 .**158** B4
Selwyn Rd, E3 . . . .**113** J2
  E13 . . . .**115** H1
  NW10 . . . .**88** D7
  New Malden KT3 . . . . .**182** D5
Semley Pl, SW1 . . . .**32** C2
Semley Rd, SW16 . . . . . .**187** E2
Senate St, SE15 . . . .**153** F2
Senator Wk, SE28
  off Broadwater Rd . . .**137** G3
Sendall Ct, SW11 . . . .**149** G3
Seneca Rd, Th.Hth. CR7 .**187** J4
Senga Rd, Wall. SM6 . . . .**200** A1
Senhouse Rd, Sutt. SM3 .**198** A3
Senior St, W2 . . . .**14** A1
Senlac Rd, SE12 . . . .**173** H1
Sennen Rd, Enf. EN1 . . . . .**44** C7
Sennen Wk, SE9 . . . .**174** B3

Senrab St, E1 . . . . .113 G6
Sentinel Cl, Nthlt. UB5 . .103 E4
Sentinel Sq, NW4 . . . . . . .71 J4
September Way, Stan.
  HA7 . . . . .53 E6
Sequoia Cl, Bushey
  (Bushey Hth.) WD23
  off Giant Tree Hill 52 A1
Sequoia Gdns, Orp. BR6 .193 J2
Sequoia Pk, Pnr. HA5 . . . .51 H6
Serbin Cl, E10 . . . . .78 C7
Serenaders Rd, SW9 . . . .151 G2
Serjeants Inn, EC4 . . . . . .19 F4
Serle St, WC2 . . . . .18 D3
Sermon La, EC4 . . . . .19 J3
★ Serpentine, The, W2 . .23 G2
★ Serpentine Gall, W2 . .23 F2
Serpentine Rd, W2 . . . . . .23 J2
Serviden Dr, Brom. BR1 .192 A1
Setchell Rd, SE1 . . . . .37 F1
Setchell Way, SE1 . . . . . . .37 F1
Seth St, SE16
  off Swan Rd 133 F2
Seton Gdns, Dag. RM9 . .100 C7
Settle Pt, E13
  off London Rd 115 G2
Settle Rd, E13
  off London Rd 115 G2
Settles St, E1 . . . . .21 J2
Settrington Rd, SW6 . . . .148 E2
Seven Acres, Cars. SM5 .199 H2
  Northwood HA6 . . . . . .50 A6
SEVEN KINGS, Ilf. 81 H7
Seven Kings Rd, Ilf. IG3 . .99 J2
Sevenoaks Cl, Bexh.
  DA7 . . . . .159 J4
Sevenoaks Ho, SE25 . . . .188 D3
Sevenoaks Rd, SE4 . . . . .153 H6
  Orpington BR6 . . . . . .207 J5
  Orpington (Grn.St.Grn.)
  BR6 . . . . .207 J7
Sevenoaks Way, Orp.
  BR5 . . . . .176 A7
  Sidcup DA14 . . . . .176 C7
Seven Sisters Rd, N4 . . . .93 F3
  N7 . . . . .93 F3
  N15 . . . . .75 J7
Seven Stars Cor, W12
  off Goldhawk Rd 127 G3
Seventh Av, E12 . . . . .98 C4
  Hayes UB3 . . . . .122 A1
Severnake Cl, E14 . . . . . .134 A4
Severn Dr, Esher KT10 . .194 D2
Severn Way, NW10 . . . . . .89 F5
Severus Rd, SW11 . . . . . .149 H4
Seville Ms, N1 . . . . .94 B7
Seville St, SW1 . . . . .24 A4
Sevington Rd, NW4 . . . . . .71 H6
Sevington St, W9 . . . . .6 A6
Seward Rd, W7 . . . . .124 D2
  Beckenham BR3 . . . . .189 G2
SEWARDSTONE, E4 . . . . . .46 C1
SEWARDSTONEBURY,
  E4 . . . . .47 E4
Sewardstone Gdns, E4 . . .46 B5
Sewardstone Grn, E4 . . . .46 E4
Sewardstone Rd, E2 . . . .113 F2
  E4 . . . . .46 B7
Seward St, EC1 . . . . .11 H5
Sewdley St, E5 . . . . .95 G3
Sewell St, SE2 . . . . .138 A3
Sewell St, E13 . . . . .115 G3
Sextant Av, E14 . . . . .134 D4
Seymour Av, N17 . . . . . . .76 D2
  Morden SM4 . . . . .184 A7
Seymour Cl, E.Mol. KT8 .179 J5
  Loughton IG10 . . . . . . .48 B6
  Pinner HA5 . . . . .67 F1
Seymour Ct, E4 . . . . .63 F2
Seymour Gdns, SE4 . . . .153 H3
  Feltham TW13 . . . . . .160 C4
  Ilford IG1 . . . . .98 C1
  Ruislip HA4 . . . . .84 D1
  Surbiton KT5 . . . . .181 J5
  Twickenham TW1 . . . .144 E7
Seymour Ms, W1 . . . . . . .16 B3
Seymour Pl, SE25 . . . . . .188 E4
  W1 . . . . .15 J2
Seymour Rd, E4 . . . . .62 B1
  E6 . . . . .116 A2
  E10 . . . . .95 J1
  N3 . . . . .57 E7
  N8 . . . . .75 G5
  N9 . . . . .61 E2
  SW18 . . . . .148 C7
  SW19 . . . . .166 A2
  W4 . . . . .126 C4
  Carshalton SM5 . . . . . .200 A5
  East Molesey KT8 . . . .179 J5

Seymour Rd, Hmptn.
  (Hmptn.H.) TW12 . . . .161 J5
  Kingston upon Thames
  KT1 . . . . .181 G1
  Mitcham CR4 . . . . .186 A7
Seymours, The, Loug.
  IG10 . . . . .48 D1
Seymour St, W1 . . . . .15 J4
  W2 . . . . .15 J4
Seymour Ter, SE20 . . . . . .188 E1
Seymour Vil, SE20 . . . . . .188 E1
Seymour Wk, SW10 . . . . . .30 C5
Seyssel St, E14 . . . . .134 C4
Shaa Rd, W3 . . . . .106 D7
Shacklegate La, Tedd.
  TW11 . . . . .162 B4
Shackleton Cl, SE23
  off Featherstone
  Av 170/171 E2
Shackleton Ct, E14
  off Maritime Quay 134 A5
  W12 . . . . .127 H7
Shackleton Rd, Sthl.
  UB1 . . . . .103 F7
SHACKLEWELL, N16 . . . . .94 C4
Shacklewell Grn, E8 . . . . .94 C4
Shacklewell La, E8 . . . . . .94 C5
Shacklewell Rd, N16 . . . . .94 C4
Shacklewell Row, E8 . . . . .94 C4
Shacklewell St, E2 . . . . . .13 G5
Shadbolt Av, E4 . . . . .61 H5
Shadbolt Cl, Wor.Pk.
  KT4 . . . . .197 F2
Shad Thames, SE1 . . . . . .29 F2
SHADWELL, E1 . . . . .113 F7
Shadwell Ct, Nthlt. UB5
  off Shadwell Dr 103 F2
Shadwell Dr, Nthlt. UB5 .103 F3
Shadwell Gdns Est, E1
  off Martha St 113 F6
Shadwell Pierhead, E1
  off Glamis Rd 113 F7
Shadwell Pl, E1
  off Sutton St 113 F7
Shaef Way, Tedd. TW11 . .162 D7
Shafter Rd, Dag. RM10 . .101 J6
Shaftesbury, Loug. IG10 . .48 A3
Shaftesbury Av, W1 . . . . . .17 H5
  WC2 . . . . .17 H5
  Barnet EN5 . . . . .41 F4
  Enfield EN3 . . . . .45 G2
  Feltham TW14 . . . . . . .142 A6
  Harrow HA2 . . . . .85 H1
  Harrow (Kenton) HA3 . .69 G6
  Southall UB2 . . . . .123 G4
Shaftesbury Circle, Har. HA2
  off Shaftesbury Av 85 J1
Shaftesbury Ct, N1
  off Shaftesbury St 112 A2
Shaftesbury Gdns,
  NW10 . . . . .107 E4
Shaftesbury Ms, SW4
  off Clapham Common S
  Side 150 C5
  W8 off Stratford Rd . . .128 D3
Shaftesbury Pl, W14
  off Warwick Rd 128 C4
Shaftesbury Pt, E13
  off High St 115 H2
Shaftesbury Rd, E4 . . . . . .62 D1
  E7 . . . . .97 J7
  E10 . . . . .96 A1
  E17 . . . . .78 B6
  N18 . . . . .60 B6
  N19 . . . . .92 E1
  Beckenham BR3 . . . . .189 J2
  Carshalton SM5 . . . . . .185 G7
  Richmond TW9 . . . . . . .145 H3
Shaftesburys, The, Bark.
  IG11 . . . . .117 F1
Shaftesbury St, N1 . . . . . .12 A2
Shaftesbury Way, Twick.
  TW2 . . . . .162 A3
Shaftesbury Waye, Hayes
  UB4 . . . . .102 B5
Shafto Ms, SW1 . . . . .23 J6
Shafton Rd, E9 . . . . .113 G1
Shakespeare Av, N11 . . . . .58 C5
  NW10 . . . . .106 D1
  Feltham TW14 . . . . . . .142 A6
  Hayes UB4 . . . . .102 B4
Shakespeare Cres, E12 . . .98 C6
  NW10 . . . . .106 D1
Shakespeare Dr, Har.
  HA3 . . . . .69 J6
Shakespeare Gdns, N2 . . .73 J4
Shakespeare Ho, N14
  off High St 58 D2
Shakespeare Rd, E17 . . . .77 G2
  N3 off Popes Dr 72 D1

Shakespeare Rd, NW7 . . . .55 F4
  SE24 . . . . .151 H5
  W3 . . . . .126 C1
  W7 . . . . .104 C7
  Bexleyheath DA7 . . . . .158 C1
★ Shakespeare's Globe
  Thea, SE1 . . . . .19 J6
Shakespeare Sq, Ilf. IG6 . .65 F6
Shakespeare Twr, EC2 . . .20 A1
Shakespeare Way, Felt.
  TW13 . . . . .160 C4
Shakspeare Ms, N16
  off Shakspeare Wk 94 B4
Shakspeare Wk, N16 . . . . .94 B4
Shalbourne Sq, E9 . . . . . .95 J6
Shalcomb St, SW10 . . . . . .30 D6
Shalden Ho, SW15
  off Tunworth Cres 147 F6
Shaldon Dr, Mord. SM4 .184 B5
  Ruislip HA4 . . . . .84 C3
Shaldon Rd, Edg. HA8 . . . .69 J1
Shalfleet Dr, W10 . . . . . . .108 A7
Shalford Cl, Orp. BR6 . . . .207 F4
Shalimar Gdns, W3 . . . . . .106 C7
Shalimar Rd, W3
  off Hereford Rd 106 C7
Shallons Rd, SE9 . . . . . . .174 E4
Shalstone Rd, SW14 . . . .146 B3
Shalston Vil, Surb. KT6 . .181 J6
Shamrock Ho, SE26
  off Talisman Sq 170 D4
Shamrock Rd, Croy. CR0 .187 F6
Shamrock St, SW4 . . . . . .150 D3
Shamrock Way, N14 . . . . . .58 B1
Shandon Rd, SW4 . . . . . .150 C6
Shand St, SE1 . . . . .28 D3
Shandy St, E1 . . . . .113 G5
Shanklin Gdns, Wat.
  WD19 . . . . .50 C4
Shanklin Rd, N8 . . . . .74 D5
  N15 . . . . .76 D4
Shanklin Way, SE15
  off Pentridge St 132 C7
Shannon Cl, NW2 . . . . . . .90 A3
  Southall UB2 . . . . .122 D5
Shannon Gro, SW9 . . . . . .151 F4
Shannon Pl, NW8 . . . . .7 H1
Shannon Way, Beck.
  BR3 . . . . .172 B6
Shap Cres, Cars. SM5 . . .199 J1
Shapland Way, N13 . . . . . .59 F5
Shapwick Cl, N11
  off Friern Barnet Rd . . .57 J5
Shardcroft Av, SE24 . . . . .151 H5
Shardeloes Rd, SE14 . . . .153 J3
Sharland Cl, Th.Hth. CR7
  off Dunheved Rd N . .187 G6
Sharman Ct, Sid. DA14 . .176 A4
Sharnbrooke Cl, Well.
  DA16 . . . . .158 C3
Sharon Cl, Surb. KT6 . . . .195 F1
Sharon Gdns, E9 . . . . . . .113 F1
Sharon Rd, W4 . . . . .126 D5
  Enfield EN3 . . . . .45 H2
Sharpe Cl, W7
  off Templeman Rd 104 C5
Sharpleshall St, NW1 . . . . .91 J7
Sharpness Cl, Hayes
  UB4 . . . . .102 E5
Sharratt St, SE15 . . . . . . .133 F6
Sharsted St, SE17 . . . . . . .35 G4
Sharvel La, Nthlt. UB5 . . .102 A1
Shavers Pl, SW1 . . . . .17 H6
Shaw Av, Bark. IG11 . . . . .118 E2
Shawbrooke Rd, SE9 . . . .155 J5
Shawbury Rd, SE22 . . . . .152 C5
Shaw Cl, SE28 . . . . .138 B1
  Bushey (Bushey Hth.)
  WD23 . . . . .52 B2
Shaw Ct, SW11 . . . . .149 G3
Shaw Dr, Walt. KT12 . . . . .178 C7
Shawfield Ct, West Dr.
  UB7 . . . . .120 B3
Shawfield Pk, Brom.
  BR1 . . . . .192 A2
Shawfield St, SW3 . . . . . . .31 H4
Shawford Ct, SW15 . . . . .147 G7
Shawford Rd, Epsom
  KT19 . . . . .196 D6
Shaw Gdns, Bark. IG11 . .118 E2
Shaw Rd, SE22 . . . . .152 B4
  Bromley BR1 . . . . .173 F3
  Enfield EN3 . . . . .45 G1
Shaws Cotts, SE23 . . . . . .171 H3
Shaw Sq, E17 . . . . .77 H1
Shaw Way, Wall. SM6 . . . .200 E7
Shearing Dr, Cars. SM5
  off Stavordale Rd 185 F7
Shearling Way, N7 . . . . . . .93 E6
Shearman Rd, SE3 . . . . . .155 F4

Shearsmith Ho, E1 . . . . . .21 J5
Shearwater Cl, Bark.
  IG11 . . . . .118 A3
Shearwater Rd, Sutt.
  SM1 . . . . .198 C5
Shearwater Way, Hayes
  UB4 . . . . .102 D6
Sheaveshill Av, NW9 . . . . .71 E4
Sheen Common Dr, Rich.
  TW10 . . . . .146 A4
Sheen Ct, Rich. TW10 . . .146 A4
Sheen Ct Rd, Rich. TW10 .146 A4
Sheendale Rd, Rich.
  TW9 . . . . .145 J4
Sheenewood, SE26 . . . . . .171 E5
Sheen Gate Gdns,
  SW14 . . . . .146 C4
Sheen Gro, N1
  off Richmond Av 111 G1
Sheen La, SW14 . . . . .146 C3
Sheen Pk, Rich TW9 . . . .145 J4
Sheen Rd, Orp. BR5 . . . . .193 J4
  Richmond TW9, TW10 .145 H5
Sheen Way, Wall. SM6 . . .201 F5
Sheen Wd, SW14 . . . . . . .146 C5
Sheepcote Cl, Houns.
  TW5 . . . . .122 A7
Sheepcote La, SW11 . . . .149 J2
Sheepcote Rd, Har. HA1 . .68 C6
Sheepcotes Rd, Rom.
  RM6 . . . . .82 D4
Sheephouse Way, N.Mal.
  KT3 . . . . .182 E7
Sheep La, E8 . . . . .112 E1
Sheep Wk Ms, SW19 . . . .166 A6
Sheerness Ms, E16 . . . . . .137 E2
Sheerwater Rd, E16 . . . . .116 A5
Sheffield Rd, Houns.
  (Hthrw.Air.) TW6
  off Southern Perimeter
  Rd 141 G5
Sheffield Sq, E3
  off Malmesbury Rd 113 J3
Sheffield St, WC2 . . . . .18 C4
Sheffield Ter, W8 . . . . .128 D1
Shefton Ri, Nthwd. HA6 . .50 A7
Shelbourne Cl, Pnr. HA5 . .67 F3
Shelbourne Pl, Beck.
  BR3 . . . . .171 J7
Shelbourne Rd, N17 . . . . .76 E2
Shelburne Dr, Houns. TW4
  off Hanworth Rd 143 G6
Shelburne Rd, N7 . . . . .93 F4
Shelbury Cl, Sid. DA14 . .176 A3
Shelbury Rd, SE22 . . . . . .153 E5
Sheldon Av, N6 . . . . .73 H7
  Ilford IG5 . . . . .80 E2
Sheldon Cl, SE12 . . . . . . .155 H5
  SE20 . . . . .189 E1
Sheldon Rd, N18 . . . . .60 B4
  NW2 . . . . .90 A4
  Bexleyheath DA7 . . . . .159 F1
  Dagenham RM9 . . . . . .100 E7
Sheldon St, Croy. CR0
  off Wandle Rd 201 J3
Sheldrake Cl, E16 . . . . . . .136 C1
Sheldrake Pl, W8 . . . . . . .128 C2
Sheldrick Cl, SW19 . . . . .185 G2
Shelduck Cl, E15 . . . . .97 F5
Sheldwich Ter, Brom.
  BR2 . . . . .192 B6
Shelford Pl, N16
  off Stoke Newington
  Ch St 94 A3
Shelford Ri, SE19 . . . . . . .170 C7
Shelford Rd, Barn. EN5 . . .39 J6
Shelgate Rd, SW11 . . . . . .149 H5
★ Shell Cen, SE1 . . . . .26 D2
Shell Cl, Brom. BR2 . . . . .192 C6
Shellduck Cl, NW9
  off Swan Dr 70/71 E2
Shell St, N16 . . . . .94 B5
Shelley Av, E12 . . . . .98 B6
  Greenford UB6 . . . . . . .104 A3
Shelley Cl, SE15 . . . . .153 E2
  Edgware HA8 . . . . .54 A4
  Greenford UB6 . . . . . . .104 A3
  Hayes UB4 . . . . .102 A5
  Orpington BR6 . . . . . . .207 H3
Shelley Cres, Houns.
  TW5 . . . . .142 D2
  Southall UB1 . . . . .103 F6
Shelley Dr, Well. DA16 . . .157 H1
Shelley Gdns, Wem. HA0 . .87 F2
Shelley Gro, Loug. IG10 . .48 C4
Shelley Rd, NW10 . . . . . . .106 D1
Shelley Way, SW19 . . . . . .167 G6
Shellness Rd, E5 . . . . .94 E5
Shell Rd, SE13 . . . . .154 B3
Shellwood Rd, SW11 . . . .149 J2

Shelmerdine CI, E3 . . . . . .114 A5
Shelton Rd, SW19 . . . . . .184 D1
Shelton St, WC2 . . . . .18 A4
Shenfield Ho, SE18
off Shooter's Hill Rd . .136 A7
Shenfield Rd, Wdf.Grn.
IG8 . . . . .63 H7
Shenfield St, N1 . . . . .12 E2
Shenley Rd, SE5 . . . . . . .152 B1
Borehamwood WD6 . . . .38 A4
Hounslow TW5 . . . . . . .142 E1
Shepcot Ho, N14 . . . . . . .42 C6
Shepherd CI, W1
off Lees PI 110 A7
Shepherdess PI, N1 . . . . . .12 A3
Shepherdess Wk, N1 . . . . .12 A1
Shepherd Mkt, W1 . . . . . .24 D1
SHEPHERD'S BUSH,
W12 . . . . .127 J1
Shepherds Bush Grn,
W12 . . . . .127 J2
Shepherds Bush Mkt,
W12 . . . . .127 J2
Shepherds Bush PI, W12 .128 A2
Shepherds Bush Rd, W6 .127 J4
Shepherds CI, N6 . . . . . . .74 B6
Orpington BR6
off Stapleton Rd 207 J3
Romford RM6 . . . . .82 D5
Shepherds Ct, W12
off Shepherds Bush
Grn 128 A2
Shepherds Grn, Chis.
BR7 . . . . .175 G7
Shepherds Hill, N6 . . . . . .74 B6
Shepherds La, E9 . . . . . . .95 G5
Shepherds Path, N6
off Fortunes Mead .84/85 E6
Shepherd's PI, W1 . . . . . . .16 B5
Shepherd St, W1 . . . . . . .24 D2
Shepherds Wk, NW2 . . . . .89 G2
NW3 . . . . .91 G5
Bushey (Bushey Hth.)
WD23 . . . . .52 A1
Shepherds Way, S.Croy.
CR2 . . . . .203 G2
Shepiston La, Hayes
UB3 . . . . .121 G4
West Drayton UB7 . . . .121 F4
Shepley CI, Cars. SM5 . . .200 A3
Sheppard CI, Enf. EN1 . . . .45 E1
Kingston upon Thames KT1
off Beaufort Rd 181 H4
Sheppard Dr, SE16 . . . . .132 E4
Sheppard St, E16 . . . . . .115 F4
Shepperton CI, Borwd.
WD6 . . . . .38 D1
Shepperton Rd, N1 . . . . .111 J1
Orpington BR5 . . . . . . .193 F6
Sheppey Gdns, Dag. RM9
off Sheppey Rd 100 C7
Sheppey Rd, Dag. RM9 . .100 B7
Sheppey Wk, N1
off Clephane Rd 93 J7
Sherard Ct, N7
off Manor Gdns 92/93 E3
Sherard Rd, SE9 . . . . . . .156 B5
Sheraton Business Cen, Grnf.
UB6 . . . . .105 E2
Sheraton St, W1 . . . . . . .17 H4
Sherborne Av, Enf. EN3 . . .45 F2
Southall UB2 . . . . .123 G4
Sherborne CI, Hayes
UB4 . . . . .102 C6
Sherborne Cres, Cars.
SM5 . . . . .185 H7
Sherborne Gdns, NW9 . . .70 A3
W13 . . . . .105 E6
Sherborne La, EC4 . . . . . .20 B5
Sherborne Rd, Chess.
KT9 . . . . .195 H5
Feltham TW14 . . . . . . .141 G7
Orpington BR5 . . . . . . .193 J4
Sutton SM3 . . . . .198 D2
Sherborne St, N1 . . . . . .112 A1
Sherboro Rd, N15
off Ermine Rd 76 C6
Sherbourne PI, Stan. HA7 .52 D6
Sherbrooke CI, Bexh.
DA6 . . . . .159 G4
Sherbrooke Rd, SW6 . . . .128 C7
Sherbrook Gdns, N21 . . . .43 H7
Shere CI, Chess. KT9 . . . .195 G5
Sheredan Rd, E4 . . . . .62 D5
Shere Rd, Ilf. IG2 . . . . . . .80 D5
Sherfield CI, N.Mal. KT3 .182 B4
Sherfield Gdns, SW15 . . .147 F6
Sheridan Ct, Houns. TW4
off Vickers Way 143 F5
Northolt UB5 . . . . .85 H5

Sheridan Cres, Chis.
BR7 . . . . .192 E2
Sheridan Gdns, Har.
HA3 . . . . .69 G6
Sheridan Ms, E11
off Woodbine PI 79 G6
Sheridan PI, SW13
off Brookwood Av 147 F2
Hampton TW12 . . . . . .179 H1
Sheridan Rd, E7 . . . . .97 F3
E12 . . . . .98 B5
SW19 . . . . .184 C1
Belvedere DA17 . . . . . .139 G4
Bexleyheath DA7 . . . . .158 E3
Richmond TW10 . . . . .163 F3
Sheridan St, E1
off Watney St 112/113 E6
Sheridan Ter, Nthlt. UB5
off Whitton Av W 85 H5
Sheridan Wk, NW11 . . . . .72 D6
Carshalton SM5
off Carshalton Pk Rd .199 J5
Sheridan Way, Beck. BR3
off Turners Meadow
Way 189 J1
Sheringham Av, E12 . . . . .98 C4
N14 . . . . .42 D5
Feltham TW13 . . . . . . .160 A3
Romford RM7 . . . . .83 J6
Twickenham TW2 . . . . .161 F1
Sheringham Dr, Bark.
IG11 . . . . .99 J5
Sheringham Rd, N7 . . . . .93 F6
SE20 . . . . .189 E3
Sheringham Twr, Sthl.
UB1 . . . . .103 H7
Sherington Av, Pnr. HA5 . .51 G7
Sherington Rd, SE7 . . . . .135 H6
Sherland Rd, Twick. TW1 .162 C1
Sherlies Av, Orp. BR6 . . .207 H2
★ Sherlock Holmes Mus,
NW1 . . . . .8 A6
Sherlock Ms, W1 . . . . . . .16 B1
Sherman Rd, Brom. BR1 .191 G1
Shernhall St, E17 . . . . . . .78 C5
Sherrard Rd, E7 . . . . .97 J6
E12 . . . . .98 A6
Sherrards Way, Barn. EN5 .40 D5
Sherrick Grn Rd, NW10 . . .89 H5
Sherriff Rd, NW6 . . . . .90 D6
Sherringham Av, N17 . . . .76 D2
Sherrin Rd, E10 . . . . .96 A4
Sherrock Gdns, NW4 . . . .71 G4
Sherry Ms, Bark. IG11
off Cecil Av 99 G7
Sherwin Rd, SE14 . . . . . .153 G1
Sherwood Av, E18 . . . . . .79 H3
SW16 . . . . .168 D2
Greenford UB6 . . . . . . .86 B6
Hayes UB4 . . . . .102 B4
Sherwood CI, SW13
off Lower Common
S 147 H3
W13 . . . . .124 E1
Bexley DA5 . . . . .158 C6
Sherwood Gdns, E14 . . . .134 A4
SE16 . . . . .37 J4
Barking IG11 . . . . .99 G7
Sherwood Pk Av, Sid.
DA15 . . . . .158 A7
Sherwood Pk Rd, Mitch.
CR4 . . . . .186 C4
Sutton SM1 . . . . .198 D5
Sherwood Rd, NW4 . . . . .71 J3
SW19 . . . . .166 C7
Croydon CR0 . . . . .188 E7
Hampton (Hmptn.H.)
TW12 . . . . .161 J5
Harrow HA2 . . . . .85 J2
Ilford IG6 . . . . .81 G4
Welling DA16 . . . . . . .157 H2
Sherwood St, N20 . . . . . .57 G3
W1 . . . . .17 G5
Sherwood Ter, N20
off Green Rd 57 G3
Sherwood Way, W.Wick.
BR4 . . . . .204 B2
Shetland CI, Borwd. WD6
off Percheron Rd 38 D6
Shetland Rd, E3 . . . . .113 J2
Shield Dr, Brent. TW8 . . .124 D6
Shieldhall St, SE2 . . . . . .138 C4
Shifford Path, SE23 . . . . .171 G3
Shillibeer PI, W1 . . . . .15 H1
Shillibeer Wk, Chig. IG7 . .65 J3
Shillingford CI, NW7
off Bittacy Hill 56 B7
Shillingford St, N1
off Cross St 93 H7
Shinfield St, W12 . . . . . . .107 J6

Shinglewell Rd, Erith
DA8 . . . . .139 G7
Shinners CI, SE25 . . . . . .188 D5
Ship All, W4
off Thames Rd 126 A6
Shipka Rd, SW12 . . . . . . .168 B1
Ship La, SW14 . . . . .146 C2
Shipman Rd, E16 . . . . . . .115 H6
SE23 . . . . .171 G2
Ship St, SE8 . . . . .154 A1
Ship Tavern Pas, EC3 . . . .20 D5
Shipton CI, Dag. RM8 . . .100 D3
Shipton St, E2 . . . . .13 G3
Shipwright Rd, SE16 . . . .133 H2
Ship Yd, E14
off Napier Av 134 B5
Shirburn CI, SE23
off Tyson Rd 153 F7
Shirbutt St, E14 . . . . . . .114 B7
Shirebrook Rd, SE3 . . . . .156 A3
Shire Ct, Epsom KT17 . . .197 F7
Erith DA18
off St. John Fisher
Rd 138 D3
Shirehall CI, NW4 . . . . . . .72 A6
Shirehall Gdns, NW4 . . . .72 A6
Shirehall La, NW4 . . . . . . .72 A6
Shirehall Pk, NW4 . . . . . . .72 A6
Shire Horse Way, Islw.
TW7 . . . . .144 C3
Shire La, Kes. BR2 . . . . . .206 C7
Orpington BR6 . . . . . . .207 G6
Shire PI, SW18
off Whitehead CI 149 F7
Shires, The, Rich. TW10 . .163 H4
Shirland Ms, W9 . . . . . . .108 C3
Shirland Rd, W9 . . . . . . .108 D3
SHIRLEY, Croy. 203 G3
Shirley Av, Bex. DA5 . . . .158 D7
Croydon CR0 . . . . .203 F1
Sutton SM1 . . . . .199 H4
Shirley Ch Rd, Croy.
CR0 . . . . .203 G3
Shirley CI, E17
off Addison Rd 78 B5
Hounslow TW3 . . . . . .143 J5
Shirley Ct, Croy. CR0 . . . .203 G3
Shirley Cres, Beck. BR3 . .189 H4
Shirley Dr, Houns. TW3 . .143 J5
Shirley Gdns, W7 . . . . . . .124 C1
Barking IG11 . . . . .99 H6
Shirley Gro, N9 . . . . .45 F7
SW11 . . . . .150 A3
Shirley Hills Rd, Croy.
CR0 . . . . .203 G5
Shirley Ho Dr, SE7 . . . . .135 J7
Shirley Oaks Rd, Croy.
CR0 . . . . .203 G1
Shirley Pk Rd, Croy. CR0 .203 E1
Shirley Rd, E15 . . . . .97 E7
W4 . . . . .126 D2
Croydon CR0 . . . . .189 E7
Enfield EN2 . . . . .43 J3
Sidcup DA15 . . . . .175 H3
Shirley St, E16 . . . . .115 F6
Shirley Way, Croy. CR0 . .203 H3
Shirlock Rd, NW3 . . . . . . .91 J4
Shirwell CI, NW7
off Bittacy Hill 56 B7
Shobden Rd, N17 . . . . . . .76 A1
Shobroke CI, NW2 . . . . . .89 J3
Shoebury Rd, E6 . . . . . . .98 C7
Shoe La, EC4 . . . . .19 F3
Sholto Rd, Houns.
(Hthrw.Air.) TW6 . . . .140 C5
Shooters Av, Har. HA3 . . . .69 F4
SHOOTER'S HILL, SE18 .156 F1
Shooter's Hill, SE18 . . . . .156 D1
Welling DA16 . . . . .156 D1
Shooter's Hill Rd, SE3 . . .155 F1
SE10 . . . . .154 D1
SE18 . . . . .135 H7
Shooters Rd, Enf. EN2 . . . .43 H1
Shoot Up Hill, NW2 . . . . .90 B5
Shore CI, Felt. TW14 . . . .142 A7
Hampton TW12
off Stewart CI 160/161 E5
SHOREDITCH, E1 . . . . . . .13 F6
Shoreditch High St, E1 . . .13 E4
Shoreditch Ho, N1 . . . . . .12 C4
Shore Gro, Felt. TW13 . . .161 G2
Shoreham CI, SW18
off Ram St 148/149 E5
Bexley DA5
off Stansted Cres 176 D1
Croydon CR0 . . . . .189 F6
Shoreham Rd E, Houns.
(Hthrw.Air.) TW6 . . . .140 B5

Shoreham Rd W, Houns.
(Hthrw.Air.) TW6 . . . .140 B5
Shoreham Way, Brom.
BR2 . . . . .191 G6
Shore PI, E9 . . . . .95 F7
Shore Rd, E9 . . . . .95 F7
Shorncliffe Rd, SE1 . . . . .37 F3
Shorndean St, SE6 . . . . .172 C1
Shorne CI, Sid. DA15 . . . .158 B6
Shornefield CI, Brom.
BR1 . . . . .192 D3
Shornells Way, SE2
off Willrose Cres 138 C5
Shorrolds Rd, SW6 . . . . .128 C7
Shortcroft Rd, Epsom
KT17 . . . . .197 F7
Shortcrofts Rd, Dag.
RM9 . . . . .101 F6
Shorter St, E1 . . . . .21 F5
Shortgate, N12 . . . . .56 C4
Short Hedges, Houns.TW3,
TW5 . . . . .143 H1
Short Hill, Har. HA1
off High St 86 B1
SHORTLANDS, Brom. . . .190 E3
Shortlands, W6 . . . . .128 A4
Hayes UB3 . . . . .121 G6
Shortlands CI, N18 . . . . . .60 A3
Belvedere DA17 . . . . . .139 F3
Shortlands Gdns, Brom.
BR2 . . . . .191 E2
Shortlands Gro, Brom.
BR2 . . . . .190 D3
Shortlands Rd, E10 . . . . .78 B7
Bromley BR2 . . . . .190 D3
Kingston upon Thames
KT2 . . . . .163 J7
Short Path, SE18
off Westdale Rd . .136/137 E6
Short Rd, E11 . . . . .96 E2
E15 . . . . .114 D1
W4 . . . . .126 E6
Hounslow (Hthrw.Air.)
TW6 . . . . .140 B6
Shorts CI, NW9 . . . . .70 B4
Shorts Gdns, WC2 . . . . . .18 A4
Shorts Rd, Cars. SM5 . . .199 H4
Short St, NW4
off New Brent St 71 J4
SE1 . . . . .27 F3
Short Wall, E15 . . . . .114 C3
Shortway, N12 . . . . .57 H6
Short Way, SE9 . . . . .156 B3
Twickenham TW2 . . . . .143 J7
Shotfield, Wall. SM6 . . . .200 B6
Shott CI, Sutt. SM1
off Turnpike La 199 F5
Shottendane Rd, SW6 . . .148 D1
Shottery CI, SE9 . . . . . . .174 B3
Shottfield Av, SW14 . . . .146 E4
Shoulder of Mutton All, E14
off Narrow St 113 H7
Shouldham St, W1 . . . . . .15 H2
Showers Way, Hayes
UB3 . . . . .122 A1
Shrapnel CI, SE18 . . . . . .136 B7
Shrapnel Rd, SE9 . . . . . .156 C3
Shrewsbury Av, SW14 . . .146 C4
Harrow HA3 . . . . .69 H4
Shrewsbury CI, Surb.
KT6 . . . . .195 H2
Shrewsbury Ct, EC1
off Whitecross St 11 J4
Shrewsbury Cres, NW10 .106 D1
Shrewsbury La, SE18 . . .156 E1
Shrewsbury Ms, W2
off Chepstow Rd 108 D5
Shrewsbury Rd, E7 . . . . . .98 A5
N11 . . . . .58 C6
W2 . . . . .108 D6
Beckenham BR3 . . . . . .189 H3
Carshalton SM5 . . . . . .185 H6
Hounslow (Hthrw.Air.)
TW6 . . . . .141 F6
Shrewsbury St, W10 . . . .107 J4
Shrewsbury Wk, Islw.TW7
off South St 144 D3
Shrewton Rd, SW17 . . . .167 J7
Shroffold Rd, Brom.
BR1 . . . . .173 E4
Shropshire CI, Mitch.
CR4 . . . . .187 E4
Shropshire Ho, N18
off Cameron CI 60/61 E5
Shropshire PI, WC1 . . . . . .9 G6
Shropshire Rd, N22 . . . . .59 F7
Shroton St, NW1 . . . . . . .15 G1
Shrubberies, The, E18 . . .79 G2
Chigwell IG7 . . . . .65 F5
Shrubbery, The, E11 . . . . .79 H5

Shrubbery Cl, N1
   off St. Paul St **111** J1
Shrubbery Gdns, N21 ....**43** H7
Shrubbery Rd, N9 ....**60** D3
  SW16 ....**168** E4
  Southall UB1 ....**123** F1
Shrubland Gro, Wor.Pk.
  KT4 ....**197** J3
Shrubland Rd, E8 ....**112** D1
  E10 ....**78** A7
  E17 ....**78** A5
Shrublands Av, Croy.
  CR0 ....**204** A4
Shrublands Cl, N20 ....**57** G5
  SE26 ....**171** F3
  Chigwell IG7 ....**65** F6
Shrubsall Cl, SE9 ....**174** B1
Shuna Wk, N1
  off St. Paul's Rd **94** A6
Shurland Av, Barn. EN4 ...**41** G6
Shurland Gdns, SE15 ....**37** G7
Shurlock Dr, Orp. BR6 ...**207** F4
Shuters Sq, W14 ....**128** C5
  off Sun Rd
Shuttle Cl, Sid. DA15 ....**157** J7
Shuttlemead, Bex. DA5 ..**159** F7
Shuttle St, E1 ....**13** H6
Shuttleworth Rd, SW11 ..**149** H2
Siamese Ms, N3
  off Station Rd **72** D1
Sibella Rd, SW4 ....**150** D2
Sibley Cl, Bexh. DA6 ....**159** E5
Sibley Gro, E12 ....**98** B7
Sibthorpe Rd, SE12 ......**155** H6
Sibton Rd, Cars. SM5 ...**185** H7
Sicilian Av, WC1 ....**18** B2
Sidbury St, SW6 ....**148** B1
SIDCUP **175** J4
Sidcup Bypass, Chis.
  BR7 ....**174** E2
  Orpington BR5 ......**176** D7
  Sidcup DA14 ....**175** H4
Sidcup High St, Sid.
  DA14 ....**176** A4
Sidcup Hill, Sid. DA14 ...**176** B4
Sidcup Hill Gdns, Sid.
  DA14 *off Sidcup Hill* ...**176** C5
Sidcup Pl, Sid. DA14 ....**176** A5
Sidcup Rd, SE9 ....**156** A7
  SE12 ....**155** H5
Sidcup Technology Cen, Sid.
  DA14 ....**176** D7
Siddeley Dr, Houns.
  TW4 ....**142** E3
Siddons La, NW1 ....**8** A6
Siddons Rd, N17 ....**76** D1
  SE23 ....**171** H2
  Croydon CR0 ....**201** G3
Side Rd, E17 ....**77** J5
Sidewood Rd, SE9 ....**175** G1
Sidford Pl, SE1 ....**26** D6
Sidings, The, E11 ....**96** C1
  Loughton IG10 ....**48** B6
Sidings Ms, N7 ....**93** G3
Sidmouth Av, Islw. TW7 .**144** B2
Sidmouth Cl, Wat. WD19 .**50** B2
Sidmouth Dr, Ruis. HA4 ..**84** A3
Sidmouth Par, NW2
  off Sidmouth Rd **89** J7
Sidmouth Rd, E10 ....**96** C3
  NW2 ....**89** J7
  Welling DA16 ....**138** C7
Sidmouth St, WC1 ....**10** B4
Sidney Av, N13 ....**59** F5
Sidney Elson Way, E6
  off Edwin Av **116** D2
Sidney Gdns, Brent.
  TW8 ....**125** F6
Sidney Gro, EC1 ....**11** G2
Sidney Rd, E7 ....**97** G3
  N22 ....**59** F7
  SE25 ....**188** D5
  SW9 ....**151** F2
  Beckenham BR3 ....**189** H2
  Harrow HA2 ....**67** J3
  Twickenham TW1 ..**144** D6
  Walton-on-Thames
  KT12 ....**178** A7
Sidney Sq, E1 ....**113** F6
Sidney St, E1 ....**113** E5
Sidworth St, E8 ....**95** E7
Siebert Rd, SE3 ....**135** G6
Siemens Rd, SE18 ....**136** A3
Sigdon Rd, E8 ....**94** D5
Sigers, The, Pnr. HA5 ....**66** B6
Signmakers Yd, NW1
  off Delancey St **110** B1
Sigrist Sq, Kings.T. KT2 .**181** H1
Silbury Av, Mitch. CR4 ..**185** H1
Silbury St, N1 ....**12** B3

Silchester Rd, W10 ......**108** A6
Silecroft Rd, Bexh. DA7 .**159** G1
Silesia Bldgs, E8
  off London La **94/95** E7
Silex St, SE1 ....**27** H4
Silk Cl, SE12 ....**155** G5
Silkfield Rd, NW9 ....**71** E5
Silkin Ho, Wat. WD19 ....**50** C3
Silk Mills Path, SE13
  off Lewisham Rd **154** C2
Silkmills Sq, E9 ....**95** J6
Silkstream Rd, Edg. HA8 .**70** C1
Silk St, EC2 ....**20** A1
Silsoe Rd, N22 ....**75** F2
Silver Birch Av, E4 ....**61** J6
Silver Birch Cl, N11 ......**58** A6
  SE28 ....**138** A1
Silver Birch Gdns, E6 ...**116** C4
Silver Birch Ms, Ilf. IG6
  off Fencepiece Rd **65** F6
Silverbirch Wk, NW3
  off Queen's Cres **92** A6
Silvercliffe Gdns, Barn.
  EN4 ....**41** H4
Silver Cl, SE14
  off Southerngate
  Way **133** H7
  Harrow HA3 ....**52** A7
Silver Cres, W4 ....**126** B4
Silverdale, SE26 ....**171** F4
  Enfield EN2 ....**43** E4
Silverdale Av, Ilf. IG3 ....**81** H5
Silverdale Cl, W7 ....**124** B1
  Northolt UB5 ....**85** F5
  Sutton SM1 ....**198** C4
Silverdale Dr, SE9 ....**174** B2
  Sunbury-on-Thames
  TW16 ....**178** B2
Silverdale Gdns, Hayes
  UB3 ....**122** A2
Silverdale Rd, E4 ....**62** D6
  Bexleyheath DA7 ...**159** H2
  Hayes UB3 ....**122** A2
  Orpington (Petts Wd)
  BR5 ....**193** F4
Silverhall St, Islw. TW7 .**144** D3
Silverholme Cl, Har. HA3 .**69** G7
Silver Jubilee Way, Houns.
  TW4 ....**142** B2
Silverland St, E16 ....**136** C1
Silver La, W.Wick. BR4 .**204** D2
Silverleigh Rd, Th.Hth.
  CR7 ....**187** F4
Silvermead, E18
  off Churchfields **63** G7
Silvermere Rd, SE6 .....**154** B6
Silver Pl, W1 ....**17** G5
Silver Rd, SE13
  off Elmira St **154** B3
  W12 ....**108** A7
Silver Spring Cl, Erith
  DA8 ....**139** H6
Silverston Way, Stan.
  HA7 ....**53** F6
Silver St, N18 ....**60** B4
  Enfield EN1 ....**44** A3
Silverthorne Rd, SW8 ..**150** B2
Silverthorn Gdns, E4 ....**62** A2
Silverton Rd, W6 ....**128** A6
SILVERTOWN, E16 .....**135** J2
Silvertown Way, E16 ...**115** E6
Silvertree La, Grnf. UB6
  off Cowgate Rd **104** A3
Silver Wk, SE16 ....**133** J1
Silver Way, Rom. RM7 ...**83** H3
Silverwood Cl, Beck.
  BR3 ....**172** A7
Silvester Rd, SE22 ......**152** C5
Silvester St, SE1 ....**28** A4
Silvocea Way, E14 ......**114** D6
Silwood Est, SE16 ......**133** F4
Silwood St, SE16 ....**133** F4
Simla Cl, SE14 ....**133** H6
Simla Ho, SE1 ....**28** C4
Simmil Rd, Esher (Clay.)
  KT10 ....**194** B5
Simmons Cl, N20 ....**57** H1
  Chessington KT9 ...**195** F7
Simmons La, E4 ....**62** D2
Simmons Rd, SE18 .....**136** E5
Simmons Way, N20 ....**57** H2
Simms Cl, Cars. SM5 ...**199** H2
Simms Gdns, N2 ....**73** F2
Simms Rd, SE1 ....**37** H2
Simnel Rd, SE12 ....**155** H7
Simon Cl, W11
  off Portobello Rd **108** C7
Simonds Rd, E10 ....**96** A2
Simone Cl, Brom.
  BR1 ....**192** A1

Simons Wk, E15
  off Waddington Rd **96** D5
Simpson Cl, N21
  off Macleod Rd **42/43** E5
Simpson Dr, W3 ....**106** D6
Simpson Rd, Houns.
  TW4 ....**143** F6
  Richmond TW10 ....**163** F4
Simpsons Rd, E14 ......**114** B7
  Bromley BR2 ....**191** G3
Simpson St, SW11 .....**149** H2
Simrose Ct, SW18
  off Wandsworth High
  St **148** D5
Sims Wk, SE3 ....**155** F4
Sinclair Ct, Beck. BR3 ..**172** A7
Sinclair Gdns, W14 .....**128** A2
Sinclair Gro, NW11 ......**72** A6
Sinclair Rd, E4 ....**61** J5
  W14 ....**128** A2
Sinclare Cl, Enf. EN1 ....**44** C1
Singapore Rd, W13 .....**124** D1
Singer St, EC2 ....**12** C4
Singleton Cl, SW17 .....**167** J7
  Croydon CR0
  off St. Saviours Rd ...**187** J7
Singleton Rd, Dag. RM9 .**101** F5
Singleton Scarp, N12 ....**56** D5
Sinnott Rd, E17 ....**77** G1
Sion Rd, Twick. TW1 ....**162** E1
SIPSON, West Dr. **120** D6
Sipson Cl, West Dr. UB7 .**120** D6
Sipson La, Hayes UB3 .**120** D6
  West Drayton UB7 ..**120** D6
Sipson Rd, West Dr. UB7 **120** D5
Sipson Way, West Dr.
  UB7 ....**120** D7
Sir Alexander Cl, W3 ...**127** F1
Sir Alexander Rd, W3 ..**127** F1
Sir Cyril Black Way,
  SW19 ....**166** D7
Sirdar Rd, N22 ....**75** H3
  W11 ....**108** A7
  Mitcham CR4
Sirinham Pt, SW8 ....**34** D6
Sirius Rd, Nthwd. HA6 ...**50** A5
★ Sir John Soane's Mus, WC2
  off Lincoln's Inn Flds .**18** D3
Sir Thomas More Est,
  SW3 ....**31** F6
Sise La, EC4 ....**20** B4
Siskin Cl, Borwd. WD6 ...**38** A4
Sisley Rd, Bark. IG11 ...**117** H1
Sispara Gdns, SW18 ...**148** C6
Sissinghurst Rd, Croy.
  CR0 ....**188** D7
Sissulu Ct, E6 ....**115** J1
Sister Mabel's Way, SE15 .**37** H7
Sisters Av, SW11 ....**149** J4
Sistova Rd, SW12 ......**168** B1
Sisulu Pl, SW9 ....**151** G3
Sittingbourne Av, Enf.
  EN1 ....**44** A6
Sitwell Gro, Stan. HA7 ...**52** C5
Siverst Cl, Nthlt. UB5 ....**85** H6
Sivill Ho, E2 ....**13** G3
Siviter Way, Dag. RM10 .**101** H7
Siward Rd, N17 ....**76** A1
  SW17 ....**167** F3
  Bromley BR2 ....**191** H3
Six Acres Est, N4 ....**93** G2
Six Bridges Trd Est, SE1 ..**37** J4
Sixth Av, E12 ....**98** C4
  W10 ....**108** B3
  Hayes UB3 ....**121** J1
Sixth Cross Rd, Twick.
  TW2 ....**161** J3
Skardu Rd, NW2 ....**90** B5
Skeena Hill, SW18 ......**148** B7
Skeffington Rd, E6 ......**116** B1
Skelbrook St, SW18 ....**167** E2
Skelgill Rd, SW15 ......**148** C4
Skelley Rd, E15 ....**97** F7
Skelton Cl, E8
  off Buttermere Wk **94** C6
Skelton Rd, E7 ....**97** G6
Skeltons La, E10 ....**78** B7
Skelwith Rd, W6 ....**127** J6
Skenfrith Ho, SE15
  off Commercial
  Way **132/133** E6
Skerne Rd, Kings.T. KT2 **181** G1
Sketchley Gdns, SE16 .**133** G5
Sketty Rd, Enf. EN1 .....**44** B3
Skiers St, E15 ....**114** E1
Skiffington Cl, SW2 ....**169** G1
Skinner Ct, E2
  off Parmiter St ...**112/113** E2
Skinner Pl, SW1 ....**32** B2

★ Skinners' Hall, EC4
  off Dowgate Hill **20** B5
Skinners La, EC4 ....**20** A5
  Hounslow TW5 .....**143** H1
Skinner St, EC1 ....**11** F4
Skipsea Ho, SW18
  off Fitzhugh Gro **149** G6
Skipsey Av, E6 ....**116** C3
Skipton Cl, N11
  off Ribblesdale Av ...**58** A6
Skipton Dr, Hayes UB3 .**121** F3
Skipworth Rd, E9 ....**113** F1
Skomer Wk, N1
  off Clephane Rd **93** J6
Skylines Village, E14 ...**134** C2
Sky Peals Rd, Wdf.Grn.
  IG8 ....**78** D1
Skyport Dr, West Dr.
  UB7 ....**120** A7
Slade, The, SE18 ....**137** H6
Sladebrook Rd, SE3 ...**156** A3
Sladedale Rd, SE18 ....**137** H5
Slade Ho, Houns. TW4 .**143** F6
Slades Cl, Enf. EN2 ......**43** G3
Slades Dr, Chis. BR7 ...**175** F3
Slades Gdns, Enf. EN2 ..**43** G2
Slades Hill, Enf. EN2 ....**43** G3
Slades Ri, Enf. EN2 ......**43** G3
Slade Twr, E10 ....**96** B2
Slade Wk, SE17 ....**35** H6
Slagrove Pl, SE13 ......**154** B5
Slaidburn St, SW10 .....**30** D6
Slaithwaite Rd, SE13 ..**154** C4
Slaney Pl, N7
  off Hornsey Rd **93** G5
Slater Cl, SE18
  off Woolwich New Rd **136** D5
Slattery Rd, Felt. TW13 .**160** C1
Sleaford Grn, Wat. WD19 .**50** D3
Sleaford St, SW8 ....**33** F7
Slievemore Cl, SW4
  off Voltaire Rd **150** D3
Slingsby Pl, WC2 ....**18** A5
Slippers Pl, SE16 ......**133** E3
Sloane Av, SW3 ....**31** G1
Sloane Ct E, SW3 ....**32** B3
Sloane Ct W, SW3 ......**32** B3
Sloane Gdns, SW1 ......**32** B2
  Orpington BR6 ......**207** F3
Sloane Sq, SW1 ....**32** A2
Sloane St, SW1 ....**24** A5
Sloane Ter, SW1 ....**32** A1
Sloane Wk, Croy. CR0 .**189** J6
Slocum Cl, SE28 ....**118** C7
Slough La, NW9 ....**70** C6
Sly St, E1
  off Cannon St Rd .112/113 E6
Smaldon Cl, West Dr. UB7
  off Walnut Av **120** D3
Smallberry Av, Islw.
  TW7 ....**144** C2
Smallbrook Ms, W2 ......**14** E4
Smalley Cl, N16 ....**94** C3
Smalley Rd Est, N16
  off Smalley Cl **94** C3
Smallwood Rd, SW17 ..**167** G4
Smardale Rd, SW18
  off Alma Rd **149** F5
Smarden Cl, Belv. DA17
  off Essenden Rd **139** G5
Smarden Gro, SE9 .....**174** C4
Smarts La, Loug. IG10 ...**48** A4
Smarts Pl, N18
  off Fore St **60** D5
Smart's Pl, WC2 ....**18** B3
Smart St, E2 ....**113** G3
Smeaton Cl, Chess. KT9
  off Merritt Gdns **195** G6
Smeaton Rd, SW18 ....**148** D7
  Woodford Green IG8 .**64** C5
Smeaton St, E1 ....**132** E1
Smedley St, SW4 ....**150** D2
  SW8 ....**150** D2
Smeed Rd, E3 ....**96** A4
Smiles Pl, SE13 ....**154** C2
Smith Cl, SE16 ....**133** G1
★ Smithfield Cen Mkt,
  EC1 ....**19** H2
Smithfield St, EC1 ....**19** G2
Smithies Ct, E15 ....**96** C5
Smithies Rd, SE2 ......**138** B4
Smith's Ct, W1 ....**17** G5
Smiths Fm Est, Nthlt.
  UB5 ....**103** G2
Smithson Rd, N17 ....**76** A1
Smiths Pt, E13
  off Brooks Rd **115** G1
Smith Sq, SW1 ....**26** A6
Smith St, SW3 ....**31** J3
  Surbiton KT5 ....**181** J6

Smiths Yd, SW18
  off Summerley St 167 F2
Smith's Yd, Croy. CR0
  off St. Georges Wk . .201 J3
Smith Ter, SW3 . . . . .31 J4
Smithwood Cl, SW19 . .166 B1
Smithy St, E1 . . . . .113 F5
Smock Wk, Croy. CR0 . .187 J6
Smokehouse Yd, EC1 . . .19 H1
Smugglers Way, SW18 . .149 E4
Smyrks Rd, SE17 . . . . . . .36 E4
Smyrna Rd, NW6 . . . . . .90 D7
Smythe St, E14 . . . . . . .114 B7
Snakes La, Barn. EN4 . . .42 B3
Snakes La E, Wdf.Grn.
  IG8 . . . . .63 J6
Snakes La W, Wdf.Grn.
  IG8 . . . . .63 G6
SNARESBROOK, E11 . . . .79 E5
Snaresbrook Dr, Stan.
  HA7 . . . . .53 G4
Snaresbrook Rd, E11 . . . .78 E4
Snarsgate St, W10 . . . . .107 J5
Sneath Av, NW11 . . . . . .72 C7
Snells Pk, N18 . . . . .60 C6
Sneyd Rd, NW2 . . . . . . .89 J4
Snowberry Cl, E15 . . . . .96 D4
Snowbury Rd, SW6 . . . .149 E2
Snowden St, EC2 . . . . . .12 D6
Snowdon Cres, Hayes
  UB3 . . . . .121 F3
Snowdon Dr, NW9 . . . . .70 E6
Snowdon Rd, Houns.
(Hthrw.Air.) TW6
  off Southern Perimeter
  Rd 141 F5
Snowdown Cl, SE20 . . . .189 G1
Snowdrop Cl, Hmptn. TW12
  off Gresham Rd 161 G6
Snow Hill, EC1 . . . . .19 G2
Snow Hill Ct, EC1 . . . . . .19 H3
Snowman Ho, NW6 . . . .109 E1
Snowsfields, SE1 . . . . . .28 C3
Snowshill Rd, E12 . . . . . .98 B5
Snowy Fielder Waye, Islw.
  TW7 . . . . .144 E2
Soames St, SE15 . . . . . .152 C3
Soames Wk, N.Mal. KT3 .182 E1
Soap Ho La, Brent. TW8 .125 H7
Socket La, Brom. BR2 . .191 H6
SOHO, W1 . . . . .17 H5
Soho Sq, W1 . . . . .17 H3
Soho St, W1 . . . . .17 H3
Sojourner Truth Cl, E8
  off Richmond Rd . .94/95 E6
Solander Gdns, E1
  off Dellow St 112/113 E7
Solebay St, E1 . . . . .113 H4
Solent Ri, E13 . . . . .115 G3
Solent Rd, NW6 . . . . . . .90 D5
Hounslow (Hthrw.Air.)
  TW6 . . . . .140 C6
Soley Ms, WC1 . . . . . . .10 E3
Solna Av, SW15 . . . . . . .147 J5
Solna Rd, N21 . . . . .60 A1
Solomon Av, N9 . . . . . . .60 D4
Solomon's Pas, SE15 . . .152 E4
Solon New Rd, SW4 . . . .150 E4
Solon New Rd Est, SW4
  off Solon New Rd.150/151 E4
Solon Rd, SW2 . . . . . . .151 E4
Solway Cl, E8
  off Buttermere Wk . . .94 C6
Hounslow TW4 . . . . . . .143 E3
Solway Rd, N22 . . . . . . .75 H1
SE22 . . . . .152 D4
Somaford Gro, Barn. EN4 .41 G6
Somali Rd, NW2 . . . . . . .90 C4
Somborne Ho, SW15
  off Fontley Way 147 G7
Somerby Rd, Bark. IG11 . .99 G7
Somercoates Cl, Barn.
  EN4 . . . . .41 H3
Somerfield Rd, N4 . . . . . .93 H2
Somerford Cl, Pnr. HA5 . .66 A4
Somerford Gro, N16 . . . .94 C4
  N17 . . . . .60 D7
Somerford Gro Est, N16
  off Somerford Gro . . .94 C4
Somerford St, E1 . . . . . .112 E4
Somerford Way, SE16 . . .133 H2
Somerhill Av, Sid.
  DA15 . . . . .158 B7
Somerhill Rd, Well.
  DA16 . . . . .158 B2
Somerleyton Pas, SW9 .151 H4
Somerleyton Rd, SW9 . .151 G4
Somersby Gdns, Ilf. IG4 . .80 C5
Somers Cl, NW1 . . . . .9 H1
Somers Cres, W2 . . . . . .15 G4

Somerset Av, SW20 . . . .183 H2
Chessington KT9 . . . . .195 G4
Welling DA16 . . . . . . .157 J5
Somerset Cl, N17 . . . . . .76 A2
New Malden KT3 . . . . .183 E6
Woodford Green IG8 . . .79 G1
Somerset Est, SW11 . . . .149 G1
Somerset Gdns, N6 . . . . .74 A7
  N17 . . . . .60 B7
SE13 . . . . .154 B2
SW16 . . . . .187 F3
Teddington TW11 . . . . .162 B5
★ Somerset Ho, WC2 . . . .18 C5
Somerset Ho, SW19 . . . .166 A3
Somerset Rd, E17 . . . . . .78 A5
  N17 . . . . .76 C3
  N18 . . . . .60 C5
NW4 . . . . .71 J4
SW19 . . . . .166 B4
W4 . . . . .126 D3
W13 . . . . .125 E1
Barnet EN5 . . . . .41 E5
Brentford TW8 . . . . . . .125 F6
Harrow HA1 . . . . .67 J5
Kingston upon Thames
  KT1 . . . . .181 J2
Southall UB1 . . . . .103 F5
Teddington TW11 . . . . .162 B5
Somerset Sq, W14 . . . . .128 B2
Somerset Waye, Houns.
  TW5 . . . . .122 C6
Somersham Rd, Bexh.
  DA7 . . . . .159 E2
Somers Ms, W2 . . . . . . .15 G4
Somers Pl, SW2 . . . . . . .151 F7
Somers Rd, E17 . . . . . . .77 J4
SW2 . . . . .151 F6
SOMERS TOWN, NW1 . . . .9 H3
Somerton Av, Rich.
  TW9 . . . . .146 B3
Somerton Rd, NW2 . . . . .90 B3
SE15 . . . . .153 E4
Somertrees Av, SE12 . . .173 H2
Somervell Rd, Har. HA2 . .85 F5
Somerville Av, SW13 . . .127 H6
Somerville Rd, SE20 . . . .171 G7
Romford RM6 . . . . . . .82 C6
Sonderburg Rd, N7 . . . . .93 F2
Sondes St, SE17 . . . . . . .36 B5
Sonia Ct, Har. HA1 . . . . . .68 C6
Sonia Gdns, N12
  off Woodside Av 57 F4
NW10 . . . . .89 F4
Hounslow TW5 . . . . . . .123 G7
Sonning Gdns, Hmptn.
  TW12 . . . . .161 E6
Sonning Rd, SE25 . . . . . .188 D6
Soper Cl, E4 . . . . .61 J5
Sophia Cl, N7 . . . .
  off Mackenzie Rd 93 F6
Sophia Rd, E10 . . . . .96 B1
  E16 . . . . .115 H6
Sophia Sq, SE16
  off Rotherhithe St 113 H7
Sopwith Av, Chess.
  KT9 . . . . .195 H5
Sopwith Cl, Kings.T.
  KT2 . . . . .163 J5
Sopwith Rd, Houns.
  TW5 . . . . .122 C7
Sopwith Way, SW8 . . . . .32 D7
Kingston upon Thames
  KT2 . . . . .181 H1
Sorrel Cl, SE28 . . . . .138 A1
Sorrel Gdns, E6 . . . . . . .116 B5
Sorrel La, E14 . . . . .114 D6
Sorrell Cl, SE14
  off Southerngate
  Way 133 H7
Sorrento Rd, Sutt. SM1 . .198 E3
Sotheby Rd, N5 . . . . . . .93 H3
Sotheran Cl, E8 . . . . . . .112 D1
Sotheron Rd, SW6 . . . . .129 E7
Soudan Rd, SW11 . . . . . .149 J1
Souldern Rd, W14 . . . . . .128 A3
South Access Rd, E17 . . .77 H7
Southacre Way, Pnr. HA5 . .66 C1
SOUTH ACTON, W3 . . . . .126 A3
South Africa Rd, W12 . . .127 H1
SOUTHALL 122 D1
Southall La, Houns.
  TW5 . . . . .122 B6
Southall UB2 . . . . .122 B6
Southall Pl, SE1 . . . . . . .28 B4
Southampton Bldgs,
  WC2 . . . . .18 E3
Southampton Gdns, Mitch.
  CR4 . . . . .186 E5
Southampton Ms, E16
  off Wesley Av 135 H1

Southampton Pl, WC1 . . .18 B2
Southampton Rd, NW5 . . .91 J5
Hounslow (Hthrw.Air.)
  TW6 . . . . .140 D6
Southampton Row, WC1 . .18 B1
Southampton St, WC2 . . .18 B5
Southampton Way, SE5 . . .36 C7
Southam St, W10 . . . . . .108 B4
South Audley St, W1 . . . . .16 C6
South Av, E4 . . . . .46 B7
Carshalton SM5 . . . . . .199 J7
Richmond TW9
  off Sandycombe Rd . .146 A2
Southall UB1 . . . . .103 F7
South Av Gdns, Sthl.
  UB1 . . . . .103 F7
South Bk, Chis. BR7 . . . .175 F4
Surbiton KT6 . . . . .181 H6
Southbank, T.Ditt. KT7 . .180 E7
South Bk Ter, Surb. KT6 .181 H6
SOUTH BEDDINGTON,
  Wall. 200 D6
South Birkbeck Rd, E11 . . .96 D3
South Black Lion La, W6 .127 G5
South Bolton Gdns, SW5 . .30 B3
SOUTHBOROUGH,
  Brom. 192 C6
Southborough Cl, Surb.
  KT6 . . . . .195 G1
Southborough La, Brom.
  BR2 . . . . .192 B5
Southborough Rd, E9 . . .113 F1
Bromley BR1 . . . . .192 B3
Surbiton KT6 . . . . .195 H1
Southbourne, Brom.
  BR2 . . . . .191 G7
Southbourne Av, NW9 . . .70 C2
Southbourne Cl, Pnr.
  HA5 . . . . .67 E7
Southbourne Cres, NW4 . .72 B4
Southbourne Gdns,
  SE12 . . . . .155 H5
Ilford IG1 . . . . .99 F5
Ruislip HA4 . . . . .84 B1
Southbridge Pl, Croy.
  CR0 . . . . .201 J4
Southbridge Rd, Croy.
  CR0 . . . . .201 J4
Southbridge Way, Sthl.
  UB2 . . . . .123 E2
Southbrook Ms, SE12 . . .155 F6
Southbrook Rd, SE12 . . .155 F6
SW16 . . . . .187 E1
Southbury Av, Enf. EN1 . . .44 D5
Southbury Rd, Enf. EN1,
  EN3 . . . . .44 A3
South Carriage Dr, SW1 . .23 F3
  SW7 . . . . .23 F4
SOUTH CHINGFORD, E4 . .61 J5
Southchurch Rd, E6 . . . .116 C2
South Cl, N6 . . . . .74 B6
Barnet EN5 . . . . .40 C3
Bexleyheath DA6 . . . . .158 D4
Dagenham RM10 . . . . .119 G1
Morden SM4
  off Green La 184/185 E6
Pinner HA5 . . . . .67 F7
Twickenham TW2 . . . . .161 G3
West Drayton UB7 . . . .120 C3
South Colonnade, E14 . . .134 A1
Southcombe St, W14 . . .128 B4
Southcote Av, Surb.
  KT5 . . . . .182 B7
Southcote Rd, E17 . . . . .77 G5
  N19 . . . . .92 C4
SE25 . . . . .189 E6
South Countess Rd, E17 . .77 J3
South Cres, E16 . . . . . . .114 D4
  WC1 . . . . .17 H2
Southcroft Av, Well.
  DA16 . . . . .157 H3
West Wickham BR4 . . . .204 C2
Southcroft Rd, SW16 . . .168 A6
SW17 . . . . .168 A6
Orpington BR6 . . . . . . .207 H3
South Cross Rd, Ilf. IG6 . .81 F5
South Croxted Rd, SE21 .170 A3
SOUTH CROYDON 201 J6
Southdale, Chig. IG7 . . . . .65 H6
Southdean Gdns, SW19 .166 C2
South Dene, NW7 . . . . . .54 D3
Southdown Av, W7 . . . . .124 D3
Southdown Cres, Har.
  HA2 . . . . .85 H1
Ilford IG2 . . . . .81 H5
Southdown Dr, SW20
  off Crescent Rd 166 A7
Southdown Rd, SW20 . . .184 A1
South Dr, Orp. BR6 . . . . .207 H5
South Ealing Rd, W5 . . . .125 G2

South Eastern Av, N9 . . . .60 C3
BR3 . . . . .190 B6
South Edwardes Sq, W8 .128 C3
SOUTHEND, SE6 . . . . . . .172 B4
South End, W8 . . . . .22 B5
Croydon CR0 . . . . .201 J4
South End Cl, NW3 . . . . . .91 H4
South End Cl, SE9 . . . . . .156 E6
Southend Cres, SE9 . . . .156 D6
South End Grn, NW3
  off South End Rd 91 H4
Southend La, SE6 . . . . . .171 J4
SE26 . . . . .171 J4
Southend Rd, E4 . . . . . . .61 H5
  E6 . . . . .98 C2
  E17 . . . . .78 B1
  E18 . . . . .79 G1
South End Rd, NW3 . . . . .91 H4
Southend Rd, Beck. BR3 .172 A2
Woodford Green IG8 . . .79 J2
South End Row, W8 . . . . .22 B5
Southern Av, SE25 . . . . .188 C3
Feltham TW14 . . . . . . .160 A1
Southern Dr, Loug. IG10 . .48 C6
Southern Gro, E3 . . . . . .113 J3
Southernhay, Loug. IG10 . .48 A5
Southern Perimeter Rd, Houns.
(Hthrw.Air.) TW6 . . . . .141 G5
Southern Rd, E13 . . . . . .115 H2
  N2 . . . . .73 J4
Southern Row, W10 . . . .108 B4
Southern St, N1 . . . . .10 C1
Southern Way, SE10 . . . .135 F4
Romford RM7 . . . . .83 G6
Southerton Rd, W6 . . . . .127 J3
South Esk Rd, E7 . . . . . . .97 J6
Southey Ms, E16
  off Wesley Av 135 G1
Southey Rd, N15 . . . . . . .76 B5
SW9 . . . . .151 G1
SW19 . . . . .166 D7
Southey St, SE20 . . . . . .171 G7
Southfield, Barn. EN5 . . . .40 A6
Southfield Cotts, W7
  off Oaklands Rd 124 C2
Southfield Gdns, Twick.
  TW1 . . . . .162 C4
Southfield Pk, Har. HA2 . . .67 H4
Southfield Rd, N17
  off The Avenue 76 B2
  W4 . . . . .126 E3
Chislehurst BR7 . . . . . .193 J3
Enfield EN3 . . . . .45 E6
SOUTHFIELDS, SW18 . . .166 D1
Southfields, NW4 . . . . . .71 G3
East Molesey KT8 . . . . .180 B6
Southfields Ct, SW19 . . .166 B1
Sutton SM1
  off Sutton Common
  Rd 198 D2
Southfields Pas, SW18 . .148 D6
Southfields Rd, SW18 . . .148 D6
Southfleet Rd, Orp. BR6 .207 H3
South Gdns, SW19 . . . . .167 G7
SOUTHGATE, N14 . . . . . . .58 C2
Southgate Circ, N14
  off The Bourne 58 D1
Southgate Gro, N1 . . . . . .94 A7
Southgate Rd, N1 . . . . . .112 A1
South Gipsy Rd, Well.
  DA16 . . . . .158 D3
South Glade, The, Bex.
  DA5 . . . . .177 F1
South Grn, NW9
  off Clayton Fld 70/71 E1
South Gro, E17 . . . . .77 J5
  N6 . . . . .92 A1
  N15 . . . . .76 A5
South Gro Ho, N6
  off Highgate W Hill 92 A1
SOUTH HACKNEY, E9 . . . .95 F7
SOUTH HAMPSTEAD,
  NW6 . . . . .91 E7
SOUTH HARROW, Har. 85 H3
South Hill, Chis. BR7 . . . .174 C6
South Hill Av, Har. HA1,
  HA2 . . . . .85 J3
South Hill Gro, Har. HA1 . .86 B4
South Hill Pk, NW3 . . . . . .91 H4
South Hill Pk Gdns, NW3 . .91 H4
South Hill Rd, Brom.
  BR2 . . . . .190 E3
Southholme Cl, SE19 . . .188 B1
South Huxley, N18 . . . . . .60 A5
Southill La, Pnr. HA5 . . . .66 A4
Southill Rd, Chis. BR7 . . .174 B7

Southill St, E14 . . . . **114** B6
 off Chrisp St **114** B6
South Island Pl, SW9 . . .**131** F7
SOUTH KENSINGTON,
 SW7 . . . .**30** C2
South Kensington Sta Arc,
 SW7 off Pelham St . .**129** G4
SOUTH LAMBETH, SW8 .**151** E1
South Lambeth Pl, SW8 . .**34** B5
South Lambeth Rd,
 SW8 . . . .**131** E6
Southland Rd, SE18 . . . .**137** J7
Southlands Av, Orp.
 BR6 . . . .**207** G4
Southlands Dr, SW19 . . .**166** A2
Southlands Gro, Brom.
 BR1 . . . .**192** B3
Southlands Rd, Brom. BR1,
 BR2 . . . .**191** J3
Southland Way, Houns.
 TW3 . . . .**144** A5
South La, Kings.T. KT1 . .**181** G3
 New Malden KT3 . . . . .**182** D4
South La W, N.Mal. KT3 .**182** D4
South Lo Av, Mitch. CR4 .**186** E4
South Lo Cres, Enf. EN2 . .**42** D4
South Lo Dr, N14 . . . .**42** E5
★ South London Art Gall,
 SE5 . . . .**152** B1
Southly Cl, Sutt. SM1 . . .**198** D3
South Mall, N9
 off Plevna Rd **60** D3
South Mead, NW9 . . . . . .**71** F1
 Epsom KT19 . . . .**197** E7
South Meadows, Wem.
 HA9 . . . .**87** J5
Southmead Rd, SW19 . . .**166** B1
South Molton La, W1 . . . .**16** D4
South Molton Rd, E16 . . .**115** G6
South Molton St, W1 . . . .**16** D4
Southmoor Ho, Esher
 KT10 . . . .**194** B2
Southmoor Way, E9 . . . . .**95** J6
SOUTH NORWOOD,
 SE25 . . . .**188** C3
South Norwood Hill,
 SE25 . . . .**188** B2
South Oak Rd, SW16 . . .**169** F4
Southold Ri, SE9 . . . . . .**174** C3
Southolm St, SW11 . . . .**150** B1
Southover, N12 . . . .**56** D4
 Bromley BR1 . . . .**173** G5
SOUTH OXHEY, Wat. **50** C3
South Par, SW3 . . . .**31** F3
 W4 . . . .**126** D4
South Pk, SW6 . . . .**148** D2
South Pk Cres, SE6 . . . .**173** F1
 Ilford IG1 . . . .**99** G3
South Pk Dr, Bark. IG11 . .**99** H4
 Ilford IG3 . . . .**99** H4
South Pk Gro, N.Mal.
 KT3 . . . .**182** C4
South Pk Hill Rd, S.Croy.
 CR2 . . . .**202** A5
South Pk Ms, SW6 . . . . .**148** E3
South Pk Rd, SW19 . . . .**166** D6
 Ilford IG1 . . . .**99** G3
South Pk Ter, Ilf. IG1 . . . .**99** G3
South Pk Way, Ruis. HA4 . .**84** C6
South Penge Est,
 SE20 . . . .**188** E2
South Pl, EC2 . . . .**20** C1
 Enfield EN3 . . . .**45** F5
 Surbiton KT5 . . . .**181** J7
South Pl Ms, EC2 . . . .**20** C2
South Pt, Sutt. SM1 . . . .**199** F6
Southport Rd, SE18 . . . .**137** G4
Southridge Pl, SW20 . . .**166** A7
South Ri Way, SE18 . . . .**137** G5
South Rd, N9 . . . .**60** D1
 SE23 . . . .**171** G2
 SW19 . . . .**167** F6
 W5 . . . .**125** G4
 Edgware HA8 . . . .**70** B1
 Feltham TW13 . . . .**160** D5
 Hampton TW12 . . . . . .**161** E6
 Romford (Chad.Hth.)
 RM6 . . . .**82** E6
 Romford (Lt.Hth.) RM6 . .**82** C5
 Southall UB1 . . . .**123** F2
 Twickenham TW2 . . . .**162** A3
 West Drayton UB7 . . . .**120** C3
South Row, SE3 . . . .**155** F2
SOUTH RUISLIP, Ruis. . . .**84** C4
Southsea Rd, Kings.T.
 KT1 . . . .**181** H4
South Sea St, SE16 . . . .**133** J3
South Side, W6 . . . .**127** F3
Southside Common,
 SW19 . . . .**165** J6

Southspring, Sid. DA15 .**157** G7
South Sq, NW11 . . . .**72** E6
 WC1 . . . .**18** E2
South St, W1 . . . .**24** C1
 Bromley BR1 . . . .**191** G2
 Enfield EN3 . . . .**45** G5
 Isleworth TW7 . . . .**144** D3
 Rainham RM13 . . . . . .**119** J2
South Tenter St, E1 . . . . .**21** G5
South Ter, SW7 . . . .**31** G1
 Surbiton KT6 . . . .**181** H6
SOUTH TOTTENHAM,
 N15 . . . .**76** B5
South Vale, SE19 . . . . . .**170** B6
 Harrow HA1 . . . .**86** B4
Southvale Rd, SE3 . . . . .**155** C2
South Vw, Brom. BR1 . . .**191** H2
Southview Av, NW10 . . . .**89** F5
Southview Cl, SW17 . . . .**168** A5
 Bexley DA5 . . . .**159** F6
Southview Cres, Ilf. IG2 . .**80** E6
South Vw Dr, E18 . . . .**79** H3
Southview Gdns, Wall.
 SM6 . . . .**200** C7
South Vw Rd, N8 . . . .**74** D3
Southview Rd, Brom.
 BR1 . . . .**172** D4
South Vw Rd, Loug. IG10 .**48** C6
 Pinner HA5 . . . .**50** B6
South Vil, NW1 . . . .**92** D6
Southville, SW8 . . . .**150** D1
Southville Rd, T.Ditt.
 KT7 . . . .**180** E7
South Wk, W.Wick. BR4 .**204** E3
SOUTHWARK, SE1 . . . . .**27** H2
 Southwark Br, EC4 . . . .**28** A1
 SE1 . . . .**28** A1
Southwark Br Rd, SE1 . . .**27** H5
★ Southwark Cathedral,
 SE1 . . . .**28** B1
Southwark Gro, SE1 . . . .**27** J2
Southwark Pk Est, SE16 .**133** E4
Southwark Pk Rd, SE16 . .**37** G1
Southwark Pl, Brom. BR1
 off St. Georges Rd . . .**192** C3
Southwark St, SE1 . . . . .**27** H1
Southwater Cl, E14 . . . .**113** J6
 Beckenham BR3 . . . . .**172** B7
South Way, N9 . . . .**61** F2
 N11 off Ringway **58** C7
Southway, N20 . . . .**56** D2
 NW11 . . . .**72** E6
 SW20 . . . .**183** J4
South Way, Brom. BR2 . .**191** G5
 Croydon CR0 . . . .**203** H3
 Harrow HA2 . . . .**67** G4
Southway, Wall. SM6 . . .**200** C4
South Way, Wem. HA9 . . .**88** A5
Southwell Av, Nthlt. UB5 .**85** G6
Southwell Gdns, SW7 . . .**30** C1
Southwell Gro Rd, E11 . . .**96** E2
Southwell Rd, SE5 . . . . .**151** J3
 Croydon CR0 . . . .**187** G6
 Harrow HA3 . . . .**69** G6
South Western Rd, Twick.
 TW1 . . . .**144** D6
Southwest Rd, E11 . . . . . .**96** D1
South Wf Rd, W2 . . . .**15** E3
Southwick Ms, W2 . . . . . .**15** F3
Southwick Pl, W2 . . . .**15** G4
Southwick St, W2 . . . .**15** G3
SOUTH WIMBLEDON,
 SW19 . . . .**166** E7
Southwold Dr, Bark.
 IG11 . . . .**100** A5
Southwold Rd, E5 . . . .**95** E2
 Bexley DA5 . . . .**159** H6
Southwood Av, N6 . . . . . .**74** B7
 Kingston upon Thames
 KT2 . . . .**182** C1
Southwood Cl, Brom.
 BR1 . . . .**192** C4
 Worcester Park KT4 . . .**198** A1
Southwood Dr, Surb.
 KT5 . . . .**182** C7
SOUTH WOODFORD,
 E18 . . . .**79** F2
South Woodford to Barking
 Relief Rd, E11 . . . .**79** J4
 E12 . . . .**98** D3
 E18 . . . .**79** J4
 Barking IG11 . . . .**98** D3
 Ilford IG1, IG4 . . . .**98** D3
Southwood Gdns, Esher
 KT10 . . . .**194** D3
 Ilford IG2 . . . .**80** E4
Southwood La, N6 . . . . . .**74** A7
Southwood Lawn Rd, N6 .**74** A7
Southwood Rd, SE9 . . . .**174** E2
 SE28 . . . .**138** B1

Southwood Smith St, N1
 off Old Royal Free Sq .**111** G1
South Worple Av, SW14 .**146** E3
South Worple Way,
 SW14 . . . .**146** D3
Sovereign Cl, E1 . . . . . .**113** E7
 W5 . . . .**105** F5
Sovereign Ct, Brom.
 BR2 . . . .**192** C5
 West Molesey KT8 . . .**179** F4
Sovereign Cres, SE16
 off Rotherhithe St **133** H1
Sovereign Gro, Wem.
 HA0 . . . .**87** G3
Sovereign Ms, E2 . . . . . .**13** F1
 Barnet EN4
 off Bournwell Cl **41** J3
Sovereign Pk, NW10 . . .**106** B4
Sovereign Rd, Bark. IG11 .**118** C3
Sowerby Cl, SE9 . . . . . .**156** B5
Space Waye, Felt. TW14 .**142** A4
Spa Cl, SE25 . . . .**188** B1
Spafield St, EC1 . . . .**11** E5
Spa Grn Est, EC1 . . . .**11** F3
Spa Hill, SE19 . . . .**188** A1
Spalding Cl, Edg. HA8
 off Blundell Rd **54**/**55** E7
Spalding Rd, NW4 . . . . . .**71** J6
 SW17 . . . .**168** B5
Spanby Rd, E3 . . . .**114** A4
Spaniards Cl, NW11 . . . . .**91** G1
Spaniards End, NW3 . . . .**91** F1
Spaniards Rd, NW3 . . . . .**91** F2
Spanish Pl, W1 . . . .**16** C3
Spanish Rd, SW18 . . . . .**149** F5
Spareleaze Hill, Loug.
 IG10 . . . .**48** C5
Sparkbridge Rd, Har.
 HA1 . . . .**68** B4
Sparkford Gdns, N11
 off Friern Barnet Rd . . .**58** A5
Sparkford Ho, SW11 . . .**149** G1
Sparks Cl, W3
 off Joseph Av **106** D6
 Dagenham RM8 . . . . .**100** D2
 Hampton TW12
 off Victors Dr . . .**160**/**161** E6
Spa Rd, SE16 . . . .**29** F6
Sparrow Cl, Hmptn.
 TW12 . . . .**160** E6
Sparrow Dr, Orp. BR5 . .**207** F1
Sparrow Fm Dr, Felt.
 TW14 . . . .**142** D7
Sparrow Fm Rd, Epsom
 KT17 . . . .**197** G4
Sparrow Grn, Dag.
 RM10 . . . .**101** H3
Sparrows La, SE9 . . . . . .**157** F7
Sparsholt Rd, N19 . . . . . .**93** F1
 Barking IG11 . . . .**117** H1
Sparta St, SE10 . . . .**154** B1
★ Speaker's Cor, W2 . . . .**16** A5
Speaker's Ct, Croy. CR0
 off St. James's Rd . . .**202** A1
Spearman St, SE18 . . . .**136** D6
Spear Ms, SW5 . . . .**128** D4
Spearpoint Gdns, Ilf. IG2 .**81** J4
Spears Rd, N19 . . . .**92** E1
Speart La, Houns. TW5 . .**122** E7
Spedan Cl, NW3 . . . .**91** E3
Speechly Ms, E8
 off Alvington Cres **94** C5
Speed Highwalk, EC2
 off Beech St **111** J5
Speed Ho, EC2 . . . .**20** B1
Speedwell St, SE8
 off Comet St **134** A7
Speedy Pl, WC1 . . . .**10** A4
Speer Rd, T.Ditt. KT7 . . .**180** C5
Speirs Cl, N.Mal. KT3 . . .**183** F6
Spekehill, SE9 . . . .**174** C3
Speke Ho, SE5 . . . .**131** J7
Speke Rd, Th.Hth. CR7 . .**188** A2
Speldhurst Cl, Brom.
 BR2 . . . .**191** F5
Speldhurst Rd, E9 . . . . . .**95** G7
 W4 . . . .**126** D3
Spellbrook Wk, N1
 off Basire St **111** J1
Spelman St, E1 . . . .**21** H1
Spence Cl, SE16
 off Vaughan St **133** J2
Spencer Av, N13 . . . .**59** F6
 Hayes UB4 . . . .**102** A5
Spencer Cl, N3 . . . .**72** C2
 NW10 . . . .**105** J3
 Orpington BR6 . . . . . .**207** H2
 Woodford Green IG8 . . .**63** J5
Spencer Ct, NW8
 off Marlborough Pl . . .**109** F2

Spencer Dr, N2 . . . .**73** F6
Spencer Gdns, SE9 . . . .**156** C5
 SW14 . . . .**146** C5
Spencer Hill, SW19 . . . .**166** B6
Spencer Hill Rd, SW19 . .**166** B7
★ Spencer Ho, SW1 . . . .**25** F2
Spencer Ms, SW8
 off Lansdowne Way . .**151** F1
 W6 off Greyhound Rd .**128** B6
Spencer Pk, SW18 . . . . .**149** G5
Spencer Pas, E2
 off Pritchard's Rd .**112**/**113** E2
Spencer Pl, N1
 off Canonbury La **93** H7
 Croydon CR0
 off Gloucester Rd **188** A7
Spencer Ri, NW5 . . . .**92** B4
Spencer Rd, E6 . . . .**116** A1
 E17 . . . .**78** C1
 N8 . . . .**75** F5
 N11 . . . .**58** B4
 N17 . . . .**76** D1
 SW18 . . . .**149** G4
 SW20 . . . .**183** H1
 W3 . . . .**126** C1
 W4 . . . .**126** C7
 Bromley BR1 . . . .**173** E7
 East Molesey KT8 . . . .**179** J5
 Harrow HA3 . . . .**68** B2
 Ilford IG3 . . . .**99** J1
 Isleworth TW7 . . . .**144** A1
 Mitcham CR4 . . . .**186** A3
 Mitcham (Bedd.Cor.)
 CR4 . . . .**186** A7
 South Croydon CR2 . .**202** B5
 Twickenham TW2 . . . .**162** B3
 Wembley HA0 . . . .**87** F2
Spencer St, EC1 . . . .**11** G4
 Southall UB2 . . . .**122** D2
Spencer Wk, NW3
 off Hampstead
 High St **91** F4
 SW15 . . . .**148** A4
Spencer Yd, SE3
 off Blackheath Village .**155** F2
Spenser Gro, N16 . . . . . .**94** B4
Spenser Ms, SE21
 off Croxted Rd **170** A1
Spenser Rd, SE24 . . . . .**151** G5
Spenser St, SW1 . . . .**25** G5
Spensley Wk, N16
 off Clissold Rd **94** A3
Speranza St, SE18 . . . . .**137** J5
Sperling Rd, N17 . . . .**76** B2
Spert St, E14 . . . .**113** H7
Speyside, N14 . . . .**42** C6
Spey St, E14 . . . .**114** C5
Spezia Rd, NW10 . . . . . .**107** G2
Spice Quay Hts, SE1 . . . .**29** G2
Spicer Cl, SW9 . . . .**151** H2
 Walton-on-Thames
 KT12 . . . .**178** C6
Spice's Yd, Croy. CR0 . . .**201** J4
Spigurnell Rd, N17 . . . . . .**76** A1
Spikes Br Rd, Sthl. UB1 .**103** E6
Spilsby Cl, NW9
 off Kenley Av **70**/**71** E2
Spindle Cl, SE18 . . . . . .**136** B3
Spindlewood Gdns, Croy.
 CR0 . . . .**202** B4
Spindrift Av, E14 . . . .**134** A4
Spinel Cl, SE18 . . . .**137** J5
Spinnaker Cl, Bark. IG11 .**118** B3
Spinnells Rd, Har. HA2 . . .**85** F1
Spinney, The, N21 . . . .**43** G7
 SW16 . . . .**168** D3
 Barnet EN5 . . . .**41** E2
 Sidcup DA14 . . . .**176** E5
 Stanmore HA7 . . . .**53** H4
 Sunbury-on-Thames
 TW16 . . . .**178** A1
 Sutton SM3 . . . .**197** J4
 Wembley HA0 . . . .**86** D3
Spinney Cl, Beck. BR3 . .**190** B4
 New Malden KT3 . . . .**182** E5
 Worcester Park KT4 . .**197** F3
Spinney Dr, Felt. TW14 . .**141** F7
Spinney Gdns, SE19 . . .**170** C5
 Dagenham RM9 . . . . .**101** E5
Spinney Oak, Brom.
 BR1 . . . .**192** B2
Spinneys, The, Brom.
 BR1 . . . .**192** C2
Spires Shop Cen, The,
 Barn. EN5 . . . .**40** B3
Spirit Quay, E1 . . . .**29** J1
★ Spitalfields Comm Fm,
 E1 . . . .**13** H6
Spital Sq, E1 . . . .**21** E1
Spital St, E1 . . . .**21** H1

Spital Yd, E1 . . . . .21 E1
Spitfire Est, Houns.TW5 .122 C5
Spitfire Rd, Wall. SM6
  off Lancastrian Rd 201 F7
Spitfire Way, Houns.
  TW5 . . . . .122 C5
Spode Wk, NW6
  off Lymington Rd . .90/91 E6
Spondon Rd, N15 . . . . . .76 D4
Spoonbill Way, Hayes
  UB4 . . . . .102 D5
Spooners Ms, W3
  off Churchfield Rd 126 D1
Spooner Wk, Wall.
  SM6 . . . . .200 D5
Sporle Ct, SW11 . . . . . . .149 G3
Sportsbank St, SE6 . . . . .154 C7
Spotted Dog Path, E7
  off Upton La 97 G6
Spottons Gro, N17
  off Gospatrick Rd 75 J1
Spout Hill, Croy. CR0 . . .204 A5
Spratt Hall Rd, E11 . . . . . .79 G5
Spray La, Twick. TW2 . . .144 B6
Spray St, SE18 . . . . .137 E4
Spreighton Rd, W.Mol.
  KT8 . . . . .179 H4
Sprimont Pl, SW3 . . . . . . .31 J3
Springall St, SE15 . . . . . .133 E7
Springbank, N21 . . . . .43 F6
Springbank Rd, SE13 . . . .154 D6
Springbank Wk, NW1
  off St. Paul's Cres 92 D7
Springbourne Ct, Beck.
  BR3 . . . . .190 C1
Spring Br Ms, W5
  off Spring Br Rd 105 G7
Spring Br Rd, W5 . . . . . .105 G7
Spring Cl, Barn. EN5 . . . . .40 A5
  Borehamwood WD6 . . .38 A1
  Dagenham RM8 . . . . . .100 D1
Springclose La, Sutt.
  SM3 . . . . .198 B6
Spring Cotts, Surb. KT6
  off St. Leonard's Rd .181 G5
Spring Ct, Sid. DA15
  off Station Rd 176 A3
Springcroft Av, N2 . . . . . .73 J4
Springdale Ms, N16
  off Springdale Rd 94 A4
Springdale Rd, N16 . . . . . .94 A4
Spring Dr, Pnr. HA5
  off Eastcote Rd 66 A6
Springfield, E5 . . . . .94 E1
  Bushey (Bushey Hth.)
  WD23 . . . . .52 A1
Springfield Av, N10 . . . . .74 C3
  SW20 . . . . .184 C3
  Hampton TW12 . . . . . .161 H6
Springfield Cl, N12 . . . . . .56 E5
  Stanmore HA7 . . . . . . .52 D3
Springfield Ct, Wall. SM6
  off Springfield Rd 200 B5
Springfield Dr, Ilf. IG2 . . . .81 G5
Springfield Gdns, E5 . . . . .95 E1
  NW9 . . . . .70 D5
  Bromley BR1 . . . . .192 C4
  Ruislip HA4 . . . . .84 B1
  West Wickham BR4 . . .204 B2
  Woodford Green IG8 . .63 J7
Springfield Gro, SE7 . . . .135 J6
Springfield La, NW6 . . . . .108 E1
Springfield Mt, NW9 . . . . .70 E5
Springfield Pl, N.Mal.
  KT3 . . . . .182 C4
Springfield Ri, SE26 . . . . .170 E3
Springfield Rd, E4 . . . . . . .62 E1
  E6 . . . . .98 C7
  E15 . . . . .115 E3
  E17 . . . . .77 J6
  N11 . . . . .58 B5
  N15 . . . . .76 D4
  NW8 . . . . .109 F1
  SE26 . . . . .171 E5
  SW19 . . . . .166 C5
  W7 . . . . .124 B1
  Bexleyheath DA7 . . . .159 H3
  Bromley BR1 . . . . .192 C4
  Harrow HA1 . . . . .68 B6
  Hayes UB4 . . . . .122 C1
  Kingston upon Thames
  KT1 . . . . .181 H3
  Teddington TW11 . . . .162 D5
  Thornton Heath CR7 . .187 J1
  Twickenham TW2 . . . .161 G1
  Wallington SM6 . . . . . .200 B5
  Welling DA16 . . . . . . .158 B3
Springfield Wk, NW6 . . . .108 E1
  Orpington BR6
  off Place Fm Av 207 G1

Spring Gdns, N5
  off Grosvenor Av 93 J5
  SE11 . . . . .34 C3
  SW1 . . . . .25 J1
  Romford RM7 . . . . .83 J5
  Wallington SM6 . . . . . .200 C5
  West Molesey KT8 . . .179 J5
  Woodford Green IG8 . .63 J7
Spring Gdns Ind Est, Rom.
  RM7 . . . . .83 J5
SPRING GROVE, Islw. . . .144 C1
Spring Gro, SE19
  off Alma Pl 170 C7
  W4 . . . . .126 A5
  Hampton TW12
  off Plevna Rd 179 H1
  Loughton IG10 . . . . . . .48 A6
  Mitcham CR4 . . . . . . .186 A1
Spring Gro Cres, Houns.
  TW3 . . . . .143 J1
Spring Gro Rd, Houns.
  TW3 . . . . .143 H1
  Isleworth TW7 . . . . . .143 H1
  Richmond TW10 . . . . .145 J5
Spring Hill, E5 . . . . .76 D7
  SE26 . . . . .171 F4
Springhill Cl, SE5 . . . . . .152 A3
Springhurst Cl, Croy.
  CR0 . . . . .203 J4
Spring Lake, Stan. HA7 . .52 E4
Spring La, E5 . . . . .95 E1
  N10 . . . . .74 A3
  SE25 . . . . .188 E6
Spring Ms, W1 . . . . .16 A1
  Richmond TW9
  off Rosedale Rd 145 H4
Spring Pk Av, Croy.
  CR0 . . . . .203 G2
Spring Pk Dr, N4 . . . . . . .93 J1
Springpark Dr, Beck.
  BR3 . . . . .190 C3
Spring Pk Rd, Croy.
  CR0 . . . . .203 G2
Spring Pas, SW15
  off Embankment 148 A3
Spring Path, NW3 . . . . . . .91 G5
Spring Pl, N3
  off Windermere Av 72 D2
  NW5 . . . . .92 B5
Springpond Rd, Dag.
  RM9 . . . . .101 E5
Springrice Rd, SE13 . . . .154 C6
Spring St, W2 . . . . .15 E4
Spring Ter, Rich.TW9 . . . .145 H5
Spring Vale, Bexh. DA7 . .159 H4
Springvale Av, Brent.
  TW8 . . . . .125 G5
Springvale Est, W14
  off Blythe Rd 128 B3
Springvale Ter, W14 . . . .128 A3
Spring Vil Rd, Edg. HA8 . .54 A7
Spring Wk, E1 . . . . .21 H1
Springwater Cl, SE18 . . .156 D1
Springway, Har. HA1 . . . . .68 A7
Springwell Av, NW10 . . .107 F1
Springwell Cl, SW16
  off Etherstone Rd . . .169 G4
Springwell Ct, Houns.
  TW4 . . . . .142 D2
Springwell Rd, SW16 . . .169 G4
  Hounslow TW4, TW5 . .142 D1
Springwood Cres, Edg.
  HA8 . . . . .54 B2
Sprowston Ms, E7 . . . . . .97 G6
Sprowston Rd, E7 . . . . . .97 G5
Spruce Ct, W5
  off Elderberry Rd 125 H3
Sprucedale Gdns, Croy.
  CR0 . . . . .203 G4
Spruce Hills Rd, E17 . . . .78 C2
Spruce Pk, Brom. BR2
  off Cumberland Rd . .191 F4
Sprules Rd, SE4 . . . . . . .153 H2
Spurfield, W.Mol. KT8 . . .179 H3
Spurgeon Av, SE19 . . . . .188 A1
Spurgeon Rd, SE19 . . . . .188 A1
Spurgeon St, SE1 . . . . . . .28 B6
Spurling Rd, SE22 . . . . . .152 C4
  Dagenham RM9 . . . . .101 F6
Spur Rd, N15
  off Philip La 76 A4
  SE1 . . . . .26 E3
  SW1 . . . . .25 F4
  Barking IG11 . . . . . . .117 F3
  Edgware HA8 . . . . .53 H4
  Feltham TW14 . . . . . .142 B5
  Isleworth TW7 . . . . . .124 E7
Spur Rd Est, Edg. HA8 . . .53 J4
Spurstowe Rd, E8
  off Marcon Pl 94/95 E6

Spurstowe Ter, E8 . . . . . .94 E5
Square, The, W6 . . . . . . .127 J5
  Carshalton SM5 . . . . .200 A5
  Hayes UB3 . . . . .121 G1
  Ilford IG1 . . . . .80 D7
  Richmond TW9 . . . . . .145 G5
  Woodford Green IG8 . .63 G5
Square Rigger Row, SW11
  off York Pl 149 F3
Squarey St, SW17 . . . . . .167 F3
Squire Gdns, NW8 . . . . . . .7 E4
Squires, The, Rom. RM7 . .83 J6
Squires Ct, SW19 . . . . . .166 D4
Squires La, N3 . . . . .73 E2
Squires Mt, NW3
  off East Heath Rd 91 G3
Squires Wd Dr, Chis.
  BR7 . . . . .174 B7
Squirrel Cl, Houns.
  TW4 . . . . .142 C2
Squirrel Ms, W13 . . . . . .104 D7
Squirrels, The, SE13 . . . . .154 D3
  Pinner HA5 . . . . .67 F3
Squirrels Cl, N12
  off Woodside Av 57 F4
Squirrels Grn, Wor.Pk.
  KT4 . . . . .197 F1
Squirrels La, Buck.H. IG9 .64 A3
Squirrels Trd Est, The, Hayes
  UB3 . . . . .122 A3
Squirries St, E2 . . . . .13 J3
Stable Cl, Nthlt. UB5 . . . .103 G2
Stables, The, Buck.H.
  IG9 . . . . .47 J7
Stables End, Orp. BR6 . . .207 F3
Stables Ms, SE27 . . . . . .169 J5
Stables Way, SE11 . . . . . .35 E3
Stable Wk, N2
  off Old Fm Rd 73 G1
Stable Way, W10
  off Latimer Rd 107 J6
Stable Yd, SW1 . . . . .25 F3
  SW9 off Broomgrove
  Rd 151 F2
  SW15 off Danemere
  St 147 J3
Stable Yd Rd, SW1 . . . . . .25 F2
Stacey Av, N18 . . . . .61 F4
Stacey Cl, E10
  off Halford Rd 78 D5
Stacey St, N7 . . . . .93 G3
  WC2 . . . . .17 J4
Stackhouse St, SW3 . . . . .23 J5
Stacy Path, SE5
  off Harris St 132 B7
Stadium Business Cen, Wem.
  HA9 . . . . .88 B3
Stadium Retail Pk, Wem. HA9
  off Wembley Pk Dr . . .88 A3
Stadium Rd, NW2 . . . . . . .71 J7
  SE18 . . . . .136 B7
Stadium St, SW10 . . . . . .129 F7
Stadium Way, Wem.
  HA9 . . . . .87 J4
Staffa Rd, E10 . . . . .95 H1
Stafford Cl, E17 . . . . .77 J6
  N14 . . . . .42 C5
  NW6 . . . . .108 D3
  Sutton SM3 . . . . .198 B6
Stafford Ct, W8 . . . . .128 D3
Stafford Cross, Croy.
  CR0 . . . . .201 F5
Stafford Gdns, Croy.
  CR0 . . . . .201 F5
Stafford Pl, SW1 . . . . .25 F5
  Richmond TW10 . . . . .145 J7
Stafford Rd, E3 . . . . .113 J2
  E7 . . . . .97 J7
  NW6 . . . . .108 D3
  Croydon CR0 . . . . .201 G4
  Harrow HA1 . . . . .51 J7
  New Malden KT3 . . . . .182 C3
  Sidcup DA14 . . . . .175 H4
  Wallington SM6 . . . . . .200 C6
Staffordshire St, SE15 . . .152 D1
Stafford St, W1 . . . . .25 F1
Stafford Ter, W8 . . . . . . .128 D3
Staff St, EC1 . . . . .12 C4
Stag Cl, Edg. HA8 . . . . . . .70 B2
Staggart Grn, Chig. IG7 . .65 J6
Stag La, NW9 . . . . .70 C3
  SW15 . . . . .165 F2
  Buckhurst Hill IG9 . . . .63 H2
  Edgware HA8 . . . . .70 B2
Stag Pl, SW1 . . . . .25 F5
Stag Ride, SW19 . . . . . . .165 F3
Stags Way, Islw.TW7 . . . .124 C6
Stainbank Rd, Mitch.
  CR4 . . . . .186 B3

Stainby Cl, West Dr.
  UB7 . . . . .120 B3
Stainby Rd, N15 . . . . .76 C4
Stainer Ho, SE3
  off Ryan Cl 155 J4
Stainer St, SE1 . . . . .28 C3
Staines Av, Sutt. SM3 . . .198 A2
Staines Rd, Felt.TW14 . . .141 G7
  Hounslow TW3, TW4 . .143 H3
  Ilford IG1 . . . . .99 F4
  Twickenham TW2 . . . .161 G3
Staines Rd E, Sun.
  TW16 . . . . .160 A7
Staines Wk, Sid. DA14
  off Evry Rd 176 C6
Stainforth Rd, E17 . . . . . .78 A4
  Ilford IG2 . . . . .81 G7
Staining La, EC2 . . . . .20 A3
Stainmore Cl, Chis.
  BR7 . . . . .193 G1
Stainsbury St, E2
  off Royston St 113 F2
Stainsby Pl, E14
  off Stainsby Rd 114 A6
Stainsby Rd, E14 . . . . . . .114 A6
Stainton Rd, SE6 . . . . . . .154 D6
  Enfield EN3 . . . . .45 F1
Stalbridge St, NW1 . . . . . .15 H1
Stalham St, SE16 . . . . . . .133 E3
Stambourne Way, SE19 . .170 B7
  West Wickham BR4 . . .204 C3
Stamford Brook Av, W6 . .127 F3
Stamford Brook Rd, W6 . .127 F3
Stamford Cl, N15 . . . . . . .76 D4
  NW3 off Heath St 91 F4
  Harrow HA3 . . . . .52 B7
  Southall UB1 . . . . .103 G7
Stamford Cotts, SW10
  off Billing St 128/129 E7
Stamford Ct, W6
  off Goldhawk Rd 127 F4
Stamford Dr, Brom.
  BR2 . . . . .191 F4
Stamford Gdns, Dag.
  RM9 . . . . .100 C7
Stamford Gro E, N16
  off Oldhill St 94 D1
Stamford Gro W, N16
  off Oldhill St 94 D1
STAMFORD HILL, N16 . . . .94 B1
Stamford Hill, N16 . . . . . .94 B1
Stamford Hill Est, N16 . . .94 C1
Stamford Rd, E6 . . . . .116 B1
  N1 . . . . .94 B7
  N15 . . . . .76 D5
  Dagenham RM9 . . . . . .118 B1
Stamford St, SE1 . . . . .26 E2
Stamp Pl, E2 . . . . .13 F3
Stanard Cl, N16 . . . . .76 B7
Stanborough Cl, Hmptn.
  TW12 . . . . .161 F6
Stanborough Pas, E8
  off Abbot St 94 C6
Stanborough Rd, Houns.
  TW3 . . . . .144 A3
Stanbridge Pl, N21 . . . . . .59 H2
Stanbridge Rd, SW15 . . .147 J3
Stanbrook Rd, SE2 . . . . . .138 B2
Stanbury Rd, SE15 . . . . . .153 E1
Stancroft, NW9 . . . . .70 E4
Standard Ind Est, E16 . . .136 C2
Standard Pl, EC2 . . . . .12 E4
Standard Rd, NW10 . . . . .106 C4
  Belvedere DA17 . . . . .139 G5
  Bexleyheath DA6 . . . . .159 E4
  Hounslow TW4 . . . . . .143 E3
Standen Rd, SW18 . . . . . .148 C7
Standfield Gdns, Dag. RM10
  off Standfield Rd 101 G6
Standfield Rd, Dag.
  RM10 . . . . .101 G5
Standish Ho, SE3
  off Elford Cl 155 J4
Standish Rd, W6 . . . . . . .127 G4
Standlake Pt, SE23 . . . . .171 G3
Stane Cl, SW19
  off Hayward Cl . .184/185 E1
Stane Way, SE18 . . . . . . .136 A7
Stanfield Rd, E3 . . . . .113 H2
Stanford Cl, Hmptn.
  TW12 . . . . .161 F6
  Romford RM7 . . . . .83 H6
  Woodford Green IG8 . .64 B5
Stanford Ct, SW6
  off Bagley's La . .148/149 E1
Stanford Ho, Bark. IG11 . .118 B2
Stanford Pl, SE17 . . . . . . .36 D2
Stanford Rd, N11 . . . . . . .57 J5
  SW16 . . . . .186 D2
  W8 . . . . .22 B5

Stanford St, SW1 . . . . . . .33 H2
Stanford Way, SW16 . . . .186 D2
Stangate Cres, Borwd.
WD6 . . . . .38 E5
Stangate Gdns, Stan.
HA7 . . . . .53 E4
Stanger Rd, SE25 . . . . . .188 D4
Stanhope Av, N3 . . . . . . .72 C3
Bromley BR2 . . . . .205 F1
Harrow HA3 . . . . .68 A1
Stanhope CI, SE16
off Middleton Dr 133 G2
Stanhope Gdns, N4 . . . . .75 H6
N6 . . . . .74 B6
NW7 . . . . .55 F5
SW7 . . . . .30 D1
Dagenham RM8 . . . . . .101 F3
Ilford IG1 . . . . .98 C1
Stanhope Gate, W1 . . . . .24 C1
Stanhope Gro, Beck.
BR3 . . . . .189 J3
Stanhope Ms E, SW7 . . . .30 D1
Stanhope Ms S, SW7 . . . .30 D2
Stanhope Ms W, SW7 . . . .30 D1
Stanhope Par, NW1 . . . . . .9 F3
Stanhope Pk Rd, Grnf.
UB6 . . . . .103 J4
Stanhope PI, W2 . . . . . . .15 J4
Stanhope Rd, E17 . . . . . .78 B5
N6 . . . . .74 C6
N12 . . . . .57 F5
Barnet EN5 . . . . .39 J6
Bexleyheath DA7 . . . . .159 E2
Carshalton SM5 . . . . . .200 A7
Croydon CR0 . . . . .202 B3
Dagenham RM8 . . . . . .101 F2
Greenford UB6 . . . . . .103 J5
Sidcup DA15 . . . . .176 A4
Stanhope Row, W1 . . . . . .24 D2
Stanhope St, NW1 . . . . . . .9 F4
Stanhope Ter, W2 . . . . . .15 F5
Stanier CI, W14
off Aisgill Av 128 C5
Stanlake Ms, W12 . . . . . .127 J1
Stanlake Rd, W12 . . . . . .127 H1
Stanlake Vil, W12 . . . . . .127 H1
Stanley Av, Bark. IG11 . . .117 J2
Beckenham BR3 . . . . . .190 C2
Dagenham RM8 . . . . . .101 F1
Greenford UB6 . . . . . .103 J1
New Malden KT3 . . . . .183 G5
Wembley HA0 . . . . . . .87 H7
Stanley CI, SW8 . . . . .34 C6
Wembley HA0 . . . . . . .87 H7
Stanley Ct, Cars. SM5
off Stanley Pk Rd 200 A7
Stanley Cres, W11 . . . . . .108 C7
Stanleycroft CI, Islw.
TW7 . . . . .144 B1
Stanley Gdns, NW2 . . . . .89 J5
W3 . . . . .126 E1
W11 . . . . .108 C7
Mitcham CR4
off Ashbourne Rd 168 A6
Wallington SM6 . . . . . .200 C6
Stanley Gdns Ms, W11
off Stanley Cres 108 C7
Stanley Gdns Rd, Tedd.
TW11 . . . . .162 B5
Croydon CR0 . . . . .187 G6
Stanley Gro, SW8 . . . . . .150 A2
Croydon CR0 . . . . .187 G6
Stanley Pas, NW1 . . . . . .10 A2
Stanley Pk, E4 . . . . .62 D1
E10 . . . . .78 B6
E12 . . . . .98 B5
E15 . . . . .114 D1
E18 . . . . .79 F1
N2 . . . . .73 G3
N9 . . . . .60 C1
N10 . . . . .58 B7
N11 . . . . .58 D6
N15 . . . . .75 H4
NW9 off West Hendon
Bdy 71 G7
SW14 . . . . .146 B4
SW19 . . . . .166 D7
W3 . . . . .126 C3
Bromley BR2 . . . . .191 H4
Carshalton SM5 . . . . . .200 A7
Croydon CR0 . . . . .187 G2
Enfield EN1 . . . . .44 B3
Harrow HA2 . . . . .85 J2
Hounslow TW3 . . . . . .143 J4
Ilford IG1 . . . . .99 G2
Mitcham CR4 . . . . .168 A7

Stanley Rd, Mord. SM4 . .184 D4
Northwood HA6 . . . . . .66 A1
Sidcup DA14 . . . . .176 A3
Southall UB1 . . . . .102 E7
Sutton SM2 . . . . .198 E6
Teddington TW11 . . . . .162 B4
Twickenham TW2 . . . . .162 A3
Wembley HA9 . . . . . . .87 J6
Stanley St, SE8 . . . . .133 J7
Stanley Ter, N19 . . . . . . .92 E2
Stanmer St, SW11 . . . . . .149 H1
STANMORE 52 D5
Stanmore Gdns, Rich.
TW9 . . . . .145 J3
Sutton SM1 . . . . .199 F3
Stanmore Hall, Stan.
HA7 . . . . .52 D3
Stanmore Hill, Stan. HA7 .52 D3
Stanmore Pk, Stan. HA7 . .52 E5
Stanmore PI, NW1
off Arlington Rd 110 B1
Stanmore Rd, E11 . . . . . .97 F1
N15 . . . . .75 H4
Belvedere DA17 . . . . . .139 J4
Richmond TW9 . . . . . .145 J3
Stanmore St, N1
off Caledonian Rd 111 F1
Stanmore Ter, Beck. BR3 .190 A2
Stanmore Way, Loug.
IG10 . . . . .48 D1
Stannard Ms, E8 . . . . . . .94 D6
Stannard Rd, E8 . . . . . . .94 D6
Stannary PI, SE11 . . . . . .35 F4
Stannary St, SE11 . . . . . .35 F5
Stannet Way, Wall. SM6 . .200 C4
Stannington Path, Borwd.
WD6 . . . . .38 A1
Stansfeld Rd, E6 . . . . . . .116 A5
Stansfield Rd, SW9 . . . . .151 F3
Hounslow TW4 . . . . . .142 B2
Stansgate Rd, Dag.
RM10 . . . . .101 G2
Stanstead CI, Brom.
BR2 . . . . .191 F5
Stanstead Gro, SE6
off Catford Hill 171 J1
Stanstead Manor, Sutt.
SM1 . . . . .198 D6
Stanstead Rd, E11 . . . . . .79 H5
SE6 . . . . .171 G1
SE23 . . . . .171 G1
Hounslow (Hthrw.Air.)
TW6 . . . . .140 C6
Stansted Cres, Bex.
DA5 . . . . .176 D1
Stanswood Gdns, SE5
off Sedgmoor PI 132 B7
Stanthorpe CI, SW16 . . . .168 E5
Stanthorpe Rd, SW16 . . .168 E5
Stanton Av, Tedd. TW11 . .162 B5
Stanton CI, Epsom KT19 .196 B5
Worcester Park KT4 . . .198 A1
Stanton Ho, SE16
off Rotherhithe St 133 J2
Stanton Rd, SE26
off Stanton Way 171 J4
SW13 . . . . .147 F2
SW20 . . . . .184 A2
Croydon CR0 . . . . .187 J7
Stanton Sq, SE26
off Stanton Way 171 J4
Stanton Way, SE26 . . . . .171 J4
Stanway CI, Chig. IG7 . . . .65 H5
Stanway Ct, N1 . . . . .13 E2
Stanway Gdns, W3 . . . . . .126 A1
Edgware HA8 . . . . .54 C5
Stanway St, N1 . . . . .12 E1
STANWELL, Stai. (Stanw.) .140 B7
Stanwell CI, Stai. (Stanw.)
TW19 . . . . .140 A6
Stanwell Gdns, Stai. (Stanw.)
TW19 . . . . .140 A6
Stanwell Rd, Felt. TW14 . .141 F7
Stanwick Rd, W14 . . . . . .128 C4
Stanworth St, SE1 . . . . . .29 F4
Stanwyck Dr, Chig. IG7 . . .65 F5
Stapenhill Rd, Wem. HA0 .86 E3
Stapfield CI, SW2 . . . . . .169 E1
Pinner HA5 . . . . .50 E7
Stapleford Av, Ilf. IG2 . . . .81 H5
Stapleford CI, E4 . . . . . . .62 C3
SW19 . . . . .148 B7
Kingston upon Thames
KT1 . . . . .182 A3
Stapleford Rd, Wem.
HA0 . . . . .87 G7
Stapleford Way, Bark.
IG11 . . . . .118 B3
Staplehurst Rd, SE13 . . . .154 E5
Carshalton SM5 . . . . . .199 H7

Staple Inn, WC1 . . . . .19 E2
Staple Inn Bldgs, WC1 . . .18 E2
Staples CI, SE16 . . . . . . .133 H1
Staples Cor, NW2 . . . . . . .89 H1
Staples Cor Business Pk,
NW2 . . . . .89 H1
Staples Rd, Loug. IG10 . . .48 B3
Staple St, SE1 . . . . .28 C4
Stapleton Gdns, Croy.
CR0 . . . . .201 G5
Stapleton Hall Rd, N4 . . . .75 F7
Stapleton Rd, SW17 . . . . .168 A3
Bexleyheath DA7 . . . . .139 F7
Orpington BR6 . . . . . . .207 J3
Stapley Rd, Belv. DA17 . . .139 G5
Stapylton Rd, Barn. EN5 . .40 B3
Star All, EC3 . . . . .20 E5
Star & Garter Hill, Rich.
TW10 . . . . .163 H1
Starboard Way, E14 . . . . .134 A3
Starch Ho La, Ilf. IG6 . . . .81 G2
Starcross St, NW1 . . . . . . .9 G4
Starfield Rd, W12 . . . . . . .127 G2
Star La, E16 . . . . .115 E4
Starling CI, Buck.H. IG9 . . .63 G1
Pinner HA5 . . . . .66 C3
Starling Ms, SE28
off Whinchat Rd 137 G2
Starling Wk, Hmptn. TW12
off Oak Av 160/161 E6
Starmans CI, Dag. RM9 . . .119 E1
Star Path, Nthlt. UB5
off Brabazon Rd 103 G2
Star PI, E1 . . . . .21 G6
Star Rd, W14 . . . . .128 C6
Isleworth TW7 . . . . . . .144 A2
Star St, E16 . . . . .115 F5
W2 . . . . .15 F3
Starts CI, Orp. BR6 . . . . . .206 D3
Starts Hill Av, Orp. BR6 . . .207 E4
Starts Hill Rd, Orp. BR6 . .206 D3
Starveall CI, West Dr.
UB7 . . . . .120 C3
Star Yd, WC2 . . . . .18 E3
State Fm Av, Orp. BR6 . . .207 E4
Staten Gdns, Twick.
TW1 . . . . .162 C1
Statham Gro, N16
off Green Las 93 J4
N18 . . . . .60 B5
Station App, E4 (Highams Pk.)
The Avenue 62 D6
E7 off Woodford Rd . . .97 H4
E11 (Snaresbrook)
off High St 79 G5
N11
off Friern Barnet Rd . . .58 B5
N12 (Woodside Pk.) . . .56 E4
N16 (Stoke Newington)
off Stamford Hill 94 C2
NW10 off Station Rd . .107 F3
SE1 . . . . .26 D4
SE3
off Kidbrooke Pk Rd . . .155 H3
SE9 (Mottingham) 174 C1
SE26 (Lwr.Sydenham)
off Worsley Br Rd 171 J5
SE26 (Sydenham)
off Sydenham Rd 171 H4
SW6 . . . . .148 B3
SW16 . . . . .168 D5
W7 . . . . .124 B1
Barnet EN5 . . . . .41 F4
Bexley DA5
off Bexley High St 159 G7
Bexleyheath DA7
off Avenue Rd . . .158/159 E2
Bexleyheath (Barne.)
DA7 . . . . .159 J2
Bromley (Hayes) BR2 . .205 G4
Buckhurst Hill IG9
off Cherry Tree Ri 64 A4
Chislehurst BR7 . . . . . .192 D1
Chislehurst (Elm.Wds.)
BR7 . . . . .174 B6
Epsom (Stoneleigh)
KT19 . . . . .197 G5
Esher (Hinch.Wd.)
KT10 . . . . .194 C3
Greenford UB6 . . . . . .86 A7
Hampton TW12
off Milton Rd 179 G1
Harrow HA1 . . . . .68 B7
Hayes UB3 . . . . .121 J2
Kingston upon Thames
KT1 . . . . .182 A1
Loughton IG10 . . . . . . .48 B5
Loughton (Debden)
IG10 . . . . .49 F4
Orpington BR6 . . . . . . .207 J2

Station App, Pnr. HA5 . . . .66 E3
Pinner (Hatch End) HA5
off Uxbridge Rd 51 G7
Richmond TW9 . . . . . .146 A1
Ruislip (S.Ruis.) HA4 . . .84 B5
Sunbury-on-Thames
TW16 . . . . .178 A1
Sutton (Cheam) SM2 . .198 B7
Watford (Carp.Pk.) WD19
off Prestwick Rd 50 D3
Welling DA16 . . . . .157 J2
Wembley HA0 . . . . . . .87 E6
West Drayton UB7 . . . .120 B1
Station App N, Sid.
DA15 . . . . .176 A2
Station App Rd, W4 . . . . .126 C7
Station Av, SW9
off Coldharbour La . . .151 H3
New Malden KT3 . . . . .183 E3
Richmond TW9 . . . . . .146 A1
Station CI, N3 . . . . .72 D1
N12 (Woodside Pk.) . . .56 E4
Hampton TW12 . . . . . .179 H1
Station Cres, N15 . . . . . . .76 A4
SE3 . . . . .135 G5
Wembley HA0 . . . . . . .87 E6
Stationers Hall Ct, EC4
off Ludgate Hill 111 H6
Station Est, Beck. BR3
off Elmers End Rd 189 G4
Station Est Rd, Felt.
TW14 . . . . .160 B1
Station Garage Ms, SW16
off Estreham Rd 168 D6
Station Gdns, W4 . . . . . . .126 C7
Station Gro, Wem. HA0 . . .87 H6
Station Hill, Brom. BR2 . . .205 G2
Station Ho Ms, N9
off Fore St 60 D4
Station Par, E11 . . . . .79 G5
N14 off High St 58 D1
NW2 . . . . .89 J6
SW12
off Balham High Rd . .168 A1
W3 . . . . .106 A6
Barking IG11 . . . . .99 F7
Feltham TW14 . . . . . . .142 B7
Richmond TW9 . . . . . .146 A1
Station Pas, E18
off Maybank Rd 79 H2
Station Path, E8
off Amhurst Rd 94/95 E6
Station PI, N4
off Seven Sisters Rd . .93 G2
Station Ri, SE27
off Norwood Rd 169 H2
Station Rd, E4
(Chingford) 62 D1
E7 . . . . .97 G4
E12 . . . . .98 A4
E17 . . . . .77 H6
N3 . . . . .72 D1
N11 . . . . .58 B5
N17 . . . . .76 D3
N19 . . . . .92 C3
N21 . . . . .59 H1
N22 . . . . .75 F2
NW4 . . . . .71 G6
NW7 . . . . .55 E5
NW10 . . . . .107 F2
SE13 . . . . .154 C3
SE20 . . . . .171 F6
SE25
(Norwood Junct.) 188 C4
SW13 . . . . .147 G2
SW19 . . . . .185 F1
W5 . . . . .105 J6
W7 (Hanwell) 124 B1
Barnet EN5 . . . . .40 C5
Belvedere DA17 . . . . . .139 G3
Bexleyheath DA7 . . . . .159 E3
Borehamwood WD6 . . .38 A4
Brentford TW8 . . . . . .125 F6
Bromley BR1 . . . . .191 G1
Bromley (Short.) BR2 . .191 E2
Carshalton SM5 . . . . . .199 J4
Chessington KT9 . . . . .195 H5
Chigwell IG7 . . . . .64 E3
Croydon (E.Croy.)
CR0 . . . . .202 A2
Croydon (W.Croy.)
CR0 . . . . .201 J1
Edgware HA8 . . . . .54 A6
Esher KT10 . . . . .194 A2
Esher (Clay.) KT10 . . . .194 A4
Hampton TW12 . . . . . .179 G1
Harrow HA1 . . . . .68 C7
Harrow (N.Har.) HA2 . . .67 H5
Hayes UB3 . . . . .121 J3
Hounslow TW3 . . . . . .143 H4

Station Rd, Ilford IG1 . . . . .98 E3
Ilford (Barkingside) IG6 . .81 G3
Kingston upon Thames
KT2 . . . . .182 A1
Kingston upon Thames
(Hmptn.W.) KT1 . . . . .181 F1
Loughton IG10 . . . . .48 B4
New Malden (Mots.Pk.)
KT3 . . . . .183 H5
Orpington BR6 . . . . . . .207 J2
Romford (Chad.Hth.)
RM6 . . . . .82 D7
Sidcup DA15 . . . . .176 A4
Sunbury-on-Thames
TW16 . . . . .160 A7
Teddington TW11 . . . . .162 C5
Thames Ditton KT7 . . . .180 C7
Twickenham TW1 . . . . .162 C1
West Drayton UB7 . . . .120 A1
West Wickham BR4 . . .204 C1
Station Rd N, Belv.
DA17 . . . . .139 H3
Station Sq, Orp. (Petts Wd)
BR5 . . . . .193 F5
Station St, E15 . . . . .96 D7
E16 . . . . .136 E1
Station Ter, NW10 . . . . .108 A2
SE5 . . . . .151 J1
Station Vw, Grnf. UB6 . .104 A1
Station Way, Buck.H.
(Rod.Val.) IG9 . . . . .63 J4
Esher (Clay.) KT10 . . . .194 B6
Sutton (Cheam) SM3 . .198 B6
Station Yd, Twick. TW1 . .144 D7
Staunton Rd, Kings.T.
KT2 . . . . .163 H6
Staunton St, SE8 . . . . . .133 J6
★ Stave Hill Ecological Pk,
SE16 . . . . .133 H2
Staveley Cl, E9
off Churchill Wk 95 F5
N7 off Penn Rd 92/93 E4
SE15 off Asylum
Rd 152/153 E1
Staveley Gdns, W4 . . . . .146 D1
Staveley Rd, W4 . . . . . . .126 D7
Staverton Rd, NW2 . . . . . .89 J7
Stave Yd Rd, SE16 . . . . .133 H1
Stavordale Rd, N5 . . . . . .93 H4
Carshalton SM5 . . . . . .185 F7
Stayner's Rd, E1 . . . . . . .113 G4
Stayton Rd, Sutt. SM1 . .198 D3
Steadfast Rd, Kings.T.
KT1 . . . . .181 G1
Stead St, SE17 . . . . .36 B2
Steam Fm La, Felt.
TW14 . . . . .141 J4
Stean St, E8 . . . . .112 C1
Stebbing Ho, W11 . . . . . .128 A1
Stebbing Way, Bark.
IG11 . . . . .118 A2
Stebondale St, E14 . . . . .134 C5
Stedham Pl, WC1 . . . . . . .18 A3
Steedman St, SE17 . . . . . .35 J2
Steeds Rd, N10 . . . . .73 J1
Steeds Way, Loug. IG10 . .48 B3
Steele Rd, E11 . . . . .96 E4
N17 . . . . .76 B3
NW10 . . . . .106 C2
W4 . . . . .126 C3
Isleworth TW7 . . . . . . .144 D4
Steeles Ms N, NW3
off Steeles Rd 91 J6
Steeles Ms S, NW3
off Steeles Rd 91 J6
Steeles Rd, NW3 . . . . . . .91 J6
Steele Wk, Erith DA8 . . .139 H6
Steel's La, E1
off Coventry Rd . .112/113 E6
Steeplestone Cl, N18 . . . .59 J5
Steeple Wk, N1
off Basire St 111 J1
Steerforth St, SW18 . . . .167 E2
Steers Mead, Mitch.
CR4 . . . . .185 J1
Steers Way, SE16 . . . . . .133 H2
Stellar Ho, N17 . . . . .60 C7
Stella Rd, SW17 . . . . . . .167 J6
Stellman Cl, E5 . . . . .94 D3

Stembridge Rd, SE20 . . . .188 E2
Stephan Cl, E8 . . . . .112 D1
Stephen Cl, Orp. BR6 . . . .207 J3
Stephendale Rd, SW6 . . .149 E2
Stephen Ms, W1 . . . . .17 H2
Stephen Pl, SW4
off Rectory Gro 150 C3
Stephen Rd, Bexh. DA7 . .159 J3
Stephenson Rd, E17 . . . . .77 H5
W7 . . . . .104 C6
Twickenham TW2 . . . . .143 G7
Stephenson St, E16 . . . . .114 E4
NW10 . . . . .107 E3
Stephenson Way, NW1 . . . .9 G5
Stephen's Rd, E15 . . . . . .115 E1
Stephen St, W1 . . . . .17 H2
STEPNEY, E1 . . . . .113 F5
Stepney Causeway, E1 . .113 G6
Stepney Grn, E1 . . . . . . .113 F5
Stepney High St, E1 . . . .113 G5
Stepney Way, E1 . . . . . . .112 E5
Sterling Av, Edg. HA8 . . . .53 J4
Pinner HA5 . . . . .66 E7
Sterling Cl, NW10 . . . . . . .89 G6
Pinner HA5 . . . . .84 D1
Sterling Gdns, SE14 . . . .133 H6
Sterling Ho, SE3
off Cambert Way 155 H4
Sterling Ind Est, Dag.
RM10 . . . . .101 H4
Sterling Pl, W5 . . . . .125 H4
Sterling St, SW7 . . . . .23 H5
Sterling Way, N18 . . . . . . .60 A5
Sternberg Cen, N3
(Finchley) . . . . .72 E2 ★
Stern Cl, Bark. IG11 . . . . .118 C2
Sterndale Rd, W14 . . . . . .128 A3
Sterne St, W12 . . . . .128 A2
Sternhall La, SE15 . . . . . .152 D3
Sternhold Av, SW2 . . . . .168 D2
Sterry Cres, Dag. RM10
off Alibon Rd 101 G5
Sterry Dr, Epsom KT19 .196 E4
Thames Ditton KT7 . . . .180 B6
Sterry Gdns, Dag. RM10 .101 G6
Sterry Rd, Bark. IG11 . . . .117 J1
Dagenham RM10 . . . . .101 G4
Sterry St, SE1 . . . . .28 B4
Steucers La, SE23 . . . . . .153 H7
Steve Biko La, SE6 . . . . .172 A4
Steve Biko Rd, N7 . . . . . .93 G3
Steve Biko Way, Houns.
TW3 . . . . .143 G3
Stevedale Rd, Well. 158 C2
DA16 . . . . .158 C2
Stevedore St, E1
off Waterman
Way 132/133 E1
Stevenage Rd, E6 . . . . . . .98 D6
SW6 . . . . .128 A7
Stevens Av, E9 . . . . .95 F6
Stevens Cl, Beck. BR3 . . .172 A6
Hampton TW12 . . . . . .161 E6
Pinner HA5
off Bridle Rd 66 C5
Stevens Grn, Bushey
(Bushey Hth.) WD23 . . .51 J1
Stevens La, Esher (Clay.)
KT10 . . . . .194 D7
Stevenson Cl, Barn. EN5 . .41 G6
Stevenson Cres, SE16 . . . .37 J3
Stevens Rd, Dag. RM8 . . .100 B3
Stevens St, SE1 . . . . .29 E5
Stevens Way, Chig. IG7 . . .65 H4
Steventon Rd, W12 . . . . .107 F7
Stewards Holte Wk, N11
off Coppies Gro 58 B4
Steward St, E1 . . . . .21 E2
Stewart Cl, NW9 . . . . .70 C6
Chislehurst BR7 . . . . . .175 E5
Hampton TW12 . . . . . .161 E5
Stewart Rainbird Ho,
E12 . . . . .98 D5
Stewart Rd, E15 . . . . .96 C4
Stewartsby Cl, N18 . . . . . .59 J5
Stewart's Gro, SW3 . . . . . .31 F3
Stewart's Rd, SW8 . . . . . .130 C7
Stewart St, E14 . . . . .134 C2
Stew La, EC4 . . . . .19 J5
Steyne Rd, W3 . . . . .126 C1
Steyning Gro, SE9 . . . . . .174 C4
Steynings Way, N12 . . . . . .56 D5
Steyning Way, Houns.
TW4 . . . . .142 C4
Steynton Av, Bex. DA5 . .176 D2
Stickland Rd, Belv. DA17
off Picardy Rd 139 G4
Stickleton Cl, Grnf. UB6 .103 H3
Stilecroft Gdns, Wem.
HA0 . . . . .86 E3

Stile Hall Gdns, W4 . . . . .126 A5
Stile Hall Par, W4
off Chiswick High Rd .126 A5
Stile Path, Sun. TW16 . . .178 A4
Stiles Cl, Brom. BR2 . . . .192 C6
Erith DA8
off Riverdale Rd 139 H5
Stillingfleet Rd, SW13 . . .127 G6
Stillington St, SW1 . . . . . .33 G1
Stillness Rd, SE23 . . . . . .153 H6
Stilton Cres, NW10 . . . . . .88 C7
Stipularis Dr, Hayes
UB4 . . . . .102 D4
Stirling Cl, SW16 . . . . . . .186 C1
Stirling Cor, Barn. EN5 . . . .38 C2
Borehamwood WD6 . . . .38 C2
Stirling Gro, Houns.
TW3 . . . . .143 J2
Stirling Rd, E13 . . . . .115 H2
E17 . . . . .77 H3
N17 . . . . .76 D1
N22 . . . . .75 H1
SW9 . . . . .150 E2
W3 . . . . .126 B3
Harrow HA3 . . . . .68 C3
Hayes UB3 . . . . .102 B7
Hounslow (Hthrw.Air.)
TW6 . . . . .140 C6
Twickenham TW2 . . . . .143 G7
Stirling Rd Path, E17 . . . .77 H3
Stirling Wk, N.Mal. KT3 . .182 C5
Surbiton KT5 . . . . .182 B6
Stirling Way, Borwd.
WD6 . . . . .38 D6
Croydon CR0 . . . . .186 E7
Stiven Cres, Har. HA2 . . . .85 F3
Stockbury Rd, Croy.
CR0 . . . . .189 F6
Stockdale Rd, Dag. RM8 .101 F2
Stockdove Way, Grnf.
UB6 . . . . .104 C3
Stocker Gdns, Dag.
RM9 . . . . .100 C7
★ Stock Exchange, EC2 . .20 C4
Stockfield Rd, SW16 . . . .169 F3
Esher (Clay.) KT10 . . . .194 B5
Stockholm Ho, E1 . . . . . .112 D7
Stockholm Rd, SE16 . . . .133 F5
Stockholm Way, E1 . . . . . .29 H1
Stockhurst Cl, SW15 . . . .147 J2
Stockingswater La, Enf.
EN3 . . . . .45 H3
Stockley Cl, West Dr.
UB7 . . . . .120 E2
Stockley Fm Rd, West Dr. UB7
off Stockley Rd . .120/121 E3
Stockley Pk, Uxb. UB11 .121 E1
Stockley Pk Roundabout,
Uxb. UB11 . . . . .120 E1
Stockley Rd, West Dr.
UB7 . . . . .120 E2
Stock Orchard Cres, N7 . .93 F5
Stock Orchard St, N7 . . . .93 F5
Stockport Rd, SW16 . . . .186 D1
Stocksfield Rd, E17 . . . . . .78 C3
Stocks Pl, E14
off Grenade St 113 J7
Stock St, E13 . . . . .115 G2
Stockton Cl, Barn. EN5 . . .41 F4
Stockton Gdns, N17
off Stockton Rd 59 J7
NW7 . . . . .54 D7
Stockton Rd, N17 . . . . . . .59 J7
N18 . . . . .60 D6
STOCKWELL, SW9 . . . . . .150 D3
Stockwell Av, SW9 . . . . . .151 F3
Stockwell Cl, Brom. BR1 .191 H2
Stockwell Gdns, SW9 . . .151 F2
Stockwell Gdns Est,
SW9 . . . . .151 E2
Stockwell Grn, SW9 . . . . .151 F2
Stockwell La, SW9 . . . . . .151 F2
Stockwell Ms, SW9
off Stockwell Rd 151 F2
Stockwell Pk Cres, SW9 .151 F1
Stockwell Pk Est, SW9 . .151 G2
Stockwell Pk Rd, SW9 . . .151 F1
Stockwell Pk Wk, SW9 . .151 F3
Stockwell Rd, SW9 . . . . . .151 F2
Stockwell St, SE10 . . . . . .134 C6
Stockwell Ter, SW9 . . . . .151 F1
Stodart Rd, SE20 . . . . . . .189 F1
Stofield Gdns, SE9
off Aldersgrove Av 174 A3
Stoford Cl, SW19 . . . . . . .148 B7
Stokenchurch St, SW6 . .148 E1
STOKE NEWINGTON,
N16 . . . . .94 B2
Stoke Newington Ch St,
N16 . . . . .94 A3

Stoke Newington Common,
N16 . . . . .94 C3
Stoke Newington High St,
N16 . . . . .94 C3
Stoke Newington Rd,
N16 . . . . .94 C5
Stoke Pl, NW10 . . . . .107 F3
Stoke Rd, Kings.T. KT2 . .164 C7
Stokesby Rd, Chess.
KT9 . . . . .195 J6
Stokesley St, W12 . . . . . .107 F6
Stokes Rd, E6 . . . . .116 B4
Croydon CR0 . . . . .189 G6
Stoll Cl, NW2 . . . . .89 J3
Stonard Rd, N13 . . . . .59 G3
Dagenham RM8 . . . . . .100 B5
Stonards Hill, Loug.
IG10 . . . . .48 C6
Stondon Pk, SE23 . . . . . .153 H7
Stondon Wk, E6 . . . . .116 A2
Stonebanks, Walt. KT12 .178 A7
STONEBRIDGE, NW10 . .106 B1
Stonebridge Common, E8
off Mayfield Rd 94 C7
Stonebridge Pk, NW10 . . .88 D7
Stonebridge Rd, N15 . . . .76 B5
Stonebridge Way, Wem.
HA9 . . . . .88 B6
Stone Bldgs, WC2 . . . . . . .18 D2
Stonechat Sq, E6
off Peridot St 116 B5
Stone Cl, SW4
off Larkhall Ri 150 C2
Dagenham RM8 . . . . . .101 F2
West Drayton UB7 . . . .120 C1
Stonecot Cl, Sutt. SM3 . .198 B1
Stonecot Hill, Sutt. SM3 .198 B1
Stone Cres, Felt. TW14 . .141 J7
Stonecroft Cl, Barn. EN5 . .39 H4
Stonecroft Rd, Erith
DA8 . . . . .139 J7
Stonecroft Way, Croy.
CR0 . . . . .187 E7
Stonecrop Cl, NW9 . . . . . .70 D3
Stonecutter Ct, EC4
off Stonecutter St 111 H6
Stonecutter St, EC4 . . . . .19 G3
Stonefield Cl, Bexh.
DA7 . . . . .159 G3
Ruislip HA4 . . . . .84 E5
Stonefield St, N1 . . . . . . .111 G1
Stonefield Way, SE7
off Greenbay Rd 136 A7
Ruislip HA4 . . . . .84 A7
Stonegrove, Edg. HA8 . . . .53 H4
Stonegrove Est, Edg.
HA8 . . . . .53 J4
Stonegrove Gdns, Edg.
HA8 . . . . .53 J5
Stonehall Av, Ilf. IG1 . . . . .80 B6
Stone Hall Gdns, W8 . . . . .22 A6
Stone Hall Pl, W8 . . . . . . .22 A6
Stone Hall Rd, N21 . . . . . .43 F7
Stoneham Rd, N11 . . . . . . .58 C6
Stonehill Cl, SW14 . . . . . .146 D5
Stonehill Grn, Dart. DA2 .177 J7
Stonehill Rd, SW14 . . . . .146 C5
W4 off Wellesley Rd . . .126 A5
Stonehills Ct, SE21 . . . . . .170 B3
Stonehill Wds Pk, Sid.
DA14 . . . . .177 H6
Stonehorse Rd, Enf. EN3 . .45 F5
Stone Ho Ct, EC3 . . . . . . .20 D3
Stone Lake Retail Pk,
SE7 . . . . .135 H4
STONELEIGH, Epsom 197 G5
Stoneleigh Av, Enf. EN1 . . .45 E1
Worcester Park KT4 . . .197 G4
Stoneleigh Bdy, Epsom
KT17 . . . . .197 G5
Stoneleigh Cres, Epsom
KT19 . . . . .197 F5
Stoneleigh Pk Av, Croy.
CR0 . . . . .189 G6
Stoneleigh Pk Rd, Epsom
KT19 . . . . .197 F6
Stoneleigh Pl, W11 . . . . . .108 A7
Stoneleigh Rd, N17 . . . . . .76 C3
Carshalton SM5 . . . . . .185 H7
Ilford IG5 . . . . .80 B3
Stoneleigh St, W11 . . . . .108 A7
Stoneleigh Ter, N19 . . . . . .92 B2
Stonells Rd, SW11
off Chatham Rd 149 J5
Stonemasons Cl, N15 . . . .76 A4
Stonenest St, N4 . . . . .93 F1
Stone Pk Av, Beck. BR3 .190 A4
Stone Pl, Wor.Pk. KT4 . . .197 G2
Stone Rd, Brom. BR2 . . . .191 F5
Stones End St, SE1 . . . . . .27 J4

Stone St, Croy. CR0 . . . .201 G5
Stonewall, E6 . . . . .116 D5
Stoney All, SE18 . . . . . . .156 D2
Stoneyard La, E14
  off Poplar High St 114 B7
Stoneycroft Cl, SE12 . . . .155 F7
Stoneycroft Rd, Wdf.Grn.
  IG8 . . . . .64 B6
Stoneydeep, Tedd. TW11
Stoneydown, E17 . . . . . . .77 H4
Stoneydown Av, E17 . . . . .77 H4
Stoneyfields Gdns, Edg.
  HA8 . . . . .54 C4
Stoneyfields La, Edg.
  HA8 . . . . .54 C5
Stoney La, E1 . . . . .21 E3
  SE19 off Church Rd . . .170 C6
Stoney St, SE1 . . . . .28 B1
Stonhouse St, SW4 . . . . .150 D3
Stonor Rd, W14 . . . . . . .128 C4
Stonycroft Cl, Enf. EN3
  off Brimsdown Av 45 H2
Stony Path, Loug. IG10 . . .48 C2
Stopes St, SE15 . . . . . . .132 C7
Stopford Rd, E13 . . . . . .115 G1
  SE17 . . . . .35 H4
Store Rd, E16 . . . . .136 D2
Storers Quay, E14 . . . . . .134 D4
Store St, E15 . . . . .96 D5
  WC1 . . . . .17 H2
Storey Rd, E17 . . . . .77 J4
  N6 . . . . .73 J6
Storey's Gate, SW1 . . . . .25 J4
Storey St, E16 . . . . .136 D1
Stories Ms, SE5 . . . . . . .152 B2
Stories Rd, SE5 . . . . . . .152 B3
Stork Rd, E7 . . . . .97 F6
Storksmead Rd, Edg.
  HA8 . . . . .54 E7
Storks Rd, SE16 . . . . .29 J6
Stormont Rd, N6 . . . . . . .73 J7
  SW11 . . . . .150 A3
Stormont Way, Chess.
  KT9 . . . . .195 F5
Stormount Dr, Hayes
  UB3 . . . . .121 F2
Storrington Rd, Croy.
  CR0 . . . . .202 C1
Story St, N1
  off Carnoustie Dr 93 F7
Stothard Pl, EC2
  off Bishopsgate 112 B5
Stothard St, E1
  off Colebert Av 113 F4
Stott Cl, SW18 . . . . .149 G6
Stoughton Av, Sutt.
  SM3 . . . . .198 A5
Stoughton Cl, SE11 . . . . .34 D2
  SW15
  off Bessborough Rd . . .165 G1
Stour Av, Sthl. UB2 . . . . .123 G3
Stourcliffe St, W1 . . . . . . .15 J4
Stour Cl, Kes. BR2 . . . . . .205 J4
Stourhead Cl, SW19
  off Castlecombe Dr . . .148 A7
Stourhead Gdns, SW20 .183 G3
Stour Rd, E3 . . . . .96 A7
  Dagenham RM10 . . . .101 G2
Stourton Av, Felt. TW13 .161 F4
Stowage, SE8 . . . . .134 A6
Stow Cres, E17 . . . . .61 H7
Stowe Gdns, N9 . . . . .60 C1
Stowe Pl, N15 . . . . .76 B3
Stowe Rd, W12 . . . . .127 H2
Stowting Rd, Orp. BR6 . .207 H4
Stox Mead, Har. HA3 . . . .68 A1
Stracey Rd, E7 . . . . .97 G4
  NW10 . . . . .106 D1
Strachan Pl, SW19
  off Woodhayes Rd 165 J6
Stradbroke Dr, Chig. IG7 .64 D6
Stradbroke Gro, Buck.H.
  IG9 . . . . .64 A1
  Ilford IG5 . . . . .80 B3
Stradbroke Pk, Chig.
  IG7 . . . . .64 E6
Stradbroke Rd, N5 . . . . . .93 J4
Stradbrook Cl, Har. HA2
  off Stiven Cres 85 F3
Stradella Rd, SE24 . . . . .151 J6
Strafford Av, Ilf. IG5 . . . . .80 D2
Strafford Rd, W3 . . . . . .126 C2
  Barnet EN5 . . . . .40 B3
  Hounslow TW3 . . . . . .143 F3
  Twickenham TW1 . . . .144 D7
Strafford St, E14 . . . . . . .134 A2
Strahan Rd, E3 . . . . .113 H3
Straight, The, Sthl. UB1 .122 D2
Straightsmouth, SE10 . .134 C7

Strait Rd, E6 . . . . .116 B7
Straker's Rd, SE22 . . . . .152 E4
STRAND, WC2 . . . . .18 A5
Strand, WC2 . . . . .18 A6
Strand Ct, SE18
  off Strandfield Cl 137 H5
Strandfield Cl, SE18 . . . .137 H5
Strand La, WC2 . . . . .18 D5
Strand on the Grn, W4 . .126 A6
Strand Pl, N18 . . . . .60 A4
Strand Sch App, W4
  off Thames Rd 126 A6
Strangways Ter, W14
  off Melbury Rd 128 C3
Stranraer Rd, Houns.
  (Hthrw.Air.) TW6 . . . .140 B6
Stranraer Way, N1 . . . . . .93 E7
Strasburg Rd, SW11 . . . .150 B1
Stratfield Pk Cl, N21 . . . . .43 H7
Stratfield Rd, Borwd.
  WD6 . . . . .38 A3
STRATFORD, E15 . . . . . . .96 C6
Stratford Av, W8
  off Stratford Rd 128 D3
Stratford Cen, The, E15 . .96 D7
Stratford Ct, Bark. IG11 .100 A7
  Dagenham RM10 . . . .101 J7
Stratford Ct, N.Mal. KT3
  off Kingston Rd 182 D4
Stratford Gro, SW15 . . . .148 A4
Stratford Ho Av, Brom.
  BR1 . . . . .192 B3
Stratford Pl, W1 . . . . .16 D4
Stratford Rd, E13 . . . . . .115 F1
  NW4 . . . . .72 A4
  W8 . . . . .128 D3
  Hayes UB4 . . . . .102 B4
  Hounslow (Hthrw.Air.)
  TW6 . . . . .141 E6
  Southall UB2 . . . . .122 E4
  Thornton Heath CR7 . .187 G4
Stratford Vil, NW1 . . . . . . .92 C7
Strathan Cl, SW18 . . . . .148 B6
Strathaven Rd, SE12 . . . .155 H6
Strathblaine Rd, SW11 . .149 G4
Strathbrook Rd, SW16 . .169 F7
Strathcona Rd, Wem.
  HA9 . . . . .87 G2
Strathdale, SW16 . . . . . .169 F5
Strathdon Dr, SW17 . . . .167 G3
Strathearn Av, Hayes
  UB3 . . . . .121 J7
  Twickenham TW2 . . . .161 H1
Strathearn Pl, W2 . . . . . . .15 F5
Strathearn Rd, SW19 . . .166 D5
  Sutton SM1 . . . . .198 D5
Stratheden Par, SE3
  off Stratheden Rd 135 G2
Stratheden Rd, SE3 . . . .155 G1
Strathfield Gdns, Bark.
  IG11 . . . . .99 G6
Strathleven Rd, SW2 . . . .151 E5
Strathmore Gdns, N3 . . . .72 E1
  W8
  off Palace Gdns Ter . . .128 D1
  Edgware HA8 . . . . .70 B2
Strathmore Rd, SW19 . .166 D3
  Croydon CR0 . . . . .187 J7
  Teddington TW11 . . . .162 B4
Strathnairn St, SE1 . . . . . .37 J2
Strathray Gdns, NW3 . . . .91 H6
Strath Ter, SW11 . . . . . . .149 H4
Strathville Rd, SW18 . . . .166 E2
Strathyre Av, SW16 . . . . .187 G3
Stratton Cl, SW19 . . . . . .184 D2
  Bexleyheath DA7 . . . . .159 E3
  Edgware HA8 . . . . .53 J6
  Hounslow TW3 . . . . . .143 F1
Strattondale St, E14 . . . .134 C3
Stratton Dr, Bark. IG11 . . .99 J5
Stratton Gdns, Sthl.
  UB1 . . . . .103 F6
Stratton Rd, SW19 . . . . .184 D2
  Bexleyheath DA7 . . . . .159 E3
Stratton St, W1 . . . . .25 E1
Strauss Rd, W4 . . . . .126 D2
STRAWBERRY HILL,
  Twick. 162 B3
Strawberry Hill, Twick.
  TW1 . . . . .162 C3
Strawberry Hill Cl, Twick.
  TW1 . . . . .162 C3
Strawberry Hill Rd, Twick.
  TW1 . . . . .162 C3
Strawberry La, Cars.
  SM5 . . . . .199 J3
Strawberry Vale, N2 . . . . .73 G1
  Twickenham TW1 . . . .162 D3
Streakes Fld Rd, NW2 . . .89 G2
Streamdale, SE2 . . . . . . .138 A6

Stream La, Edg. HA8 . . . .54 B5
Streamside Cl, N9 . . . . . . .60 C1
  Bromley BR2 . . . . .191 G4
Streamway, Belv. DA17 . .139 G6
Streatfield Av, E6 . . . . . .116 C1
Streatfield Rd, Har. HA3 . .69 G3
STREATHAM, SW16 . . . .169 E4
Streatham Cl, SW16 . . . .169 E2
Streatham Common N,
  SW16 . . . . .168 E5
Streatham Common S,
  SW16 . . . . .169 E6
Streatham Ct, SW16 . . . .168 E3
Streatham High Rd,
  SW16 . . . . .168 E5
STREATHAM HILL, SW2 .151 F7
Streatham Hill, SW2 . . . .169 E2
STREATHAM PARK,
  SW16 . . . . .168 C4
Streatham Pl, SW2 . . . . .150 E7
Streatham Rd, SW16 . . . .186 A1
  Mitcham CR4 . . . . .186 A1
Streatham St, WC1 . . . . . .17 J3
STREATHAM VALE,
  SW16 . . . . .168 D7
Streatham Vale, SW16 . .168 C7
Streathbourne Rd,
  SW17 . . . . .168 A2
Streatley Pl, NW3
  off New End Sq 91 F4
Streatley Rd, NW6 . . . . . .90 C7
Streeters La, Wall.
  SM6 . . . . .200 D3
Streetfield Ms, SE3 . . . . .155 G3
Streimer Rd, E15 . . . . . .114 C2
Strelley Way, W3 . . . . . . .106 E7
Stretton Rd, Croy. CR0 . .188 B7
  Richmond TW10 . . . . .163 F2
Strickland Row, SW18 . .149 G7
Strickland St, SE8 . . . . . .154 A2
Strickland Way, Orp.
  BR6 . . . . .207 J4
Stride Rd, E13 . . . . .115 F2
Strode Cl, N10
  off Pembroke Rd 58 A7
Strode Rd, E7 . . . . .97 G4
  N17 . . . . .76 B2
  NW10 . . . . .89 G6
  SW6 . . . . .128 A7
Strone Rd, E7 . . . . .97 J6
  E12 . . . . .98 A6
Strone Way, Hayes
  UB4 . . . . .102 E4
Strongbow Cres, SE9 . . .156 C5
Strongbow Rd, SE9 . . . . .156 C5
Strongbridge Cl, Har.
  HA2 . . . . .85 G1
Stronsa Rd, W12 . . . . . . .127 F2
Stroud Cres, SW15 . . . . .165 G3
Stroudes Cl, Wor.Pk.
  KT4 . . . . .183 E7
Stroud Fld, Nthlt. UB5 . . . .84 E6
Stroud Gate, Har. HA2 . . . .85 H4
STROUD GREEN, N4 . . . . .75 F6
Stroud Grn Gdns, Croy.
  CR0 . . . . .189 F7
Stroud Grn Rd, N4 . . . . . .93 F1
Stroud Grn Way, Croy.
  CR0 . . . . .189 E7
Stroudley Wk, E3 . . . . . .114 B3
Stroud Rd, SE25 . . . . . . .188 D6
  SW19 . . . . .166 D3
Strouds Cl, Rom.
  (Chad.Hth.) RM6 . . . . .82 B5
Strouts Pl, E2 . . . . .13 F3
Strutton Grd, SW1 . . . . . .25 H5
Strype St, E1 . . . . .21 F2
Stuart Av, NW9 . . . . .71 G7
  W5 . . . . .125 J1
  Bromley BR2 . . . . .205 G1
  Harrow HA2 . . . . .85 F3
Stuart Cres, N22 . . . . . . .75 F1
  Croydon CR0 . . . . .203 J3
Stuart Evans Cl, Well.
  DA16 . . . . .158 C3
Stuart Gro, Tedd. TW11 .162 B5
Stuart Pl, Mitch. CR4 . . .185 J1
Stuart Rd, NW6 . . . . . . .108 D3
  SE15 . . . . .153 F4
  SW19 . . . . .166 D3
  W3 . . . . .126 C1
  Barking IG11 . . . . .99 J7
  Barnet EN4 . . . . .41 H7
  Harrow HA3 . . . . .68 C2
  Richmond TW10 . . . . .163 E2
  Thornton Heath CR7 . .187 J4
  Welling DA16 . . . . .158 B1
Stuart Twr, W9 . . . . .6 C7
Stubbs Cl, NW9 . . . . .70 C5
Stubbs Dr, SE16 . . . . . . .132 E5

Stubbs Ms, Dag. RM8
  off Marlborough Rd . . .100 B4
Stubbs Pt, E13 . . . . .115 H4
Stubbs Way, SW19
  off Brangwyn Cres . . .185 G1
Stucley Pl, NW1
  off Hawley Cres 92 B7
Stucley Rd, Houns. TW5 .123 J7
Studdridge St, SW6 . . . .148 D2
Studd St, N1 . . . . .111 H1
Studholme Ct, NW3 . . . . .90 D4
Studholme St, SE15 . . . .132 E7
Studio Pl, SW1 . . . . .24 A4
Studio Way, Borwd.
  WD6 . . . . .38 C2
Studland, SE17 . . . . .36 B3
Studland Cl, Sid. DA15 . .175 J3
Studland Rd, SE26 . . . . .171 G5
  W7 . . . . .104 A6
  Kingston upon Thames
  KT2 . . . . .163 H6
Studland St, W6 . . . . . . .127 H4
Studley Av, E4 . . . . .62 D7
Studley Cl, E5 . . . . .95 H5
Studley Ct, Sid. DA14 . . .176 E5
Studley Dr, Ilf. IG4 . . . . . .80 A6
Studley Est, SW4 . . . . . . .151 E1
Studley Gra Rd, W7 . . . .124 B2
Studley Rd, E7 . . . . .97 H6
  SW4 . . . . .150 E1
  Dagenham RM9 . . . . .100 D7
Stukeley Rd, E7 . . . . .97 H7
Stukeley St, WC2 . . . . . . .18 B3
Stumps Hill La, Beck.
  BR3 . . . . .172 A6
Sturdy Rd, SE15 . . . . . . .153 E2
Sturge Av, E17 . . . . .78 B2
Sturgeon Rd, SE17 . . . . . .35 J4
Sturges Fld, Chis. BR7 . .175 G6
Sturgess Av, NW4 . . . . . .71 H7
Sturge St, SE1 . . . . .27 J3
Sturmer Way, N7 . . . . . . .93 F5
Sturminster Cl, Hayes
  UB4 . . . . .102 C6
Sturrock Cl, N15 . . . . .76 A4
Sturry St, E14 . . . . .114 B6
Sturt St, N1 . . . . .12 A2
Stutfield St, E1 . . . . .21 J4
Styles Gdns, SW9 . . . . . .151 H3
Styles Way, Beck. BR3 . .190 C4
Sudbourne Rd, SW2 . . . .151 E5
Sudbrooke Rd, SW12 . . .149 J6
Sudbrook Gdns, Rich.
  TW10 . . . . .163 G3
Sudbrook La, Rich.
  TW10 . . . . .163 H1
SUDBURY, Wem. 86 D5
Sudbury, E6
  off Newark Knok 116 D6
Sudbury Av, Wem. HA0 . . .87 G3
Sudbury Ct, E5 . . . . .95 H4
Sudbury Ct Dr, Har. HA1 . .86 C3
Sudbury Ct Rd, Har. HA1 . .86 C3
Sudbury Cres, Brom.
  BR1 . . . . .173 G6
  Wembley HA0 . . . . .87 E5
Sudbury Cft, Wem. HA0 . .86 C4
Sudbury Gdns, Croy. CR0
  off Langton Way 202 B4
Sudbury Hts Av, Grnf.
  UB6 . . . . .86 C3
Sudbury Hill, Har. HA1 . . .86 B2
Sudbury Hill Cl, Wem.
  HA0 . . . . .86 C4
Sudbury Rd, Bark. IG11 . .99 J5
Sudeley St, N1 . . . . .11 H2
Sudlow Rd, SW18 . . . . . .148 D4
Sudrey St, SE1 . . . . .27 J4
Suez Av, Grnf. GB6 . . . . .104 C2
Suez Rd, Enf. EN3 . . . . . .45 H4
Suffield Rd, E4 . . . . .62 B3
  N15 . . . . .76 C5
  SE20 . . . . .189 F2
Suffolk Cl, Borwd. WD6
  off Clydesdale Cl 38 D5
Suffolk Ct, E10 . . . . .78 A7
  Ilford IG3 . . . . .81 H6
Suffolk La, EC4 . . . . .20 B5
Suffolk Pk Rd, E17 . . . . . .77 H4
Suffolk Pl, SW1 . . . . .25 J1
Suffolk Rd, E13 . . . . .115 F3
  N15 . . . . .76 A6
  NW10 . . . . .89 E7
  SE25 . . . . .188 C4
  SW13 . . . . .127 F7
  Barking IG11 . . . . .99 G7
  Dagenham RM10 . . . .101 J5
  Enfield EN3 . . . . .45 E5
  Harrow HA2 . . . . .67 F6
  Ilford IG3 . . . . .81 H6

Suffolk Rd, Sid. DA14 . . . . .**176** C6
Worcester Park KT4 . . . .**197** F2
Suffolk St, E7 . . . .**97** G5
SW1 . . . .**25** J1
Sugar Bakers Ct, EC3
off Creechurch La **112** B6
Sugar Ho La, E15 . . . .**114** C2
Sugar Loaf Wk, E2
off Victoria Pk Sq **113** F3
Sugar Quay Wk, EC3 . . . . . .**20** E6
Sugden Rd, SW11 . . . .**150** A3
Thames Ditton KT7 . . . . .**194** E1
Sugden Way, Bark. IG11 . . .**117** J2
Sulgrave Gdns, W6
off Sulgrave Rd **127** J2
Sulgrave Rd, W6 . . . .**127** J2
Sulina Rd, SW2 . . . .**150** E7
Sulivan Ct, SW6 . . . .**148** D3
Sulivan Rd, SW6 . . . .**148** D3
Sullivan Av, E16 . . . .**116** A5
Sullivan Cl, SW11 . . . .**149** H3
Hayes UB4 . . . .**102** C5
West Molesey KT8
off Victoria Av **179** G3
Sullivan Rd, SE11 . . . .**35** F1
Sultan Rd, E11 . . . .**79** H4
Sultan St, SE5 . . . .**35** J7
Beckenham BR3 . . . .**189** G2
Sumatra Rd, NW6 . . . .**90** D5
Sumburgh Rd, SW12 . . . . .**150** A6
Summer Av, E.Mol.
KT8 . . . .**180** B5
Summercourt Rd, E1 . . . . .**113** F6
Summerene Cl, SW16 . . . . .**168** C7
Summerfield Av, NW6 . . . . .**108** B2
Summerfield La, Surb.
KT6 . . . .**195** G2
Summerfield Rd, W5 . . . . .**105** E4
Loughton IG10 . . . .**48** A6
Summerfields Av, N12 . . . . .**57** H6
Summerfield St, SE12 . . . .**155** F7
Summer Gdns, E.Mol.
KT8 . . . .**180** B5
Summer Hill, Borwd.
(Elstree) WD6 . . . .**38** A5
Chislehurst BR7 . . . .**192** D2
Summerhill Cl, Orp. BR6 .**207** H4 D
Summerhill Gro, Enf.
EN1 . . . .**44** B6
Summerhill Rd, N15 . . . . . .**76** A4
Summer Hill Vil, Chis.
BR7 . . . .**192** D1
Summerhill Way, Mitch.
CR4 . . . .**186** A1
Summerhouse Av, Houns.
TW5 . . . .**142** E1
Summerhouse La, West Dr.
UB7 . . . .**120** A6
Summerhouse Rd, N16 . . . .**94** B2
Summerland Gdns, N10 . . . .**74** B3
Summerlands Av, W3 . . . . .**106** C7
Summerlee Av, N2 . . . .**73** J4
Summerlee Gdns, N2 . . . . . .**73** J4
Summerley St, SW18 . . . . .**167** E2
Summer Rd, E.Mol. KT8 .**180** B5
Thames Ditton KT7 . . . . .**180** C5
Summersby Rd, N6 . . . .**74** B6
Summers Cl, Sutt. SM2
off Overton Rd **198** D7
Wembley HA9 . . . .**88** B1
Summers La, N12 . . . .**57** G7
Summers Row, N12 . . . .**57** H6
SUMMERSTOWN,
SW17 . . . .**166** E3
Summerstown, SW17 . . . . .**167** F3
Summer St, EC1 . . . .**11** E6
Summerton Way, SE28 . . . .**118** D6
Summer Trees, Sun. TW16
off The Avenue **178** B1
Summerville Gdns, Sutt.
SM1 . . . .**198** C6
Summerwood Rd, Islw.
TW7 . . . .**144** C6
Summit, The, Loug. I
G10 . . . .**48** C1
Summit Av, NW9 . . . .**70** D5
Summit Cl, N14 . . . .**58** C2
NW9 . . . .**70** D4
Edgware HA8 . . . .**54** A7
Summit Dr, Wdf.Grn.
IG8 . . . .**80** A2
Summit Est, N16 . . . .**76** D7
Summit Rd, E17 . . . .**78** B4
Northolt UB5 . . . .**85** G7
Summit Way, N14 . . . .**58** B2
SE19 . . . .**170** B7
Sumner Av, SE15
off Sumner Rd **152** C1
Sumner Cl, Orp. BR6 . . .**207** F4

Sumner Est, SE15 . . . . . .**132** C7
Sumner Gdns, Croy.
CR0 . . . .**201** G1
Sumner Pl, SW7 . . . .**31** F2
Sumner Pl Ms, SW7 . . . . . .**31** F2
Sumner Rd, SE15 . . . .**37** G6
Croydon CR0 . . . .**201** G1
Harrow HA1 . . . .**67** J7
Sumner Rd S, Croy. CR0 .**201** G1
Sumner St, SE1 . . . .**27** H1
Sumpter Cl, NW3 . . . .**91** F6
Sun All, Rich. TW9
off Kew Rd **145** H4
Sunbeam Rd, W10 . . . . . .**107** J4
Sunbeam Rd, NW10 . . . . .**106** C4
Sunbury Av, NW7 . . . .**54** D5
SW14 . . . .**146** D4
Sunbury Ct, Sun. TW16 . . .**178** D2
Sunbury Ct Island, Sun.
TW16 . . . .**178** D3
Sunbury Ct Ms, Sun. TW16
off Lower Hampton
Rd **178** D2
Sunbury Ct Rd, Sun.
TW16 . . . .**178** C2
Sunbury Gdns, NW7 . . . . . .**54** D5
Sunbury La, SW11 . . . . . .**149** G1
Walton-on-Thames
KT12 . . . .**178** A6
Sunbury Lock Ait, Walt.
KT12 . . . .**178** B4
Sunbury Rd, Sutt. SM3 . .**198** A3
Sunbury St, SE18 . . . .**136** C3
Sunbury Way, Felt.
TW13 . . . .**160** C5
Sun Ct, EC3 . . . .**20** C4
Suncroft Pl, SE26 . . . .**171** F3
Sunderland Ct, SE22 . . . . .**152** D7
Sunderland Mt, SE23
off Sunderland Rd **171** G2
Sunderland Rd, SE23 . . . .**171** G1
W5 . . . .**125** G3
Sunderland Ter, W2 . . . .**14** A3
Sunderland Way, E12 . . . . . .**98** A2
Sundew Av, W12 . . . .**107** G7
Sundial Av, SE25 . . . .**188** C3
Sundorne Rd, SE7 . . . .**135** H5
Sundra Wk, E1
off Beaumont Gro **113** G4
SUNDRIDGE, Brom. **173** J6
Sundridge Av, Brom.
BR1 . . . .**192** A1
Chislehurst BR7 . . . .**174** A7
Welling DA16 . . . .**157** G2
Sundridge Ho, Brom. BR1
off Burnt Ash La **173** H5
Sundridge Pl, Croy. CR0
off Inglis Rd **202** D1
Sundridge Rd, Croy. CR0 **188** C7
Sunfields Pl, SE3 . . . .**135** H7
Sunken Rd, Croy. CR0
off Coombe La **203** F5
Sunland Av, Bexh. DA6 . .**159** E4
Sun La, SE3 . . . .**135** H7
Sunleigh Rd, Wem. HA0 . .**105** H1
Sunley Gdns, Grnf. UB6 . .**104** D1
Sunlight Cl, SW19 . . . .**167** F6
Sunlight Sq, E2 . . . .**113** E3
Sunmead Rd, Sun.
TW16 . . . .**178** A3
Sunna Gdns, Sun. TW16 . .**178** B2
Sunningdale, N14
off Wilmer Way **58** D5
Sunningdale Av, W3 . . . . .**107** E7
Barking IG11 . . . .**117** G1
Feltham TW13 . . . .**160** E2
Ruislip HA4 . . . .**84** C1
Sunningdale Cl, E6 . . . . . .**116** C3
SE16 off Ryder Dr .**132/133** E5
SE28 . . . .**118** E6
Stanmore HA7 . . . .**52** D7
Surbiton KT6
off Culsac Rd **195** H2
Sunningdale Gdns, NW9 .**70** C5
W8 off Lexham Ms **128** D3
Sunningdale Rd, Brom.
BR1 . . . .**192** B4
Sutton SM1 . . . .**198** C4
Sunningfields Cres,
NW4 . . . .**71** H2
Sunningfields Rd, NW4 . . .**71** H2
Sunninghill Rd, SE13 . . . .**154** B2
Sunny Bk, SE25 . . . .**188** D3
Sunny Cres, NW10 . . . .**88** C7
Sunnycroft Rd, SE25 . . . .**188** D3
Hounslow TW3 . . . .**143** H2
Southall UB1 . . . .**103** G5
Sunnydale, Orp. BR6 . . . .**206** D2
Sunnydale Gdns, NW7 . . . .**54** D6
Sunnydale Rd, SE12 . . . . .**155** H5

Sunnydene Av, E4 . . . .**62** D5
Ruislip HA4 . . . .**84** A2
Sunnydene Gdns, Wem.
HA0 . . . .**87** F6
Sunnydene St, SE26 . . . . .**171** H4
Sunnyfield, NW7 . . . .**55** F4
Sunny Gdns Par, NW4
off Great N Way **71** J2
Sunny Gdns Rd, NW4 . . . . .**71** H2
Sunny Hill, NW4 . . . .**71** H3
Sunnyhill Cl, E5 . . . .**95** H4
Sunnyhill Rd, SW16 . . . . .**168** E4
Sunnyhurst Cl, Sutt.
SM1 . . . .**198** D3
Sunnymead Av, Mitch.
CR4 . . . .**186** C3
Sunnymead Rd, NW9 . . . . .**70** D7
SW15 . . . .**147** H5
Sunnymede Dr, Ilf. IG6 . . .**80** E4
Sunny Nook Gdns, S.Croy.
CR2 off Selsdon Rd **202** A6
Sunny Rd, The, Enf. EN3 . .**45** G1
Sunnyside, NW2 . . . .**90** C3
SW19 . . . .**166** B6
Walton-on-Thames
KT12 . . . .**178** C5
Sunnyside Dr, E4 . . . .**46** C7
Sunnyside Pas, SW19 . . . .**166** B6
Sunnyside Pl, SW19
off Sunnyside **166** B6
Sunnyside Rd, E10 . . . .**96** A1
N19 . . . .**74** D7
W5 . . . .**125** G1
Ilford IG1 . . . .**99** F3
Teddington TW11 . . . . . .**162** A4
Sunnyside Rd E, N9 . . . . . .**60** D3
Sunnyside Rd N, N9 . . . . . .**60** C3
Sunnyside Rd S, N9 . . . . . .**60** C3
Sunnyside Ter, NW9
off Edgware Rd **70** D3
Sunny Vw, NW9 . . . .**70** D5
Sunny Way, N12 . . . .**57** H7
Sun Pas, SE16 . . . .**29** H5
Sunray Av, SE24 . . . .**152** A4
Bromley BR2 . . . .**192** B6
Surbiton KT5 . . . .**196** B2
West Drayton UB7 . . . . .**120** A2
Sunrise Cl, Felt. TW13
off Exeter Rd **161** F3
Sun Rd, W14 . . . .**128** C5
Sunset Av, E4 . . . .**62** B1
Woodford Green IG8 . . . . .**63** F4
Sunset Cl, Wdf.Grn. IG8
off Navestock Cres **63** J7
Sunset Gdns, SE25 . . . . . .**188** C2
Sunset Rd, SE5 . . . .**151** J4
SE28 . . . .**138** A2
Sunset Vw, Barn. EN5 . . . . .**40** B2
Sunshine Way, Mitch.
CR4 . . . .**185** J2
Sun St, EC2 . . . .**20** D2
Sun St Pas, EC2 . . . .**20** D2
Sun Wk, E1 . . . .**21** H6
Sunwell Cl, SE15
off Cossall Wk **152/153** E1
Superior Dr, Orp. BR6 . . .**207** J6
SURBITON **181** J7
Surbiton Ct, Surb. KT6 . . .**181** F6
Surbiton Cres, Kings.T.
KT1 . . . .**181** H4
Surbiton Hall Cl, Kings.T.
KT1 . . . .**181** H4
Surbiton Hill Pk, Surb. **182** A5
Surbiton Hill Rd, Surb.
KT6 . . . .**181** H4
Surbiton Par, Surb. KT6
off St. Mark's Hill **181** H6
Surbiton Rd, Kings.T.
KT1 . . . .**181** H4
Surlingham Cl, SE28 . . . . .**118** D7
Surma Cl, E1 . . . .**112** E4
Surmans Cl, Dag. RM9
off Goresbrook Rd **118** B1
Surrendale Pl, W9 . . . .**108** D4
Surrey Canal Rd, SE14 . . .**133** F6
SE15 . . . .**133** F6
Surrey Cres, W4 . . . .**126** A5
★ Surrey Docks Fm,
SE16 . . . .**133** J2
Surrey Gdns, N4
off Finsbury Pk Av **75** J6
Surrey Gro, SE17 . . . .**36** D4
Sutton SM1 . . . .**199** G3
Surrey La, SW11 . . . .**149** H1
Surrey La Est, SW11 . . . . .**149** H1
Surrey Lo, SE1 . . . .**26** E6
Surrey Ms, SE27
off Hamilton Rd **170** B4
Surrey Mt, SE23 . . . .**171** E1

Surrey Quays Retail Cen,
SE16 . . . .**133** G3
Surrey Quays Rd, SE16 . .**133** G2
Surrey Rd, SE15 . . . .**153** G5
Barking IG11 . . . .**117** H1
Dagenham RM10 . . . . . .**101** H5
Harrow HA1 . . . .**67** J5
West Wickham BR4 . . . .**204** B1
Surrey Row, SE1 . . . .**27** G3
Surrey Sq, SE17 . . . .**36** D3
Surrey St, E13 . . . .**115** H3
WC2 . . . .**18** D5
Croydon CR0 . . . .**201** J3
Surrey Ter, SE17 . . . .**36** E3
Surrey Twr, SE20 . . . .**171** F7
Surrey Water Rd, SE16 . .**133** G1
Surridge Gdns, SE19
off Hancock Rd **170** A6
Surr St, N7 . . . .**92** E5
Susan Cl, Rom. RM7 . . . . . .**83** J3
Susannah St, E14 . . . .**114** B6
Susan Rd, SE3 . . . .**155** H2
Susan Wd, Chis. BR7 . . . .**192** D1
Sussex Av, Islw. TW7 . . . .**144** B3
Sussex Cl, N19
off Cornwallis Rd . . .**92/93** E2
Ilford IG4 . . . .**80** C6
New Malden KT3 . . . . . .**183** E4
Twickenham TW1
off Westmorland
Cl **144/145** E6
Sussex Cres, Nthlt. UB5 . .**85** G6
Sussex Gdns, N4 . . . .**75** J5
N6 off Great N Rd **73** J5
W2 . . . .**15** E5
Chessington KT9 . . . . . .**195** G6
Sussex Ms, SE6
off Ravensbourne Pk .**154** A7
Sussex Ms E, W2 . . . .**15** F4
Sussex Ms W, W2 . . . .**15** F5
Sussex Pl, NW1 . . . .**7** J4
W2 . . . .**15** F4
W6 . . . .**127** J5
Erith DA8 . . . .**139** H7
New Malden KT3 . . . . . .**183** E4
Sussex Ring, N12 . . . .**56** D5
Sussex Rd, E6 . . . .**116** D1
Carshalton SM5 . . . .**199** J6
Erith DA8 . . . .**139** H7
Harrow HA1 . . . .**67** J5
Mitcham CR4
off Lincoln Rd . . .**186/187** E5
New Malden KT3 . . . . . .**183** E4
Sidcup DA14 . . . .**176** B5
South Croydon CR2 . .**202** A6
Southall UB2 . . . .**122** D3
West Wickham BR4 . . . .**204** B1
Sussex Sq, W2 . . . .**15** F5
Sussex St, E13 . . . .**115** H3
SW1 . . . .**32** E4
Sussex Wk, SW9 . . . .**151** H4
Sussex Way, N7 . . . .**93** E2
N19 . . . .**92** E1
Barnet EN4 . . . .**42** A5
Sutcliffe Cl, NW11 . . . .**73** E5
Sutcliffe Ho, Hayes
UB3 . . . .**102** A6
Sutcliffe Rd, SE18 . . . . . .**137** H6
Welling DA16 . . . .**158** C2
Sutherland Av, W9 . . . .**6** C4
W13 . . . .**104** E6
Hayes UB3 . . . .**122** A4
Orpington BR5 . . . .**193** J6
Welling DA16 . . . .**157** H4
Sutherland Cl, Barn.
EN5 . . . .**40** B4
Sutherland Ct, NW9 . . . . . .**70** B5
Sutherland Dr, SW19 . . . .**185** G1
Sutherland Gdns,
SW14 . . . .**147** E3
Worcester Park KT4 . . . .**197** H1
Teddington TW11 . . . . . .**162** B5
Sutherland Gro, SW18 . . .**148** B6
Teddington TW11 . . . . . .**162** B5
Sutherland Pl, W2 . . . .**108** D6
Sutherland Rd, E17 . . . .**77** G2
N9 . . . .**60** D1
N17 . . . .**60** D7
W4 . . . .**126** E6
W13 . . . .**104** D6
Belvedere DA17 . . . . . .**139** G3
Croydon CR0 . . . .**187** G7
Enfield EN3 . . . .**45** G5
Southall UB1 . . . .**103** H6
Sutherland Rd Path, E17 .**77** G3
Sutherland Row, SW1 . . . . .**32** E3
Sutherland Sq, SE17 . . . . .**35** J4
Sutherland St, SW1 . . . .**32** D3
Sutherland Wk, SE17 . . . . .**36** A4
Sutlej Rd, SE7 . . . .**135** J7
Sutterton St, N7 . . . .**93** F6

SUTTON 198 E6
Sutton Cl, Beck. BR3
off Albemarle Rd 190 B1
Loughton IG10 . . . . . . .48 B7
Pinner HA5 . . . . .66 A5
Sutton Common Rd, Sutt.
SM1, SM3 . . . . .184 C7
Sutton Ct, W4 . . . . .126 C6
Sutton Ct Rd, E13 . . . . .115 J3
W4 . . . . .126 C7
Sutton SM1 . . . . .199 F6
Sutton Cres, Barn. EN5 . .40 A5
Sutton Dene, Houns.
TW3 . . . . .143 H1
Sutton Est, SW3 . . . . . . .31 H3
W10 . . . . .107 J5
Sutton Est, The, N1 . . . . .93 H7
Sutton Gdns, Bark. IG11
off Sutton Rd 117 H1
Croydon CR0 . . . . .188 C5
Sutton Grn, Bark. IG11
off Sutton Rd 117 H1
Sutton Gro, Sutt. SM1 . .199 G4
Sutton Hall Rd, Houns.
TW5 . . . . .123 G7
★ Sutton Heritage Cen, Cars.
SM5 . . . . .199 J4
★ Sutton Ho, E9 . . . . .95 F5
Sutton La, Houns. TW3 . .143 F3
Sutton La N, W4 . . . . . .126 C5
Sutton La S, W4 . . . . . .126 C6
Sutton Par, NW4
off Church Rd 71 J4
Sutton Pk Rd, Sutt.
SM1 . . . . .198 E6
Sutton Path, Borwd. WD6
off Stratfield Rd 38 A2
Sutton Pl, E9 . . . . .95 F5
Sutton Rd, E13 . . . . . . .115 F4
E17 . . . . .77 G1
N10 . . . . .74 A2
Barking IG11 . . . . .117 H2
Hounslow TW5 . . . . . .143 G1
Sutton Row, W1 . . . . . . .17 J3
Sutton Sq, E9
off Urswick Rd 95 F5
Hounslow TW5 . . . . . .143 F1
Sutton St, E1 . . . . .113 F6
Sutton's Way, EC1 . . . . . .12 A6
Sutton Wk, SE1
off York Rd 131 F1
Sutton Way, W10 . . . . . .107 J5
Hounslow TW5 . . . . . .143 F1
Swaby Rd, SW18 . . . . . .167 F1
Swaffham Way, N22
off White Hart La 59 H7
Swaffield Rd, SW18 . . . .149 E7
Swain Cl, SW16 . . . . . . .168 B6
Swain Rd, Th.Hth. CR7 . .187 J5
Swains Cl, West Dr.
UB7 . . . . .120 B2
Swains La, N6 . . . . .92 A3
Swainson Rd, W3 . . . . . .127 F2
Swains Rd, SW17 . . . . . .167 J7
Swain St, NW8 . . . . .7 G5
Swaledale Cl, N11
off Ribblesdale Av 58 A6
Swallands Rd, SE6 . . . . .172 A3
Swallow Cl, SE14 . . . . . .153 F1
Bushey WD23 . . . . .51 J1
Swallow Dr, NW10
off Kingfisher Way 88 D6
Northolt UB5 . . . . .103 G2
Swallowfield Rd, SE7 . . .135 H5
Swallowfield Way, Hayes
UB3 . . . . .121 G2
Swallow Gdns, SW16 . . .168 D5
Swallow Pas, W1 . . . . . . .17 E4
Swallow Pl, W1 . . . . .17 E4
Swallow St, E6 . . . . .116 B5
W1 . . . . .17 G6
Swanage Rd, E4 . . . . . . .62 C7
SW18 . . . . .149 F6
Swanage Waye, Hayes
UB4 . . . . .102 C6
Swan App, E6 . . . . .116 B5
Swanbridge Rd, Bexh.
DA7 . . . . .159 G1
Swan Cl, E17 . . . . .77 H1
Croydon CR0 . . . . .188 B7
Feltham TW13 . . . . . . .161 E4
Swan Ct, SW3 . . . . .31 H4
Swandon Way, SW18 . . .149 E4
Swan Dr, NW9 . . . . .70 E2
Swanfield St, E2 . . . . . . .13 F4
Swan La, EC4 . . . . .20 B6
N20 . . . . .57 F3
Loughton IG10 . . . . . . .47 J7
Swanley Rd, Well. DA16 .158 C1
Swan Mead, SE1 . . . . . . .28 D6

Swan Pas, E1
off Cartwright St 112 C7
Swan Path, E10
off Jesse Rd 96 C1
Swan Pl, SW13 . . . . .147 F2
Swan Rd, SE16 . . . . .133 F2
SE18 . . . . .136 A3
Feltham TW13 . . . . . . .160 E5
Southall UB1 . . . . .103 H6
West Drayton UB7 . . . .120 A2
Swanscombe Ho, W11
off St. Anns Rd 128 A1
Swanscombe Rd, W4 . . .127 E5
W11 . . . . .128 A1
Swansea Ct, E16
off Fishguard
Way 136/137 E1
Swansea Rd, Enf. EN3 . . .45 F4
Hounslow (Hthrw.Air.) TW6
off Southern Perimeter
Rd 141 F6
Swanshope, Loug. IG10 . .49 E2
Swansland Gdns, E17
off McEntee Av 77 H1
Swanston Path, Wat.
WD19 . . . . .50 C3
Swan St, SE1 . . . . .28 A5
Isleworth TW7 . . . . . . .144 E3
Swanton Gdns, SW19 . . .166 A1
Swanton Rd, Erith DA8 . .139 H7
Swan Wk, SW3 . . . . .31 J5
Swan Way, Enf. EN3 . . . . .45 G2
Swanwick Cl, SW15 . . . . .147 F7
Swan Yd, N1
off Highbury Sta Rd . . .93 H6
Swaton Rd, E3 . . . . .114 A4
Swaylands Rd, Belv.
DA17 . . . . .139 G6
Swaythling Cl, N18 . . . . . .61 E4
Swaythling Ho, SW15
off Tunworth Cres 147 F6
Swedenborg Gdns, E1 . . .21 J5
Sweden Gate, SE16 . . . .133 H3
Sweeney Cres, SE1 . . . . .29 G4
Sweet Briar Grn, N9 . . . . .60 C3
Sweet Briar Gro, N9 . . . . .60 C3
Sweet Briar Wk, N18 . . . .60 C4
Sweetmans Av, Pnr. HA5 .66 D3
Sweets Way, N20 . . . . . . .57 G2
Swetenham Wk, SE18
off Sandbach Pl 137 F5
Swete St, E13 . . . . .115 G2
Sweyn Pl, SE3 . . . . .155 G2
Swift Cl, E17 . . . . .61 H7
Harrow HA2 . . . . .85 H2
Swift Rd, Felt. TW13 . . . .161 E3
Southall UB2 . . . . .123 F3
Swiftsden Way, Brom.
BR1 . . . . .173 E6
Swift St, SW6 . . . . .148 C1
Swinbrook Rd, W10 . . . .108 B5
Swinburne Ct, SE5
off Basingdon Way 152 A4
Swinburne Cres, Croy.
CR0 . . . . .189 F6
Swinburne Rd, SW15 . . .147 G4
Swinderby Rd, Wem.
HA0 . . . . .87 H6
Swindon Cl, Ilf. IG3
off Salisbury Rd 99 H2
Swindon Rd, Houns.
(Hthrw.Air.) TW6 . . . . .141 F5
Swindon St, W12 . . . . . .127 H1
Swinfield Cl, Felt. TW13 .160 E4
Swinford Gdns, SW9 . . . .151 H3
Swingate La, SE18 . . . . . .137 H6
Swinnerton St, E9 . . . . . .95 H5
Swinton Cl, Wem. HA9 . . .88 B1
Swinton Pl, WC1 . . . . . . .10 C3
Swinton St, WC1 . . . . . . .10 C3
Swires Shaw, Kes. BR2 . .206 A4
Swiss Ct, W1 . . . . .17 J6
Swiss Ter, NW6 . . . . .91 G7
Swithland Gdns, SE9 . . .174 D4
Swyncombe Av, W5 . . . .125 E4
Swynford Gdns, NW4
off Handowe Cl 71 G4
Sybil Ms, N4
off Lothair Rd N 75 H6
Sybil Phoenix Cl, SE8 . . .133 G5
Sybil Thorndike Ho, N1
off Clephane Rd 93 J6
Sybourn St, E17 . . . . . . .77 J7
Sycamore Av, E3 . . . . . . .113 J1
W5 . . . . .125 G3
Sidcup DA15 . . . . .157 J6
Sycamore Cl, E16
off Clarence Rd 114/115 E4
N9 off Pycroft Way 60 D4
SE9 . . . . .174 B2

Sycamore Cl, W3
off Bromyard Av .126/127 E1
Barnet EN4 . . . . .41 G6
Carshalton SM5 . . . . . .199 J4
Edgware HA8
off Ash Cl 54 C4
Feltham TW13 . . . . . . .160 A3
Loughton IG10
off Cedar Dr 48/49 E2
Northolt UB5 . . . . .103 E1
Sycamore Ct, Surb. KT6
off Penners Gdns 181 H7
Sycamore Gdns, W6 . . . .127 H2
Mitcham CR4 . . . . .185 G2
Sycamore Gro, NW9 . . . . .70 C7
SE6 . . . . .154 C6
SE20 . . . . .170 D7
New Malden KT3 . . . . .182 D3
Sycamore Hill, N11 . . . . . .58 A6
Sycamore Ms, SW4 . . . . .150 C3
Sycamore Rd, SW19 . . . .165 J6
Sycamore St, EC1 . . . . . . .11 J6
Sycamore Wk, W10
off Fifth Av 108 B4
Ilford IG6
off Civic Way 81 F4
Sycamore Way, Tedd.
TW11 . . . . .163 F6
Thornton Heath CR7 . . .187 G5
SYDENHAM, SE26 . . . . . .171 F3
Sydenham Av, N21 . . . . . .43 F5
off Chadwick Av 43 F5
SE26 . . . . .171 J5
Sydenham Cotts, SE12 . .173 J2
Sydenham Hill, SE23 . . .170 D3
SE26 . . . . .170 D3
Sydenham Hill Est,
SE26 . . . . .170 D3
Sydenham Pk, SE26 . . . .171 F3
Sydenham Pk Rd, SE26 . .171 F3
Sydenham Ri, SE23 . . . . .170 E2
Sydenham Rd, SE26 . . . .171 F5
Croydon CR0 . . . . .188 A7
Sydmons Ct, SE23 . . . . .153 F7
Sydner Ms, N16
off Sydner Rd 94 C4
Sydner Rd, N16 . . . . .94 C4
Sydney Cl, SW3 . . . . .31 F2
Sydney Gro, NW4 . . . . . . .71 J5
Sydney Ms, SW3 . . . . . . .31 F2
Sydney Pl, SW7 . . . . .31 F2
Sydney Rd, E11
off Mansfield Rd 79 H6
N8 . . . . .75 G4
N10 . . . . .74 A1
SE2 . . . . .138 C3
SW20 . . . . .184 A2
W13 . . . . .124 D1
Bexleyheath DA6 . . . . .158 D4
Enfield EN2 . . . . .44 A4
Feltham TW14 . . . . . . .160 A1
Ilford IG6 . . . . .81 F2
Richmond TW9 . . . . . .145 H4
Sidcup DA14 . . . . .175 H4
Sutton SM1 . . . . .198 D4
Teddington TW11 . . . . .162 C5
Woodford Green IG8 . . .63 G4
Sydney St, SW3 . . . . .31 G3
Sylvan Av, N3 . . . . .72 D2
N22 . . . . .59 F7
NW7 . . . . .55 F6
Romford RM6 . . . . .83 F6
Sylvan Ct, N12
off Holden Rd 56/57 E4
Sylvan Est, SE19 . . . . . .188 C1
Sylvan Gdns, Surb. KT6 .181 G7
Sylvan Gro, NW2 . . . . . . .90 A4
SE15 . . . . .133 E7
Sylvan Hill, SE19 . . . . . .188 B1
Sylvan Rd, E7 . . . . .97 G6
E11 . . . . .79 G5
E17 . . . . .78 A5
SE19 . . . . .188 C1
Ilford IG1
off Hainault St 99 F2
Sylvan Wk, Brom. BR1 . .192 C3
Sylvan Way, Dag. RM8 . .100 B3
West Wickham BR4 . . . .204 E4
Sylverdale Rd, Croy.
CR0 . . . . .201 H3
Sylvester Av, Chis. BR7 . .174 C6
Sylvester Path, E8
off Sylvester Rd . . .94/95 E6
Sylvester Rd, E8 . . . . . . .95 E6
E17 . . . . .77 J7
N2 . . . . .73 F2
Wembley HA0 . . . . .87 F5
Sylvestrus Cl, Kings.T.
KT1 . . . . .182 A1
Sylvia Av, Pnr. HA5 . . . . .51 F6

Sylvia Ct, Wem. HA9
off Harrow Rd 88 B7
Sylvia Gdns, Wem. HA9 . .88 B7
Symes Ms, NW1 . . . . .9 F1
Symons St, SW3 . . . . . . .32 A2
Symphony Ms, W10
off Third Av 108 B3
Syon Gate Way, Brent.
TW8 . . . . .124 D7
★ Syon Ho & Pk, Brent.
TW8 . . . . .145 F1
Syon La, Islw. TW7 . . . . .124 E7
Syon Pk Gdns, Islw.
TW7 . . . . .124 C7
Syon Vista, Rich. TW9 . . .145 G1

T

Tabard Cen, SE1
off Prioress St 132 A3
Tabard Gdn Est, SE1 . . . .28 C4
Tabard St, SE1 . . . . .28 B4
Tabernacle Av, E13
off Barking Rd 115 G4
Tabernacle St, EC2 . . . . . .12 C6
Tableer Av, SW4 . . . . . . .150 D5
Tabley Rd, N7 . . . . .92 E4
Tabor Gdns, Sutt. SM3 . .198 C6
Tabor Gro, SW19 . . . . . .166 B7
Tabor Rd, W6 . . . . .127 H3
Tachbrook Est, SW1 . . . . .33 J4
Tachbrook Ms, SW1 . . . . .33 F1
Tachbrook Rd, Felt.
TW14 . . . . .141 J7
Southall UB2 . . . . .122 D4
Tachbrook St, SW1 . . . . . .33 G2
Tack Ms, SE4 . . . . .154 A3
Tadema Rd, SW10 . . . . . .30 D7
Tadmor St, W12 . . . . . . .128 A1
Tadworth Av, N.Mal.
KT3 . . . . .183 F5
Tadworth Rd, NW2 . . . . . .89 G2
Taeping St, E14 . . . . . . .134 B4
Taffy's How, Mitch.
CR4 . . . . .185 H3
Taft Way, E3
off St. Leonards St . . .114 B3
Tagg's Island, Hmptn.
TW12 . . . . .180 A2
Tailworth St, E1 . . . . .21 H2
Tait Rd, Croy. CR0 . . . . . .188 B7
Takhar Ms, SW11
off Cabul Rd 149 H2
Talacre Rd, NW5 . . . . . . .92 A6
Talbot Av, N2 . . . . .73 G3
Talbot Cl, N15 . . . . .76 C4
Talbot Ct, EC3 . . . . .20 C5
Talbot Cres, NW4 . . . . . .71 G5
Talbot Gdns, Ilf. IG3 . . . .100 A2
Talbot Ho, E14
off Giraud St 114 B6
N7 off Harvist Est 93 G3
Talbot Pl, SE3 . . . . .154 E2
Talbot Rd, E6 . . . . .116 D2
E7 . . . . .97 G4
N6 . . . . .74 A6
N15 . . . . .76 C4
N22 . . . . .74 C2
SE22 . . . . .152 B4
W2 . . . . .108 C6
W11 . . . . .108 C6
W13 . . . . .104 D7
Bromley BR2
off Masons Hill 191 H4
Carshalton SM5 . . . . . .200 A5
Dagenham RM9 . . . . . .101 F6
Harrow HA3 . . . . .68 C2
Isleworth TW7 . . . . . . .144 D4
Southall UB2 . . . . .123 E4
Thornton Heath CR7 . . .188 A4
Twickenham TW2 . . . . .162 B1
Wembley HA0 . . . . .87 G5
Talbot Sq, W2 . . . . .15 F4
Talbot Wk, NW10
off Garnet Rd 88/89 E6
W11 . . . . .108 B6
Talbot Yd, SE1 . . . . .28 B2
Talfourd Pl, SE15 . . . . . .152 C1
Talfourd Rd, SE15 . . . . . .152 C1
Talgarth Rd, W6 . . . . . . .128 B5
W14 . . . . .128 B5
Talgarth Wk, NW9 . . . . . .70 E5
Talisman Cl, Ilf. IG3 . . . .100 B1
Talisman Sq, SE26 . . . . .170 D4
Talisman Way, Wem.
HA9 . . . . .87 J3
Tallack Cl, Har. HA3
off College Hill Rd 52 B7
Tallack Rd, E10 . . . . .95 J1

Tall Elms Cl, Brom. BR2 .191 F5
Tallis Cl, E16 ....115 H6
Tallis Gro, SE7 ....135 H6
Tallis St, EC4 ....19 F5
Tallis Vw, NW10 ......88 D6
Tall Trees, SW16 .....187 F3
Tally Ho Cor, N12 ......57 F5
Talma Gdns, Twick. TW2 .144 B6
Talmage Cl, SE23
   off Tyson Rd 153 F7
Talman Gro, Stan. HA7 . .53 G6
Talma Rd, SW2 ....151 G4
Talwin St, E3 ....114 B3
Tamar Cl, E3
   off Lefevre Wk 113 J1
Tamarind Yd, E1 ....29 J1
Tamarisk Sq, W12 .....107 F7
Tamar Sq, Wdf.Grn. IG8 . .63 H6
Tamar St, SE7
   off Woolwich Rd 136 H3
Tamar Way, N17 ....76 D3
Tamesis Gdns, Wor.Pk.
   KT4 ....196 E1
Tamian Way, Houns.
   TW4 ....142 C4
Tamworth Av, Wdf.Grn.
   IG8 ....63 E6
Tamworth La, Mitch.
   CR4 ....186 B2
Tamworth Pk, Mitch.
   CR4 ....186 B4
Tamworth Pl, Croy. CR0 .201 J2
Tamworth Rd, Croy. CR0 .201 H2
Tamworth St, SW6 .....128 D6
Tancred Rd, N4 ....75 H6
Tandem Cen, SW19
   off Prince George's
   Rd 185 G1
Tandem Way, SW19 ....185 G1
Tandridge Dr, Orp. BR6 .207 G1
Tandridge Pl, Orp. BR6
   off Tandridge Dr 193 G2
Tanfield Av, NW2 ....89 F4
Tanfield Rd, Croy. CR0 . .201 J4
Tangier Rd, Rich.TW10 .146 B3
Tanglebury Cl, Brom.
   BR1 ....192 C4
Tangle Tree Cl, N3 ......73 E2
Tanglewood Cl, Croy.
   CR0 ....203 F3
   Stanmore HA7 ....52 B2
Tanglewood Way, Felt.
   TW13 ....160 B3
Tangley Gro, SW15 ....147 F6
Tangley Pk Rd, Hmptn.
   TW12 ....161 F6
Tangmere Gdns, Nthlt.
   UB5 ....102 C2
Tangmere Gro, Kings.T.
   KT2 ....163 G5
Tangmere Way, NW9 . . .71 E2
Tanhurst Wk, SE2
   off Alsike Rd 138 D3
Tankerton Rd, Surb. KT6 .195 J2
Tankerton St, WC1 ......10 B4
Tankerville Rd, SW16 . .168 D6
Tankridge Rd, NW2 .....89 H2
Tanner Pt, E13
   off Pelly Rd 115 G1
Tanners Cl, Walt. KT12 . .178 B6
Tanners End La, N18 .....60 B4
Tanners Hill, SE8 ......153 J1
Tanners La, Ilf. IG6 ......81 F3
Tanner St, SE1 ....28 E4
   Barking IG11 ....99 F6
Tannery Cl, Beck. BR3 . .189 G5
   Dagenham RM10 ....101 H3
Tannington Ter, N5 ......93 G3
Tannsfeld Rd, SE26 ....171 G5
Tansley Cl, N7
   off Hilldrop Rd 92 D5
Tanswell Est, SE1 ....27 F4
Tanswell St, SE1 ....27 E4
Tansy Cl, E6 ....116 D6
Tantallon Rd, SW12 . . .168 A1
Tant Av, E16 ....115 F6
Tantony Gro, Rom. RM6 . .82 D3
Tanworth Gdns, Pnr.
   HA5 ....66 B2
Tanyard La, Bex. DA5
   off Bexley High St . . .159 G2
Tanza Rd, NW3 ....91 J4
Tapestry Cl, Sutt. SM2 . .198 E7
Taplow, NW3 ....91 G7
   SE17 ....36 D4
Taplow Rd, N13 ....59 J4
Taplow St, N1 ....12 A2
Tappesfield Rd, SE15 . .153 F3
Tapp St, E1 ....113 E4
Tapster St, Barn. EN5 . . .40 C4

Tara Ms, N8
   off Edison Rd 74 D6
Taransay Wk, N1
   off Marquess Rd 94 A6
Tarbert Rd, SE22 ......152 B5
Tarbert Wk, E1
   off Juniper St 113 F7
Target Cl, Felt.TW14 . .141 H6
Tariff Cres, SE8 ....133 J4
Tariff Rd, N17 ....60 D6
Tarleton Gdns, SE23 . .171 E1
Tarling Cl, Sid. DA14 . .176 B3
Tarling Rd, E16 ....115 F6
   N2 ....73 F2
Tarling St, E1 ....113 E6
Tarling St Est, E1 ......113 F6
Tarn St, SE1 ....27 J6
Tarnwood Pk, SE9 ....174 C1
Tarquin Ho, SE26 .....170 D4
Tarragon Cl, SE14 .....133 H7
Tarragon Gro, SE26 . . .171 G6
Tarrant Pl, W1 ....15 J2
Tarrington Cl, SW16 . .168 D3
Tarry La, SE8 ....133 H4
Tarver Rd, SE17 ....35 H4
Tarves Way, SE10 ....134 B7
Tash Pl, N11
   off Woodland Rd 58 B5
Tasker Cl, Hayes UB3 . .121 F7
Tasker Ho, Bark. IG11
   off Dovehouse Mead .117 G2
Tasker Rd, NW3 ....91 J5
Tasman Ct, E14
   off Westferry Rd 134 B4
Tasmania Ter, N18 ......59 J6
Tasman Rd, SW9 ......151 E3
Tasman Wk, E16
   off Royal Rd 116 A6
Tasso Rd, W6 ....128 B6
Tatam Rd, NW10 ....88 C7
Tatchbury Ho, SW15
   off Tunworth Cres . .147 F6
Tate & Lyle Jetty, E16 . .136 B2
★ Tate Britain, SW1 . . . .34 A2
★ Tate Modern, SE1 . . . .27 H1
Tate Rd, E16
   off Newland St 136 C1
   Sutton SM1 ....198 D5
Tatnell Rd, SE23 ......153 H6
Tattersall Cl, SE9 ......156 B5
Tatton Cres, N16
   off Clapton Common .76 C7
Tatum St, SE17 ....36 C2
Tauheed Cl, N4 ....93 J2
Taunton Av, SW20 ....183 H2
   Hounslow TW3 ......143 J2
Taunton Cl, Ilf. IG6 .....65 J6
   Sutton SM3 ....198 D1
Taunton Dr, N2 ....73 F2
   Enfield EN2 ....43 G3
Taunton Ms, NW1 ......7 J5
Taunton Pl, NW1 ....7 J5
Taunton Rd, SE12 .....155 E5
   Greenford UB6 ......103 H1
Taunton Way, Stan. HA7 .69 H3
Tavern Cl, Cars. SM5 . .185 H7
Taverners Cl, W11
   off Addison Av 128 B1
Taverner Sq, N5
   off Highbury Gra 93 J4
Taverners Way, E4
   off Douglas Rd 62/63 E1
Tavern La, SW9 ....151 G2
Tavistock Av, E17 ....77 H3
   NW7 off Bittacy Hill . .56 B7
   Greenford UB6 ......104 D2
Tavistock Cl, N16
   off Crossway 94 B5
Tavistock Ct, WC2
   off Tavistock St 110/111 E7
Tavistock Cres, W11 . . .108 C5
   Mitcham CR4 ....187 E4
Tavistock Gdns, Ilf. IG3 . .99 H4
Tavistock Gate, Croy.
   CR0 ....202 A1
Tavistock Gro, Croy. CR0 .188 A7
Tavistock Ms, E18
   off Avon Way 79 G3
   W11 off Lancaster Rd .108 C6
Tavistock Pl, E18
   off Avon Way 79 G3
   N14 off Chase Side . . .42 B7
   WC1 ....9 J5
Tavistock Rd, E7 ....97 F4
   E15 ....97 F6
   E18 ....79 G3
   N4 ....76 A6
   NW10 ....107 F2
   W11 ....108 C6

Tavistock Rd, Brom.
   BR2 ....191 F4
   Carshalton SM5 .....199 G1
   Croydon CR0 ....202 A1
   Edgware HA8 ....70 A1
   Welling DA16 ....158 C1
   West Drayton UB7 . . .120 A1
Tavistock Sq, WC1 ......9 J5
Tavistock St, WC2 ......18 B5
Tavistock Ter, N19 ......92 D3
Tavistock Twr, SE16
   off Finland St 133 H3
Tavistock Wk, Cars. SM5
   off Tavistock Rd 199 G1
Taviton St, WC1 ....9 H5
Tavy Cl, SE11 ....35 F3
Tawney Rd, SE28 ......118 B7
Tawny Cl, W13 ....124 E1
   Feltham TW13
   off Chervil Cl 160 A3
Tawny Way, SE16 .....133 G4
Taybridge Rd, SW11 . . .150 A3
Tayben Av, Twick. TW2 .144 B6
Tayburn Cl, E14 ....114 C6
Taylor Av, Rich.TW9 . . .146 B2
Taylor Cl, N17 ....60 D7
   SE8 ....133 J6
   Hampton (Hmptn.H.)
   TW12 ....161 J5
   Hounslow TW3 ......143 J1
   Orpington BR6 ......207 J4
Taylor Ct, E15
   off Clays La 96 C5
Taylor Rd, Mitch. CR4 . .167 H7
   Wallington SM6 .....200 B5
Taylors Bldgs, SE18
   off Spray St 136/137 E4
Taylors Cl, Sid. DA14 . .175 J4
Taylors Grn, W3
   off Long Dr 106/107 E6
Taylors La, NW10 ......88 E7
   SE26 ....170 E4
   Barnet EN5 ....40 C1
Taymount Ri, SE23 ....171 F2
Tayport Cl, N1 ....93 E7
Tayside Dr, Edg. HA8 . . .54 B3
Taywood Rd, Nthlt. UB5 .103 F3
Teak Cl, SE16 ....133 H1
Teal Cl, E16
   off Fulmer Rd 116 A5
Teal Ct, Wall. SM6
   off Carew Rd 200 C6
Teale St, E2 ....13 J1
Tealing Dr, Epsom KT19 .196 D4
Teal Pl, Sutt. SM1
   off Sandpiper Rd 198 C5
Teal St, SE10 ....135 F3
Teasel Cl, Croy. CR0 . . .203 G1
Teasel Way, E15 ....114 E3
Tebworth Rd, N17 ......60 C7
Teck Cl, Islw. TW7 .....144 D2
Tedder Cl, Chess. KT9 . .195 F5
   Ruislip HA4
   off West End Rd 84 B5
Tedder Rd, S.Croy. CR2 .203 F7
TEDDINGTON 162 D6
Teddington Lock, Tedd.
   TW11 ....162 E4
Teddington Pk, Tedd.
   TW11 ....162 C5
Teddington Pk Rd, Tedd.
   TW11 ....162 C4
Tedworth Gdns, SW3 . . .31 J4
Tedworth Sq, SW3 .....31 J4
Tee, The, W3 ....106 E6
Tees Av, Grnf. UB6 ....104 B2
Teesdale Av, Islw.TW7 .144 D1
Teesdale Cl, E2 ....13 J2
Teesdale Gdns, SE25 . .188 B2
   Isleworth TW7 ......144 D1
Teesdale Rd, E11 ....79 F6
Teesdale St, E2 ....112 E2
Teesdale Yd, E2 ....13 J1
Teeswater Ct, Erith DA18
   off Middle Way 138 D3
Teevan Cl, Croy. CR0 . .188 D7
Teevan Rd, Croy. CR0 . .188 D7
Teignmouth Cl, SW4 . .150 D4
   Edgware HA8 ....69 J2
Teignmouth Gdns, Grnf.
   UB6 ....104 C2
Teignmouth Rd, NW2 . .90 A5
   Welling DA16 ....158 C2
Telcote Way, Ruis. HA4
   off Woodlands Av . . .66 C7
★ Telecom Twr, W1 .....17 F1
Telegraph Hill, NW3 .....90 E3
Telegraph La, Esher (Clay.)
   KT10 ....194 C6
Telegraph Ms, Ilf. IG3 . .100 A1

Telegraph Path, Chis.
   BR7 ....174 E5
Telegraph Pl, E14 .....134 B4
Telegraph Rd, SW15 . .147 H7
Telegraph St, EC2 ......20 B3
Telemann Sq, SE3 .....155 H3
Telephone Pl, SW6
   off Lillie Rd 128 C6
Telfer Cl, W3
   off Church Rd 126 C2
Telferscot Rd, SW12 . .168 D1
Telford Av, SW2 ....168 E1
Telford Cl, E17 ....77 H7
   SE19
   off St. Aubyn's Rd . . .170 C6
   Watford. KT12 ....178 C7
Telford Rd, N11 ....58 C6
   NW9
   off West Hendon Bdy . .71 G1
   SE9 ....175 G2
   W10 ....108 B5
   Southall UB1 ....103 H7
   Twickenham TW2 . . .143 G2
Telfords Yd, E1 ....21 J6
Telford Ter, SW1 ....33 F5
Telford Way, W3 ......106 E5
   Hayes UB4 ....102 E5
Telham Rd, E6 ....116 D2
Tell Gro, SE22 ....152 C4
Tellson Av, SE18 ......156 B1
Telscombe Cl, Orp.
   BR6 ....207 H2
Temeraire St, SE16
   off Albion St 133 F2
Temperley Rd, SW12 . .150 A7
Templar Dr, SE28 ......118 D6
Templar Ho, NW2
   off Shoot Up Hill 90 C6
Templar Pl, Hmptn.
   TW12 ....161 G7
Templars Av, NW11 .....72 C6
Templars Cres, N3 ......72 D2
Templars Dr, Har. HA3 . .52 A6
Templar St, SE5 ....151 H2
★ Temple, The, EC4 ......18 E5
Temple Av, EC4 ....111 G7
   N20 ....41 G5
   Croydon CR0 ....203 J2
   Dagenham RM8 .....101 G1
★ Temple Bar, EC4 ....18 E4
Temple Cl, E11
   off Wadley Rd 78/79 E7
   N3 off Cyprus Rd 72 C2
   SE28 ....137 F3
Templecombe Rd, E9 . .113 F1
Templecombe Way, Mord.
   SM4 ....184 B5
Temple Cl, E1
   off Rectory Sq 113 G5
Temple Fortune Hill,
   NW11 ....72 D5
Temple Fortune La,
   NW11 ....72 D6
Temple Fortune Par, NW11
   off Finchley Rd 72 C5
Temple Gdns, N21
   off Barrowell Grn 59 H2
   NW11 ....72 C6
   Dagenham RM8 .....100 D3
Temple Gro, NW11 .....72 D6
   Enfield EN2 ....43 H3
Templehof Av, NW2 .....71 J7
Temple La, EC4 ....19 F4
Templeman Rd, W7 ....104 C5
Templemead Cl, W3 . . .106 E6
Temple Mead Cl, Stan.
   HA7 ....52 E6
Temple Mill La, E15 ....96 B4
★ Temple of Mithras, EC4
   off Queen Victoria St . .20 A4
Temple Pl, WC2 ....18 D5
Temple Rd, E6 ....116 B1
   N8 ....75 F4
   NW2 ....89 J4
   W4 ....126 C3
   W5 ....125 G3
   Croydon CR0 ....202 A4
   Hounslow TW3 ......143 H4
   Richmond TW9 ......145 J3
Temple Sheen, SW14 . .146 C5
Temple Sheen Rd,
   SW14 ....146 B4
Temple St, E2 ....112 E2
Templeton Av, E4 ....62 A4
Templeton Cl, N16
   off Truman's Rd 94 B5
   SE19 ....188 A1
Templeton Ct, NW7
   off Bittacy Hill 56 B7

Templeton Pl, SW5 . . . . .128 D4
Templeton Rd, N15 . . . . . .76 A6
Temple Way, Sutt. SM1 . .199 G3
Templewood, W13 . . . . . .105 E5
Templewood Av, NW3 . . . .90 E3
Templewood Gdns,
NW3 . . . . .91 E3
Templewood Pt, NW2
off Granville Rd 90 C2
Tempsford Cl, Enf. EN2
off Gladbeck Way 43 J3
Temsford Cl, Har. HA2 . . .67 J2
Tenbury Cl, E7
off Romford Rd 98 A5
Tenbury Ct, SW2 . . . . . .168 D1
Tenby Av, Har. HA3 . . . . .68 E2
Tenby Cl, N15
off Hanover Rd 76 C4
Romford RM6 . . . . .82 E6
Tenby Gdns, Nthlt. UB5 . .85 G6
Tenby Rd, E17 . . . . .77 H5
Edgware HA8 . . . . .69 J1
Enfield EN3 . . . . .45 F3
Romford RM6 . . . . .83 E6
Welling DA16 . . . . .158 D1
Tench St, E1 . . . . .132 E1
Tenda Rd, SE16
off Roseberry St .132/133 E4
Tendring Way, Rom.
RM6 . . . . .82 C5
Tenham Av, SW2 . . . . . .168 D1
Tenison Ct, W1 . . . . .17 F5
Tenison Way, SE1 . . . . . .26 C2
Tenniel Cl, W2 . . . . .14 C4
Tennis Ct La, E.Mol. KT8
off Hampton Ct Way . .180 C3
Tennison Av, Borwd.
WD6 . . . . .38 B5
Tennison Rd, SE25 . . . . .188 C4
Tennis St, SE1 . . . . .28 B3
Tenniswood Rd, Enf.
EN1 . . . . .44 C1
Tennyson Av, E11 . . . . . .79 G7
E12 . . . . .98 B7
NW9 . . . . .70 C3
New Malden KT3 . . . . .183 H5
Twickenham TW1 . . . . .162 C1
Tennyson Cl, Enf. EN3 . . .45 G5
Feltham TW14 . . . . . . .141 J6
Welling DA16 . . . . .157 H1
Tennyson Rd, E10 . . . . . .96 B2
E15 . . . . .96 E7
E17 . . . . .77 J6
NW6 . . . . .108 C1
NW7 . . . . .55 G5
SE20 . . . . .171 G7
SW19 . . . . .167 F6
W7 . . . . .104 C7
Hounslow TW3 . . . . . . .143 J2
Tennyson St, SW8 . . . . .150 B2
Tensing Rd, Sthl. UB2 . .123 G3
Tentelow La, Sthl. UB2 . .123 G3
Tenterden Cl, NW4 . . . . .72 A3
SE9 . . . . .174 C4
Tenterden Dr, NW4 . . . . .72 A3
Tenterden Gdns, NW4 . . .72 A3
Croydon CR0 . . . . .188 D7
Tenterden Gro, NW4 . . . .72 A4
Tenterden Rd, N17 . . . . . .60 C7
Croydon CR0 . . . . .188 D7
Dagenham RM8 . . . . . .101 F2
Tenterden St, W1 . . . . . . .16 E4
Tenter Grd, E1 . . . . .21 F2
Tenter Pas, E1 . . . . .21 G4
Tent Peg La, Orp. BR5 . .193 F5
Tent St, E1 . . . . .112 E4
Terborch Way, SE22
off East Dulwich Gro .152 B5
Teredo St, SE16 . . . . . . .133 G3
Terence Ct, Belv. DA17
off Nuxley Rd 139 F6
Teresa Ms, E17 . . . . .78 A4
Teresa Wk, N10
off Connaught Gdns . . .74 B5
Terling Cl, E11 . . . . .97 F3
Terling Rd, Dag. RM8 . . .101 G2
Terling Wk, N1
off Britannia Row 111 J1
Terminus Pl, SW1 . . . . . .25 E6
Terrace, The, E4
off Chingdale Rd . .62/63 E3
N3 off Hendon La 72 C2
NW6 . . . . .108 D1
SW13 . . . . .147 E2
Woodford Green IG8
off Broadmead Rd 63 G6
Terrace Gdns, SW13 . . . .147 F2

Terrace La, Rich. TW10 . . .145 H6
Terrace Rd, E9 . . . . .95 F7
E13 . . . . .115 G1
Walton-on-Thames
KT12 . . . . .178 A7
Terrace Wk, Dag. RM9 . . .101 E5
Terrapin Rd, SW17 . . . . .168 B3
Terretts Pl, N1
off Upper St 93 H7
Terrick Rd, N22 . . . . .75 E1
Terrick St, W12 . . . . .107 H6
Terrilands, Pnr. HA5 . . . .67 F3
Terront Rd, N15 . . . . .75 J5
Tersha St, Rich. TW9 . . . .145 J4
Tessa Sanderson Pl,
SW8 . . . . .150 B3
Tessa Sanderson Way, Grnf.
UB6 off Lilian Board
Way 86 A5
Testerton Wk, W11 . . . . .108 A7
Tetbury Pl, N1
off Upper St 111 H1
Tetcott Rd, SW10 . . . . . . .30 C7
Tetherdown, N10 . . . . . . .74 A3
Tetty Way, Brom. BR2 . . .191 G2
Teversham La, SW8 . . . .151 E1
Teviot Cl, Well. DA16 . . . .158 B1
Teviot St, E14 . . . . .114 C5
Tewkesbury Av, SE23 . . .171 E1
Pinner HA5 . . . . .67 E5
Tewkesbury Cl, N15
off Tewkesbury Rd 76 A6
Loughton IG10 . . . . . . .48 B6
Tewkesbury Gdns, NW9 . .70 B3
Tewkesbury Rd, N15 . . . .76 A6
W13 . . . . .104 D7
Carshalton SM5 . . . . . .199 G1
Tewkesbury Ter, N11 . . . .58 C6
Tewson Rd, SE18 . . . . . .137 H5
Teynham Av, Enf. EN1 . . .44 A6
Teynham Grn, Brom.
BR2 . . . . .191 G5
Teynton Ter, N17 . . . . . . .75 J1
Thackeray Av, N17 . . . . . .76 D2
Thackeray Cl, SW19 . . . .166 A7
Harrow HA2 . . . . .85 G1
Isleworth TW7 . . . . . . .144 D2
Thackeray Dr, Rom.
RM6 . . . . .82 A7
Thackeray Rd, E6 . . . . . .116 A2
SW8 . . . . .150 B2
Thackeray St, W8 . . . . . . .22 B4
Thakeham Cl, SE26 . . . . .170 E5
Thalia Cl, SE10 . . . . .134 D6
Thame Rd, SE16 . . . . . . .133 G2
Thames Av, SW10 . . . . . .149 F1
Dagenham RM9 . . . . . .119 H4
Greenford UB6 . . . . . . .104 C2
Thames Bk, SW14 . . . . . .146 C2
Thamesbank Pl, SE28 . . .118 C6
Thames Circle, E14
off Westferry Rd 134 A4
Thames Cl, Hmptn.
TW12 . . . . .179 H2
Thames Ct, W.Mol. KT8 . .179 H2
Thames Cres, W4
off Corney Rd . .126/127 E7
THAMES DITTON 180 C6
Thames Ditton Island, T.Ditt.
KT7 . . . . .180 D5
★ Thames Flood Barrier &
Visitors Cen, SE18 . .136 A3
Thamesgate Cl, Rich. TW10
off Locksmeade
Rd 162/163 E4
Thames Gateway, Dag.
RM9 . . . . .119 F2
Thameshill Av, Rom.
RM5 . . . . .83 J2
★ Thames Ho, SW1 . . . . .34 A1
Thameside, Tedd. TW11 . .163 G7
Thameside Ind Est, E16 . .136 B2
Thameside Wk, SE28 . . . .117 J6
THAMESMEAD, Walt.
KT12 . . . . .178 A7
THAMESMEAD NORTH,
SE28 . . . . .118 C6
Thames Meadow, W.Mol.
KT8 . . . . .179 G2
Thamesmead Spine Rd, Belv.
DA17 . . . . .139 H2
THAMESMEAD WEST,
SE18 . . . . .137 F3
Thamesmere Dr, SE28 . . .118 A7
Thames Path, SE1 . . . . . .19 F6
SE7 . . . . .135 G3
SE10 . . . . .135 G3
W6 . . . . .127 J6
Thames Pl, SW15 . . . . . .148 A3

Thames Quay, SW10
off Harbour Av 149 F1
Thames Rd, E16 . . . . . . .136 A1
W4 . . . . .126 A6
Barking IG11 . . . . .117 J3
Thames Side, Kings.T.
KT1 . . . . .181 G1
Thames St, SE10 . . . . . . .134 B6
Hampton TW12 . . . . . .179 H1
Kingston upon Thames
KT1 . . . . .181 G2
Sunbury-on-Thames
TW16 . . . . .178 B4
Thamesvale Cl, Houns.
TW3 . . . . .143 G3
Thames Village, W4 . . . .146 C1
Thames Wf, E16 . . . . . . .135 F1
Thanescroft Gdns, Croy.
CR0 . . . . .202 B3
Thanet Dr, Kes. BR2
off Phoenix Dr 206 A3
Thanet Pl, Croy. CR0 . . . .201 J4
Thanet Rd, Bex. DA5 . . . .159 G7
Thanet St, WC1 . . . . .10 A4
Thane Vil, N7 . . . . .93 F3
Thane Wks, N7 . . . . .93 F3
Thanington Ct, SE9 . . . . .157 H6
Thant Cl, E10 . . . . .96 B3
Tharp Rd, Wall. SM6 . . . .200 D5
Thatcham Gdns, N20 . . . .41 F7
Thatcher Cl, West Dr. UB7
off Classon Cl 120 B2
Thatchers Cl, Loug. IG10 . .49 F2
Thatchers Way, Islw.
TW7 . . . . .144 A5
Thatches Gro, Rom.
RM6 . . . . .82 E4
Thavies Inn, EC1 . . . . . . .19 F3
Thaxted Ct, N1 . . . . .12 B2
Thaxted Ho, Dag. RM10 . .101 H7
Thaxted Pl, SW20 . . . . . .166 A7
Thaxted Rd, SE9 . . . . . . .175 F2
Buckhurst Hill IG9 . . . . .48 B7
Thaxton Rd, W14 . . . . . . .128 C6
Thayers Fm Rd, Beck.
BR3 . . . . .189 H1
Thayer St, W1 . . . . .16 C2
★ Theatre Royal, WC2 . . .18 B4
Theatre Sq, E15
off Great Eastern Rd . . .96 D6
Theatre St, SW11 . . . . . . .149 J3
Theberton St, N1 . . . . . . .111 G1
Theed St, SE1 . . . . .27 E2
Thelma Gdns, SE3 . . . . . .156 A1
Feltham TW13 . . . . . . .161 E3
Thelma Gro, Tedd. TW11 . .162 D6
Theobald Cres, Har.
HA3 . . . . .67 H1
Theobald Rd, E17 . . . . . . .77 J7
Croydon CR0 . . . . .201 H2
Theobalds Av, N12 . . . . . .57 F4
Theobalds Ct, N4
off Queens Dr 93 J2
Theobald's Rd, WC1 . . . . .18 C1
Theobald St, SE1 . . . . . . .28 B6
Theodore Rd, SE13 . . . . .154 C6
Therapia La, Croy. CR0 . .187 E6
Therapia Rd, SE22 . . . . . .153 F6
Theresa Rd, W6 . . . . .127 G4
Therfield Ct, N4
off Brownswood Rd . . .93 J2
Thermopylae Gate, E14 . .134 B4
Theseus Wk, N1 . . . . .11 H2
Thesiger Rd, SE20 . . . . . .171 G7
Thessaly Rd, SW8 . . . . . .130 C7
Thetford Cl, N13 . . . . .59 H6
Thetford Gdns, Dag.
RM9 . . . . .100 D7
Thetford Rd, Dag. RM9 . .118 D1
New Malden KT3 . . . . .182 D6
Thetis Ter, Rich. TW9
off Kew Grn 126 A6
Theydon Gro, Wdf.Grn.
IG8 . . . . .63 J6
Theydon Pk Rd, Epp.
(They.B.) CM16 . . . . . . .49 H1
Theydon Rd, E5 . . . . .95 F2
Theydon St, E17 . . . . .77 J7
Thicket Cres, Sutt. SM1 . .199 F4
Thicket Gro, SE20
off Anerley Rd 170 D7
Dagenham RM9 . . . . . .100 C6
Thicket Rd, SE20 . . . . . . .170 D7
Sutton SM1 . . . . .199 F4
Third Av, E12 . . . . .98 B4
E13 . . . . .115 G3
E17 . . . . .78 A5
W3 . . . . .127 F1
W10 . . . . .108 B3
Dagenham RM10 . . . . .119 H1

Third Av, Enf. EN1 . . . . . . .44 C5
Hayes UB3 . . . . .121 J1
Romford RM6 . . . . .82 C6
Wembley HA9 . . . . .87 G2
Third Cl, W.Mol. KT8 . . . .179 H4
Third Cross Rd, Twick.
TW2 . . . . .162 A2
Third Way, Wem. HA9 . . . .88 B4
Thirleby Rd, SW1 . . . . . . .25 G6
Edgware HA8 . . . . .70 D1
Thirlmere Av, Grnf. UB6 . .105 F3
Thirlmere Gdns, Wem.
HA9 . . . . .87 F1
Thirlmere Ho, Islw. TW7
off Summerwood Rd . .144 C5
Thirlmere Ri, Brom. BR1 . .173 F6
Thirlmere Rd, N10 . . . . . . .74 B1
SW16 . . . . .168 D4
Bexleyheath DA7 . . . . .159 J2
Thirsk Cl, Nthlt. UB5 . . . . .85 G6
Thirsk Rd, SE25 . . . . .188 A4
SW11 . . . . .150 A3
Mitcham CR4 . . . . .168 A7
Thirston Path, Borwd.
WD6 . . . . .38 A2
Thistlebrook, SE2 . . . . . .138 C3
Thistlebrook Ind Est,
SE2 . . . . .138 C2
Thistlecroft Gdns, Stan.
HA7 . . . . .69 G1
Thistledene, T.Ditt. KT7 . .180 B6
Thistledene Av, Har. HA2 . .85 E3
Thistle Gro, SW10 . . . . . . .30 D3
Thistlemead, Chis. BR7 . .192 E2
Thistle Mead, Loug. IG10 . .48 D3
Thistlewaite Rd, E5 . . . . . .95 E3
Thistlewood Cl, N7 . . . . . .93 F2
Thistleworth Cl, Islw.
TW7 . . . . .124 A7
Thistley Cl, N12
off Summerfields Av . . .57 H6
Thomas a'Beckett Cl, Wem.
HA0 . . . . .86 C4
Thomas Baines Rd,
SW11 . . . . .149 G3
Thomas Cribb Ms, E6 . . .116 C6
Thomas Darby Ct, W11 . .108 B6
Thomas Dean Rd, SE26
off Kangley Br Rd 171 J4
Thomas Dinwiddy Rd,
SE12 . . . . .173 H2
Thomas Doyle St, SE1 . . .27 G5
Thomas Hardy Ho, N22 . .59 F7
Thomas La, SE6 . . . . .154 A7
Thomas More Ho, EC2
off The Barbican 111 J5
Thomas More St, E1 . . . . .21 H6
Thomas More Way, N2 . . .73 F3
Thomas Pl, W8 . . . . .22 A6
Thomas Rd, E14 . . . . .113 J6
Thomas Wall Cl, Sutt. SM1
off Clarence Rd .198/199 E5
Thompson Av, Rich.
TW9 . . . . .146 A3
Thompson Cl, Ilf. IG1
off High Rd 99 F2
Sutton SM3
off Barrington Rd 198 D1
Thompson Rd, SE22 . . . .152 C6
Dagenham RM9 . . . . . .101 F3
Hounslow TW3 . . . . . . .143 H4
Thompson's Av, SE5 . . . . .35 J7
Thompson's La, Loug.
(High Beach) IG10 . . . . .47 F1
Thomson Cres, Croy.
CR0 . . . . .201 G1
Thomson Rd, Har. HA3 . . .68 B3
Thorburn Sq, SE1 . . . . . . .37 H2
Thorburn Way, SW19 . . . .185 F1
Thoresby St, N1 . . . . .12 A3
Thorkhill Gdns, T.Ditt.
KT7 . . . . .194 D1
Thorkhill Rd, T.Ditt. KT7 . .180 E7
Thornaby Gdns, N18 . . . . .60 D6
Thorn Av, Bushey
(Bushey Hth.) WD23 . . .51 J1
Thornbury Av, Islw.
TW7 . . . . .124 A7
Thornbury Cl, N16
off Truman's Rd 94 B5
NW7 off Bittacy Hill . . .56 B7
Thornbury Gdns, Borwd.
WD6 . . . . .38 C4
Thornbury Rd, SW2 . . . . .150 E6
Isleworth TW7 . . . . . . .144 A1
Thornbury Sq, N6 . . . . . . .92 C1
Thornby Rd, E5 . . . . .95 F3
Thorncliffe Rd, SW2 . . . . .150 E6
Southall UB2 . . . . .123 F5

Thorn Cl, Brom. BR2 . . . .**192** D6
  Northolt UB5 . . . .**103** F3
Thorncombe Rd, SE22 . . .**152** B5
Thorncroft Rd, Sutt.
  SM1 . . . .**198** E4
Thorncroft St, SW8 . . . . .**130** E7
Thorndean St, SW18 . . . .**167** F2
Thorndene Av, N11 . . . . . .**58** A1
Thorndike Av, Nthlt.
  UB5 . . . .**102** D1
Thorndike Cl, SW10 . . . . .**30** C7
Thorndike St, SW1 . . . . . .**33** H3
Thorndon Cl, Orp. BR5 . . .**193** J2
Thorndon Gdns, Epsom
  KT19 . . . .**196** E4
Thorndon Rd, Orp. BR5 . . .**193** J2
Thorndyke Ct, Pnr. HA5
  off Westfield Pk **51** F7
Thorne Cl, E11 . . . .**96** E4
  E16 . . . .**115** G6
  Erith DA8 . . . .**139** J6
Thorneloe Gdns, Croy.
  CR0 . . . .**201** G5
Thorne Pas, SW13 . . . . . .**147** E2
Thorne Rd, SW8 . . . .**130** E7
Thornes Cl, Beck. BR3 . . .**190** C3
Thorne St, E16 . . . .**115** F6
  SW13 . . . .**147** E3
Thornet Wd Rd, Brom.
  BR1 . . . .**192** D3
Thorney Cres, SW11 . . . .**129** G7
Thorneycroft Cl, Walt.
  KT12 . . . .**178** C6
Thorney Hedge Rd, W4 . .**126** B4
Thorney St, SW1 . . . .**34** A1
Thornfield Rd, W12 . . . . .**127** H2
Thornford Rd, SE13 . . . . .**154** C5
Thorngate Rd, W9 . . . . . .**108** D4
Thorngrove Rd, E13 . . . . .**115** H1
Thornham Gro, E15 . . . . . .**96** D5
Thornham St, SE10 . . . . .**134** B6
Thornhaugh Ms, WC1 . . . . .**9** J6
Thornhaugh St, WC1 . . . .**17** J1
Thornhill Av, SE18 . . . . . .**137** H7
  Surbiton KT6 . . . .**195** H2
Thornhill Br Wf, N1
  off Caledonian Rd **111** F1
Thornhill Cres, N1 . . . .**93** F7
Thornhill Gdns, E10 . . . . . .**96** B2
  Barking IG11 . . . .**99** H7
Thornhill Gro, N1
  off Lofting Rd **93** F7
Thornhill Rd, E10 . . . .**96** B2
  N1 . . . .**93** G7
  Croydon CR0 . . . .**187** J7
  Surbiton KT6 . . . .**195** H2
Thornhill Sq, N1 . . . .**93** F7
Thorn Ho, Beck. BR3 . . . .**189** H1
Thornlaw Rd, SE27 . . . . .**169** G4
Thornley Cl, N17 . . . .**60** D7
Thornley Dr, Har. HA2 . . . .**85** H2
Thornley Pl, SE10
  off Caradoc St **134/135** E5
Thornsbeach Rd, SE6 . . . .**172** C1
Thornsett Pl, SE20 . . . . . .**188** E2
Thornsett Rd, SE20 . . . . .**188** E2
  SW18 . . . .**167** E2
Thornside, Edg. HA8
  off High St **54** A4
Thorn Ter, SE15
  off Nunhead Gro **153** F3
Thornton Av, SW2 . . . . . .**168** D1
  W4 . . . .**127** E4
  Croydon CR0 . . . .**187** F6
  West Drayton UB7 . . . .**120** C3
Thornton Cl, West Dr.
  UB7 . . . .**120** C3
Thornton Ct, SW20 . . . . .**184** A5
Thornton Dene, Beck.
  BR3 . . . .**190** A2
Thornton Gdns, SW12 . . .**168** D1
Thornton Gro, Pnr. HA5 . . .**51** G6
THORNTON HEATH **187** H4
Thornton Hill, SW19 . . . . .**166** B7
Thornton Pl, W1 . . . .**16** A1
Thornton Rd, E11 . . . .**96** D2
  N18 . . . .**61** F3
  SW12 . . . .**150** D7
  SW14 . . . .**146** D3
  SW19 . . . .**166** A6
  Barnet EN5 . . . .**40** B3
  Belvedere DA17 . . . . . .**139** H4
  Bromley BR1 . . . .**173** G5
  Carshalton SM5 . . . . . .**199** G1
  Croydon CR0 . . . .**187** F7
  Ilford IG1 . . . .**98** E4
  Thornton Heath CR7 . . .**187** F7
Thornton Rd E, SW19
  off Thornton Rd **166** A6

Thornton Rd Retail Pk, Croy.
  CR0 . . . .**187** F6
Thornton Row, Th.Hth. CR7
  off London Rd **187** G5
Thornton St, SW9 . . . . . .**151** G2
Thornton Way, NW11 . . . .**73** E5
Thorntree Rd, SE7 . . . . . .**136** A5
Thornville Gro, Mitch.
  CR4 . . . .**185** F2
Thornville St, SE8 . . . . . .**154** A1
Thornwood Cl, E18 . . . . . .**79** H2
Thornwood Rd, SE13 . . . .**154** E5
Thorogood Gdns, E15 . . . .**97** E5
Thorold Rd, N22 . . . .**59** E7
  Ilford IG1 . . . .**98** E2
Thorparch Rd, SW8 . . . . .**150** D1
Thorpebank Rd, W12 . . . .**127** G1
Thorpe Cl, W10
  off Cambridge Gdns . .**108** B6
  Orpington BR6 . . . .**207** H2
Thorpe Cres, E17 . . . .**77** J2
Thorpedale Gdns, Ilf. IG2,
  IG6 . . . .**80** D4
Thorpedale Rd, N4 . . . . . .**93** E1
Thorpe Hall Rd, E17 . . . . .**78** C1
Thorpe Rd, E6 . . . .**116** C1
  E7 . . . .**97** F4
  E17 . . . .**78** C2
  N15 . . . .**76** B6
  Barking IG11 . . . .**99** G3
  Kingston upon Thames
  KT2 . . . .**163** H7
Thorpewood Av, SE26 . . .**171** E2
Thorsden Way, SE19
  off Oaks Av **170** B4
Thorverton Rd, NW2 . . . . .**90** B3
Thoydon Rd, E3 . . . .**113** H2
Thrale Rd, SW16 . . . .**168** C5
Thrale St, SE1 . . . .**28** A2
Thrasher Cl, E8
  off Stean St **112** C1
Thrawl St, E1 . . . .**21** G2
Threadneedle St, EC2 . . . .**20** C4
Three Barrels Wk, EC4 . . . .**20** A5
Three Colts Cor, E2 . . . . . .**13** H5
Three Colts La, E2 . . . . . .**113** E4
Three Colt St, E14 . . . . . .**113** J7
Three Cors, Bexh. DA7 . . .**159** H2
Three Cups Yd, WC1 . . . . .**18** D2
Three Kings Rd, Mitch.
  CR4 . . . .**186** A3
Three Kings Yd, W1 . . . . . .**16** D5
Three Mill La, E3 . . . .**114** C3
Three Oak La, SE1 . . . .**29** F3
Three Quays Wk, EC3 . . . .**20** E6
Threshers Pl, W11 . . . . . .**108** B7
Thriffwood, SE26 . . . .**171** F3
Thrift Fm La, Borwd.
  WD6 . . . .**38** B2
Thrigby Rd, Chess. KT9 . .**195** J6
Throckmorten Rd, E16 . . .**115** H6
Throgmorton Av, EC2 . . . .**20** C3
Throgmorton St, EC2 . . . .**20** C3
Throwley Cl, SE2 . . . .**138** C3
Throwley Rd, Sutt. SM1 . .**199** E5
Throwley Way, Sutt.
  SM1 . . . .**199** E4
Thrupp Cl, Mitch. CR4 . . .**186** B2
Thrush Grn, Har. HA2 . . . .**67** G4
Thrush St, SE17 . . . .**35** J3
Thruxton Way, SE15 . . . . .**37** G7
Thunderer Rd, Dag.
  RM9 . . . .**118** E4
Thurbarn Rd, SE6 . . . . . .**172** B5
Thurland Rd, SE16 . . . . . .**29** H5
Thurlby Cl, Har. HA1
  off Gayton Rd **68** D6
  Woodford Green IG8 . . .**64** C5
Thurlby Rd, SE27 . . . .**169** G4
  Wembley HA0 . . . .**87** G6
Thurleigh Av, SW12 . . . . .**150** A6
Thurleigh Rd, SW12 . . . . .**150** A6
Thurlestone Av, N12 . . . . .**57** J6
  Ilford IG3 . . . .**99** J4
Thurlestone Rd, SE27 . . .**169** G3
Thurloe Cl, SW7 . . . .**31** G1
Thurloe Pl, SW7 . . . .**31** F1
Thurloe Pl Ms, SW7 . . . . .**31** F1
Thurloe Sq, SW7 . . . .**31** G1
Thurloe St, SW7 . . . .**31** F1
Thurlow Cl, E4
  off Higham Sta Av **62** B6
Thurlow Gdns, Ilf. IG6 . . . .**65** G6
  Wembley HA0 . . . .**87** G5
Thurlow Hill, SE21 . . . . . .**169** J1
Thurlow Pk Rd, SE21 . . . .**169** H1
Thurlow Rd, NW3 . . . .**91** G5
  W7 . . . .**124** D2

Thurlow St, SE17 . . . .**36** C3
Thurlow Ter, NW5 . . . .**92** A5
Thurlstone Rd, Ruis.
  HA4 . . . .**84** A3
Thurnby Ct, Twick. TW2 . .**162** B3
Thursland Rd, Sid.
  DA14 . . . .**176** E5
Thursley Cres, Croy.
  (New Adgtn.) CR0 . . . .**204** D7
Thursley Gdns, SW19 . . .**166** A2
Thursley Rd, SE9 . . . .**174** C3
Thurso St, SW17 . . . .**167** G4
Thurstan Rd, SW20 . . . . .**165** H7
Thurston Rd, SE13 . . . . . .**154** B2
  Southall UB1 . . . .**103** F6
Thurston Rd Ind Est, SE13
  off Jerrard St **154** B3
Thurtle Rd, E2 . . . .**112** C1
Thwaite Cl, Erith DA8 . . . .**139** J6
Thyer Cl, Orp. BR6
  off Isabella Dr **207** F4
Thyra Gro, N12 . . . .**57** E6
Tibbatts Rd, E3 . . . .**114** B4
Tibbenham Wk, E13 . . . . .**115** F2
Tibberton Sq, N1
  off Popham Rd **93** J7
Tibbets Cl, SW19 . . . .**166** A1
Tibbet's Cor, SW15 . . . . .**148** A7
Tibbet's Cor Underpass,
  SW15 off West Hill . . .**148** A7
Tibbet's Ride, SW15 . . . . .**148** A7
Tiber Gdns, N1
  off Treaty St **111** F1
Ticehurst Cl, Orp. BR5
  off Grovelands Rd **176** A7
Ticehurst Rd, SE23 . . . . .**171** H2
Tickford Cl, SE2
  off Ampleforth Rd **138** C2
Tidal Basin Rd, E16 . . . . .**115** F7
Tidenham Gdns, Croy.
  CR0 . . . .**202** B3
Tideswell Rd, SW15 . . . . .**147** J5
  Croydon CR0 . . . .**204** A3
Tideway Cl, Rich. TW10
  off Locksmeade
  Rd **162/163** E4
Tidey St, E3 . . . .**114** A5
Tidford Rd, Well. DA16 . . .**157** J2
Tidworth Rd, E3 . . . .**114** A4
Tiepigs La, Brom. BR2 . . .**205** E2
  West Wickham BR4 . . .**205** E2
Tierney Rd, SW2 . . . .**168** E1
Tiger La, Brom. BR2 . . . . .**191** H4
Tiger Way, E5 . . . .**94** E4
Tilbrook Rd, SE3 . . . .**155** J3
Tilbury Cl, SE15 . . . .**37** G7
Tilbury Rd, E6 . . . .**116** C2
  E10 . . . .**78** C7
Tildesley Rd, SW15 . . . . .**147** J6
Tile Fm Rd, Orp. BR6 . . . .**207** G3
Tilehurst Pt, SE2
  off Yarnton Way **138** C2
Tilehurst Rd, SW18 . . . . .**167** G1
  Sutton SM3 . . . .**198** B5
Tile Kiln La, N6
  off Winchester Rd **92** B1
  N13 . . . .**59** J5
  Bexley DA5 . . . .**177** J2
Tile Yd, E14
  off Commercial Rd **113** J6
Tileyard Rd, N7 . . . .**92** E7
Tilford Gdns, SW19 . . . . .**166** A2
Tilia Cl, Sutt. SM1 . . . . . .**198** C5
Tilia Rd, E5
  off Clarence Rd **94/95** E4
Tilia Wk, SW9
  off Moorland Rd **151** H4
Tiller Rd, E14 . . . .**134** A3
Tillett Cl, NW10 . . . .**88** C6
Tillett Sq, SE16
  off Howland Way **133** H2
Tillett Way, E2 . . . .**13** H3
Tillingbourne Gdns, N3 . . .**72** C3
Tillingbourne Way, N3
  off Tillingbourne Gdns .**72** C3
Tillingham Way, N12 . . . . .**56** D4
Tilling Rd, NW2 . . . .**89** J1
Tilling Way, Wem. HA9 . . .**87** G2
Tillman St, E1
  off Bigland St **112/113** E6
Tilloch St, N1
  off Carnoustie Dr **93** F7
Tillotson Rd, N9 . . . .**60** C2
  Harrow HA3 . . . .**51** H7
  Ilford IG1 . . . .**80** D7
Tilney Ct, EC1 . . . .**12** A5
Tilney Dr, Buck.H. IG9 . . . .**63** G2
Tilney Gdns, N1 . . . .**94** A6
Tilney Rd, Dag. RM9 . . . .**101** F6
  Southall UB2 . . . .**122** C4

Tilney St, W1 . . . .**24** C1
Tilson Gdns, SW2 . . . . . .**150** E7
Tilson Ho, SW2
  off Tilson Gdns . . .**150/151** E7
Tilson Rd, N17 . . . .**76** D1
Tilston Cl, E11
  off Matcham Rd **97** F3
Tilton St, SW6 . . . .**128** B6
Tiltwood, The, W3
  off Acacia Rd **106** C7
Tilt Yd App, SE9 . . . .**156** C6
Timber Cl, Chis. BR7 . . . .**192** D2
Timbercroft, Epsom
  KT19 . . . .**196** E4
Timbercroft La, SE18 . . . .**137** H6
Timberdene, NW4 . . . .**72** A2
Timberdene Av, Ilf. IG6 . . .**81** E1
Timberland Rd, E1 . . . . . .**113** E6
Timber Mill Way, SW4 . . .**150** D3
Timber Pond Rd, SE16 . . .**133** G2
Timber St, EC1 . . . .**11** J5
Timberwharf Rd, N16 . . . .**76** D6
Timbrell Pl, SE16
  off Silver Wk **133** J1
Time Sq, E8 . . . .**94** C5
Times Sq, Sutt. SM1 . . . .**199** E5
Timothy Cl, SW4
  off Elms Rd **150** C5
  Bexleyheath DA6 . . . . .**158** E5
Timothy Ho, Erith DA18
  off Kale Rd **138/139** E2
Timothy Rd, E3 . . . .**113** J5
Timsbury Wk, SW15 . . . .**165** G1
Tindal St, SW9 . . . .**151** H1
Tinderbox All, SW14 . . . .**146** D3
Tine Rd, Chig. IG7 . . . .**65** H5
Tinniswood Cl, N5
  off Drayton Pk **93** G5
Tinsley Rd, E1 . . . .**113** F5
Tintagel Cres, SE22 . . . . .**152** C4
Tintagel Dr, Stan.
  HA7 . . . .**53** G4
Tintagel Gdns, SE22
  off Oxonian St **152** C4
Tintagel Ho, N9
  off Salisbury Rd **60** D3
Tintern Av, NW9 . . . .**70** B3
Tintern Cl, SW15 . . . .**148** B5
  SW19 . . . .**167** F7
Tintern Gdns, N14 . . . .**43** E7
Tintern Path, NW9
  off Ruthin Cl **70/71** E6
Tintern Rd, N22 . . . .**75** J1
  Carshalton SM5 . . . . . .**199** G1
Tintern St, SW4 . . . .**151** E4
Tintern Way, Har. HA2 . . . .**85** H1
Tinto Rd, E16 . . . .**115** G4
Tinwell Ms, Borwd. WD6
  off Cranes Way **38** C5
Tinworth St, SE11 . . . .**34** B3
Tippetts Cl, Enf. EN2 . . . . .**43** J1
Tipthorpe Rd, SW11 . . . .**150** A3
Tipton Dr, Croy. CR0 . . . .**202** B4
Tiptree Cl, E4
  off Mapleton Rd **62** C3
Tiptree Cres, Ilf. IG5 . . . . .**80** D3
Tiptree Dr, Enf. EN2 . . . . .**44** A4
Tiptree Est, Ilf. IG5 . . . . . .**80** D3
Tiptree Rd, Ruis. HA4 . . . .**84** B4
Tirlemont Rd, S.Croy.
  CR2 . . . .**201** J7
Tirrell Rd, Croy. CR0 . . . .**187** J6
Tisbury Ct, W1
  off Rupert St **110** D7
Tisbury Rd, SW16 . . . . . .**186** E2
Tisdall Pl, SE17 . . . .**36** C2
Titchborne Row, W2 . . . . .**15** H4
Titchfield Rd, NW8 . . . . . .**109** J1
  Carshalton SM5 . . . . . .**199** G1
Titchfield Wk, Cars. SM5
  off Titchfield Rd **185** G7
Titchwell Rd, SW18 . . . . .**149** G7
Tite St, SW3 . . . .**31** J4
Tithe Barn Cl, Kings.T.
  KT2 . . . .**181** J1
Tithe Barn Way, Nthlt.
  UB5 . . . .**102** B3
Tithe Cl, NW7 . . . .**71** G1
  Walton-on-Thames
  KT12 . . . .**178** B6
Tithe Fm Av, Har. HA2 . . . .**85** G3
Tithe Fm Cl, Har. HA2 . . . .**85** G3
Tithe Wk, NW7 . . . .**71** G1
Titley Cl, E4 . . . .**62** A5
Titmuss Av, SE28 . . . . . .**118** B7
Titmuss St, W12
  off Goldhawk Rd **127** J2
Tiverton Av, Ilf. IG5 . . . . . .**80** D3
Tiverton Dr, SE9 . . . .**175** F1
Tiverton Ho, Enf. EN3 . . . .**45** G3

Tiverton Rd, N15 . . . . .76 A6
N18 . . . . .60 B5
NW10 . . . . .108 A1
Edgware HA8 . . . . .69 J2
Hounslow TW3 . . . . . . .143 J2
Ruislip HA4 . . . . .84 A3
Thornton Heath CR7
off Willett Rd 187 G5
Wembley HA0 . . . . .105 H2
Tiverton St, SE1 . . . . .27 J6
Tiverton Way, NW7
off Bittacy Hill 56 B7
Chessington KT9 . . . . . .195 F5
Tivoli Ct, SE16 . . . . .133 J2
Tivoli Gdns, SE18 . . . . . .136 B4
Tivoli Rd, N8 . . . . .74 D5
SE27 . . . . .169 J5
Hounslow TW4 . . . . . . .142 E4
Toad La, Houns.TW4 . . . .143 F4
Tobacco Dock, E1 . . . . . .112 E7
Tobacco Quay, E1
off Wapping La . . .112/113 E7
Tobago St, E14
off Manilla St 134 A2
Tobin Cl, NW3 . . . . .91 H7
Toby La, E1 . . . . .113 H4
Toby Way, Surb. KT5 . . . .196 B2
Todds Wk, N7
off Andover Rd 93 F2
Tokenhouse Yd, EC2 . . . . .20 B3
Token Yd, SW15
off Montserrat Rd 148 B4
TOKYNGTON, Wem. 88 B6
Tokyngton Av, Wem.
HA9 . . . . .88 A6
Toland Sq, SW15 . . . . . .147 G5
Tolcarne Dr, Pnr. HA5 . . . .66 B3
Toley Av, Wem. HA9 . . . . .69 H7
Tollbridge Cl, W10
off Kensal Rd 108 B4
Tollesbury Gdns, Ilf.
IG6 . . . . .81 G3
Tollet St, E1 . . . . .113 G4
Tollgate Dr, SE21 . . . . . .170 B2
Hayes UB4 . . . . .102 D7
Tollgate Gdns, NW6 . . . . . .6 A1
Tollgate Rd, E6 . . . . .116 A5
E16 . . . . .115 J5
Tollhouse Way, N19 . . . . . .92 C2
Tollington Pk, N4 . . . . . . .93 F2
Tollington Pl, N4 . . . . .93 F2
Tollington Rd, N7 . . . . . . .93 F4
Tollington Way, N7 . . . . . .92 E3
Tolmers Sq, NW1 . . . . .9 G5
Tolpuddle Av, E13
off Rochester Av 115 J1
Tolpuddle St, N1 . . . . .10 E1
Tolsford Rd, E5 . . . . .95 E5
Tolson Rd, Islw.TW7 . . . .144 D3
Tolverne Rd, SW20 . . . . .183 J1
TOLWORTH, Surb. 196 A2
Tolworth Cl, Surb. KT6 . . .196 B1
Tolworth Gdns, Rom.
RM6 . . . . .82 D5
Tolworth Pk Rd, Surb.
KT6 . . . . .195 J2
Tolworth Ri N, Surb. KT5
off Elmbridge Av 182 C7
Tolworth Ri S, Surb. KT5
off Warren Dr S 196 C1
Tolworth Rd, Surb. KT6 . .195 H2
Tolworth Twr, Surb. KT6 .196 B2
Tomahawk Gdns, Nthlt. UB5
off Javelin Way 102 D3
Tom Coombs Cl, SE9
off Well Hall Rd 156 B4
Tom Cribb Rd, SE28 . . . .137 F3
Tom Gros Cl, E15
off Maryland St 96 D5
Tom Hood Cl, E15
off Maryland St 96 D5
Tom Jenkinson Rd, E16 . .135 G1
Tomlins Gro, E3 . . . . . . .114 A3
Tomlinson Cl, E2 . . . . .13 G4
W4 *off Oxford Rd N* . .126 B5
Tomlins Orchard, Bark.
IG11 . . . . .117 F1
Tomlins Ter, E14
off Rhodeswell Rd 113 J3
Tomlins Wk, N7
off Briset Way 93 F2
Tom Mann Cl, Bark.
IG11 . . . . .117 H1
Tom Nolan Cl, E15 . . . . .114 E2
Tompion St, EC1 . . . . .11 G4
Tom Smith Cl, SE10
off Maze Hill 134 E6
Tomswood Ct, Ilf. IG6 . . . .81 F1
Tomswood Hill, Ilf. IG6 . . .65 E7
Tomswood Rd, Chig. IG7 . .64 D6

Tom Thumbs Arch, E3
off Malmesbury Rd . .114 A2
Tom Williams Ho, SW6
off Clem Attlee Ct 128 C6
Tonbridge Cres, Har. HA3 . .69 H4
Tonbridge Ho, SE25 . . . . .188 D3
Tonbridge Rd, W.Mol.
KT8 . . . . .179 E4
Tonbridge St, WC1 . . . . . .10 A3
Tonbridge Wk, WC1
off Tonbridge St . .110/111 E3
Tonfield Rd, Sutt. SM3 . . .198 C1
Tonge Cl, Beck. BR3 . . . . .190 A5
Tonsley Hill, SW18 . . . . . .149 E5
Tonsley Pl, SW18 . . . . . . .149 E5
Tonsley Rd, SW18 . . . . . .149 E5
Tonsley St, SW18 . . . . . . .149 E5
Tonstall Rd, Mitch. CR4 . . .186 A2
Tony Cannell Ms, E3
off Maplin St 113 J3
Tooke Cl, Pnr. HA5 . . . . . .66 E1
Tookey Cl, Har. HA3 . . . . .69 J7
Took's Ct, EC4 . . . . .19 E3
Tooley St, SE1 . . . . .28 C1
Toorack Rd, Har. HA3 . . . .68 A2
Tooting Bec Gdns,
SW16 . . . . .168 D4
Tooting Bec Rd, SW16 . . .168 A3
SW17 . . . . .168 A3
TOOTING GRAVENEY,
SW17 . . . . .167 H6
Tooting Gro, SW17 . . . . . .167 H5
Tooting High St, SW17 . . .167 H6
Tootswood Rd, Brom.
BR2 . . . . .190 E5
Topaz Wk, NW2
off Marble Dr 72 A7
Topcliffe Dr, Orp. BR6 . . .207 G4
Topham Sq, N17 . . . . .75 J1
Topham St, EC1 . . . . .11 E5
Top Ho Ri, E4
off Parkhill Rd 46 C7
Topiary Sq, Rich. TW9 . . .145 J3
Topley St, SE9 . . . . .156 A4
Topmast Pt, E14 . . . . .134 A2
Top Pk, Beck. BR3 . . . . . .190 E4
Topp Wk, NW2 . . . . .89 J2
Topsfield Cl, N8
off Wolseley Rd 74 D5
Topsfield Par, N8
off Tottenham La . . .74/75 E5
Topsfield Rd, N8 . . . . .74 E5
Topsham Rd, SW17 . . . . .167 J3
Torbay Rd, NW6 . . . . .90 C7
Harrow HA2 . . . . .84 E2
Torbay St, NW1
off Hawley Rd 92 B7
Torbitt Way, Ilf. IG2 . . . . .81 J5
Torbridge Cl, Edg. HA8 . . .53 H7
Torbrook Cl, Bex. DA5 . . .159 E6
Torcross Dr, SE23 . . . . . .171 F2
Torcross Rd, Ruis. HA4 . . .84 B3
Tor Gdns, W8 . . . . .128 D2
Tormead Cl, Sutt. SM1 . . .198 D6
Tormount Rd, SE18 . . . . .137 H6
Toronto Av, E12 . . . . .98 C4
Toronto Rd, E11 . . . . .96 D4
Ilford IG1 . . . . .99 E1
Torquay Gdns, Ilf. IG4 . . . .80 A4
Torquay St, W2 . . . . .14 A2
Torrance Cl, SE7 . . . . .136 A6
Torrens Rd, E15 . . . . .97 F6
SW2 . . . . .151 F5
Torrens Sq, E15 . . . . .97 F6
Torrens St, EC1 . . . . .11 F2
Torres Sq, E14
off Maritime Quay . . .134 A5
Torre Wk, Cars. SM5 . . . .199 H1
Torriano Av, NW5 . . . . . . .92 D5
Torriano Cotts, NW5
off Torriano Av 92 C5
Torriano Ms, NW5
off Torriano Av 92 D5
Torridge Gdns, SE15 . . . .153 F4
Torridge Rd, Th.Hth.
CR7 . . . . .187 H5
Torridon Rd, SE6 . . . . . . .172 D1
SE13 . . . . .154 D7
Torrington Av, N12 . . . . . .57 G5
Torrington Cl, N12 . . . . . .57 G4
Esher (Clay.) KT10 . . . . .194 B6
Torrington Dr, Har. HA2 . . .85 H4
Loughton IG10 . . . . .49 F4
Torrington Gdns, N11 . . . .58 C6
Greenford UB6 . . . . .87 F7
Loughton IG10 . . . . .49 F4
Torrington Gro, N12 . . . . .57 H5
Torrington Pk, N12 . . . . . .57 F5
Torrington Pl, E1 . . . . .29 J1
WC1 . . . . .17 G1

Torrington Rd, E18 . . . . . .79 G3
Dagenham RM8 . . . . . .101 F1
Esher (Clay.) KT10 . . . . .194 B6
Greenford UB6 . . . . . . .105 F1
Torrington Sq, WC1 . . . . . .9 J6
Croydon CR0
off Tavistock Gro 188 A7
Torrington Way, Mord.
SM4 . . . . .184 D6
Tor Rd, Well. DA16 . . . . . .158 C1
Torr Rd, SE20 . . . . .171 G2
Torver Rd, Har. HA1 . . . . .68 B4
Torver Way, Orp. BR6 . . .207 G3
Torwood Rd, SW15 . . . . .147 G5
Tothill St, SW1 . . . . .25 H4
Totnes Rd, Well. DA16 . . .138 B7
Totnes Wk, N2 . . . . .73 G4
Tottan Ter, E1 . . . . .113 G6
Tottenhall Rd, N13 . . . . . .59 G6
TOTTENHAM, N17 . . . . . .76 B1
Tottenham Ct Rd, W1 . . . . .9 G6
Tottenham Grn E, N15 . . . .76 C4
TOTTENHAM HALE, N17 . .76 E3
Tottenham La, N8 . . . . . . .74 E5
Tottenham Ms, W1 . . . . . .17 G1
Tottenham Rd, N1 . . . . . . .94 B6
Tottenham St, W1 . . . . . . .17 G2
Totterdown St, SW17 . . . .167 J4
TOTTERIDGE, N20 . . . . . .56 B1
Totteridge Common,
N20 . . . . .55 G2
Totteridge Grn, N20 . . . . .56 D2
Totteridge Ho, SW11 . . . .149 G2
Totteridge La, N20 . . . . . .56 D2
Totteridge Village, N20 . . .56 B1
Totternhoe Cl, Har. HA3 . . .69 F5
Totton Rd, Th.Hth. CR7 . .187 G3
Toulmin St, SE1 . . . . .27 J4
Toulon St, SE5 . . . . .35 J7
Tournay Rd, SW6 . . . . . . .128 C7
Tours Pas, SW11 . . . . . . .149 F4
Toussaint Wk, SE16 . . . . . .29 J5
Tovil Cl, SE20 . . . . .188 D2
Towcester Rd, E3 . . . . . . .114 B4
★ Tower 42, EC2 . . . . .112 B6
Tower 42, EC2 . . . . .20 D3
Tower Br, E1 . . . . .29 F2
SE1 . . . . .29 F2
Tower Br App, E1 . . . . . . .29 F1
★ Tower Bridge Experience,
SE1 . . . . .29 F2
Tower Br Piazza, SE1 . . . .29 F2
Tower Br Rd, SE1 . . . . . . .28 D6
Tower Br Wf, E1 . . . . .29 H2
Tower Cl, NW3
off Lyndhurst Rd 91 G5
SE20 . . . . .170 E7
Ilford IG6 . . . . .65 E6
Orpington BR6 . . . . . . .207 J2
Tower Ct, WC2 . . . . .18 A4
Esher (Clay.)
KT10 . . . . .194 D7
Tower Gdns Rd, N17 . . . . .75 J1
Tower Hamlets Rd, E7 . . . .97 F4
E17 . . . . .78 A3
Tower Hill, EC3 . . . . .21 E6
Tower Hill Ter, EC3
off Tower Hill 112 B7
Tower La, Wem. HA9
off Main Dr 87 G3
Tower Ms, E17 . . . . .78 A4
Tower Mill Rd, SE15 . . . . .36 D6
★ Tower of London,
EC3 . . . . .21 F6
★ Tower Pier, EC3 . . . . . . .29 E1
Tower Pier, EC3 . . . . .29 E1
Tower Pt, Enf. EN2 . . . . . .44 A4
Tower Ri, Rich. TW9
off Jocelyn Rd 145 H3
Tower Rd, NW10 . . . . .89 G7
Belvedere DA17 . . . . . . .139 J4
Bexleyheath DA7 . . . . . .159 H4
Orpington BR6 . . . . . . .207 J2
Twickenham TW1 . . . . .162 C3
Tower Royal, EC4 . . . . . . .20 A5
Towers Pl, Rich. TW9
off Eton St 145 H5
Towers Rd, Pnr. HA5 . . . . .66 E1
Southall UB1 . . . . .103 G4
Tower St, WC2 . . . . .17 J4
Tower Ter, N22
off Mayes Rd 75 F2
Tower Vw, Croy. CR0 . . . .189 G7
Towfield Rd, Felt. TW13 . .161 F2
Towing Path Wk, N1 . . . . .10 A1
Town, The, Enf. EN2 . . . . .44 A3
Towncourt Cres, Orp.
BR5 . . . . .193 F5

Towncourt La, Orp. BR5 .193 G6
Town Ct Path, N4 . . . . . . .93 J1
Towney Mead, Nthlt.
UB5 . . . . .103 F2
Towney Mead Ct, Nthlt. UB5
off Towney Mead 103 F2
Town Fm Way, Stai. (Stanw.)
TW19 *off Town La* . . .140 A7
Townfield Rd, Hayes
UB3 . . . . .121 J1
Townfield Sq, Hayes
UB3 . . . . .121 J1
Town Fld Way, Islw.
TW7 . . . . .144 D2
Town Hall App, N16
off Milton Gro 94 B4
Town Hall App Rd, N15 . .76 C4
Town Hall Av, W4 . . . . . .126 D5
Town Hall Rd, SW11 . . . .149 J3
Townholm Cres, W7 . . . . .124 C3
Town La, Stai. (Stanw.)
TW19 . . . . .140 A6
Townley Ct, E15 . . . . .97 F6
Townley Rd, SE22 . . . . . .152 B5
Bexleyheath DA6 . . . . . .159 F5
Townley St, SE17 . . . . . . .36 B3
Town Meadow, Brent.
TW8 . . . . .125 G7
Townmead Rd, SW6 . . . . .149 F2
Richmond TW9 . . . . . . .146 B2
Town Quay, Bark. IG11 . . .117 E1
Town Rd, N9 . . . . .60 E2
Townsend Av, N14 . . . . . .58 D4
Townsend Ind Est,
NW10 . . . . .106 D2
Townsend La, NW9 . . . . . .70 D7
Townsend Rd, N15 . . . . . .76 C5
Southall UB1 . . . . .122 E1
Townsend St, SE17 . . . . . .36 C2
Townsend Yd, N6 . . . . . . .92 B1
Townshend Cl, Sid.
DA14 . . . . .176 B6
Townshend Est, NW8 . . . . .7 G1
Townshend Rd, NW8 . . . .109 H1
Chislehurst BR7 . . . . . . .174 E5
Richmond TW9 . . . . . . .145 J4
Townshend Ter, Rich.
TW9 . . . . .145 J4
Townson Av, Nthlt. UB5 . .102 A3
Townson Way, Nthlt. UB5
off Townson Av 102 A2
Towpath Wk, E9 . . . . .95 J5
Towpath Way, Croy.
CR0 . . . . .188 C6
Towton Rd, SE27 . . . . . . .169 J2
Toynbee Cl, Chis. BR7
*off Beechwood
Ri* 174/175 E4
★ Toynbee Hall, E1 . . . . . .21 G3
Toynbee Rd, SW20 . . . . .184 B1
Toynbee St, E1 . . . . .21 F2
Toyne Way, N6
off Gaskell Rd 73 J6
Tracey Av, NW2 . . . . .89 J5
Tracy Ct, Stan. HA7 . . . . .53 F7
Trade Cl, N13 . . . . .59 G4
Trader Rd, E6 . . . . .116 E6
Tradescant Rd, SW8 . . . . .131 E7
Trading Est Rd, NW10 . . .106 C4
Trafalgar Av, N17 . . . . . . .60 B6
SE15 . . . . .37 G4
Worcester Park KT4 . . . .198 A1
Trafalgar Business Cen,
Bark. IG11 . . . . .117 J4
Trafalgar Cl, SE16
off Greenland Quay . . .133 H4
Trafalgar Ct, E1
off Glamis Rd 113 F7
Trafalgar Gdns, E1 . . . . . .113 G5
W8 . . . . .22 B5
Trafalgar Gro, SE10 . . . . .134 D6
Trafalgar Pl, E11 . . . . .79 G4
N18 . . . . .60 D5
Trafalgar Rd, SE10 . . . . . .134 D6
SW19 . . . . .167 E7
Twickenham TW2 . . . . . .162 A2
Trafalgar Sq, SW1 . . . . . .25 J1
WC2 . . . . .25 J1
Trafalgar St, SE17 . . . . . . .36 B3
Trafalgar Ter, Har. HA1
off Nelson Rd 86 B1
Trafalgar Way, E14 . . . . . .134 C1
Croydon CR0 . . . . .201 F2
Trafford Cl, E15 . . . . .96 B5
Ilford IG6 . . . . .65 J6
Trafford Rd, Th.Hth. CR7 .187 F5
Tralee Ct, SE16
off Masters Dr . . .132/133 E5
Tramsheds Ind Est, Croy. CR0
off Coomber Way 186 D7

Tramway Av, E15 . . . . **.96** E7
N9 . . . . **.45** E7
Tramway Cl, SE20
off Oak Gro Rd . . . . . . **.189** F2
Tramway Path, Mitch.
CR4 . . . . **185** J5
Tranby Pl, E9
off Homerton High St . **.95** G5
Tranley Ms, NW3
off Fleet Rd . . . . **.91** H5
Tranmere Rd, N9 . . . . . . **.44** C7
SW18 . . . . **167** F2
Twickenham TW2 . . . . **143** H7
Tranquil Pas, SE3
off Tranquil Vale **155** F2
Tranquil Vale, SE3 . . . . . **155** E2
Transay Wk, N1
off Marquess Rd . . . . . **.94** A6
Transept St, NW1 . . . . . . **.15** G2
Transmere Cl, Orp. BR5 . **193** F6
Transmere Rd, Orp.
BR5 . . . . **193** F6
Transom Cl, SE16
off Plough Way **133** H4
Transom Sq, E14 . . . . . . **134** B4
Transport Av, Brent.
TW8 . . . . **124** D5
Tranton Rd, SE16 . . . . . . **.29** J5
Traps Hill, Loug. IG10 . . . **.48** C3
Traps La, N.Mal. KT3 . . . **182** E1
Travellers Way, Houns.
TW4 . . . . **142** C2
Travers Cl, E17 . . . . **.77** G1
Travers Rd, N7 . . . . **.93** G3
Treacy Cl, Bushey
(Bushey Hth.) WD23 . . **.51** J2
Treadgold St, W11 . . . . . **108** A7
Treadway St, E2 . . . . **112** E2
Treaty Cen, Houns. TW3 . **143** H3
Treaty Rd, Houns. TW3
off Hanworth Rd **143** H3
Treaty St, N1 . . . . **111** F1
Trebeck St, W1 . . . . **.24** D1
Trebovir Rd, SW5 . . . . . . **128** D5
Treby St, E3 . . . . **113** J4
Trecastle Way, N7
off Carleton Rd . . . . . . **.92** D4
Tredegar Ms, E3
off Tredegar Ter **113** J2
Tredegar Rd, E3 . . . . **113** J2
N11 . . . . **.58** D7
Tredegar Sq, E3 . . . . **113** J3
Tredegar Ter, E3 . . . . **113** J3
Trederwen Rd, E8 . . . . . . **112** D1
Tredown Rd, SE26 . . . . . **171** F5
Tredwell Cl, SW2
off Hillside Rd **169** F2
Bromley BR2 . . . . **191** F7
Tredwell Rd, SE27 . . . . . **169** H4
Tree Cl, Rich. TW10 . . . . **163** G1
Treen Av, SW13 . . . . **147** F3
Tree Rd, E16 . . . . **115** J6
Treeside Cl, West Dr.
UB7 . . . . **120** A4
Treetops Cl, SE2 . . . . . . **139** E5
Treetops Vw, Loug. IG10 . **.48** A4
Treeview Cl, SE19 . . . . . **188** B1
Treewall Gdns, Brom.
BR1 . . . . **173** H4
Trefgarne Rd, Dag. RM10 **101** G2
Trefil Wk, N7 . . . . **.93** E4
Trefoil Ho, Erith DA18
off Kale Rd **138/139** E2
Trefoil Rd, SW18 . . . . . . **149** F5
Tregaron Av, N8 . . . . **.74** E6
Tregaron Gdns, N.Mal. KT3
off Avenue Rd **182/183** E4
Tregarvon Rd, SW11 . . . **150** A4
Tregenna Av, Har. HA2 . . **.85** F4
Tregenna Cl, N14 . . . . . . **.42** C5
Tregenna Ct, Har. HA2 . . **.85** F4
Tregony Rd, Orp. BR6 . . **207** J4
Trego Rd, E9 . . . . **.96** A7
Tregothnan Rd, SW9 . . . **151** E3
Tregunter Rd, SW10 . . . . **.30** C5
Trehearn Rd, Ilf. IG6 . . . . **.65** G7
Treherne Ct, SW9
off Eythorne Rd **151** G1
SW17 . . . . **168** A4
Trehern Rd, SW14 . . . . . **146** D3
Trehurst St, E5 . . . . **.95** H5
Trelawney Cl, E17
off Orford Rd . . . . **.78** B4
Trelawney Est, E9 . . . . . . **.95** F6
Trelawney Rd, Ilf. IG6 . . . **.65** H7
Trelawn Rd, E10 . . . . **.96** C3
SW2 . . . . **151** G5
Trellick Twr, W10 . . . . . . **108** C4
Trellis Sq, E3
off Malmesbury Rd . . . **113** J3

Treloar Gdns, SE19
off Hancock Rd **170** A6
Tremadoc Rd, SW4 . . . . **150** D4
Tremaine Cl, SE4 . . . . . . **154** A2
Tremaine Rd, SE20 . . . . **189** E2
Tremadoc Pl, Tedd. TW11 **163** F7
Tremlett Gro, N19 . . . . . . **.92** C3
Tremlett Ms, N19 . . . . . . **.92** C3
Trenance Gdns, Ilf. IG3 . **100** A3
Trenchard Av, Ruis. HA4 . **.84** B4
Trenchard Ct, NW9
off Fulbeck Dr . . . . . . **.70/71** E1
Stanmore HA7 . . . . **.52** D6
Trenchard Cl, Mord. SM4
off Green La **184/185** E6
Trenchard St, SE10 . . . . **134** D5
SW8 . . . . **.34** A6
Trench Yd Ct, Mord. SM4
off Green La **184/185** E6
Trenholme Cl, SE20 . . . . **171** E7
Trenholme Rd, SE20 . . . **170** E7
Trenholme Ter, SE20 . . . **170** E7
Trenmar Gdns, NW10 . . . **107** H3
Trent Av, W5 . . . . **125** F3
Trentbridge Cl, Ilf. IG6 . . . **.65** J6
Trent Gdns, N14 . . . . **.42** B6
Trentham St, SW18 . . . . **166** D1
★ Trent Park Country Pk,
Barn. EN4 . . . . **.42** B2
Trent Rd, SW2 . . . . **151** F5
Buckhurst Hill IG9 . . . . **.63** H1
Trent Way, Wor.Pk. KT4 . **197** J3
Trentwood Side, Enf.
EN2 . . . . **.43** F3
Treport St, SW18 . . . . . . **149** E7
Tresco Cl, Brom. BR1 . . . **172** E6
Trescoe Gdns, Har. HA2 . **.67** E7
Tresco Gdns, Ilf. IG3 . . . **100** A3
Tresco Rd, SE15 . . . . . . **153** E4
Tresham Cres, NW8 . . . . . **.7** G5
Tresham Rd, Bark. IG11 . **.99** J7
Tresham Wk, E9
off Churchill Wk . . . . . **.95** F5
Tresilian Av, N21 . . . . . . **.43** F5
Tressell Cl, N1
off Sebbon St . . . . **.93** H7
Tressillian Cres, SE4 . . . **154** A3
Tressillian Rd, SE4 . . . . . **153** J4
Trestis Cl, Hayes UB4
off Jollys La **102/103** E5
Treswell Rd, Dag. RM9 . . **119** E1
Tretawn Gdns, NW7 . . . . **.55** E4
Tretawn Pk, NW7 . . . . . . **.55** E4
Trevanion Rd, W14 . . . . . **128** B5
Treve Av, Har. HA1 . . . . . **.67** J7
Trevelyan Av, E12 . . . . . . **.98** C4
Trevelyan Cres, Har. HA3 **.69** E7
Trevelyan Gdns, NW10 . . **107** J1
Trevelyan Rd, E15 . . . . . . **.97** F4
SW17 . . . . **167** H5
Treveris St, SE1 . . . . **.27** G2
Treverton St, W10 . . . . . **108** A4
Treves Cl, N21 . . . . **.43** F5
Treville St, SW15 . . . . . . **147** H7
Treviso Rd, SE23
off Farren Rd **171** G2
Trevithick St, SE8 . . . . . **134** A5
Trevone Gdns, Pnr. HA5 . **.67** E6
Trevor Cl, Barn. EN4 . . . . **.41** G5
Bromley BR2 . . . . **191** F7
Harrow HA3
off Kenton La . . . . **.52** C7
Isleworth TW7 . . . . **144** C5
Northolt UB5 . . . . **102** C2
Trevor Gdns, Edg. HA8 . . **.70** D1
Northolt UB5 . . . . **102** C2
Trevor Pl, SW7 . . . . **.23** H4
Trevor Rd, SW19 . . . . . . **166** B7
Edgware HA8 . . . . **.70** D1
Hayes UB3 . . . . **121** H2
Woodford Green IG8 . . . **.63** J7
Trevor Sq, SW7 . . . . **.23** J4
Trevor St, SW7 . . . . **.23** H4
Trevor Wk, SW7
off Trevor Sq **129** J2
Trevose Ho, E17 . . . . **.78** D1
Trevose Way, Wat. WD19 . **.50** C3
Trewenna Dr, Chess.
KT9 . . . . **195** G5
Trewince Rd, SW20 . . . . **183** J1
Trewint St, SW18 . . . . . . **167** F2
Trewsbury Ho, SE2
off Hartslock Dr **138** D2
Trewsbury Rd, SE26 . . . **171** G5
Triandra Way, Hayes
UB4 . . . . **102** D5
Triangle, The, EC1
off Goswell Rd **111** H4
N13 off Lodge Dr . . . . . **.59** G4
Barking IG11

Triangle, The,
off Tanner St . . . . **.99** F6
Hampton TW12
off High St **179** J1
Kingston upon Thames KT1
off Kenley Rd **182** C2
Triangle Business Cen, NW10
off Enterprise Way . . . **107** G3
Triangle Ct, E16
off Tollgate Rd **116** A5
Triangle Est, SE11 . . . . . **.35** E4
Triangle Pas, Barn. EN4
off Station App . . . . . . **.41** F4
Triangle Pl, SW4 . . . . . . **150** D4
Triangle Rd, E8 . . . . **112** E1
Trident Gdns, Nthlt. UB5
off Jetstar Way **102** D3
Trident St, SE16 . . . . **133** G4
Trident Way, Sthl. UB2 . . **122** B3
Trig La, EC4 . . . . **.19** J5
Trigon Rd, SW8 . . . . **.34** D7
Trilby Rd, SE23 . . . . **171** G2
Trimmer Wk, Brent. TW8 . **125** H6
Trim St, SE14 . . . . **133** J6
Trinder Gdns, N19
off Trinder Rd . . . . . . **.92/93** E1
Trinder Rd, N19 . . . . **.93** E1
Barnet EN5 . . . . **.39** J5
Tring Av, W5 . . . . **125** J1
Southall UB1 . . . . **103** F6
Wembley HA9 . . . . **.88** A6
Tring Cl, Ilf. IG2 . . . . **.81** F5
Trinidad Gdns, Dag. RM10
off Heathway **119** J2
Trinidad St, E14 . . . . **113** J7
Trinity Av, N2 . . . . **.73** G3
Enfield EN1 . . . . **.44** C6
Trinity Buoy Wf, E14 . . . . **115** F7
Trinity Ch Pas, SW13 . . . **127** H6
Trinity Ch Rd, SW13 . . . . **127** H6
Trinity Ch Sq, SE1 . . . . . **.28** A5
Trinity Cl, E8 . . . . **.94** C6
E11 . . . . **.97** E2
NW3 off Hampstead
High St . . . . **.91** G4
SE13 off Wisteria Rd . . **154** D4
SW4 off The Pavement .**150** C4
Bromley BR2 . . . . **206** B1
Hounslow TW4 . . . . . . **143** E4
Trinity Cotts, Rich. TW9
off Trinity Rd **145** J3
Trinity Ct, N1
off Downham Rd . . . . . **.94** B7
NW2 off Anson Rd . . . . **.89** J5
SE7 off Charlton La . . . **136** A4
Trinity Cres, SW17 . . . . . **167** J2
Trinity Gdns, E16
off Cliff Wk **115** F4
SW9 . . . . **151** F4
Trinity Gro, SE10 . . . . . . **154** C1
★ Trinity Ho, EC3 . . . . . . **.21** E5
Trinity Ms, SE20 . . . . . . **189** E1
W10
off Cambridge Gdns . . **108** A6
Trinity Path, SE26 . . . . . . **171** F3
Trinity Pl, Bexh. DA6 . . . . **159** F4
Trinity Ri, SW2 . . . . **169** G1
Trinity Rd, N2 . . . . **.73** G3
N22 . . . . **.75** E1
SW17 . . . . **167** J2
SW18 . . . . **149** G5
SW19 . . . . **166** D6
Ilford IG6 . . . . **.81** F3
Richmond TW9 . . . . . . **145** J3
Southall UB1 . . . . **122** E1
Trinity Sq, EC3 . . . . **.21** E6
Trinity St, E16
off Vincent St **115** G5
SE1 . . . . **.28** A4
Enfield EN2 . . . . **.43** J2
Trinity Wk, NW3 . . . . **.91** F6
Trinity Way, E4 . . . . **.61** J6
W3 . . . . **107** F2
Trio Pl, SE1 . . . . **.28** A4
Tristan Sq, SE3 . . . . **155** E3
Tristram Cl, E17 . . . . **.78** D3
Tristram Rd, Brom. BR1 . **173** F4
Triton Sq, NW1 . . . . **.9** F5
Tritton Av, Croy. CR0 . . . **201** E4
Tritton Rd, SE21 . . . . **170** A3
Triumph Cl, Hayes UB3 . **121** F7
Triumph Ho, Bark. IG11 . **118** B3
Triumph Rd, E6 . . . . **116** C6
★ Trocadero Cen, W1 . . . **.17** H6
Trocadero Shop Cen, W1 .**110** D7
Trojan Ct, NW6
off Willesden La . . . . . **.90** B7
Trojan Way, Croy. CR0 . . **201** F3
Troon Cl, SE16
off Masters Dr . . **132/133** E5
SE28 off Fairway Dr . . **118** D6
Troon St, E1 . . . . **113** H6

Trosley Rd, Belv. DA17 . . **139** G6
Trossachs Rd, SE22 . . . . **152** B5
Trothy Rd, SE1 . . . . **.37** J1
Trott Rd, N10 . . . . **.57** J7
Trott St, SW11 . . . . **149** H1
Trotwood, Chig. IG7 . . . . **.65** G6
Troughton Rd, SE7 . . . . . **135** H5
Troutbeck Rd, SE14 . . . . **153** H1
Trout Rd, West Dr. UB7 . . **120** A1
Trouville Rd, SW4 . . . . . . **150** C6
Trowbridge Est, E9
off Osborne Rd . . . . . . **.95** J6
Trowbridge Rd, E9 . . . . . **.95** J6
Trowlock Av, Tedd. TW11 .**163** F6
Trowlock Island, Tedd.
TW11 . . . . **163** G5
Trowlock Way, Tedd.
TW11 . . . . **163** G6
Troy Ct, SE18 . . . . **137** E4
Troy Rd, SE19 . . . . **170** A6
Troy Town, SE15 . . . . . . **152** D3
Trubshaw Rd, Sthl. UB2
off Havelock Rd **123** H3
Truesdale Rd, E6 . . . . . . **116** C6
Trulock Ct, N17 . . . . **.60** D7
Trulock Rd, N17 . . . . **.60** D7
Truman Cl, Edg. HA8
off Pavilion Way . . . . . **.54** B7
Truman's Rd, N16 . . . . . . **.94** B5
Trumpers Way, W7 . . . . . **124** B3
Trumpington Rd, E7 . . . . **.97** F4
Trump St, EC2 . . . . **.20** A4
Trundlers Way, Bushey
(Bushey Hth.) WD23 . . **.52** B1
Trundle St, SE1 . . . . **.27** J3
Trundleys Rd, SE8 . . . . . **133** G5
Trundleys Ter, SE8 . . . . . **133** G4
Truro Gdns, Ilf. IG1 . . . . . **.80** B7
Truro Rd, E17 . . . . **.77** J4
N22 . . . . **.59** E7
Truro St, NW5 . . . . **.92** A6
Truslove Rd, SE27 . . . . . **169** G5
Trussley Rd, W6 . . . . **127** J3
Trust Wk, SE21
off Peabody Hill **169** H1
Tryfan Cl, Ilf. IG4 . . . . **.80** A5
Tryon Cres, E9 . . . . **113** F1
Tryon St, SW3 . . . . **.31** J3
Trystings Cl, Esher (Clay.)
KT10 . . . . **194** D6
Tuam Rd, SE18 . . . . **137** G6
Tubbenden Cl, Orp.
BR6 . . . . **207** H2
Tubbenden Dr, Orp.
BR6 . . . . **207** G4
Tubbenden La, Orp.
BR6 . . . . **207** H3
Tubbenden La S, Orp.
BR6 . . . . **207** G5
Tubbs Rd, NW10 . . . . . . **107** F2
Tudor Av, Hmptn. TW12 . **161** G6
Worcester Park KT4 . . . **197** H3
Tudor Cl, N6 . . . . **.74** C7
NW3 . . . . **.91** H5
NW7 . . . . **.55** G6
NW9 . . . . **.88** C2
SW2 off Elm Pk **151** F6
Chessington KT9 . . . . . **195** H5
Chigwell IG7 . . . . **.64** D4
Chislehurst BR7 . . . . . **192** C1
Pinner HA5 . . . . **.66** A5
Sutton SM3 . . . . **198** A5
Wallington SM6 . . . . . **200** C7
Woodford Green IG8 . . . **.63** H5
Tudor Ct, E17 . . . . **.77** H7
Feltham TW13 . . . . **160** C4
Tudor Ct N, Wem. HA9 . . **.88** A5
Tudor Ct S, Wem. HA9 . . **.88** A5
Tudor Cres, Enf. EN2 . . . **.43** H1
Ilford IG6 . . . . **.65** E6
Tudor Dr, Kings.T. KT2 . . **163** H5
Morden SM4 . . . . **184** A6
Tudor Est, NW10 . . . . . . **106** B2
Tudor Gdns, NW9 . . . . . . **.88** C2
SW13 off Treen
Av **146/147** E3
W3 . . . . **106** A6
Harrow HA3
off Tudor Rd . . . . **.68** A2
Twickenham TW1 . . . . **162** C1
West Wickham BR4 . . . **204** C3
Tudor Gro, E9 . . . . **.95** F7
N20 off Church Cres . . . **.57** H3
Tudor Ho, Surb. KT6
off Lenelby Rd **196** A1
E9 . . . . **.95** F7
Mitcham CR4 . . . . **167** H7
Tudor Pl, W1 . . . . **.17** H3
Mitcham CR4 . . . . **167** H7
Tudor Rd, E4 . . . . **.62** B6
E6 . . . . **115** J1
E9 . . . . **113** E1

Tudor Rd, N9 . . . . .45 E7
SE19 . . . . .170 C7
SE25 . . . . .189 E5
Barking IG11 . . . . .117 J1
Barnet EN5 . . . . .40 D3
Beckenham BR3 . . . . . .190 B3
Hampton TW12 . . . . . .161 G7
Harrow HA3 . . . . .68 A2
Hounslow TW3 . . . . . .144 A4
Kingston upon Thames
KT2 . . . . .164 A2
Pinner HA5 . . . . .66 C2
Southall UB1 . . . . .102 E7
Tudor St, EC4 . . . . .19 F5
Tudor Wk, Bex. DA5 . . . .159 E6
Tudor Way, N14 . . . . .58 D1
W3 . . . . .126 A2
Orpington BR5 . . . . . .193 G6
Tudor Well Cl, Stan.
HA7 . . . . .53 E5
Tudway Rd, SE3 . . . . . .155 H3
TUFNELL PARK, N7 . . . . .92 D4
Tufnell Pk Rd, N7 . . . . . .92 C4
N19 . . . . .92 C4
Tufter Rd, Chig. IG7 . . . . .65 J5
Tufton Gdns, W.Mol.
KT8 . . . . .179 H2
Tufton Rd, E4 . . . . .62 A4
Tufton St, SW1 . . . . .25 J5
Tugboat St, SE28 . . . . . .137 H2
Tugela Rd, Croy. CR0 . . .188 A6
Tugela St, SE6 . . . . .171 J2
Tugmutton Cl, Orp. BR6
off Acorn Way . . .206/207 E4
Tuilerie St, E2 . . . . .13 H1
Tulip Cl, E6
off Bradley Stone Rd .116 C5
Croydon CR0 . . . . . . .203 G1
Hampton TW12
off Partridge Rd 161 F6
Southall UB2
off Chevy Rd 123 J2
Tulip Ct, Pnr. HA5 . . . . . .66 C3
Tulip Gdns, Ilf. IG1 . . . . . .98 E6
Tulip Way, West Dr.
UB7 . . . . .120 A4
Tull St, Mitch. CR4 . . . . .185 J7
Tulse Cl, Beck. BR3 . . . .190 C4
TULSE HILL, SE21 . . . . .169 J1
Tulse Hill, SW2 . . . . . . .151 G6
Tulse Hill Est, SW2 . . . . .151 G6
Tulsemere Rd, SE27 . . . .169 J2
Tumbling Bay, Walt.
KT12 . . . . .178 A6
Tummons Gdns, SE25 . . .188 B2
Tuncombe Rd, N18 . . . . .60 B4
Tunis Rd, W12 . . . . .127 H1
Tunley Grn, E14
off Burdett Rd 113 J5
Tunley Rd, NW10 . . . . . .106 E1
SW17 . . . . .168 A1
Tunmarsh La, E13 . . . . . .115 J3
Tunnan Leys, E6 . . . . . . .116 D6
Tunnel Av, SE10 . . . . . . .134 D2
Tunnel Gdns, N11 . . . . . .58 C7
Tunnel Rd, SE16
off St. Marychurch St .133 F2
Tunstall Cl, Orp. BR5 . . .207 H4
Tunstall Rd, SW9 . . . . . .151 F4
Croydon CR0 . . . . . . .202 B1
Tunstall Wk, Brent. TW8 .125 H6
Tunstock Way, Belv.
DA17 . . . . .139 E3
Tunworth Cl, NW9 . . . . . .70 C6
Tunworth Cres, SW15 . . .147 F6
Tun Yd, SW8
off Peardon St 150 B2
Tupelo Rd, E10 . . . . .96 B2
Turenne Cl, SW18 . . . . .149 F4
Turin Rd, N9 . . . . .45 F7
Turin St, E2 . . . . .13 H4
Turkey Oak Cl, SE19 . . . .188 B1
Turk's Head Yd, EC1 . . . .19 G1
Turks Row, SW3 . . . . . . .32 A3
Turle Rd, N4 . . . . .93 F1
SW16 . . . . .186 E2
Turlewray Cl, N4 . . . . . . .93 F1
Turley Cl, E15 . . . . .115 E1
Turnagain La, EC4 . . . . . .19 G3
Turnage Rd, Dag. RM8 . .100 E1
Turnberry Cl, NW4 . . . . . .72 A2
SE16 off Ryder Dr .132/133 E5
Turnberry Ct, Wat. WD19 .50 C3
Turnberry Quay, E14
off Pepper St 134 B3
Turnberry Way, Orp.
BR6 . . . . .207 G1
Turnbury Cl, SE28 . . . . . .118 D6
Turnchapel Ms, SW4
off Cedars Rd 150 B3

Turner Av, N15 . . . . .76 B4
Mitcham CR4 . . . . . . .185 J1
Twickenham TW2 . . . . .161 J3
Turner Cl, NW11 . . . . . . .72 E6
SW9 . . . . .151 H1
Wembley HA0 . . . . . . .87 G5
Turner Dr, NW11 . . . . . . .72 E6
Turner Pl, SW11
off Cairns Rd 149 H6
Turner Rd, E17 . . . . .78 C3
Edgware HA8 . . . . . . .69 J3
New Malden KT3 . . . . .182 D7
Turners Meadow Way, Beck.
BR3 . . . . .189 J1
Turners Rd, E3 . . . . .113 J5
Turner St, E1 . . . . .112 E5
E16 . . . . .115 F6
Turners Way, Croy. CR0 .201 G2
Turners Wd, NW11 . . . . . .73 F7
Turneville Rd, W14 . . . . .128 C6
Turney Grn, E14
off Wallwood St 113 J5
Turney Rd, SE21 . . . . . . .152 A7
Turnham Grn Ter, W4 . . .126 E4
Turnham Grn Ter Ms, W4
off Turnham Grn
Ter 126/127 E4
Turnham Rd, SE4 . . . . . .153 H5
Turnmill St, EC1 . . . . . . .11 F6
Turnpike Cl, SE8
off Amersham Vale . . .133 J7
Turnpike Ho, EC1 . . . . . .11 H4
Turnpike La, N8 . . . . .75 F4
Sutton SM1 . . . . .199 F5
Turnpike Link, Croy. CR0 .202 B2
Turnpike Way, Islw. TW7 .144 D1
Turnpin La, SE10 . . . . . .134 C6
Turnstone Cl, E13 . . . . . .115 G3
NW9 off Kestrel Cl .70/71 E2
Turpentine La, SW1 . . . . .32 E3
Turpington Cl, Brom.
BR2 . . . . .192 B6
Turpington La, Brom.
BR2 . . . . .192 B7
Turpin Rd, Felt. TW14
off Staines Rd 141 J6
Turpins La, Wdf.Grn. IG8 .64 C5
Turpin Way, N19 . . . .
off Elthorne Rd 92 D2
Wallington SM6 . . . . .200 B7
Turquand St, SE17 . . . . . .36 A2
Turret Gro, SW4 . . . . . . .150 C3
Turton Rd, Wem. HA0 . . . .87 H5
Turville St, E2 . . . . .13 F5
Tuscan Rd, SE18 . . . . . . .137 G5
Tuskar St, SE10 . . . . . . .134 E6
Tustin St, SE15 . . . . .133 F6
Tuttlebee La, Buck.H.
IG9 . . . . .63 G2
Tweedale Ct, E15 . . . . . . .96 C5
Tweeddale Rd, Cars.
SM5 . . . . .199 G1
Tweedmouth Rd, E13 . . . .115 H2
Tweedy Cl, Enf. EN1 . . . .44 C5
Tweedy Rd, Brom. BR1 . .191 F1
Tweezer's All, WC2 . . . . . .18 E5
Twelvetrees Cres, E3 . . . .114 C4
Twentyman Cl, Wdf.Grn.
IG8 . . . . .63 G5
TWICKENHAM 162 D2
Twickenham Br, Rich.
TW9 . . . . .145 F5
Twickenham TW1 . . . . .145 F5
Twickenham Cl, Croy.
CR0 . . . . .201 F3
Twickenham Gdns, Grnf.
UB6 . . . . .86 D5
Harrow HA3 . . . . .52 B7
Twickenham Rd, E11 . . . .96 D2
Feltham TW13 . . . . . .161 F3
Isleworth TW7 . . . . . .144 D3
Richmond TW9 . . . . . .145 F4
Teddington TW11 . . . .162 D5
Twickenham Trd Est, Twick.
TW1 . . . . .144 C6
Twig Folly Cl, E2
off Roman Rd 113 G2
Twilley St, SW18 . . . . . . .148 E7
Twine Cl, Bark. IG11
off Thames Rd 118 B3
Twine Ct, E1 . . . . .113 F7
Twineham Grn, N12
off Tillingham Way . . .56 D4
Twine Ter, E3
off Ropery St 113 J4
Twining Av, Twick. TW2 . .161 J3
Twinn Rd, NW7 . . . . .56 B6
Twin Tumps Way, SE28 . .118 A7
Twisden Rd, NW5 . . . . . . .92 B4
Twybridge Way, NW10 . . .88 C7

Twycross Ms, SE10 . . . . .
off Blackwall La .134/135 E4
Twyford Abbey Rd,
NW10 . . . . .105 J3
Twyford Av, N2 . . . . .73 J3
W3 . . . . .106 A7
Twyford Cres, W3 . . . . . .126 A1
Twyford Ho, N15
off Chisley Rd 76 B6
Twyford Pl, WC2 . . . . . . .18 C3
Twyford Rd, Cars. SM5 . .199 G1
Harrow HA2 . . . . .85 H1
Ilford IG1 . . . . .99 F5
Twyford St, N1 . . . . .111 F1
Tyas Rd, E16 . . . . .115 F4
Tybenham Rd, SW19 . . . .184 D3
Tyberry Rd, Enf. EN3 . . . .45 E3
Tyburn La, Har. HA1 . . . . .68 B7
Tyburn Way, W1 . . . . .16 A5
Tycehurst Hill, Loug.
IG10 . . . . .48 C4
Tye La, Orp. BR6 . . . . . . .207 F5
Tyers Est, SE1 . . . . .28 D3
Tyers Gate, SE1 . . . . .28 D3
Tyers St, SE11 . . . . .34 C3
Tyers Ter, SE11 . . . . .34 C4
Tyeshurst Cl, SE2 . . . . . .139 E5
Tylecroft Rd, SW16 . . . . .186 E2
Tylehurst Gdns, Ilf. IG1 . .99 F5
Tyler Cl, E2 . . . . .13 F1
Tyler Rd, Sthl. UB2
off McNair Rd 123 H3
Tylers Cl, Loug. IG10 . . . .48 B7
Tyler's Ct, W1 . . . . .17 H4
Tylers Gate, Har. HA3 . . . .69 H6
Tylers Path, Cars. SM5
off Rochester Rd 199 J4
Tyler St, SE10 . . . . .135 E5
Tylney Av, SE19 . . . . .170 C5
Tylney Rd, E7 . . . . .97 J4
Bromley BR1 . . . . .192 A2
Tymperley Ct, SW19
off Windlesham Gro .166 B1
Tynan Cl, Felt. TW14
off Sandycombe Rd .160 A1
Tyndale Ct, E14 . . . . .134 B5
Tyndale La, N1
off Upper St 93 H7
Tyndale Ter, N1
off Canonbury La 93 H7
Tyndall Rd, E10 . . . . .96 C2
Welling DA16 . . . . . . .157 J3
Tyneham Cl, SW11
off Shirley Gro 150 A3
Tyneham Rd, SW11 . . . . .150 A2
Tynemouth Cl, E6
off Covelees Wall .116/117 E6
Tynemouth Rd, N15 . . . . .76 C4
SE18 . . . . .137 J5
Mitcham CR4 . . . . . . .168 A7
Tynemouth St, SW6 . . . . .149 F2
Tyne St, E1 . . . . .21 G3
Type St, E2 . . . . .113 G2
Tyrawley Rd, SW6 . . . . . .148 E1
Tyre La, NW9
off Sheavesvill Av .70/71 E4
Tyrell Cl, Har. HA1 . . . . . .86 B4
Tyrell Ct, Cars. SM5 . . . . .199 J4
Tyrols Rd, SE23
off Wastdale Rd 171 G1
Tyrone Rd, E6 . . . . .116 C2
Tyron Way, Sid. DA14 . . .175 H4
Tyrrell Av, Well. DA16 . . .158 A5
Tyrrell Rd, SE22 . . . . . . .152 D4
Tyrrell Sq, Mitch. CR4 . . .185 H1
Tyrrel Way, NW9 . . . . . . .71 F7
Tyrwhitt Rd, SE4 . . . . . . .154 A3
Tysoe St, EC1 . . . . .11 E4
Tyson Rd, SE23 . . . . .153 F7
Tyssen Pas, E8 . . . . .94 C6
Tyssen Rd, N16 . . . . .94 C3
Tyssen St, E8 . . . . .94 C6
N1 . . . . .12 E1
Tytherton Rd, N19 . . . . . .92 D3

U

Uamvar St, E14 . . . . .114 B5
Uckfield Gro, Mitch.
CR4 . . . . .186 A1
Udall St, SW1 . . . . .33 G2
Udney Pk Rd, Tedd.
TW11 . . . . .162 D5
Uffington Rd, NW10 . . . .107 G1
SE27 . . . . .169 G4
Ufford Cl, Har. HA3
off Ufford Rd 51 H7
Ufford Rd, Har. HA3 . . . . .51 H7
Ufford St, SE1 . . . . .27 F3

Ufton Gro, N1 . . . . .94 A7
Ufton Rd, N1 . . . . .94 A7
Uhura Sq, N16 . . . . .94 B3
Ujima Ct, SW16
off Sunnyhill Rd .168/169 E4
Ullathorne Rd, SW16 . . . .168 C4
Ulleswater Rd, N14 . . . . .59 E4
Ullin St, E14
off St. Leonards Rd . . .114 C5
Ullswater Cl, SW15 . . . . .164 D4
Bromley BR1 . . . . .173 E6
Ullswater Ct, Har. HA2
off Oakington Av 67 G7
Ullswater Cres, SW15 . . .164 D4
Ullswater Rd, SE27 . . . . .169 H2
SW13 . . . . .127 G7
Ulster Gdns, N13 . . . . . . .59 J4
Ulster Pl, NW1 . . . . .8 D6
Ulster Ter, NW1 . . . . .8 D6
Ulundi Rd, SE3 . . . . .135 E6
Ulva Rd, SW15
off Ravenna Rd 148 A5
Ulverscroft Rd, SE22 . . . .152 C5
Ulverstone Rd, SE27 . . . .169 H2
Ulverston Rd, E17 . . . . . .78 D2
Ulysses Rd, NW6 . . . . . . .90 C5
Umberston St, E1
off Hessel St 112/113 E6
Umbria St, SW15 . . . . . . .147 G6
Umfreville Rd, N4 . . . . . . .75 H6
Undercliff Rd, SE13 . . . . .154 A3
UNDERHILL, Barn. 40 D5
Underhill, Barn. EN5 . . . .40 D5
Underhill Pas, NW1
off Camden High St . . .110 B1
Underhill Rd, SE22 . . . . . .152 E6
Underhill St, NW1
off Camden High St . . .110 B1
Underne Av, N14 . . . . . . .58 B2
Undershaft, EC3 . . . . .20 D4
Undershaw Rd, Brom.
BR1 . . . . .173 E3
Underwood, Croy.
(New Adgtn.) CR0 . . . .204 C5
Underwood, The, SE9 . . .174 C2
Underwood Rd, E1 . . . . . .13 H6
E4 . . . . .62 A5
Woodford Green IG8 . . .64 A7
Underwood Row, N1 . . . .12 A3
Underwood St, N1 . . . . . .12 A3
Undine Rd, E14 . . . . .134 B4
Undine St, SW17 . . . . . . .167 J5
Uneeda Dr, Grnf. UB6 . . .104 A1
Unicorn Ho, Brom. BR1
off Elmfield Rd 191 G3
Union Cl, E11 . . . . .96 D4
Union Cotts, E15
off Welfare Rd 96/97 E7
Union Ct, EC2 . . . . .20 D3
Richmond TW9
off Eton St 145 H5
Union Dr, E1
off Canal Cl 113 H4
Union Gro, SW8 . . . . .150 D2
Union Rd, N11 . . . . .58 D6
SW4 . . . . .150 D2
SW8 . . . . .150 D2
Bromley BR2 . . . . .192 A5
Croydon CR0 . . . . . . .187 J7
Northolt UB5 . . . . . . .103 G2
Wembley HA0 . . . . . . .87 H6
Union Sq, N1 . . . . .111 J1
Union St, E15 . . . . .114 C1
SE1 . . . . .27 H2
Barnet EN5 . . . . .40 B4
Kingston upon Thames
KT1 . . . . .181 G2
Union Wk, E2 . . . . .13 E3
Unity Cl, NW10 . . . . .89 G6
SE19 off Crown Dale .169 J5
Unity Trd Est, Wdf.Grn.
IG8 . . . . .80 A3
Unity Way, SE18 . . . . . . .136 A3
Unity Wf, SE1 . . . . .29 G3
University Cl, NW7 . . . . . .55 F7
NW9 . . . . .9 H5
University Gdns, Bex.
DA5 . . . . .159 F7
★ University of London,
WC1 . . . . .9 J6
University Pl, Erith DA8
off Belmont Rd 139 H7
University Rd, SW19 . . . .167 G6
University St, WC1 . . . . . .9 G6
University Way, E16 . . . . .116 D7
Unwin Av, Felt. TW14 . . .141 H5
Unwin Cl, SE15 . . . . .37 H6
Unwin Rd, SW7 . . . . .23 F5
Isleworth TW7 . . . . . .144 B3

Upbrook Ms, W2 . . . . .14 D4
Upcerne Rd, SW10 . . . . .129 F7
Upchurch Cl, SE20 . . . . .171 E7
Upcroft Av, Edg. HA8 . . . . .54 C5
Updale Rd, Sid. DA14 . . . .175 J4
Upfield, Croy. CR0 . . . . . .203 E2
Upfield Rd, W7 . . . . .104 C4
Upgrove Manor Way, SW2
   off Trinity Ri 151 G7
Uphall Rd, Ilf. IG1 . . . . . . .99 E5
Upham Pk Rd, W4 . . . . .127 E4
Uphill Dr, NW7 . . . . .55 E5
   NW9 . . . . .70 C5
Uphill Gro, NW7 . . . . . . .55 E4
Uphill Rd, NW7 . . . . .54 E4
Upland Ms, SE22
   off Upland Rd 152 D5
Upland Rd, E13
   off Sutton Rd 115 F4
   SE22 . . . . .152 D5
   Bexleyheath DA7 . . . . .159 F3
   South Croydon CR2 . . .202 A5
   Sutton SM2 . . . . .199 G7
Uplands, Beck. BR3 . . . . .190 A2
Uplands, The, Loug.
   IG10 . . . . .48 C3
   Ruislip HA4 . . . . .84 A1
Uplands Av, E17
   off Blackhorse La 77 G2
Uplands Business Pk,
   E17 . . . . .77 G2
Uplands Cl, SW14
   off Monroe Dr 146 B5
Uplands End, Wdf.Grn.
   IG8 . . . . .64 B7
Uplands Pk Rd, Enf.
   EN2 . . . . .43 G3
Uplands Rd, N8 . . . . . . .75 F5
   Barnet EN4 . . . . .58 A1
   Romford RM6 . . . . .82 D3
   Woodford Green IG8 . . . .64 B7
Uplands Way, N21 . . . . . .43 G5
Upney La, Bark. IG11 . . . . .99 H6
Upnor Way, SE17 . . . . . . .37 E3
Uppark Dr, Ilf. IG2 . . . . . .81 F6
Upper Abbey Rd, Belv.
   DA17 . . . . .139 F4
Upper Addison Gdns,
   W14 . . . . .128 B2
Upper Bk St, E14 . . . . . .134 B1
Upper Bardsey Wk, N1
   off Clephane Rd 93 J6
Upper Belgrave St, SW1 . .24 C5
Upper Berkeley St, W1 . . .15 J4
Upper Beulah Hill, SE19 .188 B1
Upper Brighton Rd, Surb.
   KT6 . . . . .181 G6
Upper Brockley Rd, SE4 .153 J2
Upper Brook St, W1 . . . . . .16 B6
Upper Butts, Brent. TW8 .125 F6
Upper Caldy Wk, N1
   off Clephane Rd 93 J6
Upper Camelford Wk, W11
   off Lancaster Rd 108 B6
Upper Cavendish Av, N3 . .72 D3
Upper Cheyne Row, SW3 .31 G6
UPPER CLAPTON, E5 . . . .94 E1
Upper Clapton Rd, E5 . . . .94 E1
Upper Clarendon Wk, W11
   off Lancaster Rd 108 B6
Upper Dengie Wk, N1
   off Popham Rd 111 J1
UPPER EDMONTON,
   N18 . . . . .60 D6
UPPER ELMERS END,
   Beck. 189 J6
Upper Elmers End Rd,
   Beck. BR3 . . . . .189 H4
Upper Fm Rd, W.Mol.
   KT8 . . . . .179 F4
Upper Fosters, NW4
   off New Brent St 71 J5
Upper Grn E, Mitch.
   CR4 . . . . .185 J3
Upper Grn W, Mitch. CR4
   off London Rd 185 J3
Upper Grenfell Wk, W11
   off Whitchurch Rd 108 A7
Upper Grosvenor St, W1 . .16 B6
Upper Grotto Rd, Twick.
   TW1 . . . . .162 C2
Upper Grd, SE1 . . . . .26 E1
Upper Gro, SE25 . . . . . .188 B4
Upper Gro Rd, Belv.
   DA17 . . . . .139 F6
Upper Gulland Wk, N1
   off Clephane Rd 93 J6
Upper Ham Rd, Kings.T.
   KT2 . . . . .163 G4
   Richmond TW10 . . . . . .163 G4

Upper Handa Wk, N1
   off Clephane Rd 94 A6
Upper Hawkwell Wk, N1
   off Popham Rd 111 J1
Upper Hitch, Wat. WD19 . .51 E1
UPPER HOLLOWAY, N19 . .92 C3
Upper Holly Hill Rd, Belv.
   DA17 . . . . .139 H5
Upper James St, W1 . . . . .17 G5
Upper John St, W1 . . . . . .17 G5
Upper Lismore Wk, N1
   off Clephane Rd 93 J6
Upper Mall, W6 . . . . . . .127 G5
Upper Marsh, SE1 . . . . . . .26 D5
Upper Montagu St, W1 . . .15 J1
Upper Mulgrave Rd, Sutt.
   SM2 . . . . .198 B7
Upper N St, E14 . . . . . . .114 A5
UPPER NORWOOD,
   SE19 . . . . .170 A7
Upper Palace Rd, E.Mol.
   KT8 . . . . .179 J3
Upper Pk, Loug. IG10 . . . .48 A4
Upper Pk Rd, N11 . . . . . . .58 B5
   NW3 . . . . .91 J5
   Belvedere DA17 . . . . . .139 H4
   Bromley BR1 . . . . .191 H1
   Kingston upon Thames
   KT2 . . . . .164 A6
Upper Phillimore Gdns,
   W8 . . . . .128 D2
Upper Ramsey Wk, N1
   off Clephane Rd 94 A6
Upper Rawreth Wk, N1
   off Popham Rd 111 J1
Upper Richmond Rd,
   SW15 . . . . .148 B4
Upper Richmond Rd W,
   SW14 . . . . .146 A4
   Richmond TW10 . . . . . .146 A4
Upper Rd, E13 . . . . .115 G3
   Wallington SM6 . . . . . .200 D5
Upper St. Martin's La,
   WC2 . . . . .18 A5
Upper Selsdon Rd, S.Croy.
   CR2 . . . . .202 C7
Upper Sheppey Wk, N1
   off Clephane Rd 93 J7
Upper Sheridan Rd, Belv. DA17
   off Coleman Rd 139 G4
Upper Shirley Rd, Croy.
   CR0 . . . . .203 F2
Upper Sq, Islw. TW7 . . . .144 D3
Upper St, N1 . . . . .11 F1
Upper Sunbury Rd, Hmptn.
   TW12 . . . . .179 E1
Upper Sutton La, Houns.
   TW5 . . . . .123 G7
UPPER SYDENHAM,
   SE26 . . . . .170 D4
Upper Tachbrook St,
   SW1 . . . . .33 F1
Upper Tail, Wat. WD19 . . .51 E3
Upper Talbot Wk, W11
   off Lancaster Rd 108 B6
Upper Teddington Rd, Kings.T.
   KT1 . . . . .181 F1
Upper Ter, NW3 . . . . .91 F3
Upper Thames St, EC4 . . .19 H5
Upper Tollington Pk, N4 . .93 G1
Upperton Rd, Sid.
   DA14 . . . . .175 J5
Upperton Rd E, E13
   off Inniskilling Rd 115 J3
Upperton Rd W, E13 . . . .115 J3
UPPER TOOTING, SW17 .167 H3
Upper Tooting Pk, SW17 .167 J2
Upper Tooting Rd, SW17 .167 J4
Upper Town Rd, Grnf.
   UB6 . . . . .103 H4
Upper Tulse Hill, SW2 . . .151 F7
Upper Vernon Rd, Sutt.
   SM1 . . . . .199 G5
UPPER WALTHAMSTOW,
   E17 . . . . .78 B4
Upper Walthamstow Rd,
   E17 . . . . .78 D4
Upper Wickham La, Well.
   DA16 . . . . .138 B7
Upper Wimpole St, W1 . . .16 D1
Upper Woburn Pl, WC1 . . .9 J4
Uppingham Av, Stan.
   HA7 . . . . .69 E1
Upsdell Av, N13 . . . . .59 G6
Upstall St, SE5 . . . . .151 H1
UPTON, E7 . . . . .97 H7
Upton Av, E7 . . . . .97 G7
Upton Cl, NW2
   off Somerton Rd 90 B3
   Bexley DA5 . . . . .159 F6

Upton Ct, SE20
   off Blean Gro 171 F7
Upton Dene, Sutt. SM2 . .198 E7
Upton Gdns, Har. HA3 . . . .69 E5
Upton La, E7 . . . . .97 G7
UPTON PARK, E6 . . . . . .115 J1
Upton Pk Rd, E7 . . . . .97 H7
Upton Rd, N18 . . . . .60 D5
   SE18 . . . . .137 F6
   Bexley DA5 . . . . .159 F6
   Bexleyheath DA6 . . . . .158 E4
   Hounslow TW3 . . . . . . .143 G3
   Thornton Heath CR7 . . .188 A2
Upton Rd S, Bex. DA5 . . .159 F6
Upway, N12 . . . . .57 H7
Upwood Rd, SE12 . . . . . .155 G6
   SW16 . . . . .187 E1
Urlwin St, SE5 . . . . .35 J6
Urlwin Wk, SW9 . . . . . . .151 G2
Urmston Dr, SW19 . . . . .166 B1
Ursula Ms, N4
   off Portland Ri 93 J1
Ursula St, SW11 . . . . . . .149 H1
Urswick Gdns, Dag. RM9
   off Urswick Rd 100/101 E7
Urswick Rd, E9 . . . . .95 F5
   Dagenham RM9 . . . . . .100 D7
Usborne Ms, SW8 . . . . . . .34 C7
Usher Rd, E3 . . . . .113 J2
Usk Rd, SW11 . . . . .149 F4
Usk St, E2 . . . . .113 G3
Utopia Village, NW1
   off Chalcot Rd 110 A1
Uvedale Rd, Dag. RM10 .101 G3
   Enfield EN2 . . . . .44 A5
Uverdale Rd, SW10 . . . . .129 F7
Uxbridge Gdns, Felt. TW13
   off Marlborough Rd . . .160 D2
Uxbridge Rd, W3 . . . . . . .105 H7
   W5 . . . . .105 H7
   W7 . . . . .124 C1
   W12 . . . . .127 G1
   W13 . . . . .124 C1
   Feltham TW13 . . . . . . .160 C2
   Hampton (Hmptn.H.)
   TW12 . . . . .161 G4
   Harrow HA3 . . . . .51 J7
   Hayes UB4 . . . . .102 C7
   Kingston upon Thames
   KT1 . . . . .181 G4
   Pinner HA5 . . . . .51 H7
   Southall UB1 . . . . .123 G1
   Stanmore HA7 . . . . .52 C6
Uxbridge St, W8 . . . . . . .128 D1
Uxendon Cres, Wem.
   HA9 . . . . .87 H1
Uxendon Hill, Wem.
   HA9 . . . . .87 J1

Valance Av, E4 . . . . .63 F1
Valan Leas, Brom. BR2 . .191 E3
Vale, The, N10 . . . . .74 A1
   N14 . . . . .42 D7
   NW11 . . . . .90 A3
   SW3 . . . . .31 E5
   W3 . . . . .126 D1
   Croydon CR0 . . . . .203 G2
   Feltham TW14 . . . . . . .142 B6
   Hounslow TW5 . . . . . . .122 E6
   Ruislip HA4 . . . . .84 C4
   Sunbury-on-Thames TW16
   off Ashridge Way 160 A6
   Woodford Green IG8 . . . .63 G7
Vale Av, Borwd. WD6 . . . .38 B5
Vale Cl, N2
   off Church Vale 73 J3
   W9 . . . . .6 C4
   Orpington BR6 . . . . . . .206 D4
Vale Cotts, SW15
   off Kingston Vale 164 D4
Vale Ct, W9 . . . . .6 C4
Vale Cres, SW15 . . . . . . .165 E3
Vale Cft, Esher (Clay.)
   KT10 . . . . .194 B7
   Pinner HA5 . . . . .66 E5
Vale Dr, Barn. EN5 . . . . . .40 C4
Vale End, SE22
   off Grove Vale 152 B4
Vale Gro, N4 . . . . .75 J7
   W3 off The Vale 126 D1
Vale La, W3 . . . . .106 A5
Valence Av, Dag. RM8 . . .100 D3
Valence Circ, Dag. RM8 . .100 D3
★ Valence Ho Mus, Dag.
   RM8 . . . . .100 E2
Valence Wd Rd, Dag.
   RM8 . . . . .100 D3
Valencia Rd, Stan. HA7 . . .53 F4
Valentia Pl, SW9
   off Brixton Sta Rd 151 G4
Valentine Av, Bex. DA5 . .176 E2

Valentine Ct, SE23 . . . . .171 G2
Valentine Pl, SE1 . . . . . . .27 G3
Valentine Rd, E9 . . . . .95 G6
   Harrow HA2 . . . . .85 J3
Valentine Row, SE1 . . . . . .27 G4
Valentines Rd, Ilf. IG1 . . . .98 E1
Vale of Health, NW3
   off East Heath Rd 91 G3
Vale Par, SW15
   off Kingston Vale 164 D4
Valerian Way, E15 . . . . . .115 E3
Valerie Ct, Sutt. SM2
   off Stanley Rd 198/199 E7
Vale Ri, NW11 . . . . .90 C1
Vale Rd, E7 . . . . .97 H6
   N4 . . . . .75 J7
   Bromley BR1 . . . . .192 D2
   Epsom KT19 . . . . .197 F4
   Mitcham CR4 . . . . .186 D3
   Sutton SM1 . . . . .198 E4
   Worcester Park KT4 . . .197 F4
Vale Rd N, Surb. KT6 . . .195 H2
Vale Rd S, Surb. KT6 . . . .195 H2
Vale Row, N5
   off Gillespie Rd 93 H3
Vale Royal, N7 . . . . .92 E7
Vale St, SE27 . . . . .170 A3
Valeswood Rd, Brom.
   BR1 . . . . .173 F5
Vale Ter, N4 . . . . .75 J6
Valetta Gro, E13 . . . . . . .115 G2
Valetta Rd, W3 . . . . .126 E2
Valette St, E9 . . . . .95 E6
Valiant Cl, Nthlt. UB5
   off Ruislip Rd 102 D3
   Romford RM7 . . . . .83 G2
Valiant Ho, SE7 . . . . . . .135 J5
Valiant Path, NW9
   off Blundell Rd 54/55 E7
Valiant Way, E6 . . . . .116 C5
Vallance Rd, E1 . . . . .13 J4
   E2 . . . . .13 J4
   N22 . . . . .74 C2
Vallentin Rd, E17 . . . . . . .78 C4
Valley Av, N12 . . . . .57 G4
Valley Cl, Loug. IG10 . . . . .48 C6
   Pinner HA5
   off Alandale Dr 66 B2
Valley Dr, NW9 . . . . .70 A6
Valleyfield Rd, SW16 . . . .169 F5
Valley Flds Cres, Enf.
   EN2 . . . . .43 G2
Valley Gdns, SW19 . . . . .167 G2
   Wembley HA0 . . . . .87 J7
Valley Gro, SE7 . . . . .135 J5
Valley Hill, Loug. IG10 . . . .48 B7
Valley Link Ind Est, Enf.
   EN3 . . . . .45 H6
Valley Ms, Twick. TW1
   off Cross Deep 162 D2
Valley Rd, SW16 . . . . . . .169 F4
   Belvedere DA17 . . . . . .139 H4
   Bromley BR1 . . . . .191 E2
Valley Side, E4 . . . . .62 A2
Valley Side Par, E4
   off Valley Side 62 A2
Valley Vw, Barn. EN5 . . . . .40 B6
Valley Wk, Croy. CR0 . . . .203 F2
Valliere Rd, NW10 . . . . . .107 H3
Valliers Wd Rd, Sid.
   DA15 . . . . .175 G1
Vallis Way, W13 . . . . .104 D5
   Chessington KT9 . . . . .195 G4
Valmar Rd, SE5 . . . . .151 J1
Val McKenzie Av, N7
   off Parkside Cres 93 G3
Valnay St, SW17 . . . . . . .167 J5
Valognes Av, E17 . . . . . . .77 H1
Valonia Gdns, SW18 . . . .148 C6
Vambery Rd, SE18 . . . . . .137 F6
Vanbrough Cres, Nthlt.
   UB5 . . . . .102 C1
Vanbrugh Cl, E16 . . . . . .116 A5
Vanbrugh Dr, Walt.
   KT12 . . . . .178 C7
Vanbrugh Flds, SE3 . . . . .135 F7
Vanbrugh Hill, SE3 . . . . .135 F5
   SE10 . . . . .135 F5
Vanbrugh Pk, SE3 . . . . . .135 F7
Vanbrugh Pk Rd, SE3 . . .135 F7
Vanbrugh Pk Rd W, SE3 .135 F7
Vanbrugh Rd, W4 . . . . . .126 D3
Vanbrugh Ter, SE3 . . . . . .155 F1
Vanburgh Cl, Orp. BR6 . .207 H1
Vancouver Cl, Orp. BR6 . .207 J4
Vancouver Rd, SE23 . . . .171 H2
   Edgware HA8 . . . . .70 B1
   Hayes UB4 . . . . .102 B4
   Richmond TW10 . . . . . .163 F4

Vanderbilt Rd, SW18 . . . .167 F1
Vanderville Gdns, N2
  off Tarling Rd 73 F2
Vandome CI, E16 . . . . . .115 H6
Vandon Pas, SW1 . . . . . .25 G5
Vandon St, SW1 . . . . . . .25 G5
Van Dyck Av, N.Mal.
  KT3 . . . . .182 D7
Vandyke CI, SW15 . . . . .148 A7
Vandyke Cross, SE9 . . . .156 B5
Vandy St, EC2 . . . . .12 D6
Vane CI, NW3 . . . . .91 G4
  Harrow HA3 . . . . .69 J6
Vanessa CI, Belv. DA17 .139 G5
Vane St, SW1 . . . . .33 G1
Vanguard CI, E16 . . . . . .115 G5
  Croydon CR0 . . . . . . .201 H1
  Romford RM7 . . . . . . .83 H2
Vanguard St, SE8 . . . . . .154 A1
Vanguard Way, Wall.
  SM6 . . . . .200 E7
Vanneck Sq, SW15 . . . . .147 G5
Vanner Pt, E9
  off Wick Rd 95 G6
Vanoc Gdns, Brom. BR1 .173 G3
Vansittart Rd, E7 . . . . . . .97 F4
Vansittart St, SE14 . . . . .133 H7
Vanston PI, SW6 . . . . . . .128 D7
Vantage Ms, E14
  off Prestons Rd 134 C1
Vantage PI, W8
  off Abingdon Rd 128 D3
Vant Rd, SW17 . . . . .167 J5
Varcoe Rd, SE16 . . . . . . .133 E5
Vardens Rd, SW11 . . . . .149 G4
Varden St, E1 . . . . .112 E6
Vardon CI, W3 . . . . .106 D6
Varley Par, NW9 . . . . . . .70 E4
Varley Rd, E16 . . . . .115 H6
Varley Way, Mitch. CR4 . .185 G2
Varna Rd, SW6 . . . . .128 B7
  Hampton TW12 . . . . . .179 H1
Varndell St, NW1 . . . . . . .9 F3
Varsity Dr, Twick. TW1 . .144 B5
Varsity Row, SW14
  off William's La 146 C2
Vartry Rd, N15 . . . . .76 A6
Vassall Rd, SW9 . . . . . . .131 G7
Vauban Est, SE16 . . . . . .29 G6
Vauban St, SE16 . . . . . . .29 G6
Vaughan Av, NW4 . . . . . .71 G5
  W6 . . . . .127 F4
Vaughan CI, Hmptn. TW12
  off Oak Av 160/161 E6
Vaughan Gdns, Ilf. IG1 . .80 C7
Vaughan Rd, E15 . . . . . . .97 F6
  SE5 . . . . .151 J3
  Harrow HA1 . . . . .67 J7
  Thames Ditton KT7 . . .180 E7
  Welling DA16 . . . . . . .157 J2
Vaughan St, SE16 . . . . . .133 J2
Vaughan Way, E1 . . . . . .21 H6
Vaughan Williams CI, SE8
  off Watson's St 134 A7
VAUXHALL, SE11 . . . . . .34 B4
Vauxhall Br, SE1 . . . . . . .34 A4
  SW1 . . . . .34 A4
Vauxhall Br Rd, SW1 . . . .33 G1
Vauxhall Gdns, S.Croy.
  CR2 . . . . .201 J6
Vauxhall Gdns Est, SE11 .34 D4
Vauxhall Gro, SW8 . . . . .34 C5
Vauxhall St, SE11 . . . . . .34 D3
Vauxhall Wk, SE11 . . . . .34 C3
Vawdrey CI, E1 . . . . .113 F4
Veals Mead, Mitch. CR4 .185 H1
Vectis Gdns, SW17
  off Vectis Rd 168 B6
Vectis Rd, SW17 . . . . . . .168 B6
Veda Rd, SE13 . . . . .154 A4
Veldene Way, Har. HA2 . .85 F3
Velde Way, SE22
  off East Dulwich Gro . .152 B5
Velletri Ho, E2 . . . . .113 G2
Vellum Dr, Cars. SM5 . . .200 A3
Venables St, Dag. RM10 .101 H4
Venables St, NW8 . . . . . .15 F1
Vencourt PI, W6 . . . . . . .127 G5
Venetian Rd, SE5 . . . . . .151 J2
Venetia Rd, N4 . . . . .75 H6
  W5 . . . . .125 G2
Venner Rd, SE26 . . . . . . .171 F6
Venn St, SW4 . . . . .150 C4
Ventnor Av, Stan. HA7 . . .69 E1
Ventnor Dr, N20 . . . . . . .56 E3
Ventnor Gdns, Bark. IG11 .99 H6
Ventnor Rd, SE14 . . . . . .133 G7
  Sutton SM2 . . . . .199 E7
Venture CI, Bex. DA5 . . .158 E7
Venue St, E14 . . . . .114 C5

Venus Rd, SE18 . . . . . . .136 C3
Vera Av, N21 . . . . .43 G5
Vera Lynn CI, E7
  off Dames Rd 97 G4
Vera Rd, SW6 . . . . .148 B1
Verbena CI, E16
  off Pretoria Rd 115 F4
  West Drayton UB7
  off Magnolia St 120 A5
Verbena Gdns, W6 . . . . .127 G5
Verdant La, SE6 . . . . . . .173 E1
Verdayne Av, Croy. CR0 .203 G1
Verdun Rd, SE18 . . . . . .138 A6
  SW13 . . . . .127 G6
Vereker Dr, Sun. TW16 . .178 A3
Vereker Rd, W14 . . . . . .128 B5
Vere Rd, Loug. IG10 . . . .49 F4
Vere St, W1 . . . . .16 D4
Verity CI, W11 . . . . .108 B6
Vermeer Gdns, SE15
  off Elland Rd 153 F4
Vermont CI, Enf. EN2 . . .43 H4
Vermont Rd, SE19 . . . . .170 A6
  SW18 . . . . .149 E6
  Sutton SM1 . . . . .198 E3
Verney Gdns, Dag. RM9 .100 E4
Verney Rd, SE16 . . . . . . .37 J5
  Dagenham RM9 . . . . .100 E4
Verney St, NW10 . . . . . . .88 D3
Verney Way, SE16 . . . . .132 E5
Vernham Rd, SE18 . . . . .137 F6
Vernon Av, E12 . . . . .98 C4
  SW20 . . . . .184 A2
  Woodford Green IG8 . .63 H7
Vernon CI, Epsom KT19 .196 C6
Vernon Ct, Stan. HA7
  off Vernon Dr 68/69 E1
Vernon Cres, Barn. EN4 . .42 A6
Vernon Dr, Stan. HA7 . . .68 D1
Vernon Ms, E17
  off Vernon Rd 77 J4
  W14 off Vernon St . . .128 B4
Vernon PI, WC1 . . . . . . .18 B2
Vernon Ri, WC1 . . . . . . .10 D3
  Greenford UB6 . . . . . .86 A5
Vernon Rd, E3 . . . . .113 J2
  E11 . . . . .97 E1
  E15 . . . . .97 E7
  E17 . . . . .77 J5
  N8 . . . . .75 G3
  SW14 . . . . .146 D3
  Ilford IG3 . . . . .99 J1
  Sutton SM1 . . . . .199 F5
Vernon Sq, WC1 . . . . . . .10 D3
Vernon St, W14 . . . . . . .128 B4
Vernon Yd, W11
  off Portobello Rd 108 C7
Veroan Rd, Bexh. DA7 . .158 E2
Verona Dr, Surb. KT6 . . .195 H2
Verona Rd, E7
  off Upton La 97 G7
Veronica Gdns, SW16 . .186 C1
Veronica Rd, SW17 . . . .168 B3
Veronique Gdns, Ilf. IG6 . .81 E5
Verran Rd, SW12
  off Balham Gro 150 B7
Versailles Rd, SE20 . . . .170 D7
Verulam Av, E17 . . . . . . .77 J6
Verulam Bldgs, WC1 . . . .18 D1
Verulam Rd, Grnf. UB6 . .103 G4
Verulam St, WC1 . . . . . .18 E1
Verwood Dr, Barn. EN4 . .41 J3
Verwood Rd, Har. HA2 . . .67 J2
Vesey Path, E14
  off East India Dock
  Rd 114 B6
Vespan Rd, W12 . . . . . . .127 G2
Vesta Rd, SE4 . . . . .153 H2
Vestris Rd, SE23 . . . . . .171 G2
Vestry Ms, SE5 . . . . . . .152 B1
Vestry Rd, E17 . . . . .78 B4
  SE5 . . . . .152 B1
Vestry St, N1 . . . . .12 B3
Vevey St, SE6 . . . . .171 J2
Veysey Gdns, Dag.
  RM10 . . . . .101 G3
Viaduct PI, E2
  off Viaduct St 112/113 E3
Viaduct St, E2 . . . . .112 E3
Vian St, SE13 . . . . .154 B3
Vibart Gdns, SW2 . . . . .151 F7
Vibart Wk, N1
  off Outram PI 110/111 E1
Vicarage Av, SE3 . . . . . .155 G1
Vicarage CI, Erith DA8 . .139 J6
  Northolt UB5 . . . . .85 F7
  Worcester Park KT4 . .196 E1
Vicarage Ct, W8 . . . . . . .22 A3
  Feltham TW14 . . . . . .141 F7
Vicarage Cres, SW11 . . .149 G1

Vicarage Dr, SW14 . . . . .146 D5
  Barking IG11 . . . . .99 F7
  Beckenham BR3 . . . . .190 A1
Vicarage Fm Rd, Houns. TW3,
  TW5 . . . . .142 E2
Vicarage Flds, Walt.
  KT12 . . . . .178 C6
Vicarage Fld Shop Cen, Bark.
  IG11 . . . . .99 F7
Vicarage Gdns, SW14
  off Vicarage Rd 146 C5
  W8 . . . . .128 D1
  Mitcham CR4 . . . . . . .185 H3
Vicarage Gate, W8 . . . . .22 A3
Vicarage Gro, SE5 . . . . .152 A1
Vicarage La, E6 . . . . . . .116 C3
  E15 . . . . .97 E7
  Chigwell IG7 . . . . .65 F2
  Ilford IG1 . . . . .99 G1
Vicarage Pk, SE18 . . . . .137 F5
Vicarage Path, N8 . . . . . .74 E7
Vicarage Rd, E10 . . . . . . .96 B1
  E15 . . . . .97 F7
  N17 . . . . .60 D7
  NW4 . . . . .71 G6
  SE18 . . . . .137 F5
  SW14 . . . . .146 C5
  Bexley DA5 . . . . .177 H1
  Croydon CR0 . . . . . . .201 G3
  Dagenham RM10 . . . .101 H6
  Kingston upon Thames
  KT1 . . . . .181 G2
  Kingston upon Thames
  (Hmptn.W.) KT1 . . . . .181 F1
  Sutton SM1 . . . . .198 E4
  Teddington TW11 . . . .162 D5
  Twickenham TW2 . . . .162 B2
  Twickenham (Whitton)
  TW2 . . . . .143 J6
  Woodford Green IG8 . .64 B7
Vicarage Way, NW10 . . . .88 D3
  Harrow HA2 . . . . .67 G7
Vicars CI, E9
  off Northiam St 113 F1
  E15 . . . . .115 G1
  Enfield EN1 . . . . .44 B2
Vicars Hill, SE13 . . . . . .154 B4
Vicars Moor La, N21 . . . .43 G7
Vicars Oak Rd, SE19 . . . .170 B6
Vicars Rd, NW5 . . . . . . .92 A5
Vicars Wk, Dag. RM8 . . .100 B3
Viceroy CI, N2
  off Market PI 73 H4
Viceroy Ct, NW8 . . . . . . .7 H1
Viceroy Par, N2
  off High Rd 73 H3
Viceroy Rd, SW8 . . . . . .150 E1
Vickers CI, Wall. SM6
  off Hurricane Rd 201 F7
Vickers Way, Houns.
  TW4 . . . . .143 E5
Victor Gro, Wem. HA0 . . .87 H7
★ Victoria & Albert Mus,
  SW7 . . . . .23 F6
Victoria Arc, SW1
  off Terminus PI 130 B3
Victoria Av, E6 . . . . .116 A1
  EC2 . . . . .20 E2
  N3 . . . . .72 C1
  Barnet EN4 . . . . .41 G4
  Hounslow TW3 . . . . . .143 F5
  Surbiton KT6 . . . . . . .181 G7
  Wallington SM6 . . . . .200 A3
  Wembley HA9 . . . . . . .88 B6
  West Molesey KT8 . . .179 G3
Victoria CI, Barn. EN4 . . .41 G4
  West Molesey KT8
  off Victoria Av 179 G3
★ Victoria Coach Sta,
  SW1 . . . . .32 D2
Victoria Cotts, Rich.
  TW9 . . . . .145 J1
Victoria Ct, Wem. HA9 . .88 A6
Victoria Cres, N15 . . . . . .76 B5
  SE19 . . . . .170 B6
  SW19 . . . . .166 C7
Victoria Dock Rd, E16 . .115 G6
Victoria Dr, SW19 . . . . .148 A7
Victoria Embk, EC4 . . . .18 C6
  SW1 . . . . .26 B3
  WC2 . . . . .18 C6
★ Victoria Embankment
  Gdns, WC2 . . . . .18 B6
Victoria Gdns, W11 . . . .128 D1
  Hounslow TW5 . . . . . .142 E1
Victoria Gro, N12 . . . . . .57 F5
  W8 . . . . .22 C5
Victoria Gro Ms, W2
  off Ossington St . .108/109 E7

Victoria Ind Est, NW10 . .106 E3
Victoria La, Barn. EN5 . . .40 C4
  Hayes UB3 . . . . .121 F5
Victoria Ms, NW6 . . . . . .108 D1
  SW4 off Victoria Ri . . .150 B4
  SW18 . . . . .167 F1
Victorian Gro, N16 . . . . . .94 B3
Victorian Rd, N16 . . . . . . .94 B3
★ Victoria Park, E9 . . . . .95 H7
Victoria Pk, E9 . . . . .95 H7
Victoria Pk Rd, E9 . . . . . .113 F1
Victoria Pk Sq, E2 . . . . . .113 F3
Victoria Pas, NW8 . . . . . .7 E5
Victoria PI, SW1 . . . . . . .32 E1
  Richmond TW9 . . . . . .145 G5
Victoria Pt, E13
  off Victoria Rd 115 G2
Victoria Retail Pk, Ruis.
  HA4 . . . . .84 E5
Victoria Ri, SW4 . . . . . . .150 B3
Victoria Rd, E4 . . . . .63 E1
  E11 . . . . .96 E4
  E13 . . . . .115 G2
  E17 . . . . .78 C2
  E18 . . . . .79 H2
  N4 . . . . .75 F7
  N9 . . . . .60 C4
  N15 . . . . .76 D4
  N18 . . . . .60 D4
  N22 . . . . .74 C1
  NW4 . . . . .71 J4
  NW6 . . . . .108 C1
  NW7 . . . . .55 F5
  NW10 . . . . .106 D5
  SW14 . . . . .146 D3
  W3 . . . . .106 D5
  W5 . . . . .105 E5
  W8 . . . . .22 C6
  Barking IG11 . . . . .99 E6
  Barnet EN4 . . . . .41 G4
  Bexleyheath DA6 . . . .159 G4
  Bromley BR2 . . . . . . .192 A5
  Buckhurst Hill IG9 . . . .64 A2
  Bushey WD23 . . . . . . .51 H1
  Chislehurst BR7 . . . . .174 D5
  Dagenham RM10 . . . .101 H5
  Feltham TW13 . . . . . .160 B1
  Kingston upon Thames
  KT1 . . . . .181 J2
  Mitcham CR4 . . . . . . .167 H7
  Ruislip HA4 . . . . .84 C5
  Sidcup DA15 . . . . . . .175 J3
  Southall UB2 . . . . . . .123 F3
  Surbiton KT6 . . . . . . .181 G6
  Sutton SM1 . . . . .199 G5
  Teddington TW11 . . . .162 D6
  Twickenham TW1 . . . .144 D7
Victoria Sq, SW1 . . . . . .24 E5
Victoria Sta, SW1 . . . . . .33 E1
Victoria Steps, Brent. TW8
  off Kew Br Rd 125 J6
Victoria St, E15 . . . . .96 E7
  SW1 . . . . .25 F6
  Belvedere DA17 . . . . .139 F5
Victoria Ter, N4 . . . . .93 G1
  NW10 off Old Oak
  La 106/107 E3
  Harrow HA1 . . . . .86 B1
★ Victoria Twr, SW1 . . . .26 A5
Victoria Vil, Rich. TW9 . .145 J3
Victoria Way, SE7 . . . . .135 H5
Victoria Wf, E14 . . . . . . .113 H7
Victoria Yd, E1
  off Fairclough St 112 D6
Victor Rd, NW10 . . . . . . .107 H3
  SE20 . . . . .171 G7
  Harrow HA2 . . . . .67 J3
  Teddington TW11 . . . .162 B4
Victors Dr, Hmptn.
  TW12 . . . . .161 E6
Victors Way, Barn. EN5 . .40 C3
Victor Vil, N9 . . . . .60 A3
Victor Wk, NW9 . . . . . . .70 E1
Victory Av, Mord.
  SM4 . . . . .185 F5
Victory Business Cen, Islw.
  TW7 . . . . .144 C3
Victory PI, E14
  off Northey St 113 H7
  SE17 . . . . .36 A1
  SE19 off Westow St . .170 B6
Victory Rd, E11 . . . . .79 H4
  SW19 . . . . .167 F7
Victory Rd Ms, SW19
  off Victory Rd 167 F7
Victory Wk, SE8
  off Ship St 154 A1
Victory Way, SE16 . . . . .133 H2
  Hounslow TW5 . . . . . .122 C5
  Romford RM7 . . . . . . .83 H2

Vidler Cl, Chess. KT9
  off Merritt Gdns 195 F6
Vienna Cl, Ilf. IG5 ....80 A3
View, The, SE2 ....139 E5
View Cl, N6 ....73 J7
  Chigwell IG7 ....65 G5
  Harrow HA1 ....68 A4
Viewfield Cl, Har. HA3 ...69 H7
Viewfield Rd, SW18 ....148 C6
  Bexley DA5 ....176 C1
Viewland Rd, SE18 .....137 J5
View Rd, N6 ....73 J7
Viga Rd, N21 ....43 G6
Vigilant Cl, SE26 ......170 D4
Vignoles Rd, Rom.
  RM7 ....83 G7
Vigo St, W1 ....17 F6
Viking Cl, E3
  off Selwyn Rd 113 H2
Viking Ct, SW6 ....128 D6
Viking Gdns, E6
  off Jack Dash Way ...116 B4
Viking Pl, E10 ....95 J1
Viking Rd, Sthl. UB1 ...103 E7
Viking Way, Erith DA8 ..139 J3
Villacourt Rd, SE18 ....138 A7
Village, The, SE7 ......135 J6
Village Arc, E4
  off Station Rd 62 D1
Village Cl, E4 ....62 C5
  NW3 off Ornan Rd 91 H5
Village Ct, E17
  off Eden Rd 78 B5
Village Hts, Wdf.Grn.
  IG8 ....63 F5
Village Ms, NW9 ....88 D2
Village Pk Cl, Enf. EN1 ..44 B6
Village Rd, N3 ....72 B1
  Enfield EN1 ....44 B6
Village Row, Sutt. SM2 .198 D7
Village Way, NW10 .....88 D4
  SE21 ....152 A6
  Beckenham BR3 .....190 A2
  Pinner HA5 ....67 E7
Village Way E, Har. HA2 ..67 F7
Villa Rd, SW9 ....151 G3
Villas Rd, SE18 ....137 F4
Villa St, SE17 ....36 C4
Villiers Av, Surb. KT5 ..181 J5
  Twickenham TW2 ....161 F1
Villiers Cl, E10 ....96 A2
  Surbiton KT5 ....181 J4
Villiers Ct, N20
  off Buckingham Av 41 F7
Villiers Path, Surb. KT5 .181 H5
Villiers Rd, NW2 ....89 G6
  Beckenham BR3 .....189 G2
  Isleworth TW7 ....144 B2
  Kingston upon Thames
  KT1 ....181 J3
  Southall UB1 ....123 F1
Villiers St, WC2 ....18 A6
Vincam Cl, Twick. TW2 .143 G7
Vincent Av, Surb. KT5 ..196 B1
Vincent Cl, SE16 ......133 H2
  Barnet EN5 ....40 D3
  Bromley BR2 ....191 H4
  Ilford IG6 ....65 F6
  Sidcup DA15 ....175 H1
  West Drayton UB7 ...120 D4
Vincent Gdns, NW2 .....89 F3
Vincent Ms, E3 ....114 A2
Vincent Rd, E4 ....62 D6
  N15 ....75 J4
  N22 ....75 G2
  SE18 ....137 E4
  W3 ....126 C3
  Croydon CR0 ....188 B7
  Dagenham RM9 .....100 E7
  Hounslow TW4 ......142 D2
  Isleworth TW7 ....144 A1
  Kingston upon Thames
  KT1 ....182 A3
  Wembley HA0 ....87 J7
Vincent Row, Hmptn.
  (Hmptn.H.) TW12 ....161 J4
Vincents Path, Nthlt. UB5
  off Arnold Rd 84/85 E6
Vincent Sq, SW1 ....33 G1
Vincent St, E16 ....115 F5
  SW1 ....33 H1
Vincent Ter, N1 ....11 G1
Vince St, EC1 ....12 C4
  West Drayton UB7 ...120 D4
Vine Cl, E1 ....21 J2
  Harrow HA3 ....69 H6
Vinegar All, E17 ....78 B4
Vine Gdns, Ilf. IG1 ......99 F5

Vinegar St, E1
  off Reardon St ...132/133 E1
Vinegar Yd, SE1 ....28 D3
Vine Hill, EC1 ....10 E6
Vine La, SE1 ....28 E2
Vine Pl, W5
  off The Common 125 H1
  Hounslow TW3 ......143 H4
Vine Rd, Walt. KT12 ...178 C6
Vineries, The, N14 ......42 C6
  Enfield EN1 ....44 B3
Vineries Bk, NW7 ....55 H5
Vineries Cl, Dag. RM9
  off Heathway 101 G6
  West Drayton UB7 ...120 D6
Vine Rd, E15 ....97 F7
  SW13 ....147 F3
  East Molesey KT8 ...179 J4
  Orpington BR6 ......207 J6
Vines Av, N3 ....72 E1
Vine Sq, W14 ....128 C5
Vine St, EC3 ....21 F5
  W1 ....17 G6
  Romford RM7 ....83 J5
Vine St Br, EC1 ....11 F6
Vine Yd, SE1 ....28 A3
Vineyard, The, Rich.
  TW10 ....145 H5
Vineyard Av, NW7 ......56 B7
Vineyard Cl, SE6 ......172 A1
  Kingston upon Thames
  KT1 ....181 J3
Vineyard Gro, N3 ....73 E1
Vineyard Hill Rd, SW19 .166 D4
Vineyard Pas, Rich. TW9
  off Paradise Rd 145 H5
Vineyard Path, SW14 ..146 D3
Vineyard Rd, Felt. TW13 .160 A3
Vineyard Row, Kings.T.
  KT1 ....181 F1
Vineyard Wk, EC1 ....11 E5
Viney Rd, SE13 ....154 B3
Vining St, SW9 ....151 G4
Vinson Cl, Orp. BR6 ...207 J1
Vintners Pl, EC4
  off Upper Thames St .111 J7
Vintry Ms, E17
  off Cleveland Pk Cres .78 A4
Viola Av, SE2 ....138 B4
  Feltham TW14 ......142 C6
Viola Sq, W12 ....107 F7
Violet Cl, E16 ....115 E4
  SE8 off Dorking Cl ..133 J6
  Wallington SM6 .....200 B1
Violet Gdns, Croy. CR0 .201 H5
Violet Hill, NW8 ....6 C2
Violet La, Croy. CR0 ...201 H5
Violet Rd, E3 ....114 B4
  E17 ....78 A6
  E18 ....79 H2
Violet St, E2 off Three Colts
  La 112/113 E4
Virgil Pl, W1 ....15 J2
Virgil St, SE1 ....26 D5
Virginia Cl, N.Mal. KT3
  off Willow Rd 182 C4
Virginia Gdns, Ilf. IG6 ...81 F2
Virginia Rd, E2 ....13 F4
  Thornton Heath CR7 .187 H1
Virginia St, E1 ....21 J6
Virginia Wk, SW2 .....151 F6
Viscount Cl, N11 ....58 B5
Viscount Dr, E6 ....116 C5
Viscount Gro, Nthlt. UB5
  off Wayfarer Rd 102 D3
Viscount St, EC1 ....11 J6
Viscount Way, Houns.
  (Hthrw.Air.) TW6 ....141 H4
Vista, The, SE9 ....156 A6
  Sidcup DA14
  off Langdon Shaw ...175 J5
Vista Av, Enf. EN3 ......45 G2
Vista Dr, Ilf. IG4 ....80 A5
Vista Way, Har. HA3 ....69 H6
Viveash Cl, Hayes UB3 .121 J3
Vivian Av, NW4 ....71 H5
  Wembley HA9 ....88 A5
Vivian Cl, Wat. WD19 ...50 A1
Vivian Comma Cl, N4
  off Blackstock Rd 93 H3
Vivian Gdns, Wat. WD19 .50 A1
  Wembley HA9 ....88 A5
Vivian Rd, E3 ....113 H2
Vivian Sq, SE15
  off Scylla Rd 152/153 E3
Vivian Way, N2 ....73 G5
Vivien Cl, Chess. KT9 ..195 H7
Vivienne Cl, Twick. TW1 .145 F6
Voce Rd, SE18 ....137 G7
Voewood Cl, N.Mal. KT3 .183 F6

Voltaire Rd, SW4 ....150 D3
Volt Av, NW10 ....106 D3
Volta Way, Croy. CR0 ...201 F1
Voluntary Pl, E11 ....79 G6
Vorley Rd, N19 ....92 C2
Voss Ct, SW16 ....169 E6
Voss St, E2 ....13 J4
Voyagers Cl, SE28 ....118 C6
Voysey Cl, N3 ....72 B3
Vulcan Cl, E6 ....116 D6
  Wallington SM6
  off De Havilland Rd ..201 F7
Vulcan Gate, Enf. EN2 ...43 G2
Vulcan Rd, SE4 ....153 J2
Vulcan Sq, E14
  off Britannia Rd 134 A4
Vulcan Ter, SE4 ....153 J2
Vulcan Way, N7 ....93 F6
Vyne, The, Bexh. DA7 ..159 H3
Vyner Rd, W3 ....106 D7
Vyner St, E2 ....113 E1
Vyse Cl, Barn. EN5 .....39 J4

W

Wadbrook St, Kings.T.
  KT1 ....181 G2
Wadding St, SE17 ......36 B2
Waddington Cl, Enf.
  EN1 ....44 B4
Waddington Rd, E15 .....96 D5
Waddington St, E15 .....96 D6
Waddington Way, SE19 .169 J7
WADDON, Croy. 201 G3
Waddon Cl, Croy. CR0 .201 G3
Waddon Ct Rd, Croy.
  CR0 ....201 G4
Waddon Marsh Way, Croy.
  CR0 ....201 F1
Waddon New Rd, Croy.
  CR0 ....201 H3
Waddon Pk Av, Croy.
  CR0 ....201 G4
Waddon Rd, Croy. CR0 .201 G3
Waddon Way, Croy. CR0 .201 H6
Wades Gro, N21 ....43 G7
Wades Hill, N21 ....43 G6
Wades La, Tedd. TW11
  off High St 162 D5
Wades Ms, N21
  off Wades Hill 43 G7
Wadeson St, E2 ....113 E2
Wades Pl, E14 ....114 B7
Wadeville Av, Rom.
  RM6 ....83 F7
Wadeville Cl, Belv.
  DA17 ....139 G6
Wadham Av, E17 ....62 B7
Wadham Gdns, NW3 ...109 H1
  Greenford UB6 ....86 A6
Wadham Rd, E17 ....78 B1
  SW15 ....148 B4
Wadhurst Cl, SE20 ....188 E2
Wadhurst Rd, SW8 ....150 C1
  W4 ....126 D3
Wadley Rd, E11 ....78 E7
Wadsworth Business Cen,
  Grnf. UB6 ....105 F2
Wadsworth Cl, Enf. EN3 ..45 G5
  Greenford UB6 ......105 F2
Wadsworth Rd, Grnf.
  UB6 ....105 E2
Wager St, E3 ....113 J4
Waggon Ms, N14
  off Chase Side 58 C1
Waghorn Rd, E13 .....115 J1
  Harrow HA3 ....69 G3
Waghorn St, SE15 ....152 D3
Wagner St, SE15 .....133 F7
Wagstaff Gdns, Dag.
  RM9 ....100 C7
Wagtail Cl, NW9
  off Swan Dr 70/71 E2
Wagtail Wk, Beck. BR3 .190 C5
Waights Ct, Kings.T. KT2 .181 H1
Wainfleet Av, Rom. RM5 .83 J2
Wainford Cl, SW19
  off Windlesham Gro .166 A1
Wainwright Gro, Islw.
  TW7 ....144 A4
Waite Davies Rd, SE12 .155 F7
Waite St, SE15 ....37 F5
Waithman St, EC4 ......19 G4
Wakefield Gdns, SE19 .170 B7
  Ilford IG1 ....80 B6
Wakefield Ms, WC1 .....10 B4
Wakefield Rd, N11 ......58 D5
  N15 ....76 C5
  Richmond TW10 .....145 G5

Wakefield St, E6 ....116 A1
  N18 ....60 D5
  WC1 ....10 B5
Wakehams Hill, Pnr. HA5 .67 F3
Wakeham St, N1 ....94 A6
Wakehurst Rd, SW11 ..149 H5
Wakeling Rd, W7 ......104 C5
Wakeling St, E14 .....113 H6
Wakelin Rd, E15 ....114 E2
Wakeman Rd, NW10 ...107 J3
Wakemans Hill Av, NW9 .70 D5
Wakering Rd, Bark. IG11 .99 F6
Wakerley Cl, E6
  off Truesdale Rd 116 C6
Wakley St, EC1 ....11 G3
Walberswick St, SW8 .131 E7
Walbrook, EC4 ....20 B5
Walbrook Ho, N9 ....61 F1
Walbrook Wf, EC4
  off Upper Thames St .111 J7
Walburgh St, E1
  off Bigland St ...112/113 E6
Walcorde Av, SE17 .....36 A2
Walcot Rd, Enf. EN3 ....45 J2
Walcot Sq, SE11 ....35 F1
Walcott St, SW1 ....33 G1
Waldair Ct, E16
  off Barge Ho Rd .136/137 E2
Waldair Wf, E16 ....136 E2
Waldeck Gro, SE27 ...169 H3
Waldeck Rd, N15 ....75 H4
  SW14 off Lower Richmond
  Rd 146 C3
  W4 ....126 A6
  W13 ....104 E6
Waldeck Ter, SW14
  off Lower Richmond
  Rd 146 C3
Waldegrave Av, Tedd. TW11
  off Waldegrave Rd ..162 C5
Waldegrave Gdns, Twick.
  TW1 ....162 C2
Waldegrave Pk, Twick.
  TW1 ....162 C4
Waldegrave Rd, N8 .....75 G3
  SE19 ....170 C7
  W5 ....105 J6
  Bromley BR1 ....192 B4
  Dagenham RM8 .....100 C2
  Teddington TW11 ...162 C4
  Twickenham TW1 ...162 C4
Waldegrove, Croy. CR0 .202 C3
Waldemar Av, SW6 ....148 B1
  W13 ....125 F1
Waldemar Rd, SW19 ..166 D5
Walden Av, N13 ....59 J4
  Chislehurst BR7 .....174 C4
Walden Gdns, Th.Hth.
  CR7 ....187 F3
Walden Par, Chis. BR7
  off Walden Rd 174 C6
Walden Rd, N17 ....76 A1
  Chislehurst BR7 .....174 C6
Waldenshaw Rd, SE23 .171 F1
Walden St, E1 ....112 E6
Walden Way, NW7 ......56 A6
  Ilford IG6 ....65 H7
Waldo Cl, SW4 ....150 C5
Waldo Pl, Mitch. CR4 ..167 H7
Waldo Rd, NW10 ......107 G3
  Bromley BR1 ....192 A3
Waldram Cres, SE23 ..171 F1
Waldram Pk Rd, SE23 .171 G1
Waldram Pl, SE23
  off Waldram Cres ...171 F1
Waldrist Way, Erith
  DA18 ....139 F2
Waldron Gdns, Brom.
  BR2 ....190 D3
Waldronhyrst, S.Croy.
  CR2 ....201 H4
Waldron Ms, SW3 ......31 F5
Waldron Rd, SW18 ....167 F3
  Harrow HA1, HA2 .....86 B1
Waldrons, The, Croy.
  CR0 ....201 H4
Waldrons Path, S.Croy.
  CR2 ....201 J4
Waldstock Rd, SE28 ..118 A7
Waleran Cl, Stan. HA7
  off Chenduit Way 52 C6
Walerand Rd, SE13 ...154 C2
Waleran Flats, SE1
  off Old Kent Rd 132 B4
Wales Av, Cars. SM5 ..199 J5
Wales Cl, SE15 ....132 E7
Wales Fm Rd, W3 .....106 D5
Waleton Acres, Wall.
  SM6 ....200 C6

Waley St, E1 . . . . .113 G5
Walfield Av, N20 . . . . .41 E7
Walford Rd, N16 . . . . .94 B4
Walfrey Gdns, Dag. RM9 .101 E7
WALHAM GREEN, SW6 .128 E7
Walham Grn Ct, SW6
  off Waterford Rd .128/129 E7
Walham Gro, SW6 . . . . . .128 D7
Walham Ri, SW19 . . . . . .166 B6
Walham Yd, SW6
  off Walham Gro 128 D7
Walkden Rd, Chis. BR7 . .174 D5
Walker Cl, N11 . . . . .58 C4
  SE18 . . . . .137 F4
  W7 . . . . .124 B1
  Hampton TW12
  off Fearnley Cres 161 F6
Walker Ms, SW2
  off Effra Rd 151 G5
Walkers Ct, E8
  off Wilton Way 94 D6
  W1 . . . . .17 H5
Walkerscroft Mead,
  SE21 . . . . .169 J1
Walkers Pl, SW15
  off Felsham Rd 148 B3
Walkford Way, SE15
  off Daniel Gdns 132 C7
Walks, The, N2 . . . . .73 G3
Walkynscroft, SE15
  off Firbank Rd . .152/153 E2
Wallace Cl, SE28
  off Haldane Rd 118 D7
★ Wallace Collection,
  W1 . . . . .16 B3
Wallace Cres, Cars.
  SM5 . . . . .199 J5
Wallace Rd, N1 . . . . .93 J6
Wallace Way, N19
  off Giesbach Rd 92 D2
Wallbutton Rd, SE4 . . . . .153 H2
Wallcote Av, NW2 . . . . . . .90 A1
Wall End Rd, E6 . . . . .98 D7
Waller Dr, Nthwd. HA6 . . . .66 A2
Waller Rd, SE14 . . . . .153 G1
Wallers Cl, Dag. RM9 . . . .119 E1
  Woodford Green IG8 . . . .64 C6
Wallers Hoppit, Loug.
  IG10 . . . . .48 B2
Waller Way, SE10
  off Greenwich High
  Rd 134 B7
Wallflower St, W12 . . . . . .107 F7
Wallgrave Rd, SW5 . . . . . .30 A1
Wallingford Av, W10 . . . . .108 A5
WALLINGTON 200 C5
Wallington Cor, Wall. SM6
  off Manor Rd N 200 B4
Wallington Rd, Ilf. IG3 . . . .81 J7
Wallington Sq, Wall. SM6
  off Woodcote Rd 200 B6
Wallis All, SE1 . . . . .28 A3
Wallis Cl, SW11 . . . . .149 G3
Wallis Ms, N22
  off Brampton Pk Rd . . .75 G3
Wallis Rd, E9 . . . . .95 J6
  Southall UB1 . . . . .103 H6
Wallis's Cotts, SW2 . . . . .151 E7
Wallman Pl, N22
  off Bounds Grn Rd 75 F1
Wallorton Gdns, SW14 . .146 D4
Wallside, EC2 . . . . .20 A2
Wall St, N1 . . . . .94 A6
Wallwood Rd, E11 . . . . . . .96 D1
Wallwood St, E14 . . . . . . .113 J5
Walmar Cl, Barn. EN4 . . . .41 G1
Walmer Cl, E4 . . . . .62 B2
  Orpington BR6
  off Tubbenden La S .207 G4
  Romford RM7 . . . . .83 H2
Walmer Gdns, W13 . . . . .124 D2
Walmer Ho, N9 . . . . .44 C7
Walmer Pl, W1 . . . . .15 J1
Walmer Rd, W10
  off Latimer Rd 107 J6
  W11 . . . . .108 B7
Walmer St, W1 . . . . .15 J1
Walmer Ter, SE18 . . . . . .137 F4
Walmgate Rd, Grnf.
  UB6 . . . . .104 E1
Walmington Fold, N12 . . .56 D2
Walm La, NW2 . . . . .90 A5
Walmsley Ho, SW16
  off Colson Way 168 C4
Walney Wk, N1
  off St. Paul's Rd 93 J6
Walnut Av, West Dr. UB7 .120 D3
Walnut Cl, SE8
  off Clyde St 133 J6
  Carshalton SM5 . . . . .199 J5

Walnut Cl, Ilf. IG6
  off Civic Way 81 F4
Walnut Ct, W5 . . . . .125 H2
Walnut Gdns, E15
  off Burgess Rd . . .96/97 E4
Walnut Gro, Enf. EN1 . . . .44 A5
Walnut Ms, Sutt. SM2 . . .199 F7
Walnut Rd, E10 . . . . .96 A2
Walnut Tree Av, Mitch. CR4
  off De'Arn Gdns 185 H3
Walnut Tree Cl, SW13 . . .147 F1
  Chislehurst BR7 . . . . .193 F1
Walnut Tree Cotts, SW19
  off Church Rd 166 B4
Walnut Tree Rd, SE10 . . .135 E5
  Brentford TW8 . . . . . . .125 H6
  Dagenham RM8 . . . . . .100 D2
  Hounslow TW5 . . . . . . .123 F6
Walnut Tree Wk, SE11 . . . .34 E1
Walnut Way, Buck.H.
  IG9 . . . . .64 A3
  Ruislip HA4 . . . . .84 C6
Walpole Av, Rich. TW9 . .145 J2
Walpole Cl, W13 . . . . .125 F2
  Pinner HA5 . . . . .51 G6
Walpole Cres, Tedd.
  TW11 . . . . .162 C5
Walpole Gdns, W4 . . . . . .126 C5
  Twickenham TW2 . . . . .162 B2
Walpole Ms, NW8
  off Queen's Gro 109 G1
  SW19 off Walpole Rd .167 G6
Walpole Pk, W5 . . . . .125 F1
Walpole Pl, SE18
  off Anglesea Rd .136/137 E4
  Teddington TW11 . . . . .162 C5
Walpole Rd, E6 . . . . .97 J7
  E17 . . . . .77 H4
  E18 . . . . .79 F1
  N17 (Downhills Way) . .75 J3
  N17 (Lordship La) 75 J2
  SW19 . . . . .167 G6
  Bromley BR2 . . . . .192 A5
  Croydon CR0 . . . . .202 A2
  Surbiton KT6 . . . . .181 H6
  Teddington TW11 . . . . .162 C5
  Twickenham TW2 . . . . .162 B2
Walpole St, SW3 . . . . .31 J3
Walrond Av, Wem. HA9 . . .87 H5
Walsham Cl, N16
  off Braydon Rd 76 D7
  SE28 . . . . .118 D7
Walsham Rd, SE14 . . . . . .153 G2
  Feltham TW14 . . . . . . .142 B7
Walsingham Gdns, Epsom
  KT19 . . . . .197 E4
Walsingham Pk, Chis.
  BR7 . . . . .193 G2
Walsingham Pl, SW4
  off Clapham Common
  W Side 149 J4
  SW11 . . . . .150 A6
Walsingham Rd, E5 . . . . . .94 D3
  W13 . . . . .124 D1
  Enfield EN2 . . . . .44 A4
  Mitcham CR4 . . . . .185 J5
Walsingham Wk, Belv.
  DA17 . . . . .139 G6
Walter Rodney Cl, E6
  off Stevenage Rd 98 C6
Walters Ho, SE17 . . . . . . .35 G6
Walters Rd, SE25 . . . . . . .188 B4
  Enfield EN3 . . . . .45 F5
Walter St, E2 . . . . .113 G3
  Kingston upon Thames KT2
  off Sopwith Way 181 H1
Walters Way, SE23 . . . . . .153 G6
Walters Yd, Brom. BR1 . .191 G2
Walter Ter, E1 . . . . .113 G6
Walterton Rd, W9 . . . . . . .108 C4
Walter Wk, Edg. HA8 . . . . .54 C6
Waltham Av, NW9 . . . . . . .70 A6
  Hayes UB3 . . . . .121 F3
Waltham Dr, Edg. HA8 . . . .70 A2
Waltham Pk Way, E17 . . . .78 A1
Waltham Rd, Cars.
  SM5 . . . . .185 G7
  Southall UB2 . . . . .122 E3
  Woodford Green IG8 . . .64 B6
WALTHAMSTOW, E17 . . . .78 B2
Walthamstow Av, E4 . . . . .62 A7
Walthamstow Business Cen,
  E17 . . . . .78 C2
Waltham Way, E4 . . . . .61 J4
Waltheof Av, N17 . . . . .76 A1
Waltheof Gdns, N17 . . . . .76 A1
Walton Av, Har. HA2 . . . . .85 F5
  New Malden KT3 . . . . .183 F4
  Sutton SM3 . . . . .198 C3
  Wembley HA9 . . . . .88 B3

Walton Cl, E5
  off Orient Way 95 G3
  NW2 . . . . .89 H2
  SW8 . . . . .34 B7
  Harrow HA1 . . . . .68 A4
Walton Cres, Har. HA2 . . . .85 F4
Walton Dr, NW10
  off Mitchellbrook Way .88 D6
  Harrow HA1 . . . . .68 A4
Walton Gdns, W3 . . . . . . .106 B5
  Wembley HA9 . . . . .87 H2
Walton Grn, Croy.
  (New Addgtn.) CR0 . . .204 C7
Walton Pl, SW3 . . . . .23 J5
Walton Rd, E12 . . . . .98 D4
  E13 . . . . .115 J2
  N15 . . . . .76 C5
  East Molesey KT8 . . . .179 G4
  Harrow HA1 . . . . .68 A4
  Sidcup DA14 . . . . .176 C2
  Walton-on-Thames
  KT12 . . . . .178 C5
  West Molesey KT8 . . . .179 E5
Walton St, SW3 . . . . .31 H1
  Enfield EN2 . . . . .44 A1
Walton Way, W3 . . . . .106 B5
  Mitcham CR4 . . . . .186 C4
Walt Whitman Cl, SE24
  off Shakespeare Rd . .151 H4
WALWORTH, SE17 . . . . . .35 J3
★ Walworth Garden Fm -
  Horticultural Training Cen,
  SE17 . . . . .35 J4
Walworth Pl, SE17 . . . . . . .36 A4
Walworth Rd, SE1 . . . . . . .35 J1
  SE17 . . . . .35 J1
Walwyn Av, Brom. BR1 . .192 A3
Wanborough Dr, SW15 . .165 H1
Wanderer Dr, Bark. IG11 .118 B3
Wandle Bk, SW19 . . . . . .167 G6
  Croydon CR0 . . . . .200 E4
Wandle Ct, Epsom KT19 .196 C4
Wandle Ct Gdns, Croy.
  CR0 . . . . .200 E4
Wandle Rd, SW17 . . . . . .167 H2
  Croydon CR0 . . . . .201 J3
  Croydon (Waddon)
  CR0 . . . . .201 E3
  Morden SM4 . . . . .185 F4
  Wallington SM6 . . . . . .200 B2
Wandle Side, Croy. CR0 .201 F3
  Wallington SM6 . . . . . .200 B3
Wandle Technology Pk, Mitch.
  CR4 off Goat Rd 185 J7
Wandle Trd Est, Mitch. CR4
  off Budge La 185 J7
Wandle Way, SW18 . . . . .166 E1
  Mitcham CR4 . . . . .185 J5
Wandon Rd, SW6 . . . . . . .129 E7
WANDSWORTH, SW18 . .148 C5
Wandsworth Br, SW6 . . . .149 E3
  SW18 . . . . .149 E3
Wandsworth Br Rd,
  SW6 . . . . .148 E1
Wandsworth Common,
  SW12 . . . . .149 H6
Wandsworth Common W
  Side, SW18 . . . . .149 F5
Wandsworth High St,
  SW18 . . . . .148 D5
★ Wandsworth Mus, SW18
  off Garratt La 148 E5
Wandsworth Plain,
  SW18 . . . . .148 E5
Wandsworth Rd, SW8 . . . .34 A5
Wandsworth Shop Cen,
  SW18 . . . . .148 E6
Wangey Rd, Rom. RM6 . . .82 D7
Wang Ho, Brent. TW8 . . .125 F5
Wanless Rd, SE24 . . . . . .151 J3
Wanley Rd, SE5 . . . . .152 A4
Wanlip Rd, E13 . . . . .115 H4
Wannock Gdns, Ilf. IG6 . . .65 E7
Wansbeck Rd, E9 . . . . .95 J7
Wansdown Pl, SW6 . . . . . .30 A7
Wansey St, SE17 . . . . .35 J2
Wansford Pk, Borwd.
  WD6 . . . . .38 E4
Wansford Rd, Wdf.Grn.
  IG8 . . . . .79 J1
WANSTEAD, E11 . . . . .79 H7
Wanstead Cl, Brom.
  BR1 . . . . .191 J2
Wanstead La, Ilf. IG1 . . . .80 A6
Wanstead Pk, E11 . . . . . . .80 A7
Wanstead Pk Av, E12 . . . .98 A2
Wanstead Pk Rd, Ilf. IG1 . .98 C1
Wanstead Pl, E11 . . . . . . .79 G6
Wanstead Rd, Brom.
  BR1 . . . . .191 J2

Wansunt Rd, Bex. DA5 . .177 J1
Wantage Rd, SE12 . . . . . .155 F5
Wantz Rd, Dag. RM10 . . .101 H4
WAPPING, E1 . . . . .29 J1
Wapping Dock St, E1
  off Cinnamon St .132/133 E1
Wapping High St, E1 . . . . .29 H2
Wapping La, E1 . . . . .113 E7
Wapping Wall, E1 . . . . . . .133 F1
Warbank La, Kings.T.
  KT2 . . . . .165 F7
Warbeck Rd, W12 . . . . . . .127 H1
Warberry Rd, N22 . . . . . . .75 F2
Warboys App, Kings.T.
  KT2 . . . . .164 B6
Warboys Cres, E4 . . . . . . .62 C5
Warboys Rd, Kings.T.
  KT2 . . . . .164 B6
Warburton Cl, N1
  off Culford Rd 94 B6
  Harrow HA3 . . . . .52 A6
Warburton Rd, E8 . . . . . . .95 E7
  Twickenham TW2 . . . . .161 H1
Warburton St, E8
  off Warburton Rd .112/113 E1
Warburton Ter, E17 . . . . . .78 B2
Wardalls Gro, SE14 . . . . .133 F7
Ward Cl, S.Croy. CR2 . . . .202 B5
Wardell Cl, NW7 . . . . .55 E7
Wardell Fld, NW9 . . . . .71 E1
Warden Av, Har. HA2 . . . . .85 F1
Warden Rd, NW5 . . . . .92 A6
Wardens Fld Cl, Orp.
  BR6 . . . . .207 H6
Wardens Gro, SE1 . . . . . . .27 J2
Wardle St, E9 . . . . .95 G5
Wardley St, SW18
  off Garratt La 148/149 E7
Wardo Av, SW6 . . . . .148 B1
Wardour Ms, W1 . . . . .17 G4
Wardour St, W1 . . . . .17 H5
Ward Rd, E15 . . . . .114 D1
  N19 . . . . .92 C3
Wardrobe Pl, EC4 . . . . . . .19 H5
Wardrobe Ter, EC4 . . . . . .19 H5
Wards Rd, Ilf. IG2 . . . . . . .81 G7
Wareham Cl, Houns.
  TW3 . . . . .143 H4
Waremead Rd, Ilf. IG2 . . . .80 D5
Warenford Way, Borwd.
  WD6 . . . . .38 A1
Ware Pt Dr, SE28 . . . . . . .137 G2
Warfield Rd, NW10 . . . . . .108 A3
  Feltham TW14 . . . . . . .141 H7
  Hampton TW12 . . . . . .179 H1
Warfield Yd, NW10
  off Warfield Rd 108 A3
Wargrave Av, N15 . . . . . . .76 C6
Wargrave Rd, Har. HA2 . . .85 J3
Warham Rd, N4 . . . . .75 G5
  Harrow HA3 . . . . .68 C2
  South Croydon CR2 . . .201 J5
Warham St, SE5 . . . . .35 H7
Waring Cl, Orp. BR6 . . . . .207 J6
Waring Dr, Orp. BR6 . . . . .207 J6
Waring Rd, Sid. DA14 . . . .176 C6
Waring St, SE27 . . . . .169 J4
Warkworth Gdns, Islw.
  TW7 . . . . .124 D7
Warkworth Rd, N17 . . . . . .60 A7
Warland Rd, SE18 . . . . . .137 G7
Warley Av, Dag. RM8 . . . . .83 F7
  Hayes UB4 . . . . .102 A5
Warley Cl, E10
  off Millicent Rd 95 J1
Warley Rd, N9 . . . . .61 F2
  Hayes UB4 . . . . .102 A6
  Ilford IG5 . . . . .80 D1
  Woodford Green IG8 . . .63 H7
Warley St, E2 . . . . .113 G3
Warlingham Rd, Th.Hth.
  CR7 . . . . .187 H4
Warlock Rd, W9 . . . . .108 D4
Warlters Cl, N7
  off Warlters Rd 92/93 E4
Warlters Rd, N7 . . . . .93 E4
Warltersville Rd, N19 . . . .74 E7
Warmington Cl, E5
  off Orient Way 95 G3
Warmington Rd, SE24 . . .151 J6
Warmington St, E13
  off Barking Rd 115 G4
Warminster Gdns, SE25 .188 D2
Warminster Rd, SE25 . . . .188 C2
Warminster Sq, SE25 . . . .188 D2
Warminster Way, Mitch.
  CR4 . . . . .186 B1
Warndon St, SE16 . . . . . .133 G4
Warneford Rd, Har. HA3 . .69 G3
Warneford St, E9 . . . . . . .113 E1

Warne Pl, Sid. DA15
  off Westerham Dr 158 B6
Warner Av, Sutt. SM3 . . .198 B2
Warner Cl, E15 . . . . .97 E5
NW9 . . . . .71 F7
Hampton TW12
  off Tangley Pk Rd 161 H5
Hayes UB3 . . . . .121 G7
Warner Ho, SE13
  off Conington Rd 154 B2
Warner Par, Hayes UB3 .121 G7
Warner Pl, E2 . . . . .13 J2
Warner Rd, E17 . . . . .77 H4
N8 . . . . .74 D4
SE5 . . . . .151 J1
Bromley BR1 . . . . .173 F7
Warners Cl, Wdf.Grn.
IG8 . . . . .63 G5
Warners La, Kings.T.
KT2 . . . . .163 G4
Warners Path, Wdf.Grn.
IG8 . . . . .63 G5
Warner St, EC1 . . . . .11 E6
Warner Ter, E14
  off Broomfield St 114 A5
Warner Yd, EC1 . . . . .10 E6
Warnford Ho, SW15
  off Tunworth Cres 147 F6
Warnford Ind Est, Hayes
UB3 . . . . .121 H2
Warnford Rd, Orp. BR6 . .207 J5
Warnham Ct Rd, Cars.
SM5 . . . . .199 J7
Warnham Rd, N12 . . . . . .57 H5
Warple Ms, W3
  off Warple Way . .126/127 J7
Warple Way, W3 . . . . . . .126 E1
Warren, The, E12 . . . . . . .98 B4
Hayes UB4 . . . . .102 A6
Hounslow TW5 . . . . . . .123 F7
Worcester Park KT4 . . .196 D4
Warren Av, E10 . . . . .96 C3
Bromley BR1 . . . . .172 E7
Orpington BR6 . . . . . . .207 J5
Richmond TW10 . . . . . .146 B4
South Croydon CR2 . . .203 G7
Warren Cl, N9 . . . . .45 G7
SE21 off Lairdale Cl . . .151 J7
Bexleyheath DA6 . . . . .159 G5
Hayes UB4 . . . . .102 C5
Wembley HA9 . . . . .87 G2
Warren Ct, Chig. IG7 . . . .65 G4
Warren Cres, N9 . . . . . . .44 C7
Warren Cutting, Kings.T.
KT2 . . . . .164 D7
Warrender Rd, N19 . . . . .92 C3
Warrender Way, Ruis.
HA4 . . . . .66 A7
Warren Dr, Grnf. UB6 . . .103 H4
Ruislip HA4 . . . . .66 D7
Warren Dr, The, E11 . . . . .79 J7
Warren Dr N, Surb. KT5 .196 B1
Warren Dr S, Surb. KT5 .196 C1
Warren Flds, Stan. HA7
  off Valencia Rd 53 F4
Warren Footpath, Twick.
TW1 . . . . .163 F1
Warren Gdns, E15
  off Ashton Rd 96 D5
Warren Gro, Borwd. WD6 .38 D4
Warren Hts, Loug. IG10
  off Warren Hill 47 J5
Warren Hill, Loug. IG10 . .47 J6
Warren Ho, E3
  off Bromley High St . .114 B3
Stanmore HA7 . . . . .52 C3
Warren Ms, W1 . . . . .9 F6
Warren Pk, Kings.T.
KT2 . . . . .164 C6
Warren Pk Rd, Sutt.
SM1 . . . . .199 G6
Warren Pl, E1
  off Pitsea St 113 G6
Warren Pond Rd, E4 . . . .63 F1
Warren Ri, N.Mal. KT3 . .182 D1
Warren Rd, E4 . . . . .62 C2
E10 . . . . .96 C3
E11 . . . . .97 J1
NW2 . . . . .89 F7
SW19 . . . . .167 H6
Bexleyheath DA6 . . . . .159 G5
Bromley BR2 . . . . .205 G2
Bushey (Bushey Hth.)
WD23 . . . . .51 J1
Croydon CR0 . . . . .202 B1
Ilford IG6 . . . . .81 G5
Kingston upon Thames
KT2 . . . . .164 C6
Orpington BR6 . . . . . . .207 J5

Warren Rd, Sid. DA14 . . .176 C3
Twickenham TW2 . . . . .143 J6
Warrens Shawe La, Edg.
HA8 . . . . .54 B1
Warren St, W1 . . . . .9 E6
Warren Ter, Rom. RM6 . . .82 D4
Warren Wk, SE7 . . . . . . .135 J6
Warren Way, NW7 . . . . . .56 B6
Warren Wd Cl, Brom.
BR2 . . . . .205 F2
Warriner Dr, N9 . . . . .60 D3
Warriner Gdns, SW11 . . .149 J1
Warrington Cres, W9 . . . . .6 C5
Warrington Gdns, W9 . . . .6 C5
Warrington Pl, E14
  off Yabsley St 134 C1
Warrington Rd, Croy.
CR0 . . . . .201 H3
Dagenham RM8 . . . . . .100 D2
Harrow HA1 . . . . .68 B5
Richmond TW10 . . . . . .145 G5
Warrington Sq, Dag.
RM8 . . . . .100 D2
Warrior Sq, E12 . . . . .98 D4
Warsaw Cl, Ruis. HA4
  off Glebe Av 84 B6
Warsdale Dr, NW9
  off Mardale Dr 70 D5
Warspite Rd, SE18 . . . . .136 B3
Warton Rd, E15 . . . . .96 C7
Warwall, E6 . . . . .116 E6
Warwick Av, W2 . . . . .6 C5
W9 . . . . .6 C6
Edgware HA8 . . . . .54 B3
Harrow HA2 . . . . .85 F4
Warwick Cl, Barn. EN4 . . .41 G5
Bexley DA5 . . . . .159 F7
Hampton TW12 . . . . . . .161 J7
Warwick Ct, SE15 . . . . . .152 D2
WC1 . . . . .18 D2
Surbiton KT6
  off Hook Rd 195 H2
Warwick Cres, W2 . . . . . .14 C1
Warwick Dene, W5 . . . . .125 H1
Warwick Dr, SW15 . . . . .147 H3
Warwick Est, W2 . . . . . . .14 B2
Warwick Gdns, N4 . . . . . .75 J5
W14 . . . . .128 C3
Ilford IG1 . . . . .99 E1
Thames Ditton KT7 . . . .180 C5
Warwick Gro, E5 . . . . .94 E1
Surbiton KT5 . . . . .181 J7
Warwick Ho St, SW1 . . . .25 J1
Warwick La, EC4 . . . . .19 H4
Warwick Pas, EC4 . . . . . .19 H3
Warwick Pl, W5
  off Warwick Rd 125 G2
W9 . . . . .14 C1
Warwick Pl N, SW1 . . . . .33 F2
Warwick Rd, E4 . . . . .62 A5
E11 . . . . .79 H5
E12 . . . . .98 B5
E15 . . . . .97 F6
E17 . . . . .77 J1
N11 . . . . .58 D6
N18 . . . . .60 B4
SE20 . . . . .189 E3
SW5 . . . . .128 C4
W5 . . . . .125 G2
W14 . . . . .128 C4
Barnet EN5 . . . . .40 E4
Borehamwood WD6 . . . .38 D3
Hounslow TW4 . . . . . . .142 B3
Kingston upon Thames
KT1 . . . . .181 F1
New Malden KT3 . . . . . .182 C3
Sidcup DA14 . . . . .176 B5
Southall UB2 . . . . .123 F3
Sutton SM1 . . . . .199 F4
Thames Ditton KT7 . . . .180 C5
Thornton Heath CR7 . . .187 G3
Twickenham TW2 . . . . .162 B1
Welling DA16 . . . . .158 C3
West Drayton UB7 . . . .120 B2
Warwick Row, SW1 . . . . .25 E5
Warwickshire Path, SE8 . .133 J7
Warwick Sq, EC4 . . . . . . .19 H3
SW1 . . . . .33 F3
Warwick Sq Ms, SW1 . . . .33 F2
Warwick St, W1 . . . . .17 G5
Warwick Ter, SE18 . . . . .137 G6
Warwick Way, SW1 . . . . . .33 F2
Warwick Yd, EC1 . . . . . . .12 A6
Washington Av, E12 . . . . .98 B4
Washington Rd, E6
  off St. Stephens Rd . . .97 J7
E18 . . . . .79 F2
SW13 . . . . .127 G7
Kingston upon Thames
KT1 . . . . .182 A2

Washington Rd, Wor. Pk.
KT4 . . . . .197 H2
Wastdale Rd, SE23 . . . . .171 G1
Watchfield Ct, W4 . . . . . .126 C5
Watcombe Cotts, Rich.
TW9 . . . . .126 A6
Watcombe Pl, SE25
  off Albert Rd 188/189 E5
Watcombe Rd, SE25 . . . .188 E5
Waterbank Rd, SE6 . . . . .172 B3
Waterbeach Rd, Dag.
RM9 . . . . .100 C6
Waterbrook La, NW4 . . . .71 J5
Watercress Pl, N1
  off Hertford Rd 94 B7
Waterdale Rd, SE2 . . . . .138 A6
Waterden Rd, E15 . . . . . .96 A5
Waterer Ri, Wall. SM6 . . .200 D6
Waterfall Cl, N14 . . . . . . .58 C3
Waterfall Cotts, SW19 . . .167 G6
Waterfall Rd, N11 . . . . . . .58 B4
N14 . . . . .58 C3
SW19 . . . . .167 G6
Waterfall Ter, SW17 . . . . .167 H6
Waterfield Cl, SE28 . . . . .138 B1
Belvedere DA17 . . . . . .139 G3
Waterfield Gdns, SE25 . .188 B5
Waterford Rd, SW6 . . . . .149 E1
Water Gdns, Stan. HA7 . . .53 E6
Water Gdns, The, W2 . . . .15 H3
Watergardens, The, Kings.T.
KT2 . . . . .164 C6
Watergate, EC4 . . . . .19 G5
Watergate, The, Wat.
WD19 . . . . .50 D2
Watergate St, SE8 . . . . . .134 A6
Watergate Wk, WC2 . . . . .26 B1
Waterhall Av, E4 . . . . .62 E4
Waterhall Cl, E17 . . . . . . .77 G1
Waterhouse Cl, E16 . . . . .116 A5
NW3 off Lyndhurst Rd . .91 G5
W6 off Great Ch La 128 A4
Waterhouse Sq, EC1 . . . .19 E2
Wateridge Cl, E14
  off Westferry Rd 134 A3
Water La, E15 . . . . .97 E6
EC3 . . . . .20 D6
N9 . . . . .60 E1
NW1
  off Kentish Town Rd . . .92 B7
SE14 . . . . .133 F7
Ilford IG3 . . . . .99 H3
Kingston upon Thames
KT1 . . . . .181 G1
Richmond TW9 . . . . . . .145 G5
Sidcup DA14 . . . . .177 F2
Twickenham TW1
  off The Embankment .162 D1
Water Lily Cl, Sthl. UB2
  off Navigator Dr 123 J2
Waterloo Br, SE1 . . . . . . .18 C6
WC2 . . . . .18 C6
Waterloo Cl, E9
  off Churchill Wk 95 F5
Waterloo Est, E2 . . . . . . .113 F2
Waterloo Gdns, E2 . . . . .113 F2
N1 off Barnsbury St 93 H7
Waterloo Pas, NW6 . . . . .90 C7
Waterloo Pl, SW1 . . . . . . .25 H1
Richmond TW9
  off Sheen Rd 145 H5
Richmond (Kew) TW9 . .126 A6
Waterloo Rd, E6 . . . . .97 J7
E7 off Wellington Rd . . .97 F5
E10 . . . . .78 A7
NW2 . . . . .89 G1
SE1 . . . . .27 E3
Ilford IG6 . . . . .81 F2
Sutton SM1 . . . . .199 G5
Waterloo Ter, N1 . . . . . . .93 H7
Waterlow Ct, NW11
  off Heath Cl 72/73 E7
Waterlow Rd, N19 . . . . . .92 C1
★ Watermans Art Cen, Brent.
TW8 . . . . .125 H6
Waterman's Cl, Kings.T. KT2
  off Woodside Rd 163 H7
Waterman St, SW15 . . . . .148 A3
Watermans Wk, SE16 . . .133 H3
Waterman Way, E1 . . . . .132 E1
Watermead La, Cars. SM5
  off Middleton Rd 185 J7
Watermeadow La, SW6 . .149 F2
Watermead Rd, SE6 . . . .172 C4
Watermead Twr, SW6 . . .149 F1
Watermead Way, N17 . . . .76 E3
Watermen's Sq, SE20 . . .171 F7
Water Ms, SE15 . . . . . . .153 F4
Watermill Cl, Rich.
TW10 . . . . .163 F3

Watermill La, N18 . . . . . . .60 B5
Watermill Way, SW19 . . .185 F1
Feltham TW13 . . . . .161 F2
Watermint Quay, N16 . . . .76 D7
Water Rd, Wem. HA0 . . . .105 J1
Watersedge, Epsom
KT19 . . . . .196 C4
Watersfield Way, Edg.
HA8 . . . . .53 G7
Waters Gdns, Dag.
RM10 . . . . .101 G5
Waterside, Beck. BR3
  off Rectory Rd 190 A1
Waterside Cl, E3 . . . . . . .113 J1
SE16 . . . . .29 J4
Barking IG11 . . . . .100 A4
Northolt UB5 . . . . .103 F3
Surbiton KT6
  off Culsac Rd 195 H2
Waterside Ct, SE13
  off Weardale Rd 154 D4
Waterside Dr, Walt.
KT12 . . . . .178 A5
Waterside Pl, NW1
  off Princess Rd 110 A1
Waterside Pt, SW11 . . . . .31 H7
Waterside Rd, Sthl.
UB2 . . . . .123 G3
Waterside Trd Cen, W7 . .124 B3
Waterside Way, SW17 . . .167 F4
Watersmeet Way, SE28 . .118 C6
Waterson St, E2 . . . . .13 E3
Waters Pl, SW15
  off Danemere St 147 J2
Watersplash Cl, Kings.T.
KT1 . . . . .181 H3
Watersplash La, Hayes
UB3 . . . . .122 A4
Hounslow TW5 . . . . . . .122 B5
Waters Rd, SE6 . . . . .172 E3
Kingston upon Thames
KT1 . . . . .182 B3
Waters Sq, Kings.T. KT1 .182 B3
Water St, WC2 . . . . .18 D5
Water Twr Hill, Croy.
CR0 . . . . .202 A4
Water Twr Pl, N1
  off Old Royal Free Sq .111 G1
Waterview Ho, E14 . . . . .113 H5
Waterworks La, E5 . . . . . .95 G2
Waterworks Rd, SW2 . . . .151 F6
Waterworks Yd, Croy. CR0
  off Surrey St 201 J3
Watery La, SW20 . . . . . .184 C2
Northolt UB5 . . . . .102 C2
Sidcup DA14 . . . . .176 B6
Wates Way, Mitch. CR4 . .185 J6
Wates Way Ind Est, Mitch.
CR4 off Wates Way 185 J6
Wateville Rd, N17 . . . . . . .75 J1
Watford Cl, SW11
  off Petworth St 149 H1
WATFORD HEATH, Wat. . .50 E1
Watford Rd, E16 . . . . . . .115 G5
Harrow HA1 . . . . .86 D2
Wembley HA0 . . . . .86 D2
Watford Way, NW4 . . . . . .71 G4
NW7 . . . . .71 G4
Watkin Rd, Wem. HA9 . . . .88 B3
Watkinson Rd, N7 . . . . . . .93 F6
Watling Av, Edg. HA8 . . . .54 D7
Watling Ct, EC4 . . . . .20 A4
Watling Fm Cl, Stan. HA7 .53 F1
Watling Gdns, NW2 . . . . .90 B6
Watlings Cl, Croy. CR0 . .189 H6
Watling St, EC4 . . . . .19 J4
SE15 . . . . .36 E6
Bexleyheath DA6 . . . . .159 H4
Watlington Gro, SE26 . . .171 H5
Watney Mkt, E1
  off Commercial
  Rd 112/113 E6
Watney Rd, SW14 . . . . . .146 C3
Watneys Rd, Mitch. CR4 .186 D5
Watney St, E1 . . . . .113 E6
Watson Av, E6 . . . . .98 D7
Sutton SM3 . . . . .198 B2
Watson Cl, N16
  off Matthias Rd 94 A5
SW19 . . . . .167 H6
Watson's Ms, W1 . . . . . . .15 H2
Watsons Rd, N22 . . . . . . .75 F1
Watson's St, SE8 . . . . . . .134 A7
Watson St, E13 . . . . .115 H2
Watsons Yd, NW2
  off North Circular Rd . .89 F2
Wattisfield Rd, E5 . . . . . . .95 F3
Watts Cl, N15
  off Seaford Rd 76 B5
Watts Gro, E3 . . . . .114 B5

Watts La, Chis. BR7 . . . . .**193** E1
  Teddington TW11 . . . . .**162** D5
Watts Pt, E13
  off Brooks Rd **115** G1
Watts Rd, T.Ditt. KT7 . . . .**180** D7
Watts St, E1 . . . .**133** E1
  SE15 . . . .**152** C1
Watts Way, SW7 . . . .**23** F5
Wat Tyler Rd, SE3 . . . . . .**154** C2
  SE10 . . . .**154** C2
Wauthier Cl, N13 . . . .**59** H5
Wavell Dr, Sid. DA15 . . . .**157** H6
Wavel Ms, N8 . . . .**74** D4
  NW6 off Acol Rd **90/91** E7
Wavel Pl, SE26
  off Sydenham Hill . . .**170** C4
Wavendon Av, W4 . . . . . .**126** D5
Waveney Av, SE15 . . . . . .**153** E4
Waveney Cl, E1 . . . .**29** J1
Waverley Av, E4 . . . .**61** J4
  E17 . . . .**78** D3
  Surbiton KT5 . . . .**182** B6
  Sutton SM1 . . . .**199** E2
  Twickenham TW2 . . . . .**161** F1
  Wembley HA9 . . . .**87** J5
Waverley Cl, E18 . . . .**79** J1
  Bromley BR2 . . . .**192** A5
  Hayes UB3 . . . .**121** G4
  West Molesey KT8 . . . .**179** G5
Waverley Cres, SE18 . . . .**137** G5
Waverley Gdns, E6
  off Oliver Gdns **116** B5
  NW10 . . . .**105** J3
  Barking IG11 . . . .**117** H2
  Ilford IG6 . . . .**81** F2
  Northwood HA6 . . . .**66** A1
Waverley Gro, N3 . . . .**72** B3
Waverley Ind Est, Har.
  HA1 . . . .**68** A3
Waverley Pl, N4
  off Adolphus Rd **93** H2
  NW8 . . . .**6** E1
Waverley Rd, E17 . . . .**78** C3
  E18 . . . .**79** J1
  N8 . . . .**74** D6
  N17 . . . .**60** E7
  SE18 . . . .**137** F5
  SE25 . . . .**188** E4
  Enfield EN2 . . . .**43** H4
  Epsom KT17 . . . .**197** H5
  Harrow HA2 . . . .**85** F1
  Southall UB1 . . . .**103** G7
Waverley Vil, N17 . . . .**76** C2
Waverley Wk, W2 . . . .**108** D5
Waverley Way, Cars.
  SM5 . . . .**199** H6
Waverton Ho, E3 . . . .**113** J1
Waverton Rd, SW18 . . . .**149** F7
Waverton St, W1 . . . .**24** C1
Wavertree Ct, SW2
  off Streatham Hill **169** F1
Wavertree Rd, E18 . . . . . .**79** G2
  SW2 . . . .**169** E1
Waxlow Cres, Sthl. UB1 . .**103** G6
Waxlow Rd, NW10 . . . . . .**106** C2
Waxwell Cl, Pnr. HA5 . . . .**66** D2
Waxwell La, Pnr. HA5 . . . .**66** D2
Waxwell Ter, SE1 . . . .**26** D4
Waye Av, Houns. TW5 . . .**142** A1
Wayfarer Rd, Nthlt. UB5 .**102** D4
Wayfield Link, E9 . . . .**157** G6
Wayford St, SW11 . . . . . .**149** H2
Wayland Av, E8 . . . .**94** D5
Waylands Mead, Beck.
  BR3 . . . .**190** B1
Wayleave, The, SE28 . . . .**118** B7
Waylett Pl, SE27 . . . .**169** H3
  Wembley HA0 . . . .**87** G4
Wayman Ct, E8 . . . .**94** E6
Wayne Cl, Orp. BR6 . . . . .**207** J3
Waynflete Av, Croy.
  CRO **201** H3
Waynflete Sq, W10 . . . . .**108** A7
Waynflete St, SW18 . . . .**167** F2
Wayside, NW11 . . . .**90** B1
  SW14 . . . .**146** C5
  Croydon CRO
  off Field Way **204** B6
Wayside Cl, N14 . . . .**42** C6
Wayside Commercial Est, Bark.
  IG11 . . . .**118** A1
Wayside Ct, Twick. TW1 .**145** F6
  Wembley HA9
  off Oakington Av **88** A3
Wayside Gdns, SE9 . . . . .**174** C4
  Dagenham RM10 . . . . .**101** G5
Wayside Gro, SE9 . . . . . .**174** C4
Wayside Ms, Ilf. IG2
  off Gaysham Av **80** D5

Weald, The, Chis. BR7 . . .**174** C6
Weald Cl, SE16
  off Stevenson
  Cres **132/133** E5
  Bromley BR2 . . . .**206** B2
Weald La, Har. HA3 . . . . . .**68** A2
Weald Ri, Har. HA3 . . . . . .**52** C7
Weald Sq, E5
  off Rossington St .**94/95** E2
WEALDSTONE, Har. **68** C3
Wealdstone Rd, Sutt.
  SM3 . . . .**198** C2
Weald Way, Rom. RM7 . . .**83** H6
Wealdwood Gdns, Pnr. HA5
  off Highbanks Rd **51** H6
Weale Rd, E4 . . . .**62** D3
Weardale Gdns, Enf. EN2 .**44** A1
Weardale Rd, SE13 . . . . .**154** D4
Wear Pl, E2 . . . .**112** E3
Wearside Rd, SE13 . . . . .**154** B4
Weatherley Cl, E3 . . . . . .**113** J5
Weaver Cl, E6
  off Trader Rd **116/117** E7
  Croydon CRO **202** C4
Weavers Cl, Islw. TW7 . .**144** B4
Weavers Ter, SW6 . . . . . .**128** D6
Weaver St, E1 . . . .**13** H6
Weavers Way, NW1 . . . . .**110** D1
Webb Cl, SW26 . . . .**169** H4
Webb Cl, W10 . . . .**107** J4
Webber Row, SE1 . . . .**27** F5
Webber St, SE1 . . . .**27** F3
Webb Est, E5 . . . .**76** D7
Webb Gdns, E13
  off Kelland Rd **115** G4
Webb Pl, NW10
  off Old Oak La **107** F3
Webb Rd, SE3 . . . .**135** F6
Webbscroft Rd, Dag.
  RM10 . . . .**101** H4
Webbs Rd, SW11 . . . .**149** J5
  Hayes UB4 . . . .**102** B3
Webb St, SE1 . . . .**28** D6
Wedderburn Rd, NW3 . . . .**91** G5
  Barking IG11 . . . .**117** G1
Wedgewood Wk, NW6
  off Lymington Rd . .**90/91** E5
Wedgwood Ms, W1 . . . . . .**17** J4
Wedgwood Way, SE19 . .**169** J7
Wedlake St, W10
  off Kensal Rd **108** B4
Wedmore Av, Ilf. IG5 . . . .**80** D1
Wedmore Gdns, N19 . . . .**92** D2
Wedmore Ms, N19
  off Wedmore St **92** D3
Wedmore Rd, Grnf. UB6 .**104** A3
Wedmore St, N19 . . . .**92** D3
Weech Rd, NW6 . . . .**90** D4
Weedington Rd, NW5 . . . .**92** A5
Weekley Sq, SW11
  off Thomas Baines
  Rd **149** G3
Weigall Rd, SE12 . . . .**155** G4
Weighhouse St, W1 . . . . .**16** C4
Weighton Rd, SE20 . . . . .**188** E2
  Harrow HA3 . . . .**68** A1
Weihurst Gdns, Sutt.
  SM1 . . . .**199** G5
Weimar St, SW15 . . . . . .**148** A3
Weir Av, E12 . . . .**150** C7
Weir Hall Av, N18 . . . .**60** A6
Weir Hall Gdns, N18 . . . . .**60** A5
Weir Hall Rd, N17 . . . .**60** A5
  N18 . . . .**60** A5
Weir Rd, SW12 . . . .**150** C7
  SW19 . . . .**167** E3
  Bexley DA5 . . . .**159** H7
  Walton-on-Thames
  KT12 . . . .**178** A6
Weirside Gdns, West Dr.
  UB7 . . . .**120** A1
Weir's Pas, NW1 . . . .**9** J3
Weiss Rd, SW15 . . . .**148** A3
Welbeck Av, Brom. BR1 . .**173** G4
  Hayes UB4 . . . .**102** B4
  Sidcup DA15 . . . .**176** A1
Welbeck Cl, N12
  off Torrington Pk **57** G5
  Borehamwood WD6 . . .**38** A3
  Epsom KT17 . . . .**197** G7
  New Malden KT3 . . . . .**183** F5
Welbeck Rd, E6 . . . .**116** A3
  Barnet EN4 . . . .**41** G6
  Carshalton SM5 . . . . .**199** H1
  Harrow HA2 . . . .**85** H1
  Sutton SM1 . . . .**199** G2

Welbeck St, W1 . . . .**16** D3
  Staines TW19
  off Welbeck Rd **199** H1
Welbeck Wk, Cars. SM5
  off Welbeck Rd **199** H1
Welbeck Way, W1 . . . .**16** D3
Welby St, SE5 . . . .**151** H1
Welch Pl, Pnr. HA5 . . . . . .**66** C1
Weldon Cl, Ruis. HA4 . . . .**84** B6
Weldon Dr, W.Mol. KT8 . .**179** F4
Weld Pl, N11 . . . .**58** B5
Welfare Rd, E15 . . . .**97** E7
Welford Cl, E5
  off Denton Way **95** G3
Welford Pl, SW19 . . . . . .**166** B4
Welham Rd, SW16 . . . . . .**168** A5
  SW17 . . . .**168** A5
Welhouse Rd, Cars.
  SM5 . . . .**199** H1
Wellacre Rd, Har. HA3 . . . .**69** E6
Welland Cl, Sid. DA15 . . .**158** B5
Welland Gdns, Grnf.
  UB6 . . . .**104** C2
Welland Ms, E1 . . . .**29** J1
Wellands Cl, Brom. BR1 .**192** C2
Welland St, SE10 . . . . . .**134** C6
Well App, Barn. EN5 . . . . .**39** J5
Wellbrook Rd, Orp.
  BR6 . . . .**206** D4
Well Cl, SW16 . . . .**169** F4
  Ruislip HA4
  off Parkfield Cres . .**84/85** E3
Wellclose Sq, E1 . . . .**21** J5
Wellclose St, E1 . . . .**21** J6
Well Cottage Cl, E11 . . . . .**79** J7
Well Ct, EC4 . . . .**20** A4
  SW16 . . . .**169** F4
Welldon Cres, Har. HA1 . .**68** B6
Weller's Ct, NW1 . . . .**10** A2
Weller St, SE1 . . . .**27** J3
Wellesley Av, W6 . . . .**127** H3
Wellesley Ct, W9 . . . .**6** C3
Wellesley Ct Rd, Croy.
  CRO **202** A2
Wellesley Cres, Twick.
  TW2 . . . .**162** B2
Wellesley Gro, Croy.
  CRO **202** A2
Wellesley Pk Ms, Enf.
  EN2 . . . .**43** H2
Wellesley Pas, Croy. CRO
  off Wellesley Rd **201** J2
Wellesley Pl, NW1 . . . .**9** H4
Wellesley Rd, E11 . . . .**79** G5
  E17 . . . .**78** A6
  N22 . . . .**75** G2
  NW5 . . . .**92** A5
  W4 . . . .**126** A5
  Croydon CRO **201** J1
  Harrow HA1 . . . .**68** B5
  Ilford IG1 . . . .**98** E2
  Sutton SM2 . . . .**199** F6
  Twickenham TW2 . . . .**162** A3
Wellesley St, E1 . . . .**113** G5
Wellesley Ter, N1 . . . .**12** A3
Wellfield Av, N10 . . . .**74** B3
Wellfield Rd, SW16 . . . . .**169** E4
Wellfields, Loug. IG10 . . . .**48** D3
Wellfield Wk, SW16 . . . . .**169** F5
Wellfit St, SE24
  off Hinton Rd **151** H3
Wellgarth, Grnf. UB6 . . . . .**86** E6
Wellgarth Rd, NW11 . . . . .**91** E1
Well Gro, N20 . . . .**41** F7
Well Hall Par, SE9
  off Well Hall Rd **156** C4
Well Hall Rd, SE9 . . . .**156** C3
Wellhouse La, Barn.
  EN5 . . . .**39** J4
Wellhouse Rd, Beck.
  BR3 . . . .**189** J4
WELLING **158** A3
Welling High St, Well.
  DA16 . . . .**158** A3
Wellings Ho, Hayes
  UB3 . . . .**122** B1
★ Wellington Arch, W1 . .**24** C3
Wellington Av, E4 . . . .**62** A2
  N9 . . . .**61** E3
  N15 . . . .**76** C6
  Hounslow TW3 . . . .**143** G5
  Pinner HA5 . . . .**67** F1
  Sidcup DA15 . . . .**158** A6
  Worcester Park KT4 . . .**197** J4
Wellington Bldgs, SW1 . .**32** C4
Wellington Cl, SE14
  off Rutts Ter **153** G1
  W11 off Ledbury Rd . .**108** D6
  Dagenham RM10 . . . . .**101** J7
  Watford WD19
  off Highfield **51** F3

Wellington Ct, NW8 . . . . . .**7** E2
  Staines TW19
  off Clare Rd **140** B7
Wellington Cres, N.Mal.
  KT3 . . . .**182** C3
Wellington Dr, Dag.
  RM10 . . . .**101** J7
Wellington Gdns, SE7 . . .**135** J6
  Twickenham TW2 . . . .**162** A4
Wellington Gro, SE10
  off Crooms Hill **134** D7
Wellington Ms, SE7 . . . . .**135** J6
  SE22 off Peckham Rye .**152** D4
  SW16
  off Woodbourne Av . . .**168** D3
Wellington Pk Est, NW2 . .**89** G2
Wellington Pas, E11
  off Wellington Rd **79** G5
Wellington Pl, N2
  off Great N Rd **73** H5
  NW8 . . . .**7** F3
Wellington Rd, E6 . . . . . .**116** C2
  E7 . . . .**97** F4
  E10 . . . .**95** H1
  E11 . . . .**79** G5
  E17 . . . .**77** H3
  NW8 . . . .**7** E1
  NW10 . . . .**108** A3
  SW19 . . . .**166** D2
  W5 . . . .**125** F3
  Belvedere DA17 . . . . .**139** F5
  Bexley DA5 . . . .**158** D5
  Bromley BR2 . . . .**191** J4
  Croydon CRO **187** H7
  Enfield EN1 . . . .**44** B4
  Feltham TW14 . . . .**141** H5
  Hampton TW12 . . . . . .**162** A5
  Harrow HA3 . . . .**68** B3
  Pinner HA5 . . . .**67** F1
  Twickenham TW2 . . . .**162** A5
Wellington Rd N, Houns.
  TW4 . . . .**143** F3
Wellington Rd S, Houns.
  TW4 . . . .**143** F4
Wellington Row, E2 . . . . .**13** G3
Wellington Sq, SW3 . . . . .**31** J3
Wellington St, SE18 . . . .**136** D4
  WC2 . . . .**18** B5
  Barking IG11
  off Axe St **117** F1
Wellington Ter, E1 . . . . . .**132** E1
  W2 off Notting Hill
  Gate **108/109** E7
  Harrow HA1
  off West St **86** A1
Wellington Way, E3 . . . . .**114** A3
Welling Way, SE9 . . . .**157** G3
  Welling DA16 . . . .**157** G3
Well La, SW14 . . . .**146** C5
Wellmeadow Rd, SE6 . . .**155** E7
  SE13 . . . .**154** E6
  W7 . . . .**124** D4
Wellow Wk, Cars.
  SM5 . . . .**199** G1
Well Pas, NW3 . . . .**91** G3
Well Rd, NW3 . . . .**91** G3
  Barnet EN5 . . . .**39** J5
Wells, The, N14 . . . .**42** D7
Wells Cl, Nthlt. UB5
  off Yeading La **102** C3
  South Croydon CR2 . .**202** B5
Wells Dr, NW9 . . . .**88** D1
Wells Gdns, Dag. RM10 . .**101** H5
  Ilford IG1 . . . .**80** B7
Wells Ho Rd, NW10 . . . . .**106** C5
Wellside Cl, Barn. EN5 . . .**39** J4
Wellside Gdns, SW14
  off Well La **146** C5
Wells Ms, W1 . . . .**17** G2
Wellsmoor Gdns, Brom.
  BR1 . . . .**192** D3
Wells Pk Rd, SE26 . . . . . .**170** D3
Wells Ri, NW8 . . . .**109** J1
Wells Rd, W12 . . . .**127** J2
  Bromley BR1 . . . .**192** C2
Wells Sq, WC1 . . . .**10** C4
Wells St, W1 . . . .**17** F2
Wellstead Av, N9 . . . .**45** F7
Wellstead Rd, E6 . . . .**116** D2
Wells Ter, N4 . . . .**93** G2
Well St, E9 . . . .**95** E7
  E15 . . . .**96** E6
Wells Way, SE5 . . . .**36** C5
  SW7 . . . .**22** E5
Wells Yd S, N7
  off George's Rd **93** G5
Well Wk, NW3 . . . .**91** G3
Wellwood Rd, Ilf. IG3 . . . .**100** A1
Welsford St, SE1 . . . .**37** H3
Welsh Cl, E13 . . . .**115** G3

Welshpool Ho, E8
  off Benjamin Cl 112 D1
Welshpool St, E8
  off Broadway
  Mkt 112/113 E1
Welshside Wk, NW9
  off Fryent Gro 70/71 E6
Welstead Way, W4 . . . . .127 F4
Weltje Rd, W6 . . . . . . .127 G5
Welton Rd, SE18 . . . . . .137 H7
Welwyn Av, Felt. TW14 .141 J6
Welwyn St, E2
  off Globe Rd 113 F3
WEMBLEY 87 H5
Wembley Commercial Cen,
  Wem. HA9 . . . . .87 G2
★ Wembley Conf Cen, Wem.
  HA9 . . . . .87 J4
Wembley Hill Rd, Wem.
  HA9 . . . . .87 J5
WEMBLEY PARK,
  Wem. 87 J2
Wembley Pk Business Cen,
  Wem. HA9 . . . . .88 B3
Wembley Pk Dr, Wem.
  HA9 . . . . .87 J3
Wembley Pt, Wem. HA9 . .88 B7
Wembley Rd, Hmptn.
  TW12 . . . . .161 G7
★ Wembley Stadium
  (under redevelopment),
  Wem. HA9 . . . . .88 A4
Wembley Way, Wem.
  HA9 . . . . .88 B6
Wemborough Rd, Stan.
  HA7 . . . . .53 F7
Wembury Ms, N6
  off Wembury Rd 74 B7
Wembury Rd, N6 . . . . . . .74 B7
Wendela Ct, Har. HA1 . . .86 B3
Wendell Rd, W12 . . . . . .127 F2
Wendle Ct, SW8 . . . . .34 A6
Wendling Rd, Sutt. SM1 .199 G1
Wendon St, E3 . . . . .113 J1
Wendover, SE17 . . . . .36 D4
Wendover Cl, Hayes UB4
  off Kingsash Dr . .102/103 E5
Wendover Dr, N.Mal.
  KT3 . . . . .183 F6
Wendover Rd, NW10 . . . .107 F2
  SE9 . . . . .156 A3
  Bromley BR2 . . . . .191 H3
Wendover Way, Well.
  DA16 . . . . .158 A5
Wendy Cl, Enf. EN1 . . . . .44 C6
Wendy Way, Wem. HA0 . .105 H1
Wenlock Ct, N1 . . . . .12 C2
Wenlock Gdns, NW4
  off Rickard Cl 71 G4
Wenlock Rd, N1 . . . . .11 J2
  Edgware HA8 . . . . .54 B7
Wenlock St, N1 . . . . .12 A2
Wennington Rd, E3 . . . . .113 G2
Wensley Av, Wdf.Grn.
  IG8 . . . . .63 F7
Wensley Cl, N11
  off Pickering Gdns 58 A6
  SE9 . . . . .156 C6
Wensleydale Av, Ilf. IG5 . .80 B2
Wensleydale Gdns, Hmptn.
  TW12 . . . . .161 H7
Wensleydale Pas, Hmptn.
  TW12 . . . . .179 G1
Wensleydale Rd, Hmptn.
  TW12 . . . . .161 G6
Wensley Rd, N18 . . . . . . .60 E6
Wentland Cl, SE6 . . . . . .172 D2
Wentland Rd, SE6 . . . . . .172 D2
Wentworth Av, N3 . . . . . .56 D7
Wentworth Cl, N3 . . . . . .56 E7
  SE28 . . . . .118 D6
  Bromley BR2
  off Hillside La 205 G2
  Morden SM4 . . . . .184 D7
  Orpington BR6 . . . . . . .207 H5
  Surbiton KT6 . . . . .195 G2
Wentworth Ct, Surb. KT6
  off Culsac Rd 195 H2
Wentworth Cres, SE15 . .132 D7
  Hayes UB3 . . . . .121 G3
Wentworth Dr, Pnr. HA5 . .66 A5
Wentworth Gdns, N13 . . .59 H4
Wentworth Hill, Wem.
  HA9 . . . . .87 J1
Wentworth Ms, E3
  off Eric St 113 J4
Wentworth Pk, N3 . . . . . .56 D7
Wentworth Pl, Stan. HA7
  off Greenacres Dr .52/53 E6

Wentworth Rd, E12 . . . . . .98 A4
  NW11 . . . . .72 C6
  Barnet EN5 . . . . .40 A3
  Croydon CR0 . . . . .187 G7
  Southall UB2 . . . . .122 C4
Wentworth St, E1 . . . . . . .21 F3
Wentworth Way, Pnr.
  HA5 . . . . .66 D4
Wenvoe Av, Bexh. DA7 . .159 H2
Wernbrook St, SE18 . . . .137 F6
Werndee Rd, SE25 . . . . .188 D4
Werneth Hall Rd, Ilf. IG5 . .80 C3
Werrington St, NW1 . . . . . .9 G2
Werter Rd, SW15 . . . . . .148 B4
Wesleyan Pl, NW5
  off Gordon Ho Rd 92 B4
Wesley Av, E16 . . . . .135 G1
  NW10 . . . . .106 D3
  Hounslow TW3 . . . . . . .143 E2
Wesley Cl, N7 . . . . .93 F2
  SE17 . . . . .35 H2
  Harrow HA2 . . . . .85 J2
Wesley Rd, E10 . . . . .78 C7
  NW10 . . . . .106 C1
  Hayes UB3 . . . . .102 A7
★ Wesley's Ho, EC1 . . . . .12 C5
Wesley Sq, W11
  off Bartle Rd 108 B6
Wesley St, W1 . . . . .16 C2
Wessex Av, SW19 . . . . . .184 D2
Wessex Cl, Ilf. IG3 . . . . . .81 H6
  Kingston upon Thames KT1
  off Gloucester Rd . . .182 B1
  Thames Ditton KT7 . . .194 C2
Wessex Dr, Pnr. HA5 . . . .51 E7
Wessex Gdns, NW11 . . . . .90 B1
Wessex La, Grnf. UB6 . . .104 A2
Wessex Rd, Houns.
  (Hthrw.Air.)TW6 . . . . .140 A2
Wessex St, E2 . . . . .113 F3
Wessex Way, NW11 . . . . .90 B1
West 12 Shop Cen, W12
  off Shepherds Bush
  Grn 128 A2
Westacott Cl, N19 . . . . . .92 D1
WEST ACTON, W3 . . . . . .106 A6
Westall Rd, Loug. IG10 . . .49 E3
West App, Orp. BR5 . . . .193 F5
West Arbour St, E1 . . . . .113 G6
West Av, E17 . . . . .78 B4
  N3 . . . . .56 D6
  NW4 . . . . .72 A5
  Pinner HA5 . . . . .67 F6
  Southall UB1 . . . . .103 F7
  Wallington SM6 . . . . . .201 E5
West Av Rd, E17 . . . . .78 A4
West 8k, N16 . . . . .76 B7
  Barking IG11 off Highbridge
  Rd 116/117 E1
  Enfield EN2 . . . . .43 J2
Westbank Rd, Hmptn.
  (Hmptn.H.)TW12 . . . . .161 J6
WEST BARNES, N.Mal. . .183 G5
West Barnes La, SW20 . .183 H3
  New Malden KT3 . . . . . .183 H3
Westbeech Rd, N22 . . . . .75 G3
Westbere Dr, Stan. HA7 . .53 G4
Westbere Rd, NW2 . . . . . .90 B4
Westbourne Av, W3 . . . . .106 D6
  Sutton SM3 . . . . .198 B2
Westbourne Br, W2 . . . . . .14 C2
Westbourne Cl, Hayes
  UB4 . . . . .102 B4
Westbourne Cres, W2 . . . .14 E5
Westbourne Cres Ms, W2 .14 E5
Westbourne Dr, SE23 . . .171 G2
Westbourne Gdns, W2 . . . .14 A3
WESTBOURNE GREEN,
  W2 . . . . .108 D5
Westbourne Gro, W2 . . . .108 D6
  W11 . . . . .108 C7
Westbourne Gro Ms, W11
  off Westbourne Gro . .108 D6
Westbourne Gro Ter, W2 . .14 A3
Westbourne Pk Ms, W2 . . .14 A3
Westbourne Pk Pas, W2
  off Westbourne Pk Vil .108 D5
  W11 . . . . .108 D5
Westbourne Pk Rd, W2 . .108 D5
  W11 . . . . .108 B6
Westbourne Pk Vil, W2 . .108 D5
Westbourne Pl, N9
  off Eastbournia Av .60/61 E3
Westbourne Rd, N7 . . . . . .93 F6
  SE26 . . . . .171 G6
  Bexleyheath DA7 . . . . .138 E7
  Croydon CR0 . . . . .188 C6
Westbourne St, W2 . . . . . .15 E5
Westbourne Ter, SE23
  off Westbourne Dr . . .171 G2
  W2 . . . . .14 D3

Westbourne Ter Ms, W2 . .14 C3
Westbourne Ter Rd, W2 . .14 C2
Westbridge Rd, SW11 . . .149 G1
WEST BROMPTON,
  SW10 . . . . .30 A5
Westbrook Av, Hmptn.
  TW12 . . . . .161 F7
Westbrook Cl, Barn. EN4 .41 G3
Westbrook Cres, Barn.
  EN4 . . . . .41 G3
Westbrooke Cres, Well.
  DA16 . . . . .158 C3
Westbrooke Rd, Sid.
  DA15 . . . . .175 G2
  Welling DA16 . . . . .158 B3
Westbrook Rd, SE3 . . . . .155 H1
  Hounslow TW5 . . . . . . .123 F7
  Thornton Heath CR7 . .188 A1
Westbrook Sq, Barn. EN4
  off Westbrook Cres . . .41 G3
Westbury Av, N22 . . . . . . .75 H3
  Esher (Clay.) KT10 . . . .194 C6
  Southall UB1 . . . . .103 G4
  Wembley HA0 . . . . .87 H7
Westbury Cl, Ruis. HA4 . . .66 A7
Westbury Gro, N12 . . . . . .56 D6
Westbury La, Buck.H.
  IG9 . . . . .63 J2
Westbury Lo Cl, Pnr.
  HA5 . . . . .66 D3
Westbury Par, SW12
  off Balham Hill 150 B6
Westbury Pl, Brent.
  TW8 . . . . .125 G6
Westbury Rd, E7 . . . . .97 H5
  E17 . . . . .78 A4
  N11 . . . . .58 E6
  N12 . . . . .56 D6
  SE20 . . . . .189 G1
  W5 . . . . .105 H6
  Barking IG11 . . . . .117 G1
  Beckenham BR3 . . . . . .189 H3
  Bromley BR1 . . . . .192 A1
  Buckhurst Hill IG9 . . . . .63 J2
  Croydon CR0 . . . . .188 A6
  Feltham TW13 . . . . . . .160 D1
  Ilford IG1 . . . . .98 C2
  New Malden KT3 . . . . . .182 D4
  Wembley HA0 . . . . .87 H7
Westbury St, SW8 . . . . . .150 C2
Westbury Ter, E7 . . . . .97 H6
West Carriage Dr, W2 . . . .23 F2
West Cen St, WC1 . . . . . . .18 A3
West Cen Av, W10
  off Harrow Rd 107 H3
West Chantry, Har. HA3
  off Chantry Rd 67 H1
Westchester Dr, NW4 . . . .72 A3
West Cl, N9 . . . . .60 C3
  Barnet EN5 . . . . .39 H5
  Barnet (Cockfos.) EN4 . .42 A4
  Greenford UB6 . . . . . . .103 J2
  Hampton TW12
  off Oak Av 160/161 E6
  Wembley HA9 . . . . .87 J1
Westcombe Av, Croy.
  CR0 . . . . .187 E6
Westcombe Ct, SE3
  off Westcombe Pk Rd .135 F7
Westcombe Dr, Barn.
  EN5 . . . . .40 D5
Westcombe Hill, SE3 . . .135 G5
  SE10 . . . . .135 G5
West Common Rd, Brom.
  BR2 . . . . .205 G2
  Keston BR2 . . . . .205 H4
Westcoombe Av, SW20 . .183 F1
Westcote Rd, SW16 . . . . .168 C5
West Cotts, NW6 . . . . .90 D5
Westcott Cl, N15
  off Ermine Rd 76 C6
  Bromley BR1
  off Ringmer Way 192 B5
Westcott Cres, W7 . . . . . .104 B6
Westcott Rd, SE17 . . . . . .35 G5
West Ct, SE18
  off Prince Imperial
  Rd 156 C1
Westcourt, Sun. TW16 . . .178 B2
West Ct, Wem. HA0 . . . . . .87 F2
Westcroft Cl, NW2 . . . . . . .90 B4
Westcroft Gdns, Mord.
  SM4 . . . . .184 C3
Westcroft Rd, Cars.
  SM5 . . . . .200 A4
  Wallington SM6 . . . . . .200 A4
Westcroft Sq, W6 . . . . . . .127 G4
Westcroft Way, NW2 . . . . .90 B4

West Cromwell Rd,
  SW5 . . . . .128 C4
  W14 . . . . .128 C4
West Cross Cen, Brent.
  TW8 . . . . .124 D6
West Cross Route, W10 . .108 A7
  W11 . . . . .108 A7
West Cross Way, Brent.
  TW8 . . . . .124 E6
Westdale Pas, SE18 . . . .136 E6
Westdale Rd, SE18 . . . . .137 E6
Westdean Av, SE12 . . . . .173 H1
Westdean Cl, SW18 . . . . .149 E6
West Dene, Sutt. SM3
  off Park La 198 B6
Westdown Rd, E15 . . . . . .96 C4
  SE6 . . . . .154 A7
WEST DRAYTON 120 A3
West Drayton Pk Av, West Dr.
  UB7 . . . . .120 B3
West Dr, SW16 . . . . .168 C4
  Harrow HA3 . . . . .52 A6
West Dr Gdns, Har. HA3 . .52 A6
WEST DULWICH, SE21 . .170 A3
West Eaton Pl, SW1 . . . . .32 B1
West Eaton Pl Ms, SW1 . .32 B1
West Ella Rd, NW10 . . . . .88 E7
West End Av, E10 . . . . . . .78 C5
  Pinner HA5 . . . . .66 D4
West End Cl, NW10 . . . . . .88 C7
West End Ct, Pnr. HA5 . . .66 D4
West End Gdns, Nthlt. UB5
  off Edward Cl 102 C2
West End La, NW6 . . . . . .108 D1
  Barnet EN5 . . . . .40 A4
  Hayes UB3 . . . . .121 F7
  Pinner HA5 . . . . .66 D4
West End Rd, Nthlt. UB5 .84 C7
  Ruislip HA4 . . . . .84 B5
  Southall UB1 . . . . .122 E1
Westerdale Rd, SE10 . . .135 G5
Westerfield Rd, N15 . . . . .76 C5
Westergate Rd, SE2 . . . .138 E5
Westerham Av, N9 . . . . . .60 A3
Westerham Dr, Sid.
  DA15 . . . . .158 B6
Westerham Rd, E10 . . . . .78 B7
  Keston BR2 . . . . .206 A6
Westerley Cres, SE26 . . .171 J5
Westerley Ware, Rich. TW9
  off Kew Grn 126 A6
Western Av, NW11 . . . . . .72 A6
  W3 . . . . .106 D5
  W5 . . . . .105 J4
  Dagenham RM10 . . . . .101 J6
  Greenford UB6 . . . . . . .105 G3
  Northolt UB5 . . . . .103 F1
Western Av Business Pk, W3
  off Mansfield Rd 106 B4
Western Av Underpass, W5
  off Western Av 105 J3
Western Beach Apartments,
  E16 off Hanover Av .135 G2
Western Ct, N3
  off Huntley Dr 56 D6
Western Gdns, W5 . . . . . .106 A7
Western La, SW12 . . . . . .150 A7
Western Ms, W9
  off Great Western Rd .108 C4
Western Par, Barn. EN5
  off Great N Rd 40 D5
Western Pl, SE16
  off Canon Beck Rd . . .133 F2
Western Rd, E13 . . . . . . .115 J1
  E17 . . . . .78 C5
  N2 . . . . .73 J4
  N22 . . . . .75 F2
  NW10 . . . . .106 C4
  SW9 . . . . .151 G3
  SW19 . . . . .185 G1
  W5 . . . . .105 G2
  Mitcham CR4 . . . . .185 G1
  Southall UB2 . . . . .122 D3
  Sutton SM1 . . . . .198 D5
Western Ter, W6
  off Chiswick Mall 127 G5
Western Trd Est, NW10 . .106 C4
Westferry Circ, E14 . . . . .133 J1
Westferry Rd, E14 . . . . . .134 A1
Westfield, Loug. IG10 . . . .47 J5
Westfield Cl, NW9 . . . . . . .70 C3
  SW10 . . . . .129 F7
  Enfield EN3 . . . . .45 H3
  Sutton SM1 . . . . .198 C4

Westfield Dr, Har. HA3 . . .69 G5
Westfield Gdns, Har.
 HA3 . . . . .69 G4
Westfield La, Har. HA3 . . .69 G4
Westfield Pk, Pnr. HA5 . . .51 F7
Westfield Pk Dr, Wdf.Grn.
 IG8 . . . . .64 B6
Westfield Rd, NW7 . . . . . .54 D3
 W13 . . . . .124 D1
 Beckenham BR3 . . . . . .189 J2
 Bexleyheath DA7 . . . . .159 J2
 Croydon CR0 . . . . .201 H2
 Dagenham RM9 . . . . . .101 E4
 Mitcham CR4 . . . . .185 J2
 Surbiton KT6 . . . . .181 G5
 Sutton SM1 . . . . .198 C4
 Walton-on-Thames
 KT12 . . . . .179 E7
Westfields, SW13 . . . . . . .147 F3
Westfields Av, SW13 . . . .147 E3
Westfields Rd, W3 . . . . . .106 B5
Westfield St, SE18 . . . . . .136 A3
Westfield Way, E1 . . . . . .113 H3
WEST GREEN, N15 . . . . . .75 J3
West Grn Pl, Grnf. UB6
 off Uneeda Dr 104 A1
West Grn Rd, N15 . . . . . . .75 H4
West Gro, SE10 . . . . .154 C1
 Woodford Green IG8 . . .63 J6
Westgrove La, SE10 . . . . .154 C1
West Halkin St, SW1 . . . . .24 B5
West Hallowes, SE9 . . . . .174 A1
West Hall Rd, Rich. TW9 .146 B1
WEST HAM, E15 . . . . .97 F7
West Ham La, E15 . . . . . . .96 E7
West Ham Pk, E7 . . . . . . .97 G7
WEST HAMPSTEAD,
 NW6 . . . . .90 E5
West Hampstead Ms,
 NW6 . . . . .90 E6
★ West Ham United FC,
 E13 . . . . .115 J2
West Harding St, EC4 . . . .19 F3
WEST HARROW, Har. 67 J7
Westhay Gdns, SW14 . . . .146 B5
WEST HEATH, SE2 . . . . . .138 D6
West Heath Av, NW11 . . . .90 D1
West Heath Cl, NW3 . . . . .90 D3
West Heath Dr, NW11 . . . .90 D1
West Heath Gdns, NW3 . . .90 D3
West Heath Rd, NW3 . . . . .90 D2
 SE2 . . . . .138 D6
WEST HENDON, NW9 . . . .71 E7
West Hendon Bdy, NW9 . .71 F6
West Hill, SW15 . . . . .148 A7
 SW18 . . . . .148 D5
 Harrow HA2 . . . . .86 B2
 Wembley HA9 . . . . .87 J1
West Hill Ct, N6 . . . . .92 A3
West Hill Pk, N6
 off Merton La 91 J2
West Hill Rd, SW18 . . . . . .148 D6
West Hill Way, N20 . . . . . .56 E1
Westholm, NW11 . . . . .72 E4
West Holme, Erith DA8 . . .159 J1
Westholme, Orp. BR6 . . . .193 H7
Westholme Gdns, Ruis.
 HA4 . . . . .84 A1
Westhorne Av, SE9 . . . . . .155 J6
 SE12 . . . . .155 G7
Westhorpe Gdns, NW4 . . .71 J3
Westhorpe Rd, SW15 . . . .147 J3
West Ho Cl, SW19 . . . . . .166 B1
Westhurst Dr, Chis. BR7 .175 E5
West India Av, E14 . . . . . .134 A1
West India Dock Rd, E14 .113 J6
West Kentish Town Est,
 NW5 . . . . .92 A5
WEST KILBURN, W9 . . . .108 C3
Westlake Cl, N13 . . . . .59 G3
 Hayes UB4
 off Lochan Cl 102/103 E4
Westlake Rd, Wem. HA9 . .87 G2
Westland Cl, Stai. (Stanw.)
 TW19 . . . . .140 B6
Westland Dr, Brom.
 BR2 . . . . .205 F2
Westland Ho, E16
 off Rymill St 136 D1

Westland Pl, N1 . . . . .12 B3
Westlands Cl, Hayes UB3
 off Granville Rd 122 A4
Westlands Ter, SW12
 off Gaskarth Rd 150 C6
West La, SE16 . . . . .132 E2
Westlea Rd, W7 . . . . .124 D3
Westleigh Av, SW15 . . . . .147 H5
Westleigh Dr, Brom.
 BR1 . . . . .192 B1
Westleigh Gdns, Edg.
 HA8 . . . . .70 A1
Westlinks, Wem. HA0
 off Alperton La 105 G3
Westlinton Cl, NW7 . . . . . .56 B6
West Lo Av, W3 . . . . .126 A1
West Mall, W8
 off Palace Gdns Ter . . .128 D1
Westmark Pt, SW15
 off Norley Vale 165 H1
Westmead, SW15 . . . . . . .147 H6
West Mead, Epsom
 KT19 . . . . .197 E6
 Ruislip HA4 . . . . .84 C4
Westmead Cor, Cars. SM5
 off Colston Av 199 H4
Westmead Rd, Sutt.
 SM1 . . . . .199 G4
Westmede, Chig. IG7 . . . . .65 F6
Westmere Dr, NW7 . . . . . .54 D3
West Mersea Cl, E16
 off Hanameel St 135 H1
West Ms, N17 . . . . .60 E6
 SW1 . . . . .33 E2
Westmill Ct, N4
 off Brownswood Rd 93 J2
WESTMINSTER, SW1 . . . .25 F5
★ Westminster Abbey,
 SW1 . . . . .26 A5
★ Westminster Abbey Mus,
 SW1 . . . . .26 A5
Westminster Av, Th.Hth.
 CR7 . . . . .187 H2
Westminster Br, SE1 . . . . .26 B4
 SW1 . . . . .26 B4
Westminster Br Rd, SE1 . .26 D4
★ Westminster Cathedral,
 SW1 . . . . .25 H6
★ Westminster City Hall,
 SW1 . . . . .25 G5
Westminster Cl, Felt.
 TW14 . . . . .160 A1
 Ilford IG6 . . . . .81 G2
 Teddington TW11 . . . . .162 D5
Westminster Dr, N13 . . . . .58 E5
Westminster Gdns, E4 . . . .63 E1
 SW1 . . . . .34 A1
 Barking IG11 . . . . .117 H2
 Ilford IG6 . . . . .81 F2
★ Westminster Pier,
 SW1 . . . . .26 B3
Westminster Rd, N9 . . . . . .61 E1
 W7 . . . . .124 B1
 Sutton SM1 . . . . .199 G2
Westmoat Cl, Beck.
 BR3 . . . . .172 C1
WEST MOLESEY, ...179 F5
Westmont Rd, Esher
 KT10 . . . . .194 B2
Westmoor Gdns, Enf.
 EN3 . . . . .45 G2
Westmoor Rd, Enf. EN3 . .45 G2
Westmoor St, SE7 . . . . . .135 J3
Westmoreland Av, Well.
 DA16 . . . . .157 H3
Westmoreland Bldgs, EC1
 off Bartholomew Cl . . .111 J5
Westmoreland Pl, SW1 . . .33 E4
 W5 off Mount Av 105 G5
 Bromley BR1 . . . . .191 G3
Westmoreland Rd, NW9 . .70 A4
 SE17 . . . . .36 A5
 SW13 . . . . .14/ F1
 Bromley BR1, BR2 . . . .191 E5
Westmoreland St, W1 . . . .16 C2
Westmoreland Ter, SW1 . .32 E4
Westmoreland Wk, SE17 .36 B5
Westmorland Cl, E12 . . . . .98 A2
 Twickenham TW1 . . . . .144 E6
Westmorland Rd, E17 . . . .78 A6
 Harrow HA1 . . . . .67 H5
Westmorland Sq, Mitch. CR4
 off Westmorland
 Way 186/187 E5
Westmorland Ter, SE20 . .171 E7
Westmorland Way, Mitch.
 CR4 . . . . .186 D4
Westmount Rd, SE9 . . . . .156 C2
WEST NORWOOD, SE27 .169 J3
West Oak, Beck. BR3 . . . .190 D1

Westoe Rd, N9 . . . . .61 E2
Weston Av, T.Ditt. KT7 . . .180 B7
West Molesey KT8 . . . . .179 E3
Weston Ct, N4
 off Queens Dr 93 J3
 N20 off Farnham Cl 41 F7
Weston Dr, Stan. HA7 . . . .68 E1
West One Shop Cen, W1
 off Oxford St 110 B6
Weston Gdns, Islw. TW7 .144 A1
WESTON GREEN, T.Ditt. .194 B1
Weston Grn, Dag. RM9 . .101 F4
 Thames Ditton KT7 . . . .194 B1
Weston Grn Rd, Esher
 KT10 . . . . .194 A1
 Thames Ditton KT7 . . . .194 A1
Weston Gro, Brom. BR1 .191 F1
Weston Pk, N8 . . . . .75 E6
 Kingston upon Thames KT1
 off Fairfield W 181 H2
 Thames Ditton KT7 . . . .194 B1
Weston Pk Cl, T.Ditt. KT7
 off Weston Pk 194 B1
Weston Ri, WC1 . . . . .10 D2
Weston Rd, W4 . . . . .126 C3
 Bromley BR1 . . . . .173 F7
 Dagenham RM9 . . . . . .101 E4
 Enfield EN2 . . . . .44 A1
 Thames Ditton KT7 . . . .194 B1
Weston St, SE1 . . . . .28 C5
Weston Wk, E8
 off Mare St 94/95 E7
Westover Hill, NW3 . . . . . .90 D2
Westover Rd, SW18 . . . . .149 F6
Westow Hill, SE19 . . . . . .170 B6
Westow St, SE19 . . . . . . .170 B6
West Pk, SE9 . . . . .174 B2
West Pk Av, Rich. TW9 . .146 A1
West Pk Cl, Houns. TW5
 off Heston Gra La 123 F6
 Romford RM6 . . . . .82 D5
West Pk Rd, Rich. TW9 . .146 A1
 Southall UB2 . . . . .123 J1
West Parkside, SE10 . . . .135 E2
West Pier, E1
 off Wapping High
 St 132/133 E1
West Pl, SW19 . . . . .165 J5
Westpoint Trd Est, W3 . . .106 B5
Westpole Av, Barn. EN4 . .42 A4
Westport Rd, E13 . . . . . . .115 H4
Westport St, E1 . . . . .113 G6
West Poultry Av, EC1 . . . .19 G2
West Quarters, W12 . . . . .107 G6
West Quay Dr, Hayes
 UB4 . . . . .102 E5
West Ramp, Houns.
 (Hthrw.Air.) TW6 . . . . .140 D1
West Ridge Gdns, Grnf.
 UB6 . . . . .103 J2
West Rd, E15 . . . . .115 F1
 N17 . . . . .60 E6
 SW3 . . . . .32 A4
 SW4 . . . . .150 D5
 W5 . . . . .105 H5
 Barnet EN4 . . . . .58 A1
 Feltham TW14 . . . . . . .141 G6
 Kingston upon Thames
 KT2 . . . . .182 C1
 Romford (Chad.Hth.)
 RM6 . . . . .82 D6
 West Drayton UB7 . . . .120 C3
Westrow, SW15 . . . . .147 J5
West Row, W10 . . . . .108 B4
Westrow Dr, Bark. IG11 . . .99 J6
Westrow Gdns, Ilf. IG3 . . .99 J2
West Sheen Vale, Rich.
 TW9 . . . . .145 J4
Westside, NW4 . . . . .71 H2
West Side Common,
 SW19 . . . . .165 J5
West Smithfield, EC1 . . . . .19 G2
West Sq, SE11 . . . . .27 G6
West St, E2 . . . . .113 E2
 E11 . . . . .96 E3
 E17 off Grove Rd 78 B5
 WC2 . . . . .17 J4
 Bexleyheath DA7 . . . . .159 F4
 Brentford TW8 . . . . . . .125 F6
 Bromley BR1 . . . . .191 G1
 Carshalton SM5 . . . . . .199 J3
 Croydon CR0 . . . . .201 J4
 Harrow HA1 . . . . .86 A1
 Sutton SM1 . . . . .198 E5
West St La, Cars. SM5 . . .199 J4
West Temple Sheen,
 SW14 . . . . .146 B4
West Tenter St, E1 . . . . . . .21 G4
West Thamesmead Business Pk,
 SE28 . . . . .137 J3

West Twrs, Pnr. HA5 . . . . .66 D6
Westvale Ms, W3 . . . . . . .127 E1
West Vw, NW4 . . . . .71 J4
 Feltham TW14 . . . . . . .141 F7
 Loughton IG10 . . . . .48 C3
Westview Cl, NW10 . . . . . .89 F5
 W7 . . . . .104 B6
 W10 . . . . .107 J6
Westview Cres, N9 . . . . . . .44 B7
Westview Dr, Wdf.Grn.
 IG8 . . . . .80 A2
Westville Rd, W12 . . . . . .127 G2
 Thames Ditton KT7 . . . .194 D1
West Wk, W5 . . . . .105 H5
 Barnet EN4 . . . . .42 A7
 Hayes UB3 . . . . .122 A1
West Walkway, The, Sutt. SM1
 off Cheam Rd 198/199 E5
Westward Rd, E4 . . . . .61 J5
Westward Way, Har. HA3 .69 H6
West Warwick Pl, SW1 . . .33 E2
West Way, N18 . . . . .60 A4
 NW10 . . . . .88 D3
Westway, SW20 . . . . .183 H3
 W2 . . . . .15 E2
 W9 . . . . .108 D5
 W10 . . . . .108 B6
 W12 . . . . .107 G7
West Way, Croy. CR0 . . . .203 H2
 Edgware HA8 . . . . .54 B6
 Hounslow TW5 . . . . . . .143 F1
Westway, Orp. BR5 . . . . .193 G5
West Way, Pnr. HA5 . . . . .66 D4
 West Wickham BR4 . . . .190 D6
Westway Cl, SW20 . . . . . .183 H3
Westway Cross Shop Pk,
 Grnf. UB6 . . . . .104 B1
West Way Gdns, Croy.
 CR0 . . . . .203 G2
Westways, Epsom KT19 .197 F4
Westwell Rd, SW16 . . . . .168 E6
Westwell Rd App, SW16
 off Westwell Rd . .168/169 E6
Westwick Gdns, W14 . . . .128 A2
 Hounslow TW4 . . . . . . .142 B2
WEST WICKHAM, ...204 C2
Westwood Av, SE19 . . . . .187 J1
 Harrow HA2 . . . . .85 H4
Westwood Cl, Brom.
 BR1 . . . . .192 A3
Westwood Gdns, SW13 . .147 F3
Westwood Hill, SE26 . . . .170 D5
Westwood La, Sid.
 DA15 . . . . .158 A5
 Welling DA16 . . . . .157 J3
Westwood Pk, SE23 . . . .153 E7
Westwood Pl, SE26 . . . . .170 D4
Westwood Rd, E16 . . . . . .135 H1
 SW13 . . . . .147 F3
 Ilford IG3 . . . . .99 J1
West Woodside, Bex.
 DA5 . . . . .159 E7
West World, W5 . . . . .105 H3
Wetheral Dr, Stan. HA7 . .69 E1
Wetherby Cl, Nthlt. UB5 . .85 H6
Wetherby Gdns, SW5 . . . .30 C2
Wetherby Ms, SW5 . . . . . .30 A3
Wetherby Pl, SW7 . . . . . . .30 C2
Wetherby Rd, Enf. EN2 . . .43 J1
Wetherby Way, Chess.
 KT9 . . . . .195 H7
Wetherden St, E17 . . . . . . .77 J7
Wetherell Rd, E9 . . . . . . .113 G1
Wetherill Rd, N10 . . . . .74 A1
★ Wetlands Cen, The,
 SW13 . . . . .127 H7
Wexford Rd, SW12 . . . . . .149 J7
Weybourne St, SW18 . . . .167 F2
Weybridge Ct, SE16 . . . . .37 J4
Weybridge Pt, SW11 . . . .150 A2
Weybridge Rd, Th.Hth.
 CR7 . . . . .187 G4
Wey Ct, Epsom KT19 . . . .196 C4
Weydown Cl, SW19 . . . . .166 B1
Weyhill Rd, E1 . . . . .21 J3
Weylond Rd, Dag. RM8 . .101 F3
Weyman Rd, SE3 . . . . . . .155 J1
Weymouth Av, NW7 . . . . . .54 E5
 W5 . . . . .125 F3
Weymouth Cl, E6
 off Covelees Wall .116/117 E6
Weymouth Ct, Sutt.
 SM2 . . . . .198 D7
Weymouth Ms, W1 . . . . . .16 D1
Weymouth St, W1 . . . . . . .16 C2
Weymouth Ter, E2 . . . . . . .13 G1
Weymouth Wk, Stan.
 HA7 . . . . .52 D6
Whadcote St, N4
 off Seven Sisters Rd . .93 G2

Whalebone Av, Rom.
RM6 . . . . .83 F6
Whalebone Ct, EC2 . . . . .20 C3
Whalebone Gro, Rom.
RM6 . . . . .83 F6
Whalebone La, E15
off West Ham La . . .96/97 E7
Whalebone La N, Rom.
RM6 . . . . .83 E5
Whalebone La S, Dag.
RM8 . . . . .83 F7
Romford RM6 . . . . .83 F7
Wharfdale Cl, N11
off Ribblesdale Av 58 A6
Wharfdale Ct, E6
off Rushmore Rd 95 G4
Wharfdale Rd, N1 . . . . . .10 B1
Wharfedale Gdns, Th.Hth.
CR7 . . . . .187 F4
Wharfedale St, SW10 . . . .30 A4
Wharf La, Twick. TW1 . . .162 D1
Wharf Pl, E2 . . . . .112 D1
Wharf Rd, E15 . . . . .114 D1
N1 . . . . .11 J1
Enfield EN3 . . . . .45 H6
Wharfside Rd, E16 . . . . .114 E5
Wharf St, E16 . . . . .114 E5
Wharncliffe Dr, Sthl.
UB1 . . . . .124 A1
Wharncliffe Gdns, SE25 .188 B2
Wharncliffe Rd, SE25 . . .188 B2
Wharton Cl, NW10 . . . . . .89 E6
Wharton Cotts, WC1
off Wharton St 111 F3
Wharton Rd, Brom. BR1 .191 H1
Wharton St, WC1 . . . . . . .10 D4
Whateley Rd, SE20 . . . . .171 G7
SE22 . . . . .152 C5
Whatley Av, SW20 . . . . .184 B3
Whatman Rd, SE23 . . . . .153 G7
Wheatfields, E6
off Oxleas 116/117 E6
Enfield EN3 . . . . .45 H2
Wheatfields Way, Kings.T.
KT1 . . . . .181 H2
Wheathill Rd, SE20 . . . . .188 E3
Wheatlands, Houns.
TW5 . . . . .123 G6
Wheatlands Rd, SW17
off Stapleton Rd 168 A3
Wheatley Cl, NW4 . . . . . .71 G2
Wheatley Cres, Hayes
UB3 . . . . .102 A7
Wheatley Gdns, N9 . . . . .60 B2
Wheatley Ho, SW15
off Tangley Gro 147 G7
Wheatley Rd, Islw. TW7 .144 C3
Wheatley's Ait, Sun.
TW16 . . . . .178 A5
Wheatley St, W1 . . . . . . .16 C2
Wheat Sheaf Cl, E14 . . . .134 B4
Wheatsheaf Cl, Nthlt.
UB5 . . . . .84 E5
Wheatsheaf La, SW6 . . . .127 J7
SW8 . . . . .34 B7
Wheatsheaf Ter, SW6 . . .128 C7
Wheatstone Cl, Mitch.
CR4 . . . . .185 H1
Wheatstone Rd, W10 . . .108 B5
Wheeler Cl, Wdf.Grn. IG8
off Chigwell Rd 64 C5
Wheeler Gdns, N1
off Outram Pl 110/111 E1
Wheelers Cross, Bark.
IG11 . . . . .117 G2
Wheel Fm Dr, Dag.
RM10 . . . . .101 J3
Wheelock Cl, Erith DA8 .139 H7
Wheelwright St, N7 . . . . .93 F7
Whelan Way, Wall. SM6 .200 D3
Wheler St, E1 . . . . .13 F6
Whellock Rd, W4 . . . . . .126 E3
Whenman Av, Bex. DA5 .177 J2
Whernside Cl, SE28 . . . .118 C7
WHETSTONE, N20 . . . . . .57 E2
Whetstone Cl, N20
off Oakleigh Rd N 57 G2
Whetstone Pk, WC2 . . . . .18 C3
Whetstone Rd, SE3 . . . . .155 J2
Whewell Rd, N19 . . . . . . .93 E2
Whichcote St, SE1 . . . . . .26 E2
Whidborne Cl, SE8
off Cliff Ter 154 A2
Whidborne St, WC1 . . . . .10 B4
Whimbrel Cl, SE28 . . . . .118 C7
Whimbrel Way, Hayes
UB4 . . . . .102 D6
Whinchat Rd, SE28 . . . . .137 G3
Whinfell Cl, SW16 . . . . .168 D5
Whinyates Rd, SE9 . . . . .156 B3

Whipps Cross Rd, E11 . . . .78 D5
Whiskin St, EC1 . . . . .11 G4
Whisperwood Cl, Har.
HA3 . . . . .52 B7
Whistler Gdns, Edg. HA8 .69 J2
Whistler Ms, SE15
off Commercial Way . .132 C7
Dagenham RM8
off Fitzstephen Rd . . .100 B5
Whistlers Av, SW11 . . . . .129 G7
Whistler St, N5 . . . . .93 H4
Whistler Wk, SW10 . . . . .30 D7
Whiston Rd, E2 . . . . .13 F1
Whitakers Way, Loug.
IG10 . . . . .48 C1
Whitbread Cl, N17 . . . . . .76 D1
Whitbread Rd, SE4 . . . . .153 H4
★ Whitbread Shire Horse
Stables, EC1
off Garrett St 12 A5
Whitburn Rd, SE13 . . . . .154 B4
Whitby Av, NW10 . . . . . .106 B3
Whitby Gdns, NW9 . . . . . .70 A3
Sutton SM1 . . . . .199 G2
Whitby Rd, SE18 . . . . . . .136 C4
Harrow HA2 . . . . .85 J3
Ruislip HA4 . . . . .84 B3
Sutton SM1 . . . . .199 G2
Whitby St, E1 . . . . .13 F5
Whitcher Cl, SE14 . . . . . .133 H6
Whitcher Pl, NW1
off Rochester Rd 92 C7
Whitchurch Av, Edg. HA8 .53 J7
Whitchurch Cl, Edg. HA8 .53 J6
Whitchurch Gdns, Edg.
HA8 . . . . .53 J6
Whitchurch La, Edg. HA8 .53 G7
Whitchurch Rd, W11 . . . .108 A7
Whitcomb Ct, WC2
off Whitcomb St 110 D7
Whitcombe Ms, Rich.
TW9 . . . . .146 B1
Whitcomb St, WC2 . . . . . .17 J6
White Acre, NW9 . . . . . . .71 E2
Whiteadder Way, E14 . . .134 B4
Whitear Wk, E15 . . . . . . .96 D6
Whitebarn La, Dag.
RM10 . . . . .119 G1
Whitebeam Av, Brom.
BR2 . . . . .192 D6
Whitebeam Cl, SW9
off Clapham Rd 131 F7
Whitebeam Twr, E17
off Hillyfield 77 H3
White Bear Pl, NW3
off New End Sq 91 G4
White Br Av, Mitch. CR4 .185 G4
Whitebridge Cl, Felt.
TW14 . . . . .141 J6
White Butts Rd, Ruis.
HA4 . . . . .84 D3
WHITECHAPEL, E1 . . . . . .21 H4
★ Whitechapel Art Gall,
E1 . . . . .21 G3
Whitechapel High St, E1 . .21 G3
Whitechapel Rd, E1 . . . . . .21 H3
White Ch La, E1 . . . . .21 H3
White Ch Pas, E1 . . . . . . .21 H3
White City Cl, W12 . . . . .107 J7
White City Est, W12 . . . .107 H7
White City Rd, W12 . . . . .107 H7
White Conduit St, N1 . . . .11 F1
Whitecote Rd, Sthl. UB1 .103 H6
White Craig Cl, Pnr. HA5 .51 G5
Whitecroft Cl, Beck. BR3 .190 D4
Whitecroft Way, Beck.
BR3 . . . . .190 C5
Whitecross Pl, EC2 . . . . . .20 C1
Whitecross St, EC1 . . . . . .12 A5
Whitefield Av, NW2 . . . . . .71 J7
Whitefield Cl, SW15 . . . .148 B6
Whitefoot La, Brom.
BR1 . . . . .172 C4
Whitefoot Ter, Brom.
BR1 . . . . .173 E3
Whitefriars Av, Har. HA3 . .68 B2
Whitefriars Dr, Har. HA3 . .68 A2
Whitefriars St, EC4 . . . . . .19 F4
White Gdns, Dag. RM10 .101 G6
Whitegate Gdns, Har.
HA3 . . . . .52 C7
Whitehall, SW1 . . . . .26 A1
Whitehall Ct, SW1 . . . . . .26 A2
Whitehall Cres, Chess.
KT9 . . . . .195 G5
Whitehall Gdns, E4 . . . . . .62 E1
SW1 . . . . .26 A2
W3 . . . . .126 A1
W4 . . . . .126 B6
Whitehall La, Buck.H. IG9 .63 G2

Whitehall Pk, N19 . . . . . .92 C1
Whitehall Pk Rd, W4 . . . .126 B6
Whitehall Pl, E7
off Station Rd 97 G5
SW1 . . . . .26 A2
Wallington SM6
off Bernard Rd 200 B4
Whitehall Rd, E4 . . . . .62 E2
W7 . . . . .124 D2
Bromley BR2 . . . . .192 A5
Harrow HA1 . . . . .68 B7
Thornton Heath CR7 . .187 G5
Woodford Green IG8 . . .62 E2
Whitehall St, N17 . . . . . . .60 C7
White Hart Ct, EC2
off Bishopsgate 112 B6
White Hart La, N17 . . . . . .60 A7
N22 . . . . .75 G1
NW10 off Church Rd . . .89 F6
SW13 . . . . .147 E3
Romford RM7 . . . . .83 G1
White Hart Rd, SE18 . . . .137 H4
White Hart Slip, Brom. BR1
off Market Sq 191 G2
White Hart St, SE11 . . . . .35 F3
White Hart Yd, SE1 . . . . . .28 B2
Whitehaven Cl, Brom.
BR2 . . . . .191 G4
Whitehaven St, NW8 . . . . .7 G6
Whitehead Cl, N18 . . . . . .60 A5
SW18 . . . . .149 F7
Whitehead's Gro,
SW3 . . . . .31 H3
White Heron Ms, Tedd.
TW11 . . . . .162 C6
Whitehills Rd, Loug.
IG10 . . . . .48 D3
White Horse All, EC1
off Cowcross St 111 H5
Whitehorse Hill, Chis.
BR7 . . . . .174 D4
White Horse La, E1 . . . . .113 G4
Whitehorse La, SE25 . . . .188 A4
White Horse Ms, SE1 . . . .27 F5
White Horse Rd, E1 . . . . .113 H6
E6 . . . . .116 C3
Whitehorse Rd, Croy.
CR0 . . . . .188 A6
Thornton Heath CR7 . .188 A6
White Horse St, W1 . . . . .24 D2
White Horse Yd, EC2 . . . .20 B3
Whitehouse Av, Borwd.
WD6 . . . . .38 B3
White Ho, Stan.
HA7 . . . . .53 F4
Whitehouse Way, N14 . . . .58 B2
White Kennett St, E1 . . . . .21 E3
Whitelegg Rd, E13 . . . . .115 F2
Whiteley Rd, SE19 . . . . . .170 A5
Whiteleys Cotts, W14 . . .128 C4
Whiteleys Shop Cen,
W2 . . . . .109 E6
Whiteleys Way, Felt.
TW13 . . . . .161 G3
White Lion Ct, EC3 . . . . . .20 D4
White Lion Hill, EC4 . . . . .19 H5
White Lion St, N1 . . . . . . .11 E2
White Lo, SE19 . . . . .169 H7
White Lo Cl, N2 . . . . .73 G6
Sutton SM2 . . . . .199 F7
White Lyon Ct, EC2
off Fann St 111 J4
White Oak Dr, Beck.
BR3 . . . . .190 C2
White Oak Gdns, Sid.
DA15 . . . . .157 J7
Whiteoaks La, Grnf.
UB6 . . . . .104 A2
White Orchards, N20 . . . . .40 C7
Stanmore HA7 . . . . . . .52 D5
White Post La, E9 . . . . . . .95 J7
SE13 . . . . .154 A3
White Post St, SE15 . . . .133 F7
White Rd, E15 . . . . .97 E7
Whites Av, Ilf. IG2 . . . . . . .81 H6
Whites Grds, SE1 . . . . . . .28 E4
Whites Grds Est, SE1 . . . .28 E3
White's Row, E1 . . . . .21 F2
White's Sq, SW4
off Nelson's Row 150 D4
Whitestile Rd, Brent.
TW8 . . . . .125 F5
Whitestone La, NW3
off Heath St 91 F3
Whitestone Wk, NW3
off North End Way 91 F3
White St, Sthl. UB1 . . . . .122 D2
White Swan Ms, W4
off Bennett St . . .126/127 E6

Whitethorn Gdns, Croy.
CR0 . . . . .203 E2
Enfield EN2 . . . . .44 A5
Whitethorn St, E3 . . . . . .114 A4
Whitewebbs Way, Orp.
BR5 . . . . .193 J1
Whitfield Pl, W1 . . . . .9 F6
Whitfield Rd, E6 . . . . .97 J7
SE3 . . . . .154 D1
Bexleyheath DA7 . . . . .139 F7
Whitfield St, W1 . . . . .17 H2
Whitford Gdns, Mitch.
CR4 . . . . .185 J3
Whitgift Av, S.Croy.
CR2 . . . . .201 J5
Whitgift Cen, Croy.
CR0 . . . . .201 J2
Whitgift St, SE11 . . . . . . .34 C1
Croydon CR0 . . . . .201 J3
Whiting Av, Bark. IG11 . . .98 F7
Whitings, Ilf. IG2 . . . . .81 G5
Whitings Rd, Barn. EN5 . . .39 J5
Whitings Way, E6 . . . . . .116 D5
Whitland Rd, Cars. SM5 .199 G1
Whitley Cl, Stai. (Stanw.)
TW19 . . . . .140 B6
Whitley Rd, N17 . . . . .76 B2
Whitlock Dr, SW19 . . . . .148 B7
Whitman Rd, E3
off Mile End Rd 113 H4
Whitmead Cl, S.Croy.
CR2 . . . . .202 B6
Whitmore Cl, N11 . . . . . . .58 B5
Whitmore Est, N1 . . . . . .112 B1
Whitmore Gdns, NW10 . .107 J2
Whitmore Rd, N1 . . . . . . .112 B1
Beckenham BR3 . . . . . .189 J3
Harrow HA1 . . . . .67 J7
Whitnell Way, SW15 . . . .148 A5
Whitney Av, Ilf. IG4 . . . . . .80 A4
Whitney Rd, E10 . . . . .78 B7
Whitney Wk, Sid. DA14 . .176 E6
Whitstable Cl, Beck.
BR3 . . . . .189 J1
Whitstable Ho, W10 . . . .108 A6
Whitstable Pl, Croy.
CR0 . . . . .201 J4
Whittaker Av, Rich. TW9
off Hill St 145 G5
Whittaker Rd, E6 . . . . .97 J7
Sutton SM3 . . . . .198 C3
Whittaker St, SW1 . . . . . .32 B2
Whittaker Way, SE1 . . . . . .37 J2
Whitta Rd, E12 . . . . .98 A4
Whittell Gdns, SE26 . . . .171 F3
Whittingstall Rd, SW6 . .148 C1
Whittington Av, EC3 . . . . .20 D4
Whittington Ct, N2 . . . . . .73 J5
Whittington Ms, N12
off Fredericks Pl 57 F4
Whittington Rd, N22 . . . . .58 E7
Whittington Way, Pnr.
HA5 . . . . .67 E5
Whittlebury Cl, Cars.
SM5 . . . . .199 J7
Whittle Cl, E17 . . . . .77 H6
Southall UB1 . . . . .103 H6
Whittle Rd, Houns. TW5 .122 C7
Southall UB2
off Post Rd 123 H2
Whittlesea Cl, Har. HA3 . .51 J1
Whittlesea Path, Har.
HA3 . . . . .67 J1
Whittlesea Rd, Har. HA3 . .67 J1
Whittlesey St, SE1 . . . . . .27 E2
WHITTON, Twick. 143 H4
Whitton Av E, Grnf. UB6 . .86 B5
Whitton Av W, Grnf.
UB6 . . . . .85 J5
Northolt UB5 . . . . .85 J5
Whitton Cl, Grnf. UB6 . . . .87 E6
Whitton Dene, Houns.
TW3 . . . . .143 H5
Isleworth TW7 . . . . . . .144 A5
Whitton Dr, Grnf. UB6 . . . .86 D6
Whitton Manor Rd, Islw.
TW7 . . . . .143 J5
Whitton Rd, Houns.
TW3 . . . . .143 H4
Twickenham TW1,
TW2 . . . . .144 C6
Whitton Wk, E3 . . . . .114 A2
Whitton Waye, Houns.
TW3 . . . . .143 G6
Whitwell Rd, E13 . . . . . . .115 G3
Whitworth Pl, SE18 . . . . .137 E4
Whitworth Rd, SE18 . . . .136 D7
SE25 . . . . .188 B3
Whitworth St, SE10 . . . . .135 E5
Whorlton Rd, SE15 . . . . .152 E3

Whychcote Pt, NW2
  off Claremont Rd 71 J7
Whymark Av, N22 . . . . . . .75 G3
Whytecroft, Houns.
  TW5 . . . . .122 D7
Whyteville Rd, E7 . . . . . . .97 H6
Wickersley Rd, SW11 . . . .150 A2
Wickers Oake, SE19 . . . . .170 C4
Wicker St, E1
  off Burslem St . . .112/113 E6
Wicket, The, Croy. CR0 . .204 A5
Wicket Rd, Grnf. UB6 . . . .104 D3
Wickets Way, Ilf. IG6 . . . . .65 J6
Wickford St, E1 . . . . .113 F4
Wickford Way, E17 . . . . . .77 G4
Wickham Av, Croy. CR0 . .203 H2
  Sutton SM3 . . . . .197 J5
Wickham Chase, W.Wick.
  BR4 . . . . .190 D7
Wickham Cl, E1 . . . . .113 F5
  Enfield EN3 . . . . .45 E3
  New Malden KT3 . . . . . .183 F5
Wickham Ct Rd, W.Wick.
  BR4 . . . . .204 C2
Wickham Cres, W.Wick.
  BR4 . . . . .204 C2
Wickham Gdns, SE4 . . . .153 J3
  Welling DA16 . . . . .138 A5
Wickham Ms, SE4 . . . . . .153 J2
Wickham Rd, E4 . . . . .62 C7
  SE4 . . . . .153 J4
  Beckenham BR3 . . . . . .190 B2
  Croydon CR0 . . . . .203 G2
  Harrow HA3 . . . . .68 A2
Wickham St, SE11 . . . . . .34 C1
  Welling DA16 . . . . .157 H2
Wickham Way, Beck.
  BR3 . . . . .190 C4
Wick La, E3 . . . . .114 A2
Wickliffe Av, N3 . . . . .72 B2
Wickliffe Gdns, Wem.
  HA9 . . . . .88 B2
Wicklow St, WC1 . . . . . . .10 C3
Wick Rd, E9 . . . . .95 G6
  Teddington TW11 . . . . . .163 E7
Wicks Cl, SE9 . . . . .174 A4
Wick Sq, E9
  off Eastway 95 J6
Wicksteed Ho, Brent. TW8
  off Green Dragon La .125 J5
Wickwood St, SE5 . . . . . .151 H2
Widdecombe Av, Har.
  HA2 . . . . .84 E2
Widdenham Rd, N7 . . . . . .93 F4
Widdin St, E15 . . . . .96 D7
Widecombe Gdns, Ilf.
  IG4 . . . . .80 B4
Widecombe Rd, SE9 . . . .174 B3
Widecombe Way, N2 . . . . .73 G5
Widegate St, E1 . . . . .21 E2
Widenham Cl, Pnr. HA5
  off Bridle Rd 66 C5
Wide Way, Mitch. CR4 . . .186 D3
Widewing Cl, Tedd.
  TW11 . . . . .163 E7
Widgeon Cl, E16
  off Maplin Rd 115 H6
Widley Rd, W9 . . . . .108 D3
WIDMORE, Brom. 191 H3
WIDMORE GREEN,
  Brom. 191 J1
Widmore Lo Rd, Brom.
  BR1 . . . . .192 A2
Widmore Rd, Brom.
  BR1 . . . . .191 G2
Wieland Rd, Nthwd.
  HA6 . . . . .50 A7
Wigan Ho, E5
  off Warwick Gro . .94/95 E1
Wigeon Path, SE28 . . . .137 G3
Wigeon Way, Hayes
  UB4 . . . . .102 D6
Wiggins La, Rich. TW10 . .163 F2
Wiggins Mead, NW9 . . . . .55 F7
Wigginton Av, Wem.
  HA9 . . . . .88 B6
Wigham Ho, Bark. IG11 . . .99 F7
Wightman Rd, N4 . . . . . . .75 G5
  N8 . . . . .75 G4
Wigley Rd, Felt. TW13 . . .160 D1
Wigmore Pl, W1 . . . . .16 D3
Wigmore Rd, Cars.
  SM5 . . . . .199 G2
Wigmore St, W1 . . . . .16 B4
Wigmore Wk, Cars.
  SM5 . . . . .199 G2
Wigram Rd, E11 . . . . .79 J6
Wigram Sq, E17 . . . . .78 C2
Wigston Cl, N18 . . . . .60 B5

Wigston Rd, E13 . . . . . . .115 H4
Wigton Gdns, Stan.
  HA7 . . . . .69 H1
Wigton Pl, SE11 . . . . .35 F4
Wigton Rd, E17 . . . . .77 J1
Wilberforce Rd, N4 . . . . . .93 H2
  NW9 . . . . .71 G6
Wilberforce Way, SW19 . .166 A6
Wilbraham Pl, SW1 . . . . . .32 A1
Wilbury Way, N18 . . . . . . .60 A5
Wilby Ms, W11 . . . . .128 C1
Wilcox Cl, SW8 . . . . .34 B7
  Borehamwood WD6 . . . .38 C1
Wilcox Pl, SW1 . . . . .25 G6
Wilcox Rd, SW8 . . . . .34 A7
  Sutton SM1 . . . . .198 E4
  Teddington TW11 . . . . . .162 A4
Wild Ct, WC2 . . . . .18 C3
Wildcroft Gdns, Edg.
  HA8 . . . . .53 G6
Wildcroft Rd, SW15 . . . . .147 J7
Wilde Cl, E8 . . . . .112 D1
Wilde Pl, N13
  off Medesenge Way . . .59 H6
  SW18
  off Heathfield Rd 149 G7
Wilde Rd, Erith DA8 . . . .139 H7
Wilderton Rd, N16 . . . . . . .76 B7
Wildfell Rd, SE6 . . . . .154 B7
Wild Goose Dr, SE14 . . . .153 F1
Wild Hatch, NW11 . . . . . . .72 D6
Wild's Rents, SE1 . . . . . . .28 D5
Wild St, WC2 . . . . .18 B4
Wildwood Cl, SE12 . . . . . .155 F7
Wildwood Gro, NW3
  off North End Way 91 F1
Wildwood Ri, NW11 . . . . . .91 F1
Wildwood Rd, NW11 . . . . .73 F7
Wildwood Ter, NW3 . . . . . .91 F1
Wilford Cl, Enf. EN2 . . . . . .44 A3
Wilfred Owen Cl, SW19
  off Tennyson Rd 167 F6
Wilfred St, SW1 . . . . .25 F5
Wilfred Turney Est, W6
  off Hammersmith
  Gro 127 J3
Wilfrid Gdns, W3 . . . . . . .106 C5
Wilkes Rd, Brent. TW8 . . .125 H6
Wilkes St, E1 . . . . .21 G1
Wilkie Way, SE22
  off Lordship La 170 D1
Wilkins Cl, Hayes UB3 . . .121 J5
  Mitcham CR4 . . . . .185 H1
Wilkinson Rd, E16 . . . . . .115 J6
Wilkinson St, SW8 . . . . . .131 F7
Wilkinson Way, W4 . . . . . .126 D2
Wilkin St, NW5 . . . . .92 B6
Wilkin St Ms, NW5
  off Wilkin St 92 B6
Wilks Gdns, Croy. CR0 . .203 H1
Wilks Pl, N1 . . . . .12 E2
Willan Rd, N17 . . . . .76 A2
Willan Wall, E16
  off Victoria Dock Rd . .115 F7
Willard St, SW8 . . . . .150 B3
Willcocks Cl, Chess. KT9 .195 H3
Willcott Rd, W3 . . . . .126 B1
Will Crooks Gdns, SE9 . . .155 J4
Willen Fld Rd, NW10 . . . .106 C2
Willenhall Av, Barn. EN5 . .41 F6
Willenhall Rd, SE18 . . . . .136 E5
Willersley Av, Orp. BR6 . .207 G3
  Sidcup DA15 . . . . .175 J1
Willersley Cl, Sid. DA15 . .175 J1
WILLESDEN, NW10 . . . . . .89 F6
WILLESDEN GREEN,
  NW10 . . . . .89 H7
Willesden La, NW2 . . . . . .90 A6
  NW6 . . . . .90 A6
Willes Rd, NW5 . . . . .92 B6
Willett Cl, Nthlt. UB5
  off Broomcroft Av 102 C3
  Orpington BR5 . . . . . . .193 H6
Willett Pl, Th.Hth. CR7
  off Willett Rd 187 G5
Willett Rd, Th.Hth. CR7 . .187 G5
Willett Way, Orp. BR5 . . .193 G5
William Barefoot Dr,
  SE9 . . . . .174 D4
William Bonney Est,
  SW4 . . . . .150 D4
William Booth Rd,
  SE20 . . . . .188 D1

William Carey Way, Har.
  HA1 . . . . .68 B7
William Cl, N2
  off King St 73 G3
  Romford RM5 . . . . .83 J1
  Southall UB2
  off Windmill Av 123 J2
William Dunbar Ho,
  NW6 . . . . .108 C2
William Dyce Ms, SW16
  off Babington Rd 168 D4
William Ellis Way, SE16 . . .29 J6
William IV St, WC2 . . . . . .18 A6
William Gdns, SW15 . . . . .147 H5
William Guy Gdns, E3
  off Talwin St 114 B3
William Harvey Ho, SW19
  off Whitlock Dr 166 B1
William Margrie Cl, SE15
  off Moncrieff St 152 D2
William Ms, SW1 . . . . . . .24 A5
William Morley Cl, E6 . . . .116 A1
William Morris Cl, E17 . . . .77 J3
★ William Morris Gall,
  Lloyd Pk, E17 . . . . . . .78 A3
William Morris Way,
  SW6 . . . . .149 F3
William Pl, E3
  off Roman Rd . . . . .●. .113 J2
William Rd, NW1 . . . . .9 E4
  SW19 . . . . .166 B7
  Sutton SM1 . . . . .199 F5
Williams Av, E17 . . . . .77 J1
William Saville Ho,
  NW6 . . . . .108 C2
Williams Bldgs, E2 . . . . . .113 F4
Williams Cl, N8
  off Coolhurst Rd 74 D6
Williams Gro, N22 . . . . . . .75 G1
  Surbiton KT6 . . . . .181 F6
William's La, SW14 . . . . . .146 C3
Williams La, Mord.
  SM4 . . . . .185 F5
Williamson Cl, SE10
  off Lenthorp Rd 135 F4
Williamson Rd, N4 . . . . . . .75 H6
Williamson St, N7 . . . . . . .93 E4
Williamson Way, NW7 . . . .56 B6
William Sq, SE16
  off Rotherhithe St 113 H7
Williams Rd, W13 . . . . . . .104 D7
  Southall UB2 . . . . .122 E4
Williams Ter, Croy. CR0 . .201 G6
William St, E10 . . . . .78 B6
  N17 . . . . .60 C7
  SW1 . . . . .24 A4
  Barking IG11 . . . . .99 F7
  Carshalton SM5 . . . . . .199 H3
Willifield Way, NW11 . . . . .72 C4
Willingale Cl, Loug. IG10
  off Willingale Rd 49 F2
  Woodford Green IG8 . . .64 A6
Willingale Rd, Loug.
  IG10 . . . . .49 F3
Willingdon Rd, N22 . . . . . .75 H2
Willingham Cl, NW5
  off Leighton Rd 92 C5
Willingham Ter, NW5
  off Leighton Rd 92 C5
Willingham Way, Kings.T.
  KT1 . . . . .182 A3
Willington Ct, E5
  off Mandeville St 95 H3
Willington Rd, SW9 . . . . .150 E3
Willis Av, Sutt. SM2 . . . . . .199 H6
Willis Rd, E15 . . . . .115 F1
  Croydon CR0 . . . . .187 J7
  Erith DA8 . . . . .139 J4
Willis St, E14 . . . . .114 B6
Willmore End, SW19 . . . .184 E1
Willoughby Av, Croy.
  CR0 . . . . .201 F4
Willoughby Gro, N17 . . . . .60 E7
Willoughby Ho, EC2
  off The Barbican 111 J5
Willoughby La, N17 . . . . . .61 E7
Willoughby Ms, SW4
  off Wixs La 150 B4
Willoughby Pk Rd, N17 . . . .60 E7
Willoughby Pas, E14 . . . .134 A1
Willoughby Rd, N8 . . . . . . .75 G3
  NW3 . . . . .91 G4
  Kingston upon Thames
  KT2 . . . . .181 J1
  Twickenham TW1 . . . . .145 G6
Willoughbys, The, SW14
  off Upper Richmond
  Rd W 146/147 E4
Willoughby St, WC1 . . . . . .18 A2
Willoughby Way, SE7 . . . .135 H4

Willow Av, SW13 . . . . . . .147 F2
  Sidcup DA15 . . . . .158 A6
Willow Bk, SW6 . . . . .148 B3
  Richmond TW10 . . . . . .163 E3
Willow Br Rd, N1 . . . . .93 J6
Willowbrook Est, SE15
  off Sumner Rd 132 C7
Willowbrook Rd, SE15 . . . .37 G6
  Southall UB2 . . . . .123 G3
Willow Business Cen, Mitch.
  CR4 off Willow La 185 J5
Willow Cl, Bex. DA5 . . . . .159 F6
  Brentford TW8 . . . . .125 F6
  Bromley BR2 . . . . .192 C5
  Buckhurst Hill IG9 . . . . .64 A3
  Thornton Heath CR7 . . .187 H6
Willow Cotts, Mitch.
  CR4 . . . . .186 C3
  Richmond TW9
  off Kew Grn 126 A6
Willow Ct, EC2 . . . . .12 D5
  Edgware HA8 . . . . .53 H4
Willowcourt Av, Har.
  HA3 . . . . .69 E5
Willowdene, N6
  off Denewood Rd 73 J7
Willow Dene, Pnr. HA5 . . . .66 D2
Willowdene Cl, Twick.
  TW2 . . . . .143 J7
Willow Dr, Barn. EN5 . . . . .40 B4
Willow End, N20 . . . . .56 D2
  Northwood HA6 . . . . . . .50 A6
  Surbiton KT6 . . . . .195 H1
Willow Fm La, SW15
  off Queens Ride 147 H3
Willowfield Cl, SE18 . . . . .137 H5
Willow Gdns, Houns.
  TW3 . . . . .143 G1
Willow Grn, NW9
  off Clayton Fld 70/71 E1
  Borehamwood WD6 . . . .38 D5
Willow Gro, E13
  off Libra Rd 115 G2
  Chislehurst BR7 . . . . . .174 D6
Willowhayne Dr, Walt.
  KT12 . . . . .178 B7
Willowhayne Gdns, Wor.Pk.
  KT4 . . . . .197 J3
Willow La, SE18 . . . . .136 C4
  Mitcham CR4 . . . . .185 J5
Willowmead Cl, W5 . . . . . .105 G5
Willow Mt, Croy. CR0
  off Langton Way 202 B3
Willow Pl, SW1 . . . . .33 G1
Willow Rd, NW3 . . . . .91 G4
  W5 . . . . .125 H2
  Enfield EN1 . . . . .44 B3
  New Malden KT3 . . . . . .182 C4
  Romford RM6 . . . . .83 E6
  Wallington SM6 . . . . . . .200 B7
Willows, The, Buck.H.
  IG9 . . . . .64 A3
  Esher (Clay.) KT10
  off Albany Cres 194 B6
Willows Av, Mord. SM4 . .185 E5
Willows Cl, Pnr. HA5 . . . . .66 C2
Willow St, E4 . . . . .46 D7
  EC2 . . . . .12 D5
  Romford RM7 . . . . .83 J4
Willow Tree Cl, E3
  off Birdsfield La 113 J1
  SW18 off Cargill
  Rd 166/167 E1
  Hayes UB4 . . . . .102 C4
Willow Tree La, Hayes
  UB4 . . . . .102 C4
Willowtree Marina, Hayes
  UB4 . . . . .103 E6
Willow Tree Wk, Brom.
  BR1 . . . . .191 H1
Willowtree Way, Th.Hth. CR7
  off Kensington Av 187 G1
Willow Vale, W12 . . . . . . .127 G1
  Chislehurst BR7 . . . . . .174 E6
Willow Vw, SW19 . . . . . . .185 G1
Willow Wk, E17 . . . . .77 J5
  N2 . . . . .73 G2
  N15 . . . . .75 H4
  N21 . . . . .43 F6
  SE1 . . . . .37 E1
  Orpington BR6 . . . . . . .206 E3
  Sutton SM3 . . . . .198 C3
Willow Way, N3 . . . . .56 E7
  SE26 . . . . .171 E3
  W11 off Freston Rd . . .128 A1
  Epsom KT19 . . . . .196 D6
  Sunbury-on-Thames
  TW16 . . . . .178 A4
  Twickenham TW2 . . . . .161 H2
  Wembley HA0 . . . . .86 D3

Willow Wd Cres, SE25 . . .188 B6
Willrose Cres, SE2 . . . . . .138 C5
Wills Cres, Houns. TW3 . .143 H6
Wills Gro, NW7 . . . . .55 G5
Wilman Gro, E8 . . . . .94 D7
Wilmar Gdns, W.Wick.
   BR4 . . . . .204 B1
Wilmcote Ho, W2 . . . . .14 A1
Wilmer Cl, Kings.T.
   KT2 . . . . .163 J5
Wilmer Cres, Kings.T.
   KT2 . . . . .163 J5
Wilmer Gdns, N1 . . . . . . .112 B1
Wilmer Lea Cl, E15 . . . . . .96 C7
Wilmer Pl, N16
   off Stoke Newington
   Ch St 94 C2
Wilmer Way, N14 . . . . . . .58 D5
Wilmington Av, W4 . . . . .126 D7
Wilmington Gdns, Bark.
   IG11 . . . . .99 G6
Wilmington Sq, WC1 . . . . .11 E4
Wilmington St, WC1 . . . . .11 E4
Wilmot Cl, N2 . . . . .73 F2
   SE15 . . . . .132 D7
Wilmot Pl, NW1 . . . . .92 C7
   W7 off Boston Rd 124 B1
Wilmot Rd, E10 . . . . .96 B2
   N17 . . . . .76 A3
   Carshalton SM5 . . . . . .199 J5
Wilmot St, E2 . . . . .112 E4
Wilmount St, SE18 . . . . . .136 E4
Wilna Rd, SW18 . . . . .149 F7
Wilsham St, W11 . . . . . . .128 A1
Wilshaw Cl, NW4 . . . . .71 G3
Wilshaw St, SE14 . . . . . . .154 A1
Wilsmere Dr, Har. HA3 . . .52 C7
   Northolt UB5 . . . . .85 E6
Wilson Av, Mitch. CR4 . . .167 H7
Wilson Cl, S.Croy. CR2
   off Bartlett St 202 A5
   Wembley HA9 . . . . .69 J7
Wilson Dr, Wem. HA9 . . . .69 J7
Wilson Gdns, Har. HA1 . . .67 J7
Wilson Rd, SE16 . . . . . . .132 E2
   E6 . . . . .116 A3
   SE5 . . . . .152 B1
   Chessington KT9 . . . . .195 J6
   Ilford IG1 . . . . .80 C7
Wilsons Pl, E14
   off Salmon La 113 J4
Wilsons Rd, W6 . . . . .128 A5
Wilson St, E17 . . . . .78 C5
   EC2 . . . . .20 C1
   N21 . . . . .43 G7
Wilstone Cl, Hayes UB4
   off Kingsash Dr . .102/103 E4
Wilthorne Gdns, Dag. RM10
   off Acre Rd 101 H7
Wilton Av, W4 . . . . .127 E5
Wilton Cl, West Dr.
   UB7 . . . . .120 A6
Wilton Cres, SW1 . . . . . . .24 B4
   SW19 . . . . .184 C1
Wilton Gdns, W.Mol.
   KT8 . . . . .179 G3
Wilton Gro, SW19 . . . . . .184 C1
   New Malden KT3 . . . . .183 F6
Wilton Ms, SW1 . . . . .24 C5
Wilton Par, Felt. TW13
   off Highfield Rd 160 A2
Wilton Pk Ct, SE18
   off Prince Imperial
   Rd 156 D1
Wilton Pl, SW1 . . . . .24 B4
Wilton Rd, N10 . . . . .74 A2
   SE2 . . . . .138 C3
   SW1 . . . . .25 E6
   SW19 . . . . .167 H7
   Barnet (Cockfs.) EN4 . .41 J4
   Hounslow TW4 . . . . . .142 D3
   Ilford IG1
   off Ilford La 98/99 E3
Wilton Row, SW1 . . . . . . .24 B4
Wilton Sq, N1 . . . . .112 A1
Wilton St, SW1 . . . . .24 D5
Wilton Ter, SW1 . . . . .24 B5
Wilton Vil, N1 . . . . .112 A1
Wilton Way, E8 . . . . .94 D6
Wiltshire Cl, NW7 . . . . . . .55 F5
   SW3 . . . . .31 J1
Wiltshire Gdns, N4 . . . . . .75 J6
   Twickenham TW2 . . . . .161 J1
Wiltshire Rd, SW9 . . . . . .151 G3
   Thornton Heath CR7 . .187 G3
Wiltshire Row, N1 . . . . . .112 A1
Wilverley Cres, N.Mal.
   KT3 . . . . .183 E6
Wimbart Rd, SW2 . . . . . .151 F7
WIMBLEDON, SW19 . . . .166 B6

★ Wimbledon (All England
   Tennis & Croquet Club),
   SW19 . . . . .166 B4
Wimbledon Br, SW19 . . .166 C6
★ Wimbledon Common,
   SW19 . . . . .165 F4
Wimbledon Common,
   SW19 . . . . .165 G4
★ Wimbledon FC (share
   Selhurst Pk with Crystal
   Palace FC), SE25 . . . .188 B4
Wimbledon Hill Rd,
   SW19 . . . . .166 B6
WIMBLEDON PARK,
   SW19 . . . . .166 C3
Wimbledon Pk, SW19 . . .166 C2
Wimbledon Pk Est,
   SW19 . . . . .166 B1
Wimbledon Pk Rd,
   SW18 . . . . .148 C7
   SW19 . . . . .166 C1
Wimbledon Pk Side,
   SW19 . . . . .166 A2
Wimbledon Rd, SW17 . . .167 F4
Wimbledon Sta, SW19 . .166 C6
★ Wimbledon Windmill Mus,
   SW19 . . . . .165 H2
Wimbolt St, E2 . . . . .13 H3
Wimborne Av, Hayes
   UB4 . . . . .102 B6
   Southall UB2 . . . . .123 G4
Wimborne Cl, SE12 . . . . .155 F5
   Buckhurst Hill IG9 . . . . .63 H2
   Worcester Park KT4 . . .197 J1
Wimborne Dr, NW9 . . . . . .70 A3
   Pinner HA5 . . . . .66 D7
Wimborne Gdns, W13 . . .105 E6
Wimborne Rd, N9 . . . . . . .60 D2
   N17 . . . . .76 B2
Wimborne Way, Beck.
   BR3 . . . . .189 G3
Wimbourne Av, Chis.
   BR7 . . . . .193 J4
   Orpington BR5 . . . . . . .193 J4
Wimbourne Ct, N1 . . . . . .12 B1
Wimbourne St, N1 . . . . . .12 B1
Wimpole Cl, Brom. BR2 . .191 J4
   Kingston upon Thames
   KT1 . . . . .181 J2
Wimpole Ms, W1 . . . . . . .16 D1
Wimpole Rd, West Dr.
   UB7 . . . . .120 A1
Wimpole St, W1 . . . . .16 D3
Wimshurst Cl, Croy.
   CR0 . . . . .201 E1
Winans Wk, SW9 . . . . . . .151 G2
Wincanton Cres, Nthlt.
   UB5 . . . . .85 G5
Wincanton Gdns, Ilf. IG6 . .80 E3
Wincanton Rd, SW18 . . .148 C7
Winchcombe Rd, Cars.
   SM5 . . . . .185 G7
Winchcomb Gdns, SE9 . .156 A3
Winchelsea Av, Bexh.
   DA7 . . . . .139 F7
Winchelsea Cl, SW15 . . .148 A5
Winchelsea Rd, E7 . . . . . .97 G3
   N17 . . . . .76 B3
   NW10 . . . . .106 D1
Winchelsey Ri, S.Croy.
   CR2 . . . . .202 C6
Winchendon Rd, SW6 . . .128 C7
   Teddington TW11 . . . . .162 A4
Winchester Av, NW6 . . . .108 B1
   NW9 . . . . .70 A3
   Hounslow TW5 . . . . . .123 F6
Winchester Cl, E6
   off Boultwood Rd 116 B6
   SE17 . . . . .35 H2
   Bromley BR2 . . . . .191 F3
   Enfield EN1 . . . . .44 B5
   Kingston upon Thames
   KT2 . . . . .164 B7
Winchester Ct, E17
   off Billet Rd 77 H1
Winchester Dr, Pnr. HA5 . .66 D5
Winchester Ho, SE18
   off Shooter's Hill Rd . .136 A7
Winchester Ms, NW3
   off Winchester Rd 91 G7
Winchester Pk, Brom.
   BR2 . . . . .191 F3
Winchester Pl, E8
   off Kingsland High St . .94 C5
   N6 . . . . .92 B1
   W3 off Avenue Rd 126 C2
Winchester Rd, E4 . . . . . .62 C7
   N6 . . . . .74 B7
   N9 . . . . .60 D1
   NW3 . . . . .91 G7

Winchester Rd, Bexh.
   DA7 . . . . .158 D2
   Bromley BR2 . . . . .191 F3
   Feltham TW13 . . . . . . .161 F3
   Harrow HA3 . . . . .69 H4
   Hayes UB3 . . . . .121 H7
   Ilford IG1 . . . . .99 G3
   Twickenham TW1 . . . . .144 E6
Winchester Sq, SE1 . . . . .28 B1
Winchester St, SW1 . . . . .32 E3
   W3 . . . . .126 C1
Winchester Wk, SE1 . . . . .28 B1
Winchet Wk, Croy. CR0 . .189 F6
Winchfield Cl, Har. HA3 . .69 F6
Winchfield Ho, SW15
   off Highcliffe Dr 147 F6
Winchfield Rd, SE26 . . . .171 H5
Winchilsea Cres, W.Mol.
   KT8 . . . . .179 J2
WINCHMORE HILL, N21 . .43 F7
Winchmore Hill Rd, N14 . .58 D1
   N21 . . . . .58 D1
Winckley Cl, Har. HA3 . . . .69 J5
Wincott St, SE11 . . . . .35 F1
Wincrofts Dr, SE9 . . . . . .157 G4
Windall Cl, SE19 . . . . . . .188 D1
Windborough Rd, Cars.
   SM5 . . . . .200 A7
Windermere Av, N3 . . . . .72 D3
   NW6 . . . . .108 B1
   SW19 . . . . .184 E3
   Harrow HA3 . . . . .69 F7
   Ruislip HA4 . . . . .66 C7
   Wembley HA9 . . . . .69 F7
Windermere Cl, Orp.
   BR6 . . . . .206 E3
Windermere Ct, SW13 . .127 F6
   Wembley HA9
   off Windermere Av 69 F7
Windermere Gdns, Ilf.
   IG4 . . . . .80 B5
Windermere Gro, Wem. HA9
   off Windermere Av 87 F1
Windermere Ho, Islw. TW7
   off Summerwood Rd .144 C5
Windermere Pt, SE15
   off Ilderton Rd 133 F7
Windermere Rd, N10 . . . .74 B1
   N19 off Holloway Rd . .92 C2
   SW15 . . . . .164 E4
   SW16 . . . . .186 C1
   W5 . . . . .125 F3
   Bexleyheath DA7 . . . . .159 J2
   Croydon CR0 . . . . .202 C1
   Southall UB1 . . . . .103 F5
   West Wickham BR4 . . .204 E2
Windermere Way, West Dr. UB7
   off Providence Rd 120 C1
Winders Rd, SW11 . . . . . .149 H2
Windfield Cl, SE26 . . . . . .171 G4
Windham Rd, Rich. TW9 .145 J3
Winding Way, Dag. RM8 .100 C3
   Harrow HA1 . . . . .86 B4
Windlass Pl, SE8 . . . . . . .133 H4
Windlesham Gro,
   SW19 . . . . .166 A1
Windley Cl, SE23 . . . . . . .171 F2
Windmill All, W4
   off Windmill Rd . .126/127 E4
Windmill Av, Sthl. UB2 . .123 J2
Windmill Br Ho, Croy.
   CR0 . . . . .202 B1
Windmill Cl, SE1 . . . . .37 J1
   SE13 . . . . .154 C2
   Surbiton KT6 . . . . .195 E1
Windmill Ct, NW2 . . . . . . .90 B6
Windmill Dr, NW2 . . . . . . .90 B3
   SW4 . . . . .150 C5
   Keston BR2 . . . . .205 J4
Windmill Gdns, Enf.
   EN2 . . . . .43 G3
Windmill Gro, Croy.
   CR0 . . . . .187 J7
Windmill Hill, NW3 . . . . . .91 F3
   Enfield EN2 . . . . .43 H3
Windmill Ho, E14
   off Westferry Rd 134 A4
Windmill La, E15 . . . . .96 D6
   Barnet EN5 . . . . .39 F6
   Bushey (Bushey Hth.)
   WD23 . . . . .52 B1
   Greenford UB6 . . . . . .103 J5
   Isleworth TW7 . . . . . . .124 B4
   Southall UB2 . . . . .123 J3
   Surbiton KT6 . . . . .181 E6
Windmill Ms, W4
   off Windmill Rd . .126/127 E4
Windmill Pas, W4 . . . . . .126 E4
Windmill Ri, Kings.T.
   KT2 . . . . .164 B7

Windmill Rd, N18 . . . . . . .60 A4
   SW18 . . . . .149 G6
   SW19 . . . . .165 H1
   W4 . . . . .126 E4
   W5 . . . . .125 F4
   Brentford TW8 . . . . . . .125 G5
   Croydon CR0 . . . . .187 J7
   Hampton (Hmptn.H.)
   TW12 . . . . .161 H5
   Mitcham CR4 . . . . .186 C5
Windmill Row, SE11 . . . . .35 E4
Windmill St, W1 . . . . .17 H2
   Bushey (Bushey Hth.)
   WD23 . . . . .52 B1
Windmill Wk, SE1 . . . . . . .27 F2
Windover Av, NW9 . . . . . .70 D4
Windrose Cl, SE16 . . . . . .133 G2
Windrush, N.Mal. KT3 . . .182 B4
Windrush Cl, SW11
   off Maysoule Rd 149 G4
   W4 . . . . .126 C1
   Uxbridge La, SE23 . . . .171 G3
Windrush Rd, NW10
   off Milton Av 106 D1
Windrush Sq, SW2
   off Rushcroft Rd 151 G4
Windsock Cl, SE16 . . . . .133 J4
Windsor Av, E17 . . . . .77 H2
   SW19 . . . . .185 F1
   Edgware HA8 . . . . .54 B4
   New Malden KT3 . . . . .182 C5
   Sutton SM3 . . . . .198 B3
   West Molesey KT8 . . . .179 G3
Windsor Cen, The, SE27
   off Advance Rd 169 J4
Windsor Cl, N3 . . . . .72 B2
   SE27 . . . . .169 J4
   Borehamwood WD6 . . .38 A1
   Brentford TW8 . . . . . . .124 E6
   Chislehurst BR7 . . . . . .175 E5
   Harrow HA2 . . . . .85 G3
   Northwood HA6 . . . . . .66 A2
Windsor Ct, N14 . . . . .42 C7
   Sunbury-on-Thames TW16
   off Windsor Rd 160 A6
Windsor Cres, Har. HA2 . .85 G4
   Wembley HA9 . . . . .88 B3
Windsor Dr, Barn. EN4 . . .41 J6
Windsor Gdns, W9 . . . . .108 D5
   Croydon CR0
   off Richmond Rd .200/201 E3
   Hayes UB3 . . . . .121 G3
Windsor Gro, SE27 . . . . .169 J4
Windsor Pk Rd, Hayes
   UB3 . . . . .121 J7
Windsor Pl, SW1 . . . . .25 G6
Windsor Rd, E4
   off Chivers Rd 62 B4
   E7 . . . . .97 H5
   E10 . . . . .96 B2
   E11 . . . . .97 G1
   N3 . . . . .72 B2
   N7 . . . . .93 E3
   N13 . . . . .59 G3
   N17 . . . . .76 D2
   NW2 . . . . .89 H6
   W5 . . . . .105 H7
   Barnet EN5 . . . . .40 B6
   Bexleyheath DA6 . . . . .158 E4
   Dagenham RM8 . . . . . .101 E3
   Harrow HA3 . . . . .68 A1
   Hounslow TW4 . . . . . .142 B2
   Ilford IG1 . . . . .99 E4
   Kingston upon Thames
   KT2 . . . . .163 H7
   Richmond TW9 . . . . . .145 J2
   Southall UB2 . . . . .123 F3
   Sunbury-on-Thames
   TW16 . . . . .160 A6
   Teddington TW11 . . . . .162 A5
   Thornton Heath CR7 . .187 H2
   Worcester Park KT4 . . .197 G2
Windsors, The, Buck.H.
   IG9 . . . . .64 B2
Windsor St, N1 . . . . .111 H1
Windsor Ter, N1 . . . . .12 A3
Windsor Wk, SE5 . . . . . . .152 A2
Windsor Way, W14 . . . . . .128 A4
Windsor Wf, E9 . . . . .95 J5
Windspoint Dr, SE15
   off Ethnard Rd . . .132/133 E6
Windus Rd, N16 . . . . .94 C1
Windus Wk, N16 . . . . .94 C1
Windy Ridge, Brom.
   BR1 . . . . .192 B1
Windyridge Cl, SW19 . . .166 A5
Wine Cl, E1 . . . . .113 F7
Wine Office Ct, EC4 . . . . .19 F3
Winery La, Kings.T.
   KT1 . . . . .181 J3

Winey Cl, Chess. KT9
  off Nigel Fisher Way . .**195** F7
Winford Ho, E3 . . . .**95** J7
Winford Par, Sthl. UB1
  off Telford Wk **103** H6
Winforton St, SE10 . . . . . .**154** C1
Winfrith Rd, SW18 . . . . . .**149** F7
Wingate Cres, Croy.
  CR0 . . . .**186** D6
Wingate Rd, W6 . . . .**127** H3
  Ilford IG1 . . . .**99** E5
  Sidcup DA14 . . . .**176** C5
Wingate Trd Est, N17 . . . . .**60** D7
Wingfield Ms, SE15
  off Wingfield St **152** D3
Wingfield Rd, E15 . . . .**96** E5
  E17 . . . .**78** B5
  Kingston upon Thames
  KT2 . . . .**164** A5
Wingfield St, SE15 . . . . . .**152** D3
Wingfield Way, Ruis.
  HA4 . . . .**84** B6
Wingford Rd, SW2 . . . . . .**150** E6
Wingmore Rd, SE24 . . . . .**151** J3
Wingrave Rd, W6 . . . .**127** J6
Wingrove Rd, SE6 . . . . . .**173** E2
Wings Cl, Sutt. SM1 . . . . .**198** D4
Winifred Gro, SW11 . . . . .**149** J4
Winifred Pl, N12
  off High Rd **57** F5
Winifred Rd, SW19 . . . . .**184** D1
  Dagenham RM8 . . . .**101** E2
  Hampton (Hmptn.H.)
  TW12 . . . .**161** G4
Winifred St, E16 . . . .**136** C1
Winifred Ter, E13
  off Victoria Rd **115** G2
  Enfield EN1
  off Great Cambridge
  Rd **44** C7
Winkfield Rd, E13 . . . . . .**115** H2
  N22 . . . .**75** G1
Winkley St, E2 . . . .**112** E2
Winlaton Rd, Brom.
  BR1 . . . .**172** D4
Winmill Rd, Dag.
  RM8 . . . .**101** F3
Winn Common Rd,
  SE18 . . . .**137** H6
Winnett St, W1 . . . .**17** H5
Winningales Ct, Ilf. IG5
  off Vienna Cl **80** B3
Winnings Wk, Nthlt. UB5
  off Arnold Rd **84/85** E6
Winnington Cl, N2 . . . .**73** G6
Winnington Rd, N2 . . . . . .**73** G7
Winnipeg Dr, Orp.
  BR6 . . . .**207** J6
Winnock Rd, West Dr.
  UB7 . . . .**120** A1
Winn Rd, SE12 . . . .**173** G1
Winns Av, E17 . . . .**77** H3
Winns Ms, N15
  off Grove Pk Rd **76** B4
Winns Ter, E17 . . . .**78** A2
Winsbeach, E17 . . . .**78** D3
Winscombe Cres, W5 . . . .**105** G4
Winscombe St, N19 . . . . . .**92** B2
Winscombe Way, Stan.
  HA7 . . . .**52** D5
Winsford Rd, SE6 . . . . . .**171** J3
Winsford Ter, N18 . . . .**60** A5
Winsham Gro, SW11 . . . . .**150** A5
Winslade Rd, SW2 . . . . . .**151** E5
Winslade Way, SE6
  off Rushey Grn **154** B7
Winsland Ms, W2 . . . .**15** E3
Winsland St, W2 . . . .**15** E3
Winsley St, W1 . . . .**17** F3
Winslow, SE17 . . . .**36** D4
Winslow Cl, NW10
  off Neasden La N . .**88/89** E3
  Pinner HA5 . . . .**66** B6
Winslow Gro, E4 . . . .**62** E2
Winslow Rd, W6 . . . .**127** J6
Winslow Way, Felt.
  TW13 . . . .**160** D3
Winsor Ter, E6 . . . .**116** D5
Winsor Ter Roundabout, E6
  off Royal Docks
  Rd **116/117** E5
Winstanley Est, SW11 . .**149** G3
Winstanley Rd, SW11 . . .**149** G3
Winstead Gdns, Dag.
  RM10 . . . .**101** J5
Winston Av, NW9 . . . .**70** E7
Winston Cl, Har. HA3 . . . . .**52** C6
  Romford RM7 . . . .**83** H4
Winston Ct, Har. HA3 . . . . .**51** H7
Winston Rd, N16 . . . .**94** A4

Winston Wk, W4
  off Beaconsfield Rd . . .**126** D4
Winston Way, Ilf. IG1 . . . . .**99** E3
Winstre Rd, Borwd. **38** A1
Winston Way, Ilf. IG1 . . . . .**99** E3
Winterborne Av, Orp.
  BR6 . . . .**207** G3
Winterbourne Rd, SE6 . . .**171** J1
  Dagenham RM8 . . . .**100** C2
  Thornton Heath CR7 . . .**187** G3
Winter Box Wk, Rich.
  TW10 . . . .**145** J4
Winterbrook Rd, SE24 . . .**151** J6
Winterburn Cl, N11 . . . . . .**58** A6
Winterfold Cl, SW19 . . . .**166** B2
Wintergreen Cl, E6
  off Yarrow Cres **116** B5
Winters Rd, T.Ditt. KT7 . . .**180** E7
Winterstoke Gdns, NW7 . .**55** G5
Winterstoke Rd, SE6 . . . .**171** J1
Winterton Ho, E1 . . . .**113** E6
Winterton Pl, SW10 . . . . . .**30** D5
Winterwell Rd, SW2 . . . . .**151** E5
Winthorpe Rd, SW15 . . . .**148** B4
Winthrop St, E1 . . . .**112** E5
Winthrop Wk, Wem. HA9
  off Everard Way **87** H3
Winton Av, N11 . . . .**58** C7
Winton Cl, N9 . . . .**45** G7
Winton Gdns, Edg. HA8 . . .**53** J7
Winton Rd, Orp. BR6 . . . .**206** E4
Winton Way, SW16 . . . . .**169** G5
Wisbeach Rd, Croy. CR0 .**188** A5
Wisdons Cl, Dag. RM10 . .**101** H1
Wise La, NW7 . . . .**55** H6
  West Drayton UB7 . . . . .**120** A4
Wiseman Ct, SE19 . . . . . .**170** B5
Wiseman Rd, E10 . . . .**96** A2
Wise Rd, E15 . . . .**114** D1
Wiseton Rd, SW17 . . . . . .**167** H1
Wishart Rd, SE3 . . . .**156** A1
Wisley Rd, SW11 . . . .**150** A5
  Orpington BR5 . . . .**176** A2
Wisteria Cl, NW7 . . . .**55** F6
  Ilford IG1 . . . .**98** E5
  Orpington BR6 . . . .**207** E2
Wisteria Rd, SE13 . . . . . .**154** D4
Witan St, E2 . . . .**113** E3
Witham Cl, Loug. IG10 . . . .**48** B6
Witham Rd, SE20 . . . .**189** F3
  W13 . . . .**124** D1
  Dagenham RM10 . . . . . .**101** G5
  Isleworth TW7 . . . .**144** A1
Witherby Cl, Croy. CR0 . .**202** B5
Witherington Rd, N5 . . . . .**93** G5
Withers Cl, Chess. KT9
  off Coppard Gdns **195** F6
Withers Mead, NW9 . . . . . .**71** F1
Witherston Way, SE9 . . . .**174** D2
Withycombe Rd, SW19 . . .**148** A7
Withy Mead, E4 . . . .**62** D3
Witley Cl, Croy.
  (New Adgtn.) CR0 . . . . .**204** C6
Witley Gdns, Sthl. UB2 . . .**123** F4
Witley Pt, SW15
  off Wanborough Dr **165** H1
Witley Rd, N19
  off Holloway Rd **92** C2
Witney Cl, Pnr. HA5 . . . . .**51** F6
Witney Path, SE23 . . . . .**171** G3
Wittenham Way, E4 . . . . . .**62** D3
Wittering Cl, Kings.T.
  KT2 . . . .**163** G5
Wittersham Rd, Brom.
  BR1 . . . .**173** F5
Wivenhoe Cl, SE15 . . . . .**152** E3
Wivenhoe Ct, Houns.
  TW3 . . . .**143** F4
Wivenhoe Rd, Bark.
  IG11 . . . .**118** A2
Wiverton Rd, SE26 . . . . . .**171** F6
Wixom Ho, SE3
  off Romero Sq **155** J4
Wix Rd, Dag. RM9 . . . . . .**118** D1
Wixs La, SW4 . . . .**150** B4
Woburn Cl, SE28
  off Summerton Way . . .**118** D6
  SW19 *off Tintern Cl* . . .**167** F6
  SE16 . . . .**133**
  off Masters Dr . . .**132/133** E5
Woburn Pl, WC1 . . . .**9** J5
Woburn Rd, Cars. SM5 . .**199** H1
  Croydon CR0 . . . .**201** J1
Woburn Sq, WC1 . . . .**9** J6
Woburn Wk, WC1 . . . .**9** J4
Wodehouse Av, SE5 . . . . .**152** C1
Woffington Cl, Kings.T.
  KT1 . . . .**181** F1
Woking Cl, SW15 . . . .**147** F4

Woldham Pl, Brom.
  BR2 . . . .**191** J4
Woldham Rd, Brom.
  BR2 . . . .**191** J4
Wolds Dr, Orp. BR6 . . . . .**206** D4
Wolfe Cl, Brom. BR2 . . . .**191** G6
  Hayes UB4
  off Ayles Rd **102** B3
Wolfe Cres, SE7 . . . .**136** A5
  SE16 . . . .**133** G2
Wolferton Rd, E12 . . . .**98** C4
Wolffe Gdns, E15 . . . .**97** F6
Wolffram Cl, SE13 . . . . . .**154** E5
Wolfington Rd, SE27 . . . .**169** H4
Wolftencroft Cl, SW11 . . .**149** G3
Wollaston Cl, SE1 . . . .**35** J1
Wolmer Cl, Edg. HA8 . . . . .**54** B4
Wolmer Gdns, Edg. HA8 . .**54** A3
Wolseley Av, SW19 . . . . .**166** D2
Wolseley Gdns, W4 . . . . .**126** B6
Wolseley Rd, E7 . . . .**97** H7
  N8 . . . .**74** D6
  N22 . . . .**75** F1
  W4 . . . .**126** C4
  Harrow HA3 . . . .**68** B3
  Mitcham CR4 . . . .**186** A7
Wolseley St, SE1 . . . .**29** G4
Wolsey Av, E6 . . . .**116** D3
  E17 . . . .**77** J3
  Thames Ditton KT7 . . . .**180** C5
Wolsey Cl, SW20 . . . .**165** H7
  Hounslow TW3 . . . .**143** J4
  Kingston upon Thames
  KT2 . . . .**182** B1
  Southall UB2 . . . .**123** J3
  Worcester Park KT4 . . . .**197** G4
Wolsey Cres, Mord.
  SM4 . . . .**184** B7
Wolsey Dr, Kings.T.
  KT2 . . . .**163** H5
  Walton-on-Thames
  KT12 . . . .**178** C7
Wolsey Gdns, Ilf. IG6 . . . . .**65** F6
Wolsey Gro, Edg. HA8 . . . .**54** D7
Wolsey Ms, NW5 . . . .**92** C6
  Orpington BR6
  off Osgood Av **207** J5
Wolsey Rd, N1 . . . .**94** A5
  East Molesey KT8 . . . . .**180** A4
  Enfield EN1 . . . .**45** E2
  Hampton (Hmptn.H.)
  TW12 . . . .**161** H6
Wolsey St, E1
  off Sidney St **113** F5
Wolsey Way, Chess.
  KT9 . . . .**196** A5
Wolstonbury, N12 . . . .**56** D5
Wolvercote Rd, SE2 . . . . .**138** D2
Wolverley St, E2
  off Bethnal Grn
  Rd **112/113** E3
Wolverton Av, Kings.T.
  KT2 . . . .**182** A1
Wolverton Gdns, W5 . . . .**105** J7
  W6 . . . .**128** A4
Wolverton Rd, Stan.
  HA7 . . . .**53** E6
Wolverton Way, N14 . . . . .**42** C5
Wolves La, N13 . . . .**59** G7
  N22 . . . .**59** G7
Womersley Rd, N8 . . . .**75** F6
Wonford Cl, Kings.T.
  KT2 . . . .**183** E1
Wontner Cl, N1
  off Greenman St **93** J7
Wontner Rd, SW17 . . . . . .**167** J2
Woodall Cl, E14
  off Lawless St **114** B7
Woodall Rd, Enf. EN3 . . . . .**45** G6
Woodbank Rd, Brom.
  BR1 . . . .**173** F3
Woodbastwick Rd,
  SE26 . . . .**171** G5
Woodberry Av, N21 . . . . . .**59** G2
  Harrow HA2 . . . .**67** H4
Woodberry Cl, NW7
  off Bittacy Hill **56** B7
  Sunbury-on-Thames TW16
  off Ashridge Way **160** A6
Woodberry Cres, N10 . . . .**74** B3
Woodberry Down, N4 . . . .**75** J7
Woodberry Down Est,
  N4 . . . .**75** J7
Woodberry Gdns, N12 . . . .**57** F6
Woodberry Gro, N12 . . . . .**57** F6
  N12 . . . .**57** F6
Woodberry Way, E4 . . . . . .**62** C1
  N12 . . . .**57** F6
Woodbine Cl, Twick.
  TW2 . . . .**162** A2
Woodbine Gro, SE20 . . . .**171** E7

Woodbine La, Wor.Pk.
  KT4 . . . .**197** G3
Woodbine Pl, E11 . . . .**79** G6
Woodbine Rd, Sid.
  DA15 . . . .**175** H1
Woodbines Av, Kings.T.
  KT1 . . . .**181** G3
Woodbine Ter, E9
  off Morning La **95** F6
Woodborough Rd,
  SW15 . . . .**147** H4
Woodbourne Av, SW16 . .**168** D3
Woodbourne Cl, SW16
  off Woodbourne
  Av **168/169** E3
Woodbourne Dr, Esher (Clay.)
  KT10 . . . .**194** C6
Woodbourne Gdns, Wall.
  SM6 . . . .**200** B7
Woodbridge Cl, N7 . . . . . .**93** F2
  NW2 . . . .**89** G3
Woodbridge Ct, Wdf.Grn.
  IG8 . . . .**64** B7
Woodbridge Rd, Bark.
  IG11 . . . .**99** J5
Woodbridge St, EC1 . . . . .**11** G5
Woodbrook Rd, SE2 . . . . .**138** A6
Woodburn Cl, NW4 . . . . . .**72** A5
Woodbury Cl, E11 . . . .**79** H4
  Croydon CR0 . . . .**202** C2
Woodbury Hill, Loug.
  IG10 . . . .**48** B3
Woodbury Hollow, Loug.
  IG10 . . . .**48** B2
Woodbury Pk Rd, W13 . . .**104** E4
Woodbury Rd, E17 . . . .**78** B4
Woodbury St, SW17 . . . . .**167** H5
Woodchester Sq, W2 . . . . .**14** A1
Woodchurch Cl, Sid.
  DA14 . . . .**175** G3
Woodchurch Dr, Brom.
  BR1 . . . .**174** A7
Woodchurch Rd, NW6 . . . .**90** D7
Wood Cl, E2 . . . .**13** H5
  NW9 . . . .**70** D7
  Harrow HA1 . . . .**68** A7
Woodclyffe Dr, Chis.
  BR7 . . . .**192** D2
Woodcock Ct, Har. HA3 . . .**69** H7
Woodcock Dell Av, Har.
  HA3 . . . .**69** G7
Woodcock Hill, Har. HA3 . .**69** G7
Woodcocks, E16 . . . .**115** J5
Woodcombe Cres, SE23 .**171** F1
Woodcote Av, NW7 . . . . . .**55** J6
  Thornton Heath CR7 . . .**187** H4
  Wallington SM6 . . . .**200** B7
Woodcote Cl, Enf. EN3 . . . .**45** F6
  Kingston upon Thames
  KT2 . . . .**163** J5
Woodcote Dr, Orp. BR6 . .**207** G1
Woodcote Ms, Loug.
  IG10 . . . .**48** A7
  Wallington SM6 . . . .**200** B6
Woodcote Pl, SE27 . . . . .**169** H5
Woodcote Rd, E11 . . . .**79** G7
  Wallington SM6 . . . .**200** B6
Woodcott Ho, SW15
  off Ellisfield Dr **147** G7
Woodcroft, N21 . . . .**59** F1
  SE9 . . . .**174** C3
  Greenford UB6 . . . .**86** D6
Woodcroft Av, NW7 . . . . . .**55** E7
  Stanmore HA7 . . . .**68** C1
Woodcroft Ms, SE8
  off Croft St **133** H4
Woodcroft Rd, Th.Hth.
  CR7 . . . .**187** H5
Wood Dr, Chis. BR7 . . . . .**174** B6
Woodedge Cl, E4 . . . .**63** F1
Woodend, SE19 . . . .**169** J6
  Sutton SM1 . . . .**199** F2
Wood End Av, Har. HA2 . . .**85** H4
Wood End Cl, Nthlt. UB5 . . .**86** A5
Woodend Gdns, Enf.
  EN2 . . . .**42** E4
Wood End Gdns, Nthlt.
  UB5 . . . .**85** J5
Wood End La, Nthlt.
  UB5 . . . .**85** H6
Woodend Rd, E17 . . . .**78** C2
Wood End Rd, Har. HA1 . . .**86** A4
Wood End Way, Nthlt.
  UB5 . . . .**85** J5
Wooder Gdns, E7 . . . .**97** F4
Wooderson Cl, SE25 . . . .**188** B4
Woodfall Av, Barn. EN5 . . .**40** C5
Woodfall Rd, N4 . . . .**93** G1
Woodfall St, SW3 . . . .**31** J4
Woodfarrs, SE5 . . . .**152** A4

Woodfield Av, NW9 . . . . .**71** E4
SW16 . . . .**168** D3
W5 . . . .**105** F4
Carshalton SM5 . . . . . .**200** A6
Wembley HA0 . . . .**87** F3
Woodfield Cl, SE19 . . . . .**169** J7
Enfield EN1 . . . .**44** B4
Woodfield Cres, W5 . . . . .**105** F4
Woodfield Dr, Barn.
EN4 . . . .**58** A1
Woodfield Gdns, W9
off Woodfield Rd **108** C5
New Malden KT3 . . . . . .**183** F5
Woodfield Gro, SW16 . . . .**168** D3
Woodfield La, SW16 . . . . .**168** D3
Woodfield Pl, W9 . . . .**108** C4
Woodfield Rd, W5 . . . . . .**105** F4
W9 . . . .**108** C5
Hounslow TW4 . . . .**142** B2
Thames Ditton KT7 . . . . .**194** C2
Woodfield Way, N11 . . . . .**58** D7
WOODFORD, Wdf.Grn. **63** H6
Woodford Av, Ilf. IG2,
IG4 . . . .**80** C5
Woodford Green IG8 . . . .**80** A3
WOODFORD BRIDGE,
Wdf.Grn. **64** C7
Woodford Br Rd, Ilf. IG4 . .**80** A3
Woodford Ct, W12
off Shepherds Bush
Grn **128** A2
Woodford Cres, Pnr.
HA5 . . . .**66** B2
WOODFORD GREEN **63** F4
Woodford New Rd, E17 . . .**78** E4
E18 . . . .**79** E1
Woodford Green IG8 . . . . .**79** E1
Woodford Pl, Wem. HA9 . . .**87** H1
Woodford Rd, E7 . . . .**97** H4
E18 . . . .**79** G4
WOODFORD WELLS,
Wdf.Grn. **63** H4
Woodgate Av, Chess.
KT9 . . . .**195** G5
Woodgate Cres, Nthwd.
HA6 . . . .**50** A6
Woodgate Dr, SW16 . . . .**168** D7
Woodger Rd, W12
off Goldhawk Rd **127** J2
Woodget Cl, E6
off Remington Rd **116** B6
Woodgrange Av, N12 . . . . .**57** G6
W5 . . . .**126** A1
Enfield EN1 . . . .**44** D6
Harrow HA3 . . . .**69** F5
Woodgrange Cl, Har.
HA3 . . . .**69** G5
Woodgrange Gdns, Enf.
EN1 . . . .**44** D6
Woodgrange Rd, E7 . . . . .**97** H4
Woodgrange Ter, Enf. EN1
off Great Cambridge
Rd **44** D6
WOOD GREEN, N22 . . . . .**75** E1
Wood Grn Shop City, N22
off High Rd **75** G2
Woodhall Av, SE21 . . . . .**170** C3
Pinner HA5 . . . .**66** E2
Woodhall Cl, Chess. KT9
off Ashlyns Way **195** G6
Woodhall Dr, SE21 . . . . .**170** C3
Pinner HA5 . . . .**66** D1
Woodhall Gate, Pnr.
HA5 . . . .**50** D7
Woodhall Ho, SW18
off Fitzhugh Gro **149** G6
Woodhall La, Wat. WD19 . .**50** D4
Woodhall Rd, Pnr. HA5 . . .**50** D7
Woodham Ct, E18 . . . .**79** F4
Woodham Rd, SE6 . . . . . .**172** C3
Woodhatch Cl, E6
off Remington Rd **116** B6
Woodhaven Gdns, Ilf. IG6
off Brandville Gdns . . .**81** F3
Woodhayes Rd, SW19 . . . .**165** J7
Woodhead Dr, Orp. BR6
off Sherlies Av **207** H2
Woodheyes Rd, NW10 . . . .**88** D5
Woodhill, SE18 . . . .**136** B4
Woodhill Cres, Har. HA3 . .**69** G6
Wood Ho, SW17
off Laurel Cl **167** H5
Woodhouse Av, Grnf.
UB6 . . . .**104** C2
Woodhouse Cl, Grnf.
UB6 . . . .**104** C2
Hayes UB3 . . . .**121** H3
Woodhouse Eaves, Nthwd.
HA6 . . . .**50** A6
Woodhouse Gro, E12 . . . . .**98** B6

Woodhouse Rd, E11 . . . . .**97** F3
N12 . . . .**57** G6
Woodhurst Av, Orp.
BR5 . . . .**193** F6
Woodhurst Rd, SE2 . . . . .**138** A5
W3 . . . .**106** C7
Woodington Cl, SE9 . . . . .**156** D6
Woodknoll Dr, Chis.
BR7 . . . .**192** C1
Woodland App, Grnf.
UB6 . . . .**86** D6
Woodland Cl, NW9 . . . . . .**70** C6
SE19
off Woodland Hill **170** B6
Epsom KT19 . . . .**197** E6
Woodford Green IG8 . . . .**63** H3
Woodland Cres, SE10 . . . .**134** E6
SE16 . . . .**133** G2
Woodland Gdns, N10 . . . . .**74** B5
Isleworth TW7 . . . .**144** B3
Woodland Gro, SE10 . . . .**134** E5
Woodland Hill, SE19 . . . .**170** B6
Woodland Ri, N10 . . . .**74** B4
Greenford UB6 . . . .**86** D6
Woodland Rd, E4 . . . .**62** C1
N11 . . . .**58** B5
SE19 . . . .**170** B5
Loughton IG10 . . . .**48** B3
Thornton Heath CR7 . . .**187** G4
WOODLANDS, Islw. **144** B2
Woodlands, NW11 . . . .**72** B6
SW20 . . . .**183** J4
Harrow HA2 . . . .**67** G4
Woodlands, The, N14 . . . . .**58** B1
SE13 . . . .**154** D7
SE19 . . . .**169** J7
Beckenham BR3 . . . . . .**190** C1
Isleworth TW7 . . . .**144** C2
Woodlands Av, E11 . . . . . .**97** H1
N3 . . . .**57** F7
W3 . . . .**126** B1
New Malden KT3 . . . . . .**182** C1
Romford RM6 . . . .**82** E6
Ruislip HA4 . . . .**84** C1
Sidcup DA15 . . . .**175** H1
Worcester Park KT4 . . . .**197** F2
Woodlands Cl, NW11 . . . . .**72** B5
Borehamwood WD6 . . . .**38** B4
Bromley BR1 . . . .**192** C2
Esher (Clay.) KT10 . . . .**194** C7
Woodlands Dr, Stan.
HA7 . . . .**52** C6
Sunbury-on-Thames
TW16 . . . .**178** C2
Woodlands Gro, Islw.
TW7 . . . .**144** B2
Woodlands Pk, Bex.
DA5 . . . .**177** J4
Woodlands Pk Rd, N15 . . .**75** H5
SE10 . . . .**134** E6
Woodlands Rd, E11 . . . . . .**96** E2
E17 . . . .**78** C3
N9 . . . .**61** F1
SW13 . . . .**147** F3
Bexleyheath DA7 . . . . .**159** E3
Bromley BR1 . . . .**192** B2
Enfield EN2 . . . .**44** A1
Harrow HA1 . . . .**68** C5
Ilford IG1 . . . .**99** F3
Isleworth TW7 . . . .**144** B1
Southall UB1 . . . .**122** D1
Surbiton KT6 . . . .**181** G7
Woodlands St, SE13 . . . . .**154** D7
Woodland St, E8
off Dalston La **94** C6
Woodlands Way, SW15
off Oakhill Rd **148** C5
Woodland Ter, SE7 . . . . .**136** B4
Woodland Wk, NW3 . . . . . .**91** H5
SE10 off Woodland
Gro **134/135** E5
Bromley BR1 . . . .**172** E4
Woodland Way, N21 . . . . . .**59** G2
NW7 . . . .**55** E6
SE2 . . . .**138** D4
Croydon CR0 . . . .**203** H1
Mitcham CR4 . . . .**168** A7
Morden SM4 . . . .**184** C4
Orpington BR5 . . . .**193** F4
Surbiton KT5 . . . .**196** B2
West Wickham BR4 . . . .**204** B4
Woodford Green IG8 . . . .**63** H3
Wood La, N6 . . . .**74** B6
NW9 . . . .**70** E7
W12 . . . .**107** J6
Dagenham RM8, RM9,
RM10 . . . .**100** C4
Isleworth TW7 . . . .**124** C7
Stanmore HA7 . . . .**52** D3
Woodford Green IG8 . . . .**63** F5

Woodlawn Cl, SW15 . . . .**148** C5
Woodlawn Cres, Twick.
TW2 . . . .**161** H2
Woodlawn Dr, Felt.
TW13 . . . .**160** C1
Woodlawn Rd, SW6 . . . . .**128** A7
Woodlea Dr, Brom.
BR2 . . . .**191** E5
Woodlea Rd, N16 . . . .**94** B3
Woodleigh, E18
off Churchfields **79** G1
Woodleigh Av, N12 . . . . . .**57** H6
Woodleigh Gdns, SW16 . .**169** E3
Woodley Cl, SW17
off Arnold Rd **167** J7
Woodley La, Cars. SM5 . .**199** G3
Wood Lo Gdns, Brom.
BR1 . . . .**174** B7
Wood Lo La, W.Wick.
BR4 . . . .**204** C3
Woodman La, E4 . . . .**46** E5
Woodman Path, Ilf. IG6 . . .**65** H6
Woodmans Gro, NW10 . . . .**89** F5
Woodmans Ms, W12 . . . .**107** H5
Woodmansterne Rd,
SW16 . . . .**186** D1
Woodman St, E16 . . . . . .**136** D1
Woodmere, SE9 . . . .**174** C1
Woodmere Av, Croy.
CR0 . . . .**189** G7
Woodmere Cl, SW11 . . . . .
off Lavender Hill **150** A3
Croydon CR0 . . . .**189** G7
Woodmere Gdns, Croy.
CR0 . . . .**189** G7
Woodmere Way, Beck.
BR3 . . . .**190** D5
Woodnook Rd, SW16 . . . .**168** B5
Woodpecker Cl, N9 . . . . . .**44** E6
Bushey WD23 . . . .**51** J1
Harrow HA3 . . . .**68** C1
Woodpecker Rd, SE14 . . .**133** H6
SE28 . . . .**118** C7
Wood Pt, E16
off Fife Rd **115** G5
Woodquest Av, SE24 . . . .**151** J5
Wood Retreat, SE18 . . . .**137** G7
Wood Ride, Barn. EN4 . . . .**41** G1
Orpington BR5 . . . .**193** G4
Woodridge Cl, Enf. EN2 . . .**43** G1
Woodridings Av, Pnr.
HA5 . . . .**67** F1
Woodridings Cl, Pnr.
HA5 . . . .**51** E7
Woodriffe Rd, E11 . . . .**78** D7
Wood Ri, Pnr. HA5 . . . . . .**66** A5
Wood Rd, NW10
off Fawood Av **88** D7
Woodrow, SE18 . . . .**136** C4
Woodrow Cl, Grnf. UB6 . . .**87** E7
Woodrow Ct, N17
off Heybourne Rd . .**60/61** E7
Woodrush Cl, SE14
off Southerngate
Way **133** H7
Woodrush Way, Rom.
RM6 . . . .**82** D4
Woods, The, Nthwd.
HA6 . . . .**50** A5
Wood's Bldgs, E1
off Whitechapel
Rd **112/113** E5
Woodseer St, E1 . . . .**21** G1
Woodsford, SE17 . . . .**36** B4
Woodsford Sq, W14 . . . . .**128** B2
Woodshire Rd, Dag.
RM10 . . . .**101** H3
WOODSIDE, Croy. **188** D6
Woodside, NW11 . . . .**72** D5
SW19 . . . .**166** C6
Buckhurst Hill IG9 . . . . .**63** J2
Woodside Av, N6 . . . .**73** J5
N10 . . . .**73** J5
N12 . . . .**57** F4
SE25 . . . .**188** E6
Chislehurst BR7 . . . . . .**175** F5
Esher KT10 . . . .**180** B7
Wembley HA0 . . . .**105** H1
Woodside Cl, Stan.
HA7 . . . .**52** E5
Surbiton KT5 . . . .**182** C7
Wembley HA0 . . . .**105** H1
Woodside Ct, N12
off Woodside Av **57** F4
Woodside Ct Rd, Croy.
CR0 . . . .**188** D7
Woodside Cres, Sid.
DA15 . . . .**175** H3
Woodside End, Wem.
HA0 . . . .**105** H1

Woodside Gdns, E4 . . . . . .**62** B5
N17 . . . .**76** B2
Woodside Gra Rd, N12 . . .**57** E4
Woodside Grn, SE25 . . . .**188** E6
Woodside Gro, N12 . . . . . .**57** F3
Woodside La, N12 . . . .**57** E3
Bexley DA5 . . . .**158** D6
Woodside Ms, SE22
off Heber Rd **152** C6
Woodside Pk, SE25 . . . . .**188** D5
Woodside Pk Av, E17 . . . . .**78** D4
Woodside Pk Rd, N12 . . . .**57** E4
Woodside Pl, Wem.
HA0 . . . .**105** H1
Woodside Rd, E13 . . . . . .**115** J4
N22 . . . .**59** F7
SE25 . . . .**188** E6
Bromley BR1 . . . .**192** B5
Kingston upon Thames
KT2 . . . .**163** H7
New Malden KT3 . . . . . .**182** D2
Sidcup DA15 . . . .**175** H3
Sutton SM1 . . . .**199** F3
Woodford Green IG8 . . . .**63** G4
Woodside Way, Croy.
CR0 . . . .**189** E6
Mitcham CR4 . . . .**186** B1
Woods Ms, W1 . . . .**16** A5
Woodsome Rd, NW5 . . . . .**92** A3
Woods Pl, SE1 . . . .**28** E6
Woodspring Rd, SW19 . . .**166** B2
Woods Rd, SE15 . . . .**152** E1
Woodstead Gro, Edg.
HA8 . . . .**53** H6
Woodstock Av, NW11 . . . . .**72** B7
W13 . . . .**124** D3
Isleworth TW7 . . . .**144** D5
Southall UB1 . . . .**103** F3
Sutton SM3 . . . .**184** C7
Woodstock Cl, Bex.
DA5 . . . .**177** F1
Stanmore HA7 . . . .**69** H2
Woodstock Ct, SE12 . . . . .**155** G6
Woodstock Cres, N9 . . . . .**44** E6
Woodstock Gdns, Beck.
BR3 . . . .**190** B1
Ilford IG3 . . . .**100** A2
Woodstock Gro, W12 . . . .**128** A2
Woodstock La N, Surb.
KT6 . . . .**195** F2
Woodstock La S, Chess.
KT9 . . . .**195** F4
Esher (Clay.) KT10 . . . .**194** E5
Woodstock Ms, W1 . . . . . .**16** C2
Woodstock Ri, Sutt.
SM3 . . . .**184** C7
Woodstock Rd, E7 . . . .**97** J7
E17 . . . .**78** D2
N4 . . . .**93** G1
NW11 . . . .**72** C7
W4 . . . .**127** E3
Carshalton SM5 . . . . . .**200** A5
Croydon CR0 . . . .**202** A3
Wembley HA0 . . . .**87** J7
Woodstock St, E16
off Victoria Dock
Rd **114/115** E6
W1 . . . .**16** D4
Woodstock Ter, E14 . . . . .**114** B7
Woodstock Way, Mitch.
CR4 . . . .**186** B2
Woodstone Av, Epsom
KT17 . . . .**197** G5
Wood St, E17 . . . .**78** C3
EC2 . . . .**20** A4
W4 . . . .**126** E5
Barnet EN5 . . . .**39** J4
Kingston upon Thames
KT1 . . . .**181** G1
Mitcham CR4 . . . .**186** A7
Woodsyre, SE26 . . . .**170** C4
Woodthorpe Rd, SW15 . . .**147** H4
Woodtree Cl, NW4
off Ashley La **71** J2
Wood Vale, N10 . . . .**74** C5
SE23 . . . .**170** E1
Woodvale Av, SE25 . . . . .**188** C3
Wood Vale Est, SE23 . . . .**153** F6
Woodvale Wk, SE27
off Elder Rd **169** J5
Woodvale Way, NW11
off The Vale **90** A3
Woodview Av, E4 . . . .**62** C4
Woodview Cl, N4 . . . .**75** H7
SW15 . . . .**164** D4
Orpington BR6
off Crofton Rd **207** F2
Woodville, SE3 . . . .**155** H1
Woodville Cl, SE12 . . . . . .**155** G5
Teddington TW11 . . . . . .**162** D4

Woodville Gdns, NW11 . . .72 A7
W5 . . . . .105 H6
Ilford IG6 . . . . .80 E3
Woodville Gro, Well.
DA16 . . . . .158 A3
Woodville Rd, E11 . . . . .97 F1
E17 . . . . .77 H4
E18 . . . . .79 H2
N16 . . . . .95 H5
NW6 . . . . .108 C2
NW11 . . . . .72 A7
W5 . . . . .105 G6
Barnet EN5 . . . . .40 E3
Morden SM4 . . . . .184 D4
Richmond TW10 . . . .163 E3
Thornton Heath CR7 . .187 J4
Woodville St, SE18
off Woodhill 136 B4
Woodward Av, NW4 . . . . . .71 G5
Woodward Cl, Esher (Clay.)
KT10 . . . . .194 C6
Woodwarde Rd, SE22 . .152 B6
Woodward Gdns, Dag. RM9
off Woodward Rd 100 C7
Stanmore HA7 . . . . . . .52 C7
Woodward Rd, Dag.
RM9 . . . . .100 B7
Wood Way, Orp. BR6 . . .206 D2
Woodway Cres, Har.
HA1 . . . . .68 D6
Woodwell St, SW18
off Huguenot Pl 149 F5
Wood Wf, Sel10 . . . . . . .134 B6
Woodyard Cl, NW5
off Gillies St 92 A5
Woodyard La, SE21 . . . .152 B7
Woodyates Rd, SE12 . . .155 G6
Woolacombe Rd, SE3 . . .155 J1
Woolacombe Way, Hayes
UB3 . . . . .121 H4
Wooler St, SE17 . . . . . . .36 B4
Woolf Cl, SE28 . . . . .138 B1
Woolf Ms, WC1
off Burton St 110 D4
Woollaston Rd, N4 . . . . . .75 H6
Woolmead Av, NW9 . . . . .71 G7
Woolmer Gdns, N18 . . . . .60 D5
Woolmer Rd, N18 . . . . . . .60 D5
Woolmore St, E14 . . . . .114 C7
Woolneigh St, SW6 . . . .148 E3
Wool Rd, SW20 . . . . . . .165 H6
Woolstaplers Way, SE16 . .29 H6
Woolston Cl, E17
off Riverhead Cl 77 G2
Woolstone Rd, SE23 . . .171 H2
WOOLWICH, SE18 . . . . .136 D5
Woolwich Ch St, SE18 . .136 B3
★ Woolwich Common,
SE18 . . . . .136 C7
Woolwich Common,
SE18 . . . . .136 D6
Woolwich Ferry Pier,
E16 . . . . .136 D2
Woolwich Foot Tunnel,
E16 . . . . .136 D2
SE18 . . . . .136 D2
Woolwich Garrison,
SE18 . . . . .136 C6
Woolwich High St,
SE18 . . . . .136 D3
Woolwich Ind Est, SE28
off Hadden Rd 137 H3
Woolwich Manor Way,
E6 . . . . .116 C4
E16 . . . . .136 E2
Woolwich Mkt, SE18 . . .136 E4
Woolwich New Rd,
SE18 . . . . .136 D5
Woolwich Rd, SE2 . . . . .138 D6
SE7 . . . . .135 G5
SE10 . . . . .135 F5
Belvedere DA17 . . . . .138 D6
Bexleyheath DA7 . . . .159 G4
Wooster Gdns, E14 . . . .114 D6
Wooster Ms, Har. HA2
off Fairfield Dr 67 J3
Wooster Pl, SE1 . . . . .36 C1
Wootton St, SE1 . . . . .27 F3
Worbeck Rd, SE20 . . . . .189 E2
Worcester Av, N17 . . . . . .60 D7
Worcester Cl, NW2
off Newfield Ri 89 H3
Croydon CR0 . . . . . . .203 J2
Mitcham CR4 . . . . . . .186 B3
Worcester Cres, NW7 . . . .54 E3
Woodford Green IG8 . . .63 H5
Worcester Dr, W4 . . . . . .127 E2
Worcester Gdns, SW11
off Grandison Rd 149 J5

Worcester Gdns, Grnf.
UB6 . . . . .85 J6
Ilford IG1 . . . . .80 B7
Worcester Park KT4 . . .197 E3
Worcester Ms, NW6
off Lymington Rd . .90/91 E6
WORCESTER PARK 197 F2
Worcester Pk Rd, Wor.Pk.
KT4 . . . . .196 C3
Worcester Rd, E12 . . . . . .98 C4
E17 . . . . .77 G2
SW19 . . . . .166 C5
Sutton SM4 . . . . .199 E6
Wordsworth Av, E12 . . . .98 B6
E18 . . . . .79 F3
Greenford UB6 . . . . . .104 A2
Wordsworth Dr, Sutt.
SM3 . . . . .197 J4
Wordsworth Rd, N16 . . . .94 B4
SE1 . . . . .37 F2
SE20 . . . . .171 G7
Hampton TW12 . . . . . .161 F4
Wallington SM6 . . . . .200 C6
Welling DA16 . . . . . . .157 H1
Wordsworth Wk, NW11 . .72 D4
Wordsworth Way, West Dr.
UB7 . . . . .120 B4
Worfield St, SW11 . . . . .129 H7
Worgan St, SE11 . . . . . . .34 C3
SE16 . . . . .133 G3
Worland Rd, E15 . . . . . . .97 E7
WORLD'S END, Enf. 43 G3
World's End Est, SW10 . .30 E7
Worlds End La, N21 . . . . .43 F5
Enfield EN2 . . . . .43 F5
Orpington BR6 . . . . . .207 J6
World's End Pl, SW10
off King's Rd 129 F7
Worlidge St, W6 . . . . . . .127 J5
Worlingham Rd, SE22 . .152 C4
Wormholt Rd, W12 . . . . .107 G7
Wormwood St, EC2 . . . . .20 D3
Wornington Rd, W10 . . .108 B5
Woronzow Rd, NW8 . . . .109 G1
Worple Av, SW19 . . . . . .166 A7
Isleworth TW7 . . . . . .144 D5
Worple Cl, Har. HA2 . . . . .85 F1
Worple Rd, SW19 . . . . . .166 B7
SW20 . . . . .183 J2
Isleworth TW7 . . . . . .144 D4
Worple Rd Ms, SW19 . .166 C6
Worple St, SW14 . . . . . .146 D3
Worple Way, Har. HA2 . . .85 F1
Richmond TW10 . . . . .145 H5
Worship St, EC2 . . . . . . .12 C6
Worslade Rd, SW17 . . . .167 G4
Worsley Br Rd, SE26 . . .171 J4
Beckenham BR3 . . . . .171 J5
Worsley Gro, E5 . . . . .94 D4
Worsley Rd, E11 . . . . . . .96 E4
Worsopp Dr, SW4 . . . . .150 C5
Worth Cl, Orp. BR6 . . . .207 H4
Worthfield Cl, Epsom
KT19 . . . . .196 D7
Worth Gro, SE17 . . . . . . .36 B4
Worthing Cl, E15 . . . .
off Mitre Rd 114/115 E2
Worthing Rd, Houns.
TW5 . . . . .123 F6
Worthington Cl, Mitch.
CR4 . . . . .186 B3
Worthington Rd, Surb.
KT6 . . . . .195 J1
Worthy Down Ct, SE18
off Prince Imperial
Rd 156 D1
Wortley Rd, E6 . . . . .98 A7
Croydon CR0 . . . . . . .187 G2
Worton Gdns, Islw. TW7 .144 A2
Worton Hall Ind Est, Islw.
TW7 . . . . .144 B4
Worton Rd, Islw. TW7 . .144 B3
Worton Way, Houns.
TW3 . . . . .144 A2
Isleworth TW7 . . . . . .143 J1
Wotton Rd, NW2 . . . . . . .89 J4
SE8 . . . . .133 J6
Wouldham Rd, E16 . . . .115 F6
Wragby Rd, E11 . . . . .97 E3
Wrampling Pl, N9 . . . . . . .60 D1
Wrangthorn Wk, Croy. CR0
off Epsom Rd 201 G4
Wray Av, Ilf. IG5 . . . . .80 D3
Wray Cres, N4 . . . . .93 E2
Wrayfield Rd, Sutt.
SM3 . . . . .198 A3
Wraysbury Cl, Houns. TW4
off Dorney Way . . .142/143 E5
Wrekin Rd, SE18 . . . . . .137 F7

Wren Av, NW2 . . . . .89 J5
Southall UB2 . . . . . . .123 F4
Wren Cl, E16
off Ibbotson Av 115 F6
N9 off Chaffinch Cl 61 G1
Wren Cres, Bushey
WD23 . . . . .51 J1
Wren Dr, West Dr. UB7 . .120 A3
Wren Gdns, Dag. RM9 . .100 D5
Wren Landing, E14
off Cabot Sq 133 J1
Wren Ms, SE13
off Lee High Rd . .154/155 E4
Wren Path, SE28 . . . . . .137 G3
Wren Rd, SE5 . . . . .152 A1
Dagenham RM9 . . . . .100 D5
Sidcup DA14 . . . . . . .176 C4
Wren St, WC1 . . . . .10 D5
Wren Ter, Ilf. IG5
off Tiptree Cres 80 D3
Wrentham Av, NW10 . . .108 A2
Wrenthorpe Rd, Brom.
BR1 . . . . .172 E4
Wrenwood Way, Pnr.
HA5 . . . . .66 B4
Wrestlers Ct, EC3
off Camomile St 112 B6
Wrexham Rd, E3 . . . . . .114 A2
Wricklemarsh Rd, SE3 . .155 H1
Wrigglesworth St, SE14 .133 G7
Wright Rd, N1
off Burder Cl 94 B6
Hounslow TW5 . . . . . .122 C7
Wrights All, SW19 . . . . .165 J6
Wrights Cl, SE13
off Wisteria Rd 154 D4
Dagenham RM10 . . . .101 H3
Wrights Grn, SW4
off Nelson's Row 150 D4
Wrights La, W8 . . . . .22 A5
Wrights Pl, NW10
off Mitchell Way 88 C6
Wrights Rd, E3 . . . . .113 J2
SE25 . . . . .188 B3
Wrights Row, Wall.
SM6 . . . . .200 B4
Wrights Wk, SW14 . . . .146 D3
Wrigley Cl, E4 . . . . .62 D5
Wrotham Rd, NW1
off Agar Pl 92 C7
W13 off Mattock
La 124/125 E1
Barnet EN5 . . . . .40 B2
Welling DA16 . . . . . . .158 C1
Wroths Path, Loug. IG10 . .48 C1
Wrottesley Rd, NW10 . . .107 G2
SE18 . . . . .137 F6
Wroughton Rd, SW11 . .149 J6
Wroughton Ter, NW4 . . . .71 J4
Wroxall Rd, Dag. RM9 . .100 C6
Wroxham Gdns, N11 . . . .58 C7
Wroxham Rd, SE28 . . . .118 D7
Wroxton Rd, SE15 . . . . .153 E2
WRYTHE, THE, Cars. . . .199 H2
Wrythe Grn, Cars. SM5
off Wrythe Grn Rd . . .199 J3
Wrythe Grn Rd, Cars.
SM5 . . . . .199 J3
Wrythe La, Cars. SM5 . .199 F1
Wulfstan St, W12 . . . . . .107 F6
Wyatt Cl, SE16 . . . . .133 J2
Feltham TW13 . . . . . .160 C1
Hayes UB4 . . . . .102 A5
Wyatt Dr, SW13 . . . . . . .127 J7
Wyatt Pk Rd, SW2 . . . . .169 E2
Wyatt Rd, E7 . . . . .97 G6
N5 . . . . .93 J3
Wyatts La, E17 . . . . .78 C3
Wybert St, NW1 . . . . .9 E5
Wyborne Way, NW10 . . . .88 C7
Wyburn Av, Barn. EN5 . . .40 C3
Wyche Gro, S.Croy. CR2 .201 J7
Wych Elm Dr, Brom. BR1
off London La 173 F7
Wych Elm Pas, Kings.T.
KT2 . . . . .163 J7
Wycherley Cl, SE3 . . . . .135 F7
Wycherley Cres, Barn.
EN5 . . . . .40 E6
Wychwood Av, Edg.
HA8 . . . . .53 G6
Thornton Heath CR7 . .187 J3
Wychwood Cl, Edg. HA8 . .53 G6
Sunbury-on-Thames
TW16 . . . . .160 A6
Wychwood End, N6 . . . . .74 C7
Wychwood Gdns, Ilf.
IG5 . . . . .80 C4
Wychwood Way, SE19
off Roman Ri 170 A6

Wycliffe Cl, Well. DA16 . .157 J1
Wycliffe Rd, SW11 . . . . .150 A3
SW19 . . . . .167 E6
Wyclif St, EC1 . . . . .11 G4
Wycombe Gdns, NW11 . . .90 D2
Wycombe Pl, SW18 . . . .149 F6
Wycombe Rd, N17 . . . . . .76 D1
Ilford IG2 . . . . .80 C5
Wembley HA0 . . . . . . .106 A1
Wydehurst Rd, Croy.
CR0 . . . . .188 D7
Wydell Cl, Mord. SM4 . .183 J6
Wydeville Manor Rd,
SE12 . . . . .173 H4
Wye Cl, Orp. BR6 . . . . . .193 J7
Wyemead Cres, E4 . . . . . .62 E2
Wye St, SW11 . . . . .149 G2
Wyevale Cl, Pnr. HA5 . . . .66 A3
Wyfields, Ilf. IG5
off Ravensbourne
Gdns 80/81 E1
Wyfold Ho, SE2
off Wolvercote Rd . . .138 D2
Wyfold Rd, SW6 . . . . . . .128 B7
Wyhill Wk, Dag. RM10 . .101 J6
Wyke Cl, Islw. TW7 . . . .124 C6
Wyke Gdns, W7 . . . . . . .124 D3
Wykeham Av, Dag.
RM9 . . . . .100 C6
Wykeham Cl, West Dr.
UB7 . . . . .120 D7
Wykeham Grn, Dag.
RM9 . . . . .100 C6
Wykeham Hill, Wem.
HA9 . . . . .87 J1
Wykeham Ri, N20 . . . . . .56 B1
Wykeham Rd, NW4 . . . . .71 J5
Harrow HA3 . . . . .68 E4
Wyke Rd, E3 . . . . .96 A7
SW20 . . . . .183 J2
Wyldes Cl, NW11
off Wildwood Rd 91 F1
Wyldfield Gdns, N9 . . . . .60 C2
Wyld Way, Wem. HA9 . . . .88 B6
Wyleu St, SE23 . . . . . . .153 H7
Wylie Rd, Sthl. UB2 . . . .123 G3
Wyllen Cl, E1 . . . . .113 F4
Wylo Dr, Barn. EN5 . . . . .39 G6
Wymering Rd, W9 . . . . . .108 D3
Wymond St, SW15 . . . . .147 J3
Wynan Rd, E14 . . . . .134 B5
Wynash Gdns, Cars.
SM5 . . . . .199 H5
Wynaud Ct, N22
off Palmerston Rd 59 F6
Wyncham Av, Sid. DA15 .175 H1
Wynchgate, N14 . . . . . . .58 D1
N21 . . . . .58 E1
Harrow HA3 . . . . .52 B7
Wyncroft Cl, Brom. BR1 .192 C3
Wyndale Av, NW9 . . . . . .70 A6
Wyndcliff Rd, SE7 . . . . .135 H6
Wyndcroft Cl, Enf. EN2 . . .43 H3
Wyndham Cl, Orp. BR6 . .207 F1
Sutton SM2 . . . . .198 D7
Wyndham Cres, N19 . . . .92 C3
Hounslow TW4 . . . . . .143 G6
Wyndham Est, SE5 . . . . .36 A7
Wyndham Ms, W1 . . . . . .15 J2
Wyndham Pl, W1 . . . . . . .15 J2
Wyndham Rd, E6 . . . . . . .98 A7
SE5 . . . . .131 H7
W13 . . . . .124 E3
Barnet EN4 . . . . .57 J1
Kingston upon Thames
KT2 . . . . .163 J7
Wyndham St, W1 . . . . . . .15 J1
Wyndham Yd, W1 . . . . . .15 J2
Wyneham Rd, SE24 . . . .152 A5
Wynell Rd, SE23 . . . . . .171 G3
Wynford Pl, Belv. DA17 .139 G6
Wynford Rd, N1 . . . . . . .10 C1
Wynford Way, SE9 . . . . .174 C3
Wynlie Gdns, Pnr. HA5 . . .66 B2
Wynn Br Cl, Wdf.Grn. IG8
off Chigwell Rd 79 J1
Wynndale Rd, E18 . . . . . .79 H1
Wynne Rd, SW9 . . . . . . .151 G2
Wynns Av, Sid. DA15 . . .158 A5
Wynnstay Gdns, W8 . . . .128 D3
Wynter St, SW11 . . . . . .149 F4
Wynton Gdns, SE25 . . . .188 C5
Wynton Pl, W3 . . . . .106 B6
Wynyard Ter, SE11 . . . . .34 D3
Wynyatt St, EC1 . . . . . . .11 G4
Wyre Gro, Edg. HA8 . . . . .54 B3
Hayes UB3 . . . . .122 A4
Wyresdale Cres, Grnf.
UB6 . . . . .104 C3
Wythburn Pl, W1 . . . . . . .15 J4

Wythenshawe Rd, Dag.
RM10 . . . .**101** G3
Wythens Wk, SE9 . . . . . .**156** E6
Wythes Cl, Brom. BR1 . .**192** C2
Wythes Rd, E16 . . . .**136** B1
Wythfield Rd, SE9 . . . . . .**156** C6
Wyvenhoe Rd, Har. HA2 . .**85** J3
Wyvern Est, N.Mal. KT3 .**183** G4
Wyvern Gro, Hayes UB3 .**121** E7
Wyvil Est, SW8 . . . .**34** A7
Wyvil Rd, SW8 . . . .**34** A6
Wyvis St, E14 . . . .**114** B5

Y

Yabsley St, E14 . . . .**134** C1
Yalding Rd, SE16 . . . .**29** H6
Yale Cl, Houns. TW4
off Bramley Way **143** F5
Yaohan Plaza, NW9 . . . . . .**70** D3
Yarborough Rd, SW19 . .**185** G1
Yardley Cl, E4 . . . .**46** B5
Yardley Ct, Sutt. SM3
off Hemingford Rd . . .**197** J4
Yardley La, E4 . . . .**46** B5
Yardley St, WC1 . . . .**10** E4
Yarmouth Cres, N17 . . . .**76** E5
Yarmouth Pl, W1 . . . .**24** D2
Yarnfield Sq, SE15
off Clayton Rd **152** D1
Yarnton Way, SE2 . . . . . .**138** D2
Erith DA18 . . . .**139** F3
Yarrow Cres, E6 . . . .**116** B5
Yateley St, SE18 . . . .**136** A3
Yates Ct, NW2 . . . .**90** A6
YEADING, Hayes **102** B3
Yeading Av, Har. HA2 . . . .**84** E2
Yeading Fork, Hayes
UB4 . . . .**102** C5
Yeading Gdns, Hayes
UB4 . . . .**102** B5
Yeading La, Hayes
UB4 . . . .**102** B6
Northolt UB5 . . . .**102** C3
Yeames Cl, W13 . . . .**104** D6
Yeate St, N1 . . . .**94** A7
Yeatman Rd, N6 . . . .**73** J6
Yeats Cl, NW10 . . . .**88** E6
SE13 off Eliot Pk **154** D2
Yeats Ct, N15
off Tynemouth Rd **76** C4
Yeend Cl, W.Mol. KT8 . . .**179** G4
Yeldham Rd, W6 . . . .**128** A5

Yellow Hammer Ct, NW9
off Eagle Dr **70/71** E2
Yelverton Rd, SW11 . . . .**149** G2
Yenston Cl, Mord. SM4 . .**184** D6
Yeoman Cl, E6
off Ferndale St . . .**116/117** E7
SE27 . . . .**169** H3
Yeoman Rd, Nthlt. UB5 . .**85** E7
Yeomans Acre, Ruis. HA4 .**66** A6
Yeoman's Ms, Islw. TW7
off Queensbridge Pk .**144** B5
Yeoman's Row, SW3 . . . .**23** H6
Yeoman St, SE8 . . . .**133** H4
Yeomans Yd, E1 . . . .**21** G5
Yeomen Way, Ilf. IG6 . . . .**65** F6
Yeovil Cl, Orp. BR6 . . . . .**207** H2
Yeovilton Pl, Kings.T.
KT2 . . . .**163** F5
Yerbury Rd, N19 . . . .**92** D3
Yester Dr, Chis. BR7 . . . .**174** B7
Yester Pk, Chis. BR7 . . . .**174** C7
Yester Rd, Chis. BR7 . . . .**174** C7
Yew Cl, Buck.H. IG9 . . . . .**64** A2
Yewdale Cl, Brom. BR1 . .**173** E6
Yewfield Rd, NW10 . . . . .**89** F7
Yew Gro, NW2 . . . .**90** A4
Yew Tree Cl, N21 . . . .**43** G7
Yewtree Cl, N22 . . . .**74** C1
Harrow HA2 . . . .**67** H4
Yew Tree Cl, Well. DA16 .**158** A1
Worcester Park KT4 . . .**197** E1
Yew Tree Gdns, Rom.
(Chad.Hth.) RM6 . . . . .**83** E5
Yew Tree Rd, W12 . . . . . .**107** F7
Yewtree Rd, Beck. BR3 . .**189** J3
Yew Tree Wk, Houns.
TW4 . . . .**143** F5
Yew Wk, Har. HA1 . . . . . .**86** B1
YIEWSLEY, West Dr. **120** B1
Yoakley Rd, N16 . . . .**94** B2
Yoke Cl, N7
off Ewe Cl **92/93** E6
Yolande Gdns, SE9 . . . . .**156** B5
Yonge Pk, N4 . . . .**93** G3
York Av, SW14 . . . .**146** C5
W7 . . . .**124** B1
Sidcup DA15 . . . .**175** H2
Stanmore HA7 . . . .**68** E1
York Br, NW1 . . . .**8** B5
York Bldgs, WC2 . . . .**18** B6
York Cl, E6
off Boultwood Rd **116** C6

York Cl, W7 off York Av . .**124** B1
Morden SM4 . . . .**184** E4
York Cres, Borwd. WD6 . .**38** D2
Loughton IG10 . . . .**48** B3
York Gate, N14 . . . .**42** E7
NW1 . . . .**8** B6
York Gro, SE15 . . . .**153** F1
York Hill, SE27 . . . .**169** H3
Loughton IG10 . . . .**48** B3
York Hill Est, SE27 . . . . .**169** H3
York Ho, Wem. HA9 . . . . .**87** J4
York Ho Pl, W8 . . . .**22** A3
Yorkland Av, Well.
DA16 . . . .**157** J3
York Ms, NW5
off Kentish Town Rd . . .**92** B5
Ilford IG1 off York Rd . . .**98** D3
York Par, Brent. TW8 . . . .**125** G5
York Pl, SW11 . . . .**149** G3
WC2 . . . .**18** B6
Dagenham RM10 . . . . .**101** J6
Ilford IG1 off York Rd . . .**98** D2
York Ri, NW5 . . . .**92** B3
Orpington BR6 . . . . . .**207** H1
York Rd, E4 . . . .**62** A5
E7 . . . .**97** G6
E10 . . . .**96** C3
E17 . . . .**77** G5
N11 . . . .**58** D6
N18 . . . .**60** E6
N21 . . . .**44** A7
SE1 . . . .**26** D3
SW11 . . . .**149** F3
SW18 . . . .**149** F3
SW19 . . . .**167** F6
W3 . . . .**106** C6
W5 . . . .**125** F3
Barnet EN5 . . . .**41** G5
Brentford TW8 . . . .**125** G5
Croydon CR0 . . . .**187** G2
Hounslow TW3 . . . . . .**143** H3
Ilford IG1 . . . .**98** D3
Kingston upon Thames
KT2 . . . .**163** J7
Northwood HA6 . . . . . .**66** A2
Richmond TW10
off Albert Rd **145** J5
Sutton SM2 . . . .**198** D6
Teddington TW11 . . . .**162** B4
Yorkshire Cl, N16 . . . .**94** B3
Yorkshire Gdns, N18 . . . .**60** E5
Yorkshire Grey Pl, NW3
off Heath St **91** F4
Yorkshire Grey Yd, WC1 . .**18** C2

Yorkshire Rd, E14 . . . . . .**113** H6
Mitcham CR4 . . . .**186** E5
York Sq, E14 . . . .**113** H6
York St, W1 . . . .**16** A1
Barking IG11
off Abbey Rd **117** F1
Mitcham CR4 . . . .**186** A7
Twickenham TW1 . . . .**162** D1
York Ter, Erith DA8 . . . . .**159** J1
York Ter E, NW1 . . . .**8** C6
York Ter W, NW1 . . . .**8** B6
Yorkton St, E2 . . . .**13** H2
York Way, N1 . . . .**111** E1
N7 . . . .**92** D6
N20 . . . .**57** J3
Borehamwood WD6 . . .**38** D2
Chessington KT9 . . . . .**195** H7
Feltham TW13 . . . .**161** F3
York Way Ct, N1 . . . .**111** E1
York Way Est, N7
off York Way **92/93** E6
Youngmans Cl, Enf. EN2 . .**43** J1
Young Rd, E16 . . . .**115** J6
Young's Bldgs, EC1 . . . . .**12** A5
★ Young's Ram Brewery,
SW18 . . . .**148** E5
Youngs Rd, Ilf. IG2 . . . . .**81** G5
Young St, W8 . . . .**22** A4
Yoxley App, Ilf. IG2 . . . . .**81** F6
Yoxley Dr, Ilf. IG2 . . . . . .**81** F6
Yukon Rd, SW12 . . . .**150** B7
Yuletide Cl, NW10 . . . . . .**88** E7
Yunus Khan Cl, E17 . . . . .**78** A5

Z

Zampa Rd, SE16 . . . .**133** F5
Zander Ct, E2 . . . .**13** J2
Zangwill Rd, SE3 . . . . . .**156** A1
Zealand Av, West Dr.
UB7 . . . .**120** A7
Zealand Rd, E3 . . . .**113** H2
Zeland Cl, NW2 . . . .**89** J1
Zennor Rd, SW12 . . . . . .**168** C1
Zenoria St, SE22 . . . .**152** C4
Zermatt Rd, Th.Hth.
CR7 . . . .**187** J4
Zetland St, E14 . . . .**114** B5
Zion Pl, Th.Hth. CR7 . . . .**188** A4
Zion Rd, Th.Hth. CR7 . . . .**188** A4
Zoar St, SE1 . . . .**27** J1
Zoffany St, N19 . . . .**92** D2